# Being Ethical

# Being Ethical

## Classic and New Voices on Contemporary Issues

**Edited by Shari Collins, Bertha Alvarez Manninen, Jacqueline M. Gately, and Eric Comerford**

broadview press

BROADVIEW PRESS – www.broadviewpress.com
Peterborough, Ontario, Canada

Founded in 1985, Broadview Press remains a wholly independent publishing house. Broadview's focus is on academic publishing; our titles are accessible to university and college students as well as scholars and general readers. With over 600 titles in print, Broadview has become a leading international publisher in the humanities, with world-wide distribution. Broadview is committed to environmentally responsible publishing and fair business practices.

This book is made of paper from well-managed FSC® - certified
forests, recycled materials, and other controlled sources.

**Library and Archives Canada Cataloguing in Publication**

Being ethical : classic and new voices on contemporary issues / edited by Shari Collins, Bertha Alvarez Manninen, Jacqueline M. Gately, and Eric Comerford.

Includes bibliographical references.
ISBN 978-1-55481-298-1 (paperback)

1. Ethics—Textbooks. 2. Applied ethics—Textbooks. I. Collins-Chobanian, Shari, editor

BJ1012.B428 2016      170      C2016-906680-0

Broadview Press handles its own distribution in North America
PO Box 1243, Peterborough, Ontario K9J 7H5, Canada
555 Riverwalk Parkway, Tonawanda, NY 14150, USA
Tel: (705) 743-8990; Fax: (705) 743-8353
email: customerservice@broadviewpress.com

Distribution is handled by Eurospan Group in the UK, Europe, Central Asia, Middle East, Africa, India, Southeast Asia, Central America, South America, and the Caribbean. Distribution is handled by Footprint Books in Australia and New Zealand.

Broadview Press acknowledges the financial support of the Government of Canada through the Canada Book Fund for our publishing activities.

Canada

Copy edited by Martin R. Boyne
Book Designed by George Kirkpatrick

PRINTED IN CANADA

# Contents

# Preface

AS A DISCIPLINE, PHILOSOPHY sometimes has a bad reputation. It is occasionally derided as lofty, in the ivory tower, or navel-gazing – academic work with little relevance to the real world. Some see it, at best, as mental aerobics. In this book, we hope to help change that perception. Our main goal is not only to engage students in lively and thought-provoking dialogue about difficult moral issues but also to help them see that philosophy is an inescapable and invaluable part of our everyday human lives. We illustrate this by bringing together classic voices in applied ethics with new ones, and by delving into topics not often explored in other anthologies. In addition, we have taken an inter- and transdisciplinary approach: we include a wide range of robust philosophical essays along with others in, for example, psychology and sociology, in order to highlight philosophy's connections with other disciplines.

Students often mention that what they want most from a philosophy class is to gain new perspectives, and that is also one of the goals of this anthology: to provide new insights both from established sources, or "classics," and from new voices in the field that have yet to be heard from, or at least not heard from as often. Since their inception, anthologies in applied ethics have traditionally lingered on the same issues. With the exception of adding feminist and multicultural perspectives, the discussions have remained stuck where they began. While some classic topics and essays stand the test of time, many do not, and not surprisingly this can result in reader apathy (or worse, confirmation that philosophy is "out of touch") in the classroom. In this anthology we have not only honored tradition but have also brought in many new and vibrant perspectives throughout.

At its best, education, about the world and each other, is an engaging and enriching experience. One of the ways we learn is by developing and using theories. Theories are explanatory models that take information gathered from previous experiences to help us when we encounter new experiences. In order to discuss ethical dilemmas, philosophers have developed ethical theories to provide guiding principles. So this book begins with theory. Included in this section are some of the classic ethical theories, all of which are still in use today. Once these are understood, we can see how they can influence public opinion, policies, and even our own perceptions. Unlike many other ethics anthologies, however, this section also includes new and emerging theory: Iris Marion Young's work on oppression, as well as reflection on the roles that theory can and should (and shouldn't!) have, as provided by bell hooks.

With the next section on Personal and Public Identity, we introduce ethical questions that have not yet been addressed in applied ethics anthologies. These essays address many identity issues that students today grapple with, from being the first one in their family to go to college, to surviving trauma. This section touches upon the personal lives of students and others and provides fresh ways to reflect on a range of contemporary, real-life ethical issues, ideally modeling the kind of theory that hooks advocates.

Sex and sexual issues are pervasive in our lives, and in society at large, yet they rarely receive thoughtful and reflective treatment. Sex, perhaps more than any other human issue, calls forth strong opinions, has an historic association with shame, and permeates our politics, especially clashing in the public versus private domains. In Section III we first view sex from a virtue perspective and then examine how an integrated view can be edifying. We also look at promiscuity, sexual autonomy, transgender marriage, and prostitution. The authors' rich and provocative essays provide opportunities for readers to question their own sexual values, prejudices, and autonomy.

Many people claim, and often rightly so, that they are oppressed, and it is a weighty ethical claim that deserves care and attention. Whether one thinks certain groups are indeed oppressed will make a significant difference in one's outlooks, understanding of society, and actions. It is important, therefore, to consider people's claims of oppression and to weigh these claims in light of our ethical formation. As mentioned, Section I includes a piece by Iris Marion Young entitled "Five Faces of Oppression," these five "faces" being the five kinds of oppression that Young claims encompass all types of modern oppression. It is important to note that Young does not set out to explain what *causes* oppression, but rather to outline the multiple ways in which oppression can manifest. In Section IV we make use of Young's classification of oppression by including pieces which claim that

certain groups are oppressed in ways corresponding approximately to Young's analysis. While these pieces merely scratch the surface of this important area, they invite the reader to consider whether oppression exists and, from that point onward, what responses might be called for.

The physical environment is the basis for all life and for all that we do, yet it is often taken for granted and horribly neglected through pollution and other human activities. In Section V we begin with the classic environmentalist Aldo Leopold, who argues that we need to extend ethics to the physical environment via his "Land Ethic." If we took Leopold's approach to heart, we would not live our current lifestyles and our moral landscape would enlarge to include nonhumans. Regarding the latter, we also include an essay on factory farming in which the author warns that our failure to consider the plight of nonhuman animals puts us at moral risk. Another kind of risk is posed from climate change and what are called "Genetically Modified Organisms," both of which are explored in this section. Further, we look at the issue of human consumption in an essay by Guy Claxton, who proposes that we practice mindfulness in order to reduce our consumption – and thus our environmental footprints.

This anthology transcends the typical "pro-con" approach in favor of breadth and the exchange of multiple ideas. In Section VI, on reproductive ethics, for example, two classic pieces are included that defend the traditional "pro-choice" or "pro-life" perspective, but we have added more nuanced voices as well. For example, there is a selection by a Christian thinker who, while defending the pro-life perspective, also discusses how we must both accord sympathy to women who get abortions and understand how health disparities that affect women in different socioeconomic strata play a direct role in the number of abortions procured in the US, such that social justice becomes vital to both sides of the debate. We have also included an essay that attempts to bring men back into the abortion discussion by asking what rights, if any, they have when faced with wanting to keep a fetus that their female partner has chosen to abort. Thus, this section offers the opportunity to teach abortion ethics in both a traditional and a nontraditional manner.

Health care is important to us all, for it is not something any of us can go without. But how many of us regularly think about health care from an ethical perspective? Often in the US, health care is discussed in organizational or financial terms (or in terms defined by political party affiliation). But we cannot talk about technical aspects of health care without first getting straight the moral aspects of health care – just as it would be bizarre to think about how to *organize* a day-care without first considering what the *moral* aims and function of a daycare ought to be, it is equally bizarre that people should make evaluative claims about health care without first explaining what their values are. Our section on health care, Section VII, invites readers to think ethically about health care by considering whether health care ought to be conceived of as a right and whether health-care policy ought to be subject to democratic deliberation. We also consider the health and human rights of those living in harmful circumstances set in place by power, and we confront the important issue of how best to deal with end-of-life situations in the context of modern medicine.

War and terrorism seem to be an intractable part of the human condition in the twenty-first century. What justifies war? Are there better ways to address and solve conflict? What are the costs of war? In the absence of a strong objective notion of terrorism, who may we call "terrorists"? These questions are addressed in Section VIII, using texts from both classic and contemporary authors – from Aquinas and Gandhi to Brian Orend and Claudia Card – who challenge us to reflect and consider the paths of war and terrorism.

In a world plagued by so much violence, our final section, on caring for the "other," asks us to question and analyze our propensity to dehumanize our fellow human being, and to consider the practical consequences of this tendency. While this section includes a secular perspective of what it means to care for the other, through Nel Noddings's appeal to care ethics, Søren Kierkegaard's *Works of Love* provides an avenue for discussing what religious moral obligations arise from the commandment to love one's neighbor. Then students are asked to put these moral obligations to practical use by taking certain moral issues – such as our treatment of the poor, our silence in the face of genocide, and the exploitation of people in developing countries – and considering what it would mean to treat these "others" with the same care and love we would want for ourselves and for our family and friends.

## Acknowledgments

We would all like to thank Broadview Press and their many editors, especially Martin Boyne, whose comments have helped improve this anthology. We would like to extend a very special and heartfelt note of thanks to Stephen Latta, whose guidance has been an indispensable part of seeing this book come to fruition. In addition, we thank the authors whose work has moved us to include them and has created a pedagogical tool for moving the discussion in applied ethics forward. It is time.

Shari Collins would like to thank her co-editors and colleagues for the rich intellectual and synergistic exchanges that have contributed to this anthology. She came to this field

23 years ago and felt a desire to hear voices from more perspectives and to help bring multicultural voices to the fore. This anthology represents a further honoring, not only of that tradition but of new topics as well. She thanks Stephen Latta for sharing that vision.

Bertha Alvarez Manninen would like to thank her three colleagues for an extraordinary working relationship and for the privilege of allowing her to share this experience with them. She would also like to thank her husband, Tuomas Manninen, and her girls, Michelle and Julia, for being patient as she wrote, and for always greeting her with hugs and kisses upon her return.

Jackie Gately is truly delighted for having the opportunity to work with her three colleagues on this project. It has been a joy! She is also wildly appreciative of all the support, kindness, and work (!) from Ruediger Volk as they traveled along this path, and of the generous spirit of Felipe, who remains cheerful and patient even when the adults are working.

Eric Comerford would like to thank Bertha Manninen and Shari Collins for being exceptional philosophy teachers, and Jackie Gately for her many contributions.

# Section I:
# Theoretical Foundations

ETHICS IS ONE OF the main branches of philosophy, so it is helpful to start with a word or two about philosophy in order to situate what applied ethics involves. It's probably not unfair to say that if you ask ten philosophers what philosophy is, you'll receive at least ten answers. Nonetheless, there are some relatively uncontroversial claims one can make about the discipline. One is that the term in English comes from two Greek roots, *philo-* (love) and *sophia* (wisdom or truth), and that together the word is often translated as "love of wisdom (or truth)." Philosophers, then, are "lovers of wisdom," and those who seek truth.

If a philosopher is tempted to claim that this implies that they are wise, it is helpful to remind them of Plato, an ancient Greek philosopher, and one of his discussions about love. Plato makes the point that love is a form of desire, and when we say that we desire something, that implies we don't have it (if we had it, we wouldn't want it – we'd just have it). So the emphasis in philosophy, according to this classic model, is on the desire for, not necessarily the attainment of, truth. It is a discipline that seeks out answers. This does not mean that it never finds them; in fact, one of the benefits of engaging in applied ethics is that one has to come to some sort of answer, even if it is provisional. That is, one

must ultimately decide how to act (or not to act, which is a decision of its own). But philosophers will always be open to re-evaluating their answers in light of new evidence or perspectives. So how does one arrive at these provisional answers? In doing philosophy, one is engaging in a sustained form of reflection. This will frequently include analyzing and clarifying concepts and definitions, constructing arguments, and presenting and assessing evidence to support a particular position or claim. As discussed below, it will also include examining and developing theories. In short, philosophy uses critical thinking skills.

## Ethics

Ethics, as a word in English, is derived from the Greek word *ethos*. Ethos can be understood as one's character, or as a way of living, either of which is designed to bring about a good life – ideally, in fact, the best possible life one could lead. The working assumption is that everyone would like to lead their best possible life. The question, then, is how? That is what the discipline of ethics was set up to determine.

In addressing the question of how to live one's life as a good life, questions about how we should interact with each other, and how we should treat others and ourselves in order to do this, arise naturally. This also leads to the more common understanding of ethics as making determinations about good and bad, right and wrong. These determinations are part of the larger question about living one's life. Technically, the terms *moral* and *morality* are usually reserved for systems of these determinations (i.e., if a particular action is valued as good within a society or group, then that action is referred to as a moral action), while ethics implies a justification for these determinations, so an ethical action is an action that has been shown to be good, independent of the social codes of value. Practically speaking, though, the terms *morality* and *ethics* (and *moral* and *ethical*) are often used interchangeably. What is important to remember is that one of the key tasks for the person using applied ethics is not only to make a determination of whether something is good to do, but to provide a solid reason for that decision.

To state the obvious: you are the only one who can live your life. All the good, the bad, and the ugly in your life, while it will directly and indirectly involve many others, always involves you. How can you live your best possible life? How can you live a good life? Those are the leading questions driving this book. The topics discussed are designed to get you to think about the values you hold, to examine them closely, and to develop solid reasons for holding them – or perhaps to replace them if others are better justified.

### What Happened to Religion? And the Law?

Two common sources of people's sense of what is right and wrong are religious beliefs and the legal system. There is a lot of overlap between ethics and both religious and legal perspectives, but it is important here to separate out the role that ethics plays. As mentioned above, ethics (as distinct from

morality) is set up to give a justification for its determinations about values; furthermore, the justifications (and arguments) within philosophy are always geared toward convincing those who do not agree with one's own position. Certainly, religious systems offer such determinations about values, as well as justifications for them. Nonetheless, the justifications are often seen as being compelling only for those who already believe in some basic tenets of the religion itself. So religious claims can be compatible with ethical claims, but they are generally not compelling for nonbelievers (which doesn't mean they aren't compelling and meaningful in and of themselves for those who do believe). Ethics provides a way for claims based on religious beliefs to be compelling to nonbelievers. We have included several of these types of arguments in the readings offered in this book.

In examining claims based on the legal system, let us consider the distinction between description and prescription. Description gives an account of an existing action, state of affairs, object, situation, event, and so forth. It tells how things are. Prescription, on the other hand, gives an account of a better or ideal action, state of affairs, object, situation, event, and so forth. It tells how things should be. When people are discussing whether something is legal or illegal, they are offering a description. For example, if someone is trying to figure out whether medical marijuana is legal, this is a descriptive account. Now it can be complicated to figure out, since there are American states in which medical marijuana is legal, yet it remains illegal based on federal laws. This apparent paradox is related to the notion of clarification of concepts mentioned earlier: in this case, one would do well to determine whether, when one is using the term *legal*, one means legal within the state or legal within both state and federal laws. But notice that one is not determining here whether it should be legal (in whatever sense of the word one has landed on) – that would involve prescription. And this is the question ethics is always asking: should something be the way it is, or act the way it does? Presumably, when laws are established, discussions about ethical dimensions are informing these determinations. But this is a separate activity from determining the legality of something. To say that something is legal or illegal, then, is not the end of the discussion for the philosopher, but the beginning; that is, once one has accepted that an action is legal, for example, one then asks if it *should* be legal.

### Theory: What Is It? And Why Use It?

Generally speaking, a theory (ethical or otherwise) provides an explanatory model of ideas or phenomena that is not dependent on what is being explained. It is more abstract than a general description because it is supposed to illuminate underlying patterns and/or principles driving the things we see and do, not just the things themselves. For example, one might observe that a particular medicine cures various individuals of a disease. The explanation of why that occurs provides the theoretical foundation, which can then be used in similar cases.

Theory is sometimes presented in terms of its opposition to practice. Practice focuses on specific situations or things at hand, while theory focuses on the generalized principles or patterns of many specific situations or things considered together. It is best to view theory and practice as not being in opposition, however, since they rely on each other. Practice provides the important details (and the reality check!), while theory provides the "bigger picture."

Applied ethics uses ethical theories to provide the justification for someone to maintain a particular ethical claim. Developing a theory

allows one to justify one's claims to others, to be consistent with one's own decisions, and to have a better understanding of situations and other people, as well as one's responses to them. More succinctly, as bell hooks writes in "Theory as Liberatory Practice" (selection I.7), theory can be used for "making sense out of what [is] happening." Because theoretical claims are necessarily abstract, though, theory can be very challenging to read. It is worth emphasizing, however, that this theory is meant for you to use, but you might not accept it uncritically.

### Ethical Theory

Ethical theory, then, is theory that has been developed to provide an underlying principle (or principles) that can justify making determinations about what are right or wrong actions (or inactions). People often expect that readings in ethical theory will attempt to convince them to act in a certain way. That may, ultimately, play a role, but it may be better not to think of them as motivational – that is, not to think of them as trying to convince readers to be ethical. It may be more helpful to envision the authors of these readings asking themselves, "Assuming that I want to be ethical (and I do!), how would I do it?"

To answer this question, many theorists expect that there will be one underlying principle driving ethical determinations. That is the ideal, because, as with any theory, the more particular cases I can cover with my principle, the better and more useful my theory will be. If my principle can cover *all* possible cases of ethical decision making, it is the most comprehensive and consistent it can be. For example, in the sciences, if one principle works only for some things, without providing an explanation of which things these are, or why (which itself would be another principle), it isn't terribly useful, comprehensive, or consistent – all qualities that one looks for in a theory. Imagine that my own theory of gravity – based on motion and weight – applies to apples falling out of trees and to tumbling rocks, but not to pencils and computers that accidentally get pushed off a counter. I will be in line for many unpleasant surprises because my theory is too limited (and apparently doesn't recognize the downward trajectory of sidewise motion). In order to get the desired comprehensive and complete theory, philosophers look for the most basic principle that can then explain all other decisions.

In order to determine if the chosen principle is truly the one that guides all such decisions, the principle needs to be applied to various situations. We are probably all familiar with the old "sounds good on paper" problem: if an ethical theory sounds promising but consistently generates results that are not in keeping with one's initial sense of right and wrong actions, then there is a problem with the theory. Note, however, that if the principle generally produces results that are consistent with one's already established sense of ethics, but on occasion generates something that does not fall in line with one's initial response, the initial response may be the problem. In these cases, both the situation and the response warrant more examination.

## The Rock and the Hard Place

When discussing ethics and ethical theories, two competing concerns frequently come to the surface and therefore deserve specific mention. On the one hand, there are claims that there are absolute moral truths (what is called an absolutist position) – that determinations of right and wrong are universal and always true. The major concern that arises from such claims is that, empirically (i.e., based on observation), it does not appear to

be the case that everyone agrees on these determinations of right and wrong. Without that consensus, one is left with the daunting tasks of explaining what one's source is and of justifying convincingly to everyone how one knows what these values are.

On the other hand, there are various claims that there are no moral truths (what is called a relativist position) – that these determinations are always dependent on such things as social rules or personal interpretations. The major concern that arises from such claims is that, without some kind of anchor, it apparently becomes impossible to make any kind of ethical claim. If it's always true, for example, that these determinations are derived from social rules, if a society or even subgroup within a society determines that something is right that typically is not deemed that way (e.g., killing others whom they perceive as "impure"), there is no sufficient argument against these actions. Most (if not all) people generally have at least some actions that they want to claim really are right or wrong, and a relativist has to either stake the claim that this is not possible or explain how any particular claim can be supported.

These two positions represent the extremes of a spectrum of ethical theories. And there are ways to respond to the concerns raised in response to each position, more and less convincingly. But these concerns often tend to "haunt" much of ethics, so it is helpful to recognize and address them as they appear.

## The Field of Ethical Theory

There is a long-established tradition of ethical theory within Western philosophy that informs the dominant ethical discourse in the US (and has international influence as well). For anyone investigating ethics within this context, it is important to articulate this tradition, along with its dominant players, if only because of the influence it continues to have on how people think about various matters. Additionally, of course, established theorists have spent a lot of time contemplating and then proposing the driving principles in ethical decisions and have engaged in a lot of conceptual work from which we can benefit.

Looking at a very brief overview of the history of Western ethical theory is especially helpful at this point because of the self-referential nature of the field. Philosophers will address issues that previous philosophers have brought up, philosophers who are themselves responding to issues that philosophers before them have brought up (this can go on for millennia), so reading philosophy can sometimes seem like walking into the middle of a conversation. Often, one theorist is responding to criticisms of another theorist (as, for example, when John Stuart Mill defends utilitarianism and addresses how his theory relates to both virtue and to justice; as indicated below, ethical theories based on virtue and justice preceded Mill historically, and this gives a context for Mill's arguments). The overview below attempts to bring you up to speed with the conversation (in a very quick recap).

Additionally, it is helpful to recognize some of the working assumptions at play in these theories. One notable example is that most traditional accounts of ethics place a significant emphasis on the role of rationality. This is frequently linked to an assumption that what separates humans from nonhuman animals is their capacity for rationality. Rationality is seen as crucial for the very ability to distinguish right from wrong, and to understand the implications of these differences as well as the consequences of one's actions. This is tied to an understanding of responsibility. The ability to make a choice (in terms of both the capacity to make a choice and the circumstances allowing one to act on one's decision) is seen as requisite to being responsible for

that choice. For example, within American court systems, one can be found "not guilty by reason of insanity [an inability to use rationality]." Current critiques, however, ask questions such as "Who determines what is rational/a rational choice?" and "Aren't there choices made through such phenomena as instinct that are just as legitimate?" There are also questions about whether other animals might in fact have the capacity for rationality, about the status of humans who do not have this capacity, and about the significance this might have for ethics.

Because the ethical tradition has been such a white- and male-dominated discussion, many people who are not members of one or both of these groups have felt that ethical theory, and indeed theory in general, speaks only to and for the privileged. Some have felt that it is both unhelpful and indeed harmful to those who are not affiliated with all of those groups, because it serves to bolster and justify the power of those who are within the dominant groups. This is why bell hooks (who intentionally uses lowercase letters in her name to place the reader's attention on what she is writing, rather than who she is), an African-American woman, offers an explanation of why she *does* find theory helpful. It is with the philosophical spirit that remains open to re-evaluation that we present the traditional ethical theories, as well as contemporary revisitations of them.

## The Classic Players

Within American culture, three major types of ethical theory are relied on most frequently: virtue-based theories, deontological theories, and consequentialist (also known as teleological) theories. The type of theory indicates the general approach that the theory uses to make ethical determinations. Let us consider that in any given situation, a person acts (or doesn't), and those actions (or non-actions) have certain consequences. The virtue-based theories will focus primarily on the person who acts and on her or his character. Deontological theories will focus primarily on the actions themselves and on the motives for doing them. Consequentialist or teleological theories will focus primarily on the consequences of the actions. Each of these major types of theory has a corresponding predominant theory representative of its approach, discussed below.

Virtue ethics is one of the leading virtue-based theories and the oldest of the major Western ethical theories, having been outlined by Aristotle, an ancient Greek philosopher who lived c. 384–322 BCE. The basic principle at work here is that if one is to be ethical, one should cultivate good or virtuous traits (as opposed to vices) – that is to say, one should develop a good character or be a good person. This is done through practice so that one develops habits that make being virtuous something "natural." As the name indicates, this theory evaluates the virtues of the person who is acting. To act virtuously, one is advised to follow the "mean between extremes" of character traits. So, for example, one should not be too cowardly, but one should also not be too rash, rushing into dangerous situations too quickly. In the former case there is a deficit (one doesn't act when one should because one is too fearful – that is, one has a deficiency of confidence), and in the latter there is an excess (one acts when one shouldn't, because one isn't fearful enough – that is, one has an excess of confidence). The virtuous trait here is courage, and one is courageous when one is not afraid to act but does take some caution. According to Aristotle, humans are at their best when they are exercising their rationality, and since we use our rationality to figure out what the mean between the extremes is, being rational involves being virtuous (and vice versa). Other virtue-based theories include the ethics of care, Hindu values, and certain forms of Christian ethics.

Kantian ethics is the primary example of deontological theories, developed by the eighteenth-century German philosopher Immanuel Kant. The basic principle of Kantian ethics is that one should always perform one's duty with the correct motivation. According to deontological theories, certain actions in themselves are always going to be wrong (e.g., murder), no matter what the person's character is. It is one's duty to perform certain actions and to avoid others – which is why the name *deontological*, which means "duty-based," is appropriate for this theory. Deontological theories will usually generate some kind of list (based on a general principle) of acceptable or unacceptable actions. Kant does this by using what he calls the Categorical Imperative, which generates a list of actions that one must always do or not do ("imperative") under all circumstances ("categorical"). While Kant gives several versions of the Categorical Imperative, he insists that these different versions are really just different ways of saying the same thing, and that they will always generate the same list. Such a list would include actions that you could will that everyone do or, as he puts, that you will that it should become a universal law. The practical application of this, Kant further claims, is that one should always treat people as ends in themselves (that is, one should not use them as only a means to one's own goals, but rather recognize that they have their own goals – or "ends" – in life). Also for Kant, rationality plays a key role in ethics. It is because we humans are rational beings that we see the importance of duty, and it is also because we are rational beings that we are worthy of being treated as ends in ourselves. Other deontological theories include certain forms of Christian ethics and rights theory.

Utilitarianism, developed in eighteenth- and nineteenth-century Britain, is the most prevalent example of consequentialist theories. The key principle is that in order to be ethical, one should do what creates the greatest happiness for the greatest number (known as both the Happiness Principle and the Utility Principle). It is important to note that this principle also includes the idea of bringing about the least harm to the least number. From a utilitarian perspective, if there are good consequences to an action (bringing the greatest possible happiness to everyone involved, while minimizing harms), then it doesn't particularly matter whether one is a good person while doing it. Utilitarianism thus distinguishes itself from virtue ethics, although John Stuart Mill does make the claim that virtuous people will be good utilitarians. Also, under this view there are no actions that in theory couldn't be ethical under certain circumstances. Utilitarianism thus distinguishes itself from Kantian Ethics too; for example, murder can perhaps be ethical if it is the murder of someone like Adolf Hitler, in which case one can argue that the action brings about good consequences. This is true, against virtue ethics, even if the person committing the murder is a cold-hearted killer. Another common consequentialist theory is ethical egoism, in which what is considered ethical is whatever creates the greatest happiness for the individual herself. However, many people debate whether this is an ethical theory at all!

Of these three major theories, Kantian ethics and utilitarianism are the most predominant. They are sometimes seen as rival theories; often, for key decisions, people will find that they lean more toward one than the other. This is because the two theories can be seen to represent absolutist and relativist positions (described above), respectively, which in turn can be seen as mutually exclusive (although utilitarians would probably argue that their theory is not relativist but contextual). While there are some cases where these different types of theory do appear to diverge – and they certainly do take a different approach to arrive at their conclusions – it is worth noting how frequently the various theories generate similar responses to a multitude of situations.

Social contract theory is another predominant theory used in the US, one that, as the name suggests, looks explicitly at the interactions individuals have with their society. A "social contract" is understood as a tacit agreement that people make with the society in which they live. The basic idea, which dates back at least as far as Plato (fifth–fourth centuries BCE), is that in exchange for the benefits that one gains from participating in a society (e.g., public roads, public education, etc.), one is willing to limit one's own behavior by following rules established within that society (e.g., laws, moral codes, etc.). To reap the benefits without taking on the social responsibilities attached to them is considered as a violation of "fair play." Unlike the theories described above, social contract theory is categorized differently depending on the emphasis placed on its approach. Sometimes it is understood as a deontological theory because of the rules generated by the contract; sometimes it is understood as a consequentialist theory because individuals presumably join a social contract based on the better results expected from that contract than from living entirely on their own. In both perspectives, however, the main focus of social contract theory is understood to be that of establishing justice.

# I.  Aristotle, *Nicomachean Ethics*

ARISTOTLE'S DESCRIPTION OF VIRTUE ethics comes from his classic work *Nicomachean Ethics* (said to be named after his son, Nicomachus). In this work he describes in detail what he means by a virtue, and how virtues can be attained by following the mean between extremes. Aristotle (c. 384–322 BCE) explains that the "mean" is not simply the average between two extremes but rather takes into account the various conditions and situations at hand. We see that for virtue ethics, context is extremely important in determining ethical actions. Aristotle offers many examples to more fully illustrate what a virtue is. He is careful to note that certain behaviors, such as murder, do not have a "mean," as they are already understood as bad in and of themselves. For Aristotle, virtue is cultivated over the course of a lifetime, developed in adulthood through habits that need to be instilled in childhood. Being ethical, therefore, is not simply a matter of any one action or behavior but instead comes from a well-developed character established through a repeated pattern of good actions.

---

## Book II [Virtue of Character]

### 1 [How a Virtue of Character Is Acquired]

VIRTUE, THEN, IS OF two sorts, virtue of thought and virtue of character. Virtue of thought arises and grows mostly from teaching; that is why it needs experience and time. Virtue of character [i.e., of ēthos] results from habit [ethos]; hence its name "ethical," slightly varied from "ethos."

§2 Hence it is also clear that none of the virtues of character arises in us naturally. For if something is by nature in one condition, habituation cannot bring it into another condition. A stone, for instance, by nature moves downwards, and habituation could not make it move upwards, not even if you threw it up ten thousand times to habituate it; nor could habituation make fire move downwards, or bring anything that is by nature in one condition into another condition. §3 And so the virtues arise in us neither by nature nor against nature. Rather, we are by nature able to acquire them, and we are completed through habit.

§4 Further, if something arises in us by nature, we first have the capacity for it, and later perform the activity. This is clear in the case of the senses; for we did not acquire them by frequent seeing or hearing, but we already had them when we exercised them, and did not get them by exercising them. Virtues, by contrast, we acquire, just as we acquire crafts, by having first activated them. For we learn a craft by producing the same product that we must produce when we have learned it; we become builders, for instance, by building, and we become harpists by playing the harp. Similarly, then, we become just by doing just actions, temperate by doing temperate actions, brave by doing brave actions.

§5 What goes on in cities is also evidence for this. For the legislator makes the citizens good by habituating them, and this is the wish of every legislator; if he fails to do it well he misses his goal. Correct habituation distinguishes a good political system from a bad one.

§6 Further, the sources and means that develop each virtue also ruin it, just as they do in a craft. For playing the harp makes both good and bad harpists, and it is analogous in the case of builders and all the rest; for building well makes good builders, and building badly makes bad ones. §7 Otherwise no teacher would be needed, but everyone would be born a good or a bad craftsman.

It is the same, then, with the virtues. For what we do in our dealings with other people makes some of us just, some unjust; what we do in terrifying situations, and the habits of fear or confidence that we acquire, make some of us brave and others cowardly. The same is true of situations involving appetites and anger; for one or another sort of conduct in these situations makes some temperate and mild, others intemperate and irascible. To sum it up in a single account: a state [of character] results from [the repetition of] similar activities.

§8 That is why we must perform the right activities, since differences in these imply corresponding differences in the states. It is not unimportant, then, to acquire one sort of habit or another, right from our youth. On the contrary, it is very important, indeed all-important.

## 2 [Habituation]

Our present discussion does not aim, as our others do, at study; for the purpose of our examination is not to know what virtue is, but to become good, since otherwise the inquiry would be of no benefit to us. And so we must examine the right ways of acting; for, as we have said, the actions also control the sorts of states we acquire.

§2 First, then, actions should accord with the correct reason. That is a common [belief], and let us assume it. We shall discuss it later, and say what the correct reason is and how it is related to the other virtues.

§3 But let us take it as agreed in advance that every account of the actions we must

do has to be stated in outline, not exactly. As we also said at the beginning, the type of accounts we demand should accord with the subject matter; and questions about actions and expediency, like questions about health, have no fixed answers.

§4 While this is the character of our general account, the account of particular cases is still more inexact. For these fall under no craft or profession; the agents themselves must consider in each case what the opportune action is, as doctors and navigators do. §5 The account we offer, then, in our present inquiry is of this inexact sort; still, we must try to offer help.

§6 First, then, we should observe that these sorts of states naturally tend to be ruined by excess and deficiency. We see this happen with strength and health – for we must use evident cases [such as these] as witnesses to things that are not evident. For both excessive and deficient exercise ruin bodily strength, and, similarly, too much or too little eating or drinking ruins health, whereas the proportionate amount produces, increases, and preserves it.

§7 The same is true, then, of temperance, bravery, and the other virtues. For if, for instance, someone avoids and is afraid of everything, standing firm against nothing, he becomes cowardly; if he is afraid of nothing at all and goes to face everything, he becomes rash. Similarly, if he gratifies himself with every pleasure and abstains from none, he becomes intemperate; if he avoids them all, as boors do, he becomes some sort of insensible person. Temperance and bravery, then, are ruined by excess and deficiency, but preserved by the mean.

§8 But these actions are not only the sources and causes both of the emergence and growth of virtues and of their ruin; the activities of the virtues [once we have acquired them] also consist in these same actions. For this is also true of more evident cases; strength, for instance, arises from eating a lot and from withstanding much hard labor, and it is the strong person who is most capable of these very actions. §9 It is the same with the virtues. For abstaining from pleasures makes us become temperate, and once we have become temperate we are most capable of abstaining from pleasures. It is similar with bravery; habituation in disdain for frightening situations and in standing firm against them makes us become brave, and once we have become brave we shall be most capable of standing firm.

3 [The Importance of Pleasure and Pain]

But we must take someone's pleasure or pain following on his actions to be a sign of his state. For if someone who abstains from bodily pleasures enjoys the abstinence itself, he is temperate; if he is grieved by it, he is intemperate. Again, if he stands firm against terrifying situations and enjoys it, or at least does not find it painful, he is brave; if he finds it painful, he is cowardly. For virtue of character is about pleasures and pains.

For pleasure causes us to do base actions, and pain causes us to abstain from fine ones. §2 That is why we need to have had the appropriate upbringing – right from early youth, as Plato says – to make us find enjoyment or pain in the right things; for this is the correct education.

§3 Further, virtues are concerned with actions and feelings; but every feeling and every action implies pleasure or pain; hence, for this reason too, virtue is about pleasures and pains. §4 Corrective treatments also indicate this, since they use pleasures and pains; for correction is a form of medical treatment, and medical treatment naturally operates through contraries.

§5 Further, as we said earlier, every state of soul is naturally related to and about whatever naturally makes it better or worse; and pleasures and pains make people base, from pursuing and avoiding the wrong ones, at the wrong time, in the wrong ways, or whatever other distinctions of that sort are needed in an account. These [bad effects of pleasure and pain] are the reason why people actually define the virtues as ways of being unaffected and undisturbed [by pleasures and pains]. They are wrong, however, because they speak of being unaffected without qualification, not of being unaffected in the right or wrong way, at the right or wrong time, and the added qualifications.

§6 We assume, then, that virtue is the sort of state that does the best actions concerning pleasures and pains, and that vice is the contrary state.

§7 The following will also make it evident that virtue and vice are about the same things. For there are three objects of choice – fine, expedient, and pleasant – and three objects of avoidance – their contraries, shameful, harmful, and painful. About all these, then, the good person is correct and the bad person is in error, and especially about pleasure. For pleasure is shared with animals, and implied by every object of choice, since what is fine and what is expedient appear pleasant as well.

§8 Further, pleasure grows up with all of us from infancy on. That is why it is hard to rub out this feeling that is dyed into our lives. We also estimate actions [as well as feelings] – some of us more, some less – by pleasure and pain. §9 For this reason, our whole discussion must be about these; for good or bad enjoyment or pain is very important for our actions.

§10 Further, it is more difficult to fight pleasure than to fight spirit – and Heracleitus[1] tells us [how difficult it is to fight spirit]. Now both craft and virtue are in every case about what is more difficult, since a good result is even better when it is more difficult. Hence, for this reason also, the whole discussion, for virtue and political science alike, must consider pleasures and pains; for if we use these well, we shall be good, and if badly, bad.

§11 To sum up: Virtue is about pleasures and pains; the actions that are its sources also increase it or, if they are done badly, ruin it; and its activity is about the same actions as those that are its sources.

## 4 [Virtuous Actions versus Virtuous Character]

Someone might be puzzled, however, about what we mean by saying that we become just by doing just actions and become temperate by doing temperate actions. For [one might suppose that] if we do grammatical or musical actions, we are grammarians or musicians, and, similarly, if we do just or temperate actions, we are thereby just or temperate.

§2 But surely actions are not enough, even in the case of crafts; for it is possible to produce a grammatical result by chance, or by following someone else's instructions. To be grammarians, then, we must both produce a grammatical result and produce it grammatically – that is to say, produce it in accord with the grammatical knowledge in us.

§3 Moreover, in any case, what is true of crafts is not true of virtues. For the products of a craft determine by their own qualities whether they have been produced well; and so it suffices that they have the right qualities when they have been produced. But for actions in accord with the virtues to be done temperately or justly it does not suffice that they themselves have the right qualities. Rather, the agent must also be in the right state when he does them. First, he must know [that he is doing virtuous actions]; second, he must decide on them, and decide on them for themselves; and, third, he must also do them from a firm and unchanging state.

As conditions for having a craft, these three do not count, except for the bare knowing. As a condition for having a virtue, however, the knowing counts for nothing, or [rather] for only a little, whereas the other two conditions are very important, indeed all-important. And we achieve these other two conditions by the frequent doing of just and temperate actions.

§4 Hence actions are called just or temperate when they are the sort that a just or temperate person would do. But the just and temperate person is not the one who [merely] does these actions, but the one who also does them in the way in which just or temperate people do them.

§5 It is right, then, to say that a person comes to be just from doing just actions and temperate from doing temperate actions; for no one has the least prospect of becoming good from failing to do them.

§6 The many, however, do not do these actions. They take refuge in arguments, thinking that they are doing philosophy, and that this is the way to become excellent people. They are like a sick person who listens attentively to the doctor, but acts on none of his instructions. Such a course of treatment will not improve the state of the sick person's body; nor will the many improve the state of their souls by this attitude to philosophy.

## 5 [Virtue of Character: Its Genus]

Next we must examine what virtue is. Since there are three conditions arising in the soul – feelings, capacities, and states – virtue must be one of these.

§2 By feelings I mean appetite, anger, fear, confidence, envy, joy, love, hate, longing, jealousy, pity, and in general whatever implies pleasure or pain. By capacities I mean what we have when we are said to be capable of these feelings – capable of being angry, for instance, or of being afraid or of feeling pity. By states I mean what we have when we are well or badly off in relation to feelings. If, for

SECTION I: THEORETICAL FOUNDATIONS

instance, our feeling is too intense or slack, we are badly off in relation to anger, but if it is intermediate, we are well off; the same is true in the other cases.

§3 First, then, neither virtues nor vices are feelings. For we are called excellent or base insofar as we have virtues or vices, not insofar as we have feelings. Further, we are neither praised nor blamed insofar as we have feelings; for we do not praise the angry or the frightened person, and do not blame the person who is simply angry, but only the person who is angry in a particular way. We are praised or blamed, however, insofar as we have virtues or vices. §4 Further, we are angry and afraid without decision; but the virtues are decisions of some kind, or [rather] require decision. Besides, insofar as we have feelings, we are said to be moved; but insofar as we have virtues or vices, we are said to be in some condition rather than moved.

§5 For these reasons the virtues are not capacities either; for we are neither called good nor called bad, nor are we praised or blamed, insofar as we are simply capable of feelings. Further, while we have capacities by nature, we do not become good or bad by nature; we have discussed this before.

§6 If, then, the virtues are neither feelings nor capacities, the remaining possibility is that they are states. And so we have said what the genus of virtue is.

6 [Virtue of Character: Its Differentia]

But we must say not only, as we already have, that it is a state, but also what sort of state it is.

§2 It should be said, then, that every virtue causes its possessors to be in a good state and to perform their functions well. The virtue of eyes, for instance, makes the eyes and their functioning excellent, because it makes us see well; and similarly, the virtue of a horse makes the horse excellent, and thereby good

at galloping, at carrying its rider, and at standing steady in the face of the enemy. §3 If this is true in every case, the virtue of a human being will likewise be the state that makes a human being good and makes him perform his function well.

§4 We have already said how this will be true, and it will also be evident from our next remarks, if we consider the sort of nature that virtue has.

In everything continuous and divisible we can take more, less, and equal, and each of them either in the object itself or relative to us; and the equal is some intermediate between excess and deficiency. §5 By the intermediate in the object I mean what is equidistant from each extremity; this is one and the same for all. But relative to us the intermediate is what is neither superfluous nor deficient; this is not one, and is not the same for all.

§6 If, for instance, ten are many and two are few, we take six as intermediate in the object, since it exceeds [two] and is exceeded [by ten] by an equal amount, [four]. §7 This is what is intermediate by numerical proportion. But that is not how we must take the intermediate that is relative to us. For if ten pounds [of food], for instance, are a lot for someone to eat, and two pounds a little, it does not follow that the trainer will prescribe six, since this might also be either a little or a lot for the person who is to take it – for Milo [the athlete] a little, but for the beginner in gymnastics a lot; and the same is true for running and wrestling. §8 In this way every scientific expert avoids excess and deficiency and seeks and chooses what is intermediate – but intermediate relative to us, not in the object.

§9 This, then, is how each science produces its product well, by focusing on what is intermediate and making the product conform to that. This, indeed, is why people regularly comment on well-made products that nothing could be added or subtracted; they assume that excess or deficiency ruins a good [result], whereas the mean preserves it. Good craftsmen also, we say, focus on what is intermediate when they produce their product. And since virtue, like nature, is better and more exact than any craft, it will also aim at what is intermediate.

§10 By virtue I mean virtue of character; for this is about feelings and actions, and these admit of excess, deficiency, and an intermediate condition. We can be afraid, for instance, or be confident, or have appetites, or get angry, or feel pity, and in general have pleasure or pain, both too much and too little, and in both ways not well. §11 But having these feelings at the right times, about the right things, toward the right people, for the right end, and in the right way, is the intermediate and best condition, and this is proper to virtue. §12 Similarly, actions also admit of excess, deficiency, and an intermediate condition.

Now virtue is about feelings and actions, in which excess and deficiency are in error and incur blame, whereas the intermediate condition is correct and wins praise, which are both proper to virtue. §13 Virtue, then, is a mean, insofar as it aims at what is intermediate.

§14 Moreover, there are many ways to be in error – for badness is proper to the indeterminate, as the Pythagoreans[2] pictured it, and good to the determinate. But there is only one way to be correct. That is why error is easy and correctness is difficult, since it is easy to miss the target and difficult to hit it. And so for this reason also excess and deficiency are proper to vice, the mean to virtue; "for we are noble in only one way, but bad in all sorts of ways."

§15 Virtue, then, is a state that decides, consisting in a mean, the mean relative to us, which is defined by reference to reason, that is to say, to the reason by reference to which the prudent person would define it. It is a mean between two vices, one of excess and one of deficiency.

§16 It is a mean for this reason also: Some vices miss what is right because they are deficient, others because they are excessive, in feelings or in actions, whereas virtue finds and chooses what is intermediate.

§17 That is why virtue, as far as its essence and the account stating what it is are concerned, is a mean, but, as far as the best [condition] and the good [result] are concerned, it is an extremity.

§18 Now not every action or feeling admits of the mean. For the names of some automatically include baseness – for instance, spite, shamelessness, envy [among feelings], and adultery, theft, murder, among actions. For all of these and similar things are called by these names because they themselves, not their excesses or deficiencies, are base. Hence in doing these things we can never be correct, but must invariably be in error. We cannot do them well or not well – by committing adultery, for instance, with the right woman at the right time in the right way. On the contrary, it is true without qualification that to do any of them is to be in error.

§19 [To think these admit of a mean], therefore, is like thinking that unjust or cowardly or intemperate action also admits of a mean, an excess and a deficiency. If it did, there would be a mean of excess, a mean of deficiency, an excess of excess and a deficiency of deficiency. §20 On the contrary, just as there is no excess or deficiency of temperance or of bravery (since the intermediate is a sort of extreme), so also there is no mean of these vicious actions either, but whatever way anyone does them, he is in error. For in general there is no mean of excess or of deficiency, and no excess or deficiency of a mean.

7 [The Particular Virtues of Character]

However, we must not only state this general account but also apply it to the particular cases. For among accounts concerning actions, though the general ones are common to more cases, the specific ones are truer, since actions are about particular cases, and our account must accord with these....

§2 First, then, in feelings of fear and confidence the mean is bravery. The excessively fearless person is nameless (indeed many cases are nameless), and the one who is excessively confident is rash. The one who is excessive in fear and deficient in confidence is cowardly.

§3 In pleasures and pains – though not in all types, and in pains less than in pleasures – the mean is temperance and the excess intemperance. People deficient in pleasure are not often found, which is why they also lack even a name; let us call them insensible.

§4 In giving and taking money the mean is generosity, the excess wastefulness and the deficiency ungenerosity. Here the vicious people have contrary excesses and defects; for the wasteful person is excessive in spending and deficient in taking, whereas the ungenerous person is excessive in taking and deficient in spending. §5 At the moment we are speaking in outline and summary, and that is enough; later we shall define these things more exactly.

§6 In questions of money there are also other conditions. Another mean is magnificence; for the magnificent person differs from the generous by being concerned with large matters, while the generous person is concerned with small. The excess is ostentation and vulgarity, and the deficiency is stinginess. These differ from the vices related to generosity in ways we shall describe later.

§7 In honor and dishonor the mean is magnanimity, the excess something called a sort of vanity, and the deficiency pusillanimity. §8 And just as we said that generosity differs from magnificence in its concern with small matters, similarly there is a virtue concerned with small honors, differing in the same way from magnanimity, which is concerned with great honors. For honor can be desired either in the right way or more or less than is right. If someone desires it to excess, he is called an honor-lover, and if his desire is deficient he is called indifferent to honor, but if he is intermediate he has no name. The corresponding conditions have no name either, except the condition of the honor-lover, which is called honor-loving.

This is why people at the extremes lay claim to the intermediate area. Moreover, we also sometimes call the intermediate person an honor-lover, and sometimes call him indifferent to honor; and sometimes we praise the honor-lover, sometimes the person indifferent to honor. §9 We will mention later the reason we do this; for the moment, let us speak of the other cases in the way we have laid down.

§10 Anger also admits of an excess, deficiency, and mean. These are all practically nameless; but since we call the intermediate person mild, let us call the mean mildness. Among the extreme people, let the excessive person be irascible, and his vice irascibility, and let the deficient person be a sort of inirascible person, and his deficiency inirascibility.

§11 There are also three other means, somewhat similar to one another, but different. For they are all concerned with common dealings in conversations and actions, but differ insofar as one is concerned with truth telling in these areas, the other two with sources of pleasure, some of which are found in amusement, and the others in daily life in general. Hence we should also discuss these states, so that we can better observe that in every case the mean is praiseworthy, whereas the extremes are neither praiseworthy nor correct, but blameworthy. Most of these cases are also nameless, and we must try, as in the other cases also, to supply names ourselves, to make things clear and easy to follow.

§12 In truth-telling, then, let us call the intermediate person truthful, and the mean truthfulness; pretense that overstates will be boastfulness, and the person who has it boastful; pretense that understates will be self-deprecation, and the person who has it self-deprecating.

§13 In sources of pleasure in amusements let us call the intermediate person witty, and the condition wit; the excess buffoonery and the person who has it a buffoon; and the deficient person a sort of boor and the state boorishness.

In the other sources of pleasure, those in daily life, let us call the person who is pleasant in the right way friendly, and the mean state friendliness. If someone goes to excess with no [ulterior] aim, he will be ingratiating; if he does it for his own advantage, a flatterer. The deficient person, unpleasant in everything, will be a sort of quarrelsome and ill-tempered person.

§14 There are also means in feelings and about feelings. Shame, for instance, is not a virtue, but the person prone to shame as well as [the virtuous people we have described] receives praise. For here also one person is called intermediate, and another – the person excessively prone to shame, who is ashamed about everything – is called excessive; the person who is deficient in shame or never feels shame at all is said to have no sense of disgrace; and the intermediate one is called prone to shame.

§15 Proper indignation is the mean between envy and spite; these conditions are concerned with pleasure and pain at what happens to our neighbors. For the properly indignant person feels pain when someone does well undeservedly; the envious person exceeds him by feeling pain when anyone does well, while the spiteful person is so deficient in feeling pain that he actually enjoys [other people's misfortunes].

§16 There will also be an opportunity elsewhere to speak of these. We must consider justice after these. Since it is spoken of

in more than one way, we shall distinguish its two types and say how each of them is a mean. Similarly, we must also consider the virtues that belong to reason.

8 [Relations between Mean and Extreme States]

Among these three conditions, then, two are vices – one of excess, one of deficiency – and one, the mean, is virtue. In a way, each of them is opposed to each of the others, since each extreme is contrary both to the intermediate condition and to the other extreme, while the intermediate is contrary to the extremes.

§2 For, just as the equal is greater in comparison to the smaller, and smaller in comparison to the greater, so also the intermediate states are excessive in comparison to the deficiencies and deficient in comparison to the excesses – both in feelings and in actions. For the brave person, for instance, appears rash in comparison to the coward, and cowardly in comparison to the rash person; the temperate person appears intemperate in comparison to the insensible person, and insensible in comparison with the intemperate person; and the generous person appears wasteful in comparison to the ungenerous, and ungenerous in comparison to the wasteful person. §3 That is why each of the extreme people tries to push the intermediate person to the other extreme, so that the coward, for instance, calls the brave person rash, and the rash person calls him a coward, and similarly in the other cases.

§4 Since these conditions of soul are opposed to each other in these ways, the extremes are more contrary to each other than to the intermediate. For they are further from each other than from the intermediate, just as the large is further from the small, and the small from the large, than either is from the equal.

§5 Further, sometimes one extreme – rashness or wastefulness, for instance – appears

27

somewhat like the intermediate state, bravery or generosity. But the extremes are most unlike one another; and the things that are furthest apart from each other are defined as contraries. And so the things that are further apart are more contrary.

§6 In some cases the deficiency, in others the excess, is more opposed to the intermediate condition. For instance, cowardice, the deficiency, not rashness, the excess, is more opposed to bravery, whereas intemperance, the excess, not insensibility, the deficiency, is more opposed to temperance.

§7 This happens for two reasons: One reason is derived from the object itself. Since sometimes one extreme is closer and more similar to the intermediate condition, we oppose the contrary extreme, more than this closer one, to the intermediate condition. Since rashness, for instance, seems to be closer and more similar to bravery, and cowardice less similar, we oppose cowardice, more than rashness, to bravery; for what is further from the intermediate condition seems to be more contrary to it. This, then, is one reason, derived from the object itself.

§8 The other reason is derived from ourselves. For when we ourselves have some natural tendency to one extreme more than to the other, this extreme appears more opposed to the intermediate condition. Since, for instance, we have more of a natural tendency to pleasure, we drift more easily toward intemperance than toward orderliness. Hence we say that an extreme is more contrary if we naturally develop more in that direction; and this is why intemperance is more contrary to temperance, since it is the excess [of pleasure].

9 [How Can We Reach the Mean?]

We have said enough, then, to show that virtue of character is a mean and what sort of mean it is; that it is a mean between two vices,

one of excess and one of deficiency; and that it is a mean because it aims at the intermediate condition in feelings and actions.

§2 That is why it is also hard work to be excellent. For in each case it is hard work to find the intermediate; for instance, not everyone, but only one who knows, finds the midpoint in a circle. So also getting angry, or giving and spending money, is easy and everyone can do it; but doing it to the right person, in the right amount, at the right time, for the right end, and in the right way is no longer easy, nor can everyone do it. Hence doing these things well is rare, praiseworthy, and fine.

§3 That is why anyone who aims at the intermediate condition must first of all steer clear of the more contrary extreme, following the advice that Calypso also gives: "Hold the ship outside the spray and surge."[3] For one extreme is more in error, the other less. §4 Since, therefore, it is hard to hit the intermediate extremely accurately, the second-best tack, as they say, is to take the lesser of the evils. We shall succeed best in this by the method we describe.

We must also examine what we ourselves drift into easily. For different people have different natural tendencies toward different goals, and we shall come to know our own tendencies from the pleasure or pain that arises in us. §5 We must drag ourselves off in the contrary direction; for if we pull far away from error, as they do in straightening bent wood, we shall reach the intermediate condition.

§6 And in everything we must beware above all of pleasure and its sources; for we are already biased in its favor when we come to judge it. Hence we must react to it as the elders reacted to Helen,[4] and on each occasion repeat what they said; for if we do this, and send it off, we shall be less in error.

§7 In summary, then, if we do these things we shall best be able to reach the intermediate condition. But presumably this is difficult, especially in particular cases, since it is not easy to define the way we should be angry, with whom, about what, for how long. For sometimes, indeed, we ourselves praise deficient people and call them mild, and sometimes praise quarrelsome people and call them manly.

§8 Still, we are not blamed if we deviate a little in excess or deficiency from doing well, but only if we deviate a long way, since then we are easily noticed. But how great and how serious a deviation receives blame is not easy to define in an account; for nothing else perceptible is easily defined either. Such things are among particulars, and the judgment depends on perception.

§9 This is enough, then, to make it clear that in every case the intermediate state is praised, but we must sometimes incline toward the excess, sometimes toward the deficiency; for that is the easiest way to hit the intermediate and good condition.

## Study Questions

1. Are humans naturally virtuous, according to Aristotle? What makes us virtuous? What is a virtue? What are some examples of virtue? Do you agree that these are good character traits to have? Do you think everyone would agree which traits are virtuous?

2. One of the major concerns about virtue ethics is that, because it takes the context of the situation into account (often considered a positive aspect of the theory), it doesn't really provide specific guidance about how to act ethically. What might be examples of situations in which virtue ethics can or cannot provide guidance? If there are cases in which it doesn't, does that indicate a weakness in the theory, or does it simply point to the complicated nature of ethical situations?

3. What is your understanding of what Aristotle means when he writes, "Actions, then, are called just and temperate when they are such as the just or temperate man would do; but it is not the man who does these that is just and temperate, but the man who also does them as just and temperate men do them"? Do you agree with his point here? Is it possible that the same action in the same situation could be virtuous if done by one person but not virtuous if done by another? What is an example to support your answer?

4. Do you agree that living a life of moderation would be a happy life?

## Notes

1 Heracleitus, or Heraclitus (c. 535–c. 475 BCE), was a pre-Socratic Greek philosopher.
2 Followers of the Greek philosopher and mathematician Pythagoras (c. 570–c. 490 BCE).
3 Calypso is a nymph in Homer's *Odyssey* (Book V). She detains Odysseus on her island for seven years before helping him build a boat and sending him on his way.
4 In Greek mythology, Helen, wife of king Menelaus of Sparta, was abducted by the Trojan prince Paris, which ultimately led to the Trojan War and the destruction of Troy by the Greeks. The elders are Oucalegaon and Antenor, mentioned in Homer's *Iliad* III.156–60.

## 2. Immanuel Kant, *Groundwork of the Metaphysics of Morals*

IN *GROUNDWORK OF THE* Metaphysics of Morals (1785), Immanuel Kant (1724–1804) describes his version of deontological ethics, which is now so famous that it is actually better known as Kantian ethics. Kant defines his ethical principle, the Categorical Imperative, as that which is good in and of itself, that is, without reference to anything else. For Kant, this means that if an action is such that we would want it to become a universal law, then that action is ethical. He further develops this rule into what he calls the "practical imperative," which states that we must always treat all people as an end and never as a means only. In other words, we must not use people; people should not be treated as a means to some other goal we have in mind, but they should be respected in and of themselves, as the rational creatures they are. These formulas can be employed to generate the duties we have. Because by definition he is focusing on actions that are ethical for everyone, he claims that these ethical determinations are objective, or absolute. Kant also emphasizes the role of good intentions in performing our duties. Since according to Kant we have control over our intentions for choosing an action but not over the consequences of our actions, he argues that we must be concerned with intentions when determining whether we are acting ethically.

### Section II

EVERYTHING IN NATURE WORKS according to laws. Rational beings alone have the capacity to act *in accordance with the representation* of laws – that is, according to principles, that is, have a *will*. Since the deduction of actions from principles requires *reason*, the will is nothing but practical reason. If reason infallibly determines the will, then the actions of such a being which are recognized as objectively necessary are subjectively necessary also, that is, the will is a capacity to choose *that only* which reason independent of inclination recognizes as practically necessary, that is, as good. But if reason of itself does not sufficiently determine the will, if the latter is subject also to subjective conditions (particular incentives) which do not always coincide with the objective conditions, in a word, if the will does not *in itself* completely accord with reason (which is actually the case with human beings), then the actions which objectively are recognized as necessary are subjectively contingent, and the determination of such a will according to objective laws is *necessitation*, that is to say, the relation of the objective laws to a will that is not thoroughly good is conceived as the determination of the will of a rational being by principles of reason, but which the will from its nature does not necessarily follow.

The conception of an objective principle, in so far as it is obligatory for a will, is called a command (of reason), and the formula of the command is called an **imperative**.

All imperatives are expressed through an *ought*, and thereby indicate the relation of an objective law of reason to a will which from its subjective constitution is not necessarily determined by it (a necessitation). They say that something would be good to do or to forbear, but they say it to a will which does not always do a thing because it is represented to be good to do it. That is *practically good*, however, which determines the will by means of the representations of reason, and consequently not from subjective causes, but objectively, that is, on principles which are valid for every rational being as such. It is distinguished from the agreeable as that which influences the will only by means of feeling from merely subjective causes, valid only for the senses of this or that one, and not as a principle of reason which holds for everyone.[1]

A perfectly good will would therefore be equally subject to objective laws (viz. laws of good), but could not be conceived as *necessitated* thereby to act lawfully, because of itself from its subjective constitution it can only be determined by the conception of good. Therefore no imperatives hold for the Divine will, or in general for a *holy* will; *ought* is here out of place because the volition is already of itself necessarily in unison with the law. Therefore imperatives are only formulae to express the relation of objective laws of all volition to the subjective imperfection of the will of this or that rational being, for example, a human will.

Now all imperatives command either *hypothetically* or *categorically*. The former represent the practical necessity of a possible action as means to something else that is willed (or at least which one might possibly will). The categorical imperative would be that which represented an action as necessary of itself without reference to another end, that is, as objectively necessary.

Since every practical law represents a possible action as good, and on this account, for a subject who is practically determinable by reason, as necessary, all imperatives are formulae determining an action which is necessary according to the principle of a will good in some respects. If now the action is good only as a means *to something else*, then the imperative is *hypothetical*; if it is conceived as good *in itself* and consequently as being necessarily the principle of a will which of itself conforms to reason, then it is *categorical*.

Thus the imperative declares what action possible by me would be good, and presents the practical rule in relation to a will which does not forthwith perform an action simply because it is good, whether because the subject does not always know that it is good, or because, even if it know this, yet its maxims might be opposed to the objective principles of practical reason.

Accordingly the hypothetical imperative only says that the action is good for some purpose, *possible* or *actual*. In the first case, it is a **problematic**, in the second an **assertoric**, practical principle. The categorical imperative which declares an action to be objectively necessary in itself without reference to any purpose, without any other end, is valid as an **apodictic** (practical) principle.

Whatever is possible only by the power of some rational being may also be conceived as a possible purpose of some will; and therefore the principles of action as regards the means necessary to attain some possible purpose are in fact infinitely numerous. All sciences have a practical part consisting of problems expressing that some end is possible for us, and of imperatives directing how it may be attained. These may, therefore, be called in general imperatives of **skill**. Here there is no question whether the end is rational and good, but only what one must do in order to attain it. The precepts for the physician to make his patient thoroughly healthy, and for a poisoner to ensure certain death, are of equal value in this respect, that each serves to effect its purpose perfectly. Since in early youth it cannot be known what ends are likely to occur to us in the course of life, parents seek to have their children taught a *great many things*, and provide for their *skill* in the use of means for all sorts of *discretionary* ends, of none of which can they determine whether it may not perhaps hereafter be an object to their pupil, but which it is at all events *possible* that he might aim at; and this anxiety is so great that they commonly neglect to form and correct their children's judgment of the value of the things which may be chosen as ends.

There is *one* end, however, which may be assumed to be actually such to all rational beings (so far as imperatives apply to them, viz. as dependent beings), and therefore, one purpose which they not merely *may* have, but which we may with certainty assume that they all actually *do have* by a natural necessity, and this is *happiness*. The hypothetical imperative which expresses the practical necessity of an action as means to the advancement of happiness is *assertoric*. We are not to present it as necessary for an uncertain and merely possible purpose, but for a purpose which we may presuppose with certainty and *a priori* in every human being, because it belongs to his being. Now skill in the choice of means to his own greatest well-being may be called *prudence*,[2] in the narrowest sense. And thus the imperative which refers to the choice of means to one's own happiness, that is, the precept of prudence, is still always *hypothetical*; the action is not commanded absolutely, but only as means to another purpose.

Finally, there is an imperative which commands a certain conduct immediately, without having as its condition any other purpose to be attained by it. This imperative is **categorical**. It concerns not the matter of the action, or its intended result, but its form and the principle of which it is itself a result; and what is essentially good in it consists in the mental disposition, let the consequence be what it may. This imperative may be called that of **morality**.

There is a marked distinction also between the volitions on these three sorts of principles in the *dissimilarity* of the necessitation of the will. In order to mark this difference more clearly, I think they would be most suitably named in their order if we said they are either *rules* of skill, or *counsels* of prudence, or *commands* (*laws*) of morality. For it is law only that involves the concept of an *unconditional* and objective necessity, which is consequently universally valid; and commands are laws which must be obeyed, that is, must be followed, even in opposition to inclination. *Counsels*, indeed, involve necessity, but one which can only hold under a contingent subjective condition, viz., they depend on whether this or that human being counts this or that as part of his happiness; the categorical imperative, on the contrary, is not limited by any condition, and as being absolutely, although practically, necessary may be quite properly called a command. We might also call the first kind of imperatives *technical* (belonging to art), the second *pragmatic*[3] (belonging to welfare), and the third *moral* (belonging to free conduct as such, that is, to morals).

Now arises the questions, how are all these imperatives possible? This question does not seek to know how we can conceive the performance of the action which the imperative ordains, but merely how we can conceive the necessitation of the will which the imperative expresses. No special explanation is needed to show how an imperative of skill is possible. Whoever wills the end wills also (so far as reason has decisive influence on his action) the means in his power which are indispensably necessary to it. This proposition is, as regards the volition, analytic; for in willing an object as my effect there is already thought the causality of myself as an acting cause, that is to say, the use of the means; and the imperative educes from the concept of a volition of an end the concept of actions necessary to this end. Synthetic propositions must no doubt be employed in defining the means to a proposed end; but they do not concern the principle, the act of the will, but the object and its real-ization.[4] For example, that in order to bisect a line on an unerring principle I must draw from its extremities two intersecting arcs; this no doubt is taught by mathematics only in synthetic propositions; but if I know that it is only by this process that the intended op-eration can be performed, then to say that if I fully will the operation, I also will the action required for it, is an analytic proposition; for it is one and the same thing to represent some-thing as an effect which I can produce in a certain way, and to represent myself as acting in this way.

If it were only equally easy to give a defi-nite conception of happiness, the imperatives of prudence would correspond exactly with those of skill, and would likewise be analytic. For in this case as in that, it could be said whoever wills the end wills also (necessarily in accordance with reason) the indispensable means thereto which are in his power. But, unfortunately, the notion of happiness is so indeterminate that although every human being wishes to attain it, yet he never can say definitely and consistently what it is that he really wishes and wills. The reason for this is that all the elements which belong to the concept of happiness are altogether empirical, that is, they must be borrowed from experi-ence, and nevertheless the idea of happiness requires an absolute whole, a maximum of welfare in my present and all future cir-cumstances. Now it is impossible that the most clear-sighted and at the same time most powerful being (supposed finite) should frame for himself a definite conception of what he really wills in this. If he wills riches, how much anxiety, envy, and snares might he not thereby draw upon his shoulders? If he wills knowledge and discernment, perhaps it might prove to be only an eye so much sharper to show him so much the more fearfully the evils that are now concealed from him and that

cannot be avoided, or to impose more wants on his desires, which already give him con-cern enough. Would he have long life? Who guarantees to him that it would not be a long misery? Would he at least have health? How often has uneasiness of the body restrained from excesses into which perfect health would have allowed one to fall, and so on? In short, he is unable, on any principle, to determine with certainty what would make him truly happy; because to do so he would need to be omniscient. We cannot therefore act on any definite principles to secure happiness, but only on empirical counsels, for example, of regimen, frugality, courtesy, reserve, etc., which experience teaches do, on the average, most promote well-being. Hence it follows that the imperatives of prudence do not, strictly speaking, command at all, that is, they cannot present actions objectively as practical-ly *necessary*; that they are rather to be regarded as counsels (*consilia*) than precepts (*praecepta*) of reason, that the problem to determine certainly and universally what action would promote the happiness of a rational being is completely insoluble, and consequently no imperative respecting it is possible which would, in the strict sense, command him to do what makes him happy; because happiness is not an ideal of reason but of imagination, resting solely on empirical grounds, and it is vain to expect that these should determine an action by which one could attain the total-ity of a series of consequences which is really endless. This imperative of prudence would, however, be an analytic proposition if we as-sume that the means to happiness could be certainly assigned; for it is distinguished from the imperative of skill only by this, that in the latter the end is merely *possible*, in the former it is *given*; as, however, both only ordain the means to that which we suppose to be willed as an end, it follows that the imperative which ordains the willing of the means to him who wills the end is in both cases analytic. Thus there is no difficulty in regard to the possibility of an imperative of this kind either.

On the other hand, the question, how the imperative of *morality* is possible, is undoubtedly one, the only one, demanding a solution, as this is not at all hypothetical, and the objective necessity which it presents cannot rest on any hypothesis, as is the case with the hypothetical imperatives. Only here we must never leave out of consideration that we *cannot* make out *by means of any example*, in other words, empirically, whether there is such an imperative at all; but it is rather to be feared that all those which seem to be categorical may yet be at bottom hypothetical. For instance, when the precept is: "You ought not to promise deceitfully," and it is assumed that the necessity of this is not a mere counsel to avoid some other ill, so that it should mean: "You shall not make a lying promise, lest if it become known you should destroy your credit," but that an action of this kind must be regarded as evil in itself, so that the imperative of the prohibition is categorical; then we cannot show with certainty in any example that the will was determined merely by the law, without any other incentives, although it may appear to be so. For it is always possible that fear of disgrace, perhaps also obscure dread of other dangers, may have a secret influence on the will. Who can prove by experience the non-existence of a cause when all that experience tells us is that we do not perceive it? But in such a case the so-called moral imperative, which as such appears to be categorical and unconditional, would in reality be only a pragmatic precept, drawing our attention to our own interests, and merely teaching us to take these into consideration.

We will therefore have to investigate *a priori* the possibility of a *categorical* imperative, as we have not in this case the advantage of its reality being given in experience, so that

[the elucidation of] its possibility should be requisite only for its explanation, not for its establishment. In the meantime it may be discerned beforehand that the categorical imperative alone has the purport of a practical law; and the rest may indeed be called *principles* of the will but not laws, since whatever is only necessary for the attainment of some discretionary purpose may be considered as in itself contingent, and we can at any time be free from the precept if we give up the purpose; on the contrary, the unconditional command leaves the will no liberty to choose the opposite, consequently it alone carries with it that necessity which we require of a law.

Secondly, in the case of this categorical imperative or law of morality, the difficulty (of describing its possibility) is a very profound one. It is an *a priori* synthetic practical proposition;[5] and as there is so much difficulty in discerning the possibility of speculative propositions of this kind, it may readily be supposed that the difficulty will be no less with the practical.

In this problem we will first inquire whether the mere concept of a categorical imperative may not perhaps supply us also with the formula of it, containing the proposition which alone can be a categorical imperative; for even if we know the tenor of such an absolute command, yet how it is possible will require further special and laborious study, which we postpone to the last section.[6]

When I conceive a hypothetical imperative, in general I do not know beforehand what it will contain until I am given the condition. But when I conceive a categorical imperative, I know at once what it contains. For as the imperative contains besides the law only the necessity that the maxims[7] shall conform to this law, while the law contains no conditions restricting it, there remains nothing but the general statement that the maxim of the action should conform to universal law, and it is this conformity alone that the imperative properly represents as necessary.

There is therefore but one categorical imperative, namely, this: *Act only on that maxim whereby you can at the same time will that it become a universal law.*[8]

Now if all imperatives of duty can be deduced from this one imperative as their principle, then, although it should remain undecided whether what is called duty is not merely a vain notion, yet at least we shall be able to show what we understand by it and what this notion means.

Since the universality of the law according to which effects are produced constitutes what is properly called *nature* in the most general sense (as to form) – that is, the existence of things so far as it is determined by general laws – the imperative of duty may be expressed thus: *Act as if the maxim of your action were to become by your will a **universal law of nature**.*

We will now enumerate a few duties, adopting the usual division of them into duties to ourselves and duties to others, and into perfect and imperfect duties.[9]

1. Someone reduced to despair by a series of misfortunes feels wearied of life, but is still so far in possession of his reason that he can ask himself whether it would not be contrary to his duty to himself take his own life. Now he inquires whether the maxim of his action could become a universal law of nature. His maxim is: From self love I adopt it as my principle to shorten my life when its longer duration is likely to bring more ill than satisfaction. It is asked then simply whether this principle founded on self-love can become a universal law of nature. Now we can see at once that a system of nature of which it should be a law to destroy life by means of the very feeling whose vocation it is to impel to the improvement of life would contradict itself, and therefore could not exist as a system of nature; hence that maxim cannot possibly

exist as a universal law of nature, and consequently would be wholly inconsistent with the supreme principle of all duty.

2. Another finds himself forced by necessity to borrow money. He knows that he will not be able to repay it, but sees also that nothing will be lent to him unless he promises firmly to repay it within in a determinate time. He wants to make this promise, but he has still so much conscience as to ask himself: Is it not unlawful and inconsistent with duty to get out of a difficulty this way? Suppose, however, that he resolves to do so, then the maxim of his action would be expressed thus: When I think myself in want of money, I will borrow money and promise to repay it, although I know that I never can do so. Now this principle of self-love or of one's own advantage may perhaps be consistent with my whole future welfare; but the question now is, Is it right? I change then the suggestion of self-love into a universal law, and state the question thus: How would it be if my maxim were a universal law? Then I see at once that it could never hold as a universal law of nature, but would necessarily contradict itself. For supposing it to be a universal law that everyone when he thinks himself in a difficulty should be able to promise whatever he pleases, with the purpose of not keeping his promise, the promise itself would become impossible, as well as the end that he might have in view in it, since no one would consider that anything was promised to him, but would ridicule all such statements as vain pretenses.

3. A third finds in himself a talent which with the help of some culture might make him a useful human being in many respects. But he finds himself in comfortable circumstances and prefers to indulge in pleasure rather than to take pain in enlarging and improving his fortunate natural predispositions. He asks, however, whether his maxim of neglect of his natural gifts, besides agreeing with

his inclination to indulgence, agrees also with what is called duty. He sees then that a system of nature could indeed subsist with such a universal law, although human beings (like the South Sea islanders) should let their talents rust and resolve to devote their lives merely to idleness, amusement, and propagation of their species – in a word, to enjoyment; but he cannot possibly **will** that this should be a universal law of nature, or be implanted in us as such by a natural instinct. For as a rational being, he necessarily wills that his faculties be developed, since they serve him, and have been given him, for all sorts of purposes.

4. Yet a fourth, who is in prosperity, while he sees that others have to contend with great wretchedness and that he could help them, thinks: What concern is it of mine? Let everyone be as happy as heaven pleases, or as he can make himself; I will take nothing from him nor even envy him, only I do not wish to contribute anything to his welfare or to his assistance in need! Now no doubt, if such a mode of thinking were a universal law, the human race might very well subsist, and doubtless even better than in a state in which everyone talks of sympathy and good-will, or even takes care occasionally to put it into practice, but, on the other side, also cheats when he can, betrays the rights of human beings, or otherwise violates them. But although it is possible that a universal law of nature might exist in accordance with that maxim, it is impossible to **will** that such a principle should have the universal validity of a law of nature. For a will which resolved this would contradict itself, inasmuch as many cases might occur in which one would have need of the love and sympathy of others, and in which, by such a law of nature, sprung from his own will, he would deprive himself of all hope of the aid he desires.

These are a few of the many actual duties, or at least what we regard as such, which

obviously fall into two classes on the one principle that we have laid down. We must *be able to will* that a maxim of our action should be a universal law. This is the canon of the moral judgment of the action generally. Some actions are of such a character that their maxim cannot without contradiction be even *conceived* as a universal law of nature, far from it being possible that we should *will* that it *should* be so. In others, this intrinsic impossibility is not found, but still it is impossible to *will* that their maxim should be raised to the universality of a law of nature, since such a will would contradict itself. It is easily seen that the former violate strict or rigorous (inflexible) duty; the latter only wide (meritorious) duty. Thus it has been completely shown by these examples how all duties depend as regards the nature of the obligation (not the object of the action) on the same principle.

If now we attend to ourselves on occasion of any transgression of duty, we will find that we in fact do not will that our maxim should be a universal law, for that is impossible for us; on the contrary, we will that the opposite should remain a universal law, only we assume the liberty of making an *exception* in our own favor or (just for this time only) in favor of our inclination. Consequently, if we considered all cases from one and the same point of view, namely, that of reason, we should find a contradiction in our own will, namely, that a certain principle should be objectively necessary as a universal law, and yet subjectively should not be universal, but admit of exceptions. As, however, we at one moment regard our action from the point of view of a will wholly conformed to reason, and then again look at the same action from the point of view of a will affected by inclination, there is not really any contradiction, but an opposition (*antagonismus*) of inclination to the precept of reason, whereby the universality (*universalitas*) of the principle is changed into a mere generality (*generalitas*), so that the practical principle of reason shall meet the maxim half way. Now, although this cannot be justified in our own impartial judgment, yet it proves that we do really recognize the validity of the categorical imperative and (with all respect for it) only allow ourselves a few exceptions which we think unimportant and forced upon us.

We have thus established at least this much – that if duty is a conception which is to have any import and real legislative authority for our actions, it can only be expressed in categorical, and not at all in hypothetical, imperatives. We have also, which is of great importance, exhibited clearly and definitely for every practical application the content of the categorical imperative, which must contain the principle of all duty if there is such a thing at all. We have not yet, however, advanced so far as to prove *a priori* that there actually is such an imperative, that there is a practical law which commands absolutely of itself and without any other incentive, and that the following of this law is duty.

With the view of attaining to this it is of extreme importance to remember that we must not allow ourselves to think of deducing the reality of this principle from the *particular attributes of human nature*. For duty is to be a practical, unconditional necessity of action; it must therefore hold for all rational beings (to whom an imperative can apply at all), and *for this reason only* be also a law for all human wills. On the contrary, whatever is deduced from the particular natural characteristics of humanity, from certain feelings and propensities, or even, if possible, from any particular tendency proper to human reason, and which need not necessarily hold for the will of every rational being – this may indeed supply us with a maxim but not with a law; with a subjective principle on which we may have a propensity and inclination to act, but not with an objective principle on which we

should be *enjoined* to act, even though all our propensities, inclinations, and natural dispositions were opposed to it. In fact, the sublimity and intrinsic dignity of the command in duty are so much the more evident, the less the subjective impulses favor it and the more they oppose it, without being able in the slightest degree to weaken the obligation of the law or to diminish its validity.

Here then we see philosophy brought to a critical position, since it has to be firmly fixed, notwithstanding that it has nothing to support it in heaven or on earth. Here it must show its purity as absolute director of its own laws, not the herald of those which are whispered to it by an implanted sense or who knows what tutelary nature. Although these may be better than nothing, yet they can never afford principles dictated by reason, which must have their source wholly *a priori* and, at the same time, their commanding authority from this, expecting everything from the supremacy of the law and the due respect for it, nothing from inclination, or else condemning the human being to self-contempt and inward abhorrence.

Thus every empirical element is not only quite incapable of being an aid to the principle of morality, but is even highly prejudicial to the purity of morals; for the proper and inestimable worth of an absolutely good will consists just in this, that the principle of action is free from all influence of contingent grounds, which alone experience can furnish. We cannot too much or too often repeat our warning against this lax and even mean habit of thought which seeks for its principle among empirical motives and laws; for human reason in its weariness is glad to rest on this pillow, and in a dream of sweet illusions (in which, instead of Juno, it embraces a cloud) it substitutes for morality a bastard patched up from limbs of various derivation, which looks like anything one chooses to see in it; only not like virtue to one who has once beheld her in her true form.[10]

The question then is this: Is it a necessary law *for all rational beings* that they should always judge their actions by maxims of which they can themselves will that they should serve as universal laws? If there is such a law, then it must be connected (altogether a priori) with the very concept of the will of a rational being as such. But in order to discover this connection we must, however reluctantly, take a step into metaphysics, although into a domain of it which is distinct from speculative philosophy – namely, the metaphysics of morals. In a practical philosophy, where it is not the grounds of what *happens* that we have to ascertain, but the laws of what *ought to happen*, even though it never does, that is, objective practical laws, there it is not necessary to inquire into the grounds why anything pleases or displeases, how the pleasure of mere sensation differs from taste, and whether the latter is distinct from a general satisfaction of reason; on what the feeling of pleasure or pain rests, and how from it desires and inclinations arise, and from these again maxims by the cooperation of reason; for all this belongs to an empirical psychology, which would constitute the second part of the doctrine of nature, if we regard physics as the *philosophy of nature*, so far as it is based *on empirical laws*. But there we are concerned with objective practical laws, and consequently with the relation of the will to itself so far as it is determined by reason alone, in which case whatever has reference to anything empirical is necessarily excluded; since if *reason of itself alone* determines the conduct (and it is the possibility of this that we are now investigating), it must necessarily do so a priori.

The will is conceived as a capacity of determining itself to action in accordance with the *representation of certain laws*. And such a capacity can be found only in rational beings. Now that which serves the will as the objective

ground of its self-determination is the *end*, and if this is assigned by reason alone, it must hold for all rational beings. On the other hand, that which merely contains the ground of possibility of the action of which the effect is the end, this is called the *means*. The subjective ground of the desire is the *incentive*, the objective ground of the volition is the *motive*; hence the distinction between subjective ends which rest on incentives, and objective ends which depend on motives valid for every rational being. Practical principles are *formal* when they abstract from all subjective ends; they are *material* when they assume these, and therefore particular incentives. The ends which a rational being proposes to himself at pleasure as *effects* of his actions (material ends) are all only relative, for it is only their relation to the particular desires of the subject that gives them their worth, which therefore cannot furnish principles universal and necessary for all rational beings and for every volition, that is to say, practical laws. Hence all these relative ends can give rise only to hypothetical imperatives.

Supposing, however, that there were something *whose existence* has *in itself* an absolute worth, something which, being *an end in itself*, could be a source of definite laws, then in this and this alone would lie the source of a possible categorical imperative, that is, a practical law.

Now I say: the human being and in general every rational being exists as an end in itself, *not merely as a means* to be arbitrarily used by this or that will, but in all his actions, whether they concern himself or other rational beings, must be always regarded at the same time as an end. All objects of the inclinations have only a conditional worth; for if the inclinations and the needs founded on them did not exist, then their object would be without any value. But the inclinations themselves, being sources of needs, are so far from having an absolute worth for which they should be desired that, on the contrary, it must be the universal wish of every rational being to be wholly free from them. Thus the worth of any object which is *to be acquired* by our action is always conditional. Beings whose existence depends not on our will but on nature's, have nevertheless, if they are nonrational beings, only a relative value as means, and are therefore called *things*; rational beings, on the contrary, are called *persons*, because their very nature restricts all choice (and is an object of respect).[11] These, therefore, are not merely subjective ends whose existence has a worth *for us* as an effect of our action, but *objective ends*, that is, things whose existence is an end in itself – an end, moreover, for which no other can be substituted, to which they should serve *merely* as means, for otherwise nothing whatever would possess *absolute worth*; but if all worth were conditioned and therefore contingent, then there would be no supreme practical principle of reason whatever.

If then there is a supreme practical principle or, with respect to the human will, a categorical imperative, it must be one which, being drawn from the conception of that which is necessarily an end for everyone because it is *an end in itself*, constitutes an *objective* principle of will, and can therefore serve as a universal practical law. The foundation of this principle is: *rational nature exists as an end in itself*. The human being necessarily conceives of his own existence as being so; so far then this is a *subjective* principle of human actions. But every other rational being regards its existence similarly, just on the same rational principle that holds for me;[12] so that it is at the same time an objective principle from which as a supreme practical law all laws of the will must be capable of being deduced. Accordingly the practical imperative will be as follows: *So act as to treat humanity, whether in your own person or in that of any other, in every case at the same time as an end, never as a means only.*[13] We will now inquire whether this can be practically carried out.

To abide by the previous examples:

*First*, under the head of necessary duty to oneself: Someone who contemplates suicide should ask himself whether his action can be consistent with the idea of humanity *as an end in itself*. If he destroys himself in order to escape from painful circumstances, he uses a person merely as a *means* to maintain a tolerable condition up to the end of life. But a human being is not a thing, that is to say, something which can be used merely as a means, but must in all his actions be always considered as an end in itself. I cannot, therefore, dispose in any way of a human being in my own person by mutilating, damaging, or killing him. (It belongs to morals proper to define this principle more precisely, so as to avoid all misunderstanding, for example, as to the amputation of the limbs in order to preserve myself; as to exposing my life to danger with a view to preserve it, etc. This question is therefore omitted here.)[14]

*Second*, as regards necessary duties, or those of strict obligation, towards others: He who is thinking of making a lying promise to others will see at once that he would be using another human being *merely as a means*, without the latter at the same time containing in himself the end. For he whom I propose by such a promise to use for my own purposes cannot possibly assent to my mode of acting toward him, and therefore cannot himself contain the end of this action. This violation of the principle of humanity in other human beings is more obvious if we take in examples of attacks on the freedom and property of others. For then it is clear that he who transgresses the rights of human beings intends to use the person of others merely as means, without considering that as rational beings they ought always to be esteemed also as ends, that is, as beings who must be capable of containing in themselves the end of the very same action.[15]

*Third*, as regards contingent (meritorious) duties to oneself: It is not enough that the action does not violate humanity in our own person as an end in itself, it must also *harmonize with* it. Now there are in humanity capacities of greater perfection which belong to the end that nature has in view with regard to humanity in ourselves as the subject; to neglect these might perhaps be consistent with the *maintenance* of humanity as an end in itself, but not with the *advancement* of this end.

*Fourth*, as regards meritorious duties toward others: The natural end which all human beings have is their own happiness. Now humanity might indeed subsist although no one should contribute anything to the happiness of others, provided he did not intentionally withdraw anything from it; but after all, this would only harmonize negatively, not positively, with *humanity as an end in itself*, if everyone does not also endeavor, as far as he can, to forward the ends of others. For the ends of any subject which is an end in itself ought as far as possible to be *my* ends also, if that conception is to have its *full* effect in me.

This principle that humanity and generally every rational nature is *an end in itself* (which is the supreme limiting condition of every human being's freedom of action), is not borrowed from experience, *first*, because it is universal, applying as it does to all rational beings whatever, and experience is not capable of determining anything about them; *second*, because it does not present humanity as an end to human beings (subjectively), that is, as an object which human beings do of themselves actually adopt as an end; but as an objective end which must as a law constitute the supreme limiting condition of all our subjective ends, let them be what they will; it must therefore spring from pure reason. In fact the ground of all practical legislation lies (according to the first principle) *objectively in the rule* and its form of universality which makes it capable of being a law (say, for example, a law of nature); but *subjectively* in the *end*; now by the second principle, the subject of all ends is each rational being inasmuch as it is an end in itself. From this follows the third practical principle of the will, which is the ultimate condition of its harmony with the universal practical reason, viz., the idea of *the will of every rational being as a will giving universal law*.[16]

On this principle all maxims are rejected which are inconsistent with the will being itself universal legislator. Thus the will is not merely subject to the law, but subject to it so that it must be regarded *as itself giving the law*, and on this ground only subject to the law (of which it can regard itself as the author).

## Study Questions

1. What does Kant mean by a "categorical imperative"? Do you agree that there are some actions that are unethical universally? What are the benefits to disregarding the context of an action when evaluating whether it is ethical?

2. What is Kant's argument against suicide? Is this a compelling argument? Do you think there could ever be cases in which committing suicide would be ethical? Do we have a duty to maintain our own lives?

3. Do you think that Kant's principle that we should never use other people is a good place to start an ethical theory?

## Notes

1  [Kant's note:] The dependence of the faculty of desire on sensations is called inclination, and this accordingly always indicates a *need*. The dependence of a contingently determinable will on principles of reason is called an *interest*. This, therefore, is found only in the case of a dependent will which does not always of itself conform to reason; in the Divine will we cannot conceive any interest. But the human will can also *take an interest* in a thing without therefore acting *from interest*. The former signifies the *practical* interest in the action, the latter the *pathological* interest in the object of the action. The former indicates only dependence on principles of reason for the sake of inclination, reason supplying only the practical rules how the requirement of the inclination may be satisfied. In the first case the action interests me; in the second the object of the action (because it is pleasant to me). We have seen in the first section that in an action done from duty we must look not to the interest in the object, but only to that in the action itself, and in its rational principle (viz., the law).

2  [Kant's note:] The word *prudence* is taken in two senses: in the one it may bear the name of knowledge of the world, in the other that of private prudence. The former is a human being's ability to influence others so as to use them for his own purposes. The latter is the sagacity to combine all these purposes for his own lasting benefit. This latter is properly that to which the value even of the former is reduced, and when someone is prudent in the former sense but not in the latter, we might better say of him that he is clever and cunning, but, on the whole, imprudent.

3  [Kant's note:] It seems to me that the proper signification of the word *pragmatic* may be most accurately defined this way. For *sanctions* are called pragmatic which flow properly, not from the law of the states as necessary enactments, but from *precaution* for the general welfare. A history is composed pragmatically when it teaches *prudence*, that is, instructs the world how it can provide for its interests better, or at least as well as the human beings of former time.

4  As Kant here implies, analytic propositions state a subject-predicate relationship in which the predicate is already contained in the thought of the subject, and (at most) needs to be drawn out through analysis; synthetic propositions add something new to the subject – something not already contained in its concept.

5  [Kant's note:] I connect the act with the will without presupposing any condition resulting from any inclination, but *a priori*, and therefore necessarily (though only objectively, that is, assuming the idea of a reason possessing full power over all subjective motives). This is accordingly a practical proposition which does not deduce the willing of an action by mere analysis from another already presupposed (for we have not such a perfect will), but connects it immediately with the conception of the will of a rational being, as something not contained in it.

6  Kant now shifts his focus to the content of a categorical imperative, suspending the discussion of how a categorical imperative is possible.

7  [Kant's note:] A *maxim* is a subjective principle of action, and must be distinguished from the *objective principle*, namely, the practical law. The former contains the practical rule set by reason according to the conditions of the subject (often its ignorance or its inclinations), so that it is the principle on which the subject acts; but the law is the objective principle valid for every rational being, and is the principle on which it *ought to act* – that is, an imperative.

8  This formulation of the categorical imperative, the "formula of universal law" (along with its variant, the "formula of the law of nature") has been a primary target for criticism.

9  [Kant's note:] It must be noted here that I reserve the division of duties for a future *metaphysics of morals*; so that I give it here only as an arbitrary one (in order to arrange my examples). For the rest, I understand by a perfect duty one that admits no exception in favor of inclination,

and then I have not merely external but also internal perfect duties. This is contrary to the use of the word adopted in the schools; but I do not intend to justify it here, as it is all one for my purpose whether it is admitted or not.

10 [Kant's note:] To behold virtue in her proper form is nothing else but to contemplate morality stripped of all admixture or sensible things and of every spurious ornament of reward or self-love. How much she then eclipses everything else that appears charming to the affections, every one may readily perceive with the least exertion of his reason, if his reason is not wholly spoiled for abstraction.

11 This passage makes explicit Kant's view that nonrational animals lack the dignity that Kant attributes to persons, and thus cannot be owed respect or consequent duties. For Kant's account of our duties regarding animals, and his rationale for them, see *Metaphysics of Morals* 6:433.

12 [Kant's note:] This proposition is here stated as a postulate. The ground of it will be found in the concluding section.

13 This formulation, the "formula of humanity," is criticized by [German philosopher Johann Gottlieb] Fichte [1762–1814]. Note the similarities between this formulation and the "supreme principle of the doctrine of virtue" in *Metaphysics of Morals* 6:395. The latter principle also contains traces of the formula of universal law.

14 See *Metaphysics of Morals* 6:422–44 for Kant's promised, fuller exposition of this duty.

15 [Kant's note:] Let it not be thought that the common: *quod tibi non vis fieri, etc.*, [i.e., what you do not want others to do to you, do not do to them] could serve here as the rule or principle. For it is only a deduction from the former, though with several limitations; it cannot be a universal law, for it does not contain the principle of duties to oneself, nor of the duties of benevolence to others (for many a one would gladly consent that others should not benefit him, provided only that he might be excused from showing benevolence to them), nor finally that of duties of strict obligation to one another, for on this principle the criminal might argue against the judge who punishes him, and so on.

16 This is called the "formula of autonomy."

# 3. W.D. Ross, "What Makes Right Action Right?"

ONE OF THE CONCERNS frequently mentioned when examining Kantian ethics stems from Kant's insistence that certain duties are always required. The problem is that it appears that duties sometimes conflict with each other. For example, according to Kant I have a duty not to lie, but I also have a duty to refrain from harming innocent others. There do appear to be circumstances, such as if a terrorist were asking me where my friend (whom they want to kill) is, and I knew where she was at that moment, in which fulfilling one duty would require not fulfilling another duty. Rejecting the idea that duties never conflict, Scottish philosopher W.D. Ross (1877–1971) develops the idea of *prima facie* duties in his well-known work *The Right and the Good* (1930). *Prima facie* duties are those that we must fulfill, unless there are compelling reasons not to do so. Ross offers a provisional list of these duties, including duties of fidelity (not lying, keeping promises, etc.), reparation, gratitude, justice, beneficence (actively seeking to help others), self-improvement, and non-maleficence (avoiding harming others). He makes no claim to a universal principle, and in this way he sets himself apart from both Kantian ethics and utilitarianism, but rather states that his list is based on reflection of what we generally consider to be ethical. We must navigate through these duties, giving sufficient weight to each as is fitting for the circumstances in which we find ourselves.

---

THE REAL POINT AT issue between hedonism and utilitarianism on the one hand and their opponents on the other is not whether "right" means "productive of so and so"; for it cannot with any plausibility be maintained that it does. The point at issue is that to which we now pass, viz. whether there is any general character which makes right acts right, and if so, what it is. Among the main historical attempts to state a single characteristic of all right actions which is the foundation of their rightness are those made by egoism and utilitarianism. But I do not propose to discuss these, not because the subject is unimportant, but because it has been dealt with so often and so well already, and because there has come to be so much agreement among moral philosophers that neither of these theories is satisfactory. A much more attractive theory has been put forward by Professor [G.E.] Moore [1873–1958]: that what makes actions right is that they are productive of more *good* than could have been produced by any other action open to the agent.[1]

This theory is in fact the culmination of all the attempts to base rightness on productivity of some sort of result. The first form this attempt takes is the attempt to base rightness on conduciveness to the advantage or pleasure of the agent. This theory comes to grief over the fact, which stares us in the face, that a great part of duty consists in an observance of the rights and a furtherance of the interests of others, whatever the cost to ourselves may be. Plato and others may be right in holding that a regard for the rights of others never in the long run involves a loss of happiness for the agent, that "the just life profits a man." But this, even if true, is irrelevant to the rightness of the act. As soon as a man does an action *because* he thinks he will promote his own interests thereby, he is acting not from a sense of its rightness but from self-interest.

SECTION I: THEORETICAL FOUNDATIONS

To the egoistic theory hedonistic utilitarianism supplies a much-needed amendment. It points out correctly that the fact that a certain pleasure will be enjoyed by the agent is no reason why he *ought* to bring it into being rather than an equal or greater pleasure to be enjoyed by another, though, human nature being what it is, it makes it not unlikely that he *will* try to bring it into being. But hedonistic utilitarianism in its turn needs a correction. On reflection it seems clear that pleasure is not the only thing in life that we think good in itself, that for instance we think the possession of a good character, or an intelligent understanding of the world, as good or better. A great advance is made by the substitution of "productive of the greatest good" for "productive of the greatest pleasure."

Not only is this theory more attractive than hedonistic utilitarianism, but its logical relation to that theory is such that the latter could not be true unless *it* were true, while it might be true though hedonistic utilitarianism were not. It is in fact one of the logical bases of hedonistic utilitarianism. For the view that what produces the maximum pleasure is right has for its bases the views (1) that what produces the maximum good is right, and (2) that pleasure is the only thing good in itself. If they were not assuming that what produces the maximum *good* is right, the utilitarians' attempt to show that pleasure is the only thing good in itself, which is in fact the point they take most pains to establish, would have been quite irrelevant to their attempt to prove that only what produces the maximum *pleasure* is right. If, therefore, it can be shown that productivity of the maximum good is not what makes all right actions right, we shall *a fortiori* have refuted hedonistic utilitarianism.

When a plain man fulfils a promise because he thinks he ought to do so, it seems clear that he does so with no thought of its total consequences, still less with any opinion that these are likely to be the best possible. He thinks in fact much more of the past than of the future. What makes him think it right to act in a certain way is the fact that he has promised to do so – that and, usually, nothing more. That his act will produce the best possible consequences is not his reason for calling it right. What lends color to the theory we are examining, then, is not the actions (which form probably a great majority of our actions) in which some such reflection as "I have promised" is the only reason we give ourselves for thinking a certain action right, but the exceptional cases in which the consequences of fulfilling a promise (for instance) would be so disastrous to others that we judge it right not to do so. It must of course be admitted that such cases exist. If I have promised to meet a friend at a particular time for some trivial purpose, I should certainly think myself justified in breaking my engagement if by doing so I could prevent a serious accident or bring relief to the victims of one. And the supporters of the view we are examining hold that my thinking so is due to my thinking that I shall bring more good into existence by the one action than by the other. A different account may, however, be given of the matter, an account which will, I believe, show itself to be the true one. It may be said that besides the duty of fulfilling promises I have and recognize a duty of relieving distress,[2] and that when I think it right to do the latter at the cost of not doing the former, it is not because I think I shall produce more good thereby but because I think it the duty which is in the circumstances more of a duty. This account surely corresponds much more closely with what we really think in such a situation. If, so far as I can see, I could bring equal amounts of good into being by fulfilling my promise and by helping some one to whom I had made no promise, I should not hesitate to regard the former as my duty. Yet on the view that what is right is right because it is productive of the most good I should not so regard it.

There are two theories, each in its way simple, that offer a solution of such cases of conscience. One is the view of Kant, that there are certain duties of perfect obligation, such as those of fulfilling promises, of paying debts, of telling the truth, which admit of no exception whatever in favor of duties of imperfect obligation, such as that of relieving distress. The other is the view of, for instance, Professor Moore and Dr. [Hastings] Rashdall [1858–1924], that there is only the duty of producing good, and that all "conflicts of duties" should be resolved by asking "by which action will most good be produced?" But it is more important that our theory fit the facts than that it be simple, and the account we have given above corresponds (it seems to me) better than either of the simpler theories with what we really think, viz. that normally promise-keeping, for example, should come before benevolence, but that when and only when the good to be produced by the benevolent act is very great and the promise comparatively trivial, the act of benevolence becomes our duty.

In fact the theory of "ideal utilitarianism," if I may for brevity refer so to the theory of Professor Moore, seems to simplify unduly our relations to our fellows. It says, in effect, that the only morally significant relation in which my neighbors stand to me is that of being possible beneficiaries by my action.[3] They do stand in this relation to me, and this relation is morally significant. But they may also stand to me in the relation of promisee to promiser, of creditor to debtor, of wife to husband, of child to parent, of friend to friend, of fellow countryman to fellow countryman, and the like; and each of these relations is the foundation of a *prima facie* duty, which is more or less incumbent on me according to the circumstances of the case. When I am in a situation, as perhaps

I always am, in which more than one of these *prima facie* duties is incumbent on me, what I have to do is to study the situation as fully as I can until I form the considered opinion (it is never more) that in the circumstances one of them is more incumbent than any other; then I am bound to think that to do this *prima facie* duty is my duty *sans phrase* in the situation.

I suggest "*prima facie* duty" or "conditional duty" as a brief way of referring to the characteristic (quite distinct from that of being a duty proper) which an act has, in virtue of being of a certain kind (e.g., the keeping of a promise), of being an act which would be a duty proper if it were not at the same time of another kind which is morally significant. Whether an act is a duty proper or actual duty depends on *all* the morally significant kinds it is an instance of. The phrase "*prima facie* duty" must be apologized for, since ... it suggests that what we are speaking of is a certain kind of duty, whereas it is in fact not a duty, but something related in a special way to duty....

There is nothing arbitrary about these *prima facie* duties. Each rests on a definite circumstance which cannot seriously be held to be without moral significance. Of *prima facie* duties I suggest, without claiming completeness or finality for it, the following division.[4]

(1) Some duties rest on previous acts of my own. These duties seem to include two kinds, (*a*) those resting on a promise or what may fairly be called an implicit promise, such as the implicit undertaking not to tell lies which seems to be implied in the act of entering into conversation (at any rate by civilized men), or of writing books that purport to be history and not fiction. These may be called the duties of fidelity. (*b*) Those resting on a previous wrongful act. These may be called the duties of reparation. (2) Some rest on previous acts of other men, i.e., services done by them to me. These may be loosely described as the duties of gratitude.... (3) Some rest on the fact

or possibility of a distribution of pleasure or happiness (or of the means thereto) which is not in accordance with the merit of the persons concerned; in such cases there arises a duty to upset or prevent such a distribution. These are the duties of justice. (4) Some rest on the mere fact that there are other beings in the world whose condition we can make better in respect of virtue, or of intelligence, or of pleasure. These are the duties of beneficence. (5) Some rest on the fact that we can improve our own condition in respect of virtue or of intelligence. These are the duties of self-improvement. (6) I think that we should distinguish from (4) the duties that may be summed up under the title of "not injuring others." No doubt to injure others is incidentally to fail to do them good; but it seems to me clear that non-maleficence is apprehended as a duty distinct from that of beneficence, and as a duty of a more stringent character. It will be noticed that this alone among the types of duty has been stated in a negative way. An attempt might no doubt be made to state this duty, like the others, in a positive way. It might be said that it is really the duty to prevent ourselves from acting either from an inclination to harm others or from an inclination to seek our own pleasure, in doing which we should incidentally harm them. But on reflection it seems clear that the primary duty here is the duty not to harm others, this being a duty whether or not we have an inclination that if followed would lead to our harming them; and that when we have such an inclination the primary duty not to harm others gives rise to a consequential duty to resist the inclination. The recognition of this duty of non-maleficence is the first step on the way to the recognition of the duty of beneficence; and that accounts for the prominence of the commands "thou shalt not kill," "thou shalt not commit adultery," "thou shalt not steal," "thou shalt not bear false witness," in so early a code as the Decalogue [i.e., the Ten Commandments]. But even when we have come to recognize the duty of beneficence, it appears to me that the duty of non-maleficence is recognized as a distinct one, and as *prima facie* more binding. We should not in general consider it justifiable to kill one person in order to keep another alive, or to steal from one in order to give alms to another.

The essential defect of the "ideal utilitarian" theory is that it ignores, or at least does not do full justice to, the highly personal character of duty. If the only duty is to produce the maximum of good, the question who is to have the good – whether it is myself, or my benefactor, or a person to whom I have made a promise to confer that good on him, or a mere fellow man to whom I stand in no such special relation – should make no difference to my having a duty to produce that good. But we are all in fact sure that it makes a vast difference....

I would contend that in principle there is no reason to anticipate that every act that is our duty is so for one and the same reason. Why should two sets of circumstances, or one set of circumstances, *not* possess different characteristics, any one of which makes a certain act our *prima facie* duty? When I ask what it is that makes me in certain cases sure that I have a *prima facie* duty to do so and so, I find that it lies in the fact that I have made a promise; when I ask the same question in another case, I find the answer lies in the fact that I have done a wrong. And if on reflection I find (as I think I do) that neither of these reasons is reducible to the other, I must not on any *a priori* ground assume that such a reduction is possible.

An attempt may be made to arrange in a more systematic way the main types of duty which we have indicated. In the first place it seems self-evident that if there are things that are intrinsically good, it is *prima facie* a duty to bring them into existence rather than not to do so, and to bring as much of them into existence as possible. It will be argued … that there are three main things that are intrinsically good – virtue, knowledge, and, with certain limitations, pleasure. And since a given virtuous disposition, for instance, is equally good whether it is realized in myself or in another, it seems to be my duty to bring it into existence whether in myself or in another. So too with a given piece of knowledge.

The case of pleasure is difficult; for while we clearly recognize a duty to produce pleasure for others, it is by no means so clear that we recognize a duty to produce pleasure for ourselves. This appears to arise from the following facts. The thought of an act as our duty is one that presupposes a certain amount of reflection about the act; and for that reason does not normally arise in connexion with acts towards which we are already impelled by another strong impulse. So far, the cause of our not thinking of the promotion of our own pleasure as a duty is analogous to the cause which usually prevents a highly sympathetic person from thinking of the promotion of the pleasure of others as a duty. He is impelled so strongly by direct interest in the well-being of others towards promoting their pleasure that he does not stop to ask whether it is his duty to promote it; and we are all impelled so strongly towards the promotion of our own pleasure that we do not stop to ask whether it is a duty or not. But there is a further reason why even when we stop to think about the matter it does not usually present itself as a duty: viz. that, since the performance of most of our duties involves the giving up of some pleasure that we desire, the doing of duty and the getting of pleasure for ourselves come by a natural association of ideas to be thought of as incompatible things. This association of ideas is in the main salutary in its operation, since it puts a check on what but for it would be much

too strong, the tendency to pursue one's own pleasure without thought of other considerations. Yet if pleasure is good, it seems in the long run clear that it is right to get it for ourselves as well as to produce it for others, when this does not involve the failure to discharge some more stringent *prima facie* duty….

If these contentions are right, what we have called the duty of beneficence and the duty of self-improvement rest on the same ground. No different principles of duty are involved in the two cases. If we feel a special responsibility for improving our own character rather than that of others, it is not because a special principle is involved, but because we are aware that the one is more under our control than the other….

It is equally clear, and clear at an earlier stage of moral development, that if there are things that are bad in themselves we ought, *prima facie*, not to bring them upon others; and on this fact rests the duty of non-maleficence.

The duty of justice is particularly complicated, and the word is used to cover things which are really very different – things such as the payment of debts, the reparation of injuries done by oneself to another, and the bringing about of a distribution of happiness between other people in proportion to merit. I use the word to denote only the last of these three…. The bringing of this about is a duty which we owe to all men alike, though it may be reinforced by special responsibilities that we have undertaken to particular men. This, therefore, with beneficence and self-improvement, comes under the general principle that we should produce as much good as possible, though the good here involved is different in kind from any other.

But besides this general obligation, there are special obligations. These may arise, in the first place, incidentally, from acts which were not essentially meant to create such an obligation, but which nevertheless create it. From

SECTION I: THEORETICAL FOUNDATIONS

the nature of the case such acts may be of two kinds – the infliction of injuries on others, and the acceptance of benefits from them. It seems clear that these put us under a special obligation to other men, and that only these acts can do so incidentally. From these arise the twin duties of reparation and gratitude.

And finally there are special obligations arising from acts the very intention of which, when they were done, was to put us under such an obligation. The name for such acts is "promises"; the name is wide enough *if* we are willing to include under it implicit promises, i.e., modes of behavior in which without explicit verbal promise we intentionally create an expectation that we can he counted on to behave in a certain way in the interest of another person.

These seem to be, in principle, all the ways in which *prima facie* duties arise. In actual experience they are compounded together in highly complex ways. Thus, for example, the duty of obeying the laws of one's country arises partly (as Socrates contends in the *Crito* [of Plato]) from the duty of gratitude for the benefits one has received from it; partly from the implicit promise to obey which seems to be involved in permanent residence in a country whose laws we know we are *expected* to obey, and still more clearly involved when we ourselves invoke the protection of its laws (this is the truth underlying the doctrine of the social contract); and partly (if we are fortunate in our country) from the fact that its laws are potent instruments for the general good.

Or again, the sense of a general obligation to bring about (so far as we can) a just apportionment of happiness to merit is often greatly reinforced by the fact that many of the existing injustices are due to a social and economic system which we have, not indeed created, but taken part in and assented to; the duty of justice is then reinforced by the duty of reparation.

It is necessary to say something by way of clearing up the relation between *prima facie* duties and the actual or absolute duty to do one particular act in particular circumstances. If, as almost all moralists except Kant are agreed, and as most plain men think, it is sometimes right to tell a lie or to break a promise, it must be maintained that there is a difference between *prima facie* duty and actual or absolute duty. When we think ourselves justified in breaking, and indeed morally obliged to break, a promise in order to relieve some one's distress, we do not for a moment cease to recognize a *prima facie* duty to keep our promise, and this leads us to feel, not indeed shame or repentance, but certainly compunction, for behaving as we do; we recognize, further, that it is our duty to make up somehow to the promisee for the breaking of the promise. We have to distinguish from the characteristic of being our duty that of tending to be our duty. Any act that we do contains various elements in virtue of which it falls under various categories. In virtue of being the breaking of a promise, for instance, it tends to be wrong; in virtue of being an instance of relieving distress it tends to be right. Tendency to be one's duty may be called a parti-resultant attribute, i.e., one which belongs to an act in virtue of some one component in its nature. *Being* one's duty is a toti-resultant attribute, one which belongs to an act in virtue of its whole nature and of nothing less than this.... This distinction between parti-resultant and toti-resultant attributes is one which we shall meet in another context also....

Another instance of the same distinction may be found in the operation of natural laws. *Qua* subject to the force of gravitation towards some other body, each body tends to move in a particular direction with a particular velocity; but its actual movement depends on *all* the forces to which it is subject. It is only by recognizing this distinction that we can preserve

48

the absoluteness of laws of nature, and only by recognizing a corresponding distinction that we can preserve the absoluteness of the general principles of morality. But an important difference between the two cases must be pointed out. When we say that in virtue of gravitation a body tends to move in a certain way, we are referring to a causal influence actually exercised on it by another body or other bodies. When we say that in virtue of being deliberately untrue a certain remark tends to be wrong, we are referring to no causal relation, to no relation that involves succession in time, but to such a relation as connects the various attributes of a mathematical figure. And if the word "tendency" is thought to suggest too much a causal relation, it is better to talk of certain types of act as being *prima facie* right or wrong (or of different persons as having different and possibly conflicting claims upon us), than of their tending to be right or wrong.

Something should be said of the relation between our apprehension of the *prima facie* rightness of certain types of act and our mental attitude towards particular acts. It is proper to use the word "apprehension" in the former case and not in the latter. That an act, *qua* fulfilling a promise, or *qua* effecting a just distribution of good, or *qua* returning services rendered, or *qua* promoting the good of others, or *qua* promoting the virtue or insight of the agent, is *prima facie* right, is self-evident; not in the sense that it is evident from the beginning of our lives, or as soon as we attend to the proposition for the first time, but in the sense that when we have reached sufficient mental maturity and have given sufficient attention to the proposition it is evident without any need of proof, or of evidence beyond itself. It is self-evident just as a mathematical axiom, or the validity of a form of inference, is evident. The moral order expressed in these propositions is just as much part of the fundamental nature of the universe (and, we may add, of any possible universe in which there were moral agents at all) as is the spatial or numerical structure expressed in the axioms of geometry or arithmetic. In our confidence that these propositions are true there is involved the same trust in our reason that is involved in our confidence in mathematics; and we should have no justification for trusting it in the latter sphere and distrusting it in the former. In both cases we are dealing with propositions that cannot he proved, but that just as certainly need no proof....

Our judgements about our actual duty in concrete situations have none of the certainty that attaches to our recognition of the general principles of duty. A statement is certain, i.e., is an expression of knowledge, only in one or other of two cases: when it is either self-evident, or a valid conclusion from self-evident premises. And our judgements about our particular duties have neither of these characters. (1) They are not self-evident. Where a possible act is seen to have two characteristics, in virtue of one of which it is *prima facie* right, and in virtue of the other *prima facie* wrong, we are (I think) well aware that we are not certain whether we ought or ought not to do it; that whether we do it or not, we are taking a moral risk. We come in the long run, after consideration, to think one duty more pressing than the other, but we do not feel certain that it is so. And though we do not always recognize that a possible act has two such characteristics, and though there *may* be cases in which it has not, we are never certain that any particular possible act has not, and therefore never certain that it is right, nor certain that it is wrong. For, to go no further in the analysis, it is enough to point out that any particular act will in all probability in the course of time contribute to the bringing about of good or of evil for many human beings, and thus have a *prima facie* rightness or wrongness

SECTION I: THEORETICAL FOUNDATIONS

of which we know nothing. (2) Again, our judgements about our particular duties are not logical conclusions from self-evident premisses. The only possible premises would be the general principles stating their *prima facie* rightness or wrongness *qua* having the different characteristics they do have; and even if we could (as we cannot) apprehend the extent to which an act will tend on the one hand, for example, to bring about advantages for our benefactors, and on the other hand to bring about disadvantages for fellow men who are not our benefactors, there is no principle by which we can draw the conclusion that it is on the whole right or on the whole wrong. In this respect the judgement as to the rightness of a particular act is just like the judgement as to the beauty of a particular natural object or work of art. A poem is, for instance, in respect of certain qualities beautiful and in respect of certain others not beautiful; and our judgement as to the degree of beauty it possesses on the whole is never reached by logical reasoning from the apprehension of its particular beauties or particular defects. Both in this and in the moral case we have more or less probable opinions which are not logically justified conclusions from the general principles that are recognized as self-evident.

There is therefore much truth in the description of the right act as a fortunate act. If we cannot be certain that it is right, it is our good fortune if the act we do is the right act. This consideration does not, however, make the doing of our duty a mere matter of chance. There is a parallel here between the doing of duty and the doing of what will be to our personal advantage. We never *know* what act will in the long run be to our advantage. Yet it is certain that we are more likely in general to secure our advantage if we estimate to the best of our ability the probable tendencies of our actions in this respect, than if we act on caprice. And similarly we are more likely

to do our duty if we reflect to the best of our ability on the *prima facie* rightness or wrongness of various possible acts in virtue of the characteristics we perceive them to have, than if we act without reflection. With this greater likelihood we must be content....

[I]n order that the act should be morally good, or an act I am not to be blamed for doing, it must not merely be the act which it is reasonable for me to think my duty; it must also be done for that reason, or from some other morally good motive. Thus the conception of the right act as the act which it is reasonable for me to think my duty is an unsatisfactory compromise between the true notion of the right act and the notion of the morally good action.

The general principles of duty are obviously not self-evident from the beginning of our lives. How do they come to be so? The answer is, that they come to be self-evident to us just as mathematical axioms do. We find by experience that this couple of matches and that couple make four matches, that this couple of balls on a wire and that couple make four balls: and by reflection on these and similar discoveries we come to see that it is of the nature of two and two to make four. In a precisely similar way, we see the *prima facie* rightness of an act which would be the fulfilment of a particular promise, and of another which would be the fulfilment of another promise, and when we have reached sufficient maturity to think in general terms, we apprehend *prima facie* rightness to belong to the nature of any fulfilment of promise. What comes first in time is the apprehension of the self-evident *prima facie* rightness of an individual act of a particular type. From this we come by reflection to apprehend the self-evident general principle of *prima facie* duty. From this, too, perhaps along with the apprehension of the self-evident *prima facie* rightness of the same act in virtue of its having another characteristic as well, and perhaps in spite of the apprehension of its *prima facie* wrongness in virtue of its having some third characteristic, we come to believe something not self-evident at all, but an object of probable opinion, viz. that this particular act is (not *prima facie* but) actually right.

In this respect there is an important difference between rightness and mathematical properties. A triangle which is isosceles necessarily has two of its angles equal, whatever other characteristics the triangle may have – whatever, for instance, be its area, or the size of its third angle. The equality of the two angles is a parti-resultant attribute.... And the same is true of all mathematical attributes. It is true, I may add, of *prima facie* rightness. But no act is ever, in virtue of falling under some general description, necessarily actually right; its rightness depends on its whole nature[5] and not on any element in it. The reason is that no mathematical object (no figure, for instance, or angle) ever has two characteristics that tend to give it opposite resultant characteristics, while moral acts often (as every one knows) and indeed always (as on reflection we must admit) have different characteristics that tend to make them at the same time *prima facie* right and *prima facie* wrong; there is probably no act, for instance, which does good to any one without doing harm to some one else, and *vice versa*....

## Study Questions

1. What is a prima facie duty, according to Ross? What are some examples of the prima facie duties that Ross lists?

2. Do you agree with Ross that sometimes duties conflict? Do you think his system is a good one for addressing this possible problem?

3. Is it sufficient to use reflections on and descriptions of the ways in which people act ethically to base an ethical theory? Do we come to see the rightness of an act through many experiences of that act?

## Notes

1 I take the theory which, as I have tried to show, seems to be put forward in [Moore's] *Ethics* [1912] rather than the earlier and less plausible theory put forward in [his] *Principia Ethica* [1903]. For the difference, [see above in Ross's book].
2 These are not strictly speaking duties, but things that tend to be our duty, or *prima facie* duties. Cf. [above].
3 Some will think it, apart from other considerations, a sufficient refutation of this view to point out that I also stand in that relation to myself, so that for this view the distinction of oneself from others is morally insignificant.
4 I should make it plain at this stage that I am *assuming* the correctness of some of our main convictions as to *prima facie* duties, or, more strictly, am claiming that we *know* them to be true. To me it seems as self-evident as anything could be, that to make a promise, for instance, is to create a moral claim on us in someone else. Many readers will perhaps say that they do *not* know this to be true. If so, I certainly cannot prove it to them; I can only ask them to reflect again, in the hope that they will ultimately agree that they also know it to be true. The main

moral convictions of the plain man seem to me to be, not opinions which it is for philosophy to prove or disprove, but knowledge from the start; and in my own case I seem to find little difficulty in distinguishing these essential convictions from other moral convictions which I also have, which are merely fallible opinions based on an imperfect study of the working for good or evil of certain institutions or types of action.

5  To avoid complicating unduly the statement of the general view I am putting forward, I have here rather overstated it. Any act is the origination of a great variety of things many of which make no difference to its rightness or wrongness. But there are always many elements in its nature (i.e., in what it is the origination of) that make a difference to its rightness or wrongness, and no element in its nature can be dismissed without consideration as indifferent.

# 4. John Stuart Mill, *Utilitarianism*

IN *UTILITARIANISM* (1863), ENGLISH philosopher John Stuart Mill (1806–73) offers his famous version of the theory and its principle, describing ethical actions as those that promote the greatest happiness for the greatest number, and includes the key distinction between higher and lower pleasures. For Mill, this distinction, not present in Jeremy Bentham's (1748–1832) earlier account of utilitarianism, provides a response to those who would criticize the Principle of Utility on the grounds that it is strictly pleasure-based and therefore promotes animalistic behavior. He insists that when one includes pleasures such as intellectual and emotional pleasures (the higher pleasures) in one's understanding of happiness (which includes absence of pain as well as presence of pleasure), utilitarianism actually promotes the cultivation of nobility in humans. Mill also addresses one of the most critical concerns about utilitarianism that is still pressing today: the fact that it appears to be willing to dismiss individual rights (and therefore justice) in the name of the greater good. Mill argues that people's desire for security needs to be added into any utilitarian equation and will prevent the wanton disregard for rights. In the rare cases that so-called rights are disregarded out of need for a larger concern (e.g., if one person's life has to be sacrificed for the sake of saving a nation), Mill points out that we don't actually perceive these instances as violations of rights but rather recognize their unfortunate necessity.

## Chapter 2: What Utilitarianism Is

... THE CREED WHICH ACCEPTS as the foundation of morals, Utility, or the Greatest Happiness Principle, holds that actions are right in proportion as they tend to promote happiness, wrong as they tend to produce the reverse of happiness. By happiness is intended pleasure, and the absence of pain; by unhappiness, pain, and the privation of pleasure. To give a clear view of the moral standard set up by the theory, much more requires to be said; in particular, what things it includes in the ideas of pain and pleasure; and to what extent this is left an open question. But these supplementary explanations do not affect the theory of life on which this theory of morality is grounded – namely, that pleasure, and freedom from pain, are the only things desirable as ends; and that all desirable things (which are as numerous in the utilitarian as in any other scheme) are desirable either for the pleasure inherent in themselves, or as means to the promotion of pleasure and the prevention of pain.

Now, such a theory of life excites in many minds, and among them in some of the most estimable in feeling and purpose, inveterate dislike. To suppose that life has (as they express it) no higher end than pleasure – no better and nobler object of desire and pursuit – they designate as utterly mean and grovelling; as a doctrine worthy only of swine, to whom the followers of Epicurus[1] were, at a very early period, contemptuously likened;[2] and modern holders of the doctrine are occasionally made the subject of equally polite comparisons by its German, French, and English assailants.

When thus attacked, the Epicureans have always answered, that it is not they, but their accusers, who represent human nature in a degrading light; since the accusation supposes human beings to be capable of no pleasures except those of which swine are capable. If this supposition were true, the charge could not be gainsaid,[3] but would then be no longer an imputation; for if the sources of pleasure were precisely the same to human beings and to swine, the rule of life which is good enough for the one would be good enough for the other. The comparison of the Epicurean life to that of beasts is felt as degrading, precisely because a beast's pleasures do not satisfy a human being's conceptions of happiness. Human beings have faculties more elevated than the animal appetites, and when once made conscious of them, do not regard anything as happiness which does not include their gratification. I do not, indeed, consider the Epicureans to have been by any means faultless in drawing out their scheme of consequences from the utilitarian principle. To do this in any sufficient manner, many Stoic,[4] as well as Christian elements require to be included. But there is no known Epicurean theory of life which does not assign to the pleasures of the intellect, of the feelings and imagination, and of the moral sentiments, a much higher value as pleasures than to those of mere sensation. It must be admitted, however, that utilitarian writers in general have placed the superiority of mental over bodily pleasures chiefly in the greater permanency, safety, uncostliness, etc., of the former – that is, in their circumstantial advantages rather than in their intrinsic nature. And on all these points utilitarians have fully proved their case; but they might have taken the other, and, as it may be called, higher ground, with entire consistency. It is quite compatible with the principle of utility to recognize the fact, that some *kinds* of pleasure are more desirable and more valuable than others. It would be absurd that while, in estimating all other things, quality is considered as well as

quantity, the estimation of pleasures should be supposed to depend on quantity alone.

If I am asked, what I mean by difference of quality in pleasures, or what makes one pleasure more valuable than another, merely as a pleasure, except its being greater in amount, there is but one possible answer. Of two pleasures, if there be one to which all or almost all who have experience of both give a decided preference, irrespective of any feeling of moral obligation to prefer it, that is the more desirable pleasure. If one of the two is, by those who are competently acquainted with both, placed so far above the other that they prefer it, even though knowing it to be attended with a greater amount of discontent, and would not resign it for any quantity of the other pleasure which their nature is capable of, we are justified in ascribing to the preferred enjoyment a superiority in quality, so far outweighing quantity as to render it, in comparison, of small account.

Now it is an unquestionable fact that those who are equally acquainted with, and equally capable of appreciating and enjoying, both, do give a most marked preference to the manner of existence which employs their higher faculties. Few human creatures would consent to be changed into any of the lower animals, for a promise of the fullest allowance of a beast's pleasures; no intelligent human being would consent to be a fool, no instructed person would be an ignoramus, no person of feeling and conscience would be selfish and base, even though they should be persuaded that the fool, the dunce, or the rascal is better satisfied with his lot than they are with theirs. They would not resign what they possess more than he for the most complete satisfaction of all the desires which they have in common with him. If they ever fancy they would, it is only in cases of unhappiness so extreme, that to escape from it they would exchange their lot for almost any other, however undesirable in their own eyes. A being of higher faculties requires more to make him happy, is capable probably of more acute suffering, and certainly accessible to it at more points, than one of an inferior type; but in spite of these liabilities, he can never really wish to sink into what he feels to be a lower grade of existence. We may give what explanation we please of this unwillingness; we may attribute it to pride, a name which is given indiscriminately to some of the most and to some of the least estimable feelings of which mankind are capable: we may refer it to the love of liberty and personal independence, an appeal to which was with the Stoics one of the most effective means for the inculcation of it; to the love of power, or to the love of excitement, both of which do really enter into and contribute to it: but its most appropriate appellation is a sense of dignity, which all human beings possess in one form or other, and in some, though by no means in exact, proportion to their higher faculties, and which is so essential a part of the happiness of those in whom it is strong, that nothing which conflicts with it could be, otherwise than momentarily, an object of desire to them. Whoever supposes that this preference takes place at a sacrifice of happiness – that the superior being, in anything like equal circumstances, is not happier than the inferior – confounds the two very different ideas, of happiness, and content. It is indisputable that the being whose capacities of enjoyment are low, has the greatest chance of having them fully satisfied; and a highly endowed being will always feel that any happiness which he can look for, as the world is constituted, is imperfect. But he can learn to bear its imperfections, if they are at all bearable; and they will not make him envy the being who is indeed unconscious of the imperfections, but only because he feels not at all the good which those imperfections qualify. It is better to be a human being dissatisfied than a pig satisfied; better to be Socrates dissatisfied than a fool satisfied. And if the fool, or the pig, are of a different opinion, it is because they only know their own side of the question. The other party to the comparison knows both sides.

It may be objected, that many who are capable of the higher pleasures, occasionally, under the influence of temptation, postpone them to the lower. But this is quite compatible with a full appreciation of the intrinsic superiority of the higher. Men often, from infirmity of character, make their election for[5] the nearer good, though they know it to be the less valuable; and this no less when the choice is between two bodily pleasures, than when it is between bodily and mental. They pursue sensual indulgences to the injury of health, though perfectly aware that health is the greater good.

It may be further objected, that many who begin with youthful enthusiasm for everything noble, as they advance in years sink into indolence and selfishness. But I do not believe that those who undergo this very common change, voluntarily choose the lower description of pleasures in preference to the higher. I believe that before they devote themselves exclusively to the one, they have already become incapable of the other. Capacity for the nobler feelings is in most natures a very tender plant, easily killed, not only by hostile influences, but by mere want of sustenance; and in the majority of young persons it speedily dies away if the occupations to which their position in life has devoted them, and the society into which it has thrown them, are not favorable to keeping that higher capacity in exercise. Men lose their high aspirations as they lose their intellectual tastes, because they have not time or opportunity for indulging them; and they addict themselves to inferior pleasures, not because they deliberately prefer them, but because they are either the only ones to which they have access, or the only ones which they are any longer capable of enjoying. It may be questioned whether any one who has remained equally susceptible to both classes of pleasures, ever knowingly and calmly preferred the lower; though many, in all ages, have broken down in an ineffectual attempt to combine both.

From this verdict of the only competent judges, I apprehend there can be no appeal. On a question which is the best worth having of two pleasures, or which of two modes of existence is the most grateful to the feelings, apart from its moral attributes and from its consequences, the judgment of those who are qualified by knowledge of both, or, if they differ, that of the majority among them, must be admitted as final. And there needs be the less hesitation to accept this judgment respecting the quality of pleasures, since there is no other tribunal to be referred to even on the question of quantity. What means are there of determining which is the acutest of two pains, or the intensest of two pleasurable sensations, except the general suffrage[6] of those who are familiar with both? Neither pains nor pleasures are homogeneous, and pain is always heterogeneous with pleasure. What is there to decide whether a particular pleasure is worth purchasing at the cost of a particular pain, except the feelings and judgment of the experienced? When, therefore, those feelings and judgment declare the pleasures derived from the higher faculties to be preferable *in kind*, apart from the question of intensity, to those of which the animal nature, disjoined from the higher faculties, is susceptible, they are entitled on this subject to the same regard.

I have dwelt on this point, as being a necessary part of a perfectly just conception of Utility or Happiness, considered as the directive rule of human conduct. But it is by no means an indispensable condition to the acceptance of the utilitarian standard; for that standard is not the agent's own greatest happiness, but the greatest amount of happiness altogether; and if it may possibly be doubted whether a noble character is always the happier for its nobleness, there can be no doubt that it makes other people happier, and that the world in general is immensely a gainer by it. Utilitarianism, therefore, could only attain its end by the general cultivation of nobleness of character, even if each individual were only benefited by the nobleness of others, and his own, so far as happiness is concerned, were a sheer deduction[7] from the benefit. But the bare enunciation of such an absurdity as this last, renders refutation superfluous.

According to the Greatest Happiness Principle, as above explained, the ultimate end, with reference to and for the sake of which all other things are desirable (whether we are considering our own good or that of other people), is an existence exempt as far as possible from pain, and as rich as possible in enjoyments, both in point of quantity and quality; the test of quality, and the rule for measuring it against quantity, being the preference felt by those who in their opportunities of experience, to which must be added their habits of self-consciousness and self-observation, are best furnished with the means of comparison. This, being, according to the utilitarian opinion, the end of human action, is necessarily also the standard of morality; which may accordingly be defined, the rules and precepts for human conduct, by the observance of which an existence such as has been described might be, to the greatest extent possible, secured to all mankind; and not to them only, but, so far as the nature of things admits, to the whole sentient creation.[8]
...

## Chapter 4: Of What Sort of Proof the Principle of Utility Is Susceptible

It has already been remarked, that questions of ultimate ends do not admit of proof, in the ordinary acceptation of the term. To be incapable of proof by reasoning is common to all first principles; to the first premises of our knowledge,[9] as well as to those of our conduct. But the former, being matters of fact, may be the subject of a direct appeal to the faculties which judge of fact – namely, our senses, and our internal consciousness.[10] Can an appeal be made to the same faculties on questions of practical ends? Or by what other faculty is cognisance taken of them?

Questions about ends are, in other words, questions about what things are desirable. The utilitarian doctrine is, that happiness is desirable, and the only thing desirable, as an end; all other things being only desirable as means to that end. What ought to be required of this doctrine – what conditions is it requisite that the doctrine should fulfil – to make good its claim to be believed?

The only proof capable of being given that an object is visible, is that people actually see it. The only proof that a sound is audible, is that people hear it: and so of the other sources of our experience. In like manner, I apprehend, the sole evidence it is possible to produce that anything is desirable, is that people do actually desire it. If the end which the utilitarian doctrine proposes to itself were not, in theory and in practice, acknowledged to be an end, nothing could ever convince any person that it was so. No reason can be given why the general happiness is desirable, except that each person, so far as he believes it to be attainable, desires his own happiness. This, however, being a fact, we have not only all the proof which the case admits of, but all which it is possible to require, that happiness is a good: that each person's happiness is a

good to that person, and the general happiness, therefore, a good to the aggregate of all persons. Happiness has made out its title as *one* of the ends of conduct, and consequently one of the criteria of morality.

But it has not, by this alone, proved itself to be the sole criterion. To do that, it would seem, by the same rule, necessary to show, not only that people desire happiness, but that they never desire anything else. Now it is palpable that they do desire things which, in common language, are decidedly distinguished from happiness. They desire, for example, virtue, and the absence of vice, no less really than pleasure and the absence of pain. The desire of virtue is not as universal, but it is as authentic a fact, as the desire of happiness. And hence the opponents of the utilitarian standard deem that they have a right to infer that there are other ends of human action besides happiness, and that happiness is not the standard of approbation and disapprobation.

But does the utilitarian doctrine deny that people desire virtue, or maintain that virtue is not a thing to be desired? The very reverse. It maintains not only that virtue is to be desired, but that it is to be desired disinterestedly, for itself. Whatever may be the opinion of utilitarian moralists as to the original conditions by which virtue is made virtue; however they may believe (as they do) that actions and dispositions are only virtuous because they promote another end than virtue; yet this being granted, and it having been decided, from considerations of this description, what is virtuous, they not only place virtue at the very head of the things which are good as means to the ultimate end, but they also recognize as a psychological fact the possibility of its being, to the individual, a good in itself, without looking to any end beyond it; and hold, that the mind is not in a right state, not in a state conformable to Utility, not in the state most conducive to the general happiness, unless it does love virtue in this manner — as a thing desirable in itself, even although, in the individual instance, it should not produce those other desirable consequences which it tends to produce, and on account of which it is held to be virtue. This opinion is not, in the smallest degree, a departure from the Happiness principle. The ingredients of happiness are very various, and each of them is desirable in itself, and not merely when considered as swelling an aggregate. The principle of utility does not mean that any given pleasure, as music, for instance, or any given exemption from pain, as for example health, is to be looked upon as means to a collective something termed happiness, and to be desired on that account. They are desired and desirable in and for themselves; besides being means, they are a part of the end. Virtue, according to the utilitarian doctrine, is not naturally and originally part of the end, but it is capable of becoming so; and in those who love it disinterestedly it has become so, and is desired and cherished, not as a means to happiness, but as a part of their happiness.

To illustrate this farther, we may remember that virtue is not the only thing, originally a means, and which if it were not a means to anything else, would be and remain indifferent, but which by association with what it is a means to, comes to be desired for itself, and that too with the utmost intensity. What, for example, shall we say of the love of money? There is nothing originally more desirable about money than about any heap of glittering pebbles. Its worth is solely that of the things which it will buy; the desires for other things than itself, which it is a means of gratifying. Yet the love of money is not only one of the strongest moving forces of human life, but money is, in many cases, desired in and for itself, the desire to possess it is often stronger than the desire to use it, and goes on increasing when all the desires which point to ends

beyond it, to be compassed by it, are falling off. It may, then, be said truly, that money is desired not for the sake of an end, but as part of the end. From being a means to happiness, it has come to be itself a principal ingredient of the individual's conception of happiness. The same may be said of the majority of the great objects of human life — power, for example, or fame; except that to each of these there is a certain amount of immediate pleasure annexed, which has at least the semblance of being naturally inherent in them; a thing which cannot be said of money. Still, however, the strongest natural attraction, both of power and of fame, is the immense aid they give to the attainment of our other wishes; and it is the strong association thus generated between them and all our objects of desire, which gives to the direct desire of them the intensity it often assumes, so as in some characters to surpass in strength all other desires. In these cases the means have become a part of the end, and a more important part of it than any of the things which they are means to. What was once desired as an instrument for the attainment of happiness, has come to be desired for its own sake. In being desired for its own sake it is, however, desired as *part* of happiness. The person is made, or thinks he would be made, happy by its mere possession; and is made unhappy by failure to obtain it. The desire of it is not a different thing from the desire of happiness, any more than the love of music, or the desire of health. They are included in happiness. They are some of the elements of which the desire of happiness is made up. Happiness is not an abstract idea, but a concrete whole; and these are some of its parts. And the utilitarian standard sanctions and approves their being so. Life would be a poor thing, very ill provided with sources of happiness, if there were not this provision of nature, by which things originally indifferent, but conducive to, or otherwise associated with, the satisfaction of our primitive desires, become in themselves sources of pleasure more valuable than the primitive pleasures, both in permanency, in the space of human existence that they are capable of covering, and even in intensity.

Virtue, according to the utilitarian conception, is a good of this description. There was no original desire of it, or motive to it, save its conduciveness to pleasure, and especially to protection from pain. But through the association thus formed, it may be felt a good in itself, and desired as such with as great intensity as any other good; and with this difference between it and the love of money, of power, or of fame, that all of these may, and often do, render the individual noxious to the other members of the society to which he belongs, whereas there is nothing which makes him so much a blessing to them as the cultivation of the disinterested love of virtue. And consequently, the utilitarian standard, while it tolerates and approves those other acquired desires, up to the point beyond which they would be more injurious to the general happiness than promotive of it, enjoins and requires the cultivation of the love of virtue up to the greatest strength possible, as being above all things important to the general happiness.

It results from the preceding considerations, that there is in reality nothing desired except happiness. Whatever is desired otherwise than as a means to some end beyond itself, and ultimately to happiness, is desired as itself a part of happiness, and is not desired for itself until it has become so....

## Chapter 5: On the Connection between Justice and Utility

In all ages of speculation, one of the strongest obstacles to the reception of the doctrine that Utility or Happiness is the criterion of right and wrong, has been drawn from the idea of justice. The powerful sentiment, and apparently clear perception, which that word recalls with a rapidity and certainty resembling an instinct, have seemed to the majority of thinkers to point to an inherent quality in things; to show that the just must have an existence in Nature as something absolute, generically distinct from every variety of the Expedient,[11] and, in idea, opposed to it, though (as is commonly acknowledged) never, in the long run, disjoined from it in fact....

[T]he idea of justice supposes two things; a rule of conduct, and a sentiment which sanctions the rule. The first must be supposed common to all mankind, and intended for their good. The other (the sentiment) is a desire that punishment may be suffered by those who infringe the rule. There is involved, in addition, the conception of some definite person who suffers by the infringement; whose rights (to use the expression appropriated to the case) are violated by it. And the sentiment of justice appears to me to be, the animal desire to repel or retaliate a hurt or damage to oneself, or to those with whom one sympathizes, widened so as to include all persons, by the human capacity of enlarged sympathy, and the human conception of intelligent self-interest. From the latter elements, the feeling derives its morality; from the former, its peculiar impressiveness, and energy of self-assertion.

I have, throughout, treated the idea of a *right* residing in the injured person, and violated by the injury, not as a separate element in the composition of the idea and sentiment, but as one of the forms in which the other two elements clothe themselves. These elements are, a hurt to some assignable person or persons on the one hand, and a demand for punishment on the other. An examination of our own minds, I think, will show, that these two things include all that we mean when we speak of violation of a right. When we call anything a person's right, we mean that he has a valid claim on society to protect him in the possession of it, either by the force of law, or by that of education and opinion. If he has what we consider a sufficient claim, on whatever account, to have something guaranteed to him by society, we say that he has a right to it. If we desire to prove that anything does not belong to him by right, we think this done as soon as it is admitted that society ought not to take measures for securing it to him, but should leave him to chance, or to his own exertions. Thus, a person is said to have a right to what he can earn in fair professional competition; because society ought not to allow any other person to hinder him from endeavoring to earn in that manner as much as he can. But he has not a right to three hundred a-year, though he may happen to be earning it; because society is not called on to provide that he shall earn that sum. On the contrary, if he owns ten thousand pounds three per cent stock, he *has* a right to three hundred a-year; because society has come under an obligation to provide him with an income of that amount.

To have a right, then, is, I conceive, to have something which society ought to defend me in the possession of. If the objector goes on to ask, why it ought? I can give him no other reason than general utility. If that expression does not seem to convey a sufficient feeling of the strength of the obligation, nor to account for the peculiar energy of the feeling, it is because there goes to the composition of the sentiment, not a rational only, but also an animal element, the thirst for retaliation; and this thirst derives its intensity, as well as its moral justification, from the extraordinarily important and impressive kind of utility which is concerned. The interest involved is that of security, to every one's feelings the most vital of all interests. Nearly all other earthly benefits are needed by one person, not needed by another; and many of them can, if necessary, be cheerfully foregone, or replaced by something else; but security no human being can possibly do without; on it we depend for all our immunity from evil, and for the whole value of all and every good, beyond the passing moment; since nothing but the gratification of the instant could be of any worth to us, if we could be deprived of anything the next instant by whoever was momentarily stronger than ourselves. Now this most indispensable of all necessaries, after physical nutriment, cannot be had, unless the machinery for providing it is kept unintermittedly in active play. Our notion, therefore, of the claim we have on our fellow-creatures to join in making safe for us the very groundwork of our existence, gathers feelings around it so much more intense than those concerned in any of the more common cases of utility, that the difference in degree (as is often the case in psychology) becomes a real difference in kind. The claim assumes that character of absoluteness, that apparent infinity, and incommensurability with all other considerations, which constitute the distinction between the feeling of right and wrong and that of ordinary expediency and inexpediency. The feelings concerned are so powerful, and we count so positively on finding a responsive feeling in others (all being alike interested), that *ought* and *should* grow into *must*, and recognized indispensability becomes a moral necessity, analogous to physical, and often not inferior to it in binding force.

[...]

It appears from what has been said, that justice is a name for certain moral requirements, which, regarded collectively, stand higher in the scale of social utility, and are therefore of more paramount obligation, than any others; though particular cases may occur in which some other social duty is so important, as to overrule any one of the general maxims of justice. Thus, to save a life, it may not only be allowable, but a duty, to steal, or take by force, the necessary food or medicine, or to kidnap, and compel to officiate, the only qualified medical practitioner. In such cases, as we do not call anything justice which is not a virtue, we usually say, not that justice must give way to some other moral principle, but that what is just in ordinary cases is, by reason of that other principle, not just in the particular case. By this useful accommodation of language, the character of indefeasibility[12] attributed to justice is kept up, and we are saved from the necessity of maintaining that there can be laudable injustice.

… Justice remains the appropriate name for certain social utilities which are vastly more important, and therefore more absolute and imperative, than any others are as a class (though not more so than others may be in particular cases); and which, therefore, ought to be, as well as naturally are, guarded by a sentiment not only different in degree, but also in kind; distinguished from the milder feeling which attaches to the mere idea of promoting human pleasure or convenience, at once by the more definite nature of its commands, and by the sterner character of its sanctions.

## Study Questions

1. What is the Utility (or Happiness) Principle? How does Mill define happiness? Do you think happiness is a solid basis for an ethical theory? Why or why not?

2. Mill claims that utilitarianism will not violate principles of justice or individual rights. What is his argument for this? Do you find it compelling, or do you think that being a utilitarian will involve violating people's rights? If so, is this a significant weakness of the theory?

3. What is the difference between pleasures that use humans' higher faculties (higher pleasures) and other pleasures (lower pleasures), according to Mill? What are some examples of each type of pleasure? Which are more important, according to Mill? Why? How does Mill claim to know this is true? Do you agree with his assessment of these pleasures? Why is he making this distinction?

4. What is the proof that the Principle of Utility is the correct way to evaluate ethics, according to Mill? That is, why should we use happiness to measure ethical actions? Do you agree with his argument?

## Notes

1  Epicurus (341–270 BCE) was a Greek philosopher.
2  For example, in Diogenes Laertius' *Lives of Eminent Philosophers*, written c. 230 CE.
3  Denied.
4  Stoicism was, with Epicureanism, one of the two main strands of "Hellenistic" philosophy (roughly, that associated with Greek culture during the 300 years after the death of Alexander the Great in 323 BCE). Its main ethical doctrine was that the wise and virtuous man accepts, with calm indifference, his place in the impartial, rational, inevitable order of the universe

    – even if it is his fate to suffer hardship or painful death – but also works dutifully to foster a social order that mirrors the rational order of the cosmos.

5  Choose.

6  A view expressed by voting (or the right to make such a vote).

7  I.e., subtraction (as opposed to an inference).

8  I.e., to all creatures capable of sensation (and thus of feeling pleasure and pain).

9  I.e., sense experience.

10  Mill means the memory of something previously experienced.

11  An action is "expedient" in Mill's terms when it produces utility – when, that is, it will result in the greatest happiness for the greatest number of people.

12  Inability to be annulled or made inapplicable.

# 5. John Rawls, "Distributive Justice"

AMERICAN PHILOSOPHER JOHN RAWLS (1921–2002) also takes up the issue of justice within society, and spells out his version of a just society in "Distributive Justice" (1967). For Rawls, utilitarianism cannot explain sufficiently why people should strive toward equality in a society. That is, he claims that within Utilitarianism it is entirely as possible for a society to split the total happiness such that some get much more than others, as it is for the pleasures of those who receive more to balance out the pain of those who receive much less. Yet he insists that a just society does need to strive toward equality. The way to establish a just society, according to Rawls, is to employ a rhetorical device he calls the original position, which involves a "veil of ignorance." When making choices, to determine what is just, an individual should imagine the choice she would make if she did not know what place in society she occupies. This veil is meant to ensure that individuals choose what is truly fair for all, since everyone remains unaware of where they will land in this society, and they will therefore attempt to make all situations as good as possible. He then posits two principles of justice: the "liberty" principle and the "difference" principle. The liberty principle states that all individuals in a society should have as much liberty as possible. The difference principle states that inequality is allowed only if it works out to everyone's advantage, and that benefits within a society should be capable of being shared by all. With these principles, Rawls attempts to establish a social contract that meets the demands of justice.

---

I[1]

WE MAY THINK OF a human society as a more or less self-sufficient association regulated by a common conception of justice and aimed at advancing the good of its members. As a co-operative venture for mutual advantage, it is characterized by a conflict as well as an identity of interests. There is an identity of interests since social co-operation makes possible a better life for all than any would have if everyone were to try to live by his own efforts; yet at the same time men are not indifferent as to how the greater benefits produced by their joint labors are distributed, for in order to further their own aims each prefers a larger to a lesser share. A conception of justice is a set of principles for choosing between the social arrangements which determine this division and for underwriting a consensus as to the proper distributive shares.

Now at first sight the most rational conception of justice would seem to be utilitarian. For consider: each man in realizing his own good can certainly balance his own losses against his own gains. We can impose a sacrifice on ourselves now for the sake of a greater advantage later. A man quite properly acts, as long as others are not affected, to achieve his own greatest good, to advance his ends as far as possible. Now, why should not a society act on precisely the same principle? Why is not that which is rational in the case of one man right in the case of a group of men? Surely the simplest and most direct conception of the right, and so of justice, is that of maximizing the good. This assumes a prior understanding of what is good, but we can think of the good as already given by the interests of rational individuals. Thus just as the principle of individual choice is to achieve one's greatest good, to advance so far as possible one's own system of rational desires, so the principle of social choice is to realize the greatest good (similarly defined) summed over all the members of society. We arrive at the principle of utility in a natural way: by this principle a society is rightly ordered, and hence just, when its institutions are arranged so as to realize the greatest sum of satisfactions.

The striking feature of the principle of utility is that it does not matter, except indirectly, how this sum of satisfactions is distributed among individuals, any more than it matters, except indirectly, how one man distributes his satisfactions over time. Since certain ways of distributing things affect the total sum of satisfactions, this fact must be taken into account in arranging social institutions; but according to this principle the explanation of common-sense precepts of justice and their seemingly stringent character is that they are those rules which experience shows must be strictly respected and departed from only under exceptional circumstances if the sum of advantages is to be maximized. The precepts of justice are derivative from the one end of attaining the greatest net balance of satisfactions. There is no reason in principle why the greater gains of some should not compensate for the lesser losses of others; or why the violation of the liberty of a few might not be made right by a greater good shared by many. It simply happens, at least under most conditions, that the greatest sum of advantages is not generally achieved in this way. From the standpoint of utility the strictness of common-sense notions of justice has a certain usefulness, but as a philosophical doctrine it is irrational.

If, then, we believe that as a matter of principle each member of society has an inviolability founded on justice which even the welfare of everyone else cannot over-ride, and that a loss of freedom for some is not made right by a greater sum of satisfactions enjoyed by many, we shall have to look for another account of the principles of justice. The principle of utility is incapable of explaining the fact that in a just society the liberties of equal citizenship are taken for granted, and the rights secured by justice are not subject to political bargaining nor to the calculus of social interests. Now, the most natural alternative to the principle of utility is its traditional rival, the theory of the social contract. The aim of the contract doctrine is precisely to account for the strictness of justice by supposing that its principles arise from an agreement among free and independent persons in an original position of equality and hence reflect the integrity and equal sovereignty of the rational persons who are the contractees. Instead of supposing that a conception of right, and so a conception of justice, is simply an extension of the principle of choice for one man to society as a whole, the contract doctrine assumes that the rational individuals who belong to society must choose together, in one joint act, what is to count among them as just and unjust. They are to decide among themselves once and for all what is to be their conception of justice. This decision is thought of as being made in a suitably defined initial situation one of the significant features of which is that no one knows his position in society, nor even his place in the distribution of natural talents and abilities. The principles of justice to which all are forever bound are chosen in the absence of this sort of specific information. A veil of ignorance prevents anyone from being advantaged or disadvantaged by the contingencies of social class and fortune; and hence the bargaining problems which arise in everyday life from the possession of this knowledge do not affect the choice of principles. On the contract doctrine, then, the theory of justice, and indeed ethics itself, is part of the general theory of rational choice, a fact perfectly clear in its Kantian formulation.

Once justice is thought of as arising from an original agreement of this kind, it is evident that the principle of utility is problematical. For why should rational individuals who have a system of ends they wish to advance agree to a violation of their liberty for the sake of a greater balance of satisfactions enjoyed by others? It seems more plausible to suppose that, when situated in an original position of equal right, they would insist upon institutions which returned compensating advantages for any sacrifices required. A rational man would not accept an institution merely because it maximized the sum of advantages irrespective of its effect on his own interests. It appears, then, that the principle of utility would be rejected as a principle of justice, although we shall not try to argue this important question here. Rather, our aim is to give a brief sketch of the conception of distributive shares implicit in the principles of justice which, it seems, would be chosen in the original position. The philosophical appeal of utilitarianism is that it seems to offer a single principle on the basis of which a consistent and complete conception of right can be developed. The problem is to work out a contractarian alternative in such a way that it has comparable if not all the same virtues.

## II

In our discussion we shall make no attempt to derive the two principles of justice which we shall examine; that is, we shall not try to show that they would be chosen in the original position.[2] It must suffice that it is plausible that they would be, at least in preference to the standard forms of traditional theories. Instead we shall be mainly concerned with three questions: first, how to interpret these principles so that they define a consistent and complete conception of justice; second, whether it is possible to arrange the institutions of a constitutional democracy so that these principles are satisfied, at least approximately; and third, whether the conception of distributive shares which they define is compatible with common-sense notions of justice. The significance of these principles is that they allow for the strictness of the claims of justice; and if they can be understood so as to yield a consistent and complete conception, the contractarian alternative would seem all the more attractive.

The two principles of justice which we shall discuss may be formulated as follows: first, each person engaged in an institution or affected by it has an equal right to the most extensive liberty compatible with a like liberty for all; and second, inequalities as defined by the institutional structure or fostered by it are arbitrary unless it is reasonable to expect that they will work out to everyone's advantage and provided that the positions and offices to which they attach or from which they may be gained are open to all. These principles regulate the distributive aspects of institutions by controlling the assignment of rights and duties throughout the whole social structure, beginning with the adoption of a political constitution in accordance with which they are then to be applied to legislation. It is upon a correct choice of a basic structure of society, its fundamental system of rights and duties, that the justice of distributive shares depends.

The two principles of justice apply in the first instance to this basic structure, that is, to the main institutions of the social system and their arrangement, how they are combined together. Thus this structure includes the political constitution and the principal economic and social institutions which together define a person's liberties and rights and affect his life-prospects, what he may expect to be and how well he may expect to fare. The intuitive idea here is that those born into the social system at different positions, say in different social classes, have varying life-prospects determined, in part, by the system of political liberties and personal rights, and by the economic and social opportunities which are made available to these positions. In this way the basic structure of society favors certain men over others, and these are the basic inequalities, the ones which affect their whole life-prospects. It is inequalities of this kind, presumably inevitable in any society, with which the two principles of justice are primarily designed to deal.

Now the second principle holds that an inequality is allowed only if there is reason to believe that the institution with the inequality, or permitting it, will work out for the advantage of every person engaged in it. In the case of the basic structure this means that all inequalities which affect life-prospects, say the inequalities of income and wealth which exist between social classes, must be to the advantage of everyone. Since the principle applies to institutions, we interpret this to mean that inequalities must be to the advantage of the representative man for each relevant social position; they should improve each such man's expectation. Here we assume that it is possible to attach to each position an expectation, and that this expectation is a function of the whole institutional structure: it can be raised and lowered by reassigning rights and duties throughout the system. Thus the expectation of any position depends upon the expectations of the others, and these in turn depend upon the pattern of rights and duties established by the basic structure. But it is not clear what is meant by saying that inequalities must be to the advantage of every representative man....

## IV

... [One] interpretation ... [of what is meant by saying that inequalities must be to the advantage of every representative man] is to choose some social position by reference to which the pattern of expectations as a whole is to be judged, and then to maximize with respect to the expectations of this representative man consistent with the demands of equal liberty and, equality of opportunity. Now, the one obvious candidate is the representative man of those who are least favored by the system of institutional inequalities. Thus we arrive at the following idea: the basic structure of the social system affects the life-prospects of typical individuals according to their initial places in society, say the various income classes into which they are born, or depending upon certain natural attributes, as when institutions make discriminations between men and women or allow certain advantages to be gained by those with greater natural abilities. The fundamental problem of distributive justice concerns the differences in life-prospects which come about in this way. We interpret the second principle to hold that these differences are just if and only if the greater expectations of the more advantaged, when playing a part in the working of the whole social system, improve the expectations of the least advantaged. The basic structure is just throughout when the advantages of the more fortunate promote the well-being of the least fortunate, that is, when a decrease in their advantages would make the least fortunate even worse off than they are. The basic structure is perfectly just when the prospects of the least fortunate are as great as they can be.

In interpreting the second principle (or rather the first part of it which we may, for obvious reasons, refer to as the difference principle), we assume that the first principle requires a basic equal liberty for all, and that the resulting political system, when circumstances permit, is that of a constitutional democracy in some form. There must be liberty of the person and political equality as well as liberty of conscience and freedom of thought. There is one class of equal citizens which defines a common status for all. We also assume that there is equality of opportunity and a fair competition for the available positions on the basis of reasonable qualifications. Now, given this background, the differences to be justified are the various economic and social inequalities in the basic structure which must inevitably arise in such a scheme. These are the inequalities in the distribution of income and wealth and the distinctions in social prestige and status which attach to the various positions and classes. The difference principle says that these inequalities are just if and only if they are part of a larger system in which they work out to the advantage of the most unfortunate representative man. The just distributive shares determined by the basic structure are those specified by this constrained maximum principle.

Thus, consider the chief problem of distributive justice, that concerning the distribution of wealth as it affects the life-prospects of those starting out in the various income groups. These income classes define the relevant representative men from which the social system is to be judged. Now, a son of a member of the entrepreneurial class (in a capitalist society) has a better prospect than that of the son of an unskilled laborer. This will be true, it seems, even when the social injustices which presently exist are removed and the two men are of equal talent and ability; the inequality cannot be done away with as long as something like the family is maintained. What, then, can justify this inequality in life-prospects? According to the second principle it is justified only if it is to the advantage of the representative man who is worst off, in

this case the representative unskilled laborer. The inequality is permissible because lowering it would, let's suppose, make the working man even worse off than he is. Presumably, given the principle of open offices (the second part of the second principle), the greater expectations allowed to entrepreneurs has the effect in the longer run of raising the life-prospects of the laboring class. The inequality in expectation provides an incentive so that the economy is more efficient, industrial advance proceeds at a quicker pace, and so on, the end result of which is that greater material and other benefits are distributed throughout the system. Of course, all of this is familiar, and whether true or not in particular cases, it is the sort of thing which must be argued if the inequality in income and wealth is to be acceptable by the difference principle.

We should now verify that this interpretation of the second principle gives a natural sense in which everyone may be said to be made better off. Let us suppose that inequalities are chain-connected: that is, if an inequality raises the expectations of the lowest position, it raises the expectations of all positions in between. For example, if the greater expectations of the representative entrepreneur raises [sic] that of the unskilled laborer, it [sic] also raises that of the semi-skilled. Let us further assume that inequalities are close-knit: that is, it is impossible to raise (or lower) the expectation of any representative man without raising (or lowering) the expectations of every other representative man, and in particular, without affecting one way or the other that of the least fortunate. There is no loose-jointedness, so to speak, in the way in which expectations depend upon one another. Now, with these assumptions, everyone does benefit from an inequality which satisfies the difference principle, and the second principle as we have formulated it reads correctly. For the representative man who is better off in any pair-wise comparison gains by being allowed to have his advantage, and the man who is worse off benefits from the contribution which all inequalities make to each position below. Of course, chain-connection and close-knitness may not obtain; but in this case those who are better off should not have a veto over the advantages available for the least advantaged. The stricter interpretation of the difference principle should be followed, and all inequalities should be arranged for the advantage of the most unfortunate even if some inequalities are not to the advantage of those in middle positions. Should these conditions fail, then, the second principle would have to be stated in another way.

It may be observed that the difference principle represents, in effect, an original agreement to share in the benefits of the distribution of natural talents and abilities, whatever this distribution turns out to be, in order to alleviate as far as possible the arbitrary handicaps resulting from our initial starting places in society. Those who have been favored by nature, whoever they are, may gain from their good fortune only on terms that improve the well-being of those who have lost out. The naturally advantaged are not to gain simply because they are more gifted, but only to cover the costs of training and cultivating their endowments and for putting them to use in a way which improves the position of the less fortunate. We are led to the difference principle if we wish to arrange the basic social structure so that no one gains (or loses) from his luck in the natural lottery of talent and ability, or from his initial place in society, without giving (or receiving) compensating advantages in return. (The parties in the original position are not said to be attracted by this idea and so agree to it; rather, given the symmetries of their situation, and particularly their lack of knowledge, and so on, they will find it to their interest to agree to a principle which can be understood in this way.) And we should note also that when the difference principle is perfectly satisfied, the basic structure is optimal by the efficiency principle. There is no way to make anyone better off without making someone else worse off, namely, the least fortunate representative man. Thus the two principles of justice define distributive shares in a way compatible with efficiency, at least as long as we move on this highly abstract level. If we want to say (as we do, although it cannot be argued here) that the demands of justice have an absolute weight with respect to efficiency, this claim may seem less paradoxical when it is kept in mind that perfectly just institutions are also efficient.

## V

Our second question is whether it is possible to arrange the institutions of a constitutional democracy so that the two principles of justice are satisfied, at least approximately. We shall try to show that this can be done provided the government regulates a free economy in a certain way. More fully, if law and government act effectively to keep markets competitive, resources fully employed, property and wealth widely distributed over time, and to maintain the appropriate social minimum, then if there is equality of opportunity underwritten by education for all, the resulting distribution will be just. Of course, all of these arrangements and policies are familiar. The only novelty in the following remarks, if there is any novelty at all, is that this framework of institutions can be made to satisfy the difference principle. To argue this, we must sketch the relations of these institutions and how they work together.

First of all, we assume that the basic social structure is controlled by a just constitution which secures the various liberties of equal citizenship. Thus the legal order is administered in accordance with the principle of legality, and liberty of conscience and freedom of thought are taken for granted. The political process is conducted, so far as possible, as a just procedure for choosing between governments and for enacting just legislation. From the standpoint of distributive justice, it is also essential that there be equality of opportunity in several senses. Thus, we suppose that, in addition to maintaining the usual social overhead capital, government provides for equal educational opportunities for all either by subsidizing private schools or by operating a public school system. It also enforces and underwrites equality of opportunity in commercial ventures and in the free choice of occupation. This result is achieved by policing business behavior and by preventing the establishment of barriers and restriction to the desirable positions and markets. Lastly, there is a guarantee of a social minimum which the government meets by family allowances and special payments in times of unemployment, or by a negative income tax.

In maintaining this system of institutions the government may be thought of as divided into four branches. Each branch is represented by various agencies (or activities thereof) charged with preserving certain social and economic conditions. These branches do not necessarily overlap with the usual organization of government, but should be understood as purely conceptual. Thus, the allocation branch is to keep the economy feasibly competitive, that is, to prevent the formation of unreasonable market power.... The allocation branch is also charged with identifying and correcting, say by suitable taxes and subsidies wherever possible, the more obvious departures from efficiency caused by the failure of prices to measure accurately social benefits and costs. The stabilization branch strives to maintain reasonably full employment so that there is no waste through failure to use resources and the free choice of occupation and the deployment of finance is supported by strong effective demand....

The social minimum is established through the operations of the transfer branch.... The main idea is that the workings of the transfer branch take into account the precept of need and assign it an appropriate weight with respect to the other common-sense precepts of justice. A market economy ignores the claims of need altogether. Hence there is a division of labor between the parts of the social system as different institutions answer to different common-sense precepts.... Thus it is obvious that the justice of distributive shares depends upon the whole social system and how it distributes total income, wages plus transfers....

Finally, the distribution branch is to preserve an approximately just distribution of income and wealth over time by affecting the background conditions of the market from period to period. Two aspects of this branch may be distinguished. First of all, it operates a system of inheritance and gift taxes. The aim of these levies is not to raise revenue, but gradually and continually to correct the distribution of wealth and to prevent the concentrations of power to the detriment of liberty and equality of opportunity....

The second part of the distribution branch is a scheme of taxation for raising revenue to cover the costs of public goods, to make transfer payments, and the like. This scheme belongs to the distribution branch since the burden of taxation must be justly shared....

Whatever form the distribution branch assumes, the argument for it is to be based on justice: we must hold that once it is accepted the social system as a whole – the competitive economy surrounded by a just constitutional and legal framework – can be made to satisfy the principles of justice with the smallest loss in efficiency. The long-term expectations of the least advantaged are raised to the highest level consistent with the demands of equal liberty....

## Study Questions

1. How does Rawls's original position work to secure a just society? Do you think that people would make decisions that are most just from behind a "veil of ignorance"?

2. What do Rawls's principles of equality and difference involve? Does a just society need them?

3. What might be an example of an ethical decision that would be made differently under utilitarianism than under Rawls's distributive justice model? Which assessment do you find more useful? Why?

## Notes

1   In this essay I try to work out some of the implications of the two principles of justice discussed in "Justice as Fairness" which first appeared in the *Philosophical Review*, 1958, and which is reprinted in *Philosophy, Politics and Society*, Series II, pp. 132–57.

2   This question is discussed very briefly in "Justice as Fairness," see pp. 138–41. The intuitive idea is as follows. Given the circumstances of the original position, it is rational for a man to choose as if he were designing a society in which his enemy is to assign him his place. Thus, in particular, given the complete lack of knowledge (which makes the choice one under uncertainty), the fact that the decision involves one's life-prospects as a whole and is constrained by obligations to third parties (e.g., one's descendants) and duties to certain values (e.g., to religious truth), it is rational to be conservative and so to choose in accordance with an analogue of the maximin principle. Viewing the situation in this way, the interpretation given to the principles of justice in Section IV is perhaps natural enough. Moreover, it seems clear how the principle of utility can be interpreted: it is the analogue of the Laplacean principle for choice uncertainty. (For a discussion of these choice criteria, see R.D. Luce and H. Raiffa, *Games and Decisions* [1957], pp. 275–98.) ["Laplacean" refers to French mathematician and astronomer Pierre-Simon Laplace (1749–1827).]

# 6. Iris Marion Young, "Five Faces of Oppression"

RESPONDING TO RAWLS AND theories of distributive justice, American philosopher Iris Marion Young (1949–2006) argues in this selection from *Justice and the Politics of Difference* (1990) that social justice needs to be understood in wider terms. Because distributive justice has a tendency to focus on material goods, it overlooks the crucial aspects of oppression and domination that mark injustice within a society. In this piece, Young describes what she sees as five prominent forms of oppression: exploitation, marginalization, powerlessness, cultural imperialism, and violence. In so doing, she works to challenge these forms of oppression. She points out that oppression need not be intentional, and that for every group that is oppressed there is a corresponding group that is privileged, as groups exist in relation to one another. Working under the assumption that it is impossible to hold a fully impartial view such as Rawls's original position (and that pretending to do so only serves to make the claim that one's own position is a "universal" one), Young's larger claim is that we must pay attention to the differences of our situations and the groups we find ourselves within. The categories she describes offer a means toward articulating the more general issues of social injustice, without erasing the specific differences as they are experienced by the individuals within the oppressed groups.

---

Someone who does not see a pane of glass does not know that he does not see it. Someone who, being placed differently, does see it, does not know the other does not see it.

When our will finds expression outside ourselves in actions performed by others, we do not waste our time and our power of attention in examining whether they have consented to this. This is true for all of us. Our attention, given entirely to the success of the undertaking, is not claimed by them as long as they are docile....

Rape is a terrible caricature of love from which consent is absent. After rape, oppression is the second horror of human existence. It is a terrible caricature of obedience.

– Simone Weil[1]

I HAVE PROPOSED AN ENABLING conception of justice. Justice should refer not only to distribution, but also to the institutional conditions necessary for the development and exercise of individual capacities and collective communication and cooperation. Under this conception of justice, injustice refers primarily to two forms of disabling constraints, oppression and domination. While these constraints include distributive patterns, they also involve matters which cannot easily be assimilated to the logic of distribution: decision-making procedures, division of labor, and culture.

Many people in the United States would not choose the term "oppression" to name injustice in our society. For contemporary emancipatory social movements, on the other hand – socialists, radical feminists, American Indian activists, Black activists, gay and lesbian activists – oppression is a central category of political discourse. Entering the political discourse in which oppression is a central category involves adopting a general mode of analyzing and evaluating social structures and practices....

I offer some explication of the concept of oppression as I understand its use by new social movements in the United States since the 1960s. My starting point is reflection on the conditions of the groups said by these movements to be oppressed: among others women, Blacks, Chicanos, Puerto Ricans and other Spanish-speaking Americans, American Indians, Jews, lesbians, gay men, Arabs, Asians, old people, working-class people, and the physically and mentally disabled....

Obviously the above-named groups are not oppressed to the same extent or in the same ways. In the most general sense, all oppressed people suffer some inhibition of their ability to develop and exercise their capacities and express their needs, thoughts, and feelings. In that abstract sense all oppressed people face a common condition. Beyond that, in any more specific sense, it is not possible to define a single set of criteria that describe the condition of oppression of the above groups.... [O]ppression names in fact a family of concepts and conditions, which I divide into five categories: exploitation, marginalization, powerlessness, cultural imperialism, and violence.

... Each may entail or cause distributive injustices, but all involve issues of justice beyond distribution. In accordance with ordinary political usage, I suggest that oppression is a condition of groups. Thus before explicating the meaning of oppression, we must examine the concept of a social group.

## Oppression as a Structural Concept

One reason that many people would not use the term oppression to describe injustice in our society is that they do not understand the term in the same way as do new social movements. In its traditional usage, oppression means the exercise of tyranny by a ruling group. Thus many Americans would agree with radicals in applying the term oppression to the situation of Black South Africans under apartheid. Oppression also traditionally carries a strong connotation of conquest and colonial domination....

New left social movements of the 1960s and 1970s, however, shifted the meaning of the concept of oppression. In its new usage, oppression designates the disadvantage and injustice some people suffer not because a tyrannical power coerces them, but because of the everyday practices of a well-intentioned liberal society. In this new left usage, the tyranny of a ruling group over another, as in South Africa, must certainly be called oppressive. But oppression also refers to systemic constraints on groups that are not necessarily the result of the intentions of a tyrant. Oppression in this sense is structural, rather than the result of a few people's choices or policies. Its causes are embedded in unquestioned norms, habits, and symbols, in the assumptions underlying institutional rules and the collective consequences of following those rules.... In this extended structural sense oppression refers to the vast and deep injustices some groups suffer as a consequence of often unconscious assumptions and reactions of well-meaning people in ordinary interactions, media and cultural stereotypes, and structural features of bureaucratic hierarchies and market mechanisms – in short, the normal processes of everyday life. We cannot eliminate this structural oppression by getting rid of the rulers or making some new laws, because oppressions are systematically reproduced in major economic, political, and cultural institutions.

The systemic character of oppression implies that an oppressed group need not have a correlate oppressing group. While structural oppression involves relations among groups, these relations do not always fit the paradigm of conscious and intentional oppression of one group by another. Foucault (1977) suggests that to understand the meaning and operation of power in modern society we must look beyond the model of power as "sovereignty," a dyadic relation of ruler and subject, and instead analyze the exercise of power as the effect of often liberal and "humane" practices of education, bureaucratic administration, production and distribution of consumer goods, medicine, and so on. The conscious actions of many individuals daily contribute to maintaining and reproducing oppression, but those people are usually simply doing their jobs or living their lives, and do not understand themselves as agents of oppression.

I do not mean to suggest that within a system of oppression individual persons do not intentionally harm others in oppressed groups. The raped woman, the beaten Black youth, the locked-out worker, the gay man harassed on the street, are victims of intentional actions by identifiable agents. I also do not mean to deny that specific groups are beneficiaries of the oppression of other groups, and thus have an interest in their continued oppression. Indeed, for every oppressed group there is a group that is *privileged* in relation to that group....

I offer below an explication of five faces of oppression as a useful set of categories and distinctions which I believe is comprehensive, in the sense that it covers all the groups said by new left social movements to be oppressed and all the ways they are oppressed. I derive the five faces of oppression from reflection on the condition of these groups. Because different factors, or combinations of factors, constitute the oppression of different groups, making their oppression irreducible, I believe it is not possible to give one essential definition of oppression. The five categories articulated in this chapter, however, are adequate to describe the oppression of any group, as well as its similarities with and differences from the oppression of other groups. But first we must ask what a group is.

**The Concept of a Social Group**

Oppression refers to structural phenomena that immobilize or diminish a group. But what is a group? Our ordinary discourse differentiates people according to social groups such as women and men, age groups, racial and ethnic groups, religious groups, and so on. Social groups of this sort are not simply collections of people, for they are more fundamentally intertwined with the identities of the people described as belonging to them. They are a specific kind of collectivity, with specific consequences for how people understand one another and themselves....

A social group is a collective of persons differentiated from at least one other group by cultural forms, practices, or way of life. Members of a group have a specific affinity with one another because of their similar experience or way of life, which prompts them to associate with one another more than with those not identified with the group, or in a different way. Groups are an expression of social relations; a group exists only in relation to at least one other group. Group identification arises, that is, in the encounter and interaction between social collectivities that experience some differences in their way of life and forms of association, even if they also regard themselves as belonging to the same society.

As long as they associated solely among themselves, for example, an American Indian group thought of themselves only as "the people." The encounter with other American Indians created an awareness of difference; the others were named as a group, and the first group came to see themselves as a group. But social groups do not arise only from an encounter between different societies. Social processes also differentiate groups within a single society. The sexual division of labor, for example, has created social groups of women and men in all known societies. Members of each gender have a certain affinity with others in their group because of what they do or experience, and differentiate themselves from the other gender, even when members of each gender consider that they have much in common with members of the other, and consider that they belong to the same society.

... To arrive at a specific concept of the social group it is thus useful to contrast social groups with both aggregates and associations.

An aggregate is any classification of persons according to some attribute. Persons can be aggregated according to any number of attributes – eye color, the make of car they drive, the street they live on. Some people interpret the groups that have emotional and social salience in our society as aggregates, as arbitrary classifications of persons according to such attributes as skin color, genitals, or age. George Sher, for example, treats social groups as aggregates, and uses the arbitrariness of aggregate classification as a reason not to give special attention to groups. "There are really as many groups as there are combinations of people and if we are going to ascribe claims to equal treatment to racial, sexual, and other groups with high visibility, it will be mere favoritism not to ascribe similar claims to these other groups as well" (Sher, 1987, p. 256).

But "highly visible" social groups such as Blacks or women are different from aggregates, or mere "combinations of people" (see French, 1975; Friedman and May, 1985; May, 1987, chap. 1). A social group is defined not primarily by a set of shared attributes, but by a sense of identity. What defines Black Americans as a social group is not primarily

their skin color; some persons whose skin color is fairly light, for example, identify themselves as Black. Though sometimes objective attributes are a necessary condition for classifying oneself or others as belonging to a certain social group, it is identification with a certain social status, the common history that social status produces, and self-identification that define the group as a group.

Social groups are not entities that exist apart from individuals, but neither are they merely arbitrary classifications of individuals according to attributes which are external to or accidental to their identities. Admitting the reality of social groups does not commit one to reifying collectivities, as some might argue. Group meanings partially constitute people's identities in terms of the cultural forms, social situation, and history that group members know as theirs, because these meanings have been either forced upon them or forged by them or both (cf. Fiss, 1976). Groups are real not as substances, but as forms of social relations (cf. May, 1987, pp. 22–23).

Moral theorists and political philosophers tend to elide social groups more often with associations than with aggregates (e.g., French, 1975; May, 1987, chap. 1). By an association I mean a formally organized institution, such as a club, corporation, political party, church, college, or union. Unlike the aggregate model of groups, the association model recognizes that groups are defined by specific practices and forms of association. Nevertheless it shares a problem with the aggregate model. The aggregate model conceives the individual as prior to the collective, because it reduces the social group to a mere set of attributes attached to individuals. The association model also implicitly conceives the individual as ontologically prior to the collective, as making up, or constituting, groups.

A contract model of social relations is appropriate for conceiving associations, but not groups. Individuals constitute associations, they come together as already formed persons and set them up, establishing rules, positions, and offices. The relationship of persons to associations is usually voluntary, and even when it is not, the person has nevertheless usually entered the association. The person is prior to the association also in that the person's identity and sense of self are usually regarded as prior to and relatively independent of association membership.

Groups, on the other hand, constitute individuals. A person's particular sense of history, affinity, and separateness, even the person's mode of reasoning, evaluating, and expressing feeling, are constituted partly by her or his group affinities. This does not mean that persons have no individual styles, or are unable to transcend or reject a group identity. Nor does it preclude persons from having many aspects that are independent of these group identities.

The social ontology underlying many contemporary theories of justice ... is methodologically individualist or atomist. It presumes that the individual is ontologically prior to the social. This individualist social ontology usually goes together with a normative conception of the self as independent. The authentic self is autonomous, unified, free, and self-made, standing apart from history and affiliations, choosing its life plan entirely for itself.

One of the main contributions of poststructuralist philosophy has been to expose as illusory this metaphysic of a unified self-making subjectivity, which posits the subject as an autonomous origin or an underlying substance to which attributes of gender, nationality, family role, intellectual disposition, and so on might attach. Conceiving the subject in this fashion implies conceiving consciousness as outside of and prior to language and the context of social interaction, which the subject enters. Several currents of recent philosophy challenge this deeply held Cartesian assumption.... The self is a product of social processes, not their origin....

A person joins an association, and even if membership in it fundamentally affects one's life, one does not take that membership to define one's very identity, in the way, for example, being Navaho might. Group affinity, on the other hand, has the character of what Martin Heidegger (1962) calls "thrownness": one *finds oneself* as a member of a group, which one experiences as always already having been. For our identities are defined in relation to how others identify us, and they do so in terms of groups which are always already associated with specific attributes, stereotypes, and norms.

From the thrownness of group affinity it does not follow that one cannot leave groups and enter new ones. Many women become lesbian after first identifying as heterosexual. Anyone who lives long enough becomes old. These cases exemplify thrownness precisely because such changes in group affinity are experienced as transformations in one's identity. Nor does it follow from the thrownness of group affinity that one cannot define the meaning of group identity for oneself; those who identify with a group can redefine the meaning and norms of group identity. Indeed, in Chapter 6 I will show how oppressed groups have sought to confront their oppression by engaging in just such redefinition. The present point is only that one first finds a group identity as given, and then takes it up in a certain way. While groups may come into being, they are never founded.

Groups, I have said, exist only in relation to other groups. A group may be identified by outsiders without those so identified having any specific consciousness of themselves as a group. Sometimes a group comes to exist only because one group excludes and labels a category of persons, and those labeled come to understand themselves as group members only slowly, on the basis of their shared oppression. In Vichy France, for example, Jews who had been so assimilated that they had no specifically Jewish identity were marked as Jews by others and given a specific social status by them. These people "discovered" themselves as Jews, and then formed a group identity and affinity with one another (see Sartre, 1948). A person's group identities may be for the most part only a background or horizon to his or her life, becoming salient only in specific interactive contexts.

Assuming an aggregate model of groups, some people think that social groups are invidious fictions, essentializing arbitrary attributes. From this point of view problems of prejudice, stereotyping, discrimination, and exclusion exist because some people mistakenly believe that group identification makes a difference to the capacities, temperament, or virtues of group members. This individualist conception of persons and their relation to one another tends to identify oppression with group identification. Oppression, on this view, is something that happens to people when they are classified in groups. Because others identify them as a group, they are excluded and despised. Eliminating oppression thus requires eliminating groups. People should be treated as individuals, not as members of groups, and allowed to form their lives freely without stereotypes or group norms.

… [I take] issue with that position. While I agree that individuals should be free to pursue life plans in their own way, it is foolish to deny the reality of groups. Despite the modern myth of a decline of parochial attachments and ascribed identities, in modern society group differentiation remains endemic. As both markets and social administration increase the web of social interdependency on a world scale, and as more people encounter one another as strangers in cities and states, people retain and renew ethnic, locale, age, sex, and occupational group identifications, and form new ones in the processes of encounter (cf. Ross, 1980, p. 19; Rothschild, 1981, p. 130). Even when they belong to oppressed groups, people's group identifications are often important to them, and they often feel a special affinity for others in their group. I believe that group differentiation is both an inevitable and a desirable aspect of modern social processes. Social justice, I shall argue in later chapters, requires not the melting away of differences, but institutions that promote reproduction of and respect for group differences without oppression.

Though some groups have come to be formed out of oppression, and relations of privilege and oppression structure the interactions between many groups, group differentiation is not in itself oppressive. Not all groups are oppressed. In the United States Roman Catholics are a specific social group, with distinct practices and affinities with one another, but they are no longer an oppressed group. Whether a group is oppressed depends on whether it is subject to one or more of the five conditions I shall discuss below.

The view that groups are fictions does carry an important antideterminist or antiessentialist intuition. Oppression has often been perpetrated by a conceptualization of group difference in terms of unalterable essential natures that determine what group members deserve or are capable of, and that exclude groups so entirely from one another that they have no similarities or overlapping attributes. To assert that it is possible to have social group difference without oppression, it is necessary to conceptualize groups in a much more relational and fluid fashion.

Although social processes of affinity and differentiation produce groups, they do not give groups a substantive essence. There is no common nature that members of a group share. As aspects of a process, moreover, groups are fluid; they come into being and may fade away. Homosexual practices have existed in many societies and historical periods, for example. Gay men or lesbians have been identified as specific groups and so identified themselves, however, only in the twentieth century (see Ferguson, 1989, chap. 9; Altman, 1981).

Arising from social relations and processes, finally, group differences usually cut across one another. Especially in a large, complex, and highly differentiated society, social groups are not themselves homogeneous, but mirror in their own differentiations many of the other groups in the wider society. In American society today, for example, Blacks are not a simple, unified group with a common life. Like other racial and ethnic groups, they are differentiated by age, gender, class, sexuality, region, and nationality, any of which in a given context may become a salient group identity.

This view of group differentiation as multiple, cross-cutting, fluid, and shifting implies another critique of the model of the autonomous, unified self. In complex, highly differentiated societies like our own, all persons have multiple group identifications. The culture, perspective, and relations of privilege and oppression of these various groups, moreover, may not cohere. Thus individual persons, as constituted partly by their group affinities and relations, cannot be unified, themselves are heterogeneous and not necessarily coherent.

## The Faces of Oppression

### Exploitation

The central function of Marx's theory of exploitation is to explain how class structure can exist in the absence of legally and normatively sanctioned class distinctions. In precapitalist societies domination is overt and accomplished through directly political means. In both slave society and feudal society the right to appropriate the product of the labor of others partly defines class privilege, and these societies legitimate class distinctions with ideologies of natural superiority and inferiority.

Capitalist society, on the other hand, removes traditional juridically enforced class distinctions and promotes a belief in the legal freedom of persons. Workers freely contract with employers and receive a wage; no formal mechanisms of law or custom force them to work for that employer or any employer. Thus the mystery of capitalism arises: when everyone is formally free, how can there be class domination? Why do class distinctions persist between the wealthy, who own the means of production, and the mass of people, who work for them? The theory of exploitation answers this question.

Profit, the basis of capitalist power and wealth, is a mystery if we assume that in the market goods exchange at their values. The labor theory of value dispels this mystery. Every commodity's value is a function of the labor time necessary for its production. Labor power is the one commodity which in the process of being consumed produces new value. Profit comes from the difference between the value of the labor performed and the value of the capacity to labor which the capitalist purchases. Profit is possible only because the owner of capital appropriates any realized surplus value....

The injustice of capitalist society consists in the fact that some people exercise their capacities under the control, according to the purposes, and for the benefit of other people. Through private ownership of the means of production, and through markets that allocate labor and the ability to buy goods, capitalism systematically transfers the powers of some persons to others, thereby augmenting the power of the latter. In this process of the transfer of powers, according to Macpherson, the capitalist class acquires and maintains an ability to extract benefits from workers. Not only are powers transferred from workers to capitalists, but also the powers of workers diminish by more than the amount of transfer, because workers suffer material deprivation and a loss of control, and hence are deprived of important elements of self-respect. Justice, then, requires eliminating the institutional forms that enable and enforce this process of transference and replacing them with institutional forms that enable all to develop and use their capacities in a way that does not inhibit, but rather can enhance, similar development and use in others.

The central insight expressed in the concept of exploitation, then, is that this oppression occurs through a steady process of the transfer of the results of the labor of one social group to benefit another. The injustice of class division does not consist only in the distributive fact that some people have great wealth while most people have little (cf. Buchanan; 1982, pp. 44–49; Holmstrom, 1977). Exploitation enacts a structural relation between social groups. Social rules about what work is, who does what for whom, how work is compensated, and the social process by which the results of work are appropriated operate to enact relations of power and inequality. These relations are produced and reproduced through a systematic process in which the energies of the have-nots are continuously expended to maintain and augment the power, status, and wealth of the haves....

Feminists have had little difficulty showing that women's oppression consists partly in a systematic and unreciprocated transfer of powers from women to men. Women's oppression consists not merely in an inequality of status, power, and wealth resulting from men's excluding them from privileged activities. The freedom, power, status, and self-realization of men is possible precisely because women work for them. Gender exploitation has two aspects, transfer of the fruits of material labor to men and transfer of nurturing and sexual energies to men.

Christine Delphy (1984), for example, describes marriage as a class relation in which women's labor benefits men without comparable remuneration. She makes it clear that the exploitation consists not in the sort of work that women do in the home, for this might include various kinds of tasks, but in the fact that they perform tasks for someone on whom they are dependent. Thus, for example, in most systems of agricultural production in the world, men take to market the goods women have produced, and more often than not men receive the status and often the entire income from this labor.

With the concept of sex-affective production, Ann Ferguson (1979; 1984; 1989, chap. 4) identifies another form of the transference of women's energies to men. Women provide men and children with emotional care and provide men with sexual satisfaction, and as a group receive relatively little of either from men (cf. Brittan and Maynard, 1984, pp. 142–48). The gender socialization of women makes us tend to be more attentive to interactive dynamics than men, and makes women good at providing empathy and support for people's feelings and at smoothing over interactive tensions. Both men and women look to women as nurturers of their personal lives, and women frequently complain that when they look to men for emotional support they do not receive it (Easton, 1978). The norms of heterosexuality, moreover, are oriented around male pleasure, and consequently many women receive little satisfaction from their sexual interaction with men (Gottlieb, 1984).

Most feminist theories of gender exploitation have concentrated on the institutional structure of the patriarchal family. Recently, however, feminists have begun to explore relations of gender exploitation enacted in the contemporary workplace and through the state. Carol Brown argues that as men have removed themselves from responsibility for children, many women have become dependent on the state for subsistence as they continue to bear nearly total responsibility for childrearing (Brown, 1981; cf. Boris and Bardaglio, 1983; A. Ferguson, 1984). This creates a new system of the exploitation of women's domestic labor mediated by state institutions, which she calls public patriarchy.

In twentieth-century capitalist economies the workplaces that women have been entering in increasing numbers serve as another important site of gender exploitation. David Alexander (1987) argues that typically feminine jobs involve gender-based tasks requiring sexual labor, nurturing, caring for others' bodies, or smoothing over workplace tensions. In these ways women's energies are expended in jobs that enhance the status of, please, or comfort others, usually men; and these gender-based labors of waitresses, clerical workers, nurses, and other caretakers often go unnoticed and undercompensated.

To summarize, women are exploited in the Marxist sense to the degree that they are wage workers. Some have argued that women's domestic labor also represents a form of capitalist class exploitation insofar as it is labor covered by the wages a family receives. As a group, however, women undergo specific forms of gender exploitation in which their energies and power are expended, often unnoticed and unacknowledged, usually to benefit men by releasing them for more important and creative work, enhancing their status or the environment around them, or providing them with sexual or emotional service.

Race is a structure of oppression at least as basic as class or gender. Are there, then, racially specific forms of exploitation? There is no doubt that racialized groups in the United States, especially Blacks and Latinos, are oppressed through capitalist superexploitation resulting from a segmented labor market that tends to reserve skilled, high-paying, unionized jobs for whites. There is wide disagreement about whether such superexploitation benefits whites as a group or only benefits the capitalist class (see Reich, 1981), and I do not intend to enter into that dispute here.

However one answers the question about capitalist superexploitation of racialized groups, is it possible to conceptualize a form of exploitation that is racially specific on analogy with the gender-specific forms just discussed? I suggest that the category of *menial* labor might supply a means for such conceptualization. In its derivation "menial" designates the labor of servants. Wherever there is racism, there is the assumption, more or less enforced, that members of the oppressed racial groups are or ought to be servants of those, or some of those, in the privileged group. In most white racist societies this means that many white people have dark- or yellow-skinned domestic servants, and in the United States today there remains significant racial structuring of private household service. But in the United States today much service labor has gone public: anyone who goes to a good hotel or a good restaurant can have servants. Servants often attend the daily – and nightly – activities of business executives, government officials, and other high-status professionals. In our society there remains strong cultural pressure to fill servant jobs – bellhop, porter, chambermaid, busboy, and so on – with Black and Latino workers. These jobs entail a transfer of energies whereby the servers enhance the status of the served.

Menial labor usually refers not only to service, however, but also to any servile, unskilled, low-paying work lacking in autonomy, in which a person is subject to taking orders from many people. Menial work tends to be auxiliary work, instrumental to the work of others, where those others receive primary recognition for doing the job. Laborers on a construction site, for example, are at the beck and call of welders, electricians, carpenters, and other skilled workers, who receive recognition for the job done. In the United States explicit racial discrimination once reserved menial work for Blacks, Chicanos, American Indians, and Chinese, and menial work still tends to be linked to Black and Latino workers (Symanski, 1985). I offer this category of menial labor as a form of racially specific exploitation, as a provisional category in need of exploration.

The injustice of exploitation is most frequently understood on a distributive model....

Jeffrey Reiman argues that such a distributive understanding of exploitation reduces the injustice of class processes to a function of the inequality of the productive assets classes own. This misses, according to Reiman, the relationship of force between capitalists and workers, the fact that the unequal exchange in question occurs within coercive structures that give workers few options (Reiman, 1987; cf. Buchanan, 1982, pp. 44–49; Holmstrom, 1977). The injustice of exploitation consists in social processes that bring about a transfer of energies from one group to another to produce unequal distributions, and in the way in which social institutions enable a few to accumulate while they constrain many more. The injustices of exploitation cannot be eliminated by redistribution of goods, for as long as institutionalized practices and structural relations remain unaltered, the process of transfer will re-create an unequal distribution of benefits. Bringing about justice where there is exploitation requires reorganization of institutions and practices of decision making, alteration of the division of labor, and similar measures of institutional, structural, and cultural change.

## Marginalization

Increasingly in the United States racial oppression occurs in the form of marginalization rather than exploitation. Marginals are people the system of labor cannot or will not use. Not only in Third World capitalist countries, but also in most Western capitalist societies, there is a growing underclass of people permanently confined to lives of social marginality, most of whom are racially marked – Blacks or Indians in Latin America, and Blacks, East Indians, Eastern Europeans, or North Africans in Europe.

Marginalization is by no means the fate only of racially marked groups, however. In the United States a shamefully large proportion of the population is marginal: old people, and increasingly people who are not very old but get laid off from their jobs and cannot find new work; young people, especially Black or Latino, who cannot find first or second jobs; many single mothers and their children; other people involuntarily unemployed; many mentally and physically disabled people; American Indians, especially those on reservations.

Marginalization is perhaps the most dangerous form of oppression. A whole category of people is expelled from useful participation in social life and thus potentially subjected to severe material deprivation and even extermination. The material deprivation marginalization often causes is certainly unjust, especially in a society where others have plenty. Contemporary advanced capitalist societies have in principle acknowledged the injustice of material deprivation caused by marginalization, and have taken some steps to address it by providing welfare payments and services. The continuance of this welfare state is by no means assured, and in most welfare state societies, especially the United States, welfare redistributions do not eliminate large-scale suffering and deprivation.

Material deprivation, which can be addressed by redistributive social policies, is not, however, the extent of the harm caused by marginalization. Two categories of injustice beyond distribution are associated with marginality in advanced capitalist societies. First, the provision of welfare itself produces new injustice by depriving those dependent on it of rights and freedoms that others have. Second, even when material deprivation is somewhat mitigated by the welfare state, marginalization is unjust because it blocks the opportunity to exercise capacities in socially defined and recognized ways....

Liberalism has traditionally asserted the right of all rational autonomous agents to equal citizenship. Early bourgeois liberalism explicitly excluded from citizenship all those whose reason was questionable or not fully developed, and all those not independent (Pateman, 1988, chap. 3; cf. Bowles and Gintis, 1986, chap. 2). Thus poor people, women, the mad and the feebleminded, and children were explicitly excluded from citizenship, and many of these were housed in institutions modeled on the modern prison: poorhouses, insane asylums, schools.

Today the exclusion of dependent persons from equal citizenship rights is only barely hidden beneath the surface. Because they depend on bureaucratic institutions for support or services, the old, the poor, and the mentally or physically disabled are subject to patronizing, punitive, demeaning, and arbitrary treatment by the policies and people associated with welfare bureaucracies. Being a dependent in our society implies being legitimately subject to the often arbitrary and invasive authority of social service providers and other public and private administrators, who enforce rules with which the marginal must comply, and otherwise exercise power over the conditions of their lives. In meeting needs of the marginalized, often with the aid of social scientific disciplines, welfare agencies also construct the needs themselves. Medical and social service professionals know what is good for those they serve, and the marginals and dependents themselves do not have the right to claim to know what is good for them (Fraser, 1987a; K. Ferguson, 1984, chap. 4). Dependency in our society thus implies, as it has in all liberal societies, a sufficient warrant to suspend basic rights to privacy, respect, and individual choice.

Although dependency produces conditions of injustice in our society, dependency in itself need not be oppressive. One cannot imagine a society in which some people would not need to be dependent on others at least some of the time: children, sick people, women recovering from childbirth, old people who have become frail, depressed or otherwise emotionally needy persons, have the moral right to depend on others for subsistence and support.

An important contribution of feminist moral theory has been to question the deeply held assumption that moral agency and full citizenship require that a person be autonomous and independent. Feminists have exposed this assumption as inappropriately individualistic and derived from a specifically male experience of social relations, which values competition and solitary achievement (see Gilligan, 1982; Friedman, 1985). Female experience of social relations, arising both from women's typical domestic care responsibilities and from the kinds of paid work that many women do, tends to recognize dependence as a basic human condition (cf. Hartsock, 1983, chap. 10). Whereas on the autonomy model a just society would as much as possible give people the opportunity to be independent, the feminist model envisions justice as according respect and participation in decision making to those who are dependent as well as to those who are independent (Held, 1987). Dependency should not be a reason to be deprived of choice and respect, and much of the oppression many marginals experience would be lessened if a less individualistic model of rights prevailed.

Marginalization does not cease to be oppressive when one has shelter and food. Many old people, for example, have sufficient means to live comfortably but remain oppressed in their marginal status. Even if marginals were provided a comfortable material life within institutions that respected their freedom and dignity, injustices of marginality would remain in the form of uselessness, boredom, and lack of self-respect. Most of our society's productive and recognized activities take place in contexts of organized social cooperation, and social structures and processes that close persons out of participation in such social cooperation are unjust. Thus while marginalization definitely entails serious issues of distributive justice, it also involves the deprivation of cultural, practical, and institutionalized conditions for exercising capacities in a context of recognition and interaction.

The fact of marginalization raises basic structural issues of justice, in particular concerning the appropriateness of a connection between participation in productive activities of social cooperation, on the one hand, and access to the means of consumption, on the other. As marginalization is increasing, with no sign of abatement, some social policy analysts have introduced the idea of a "social wage" as a guaranteed socially provided income not tied to the wage system. Restructuring of productive activity to address a right of participation, however, implies organizing some socially productive activity outside of the wage system (see Offe, 1985, pp. 95–100), through public works or self-employed collectives.

Powerlessness

... [T]he Marxist idea of class is important because it helps reveal the structure of exploitation: that some people have their power and wealth because they profit from the labor of others.... It remains the case that the labor of most people in the society augments the power of relatively few. Despite their differences from nonprofessional workers, most professional workers are still not members of the capitalist class. Professional labor either involves exploitative transfers to capitalists or supplies important conditions for such transfers. Professional workers are in an ambiguous class position, it is true, because ... they also benefit from the exploitation of nonprofessional workers.

While it is false to claim that a division between capitalist and working classes no longer describes our society, it is also false to say that class relations have remained unaltered since the nineteenth century. An adequate conception of oppression cannot ignore the experience of social division reflected in the colloquial distinction between the "middle class" and the "working class," a division structured by the social division of labor between professionals and nonprofessionals. Professionals are privileged in relation to nonprofessionals, by virtue of their position in the division of labor and the status it carries. Nonprofessionals suffer a form of oppression in addition to exploitation, which I call powerlessness.

In the United States, as in other advanced capitalist countries, most workplaces are not organized democratically, direct participation in public policy decisions is rare, and policy implementation is for the most part hierarchical, imposing rules on bureaucrats and citizens. Thus most people in these societies do not regularly participate in making decisions that affect the conditions of their lives and actions, and in this sense most people lack significant power. At the same time, ... domination in modern society is enacted through the widely dispersed powers of many agents mediating the decisions of others. To that extent many people have some power in relation to others, even though they lack the power to decide policies or results. The powerless are those who lack authority or power even in this mediated sense, those over whom power is exercised without their exercising it; the powerless are situated so that they must take orders and rarely have the right to give them. Powerlessness also designates a position in the division of labor and the concomitant social position that allows persons little opportunity to develop and exercise skills. The powerless have little or no work autonomy, exercise little creativity or judgment in their work, have no technical expertise or authority, express themselves awkwardly, especially in public or bureaucratic settings, and do not command respect. Powerlessness names the oppressive situations Sennett and Cobb (1972) describe in their famous study of working-class men.

This powerless status is perhaps best described negatively: the powerless lack the authority, status, and sense of self that professionals tend to have. The status privilege of professionals has three aspects, the lack of which produces oppression for nonprofessionals.

First, acquiring and practicing a profession has an expansive, progressive character. Being professional usually requires a college education and the acquisition of a specialized knowledge that entails working with symbols and concepts. Professionals experience progress first in acquiring the expertise, and then in the course of professional advancement and rise in status. The life of the nonprofessional by comparison is powerless in the sense that it lacks this orientation toward the progressive development of capacities and avenues for recognition.

Second, while many professionals have supervisors and cannot directly influence many decisions or the actions of many people, most nevertheless have considerable day-to-day work autonomy. Professionals usually have some authority over others, moreover – either over workers they supervise, or over auxiliaries, or over clients. Nonprofessionals, on the other hand, lack autonomy, and in both their working and their consumer-client lives often stand under the authority of professionals.

Though based on a division of labor between "mental" and "manual" work, the distinction between "middle class" and "working class" designates a division not only in working life, but also in nearly all aspects of social life. Professionals and nonprofessionals belong to different cultures in the United States. The two groups tend to live in segregated neighborhoods or even different towns, a process itself mediated by planners, zoning officials, and real estate people. The groups tend to have different tastes in food, decor, clothes, music, and vacations, and often different health and educational needs. Members of each group socialize for the most part with others in the same status group. While there is some intergroup mobility between generations, for the most part the children of professionals become professionals and the children of nonprofessionals do not.

Thus, third, the privileges of the professional extend beyond the workplace to a whole way of life. I call this way of life "respectability." To treat people with respect is to be prepared to listen to what they have to say or to do what they request because they have some authority, expertise, or influence. The norms of respectability in our society are associated specifically with professional culture. Professional dress, speech, tastes, demeanor, all connote respectability. Generally professionals expect and receive respect from others. In restaurants, banks, hotels, real estate offices, and many other such public places, as well as in the media, professionals typically receive more respectful treatment than non-professionals. For this reason nonprofessionals seeking a loan or a job, or to buy a house or a car, will often try to look "professional" and "respectable" in those settings.

The privilege of this professional respectability appears starkly in the dynamics of racism and sexism. In daily interchange women and men of color must prove their respectability. At first they are often not treated by strangers with respectful distance or deference. Once people discover that this woman or that Puerto Rican man is a college teacher or a business executive, however, they often behave more respectfully toward her or him. Working-class white men, on the other hand, are often treated with respect until their working-class status is revealed....

I have discussed several injustices associated with powerlessness: inhibition in the development of one's capacities, lack of decision-making power in one's working life, and exposure to disrespectful treatment because of the status one occupies. These injustices have distributional consequences, but are more fundamentally matters of the division of labor. The oppression of powerlessness brings into question the division of labor basic to all industrial societies: the social division between those who plan and those who execute....

## Cultural Imperialism

Exploitation, marginalization, and powerlessness all refer to relations of power and oppression that occur by virtue of the social division of labor – who works for whom, who does not work, and how the content of work defines one institutional position relative to others. These three categories refer to structural and institutional relations that delimit people's material lives, including but not restricted to the resources they have access to and the concrete opportunities they have or do not have to develop and exercise their capacities. These kinds of oppression are a matter of concrete power in relation to others – of who benefits from whom, and who is dispensable.

Recent theorists of movements of group liberation, notably feminist and Black liberation theorists, have also given prominence to a rather different form of oppression, which following Lugones and Spelman (1983) I shall call cultural imperialism. To experience cultural imperialism means to experience how the dominant meanings of a society render the particular perspective of one's own group invisible at the same time as they stereotype one's group and mark it out as the Other.

Cultural imperialism involves the universalization of a dominant group's experience and culture, and its establishment as the norm. Some groups have exclusive or primary access to what Nancy Fraser (1987b) calls the means of interpretation and communication in a society. As a consequence, the dominant cultural products of the society, that is, those most widely disseminated, express the experience, values, goals, and achievements of these groups. Often without noticing they do so, the dominant groups project their own experience as representative of humanity as such. Cultural products also express the dominant group's perspective on and interpretation of events and elements in the society, including other groups in the society, insofar as they attain cultural status at all.

An encounter with other groups, however, can challenge the dominant group's claim to universality. The dominant group reinforces its position by bringing the other groups under the measure of its dominant norms. Consequently, the difference of women from men, American Indians or Africans from Europeans, Jews from Christians, homosexuals from heterosexuals, workers from professionals, becomes reconstructed largely as deviance and inferiority. Since only the dominant group's cultural expressions receive wide dissemination, their cultural expressions become the normal, or the universal, and thereby the unremarkable. Given the normality of its own cultural expressions and identity, the dominant group constructs the differences which some groups exhibit as lack and negation. These groups become marked as Other.

The culturally dominated undergo a paradoxical oppression, in that they are both marked out by stereotypes and at the same time rendered invisible. As remarkable, deviant beings, the culturally imperialized are stamped with an essence. The stereotypes confine them to a nature which is often attached in some way to their bodies, and which thus cannot easily be denied. These stereotypes so permeate the society that they are not noticed as contestable. Just as everyone knows that the earth goes around the sun, so everyone knows that gay people are promiscuous, that Indians are alcoholics, and that women are good with children. White males, on the other hand, insofar as they escape group marking, can be individuals.

Those living under cultural imperialism find themselves defined from the outside, positioned, placed, by a network of dominant meanings they experience as arising from elsewhere, from those with whom they do not identify and who do not identify with them. Consequently, the dominant culture's stereotyped and inferiorized images of the group must be internalized by group members at least to the extent that they are forced to react to behavior of others influenced by those images. This creates for the culturally oppressed the experience that W.E.B. Du Bois called "double consciousness" – "this sense of always looking at one's self through the eyes of others, of measuring one's soul by the tape of a world that looks on in amused contempt and pity" (DuBois, 1969 [1903], p. 45). Double consciousness arises when the oppressed subject refuses to coincide with these devalued, objectified, stereotyped visions of herself or himself. While the subject desires recognition as human, capable of activity, full of hope and possibility, she receives from the dominant culture only the judgment that she is different, marked, or inferior.

The group defined by the dominant culture as deviant, as a stereotyped Other, *is* culturally different from the dominant group, because the status of Otherness creates specific experiences not shared by the dominant group, and because culturally oppressed groups also are often socially segregated and occupy specific positions in the social division of labor. Members of such groups express their specific group experiences and interpretations of the world to one another, developing and perpetuating their own culture. Double consciousness, then, occurs because one finds one's being defined by two cultures: a dominant and a subordinate culture. Because they can affirm and recognize one another as sharing similar experiences and perspectives on social life, people in culturally imperialized groups can often maintain a sense of positive subjectivity.

Cultural imperialism involves the paradox of experiencing oneself as invisible at the same time that one is marked out as different. The invisibility comes about when dominant groups fail to recognize the perspective embodied in their cultural expressions as a perspective. These dominant cultural expressions often simply have little place for the experience of other groups, at most only mentioning or referring to them in stereotyped or marginalized ways. This, then, is the injustice of cultural imperialism: that the oppressed group's own experience and interpretation of social life finds little expression that touches the dominant culture, while that same culture imposes on the oppressed group its experience and interpretation of social life....

## Violence

Finally, many groups suffer the oppression of systematic violence. Members of some groups live with the knowledge that they must fear random, unprovoked attacks on their persons or property, which have no motive but to damage, humiliate, or destroy the person. In American society women, Blacks, Asians, Arabs, gay men, and lesbians live under such threats of violence, and in at least some regions Jews, Puerto Ricans, Chicanos, and other Spanish-speaking Americans must fear such violence as well. Physical violence against these groups is shockingly frequent. Rape Crisis Center networks estimate that more than one-third of all American women experience an attempted or successful sexual assault in their lifetimes. Manning Marable (1984, pp. 238–41) catalogues a large number of incidents of racist violence and terror against blacks in the United States between 1980 and 1982. He cites dozens of incidents of the severe beating, killing, or rape of Blacks by police officers on duty, in which the police involved were acquitted of any wrongdoing. In 1981, moreover, there were at least five hundred documented cases of random white teenage violence against Blacks. Violence against gay men and lesbians is not only common, but has been increasing in the last five years. While the frequency of physical attack on members of these and other racially or sexually marked groups is very disturbing, I also include in this category less severe incidents of harassment, intimidation, or ridicule simply for the purpose of degrading, humiliating, or stigmatizing group members.

Given the frequency of such violence in our society, why are theories of justice usually silent about it? I think the reason is that theorists do not typically take such incidents of violence and harassment as matters of social injustice. No moral theorist would deny that such acts are very wrong. But unless all immoralities are injustices, they might wonder, why should such acts be interpreted as symptoms of social injustice? Acts of violence or petty harassment are committed by particular individuals, often extremists, deviants, or the mentally unsound. How then can they be said to involve the sorts of institutional issues I have said are properly the subject of justice?

What makes violence a face of oppression is less the particular acts themselves, though these are often utterly horrible, than the social context surrounding them, which makes them possible and even acceptable. What makes violence a phenomenon of social injustice, and not merely an individual moral wrong, is its systemic character, its existence as a social practice.

Violence is systemic because it is directed at members of a group simply because they are members of that group. Any woman, for example, has a reason to fear rape. Regardless of what a Black man has done to escape the oppressions of marginality or powerlessness, he lives knowing he is subject to attack or harassment. The oppression of violence consists not only in direct victimization, but in the daily knowledge shared by all members of oppressed groups that they are *liable* to violation, solely on account of their group identity. Just living under such a threat of attack on oneself or family or friends deprives the oppressed of freedom and dignity, and needlessly expends their energy.

Violence is a social practice. It is a social given that everyone knows happens and will happen again. It is always at the horizon of social imagination, even for those who do not perpetrate it. According to the prevailing social logic, some circumstances make such violence more "called for" than others. The idea of rape will occur to many men who pick up a hitchhiking woman; the idea of hounding or teasing a gay man on their dorm floor will occur to many straight male college students. Often several persons inflict the violence together, especially in all-male groupings. Sometimes violators set out looking for people to beat up, rape, or taunt. This rule-bound, social, and often premeditated character makes violence against groups a social practice.

Group violence approaches legitimacy, moreover, in the sense that it is tolerated. Often third parties find it unsurprising because it happens frequently and lies as a constant possibility at the horizon of the social imagination. Even when they are caught, those who perpetrate acts of group-directed violence or harassment often receive light or no punishment. To that extent society renders their acts acceptable.

An important aspect of random, systemic violence is its irrationality. Xenophobic violence differs from the violence of states or ruling-class repression. Repressive violence has a rational, albeit evil, motive: rulers use it as a coercive tool to maintain their power. Many accounts of racist, sexist, or homophobic violence attempt to explain its motivation as a desire to maintain group privilege or domination. I do not doubt that fear of violence often functions to keep oppressed groups subordinate, but I do not think xenophobic violence is rationally motivated in the way that, for example, violence against strikers is.

On the contrary, the violation of rape, beating, killing, and harassment of women, people of color, gays, and other marked groups is motivated by fear or hatred of those groups. Sometimes the motive may be a simple will to power, to victimize those marked as vulnerable by the very social fact that they are subject to violence. If so, this motive is secondary in the sense that it depends on a social practice of group violence. Violence-causing fear or hatred of the other at least partly involves insecurities on the part of the violators; its irrationality suggests that unconscious processes are at work.... I think such unconscious fears account at least partly for the oppression I have here called violence. It may also partly account for cultural imperialism.

Cultural imperialism, moreover, itself intersects with violence. The culturally imperialized may reject the dominant meanings and attempt to assert their own subjectivity, or the fact of their cultural difference may put the lie to the dominant culture's implicit claim to universality. The dissonance generated by such a challenge to the hegemonic cultural meanings can also be a source of irrational violence.

Violence is a form of injustice that a distributive understanding of justice seems ill equipped to capture. This may be why contemporary discussions of justice rarely mention it. I have argued that group-directed violence is institutionalized and systemic. To the degree that institutions and social practices encourage, tolerate, or enable the perpetration of violence against members of specific groups, those institutions and practices are unjust and should be reformed. Such reform may require the redistribution of resources or positions, but in large part can come only through a change in cultural images, stereotypes, and the mundane reproduction of relations of dominance and aversion in the gestures of everyday life....

## Applying the Criteria

... I have arrived at the five faces of oppression – exploitation, marginalization, powerlessness, cultural imperialism, and violence....

Applying these five criteria to the situation of groups makes it possible to compare oppressions without reducing them to a common essence or claiming that one is more fundamental than another. One can compare the ways in which a particular form of oppression appears in different groups. For example, while the operations of cultural imperialism are often experienced in similar fashion by different groups, there are also important differences. One can compare the combinations of oppressions groups experience, or the intensity of those oppressions. Thus with these criteria one can plausibly claim that one group is more oppressed than another without reducing all oppressions to a single scale....

## References

Alexander, David. 1987. "Gendered Job Traits and Women's Occupations." PhD dissertation, Economics, University of Massachusetts.

Altman, Dennis. 1982. *The Homosexualization of American Society*. Boston: Beacon.

Boris, Ellen and Peter Bardaglio. 1983. "The Transformation of Patriarchy: The Historic Role of the State." In Irene Diamond, ed., *Families, Politics and Public Policy*. New York: Longman.

Bowles, Samuel and Herbert Gintis. 1982. "Crisis of Liberal Democratic Capitalism: The Case of the United States." *Politics and Society* 11: 51–94.

Brittan, Arthur and Mary Maynard. 1984. *Sexism, Racism and Oppression*. Oxford: Blackwell.

Brown, Carol. 1981. "Mothers, Fathers and Children: From Private to Public Patriarchy." In Lydia Sargent, ed., *Women and Revolution*. Boston: South End.

Buchanan, Allen. 1982. *Marx and Justice*. Totowa, NJ: Rowman and Allanheld.

Delphy, Christine. 1984. *Close to Home: A Materialist Analysis of Women's Oppression*. Amherst: U of Massachusetts P.

Du Bois, W.E.B. 1969 [1903]. *The Souls of Black Folk*. New York: New American Library.

Easton, Barbara. 1978. "Feminism and the Contemporary Family." *Socialist Review* 39 (May/June): 11–36.

Ferguson, Ann. 1984. "On Conceiving Motherhood and Sexuality: A Feminist Materialist Approach." In Joyce Trebilcot, ed., *Mothering: Essays in Feminist Theory*. Totowa, NJ: Rowman and Allanheld.

____. 1989. *Blood at the Root*. London: Pandora.

Ferguson, Kathy. 1984. *The Feminist Case against Bureaucracy*. Philadelphia: Temple UP.

Fiss, Owen. 1976. "Groups and the Equal Protection Clause." *Philosophy and Public Affairs* 5 (Winter): 107–76.

Foucault, Michel. 1977. *Discipline and Punish*. New York: Pantheon.

Fraser, Nancy. 1987a. "Women, Welfare, and the Politics of Need Interpretation." *Hypatia: A Journal of Feminist Philosophy* 2 (Winter): 103–22.

____. 1987b. "Social Movements vs. Disciplinary Bureaucracies: The Discourse of Social Needs." CHS Occasional Paper No. 8 Center for Humanistic Studies. U of Minnesota.

French, Peter. 1975. "Types of Collectivities and Blame." *The Personalist* 56 (Spring): 160–69.

Friedman, Marilyn. 1985. "Care and Context ion Moral Reasoning." In Carol Harding, ed., *Moral Dilemmas: Philosophical and Psychological Issues in the Development of Moral Reasoning*. Chicago: Precedent.

____ and Larry May. 1985. "Harming Women as a Group." *Social Theory and Practice* 11 (Summer): 297–34.

Gilligan, Carol. 1982. *In a Different Voice*. Cambridge: Harvard UP.

Gottlieb, Rhonda. 1984. "The Political Economy of Sexuality." *Review of Radical Political Economy* 16 (Spring): 143–65.

Hartsock, Nancy. 1983. *Money, Sex and Power*. New York: Longman.

Heidegger, Martin. 1962. *Being and Time*. New York: Harper and Row.

Held, Virginia. 1987. "A Non-Contractual Society." In Marsha Hanen and Kai Nielsen, eds., *Science, Morality and Feminist Theory*. Calgary: U of Calgary P.

Holmstrom, Nancy. 1977. "Exploitation." *Canadian Journal of Philosophy* 7 (June): 353–69.

Lugones, Maria C. and Elizabeth V. Spelman. 1983. "Have We Got a Theory for you! Feminist Theory, Cultural Imperialism and the Demand for 'the Woman's Voice.'" *Women's Studies International Forum* 6: 573–81.

Marable, Manning. 1984. *Race, Reform and Rebellion: The Second Reconstruction in Black America, 1945–82*. Jackson: UP of Mississippi.

May, Larry. 1987. *The Morality of Groups: Collective Responsibility, Group-Based Harm, and Corporate Rights*. Notre Dame: Notre Dame UP.

Offe, Claus. 1985. *Disorganized Capitalism*. Cambridge: MIT P.

Pateman, Carole. 1988. *The Sexual Contract*. Stanford: Stanford UP.

Reich, Michael. 1981. *Racial Inequality*. Princeton: Princeton UP.

Reiman, Jeffrey. 1987. "Exploitation, Force, and the Moral Assessment of Capitalism: Thoughts on Roemer and Cohen." *Philosophy and Public Affairs* 16 (Winter): 3-41.

Ross, Jeffrey. 1980. Introduction to Jeffrey Ross and Ann Baker Cottrell, eds., *The Mobilization of Collective Identity*. Lanham, MD: UP of America.

Rothschild, Joseph. 1981. *Ethnopolitics*. New York: Columbia UP.

Sartre, Jean-Paul. 1948. *Anti-Semite and Jew*. New York: Schloken.

Sennett, Richard and Jonathan Cobb. 1972. *The Hidden Injuries of Class*. New York: Vintage.

Sher, George. 1987. "Groups and the Constitution." In Gertrude Ezorsky, ed., *Moral Rights in the Workplace*. Albany: State U of New York P.

Symanski, Al. 1985. "The Structure of Race." *Review of Radical Political Economy* 17 (Winter): 106–20.

## Study Questions

1. What are the five faces of oppression, according to Young? Explain the defining characteristics of each "face." Which type of oppression does Young claim is the most dangerous one? Why?

2. Young assumes that people cannot truly go behind a "veil of ignorance" (as Rawls suggests), and that our social position always somehow informs how we view the world. Do you agree or disagree with this assumption?

3. One of Young's main understandings is that oppression is structural; that is, it arises from everyday practices, not necessarily some tyrannical power, and that as such it can come from "a well-intentioned liberal society." What might be some examples of this type of oppression? Do you agree that it is possible for people who have good intentions to be oppressing others, often without noticing this?

## Note

1 Simone Weil (1909–43) was a French philosopher.

# 7. bell hooks, "Theory as Liberatory Practice"

BECAUSE IT IS TYPICALLY members of privileged groups who develop theories, theory itself can be seen as suspect. That is, those who have the time and the resources to reflect on and then offer their own interpretations of what is happening may be smuggling their own privileged perspectives into what are presumed to be universal claims. In this piece from 1991, bell hooks (b. 1952) argues that theory in and of itself is neither oppressive nor liberating: that it becomes so depending on what the theorist does. She is concerned specifically about feminist theory that does not serve the individuals it is presumably created for and that in fact alienates individuals through its use of abstraction and jargon. This is its own form of domination. Yet she maintains that the ideas within even these theories could become liberatory, and reduce oppression, if used differently. She reminds us of theory's power to name and transform situations, and she cautions against a type of reactionary anti-intellectualism that throws the baby out with the bathwater, as it were. Though she is looking at feminist theory, hooks offers a way to perform an ethical critique of ethical theory by simply asking in what ways the theory serves to make our lives and the world better.

---

... I CAME TO THEORY BECAUSE I was hurting – the pain within me was so intense that I could not go on living. I came to theory desperate, wanting to comprehend – to grasp what was happening around and within me. Most importantly, I wanted to make the hurt go away. I saw in theory then a location for healing.

I came to theory young, when I was still a child. In *The Significance of Theory* Terry Eagleton [1981] says:

> Children make the best theorists, since they have not yet been educated into accepting our routine social practices as "natural," and so insist on posing to those practices the most embarrassingly general and fundamental questions, regarding them with a wondering estrangement which we adults have long forgotten. Since they do not yet grasp our social practices as inevitable, they do not see why we might not do things differently.

Whenever I tried in childhood to compel folks around me to do things differently, to look at the world differently, using theory as intervention, as a way to challenge the status quo, I was punished. I remember trying to explain at a very young age to Mama why I thought it was highly inappropriate for Daddy, this man who hardly spoke to me, to have the right to discipline me, to punish me physically with whippings. Her response was to suggest I was losing my mind and in need of *more* frequent punishment.

Imagine if you will this young black couple struggling first and foremost to realize the patriarchal norm (that is of the woman staying home, taking care of the household and children while the man worked) even though such an arrangement meant that economically, they would always be living with less. Try to imagine what it must have been like for them, each of them working hard all day, struggling to maintain a family of seven children, then having to cope with one bright-eyed child relentlessly questioning, daring to challenge male authority, rebelling against the very patriarchal norm they were trying so hard to institutionalize.

It must have seemed to them that some monster had appeared in their midst in the shape and body of a child – a demonic little figure who threatened to subvert and undermine all that they were seeking to build. No wonder then that their response was to repress, contain, punish. No wonder that Mama would say to me, now and then, exasperated, frustrated, "I don't know where I got you from, but I sure wish I could give you back."

Imagine then if you will, my childhood pain. I did not feel truly connected to these strange people, to these familial folks who could not only fail to grasp my worldview but who just simply did not want to hear it. As a child, I didn't know where I had come from. And when I was not desperately seeking to belong to this family community that never seemed to accept or want me, I was desperately trying to discover the place of my belonging. I was desperately trying to find my way home. How I envied Dorothy her journey in *The Wizard of Oz*, that she could travel to her worst fears and nightmares only to find at the end that "there is no place like home." Living in childhood without a sense of home, I found a place of sanctuary in "theorizing," in making sense out of what was happening. I found a place where I could imagine possible futures, a place where life could be lived differently. This "lived" experience of critical thinking, of reflection and analysis, became a place where I worked at explaining the hurt and making it go away. Fundamentally, I learned from this experience that theory could be a healing place.

Psychoanalyst Alice Miller lets you know in her introduction to the book *Prisoners of Childhood* [1981] that it was her own personal struggle to recover from the wounds of childhood that led her to rethink and theorize

anew prevailing social and critical thought about the meaning of childhood pain, of child abuse. In her adult life, through her practice, she experienced theory as a healing place. Significantly, she had to imagine herself in the space of childhood, to look again from that perspective, to remember "crucial information, answers to questions which had gone unanswered throughout [her] study of philosophy and psychoanalysis." When our lived experience of theorizing is fundamentally linked to processes of self-recovery, of collective liberation, no gap exists between theory and practice. Indeed, what such experience makes more evident is the bond between the two – that ultimately reciprocal process wherein one enables the other.

Theory is not inherently healing, liberatory, or revolutionary. It fulfills this function only when we ask that it do so and direct our theorizing towards this end. When I was a child, I certainly did not describe the processes of thought and critique I engaged in as "theorizing." Yet, as I suggested in *Feminist Theory: From Margin to Center* [1984], the possession of a term does not bring a process or practice into being; concurrently one may practice theorizing without ever knowing/possessing the term, just as we can live and act in feminist resistance without ever using the word "feminism."

Often individuals who employ certain terms freely – terms like "theory" or "feminism" – are not necessarily practitioners whose habits of being and living most embody the action, the practice of theorizing or engaging in feminist struggle. Indeed, the privileged act of naming often affords those in power access to modes of communication and enables them to project an interpretation, a definition, a description of their work and actions, that may not be accurate, that may obscure what is really taking place. Katie King's essay "Producing Sex, Theory, and Culture: Gay/Straight Re-Mappings in Contemporary Feminism" (in *Conflicts in Feminism* [1990]) offers a very useful discussion of the way in which academic production of feminist theory formulated in hierarchical settings often enables women, particularly white women, with high status and visibility, to draw upon the works of feminist scholars who may have less or no status, less or no visibility, without giving recognition to these sources. King discusses the way work is appropriated and the way readers will often attribute ideas to a well-known scholar/feminist thinker, even if that individual has cited in her work that she is building on ideas gleaned from less well-known sources. Focusing particularly on the work of Chicana theorist Chela Sandoval, King states, "Sandoval has been published only sporadically and eccentrically, yet her circulating unpublished manuscripts are much more cited and often appropriated, even while the range of her influence is rarely understood." Though King risks positioning herself in a caretaker role as she rhetorically assumes the posture of feminist authority, determining the range and scope of Sandoval's influence, the critical point she works to emphasize is that the production of feminist theory is complex, that it is an individual practice less often than we think and usually emerges from engagement with collective sources. Echoing feminist theorists, especially women of color who have worked consistently to resist the construction of restrictive critical boundaries within feminist thought, King encourages us to have an expansive perspective on the theorizing process.

Critical reflection on contemporary production of feminist theory makes it apparent that the shift from early conceptualizations of feminist theory (which insisted that it was most vital when it encouraged and enabled feminist practice) begins to occur or at least becomes most obvious with the segregation and institutionalization of the feminist theorizing process in the academy, with the privileging of written feminist thought/theory over oral narratives. Concurrently, the efforts of black women and women of color to challenge and deconstruct the category "woman" – the insistence on recognition that gender is not the sole factor determining constructions of femaleness – was a critical intervention, one which led to a profound revolution in feminist thought and truly interrogated and disrupted the hegemonic feminist theory produced primarily by academic women, most of whom were white.

In the wake of this disruption, the assault on white supremacy made manifest in alliances between white women academics and white male peers seems to have been formed and nurtured around common efforts to formulate and impose standards of critical evaluation that would be used to define what is theoretical and what is not. These standards often led to appropriation and/or devaluation of work that did not "fit," that was suddenly deemed not theoretical – or not theoretical enough. In some circles, there seems to be a direct connection between white feminist scholars turning towards critical work and theory by white men, and the turning away of white feminist scholars from fully respecting and valuing the critical insights and theoretical offerings of black women or women of color.

Work by women of color and marginalized groups or white women (for example, lesbians, sex radicals), especially if written in a manner that renders it accessible to a broad reading public, is often de-legitimized in academic settings, even if that work enables and promotes feminist practice. Though such work is often appropriated by the very individuals setting restrictive critical standards, it is this work that they most often claim is not really theory. Clearly, one of the uses these individuals make of theory is instrumental. They use it to set up unnecessary and competing hierarchies of thought which reinscribe the politics of domination by designating work as either inferior, superior, or more or less worthy of attention. King emphasizes that "theory finds different uses in different locations." It is evident that one of the many uses of theory in academic locations is in the production of an intellectual class hierarchy where the only work deemed truly theoretical is work that is highly abstract, jargonistic, difficult to read, and containing obscure references. In Childers and hooks's "A Conversation about Race and Class" (also in *Conflicts in Feminism*) literary critic Mary Childers declares that it is highly ironic that "a certain kind of theoretical performance which only a small cadre of people can possibly understand" has come to be seen as representative of any production of critical thought that will be given recognition within many academic circles as "theory." It is especially ironic when this is the case with feminist theory. And, it is easy to imagine different locations, spaces outside academic exchange, where such theory would not only be seen as useless, but as politically nonprogressive, a kind of narcissistic, self-indulgent practice that most seeks to create a gap between theory and practice so as to perpetuate class elitism. There are so many settings in this country where the written word has only slight visual meaning, where individuals who cannot read or write can find no use for a published theory however lucid or opaque. Hence, any theory that cannot be shared in everyday conversation cannot be used to educate the public.

Imagine what a change has come about within feminist movements when students, most of whom are female, come to Women's Studies classes and read what they are told is feminist theory only to feel that what they are reading has no meaning, cannot be understood, or when understood in no way connects to "lived" realities beyond the classroom. As feminist activists we might ask ourselves, of what use is feminist theory that assaults the fragile psyches of women struggling to throw off patriarchy's oppressive yoke? We might ask ourselves, of what use is feminist theory that literally beats them down, leaves them stumbling bleary-eyed from classroom settings feeling humiliated, feeling as though they could easily be standing in a living room or bedroom somewhere naked with someone who has seduced them or is going to, who also subjects them to a process of interaction that humiliates, that strips them of their sense of value? Clearly, a feminist theory that can do this may function to legitimize Women's Studies and feminist scholarship in the eyes of the ruling patriarchy, but it undermines and subverts feminist movements. Perhaps it is the existence of this most highly visible feminist theory that compels us to talk about the gap between theory and practice. For it is indeed the purpose of such theory to divide, separate, exclude, keep at a distance. And because this theory continues to be used to silence, censor, and devalue various feminist theoretical voices, we cannot simply ignore it. Yet, despite its uses as an instrument of domination, it may also contain important ideas, thoughts, visions, that could, if used differently, serve a healing, liberatory function. However, we cannot ignore the dangers it poses to feminist struggle which must be rooted in a theory that informs, shapes, and makes feminist practice possible.

Within feminist circles, many women have responded to hegemonic feminist theory that does not speak clearly to us by trashing theory, and, as a consequence, further promoting the false dichotomy between theory and practice. Hence, they collude with those whom they would oppose. By internalizing the false assumption that theory is not a social practice, they promote the formation within feminist circles of a potentially oppressive hierarchy where all concrete action is viewed as more important than any theory written or spoken. Recently, I went to a gathering of predominantly black women where we discussed whether or not black male leaders, such as Martin Luther King and Malcolm X, should be subjected to feminist critiques that pose hard questions about their stance on gender issues. The entire discussion was less than two hours. As it drew to a close, a black woman who had been particularly silent, said that she was not interested in all this theory and rhetoric, all this talk, that she was more interested in action, in doing something, that she was just "tired" of all the talk.

This woman's response disturbed me: it is a familiar reaction. Perhaps in her daily life she inhabits a world different from mine. In the world I live in daily, there are few occasions when black women or women-of-color thinkers come together to debate rigorously issues of race, gender, class, and sexuality. Therefore, I did not know where she was coming from when she suggested that the discussion we were having was common, so common as to be something we could dispense with or do without. I felt that we were engaged in a process of critical dialogue and theorizing that has long been taboo. Hence, from my perspective we were charting new journeys, claiming for ourselves as black women an intellectual terrain where we could begin the collective construction of feminist theory.

In many black settings, I have witnessed the dismissal of intellectuals, the putting down of theory, and remained silent. I have come to see that silence is an act of complicity, one that helps perpetuate the idea that we can engage in revolutionary black liberation and feminist struggle without theory. Like many insurgent black intellectuals, whose intellectual work and teaching is often done in predominantly white settings, I am often so pleased to be engaged with a collective group of black folks that I do not want to make waves, or make myself an outsider by disagreeing with the group. In such settings, when the work of intellectuals is devalued, I have in the past rarely contested prevailing assumptions, or have spoken affirmatively or ecstatically about intellectual process. I was afraid that if I took a stance that insisted on the importance of intellectual work, particularly theorizing, or if I just simply stated that I thought it was important to read widely, I would risk being seen as uppity, or as lording it over. I have often remained silent.

These risks to one's sense of self now seem trite when considered in relation to the crises we are facing as African Americans, to our desperate need to rekindle and sustain the flame of black liberation struggle. At the gathering I mentioned, I dared to speak, saying in response to the suggestion that we were just wasting our time talking, that I saw our words as an action, that our collective struggle to discuss issues of gender and blackness without censorship was subversive practice. Many of the issues that we continue to confront as black people – low self-esteem, intensified nihilism and despair, repressed rage and violence that destroys our physical and psychological well-being – cannot be addressed by survival strategies that have worked in the past. I insisted that we needed new theories rooted in an attempt to understand both the nature of our contemporary predicament and the means by which we might collectively engage in resistance that would transform our current reality. I was, however, not as rigorous and relentless as I would have been in a different setting in my efforts to emphasize the importance of intellectual work, the production of theory as a social practice that can be liberatory. Though not afraid to speak, I did not want to be seen as the one who "spoiled" the good time, the collective sense of sweet solidarity in blackness. This fear reminded me of what it was like more than ten years ago to be in feminist settings, posing questions about theory and practice, particularly about issues of race and racism that were seen as potentially disruptive of sisterhood and solidarity....

Again and again, black women find our efforts to speak, to break silence and engage in radical progressive political debates, opposed. There is a link between the silencing we experience, the censoring, the anti-intellectualism in predominantly black settings that are supposedly supportive (like all-black woman space), and that silencing that takes place in institutions wherein black women and women of color are told that we cannot be fully heard or listened to because our work is not theoretical enough. In "Travelling Theory: Cultural Politics of Race and Representation" [1990], cultural critic Kobena Mercer reminds us that blackness is complex and multifaceted and that black people can be interpolated into reactionary and antidemocratic politics. Just as some elite academics who construct theories of "blackness" in ways that make it a critical terrain which only the chosen few can enter – using theoretical work on race to assert their authority over black experience, denying democratic access to the process of theory making – threaten collective black liberation struggle, so do those among us who react to this by promoting anti-intellectualism by declaring all theory as worthless. By reinforcing the idea that there is a split between theory and practice or by creating such a split, both groups deny the power of liberatory education for critical consciousness, thereby perpetuating conditions that reinforce our collective exploitation and repression.

I was reminded recently of this dangerous anti-intellectualism when I agreed to appear on a radio show with a group of black women and men to discuss Shahrazad Ali's *The Blackman's Guide to Understanding the Blackwoman* [1989]. I listened to speaker after speaker express contempt for intellectual work, and speak against any call for the production of theory. One black woman was vehement in her insistence that "we don't need no theory." Ali's book, through written in plain language, in a style that makes use of engaging black vernacular, has a theoretical foundation. It is rooted in theories of patriarchy (for example, the sexist, essentialist belief that male domination of females is "natural"), that misogyny is the only possible response black men can have to any attempt by women to be fully self-actualized. Many black nationalists will eagerly embrace critical theory and thought as a necessary weapon in the struggle against white supremacy, but suddenly lose the insight that theory is important when it comes to questions of gender, of analyzing sexism and sexist oppression in the particular and specific ways it is manifest in black experience. The discussion of Ali's book is one of many possible examples illustrating the way contempt and disregard for theory undermines collective struggle to resist oppression and exploitation.

Within revolutionary feminist movements, within revolutionary black liberation struggles, we must continually claim theory as necessary practice within a holistic framework of liberatory activism. We must do more than call attention to ways theory is misused. We must do more than critique the conservative and at times reactionary uses some academic women make of feminist theory. We must actively work to call attention to the importance of creating a theory that can advance renewed feminist movements, particularly highlighting that theory which seeks to further feminist opposition to sexism, and sexist oppression. Doing this, we necessarily celebrate and value theory that can be and is shared in oral as well as written narrative.

Reflecting on my own work in feminist theory, I find writing – theoretical talk – to be most meaningful when it invites readers to engage in critical reflection and to engage in the practice of feminism. To me, this theory emerges from the concrete, from my efforts to make sense of everyday life experiences, from my efforts to intervene critically in my life and the lives of others. This to me is what makes feminist transformation possible. Personal testimony, personal experience, is such fertile ground for the production of liberatory feminist theory because it usually forms the base of our theory making. While we work to resolve those issues that are most pressing in daily life (our need for literacy, an end to violence against women and children, women's health and reproductive rights, and sexual freedom, to name a few), we engage in a critical process of theorizing that enables and empowers. I continue to be amazed that there is so much feminist writing produced and yet so little feminist theory that strives to speak to women, men and children about ways we might transform our lives via a conversion to feminist practice. Where can we find a body of feminist theory that is directed toward helping individuals integrate feminist thinking and practice into daily life? What feminist theory, for example, is directed toward assisting women who live in sexist households in their efforts to bring about feminist change?

We know that many individuals in the United States have used feminist thinking to educate themselves in ways that allow them to transform their lives. I am often critical of a lifestyle-based feminism, because I fear that any feminist transformational process that seeks to change society is easily co-opted if it is not rooted in a political commitment to mass-based feminist movement. Within white supremacist capitalist patriarchy, we have already witnessed the commodification of feminist thinking (just as we experience the commodification of blackness) in ways that make it seem as though one can partake of the "good" that these movements produce without any commitment to transformative politics and practice. In this capitalist culture, feminism and feminist theory are fast becoming a commodity that only the privileged can afford. This process of commodification is disrupted and subverted when as feminist activists we affirm our commitment to a politicized revolutionary feminist movement that has as its central agenda the transformation of society....

It is not easy to name our pain, to make it a location for theorizing. Patricia Williams, in her essay "On Being the Object of Property" (in *The Alchemy of Race and Rights* [1991]), writes that even those of us who are "aware" are made to feel the pain that all forms of domination (homophobia, class exploitation, racism, sexism, imperialism) engender.

> There are moments in my life when I feel as though a part of me is missing. There are days when I feel so invisible that I can't remember what day of the week it is, when I feel so manipulated that I can't remember my own name, when I feel so lost and angry that I can't speak a civil word to the people who love me best. These are the times when I catch sight of my reflection in store windows and am surprised to see a whole person looking back ... I have to close my eyes at such times and remember myself, draw an internal pattern that is smooth and whole.

It is not easy to name our pain, to theorize from that location....

Mari Matsuda has told us that "we are fed a lie that there is no pain in war," and that patriarchy makes this pain possible. Catharine MacKinnon reminds us that "we know things with our lives and we live that knowledge, beyond what any theory has yet theorized." Making this theory is the challenge before us. For in its production lies the hope of our liberation, in its production lies the possibility of naming all our pain – of making all our hurt go away. If we create feminist theory, feminist movements that address this pain, we will have no difficulty building a mass-based feminist resistance struggle. There will be no gap between feminist theory and feminist practice.

## Study Questions

1. Do you agree with hooks that theory can be liberatory? If so, in what ways? What might be examples of this? If not, why not?

2. Do you agree that theory can be an expression of domination? Why or why not? What are some of hooks's examples of this? If a theory can be used to dominate, can one extract something important from the theory nonetheless?

3. Near the beginning of her piece, hooks offers a personal story. Why do you suppose she does this?

4. Why might people reject the use of theory? Why does hooks argue against this?

# Section II:
# Personal and Public Identity

WHO AM I? WHILE there are many an-swers to this question, they all seek to provide us with a sense of identity. Concerns about identity in Western philosophy are often seen as concerns about persistency over time, about what links the me of today to the me when I was a child and to the me I will be on my deathbed; or the essence of an individual – that is, what it is in us that does not, will not, and cannot change. For most of the general public, though, asking who I am includes both more and less than this: more, because for example perhaps who we are is a set of relations; perhaps who we are changes over time (a common assumption); less, because for example maybe there isn't any *one* identity or set of characteristics that makes us who we are (and therefore we *don't have* an essence); perhaps who we are would collapse if we were left entirely alone, as in solitary confinement (often seen as the ultimate punishment for this very reason).

In an age of metadata, in which the individual person is lucky to be but a blip on a chart, and mass production of everything from our beverage choice to the clothes we wear, it is easy to lose one's sense of self. On the other hand, we appear hyper-individual-ized in our social media and can follow the particular individuals we enjoy through their Twitter feed, "like" specific movies, artists, or books, and personalize our ringtones or just about anything else (from a given choice of options, of course). Are we our virtual selves? Are we the sum total of our choices? How do we even go about addressing that question: who am I? And what is the significance of our answers?

This section investigates the formation of various identities, as well as the privileges, experiences, and harms that can accompany this process, and the ways in which identities affect decision making and both political and everyday thinking. It begins with Jean-Paul Sartre's classic description of how others affect our own sense of self, examines the ethical significance of the recognition of others as theorized by Axel Honneth, and then moves on to consider some of the concrete identities that people either assume or are given, as well as the impact these identities can have.

## Ethics and Identity Formation

I have serious reason to believe that the planet from which the little prince came is the asteroid known as B-612.

This asteroid has only once been seen through the telescope. That was by a Turkish astronomer, in 1909. On making his discovery, the astronomer had presented it to the International Astronomical

Congress, in a great demonstration. But he was in Turkish costume, and so nobody would believe what he said.

Grown-ups are like that …

Fortunately, however, for the reputation of Asteroid B-612, a Turkish dictator made a law that his subjects, under pain of death, should change to European costume. So in 1920 the astronomer gave his demonstration all over again, dressed with impressive style and elegance. And this time everybody accepted his report.

– Antoine de Saint-Exupéry,
*The Little Prince* (1943)

Ethics involves interacting with others. As mentioned in the introduction to Section I, one large question that the field of ethics addresses is how to live one's life, but that question inevitably involves concerns about how to live one's life *with others*. Sometimes "others" involves animals or the environment and brings up issues like those discussed in Section V on environmental ethics. Sometimes the ultimate "other" is perceived as a divinity, and this raises religious concerns (e.g., how do I live my life in relation to God?). Most often, though, those "others" being considered are other people. There is much discussion within ethics about dealing with other people, particularly when other people are seen *as* "others," as examined in Section IX. But it is difficult to find explicit discussions in most ethics textbooks about intersubjectivity – that is, how others affect our very sense of self, and vice versa – and about the concerns these interconnections raise. In other words, most attention is focused on our external relations with others. But what of our internal relations, both in terms of how we perceive others, and how that might affect our actions, and in terms of how others perceive us, and the effects of this on our sense and reality of our own existence? For example, we

may help someone physically or materially, which is the kind of external action that ethicists will often evaluate, typically in a positive light. But if we do this because we perceive the other person as incapable of helping herself due to some incompetence or lack, which is viewed as a negative character trait, are we potentially inflicting harm of some sort? This is a question that is not frequently addressed.

Presumably, our thoughts drive our intentional actions. As the opening quotation from Saint-Exupéry indicates, our understandings of the identity of the person we are dealing with can substantially influence our responses to that individual. Simply put, our thoughts about other people have an impact upon how we act toward those people. Similarly, our sense of who we ourselves are affects our behavior, and that sense in large part comes from our dealings with others. There is no guarantee of the consistency of how various others see me, or of how others see me and how I see myself, but considered broadly, in terms of personality traits for example, it presumably would be very difficult to claim that I am a nice person if everyone around me claimed otherwise. And we act accordingly, trying to fulfill or avoid these impressions, as the bumper sticker proclaiming "I hope I'm as good as my dog thinks I am" suggests.

We are living in a world that is paradoxically both more interconnected and more disconnected than ever before. If we have the resources, we can correspond instantaneously with anyone in almost any place on the planet (and beyond, if you happen to be in an airplane or work for NASA), but we often don't know who our immediate neighbor is and have been known to text people sitting next to us rather than speak directly to them. On a larger scale, many national identities that used to connect people are in flux, sometimes due to much stronger preference for regional identities, but sometimes more simply because there are people who are more likely to feel an association with their sports team, their musical interests, or their consumer products than their country. What, then, constitutes the connections with and perceptions of other people, and what of them?

In Western philosophy (and Western countries more generally), there is a tendency to view humans as autonomous (or self-ruling) individuals, separated from other humans as well as from the world. They (we) are considered to be subjects, looking out on a world of objects around them (us). The image of a scientist objectively measuring objects in the world illustrates this tendency well. Here the scientist is expected to avoid interacting with the object of study; if the scientist does interfere, or asserts any of his or her influence on the material under investigation, the study is invalidated. Of course, the scientist must be separate from these objects in order to avoid this interaction. Moreover, the objective of Western science is to separate out not only the individual from the object but also the parts of the object from each other. That the subject (or any object) is wholly distinct from the world around her is a view that has been challenged, however, by a conception of the world (and the humans in it) as integrally and fundamentally interconnected.

Martin Heidegger (1889–1976), a controversial but highly influential German philosopher, described the experience of a human, or what he called "being-there" (*Dasein* in German), as "being-in-the-world." Here, Heidegger reminds us of the interconnection between the so-called self or subject and the world by linking the words together ("so-called" because the use of the terms individually implies separate entities). In this way Heidegger is more aligned with Eastern thought, which is typically more holistic in its approach.

Following Heidegger, but moving in a different and sometimes opposing direction,

Jean-Paul Sartre makes the claim that humans are at all times both subject (or consciousness) and object. Sartre is also building on one of Heidegger's predecessors, G.W.F. Hegel (1770–1831), who describes the interaction between two individuals who are autonomous subjects as a struggle for recognition. Sartre points out, however, that when it comes to other people, we are first and foremost objects. For example, we can't see each other's thoughts, but we can see others and be seen by others as a body in the world, which is to say, an object. But at the same time, we experience our own thoughts and interactions with the world through our minds, feelings, emotions, and so on – that is, as a subject, or consciousness. These two modes of being, which Sartre labels "being-in-itself" (oneself as object) and "being-for-itself" (oneself as subject), travel alongside each other but are impossible to merge: I can't fully be an object for myself, because I am also at the same time aware of myself as subject, and as a subject I can change my objective self; others do not have this difficulty and can objectify me more easily than I can myself. For Sartre, this puts us in a tense relation with others, as we must rely on their perceptions of us. Sartre has been criticized for focusing on the negative aspects of our relations with others; theoretically, however, there is no reason we can't (and in fact it appears that we do) turn to others for positive understandings of ourselves.

The significance here is that we need each other, in the most fundamental way, in order to have an identity at all. Bottom line: no others, no "self." According to Sartre, that's the reality we live in, since others provide us access to the objectifications which create that self. At any given moment, this does not require the presence of actual others, however; we can objectify our own self out of expectation once we've been exposed to other subjects. In fact, this process explains how it is that we can have the internalized oppression or constraints that various theorists speak of. Sartre's recognition of the role of others in one's own self-perception echoes the famous "double consciousness" that sociologist W.E.B. Du Bois (1868–1963) explicates regarding life as an African American: "It is a peculiar sensation, this double-consciousness, this sense of always looking at one's self through the eyes of others."[1] Sartre claims that we all live through this process, though we may not all be aware of it, particularly if we live a life of privilege in which our own subjective visions of ourselves as object go largely unchallenged.

**The Ethics of Recognition**

Sartre was never able to develop an ethical theory from his description of the dual structure of humans, despite mentioning the importance of it and making several attempts toward it. However, his lifetime partner Simone de Beauvoir (1908–86) offered what she titled *The Ethics of Ambiguity* and outlined the need to respect the freedom of other people, since it is freedom that allows us to be ethical in the first place (that is, if we didn't have any choice in our actions, there would be no need to determine the *right* action). Both she and Sartre point out that the freedom of others is also necessary to the process of our own objectification (which forms our identity). Sartre writes in the piece reproduced in this section that the imprecise expression of this objectification would be that "I see myself because somebody sees me" and goes on to explain that "these new characteristics [about myself which I now see] do not come only from the fact that I can not know the Other; they stem also and especially from the fact that the Other is free." The Other must be free in order to have another perspective that I do not (and cannot) create myself. Kant, through his practical imperative, provides a

similar theme of respect in claiming that we must recognize the rationality of others. Axel Honneth, in the selection from this chapter entitled "Integrity and Disrespect: Principles of a Conception of Morality Based on the Theory of Recognition," provides a contemporary framework that more specifically substantiates an ethics based on the recognition of identity.

Simple lack of recognition leads to a social invisibility that can also have a significant impact on real lives and the choices people make. JeeYeun Lee discusses her experience in a feminist studies class in this manner. As much as she was exhilarated by the course, she notes that

> [a]t the same time, it was an intensely uncomfortable experience. I knew "women of color" [one of the topics of the class] was supposed to include Asian American women, but I could not find any in the class readings. Were there no Asian American feminists? ... First of all, I felt jealous of African American and Chicana feminists. Their work was present at least to some degree in the readings: They had research and theories, they were eloquent and they existed.[2]

The link that Lee makes between visibility and existence is very literal (perhaps if she can't see them, Asian-American feminists really don't exist) and affects her self-perception; she recognizes that she is forming her own identity, but it is an identity displaced through the women she is reading about. Without being able to see herself in the writings, Lee feels both obscured and excluded. Her burgeoning awareness of, and excitement for, a sharing of feminist perspectives is hampered by this lack, a lack also experienced by the African-American and Chicana feminists she is writing about. For example, bell hooks (see

I.7) addresses the ways in which, historically, feminist discourse in the US has been written as if black women didn't exist.

Similarly, in his book *Blackness Visible*, in discussing why African Americans are seriously underrepresented in philosophy departments in the US, Charles Mills asks, "What, then, is the source for blacks of a likely feeling of alienness, strangeness, of not being entirely at home in this conceptual world?" and points out that the answer must be linked to "silences and invisibility." He goes on to remark that these silences are "not of tacit inclusion but rather of exclusion."[3] It does not take a negative image, but rather the lack of a positive image to hinder the formation of an individual's sense of what is a possible identity for them. In this case, the lack of recognition of black philosophers appears to influence black students in their choice of viable academic interests and careers. Along these same lines, Lewis Gordon notes that "[t]he black body lives in an antiblack world as a form of absence of human presence.... In order to see the black as a thing requires the invisibility of a black's perspective"; he goes on to invoke Ralph Ellison's description from *Invisible Man* (1952): "I am invisible, understand, simply because people refuse to see me."[4]

On the other side, there are desirable identities in which one is *not* ignored, in which one is not put under a microscope or interrogated, viewed as a token, awkwardly avoided, or considered to be a problem. This is a tacit inclusion that largely goes unnoticed. The transparency of identity afforded to certain groups is itself an invisible phenomenon, and includes what is known as "white privilege." While Honneth argues for the ability for all to pursue their own identity, there are those who benefit from positive associations with the identities they are given, regardless of whether they have made efforts toward attaining these benefits. As Peggy McIntosh points out, it is easier for privileged groups to recognize the obstructions to others than to recognize the unearned privileges they have. She speaks of an "invisible knapsack of white privilege"[5] that white people carry on their backs, illustrative of the difficulty of seeing privilege.

## The Ethics of Identities

A whole host of ethical issues arise based on the various identities we can inhabit, assume, receive, or give to others. Indeed, the forms of oppression that Young describes in her theoretical framework in Section One (I.6), also discussed in more detail in the introduction to Section IV, are based on group identities. Negatively evaluated identities can also be disrespected and can bring about the issues Honneth discusses below. But even positive identities bring challenges (for example, white privilege, as discussed above), defining one's self can involve multiple and sometimes conflicting identities, and the process can be confusing, presumably the source of the famous quest to "find oneself." Furthermore, it may not even be clear whether a particular identity is positive or negative, or this may change depending on circumstances or on how and whether an identity gets reclaimed. For example, the use of slurs against a particular group which are then reclaimed and used by that group can be quite controversial, such as the embrace of the word "queer" by some in what has been labelled the LGBT (lesbian, gay, bisexual, transgender) community. Because this word was used so negatively and caused much emotional harm to individuals, there was initial resistance to its use as an umbrella term within these groups themselves. And the notion of a homogeneous identity based on common experiences or traits can also be problematic because of the individual nature of the members of the group who purportedly share that identity.

Indeed, for several decades, much attention has been paid in the US to ethical concerns about issues related to broad identity categories such as gender, race, and class. What has been called "identity politics" wrestles with the ways in which members of certain groups experience oppressive forces. Whole fields of study – gender studies (often called women's studies), for example – examine the many ways in which having a particular identity influences our lives, the opportunities we experience, the ways we are treated, and so forth.

Traditional Western philosophical studies of identity often examine whether there is something essential about group members. Regardless of the answer (or lack thereof) to this question of essence, the reciprocal structure that Sartre describes (of perceiving and being perceived as) suggests an answer to another basic and related question regarding group identities, namely a question such as (to use gender as an example) "Is there anything that all women have in common?" Under Sartre's framework we can see that all of these individuals share the potentiality of *being seen as* a woman. That is, all women (or members of other groups) can be placed in the same set, with whatever that category is presumed to represent. The significance of that representation will vary widely and in fact may not always be seen as significant. For example, a woman who is white may not be seen in the same category as other non-white women (by a Ku Klux Klan member, perhaps). But the potential consistently exists for her to be put in a grouping, one with which she might or might not identify. There is something about identity that is always beyond our control, and this is one element that connects its members. As Maria Lugones expresses it, "You may not 'identify' with that self, but you can't help animating it."[6]

And then there are individuals who very much do not identify with the self they are perceived as. Since the recent inception of sex-reassignment surgery, known cases of transsexual individuals are on the rise, one of the most famous in the US being Caitlyn Jenner (former Olympic gold medalist Bruce Jenner) in 2015. The ability to determine one's own sex identity can be considered quite significant: Laverne Cox, the actress from the television show *Orange Is the New Black*, has said that "when we're misgendered, that is an act of violence."[7] To avoid such "misgendering" requires others to perceive individuals in the same manner as they perceive themselves.

Not only whether an individual belongs in a particular category but also the categories themselves can be examined and challenged, a theme discussed in Loren Cannon's article in Section III. For example, intersex individuals – that is, those who are born with reproductive or sexual anatomy which is not clearly "male" or "female" – raise questions about the very assignment of sex or gender. It has been common practice in the US to perform surgery on babies born with ambiguous genitalia in order to assign one of the two traditionally accepted categories, although this approach, along with certain types of cosmetic surgery (e.g., those performed on minors) and body alterations more generally, is currently considered ethically questionable. In the case of body alterations, assuming that the individual is a consenting adult, there are still issues of whether cultural norms and/or addictive personalities create undue influence on those choices (for example, what many people considered Michael Jackson's excessive use of plastic surgery and whether his surgeon was acting ethically in performing it). Because these and many other identity issues affect people on a very deep and personal level, we stand to benefit by examining them closely.

## Notes

1  W.E.B. Du Bois, *The Souls of Black Folk* (New York: Penguin, 1995), 45.
2  JeeYeun Lee, "Beyond Bean Counting," *Listen Up: Voices from the Next Feminist Generation*, ed. Barbara Findlen (Seattle: Seal Press, 1995), 206–07.
3  Charles Mills, *Blackness Visible: Essays on Philosophy and Race* (Ithaca, NY: Cornell UP, 1998), 3.
4  Lewis Gordon, *Existence in Black: An Anthology of Black Existential Philosophy* (New York: Routledge, 1997), 72–73.
5  Peggy McIntosh, "White Privilege and Male Privilege: A Personal Account of Coming to See Correspondences Through Work in Women's Studies," *Applied Ethics: A Multicultural Approach*, ed. Larry May, Shari Collins-Chobanian, and Kai Wong (Upper Saddle River, NJ: Prentice Hall, 2002), 438.
6  Maria Lugones, *Pilgrimages/Peregrinajes* (Lanham, MD: Rowman & Littlefield, 2003), 74.
7  Lila Shapiro, "Shouting Disrupts Vigil For Murdered Transgender Woman Islan Nettles," *The Huffington Post* 28 August 2013, http://www.huffingtonpost.com/2013/08/28/islan-nettles_n_3832004.html.

# I. Jean-Paul Sartre, "The Look"

IN A SECTION FROM his famous work *Being and Nothingness* (1943), in which he discusses our relations with others, Jean-Paul Sartre (1905–80) outlines the basic structure of a human as being twofold: humans are both subjects and objects in the world. Through an awareness of this structure, Sartre asserts the fundamental intersubjectivity of humans, such that we are always incorporating others' perspectives in our own sense of self-identity. The moment one experiences "the Look" is the moment one becomes aware that one is viewed (as an object) by another.

Through his description of the "Other," Sartre claims we recognize intuitively that humans are different from other objects in our world, because other people have their own perspectives – that is, they are subjects. This fact changes our fundamental relation to them, to our world, and even to ourselves. The "permanent possibility of *being seen* by the Other" means that I experience myself in certain moments as an object, an experience Sartre calls "reflective consciousness." This is a shift from when I am experiencing the world as "unreflective consciousness," that is, just looking out at objects around me, focused on the objects, without paying any attention to or being aware of myself.

---

THIS WOMAN WHOM I see coming toward me, this man who is passing by in the street, this beggar whom I hear calling before my window, all are for me *objects* – of that there is no doubt. Thus it is true that at least one of the modalities of the Other's presence to me is *object-ness*. But ... my apprehension of the Other as an object essentially refers me to a fundamental apprehension of the Other in which he will not be revealed to me as an object but as a "presence in person." ... Whether or not this consciousness exists in a separate state, the face which I see does not refer to it; it is not this consciousness which is the *truth* of the probable object which I perceive.... the problem of Others has generally been treated as if the primary relation by which the Other is discovered is object-ness; that is, as if the Other were first revealed – directly or indirectly – to our perception. But since this perception by its very nature refers to something other than to itself, ... its essence must be to refer to a primary relation between my consciousness and the Other's. This relation, in which the Other must be given to me directly as a subject although in connection with me, is the fundamental relation, the very type of my being-for-others.

... It is in the reality of everyday life that the Other appears to us.... In order to understand it I must question more exactly this ordinary appearance of the Other in the field of my perception; since this appearance refers to that fundamental relation, the appearance must be capable of revealing to us, at least as a reality aimed at, the relation to which it refers.

I am in a public park. Not far away there is a lawn and along the edge of that lawn there are benches. A man passes by those benches. I see this man; I apprehend him as an object and at the same time as a man. What does this signify? What do I mean when I assert that this object *is a man*?

If I were to think of him as being only a puppet, I should apply to him the categories which I ordinarily use to group temporal-spatial "things." That is, I should apprehend him as being "beside" the benches, two yards and twenty inches from the lawn, as exercising a certain pressure on the ground, etc. His relation with other objects would be of the purely additive type; this means that I could have him disappear without the relations of the other objects around him being perceptibly changed. In short, no new relation would appear *through him* between those things in my universe: grouped and synthesized *from my point of view* into instrumental complexes, they would *from his* disintegrate into multiplicities of indifferent relations. Perceiving him as a *man*, on the other hand, is not to apprehend an additive relation between the chair and him; it is to register an organization *without* distance of the things in my universe around that privileged object. To be sure, the lawn remains two yards and twenty inches away from him, but it is also as a lawn bound to him in a relation which at once both transcends distance and contains it. Instead of the two terms of the distance being indifferent, interchangeable, and in a reciprocal relation, the distance *is unfolded* starting from the man whom I see and extending up to the lawn as the synthetic upsurge of a univocal relation. We are dealing with a relation which is without parts, given at one stroke, inside of which there unfolds a spatiality, which is not my spatiality; for instead of a grouping toward me of the objects, there is now an orientation *which flees* from me.

[...]

The Other is first the permanent flight of things toward a goal which I apprehend as an object at a certain distance from me but which escapes me inasmuch as it unfolds about itself its own distances. Moreover this disintegration grows by degrees; if there exists between the lawn and the Other a relation which is without distance and which creates distance, then there exists necessarily a relation between the Other and the statue which stands on a pedestal in the middle of the lawn, and a relation between the Other and the big chestnut trees which border the walk; there is a total space which is grouped around the Other, and this space is made *with my* space; there is a regrouping in which I take part but which escapes me, a regrouping of all the objects which people my universe. This regrouping does not stop there. The grass is something qualified; it is *this* green grass which exists for the Other; in this sense the very quality of the object, its deep, raw green is in direct relation to this man. This green turns toward the Other a face which escapes me. I apprehend the relation of the green to the Other as an objective relation, but I can not apprehend the green as it appears to the Other. Thus suddenly an object has appeared which has stolen the world from me. Everything is in place; everything still exists for *me*; but everything is traversed by an invisible flight and fixed in the direction of a new object. The appearance of the Other in the world corresponds therefore to a fixed sliding of the whole universe, to a decentralization of the world which undermines the centralization which I am simultaneously effecting.

But the Other is still an object for me. He belongs to my distances; the man is there, twenty paces from me, he is turning his back on me. As such he is again two yards, twenty inches from the lawn, six yards from the statue; hence the disintegration of my universe is contained within the limits of this same universe; we are not dealing here with a flight of the world toward nothingness or outside itself. Rather it appears that the world has a kind of drain hole in the middle of its being and that it is perpetually flowing off through this hole....

... if the Other-as-object is defined in connection with the world, as the object which *sees* what I see, then my fundamental connection with the Other-as-subject must be able to be referred back to my permanent possibility of *being seen* by the Other. It is in and through the revelation of my being-as-object for the Other that I must be able to apprehend the presence of his being-as-subject.... I have observed that I can not be an object for an object. A radical conversion of the Other is necessary if he is to escape objectivity. Therefore I can not consider the look which the Other directs on me as one of the possible manifestations of his objective being; the Other can not look at me as he looks at the grass. Furthermore my objectivity can not itself derive for me from the objectivity of the world since I am precisely the one by whom there *is* a world; that is, the one who on principle can not be an object for himself.

... In a word, my apprehension of the Other in the world as probably being a man refers to my permanent possibility of *being-seen-by-him*; that is, to the permanent possibility that a subject who sees me may be substituted for the object seen by me. "Being-seen-by-the-Other" is the truth of "seeing-the-Other." Thus the notion of the Other can not under any circumstances aim at a solitary, extra-mundane consciousness which I can not even think. The man is defined by his relation to the world and by his relation to myself. He is that object in the world which determines an internal flow of the universe, an internal hemorrhage. He is the subject who is revealed to me in that flight of myself toward objectivation.... At each instant the Other *is* looking at me. It is easy therefore for us to attempt with concrete examples to describe this fundamental connection which must form the basis of any theory concerning the Other. If the Other is on principle the *one who looks* at me, then we must be able to explain the meaning of the Other's look.

Every look directed toward me is manifested in connection with the appearance of a sensible form in our perceptive field, but contrary to what might be expected, it is not connected with any determined form. Of course what most often manifests a look is the convergence of two ocular globes in my direction. But the look will be given just as well on occasion when there is a rustling of branches, or the sound of a footstep followed by silence, or the slight opening of a shutter, or a light movement of a curtain. During an attack men who are crawling through the brush apprehend as a *look to be avoided*, not two eyes, but a white farm-house which is outlined against the sky at the top of a little hill.... Now the bush, the farmhouse are not the look; they only represent the eye, for the eye is not at first apprehended as a sensible organ of vision but as the support for the look. They never refer therefore to the actual eye of the watcher hidden behind the curtain, behind a window in the farmhouse. In themselves they are already eyes. On the other hand neither is the look one quality among others of the object which functions as an eye, nor is it the total form of that object, nor a "worldly" relation which is established between that object and me. On the contrary, far from perceiving the look on the objects which manifest it, my apprehension of a look turned toward me appears on the ground of the destruction of the eyes which "look at me." If I apprehend the look, I cease to perceive the eyes; they are there, they remain in the field of my perception as pure presentations, but I do not make any use of them; they are neutralized, put out of play.... It is never when eyes are looking at you that you can find them beautiful or ugly, that you can remark on their color. The Other's look hides his eyes; he seems to go *in front of them*.... What I apprehend immediately when I hear the branches crackling behind me is not that there is someone there; it is that I am vulnerable, that I have a body which can be hurt, that I occupy a place and that I can not in any case escape from the space in which I am without defense – in short, that I am seen. Thus the look is first an intermediary which refers from me to myself. What is the nature of this intermediary? What does being seen mean for me?

Let us imagine that moved by jealousy, curiosity, or vice I have just glued my ear to the door and looked through a keyhole. I am alone and on the level of a non-thetic self-consciousness. This means first of all that there is no self to inhabit my consciousness, nothing therefore to which I can refer my acts in order to qualify them. They are in no way known; I am my acts and hence they carry in themselves their whole justification. I am a pure consciousness of things, and things, caught up in the circuit of my selfness, offer to me their potentialities as the proof of my non-thetic consciousness (of) my own possibilities. This means that behind that door a spectacle is presented as "to be seen," a conversation as "to be heard." The door, the keyhole are at once both instruments and obstacles; they are presented as "to be handled with care"; the keyhole is given as "to be looked through close by and a little to one side," etc. Hence from this moment "I do what I have to do." No transcending view comes to confer upon my acts the character of a given on which a judgment can be brought to bear. My consciousness sticks to my acts, it is my acts; and my acts are commanded only by the ends to be attained and by the instruments to be employed. My attitude, for example, has no "outside"; it is a pure process of relating the instrument (the keyhole) to the end to be attained (the spectacle to be seen), a pure mode of losing myself in the world, of causing myself to be drunk in by things as ink is by a blotter....

But all of a sudden I hear footsteps in the hall. Someone is looking at me! What does this mean? It means that I am suddenly affected in my being and that essential modifications appear in my structure – modifications which I can apprehend and fix conceptually by means of the reflective cogito.

First of all, I now exist as *myself* for my unreflective consciousness. It is this irruption of the self which has been most often described: I see *myself* because somebody sees me – as it is usually expressed. This way of putting it is not wholly exact.... the person is presented to consciousness *in so far as the person is an object for the Other.* This means that all of a sudden I am conscious of myself as escaping myself, not in that I am the foundation of my own nothingness but in that I have my foundation outside myself. I am for myself only as I am a pure reference to the Other.

... It is shame or pride which reveals to me the Other's look and myself at the end of that look. It is the shame or pride which makes me *live*, not *know* the situation of being looked at.

Now, shame ... is shame of *self*; it is the recognition of the fact that I am indeed that object which the Other is looking at and judging. I can be ashamed only as my freedom escapes me in order to become a given object.... Shame reveals to me that I am this being, not in the mode of "was" or of "having to be" but *in-itself*. When I am alone, I can not realize my "being-seated"; at most it can be said that I simultaneously both am it and am not it. But in order for me to be what I am, it suffices merely that the Other look at me. It is not for myself, to be sure; I myself shall never succeed at realizing this being-seated which I grasp in the Other's look. I shall remain forever a consciousness. But it is for the Other.... For the Other I am seated as this inkwell is on the table; for the Other, I am leaning over the keyhole as this tree *is* bent by the wind. Thus for the Other I have stripped myself of my transcendence. This is because my transcendence becomes for whoever makes himself a witness of it (i.e., determines himself as not being my transcendence) a purely established transcendence, a given-transcendence; that is, it acquires a nature by the sole fact that the Other confers on it an outside.... If there is an Other, whatever or whoever he may be; whatever may be his relations with me, and without his acting upon me in any way except by the pure upsurge of his being-then I have an outside, I have a nature. My original fall is the existence of the Other. Shame – like pride – is the apprehension of myself as a nature although that very nature escapes me and is unknowable as such....

## Study Questions

1. What are some of the descriptions Sartre gives of our relations with others? In this extract, these descriptions are typically negative ones. Is it possible, or necessary, given Sartre's understanding, that others can contribute positively to our sense of ourselves as well?

2. Explain your understanding of Sartre's claim that "Being-seen-by-the-Other" is the truth of "seeing-the-Other." Do you agree with this? How might this claim relate to acting ethically? That is, if everyone agreed with Sartre on this point, how might we act toward each other? Would we recognize and value each other's freedom because of this fact?

3. Sartre's explanation of "the Look" is based on in-person relations with one another (even in cases when there is no actual person present). Does this explanation apply to our virtual selves as well? If so, what are some of the implications of this for our virtual identity and behavior? How might Sartre's model relate to something like cyber-bullying?

4. Does Sartre's account of humans' intersubjectivity suggest that we have a responsibility toward all others? What might this look like? Would it involve, for example, a responsibility to avoid stereotypes or unnecessarily negative portrayals of others? Would we humans have any ethical responsibilities toward animals or the environment based on this intersubjectivity?

# 2. Axel Honneth, "Integrity and Disrespect: Principles of a Conception of Morality Based on the Theory of Recognition"

IN THIS ARTICLE FROM 1992, German philosopher Axel Honneth (b. 1949) develops a set of moral principles based on human dignity and asserts that disrespectful behavior is "injurious because it impairs ... persons in their positive understanding of self – an understanding acquired by intersubjective means." He outlines three forms of disrespect (disrespect of physical integrity, denial of rights, and evaluative forms of disrespect) and discusses the harm they do, as well as the forms of positive recognition that act against these harms (love, rights, and solidarity).

Honneth conceives of an ethical society as one that includes relations that allow for the healthy (non-repressed) self-actualization of identities. Here Honneth gives those who might have *felt* (or who have always had underlying feelings of) identity-related disrespect a theory that allows them to name that disrespect.

---

... THE LANGUAGE OF EVERYDAY life is still invested with a knowledge – which we take for granted – that we owe our integrity, in a subliminal way, to the receipt of approval or recognition from other persons. Up to the present day, when individuals who see themselves as victims of moral maltreatment describe themselves, they assign a dominant role to categories that, as with "insult" or "degradation," are related to forms of disrespect, to the denial of recognition. Negative concepts of this kind are used to characterize a form of behavior that does not represent an injustice solely because it constrains the subjects in their freedom for action or does them harm. Rather, such behavior is injurious because it impairs these persons in their positive understanding of self – an understanding acquired by intersubjective means. There can be no meaningful use whatsoever of the concepts of "disrespect" or "insult" were it not for the implicit reference to a subject's claim to be granted recognition by others....

Not only Hegel's theory of recognition but especially G.H. Mead's[1] social psychology transformed this intuitive knowledge into a basis for the framework of a systematic theory. According to this theory, human individuation is a process in which the individual can unfold a practical identity to the extent that he is capable of reassuring himself of recognition by a growing circle of partners to communication.[2] Subjects capable of language and action are constituted as individuals solely by learning, from the perspective of others who offer approval, to relate to themselves as beings who possess certain positive qualities and abilities. Thus as their consciousness of their individuality grows, they come to depend to an ever increasing extent on the conditions of recognition they are afforded by the life-world of their social environment. That particular human vulnerability signified by the concept of "disrespect" arises from this interlocking of individuation and recognition on which both Hegel and Mead based their inquiries. Since, in his normative image of self — something Mead would call his "Me" — every individual is dependent on the possibility of constant reassurance by the Other; the experience of disrespect poses the risk of an injury that can cause the identity of the entire person to collapse.

It is obvious that we use the terms "disrespect" or "insult" in everyday language to designate a variety of degrees of psychological injury to a subject. The use of a single expression would threaten to efface the categorical difference between the blatant degradation which is bound up with the deprivation of basic human rights and the subtle humiliation that accompanies public statements as to the failings of a given person. However, the fact that we are also intuitively inclined to break down the positive counterconcept of "respect" into a number of intuitive gradations already implies that internal differences exist between individual forms of disrespect.... I seek to set up a systematic classification of three forms of "disrespect." ... The differences between these forms are measured by the degree to which they can upset a person's practical relationship to self by depriving this person of the recognition of certain claims to identity.

... [I]t would appear sensible to start from a type of disrespect that pertains to a person's physical integrity. Those forms of practical maltreatment in which a person is forcibly deprived of any opportunity to dispose freely over his own body represent the most fundamental type of personal degradation. This is the case because every attempt to seize control of a person's body against his will, irrespective of the intention involved, causes a degree of humiliation, which, by comparison to other forms of disrespect, has a more profoundly destructive impact on an individual's practical relationship to self. For what is special about such forms of physical injury, as exemplified by torture or rape, is not the raw pain experienced by the body but the coupling of this pain with the feeling of being defenselessly at the mercy of another subject, to the point of being deprived of all sense of reality.[3] The physical maltreatment of a subject represents a type of disrespect that does lasting damage to the subject's confidence, acquired at an early state, that he can coordinate his own body autonomously. Hence one of the consequences, wedded to a type of social shame, is the loss of self-confidence and trust in the world, and this adversely affects all practical interaction with other subjects, even at a physical level. Through the experience of this type of disrespect, therefore, the person is deprived of that form of recognition that is expressed in unconditional respect for autonomous control over his own body, a form of respect acquired just through experiencing emotional attachment in the socialization process. The successful integration of physical and emotional qualities of behavior is thus shattered post facto from without, crippling the most fundamental form of the practical relationship to self, namely, confidence in oneself.

This extreme type of disrespect, which interrupts the continuity of a positive image of self even at the corporeal level, is to be distinguished from forms of degradation that affect a person's normative understanding of self. I am referring to those forms of personal disrespect which a subject undergoes by being structurally excluded from the possession of certain rights within a given society. We can construe the term "rights" to signify those individual claims that a person can legitimately expect society to fulfil, since, as a full-fledged member of a community, he has an equal right to participate in its institutional order. Should he now be systematically denied certain rights of this kind, the implication is that he is not deemed to possess the same degree of moral accountability as other members of society. The distinguishing feature of such forms of disrespect, as typified by the denial of rights or by social ostracism, thus lies not solely in comparative restrictions on personal autonomy but in the combination of these restrictions with the feeling that the subject lacks the status of full-fledged partners to interaction who all possess the same moral rights. For the individual, having socially valid legal rights withheld from him or her signifies a violation of the person's intersubjective expectation that he or she will be recognized as a subject capable of reaching moral judgments. To this extent, the experience of being denied rights is typically coupled with a loss of self-respect, of the ability to relate to oneself as a partner to interaction in possession of equal rights on a par with all other individuals.[4] Through the experience of this type of disrespect, therefore, the person is deprived of that form of recognition that takes the shape of cognitive respect for moral accountability. The latter, for its part, was only painstakingly acquired in the interactive processes involved in socialization.

This second type of disrespect, which has a detrimental effect on a subject's normative understanding of self, is to be set off from a third and final type of degradation, which entails negative consequences for the social value of individuals or groups. Only when we consider these, as it were, evaluative forms of disrespect, namely, the denigration of individual or collective life-styles, do we actually arrive at the form of behavior for which our everyday language provides such designations as "insult" or "degradation." The "honor," "dignity" or, to use the modem term, "status" of a person can be understood to signify the degree of social acceptance forthcoming for a person's method of self-realization within the horizon of cultural traditions in a given society.[5] If this hierarchy of societal values is structured so as to downgrade individual

forms of living and convictions for being inferior or deficient, then it robs the subjects in question of every opportunity to accord their abilities social value. Once confronted with an evaluation that downgrades certain patterns of self-realization, those who have opted for these patterns cannot relate to their mode of fulfillment as something invested with positive significance within their community. The individual who experiences this type of social devaluation typically falls prey to a loss of self esteem – that is, he is no longer in a position to conceive of himself as a being whose characteristic traits and abilities are worthy of esteem. Through the experience of this type of disrespect, therefore, the person is deprived of the form of recognition that is expressed in society's approval of a type of self-realization that the person had only been able to acquire through an arduous process involving encouragement in the form of group solidarity.

It is a standard feature of the three groups of experiences of disrespect distinguished in the foregoing analysis that their consequences for the individual are regularly described with metaphors derived from states of decay of the human body. Psychological studies investigating the personal after effects of experiencing torture or rape frequently speak of "psychological death." Research into the collective processing of being denied rights and social ostracism, which takes slavery as its example, now routinely operates with the concept of "social death." And the category of injury occupies a privileged position in discussions of the kind of disrespect associated with the cultural downgrading of a form of living.[6] These metaphorical allusions to physical suffering and death express the fact that the various forms of disrespect for psychological integrity take on the same negative role that organic diseases play in the context of body processes. The experience of social degradation and humiliation jeopardizes the identity of human beings to the same degree as the suffering of illnesses jeopardizes their physical well-being. If there is any truth in this link suggested by the conventions of our language, it follows that our survey of the various forms of disrespect should also enable us to draw conclusions as to the factors that foster what may be termed psychological "health" or human integrity. Seen in this light, the preventive treatment of illnesses would correspond to the social guarantee of relations of recognition that are capable of providing the subject with the greatest possible protection from an experience of disrespect. In the next section, I venture a brief explanation of the thesis which this connection implies.

## II

... The classification of three forms of disrespect, which has been the focal point of the present inquiry up to this point, itself contains an indirect reference to intersubjective relationships of recognition whose collective existence forms the prerequisite for human integrity. As Hegel and Mead convincingly demonstrated, subjects capable of action owe their potential for developing a positive relationship to self to the experience of mutual recognition. Since it can only learn self-confidence and self-respect from the perspective of the approving reactions of partners to interaction, their practical Ego is dependent on intersubjective relationships in which it is capable of experiencing recognition. This being the case, it must be possible to apply to these relationships of mutual recognition the same distinctions as we have observed between the various forms of social disrespect. After all, each type of insult and degradation that we examined involved the injury of a specific instance of positive relationship to self, which, in turn, it seems can only come about if the corresponding specific relation of recognition

exists. To this extent, the differentiation of three forms of disrespect provides us with the key to classifying an identical number of relationships of mutual recognition. If this argumentation is accurate, then these relationships establish the moral infrastructure of a social life-world in which individuals can both acquire and preserve their integrity as human beings.

I based my distinctions on those forms of disrespect present in acts of physical humiliation, such as torture or rape. These could be classed as the most fundamental type of human degradation because they strip a person of what has become a physical autonomy in interaction with self and thus destroy part of his basic trust in the world. What corresponds to this type of disrespect is a relation of recognition, which, because it enables the individual to develop this body-related self-confidence in the first place, takes the form of emotional attachment of the sort that Hegel, the Romantic, sought to express in the concept of "love." As needs and emotions, in a certain sense, can only receive "confirmation" by being directly satisfied or answered, recognition in this case must itself take the form of emotional approval and encouragement. This relation of recognition thus also depends on the concrete physical existence of other persons who acknowledge each other with special feelings of appreciation. The positive attitude which the individual is capable of assuming toward himself if he experiences this type of emotional recognition is that of self-confidence. I am referring, in other words, to the underlying layer of an emotional, body-related sense of security in expressing one's own needs and feelings, a layer which forms the psychological prerequisite for the development of all further attitudes of self-respect.[7] There are no more general terms for this mode of reciprocal recognition beyond the circle of primary social relationships such as are to be found in emotional ties patterned after families, friendships, and love affairs. Because attitudes of emotional affirmation are tied to the prerequisites of attraction which individuals do not have at their unique disposal, these attitudes cannot be indefinitely extended to cover a larger number of partners to interaction. Hence this relation of recognition inherently entails a moral particularism which no attempt at generalization can succeed in dissolving.

The physical maltreatment, which has as its positive counterpart the emotional attachments in primary relationships of this kind, was distinguished from a second form of disrespect, namely, denying someone rights and ostracizing them socially. With this form, a human being incurs the dishonor of having the community refuse to grant him the moral accountability that a full-fledged legal member of that community would have. Accordingly, this type of disrespect must be paired with a condition of mutual recognition in which the individual learns to see himself from the perspective of his partners to interaction as a bearer of equal rights. The mechanism by which this takes place was identified by Mead as the process of assuming the perspective of a "generalized Other," who, at the same time as prescribing certain responsibilities, guarantees the Self (as in the practical relationship to self) that specific claims will be fulfilled. It follows that, in contrast to intimate relationships, this type of relation of recognition is invested with a primarily cognitive character: ego and alter mutually recognize each other as legal persons, in that they share a knowledge of those norms by which their particular community superintends the rights and responsibilities to which they are equally entitled. The positive attitude that a subject can assume toward himself if he experiences this kind of legal recognition is that of fundamental self-respect. He is able to consider himself a person who shares with all

other members of his community the qualities of a morally accountable active subject.[8] This legal relationship contrasts with the relations of recognition in the primary relationship for it permits that medium of recognition unique to the subject to be generalized in two directions: it allows for the expansion of rights on both objective and social grounds. In the first instance, the rights are enhanced in terms of their material content; as a consequence, the individual differences in the opportunities for realizing intersubjectively guaranteed freedoms are increasingly taken into legal account. In the second instance, however, the legal relationship is universalized in the sense that a growing circle of hitherto excluded or disadvantaged groups has the same rights extended to it as are enjoyed by all other members of the community. Hence the conditions under which rights are recognized inherently entail a principle of universalism, which unfolds in the course of historical struggles.

Finally, the third type of disrespect distinguished in the foregoing proposed classification involves the downgrading of the social value of forms of self-realization. Such patterns of denigrative evaluation of certain forms of living rob the subjects in question of the potential for taking a positive view – in the sense of social acceptance – of the abilities that they have acquired in the course of their lives. Accordingly, the counterpart of this form of disrespect is a relationship of recognition that can aid the individual in acquiring this kind of self-esteem – a condition of solidarity with, and approval of, unconventional life-styles. This condition would enable the subjects to find recognition based on mutual encouragement given their special characteristics as persons whose individuality has been formed by their specific biographies. Mead had this type of relation of recognition in mind when he argued that because the Self (as in the practical relationship to self) had to reassure itself that it was not only an autonomous but an individuated being, it was also forced to assume the perspective of a "generalized Other" from whom intersubjective approval is forthcoming for its claim to uniqueness and irreplaceability.[9] The potential for this type of ethical self-reassurance is provided by a condition of mutual recognition in which ego and alter encounter one another against a horizon of values and goals, whereby these signal to the respective Other the indispensable significance of Ego's life for him or her. Insofar as this form of recognition could not exist were it not for the vital experience of commonly shared burdens and responsibilities, it always goes beyond the bounds of the cognitive moment of ethical knowledge, incorporating an emotional element of solidarity and sympathy. The positive attitude which a subject can assume toward himself if he receives recognition in this form is that of acquiring esteem for himself: since he is respected by his partners to interaction as a person whose individuality has been formed by his biography, the subject is capable of unreserved identification with his particular qualities and abilities. For Mead, then, the specific feature of such a relation of ethical recognition lies in the fact that it is geared internally toward the possibility of a successive opening to the tendencies that the Self has for self-realization....

These three patterns of recognition – love, rights, and solidarity – set down the formal requirements for conditions of interaction within which human beings can feel assured of their "dignity" or integrity. These preconditions are "formal" in the sense that they, and the types of recognition on which they are based, are meant only to distinguish structural features of forms of communication. They do not go as far as to outline the institutional framework in which these forms may be realized. By listing the three patterns of recognition, we have specified the moral infrastructures that a social life-world must exhibit if it is to be able to protect its members. Accordingly, here again "integrity" can only mean that a subject may regard society as supporting him over the entire range of his practical relationships to self. If the subject participates in a social life-world in which the tripartite hierarchy of patterns of recognition is present, regardless of the concrete form these take, he may anchor his relationship to self in the positive modes of selfconfidence, self-respect, and self-esteem.... Morality, if understood as an institution for the protection of human dignity, defends the reciprocity of love, the universalism of rights, and the egalitarianism of solidarity against their being relinquished in favor of force and repression. In other words, morality inherently contains an interest in the cultivation of those principles that provide a structural basis for the various forms of recognition.

## Study Questions

1. Honneth bases his ethical analysis in part on the idea that individuals are dependent on others to gain their sense of self-identity. What are some examples that this is or is not the case? Are we responsible for other people's development of a sense of self ethically speaking? Why or why not? Does Sartre's description of intersubjectivity from this chapter provide an answer for this? Are we responsible to see others in particular ways (as well as to treat them in particular ways)? Does Brison's description (II.6) of the role her son played in helping her heal or her account of the importance of others hearing her story confirm Honneth's claim?

2. In his discussion of a morality based on the theory of recognition, Honneth lists some problem behaviors: physical assault, denial of rights or social ostracism, and the denigration of individual or collective lifestyles. Are these actions you would typically perceive as unethical? According to Honneth, why are these behaviors forms of disrespect?

3. Honneth is using disrespect as a guide to evaluate actions as ethical or unethical. Kant's ethics is often seen as an ethics of respect, also considering disrespectful action to be unethical. Based on the Kant reading (I.2), in what other ways are Kant and Honneth similar? In what ways are they different? Can you think of an example in which the two approaches would not agree in their evaluation of whether something is ethical or not? If so, which evaluation do you prefer? Why?

4. Using Honneth's principles, would a person have to be acting in such a way that is intentionally disrespectful for that action to be unethical? That is, if a person were unaware of being disrespectful, would he or she still be unethical? What if people had genuinely different senses of identity or respect? Whose understanding of disrespect would be most relevant, the person acting or the person being potentially injured? Could Honneth's principles take cultural differences into account?

## Notes

1  George Herbert Mead (1863–1931) was a philosopher, sociologist, and psychologist. [Ed.]
2  In my *Habilitationschrift*, I undertook a detailed reconstruction of this concept; see Axel Honneth, *Kampf um Erloesung, Ein Theorieprogramm in Anschluss an Hegel und Mead* (Frankfurt, 1989).
3  For an excellent study of loss of reality as a result of torture, see Elaine Scarry, *The Body in Pain: The Making and Unmaking of the World* (New York: Oxford UP, 1985), chap. 1. A survey of the literature is provided by Guenter Frankenberg, "Politisches Asyl – ein Menschenrecht?" in *Kritische Justiz*.
4  On the connection between rights and self-respect, see Joel Feinberg, "The Nature and Value of Rights," in his *Rights, Justice and the Bounds of Liberty: Essays in Social Philosophy* (Princeton, NJ: Princeton UP, 1980), 143ff. A more differentiated version has since been provided by Andreas Wild, *Recht und Selbstachtung* (manuscript, 1990).
5  Among the exhaustive literature on the subject, the clearest exposition of this phenomenon is, in my opinion, Wilhelm Korff, *Ehre, Prestige, Gewissen* (Cologne, 1966). Of interest from the sociological perspective are Peter Berger, "On the Obsolescence of the Concept of Honor," in *European Journal of Sociology* 11 (1970): 339, and Hans Speier, "Honor and Social Structure," in *Social Order and the Risks of War: Papers in Political Sociology* (New York, 1952), 36ff.
6  Among studies pointing to the category of "psychological death" are those of Bruno Bettelheim, in *Surviving and Other Essays* (London: Thames & Hudson, 1979), especially part 1. On the category of "social death" see, among others, Orlando Patterson, *Slavery and Social Death: A Comparative Study* (Cambridge, MA: Harvard UP, 1982), and Claude Meillassoux, *Anthropologie der Sklaverei* (Frankfurt, 1989), part 1, chap. 5.
7  For a systematic analysis of "self-confidence" as the result of experiences of attachment in early childhood, see Erik H. Erikson, *Identity and the Life-Cycle* (London: 1980). For a study in terms of theory of recognition drawing on Hegelian concepts but using advanced

psychoanalytical tools, see Jessica Benjamin, *The Bonds of Love: Psychoanalysis, Feminism and the Problem of Domination* (New York, 1988), esp. chap. 1.

8  On this point, see G.H. Mead, *Geist, Identitaet und Gesellschaft* (Frankfurt, 1973), 263ff. A reconstruction from the perspective of self-respect is undertaken by Ernst Tugendhat, *Selbstbewusstsein und Selbstbestimmung* (Frankfurt, 1979), lecture 12, 282ff.

9  On this point, see Mead, 244ff. My own reconstruction focuses on this issue; see Honneth, *Kampf um Anerkennung* (Frankfort: Suhrkamp, 1992), esp. 183ff.

# 3.  Luis Plascencia, "The 'Undocumented' Mexican Migrant Question: Re-examining the Framing of Law and Illegalization in the United States"

IN THIS ARTICLE FROM the journal *Urban Anthropology* (2009), Luis Plascencia argues that there are many similarities between the terms "illegal immigrant" and "undocumented immigrant," despite many people's sense that they represent a significant conceptual distinction. Through a discussion of the historical development of the terms, Plascencia shows that both expressions are inaccurate, that they feed off of public sentiment, and that they erase the role of government in creating this status for any person.

Specifically, Plascencia is discussing the use of the term "undocumented" instead of "illegal" in regard to people crossing from Mexico into the United States. "Undocumented" is the word usually employed by those more sympathetic to the migrants. He explains that in a key way, the two terms are not different since they both imply that individuals are in a situation in which they could have documents (but don't), and that this obscures the role of the national governments in determining whether that is in fact possible. By erasing the government's role, the ethical questions about the status of the migrant are misplaced and misunderstood. This also speaks to some of the complications of national affiliation, since there are cases in which individuals do not move, but rather the borders of the countries do, thus giving a different identity to the individual – not one of his or her choosing, and not because anything about the individual person has changed, only the environment. Moreover, both labels are oxymoronic, since, as Plascencia explains, the word "immigrant" in US law actually means "persons who have been formally admitted for permanent residency," as opposed to nonimmigrants (those who have been allowed temporary entry). Nevertheless, these labels are used constantly.

## Introduction

... THE CONTEMPORARY ACADEMIC AND popular usage of the terms "illegal" and "undocumented migrant" incorporates a taken-for-granted sense about the meaning of the terms. It is not uncommon to find academic use of the terms "illegal" and "undocumented" migrant without any explanatory note or definition.[1] Journalists, advocacy organizations, and politicians engaged with the issue also commonly invoke the terms without a definition or an explanation for the selection of the respective term.[2] The result is that the two terms have become dominant signifiers that carry much political weight and signification, yet are commonly used as if their respective referent was a priori established, indexed an established exegesis, or were simply technical statutory concepts....

In this essay, I address the gap in the academic and public discourse on the illegal/undocumented migrant.... The article presents two arguments. One, insufficient

attention has been paid to the intrinsic problematic in the debate surrounding the illegal
versus undocumented migrant labels, and
that this has detracted from examining the
common assumptions and limitations in the
labels. Two, although the label undocumented
migrant emerged in explicit opposition to the
illegal migrant label, and is argued by some
as being a neutral or positive alternative, the
former also contributes to the production of
migrant "illegality." ... I discuss the common
assumptions and limitations in both terms.
In particular, I note two key problems: (a) an
overriding emphasis on the individual migrant
as a self-determining actor, and (b) the insufficient attention to the role of the State (Mexico
and the US) in shaping human migration
from the former to the latter. Subsequently, I
suggest alternative migration terminology.

### Situating the "Illegal" and "Undocumented" Migrant Begriffe

Statutory Migrant Classification and "Removable Aliens"

In order to more fully comprehend the general
academic and popular use of the terms illegal/
undocumented migrant, it is necessary to summarize the formal relevant terminology in the
nation's migration statute, the Immigration
and Nationality Act (INA), codified as Title 8
of the United States Code (8 U.S.C.), and the
determination of who is a "removable alien."
... At the core of the nation's migration statute is the concept of "alien."[3] ... Within the
Immigration and Nationality Act, an "alien"
is defined as "any person not a citizen or national of the United States" (INA § 101 [8
U.S.C. 1101]).[4] "Aliens" are subdivided into
two major categories: (a) immigrants, and
(b) nonimmigrants. The former are persons
who have been formally admitted for permanent residency, also commonly labeled LPRs

(lawful/ legal permanent residents), or green
card holders; and the latter are those who are
allowed temporary entry under one of the
more than 25 general categories of visas such
as foreign students (F-1), high-tech specialty
occupations (H-1B), temporary agricultural
workers (H-2A), inter-company transfers (L1),
and entertainers (P-1). All visas have conditions that must be adhered to in order for the
visa to remain valid. The violation of the conditions voids the visa and makes the person
subject to removal.

In the context of the aforementioned,
the academic and common use of the terms
"illegal immigrant" and "undocumented immigrant" (as well as other parallels such as
"unauthorized immigrant"), despite their frequent use, do not have a basis in US migration
law. Consequently, in a technical sense they
are oxymorons. They more accurately reflect
popular political notions of migrants and migration, than formal juridical constructs. Yet
scholars, politicians, journalists, and segments
of the general public invoke these as if they
indexed a formal or a priori established referent. A similar limitation also applies to the
use of the concepts of "illegal immigration,"
and "undocumented immigration." Under
US migration law, a person who has formally
"immigrated" is an "immigrant," and as such
has been allowed to enter and live permanently in the United States, and given a document
(i.e., a green card); thus for a migrant to be
categorized as an "immigrant" means that
the person was part of a "legal immigration"
process. On the other hand, the parallel labels
of "legal immigration" and "documented immigration" are redundant designations.

... [T]he popular term "illegal alien" and
the juridical concept of "illegal alien" are not
the same. The popular use is generally applied
to persons who are thought to have entered
the US without authorization, what Border
Patrol agents informally label EWIs (Entered

without Inspection).[5] On the other hand, the juridical term refers to a narrower and more specific categorization. The popular term "illegal alien" is closer in meaning to the formal categories regarding presence and entrance.... [T]he term "undocumented immigrant" does not exist in statute, in addition to its oxymoronic dimension.

Under US migration law and regulations, what is ultimately the determining factor of who in everyday language is an illegal/undocumented migrant is whether the person has been found to be "subject to removal" by a federal Immigration Judge.[6] And so it is critical to understand that most migrants become subject to removal because of three general reasons: (a) violating the terms of the visa, such as remaining in the US beyond the authorized time period or working when the particular visa prohibited employment (i.e., "immigration violator");[7] (b) convicted of specified crimes, including even if already granted LPR status; or (c) entering the territory without formal authorization (i.e., "not lawfully present," "illegal entrant").[8] A migrant apprehended by ICE (Immigration and Customs Enforcement) or CBP (Customs and Border Protection) is not automatically subject to immediate removal upon apprehension. If apprehended, a migrant can ask for a removal hearing, and so would be placed in detention until the hearing. However, apprehended migrants, for mutual convenience and cost-saving concerns to US authorities, are offered the option of "voluntary departure." Most apprehended migrants choose that option and are escorted as they "voluntarily" depart (are "returned"). This is not deportation/removal, although the two actions are commonly thought of as being the same.[9]

At a removal hearing, an Immigration Judge reviews the individual case and may adopt possible exceptions such as revok[ing] or suspend[ing] the removal, grant[ing] asylum, grant[ing] Temporary Protected Status, as well as grant[ing] authorization to work, depending on the particulars of the case. Thus, subject to removal means that the migrant is subject to exceptions in the law regarding removability, as well as actual removal, what can be labeled "removability," the threat of possible removal (what Sayad insightfully noted in his 1996 essay as "liability to deportation" [2004: 293], and De Genova later reiterated as "deportability" [2002]).[10] A person found to be "unlawfully present" is removed only after the judge has issued a removal order. The force of law thus rests on the threat of potential removal, not on an automatic action upon apprehension. Consequently, migrants who have been ordered removed by an Immigration Judge are ultimately persons who have been determined not to have a legal basis for being allowed to remain; they have been formally deemed as being "unlawfully present." ...

Finally, a related issue is the question: who are the "illegal/undocumented" migrants (those subject to removal)? Since the late 1920s, a southward political gaze has dominated much of the national discussion regarding "unlawful presence" and the "border" (Bustamante 1972, 1975; Cárdenas 1975; Cardoso 1980; Chávez 2001; García 1980; Heer 1990; Heyman 1998, 2001; López 1980–81; Reisler 1976). The result has been twofold. First, the Mexico-US boundary area has been coded as "the border" in the imagination of members of Congress, the media, anti- and pro-migrant activists, popular and documentary film producers, and numerous academics. Thus, when many scholars and others discuss border security, border deaths, Border Patrol abuses at the border, or border justice efforts, [etc.], it is generally not the coastal borders or the northern border that are imagined; it is the Mexico-US boundary area that is being constructed as the unmarked category.

Second, the labels illegal/undocumented migrants have come to be largely associated with Mexican-origin persons and their possible "unlawful" entry, and created a near-synonym between the concept of "illegal/undocumented immigrant/alien" and Mexican migrant.[11] Together, they have contributed to the making of the nation's "immigration problem" a Mexico-centered problem; fostered the illegalization of Mexican migrants; and correspondingly, constructed Mexican migrants as the problem population threatening the nation's sovereignty.

... Correspondingly, the logically imagined "solution" is, as President Reagan and later President Clinton would often assert, to "regain control of our border" and ensure our national sovereignty. What is overlooked in such a formulation is the fact that the population of migrants who may have entered without formal authorization may constitute about half or less of those subject to removal; "visa violators" appear to make up the other half, or more than half.[12] Yet the bulk of resources, personnel, and plans conjured to "solve" the imagined migration problem are aimed at "securing" the southern border through fences, drones, video surveillance, and increased Border Patrol personnel, as if solving the entry issue would automatically solve the entire illegal/undocumented migrant "problem." ...

[...]

## Toward a Genealogy of the Illegal/ Undocumented Migrant Nomenclature

... The end of the US-Mexican War and its aftermath contributed to the positioning of Mexicans in the acquired territory as a racialized, sociopolitical Other.... While the 1848 Treaty of Guadalupe Hidalgo granted collective US citizenship to the approximately 100,000 Mexican-descent individuals who remained in the acquired territory, this did not guarantee that they or their descendants would be granted full membership rights or be perceived as belonging in the nation (Griswold del Castillo 1990; Martínez 2001, 2006; Meeks 2007; Montejano 1987; Zamora 1993). Even individuals who trace their descent to Mexican/Spanish families settled in the territory prior to 1848 are at times thought of as possible "immigrants" to the US....

### "Illegal Immigrant, Illegal Alien, Illegals"

The terms "illegal immigrant/alien" and the noun-form "illegals," as noted above, have come to be commonly associated with Mexican-origin migrants. Yet their origins are not with that community. The entry prohibitions enacted by Congress under the 1875 "Page Law" (18 Statutes-at-Large 477) and 1882 Chinese Exclusion Act (22 Statutes-at-Large 58) were aimed at restricting primarily Chinese migration, and so in the late 19th century, public and governmental concern was with the "illegal entry" of "alien" Chinese. With the emergence of anti-Japanese sentiments on the West Coast in the early 1900s, concern shifted to the "illegal entry" of "alien" Japanese. Concern with the significant "illegal entry" of Europeans from Canada and Mexico also emerged in the early 1900s (Gutiérrez 1995; Ngai 1998, 2004; Reisler 1976).

Between 1900 and 1930, as noted by the historian George Sánchez (1993), the term "alien" began to be applied to Mexicans in the Southwest....

Within news media, the first appearance of the label "illegal alien" appears to be a New York Times article in 1926 that describes the energetic Andrew Donaldson from Ireland who entered the US from Canada on a bicycle after riding 300 miles (New York Times 1926).

Although the term "illegal immigrant"

had wide circulation in the 1930s in the context of mass deportation drives of Mexicans (Balderrama and Rodriguez 1995), the noun-form (i.e., "illegal"), now commonly invoked to label Mexican migrants, was not initially applied to Mexicans. It was applied to European Jewish migrants in the 1930s who sought to enter British controlled Palestine (Halamish 1995; Liebreich 2005; Samuel 1956)....

... Academic uses of illegal(s) in reference to Mexican migrants do not appear until the 1970s....

According to the detailed account by Leo Chávez (2001) regarding the "anti-Mexican migrant discourse" in popular magazines, and the work of Fernández and Pedroza (1981) in newspapers, the early 1970s was key in the association of Mexican migration and illegality. In the early 1970s, the labels "illegal alien" and "illegals" became common references in discussions of the migration "crisis" on the Mexico-US boundary area.... The 1970s, however, were not only important to the circulation of the term "illegal" migrant, the period was also important to the emergence of opposition to that term.

## "Undocumented Immigrant, Undocumented Worker, Undocumented"

The development of the term "undocumented immigrant" (or in Spanish, indocumentado) can be traced, though with less precision than "illegal immigrant." ...

... The term indocumentado/undocumented thus emerged in direct opposition to "illegal alien" and influenced young Chicano/Mexican-origin activists on and off campuses.

The earliest news media use of "undocumented" in reference to migrants took place in 1935. The New York Times reporter Frank George published an article about the deportation activities of the Immigration Bureau regarding Canadians, Europeans, and Mexican migrants who had overstayed their visas or entered without authorization (George 1935).

Jorge Bustamante's 1972 article in the journal *Aztlán* appears to be the first published academic essay in English that invokes the label "undocumented" in reference to Mexican migration (1972)....

A significant marker of the incorporation of the term undocumented migrant in governmental language was President Carter's news conference on April 15, 1977. At that news conference he was asked about his administration's study of the "illegal aliens coming into this country from Mexico." His response was: "My guess is that I will have a message to present on the illegal, or undocumented alien, probably within the next two weeks" (Carter 1977)....

The mid-1970s was also important in international discussions on the labeling of migrants. Although it is not often noted in academic writings on migration, the United Nations (UN) General Assembly passed an important measure at the end of 1975. The measure directs UN entities to use "nondocumented" or "irregular migrant workers" in all official documents for migrants that "illegally and/or surreptitiously enter another country to obtain work" (PICUM, Platform for International Cooperation on Undocumented Migrants, 2007: 5). Since 1975, several international and regional organizations (e.g., International Labor Organization, The Council of Europe) have rejected the term "illegal" migrant and instead adopted "irregular migrant" or "undocumented migrant" (PICUM 2007). In the US, the labels illegal migrant and undocumented migrant are part of a more than thirty-year-old oppositional discourse that continues to the present, and has become part of the conceptual cacophony that is not limited to visible commentators such as CNN's Lou Dobbs, Fox News' Linda Chavez, and radio host Rush Limbaugh, but also surfaces in academic writings in the social sciences and legal scholarship.

[...]

## Common Ground, Common Limitations

The contemporary debate on the "illegal" versus "undocumented" migrant labels is generally thought of as one involving mutually exclusive positions. Groups favoring more restrictive policies tend to favor the former and adhere fairly strictly to it, while groups proposing more welcoming policies, generally avoid the former and are fairly loyal to the latter. The oppositional development of the terms over the last four decades has fostered the perception of mutual exclusivity. This opposition, however, does not mean that they have nothing in common. Both terms share some fundamental premises and limitations.

... One element that is shared by both is a perspective regarding the link between US State action and the actions of individuals. This aspect is commonly overlooked in the academic and national debate, and its absence reinforces the perception that it is principally an individual's action that creates a "legal" or "illegal/undocumented" migrant status. Such a view obscures the central role of the State (both the US and Mexican State) in instituting rules and practices that encourage migratory movements, including the discretion regarding which laws to enforce and not enforce, as well as what label should be applied and to whom.... Ironically, the anti- and pro-migrant perspectives at times share the premise that the individual is the principal "determining actor." The former situates the "illegal" migrant as someone who consciously chose to break the law, particularly entry restrictions. The latter labels a migrant who

did not obtain, for unexamined reasons, the necessary documents to enter the US, as an "undocumented" migrant. In both cases the State (both the Mexican and US) recedes in the political horizon. In the first, the law is neutral and fixed, someone who enters US territory without authorization is a "lawbreaker," and such persons have no legal right to remain and must be expelled according to the "rule of law." In the second perspective, the role of the State in setting admission quotas, criteria for "adjustment of status," decisions on who gets and does not get "papers," the encouragement of the growth of a remittance sending population, etc., are generally eschewed.

... [I]t borders on the assumption that persons labeled "undocumented" migrant, are "undocumented" because they have selected not to obtain los papeles ("the papers") that would convert them to "documented," a perspective that excludes the paper-granting entity, the State.

Both views overlook the fact that it is the enactment of the law and its implementation that constitutes illegality.... The same body of law creates, ignores, or pardons violations. The inaction of federal prosecutors and migration officials regarding the 1885 Contract Labor Law in the Southwest, and the World War I migrant contract labor under the Ninth Proviso of the 1917 Immigration Act are two of many examples of this process. The "Open Border" incidents in 1948 and 1954, wherein US migration officials chose to disregard entry inspection procedures and applicable federal restrictions on the Mexico-US border and allowed several thousands of individuals to enter US territory (Cohen 2001; Galarza 1964; García y Griego 1983; Robinson 2007) are also noteworthy because of the blurring of whether those persons allowed entry are thought of as having been formally authorized entry, or not. The migrants were not issued any documents, so can be thought of as "undocumented" migrants; but their entry was authorized by federal officials, so they were "legally" admitted under the discretion assumed by the officials (and directives from higher authorities at INS).

... These laws and practices, as well as many others, underscore the limitation in the premise that in the US "rule of law" there is a clear and mutually exclusive categorization in the constitution of the "legal" and "illegal/undocumented" migrant. Thus, a central premise in the long-running and contentious "illegal/undocumented" migration debate has survived despite the intrinsic errors in its formulation. Both anti- and pro-migrant camps have commonly overlooked this problem.

[...]

## Alternative Nomenclature: Informally and Formally Authorized Migrants

In order to move away from the common practice of classifying persons as having or lacking "documents" (papeles), and thus explicitly bring the State back into not only the formal issuance of authorizing documents, but also into its role in the management of national economies, I propose the alternative labels of "informally authorized" and "formally authorized" migrants. As indicated, both are authorized. The former refers to persons whose presence is tacitly recognized and allowed through the discretion of federal authorities, who by the use of their discretion to not deter employers from employing such persons (i.e., not seriously enforcing "employer sanctions"), in effect authorize their physical presence and their participation in the economy.[13] ...

... "Formally authorized" persons are here defined as those individuals who have been formally allowed to enter and, for the most part, work in the US. The "formally authorized" includes persons allowed entry such as "lawful permanent residents," students, parolees, asylees, temporary agricultural workers, NAFTA Treaty workers, and athletes; and as such are subject to the perpetually shifting terrain upon which people are conferred particular statuses ("legal" and "illegal" migrant statuses), or granted or denied access to benefits (such as the 5-year limitation imposed on "lawful permanent residents"), all too often commensurate with the needs of the State and interests of capital.

## References

Acuña, Rodolfo (2004). *Occupied America: A History of Chicanos*. (5th ed.). New York: Pearson-Longman.

Anti-Defamation League (2007). "Immigrants Targeted: Extremist Rhetoric Moves into the Mainstream." www.adl.org.

Balderrama, Francisco E., and Raymond Rodríguez (1995). *Decade of Betrayal: Mexican Repatriation in the 1930s*. Albuquerque: U of New Mexico P.

Bosniak, Linda S. (1988). "Exclusion and Membership: The Dual Identity of the Undocumented Worker under United States Law." *Wisconsin Law Review*, 955–1042.

_____ (2007). "The Undocumented Immigrant: Contending Policy Approaches." In Carol M. Swain (ed.), *Debating Immigration* (pp. 85–94). New York: Cambridge UP.

Bustamante, Jorge A. (1972). "The Historical Context of Undocumented Mexican Immigration to the United States." *Aztlán* 3(2): 257–81.

_____ (1975). "Mexican Immigration and the Social Relations of Capitalism." PhD dissertation, University of Notre Dame.

_____ (1978). "Commodity Migrants: Structural Analysis of Mexican Immigration to the United States." In Stanley Ross (ed.), *Views Across the Border: The United States and Mexico* (pp. 183–203). Albuquerque: U of New Mexico P.

Cárdenas, Gilberto (1975). "United States Immigration Policy toward Mexico: An Historical Perspective." *Chicano Law Review* 2: 66–91.

Cardoso, Lawrence A. (1980). *Mexican Emigration to the United States, 1897–1931: Socio-Economic Patterns.* Tucson: The U of Arizona P.

Carter, Jimmy (1977). Transcript of the President's News Conference. *The New York Times* (April 16).

Chávez, Leo R. (1992). *Shadowed Lives: Undocumented Immigrants in American Society.* Orlando: Harcourt Brace Jovanovich.

_____ (2001). *Covering Immigration: Popular Images and the Politics of the Nation.* Berkeley: U of California P.

Cohen, Deborah (2001). "Caught in the Middle: the Mexican State's Relationship with the United States and Its Own Citizen-Workers, 1942–1954." *Journal of American Ethnic History* 20: 110–32.

Cronin, Michael D. (1999). Statement of Michael D. Cronin, Associate Commissioner for Programs, US Immigration and Naturalization Service, US House of Representatives, Subcommittee on Immigration and Claims, Committee on the Judiciary. Hearing: Illegal Aliens in the United States. 106th Congress, First Session, Serial No. 45. (March 18).

Cutler, Michael W. (2006). Statement of Michael W. Cutler, Former Senior Special Agent, US Immigration and Naturalization Service. Subcommittee on Oversight and Investigations, Committee on International Relations, House of Representatives, 109th Congress, Second Session (May 11). Washington, DC.

De Genova, Nicholas P. (2002). "Migrant 'Illegality' and Deportability in Everyday Life." *Annual Review of Anthropology* 31: 419–47.

Durand, Jorge, Douglas S. Massey, and Rene M. Zenteno (2001). "Mexican Immigration to the United States: Continuities and Changes." *Latin American Research Review* 36(1): 107–27.

Fernández, Celestino, and Lawrence R. Pedroza (1981). *The Border Patrol and News Media Coverage of Undocumented Mexican Immigration during the 1970s: A Quantitative Content Analysis in the Sociology of Knowledge.* Tucson: The U of Arizona P.

Flores, Lisa (2003). "Constructing Rhetorical Borders: Peons, Illegal Aliens, and Competing Narratives of Immigration." *Critical Studies in Media Communication* 20(4): 362–87.

Galarza, Ernesto (1964). *Merchants of Labor: The Mexican Bracero Story.* Santa Barbara: McNally and Loftin.

García, Juan Ramón (1980). *Operation Wetback: The Mass Deportation of Mexican Undocumented Workers in 1954.* Westport: Greenwood P.

García y Griego, Manuel (1983). "The Importation of Mexican Contract Laborers to the United States, 1942–1964: Antecedents, Operation, and Legacy." In Peter G. Brown and Henry Shue (eds.), *The Border that Joins: Mexican Migrants and U.S. Responsibility* (pp. 49–98). Totowa: Rowman and Littlefield.

George, Frank (1935). "Illegal Entrants Find Going Harder: Government Tightens Nets to Block an Anticipated Rush of Undocumented Aliens." *The New York Times* (February 17).

Griswold del Castillo, Richard (1990). *The Treaty of Guadalupe Hidalgo: A Legacy of Conflict.* Norman: U of Oklahoma P.

Gutiérrez, David G. (1995). *Walls and Mirrors: Mexican Americans, Mexican Immigrants, and the Politics of Ethnicity.* Berkeley: U of California P.

Halamish, Aviva (1995). "American Volunteers in Illegal Immigration to Palestine, 1946–1948." *Jewish History* 9(1): 91–106.

Heer, David M. (1990). *Undocumented Mexicans in the United States.* New York: Cambridge UP.

Heyman, Josiah McC. (1998). *Finding a Moral Heart for U.S. Immigration Policy: An Anthropological Perspective*. Arlington: American Anthropological Association.

Hing, Bill Ong (2007). "Immigration Policy: Thinking Outside the (Big) Box." *Connecticut Law Review* 30(4): 1401–41.

Hirsch, Jennifer S. (2002). "'Que, pues, con el pinche NAFTA?'; Gender, Power and Immigration Between Western Mexico and Atlanta." *Urban Anthropology and Studies of Cultural Systems and World Economic Development* 31(3–4): 351–88.

Inda, Jonathan Xavier (2006). *Targeting Immigrants: Government, Technology, and Ethics*. Malden: Blackwell.

Johnson, Kevin R. (1996–1997). "'Aliens' and the U.S. Immigration Laws: The Social and Legal Construction of Nonpersons." *Inter-American Law Review* 28(2): 263–92.

Kemper, Robert V., Julie Adkins, Marco Flores, and José Leonardo Santos (2007). "From Undocumented Camionetas (Mini-Vans) to Federally Regulated Motor Carriers: Hispanic Transportation in Dallas, Texas and Beyond." *Urban Anthropology and Studies of Cultural Systems and World Economic Development* 36(4): 381–423.

Liebreich, Fritz (2005). *Britain's Naval and Political Reaction to the Illegal Immigration of Jews to Palestine, 1945–1948*. London: Routledge.

López, Gerald P. (1980–81). "Undocumented Mexican Migration: In Search of a Just Immigration Law and Policy." *UCLA Law Review* 28: 615–714.

Martínez, Oscar J. (2001). *Mexican-Origin People in the United States: A Topical History*. Tucson: The U of Arizona P.

_____ (2006). *Troublesome Border*. Tucson: The U of Arizona P.

Meeks, Eric (2007). *Border Citizens: The Making of Indians, Mexicans, and Anglos in Arizona*. Austin: U of Texas P.

Mehan, Hugh (1997). "The Discourse of the Illegal Immigration Debate: A Case Study in the Politics of Representation." *Discourse and Society* 8(2): 249–70.

Montejano, David (1987). *Anglos and Mexicans in the Making of Texas, 1836–1986*. Austin: U of Texas P.

Nevins, Joseph (2002). *Operation Gatekeeper: The Rise of the "Illegal Alien" and the Making of the U.S.-Mexico Boundary*. New York: Routledge.

Ngai, Mae M. (1998). "Illegal Aliens and Alien Citizens: United States Immigration Policy and Racial Formation, 1924–1945." PhD dissertation, Columbia University.

_____ (2004). *Impossible Subjects: Illegal Aliens and the Making of Modern America*. Princeton: Princeton UP.

Ono, Kent A. and John M. Sloop (2002). *Shifting Borders: Rhetoric, Immigration, and California's Proposition 187*. Philadelphia: Temple UP.

Pew Hispanic Center (2006). "Modes of Entry for the Unauthorized Migrant Population." Fact Sheet (May 22). Washington, DC. www.pewhispanic.org.

PICUM (Platform for International Cooperation on Undocumented Migrants) (2007). "Undocumented Migrants Have Rights!: An Overview of International Human Rights Framework." Belgium.

Reisler, Mark (1976). *By the Sweat of Their Brow: Mexican Immigrant Labor in the United States, 1900–1940*. Westport: Greenwood P.

Robinson, Robert S. (2007). "Creating Foreign Policy Locally: Migratory Labor and the Texas Border, 1943–1952." PhD dissertation, The Ohio State University.

Samuel, Edwin (1956). "The Immigration Cycle in Palestine and Israel, 1919–1954." *The South African Journal of Economics* 24(1): 29–36.

Sánchez, George J. (1993). *Becoming Mexican American: Ethnicity, Culture and Identity in Chicano Los Angeles, 1900–1945*. New York: Oxford UP.

Sayad, Abdelmalek (2004). *The Suffering of the Immigrant*. Malden: Polity.

Southern Poverty Law Center (2002). "Intelligence Report." Summer, Issue 106.

Stull, Donald D., and Michael J. Broadway (2001). "'We Come to the Garden' ... Again: Garden City, Kansas, 1990–2000." *Urban Anthropology and Studies of Cultural Systems and World Economic Development* 30(4): 269–99.

US Department of Homeland Security, Office of Immigration Statistics (2008). 2007 Yearbook of Immigration Statistics. Washington, DC.

Wilson, Tamar Diana (2002). "Counterhegemony: Undocumented Mexican Immigrants Crossing the Border." *Urban Anthropology and Studies of Cultural Systems and World Economic Development* 31(2): 163(35).

Zamora, Emilio (1993). *The World of the Mexican Worker in Texas*. College Station: Texas A&M UP.

## Study Questions

1. Plascencia's article raises questions about evaluating individuals (e.g., "undocumented" migrants) while disregarding systematic issues (e.g., the changing regulations of governments regarding the issuance of documents). Does a strict emphasis on evaluating individual actions point us in the wrong direction or act as a distraction from policies that may be troubling? What if the laws that make an action unethical are themselves unethical? Laws in Hitler's Germany are sometimes given as an example of this problem (e.g., that it was illegal to give aid to a Jewish person). How do we evaluate whether the policies themselves are unethical?

2. Plascencia's discussion points to the role of labels in categorizing other people, in this case showing that a presumed neutral term ("undocumented") creates a negative (and inaccurate) identity. Is it unethical to use these types of labels? Do people have a responsibility to investigate the context of a label before using it?

3. There are many cases in history in which one national power takes over another region. In these cases, individuals who stay in place can find themselves with a new national identity (considered either legitimate or illegitimate), despite the fact that they have not changed at all. Does this involuntary shift in identity bring any ethical responsibilities or special concerns for these individuals?

## Notes

1 I have compiled a list of over 100 authors within anthropology, communication studies, economics, political science, social work, sociology, and legal scholarship who discuss Mexican migration and use the two keywords but do not present a rationale for their respective selection. See, for example, Bosniak 1988, 2007; Durand et al. 2001; Flores 2003; Heer 1990; Hing 2007; Hirsch 2002; Kemper et al. 2007; Mehan 1997; Stull and Broadway 2001; Wilson 2002.

2 In general, those individuals and organizations favoring removal of persons labeled "illegal immigrants" and/or stronger control measures on the Mexico-US boundary, tend to favor the term "illegal" migrant. Some of the more visible "activist" individuals and groups include those associated with John H. Tanton, MD (such as FAIR, Center for Immigration Studies, Numbers USA), the online journal Social Contract (published by Tanton), Arizona Border Watch, Mothers Against Illegal Aliens (Arizona), The Minutemen, Texas Ranch Rescue,

and others. For a discussion of Tanton's role in fostering a network of "anti-migrant" efforts and some of the links to "White supremacist" groups, see the Southern Poverty Law Center's Intelligence Report (2002). See also the Anti-Defamation League (2007) for a listing of organizations with "extremist rhetoric" against Latino migrants. Among the more visible "activists" taking a "pro-migrant" position, and generally using "undocumented," include the ACLU, Anti-Defamation League (ADL), MALDEF (Mexican American Legal Defense and Education Fund), National Council of La Raza (NCLR), National Immigration Law Center (NILC), and National Network for Immigrant and Refugee Rights (NNIRR).

3  It should be noted that US migration law is principally grounded in a binary: citizen versus alien. An alien is a person who is not a citizen, and a citizen is ultimately a person who is not an alien. There is also a third keyword, national; however, it ultimately overlaps with citizen. Thus, all citizens are US nationals, though some nationals (in certain territorial possessions) are nationals but not citizens.

4  The current INA is based on the consolidation of migration and citizenship statutes brought about by the McCarran-Walter bill of 1952 (Public Law No. 82-414), and subsequent amendments to the statute.

5  It should be noted that the label Entered Without Inspection is a descriptor for the form of entry into the US: one can enter "with inspection," meaning that the person was processed by a customs official at a port of entry (including airports); and "entered without inspection" refers to the possibility of a person entering at a point other than a port of entry. Consequently, a US citizen, permanent resident, or nonimmigrant could also enter without inspection, yet the person would not be considered an "illegal/undocumented" migrant. However, as sometimes used by migration officials, the label for an entry process is transformed into a noun and applied to persons deemed to have entered without authorization, or right to remain. The label marks a process, not a juridical migrant category; although it is used as noun to label individuals.

6  In 1996 Congress replaced the concept of "deportation" with "removal" (IIRIRA). Thus, since then persons are subject to removal, can petition for suspension of removal, or are removed from the territory (i.e., deported).

7  In the interest of simplifying the main issue, I do not include violations that take place under the Visa Waiver Program that allows persons from 35 countries (not including Mexico) to enter the US without prior obtainment of a visa; I also exclude the issue of persons entering with stolen passports.

8  For convenience, I am here including cases involving entering with fraudulent documents and persons entering under "misrepresentation of material facts" (e.g., a person claiming to be a US citizen and allowed entry, particularly before September 11, 2001). It should also be noted that even "naturalized" US citizens may have their citizenship revoked, a process known as "denaturalization."

9  According to the US Department of Homeland Security, there were 319,382 removals, and 891,390 "returns" in FY 2007 (2008: 95). Moreover, ICE frequently reports total "removals," with a qualifier or footnote noting that "returns" are included in the quoted figure.

10  In light of the conceptual change made by Congress (from deportation to removal) in 1996, a few years before De Genova's article (2002), "removability" retains consistency with the change.

11  Numerous academic articles, policy reports, and news media use the term "illegal aliens/immigrant" in their titles as a proxy for the topic being addressed: Mexican migrants alleged to have entered without formal authorization. For academic discussion of this association, see for example, Acuña 2004; Bustamante 1972a, 1978; Chávez 1992, 2001; Fernández and Pedroza 1981; Gutiérrez 1995; Inda 2006; Johnson 1996–1997; López 1980-1981, Mazon 1975; Nevins 2002; Ono and Sloop 2002.

12  Michael D. Cronin, representing the Immigration and Naturalization Service (INS), testified to Congress in 1999 that "(approximately 40–50%) of the estimated illegal alien population in the United States" were nonimmigrants who overstayed their visas (Cronin 1999: 120). A US General Accounting Office report notes that the Department of Homeland Security (DI-IS) estimate of 30% is likely low, and notes that it may be as high as 57% (2004a: 10). In 2006, a committee of Congress was told by a former INS Senior Special Agent that it "is currently estimated that more than 40% of the illegal alien population" violated the terms of their visas (Cutler 2006: 31). The Pew Hispanic Center estimates that the "overstay" migrant population makes up about 45% of "unauthorized migrant" population (2006: 1). It should be observed that irrespective of the actual "overstay" migrant population, all the estimates overlook that in addition to "overstay" violations, an unknown number of nonimmigrants have voided their visas by violating other conditions such as employment; thus they are also subject to removal if discovered. Consequently, it is possible that the number of Mexican migrants who entered without formal authorization may ultimately make up a significantly smaller share than what politicians, academics, media, and others assume to be the case.

13  There already is a parallel, though not that well known, in US statutes: PRUCOL (Permanently Residing Under Color of Law). The concept, used primarily in reference to public assistance benefits, refers to persons who federal migration authorities are aware of, in many cases know their names, addresses, etc., yet have taken no action to remove such persons. Thus courts have recognized that federal migration authorities are in fact implicitly/informally authorizing those persons to remain in the US. Prior to IRCA, and particularly after PRWORA, the list of benefits has been reduced considerably.

# 4. Mark Orbe, "Negotiating Multiple Identities within Multiple Frames: An Analysis of First-Generation College Students"

IN THIS ARTICLE FROM the journal *Communication Education* (2004), Mark Orbe (b. 1964) explains that for some first-generation college (FGC) students, this status is no big deal; for others, it weighs heavy on them. For some, it indicates ways in which their identity is or will be different from other family members. Orbe concludes that it is in the better interest of all students to "expand traditional discussions of privilege beyond that which is closely associated with gender and race" and that "[w]ith an increased awareness of the multidimensional nature of students' identities, teachers can then begin to discern what their role should be in terms of increasing their students' sense of agency." Here the ethical issues revolve around the establishment of the FGC category as an identity in order to better serve student needs. Lack of this identity category would have potentially detrimental effects.

[...]

FIRST-GENERATION COLLEGE (FGC) STUDENTS are enrolling in US colleges and universities in increasing numbers, yet we know little of how this aspect of identity is negotiated in their communication with others.... FGC students often overlap with those who fall under the rubrics of "nontraditional" (Query, Parry, and Flint, 1992), "underprepared" (Bartholomae, 1985; Rose, 1989), or "disadvantaged" students (Rodriguez, 1975). In fact, research that describes how higher education has, or has not, been true to its commitment to provide accessible public education to these groups (Shor, 1987) serves as an important backdrop for current research on FGC students. However, it is important to recognize that not all FGC students enter college from nontraditional, disadvantaged backgrounds. Some, as described by Orbe (2003), come from families with considerable "cultural capital" (Karabel and Halsey, 1977) that, in the absence of a college education, still provide significant support for FGC students.

... The small amount of research that does focus solely on FGC students typically examines statistical relations with other important variables related to college success. For instance, FGC students (as compared to students whose parents had some college experience) have lower SAT scores (Riehl, 1994), make the decision to attend college later in their high-school careers (Fallon, 1997), and choose less selective colleges (MacDermott, Conn, and Owen, 1987). Once enrolled, they tend to experience more difficulties adjusting to college and "have less commitment to the role of student" (Orozco, 1999, p. 70). Some of these difficulties can be tied to lack of support at home (Bartels, 1995; York-Anderson and Bowman, 1991). FGC students typically do not participate in student organizations, interact with other students or faculty, or study hard (Billson and Terry, 1982), when compared to those whose parents had some college experience.

Given this information, it should come as no surprise that FGC students on average have lower first-semester grades, are more likely to drop out the first semester, or do not return for their second year (Brooks-Terry, 1988; Riehl, 1994). Billson and Terry (1982) suggest that this academic achievement gap may be in part due to the tendency for FGC students to spend almost twice as much time working part-time or full-time jobs (as compared to their second-generation counterparts)....

... [E]ducation scholars explored the similarities and differences among FGC students (based on age, race/ethnicity, gender and class; Kiang, 1992; Rendon, 1992; Richardson and Skinner, 1992), and also described some existing programs designed to enhance the success of FGC students (Chaffe, 1992; Padron, 1992; Stein, 1992).... [T]he ongoing negotiation of home and college life results in "trying to live simultaneously in two vastly different worlds" (Rendon, 1992, p. 56). The consistent conclusion that FGC students may feel like outsiders at school as well as home is especially relevant to research regarding multiple-identity negotiation.

In fact, some scholars have described the experiences of FGC students as similar to entering an "alien culture" (Chaffe, 1992; Rose, 1989) complete with peculiar ways of seeing, doing, and communicating about things (Bartholomae, 1985). While the transition from high school/full-time employment to college involves some adaptation for all students (in terms of learning a new set of academic and social rules; see Terenzini et al., 1994), FGC students do not have the benefit of parental experience to guide them, either in preparing for college or in helping them understand what will be expected of them after they enroll (Riehl, 1994). In addition to attempting to learn an "alien culture" of academic and social rules, FGC students must also negotiate issues of marginality – on both

ends – as they work to bridge the worlds of their homes/families/neighborhoods and college life (Brooks-Terry, 1988; Orbe, 2003). A central aspect of this ongoing process involves negotiating multiple layers of identity.

The increasing number of FGC students on college campuses across the US therefore presents itself as a valuable point of analysis for research that seeks insight into how multiple aspects of identity are negotiated in an educational environment....

**Theoretical Framework**

Michael Hecht (1993) outlined the initial conceptualization of the Communication Theory of Identity (CTI) more than a decade ago.... According to CTI, identity is "inherently a communication process and must be understood as a transaction in which messages and values are exchanged" (Hecht et al., 2003, p. 230). Identity is located within four different "frames": (1) within individuals, (2) within relationships, (3) within groups, and (4) communicated between relational partners and group members (Golden et al., 2002). It is important to recognize that these frames permeate all discussions of identity and should not be seen as static or linear (Hecht et al., 2003). Studies of identity should include an awareness of the "interpenetration of frames" (Hecht, 1993, p. 80) – or the ways in which frames can be studied simultaneously. Such analyses can illustrate how frames of identity are competing and/or complementary with one another (Golden et al., 2002) and, consequently, capture the intricate ways that the communication of identity is a complex, multidimensional process. In this regard, each of the frames discussed here serves as a "frame of reference" for a person's identity (Hecht et al., 2003).

The first frame of identity is the personal frame. Within this context, identity is the result of a person's self-cognitions, self-concept, and sense of well-being (Golden et al., 2002). The second frame of identity involves the enactment of identity to others. According to CTI, identities are enacted to others through communication (Hecht et al., 2003); thus, the second frame focuses on messages that a person sends that express his or her identity. Individuals can use either direct or indirect messages to reveal their identity to others (Hecht 8: Faulkner, 2000). A relationship frame of identity, the third in the model, focuses on how identity emerges through our relationships with others, as well as how relationships themselves construct their own identities (Golden et al., 2002; Hecht et al., 2003). The fourth location of identity, identity as a communal frame, occurs in the context of a larger community. "Identity is something held in the collective or public memory of a group that, in turn, bonds the group together" (Hecht et al., 2003, p.237). In this regard, a community possesses a group identity that represents a shared identity of all of its members.

... [B]eing an FGC student may be highly salient to one person's identity, not important at all to another, or somewhere in between for a third, depending on the situation. (See Hecht 8: Faulkner, 2000, for a similar discussion of varying ethnic salience among Jewish Americans.) Given the lack of research on the identity messages of FGC students, and the usefulness of CTI in studying negotiations of multiple identities, the following two research questions were posed:

RQ1: How central is FGC status to the identities of FGC students on different college campuses?

RQ2: How, if at all, is FGC identity negotiated at the personal, enacted, relational, and communal frames of identity?

[...]

## Findings

[...]

### Centrality of Identity via Personal Frames

*High-salience FGC student identity.* When asked, "How conscious are you about being the first in your family to attend college?", many participants stated that it was something that they thought about "every day." One African American male FGC student attending a selective university explained:

> It sits in my head every day. It's like I know that I'm the first one to get this far for my family. I know that my mom is depending on me to make a very good example for my little brother. So, I have to do my best at all times.

Many of the participants described how their FGC student status helped to motivate them at college. Several students of color were particularly adamant in describing how this aspect of their identity is important because it serves as an important link to others in their families who can build on their collegiate success. One African American woman who was excelling at a selective Midwestern university explained:

> Sometimes it gets really hard – What keeps me going is that I am the first in my family [to attend college]. And I have four younger brothers and sisters that look up to me.... That's what keeps me going instead of just shutting down or throwing a temper tantrum. I just keep going. I can't do anything else but finish.

For some, the centrality of their FGC student

identity served as a key motivator for success. However, other participants acknowledged the pressure that this status exerted on their college experiences. Like the student who earlier described his FGC student status as "sitting in his head everyday," a Latina student from a public university also shared the weight that sometimes accompanied this aspect of her identity:

> I think about it a lot. I stress a lot about classes, knowing that it is all of my family's hopes and dreams ... everything that they couldn't do, that my brothers and sisters could not do. I'm doing it for everyone. I'm the youngest of four and the first person to graduate from high school, first and only one to attend the university. My dad is one of 12 and my mom is one of 13. Out of all of my dad's side and all of my mom's side, I'm actually the second person to go to the university.

Another European American woman at a more selective university in the same state described how she attempted to avoid the extra pressure that came with being an FGC student:

> I know that I think about it all of the time. Sometimes I try to avoid thinking about it, in terms of being a first generation college student. I just think that, okay, I'm here, I have to do this. I have to get it done. I have to do what I want [to] do – my goals. Okay, I'm the only one. I'm the last one in my family. So, I have to do this. I have to get my college degree and bring it back home to my parents.

For a number of participants, FGC student status functioned as a salient aspect of their identity because of the hardships that they experienced, compared to students who had the benefits of parents who had gone to college. While this was an issue across a number of different focus group students, it seemed most relevant to students who were attending a selective university "where students had a lot of money." Several of the students remarked that "they [had] pretty much put themselves through school," a reality that situated their FGC status as a salient part of their personal identity frame – especially when they lacked the privilege afforded to non-FGC students. One Latina student offered the following example:

> I think about it all the time, especially because they [students whose parents went to college] have so many more benefits than us [FGC students]. Take my one friend, for example. She got the same score on the ACT test that I did. But then her dad made her take that Princeton Review course – paid $800 for her – and then had her retake the test. She got a 27 on it after she scored an 18. I couldn't believe it. I just remember telling my mom, and she was like, "I wish that I could do it for you, but is it that important?"

Another Latina student at the same selective university enumerated additional privileges that non-FGC students unconsciously benefited from:

> Those kids have their own computers in their rooms ... you stand in line at the computer lab forever – late at night whenever you can get on a computer. But they can get up whenever they want and work on their computer. I don't know ... they just have that extra edge on everything. I mean they get their books right then and there, but we have to wait until the financial aid checks come in. So, we have to usually spend extra money on the

new books. I don't know … It's a lot of small things.

*Variable-salience FGC student identity.* Not all participants described their FGC student status as central to their personal frames of identity, however. A focus group comprising women at a large Midwestern public university manifested considerable difference of opinion about FGC status. For example, one European American woman stated, "If I were to describe myself, [FGC student status] wouldn't be the first thing that I would say about myself. It would come closer to the end of the list. It's not a big deal for me. When I talk with other people, it just doesn't come up." However, another European American woman confessed, "I do think about it. I think about it a lot when I start thinking about my family. I am the only one who ever went to college."

When asked directly about the salience of FGC student status on their identity, many participants described it as highly situational. In other words, it was contingent on other things that were going on in their lives. This was most evident when participants discussed different periods of their college years. For example, when asked about how central being an FGC was to her identity, one European American nontraditional student who was currently working part-time on her PhD at a mid-sized selective university said:

It depends on what is happening in my life when taking certain classes, I always felt like I didn't know what the heck they were talking about. I felt like I started on a different level than a lot of people. And I was always trying to catch up.

Another student thought about his family's lack of previous experience in college when he chose to attend a local branch campus instead of going away to college. "I thought it would be easier to be at home," he shared.

Two occasions in particular seem to trigger a greater consciousness for FGC students regarding their identities as the first in their families to attend college. The first occasion was during their initial experiences on campus. One Hispanic man, who was attending a large public university, explained the surreal nature of actually being on campus during his first semester:

I used to think about it a lot at the beginning. I kept thinking about it probably like the entire first month. "Wow, I'm in college. Wow, I'm the first one to go. Wow, I'm going to classes. I have my backpack and everything. I look like those people on TV that go to school."

Another student remembers thinking about being an FGC student during the first few days of class. The normal anxiety of being able to complete the work was magnified by feelings that "people like me don't go to college." She shared with the focus group that she "definitely felt out of place." In fact, she recalled, "looking around at all of the people in the room and thinking: 'I bet all of their parents went to college.'" For many of these participants, becoming acclimated to college life resulted in a reduced level of consciousness of their FGC student status. However, graduation was the second occasion that typically triggered a resurgence in terms of their identity of FGC students. One European American student, who relied on student loans throughout his tenure at a large public university, described how his FGC student status "hit him" when he received notification that he would be "paying the loans back until 2026!" Another FGC student, a Latina from the same university, shared that her feelings of being at a disadvantage resurfaced while she completed graduate school applications. She described "being amazed at the amount of support that [her] boyfriend [a non–FGC student] got from his family, something completely lacking from [her] own family." ... For many participants, graduation represented a time when they were able to witness exactly how much their accomplishments at college meant to their families. One European American man at a small public university reflected:

> The time that I thought about it most was at graduation. My parents and grandparents were there ... just seeing the smiles on their faces and how much they enjoyed that ... that was the most rewarding thing that I had ever gone through.

*Nonsalient FGC student status.* While the vast majority of participants described the central or variable ways in which FGC student status functioned as part of their identity, a small but significant number of participants reported that they had never really thought about being the first in their family to go to college. Most of these individuals reported that the first time they had recognized this aspect of their identities was when they were informed of the study. As one European American man, who attended a community college, explained:

> I never thought about it. When I heard about the study that was the first time I thought about [being an FGC student]. I don't think that there is a big difference. Everyone comes to college not knowing any one. And we are all here, going to class on the first day. It's all the same.

FGC students who described their status as nonsalient were attending, or had attended, less prestigious campuses (e.g., a local two-year business college). Student comments from students at these schools revealed that

being surrounded by students from similar circumstances reduced the likelihood that FGC status served as a point of differentiation in their educational experiences.

In addition, an analysis of the narratives across saliency levels revealed that certain types of students were more likely to regard their FGC status as more salient than others. Students of color, students from a lower socioeconomic status, and nontraditional female students most often described a high saliency regarding their FGC status. In comparison, those FGC students who were White, from a middle to high socioeconomic status, and of traditional college age were more likely to experience being a first-generation college student with variable salience. Interestingly, the only four-year university participants to describe their FGC status as nonsalient were traditionally aged European American male students.

### Enacted and Relational Frames of FGC Student Identity

[...]

*Identity enactment at home.* By definition, being an FGC student is initially manifested with the relational frame of identity. In other words, being a first-generation college student is contingent on the fact that those to which you are relationally tied did not attend college. This is an important consideration given that many participants described that their FGC student status was enacted at home – a context where being a FGC student often emerged as a salient point of difference for family members and friends. This section describes the identity negotiation process, sometimes mutual, sometimes not, that FGC students are challenged by within their home environments.

In several focus-group discussions, participants explained how they were given "special attention" during weekend trips home. Specifically, some FGC students explained that, while they were home, they benefited from special meals, shopping trips, monetary gifts, and extra attention from relatives. One African American student at a large public university explained how he was typically "treated like a king":

I think about it [being an FGC student] a lot, especially when I go home and visit on the weekends. When I go home, I get treated like a king! I hear that my mom hadn't cooked the whole week, but as soon as I make it in town she's in there cooking up a storm! It definitely comes with its perks. My siblings definitely think that I get more attention now.

Another African American male student from the same university explained that, during his last trip home, his church acknowledged his presence and took up a special offering for him. He went on to explain how others – past classmates and younger children in the neighborhood – always want to talk with him to see how he is doing, something that is tied to "the neighborhood that [he] grew up in only a select few make it out."

African American and Latino FGC students were especially likely to feel that they were representing the larger community back home. One African American man related a story that illustrated how many members of his community regarded him as a liaison to college life:

So, now when I go home, my mother is quick to say, "Come to work with me." I would go to work with her, but I would basically sit in a chair and watch her do people's hair. All the women will say, "Oh, you are so-so's boy. You are so handsome. You go to college?" They talk

to you like you are not a regular person any more. They talked to you like you are – not a superstar – but like you came back from outer space or something. "So what was it like there?"

For several students, additional attention from family and friends was less direct. Some, for instance, described how they would not receive direct messages from family members about the significance of their identity as college students. Instead, they would hear from others that those very family members frequently told them how proud they were. One European American man explained:

It's weird my older brothers and sisters tell me that my dad keeps telling everyone else how proud he is of me. But I've never heard it from him. It's like he's keeping a secret from me that he's proud. He'll tell my brother how proud he is of me. And then I'll walk in the room, [and he'll scream]: "Hey your football team sucks!"

While several individuals described how their FGC student status was enacted at home in positive ways, such was not the case for all participants. Some explained that college was not a topic that was discussed in their home, and they received clear messages that it was to be avoided. One woman explained that part of this, for her, related to sex roles in her culture:

When you get home, it's like, okay, you are not in this Latina college student identity any more. You are now back home where your college life doesn't matter you have to do what everyone tells you ... you have to learn to bite your lip.

Several nontraditional female FGC students also explained how they explicitly avoided behaviors that would give prominence to their college studies. For some, including one European American woman who had begun her doctoral studies at a mid-sized selective university, this included avoiding studying around certain family members:

> My husband is still against college I don't really tell him a lot about it. It's like my own little world. He complains when I stay up late studying for tests. For a while I couldn't bring a book out if he was home. He had to be at work or out.

Despite attempts to downplay their identity as FGC students, several participants described instances where it remained a point of contention with others who were perceived to be "threatened by," or "jealous of" their accomplishments. One European American woman explained how this was the case when communicating with one of her older brothers:

> I try to – to be honest with you – avoid acting like I've got all this new information in my head because they don't like it. I have a brother and we usually talk about different things. I can't remember the specific topic, but I asked him, "Where did you read that? Where did you get that statistic from?" He just got irate! "The big college woman wants proof!" He thinks that I've changed, [and am] trying to act better than the rest of them.

While FGC student identity is defined in terms of family, it also impinges on non-familial friendships. A European American woman at a mid-sized public university shared a story involving her best friend.

> I have a best friend, and she never went to college. She could paint very well and she

could have had such a great career. But I get ... I don't know if it is being resentful ... but it seems as if she just gets mad at me because I am at school trying to do things. When I do go home, she wants to go out to the bar where she works. I usually go for a little while, but when I'm ready to leave, she'll say, "Oh, are you going to get your degree? Too good to hang out with us now?" You do get that friction sometimes which make it easy to just NOT go home.

*Identity enactment on campus.* At home, being an FGC student was nearly always salient. Whether communicated overtly or covertly, family and friends would insist on identity negotiation regardless of the students' preference. On campus, however, FGC student identity was enacted mostly at the discretion of the FGC student, since there were no overt identifying markers. Out of the total number of participants, only one (a European American woman) explained that she was proud to disclose that she was an [FGC student] in her conversations with others. Being an FGC student was central to her self-concept and gave her accomplishments particular importance. In comparison, a handful of students stated that they typically did not enact their identity as FGC students to others. For some, especially those who were attending the more selective universities, coming from a family without college degrees was "embarrassing." One African American woman, for example, explained that she didn't want others to think that her parents didn't value education.

> I do think about it [being an FGC student] a lot, but I don't just go around and announce it. I do think about it a lot, and I do know and understand the reasons why neither one of my parents could go. But I don't know if others will understand

... they may think that my parents don't value what goes on at college.

For these students, a negative stigma was attached to being an FGC student. However, decisions to avoid enacting this aspect of identity were made based on other reasons as well. One European American student at a large public university was clear that the reason why he did not disclose that part of his identity is because he didn't want to be defined primarily as an FGC student.

I don't really tell other people that I'm first generation, it's something that I just keep to myself but for no particular reason. I just don't feel that they need to know. I don't feel a need to share. I don't want pity or praise for that, I want it for me. First-generation college student that's not how I want to be known. I just want to be known as me, myself.

As revealed in the transcripts, many FGC students assume that most – if not all – of the students that they come into contact with come from families with a legacy of college experience. Such was the case with one non-traditional female student who was attending a community college.

I definitely felt out of place. I'm looking around at all of the people in the classroom and thinking: "I bet all of their parents went to college." I don't want to tell them that mine didn't. I would not tell people. I still haven't told people that my mom and dad didn't graduate from high school. I bet I've only told 2–3 people total. I kinda wait to see what they are going to say. But, I don't know. I don't want to be the only one in the group whose parents didn't attend college.

Making decisions based on the situational elements inherent in the communication setting (relationship with the other person, timing, context of particular discussion) is common to the identity messages within the enacted frame of identity (Hecht and Faulkner, 2000). For FGC students, this was reflected in explicit identity messages that were enacted once they learned that others were FGC students themselves, or displayed some sensitivity to their experiences. However, in other instances, identity messages were expressed to others who were not aware of the privilege that was associated with having parents who went to college. Such was often the case for FGC students whose roommates seemed to take college less seriously because "it was handed to them on a silver platter by their parents." Within each focus group discussion, participants described their disbelief in terms of how non-FGC roommates treated their college experience. Many recounted how roommates would "sleep until noon," "miss class all the time," and "not study at all," while they "never missed a class despite holding down two jobs to help pay for school." In several instances, FGC students would get so frustrated with these types of roommates that they would confront them by "telling them how lucky they were to have so much family support." Such conversations typically included disclosures about their own backgrounds, reaffirming the vigor in which the FGC students maximized their college experiences.

**Discussion**

Results indicated considerable variability among FGC students in terms of the centrality of that aspect of their identities. One of the most important determinants of that salience may have been the demographic composition of the student body on their campus. For example, the two participants quoted in the section on nonsalient FGC student identity both attended a regional campus that served a large proportion of FGC students. In short, these two traditionally aged students – and others like them – less frequently discussed the saliency of being an FGC student than their nontraditionally aged counterparts. Especially during the morning and afternoon hours when these two participants took most of their classes, they were no different than most of the classmates: 18–25-year-old European American FGC students. In this context, they were not "others," but they were members of the predominant group.

The findings highlight three specific points of conclusion. First, the saliency of FGC student status in the overall construction of identity varied greatly. The centrality of FGC student identity was largely influenced by situational context (home versus school) and type of campus (selective, public, community college, or university). Second, FGC student status appeared to be more salient when it intersected with other aspects of a person's co-cultural identity, especially those based on race/ethnicity, age, socioeconomic status, and gender. For some FGC students, the privilege associated with being male, European American, middle/upper class, and/or within the traditional age for college students enables FGC student status to remain on the margins of their self-concepts. Third, and finally, FGC students appear to lack any sense of community with other groups of FGC students. The findings reveal that first-generation college students are more likely to feel more comfortable in sharing their experiences with other FGC students; yet, this did not occur as frequently as one would expect. When FGC students did support one another, it was most often done within the context of one or two individuals. For the vast majority of participants, being a part of the study's focus group was the very first time that they

knowingly found themselves within a large group of FGC students. In the absence of any particular form of a collective "we," individual relationships with others – family, friends, and roommates – have a greater influence in terms of how their identity is enacted. Each of these three points has clear implications in terms of research, theory, and practice.

## Theoretical Implications

… Unlike most aspects of cultural identity studied by communication scholars, FGC student status does not exist within the context of a larger community with which individuals can identify. Many of the participants of this study were conscious of the unique challenges that came with being the first in the family to attend college, yet were unaware (until learning of the study) of the existing language and research surrounding this phenomenon.…

A second pressing issue, which has not explicitly been explored in previous CTI studies, involves instances when a person has little choice to enact an aspect of their identity because it is directly or indirectly enacted by others. In more traditional identity theory terms, attributed identity as a college student is often inescapable when FGC students return to their communities of origin, regardless of whether the student chooses to avow such an identity.…

## Recognizing FGC Identity Negotiation in Classrooms

For those of us who experience higher education from the standpoint of an FGC student, it is clear that the academy changes "foreigners" who enter its culture, more so than being changed by them (Rendon, 1992). While a number of different programs have been developed to increase the enrollment and matriculation of FGC students (Chaffe,

1992; Padron, 1992; Stein, 1992), the impact of these support services on the larger cultural framework of most universities is questionable (Shor, 1987). What has been largely absent from most discussions regarding this issue is the role that faculty members can play in facilitating a cultural environment that enhances the success of FGC students....

In the past ten to 15 years, the concept of privilege has been used to enlighten educators to the small, but significant, ways in which majority group members benefit from existing social, organizational, and societal structures. Initially, this work focused on White privilege and male privilege (e.g., McIntosh, 1988).... I would argue that educators need to gain a greater awareness of various locations of privilege and conduct self-examinations of the current practices, in terms of both pedagogy

and curricula. Some current treatments (e.g., Orbe and Harris, 2001) do explain how educators can expand traditional discussions of privilege beyond that which is closely associated with gender and race. By expanding the conversation about relative privilege in society in such a manner, students of all backgrounds can achieve greater consciousness regarding the dynamics of privileges as applied to FGC student status, as well as to age, disability, socioeconomic status, and sexual orientation....

... With an increased awareness of the multidimensional nature of students' identities, teachers can then begin to discern what their role should be in terms of increasing their students' sense of agency as those students negotiate multiple aspects of their identity.

[...]

## References

Bartels, K. (1995). "Psychosocial Predictors of Adjustment to the First Year of College: A Comparison of First-Generation and SGCs." Unpublished doctoral dissertation, University of Missouri-Columbia.

Bartholomae, D. (1985). "Inventing the University." In M. Rose (ed.), *When a Writer Can't Write* (pp. 134–65). New York: Guilford.

Billson, I.M., and M.B. Terry. (1982). "In Search of the Silken Purse: Factors in Attrition among First-Generation Students." *College and University* 58: 57–75.

Brooks-Terry, M. (1988). "Tracing the Disadvantages of First-Generation College Students: An Application of Sussman's Option Sequence Model." In S.K. Steinmetz (ed.), *Family Support Systems across the Life Span* (pp. 121–34). New York: Plenum P.

Chaffe, I. (1992). "Transforming Educational Dreams into Education Reality." In L.S. Zwerling and H.B. London (eds.), *First-Generation Students: Confronting the Cultural Issues* (pp. 81–88). San Francisco: Jossey-Bass.

Fallon, M. V. (1997). "The School Counselor's Role in First Generation Students' College Plans." *The School Counselor* 44: 384–93.

Golden, D.R., T.A. Niles, and M.L. Hecht. (2002). "Jewish American Identity." In I.N. Martin, T.K. Nakayama, and L.A. Flores (eds.), *Readings in Intercultural Communication: Experiences and Contexts* (pp. 44–52). New York: McGraw-Hill.

Hecht, M.L. (1993). "2002 – A Research Odyssey: Toward the Development of a Communication Theory of Identity." *Communication Monographs*, 60: 76–81.

Hecht, M.L., and S. Faulkner. (2000). "Sometimes Jewish, Sometimes Not: The Closeting of Jewish American Identity." *Communication Studies*, 51: 372–87.

Hecht, M.L., R.L. Jackson, and S.A. Ribeau. (2003). *African American Communication: Exploring Identity and Culture*. Mahwah, NJ: Lawrence Erlbaum.

Karabel, I., and A.H. Halsey. (1977). "Educational Research: A Review and Interpretation." In I. Karabel and A.H. Halsey (eds.), *Power and Ideology in Education* (pp. 323–47). New York: Oxford UP.

Kiang, P.N. (1992). "Issues of Curriculum and Community for First-Generation Asian Americans in College." In L.S. Zwerling and H.B. London (eds.), *First-Generation Students: Confronting the Cultural Issues* (pp. 97–112). San Francisco: Jossey-Bass.

MacDermott, K.G., P.A. Conn, and I.W. Owen. (1987). "The Influence of Parental Education Level on College Choice." *Journal of College Admissions*, 115: 3–10.

McIntosh, P. (1988). "White Privilege and Male Privilege: A Personal Account of Coming to See Correspondence through Work in Women's Studies." Wellesley College Center for Research on Women Working Paper Series, 189, 1–19.

Orbe, M. (2003). "African American First Generation College Student Communicative Experiences." *Electronic Journal of Communication/La revue électronique de communication* 13 (2/3).

Orbe, M., and T.M. Harris. (2001). *Interracial Communication: Theory into Practice*. Belmont, CA: Wadsworth.

Orozco, C.D. (1999). "Factors Contributing to the Psychosocial Adjustment of Mexican American College Students." Dissertation Abstracts International, 59, 4359.

Padron, E.I. (1992). "The Challenge of First-Generation College Students: A Miami-Dade Perspective." In L.S. Zwerling and H.B. London (eds.), *First-Generation Students: Confronting the Cultural Issues* (pp. 71–80). San Francisco: Jossey-Bass.

Query, I.M., D. Parry, and L.I. Flint. (1992). "The Relationship among Social Support, Communication Competence, and Cognitive Depression for Nontraditional Students." *Journal of Applied Communication*, 20: 78–94.

Rendon, L.I. (1992). "From the Barrio to the Academy: Revelations of a Mexican American 'Scholarship Girl.'" In L.S. Zwerling and H.B. London (eds.), *First-Generation Students: Confronting the Cultural Issues* (pp. 55–64). San Francisco: Jossey-Bass.

Richardson, R.C., and E.F. Skinner. (1992). "Helping First-Generation Minority Students Achieve Degrees." In L.S. Zwerling and H.B. London (eds.), *First-Generation Students: Confronting the Cultural Issues* (pp. 29–44). San Francisco: Jossey-Bass.

Riehl, R.I. (1994). "The Academic Preparation, Aspirations, and First-Year Performance of First-Generation Students." *College and University*, 70: 14–19.

Rodriguez, R. (1975). "Going Home Again: The New American Scholarship Boy." *American Scholar*, 44: 15–28.

Rose, M. (1989). *Lives on the Boundary: The Struggles and Achievements of America's Underprepared*. New York: The Free P.

Shor, I. (1987). *Critical Teaching and Everyday Life*. Chicago: U of Chicago P.

Stein, W.I. (1992). "Tribal Colleges: A Success Story." In L.S. Zwerling and H.B. London (eds.), *First-Generation Students: Confronting the Cultural Issues* (pp. 89–96). San Francisco: Jossey-Bass.

Terenzini, P.T., L.I. Rendon, M.L. Upcraft, S.B. Millar, K.W. Allison, P.L. Gregg, and R. Jalomo. (1994). "The Transition to College: Diverse Students, Diverse Stories." *Research in Higher Education*, 35(1): 57–73.

York-Anderson, D.C., and Bowman, S.L. (1991). "Assessing the College Knowledge of First-Generation and Second-Generation College Students." *Journal of College Student Development*, 32: 116–22.

## Study Questions

1. Based on the narratives given in the article, what might be an example of an ethical issue regarding first-generation college students? Does it appear that there are special

areas to consider for this student population? Are there other concerns you are aware of for this population, either from your own experience or from that of others?

2. Does it appear to be helpful to identify the category "FGC students," even if not everyone in that group identifies with it? Would it be unethical to disregard this category? Are there other identities you can think of that might be helpful to recognize?

3. Are there any extra responsibilities we might have toward those who find themselves in an unfamiliar environment? Are there any examples you can think of regarding other situations of this same type? What responsibilities might we have in those situations?

# 5. David DiRamio and Kathryn Jarvis, "Crisis of Identity? Veteran, Civilian, Student"

IN THIS ARTICLE, FROM the ASHE Higher Education Report (2011), David DiRamio and Kathryn Jarvis discuss the specific challenges that military veterans may face when returning to the classroom in a college setting. Because the military emphasizes community identity while college encourages growth of the individual, veterans often have to develop a "new core identity" as they switch from one environment to the other. "In the military environment, the expectation is that individual identity becomes secondary to the identity of the group," the report begins, whereas the academy "has flexibility and questions regarding adherence to rules are encouraged." In this way, then, there is an inherent tension in their perception of themselves *as students*, which veterans are more likely to experience than other students. Again, awareness of this identity and the challenges associated with it works to the benefit of the students.

---

IN THE MILITARY ENVIRONMENT, the expectation is that individual identity becomes secondary to the identity of the group. One young man noted that "his real mission in life – in the Army – is being there for his troops" (Lewis et al., 2005, p. 368). The aggressive, male-dominated ethos, the rituals of wearing the uniform, the pride in belonging, all contribute to the collective identity. To thrive in the military, one must develop a "goodness of fit" and accommodate group norms. The sociologist Toennies (1957) called it *Gemeinschaft*, which refers to a culture in which belonging is pervasive. Winslow (1998) described the cultural phenomenon this way: "Individuals exhibit strong allegiance to their group and the group exerts social control over the individual member. In the military, group allegiance is seen to be essential to combat effectiveness. Strong affective ties bind soldiers into a fighting unit in which they are willing to sacrifice their lives for each other. Military culture emphasizes 'belonging.' ... *Gemeinschaft* is perceived as a positive state in the military" (p. 345).

When the term of service has ended and the veteran begins to move on, the paradigm of *Gemeinschaft* likely persists in his or her consciousness. One veteran, a junior in college who spent eight months serving in the Middle East as a translator, described it this way: "It's part of your identity. It's something you carry around with you" (Arora, 2008, p. 1). Josselson, renowned for her work on identity development (1996), conceptualizes the notion of identity: "Identity links the past, the present and the social world into a narrative that makes sense. It embodies both change and continuity" (p. 29).

So how does this "change and continuity" affect college students with military experience? Does the military identity, while still present and an integral part of "self," at some point recede and become overlaid with a post-veteran civilian identity, which in the college environment incorporates a newly acquired status as student? How does prior knowledge of self translate during the transition from veteran to student? What role does an understanding of metacognitive awareness of other's reactions to self and relationships to others play in solidifying this new student veteran identity? What challenges does "straddling" multiple roles bring to the student veteran? What are the implications of identity development for students with military experience, and how can college personnel, including administrators, staff, and faculty, assist this emerging student population? ...

## Identity Development and Knowledge of Self

The developmental path that incorporates a sense of identity is most closely tied to the work of Erikson (1968) and is defined as a psychosocial process that combines cognitive growth and environmental challenges. Chickering's framework (1969) for identity as the pivotal vector in his explanation of how students develop grew out of Erikson's theory of identity development as an evolving sense of self that changes and adapts (or maladapts) when one encounters challenges in the environment. This definition is highly salient for college student veterans, for during the transition from active duty to student, which for many may be during their young adult years, their previously determined identity is bombarded by differing relationships and external factors they may confront in a new environment. The need to reformulate an identity arises out of a state of disequilibrium and discomfort resulting from the conflicts between what established identity dictates and what changes are being faced. These changes may come from outside pressures, cultural norms and expectations, and personal life events.

In Kegan's theory of self (1994), how people understand and make meaning of the world around them determines and influences their identity, self-concept, and interpersonal relationships (Lewis et al., 2005). According to King (2009), the cognitive domain must take the lead in how a person makes meaning of

the world. Underlying a growth in cognitive development is the concept of "perspective taking" (Kegan, 1994; Lewis et al., 2005), which frames a sense of self for most college-age students, this move toward "self authorship" (Kegan, 1994; Baxter Magolda, 1992) is not accomplished until they are more advanced in college. On the return to the college environment, the student veteran who has developed a strong prior knowledge of self faces additional challenges to the military identity he or she may have established. The shift to student status for some will prove more difficult and will depend on a number of situational and support factors in the new environment.

## Self and Others

This cognitive growth parallels Perry's model (1968) of increasing levels of ambiguity in how students think and relate to the world. The younger student's thinking is more dualistic and based on absolutes; as he or she progresses, thinking takes on a less concrete worldview. As students mature cognitively, they are able to entertain others' ideas and grapple with issues from multiple perspectives. The ability to reflect on how behavior affects others and to think about thinking provides the basis for identity formation, moral decision making, and relationships with others. This domain may provide a greater challenge for the veteran in the college environment during the period of transition. Although the academy has rules, it also has flexibility and questions regarding adherence to rules are encouraged. To apply Perry's positions (1968), the military environment demands a good measure of dualistic thinking, while one goal of higher education is to adopt relativism.

In the study by Lewis et al. of identity development in early-career West Point cadets (2005, p. 369), traditional-age military students understood and expressed ideas about their world based more on concrete rewards and self interest than mutuality. Developmental changes in their thinking did occur as they got older, but the internalization necessary for mature introspective decision making was not evident in the first years of the military program.

Not surprisingly, in Chickering's framework (1969), the development of integrity is one of the last vectors to be achieved and is closely tied to the emergence of a true identity. This domain is aligned with the growth in cognitive development and the knowledge of a sense of purpose. Experiences in this domain may be limited for some student veterans, as purpose and decision making have been defined by the reliance on external authority found in a military environment. Navigating in an environment where finding a purpose is an individual task can be a struggle and requires an awareness and acceptance of independent and interdependent thinking.

The ability to interact with others who are different and not be threatened by their difference is an important part of a fully integrated identity. A certain level of metacognitive awareness is necessary to enable one to gauge responses to self and to others that requires the perspective taking discussed by Lewis and his coauthors (2005). For the student veteran, a number of relationships have been predetermined in a strict hierarchical environment, and the transition to a less programmed civilian world can present a challenge. In the military, decision making involved following the rules that were supported by outside forces. In the college environment, self-regulation is key to a successful transition. The personal relationships the veteran has developed may or may not be sustained outside the military environment, and prior civilian relationships will be affected by factors in the veteran's established identity. How these challenges are met and the environmental supports provided

contribute to successful balance as the veteran makes the transition.

## Multiple Roles and Intersecting Identities

Although a number of students may be challenged by adapting to the college environment, particularly if they function in additional roles such as parent, worker, and caregiver, the status of student veteran adds yet another layer to the complexity of intersecting identities. In addition to the social identities of race, culture, sexual orientation, and gender, other pre-entry variables such as first-generation status, officer or enlisted rank, socioeconomic status, and disability all differentially affect the veteran as he or she enters the academy. In the familiar world of the military, the social and personal context for what constitutes a visible and acceptable identity is narrow; the "dominant values dictate norms and expectations" (Torres, Jones, and Renn, 2009, p. 577). As explained by Abes, Jones, and McEwen (2007), the multidimensional filters that were effective in one context may need to be reframed and adjusted as the student veteran faces multiple intersecting domains in the college environment. When different cognitive, interpersonal, and intrapersonal influences are encountered in college, the student veteran's identity shifts and reforms to create a multidimensional model that incorporates various features into the proportionality of the "goodness of fit" for the student veteran in the "new" environment of college. How the veteran adapts and copes with these changes can be determined by the level of transition experienced; the timing, support, strategies, and sense of self that were in place before the transition (Schlossberg, 1984); and the commitment made to the development of a new core identity.

Schlossberg, Lynch, and Chickering (1989) provide a useful starting point for considering the transition of students with military experience. The Moving In, Moving Through, Moving Out model is used to study the dynamics of transition and to identify factors that individuals must cope with to succeed. When moving in and out of the phases of this model, a person evaluates each transition over time while reflecting on the likely positive or negative effects as well as considers the resources available to him or her for use in managing change. This process is not easy; as one student who spent thirty-four months in Iraq and Kuwait remarked, "I was more scared of college than I was of the Marine Corps, and that's the truth" (Tillo, 2011, p. 1).

Part of the self-analysis recommended by Schlossberg and her colleagues includes conducting an inventory of strengths and weaknesses based on personal traits, psychological factors, and social supports available. Thus, coping strategies are formulated for the individual to use in modifying the situation, controlling the meaning of the transition, and managing stressors (Schlossberg, Lynch, and Chickering, 1989). It is during the Moving Through college phase that a crisis of identity can emerge, and research confirms that such crises occur during transitions (Erikson, 1968). One former service member who experienced some measure of identity crisis described the difficulties of transitioning to college this way: "I ended my time in the Marine Corps as a platoon sergeant, and the way we deal with things in the Marines is different. I caught myself yelling at kids in discussion groups" (Arora, 2008, p. 1).

This [reading] approaches identity development in the student veteran population through a multidimensional lens that integrates self, others, and the environment. Different from a linear model, this multidimensional view of identity is fluid and is affected by a person's response in interpersonal, intrapersonal, and cognitive domains....

## Crisis, Exploration, and Commitment

Particularly applicable to student veterans at a time of transition, Marcia's theory of identity formation (1966) provides a vehicle to understand how young people navigate and reconcile crises. According to Marcia, the two variables in identity formation are exploration and commitment. In the exploration stage, a crisis is experienced, and information seeking either clarifies or challenges previous values. The commitment stage occurs when the values and beliefs are confirmed and then acted on. Four statuses in the exploration and commitment stages — foreclosure, moratorium, diffusion, and identity achievement — attempt to explain how the crises and commitments work together. Unlike Erikson's stages, they do not necessarily occur in a progressive pattern. We believe this framework has particular relevance and application to the student veteran during the period of transition from a military environment....

## Multiple Dimensions of Identity

McEwen (1996) and Jones and McEwen (2000) describe multiple dimensions of identity as the intersections of various contextual categories that make up identity development. This conceptual model, represented as a helix-like structure, contains a core identity or self, which McEwen calls the "unified self." The knowledge of self can be likened to a type of Johari window (Luft, 1969), with personal identity somewhat protected yet open in different contexts. For example, when considering one dimension of identity in a military context, the status of sexual identity had been hidden by rule of law (but repealed during this writing [Dinan, 2010]) in the "don't ask, don't tell" policy (P.L. 103–60). This new law affects both the interpersonal and intrapersonal domains and therefore a sense of self, particularly for the student with military experience who is transitioning to college.

The various social dimensions of identity such as gender, race, culture, and sexual orientation exert different influences on "self" at different times, depending on their relative importance in context. This social construction of identity involves expectations of others, societal norms, and the various dimensions of identity (Torres, Jones, and Renn, 2009). In addition to the aforementioned social dimensions, we suggest that the context of first-generation status and socioeconomic status plays an important role in the identity puzzle for the student veteran and so include these parameters in our discussion....

## Typologies

Typological models highlight differences among people based on the way they think or act. Perhaps the most familiar example of the use of typologies is the Myers-Briggs Type Indicator (Myers and McCaulley, 1985), which measures psychological preferences and categorizes individuals into sixteen possible personality types. It is important to note that no normative values are associated with typological categories; one type is no better than another type. This sort of methodological neutrality is desirable when classifying college students and is preferable to demographic stereotyping using race, gender, or other categories. Typological models also provide an alternative to traditional college student development theories such as psychosocial or cognitive approaches.

... This study adds to the literature on student typologies, with a focus on the identity development of students with military experience.

### Type I: Ambivalent

These students can be characterized by a diffused sense of self. They show little commitment to their old military identity and have not adopted a new identity or see the need to change to adapt to the new environment. They sense no crisis of identity, and their former military life exerts a modest influence, with the other dimensions of identity having an impact only as issues arise. For ambivalent students, change is effected by external rather than internal pressures. When it comes to selecting a major or getting involved in social organizations (even the student veterans organization), these students lack a desire for a commitment to any of the typical occupational or ideological areas. Perhaps the ambivalence stems from a sense that people cannot or will not understand the experiences of a veteran, a scenario evident with an art student who served three deployments to Iraq. He "usually doesn't tell fellow art students about his life in the military 'because they can't relate'" (Hancock, 2007, p. 1).

This is where a helping professional in student or academic affairs can assist the ambivalent student to move toward identity exploration and the development of internal rather than external sources of authority. Unfortunately, the lack of commitment to the exploration of a new core identity that is seen in these students is more likely to put them at risk for departure and noncompletion of a degree. If they find a connection or are challenged by a crisis, then "lost – sometimes found" students, as characterized by Josselson (1987), may move into Type III: Emerging.

The ambivalent student's situation may be exacerbated by problems with mental acuity, a symptom of injury from a concussive force such as a roadside bomb explosion, or psychological difficulties, perhaps an undiagnosed case of PTSD. In one study a student veteran remarked, "Once I got back to school, it was like I know what I need to do and it is right in front of me, but I'm just not doing it. I don't know if it [is] because I am not as focused as I was before I left…. I don't know" (Ackerman, DiRamio, and Garza Mitchell, 2009, p. 10). College personnel should be aware of the issues that a Type I student may be facing, be prepared to make a referral or referrals for qualified help, and follow up with the student.

## Type II: Skeptic

Skeptics live with a continuing commitment to a military core identity, which serves as their dominant sense of self. The other dimensions of their identity are "foreclosed," and in this state, these students experience no crisis and no need to explore other aspects of identity. The student veterans who fit this type may have achieved goals in the military by never questioning authority and continue to expect their role will be as receivers of knowledge in a culture that supports this allegiance. Although this approach may have been effective and even necessary in the male-dominated military culture, a certain amount of frustration may arise in the academic environment as the military identity is relegated to a smaller piece of the multidimensional identity puzzle. Unless a crisis is experienced in foreclosure status, no need exists to change and the commitment to the identity status quo remains static (Marcia, 1966).

The risk for skeptic veterans is how to cope when challenges arise to their established military identity…. One student, a former Army sergeant, described her focus when she remarked, "Coming back from not only being in the military but also from war, you realize all of the advantages we have here in the United States, and so you're career-oriented and driven and you want to go through school as soon as you can to get back to a

job" (Tillo, 2011, p. 1). In this example, the student does not view the collegiate experience as one where identity dimensions are to be explored but as a straightaway process where job training and vocational preparation are paramount. She is likely "foreclosed" to change at this point, viewing her military identity as a strong asset in a linear quest for a degree without detours. Unless her narrow focus is challenged, perhaps by necessity in an exigent learning environment or with the help of a caring higher education professional, she may experience frustration and depart (Tinto, 1993).

## Type III: Emerging

Those in moratorium status are not yet committed to change but sense that their military identity, which has been dominant, may not serve effectively in other contexts, particularly in the college environment. One student, a four year veteran of the Marines and a junior, may have sensed a commitment to change was necessary when he remarked, "There's a structure in the military. You know what to do. You wake up at 5:30, train, follow your set schedule for the day, go out and do your mission, and come back and do it all over again. At a university, there's no commander or structure like that" (Mangan, 2009, p. 1). Moreover, the Type III student may experience dissonance when attempting to substitute new and uncomfortable opportunities for social interaction in college for the friendship and solidarity he or she felt while in the military. One student veteran, a history major, remarked about serving in the military: "That's camaraderie. That's brotherhood. What's their [fraternity members'] idea of brotherhood? Coming back in fifteen years and reliving the fraternity college experience, the undergrad experience? Come on" (Brown, 2009, p. 1).

Having been forced to deny other social identities (for example, sexual identity as a result of "don't ask, don't tell") and push them into the background in the military, those emerging students may struggle with the crisis encountered when the voice of authority and the development of a new voice collide. As the student development literature has pointed out (for example, Evans et al., 2009), cognitive conflict forces change. Forced change on a Type III student, however, will likely require support from campus personnel, including staff and faculty members. A report by the National Survey of Student Engagement noted that "'culture shock' is the way some veterans describe their transition from military life to college life on campus. Most don't feel they fit in. And often, institutions don't make it any easier" (Chappell, 2010, p. 1). Assistance is vital at this stage as the student seeks to discover or reestablish a meaning and purpose in life apart from military service. Moreover, according to Marcia (1966), those in a moratorium status remain with this balancing act for a short time, and most move on to an achievement status where multiple identities eventually lead to a balanced core.

### Type IV: Fulfilled Civilian Self

A balanced core identity defines student veterans who have achieved a fulfilled civilian self. They have experienced crisis and questioned authority, explored identity options, grappled with the idea of change, and become comfortable with the need for interdependency (Chickering and Reisser, 1993). For example, Type IV students have established and maintained relationships with other students, faculty members, and staff (Berger and Milem, 1999; Tinto, 2000).

Moreover, this student has by now worked to renegotiate roles with family members and has reestablished interdependent relationships with friends (Schlossberg, Lynch, and Chickering, 1989). Assistance from a helping professional on campus could be critical for a student desiring to explore Type IV actions and behaviors.

Ultimately, the various aspects of their identity have balanced out, with the different dimensions appropriately influencing and fluctuating as the environment dictates while maintaining the core identity. Social and academic integration in college has helped these Type IV students make substantial progress toward a comprehensive transition from military service to civilian life through an "organized set of images, the sense of self, which expresses who or what [they] really are" (Widick, Parker, and Knefelkamp, 1978, p. 2). Cognitively and affectively they have found their own voice.

### Conclusion

Applying theories of identity development is helpful for understanding the emerging population of students with military experience. Student veterans who have served in this most recent decade of conflict are a relatively new phenomenon on college campuses, and little empirical evidence exists to support the ideas presented.... Applying ideas about identity development in both theory and practice to this unique student population is a starting point, however, for conducting future research. The use of typologies, their limitations notwithstanding, can be one path to creating variables for study in the area of student veteran transition, personal fulfillment, and academic success.

## References

Abes, E.S., S.R. Jones, and M.K. McEwen. (2007). Reconceptualizing the Model of Multiple Dimensions of Identity: The Role of Meaning-Making Capacity in the Construction of Multiple Identities." *Journal of College Student Development* 48: 1–22.

Ackerman, R., D. DiRamio, and R.L. Garza Mitchell. (2009). "Transitions: Combat Veterans as College Students." *New Directions for Student Services* 126: 5–14.

Arora, D. (2008, September 28). "Student Veterans Adapt to College Life." The Daily Californian (online). Retrieved January 8, 2011, from www.dailycal.org/article/102743/student_veterans_adapt_to_college_life.

Baxter Magolda, M. (1992). *Knowing and Reasoning in College: Gender Related Patterns in Students' Intellectual Development.* San Francisco: Jossey-Bass.

Berger, J.B., and J.F. Milem. (1999). "The Role of Student Involvement and Perceptions of Integration in a Causal Model of Student Persistence." *Research in Higher Education* 40: 641–64.

Brown, K. (2009, October 10). "Veterans Struggle to Fit into College Campuses." National Public Radio (online). Retrieved January 4, 2011, from www.npr.org/templates/story/story.php?storyId=113698227.

Chappell, B. (2010, November 4). "Veterans Who Head to College Lack Support, Study Finds." National Public Radio (online). Retrieved January 3, 2011, from www.npr.org/blogs/thetwo-way/2010/11/04/131070705/support-is-lacking-for-veterans-who-head-tocollege-study-finds.

Chickering, A.W. (1969). *Education and Identity.* San Francisco: Jossey-Bass.

Chickering, A.W., and L. Reisser. (1993). *Education and Identity* (2nd ed.). San Francisco: Jossey-Bass.

Dinan, S. (2010, December 22). "Obama Signs Bill to Repeal 'Don't Ask, Don't Tell.'" Washington Times (online). Retrieved January 9, 2011, from www.washingtontimes.com/news/2010/dec/22/obama-signs-dont-ask-dont-tell-repeal2/.

Erikson, E. (1968). *Identity: Youth and Crisis.* New York: Horton.

Evans, N.J. et al. (2009). *Student Development in College: Theory, Research, and Practice* (2nd ed.). San Francisco: Jossey-Bass.

Hancock, L. (2007, March 23). "College Can Be Struggle for Veterans." Deseret Morning News (online). Retrieved July 8, 2010, from findarticles.com/p/articles/mi_qn4188/ is_20070323/ai_n18762643/.

Jones, S., and M. McEwen. (2000). "A Conceptual Model of Multiple Dimensions of Identity." *Journal of College Student Development* 41: 405–14.

Josselson, R. (1987). *Finding Herself: Pathways to Identity Development in Women.* San Francisco: Jossey-Bass.

_____. (1996). *Revising Herself: The Story of Women's Identity from College to Midlife.* New York: Oxford UP.

Kegan, R. (1994). *In Over Our Heads: The Mental Demands of Modern Life.* Cambridge, MA: Harvard UP.

King, P.M. (2009). "Principles of Development and Developmental Change Underlying Theories of Cognitive and Moral Development." *Journal of College Student Development* 50: 597–620.

Lewis, P. et al. (2005). "Identity Development during the College Years: Findings from the West Point Longitudinal Study." *Journal of College Student Development* 46(4): 357–73.

Luft, J. (1969). *Of Human Interaction.* Palo Alto, CA: National Press Books.

Mangan, K. (2009, October 18). "Colleges Help Veterans Advance from Combat to Classroom." Chronicle of Higher Education (online). Retrieved July 9, 2010, from chronicle.com/article/Colleges-Help-Veterans-Advance/48846/.

Marcia, J.E. (1966). "Development and Validation of Ego Identity Status." *Journal of Personality and Social Psychology* 3: 551–58.

McEwen, M.K. (1996). "New Perspectives on Identity Development." In S.R. Komives and D.B. Woodard, Jr. (eds.), *Student Services: A Handbook for the Profession* (pp. 188–217). San Francisco: Jossey-Bass.

Myers, I.B., and M.H. McCaulley. (1985). *Manual: A Guide to the Development and Use of the Myers-Briggs Type Indicator.* Palo Alto, CA: Consulting Psychologists P.

Perry, W.G. (1999). *Forms of Ethical and Intellectual Development in the College Years.* San Francisco: Jossey-Bass.

Schlossberg, N.K. (1984). *Counseling Adults in Transition: Linking Practice with Theory.* New York: Springer.

Schlossberg, N.K., A.Q. Lynch, and A.W. Chickering. (1989). *Improving Higher Education Environments for Adults.* San Francisco: Jossey-Bass.

Tillo, C. (2011, January 7). "Veterans Return to College with a Lot to Adjust To." Gainesville Sun (online). Retrieved January 10, 2011, from www.gainesville.com/article/20110107/articles/110109630.

Tinto, V. (1993). *Leaving College: Rethinking the Causes and Cures of Student Attrition* (2nd ed.). Chicago: U of Chicago P.

____. (2000). "Linking Learning and Leaving." In J.M. Braxton (ed.), *Reworking the Departure Puzzle* (pp. 81–24). Nashville: Vanderbilt UP.

Toennies, F. (1957). *Community and Society.* East Lansing: Michigan State UP.

Torres, V., S.R. Jones, and K.A. Renn. (2009). "Identity Development Theories in Student Affairs: Origins, Current Status, and New Approaches." *Journal of College Student Development* 50: 577–96.

Winslow, D. (1998). "Misplaced Loyalties: The Role of Military Culture in the Breakdown of Discipline in Peace Operations." *Canadian Review of Sociology and Anthropology* 35(3): 345–67.

## Study Questions

1. How does the report describe the military and academic environments? Do these seem to be accurate descriptions? Would a person's actions be likely to be different based on these different environments? Might being in these different environments lead toward different decisions regarding the ethics of an action? If so, how can an action be evaluated? Do any of the ethical theories we have been examining provide a way to conduct this evaluation regardless of the environment? Would they be helpful to use?

2. How does this article relate to the points Honneth makes (II.2) about the need for recognizing individual identities? Should military veterans who are students be recognized as a distinct group? Can you think of any ethical concerns that would be particular to this group?

3. Because military actions are necessarily involved with violent actions by their nature, some people object both to these practices and also, sometimes more generally, to the military community. What might be some ways to evaluate whether a community-based identity (such as the military) is itself ethical or unethical? Presumably there are certain groups and group identities that most people would obviously not want to support, but what makes a community a good or bad one?

4. What is the role of personal responsibility in terms of how people behave when they are part of a community where they are told to follow orders? Individuals within the military will likely not know all of the details of the activities they are participating in for strategic purposes, and therefore will not be fully informed. How should we evaluate their actions, ethically speaking, if individuals act unethically but are following orders? Do these evaluations about a military identity extend to these same individuals in their role as a student?

# 6. Susan Brison, "Outliving Oneself"

DRAWING ON HER OWN experience of a brutal assault, as well as others' experiences, in this chapter from her 2002 book *Aftermath: Violence and the Remaking of a Self*, Susan Brison (b. 1954) analyzes how trauma affects the individual's ability to "be oneself even to oneself." Brison discusses traditional philosophical understandings of identity and how these can be enhanced by an understanding of trauma, particularly in regard to a person's body. She argues for an understanding of "the relational self," whereby "the self is both autonomous and socially dependent, vulnerable enough to be undone by violence and yet resilient enough to be reconstructed with the help of empathic others." She points to the importance of being able to make sense of one's experiences in helping to repair the damage from the shattered self-identity.

Brison is explicit in discussing the role of the body in this process, in a way that many other philosophers are not. She also describes the process by which she remakes her own identity after her previous sense of self has been shattered. Brison points to the use of narrative to do so, arguing for an understanding that "the embodied self, the self as narrative, and the autonomous self are compatible and complementary ... [and] that each of these aspects of the self is fundamentally relational." Brison offers an important construct with which to understand more specifically the ways in which our identity is constituted by our relations with others, as well as the ethical impact of these relations.

---

I died in Auschwitz, but no one knows it.
— Charlotte Delbo[1]

SURVIVORS OF TRAUMA FREQUENTLY remark that they are not the same people they were before they were traumatized. As a survivor of the Nazi death camps observes, "One can be alive after Sobibor without having survived Sobibor."[2] Jonathan Shay, a therapist who works with Vietnam veterans, has often heard his patients say, "I died in Vietnam."[3] Migael Scherer expresses a loss commonly experienced by rape survivors when she writes, "I will always miss myself as I was."[4] What are we to make of these cryptic comments?[5] How can one miss oneself? How can one die in Vietnam or fail to survive a death camp and still live to tell one's story? How does a life-threatening event come to be experienced as self-annihilating? And what self is it who remembers having had this experience?

How one answers these questions depends on, among other things, how one defines "trauma" and "the self." ... I discuss the nature of trauma, show how it affects the self, construed in several ultimately interconnected ways, and then use this analysis to elaborate and support a feminist account of the relational self.[6] On this view the self is both autonomous and socially dependent, vulnerable enough to be undone by violence and yet resilient enough to be reconstructed with the help of empathic others.

My methodology differs from that used in traditional philosophizing about the self, and yields distinctly different results. Philosophers writing about the self have, at least since [John] Locke [1632–1704], puzzled over such questions as whether persons can survive the loss or exchange of their minds, brains, consciousness, memories, characters, and/or bodies.[7] In recent years, increasingly gruesome and high-tech thought experiments involving fusion, fission, freezing, dissolution, reconstitution, and/or tele-transportation of an individual have been devised to test our intuitions about who, if anyone, survives which permutations.[8] Given philosophers' preoccupation with personal identity in extreme, life-threatening, and possibly self-annihilating situations, it is odd that they have neglected to consider the accounts of actual trauma victims who report that they are not the same people they were prior to their traumatic transformations.[9] This oversight may result from the fact that imaginary scenarios, however far-fetched, are at least *conceivable*, whereas the experiences of rape victims, Holocaust survivors, and war veterans are, for most of us, unthinkable. In addition, philosophers are trained to divert their gaze from the messy real world to the neater, more controllable, and more comprehensible realm of pure thought.

... [H]owever, feminist theorists writing in the areas of ethics and social, political, and legal philosophy have recently argued for the necessity of focusing on the actual experiences of real people and have made use of first- and third-person narratives in their attempts to do this.[10] Feminist theorists have also stressed the importance of taking context into account, recognizing that we all reason from a "positioned perspective" and that some of us, with "multiple consciousness," reason from a variety of sometimes incompatible perspectives.[11]

...

## Trauma and the Undoing of the Self

There is a much clearer professional consensus among psychologists about what counts as a traumatic event than there is among philosophers concerning the nature of the self.[12] A traumatic event is one in which a person feels utterly helpless in the face of a force that is perceived to be life-threatening.[13] The immediate psychological responses to such trauma include terror, loss of control, and intense fear of annihilation. Long-term effects include the physiological responses of hyper vigilance, heightened startle response, sleep disorders, and the more psychological, yet still involuntary, responses of depression, inability to concentrate, lack of interest in activities that used to give life meaning, and a sense of a foreshortened future. A commonly accepted explanation of these symptoms of post-traumatic stress disorder (PTSD) is that, in trauma, the ordinarily adaptive human responses to danger that prepare the body to fight or flee are of no avail. "When neither resistance nor escape is possible," Judith Herman explains, "the human system of self-defense becomes overwhelmed and disorganized. Each component of the ordinary response to danger, having lost its utility, tends to persist in an altered and exaggerated state long after the actual danger is over" (Herman 1992, 34). When the trauma is of human origin and is intentionally inflicted, ... it not only shatters one's fundamental assumptions about the world and one's safety in it, but it also severs the sustaining connection between the self and the rest of humanity. Victims of human-inflicted trauma are reduced to mere objects by their tormenters: their subjectivity is rendered useless and viewed as worthless. As Herman observes, "The traumatic event thus destroys the belief that one can be oneself in relation to others" (Herman 1992, 53). Without this belief, I argue, one can no longer be oneself even to oneself, since the self exists fundamentally in relation to others.

How one defines "self" depends in part on what explanatory work one wants the concept of a self to do. Philosophers have invoked this concept in various areas of the discipline in order to account for a wide range of phenomena. The self is, in metaphysics, whatever it is whose persistence accounts for personal identity over time. One metaphysical view of the self holds that it is bodily continuity that accounts for personal identity and the other, that it is continuity of memory, character traits, or other psychological characteristics that makes someone the same person over time. There is also the view, held by poststructuralists, that the self is a narrative, which, properly construed, is a version of the view that psychological continuity constitutes personal identity.[14] In ethics the self is viewed as the locus of autonomous agency and responsibility and, hence, is the subject of praise or blame. Most traditional accounts of the self, from [René] Descartes's [1596–1650] to contemporary theorists', have been individualistic, based on the assumption that one can individuate selves and determine the criteria for their identity over time independent of the social context in which they are situated. In contrast, feminist accounts of the self have focused on the ways in which the self is formed in relation to others and sustained in a social context. On these accounts, persons are, in [philosopher] Annette Baier's [1929–2012] words, "second persons," that is, "essentially successors, heirs to other persons who formed and cared for them?"[15] In addition, the self is viewed as related to and constructed by others in an ongoing way, not only because others continue to shape and define us throughout our lifetimes, but also because our own sense of self is couched in descriptions whose meanings are social phenomena (Scheman 1983).

[...]

## The Embodied Self

Although we recognize other persons most readily by their perceptible, that is, bodily, attributes, philosophers have been loath to identify the self with a body for a host of reasons.[16] A dead body cannot be said to be anyone's self, nor can a living, but permanently comatose, one. We do not typically use a bodily criterion of identity to determine who we ourselves are, and most of us, when imagining Locke's prince, whose soul "enters and informs" the body of a cobbler, would suppose the resulting person to be the prince (Locke 1974, 216). Some philosophers[17] have been concerned to show that the self can survive the death of the body, but perhaps the primary reason philosophers have not identified the self with the body is an ancient bias against our physical nature.[18] Plato praised philosophers for "despising the body and avoiding it," and urged that "[i]f we are ever to have pure knowledge of anything, we must get rid of the body and contemplate things by themselves with the soul by itself."[19] ...

Plato praised those "who long to beget spiritually, not physically, the progeny which it is the nature of the soul to create and bring to birth. If you ask what that progeny is, it is wisdom and virtue in general.... Everyone would prefer children such as these to children after the flesh" (quoted in Ruddick 1989, 192–93). It occurred to me that this preference was not, after all, universal, and that, in any case, one did not have to choose between pursuing wisdom and virtue, on the one hand, and having children, on the other. My husband (who never felt as compelled to make such a choice) and I started trying to conceive, or, rather, as a friend put it more aptly, stopped trying not to. It was just six months later, however, that I was jumped from behind, beaten, raped, strangled, and left for dead in a ravine. The pleasures of embodiment were suddenly replaced by the pain and terror to which being embodied makes one prey.

I was no longer the same person I had been before the assault, and one of the ways in which I seemed changed was that I had a different relationship with my body. My body was now perceived as an enemy, having betrayed my newfound trust and interest in it, and as a site of increased vulnerability. But rejecting the body and returning to the life of the mind was not an option, since body and mind had become nearly indistinguishable. My mental state (typically, depression) felt physiological, like lead in my veins, while my physical state (frequently, incapacitation by fear and anxiety) was the incarnation of a cognitive and emotional paralysis resulting from shattered assumptions about my safety in the world. The symptoms of PTSD gave the lie to a latent dualism that still informs society's most prevalent attitude to trauma, namely, that victims should buck up, put the past behind them, and get on with their lives. My hyper vigilance, heightened startle response, insomnia, and other PTSD Symptoms were no more psychological, if that is taken to mean under my conscious control, than were my heart-rate and blood pressure.[20]

The intermingling of mind and body is also apparent in traumatic memories that remain in the body, in each of the senses, in the heart that races and skin that crawls whenever something resurrects the only slightly buried terror. As Jonathan Shay writes in his study of combat trauma, "Traumatic memory is not narrative. Rather, it is experience that reoccurs, either as full sensory replay of traumatic events in dreams or flashbacks, with all things seen, heard, smelled, and felt intact, or as disconnected fragments. These fragments may be inexplicable rage, terror, uncontrollable crying, or disconnected body states and sensations" (1994, 172). The main change in the modality as well as in the content of the most salient traumatic memories is that they are more tied to the body than memories are typically considered to be.

Sensory flashbacks are not, of course, merely a clinical phenomenon, nor are they peculiar to trauma.... Trauma, however, changes the nature and frequency of sensory, emotional, and physiological flashbacks. They are reminiscent of the traumatic event itself, as Shay writes, in that "[o]nce experiencing is under way, the survivor lacks authority to stop it or put it away. The helplessness associated with the original experience is replayed in the apparent helplessness to end or modify the re-experience once it has begun" (1994, 174). Traumatic flashbacks immobilize the body by rendering the will as useless as it is in a nightmare in which one desperately tries to flee, but remains frozen.

The bodily nature of traumatic memory complicates a standard philosophical quandary concerning which of two criteria of identity – continuous body or continuous memories – should be used to determine personal identity over time. Locke's bodily transfer puzzle in which we are asked to decide who survives "should the soul of a prince ... enter and inform the body of a cobbler" (1974, 116) no longer presents us with an either/or choice, depending on which criterion we invoke. If memories are lodged in the body, the Lockean distinction between the memory criterion and that of bodily identity no longer applies.[21]

The study of trauma also replaces the traditional philosophical puzzle about whether the soul can survive the death of the body with the question of whether the self can reconstitute itself after obliteration at the hands of another, after what Cathy Winkler has labeled "social murder" (1991). Winkler describes the way in which, during a rape, the victim is defined out of existence by the attitudes and actions of the rapist, which incapacitate the victim's self. "Without our abilities to think and feel as we choose ... our existence becomes like a body on life support," Winkler writes. "During an attack, victims have confronted social death, and grappled with it to save themselves" (1991, 14). The victim's inability to be – and to assert – her self in the context of a rape constitutes at least a temporary social death, one from which a self can be resurrected only with great difficulty and with the help of others.

In the aftermath of trauma, not only is the victim's bodily awareness changed,[22] but she may also attempt to change her body itself in an effort to enhance her control over it. Eating disorders are a common reaction to sexual abuse, as is dressing in ways that disguise one's body. After my own assault, I wished I could add eyes in the back of my head, but I settled for cutting my hair so short that, when viewed from behind, I might be mistaken for a man.

The study of trauma does not lead to the conclusion that the self can be identified with the body, but it does show how the body and one's perception of it are nonetheless essential components of the self. It also reveals the ways in which one's ability to feel at home in the world is as much a physical as an epistemological accomplishment. Jean Améry writes, of the person who is tortured, that from the moment of the first blow he loses "trust in the world," More important, according to Améry, is the loss of the certainty that other persons "will respect my physical, and with it also my metaphysical, being. The boundaries of my body are also the boundaries of myself. My skin surface shields me against the external world. If I am to have trust, I must feel on it only what I want to feel. At the first blow, however, this trust in the world breaks down" (1995, 126). Améry goes on to compare torture to rape, an apt comparison, not only because both objectify and traumatize the victim, but also because the pain they inflict reduces the

victim to flesh, to the purely physical. This reduction has a particularly anguished quality for female victims of sexual violence who are already viewed as more tied to nature than men and are sometimes treated as mere flesh.[23] It is as if the tormentor says with his blows, "You are nothing but a body, a mere object for my will – here, I'll prove it!"

Those who endure long periods of repeated torture often find ways of dissociating themselves from their bodies, that part of themselves which undergoes the torture. As the research of Herman (1992) and Terr (1994) has shown, child victims of sexual and other physical abuse often utilize this defense against annihilation of the self, and, in extreme cases, even develop multiple personalities that enable one or more "selves" to emerge unscathed from the abuse. Some adult victims of rape report a kind of splitting from their bodies during the assault, as well as a separation from their former selves in the aftermath of the rape.

A number of Holocaust survivors, whose former selves were virtually annihilated in the death camps, gave themselves new names after the war, Jean Améry (formerly Hanns Mayer [1912–78]) and Paul Celan (formerly Paul Antschel [1920–70]) being among the most well-known. In a startling reappropriation of the name (literally) imposed on him during his incarceration at Auschwitz, one survivor retained and published under the name "Ka-Tzetnik 135633," meaning "concentration camp inmate number 135633."[24] Others were forced to assume new names and national and religious identifies (or, rather, the appearance of them) in order to avoid capture, and probable death, during the war. The dislocations suffered by what Rosi Braidotti has called "nomadic subjects" (1994) can be agonizing even when the migrations are voluntary or, as in the case of Eva Hoffman (1989), whose family moved from Poland to Canada when she was 13, involuntary, but unmarked by violence. Given how traumatic such relocations can be, it is almost unimaginable how people can survive self-disintegrating torture and then manage to rebuild themselves in a new country, a new culture, and a new language. Nermina Zildzo, a recent refugee from the war in Bosnia, describes her new life in America, in which she struggles to become someone who can be herself in English, as that of "a cadaver," which is to say, not a life at all.[25]

Some who survived the Holocaust, such as Delbo, have written about a distinct self that emerged in the camps and then, in some sense, stayed there after the liberation. "Auschwitz is so deeply etched in my memory that I cannot forget one moment of it. – So you are living with Auschwitz? – No. I live next to it," Delbo writes (1985, 2). "No doubt, I am very fortunate in not recognizing myself in the self that was in Auschwitz. To return from there was so improbable that it seems to me I was never there at all.... I live within a twofold being. The Auschwitz double doesn't bother me, doesn't interfere with my life. As though it weren't I at all. Without this split I would not have been able to revive" (1985, 3).

What can we conclude from these clinical studies and personal narratives of trauma concerning the relationship of one's self to one's body? Does trauma make one feel more or less tied to one's body? That may depend on one's ability to dissociate. Since I, like most victims of one-time traumatic events, did not dissociate during the assault, I felt (and continue to feel) more tied to my body than before, or, at any rate, more vulnerable to self-annihilation because of it.[26] Those who survived ongoing trauma by dissociating from their bodies may feel that an essential part of themselves was untouched by the trauma, but even they experience, in the aftermath, the physical intrusions of visceral traumatic memories.

These various responses to trauma – dissociation from one's body, separation from the self one was either before or during the trauma – have in common the attempt to distance one's (real) self from the bodily self that is being degraded, and whose survival demands that one do, or at any rate be subjected to, degrading things. But such an attempt is never wholly successful and the survivor's bodily sense of self is permanently altered by an encounter with death that leaves one feeling "marked" for life....

## The Self as Narrative

Locke famously identified the self with a set of continuous memories, a kind of ongoing narrative of one's past that is extended with each new experience (1974). The study of trauma presents a fatal challenge to this view, since memory is so drastically disrupted by traumatic events, unless one is prepared to accept the conclusion that survivors of such events are distinct from their former selves. The literature on trauma does seem to support the view, advocated by Derek Parfit (1986), that the unitary self is an illusion and that we are all composed of a series of successive selves.[27] But how does one remake a self from the scattered shards of disrupted memory? ... Not only are one's memories of an earlier life lost, along with the ability to envision a future, but one's basic cognitive and emotional capacities are gone, or radically altered, as well. This epistemological crisis leaves the survivor with virtually no bearings to navigate by. As Améry writes, "Whoever has succumbed to torture can no longer feel at home in the world" (1995, 136). Shattered assumptions about the world and one's safety in it can, to some extent, eventually be pieced back together, but this is a slow and painful process. Although the survivor recognizes, at some level, that these regained assumptions are illusory, she learns that they are necessary illusions....[28]

[...]

By constructing and telling a narrative of the trauma endured, and with the help of understanding listeners, the survivor begins not only to integrate the traumatic episode into a life with a before and an after, but also to gain control over the occurrence of intrusive memories. When I was hospitalized after my assault I experienced moments of reprieve from vivid and terrifying flashbacks when giving my account of what had happened – to the police, doctors, a psychiatrist, a lawyer, and a prosecutor. Although others apologized for putting me through what seemed to them a retraumatizing ordeal, I responded that it was, even at that early stage, therapeutic to bear witness in the presence of others who heard and believed what I told them. Two and a half years later, when my assailant was brought to trial, I found it healing to give my testimony in public and to have it confirmed by the police, the prosecutor, my lawyer, and, ultimately, the jury, who found my assailant guilty of rape and attempted murder.[29]

How might we account for this process of "mastering the trauma" through repeated telling of one's story? The residue of trauma is a kind of body memory, as Roberta Culbertson notes, "full of fleeting images, the percussion of blows, sounds, and movements of the body – disconnected, cacophonous, the cells suffused with the active power of adrenalin, or coated with the anesthetizing numbness of noradrenalin" (1995, 174). Whereas traumatic memories (especially perceptual and emotional flashbacks) feel as though they are passively endured, narratives are the result of certain obvious choices (e.g., how much to tell to whom, in what order, etc.). This is not to say that the narrator is not subject to the constraints of memory or that the story will ring true however it is told. And the telling itself may be out of control, compulsively repeated.

But one can control certain aspects of the narrative and that control, repeatedly exercised, leads to greater control over the memories themselves, making them less intrusive and giving them the kind of meaning that enables them to be integrated into the rest of life.

Not only present listeners, but also one's cultural heritage, can determine to a large extent the way in which an event is remembered and retold, and may even lead one to respond as though one remembered what one did not in fact experience.[30] Yael Tamir [b. 1954], an Israeli philosopher, told me a story illustrating cultural memory, in which she and her husband, neither of whom had been victims or had family members who had been victims of the Holocaust, literally jumped at the sound of a German voice shouting instructions at a train station in Switzerland. The experience triggered such vivid "memories" of the deportation that they grabbed their suitcases and fled the station. Marianne Hirsch (1992–93) discusses the phenomenon of "postmemory" in children of Holocaust survivors and Tom Segev writes of the ways in which the Holocaust continues to shape Israeli identity: "Just as the Holocaust imposed a posthumous collective identity on its six million victims, so too it formed the collective identity of this new country – not just for the survivors who came after the war but for all Israelis, then and now" (1993, 11). The influence of cultural memory on all of us is additional evidence of the deeply relational nature of the narrative self.

The relational nature of the self is also revealed by a further obstacle confronting trauma survivors attempting to reconstruct coherent narratives: the difficulty of regaining one's voice, one's subjectivity, after one has been reduced to silence, to the status of an object, or, worse, made into someone else's speech, an instrument of another's agency. Those entering Nazi concentration camps had the speech of their captors literally inscribed on their bodies. As Levi describes it, the message conveyed by the prisoners' tattoos was "You no longer have a name; this is your new name." It was "a non-verbal message, so that the innocent would feel his sentence written on his flesh" (1989, 119).[31]

[…]

… Piecing together a dismembered self seems to require a process of remembering in which speech and affect converge. This working through, or remastering of, the traumatic memory involves going from being the medium of someone else's (the torturer's) speech to being the subject of one's own. The results of the process of working through reveal the performative role of speech acts in recovering from trauma: saying something about a traumatic memory does something to it. As Shay notes in the case of Vietnam veterans, "Severe trauma explodes the cohesion of consciousness. When a survivor creates fully realized narrative that brings together the shattered knowledge of what happened, the emotions that were aroused by the meanings of the events, and the bodily sensations that the physical events created, the survivor pieces back together the fragmentation of consciousness that trauma has caused" (1994, 188). But one cannot recover in isolation, since "[n]arrative heals personality changes only if the survivor finds or creates a trustworthy community of listeners for it" (1994, 188). As Levi observes, "Part of our existence lies in the feelings of those near to us. This is why the experience of someone who has lived for days during which man was merely a thing in the eyes of man is non-human" (1993, 172). Fortunately, just as one can be reduced to an object through torture, one can become a human subject again through one's narrative to caring others who are able to listen.

Intense psychological pressures make it difficult, however, for others to listen to trauma narratives. Cultural repression of traumatic memories (in the United States about slavery, in Germany and Poland and elsewhere about the Holocaust) comes not only from an absence of empathy with victims, but also out of an active fear of empathizing with those whose terrifying fate forces us to acknowledge that we are not in control of our own. I recently felt my own need to distance myself from a survivor's trauma when I read the story of Ruth Elias, who was three months pregnant when she arrived in Auschwitz in December 1943. After she gave birth, Josef Mengele decided to experiment on her son to see how long a newborn could live without food. "In the beginning, the baby was crying all the time," Elias recalled. "Then only whimpering." After a week, a Jewish doctor took pity on her and gave her some morphine with which she euthanized her child. "It didn't take long before the child stopped breathing…. I didn't want to live anymore."[32] How she managed (how she manages) to continue living is incomprehensible to me. I realize, though, that I manage to bear the knowledge of such an atrocity by denying that such a thing could ever happen to a child of mine. I can (now) live with the (vivid) possibility that I might be murdered. But I cannot live with even the possibility that this kind of torture could be inflicted on my child. So I employ the usual defenses: it couldn't happen here/now/to me/and so on.

As a society, we live with the unbearable by pressuring those who have been traumatized to forget and by rejecting the testimonies of those who are forced by fate to remember. As individuals and as cultures, we impose arbitrary term limits on memory and on recovery from trauma: a century, say, for slavery, fifty years, perhaps, for the Holocaust, a decade or two for Vietnam, several months for mass rape or serial murder. Even a public memorialization can be a forgetting, a way of saying to survivors what someone said after I published my first article on sexual violence: "Now you can put this behind you." But attempting to limit traumatic memories does not make them go away; the signs and symptoms of trauma remain, caused by a source more virulent for being driven underground.

In *The Book of Laughter and Forgetting*, Milan Kundera writes that "The struggle against power is the struggle of memory against forgetting."[33] Whether the power is a fascist state or an internalized trauma, surviving the present requires the courage to confront the past, reexamine it, retell it, and thereby remaster its traumatic aspects. As Eva Hoffman, who returns repeatedly in her memoir to a past in which she was "lost in translation" after moving from Poland to Canada, explains, "Those who don't understand the past may be condemned to repeat it, but those who never repeat it are condemned not to understand it" (1989, 278).

[...]

To recover from trauma, according to psychoanalyst Dori Laub, a survivor needs to construct a narrative and tell it to an empathic listener, in order to reexternalize the event. "Bearing witness to a trauma is, in fact, a process that includes the listener" (1992, 70). And to the extent that bearing witness reestablishes the survivor's identity, the empathic other is essential to the continuation of a self. Laub writes of Chaim Guri's film, *The Eighty-First Blow* [1974], which "portrays the image of a man who narrates the story of his sufferings in the camps only to hear his audience say: 'All this cannot be true, it could not have happened. You must have made it up.' This denial by the listener inflicts, according to the film, the ultimately fateful blow, beyond the eighty

blows that man, in Jewish tradition, can sustain and survive" (1992, 68).

## The Autonomous Self

The view of the self most central to ethics, as well as to social, political, and legal philosophy (at least in the analytic tradition), is one that holds that the self is the locus of autonomous agency, that which freely makes choices and wills actions. This is a self that is considered responsible for its decisions and actions and is an appropriate subject of praise or blame. It is the transformation of the self as autonomous agent that is perhaps most apparent in survivors of trauma. First, the autonomy-undermining symptoms of PTSD reconfigure the survivor's will, rendering involuntary many responses that were once under voluntary control. Intrusive memories are triggered by things reminiscent of the traumatic event and carry a strong, sometimes overwhelming, emotional charge. Not only is one's response to items that would startle anyone heightened, but one has an involuntary startle response to things that formerly provoked no reaction or a subtler, still voluntary one. The loss of control evidenced by these and other PTSD symptoms alters who one is, not only in that it limits what one can do (and can refrain from doing), but also in that it changes what one *wants* to do.

A trauma survivor suffers a loss of control not only over herself, but also over her environment, and this, in turn, can lead to a constriction of the boundaries of her will. If a rape victim is unable to walk outside without the fear of being assaulted again, she quickly loses the desire to go for a walk. If one's self, or one's true self, is considered to be identical with one's will, then a survivor cannot be considered to be the same as her pre-trauma self, since what she is able to will post-trauma is so drastically altered. Some reactions that once were under the will's command become involuntary and some desires that once were motivating can no longer be felt, let alone acted upon.

Such loss of control over oneself can explain, to a large extent, what a survivor means in saying, "I am no longer myself." The trauma survivor identifies with her former self not only because that self was more familiar and less damaged, but also because it was more predictable. The fact that, as has been recently discovered, certain drugs, such as Prozac, give PTSD sufferers greater self-control, by making them better able to choose their reactions to things and the timing of their responses, accounts for the common response to such drugs: "they make me more myself" (Kramer 1993). It may also be that after taking Prozac such a person is better able to endorse, or identify with, her new self.[34]

In order to recover, a trauma survivor needs to be able to control herself, control her environment (within reasonable limits), and be reconnected with humanity. Whether the latter two achievements occur depends, to a large extent, on other people. Living with the memory of trauma is living with a kind of disability, and whether one is able to function with a disability depends largely on how one's social and physical environments are set up (Minow 1990). A trauma survivor makes accommodations, figuring out how to live with her limits, but she also realizes that at least some externally imposed limits can be changed. In the year after my assault, when I was terrified to walk alone, I was able to go to talks and other events on campus by having a friend walk with me. I became able to use the locker room in the gym after getting the university to put a lock on a door that led to a dark, isolated passageway, and I was able to park my car at night after lobbying the university to put a light in the parking lot.

These ways of enhancing my autonomy in the aftermath of my assault reinforced my view of autonomy as fundamentally dependent on others. Not only is autonomy compatible with socialization and with caring for and being cared for by others (Meyers 1987, 1989, 1992), but the right sort of interactions with others can be seen to be essential to autonomy. In "Jurisprudence and Gender," Robin West (1988) discusses the tension within feminist theory between, on the one hand, the desire for connection and fear of alienation (in cultural feminism)[35] and, on the other hand, the desire for autonomy and fear of invasion (in radical or "dominance" feminism).[36] Once one acknowledges the relational nature of autonomy, however, this apparent tension can be resolved by noting that the main reason all of us, especially women, have to fear violent intrusions by others is that they severely impair our ability to be connected to humanity in ways we value. It is this loss of connection that trauma survivors mourn, a loss that in turn imperils autonomous selfhood. In order to reestablish that connection in the aftermath of trauma, one must first feel able to protect oneself against invasion. The autonomous self and the relational self are thus shown to be interdependent, even constitutive of one another.

Virginia Held defends a relational account of autonomy in which autonomy does not consist of putting walls around oneself or one's property (as in Isaiah Berlin's phrase for autonomy, "the inner citadel"),[37] but instead, of forming essential relationships with others. Held cites Jennifer Nedelsky, who suggests that "the most promising model, symbol, or metaphor for autonomy is not property, but childrearing. There we have encapsulated the emergence of autonomy through relationship with others.... Interdependence [is] a constant component of autonomy" (Nedelsky 1989, 11).

Trauma survivors are dependent on empathic others who are willing to listen to their narratives. Given that the language in which such narratives are conveyed and are understood is itself a social phenomenon, this aspect of recovery from trauma also underscores the extent to which autonomy is a fundamentally relational notion.[38]

Primo Levi recalls a dream in which he is telling his sister and others about the camp and they are completely indifferent, acting as though he is not there. Many others in the camp had this dream. "Why does it happen?" he asks. "Why is the pain of every day translated so constantly into our dreams, in the ever-repeated scene of the unlistened-to story?" (1993, 60). Why is it so horrifying for survivors to be unheard? There is a scene in the film *La Famiglia* (Ettore Scola, 1987) in which a little boy's uncle pretends not to see him, a game that quickly turns from a bit of fun into a kind of torture when the man persists long beyond the boy's tolerance for invisibility. For the child, not to be seen is not to exist, to be annihilated. Not to be heard means that the self the survivor has become does not exist for these others. Since the earlier self died, the surviving self needs to be known and acknowledged in order to exist.

This illuminates a connection among the views of the self as narrative, as embodied, and as autonomous. It is not sufficient for mastering the trauma to construct a narrative of it: one must (physically, publicly) say or write (or paint or film) the narrative and others must see or hear it in order for one's survival as an autonomous self to be complete. This reveals the extent to which the self is created and sustained by others and, thus, is able to be destroyed by them. The boundaries of the will are limited, or enlarged, not only by the stories others tell, but also by the extent of their ability and willingness to listen to ours.

In the traditional philosophical literature on personal identity, one is considered to be the same person over time if one can (now) identify with that person in the past or future.

One typically identifies with a person in the past if one can remember having that person's experiences and one identifies with a person in the future if one cares in a unique way about that person's future experiences. An interesting result of group therapy with trauma survivors is that they come to have greater compassion for their earlier selves by empathizing with others who experienced similar traumas. They stop blaming themselves by realizing that others who acted or reacted similarly are not blameworthy. Rape survivors, who typically have difficulty getting angry with their assailants, find that in group therapy they are able to get angry on their own behalf by first getting angry on behalf of others (Koss and Harvey 1991).

That survivors gain the ability to reconnect with their former selves by empathizing with others who have experienced similar traumas reveals the extent to which we exist only in connection with others. It also suggests that healing from trauma takes place by a kind of splitting off of the traumatized self which one then is able to empathize with, just as one empathizes with others.[39] The loss of a trauma survivor's former self is typically described by analogy to the loss of a beloved other. And yet, in grieving for another, one often says, "It's as though a part of myself has died." It is not clear whether this circular comparison is a case of language failing us or, on the contrary, its revealing a deep truth about selfhood and connectedness. By finding (some aspects of) one's lost self in another person, one can manage (to a greater or lesser degree) to reconnect with it and to reintegrate one's various selves into a coherent personality.

The fundamentally relational character of the self is also highlighted by the dependence of survivors on others' attitudes toward them in the aftermath of trauma. Victims of rape and other forms of torture often report drastically altered senses of self-worth, resulting from their degrading treatment. That even one person – one's assailant – treated one as worthless can, at least temporarily, undo an entire lifetime of self-esteem (see Roberts 1989, 91). This effect is magnified by prolonged exposure to degradation, in a social and historical context in which the group to which one belongs is despised. Survivors of trauma recover to a greater or lesser extent depending on others' responses to them after the trauma. These aspects of trauma and recovery reveal the deeply social nature of one's sense of self and underscore the limits of the individual's capacity to control her own self-definition.

But what can others do to help a survivor recover from trauma, apart from listening empathically? Kenneth Seeskin argues, in discussing an appropriate response to the Holocaust, that we who did not experience it cannot hope to understand it and yet to remain silent in the aftermath of it would be immoral. And so, he suggests, we should move beyond theory, beyond an attempt to understand it, to a practice of resistance. As Emil Fackenheim writes, "The truth is that to grasp the Holocaust whole-of-horror is not to comprehend or transcend it, but rather *to say no to it, or resist it*."[40] The "no" of resistance is not the "no" of denial. It is the "no" of acknowledgment of what happened and refusal to let it happen again....

## References

Améry, Jean. 1995. "Torture." In *Art from the Ashes: A Holocaust Anthology*, ed. Lawrence Langer. New York: Oxford UP.

Baier, Annette. 1985. *Postures of the Mind: Essays on Mind and Morals*. Minneapolis; U of Minnesota P.

Bettelheim, Bruno. 1979. *Surviving and Other Essays*. New York: Knopf.

Bolker, Joan L. 1995. "Forgetting Ourselves." *Readings: A Journal of Reviews and Commentary in Mental Health*, June: 12–15.

Briadotti, Rosi. 1994. *Nomadic Subjects: Embodiment and Sexual Difference in Contemporary Feminist Theory*. New York: Columbia UP.

Brison, Susan. 1995a. "The Theoretical Importance of Practice." *Nomos* 37: 216–38.

———. 1995b. "On the Personal as Philosophical." *APA Newsletter* 95, no. 1: 37–40.

Culbertson, Roberta. 1995. "Embodied Memory, Transcendence, and Telling: Recounting Trauma, Re-establishing the Self." *New Literary History* 26: 169–95.

Delbo, Charlotte. 1995. *Auschwitz and After*. Trans. Rosette C. Lamont. New Haven: Yale UP.

Descartes, René. 1984 (orig. pub. 1641). *Meditations*. In *The Philosophical Writings of Descartes*, vol. II, trans. John Cottingham, Robert Stoothoff, and Dugald Murdoch. New York: Cambridge UP.

Felman, Shoshana, and Dori Laub, eds. 1992. *Testimony: Crises of Witnessing in Literature, Psychoanalysis, and History*. New York: Routledge.

Frankfurt, Harry. 1988. *The Importance of What We Care About*. New York: Cambridge UP.

Gilligan, Carol. 1982. *In a Different Voice*. Cambridge, MA: Harvard UP.

Hacking, Ian. 1995. *Rewriting the Soul. Multiple Personality and the Sciences of Memory*. Princeton: Princeton UP.

Held, Virginia. 1993. *Feminist Morality: Transforming Culture, Society, and Politics*. Chicago: U of Chicago P.

Herman, Judith Lewis. 1992. *Trauma and Recovery*. New York: Basic.

Hirsch, Marianne. 1992–93. "Family Pictures: *Maus*, Mourning, and Post-Memory." *Discourse* 15, no. 2: 3–29.

Hoffman, Eva. 1989. *Lost in Translation*. New York: Dutton.

Jaggar, Alison M. 1983. *Feminist Politics and Human Nature.* Totowa, NJ: Rowman & Allanheld.

Janoff-Bulman, Ronnie. 1992. *Shattered Assumptions: Towards a New Psychology of Trauma.* New York: The Free P.

Ka-Tzetnik 135633. 1989. *Shivitti: A Vision.* New York: Harper & Row.

King, Deborah K. 1988. "Multiple Jeopardy, Multiple Consciousness: The Context of a Black Feminist Ideology." *Signs* 14, no. 1:42–72.

Kramer, Peter. 1993. *Listening to Prozac.* New York: Viking.

Langer, Lawrence, ed. 1995. *Art from the Ashes.* New York: Oxford UP.

Levi, Primo. 1989. *The Drowned and the Saved.* New York: Random House.

____. 1993. *Survival in Auschwitz.* New York: Macmillan.

Locke, John. 1974. (This section, on personal identity, was orig. pub. 1694.) *An Essay Concerning Human Understanding,* ed. A.D. Woozley, 210–20. New York: New American Library.

Lugones, Maria. 1987. "Playfulness, 'World'-Travelling, and Loving Perception." *Hypatia* 2, no. 2: 3–19.

MacKinnon, Catharine. 1987. *Feminism Unmodified: Discourses on Life and Law.* Cambridge, MA: Harvard UP.

Matsuda, Mari. 1989a. "Public Response to racist Speech: Considering the Victim's Story." *Michigan Law Review* 87, no. 8: 2320–81.

____. 1989b. "When the First Quail Calls: Multiple Consciousness as Jurisprudential Method." *Women's Rights Law Reporter* 11, no. 1: 7–10.

Meyers, Diana Tietjens. 1987. "The Socialized Individual and Individual Autonomy: An Intersection between Philosophy and Psychology." In *Women and Moral Theory,* ed. Eva Feder Kittay and Diana Tietjens Meyers. Savage, MD: Rowman and Littlefield.

____. 1989. *Self, Society, and Personal Choice.* New York: Columbia UP.

____. 1992. "Personal Autonomy or the Deconstructed Subject? A Reply to Hekman." *Hypatia* 7, no. 1: 124–32.

____, ed. 1997. *Feminist Social Thought: A Reader.* New York: Routledge.

Minow, Martha. 1990. *Making All the Difference: Inclusion, Exclusion, and American Law.* Ithaca: Cornell UP.

Nagel, Thomas. 1975. "Brain Bisection and the Unity of Consciousness." In *Personal Identity,* ed. John Perry. Berkeley: U of California P.

Nedelsky, Jennifer. 1989. "Reconceiving Autonomy: Sources, Thoughts and Possibilities." *Yale Journal of Law and Feminism* 1, no. 7: 7–36.

Noonan, Harold W. 1989. *Personal Identity.* New York: Routledge.

Parfit, Derek. 1986. *Reasons and Persons.* Oxford: Oxford UP.

Perry, John. 1975. *Personal Identity.* Berkeley: U of California P.

Roberts, Cathy. 1989. *Women and Rape.* New York: New York UP.

Rorty, Amélie Oksenberg, ed. 1976. *The Identities of Persons.* Berkeley: U of California P.

Ruddick, Sara. 1989. *Maternal Thinking: Toward a Politics of Peace.* Boston: Beacon.

Scheman, Naomi. 1983. "Individualism and the Objects of Psychology." In *Discovering Reality: Feminist Perspectives on Epistemology, Metaphysics, Methodology, and Philosophy of Science,* ed. Sandra Harding and Merrill B. Hintikka, 225–44. Boston: D. Reidel.

____. 1993. "Though This Be Method, Yet There Is Madness in It." In *A Mind of One's Own,* ed. Louise M. Antony and Charlotte Witt. Boulder, CO: Westview.

Scherer, Migael. 1992. *Still Loved by the Sun: A Rape Survivor's Journal.* New York: Simon & Schuster.

Seeskin, Kenneth. 1988. "Coming to Terms with Failure: A Philosophical Dilemma." In *Writing and the Holocaust,* ed. Berel Lang. New York: Holmes & Meier.

Segev, Tom. 1993. *The Seventh Million.* Trans. Haim Watzman. New York: Hill and Wang.

Shay, Jonathan. 1994. *Achilles in Vietnam: Combat Trauma and the Undoing of Character*. New York: Atheneum.

Terr, Lenore. 1994. *Unchained Memories*. New York: HarperCollins.

Ungar, Peter. 1990. *Identity, Consciousness and Value*. New York: Oxford UP.

West, Robin. 1988. "Jurisprudence and Gender." *University of Chicago Law Review* 55, no. 6: 1–72.

Wilkes, Kathleen. 1988. *Real People*. New York: Oxford UP

Williams, Bernard. 1970. "The Self and the Future." *Philosophical Review* 79, no. 2: 161–80.

Winkler, Cathy. 1991. "Rape as Social Murder." *Anthropology Today* 7, no. 3: 12–14.

Young, Iris Marion. 1990. *Throwing Like a Girl and Other Essays in Feminist Philosophy and Social Theory*. Indianapolis: Indiana UP.

## Study Questions

1. How does our body play a role in creating a sense of personal identity? Brison provides an account of the embodied self, in which mind and body can "become nearly indistinguishable," as for example in her own case of depression, a mental state which felt "like lead in [her] veins." Similarly, Honneth (II.2) argues that a physical intrusion will work to block a person from developing their full sense of identity. Can you think of examples of ways in which our personal identity is related directly to our body?

2. Is there an ethical responsibility to listen to survivor stories? Is there a more general special responsibility to those who have survived trauma? If so, what would this involve? Would it be unethical to attempt to deny someone the ability to create their own understanding of a traumatic event?

3. Brison is arguing that our sense of self is established within a context, and that it is therefore important to pay attention to that context. Can we think about ethics without taking the context into account? Immanuel Kant argues that ethics must never take context into account because we must have a principle first to make the determination of what is right or wrong before applying it to situations. If we use examples to derive our ethics, accordingly, there must be something we already have in mind in choosing and interpreting those examples. What do you think of these claims about including or rejecting context? What might be benefits to the approach of studying ethics from the perspective of those who have survived what are generally understood as unethical actions?

## Notes

1   [Charlotte Delbo (1913–85) was a French writer who wrote several memoirs of her time in the Auschwitz Nazi concentration camp.] Delbo (1995, 267) attributes this statement to one of her fellow deportees.
2   Quoted in Langer (1995, 14). The irony of calling the author of the quote a "survivor" is evident, but, it seems to me, linguistically unavoidable.
3   Shay (1994, 180). Shay writes, "When a survivor of prolonged trauma loses all sense of meaningful personal narrative, this may result in a contaminated identity. 'I died in Vietnam' may express a current identity as a corpse."

4  Scherer (1992, 179).

5  I do not mean to imply that the traumas suffered by these different groups of survivors are the same, or even commensurable. However, researchers such as Judith Herman, in *Trauma and Recovery* (1992), and Ronnie Janoff-Bulman, in *Shattered Assumptions: Towards a New Psychology of Trauma* (1992), have persuasively argued that many of those who survive life-threatening traumatic events in which they are reduced to near-complete helplessness later suffer from the symptoms of post-traumatic stress disorder. I would add that they experience a similar disintegration of the self. In this essay, I use the term "victim" as well as the term "survivor" to denote someone who has been victimized by, and yet survived, such a life-threatening trauma. Clearly, many civilians are more traumatized by war (and with greater injustice) than the veterans to whom I refer in this chapter. I mention the latter simply because trauma research on survivors of war has focused on veterans – US veterans in particular – whose trauma symptoms our federal government is obliged to attempt to understand and treat.

6  In defending a feminist account of the relational self, I do not mean to imply that all relational accounts of the self are feminist. Some that are not (necessarily) feminist are those advocated by Hegel, Marx, and contemporary communitarians.

7  See Locke (1974, orig. pub. 1694), Noonan (1989), and Perry (1975) for treatments of personal identity by seventeenth- and eighteenth-century philosophers.

8  See Ungar (1990), Parfit (1986), Noonan (1989), Rorty (1976), and Perry (1975) for discussions of contemporary theories of personal identity.

9  While most philosophers writing about personal identity have neglected to consider *any* actual transformations of real persons, there are a few notable exceptions. Kathleen Wilkes argues that the "bizarre, entertaining, confusing, and inconclusive thought experiments" so common in philosophical writing about personal identity are not helpful, and, in any case, not needed, "since there are so many actual puzzle-cases which defy the *imagination*, but which we none the less have to accept as facts" (Wilkes 1988, vii). She does not discuss trauma, however, and uses third-person scientific accounts of neurological disorders rather than first person narratives in her analysis. Although he does not discuss trauma and the self either, Thomas Nagel examines the effect of commissurotomy on the self in "Brain Bisection and the unity of Consciousness" (1975). Three philosophers, however, have in recent writings departed from this tradition of ignoring trauma and have analyzed alleged cases of trauma-induced dissociation and subsequent recovered memories. Ian Hacking (1995) presents a deeply skeptical treatment of the alleged splitting of the self that occurs during severe child abuse, while Naomi Scheman considers the multiple personalities constructed by severely abused children to be "a comprehensible, perhaps even rational, response to an intolerable situation, a way of maintaining some degree of agency in the fact of profoundly soul-destroying attacks on one's ability to construct a sense of self" (1993, 164). Diana T. Meyers, in "The Family Romance" (Meyers 1997, 440–57), mediates between these two views with an account focusing, not on whether the incest trope that "figures" such recovered memories is historically accurate, but, rather, on whether such a figuration is useful to the alleged victims.

10  For discussions of the usefulness of such narratives, see Brison (1995a) and Brison (1995b).

11  See King (1988), Lugones (1978), and Matsuda (1989).

12  This is not (merely) because philosophers are a more disputatious lot, but rather because psychologists need at least the appearance of clarity and agreement in order to categorize illnesses, make diagnoses, carry out research, fill out insurance claim forms, and so on.

13  This paraphrases Judith Herman's description of traumatic events (1992, 33). This description and the following discussion of trauma are distilled from Herman's book as well as from Janoff-Bulman (1992) and Shay (1994).

14  While some poststructuralists hold that the self is a fiction, not all do, and this is not, in any case, implied by the view that it is a narrative. I think the clinical studies and narrative

accounts of trauma discussed below show that the self is not a fiction, if that is taken to mean that it is freely constructed by some narrator. No one, not even Stephen King, would voluntarily construct a self so tormented by trauma and its aftermath.

15  Baier (1985, 84). For other discussion of the relational self, see Jaggar (1983) and Meyers (1978, 1989, 1992, 1994). Virginia Held gives an excellent survey of feminist views of the relational self in so far as they bear on moral theory (Held 1993, 57–64).

16  An exception is Bernard Williams (1970), who presents a thought experiment that prompts the intuition that in at least some cases of so-called body transfer, we would identify with the surviving individual who has our body, and not the one who has our memory and other psychological characteristics.

17  Most famously, Descartes (1984).

18  In refreshing contrast to the disciplinary bias is the philosophical writing on embodiment by Iris Young (1990).

19  Plato, *Phaedo*, II65c–67d (quoted in Ruddick 1989, 188).

20  That fear, anxiety, and so on are psychological, and hence controllable, responses to trauma is an assumption underlying the view, held by many liberals, that victims of hate speech should simply toughen their emotional hides to avoid being affected adversely by it. This view presupposes a mind-body split more thoroughgoing than that defended by Descartes (1984).

21  If memories do not reside solely in the mind or in the body, but rather are a function of the way in which consciousness "inhabits" a body, then not only Locke's thought experiment, but also Sydney Shoemaker's (Perry 1975, 119–34) and Bernard Williams's (1970) appear to be incoherent as described.

22  And, in the case of the extreme trauma endured by Holocaust survivors, their bodies themselves were drastically changed, by starvation, disease, and torture.

23  An especially striking literary illustration of this is the scene is *Studs Lonigan* in which the narrator says of the woman Weary Reilly is about to rape, "She was his meat" (James T. Farrell, *Studs Lonigan*, Book II [New York: Vanguard, 1935], 396). I thank Blanche Gelfant for drawing my attention to this passage.

24  Ka-Tzetnik 135633 (1989). I thank Alexis Jetter for showing me the work of this author.

25  Nermina Zildzo, essay for English 2, Dartmouth College, Fall 1995.

26  See Terr (1994) for an account of different responses to one-time and ongoing traumas.

27  Parfit would not, however, agree with the relational account of the self I am defending here. In her comments on a draft of this chapter, Susan Dwyer wondered "how many people who have not suffered trauma have a clear sense of what it was like to be them at some earlier point in their lives." She guessed "not many," and suggested that this "explains a number of rituals we engage in, taking photographs of significant events, keeping a diary, marking anniversaries, valuing family (i.e., people who were there, too, who can tell you about your former self)."

28  Bruno Bettelheim discusses the "personality-disintegrating" effects of being in a German concentration camp (1979, 25). "Being subjected to living in an extreme situation somehow contaminates permanently the old life and the old personality. This suggests that a personality which did not protect the individual against landing in an extreme situation seems so deficient to the person that he feels in need of widespread restructuring" (1979, 123–24). In spite of this conviction, trauma survivors are forced to reacquire at least some of their earlier illusions if life is to continue to be livable.

29  Of course, not many rape survivors are fortunate enough to have such an experience with the criminal justice system, given the low rates of reporting, prosecuting, and conviction of rapists. I also had the advantage of having my assailant tried in a French court, in which the adversarial system is not practiced, so I was not cross-examined by the defense lawyer. In addition, since the facts of the case were not in dispute and my assailant's only defense was an

(ultimately unsuccessful) insanity plea, no one in the courtroom questioned my narrative of what happened.

30  I am not suggesting that for this reason the memories of trauma survivors are less reliable that others' memories. In the subsequent story, Yael Tamir did not have a false memory of actually having lived through the Holocaust. Rather, the cultural climate in which she was raised led her to respond instinctively to certain things (a shouting German voice at a train station) in ways characteristic of those who had actually been deported. In any case, since all narrative memory involves reconstruction, trauma survivors' narratives are no less likely to be accurate than anyone else's. (I thank Susan Dwyer for encouraging me to make this last point more explicit.)

31  Levi writes that "[a]t a distance of forty years, my tattoo has become a part of my body," which no longer taints his sense of self (1989, 119).

32  *Newsweek*, January 16, 1995, 54.

33  Milan Kundera, *The Book of Laughter and Forgetting* (New York: Knopf, 1980), 3. I thank Joan Bolker for reminding me of this quote, with which she begins her review (1995, 12) of Terr (1994). In this article Bolker also refers to "term limits on memory" which, she says, were what the US electorate really voted for in the November 1994 elections (1995, 15).

34  For an example of an endorsement account of autonomy, see Frankfurt (1988, chs. 5 and 12).

35  Two of the most prominent proponents of what West calls "cultural feminism" (and others have called "difference feminism") are Carol Gilligan (1982) and Sara Ruddick (1989).

36  The best-known advocate of "radical" or "dominance" feminism is Catharine MacKinnon (1987).

37  The militaristic nature of this image is brought out by an update of this notion mentioned to me by Diane Meyers: autonomy as "the inner missile silo"!

38  In addition, not simply what we are able to express, but also what we are able to feel, can be seen to be a function of one's social relations. See Scheman (1983).

39  This is one of the positive aspects of a kind of multiple consciousness. Cf. Scheman (1993), Lugones (1987), Matsuda (1989), and King (1988).

40  Seeskin (1988, 120), quoting Emil Fackenheim, *To Mend the World* (New York: Schocken, 1982), 239.

# Section III:
# Thinking Sex: Personal and Public

ETHICAL QUESTIONS ABOUT SEX are some of the most interesting questions that humans ask, and they cover the gamut of human sexual behavior, from mild curiosity to the prurient. Attitudes toward sex range from ultraconservative to ultraliberal, with nearly every behavior considered along the way. For example, is sex only ethically acceptable in order to procreate? Is it acceptable between any consenting adults? Is promiscuity unethical? And what of the traditional notion that sex is only ethically permissible within the confines of a heterosexual, monogamous marriage? There are also the perspectives of many communities to consider, including LGBTQQIAAP (Lesbian, Gay, Bisexual, Transgender, Queer, Questioning, Intersex, Asexual, Ally, Pansexual), BDSM (Bondage and Discipline, Dominance and Submission, Sadism and Masochism), and polyamorous communities. Human sexuality is extremely diverse, and while many people advocate for and/or assume monogamous heterosexuality as the norm, this norm is continually challenged.

The Supreme Court of the United States recently ruled, in *Obergefell ET AL. v. Hodges, Director, Ohio Department of Health, ET AL.* (2015) that the right to marry is a fundamental right and that same-sex marriages cannot be prohibited in the United States. This landmark decision remains controversial for approximately 40–60 per cent of the (American) population, depending upon which poll one reads, with some who are opposed refusing to perform services for same-sex couples, often citing their religious beliefs. Although marriage has changed throughout history, for example regarding such issues as consent (and the age at which one may consent) and the status of women as property, many people resist changes to the "traditional" one-man-one-woman marriage. Sex has occupied our private and public consciousness in every imaginable way.

## Personal Applied Ethics in Sex

The influential Greek philosopher Epicurus (341–270 BCE) held that moderating one's sexual activities is the best way to attain the greatest good in life, that greatest good being a steady influx of pleasure with minimal pain. Epicurus wrote that by pleasure he meant

> the absence of pain in the body and of trouble in the soul. It is not an unbroken succession of drinking-bouts and of merrymaking, not sexual love, not the enjoyment of the fish and other delicacies of a luxurious table, which produce a pleasant life; it is sober reasoning,

searching out the grounds of every choice and avoidance, and banishing those beliefs through which the greatest disturbances take possession of the soul.[1]

Pleasure, for Epicurus, is more the removal of suffering than the excitement of the senses, more about peace of mind and steering clear of activities that would disturb that peace of mind than it is about excess.

Aristotle (384–322 BCE), who engaged nearly every sphere of intellectual pursuit, rejected the view that happiness consists of pleasure. In *Nicomachean Ethics* (see I.1), Aristotle asserts that the key to the good life is the rational "mean between extremes" of character types, and so it would be for one's sex life. Thus, an even-handed, not too ascetic or sparse, and not too extravagant or indiscriminative sex life would be the main focus for an Aristotelian personal ethics for sex. The guide for finding the middle road is found in the virtues. The virtues are considered universal directors of behavior because they carry inherently worthy and good traits of conduct, so to employ them in one's life, no matter the situation, is almost a guarantee of success. Lucid and routine application of the virtues, along with the knowledge and practice of how to reason in this way, is how one can achieve the greatest good: *eudaimonia* – happiness or flourishing in one's life.

Immanuel Kant (1724–1804) maintained the position that duties were what made sex morally acceptable. Sex, said Kant, when done for itself, violates the categorical imperative by rendering someone a sexual thing for another's enjoyment. The only sex that Kant found acceptable was that within heterosexual marriage. Further, this was acceptable only if there were interpersonal feelings and values that honored the personhood of one's spouse, such that they overcame the objectifying sexual desires.

Constructing an individual, personal sexual ethic can be informed by virtue ethics and personal duties such as those discussed above. Situating a sex life in virtue ethics allows one to integrate sexual desire and acts with reason. It allows for pleasure but also requires self-governance in ways that enable personal happiness as well as the happiness of one's sexual partner. Virtue ethics can also highlight the weighty responsibilities involved in intimate dealings with others, as to act virtuously is strongly connected with how one treats another. With these considerations in mind, we can move our personal sex lives beyond passivity and desire to thoughtful and dignified relationships. The first two authors in this section, Dan Putnam and Raja Halwani, both approach sexual activity from within virtue ethics.

To position our sex lives in the realm of personal duties raises some important concerns as well. Personal duties are those that are manifest in relationships by virtue of individual options or preferences contained in them, as opposed to being under the control of legal duties. Thus there is unavoidable choice in each relationship wherein individual relationships will give rise to their own duties yet also must heed external constraints. This is terrain that must be negotiated, and to do so as an ethical activity presents a number of important considerations. For example, to delineate what personal duties one expects in a relationship means to reciprocally, responsibly, and intimately think about what kinds of expectations one has. And this means not having those duties defined by outside expectations or cultural precepts, such that we can be more autonomous and more in command of the character of our lives. Michael Warner's essay in this section delves into these outside expectations and cultural precepts and argues for a robust sexual autonomy.

## Sex and Consciences in the Public Domain

The *Declaration of Sexual Rights* (2014), produced by the World Association for Sexual Health, states that sexual rights are "universal human rights" that are "based on the inherent freedom, dignity, and equality of all human beings."[2] The *Declaration* states that sexual privacy, sexual equality, sexual expression, and sexual safety, among others, are examples of such human rights. This position is a drastic step away from many views of sexuality throughout history. In the US and the UK, for example, sex outside of marriage was traditionally seen as a grave public transgression, and laws not only addressed this but also defined other sexual deviations and penalties. For example, sodomy laws in the US, which had been so long used to prosecute homosexuals and which were rendered unconstitutional by the Supreme Court only in 2003, in *Lawrence v. Texas*, 539 U.S. 558, had severe punishments and destroyed lives. Many social factors were involved in this change, including a call for respecting the separation of church and state, a call for respecting individual freedom and equality, and the LGBT (Lesbian, Gay, Bisexual, and Transgender) movement and its allies.

Many scholars have come to see how sex and politics merge in central ways – and not just through political scandals. They have identified, as in the *Declaration*, that there is a crucial relationship between social practice and sexual freedom. They call for sexual justice that entails equality for sexual minorities, arguing that this equality is indispensable to the promise of modern democracies and hence an important political concern. One major proponent of sexual justice, Morris B. Kaplan, maintains that there is an important connection between happiness and sexual pleasure/desire.[3] When one understands happiness in this way, individual "voluntary associations" become morally important. Such relational associations, which involve consent and do not impinge on another's rights, should not suffer state interference. Valuing happiness then translates into allowing individuals the freedom to establish families, identities, and lifestyles in accordance with their desires. The Supreme Court's decision in *Obergefell* is thus a significant step toward sexual justice.

As acknowledged above, however, and as is glaringly clear in American society, not everyone is a proponent of sexual autonomy and sexual justice. And many who celebrate decisions such as *Lawrence* and *Obergefell* also note the decades of struggle required to arrive at this point. And that point is still a contentious one. Ethical questions about sex are indeed some of the most interesting one can explore; they touch on the most intimate aspects of our lives, in both public and private ways. Such questions take people to the streets and invade our bedrooms and influence our families (and the very notion of "family" itself). Philosophical and ethical reflection regarding one's personal sexual autonomy and the public, legal constraints upon that autonomy is therefore a fruitful venture.

## Reading Selections

In the readings in this section, Dan Putnam first argues that virtues help us develop as integrated persons, and help us treat our sexual partners with sensitivity, without which sex becomes divisive and results in vice. Sexual vice involves solely autoerotic or ego-centered behavior which reflects the inability to function as a full human being. This is unfortunate, whether one is culpable for failing to develop virtues or whether one has an inherent "defect" that does not allow one to develop virtues. Putnam argues for a well-integrated full life that includes a sexual relationship entailing trust, honesty, affection, and emotional presence. Thus for Putnam, sex with love, or something very close to love, is an expression of a virtuous life.

But what of sex without love? Raja Halwani addresses casual sex and promiscuity and argues that this does not necessarily result in vice. Halwani does not give a magic number of casual sexual encounters that crosses one over into intemperance, but there is a line somewhere. That somewhere depends on maintaining motives that are morally sound and on being vigilant in sexual dealings with others. Whether one is successful in a virtuous active casual sex life can be decided only on a case-by-case basis.

In contrast, Michael Warner argues for a robust sexual autonomy. Warner argues that the intrusions of absolutism and shaming around sexual norms infringe on one's dignity and freedom of expression and being, and this infringement goes beyond sexual identity and to one's core. Sexual autonomy is one vital aspect of queer ethics that allows us all to defy sexual hierarchies and move toward an integrated and liberated thriving existence.

One aspect of sexual autonomy is the full spectrum of LGBTQQIAAP experiences. Loren Cannon also challenges sexual hierarchies through the multifaceted lenses of transgender and intersex people. Cannon illustrates how the male/female binary, a societal epitome of sexual expression, resembles racism and its categories. Cannon argues for a transformative view of same-sex and trans-marriages, with the hopes that we can move beyond discriminatory social constructions.

Perhaps no other profession has faced more discriminatory social constructions than prostitution. The United States is inconsistent on its views involving pay-for-sex. The porn industry is more profitable than major league sports; on video one can view nearly any kind of sex imaginable, and the people engaged in sex are paid to perform these acts. Ironically, pay-for-sex prostitution is considered somehow different; it is illegal, with the exception of some areas of Nevada. Michelle Madden Dempsey provides three avenues from which to argue about prostitution: the empirically data-based, the philosophical, and the political.

Sex is one contentious topic that touches almost everyone's life. Whether it is the debate about being a virtuous person, or having sexual autonomy and the freedom to choose one's own identity, or the option for a profession, it captivates our attention and raises many judgments and hierarchies. Navigating these waters can be tricky, but it is always interesting and controversial.

## Notes

1  Epicurus, *Letter to Menoeceus*, trans. Robert Drew Hicks, 1994, http://classics.mit.edu/Epicurus/menoec.html.
2  *The Declaration of Sexual Rights*. 2014. http://www.worldsexology.org/wp-content/uploads/2013/08/declaration_of_sexual_rights_sep03_2014.pdf.
3  See Morris B. Kaplan, *Sexual Justice: Democratic Citizenship and the Politics of Desire* (New York: Routledge, 1997).

# I.   Dan Putnam, "Sex and Virtue"

IN THIS 1991 ESSAY from the *International Journal of Moral and Social Studies*, Dan Putnam introduces interesting and broad ways in which one can think about sex in terms of virtue, especially when virtue is concerned with the moral development of the individual. Putnam thus provides a theoretical framework in which sexual activity can be used as data for moral judgment about one's life.

[...]

## II

TWO ELEMENTS OF MODERN virtue theory are especially helpful when analyzing sex. The first is the effect of virtues on practices (MacIntyre [1981] 1984: ch. 14). We have had a tendency in the West in recent years to view the achievement of pleasure in the sex act as a matter of technique. But coinciding with the techniques of sex are certain character traits on the part of the participants which increase the richness of the sexual experience. These include sensitivity, imaginativeness, self-discipline and self-honesty. These traits, some of which are more significant virtues than others, can add considerably to the "joy of sex." Knowing technique is pointless unless one is sensitive to where one's partner is emotionally at any given time. Without sensitivity sex can become a divisive act. Imaginativeness can keep a long-term sexual relationship from becoming routine. In the sexual context imaginativeness is the ability to modify technique in creative ways as needs require. Self-discipline is a virtue especially relevant for sex because the pleasure of the other may directly depend to a great degree on disciplining one's own desire. And self-honesty as a general character trait permits one to accept feedback on one's behavior, some of which may not be easy to accept. Sex as an integral part of our self-image is an area in which self-deception can occur easily. We do not like to admit mistakes or defects and are quick to rationalize. Yet the pleasure of the experience will not be increased until we learn from our past. Self-honesty is an important virtue for improving the quality of the practice in the future.

Virtue theory can also provide a positive framework within which sex can be viewed as part of human life. This is where the greatest controversy arises. Ruddick's assumption about "disembodied" sex being generally harmful to people's mental health and development points to an underlying theory of human nature which needs to be explored. Western history provides many examples of linking sex to some concept of being human. The abuses which resulted from this approach have led some philosophers to reject virtue ethics totally as a way to judge sexual behavior (Humber 1987–88; Matthews 1988). Older theories on the role of sex relied on a priori concepts of human nature often derived from religious assumptions. Moreover, those theories that claimed to be grounded empirically such as Aristotle's relied on a limited examination of human life which led to some hasty conclusions. The perspective taken by Ruddick and many others has at least one advantage over its predecessors – it is not only based on empirical studies but is also, in theory anyway, open to modification (Jones 1987; Scruton 1984; Brod 1984).

The model underlying the moral claims alluded to above is the concept of "moral maturity" based on an analysis of human psychological development. The idea of developmental stages applied to sex was first argued by Freud (Freud 1938). While the evidence does not support many of Freud's ideas about childhood sexuality, it does support his claim that childhood sexuality is autoerotic, primarily concerned with the self. Freud's original ideas about stages of development have been corrected and refined through developmental psychology to the point where Kohlberg and Gilligan can both claim that ego-centered moral decisions in general represent a less-developed level of maturity (Kohlberg 1981; Gilligan 1982). On the developmental model of human maturity adults whose sexual behavior is solely autoerotic or ego-centered have failed to develop fully as human beings. They have what the Greeks meant by a vice, an inability or a breakdown in their total functioning as a human.

Human development involves learning how to function as an integrated person. The "parts" of one's self, whether it be the feet in walking or sexual desire, function best when they form together what might be viewed as a smoothly flowing system. If the parts fight each other, the effect on the individual is disintegrating. Energy is wasted and experiences are limited because the system cannot freely absorb new data. The individual is too busy fighting himself or herself. Carr has pointed out some of the implications of this model relative to sex (Carr 1987). As a person matures, feelings such as sex, anger and affection impinge on each other. The mature person is the one who can integrate these emotions and act appropriately and realistically in life situations. In some cases, such as a parent-child relationship, the appropriate response is affection without sex. In other cases, such as a marital relationship, affection and sex can reinforce each other and add to the strength of the marriage and the development of both partners. Carr points out that "neuroses" or personality disorders have moral dimensions. Such disorders are often expressed in the inability to integrate one's feelings which in turn may have profound moral effects. Individuals like the child molester or Peeping Tom have deep divisions between sex and other aspects of life. But this lack of integration is not limited to extreme cases; we are all prone to it. A married partner who cannot deal with a sexual problem in the marriage may begin to separate sex from the marital relationship even though he or she maintains affection toward the spouse. If this split continues, many of the positive features in the marriage may be lost. Moreover, we all share in a culture which reinforces the isolation of feelings. Advertising and the media promote sex as an isolated experience and rarely if ever show it realistically in the context of other (especially positive) feelings. The fundamental question is whether this condition of separating sex from other feelings is simply one option among others, all equal in terms of human potential, or whether this split constitutes a defect in living a human life. The developmental model claims the latter. A human life is richer if feelings are integrated and not blocked off from each other. As Carr puts it, for more extreme cases where sex cannot be integrated into larger relationships, "life presents a dismal picture and one cannot but wish ... that matters had turned out otherwise" (Carr 1987: 373).

Not all cases of poor integration result in overall negative results. Many creative artists in history, for example, have been tortured individuals when it comes to other facets of their lives. Someone deeply into a field of study may integrate himself or herself so strongly around his or her work that other areas of life are either neglected or performed poorly. If looked at from a utilitarian perspective, one might well argue that the good given to the world outweighs the disharmony of the person. The individual may also feel that the joy achieved in one area is worth the pain in others. Strongly emphasizing one "part" may be very productive. Such cases present interesting questions for both psychology and ethics. Did Beethoven have to be a tortured soul to produce what Leonard Bernstein once called the voice of an angel? In his case was the energy necessarily sublimated from other areas of life? We do not know. In terms of ethics, is there, in some people a necessary clash between working toward a well-rounded life and doing the greatest good? Given the background and social context of some people ([Mahatma] Gandhi [1869–1948], for example) the answer may be affirmative. But I do not think this constitutes a telling blow to the developmental model of virtue. Incomplete personal integration may be the price to pay for achievement of a goal of which one is capable. But it is still a price. It would be "better" as a human being if the price did not have to be so high. Conditions in life or the clash of ideals and goals may mean that developmental maturity does not occur in certain areas like sex or anger but this situation does not seem necessary in principle. People deeply behind certain causes may also have highly developed characters all-around, and not all artistic and scientific geniuses have had distorted or unhappy personal lives.

Humans may also be born with or may succumb to physiological defects which do not allow the expression of a person's capabilities or which force a person to isolate sex or other emotions from the rest of life. To an extent society imposes such limits on everyone, on some much more than others; developing one's mind or emotions may be virtually impossible if one is born into certain families or social conditions. But some of the clearest examples of the tragic element are the physiological blocks to integration and development. Handicapped students I have had claim that, in certain areas of life and at certain times, the frustrations of self-expression and the inability to tie emotions into satisfactory actions can be so unbearable that suicide becomes a serious option. What makes it especially difficult is the awareness of what they could achieve if they were not blocked physiologically. For some people the choices they make block their own development. For others the negative choices are made for them by nature, parents or society. Overcoming these obstacles has led in some individuals to a complex of virtues (courage, empathy, self-discipline) which puts them well ahead of the majority of the human race. However, many others have also been crushed as human beings. Like the other ethical theories virtue theory has to maintain a strong sense of the tragic.

Given the possibility of choice, how can the developmental model be applied to actual sexual behavior? Some forms of sexual behavior such as masturbation would be temporary (usually benign) forms of regression. Ideally one should be able to integrate sexual acts with others in a reciprocal relationship. Granting the fact that life is not ideal, the more one focuses primarily or exclusively on autoerotic behavior the more the sexual other becomes unreal, a fantasy which real life may make increasingly difficult to match. Some forms of what is traditionally called "perversion" would also fit here. Necrophilia, for example, is not just another equal sexual option. It is often (perhaps always) a symptom of a fear of relating to others, a channeling of sexuality which divorces sex from other facets of life. Other forms of traditional perversions are not perversions under the developmental model. Homosexuality, for example, would be judged positively or negatively on the same criteria heterosexuality is judged, i.e., by how much the sexual part of the relationship is tied to other aspects like affection, trust, and honesty. Unlike some of the older theories, the developmental model of excellence is not based on the supposed function of sex or sexual organs. It is rather based on levels of psychological development. An adult for whom sexual relationships were possible but for whom voyeurism was the sole sexual outlet would be fixated at a child's level whereas homosexual relationships may be as deeply affectionate, trusting and honest as heterosexual ones. Moral maturity has to do with the integration of one's life. Society may make this difficult for homosexuals but nothing in the relationship itself prevents it from being as integrating as any heterosexual relationship.

The idea of a well-integrated emotional life is closely linked to what Aristotle meant by the harmonious relationship between the virtues (Aristotle: 1144b32–39). Courage, for example, involves a particular desire to achieve a goal in the face of difficult circumstances. The desire involved in courage can, as Aristotle noted, be excessive. Courage can become foolhardiness. Courage must be tempered and refined by other virtues such as prudence and self-discipline. These virtues also involve character traits but traits which reflect different aspects of the person. Self-discipline involves the will; prudence includes a cognitive openness to the facts of a situation, an acceptance of those facts, and the ability to adjust desires accordingly. The person who has not matured on the developmental model is one in whom these parts of the self are not integrated and who cannot deal with situations in a realistic way. Such a person's "courage" may be directed at goals which run counter to his or her own best interests as a human being. The courage of a Peeping Tom or obscene phone caller in risking family and/or career for voyeuristic pleasure is a courage not tempered by self-discipline or prudence. The self which, psychologically, lacks unity is a self which, morally, lacks harmony in the virtues. Virtues become increasingly interconnected as an individual freely and reflectively connects emotions in consciousness. To block emotions from each other is at the same time to isolate virtues so that character traits can become like Plato's horses – powerful but undirected. They then become dangerous both to the self and others.

Knowledge about what constitutes the good for a species permits judgments regarding actions done by and done to that species. The actions of a child molester are evil because of their effect on the developing character of the child; such actions also point to a defect in the character of the agent as a human being. The actions of a Peeping Tom reflect an inability to integrate sex with other feelings like affection. This divided self constitutes a particular character type. In practice such character flaws lead to certain consequences involving harm to others and oneself as well as a limited or distorted recognition of rights and duties. Analysis of character is a necessary (often implicit) condition in moral judgments but it is not a sufficient one. All factors need to be considered. The special value of virtue theory in sexual ethics is that, unlike the other theories, it compels each of us to think about what kind of person we are and could be. Given the intensely personal nature of sex, virtue theory is a most appropriate method through which to examine our own sexual lives.

## References

Aristotle ([4th C BCE] 1985) *Nicomachean Ethics*. Trans. T. Irwin. Indianapolis: Hackett.
Baker, R. and F. Elliston. (1975) (Eds.) *Philosophy and Sex*. Buffalo: Prometheus.
Brod, H. (1984) "Eros Thanatized: Pornography and Male Sexuality." *Humanities in Society* Winter 1984.
Carr, D. (1987) "Freud and Sexual Ethics." *Philosophy* 62.
Freud, S. (1938) "Three Contributions to the Theory of Sex." *The Basic Writings of Sigmund Freud*. New York: Random House.
Gilligan, C. (1982) *In a Different Voice*. Cambridge: Harvard.
Humber, J. (1987–88) "Sexual Perversion and Human Nature." *Philosophy Research Archives* XII.
Jones, K. (1987) "Human Sexuality." *Irish Philosophical Quarterly* 4.
Kohlberg, L. (1981) *The Philosophy of Moral Development*. San Francisco: Harper & Row.
MacIntyre, A. ((1981) 1984) *After Virtue*. Notre Dame: U of Notre Dame P.
Matthews, E. (1988) "AIDS and Sexual Morality." *Bioethics* 2.
Ruddick, S. (1975) "Better Sex." in Baker and Elliston 1975.
Scruton, R. (1984) "Sexual Arousal." *Philosophy* 18 Supplemental.

## Study Questions

1. What is the developmental model of virtue? How does it point toward sex without feelings or love as being inferior? Is sex with love or feelings superior? If so, is physical pleasure from a consenting other with whom one does not share love or feelings a lesser pleasure? Why or why not?

2. Putnam argues that "moral maturity" is largely a result of "the integration of one's life" and is very close to Aristotle's notion of a "harmonious relationship between the virtues." Detail some of the examples of this that he provides. Do you agree with the goal of the integration of your life, first as a goal, and second as a way to reach moral maturity?

3. Putnam provides harsh examples of non-integrated persons to illustrate his perspective on virtue theory and sex, such as pedophiles and "Peeping Toms." Yet sex without love, or recreational sex, is extremely common. Is recreational sex between consenting adults a moral hazard to being a virtuous person? Why or why not? If you argue that it is not, is there a point where you would see it as a moral hazard (such as promiscuity and/or a life-long behavior and/or with myriad people)?

# 2. Raja Halwani, "Casual Sex, Promiscuity, and Temperance"

IN THIS CHAPTER FROM his book *Sex and Ethics* (2007), Raja Halwani inquires whether casual sex or promiscuity can be conducted in ways that exhibit the virtue of temperance. Halwani argues against the *prima facie* notion that casual sex and promiscuity are always intemperate. In so doing, he views casual sex and promiscuity via the lens of moral motives and desires, and challenges the notion that these acts are internally wrong. While it is possible for one who engages in both casual sex and promiscuity to remain temperate, he warns that maintaining moral motives therein is a challenging task requiring constant vigil for temperance.

## I. Introduction

AN APPARENTLY OBVIOUS ANSWER to the question "Can one be sexually promiscuous while also being sexually temperate?" is negative, for it seems that promiscuity would be high on a list of behaviors and desires incompatible with temperance (a list which would also include rape, bestiality, necrophilia, and pedophilia). I take this negative answer very seriously, if only for the reason that common sense and tradition seem to support it. But I will also argue that one can be promiscuous and engage in casual sex while being temperate.[1] After offering some working definitions of the central terms, I begin the argument.

I understand temperance as follows.[2] ... [W]hether one is temperate hinges on the rightness and wrongness of the sexual desire in question. For example, one cannot be temperate if part of one's sexual psychology is the desire to rape others or to fondle children. These are, aside from the issue of acting on them, wrong desires to have.[3] We should not confuse the issue of having certain sexual desires with that of acting on sexual desires, which involves actions that could be wrong

even if the desires themselves are "normal" or right: if X, for example, satisfies his desire for heterosexual sexual intercourse with Y by deceiving Y, then X's action would be wrong. Moreover, a sexual act could be wrong even if the usual liberal criteria, such as the genuine consent of the parties and the lack of (significant) harm to third parties (and, perhaps, even to the parties involved), are satisfied, because the act could still go against virtues other than honesty and respect or stem from vices other than dishonesty and disrespect, such as greed and vanity. It would thus be a vicious, and so wrong, act. So to tackle the issue of whether one can be temperate and yet engage in casual sex or promiscuity, we need mostly – not solely (see below) – to attend to the issue of whether the sexual desires involved in casual sex and promiscuity are morally acceptable.

I understand casual sex to be sex between two or more people such that at least one party engages in the sexual act solely for the sexual pleasure it yields, and such that the parties are not involved in love relationships *with each other*.[4] For X's sexual behavior to be promiscuous, it must constitute a series of sexual acts over time with different people (Elliston 1975, 223–24). A large number of sexual acts is crucial for characterizing promiscuity, even though it is impossible to find the threshold for this number, such that beyond, but not below, the threshold one becomes promiscuous. Thus, one can engage in casual sex only a few times in one's life without thereby being promiscuous. Moreover – and intuitions here no doubt conflict – one can be promiscuous without engaging in casual sex. Suppose that X is a serial monogamist: every sexual partner she has is one with whom she is in a relationship, but such that she has a new relationship every week. It seems that while X is promiscuous, she does not engage in casual sex.

Beginning with casual sex, I treat these two phenomena separately.

## i. Casual Sex

Is casual sex necessarily in conflict with temperance? Given the above, our first step is to ask whether desires for casual sex are morally acceptable. People who engage in casual sex do so either out of a desire to have no-strings-attached sex (NSA sex – either because NSA sex is the kind of sex that thrills them or because they wish to avoid commitments or emotional entanglements) or out of different desires (with the description "NSA sex" or something similar not crossing their minds) but such that the sex they end up having is, in fact, casual. For example, X has sex with Y without any desires having to do with whether the sex should be NSA; alternatively, X might hope that the sex will be a precursor to a relationship with Y, but in fact it will not be. The latter case should not raise philosophical difficulties, as long as the desire that prompts the sexual act is acceptable. It is the former case that concerns us, because it involves the intentional seeking of casual sex *as* casual sex. To desire casual sex is to desire to have sex with one or more people (simultaneously) with no strings attached.

Now, NSA sex can be adulterous, pedophiliac, bestial, or, I suppose, necrophiliac, to give some examples. Whether the desire for casual sex is wrong depends not merely on whether it is NSA sex, but on what *kind* of NSA sex it is.[5] If it is a desire to have NSA sex with children, then it is wrong. If it is for adulterous sex, then, if adultery is wrong or is wrong in that case, the desire for it is wrong. But, of course, the wrongness here stems not from the fact that the desired sex is NSA, but from the fact that it is with children or because it is adulterous. If the desired casual sex were to lack such usual wrong-making features (pedophilia, adultery, deception, etc.), it might very well be – and, according to secular and liberal views, is – not wrong. Moreover, and with the possible exception of objectification, it is hard to see how the desire for casual sex is morally suspect, for, if one were to argue, say, that (aside from such usual wrong-making features) casual sex has bad consequences, it seems that such consequences, such as transmitting sexual diseases, are a contingent, not an essential, aspect of casual sex (Ellis 1986, 165–67; Halwani 2006a). Henceforth, when mentioning "casual sex," I confine the discussion to casual sex that lacks these usual wrong-making features.

Objectification, however, seems to pose a problem. Many have argued that casual sex is a form of sexual activity in which the partners objectify each other.[6] If this is an essential feature of casual sex, then one cannot desire NSA sex without, *ipso facto*, desiring to objectify the other. At the very least, even if it were possible for X sexually to desire casual sex with Y without also desiring to objectify Y, the ensuing sexual act would have the feature that X actually objectifies Y, much as in desiring to have a cup of coffee I need not desire to feel the texture of the mug against my fingers but

I actually end up doing so (assuming I do not hold the mug indirectly by the use of some contraption). If this is so, then desires for casual sex would be wrong. By way of analogy, when adults desire sex with children, they do not (typically) desire them harm. However, given that usually such sexual contact does harm the children, pedophiliac desires are wrong. The point is that for a sexual desire to be wrong, it need not be the case that, logically, sexually to desire the act in question is also to desire the act's wrong-making feature.

I cannot hope to solve as thorny an issue as objectification, especially given the large literature on the subject.[7] But, generally, there are two strategies for attempting to solve the problem. The first is to accept that many types of sexual acts involve, even necessarily, objectification, but to argue that objectification is not always wrong.[8] The second is to deny that objectification characterizes a *type* of sexual activity, such as casual sex (with perhaps a few exceptions, such as rape), and to argue that whether objectification is present depends on the *particular* sexual act in question. Suppose that A1 – a particular act of casual sex, involves objectification, whereas A2, another such particular act, does not. Then one can go on to claim that at least as far as objectification is concerned, A2 is not wrong, and either that A1 is wrong (because of the objectification) *or* that it is not wrong, despite the objectification – in effect resorting to the first strategy.

But how does one argue that a particular casual sexual act does not involve objectification? Well, *if* to objectify someone sexually is to *treat* him as a sex object (or as an object during the sexual act), then paying more attention to the phenomenology involved in casual sexual acts might show that in many instances of casual sex no objectification actually occurs. Casual sex partners could be sensitive to each other's needs, desires, and sources of pleasure. They can respect each other's wishes and limits, and can desire to please their partners, even if they do not always derive pleasure from doing so. If this is possible – and, clearly, it is not only possible but also factual – then not all instances of casual sex would involve objectification, because when we treat others in these ways we are not treating them as objects. If one counters by claiming that we often treat objects as if they have boundaries, desires, and wishes,[9] so that treating sexual partners in these ways also does not get us around the charge of objectification, it is hard to see what would be wrong with objectification, since then one can argue that treating objects as if they have boundaries, desires, and wishes is to elevate the *objects* to a higher moral plane. In any case, although it might be true that we sometimes treat objects as if they have desires and wishes, casual sex partners, when they do treat each other with such forms of consideration, do not do so *as if* they had wishes and desires, but typically because they *do* have these. It is when we exhibit such forms of consideration during sex with, say, an inflated doll (and inanimate objects in general) that we treat the doll *as if* it had desires and wishes.

The above reasoning is simply a strategy and so needs augmentation. Moreover, if successful, it does not deny that some instances of casual sex are objectifying, for surely many such instances involve at least one party treating the other as being nothing but "a piece of ass."[10] But the truth in the strategy is that sexual focus on another's body should not be *identified* with objectification, and that the latter should not be inferred from the former. Even in the most anonymous sexual encounters – say, sucking a man's penis through a glory hole – there need be no objectification if the parties to the sexual encounter respectively consider the penis and the mouth, as is usually the case, as parts of another human being whose desires and wishes are being attended to in the very act of sucking the penis. The claim that casual sex acts often focus on only one bodily part of a person (or, more generally, on only the body) is true. It is the inference that some form of objectification occurs that is invalid. To make such an inference in sexual contexts, it seems to me, would commit one to inferring that in any act in which X focuses on one or a few aspects of Y (e.g., X focuses solely on a poet's ideas, tone of voice, and delivery of the poem as the poet delivers it), as opposed to focusing on many or all such features, there is objectification. This is highly implausible.

We can tentatively conclude that, as far as the first factor is concerned, the desire for casual sex is not, as such, a wrong desire. It is not a desire that a temperate person would not feel or, if he felt it, would not give any role in his life. Moreover, since having sexual desires is, in and of itself, healthy, unless a temperate person has overriding reasons (e.g., he is in a monogamous relationship, or having casual sex in a particular instance would be exploitive or would be at the expense of something else he should be doing), there is no reason for him not to seek the pleasures of casual sex if he feels the desire for them. Of course, it might be that too many casual sex acts are not good and so a temperate person would not engage in a large number. But this takes us into issues surrounding promiscuity, to which I turn in the next section.

It is worthwhile to emphasize two points. First, even though desires for casual sex can be, and often are, compatible with temperance, this does not guarantee their compatibility with other virtues (unless one subscribes to a strong version of the unity of the virtues thesis – and I do not – according to which the existence of any virtue entails the remainder, from which it follows that any activity compatible with temperance would be compatible with the rest of the virtues), for desires for

casual sex can stem from greed, envy, vindictiveness, and other bad motives and vices. When they do stem from bad motives and vices, they will be morally unacceptable and acting on them would be wrong. Second, one can have a host of physiological or psychological causes for casual (and promiscuous) sex, causes whose connections to moral traits (vices and virtues) are not clear, such that the mere possession of these does not imply that one's desires for casual sex are morally unacceptable. For example, one can engage in casual sex because one is "emotionally bruised" from a bad relationship, or a series of bad relationships, because one is "too anxious about proving something" about oneself, or simply because one has a sexually adventurous personality and likes to experiment.[11] None of these implies that one's desires for casual sex are morally unacceptable. They might be, but whether they are cannot simply be read off from such generic descriptions of these psychological causes, and the issue might need to be settled on a case-by-case basis.

## ii. Promiscuity

Promiscuous people generally fall into one of two types. There are those who are intentionally promiscuous. They desire a life of promiscuity, a life in which they are capable of experiencing a large number of sexual encounters with a large number of people (subject, of course, to all sorts of restrictions). They need not be promiscuous for their whole lives; they might be promiscuous for certain periods, until they decide to settle down, monogamously, with someone. Another type of promiscuous person is the unintentional one. This might be someone who desires to be in a long-term, monogamous relationship but who thinks that the best way, or one good way, to meet and find her special person is to sleep with him or her. As

183

a result of bad luck, the relationships quickly fail or never start to begin with. Or she might be someone who decides not to squander away potential sexual mates while she waits for Mr. or Ms. Right. She is, so to speak, a promiscuous person by default. It seems to me that it is the first type that is more interesting from a virtue point of view, for such a type adopts, as a policy or intention, a life of promiscuity. And it is interesting to see whether such a policy or basic intention is compatible with temperance. Moreover, if it turns out that intentional promiscuity is incompatible with virtue, there is a good chance that unintentional promiscuity would also be incompatible with virtue, for it intuitively seems that the reasons intentional promiscuity would be incompatible with virtue have to do with the promiscuity itself, not with the *policy* of being promiscuous. However, this might not be true, since the motives from which or the reasons the unintentionally promiscuous engage in a series of (*de facto*) casual sex acts (which add up to promiscuous behavior) could be morally acceptable. If so, and if the ensuing sexual acts are morally permissible, then unintentional promiscuity would be compatible with temperance. In any case, my discussion is confined to the intentionally promiscuous.

But here we have to be careful. Exactly what policy or basic intention does the promiscuous person of the first type adopt? To say that X intends, or adopts the policy, to be promiscuous is unhelpful because it is uninformative. We need to know the content of X's intention. One suggestion is "To sleep with as many people as possible." But this does not characterize promiscuous people, whose desire is not necessarily to *maximize* the number of sexual partners. Perhaps then the content of the basic intention or policy is, simply, to engage in a number of casual sexual encounters with different people over time, the usual overarching purpose being to enjoy sex. Note that, as with any other type of policy or intention, it might not be successfully carried out. In the case of promiscuity, the person might, despite his intentions, fail to be promiscuous (for all sorts of reasons: he chickens out at the last minute; few sexually desire him; he sexually desires only a few; he desires many, and many desire him, but the two sets do not coincide, etc.). If this happens, then, intention or no intention, the person is not promiscuous. Nonetheless, we can still ask whether there is anything morally unacceptable with his intention or policy.

Note that the intentionally promiscuous adopt, in effect, a policy of engaging in casual sex over time; its building-blocks are casual sexual acts. This yields – to complicate things – two types of intentionally promiscuous people. The first, rare, type is one whose intention is *transparent*: he explicitly desires to be promiscuous; he says to himself, "I want to be a promiscuous person." This is probably a rare type because it seems that people do not usually set out to be promiscuous. It is the second type that seems to be more common, the person who intends to engage in casual sex as a way of conducting his sexual life, but who, because of a sufficiently large number of such acts, ends up being promiscuous. I nonetheless label this type "intentionally promiscuous" because of the intention to live one's sexual life by engaging in casual sex. At some level, one must know that doing so is in effect to lead a life of sexual promiscuity. In any case, my focus is on this second type.

Now *if* desiring casual sex is permissible and so is compatible with temperance, it seems that desiring a series of such acts is also permissible and so compatible with temperance. But does this follow? From the fact that desiring this slice of apple pie is acceptable it does not follow that desiring fifty slices is; under normal circumstances, one slice will hardly make a dent in my health, but fifty surely would. But would desiring the fifty slices *over a period of time* be acceptable? This is an inference more similar to the one about casual sex. If the absence of the usual wrong-making features makes a single casual sexual act permissible, then why shouldn't fifty of them over time be permissible if these features remain absent? Indeed, even if there were something troubling about the *inference*, it seems to be permissible to desire numerous casual encounters over time as long as the usual wrong-making features are absent and provided they do not occur through deception, force, excessive harm, wrongful objectification, and so on. It then seems that desiring such acts would also be permissible. So we can conclude that a policy of promiscuity is compatible with temperance.

Note, however, that this conclusion supports at best the compatibility of promiscuity with other-oriented temperance:[12] the sexual desires are permissible because the wrongful features they lack are other-oriented – no deception, coercion, objectification, and so on. But there is still the question of whether promiscuity is compatible with agent-oriented temperance. Because this form of temperance is usually understood in terms of amounts (the issue of casual sex does not arise with respect to agent-oriented temperance, since casual sex as such is not about numbers or amounts), whereby to be temperate is to engage in moderate amounts of sex (or food or drink), the question here is whether one can be intemperate simply *in* or *by* engaging in too much sex or, alternatively, whether too much sex can somehow undermine temperance.[13] The answer to this question, however phrased, is "yes." Clearly, and assuming that there are worthwhile activities other than sex,[14] one can be intemperate if one engages in too much sex. The problem here is that it is difficult to decide what "too much" sex is: is having sex once a day, seven days a week,

too much? If not, what about twice a day? If it is, why? Despite this difficulty, some answers – such as having so much sex that one leaves little room for much else in one's life – are plausible. In this respect, one would be sexually intemperate through the sheer number of one's sexual encounters over time.[15] This applies to both intentionally and unintentionally promiscuous people.

Moreover, too much sex can undermine temperance in a different way: by pursuing sexual pleasures, one can undermine one's psychic health: one uses one's reasoning powers to secure oneself sexual partners and encounters. In this respect, one's reason becomes the tool of one's sexual desires (Halwani 2003, 217–25). These two ways in which promiscuity is incompatible with temperance are not identical. Unless sexual activity constitutes one's life vocation, then since there are activities much more worthwhile than sex, one *cannot* rationally plan one's life in such a way that one engages *only* in sexual activity (setting aside, of course, other things one needs to sustain one's life). In this respect, the use of one's reason is merely instrumental: reason exists to serve one's goal of having sex. Here, both ways in which promiscuity and temperance are incompatible are the same. However, one can use one's reason instrumentally even if one does not engage in too much sex: one can – the bizarreness of the case notwithstanding – use one's reason solely to plan one's weekly sexual encounter; everything one does, directly or indirectly, serves to bring about this encounter. In this way, promiscuity is incompatible with temperance because it undermines reason, but without involving "too much" sex.

The above, of course, entails that one can be both promiscuous and temperate if, say, one's policy of being promiscuous is acted on in such a way that it does not undermine reason (Halwani 2003, 217–25). Someone can, for example, decide to lead her life in such a way that she focuses on her work, satisfying her sexual urges by having casual sex with different people over time. She thus adopts a policy of being promiscuous as far as her sex life is concerned. Yet the policy seems to be controlled by the woman's overarching life plan, and her reason seems to be firmly in control. To give another example, one can decide not to be in a monogamous romantic relationship or in a romantic relationship, period, and to spend one's sexual life engaging in NSA sex. In these ways, promiscuity is compatible with temperance: there is not "too much" sex (sexual encounters whose sheer number rules out a life of temperance) and reason is not employed merely instrumentally.

Although such cases are *possible*, it is a question of how likely they are.[16] That is, if sexual desire is a powerful force in us, the question remains as to the likelihood of it being controlled by reason. There are two issues here, both of which, incidentally, apply to temperance in its agent-oriented and its other-oriented guises. The first is – given the force of sexual desire – the likelihood of one's *continuing* to be temperate and not becoming continent. The second issue goes beyond the first and concerns the likelihood of sexual desire and activity fostering incontinence or vice. To explain: if one is both promiscuous and temperate, there is the danger that one's reason eventually loses control. This danger is of two types. The first, milder one is that the agent becomes continent, whereby he has to struggle to keep his sexual desires at bay. If this happens, he ceases to be temperate, but his reason at least remains in control. The second, more serious danger is that he becomes incontinent or, worse, vicious. If incontinent, he succumbs to the urge to act on his sexual desires when he knows that he should not: he knows that he should not deceive X into sex or he knows that he should get a good night's

sleep instead of going out looking for sex. If vicious, he convinces himself that acting on his sexual desires is okay when, in fact, it is not (e.g., "Sure it's okay to deceive X into sex; he's so stupid he deserves it"); alternatively, he becomes indifferent to the demands of morality ("Who cares whether I deceive X or not?").[17] These dangers are likely because sexual desire is a very powerful drive. People are not usually led by the desire to eat their favorite dish or to drink their favorite beverage to engage in some seriously strange or immoral behavior. Yet people do often follow where their sexual desires lead, much to their future regret and even detriment. And it seems sensible to attribute such weakness in the face of what they know better to the power of the sexual drive, which can render people weak-willed and downright irrational. So sexual urges and desires, more than other types of desires, pose a danger to our ability to lead our lives under our own light and ideals.

Of course, issues of likelihood are hard to settle. This is, partly, because they are empirical in nature, for whether promiscuity is likely to lead to continence, incontinence, or viciousness is an issue that requires some serious empirical research. Minimally, we need, first, to be careful to show that any state of character, such as incontinence or viciousness, is a state that was indeed *caused* solely or mainly by promiscuity. Second, we need to show that it was caused by promiscuity in the proper direction, that is, from a better to a worse state of character (if one went from viciousness into incontinence because of promiscuity, promiscuity would be a good thing). Third, we need to have a large enough sample of human beings in whom we trace the effects of promiscuity, and we need to be able to control this sample in appropriate ways and to trace the effects of promiscuity over time. In all of this, we must keep in mind that people usually become promiscuous at an age when their characters have either been fully formed or are close to being fully formed, at which point they are either virtuous, continent, incontinent, or vicious, or display a mix and match of vices and virtues. If so, and if characters, once formed, are difficult to change, it is an issue to what extent one who is promiscuous is likely to have one's character changed by the promiscuity.[18]

However, and despite the difficulties in any such empirical research, we should not conclude that there is nothing to be said about these dangers. The fact that we know that sexual desire is an especially powerful desire ought to give us pause. Perhaps we need to approach this issue with a dose of realism large enough to render a somewhat pessimistic verdict, namely, that most people are not likely to be temperate about sex, and that the lucky ones would have to settle for continence, all the while guarding against slipping into incontinence and even vice. Although it is possible that temperance and promiscuity are compatible, this is a truth we should not exaggerate and allow to lead us into a sense of moral ease in our thinking about, and being, promiscuous.

## References

Baker, Robert, and Frederick Elliston, eds. 1975. *Philosophy and Sex*, first edition. Buffalo, NY: Prometheus Books.

Ellis, Anthony. 1986. "Casual Sex." *International Journal of Moral and Social Studies* 1: 157–69.

Elliston, Frederick. 1975. "In Defense of Promiscuity." In Baker and Elliston 1975.

Halwani, Raja. 2003. *Virtuous Liaisons: Care, Love, Sex, and Virtue Ethics*. Chicago: Open Court.

——. 2006a. "Casual Sex." In Soble 2006.

——. 2006b. "Ethics, Virtue." In Soble 2006.

Kristjánsson, Kristján. 1998. "Casual Sex Revisited." *Journal of Social Philosophy* 29: 97–108.

Morgan, Seiriol. 2003a. "Dark Desires." *Ethical Theory and Moral Practice* 6: 377–410.

——. 2003b. "Sex in the Head." Journal of Applied Philosophy 20: 1–16.

Nussbaum, Martha C. 1995. "Objectification." *Philosophy and Public Affairs* 24: 249–91.

Quinn, Carol. 2006. "Objectification, Sexual." In Soble 2006.

Schofield, Michael. 1976. *Promiscuity*. London: Gollancz.

Soble, Alan. 2002a. *Pornography, Sex, and Feminism*. Amherst, NY: Prometheus Books.

——. 2002b. "Sexual Use and What to Do about it: Internalist and Externalist Sexual Ethics." In Soble 2002c.

——, ed. 2002c. *The Philosophy of Sex: Contemporary Readings*, fourth edition. Lanham, MD: Rowman and Littlefield.

——, ed. 2006. *Sex from Plato to Paglia: A Philosophical Encyclopedia* (two volumes). Westport, CT: Greenwood P.

## Study Questions

1. Why do you think Halwani focuses on the virtue of temperance (engaging in moderate amounts of a behavior) regarding casual sex and promiscuity, rather than another virtue? Do you think that temperance is a chief virtue with respect to one's sexual life? How might other virtues, such as honesty, patience, and courage, play a role in the ethicality of one's sex life?

2. After a lengthy discussion on objectification, with many examples, Halwani concludes that determining whether casual sex can be temperate "might need to be settled on a case-by-case basis" due to the many possible psychological bases for engaging in casual sex. Do you agree, or do you see the issue as requiring a universal ethic regarding the behavior? Why?

3. Halwani does not demarcate the point whereby one becomes promiscuous. First, define promiscuity. Do you think that you can make an empirical determination for when casual sex crosses over into promiscuity? How does Halwani argue that one may be promiscuous and still temperate?

4. Halwani argues that if promiscuity leads to incontinence or viciousness it is now a vice. What are the potential risks to one's virtue that he describes? Do you agree with his conclusion regarding promiscuity?

## Notes

1  In so doing, I rely on and expand my account in Halwani 2003, chapter 3.
2  For elaboration, see Chapter 9 in this volume.
3  See on such issues Morgan 2003a, b.
4  Lovers often engage in sex solely for sexual pleasure, but this does not make their encounters casual. Note that sex between a prostitute and her client is still casual, for at least one party (the client) is usually in it solely for sexual pleasure. For the difficulties involved in finding an adequate definition of "casual sex," see Halwani 2006a.
5  Unless, of course, one subscribed to particular beliefs implying that *any* NSA sex is wrong in virtue of its being NSA. For example, many religious people have such beliefs.
6  I treat this issue in its non-Kantian framework, which relies on Kant's own metaphysical assumptions.
7  For a start and for further references, see Quinn 2006.
8  Nussbaum (1995) and Soble (2002a) seem to adopt this strategy, but for entirely different reasons. For a view that Kant also adopted this strategy, see Soble 2002b.
9  Nussbaum makes this point, but not as an objection (1995, 257–65).
10  If the other party were to want to be treated as nothing but a "piece of ass," it is unclear whether the one using would be objectifying the one used if he were to use the latter because of the latter's desire to be used.
11  These examples are from <http://lg.loversguide.com/content/article.3.8.550. phpx>; date of access February 7, 2006.
12  For the distinction between agent-oriented and other-oriented temperance, see Chapter 9 in this volume and Halwani 2003, 171–91; 2006b.
13  There is the further question of whether promiscuity can undermine external goods needed for the well-lived life. I have argued elsewhere that this is not necessary (Halwani 2003, 209–25). For an argument that it undermines love, see Kristjánsson 1998.
14  By "sexual activity" I mean sexual activities solely for their pleasure, not (or also) sexual activities as part of one's profession, whatever that might be.
15  Though sex workers (prostitutes, pornography actors, strippers, etc.) fit the bill, it is not clear that their promiscuity is incompatible with temperance. I have argued elsewhere that it is compatible (Halwani 2003, 242–54).

16  Both Alan Soble and Rosalind Hursthouse have, in personal correspondence, rightly pressed me on this point.

17  For different types of viciousness, see Chapter 9 in this volume.

18  A somewhat old study of promiscuous people concludes that they are not distinguished from nonpromiscuous people by their home background, education, and job type. Nor can the sample studied be labeled "sick" in any nonquestion-begging way. The sample, however, is just a sample, and the definition of "promiscuous" relied on is quite loose: one is promiscuous if one has had more than one partner in the previous year. The study is discussed in Schofield 1976, chapter 4, and the implication of its results for a discussion of virtues and vices can only be indirect, insofar as psychological, economic, and educational backgrounds have no necessary connections with any particular virtues or vices.

# 3. Michael Warner, "The Ethics of Sexual Shame"

IN THIS SELECTION FROM the first chapter of his book *The Trouble with Normal* (1999), Michael Warner (b. 1958) explores how sexual autonomy can be realized for all people. He explores this in the face of an historical trend regarding societal sexual ethics in which there is a tendency toward absolutism and making prejudicial sexual norms dominant in a society. This results in sexual minorities who have to struggle with shame, and then stigma, which crushes their freedom and dignity. In order to realize sexual autonomy, Warner argues, we need to defy values that uphold sexual hierarchies, accept varied forms of sexual experience, and foster a society that allows for sexual freedom without humiliation. This, he contends, is what queer ethics is all about.

---

... IT WOULD BE NICE if the burden of proof, in such questions of sexual morality, lay on those who want to impose their standard on someone else. Then the goal of sexual ethics would be to constrain coercion rather than shut down sexual variance. But things usually work the other way around. We do not begin with what the sports-minded like to call a level playing field. We live with sexual norms that survive from the Stone Age, including prohibitions against autoeroticism, sodomy, extramarital sex, and (for those who still take the Vatican seriously) birth control. This is a problem with any essentially conservative or traditionalist stance on sexual morality: what we have to conserve is barbaric. What we inherit from the past, in the realm of sex, is the morality of patriarchs and clansmen, souped up with Christian hostility to the flesh ("our vile body," Saint Paul called it), medieval chastity cults, virgin/whore complexes, and other detritus of ancient repression. Given these legacies of unequal moralism, nearly every civilized aspect of sexual morality has initially looked deviant, decadent, or sinful, including voluntary marriage, divorce, and nonreproductive sex.

For many people, the antiquity of sexual norms is a reason to obey them. In *Bowers v. Hardwick* (1986), for example, the Supreme Court invoked the "ancient roots" of the prohibition against sodomy. Chief Justice Warren Burger noted that "decisions of individuals relating to homosexual conduct have been subject to state intervention throughout the history of Western civilization." One might have thought that such a hoary pedigree of barbarism was all the more reason for skepticism, but of course that wasn't Burger's conclusion....

The politics of shame, in other words, includes vastly more than the overt and deliberate shaming produced by moralists. It also involves silent inequalities, unintended effects of isolation, and the lack of public access. So sexual autonomy requires more than freedom of choice, tolerance, and the liberalization of sex laws. It requires access to pleasures and possibilities, since people commonly do not know their desires until they find them. Having an ethics of sex, therefore, does not mean having a theory about what people's desires are or should be. If the goal is sexual autonomy, consistent with everyone else's sexual autonomy, then it will be impossible to say in advance what form that will take. Even bondage can be a means of autonomy – or not. Moralism cannot; it can only produce complacent satisfaction in others' shame. The taken-for-grantedness of dominant sexuality has the same effect, as does the privatization or isolation of sexual experience....

Women and gay people have been especially vulnerable to the shaming effects of isolation. Almost all children grow up in families that think of themselves and all their members as heterosexual, and for some children this produces a profound and nameless estrangement, a sense of inner secrets and hidden shame. No amount of adult "acceptance" or progress in civil rights is likely to eliminate this experience of queerness for many children and adolescents. Later in life, they will be told that they are "closeted," as though they have been telling lies. They bear a special burden of disclosure. No wonder so much of gay culture seems marked by a primal encounter with shame, from the dramas of sadomasochism to the rhetoric of gay pride, or the newer "queer" politics. Ironically, plenty of moralists will then point to this theme of shame in gay life as though it were proof of something pathological in gay people. It seldom occurs to anyone that the dominant culture and its family environment should be held accountable for creating the inequalities of access and recognition that produce this sense of shame in the first place.

Most people, I hope, have had the experience of discovering deep pleasure in something they would not have said previously that they wanted. Yet the prevalent wisdom, oddly enough, seems to be that variant desires are legitimate only if they can be shown to be immutable, natural, and innate. If that were true, then statues would be enough. People wouldn't need an accessible culture of sex to tell them anything they deserved to know. Then again, it would be hard to justify *any* kind of sexuality on these grounds. It would be hard, for example, to justify the morality of marriage by finding a gene for it; it is a conventional legal relation. Because moralism so often targets not just sex but knowledge about sex, people come to believe, nonsensically, that moral or legitimate sex must be unlearned, prereflective, present before history, isolated from the public circulation of culture.

This is one reason why so many gay people are now desperately hoping that a gay gene can be found. They think they would be more justified if they could show that they had no choice, that neither they nor gay culture in general played any role in shaping their desires. Some conservatives, meanwhile, trivialize gay experience as "lifestyle," as though that warrants interfering with it. Both sides seem to agree on an insane assumption: that only immutable and genetic sexualities could be legitimate, that if being gay could be shown to be learned, chosen, or partly chosen, then it could be reasonably forbidden....

The best historians of sexuality argue that almost everything about sex, including the idea of sexuality itself, depends on historical conditions, though perhaps at deep levels of consciousness that change slowly. "Heterosexual" and "homosexual" ... [a]s ways of classifying people's sex, [are] ... apparently neutral terms ... of relatively recent vintage, and only make sense against a certain cultural background. So however much they might involve genetic or biological factors, they also involve changes in consciousness and culture. The idea drives the moralists crazy, but it shouldn't: any sexual ethics ought to allow for change....

What would it take to make sexual autonomy possible? The answer is not simply to roll back repression, loosen all constraints, purge ourselves from all civilized shame, return to an earlier state of development, run wild through the streets. (Anyone who wants to run wild down my street has my blessing.) Sexual autonomy has grown, not just by regressing to infantile pleasure (however important that might be), but by making room for new freedoms, new experiences, new pleasures, new identities, new bodies – even if many of us turn out to live in the old ones without complaining. Variation in this way is a precondition of autonomy – as much as it is also the outcome of autonomy. Pleasures once imaginable only with disgust, if at all, become the material out of which individuals and groups elaborate themselves.

Inequalities of shame act as a drag on this process. They inhibit variation and restrict knowledge about the variations that do exist. Moralities that insist on the permanence of sexual norms have an especially stunting effect on people who lack resources of knowledge or of experiment…. The more people are isolated or privatized, the more vulnerable they are to the unequal effects of shame. Conditions that prevent variation, or prevent the knowledge of such possibilities from circulating, undermine sexual autonomy. And the moralists work very hard to make sure that this happens.

The United States Supreme Court went so far in this effort as to exempt sexual materials from First Amendment protections. In *Roth v. the United States* (1957), it allowed states and the federal government to restrict anything defined as "obscene" – a word designed to shame dissenters into silence. The Court later defined obscenity as anything having "prurient" interest in sex and "offensive" by community standards. Since community standards set the definition of obscene, the law in this area – unlike the rest of First Amendment law – allows the majority to impose its will without Constitutional check. Defenders of the law say that it imposes discretion and restraint on everyone. In fact it enlists the government in the politics of shame, making sure that nothing challenging to the tastes of the majority will be allowed to circulate.

The legal and political systems routinely produce shame simply in the pompous and corny way they force people to talk. Like many other states, for example, the state of Virginia has a law, enacted in 1950, that makes it a crime for any persons "to lewdly and lasciviously associate and cohabit together." This just means that sex outside of marriage, or merely living together, is illegal. The law is seldom enforced, and most people regard it as harmless anachronism. But it has real effects: people are denied child custody because it makes them criminal; gay men and lesbians have been fired from their jobs in some states on the same grounds; and defendants on other charges are often given tougher sentences by means of such statutes.[1] (Sodomy laws are especially popular with prosecutors for this purpose.) Archaic legal language also has an effect simply by staying on the books and helping to create the air of unreality in which medieval moral judgments are given authority. Massachusetts law still refers to the "abominable and detestable crime against nature." Florida criminalizes "any unnatural and lascivious act." …

As sexual culture changes, it creates new needs for resisting shame. Ever since the idea of autonomy was first coupled with sex during the Enlightenment, one wave of unexpected resistance has followed another, from the women's movement to psychoanalysis to the lesbian and gay movement. Each has had to resist not just violence but the more normal kinds of sexual unfreedom: moralism, law, stigma, shame, and isolation. All of these constraints on people's autonomy might be in play anytime human beings seek to dominate one another. But in the realm of sex, more than in any other area of human life, shame rules….

## Hierarchies of Shame

... In an influential 1984 essay called "Thinking Sex," Gayle Rubin suggested that the whole gamut of conflicts over sex – of the kind that crop up in every context, from office gossip and school board disputes to the highest levels of national and international policy – demonstrates a common dynamic. Sex has a politics of its own. Hierarchies of sex sometimes serve no real purpose except to prevent sexual variance. They create victimless crimes, imaginary threats, and moralities of cruelty. Rubin notes: "The criminalization of innocuous behaviors such as homosexuality, prostitution, obscenity, or recreational drug use is rationalized by portraying them as menaces to health and safety, women and children, national security, the family, or civilization itself."[2] These rationalizations obscure the intent to shut down sexual variance.

Reviewing a wide range of sexual stigmas and regulations, Rubin contended that people sort good sex from bad by a series of hierarchies:

| Good, Normal, Natural | Bad, Abnormal, Unnatural |
| --- | --- |
| Heterosexual | Homosexual |
| Married | Unmarried |
| Monogamous | Promiscuous |
| Procreative | Nonprocreative |
| Noncommercial | Commercial |
| In pairs | Alone or in groups |
| In a relationship | Casual |
| Same generation | Cross-generational |
| In private | In public |
| No pornography | Pornography |
| Bodies only | With manufactured objects |
| Vanilla | Sadomasochistic |

These distinctions between good sex and bad do not necessarily come as whole packages; most people tend to mix traits from each column. The main thing the different distinctions have in common is the simple fact that each is a hierarchy, and if you are on the wrong side of the hierarchy you will be stigmatized in a way that could entail real damage....

... As Rubin points out, some kinds of deviation have become more respectable over time. Others remain beyond the pale for all but the most radical or the most libertarian. Thus people who stray into the wrong category on one score or another may well reject with disdain any suggestion that they belong in alliance with the perverts who stand below them on the scale of disgust. The people who drift into the right-hand column do not make common cause. If they did, the left-hand column wouldn't stand a chance of survival. Those who inhabit only the left-hand column are probably a tiny minority. And yet their scheme of value dominates.

One reason why people do not unite against shame is that there are some real differences among them. Here perhaps we should make an elementary distinction between stigma of the kind that gay people endure and shame of the kind that dogs Clinton. Rubin presents these as a continuum, but they differ in kind rather than degree, and the difference will turn out to be crucial to all of the examples studied in this book.

Stigma, like its etymological kin *stigmata*, refers to a mark on the body, like a brand or a tattoo or a severed ear, identifying a person permanently with his or her disgrace. Among the Greeks, it may have been punishment for a deed such as treason or running away from a master. It marked the person, not the deed, as tainted. This is what the modern metaphor of stigma singles out. It is a kind of "spoiled identity,"[3] as Erving Goffman calls it in his classic study. Ordinary shame, by contrast, passes. One might do a perverse thing and bring scorn or loathing on oneself, only to sober up and make excuses, move to a new town and start over, stay and outlive the memory, or redeem oneself by fine deeds. This kind of shame affects one's biographical identity. The shame of a true pervert – stigma – is less delible; it is a social identity that befalls one like fate. Like the related stigmas of racial identity or disabilities, it may have nothing to do with acts one has committed. It attaches not to doing, but to being; not to conduct, but to status.

Some of the dilemmas of the gay movement become clearer when we remember that it has had to combat both shame and stigma, and that they are often confused in practice. Sexual deviance once was more a matter of shame than of stigma. Sodomy was a sin like fornication, not the sign of an identity. Anyone could do it. In the modern world that shame has deepened into stigma. It affects certain people, regardless of what they do. As moralists began concentrating not simply on deeds but on kinds of persons, mere sex became sexuality. The act of sodomy came to be only one sign of homosexual identity among many. It became possible to suffer stigma as a homosexual quite apart from any sexual acts.[4] Shame about sexual acts and the stigma on homosexual identity can be utterly distinct in some cases. But each has a tendency to blur into the other.

At first the distinction was the invention of medical experts, and worked only to the detriment of gay people. It was a way of saying that homosexuals were pathological in their very being, whether they ever committed an immoral act or not, simply by the nature of their desires. This pseudo-medical thinking raised perversion to a social identity. It fastened loathing and discrimination onto people in a way that had only a theoretical relation to any sex they might or might not have. Later, the same distinction became crucial to the gay resistance. The concept of perversion, as distinct

from perverse acts, led to the concept of sexual identity (or its close kin, sexual orientation). Each distinguishes between identity and sex, between the person and the act, status and conduct. The doctors had inadvertently made it possible for their former patients to claim that being gay is not necessarily about sex. Homosexuals could argue that any judgment about their worth as persons, irrespective of their actions, was irrational prejudice. In so doing, they could challenge the stigma of identity, without in the least challenging the shame of sexual acts. To this day, a similar logic governs much of gay politics. That is why lawyers who challenge military antigay policy or discrimination by the Boy Scouts usually take pains to find test cases in which the victim is a model victim because he or she has never done anything wrong – that is, had sex.

When Clinton set out to reform the military antigay policy after his election in 1992, he made a point of saying that the military should be allowed to punish people for their acts, but not for their identities; the focus should be on "conduct, not status." He was invoking the most central premise of lesbian and gay politics as a politics of identity: that sexual orientation is fundamental to one's personality and is not mere sexual behavior. In making this argument, he was appealing to the same kind of distinction between doing and being that emerged a century before, when it first became common to think of some people as homosexual persons, whatever their sexual acts in fact were.

But this distinction proved difficult to observe. For one thing, the Supreme Court had blurred it in *Bowers v. Hardwick*. Although the Georgia sodomy statute that was the subject of that case applied to oral and anal sex for heterosexual partners as well as homosexual ones, the Court decided to regard the issue only as one of "homosexual sodomy" and the rights of homosexuals. The act – a kind of sex that gay or straight or bi or other people could equally perform – became an identity. In a dizzying series of logical moves, the Court ruled that Georgia could ban the sexual practice because of its connection to a despised identity, even though the law banned the practice for everybody. At the same time, the Court held that the identity could be (and in subsequent lower court decisions has been) regarded as fairly subject to discrimination because the sex, which "defines the class," was criminal. Gotcha: the sex has no privacy protection because homos are immoral; homos are immoral because they commit, or want to commit, criminal sex acts. As Janet Halley has shown, lawyers for the Department of Defense introduced the same circular equivocations to the revisions of military policy, and apparently Clinton never noticed that the one moral distinction he had laid down was now useless. The result is the notorious "Don't Ask, Don't Tell" policy, which punishes both act and identity, status and conduct – and under which military discharges for homosexuality have skyrocketed.[5]

Just as the Supreme Court could utterly confuse status and conduct for legal purposes, so also lesbians and gay men often find in practice that the stigma on identity and the shame of sexual activity are hard to separate. That is not just because of the slipperiness of the Court's thinking. The prevailing ideas of sexual identity being what they are, when you come out as gay or lesbian the implication is that you have the same sexuality as all the others, including those compulsives crawling from orgasm to orgasm in the parks and gutters. The queer stigma covers us all, at least in some contexts. As a consequence, people try to protect their identities by repudiating mere sex.

This confusion results from a basic paradox in the notion of sexual identity. Identity, like

stigma, tars us all with the same brush, but it also allows us to distance ourselves from any actual manifestation of queerness. We only share the identity and its stigma, in fact, *because* identity has been distinguished from sexual acts and their shame. Pride or stigma belongs to us as a class, a recognizable kind of person, regardless of our deeds as individuals. Thus there always seem to be some gay people who are shocked, *shocked* to find that others are having deviant sex. They will have you know that their dignity is founded on being gay, which in their view has nothing to do with sex. If others are having sex – or too much sex or sex that is too deviant – then those people have every reason to be ashamed. Of course only the playwright Larry Kramer and a few other ranting moralists put it in these extreme terms, admittedly a caricature. And the distinction between stigma and shame, identity and act, is undeniable in some contexts. But to have a politics of one without the other is to doom oneself to incoherence and weakness. It is to challenge the stigma on identity, but only by reinforcing the shame of sex. And unfortunately, this has been the choice not only of individuals, but of much of the official gay movement. In too many ways, it has chosen to articulate the politics of identity rather than to become a broader movement targeting the politics of sexual shame.

The core dilemma is ethical as well as political. Erving Goffman captures its essence nicely, in a brilliant paragraph about what he calls ambivalence:

Whether closely allied with his own kind or not, the stigmatized individual may exhibit identity ambivalence when he obtains a close sight of his own kind behaving in a stereotyped way, flamboyantly or pitifully acting out the negative attributes imputed to them. The sight may repel him, since after all he supports the norms of the wider society, but his social and psychological identification with these offenders holds him to what repels him, transforming repulsion into shame, and then transforming ashamedness itself into something of which he is ashamed. In brief, he can neither embrace his group nor let it go.[6]

On top of having ordinary sexual shame, and on top of having shame for being gay, the dignified homosexual also feels ashamed of every queer who flaunts his sex and his faggotry, making the dignified homosexual's stigma all the more justifiable in the eyes of straights. On top of that he feels shame about his own shame, the fatedness of which he is powerless to redress....

The dilemma of "identity ambivalence" has been an unmistakable force in the lesbian and gay movement from its inception. For individuals, it is a profound ethical challenge. This is true for people with any stigmatized identity, such as Jews or African Americans. But the dilemma is more tempting and more complicated for lesbians and gay men, or any other stigmatized sexuality. The distinction between stigma and shame makes it seem as though an easy way to resolve the ambivalence of belonging to a stigmatized group is to embrace the identity but disavow the act. As Kramer puts it, "The only response, the only way gays can assume our political responsibility and obtain our democratic due, is to fight for our rights *as gays*. To be taught about, to be studied, to be written about ... as *gays*."[7] Kramer's distinction is not entirely mistaken. There is a real and consequential difference. But being lesbian or gay necessarily involves both stigma and shame....

## The Ethics of Queer Life

Defensiveness about sex and sexual variance is most common in public or official contexts. In many other circles, the idea of a gay man or lesbian posing as too mature or too respectable for mere sex is held to be ridiculous. For all the variety of queer culture – and all its limitations – it is possible to find, running through its development over the past century, and especially in its least organized and least "respectable" circles, an ethical vision much more at home with sex and with the indignities associated with sex. Nowhere, after all, are people more aware of the absurdity and tenacity of shame than in queer culture. That's why the official gay organizations' pious idea of a respectable, dignified gay community seems so out of keeping with the world those organizations claim to represent....

In those circles where queerness has been most cultivated, the ground rule is that one doesn't pretend to be *above* the indignity of sex. And although this usually isn't announced as an ethical vision, that's what it perversely is. In queer circles, you are likely to be teased and abused until you grasp the idea. Sex is understood to be as various as the people who have it. It is not required to be tidy, normal, uniform, or authorized by the government. This kind of culture is often denounced as relativist, self-indulgent, or merely libertine. In fact, it has its own norms, its own way of keeping people in line. I call its way of life an ethic not only because it is understood as a better kind of self-relation, but because it is the premise of the special kind of sociability that holds queer culture together. A relation to others, in these contexts, begins in an acknowledgment of all that is most abject and least reputable in oneself. Shame is bedrock. Queers can be abusive, insulting, and vile toward one another, but because abjection is understood to be the shared condition, they also know how to communicate through such camaraderie a moving and unexpected form of generosity. No one is beneath its reach, not because it prides itself on generosity, but because it prides itself on nothing. The rule is: Get over yourself. Put a wig on before you judge. And the corollary is that you stand to learn most from the people you think are beneath you. At its best, this ethic cuts against every form of hierarchy you could bring into the room. Queer scenes are the true *salons des refusés*, where the most heterogeneous people are brought into great intimacy by their common experience of being despised and rejected in a world of norms that they now recognize as false morality.

For this reason, paradoxically, the ethic of queer life is actually truer to the core of the modern notion of dignity than the usual use of the word is. Dignity has at least two radically different meanings in our culture. One is ancient, closely related to honor, and fundamentally an ethic of rank. It is historically a value of nobility. It requires soap. (Real estate doesn't hurt, either.) The other is modern and democratic. Dignity in the latter sense is not pomp and distinction; it is inherent in the human.[8] You can't, in a way, not have it. At worst, others can simply fail to recognize your dignity. These two notions of dignity have opposite implications for sex. The most common judgments about sex assign dignity to some kinds (married, heterosexual, private, loving), as long as they are out of sight, while all other kinds of sex are no more dignified than defecating in public, and possibly less so. That kind of dignity we might as well call bourgeois propriety. In what I am calling queer culture, however, there is no truck with bourgeois propriety. If sex is a kind of indignity, then we're all in it together. And the paradoxical result is that only when this

indignity of sex is spread around the room, leaving no one out, and in fact binding people together, that it begins to resemble the dignity of the human. In order to be consistent, we would have to talk about dignity in shame. That, I think, is a premise of queer culture, and one reason why people in it are willing to call themselves queer – a word that, as Eve Sedgwick notes, emblazons its connection to shame in a way that still roils the moralists. But I'm speaking now of sluts and drag queens and trannies and trolls and women who have seen a lot of life – not of the media spokesmen and respectable leaders of the gay community....

Stigma is messy and often incoherent. The received wisdom, in straight culture, is that all of its different norms line up, that one is synonymous with the others. If you are born with male genitalia, the logic goes, you will behave in masculine ways, desire women, desire feminine women, desire them exclusively, have sex in what are thought to be normally active and insertive ways and within officially sanctioned contexts, think of yourself as heterosexual, identify with other heterosexuals, trust in the superiority of heterosexuality no matter how tolerant you might wish to be, and never change any part of this package from childhood to senescence. Heterosexuality is often a name for this entire package, even though attachment to the other sex is only one element. If you deviate at any point from this program, you do so at your own cost. And one of the things straight culture hates most is any sign that the different parts of the package might be recombined in an infinite number of ways. But experience shows that this is just what tends to happen. If heterosexuality requires the entire sequence, then it is very fragile. No wonder it needs so much terror to induce compliance....

## Study Questions

1. Warner argues for a robust sexual autonomy, free of "moralism, law, stigma, shame, and isolation." What does sexual autonomy mean for Warner? Why do you think American citizens argue so vehemently for autonomy and yet are so preoccupied with sexual moralism?

2. Warner argues that homosexuals and others who do not fit the heteronormative societal criteria feel isolation and shame and have a special burden of disclosure that heterosexuals do not. How would validating sexual autonomy bring about positive changes for those who have this burden of disclosure?

3. How does Warner distinguish between shame and stigma? How does Warner trace the way in which shame can become stigma and thus identity for homosexuals and anyone appearing to be homosexual? How do "the ethics of queer life" combat this?

## Notes

1 On this and related issues in the laws of the states, see Richard Posner and Katharine Silbaugh, *A Guide to America's Sex Laws* (Chicago: U of Chicago P, 1996), pp. 98–99.
2 Gayle Rubin, "Thinking Sex: Notes for a Radical Theory of a Politics of Sexuality," in Carole S. Vance, ed., *Pleasure and Danger: Exploring Female Sexuality* (1984; reprint, London: Pandora, 1992), pp. 267–319, quote at p. 297.
3 Erving Goffman, *Stigma: Notes on the Management of Spoiled Identity* (1963; reprint, New York: Touchstone, 1986), pp. 107–08.
4 This dramatic change was first emphasized by Michel Foucault, *The History of Sexuality*, vol. 1, trans. Robert Hurley (New York: Random House, 1978).
5 See Janet Halley, *Don't: A Guide to Military Antigay Policy* (Durham: Duke UP, 1999).
6 Goffman, 108.
7 Larry Kramer, "Sex and Sensibility," *The Advocate*, May 27, 1997.
8 See Peter Berger, "On the Obsolescence of the Concept of Honour," in Stanley Hauerwas and Alasdair MacIntyre, *Revisions: Changing Perspectives in Moral Philosophy* (Notre Dame: U of Notre Dame P, 1983), pp. 172–81.

# 4. Loren Cannon, "Trans-Marriage and the Unacceptability of Same-Sex Marriage Restrictions"

IN THIS 2009 ARTICLE from the journal *Social Philosophy Today*, Loren Cannon explores the heterosexual, legal binary of male/female marriage and exposes the many empirical challenges, such as those from transgender and intersex people, that point toward its social construction. Rather than there being a tidy, exhaustive, biological basis for clear identification, there are exceptions, including hormone and genitalia variations, that problematize the binary as an objective measurement. In addition to the firm categorization failure, transgender people bring to light the fluidity of man and woman, and how one can shift between these. Cannon argues that the definition of marriage law using the heterosexual male/female binary is similar to previous racial categorization and is as inherently unjust and oppressive.

## I. Introduction

MUCH HAS BEEN WRITTEN regarding how the current restriction on same-sex marriages in the United States affects lesbian and gay couples, and rightly so. Those who are proponents of the *one man-one woman* marriage restriction are primarily targeting lesbian and gay couples for exclusion from the institution of civil marriage. Furthermore, there have been many very cogent arguments written in defense of legalizing marriage for lesbian and gay couples; some such arguments involve certain rights claims, others emphasize the level of privilege that heterosexual couples have over same-sex couples, still others focus on the political status of lesbians and gay men in the United States.

While I am sympathetic to many of the arguments of the kind identified above, they all seem to make unwarranted assumptions regarding the nature of the gendered categories upon which these restrictions rely. In what follows I wish not to focus on the fairness or unfairness of marriage restrictions, but even more basically, I argue that any statute that identifies marriage as only legal between one man and one woman *fails* as a law. The analysis that I offer does not focus on aspects of sexual orientation but of gender identity. The emphasis here is on the experience of transgender individuals, their life partners, and the same-sex marriage restrictions affecting these couples. By focusing on the experience of transpersons in the context of civil marriage, it becomes clear that marriage restrictions rely on the assumptions that men and women comprise two disjoint and exhaustive sets and that one's unambiguously determined sex makes one fit or unfit for marriage to [a certain] other. By focusing on trans-marriage it becomes obvious that these two assumptions are faulty, thus illegitimating the laws against *same-sex* marriage. Since same-sex marriage restrictions fail as legitimate law they should be abolished.[1]

## II. Trans-Marriage

The term "trans-marriage" is used herein to describe legal marriages in which at least one of the individuals in the marriage is transgender. The term "transgender" has come to be known as an umbrella term with which many gender transgressing individuals identify. For the purposes of this essay, I focus on those who choose to physically and legally transition from their originally assigned gender category to another. While these individuals sometimes identify with the word "transsexual," I will use the more general term "transgender" in this essay.[2]

While there are cases in which both members of the legal marriage are transgender, if only one identifies as such the union will fall into one of two types.[3] First, there are those couples who were married before the trans-individual underwent gender transition and who simply remained married. These types of marriages represent a distinctive challenge to those who wish to restrict marriage privileges to heterosexuals since, after transition, these couples often appear and may identify as a lesbian or gay couple. For instance, consider the fictional couple of Don and Michelle. Since they are married most assume that Don and Michelle are both heterosexual and that neither individual is transgender. However, after living as a married couple for some years, Don comes out as a male-to-female (MTF) transsexual and undergoes the physical transformation that will allow her to finally feel at home in her skin and live her life as a woman. As a transwoman, Donna completes the necessary steps to be deemed legally female. Michelle and Donna love each other and remain married. This couple may or may not identify as lesbian, but they are, nevertheless, two (legal) women who are legally married. Similarly, a heterosexual-appearing marriage may later appear as a union of two men if one member of the couple transitions from female to male. Using the names from our last example, Don and Michelle could become Don and Michael.

The second type of trans-marriage is one in which the privileges of marriage only become accessible after one member undergoes at least some aspects of physical and legal transition. Before the partner's transition the couple is assumed to identify as lesbian or gay, but are, after transition, perceived as heterosexual. For example, a couple that is assumed to be lesbian may later have access to legal marriage if one member of the couple comes out as a transman and becomes legally male or, a couple that appears to be two gay men might later wed if one individual transitions and becomes legally female. (Of course, this should not be construed as implying that individuals undergo gender transition for the primary purpose of being marriage eligible. The legal, financial, social, professional, and personal challenges involved tend to outweigh a lack of accepted marriage rights.) Furthermore, it is not uncommon for a post-transition individual to marry a person who was unacquainted with their pre-transition selves. Lastly, it should be noted that due to inconsistencies in how states determine marriage privileges, some post-transition transpersons find civil marriage eventually attainable, while others have no access at all.[4]

### III. Some Details

While each marriage is a unique entity to itself, there are some details that are worth mentioning so as to avoid later misunderstandings. First, I have been careful to stress that certain couples may *appear* lesbian, gay, or heterosexual, as opposed to using some variation of the verb *to be*, such as "the couple *is* gay, lesbian, or heterosexual." This word choice reflects the often complicated relationship some trans-individuals may have with categories of sexual orientation. Some transpersons identify strongly with a sexual orientation while others find that a given category is simply a consequence of their transition and is not an important aspect of their identity. Furthermore, it should be noted that sexual orientation is independent of one's gender identity, so a transperson may identify as heterosexual, a gay man, a lesbian, or may have a fluid or otherwise atypical sexual orientation. Lastly, some transpersons regard the aforementioned categories of sexual orientation to be presumptive of the binary sex/gender system, which at its most basic level leaves out transpersons completely. In many very significant ways, the acknowledgment of the lives and experiences of transpersons serves to shake the foundation of the meanings of categories such as bisexual, lesbian, gay, and heterosexual. As I shall argue, the categories of *man* and *woman* are just as vulnerable.

In what follows I present two cases, one of a woman growing up in apartheid South Africa and the other of a transwoman in the State of Texas. My claim is that these two cases are structurally similar, and that what goes wrong both morally and legally in the first case is comparable to that of the second. As I will argue, each of these two women's lives was unnecessarily burdened by laws that presume persons can be easily categorized in terms of racial and sexual identity. In each case, the laws involved rely on a false belief that certain social categories are both exhaustive and disjoint and can serve as the basis for awarding social privilege. First for consideration is the case of Sandra Laing.

## IV. The Story of Sandra Laing

Sandra Laing was born of white pro-apartheid parents in 1955 and was categorized as white at birth.[5] Her skin complexion can be described as a light coppery brown and her hair is black and was described by others as "frizzy." Her appearance led to her being bullied by her fellow students and mistreated by her school teachers at her all-white elementary school. She was eventually expelled from school and the Interior Ministry that investigated the

case reclassified her as legally "coloured," one of the racial categories of apartheid South Africa generally meant to refer to those of mixed race.

Abraham Laing, Sandra's father, sought a reclassification by the Race Classification Appeal Board – so that his child would again be able to live as a white Afrikaner. News of this reclassification case hit the press, and Sandra's parents, Abraham and Sarah, were interviewed about the case. The following excerpt from the newspaper the *Rand Daily Mail* makes it clear that the Laings knew what was at stake.

> If Sandra's classification is not changed then my husband and I will have to send her overseas [Mrs. Laing said.] She cannot live in South Africa as a Coloured, yet part of a White family....
>
> Sandra has been brought up as a White. She considers herself White. She is darker than we are, but in every way she has always been a White person....
>
> "If Sandra remains 'Coloured' does it mean she will have to be registered as a servant in order to live with us?" [Mr. Laing] added. "Or must she move away into a location? Will we be breaking the law if we take Sandra into a tearoom or a cinema, or take her on a train journey with us? And who would Sandra be allowed to marry?"[6]

In cases like Sandra's, racial "experts" were called in to determine one's true racial category through a series of tests. Tests generally used included measurements of the nose, nostrils, and cheekbones, and an analysis of hair texture. The latter often included the "pencil test." It was thought that a white person's hair is not so curly as to hold a pencil, whereas the hair of those designated "coloured" could do so. There were gradations of skin color to be measured in various places of the body including the fingernails and the eyelids; earlobes were squeezed to determine their degree of softness. (It was thought that a black person's earlobes were softer than others.) Individuals challenging their racial classification before the board would also be asked what they had for breakfast and what sport they most enjoyed.

Sandra's father appealed the case, but Sandra was not reclassified as white under the standards given above. To the relief of Abraham Laing, however, the Ministry of Home Affairs revised the decision-making procedure to include information regarding an individual's parentage. After submitting a blood test Mr. Laing again requested the racial re-classification of his daughter, this time with success, as it was decided that Sandra was, again, white.

Sandra's parents were relieved at their legal success, but just a few years later Sandra would again become entangled in the racial classification laws when she decided to live with her black boyfriend and his family in neighboring Swaziland. Now her racial category as a white woman meant that the custody of her children was threatened. In need of a national identification card, Sandra went to the Department of Home Affairs to apply. She recalls, "The person there said if they give me a white I.D., they're going to take my kids away because a white woman can't have kids who are not white. So I wanted to become coloured again."[7] On her application to the reclassification office Sandra wrote:

> I am happy with my boyfriend and our children. I want to obtain permission to be classified and/or reclassified as a Swazi and I do not want to be classified and/or considered white because I want to keep my children and also proceed to marry my present boyfriend. I have for all intents

and purposes lived as a Swazi woman for the last four years and I have given birth to Swazi children and I intend remaining a Swazi and I pray that I be permitted to continue living as a Swazi in which group I have been accepted as a Swazi daughter-in-law. I do not intend to go back and live as a white.[8]

Sandra would not be able to obtain her desired classification as coloured until many years later. Domestic abuse led her to flee her home in Swaziland, and the resulting lack of community (she became estranged from her parents who, it seems, saw her as a kind of traitor), coupled with illness and financial vulnerability, led to the loss of custody of her children. She spent the greater part of her adulthood trying to be financially stable enough to gain custody of her children, a goal she eventually obtained. Her white upbringing gave her few skills to predict the economic severity of the apartheid system, and her skin complexion and lack of education made the privileges of whiteness beyond her grasp.

## V. The Story of Christie Lee Littleton

Christie Lee Cavazos was married to Jonathon Mark Littleton in the Commonwealth of Kentucky in 1989, at which time she took his surname.[9] Christie and Jonathon moved back to Christie's hometown of San Antonio, Texas, and lived there happily as husband and wife until Jonathon's unexpected death in 1996. Believing that her husband did not receive proper medical treatment, she filed a medical malpractice suit against his physician under the Texas Wrongful Death and Survival Statute. The defendant in the suit became aware of Littleton's trans-status and claimed that she was not in a position to file the malpractice suit since she, as a transwoman, could not claim to be Jonathon's widow.

In deciding the case the court did not consider the nature of the commitment between Jonathon and Christie, or the years in which they functioned as a married couple in society.[10] Instead of these issues, it was, quite literally, Christie Lee Littleton's *womanhood* that was to be decided by the Texas Court. As such, her childhood, her relationship and feelings about her body, the size and shape of her genitalia and internal organs, and even the quality of her sex life with her husband were subject to the rigors of legal investigation.

As testified, Littleton's life was one of repeated assertion of her female identity even as the forces of society pressured her otherwise. It was verified that Littleton was born with (assumedly) functioning male genitalia but that she "considered herself female from the time that she was three or four years old."[11] Despite measures taken by her parents meant to support for her a male identity, Littleton eventually sought help at the University of Texas Health Science Center at the age of twenty-three. There, she underwent years of treatment by several physicians and mental health professionals who supported her decision to transition. Littleton's legal and physical transition included changing her name, feminizing her body through hormone therapy and surgery, and eventually amending her Texas birth certificate. Her doctors testified that "true male to female transsexuals are, in their opinion, psychologically and psychiatrically female before and after the sex reassignment surgery, and that Christie is a true male to female transsexual."[12] The court also verified that the couple did have regular sexual relations and that Jonathon was fully aware of Christie's history.

## VI. The Ruling

The 4th Circuit Court of Texas in the case of Christie Lee Littleton concludes:

We hold, as a matter of law, that Christie Littleton is a male. As a male, Christie cannot be married to another male. Her marriage to Jonathon was invalid, and she cannot bring a cause of action as his surviving spouse.[13]

Recall that the court maintained that their responsibility was, to the best of their ability, to identify Littleton's sexual category. They should not, they maintained, "write a protocol for when transsexuals would be recognized as having successfully changed their sex."[14] To use the popular phraseology, this, they seemed to believe, would be to *legislate from the bench*. The court seemed to disregard all information that involved aspects of Littleton's life during or post transition. Cited as significant was Littleton's original birth certificate, her lack of certain internal organs, and her (assumed) chromosomal structure. From the court's transcript:

Through surgery and hormones, a transsexual male can be made to look like a woman, including female genitalia and breasts. Transsexual medical treatment, however, does not create the internal sexual organs of a woman (except for the vaginal canal). There is no womb, cervix or ovaries in the post-operative transsexual female.

The male chromosomes do not change with either hormonal treatment or sex reassignment surgery. Biologically a post-operative female transsexual is still a male.[15]

While my intention here is to consider the Littleton case with respect to certain legal standards, it is not difficult to imagine the degree of hardship this trial and its consequences created for Christie Lee Littleton. Having her marriage annulled by the state; her identity, physicality, psychology and sexual behavior analyzed in the court of law; having the legitimacy of her marriage come to rest on the only remaining aspects of her male past; and being barred from investigating her husband's sudden death are all serious harms that should not be minimized.

## VII. The Analogy

It is undeniable that there are many ways that the cases of Sandra Laing and Christie Lee Littleton differ. It is not my claim that the harms incurred by these two women, or by the collectives that we may affiliate them with, are comparable either. Any comparisons should be done cautiously and with recognition of the vast differences between the nature of the harms suffered and the complex experiences of these two individuals. Furthermore, it should also be noted that no individual is situated within a single social category but that intersections of identities involving race or ethnicity, national citizenship, legal status, economic class, gender expression, sexual orientation, or gender identity result in a mix of social privileges and/or injustices that affect each of us daily. That said, it seems clear that in both of the cases described herein, the legal judgments involved a categorization of person that was both misguided and unjust. For Laing, experts were employed to determine into which racial categorization (white, coloured, or black) she should be classified. The social privileges that she could expect to have access to in her life were the result of this classification. This classification would affect her legal and interpersonal relationship with her parents, her partner, and her children, and could burden and even de-legitimize those relationships. There was an underlying belief that the racial categories employed were disjoint and exhaustive and could be justly used to identify degrees of social privilege.

In the Littleton case, there are a set of similar assumptions and parameters. The court assumed that the categories of *man* and *woman* are both disjoint and exhaustive and employed experts to identify Littleton's category. Like Laing, this category identification can legitimize or de-legitimize her marriage and determines whether or not she has the privilege of legally investigating the death of her spouse. Furthermore, it seems that each of these two women attempted to live lives that supported their most cherished relationships, but in each case the law got in the way. Certainly, a legal recognition and valuing of Laing's relationships with her parents, partner and children should not be determined by her complexion and neither should the legal recognition of Littleton's marriage depend on the absence or presence of certain internal organs or chromosomal structure.

## VIII. The Problem

The idea that racial categories identify different *types* of persons and can justify differing sets of social privileges is no longer commonly accepted, or at least asserted, in most arenas. Both science and common experience support the idea that while one's appearance can lead others to assume one's membership in a certain racial or ethnic category, such categories are neither well defined nor used as the basis for legally sanctioned degrees of social privilege. Unfortunately, it is still commonly assumed that the sexual categories of male and female (and their assumptive correlative gender categories of man and woman) are both disjoint and exhaustive and serve as a suitable basis for the distribution of certain social privileges. In her essay "Categories in Distress," Marilyn Frye argues that part of the problem inherent in describing the categories of *man* and *woman* involves an underlying belief regarding the *nature* of these types of categories themselves. Frye's view relies on the idea that we have been trained to think of categories, even social categories, as mathematical sets in which inclusion and exclusion in any given category is unambiguous. She writes,

> Another mind-binding consequence of conceptualizing categories as sets is its encouragement of the idea that the function of categories is *sorting.* Thinking of categories as sets, and thus as defined by necessary and sufficient conditions, one sees those conditions as constituting an algorithm for sorting individuals into members and nonmembers; using categories comes to look like chucking pieces of mail in cubby holes or sorting laundry or silverware.[16]

In the Littleton case, the judges believed that they were charged with the task of sorting Littleton into the correct category so that it could be determined whether her marriage was legally permissible, giving her the right to sue her late husband's doctor for wrongful death. In determining whether the *one man-one woman* law was infringed, the court primarily considered a selection of Littleton's biological characteristics. In doing so, they relied on two problematic assumptions. First, they assumed that the category of woman is coextensive with the category of female. In other words, despite de Beauvoir's assertion that a woman is made and not born, the court assumed that that which is a woman just is an adult person who is equipped with certain reproductive parts and chromosomal features. Their second problematic assumption involved the belief that even the categories of female and male, as identified through certain biological characteristics, are disjoint and exhaustive. I will consider problems with each of these assumptions, beginning with the one just identified.

It is a common yet false belief that human beings come in one of two sexual categories and that the criteria for being identified as a male or female involve the existence of certain necessary characteristics. Just as the experiences of transpersons call into question the relationship between biological sex and gender, those with intersex condition give testament to the idea that even the biological categories of male and female are neither exhaustive nor disjoint. In fact, of the biological characteristics of chromosomes, gonads and genital structure, as well as that of hormonal make up, all afford variation. Few individuals have their chromosomes checked, but even very typical looking individuals may have atypical chromosomal structures. Such structures can vary from the typical XX or XY combination to XO, XXX, XYY, XXY, or XXXY. Hormonal levels also vary widely among healthy adults. There are women who have a higher than average testosterone level and men whose estrogen level is uncommonly elevated. It is the severe social pressure to deny this kind of difference that often keeps it hidden and unacknowledged. Lastly, there is a degree of variation in terms of any given individual's genital make-up. While the testes-penis and ovaries-vagina combinations are considered typical, others are quite possible. In Anne Fausto-Sterling's essay, "The Five Sexes, Revisited: The Emerging Recognition that People Come in Bewildering Sexual Varieties Is Testing Medical Values and Social Norms," she provocatively suggests that instead of just two we identify five different types of sexes:

> In addition to males and females, I included "herms" (named after true hermaphrodites, people born with both a testis and an ovary); "merms" (male pseudohermaphrodites, who are born with testes and some aspect of female genitalia);

and "ferms" (female pseudohermaphrodites, who have ovaries combined with some aspect of male genitalia.)[17]

Indeed, if marriage is restricted to one *man and one woman* and if these categories are identified by the existence of internal sex organs and external genitalia in certain combinations, as was the case for Littleton, then consistency would dictate that many individuals would not be eligible to marry anyone. Furthermore, because some conditions are difficult to detect, chromosome tests and physical examinations would need to be part of any marriage application process.

Rather than simplistically and problematically assuming that that which is *female* is that which is *woman*, the court might have considered the gender category of *woman* more thoroughly. Had it done so, it would have found that, like the categories of male and female, the categories of man and woman are not the sorts that lend themselves to the identification of necessary or sufficient conditions for membership. Indeed, scholars such as Simone de Beauvoir, Monique Wittig, Judith Halberstam, Jacob Hale, Marilyn Frye, and many others have considered the meaning and potential membership criteria for the category *woman*. It is not practical to review all of these arguments here, but it is important to note that the category of *woman* is most often characterized as one that is constructed through collective belief systems that may vary through time as well as by culture, class, and other factors. Being a woman involves both how an individual identifies or sees herself and how she is seen by others. For some, it may involve adopting certain gendered roles and presenting oneself in certain socially accepted ways. In "Are Lesbians Women," Jacob Hale, in his critique of Wittig's view of the relationship between the categories of lesbianism and womanhood, offers his own analysis

of the dominant culture's view of the category woman.[18] Hale offers thirteen characteristics, none of which is necessary or sufficient for membership in the category, yet, depending on circumstances and how each characteristic is weighed in those circumstances, can combine to form a resemblance of the dominant society's image of womanhood. Hale's characteristics include some which are biologically based (absence of a penis, presence of breasts, certain chromosomal or hormonal attributes), others consist in aspects of gender as mentioned above (gender identity, presentation, role, and acceptance by others), one's sexual orientation (lesbians can be seen as less *woman* than those with similar characteristics yet heterosexual), and the constancy of such characteristics. I agree with Hale that those individuals who wish to be seen as women consciously or unconsciously navigate these expectations of womanhood. Similarly, I agree that while one may attempt to evaluate some of these characteristics individually, there is no formula that aptly weighs each of them in correspondence to their relative level of importance and identifies a fact of one's womanhood. To be clear, this argument is not one that concludes that Littleton is a *real woman* anymore than any other woman is *real*. Rather, there is no reasonable method to determine womanhood that can be used in all cases. It is not just that the Littleton court employed false assumptions in their decision making but that the questions involving Littleton's womanhood are not those that the court can reasonably answer.

While the Littleton case has been the focus here, it is important to briefly review the other type of trans-marriage whose participants are burdened by these marriage restrictions. Recall the fictional couple of Don and Michael who were married before Michael transitioned from female to male. Here, Don and Michael are two legal men who are legally married and who do not wish to divorce. It is unclear in this case whether, to remain law abiding, they should divorce; or if the State, to be consistent, should void their marriage; or, if Don and Michael happen to live in a state in which their union no longer *counts* as marriage, they should be obligated to move to a state in which it does. More broadly, it seems incomprehensible to argue that as Don and Michelle this couple had the *right stuff* for the institution of marriage but somehow lost this through Michael's legal and physical transition.

## IX. The Law's Failure

In "The Morality of Law," Lon L. Fuller rightfully argues that the purpose of law is to guide individual action.[19] To have a reciprocal respect between the law and its subjects, each subject must be able to plan a life that respects the law without undue worry that, in the end, she won't find herself legally penalized despite her best efforts. According to Fuller, forming a plan for a legal future is impossible when there are inconsistencies or contradictions in the law or when the law essentially makes citizens responsible for completing impossible tasks. The legal restriction against [what is thought to be] same-sex marriage fails in at least these two ways.

According to all legal documentation, Littleton is legally a female person. This is inconsistent with the ruling that her marriage, as a woman to a man, is illegal. Littleton faithfully abided by very known legal regulation when undergoing her transition from male to female and in obtaining her marriage certificate and yet *still* had her marriage revoked and her identity unacknowledged. She had no evidence that the state whose laws supported her physical and legal transition would be the same to void her marriage. Additionally, while the laws of San Antonio have not changed

this ruling (by the date of this publication), the State of Texas and the country itself is an odd patchwork of marriage laws affecting transpersons differently. When the *New York Times* questioned Littleton's lawyers in April, 2008 about these inconsistencies they stated:

> Taking this situation to its logical conclusion, Mrs. Littleton, while in San Antonio, Texas, is a male and has a void marriage; as she travels to Houston, Texas, and enters federal property, she is female and a widow; upon traveling to Kentucky she is female and a widow; but, upon entering Ohio, she is once again male and prohibited from marriage; entering Connecticut, she is again female and may marry; if her travel takes her north to Vermont, she is male and may marry a female; if instead she travels south to New Jersey, she may marry a male.[20]

Thus, while Littleton's home municipality may be consistent over time with regard to the legal treatment of trans-marriages, Littleton and other transpersons are still burdened by the geographic inconsistencies of these statutes. Furthermore, if one interprets the ruling of the court as stating that "post transition transsexuals can marry the 'opposite' sex only if they also change their chromosomes and internal organs to those of their target-gender," then Littleton and others are facing an impossible task. According to Fuller (and common sense), "rules that require conduct beyond the powers of the affected party" fail as law.[21]

In response to the above, some might argue that what is needed is a national law that clearly outlines the conditions under which transpersons may qualify to wed those of the presumed "opposite" sex. Toward this end some believe that undergoing sexual reassignment surgery should be the qualifier for marriage-ready legal status, but this unjustifiably connects one's privilege to marry with one's financial status since, given present circumstances, sexual reassignment surgery for US citizens is usually only available to those who can afford the out of pocket expense.[22] Furthermore, while it is possible to identify a set of internal organs or a chromosomal structure as a necessary requirement for marriage to the presumed opposite sex, any such identification would be clearly as arbitrary and as vulnerable to counterexample as the aforementioned "pencil test" for racial category. Lastly, neither of the above suggestions is reasonable for or helpful to our fictional couple, Don and Michael. It seems that what we need is not a new set of laws that deal with transpersons as a separate class of people but a recognition that the present marriage laws fail by relying on problematic and unjust categorizations.

## X. Competing Views

Legal scholar Ruthann Robson, in "A Mere Switch or a Fundamental Change? Theorizing Transgender Marriage," concludes that, "as a matter of reform, it may be expedient to argue for the recognition of transgender marriages, but as a matter of critical change, the argument fails."[23] This conclusion is based on her analysis of the arguments of the Littleton case and a number of others that involve transgender marriage and child custody issues. According to Robson, this analysis reveals that the legitimacy of trans-marriages has been upheld when the argument rests on the capacity of the involved partners for vaginal-penile intercourse[24] and denied when it is argued that the status of the marriage involves a determination of one's true gender, which, as in Littleton's case and that of the *Estate of Gardiner*,[25] is taken to be either fixed or changeable only to the designation of "transsexual." In other words, when legitimacy is denied, the arguments offered support the

belief in a binary system of sex and gender, and when such marriages are affirmed, heterosexuality is normalized and privileged.

I disagree with Robson's final conclusion and see recognition of trans-marriages as a fundamental change in our collective belief regarding the concept of marriage and of sexual orientation. It seems of little surprise that the arguments used both for and against contested trans-marriages unapologetically privilege heterosexuality and reinforce a belief in a binary sex/gender system. Lawyers, after all, choose their arguments prudently; each wishes to be as persuasive as possible to their audience. When preparing such arguments, lawyers can predict that the deciding judge(s) or jury of the case are probably heterosexuals who support the binary gender system. This, however, does not entail that a full consideration of the ramifications of trans-marriages is not transformative, only that the (legally successful) arguments to date have failed to be so. Robson refers to these legal arguments as well as the depiction of transpersons in popular media to support the view that gender transition simply reinstates the heterosexual-binary-system; that gender transition is a *mere switch* used to help maintain the heteronormative status quo. This is a common misunderstanding and, I believe, a function of being familiar with only a limited number of transgender life histories. Of course, the transgender narratives that receive the most publicity are those that are most palatable to the masses and most supportive of the dominant view. Trans-individuals who have a nontraditional gender presentation and/or are not resolutely heterosexual attract little media attention and are burdened with additional societal pressure for identifying as bisexual, lesbian, gay, or gender nonconforming. Heteronormative dominance affects both the types of legal arguments constructed and the image of transsexuals by the media. As I have argued here, a more thorough consideration of the transgender experience, including that of marriage, cannot help but be transformative of our understanding of the nature of men and women, as well as of the traditional categories of sexual orientation.

## XI. Conclusion

Between the years of 1950 and 1966, there were 267,541 individuals who could not be adequately categorized by the apartheid system of racial categorization.[26] So too are there countless individuals who cannot easily be categorized by the binary sex/gender system which is used to identify marital privileges for all Americans. Those with an intersex condition and transgender persons are counter examples to the claim that the traditional binary categories of sex/gender are descriptive of our population and can thus be used to differentiate between types of persons. Laws that limit the privilege of civil marriage to *one man and one woman* fail as laws just as the racial policies of South Africa failed as laws. Such laws as these that identify one's rights by one's assumed sexual and/or racial category are inherently unjust and serve not only to support oppressive systems of privilege but also to create a kind of special legal status available only to those individuals whose identities and physical characteristics fall neatly within these legal categories. Laws need to be such that they can be reasonably and consistently applied to all citizens and leave no citizen vulnerable to the arbitrary judgments that are often the result of legal-limbo. Given the intractability of these problems, same-sex marriage restrictions should be abolished.

## Study Questions

1. Cannon provides two cases, those of Laing and Littleton, the first regarding racial classification and the second regarding sexual classification. What are the similarities between these cases? Do you agree that, while different, they both point to inherently unjust legal status? Why or why not?

2. Cannon provides biological evidence for the inability to exhaustively classify sex into two categories due to the empirical fact of intersex persons. Furthermore, there are hormonal, chromosomal, and genital variations that exist in what otherwise are considered "normal" males or females. First, detail these facts. Next, explain how this challenges the assumed male/female binary, and thus how laws based on such a binary are problematic.

3. Cannon argues that sex and gender do not fall into two unambiguous groupings, but rather that those two groupings are socially constructed. How does he establish the social construction of sex and gender? Aside from the implications he argues regarding same-sex marriage, what other areas of society could be transformed from a serious analysis of sex and gender being socially constructed?

**Notes**

1 It might be of interest to note that my own experience with marriage as a transman (female to male transsexual) and the experiences of those in my own community have served as motivation to consider this topic more fully. Certainly, marriage, its practice or avoidance, affects nearly all of us. That said, this essay is neither autobiographical nor representative of the views of any population or community.

2 It is not my view that those who choose not to transition should do so, or that those who do make this choice are more *trans* than another. This decision is very complicated, personal, and costly.

3 Of course, two transpersons may marry. As of this writing I know of no such marriages that have been legally challenged.

4 These inconsistencies involve what documents are required as sufficient proof of one's gender category. Some civil agencies require only a driver's license or state-issued I.D. card with the required gender marker for legal marriage to another with the *opposite* such marker. Other agencies require birth certificates and sometimes one's original (non-amended) birth certificate. Furthermore, the regulations for changing one's gender marker on legal documents vary from state to state. In some states one can change the gender marker on one's driver's license by supplying certain letters from one's physician or psychologist. Obtaining a birth certificate with the gender marker amended involves meeting certain requirements of one's birth state. Some states do not allow one to change this designation under any circumstances; others will provide a birth certificate with the original gender designation crossed out and the new one also identified. In any case, meeting these requirements usually requires a high level of financial privilege.

5 Judith Stone, *When She Was White: The True Story of A Family Divided By Race* (New York: Miramax, 2007).

6 Ibid., 104.

7 Ibid., 162.

8 Ibid.

9 I originally became aware of Christie Lee Littleton's case through her website at http:// christielee.net/main2.htm.

10 It is notable that for non-transgender heterosexuals, functioning as husband and wife for an extended period of time can be seen as evidence that a marriage does exist even without history of any civil ceremony. Common law marriages are still accepted in many states.

11 *Littleton v. Prange* (No. 04-99-00010-CV, 288th Judicial District Court, Bexar County, Texas, Trial Court No. 98-CI-15220), 1997, 2.

12 Ibid.

13 Ibid., 10.

14 Ibid., 9.

15 Ibid., 9–10.

16 Marilyn Frye, "Categories in Distress," *Feminist Interventions in Ethics and Politics: Feminist Ethics and Social Theory*, ed. Barbara S. Andrew, Jean Keller, and Lisa Schwartzman (Lanham, MD: Rowman & Littlefield, 2005), 48.

17 Ann Fausto-Sterling, "The Five Sexes, Revisited: The Emerging Recognition that People Come in Bewildering Sexual Varieties is Testing Medical Values and Social Norms," *The Sciences* (July/August 2000): 19. This quote is recalling another that she wrote in *The Sciences* titled "The Five Sexes" (March/April 1993).

18 Jacob Hale, "Are Lesbians Women?" *Hypatia* 11.2 (1996): 94–121.

19 Lon L. Fuller, *The Morality of Law*, revised edition (New Haven and London: Yale UP, 1969).

20  Tina Kelly, "Through Sickness, Health and Sex Change," *The New York Times*, April 27, 2008. http://www.nytimes.com/2008/04/27/fashion/27trans. html.

21  Fuller, *The Morality of Law*, 39.

22  The American Medical Association has recently accepted Resolution 122 that is meant to remove financial barriers for trans-patients by recommending that health insurance plans support trans-health issues (including transition). While this is a positive step, it may be quite some time before insurance companies agree to such policies.

23  Ruthann Robson, "A Mere Switch or a Fundamental Change? Theorizing Transgender Marriage," *Hypatia* 22.1 (2007): 58–70, 66.

24  *M.T. v. J.T.*, New Jersey Superior Court, 1976.

25  *In re Estate of Gardiner.* 42 P.3d 120 (Kan. 2002).

26  Stone, *When She Was White*, 98.

# 5.  Michelle Madden Dempsey, "How to Argue about Prostitution"

IN THIS 2012 ARTICLE from the journal *Criminal Law and Philosophy*, Michelle Madden Dempsey provides three potential methodologies with which to argue about prostitution: the empirical (focusing on accurate real-world data), the philosophical (focusing on constructing sound and illuminating arguments), and the political (focusing on what happens in the real world with an eye toward changing it for the better). One of the main issues regarding prostitution is whether it is voluntary and consensual; Dempsey addresses the strengths and weaknesses of each methodology utilized to address this issue. In so doing, she also tackles the thorny issues of doing applied ethics.

---

[…]

AS WITH PRETTY MUCH any topic, there are different ways to argue about prostitution – by which I mean there are various methodologies one can employ to build an argument regarding prostitution law and policy. These methodologies provide the intellectual toolkit for the argument: they determine (more or less) what kinds of assumptions one brings to the table, what kinds of tasks one undertakes, and what kinds of conclusions one defends. At the risk of gross oversimplification, most arguments regarding prostitution can be categorized into three methodologies – empirical, philosophical, political – and the following chart captures the general division of labor amongst them (see Table 1).

It will be readily apparent that the distinctions drawn above are blurry and there is a great deal of cross-over between these three methodologies. Some of this cross-over is by necessity. Empirical researchers, for example, must conceptualize their subject of study both at its most basic level ("what counts as prostitution?") and at more complex, contested levels ("what is the difference between prostitution and sex trafficking?"). Thus, in order to get an empirical study of prostitution off the ground, empirical researchers must get clear about concepts, which is to say, they must engage some philosophical methodologies. It is no surprise then, that their outputs (the articles written by self-described empirical researchers) often go well beyond simply adding to the existing body of empirical data describing prostitution and add as well to the range and quality of understanding concerning relevant concepts and salient considerations regarding prostitution.[1]

There is nothing especially troubling about empirical researchers dipping into philosophical methods or offering conclusions which draw upon their philosophical insights. (As I've noted, this cross-fertilization is necessary to some extent.) The trouble comes when empirical researchers do so without any appreciation that the concepts and considerations which form the object of their *empirical* study are also the object of *philosophical* study – that many of these concepts and considerations remain quite poorly understood (or at least hotly contested) at a philosophical level – and that empirical data alone will not resolve

## Table 1: Three Methodologies for Arguing about Prostitution

| | Empirical | Philosophical | Political |
|---|---|---|---|
| **Assumptions** | What happened or is happening in the real world matters (that is, past and current observable facts matter) | What happens in the real world can be stipulated without (much) loss[a] | What *will* happen in the real world in the future matters |
| | Convincing one's audience is secondary to reporting accurate data | Convincing one's audience is secondary to constructing sound, illuminating, arguments[b] | Convincing one's audience is at least as important as employing accurate data and constructing sound arguments |
| **Tasks** | Conduct empirical research regarding prostitution, with the aim of gathering empirical facts (that is, the facts that can be observed through sensory observation) – thereby adding to our body of empirical knowledge | Construct philosophical arguments regarding prostitution, with the aim of clarifying relevant concepts and identifying potentially salient considerations, and improving one's (and perhaps others') understanding of the matters under examination | Draw upon empirical and philosophical work of others (as well as other disciplines) to craft and implement prostitution policies, with the aim of advancing the best all-things-considered policies |
| **Conclusions** | Accounts of what has [happened] or is happening in the real world – at a narrowly focused level – issuing conclusions based primarily on the observed data in the particular study at issue (as compared to findings from similar empirical studies, where such studies are available for comparison) | Accounts of how best to understand relevant concepts and weigh potentially salient considerations – at a general level – issuing conclusions qualified by the acknowledgement that if stipulations regarding the real world do not hold, then neither do one's conclusions)[c] | Accounts of what purports to be the best all-things-considered laws and policies – at a level of generality appropriate to the jurisdiction in which one offers such an account |

| **Notes** | | |
|---|---|---|
| a | A prime illustration of this assumption is the large philosophical literature on Zombies, which now has its own entry in the Stanford Encyclopedia of Philosophy: http://plato.stanford.edu/entries/zombies/ . | |
| b | "Most philosophical inquiry aims at truth and understanding, not effect on practice" (Leiter 2007: 146). | |
| c | To his credit, de Marneffe is careful to make such a concession (39). | |

the conflicts with which philosophers are grappling.

According to our best philosophical accounts of consent, the question of whether prostitution is freely chosen is a question of whether the subjects' choice is *morally transformative* under the circumstances (Feinberg 1986: chs. 22–26; Hurd 1996; Schulhoffer 1998; Wertheimer 2000; Miller and Wertheimer 2010; Hyams 2011). The key question, in other words, is whether and how the subjects' choice affects the moral permissibility of another person's conduct. As Peter Westen puts the point, "consent matters because of the normative work it does" (Westen 2004: 15). What we need to know about consent then is not simply data we can glean from empirical observations; we need to know what kind of data might be relevant and how we should evaluate that data in reaching our conclusions. Any adequate answer to the question of whether prostitution is freely chosen, in any sense that matters, thus requires not only empirical data but philosophical argumentation.

Unfortunately, however, these philosophical complexities are not often acknowledged in empirical research regarding prostitution. Philosophers who have spent any time reflecting on the nature of concepts such as choice, voluntariness, consent, etc. will understandably find themselves perplexed when encountering social science prostitution literature that purports to prove *as an empirical matter* whether prostitution is generally free chosen, voluntary and/or consensual. For one example, a recent article entitled "Working Girls: Abuse or Choice in Street-Level Sex Work?" reports on an empirical study in which the subjects (women who previously engaged in prostitution) were presented questionnaires asking whether they "made a free choice to sex work" or were "forced into it by someone else." Several subjects responded "yes" to both options. The authors characterized the

response as a "problematic combination ... (since) it does not seem possible for someone to make a free choice and to be forced at the same time" (Harding and Hamilton 2009: 1126). Undeterred by this potential hiccup in their study, the authors conclude that it was "apparent that these women had been forced into making a choice to sex work, even though they ultimately believed that they made that decision for themselves" (Harding and Hamilton 2009: 1126). Bafflingly, the authors provided no context in which to evaluate or even understand their conclusions on this point.

There are multiple ways this empirical finding could have been reported by the authors. First, they could have acknowledged that, given their chosen methodology and research design, they were in a position to report only one small piece of empirical data: post-hoc self-reports of women's views regarding whether they believe they exercised free choice or were forced into prostitution. Moreover, the authors could have noted that this data is at least two steps removed from revealing what the subjects' own views of this matter were at the time, since the reports women give to academic researchers regarding such matters might not reflect their genuinely held views (Vanwesenbeeck 2001: 259) and the self-understandings of freedom and choice that women adopt after exiting prostitution might not reflect what their views were at the time they were prostituting.[2]

Second, the authors could have acknowledged that even the best-designed and most expertly executed empirical study regarding a subject's beliefs on the matter will not fully resolve the question of whether the prostitution was free or forced. Insofar as choice and force are evaluative concepts, we need more than empirical evidence to answer these questions. Rather, we need to engage in *evaluative* arguments to determine the presence or absence of freedom or force in any given context.

Rather than adopting either of these strategies for reporting their empirical data, however, the authors reported something entirely different: they reported their *evaluative* conclusion that the women had indeed been forced, as if it were merely an *empirical* matter. I take no position here on whether the authors' evaluative conclusion was justified; I mean only to note that the conclusion is not an empirical matter, but an evaluative one. Without more information regarding the empirical data and evaluative criteria employed by the authors in reaching their conclusion, their readers are not in a position to judge whether the conclusion was justifiable.

I do not mean to suggest that all empirical prostitution researchers are naive to these concerns – but even those who do have a sophisticated appreciation of these issues have an unfortunate tendency to retreat from them, rather than engaging their complexities. This retreat typically involves a move toward rejection of the forced/free distinction on grounds that the distinction itself is untenable (Augustin 2007: 35–40; Doezema 1998), or a drift toward a more explicitly political methodology. For example, Liz Kelly, one of the most insightful and reflective empirical researchers working on prostitution today, defends the refusal to draw any distinction between forced and free prostitution in her research because, she explains, the forced-free debate "is the wrong debate to be having, if we are interested in making a difference in the lives of women and girls" (Kelly 2003: 139). Amongst the reasons Kelly offers is the concern that drawing the forced-free distinction simply "plays into the hands" of abusive pimps and traffickers "who will escape sanction except in the most extreme cases" (Kelly 2003: 139).

By avoiding philosophical debates in order to advance political ends, these empirical researchers can be understood as having drifted away from an empirical methodology and adopted a more straightforwardly political one.[3] By constructing their research projects with an eye primarily on the task of making a difference in the real world and influencing their audience to adopt particular policies, they leave behind the paradigmatic task of the empirical researcher – that is, adding to our body of empirical knowledge.

While I share Kelly's interest in making a difference in the lives of women and girls (and, of course, do not wish for abusive pimps and traffickers to escape sanction), there are at least two reasons why the adoption of a political methodology by those who claim to be doing empirical research may prove problematic. First, empirical researchers focused on achieving political ends might miss an opportunity to gather empirical data that would better inform both philosophical arguments, and ultimately, political policy-making regarding prostitution. By taking the issue head-on and gathering data that is responsive to the sorts of considerations philosophers take into account in providing our best accounts of normatively transformative consent, empirical researchers and philosophers can stand in a symbiotic relationship with one another: toiling on the same task (understanding the reality of prostitution) alongside one another, employing our distinct methodological tool kits.

As Nicola Lacey has correctly observed, philosophers who are "engaged in theorizing social phenomena which have a real existence," bear a special responsibility, insofar as their "philosophical account is … in some sense answerable … to the contours" of that social phenomena (Lacey 2007: 138). Given that prostitution is a social phenomenon which has a real existence, when philosophers take up the task of providing a philosophical account of prostitution, they are answerable to the contours of how prostitution operates in the real world. If empirical researchers remain firmly committed to the assumptions and tasks of empirical methodologies, rather than drifting into more political methodologies, they will better provide the sort of data which can keep philosophers answerable to the contours of how prostitution actually operates in the social world.

The second reason why the drift toward a political methodology may prove problematic applies to empirical researchers, philosophers, and indeed, to all academics. John Gardner captures this concern well in extolling the virtues of a "bureaucratic conception of academic life":

Those who want academics to be intentionally and extensively engaged with public life are insufficiently aware, it seems to me, of the problem of counter productivity. Of course scholars ... can be an important check on excesses of public and private power. But scholars play this role best, as a rule, when they do not try to play it. For the most part, in their academic work, they should aim at true premises, valid arguments, clear thinking, attention to detail, avoidance of banality, and so forth, without regard to the consequences of their work, if any, for the development of public policy ... In particular, they should not confuse themselves with campaigners, pundits, advocates, or government advisors. Sticking to purely intellectual objectives is usually the best way (and is certainly the distinctive way) for them to avoid becoming corrupted by the system that they help to check. (Gardner 2007: 54)

Echoing this point, Fred Schauer observes that "not only philosophy, but also much of the best academic work more generally, ... seeks to avoid being an active player in current issues precisely in order to achieve that degree of distance or detachment necessary to give academics and their enterprise a comparative advantage over what exists in day-to-day public discourse" (Schauer 2007: 205).

I confess to being somewhat on the fence regarding whether these concerns are valid. Given the strength with which I share Liz Kelly's concern positively to affect the lives of women and girls, I wonder if the concerns articulated above are sufficient to establish that academic detachment is preferable to political engagement *qua* academic. The issue is one that clearly divides prominent legal philosophers as well, with John Gardner, Fred Schauer, Leslie Green and Brian Leiter broadly in support of a bureaucratic conception of the academic enterprise, while Nicola Lacey, Doug Husak, and Andrew von Hirsch remain more open to the notion that philosophers might appropriately aim to affect practice (Nielsen 2007). Indeed, according to Lacey "it surely goes without saying that legal philosophers have a general responsibility – like all scholars – to think about the effect of their work, on practice generally and not merely on legal practice" (Lacey 2007: 139) – whereas for Gardner and his ilk, this may be one thought too many.

I suspect de Marneffe sits on this fence alongside me. My suspicion was first piqued in his introduction, where he explains his rationale for adopting a paternalistic argument. Such an argument, he claims, "might actually be the strongest argument" because it might be "the most convincing to an impartial judge" (8). I may be reading too much into the passage, but if it suggests that de Marneffe's aim was to *convince* – rather than (or in addition to) articulating true premises, crafting valid arguments, demonstrating clear thinking, and so forth – then his aim might explain, at least in part, the methodological slippage I criticized.... By occasionally helping himself to the allure of scientific certainty regarding the realities of prostitution, rather than remaining content with his stipulations, de Marneffe crafted an argument that is, admittedly, more likely to persuade his audience. If his mixed motives resulted in somewhat of a mixed methodology at times, then I am hardly one to throw stones.[4] It does, however, raise a question for de Marneffe – and for all philosophers whose "theorizing is ... in some sense answerable ... to the contours ... of social phenomena." How do we properly engage in philosophical argumentation about real world phenomena like prostitution when we do not, as a discipline, study the empirical realities of what is happening in the world?

One answer to this question should clearly be rejected: that philosophers should become empirical researchers in order to earn the right to argue about prostitution. Inexplicably, this was the answer implied by a fellow philosopher in a recent review of de Marneffe's book (Schwarzenbach 2011):[5]

Regarding its empirical assumptions, de Marneffe's book not only makes selective use of the evidence (relying heavily on the sensational "prostitute as victim" literature), but the author also seems not to have interviewed even *one* professional sex worker for it.

The reviewer's suggestions here are two-fold. First, there is the suggestion that de Marneffe based his assumptions on partial and implausible empirical evidence regarding prostitution. While I do not agree with the substance of the complaint (and indeed, I thought de Marneffe's use of the empirical literature was commendably even-handed), I acknowledge that any philosopher who bases his arguments on empirical assumptions is liable to be criticized on grounds that his assumptions are implausible. This point simply echoes the one I made earlier regarding stipulations: they come with a cost – and unfortunately for de Marneffe, his reviewer in *Ethics* was not convinced.

The second suggestion being made by the reviewer is that she would have been inclined to give de Marneffe more leeway in making his assumptions if he had shored them up with a bit of empirical research of his own. If he had "interviewed even *one* professional sex worker" for the book, it seems the reviewer would have considered this a valuable addition to de Marneffe's methodological repertoire.[6] The implicit message underpinning the reviewer's second suggestion is that a philosophical methodology is not well-suited to addressing the issue of prostitution. Instead, anyone who wishes to be taken seriously when arguing about prostitution must jump on the empirical research bandwagon and drift away from philosophical methods in order to bulk up his real-world credentials. I, for one, could not agree less. While I remain somewhat uncomfortably on the fence regarding the methodological boundaries between the philosophical and the political, I remain firmly convinced that philosophers ought not to be chided into engaging in empirical research for the sake of being cut some slack by their readers. While it is true that having practical experience in an area can prove a rich source of philosophical insight, critiques of philosophical works should focus on appraising the quality of those insights – not on how the author came to possess them.

## References

Augustin, L. (2007). *Sex at the Margins*. London: Zed Books.

Cook, J., and M.M. Fonow. (1986). "Knowledge and Women's Interests: Issues of Epistemology and Methodology in Feminist Sociological Research." *Sociological Inquiry* 56(4): 2–29.

de Marneffe, P. (2010). *Liberalism and Prostitution*. New York: Oxford UP.

Dempsey, M.M. (2010). "Sex Trafficking and Criminalization: In Defense of Feminist Abolitionism." *University of Pennsylvania Law Review* 158: 1729–78.

Doezema, J. (1998). "Forced to Choose: Beyond the Voluntary v. Forced Prostitution Dichotomy." In J. Doezema and K. Kempadoo (eds.), *Global Sex Workers: Rights, Resistance, and Redefinition* (pp. 34–50). New York: Routledge.

Farley, M. (2006). "Prostitution, Trafficking and Cultural Amnesia: What We Must Not Know in Order to Keep the Business of Sexual Exploitation Running Smoothly." *Yale Journal of Law and Feminism* 18: 109–44.

Feinberg, J. (1986). *Harms to Self* (pp. 172–342). New York: Oxford UP.

Gardner, J. (2007). Interview. In M.E.J. Nielsen (ed.), *Legal Philosophy: 5 Questions* (pp. 45–57). London: Automatic P.

Harding, R., and P. Hamilton. (2009). "Working Girls: Abuse or Choice in Street-Level Work?" *British Journal of Social Work* 39: 1118–37.

Herman, J. L. (2003). "Hidden in Plain Sight: Clinical Observations on Prostitution." In M. Farley (ed.), *Prostitution, Trafficking and Traumatic Stress* (pp. 1–16). Binghamton, NY: Haworth P.

Hurd, H. (1996). "The Moral Magic of Consent." *Legal Theory* 2: 121–46.

Hyams, K. (2011). "When Consent Doesn't Work: A Rights-Based Case for Limits to Consent's Capacity to Legitimise." *Journal of Moral Philosophy* 8: 110–38.

Kelly, L. (1989). *Surviving Sexual Violence*. Minneapolis: U of Minnesota P.

_____. (2003). "The Wrong Debate: Reflections on Why Force Is Not the Key Issue with Respect to Trafficking in Women for Sexual Exploitation." *Feminist Review* 73: 139–44.

Lacey, N. (2007). Interview. In M.E.J. Nielsen (ed.), *Legal Philosophy: 5 Questions* (pp. 125–41). London: Automatic P.

Leiter, B. (2007). Interview. In M.E.J. Nielsen (ed.), *Legal Philosophy: 5 Questions* (pp. 143–51). London: Automatic P.

Miller, F.G., and A. Wertheime (eds.). (2010). *The Ethics of Consent*. New York: Oxford UP.

Nielsen, M.E.J. (ed.). (2007). *Legal Philosophy: 5 Questions*. London: Automatic P.

Phoenix, J. (2001). *Making Sense of Prostitution*. London: Palgrave Macmillan.

Schauer, F. (2007). Interview. In M.E.J. Nielsen (ed.), *Legal Philosophy: 5 Questions* (pp. 199–208). London: Automatic P.

Schulhoffer, S. (1998). *Unwanted Sex*. Cambridge, MA: Harvard UP.

Schwarzenbach, S.A. (2011). Book review. *Ethics* 121(2): 439–43.

Vanwesenbeeck, I. (2001). "Another Decade of Social Scientific Work on Sex Work: A Review of Research 1990–2000." *Annual Review of Sex Research* 12: 242–89.

Wertheimer, A. (2000). "What Is Consent? Why Is It Important?" *Buffalo Criminal Law Review* 3: 557–83.

Westen, P. (2004). *The Logic of Consent*. Burlington, VT: Ashgate P.

## Study Questions

1. What are the three methodologies Dempsey articulates with which one can argue about prostitution? Briefly explain each one. What are the ways in which these methodologies' boundaries tend to blur and inform each other? Which methodology would you choose to argue about prostitution? Why?

2. One glaring inconsistency in the United States is that pornographic movies are legal, yet with the exception of a small part of Nevada, prostitution is not. In pornographic movies, not only do people get paid to have sex, but there is undeniable evidence of this via the film. Choose a methodology that Dempsey presents and provide an argument that this inconsistency should be reconciled, either by ending pornographic movies or by legalizing prostitution.

3. Dempsey's full essay (edited for this anthology) begins in response to Peter de Marneffe's book *Liberalism and Prostitution* (Oxford UP, 2010). In the extract above she mentions his critics' views on his failure to engage in any empirical research by not interviewing even a single sex worker, suggesting "that a philosophical methodology is not well-suited to addressing the issue of prostitution." Take a position on this, drawing from the empirical and philosophical methodologies chart.

## Notes

1  For two insightful illustrations, from two distinct points of view on how best to conceptualize prostitution, see Farley 2006 and Phoenix 2001: ch. 3.
2  For a study of this phenomenon regarding sexual violence more generally, see Kelly 1989. For discussion in the context of prostitution, see Herman 2003.
3  This drift is explicitly encouraged by much of the literature on feminist methodologies in the social sciences. See, e.g., Cook and Fonow 1986. I do not wish to suggest there is a clear demarcation between the empirical and political, but simply to suggest that there is some distinction between pursuing research with an eye primarily toward providing an account of how the world is according to sensory observations (what I am calling the empirical approach) and pursuing research with an eye primarily toward changing the world (what I am calling a political approach).
4  Arguably, I have been guilty of going too far in the other direction, relying on stipulation at the expense of empirical evidence (Dempsey 2010). For reasons I hope are now somewhat more clear, I remain (mostly) convinced that this reliance was justified by my methodological commitments, even if they come at the expense of convincing my audience.
5  Moreover, this review appeared in the journal *Ethics* – a leading journal for academic philosophers, which is particularly well-regarded for its book reviews of new philosophical works – philosophers reviewing the work of other philosophers.
6  Indeed, the reviewer goes on to ground her critique of de Marneffe's assumptions based on her own real world experiences as friend and teacher to women in prostitution – thus shoring up her own empirical credentials.

# Section IV:
# Uncovering Oppression

What if … [white politicians who identified with black Americans] launched campaigns castigating America for the racism that most whites refuse to acknowledge and few blacks can escape? What if they called on whites to give up their privileges and join with blacks for major social reforms needed by all? Would their celebrity-amplified voices move whites to explore the depth and breadth of racism that every black has experienced first-hand?

– Derrick Bell, *Paul Robeson: Doing the State Some Service*

To say that the desire to persist in one's own being depends on norms of recognition is to say that the basis of one's autonomy, one's persistence as an "I" through time, depends fundamentally on a social norm that exceeds that "I," that positions that "I" ec-statically, outside of itself in a world of complex and changing norms…. To assert sexual rights, then, takes on a specific meaning against this background. It means, for instance, that when we struggle for rights, we are not simply struggling for rights that attach to my person, but we are struggling *to be conceived as persons*.

– Judith Butler, *Undoing Gender*

IRIS MARION YOUNG, IN her 1990 book *Justice and the Politics of Difference*, developed five conceptual frameworks with which to identify and analyze oppression (see I.6). Young developed her concepts of oppression by studying the social struggles of the 1960s and the 1970s in the United States, such as "democratic socialist, environmentalist, Black, Chicano, Puerto Rican, and American Indian movements; movements against US military intervention in the Third World; gay and lesbian liberation; movements of the disabled, the old, tenants, and the poor; and the feminist movement." What all these movements have in common, says Young, is that they each "claim in varying ways that American society contains deep institutional injustices."[1]

Oppression, according to Young, is "systematic institutional processes which prevent some people from learning and using satisfying and expansive skills in socially recognized settings, or institutionalized social processes which inhibit people's ability to play and communicate with others or to express their feelings and perspective on social life in contexts where others can listen."[2] This definition is meant to be expansive so as to include the five forms of oppression that Young identifies: exploitation, marginalization, powerlessness, cultural imperialism, and violence. What it helps us see is that to be interested in addressing oppression does not mean to be exclusively concerned with the distribution of advantages and disadvantages in society but, on an even deeper level, to be concerned with "the institutional conditions necessary for the development and exercise of individual capacities and collective communication and cooperation."[3] The reason one would focus on such institutional processes, rather than on distributive patterns alone, is that we can understand unjust distributive patterns only if we take into account the background institutional conditions that cause them to exist and be sustained in the first place.

This definition also identifies oppression as systematic. Oppression does not consist merely of individual acts but rather of social patterns. While negative beliefs and attitudes about certain groups of people can certainly help create oppressive conditions, oppression becomes a social reality when certain groups of people are systematically prevented – at economic, cultural or institutional levels – from learning, expressing themselves, developing their skills, gaining recognition from others in established social settings, having access to safe and healthful social spaces, having free time, having a say in their work, and communicating their own perspectives and experiences on social life to others. If such institutional processes are systematic, then they are also sociologically verifiable realities and not mere perceptions of mistreatment.

To whom does oppression happen? Young holds that it happens to social groups on account of their group identity.[4] The groups that we will look at in specific ways in this section are African Americans, transgendered individuals, and women. To say that such groups are oppressed is to say that they experience conditions that prevent them from being full members of society in one way or another. It is also important to note that not only does oppression prevent certain groups of people from learning, developing, and speaking but also, as a consequence, it simultaneously acts to privilege other groups, since groups stand in relation to each other.[5] As Young writes, "for every oppressed group there is a group that is *privileged* in relation to that group."[6]

Serena Parekh writes that Young understands oppression as "structural and systemic constraints resulting from the everyday practices of well-meaning people, rather than the intentional coercion of individual agents or a tyrannical ruler."[7] The connection between *practices* and *constraints* is important, for to be a member of an oppressed group is to be constrained or diminished in one's person and capacities by cultural, social or institutional practices. Parekh identifies three main features of Young's concept of oppression. First, oppression is not the product of anyone's intentions. To the contrary, oppression is caused by "norms and habits embedded in everyday life," which have the result of constraining the personal growth, communicative power, and cultural life of certain groups of people. Second, oppression is not caused by particular individuals but rather "results from the unconscious, habitual actions of millions of people." Third, because oppressive conditions are created by "background conditions, norms, habits and everyday interactions," they may not be recognized for what they are.[8] According to Parekh's analysis, then, oppression for Young is non-intentional, collective (habitual), and difficult to recognize. Putting Young's definition together with Parekh's, we can say that oppression consists of not specifically intended, widespread, and often difficult to recognize social conditions that have the result of preventing members of certain social groups from adequately and freely growing, loving, existing, speaking, living or achieving at levels on par with other social groups.

The 1997 definition of oppression specifically defined by Judy H. Katz and approved of by the Equity Mission Team is helpful for expanding on and concretizing the above discussion. This handbook defines oppression as follows and identifies three levels of oppression:

[Oppression is t]he systemic subjugation of one social group by another. Oppression is having the power to carry out systematic discriminatory practices through and with the support of major societal institutions. Examples are racism, sexism, heterosexism, classism, ageism, ableism, anti-semitism.

### Levels/Types of Oppression

**Level 1 – Individual** – attitudes, beliefs, socialization, interpersonal interactions, individual behaviors.[9]

**Level 2 – Institutional** – housing, employment, education, media, religion, health services (psychological & physical), government, legal system.

**Level 3 – Cultural/systematic** – values, norm, needs, language, standards of beauty, holidays, sex roles, societal expectations, logic system.[10]

Once we start thinking about the examples of racism, sexism, heterosexism, classism, ageism and so on that exist in the world, then we can begin to see how various background conditions, norms, and habits can oppress certain groups of people with respect to the levels outlined above.

Gay men, transgendered individuals, or lesbians, for example, can experience oppression at the *individual* level because individual deviations from heterosexual gendered behavior can often result in forms of physical or emotional cruelty. The cumulative effects of living in a society with heterosexual norms can also prevent LGBTQ people from fully realizing their potential, or indeed their humanity. This illustrates some of the individual costs of being a member of an oppressed group.

For an example of oppression at the *institutional* level, women have historically had to struggle for the right to vote, to gain access to formal education, and to seek employment in areas of their choice, as well as to receive the same pay as men do for the same jobs. These struggles were against attitudes, beliefs, and laws (or the lack thereof) that held, for example, "that women were equipped with few salable skills, or that the demands of household work were sufficient for them, or that females were intellectually and physically inferior" in comparison to men.[11] As an example, Abigail Adams implored her husband, John, in a letter she wrote to him in 1776, to ensure that women were legally represented in the United States. She wrote, "in the new code of laws which I suppose it will be necessary for you to make, I desire you would remember the ladies.... If particular care and attention is not paid to the ladies, we are determined to foment a rebellion, and will not hold ourselves bound by any laws in which we have no voice or representation."[12] Even before World War I, organizations were formed to advance the occupational and professional interests of women, such as the American Home Economics Association in 1881 and the American Association of University Women in 1884.[13] While women could attend college by the end of World War II, doors to administrative positions in education, law, and medicine still all too often remained closed.[14] The efforts of the women's movement of the 1960s and 1970s, and civil rights law prohibiting discrimination on the basis of sex, helped removed such barriers, but gender stereotypes still played a role in determining what women could do and how they were treated. For example, estimates in 1980 determined that whereas there were approximately 1.5 million K-12 female educators compared to 712,000 men, women were far less represented in the areas of administration; for example, only 15 per cent of principals were women. Men still dominated leadership roles in teachers' organizations as well. In 1981, "one of [the National Educational Association's] three executive officers [was] a woman; five of its nine-member Executive Committee [were] women; 67 of its 123-member Board of Directors, 22 of its 54 state affiliate presidents and 5 of its 54 state executive directors [were] women." Phi Delta Kappa, an educational research organization, was all male until 1973.[15] Blacks have historically experienced institutional oppression as well, since, even though the belief in equity and equality of opportunity is fundamental to the American way of life, blacks have been subject to numerous and various institutional barriers to equal opportunity in education as well as employment, housing, access to adequate medical care, and fair treatment under the law.[16]

For an example of oppression at the *cultural* level, in a survey of 5,206 children's books published between 1962 and 1964, only 6.7 per cent included even one black character.[17] Since literature is an important vehicle through which children are socialized and through which culture is transmitted, the lack of positive images of blacks in children's books during this time reflected the cultural dominance of whites. The omission of black characters from children's books could cause white children, finding only children like themselves in their books, to come to believe in the universality of the white experience and to develop negative stereotypes of blacks. Research on this matter has shown that

[f]or black children, the absence of positive images in children's books was a clear signal that they themselves had little worth in the society that these books reflected. All-white books do not permit black children to develop a strong sense of their own humanity, to affirm their sense of self-worth, or to discover their own identity within a group.[18]

In a study that surveyed 150 children's books from 1965 to 1979 that included at least one black character, a very small percentage were written from a black cultural point of view. Many of these books presupposed that all Americans shared the same white, middle-class life experiences. Then there were books that portrayed "Black children and families ... as exotic or alien and too often tainted with some of the stereotypes lingering from past literary portrayals. The White protagonists are often vehicles for conveying messages about the need to be empathetic, sympathetic, or at least tolerant in their interactions with the Black children and families with whom they are coming to contact."[19] This last group of books attempted to teach white children to *tolerate* blacks.

## Oppression in the Context of the Readings

The readings included in this section look at specific ways in which certain social groups are oppressed. Tommy J. Curry addresses what Young would identify as the oppression of violence and the oppression of cultural imperialism, the latter of which we will examine below. Concerning the oppression of violence, Young holds that a social group is oppressed if it must regularly deal with violent attacks and the fear of unprovoked harassment or assault. In particular, she writes that "[t]he oppression of violence consists not only in direct victimization, but in the daily knowledge shared by all members of oppressed groups that they are *liable* to violation, solely on account of their group identity. Just living under such a threat of attack on oneself or family or friends deprives the oppressed of freedom and dignity, and needlessly expends their energy."[20] Accordingly, we can identify police violence and harassment against blacks to be an example of violent oppression.[21] Curry argues that the cultural production of negative stereotypes of African-American men is largely responsible for creating the conditions through which systematic violence against these men is realized. He also argues that anti-black racism against African-American men is of a different order than anti-black racism against African-American women (although he does not look at the latter issue).[22] What this piece uncovers is that the oppression of cultural imperialism can be intimately connected to the oppression of violence.

To introduce the reading by Shari Collins-Chobanian, we must briefly consider the form of oppression that Young identifies as "powerlessness." For Young,

> The powerless are those who lack author-
> ity or power ... the powerless are situated
> so that they must take orders and rarely
> have the right to give them. Powerlessness
> also designates a position in the division of
> labor and the concomitant social position
> that allows persons little opportunity to
> develop and exercise skills. The powerless
> have little or no work autonomy, exercise
> little creativity or judgment in their work,
> have no technical expertise or authority,
> express themselves awkwardly, especially
> in public or bureaucratic settings, and do
> not command respect.[23]

The powerless are those who are typically classified as the working class. They are those who will be threatened or financially punished by management if they exercise even minimal forms of autonomy in the labor process. They are those who cannot speak out and who cannot influence conditions surrounding their work. The powerless also do not generally have access to social respect because of their low-level jobs or lack of professional qualifications. Powerlessness is not the same kind of oppression as exploitation or marginalization, but certainly those who are powerless will also often be exploited or marginalized. Collins-Chobanian looks at how the criminal-justice system keeps African Americans powerless in the United States by disproportionately jailing them for nonviolent drug offences.

To gain an awareness of the current status of the criminal-justice system, we should briefly consult the research of Michelle Alexander, a professor of law at the Ohio State University. In her 2011 book *The New Jim Crow*, she retells the legal and political history that led to the criminal-justice system becoming an effective and widespread social mechanism for the disempowerment and disenfranchisement of black and brown persons of color. We cannot review that history here, but we can summarize her main findings. Despite the fact that, as Alexander writes, according to a government survey conducted in 2000, "white youth were actually the *most likely* of any racial or ethnic group to be guilty of illegal drug possession and sales,"[24] as she writes in another context, "[m]ore than two million African Americans are currently under the control of the criminal-justice system – in prison or jail, on probation or parole,"[25] many of whom are in the criminal-justice system because of nonviolent drug offences. As Alexander explains,

> The drug war ... has been waged almost
> exclusively in poor communities of color,
> despite the fact that studies consistently
> indicate that people of all races use and
> sell illegal drugs at remarkably similar

rates. This is not what one would guess by peeking inside our nation's prisons and jails, which are overflowing with black and brown drug offenders. In 2000, African Americans made up 80 per cent to 90 per cent of imprisoned drug offenders in some states.[26]

Drug charges can be felonies or misdemeanors. Employers frequently reject candidates if they have misdemeanors, no matter how long ago the charge was filed, and felonies can act to strip individuals of political rights or bar them from receiving social services. As Alexander writes,

> [c]urrent felon-disenfranchisement laws bar 13 per cent of African American men from casting a vote, thus making mass incarceration an effective tool in voter suppression – one reminiscent of the poll taxes and literacy tests of the Jim Crow era. Employers routinely discriminate against an applicant based on criminal history, as do landlords. In most states, it is also legal to make ex-drug offenders ineligible for food stamps. In some major urban areas ... more than half of working age African American men have criminal records and are thus subject to legalized discrimination for the rest of their lives.[27]

What Alexander concludes from this is that current incarceration practices, which affect African Americans in an overwhelmingly adverse way, have created a social system similar to Jim Crow that acts to politically and socially disenfranchise blacks. Thus she states, explaining her thesis,

> Most people appreciate that millions of African Americans were locked into a second-class status during slavery and Jim Crow, and that these earlier systems of

racial control created a legacy of political, social, and economic inequality that our nation is still struggling to overcome. Relatively few, however, seem to appreciate that millions of African Americans are subject to a new system of control – mass incarceration – which also has a devastating effect on families and communities.[28]

Collins-Chobanian argues that because the criminal-justice system has the institutional effect of disproportionately disadvantaging African Americans, nonviolent drug charges raised against African Americans should be dismissed when brought to a jury. It is important to keep in mind, as Alexander says, that the high percentage of people of color in the criminal-justice system for drug offences cannot be explained by the prejudiced assumption that blacks or Hispanics use or sell drugs more than other racial or ethnic groups; this may well be a faulty inference based on the fact that law-enforcement practices target communities of color to make drug arrests. The criminal-justice system currently acts as a social mechanism which ensures that African Americans as a group, especially if they are from poor communities, remain poor and powerless; it thus acts as a very powerful agent of their oppression. Collins-Chobanian's support of race-based jury nullification could act as a means by which to combat such oppression.

Moya Lloyd looks at a type of oppression that Young would classify as both cultural imperialism and violence. Most basically considered, cultural imperialism

> involves the universalization of a dominant group's experience and culture, and its establishment as the norm. [Because the dominant cultural group has "exclusive or primary" access to public means of communication] ... the dominant cultural

products of the society, that is, those most widely disseminated, express the experiences, values, goals, and achievements of these groups. Often without noticing they do so, the dominant groups project their own experience as representative of humanity as such. Cultural products also express the dominant group's perspective on and interpretation of events and elements in the society, including other groups in the society, insofar as they attain cultural status at all.[29]

Lloyd argues that the 2002 killing of 17-year-old Gwen Araujo,[30] a transgender woman, was elicited by culturally dominant norms that can generally be identified as "heterosexist" and "homophobic." The Equity Mission Team (1997) approved of this definition of heterosexism as articulated by Cooper Thompson:

The belief in the inherent superiority of one pattern of loving and thereby its right to dominance. [Heterosexism can also be identified as] Social standards and norms which dictate that being heterosexual is better or more moral than being lesbian, gay or bisexual, and that everyone is heterosexual or should be.[31]

The handbook defines "homophobia" as "[t]he fear of feelings of love for members of one's own sex and therefore the hatred of those feelings in others."[32] Lloyd analyzes both Araujo's killing and the legal strategy that was used by defense lawyers in the trials following her killing. Instead of analyzing the defense lawyers' legal strategy in terms of heterosexism or homophobia, she does so in terms of "heteronormativity," the basic belief that the possession of male or female genitalia should designate one's sexual attraction to the "opposite" sex, which should be coupled

with corresponding, heterosexual gendered behavior and presentation. Lloyd believes that heteronormativity was a factor both in the defense lawyers' legal strategy to defend Araujo's killers and in the motivations of Araujo's killers. Like Curry, Lloyd draws close connections between the oppression of cultural imperialism, in this case, heteronormativity, and the oppression of violence, in this case, attacking, raping or killing transgendered individuals because they elicit in others feelings of normative outrage and panic.

The final reading is by Catharine MacKinnon, who was co-counsel for Mechelle Vinson in the 1986 US Supreme Court case *Meritor Savings Bank v. Vinson*, which questioned whether sexual harassment was in violation of Title VII of the Civil Rights Act of 1964 and thus constituted sex discrimination. The Court found that sexual harassment did violate Title VII. MacKinnon was one of the first legal scholars to employ the term "sexual harassment"; she uncovered the phenomenon of systematic sexual harassment against women in her 1979 book *Sexual Harassment of Working Women: A Case of Sex Discrimination*. She has also written influential pieces on prostitution, rape, hate speech, sex atrocities, race-based discrimination and pornography. Before reading her piece, one should review the definition of sexual harassment as defined by the US Equal Employment Opportunity Commission,[33] as well as the early efforts to enforce it as an attempt to address discriminatory practices in employment.[34] MacKinnon's article discusses the ideas she developed while representing Vinson. She explains why sexual harassment is something that systematically happens to women as women, whom she thinks belong to an oppressed group on account of their sex. She explains that sexual harassment was a long-standing and deep-rooted harm that women were well acquainted with but, prior to sexual harassment law, they could do nothing about nor even name. MacKinnon, in contrasting the times before and after sexual harassment law, brings to light the previously accepted powerlessness and assumed sexual availability of women and their incapacity to react against harms perpetrated against them by men often in positions of power.

The section begins with Charles Taylor's article "The Politics of Recognition." Taylor looks at civil or political oppression, which usually manifests in some form of discrimination, and at the oppression of one's cultural identity (what Young would call cultural imperialism), which usually manifests when, because one is a member of a certain culture, one is assimilated into, silenced by, or mispresented by a dominant cultural group. Taylor holds that these two political ideals – the ideal of nondiscrimination and the ideal of recognizing others in light of their difference – are both legitimate but can come into conflict, and states that the two ideals need to be balanced carefully in specific contexts.

## Notes

1   Iris Marion Young, *Justice and the Politics of Difference* (Princeton, NJ: Princeton UP), 7.
2   Young 38.
3   Young 39.
4   Young 9.
5   Fred L. Pincus and Natalie J. Sokoloff define oppression as "a dynamic process by which one segment of society achieves power and privilege through the control and exploitation of other groups, which are burdened and pushed down into the lower levels of the social order" (10). They go on to say that "Generally, systems of oppression includ[e] a combination of attitudes (prejudices), behaviors (discrimination), policies, social structures and ideologies" (10). Fred L. Pincus and Natalie J. Sokoloff, "Does 'Classism' Help Us to Understand Class Oppression?" *Race, Gender and Class* 15.1/2 (2008): 9–23.
6   Young 42; emphasis in original.
7   Serena Parekh, "Getting to the Root of Gender Inequality: Structural Injustice and Political Responsibility," *Hypatia* 26.4 (2011): 672–89, at 676.
8   Parekh 676–77.
9   These may be intentional by individuals or systematic.
10  Barbara A. Bitters, *Useful Definitions for Exploring Educational Equity* (Madison: Equity Mission Team, Wisconsin Department of Public Instruction, 1997), 12–13.
11  Mary Hatwood Futrell, "Organizing for Equal Opportunity in Education and Employment," *Educational Horizons* 60.1 (1981): 26–29, at 26.
12  "Letters Between Abigail Adams And Her Husband John Adams," The Liz Library, http://www.thelizlibrary.org/suffrage/abigail.htm.
13  Futrell 27.
14  Futrell 27.
15  Furtell 28.
16  For a review of discrimination in housing against African Americans, for example, see Ta-Nehisi Coates, "The Case for Reparations," *The Atlantic* June 2015, http://www.theatlantic.com/features/archive/2014/05/the-case-for-reparations/361631/.
17  Rudine Sims, "What Has Happened to the 'All-White' World of Children's Books?" *The Phi Delta Kappan* 64.9 (1983): 650–53, at 650.
18  Sims 650.
19  Rudine Sims Bishop, "Reflections on the Development of African American Children's Literature." *Journal of Children's Literature* 38.2 (2012): 5–13, at 7.

20  Young 62.

21  See Claudia Card's essay in in Section VIII. Card analyzes domestic violence and the stalking of women not in terms of oppression but in terms of terrorism. In that case, we may want to say that blacks who, by virtue of their group identity, are subject to violent oppression from police officers on account of law-enforcement practices are also subject to police terrorism.

22  Black women are killed by police officers, too. For a list of some recent victims, see Kate Abbey-Lambertz, "These 15 Black Women Were Killed during Police Encounters. Their Lives Matter, Too." *Huffington Post* 13 Feb. 2015, http://www.huffingtonpost.com/2015/02/13/black-womens-lives-matter-police-shootings_n_6644276.html.

23  Young 56–57.

24  Michelle Alexander, *The New Jim Crow: Mass Incarceration in the Age of Colorblindness* New York: The New P, 2011), 99.

25  Michelle Alexander, "The New Jim Crow: How Mass Incarceration Turns People of Color into Permanent Second-Class Citizens," *The American Prospect*, January/February 2011: A19–A21 at A20.

26  Alexander, "The New Jim Crow" A21.

27  Alexander, "The New Jim Crow" A20.

28  Alexander, "The New Jim Crow" A20.

29  Young 59.

30  Gwen Araujo's life has been dramatized on film. See Braun Entertainment Group (production co.) and Agnieszka Holland (director), *A Girl like Me: The Gwen Araujo Story*. New York: Lifetime, 2006.

31  Bitters 9.

32  Bitters 9.

33  See US Equal Employment Opportunity Commission, "Sexual Harassment," https://www.eeoc.gov/laws/types/sexual_harassment.cfm.

34  See US Equal Employment Opportunity Commission, "Enforcement Efforts in the 1980s: Early Aims at Eliminating Systemic Discrimination Generally," http://www.eeoc.gov/eeoc/history/35th/1980s/enforcement.html.

# 1. Charles Taylor, "The Politics of Recognition"

ONE OF THE MOST pre-eminent Canadian philosophers, Charles Taylor (b. 1931) is professor emeritus of philosophy at McGill University. He has written extensively on political philosophy and the history of philosophy. In this essay, from his edited volume *Multiculturalism: Examining the Politics of Recognition* (1994), Taylor discusses the modern politics of equal respect/dignity, which requires that everyone be treated equally under the law and be afforded the same basic rights and liberties, and the politics of difference, which maintains that members of non-dominant cultural groups should be afforded forms of public recognition and should not be erased, persecuted or suppressed by culturally dominant groups. He looks specifically at how the 1982 Canadian Charter of Rights and Freedoms, which speaks to the politics of equal respect/dignity, conflicted with Quebeckers' claim that French-Canadian culture should not be erased or suppressed by prioritizing individual freedoms and rights over the collective goal of cultural survival. At stake here is whether denying certain individuals freedoms would constitute a violation of their rights and whether the collective goal of cultural survival necessarily oppresses those who are not members of the dominant culture. Taylor asserts that there are models of liberalism that could justly uphold collective goals over some individual privileges.

---

I

A NUMBER OF STRANDS IN contemporary politics turn on the need, sometimes the demand, for *recognition*. The need, it can be argued, is one of the driving forces behind nationalist movements in politics. And the demand comes to the fore in a number of ways in today's politics, on behalf of minority or "subaltern" groups, in some forms of feminism and in what is today called the politics of "multiculturalism."

The demand for recognition in these latter cases is given urgency by the supposed links between recognition and identity, where this latter term designates something like a person's understanding of who they are, of their fundamental defining characteristics as a human being. The thesis is that our identity is partly shaped by recognition or its absence, often by the *misrecognition* of others, and so a person or group of people can suffer real damage,

real distortion, if the people or society around them mirror back to them a confining or demeaning or contemptible picture of themselves. Nonrecognition or misrecognition can inflict harm, can be a form of oppression, imprisoning someone in a false, distorted, and reduced mode of being.

Thus some feminists have argued that women in patriarchal societies have been induced to adopt a depreciatory image of themselves. They have internalized a picture of their own inferiority, so that even when some of the objective obstacles to their advancement fall away, they may be incapable of taking advantage of the new opportunities. And beyond this, they are condemned to suffer the pain of low self-esteem. An analogous point has been made in relation to blacks: that white society has for generations projected a demeaning image of them, which some of them have been unable to resist adopting. Their own self-depreciation, on this view, becomes one of the most potent instruments of their own oppression. Their first task ought to be to purge themselves of this imposed and destructive identity. Recently, a similar point has been made in relation to indigenous and colonized people in general. It is held that since 1492 Europeans have projected an image of such people as somehow inferior, "uncivilized," and through the force of conquest have often been able to impose this image on the conquered. The figure of Caliban [from Shakespeare's *The Tempest*] has been held to epitomize this crushing portrait of contempt of New World aboriginals.

Within these perspectives, misrecognition shows not just a lack of due respect. It can inflict a grievous wound, saddling its victims with a crippling self-hatred. Due recognition is not just a courtesy we owe people. It is a vital human need....

The importance of recognition is now universally acknowledged in one form or another; on an intimate plane, we are all aware of how identity can be formed or malformed through the course of our contact with significant others. On the social plane, we have a continuing politics of equal recognition. Both planes have been shaped by the growing ideal of authenticity, and recognition plays an essential role in the culture that has arisen around this ideal.

On the intimate level, we can see how much an original identity needs and is vulnerable to the recognition given or withheld by significant others. It is not surprising that in the culture of authenticity, relationships are seen as the key loci of self-discovery and self-affirmation. Love relationships are not just important because of the general emphasis in modern culture on the fulfillments of ordinary needs. They are also crucial because they are the crucibles of inwardly generated identity.

On the social plane, the understanding that identities are formed in open dialogue, unshaped by a predefined social script, has made the politics of equal recognition more central and stressful. It has, in fact, considerably raised the stakes. Equal recognition is not just the appropriate mode for a healthy democratic society. Its refusal can inflict damage on those who are denied it, according to a widespread modern view, as I indicated at the outset. The projection of an inferior or demeaning image on another can actually distort and oppress, to the extent that the image is internalized. Not only contemporary feminism but also race relations and discussions of multiculturalism are undergirded by the premise that the withholding of recognition can be a form of oppression....

## II

I want to concentrate here on the public sphere, and try to work out what a politics of equal recognition has meant and could mean.

... [T]he content of this politics has been the equalization of rights and entitlements. What is to be avoided at all costs is the existence of "first-class" and "second-class" citizens. Naturally, the actual detailed measures justified by this principle have varied greatly, and have often been controversial. For some, equalization has affected only civil rights and voting rights; for others, it has extended into the socioeconomic sphere. People who are systematically handicapped by poverty from making the most of their citizenship rights are deemed on this view to have been relegated to second-class status, necessitating remedial action through equalization. But through all the differences of interpretation, the principle of equal citizenship has come to be universally accepted. Every position, no matter how reactionary, is now defended under the colors of this principle. Its greatest, most recent victory was won by the civil rights movement of the 1960s in the United States. It is worth noting that even the adversaries of extending voting rights to blacks in the southern states found some pretext consistent with universalism, such as "tests" to be administered to would-be voters at the time of registration.

By contrast, the second change, the development of the modern notion of identity, has given rise to a politics of difference. There is, of course, a universalist basis to this as well, making for the overlap and confusion between the two. *Everyone* should be recognized for his or her unique identity. But recognition here means something else. With the politics of equal dignity, what is established is meant to be universally the same, an identical basket of rights and immunities; with the politics of difference, what we are asked to recognize is the unique identity of this individual or group, their distinctness from everyone else. The idea is that it is precisely this distinctness that has been ignored, glossed over, assimilated to a dominant or majority identity. And this assimilation is the cardinal sin against the ideal of authenticity.[1]

Now underlying the demand is a principle of universal equality. The politics of difference is full of denunciations of discrimination and refusals of second-class citizenship. This gives the principle of universal equality a point of entry within the politics of dignity. But once inside, as it were, its demands are hard to assimilate to that politics. For it asks that we give acknowledgment and status to something that is not universally shared. Or, otherwise put, we give due acknowledgment only to what is universally present – everyone has an identity – through recognizing what is peculiar to each. The universal demand powers an acknowledgment of specificity.

The politics of difference grows organically out of the politics of universal dignity through one of those shifts with which we

are long familiar, where a new understanding of the human social condition imparts a radically new meaning to an old principle. Just as a view of human beings as conditioned by their socioeconomic plight changed the understanding of second-class citizenship, so that this category came to include, for example, people in inherited poverty traps, so here the understanding of identity as formed in interchange, and as possibly so malformed, introduces a new form of second-class status into our purview. As in the present case, the socioeconomic redefinition justified social programs that were highly controversial. For those who had not gone along with this changed definition of equal status, the various redistributive programs and special opportunities offered to certain populations seemed a form of undue favoritism....

The politics of equal dignity is based on the idea that all humans are equally worthy of respect. It is underpinned by a notion of what in human beings commands respect, however we may try to shy away from this "metaphysical" background. For Kant, whose use of the term *dignity* was one of the earliest influential evocations of this idea, what commanded respect in us was our status as rational agents, capable of directing our lives through principles.[2] Something like this has been the basis for our intuitions of equal dignity ever since, though the detailed definition of it may have changed.

Thus, what is picked out as of worth here is a *universal human potential*, a capacity that all humans share. This potential, rather than anything a person may have made of it, is what ensures that each person deserves respect. Indeed, our sense of the importance of potentiality reaches so far that we extend this protection even to people who through some circumstance that has befallen them are incapable of realizing their potential in the normal way – handicapped people, or those in a coma, for instance.

In the case of the politics of difference, we might also say that a universal potential is at its basis, namely, the potential for forming and defining one's own identity, as an individual, and also as a culture. This potentiality must be respected equally in everyone. But at least in the intercultural context, a stronger demand has recently arisen: that one accord equal respect to actually evolved cultures. Critiques of European or white domination, to the effect that they have not only suppressed but failed to appreciate other cultures, consider these depreciatory judgments not only factually mistaken but somehow morally wrong. When Saul Bellow is famously quoted as saying something like, "When the Zulus produce a Tolstoy we will read him,"[3] this is taken as a quintessential statement of European arrogance, not just because Bellow is allegedly being de facto insensitive to the value of Zulu culture, but frequently also because it is seen to reflect a denial in principle of human equality. The possibility that the Zulus, while having the same potential for culture formation as anyone else, might nevertheless have come up with a culture that is less valuable than others is ruled out from the start. Even to entertain this possibility is to deny human equality. Bellow's error here, then, would not be a (possibly insensitive) particular mistake in evaluation, but a denial of a fundamental principle.

To the extent that this stronger reproach is in play, the demand for equal recognition extends beyond an acknowledgment of the equal value of all humans potentially, and comes to include the equal value of what they have made of this potential in fact. This creates a serious problem, as we shall see below.

These two modes of politics, then, both based on the notion of equal respect, come into conflict. For one, the principle of equal respect requires that we treat people in a difference-blind fashion. The fundamental intuition that humans command this respect focuses on what is the same in all. For the other, we have to recognize and even foster particularity. The reproach the first makes to the second is just that it violates the principle of nondiscrimination. The reproach the second makes to the first is that it negates identity by forcing people into a homogeneous mold that is untrue to them. This would be bad enough if the mold were itself neutral – nobody's mold in particular. But the complaint generally goes further. The claim is that the supposedly neutral set of difference-blind principles of the politics of equal dignity is in fact a reflection of one hegemonic culture. As it turns out, then, only the minority or suppressed cultures are being forced to take alien form. Consequently, the supposedly fair and difference-blind society is not only inhuman (because suppressing identities) but also, in a subtle and unconscious way, itself highly discriminatory.[4]

This last attack is the cruelest and most upsetting of all. The liberalism of equal dignity seems to have to assume that there are some universal, difference-blind principles. Even though we may not have defined them yet, the project of defining them remains alive and essential. Different theories may be put forward and contested – and a number have been proposed in our day[5] – but the shared assumption of the different theories is that one such theory is right.

The charge leveled by the most radical forms of the politics of difference is that "blind" liberalisms are themselves the reflection of particular cultures. And the worrying thought is that this bias might not just be a contingent weakness of all hitherto proposed theories, that the very idea of such a liberalism may be a kind of pragmatic contradiction, a particularism masquerading as the universal.

I want now to try to move, gently and gingerly, into this nest of issues.... I will first look at the politics of equal dignity....

## IV

... The notion that any of the standard schedules of rights might apply differently in one cultural context than they do in another, that their application might have to take account of different collective goals, is considered quite unacceptable. The issue, then, is whether this restrictive view of equal rights is the only possible interpretation. If it is, then it would seem that the accusation of homogenization is well founded. But perhaps it is not. I think it is not, and perhaps the best way to lay out the issue is to see it in the context of the Canadian case, where this question has played a role in the impending breakup of the country. In fact, two conceptions of rights-liberalism have confronted each other, albeit in confused fashion, throughout the long and inconclusive constitutional debates of recent years.

The issue came to the fore because of the adoption in 1982 of the Canadian Charter of Rights, which aligned our political system in this regard with the American one in having a schedule of rights offering a basis for judicial review of legislation at all levels of government. The question had to arise how to relate this schedule to the claims for distinctness put forward by French Canadians, and particularly Quebeckers, on the one hand, and aboriginal peoples on the other. Here what was at stake was the desire of these peoples for survival, and their consequent demand for certain forms of autonomy in their self-government, as well as the ability to adopt certain kinds of legislation deemed necessary for survival.

For instance, Quebec has passed a number of laws in the field of language. One regulates who can send their children to English-language schools (not francophones or immigrants); another requires that businesses with more than fifty employees be run in French; a third outlaws commercial signage in any language other than French. In other words, restrictions have been placed on Quebeckers by their government, in the name of their collective goal of survival, which in other Canadian communities might easily be disallowed by virtue of the Charter.[6] The fundamental question was: Is this variation acceptable or not?

The issue was finally raised by a proposed constitutional amendment, named after the site of the conference where it was first drafted, Meech Lake. The Meech amendment proposed to recognize Quebec as a "distinct society," and wanted to make this recognition one of the bases for judicial interpretation of the rest of the constitution, including Charter. This seemed to open up the possibility for variation in its interpretation in different parts of the country. For many, such variation was fundamentally unacceptable. Examining why brings us to the heart of the question of how rights-liberalism is related to diversity.

The Canadian Charter follows the trend of the last half of the twentieth century, and gives a basis for judicial review on two basic scores. First, it defines a set of individual rights that are very similar to those protected in other charters and bills of rights in Western democracies, for example, in the United States and Europe. Second, it guarantees equal treatment of citizens in a variety of respects, or, alternatively put, it protects against discriminatory treatment on a number of irrelevant grounds, such as race or sex. There is a lot more in our Charter, including provisions for linguistic rights and aboriginal rights, that could be understood as according powers to collectivities, but the two themes I singled out dominate in the public consciousness.

This is no accident. These two kinds of provisions are now quite common in entrenched schedules of rights that provide the basis for judicial review. In this sense, the Western world, perhaps the world as a whole, is following American precedent. The Americans were the first to write out and entrench a bill of rights, which they did during the ratification of their Constitution and as a condition of its successful outcome. One might argue that they weren't entirely clear on judicial review as a method of securing those rights, but this rapidly became the practice. The first amendments protected individuals, and sometimes state governments,[7] against encroachment by the new federal government. It was after the Civil War, in the period of triumphant Reconstruction, and particularly with the Fourteenth Amendment, which called for "equal protection" for all citizens under the laws, that the theme of nondiscrimination became central to judicial review. But this theme is now on a par with the older norm of the defense of individual rights, and in public consciousness perhaps even ahead.

For a number of people in "English Canada," a political society's espousing certain collective goals threatens to run against both of these basic provisions of our Charter, or indeed any acceptable bill of rights. First, the collective goals may require restrictions on the behavior of individuals that may violate their rights. For many nonfrancophone Canadians, both inside and outside Quebec, this feared outcome had already materialized with Quebec's language legislation. For instance, Quebec legislation prescribes, as already mentioned, the type of school to which parents can send their children; and in the most famous instance, it forbids certain kinds of commercial signage. This latter provision was actually struck down by the Supreme Court as contrary to the Quebec Bill of Rights, as well as the Charter, and only reenacted through the invocation of a clause in the Charter that permits legislatures in certain cases to override decisions of the courts relative to the Charter for a limited period of time (the so-called notwithstanding clause).

But second, even if overriding individual rights were not possible, espousing collective goals on behalf of a national group can be thought to be inherently discriminatory. In the modern world it will always be the case that not all those living as citizens under a certain jurisdiction will belong to the national group thus favored. This in itself could be thought to provoke discrimination. But beyond this, the pursuit of the collective end will probably involve treating insiders and outsiders differently. Thus the schooling provisions of Law 101 forbid (roughly speaking) francophones and immigrants to send their children to English-language schools, but allow Canadian anglophones to do so.

This sense that the Charter clashes with basic Quebec policy was one of the grounds of opposition in the rest of Canada to the Meech Lake accord. The cause for concern was the distinct society clause, and the common demand for amendment was that the Charter be "protected" against this clause, or take precedence over it. There was undoubtedly in this opposition a certain amount of old-style anti-Quebec prejudice, but there was also a serious philosophical point, which we need to articulate here.

Those who take the view that individual rights must always come first, and, along with nondiscrimination provisions, must take precedence over collective goals, are often speaking from a liberal perspective that has become more and more widespread in the Anglo-American world. Its source is, of course, the United States, and it has recently been elaborated and defended by some of the best philosophical and legal minds in that society, including John Rawls [1921–2002], Ronald Dworkin [1931–2013], Bruce Ackerman [b. 1943], and others.[8] There are various formulations of the main idea, but perhaps the one that encapsulates most clearly the point that is relevant to us is the one expressed by Dworkin in his short paper entitled "Liberalism."[9]

Dworkin makes a distinction between two kinds of moral commitment. We all have views about the ends of life, about what constitutes a good life, which we and others ought to strive for. But we also acknowledge a commitment to deal fairly and equally with each other, regardless of how we conceive our ends. We might call this latter commitment "procedural," while commitments concerning the ends of life are "substantive." Dworkin claims that a liberal society is one that as a society adopts no particular substantive view about the ends of life. The society is, rather, united around a strong procedural commitment to treat people with equal respect. The reason that the polity as such can espouse no substantive view, cannot, for instance, allow that one of the goals of legislation should be to make people virtuous in one or another meaning of that term, is that this would involve a violation of its procedural norm. For, given the diversity of modern societies, it would unfailingly be the case that some people and not others would be committed to the favored conception of virtue. They might be in a majority; indeed, it is very likely that they would be, for otherwise a democratic society probably would not espouse their view. Nevertheless, this view would not be everyone's view, and in espousing this substantive outlook the society would not be treating the dissident minority with equal respect. It would be saying to them, in effect, "your view is not as valuable, in the eyes of this polity, as that of your more numerous compatriots."

There are very profound philosophical assumptions underlying this view of liberalism, which is rooted in the thought of Immanuel Kant [1724–1804]. Among other features, this view understands human dignity to consist largely in autonomy, that is, in the ability of each person to determine for himself or herself a view of the good life. Dignity is associated less with any particular understanding of the good life, such that someone's departure from this would detract from his or her own dignity, than with the power to consider and espouse for oneself some view or other. We are not respecting this power equally in all subjects, it is claimed, if we raise the outcome of some people's deliberations officially over that of others. A liberal society must remain neutral on the good life, and restrict itself to ensuring that however they see things, citizens deal fairly with each other and the state deals equally with all.

The popularity of this view of the human agent as primarily a subject of self-determining or self-expressive choice helps to explain why this model of liberalism is so strong. But we must also consider that it has been urged with great force and intelligence by liberal thinkers in the United States, and precisely in the context of constitutional doctrines of judicial review.[10] Thus it is not surprising that the idea has become widespread, well beyond those who might subscribe to a specific Kantian philosophy, that a liberal society cannot accommodate publicly espoused notions of the good. This is the conception, as Michael Sandel has noted, of the "procedural republic," which has a very strong hold on the political agenda in the United States, and which has helped to place increasing emphasis on judicial review on the basis of constitutional texts at the expense of the ordinary political process of building majorities with a view to legislative action.[11]

But a society with collective goals like Quebec's violates this model. It is axiomatic for Quebec governments that the survival and flourishing of French culture in Quebec is a good. Political society is not neutral between those who value remaining true to the culture of our ancestors and those who might want to cut loose in the name of some individual goal of self-development. It might be argued that one could after all capture a goal like *survivance* for a proceduralist liberal society. One could consider the French language, for instance, as a collective resource that individuals might want to make use of, and act for its preservation, just as one does for clean air or green spaces. But this can't capture the full thrust of policies designed for cultural survival. It is not just a matter of having the French language available for those who might choose it. This might be seen to be the goal of some of the measures of federal bilingualism over the last twenty years. But it also involves making sure that there is a community of people here in the future that will want to avail itself of the opportunity to use the French language. Policies aimed at survival actively seek to *create* members of the community, for instance, in their assuring that future generations continue to identify as French-speakers. There is no way that these policies could be seen as just providing a facility to already existing people.

Quebeckers, therefore, and those who give similar importance to this kind of collective goal, tend to opt for a rather different model of a liberal society. On their view, a society can be organized around a definition of the good life, without this being seen as a depreciation of those who do not personally share this definition. Where the nature of the good requires that it be sought in common, this is the reason for its being a matter of public policy. According to this conception, a liberal society singles itself out as such by the way in which it treats minorities, including those who do not share public definitions of the good, and above all by the rights it accords to all of its members. But now the rights in question are conceived to be the fundamental and crucial ones that have been recognized as such from the very beginning of the liberal tradition: rights to life, liberty, due process,

free speech, free practice of religion, and so on. On this model, there is a dangerous over-looking of an essential boundary in speaking of fundamental rights to things like commercial signage in the language of one's choice. One has to distinguish the fundamental liberties, those that should never be infringed and therefore ought to be unassailably entrenched, on one hand, from privileges and immunities that are important, but that can be revoked or restricted for reasons of public policy – although one would need a strong reason to do this – on the other.

A society with strong collective goals can be liberal, on this view, provided it is also capable of respecting diversity, especially when dealing with those who do not share its common goals; and provided it can offer adequate safeguards for fundamental rights. There will undoubtedly be tensions and difficulties in pursuing these objectives together, but such a pursuit is not impossible, and the problems are not in principle greater than those encountered by any liberal society that has to combine, for example, liberty and equality, or prosperity and justice.

Here are two incompatible views of liberal society. One of the great sources of our present disharmony is that the two views have squared off against each other in the last decade. The resistance to the "distinct society" that called for precedence to be given to the Charter came in part from a spreading procedural outlook in English Canada. From this point of view, attributing the goal of promoting Quebec's distinct society to a government is to acknowledge a collective goal, and this move had to be neutralized by being subordinated to the existing Charter. From the standpoint of Quebec, this attempt to impose a procedural model of liberalism not only would deprive the distinct society clause of some of its force as a rule of interpretation, but bespoke a rejection of the model of liberalism on which this society was founded. Each society misperceived the other throughout the Meech Lake debate. But here both perceived each other accurately – and didn't like what they saw. The rest of Canada saw that the distinct society clause legitimated collective goals. And Quebec saw that the move to give the Charter precedence imposed a form of liberal society that was alien to it, and to which Quebec could never accommodate itself without surrendering its identity.[12]

I have delved deeply into this case because it seems to me to illustrate the fundamental questions. There is a form of the politics of equal respect, as enshrined in a liberalism of rights, that is inhospitable to difference, because (a) it insists on uniform application of the rules defining these rights, without exception, and (b) it is suspicious of collective goals. Of course, this doesn't mean that this model seeks to abolish cultural differences. This would be an absurd accusation. But I call it inhospitable to difference because it can't accommodate what the members of distinct societies really aspire to, which is survival. This is (b) a collective goal, which (a) almost inevitably will call for some variations in the kinds of law we deem permissible from one cultural context to another, as the Quebec case clearly shows.

I think this form of liberalism is guilty as charged by the proponents of a politics of difference. Fortunately, however, there are other models of liberal society that take a different line on (a) and (b). These forms do call for the invariant defense of *certain* rights, of course. There would be no question of cultural differences determining the application of *habeas corpus*, for example. But they distinguish these fundamental rights from the broad range of immunities and presumptions of uniform treatment that have sprung up in modern cultures of judicial review. They are willing to weigh the importance of certain forms of uniform treatment against the importance of cultural survival, and opt sometimes in favor of the latter. They are thus in the end not procedural models of liberalism, but are grounded very much on judgments about what makes a good life – judgments in which the integrity of cultures has an important place.

Although I cannot argue it here, obviously I would endorse this kind of model. Indisputably, though, more and more societies today are turning out to be multicultural, in the sense of including more than one cultural community that wants to survive. The rigidities of procedural liberalism may rapidly become impractical in tomorrow's world....

## Study Questions

1. Define the politics of difference and the politics of equal respect/dignity and provide examples of each. What is the moral grounding of the politics of difference and the politics of equal dignity? How are these moral groundings similar? Do you think there might be a way to fuse these two politics together or must they always conflict with each other?

2. According to Taylor, how can collective goals threaten individual rights, especially those enumerated in the Canadian Charter of Rights? What is the nature of such threats?

3. Identify the philosophical views of Dworkin and Kant which justify the claim that individual rights should have priority over collective goals. What do you find important about such reasoning? Do you think such reasons should be primary in determining how a society is politically structured?

4. Do you think Taylor can hold true to liberalism while upholding Quebec's interest in producing new members of the French-Canadian community?

## Notes

1 A prime example of this charge from a feminist perspective is Carol Gilligan's critique of Lawrence Kohlberg's theory of moral development, for presenting a view of human development that privileges only one facet of moral reasoning, precisely the one that tends to predominate in boys rather than girls. See Gilligan, *In a Different Voice* (Cambridge, MA: Harvard UP, 1982).

2 See Kant, *Grundlegung der Metaphysik der Sitten* (Berlin: Gruyter, 1968; reprint of the Berlin Academy edition), p. 434.

3 I have no idea whether this statement was actually made in this form by [Canadian-American writer] Saul Bellow [1915–2005], or by anyone else. I report it only because it captures a widespread attitude, which is, of course, why the story had currency in the first place.

4 One hears both kinds of reproach today. In the context of some modes of feminism and multiculturalism, the claim is the strong one, that the hegemonic culture discriminates. In the Soviet Union, however, alongside a similar reproach leveled at the hegemonic Great Russian culture, one also hears the complaint that Marxist-Leninist communism has been an alien imposition on all equally, even on Russia itself. The communist mold, on this view, has been truly nobody's. [Russian writer Aleksandr] Solzhenitsyn [1918–2008] has made this claim, but it is voiced by Russians of a great many different persuasions today, and has something to do with the extraordinary phenomenon of an empire that has broken apart through the quasi-secession of its metropolitan society.

5 See John Rawls, *A Theory of Justice* (Cambridge, MA: Harvard UP, 1971); Ronald Dworkin, *Taking Rights Seriously* (London: Duckworth, 1977) and *A Matter of Principle* (Cambridge, MA: Harvard UP, 1985); and Jürgen Habermas, *Theorie des kommunikativen Handelns* (Frankfurt: Suhrkamp, 1981).

6 The Supreme Court of Canada did strike down one of these provisions, the one forbidding commercial signage in languages other than French. But in their judgment the justices agreed that it would have been quite reasonable to demand that all signs be in French, even though accompanied by another language. In other words, it was permissible in their view for Quebec to outlaw unilingual English signs. The need to protect and promote the French language in the Quebec context would have justified it. Presumably this would mean that legislative restrictions on the language of signs in another province might well be struck down for some quite other reason.

Incidentally, the signage provisions are still in force in Quebec, because of a provision of the Charter that in certain cases allows legislatures to override judgments of the courts for a restricted period.

7 For instance, the First Amendment, which forbade Congress to establish any religion, was not originally meant to separate church and state as such. It was enacted at a time when many states had established churches, and it was plainly meant to prevent the new federal

government from interfering with or overruling these local arrangements. It was only later, after the Fourteenth Amendment, following the so-called Incorporation doctrine, that these restrictions on the federal government were held to have been extended to all governments, at any level.

8 Rawls, *A Theory of Justice* and "Justice as Fairness: Political Not Metaphysical," *Philosophy & Public Affairs* 14 (1985): 223–51; Dworkin, *Taking Rights Seriously* and "Liberalism," in *Public and Private Morality*, ed. Stuart Hampshire (Cambridge: Cambridge UP, 1978); Bruce Ackerman, *Social Justice in the Liberal State* (New Haven: Yale UP, 1980).

9 Dworkin, "Liberalism."

10 See, for instance, the arguments deployed by Lawrence Tribe in his *Abortion: The Clash of Absolutes* (New York: Norton, 1990).

11 Michael Sandel, "The Procedural Republic and the Unencumbered Self," *Political Theory* 12 (1984): 81–96.

12 See Guy Laforest, "L'esprit de 1982," in *Le Québec et la restructuration du Canada, 1980–1992*, ed. Louis Balthasar, Guy Laforest, and Vincent Lemieux (Quebec: Septentrion, 1991).

## 2. Tommy J. Curry, "Michael Brown and the Need for a Genre Study of Black Male Death and Dying"

TOMMY J. CURRY SPECIALIZES in Africana philosophy, the history of African American political philosophy, critical race theory, and anti-colonial theory, among other areas. In this article from the journal *Theory & Event* (2014), Curry theorizes that "anti-black chauvinism" contributes to specifically black male death in the United States and that this form of racism remains hidden from view even though its webs are dispersed and constant in the American mind. His writing corresponded to the outrage and sadness that spread across the United States in response to the police killing of unarmed 18-year-old Michael Brown, a black male, on 9 August 2014 in Ferguson, Missouri.

But say to a people: "The one virtue is to be white," and the people rush to the inevitable conclusion, "Kill the 'nigger'!"

— W.E.B. Du Bois, *Darkwater* (1920)

### Introduction

MICHAEL BROWN IS DEAD. His life was taken, August 9, 2014 by a police officer named Darren Wilson for jaywalking. He was executed in broad daylight with his hands up; his final moments being described by his friend Dorian Johnson as frightening, terror-filled, and violent.[1] Like the deaths of many Black men before him, Michael Brown was executed by a police officer and then blamed for his own death.[2] Justifications for the murder of Michael Brown ranged from him attacking the officer which resulted in the "broken eye-socket of Darren Wilson" to police propaganda directed at painting Mr. Brown as a robbery suspect posthumously.[3] This is not the first time nor will it be the last that Black men will be thought to deserve death for the danger they pose to society and the fear they inspire in the white imagination.

The unabated murder of Black males in America has a long history, a history whose study is now taken to be decadent and exclusionary. Despite Black males occupying the bottom of every measure of a population's health and prosperity, this reality is largely displaced by calls like that of Paul Butler urging us to deemphasize the actual depravations of Black males because attention to their specific ills risks perpetuating patriarchy. "Black men are still men," says Butler, "They don't have access to all the 'benefits' of the patriarchy, but they have some of them. To the extent that Black male exceptionalism allocates gender-based benefits, there is the danger that it reinforces gender-based hierarchy. In a patriarchal system, empowering men poses potential dangers."[4] But such a perspective does little to arrest the actual deaths of Black males in America or advance our understandings of the causes underlying their murder at the hands of an increasingly militarized police state. The disciplinary division asserted between Black men and boys and every other raced, gendered, and classed

241

subject, which is presumed to be "more op-pressed" purely from an arithmetic conducted upon race, class, and gender categories *a priori*, prevents a serious study of the relationship between the historical and political causes of the seemingly endless violence against Black males.... In failing to address the deeper causes responsible for the death of so many Black men, often at the hands of those seem-ingly charged with their protection, we fail to address America's long-standing predilection towards killing Black males that is not easily reduced to the fact of racism.[5]

While Black men and boys continue to die at the hands of the state and white vigilantes, disciplinary morality asserts that scholars should resist the urge to theoretically account for these deaths through any seri-ous philosophical or conceptual study. Black male scholars throughout the university have noted the resistance of journals and various disciplines to seriously consider Black male vulnerability beyond Black feminism or other paradigms which assume Black males to be culturally maladjusted and pathologically vio-lent.[6] Any study of Black male vulnerability is taken to be at odds with and thereby eras-ing Black female suffering. Conferences are reluctant to accept papers, editors discourage submitting such work for review, and there is a permissible vitriol towards the authors of such work allowing "booing," ridicule, and intimidation throughout the academy.... Black men are disproportionately affected by violence, incarceration, poverty, unemploy-ment, and suicide in this country, yet there is an insistence that the deaths of Black men need not be accounted for beyond "racism" in our current political milieu.[7] This mora-torium discourages research into dilemmas peculiar to Black males, ultimately coercing Black men into accepting their erasure as a matter of disciplinarity. This silence takes ad-vantage of the deaths which make Black men

underrepresented throughout society, and the racism making it unlikely that they will matriculate from high school, college, and ultimately *be* present and considered in the academy.[8]

Michael Brown's death, like that of Vonderitt Myers, Oscar Grant, John Crawford, Jordan Davis, and Stephen Watts, represents the accumulation of an intellec-tual failure to grasp the complexities and the motivations implicated within the genocidal logics of American racism. The negrophobia that drove white America to endorse lynching as a technology of murder is the same anxiety and fear that now allows the white public to endorse the murder of Black men and boys as "justifiable homicides." Black males are often killed by police officers because the officer claims they fear for their lives. This phobia is a normalized and institutional program used to justify police violence, ostracism, and in-carceration – it is a fear that is given so much weight in individual cases precisely because it is a fear that both white America and many racial and ethnic groups in America share as well. The vulnerability of Black men and boys lie in this consensus. The agreement that Black males can be killed and that the individuals responsible for these murders will be ideo-logically supported in their rationalizations and financially rewarded for their actions.[9] I am particularly concerned by the myth of the super-predator, and the disciplinary prolif-eration of similar pathological concepts about Black masculinity used to justify the murder of Black males in society and obscure the full viewing of Black male oppression in America.

## Lil Niggers: Black Masculinity and Negrophobia

The death of Michael Brown was not an aberration to American democracy, but the fulfillment of its promises of order and stabil-ity for the (white) majority. As historian A.J.

William-Myers notes in *Destructive Impulses: An Examination of an American Secret in Race Relations: White Violence*, "white violence … was part and parcel of the socioeconomic and political structure of the American democratic process."[10] Pointing to the "enormous capacity of American democracy to absorb unprecedented levels of violence and not be structurally damaged by it," Williams- Myers concludes that anti-Black violence and the societal legitimation of the white agents responsible for the death of Black people serve to maintain societal order, and bolster the implicit ideological power of white supremacy in America. *Stated differently, contrary to the democratic calls for justice currently insisted upon by activists and scholars alike, the deaths of Black men and boys in America serve to indicate the health of American democracy, not its malaise.*

For young Black boys, maleness in a white supremacist society is fraught with difficulty and the all too likely outcome of death. Even as men, this racialized masculinity is not thought to result in a recognizable intellectual maturity, and social standing of a citizen; rather the masculinity impressed upon these Black-male-bodies is known only through its uncontrollable excess, its lack of maturation, where any and all transgressions (no matter how small or idiosyncratic) are understood to be demonstrations of the more primitive and uncivilized aspects of a not yet evolved savagery. As Geoffrey Canada, President of the Harlem Children Zone, remarks, "The image of the male as strong is mixed with the image of male as violent. Male as virile gets confused with male as promiscuous. Male as adventurous equals male as reckless. Male as intelligent often gets mixed with male as arrogant, racist, and sexist … Boys find themselves pulled and tugged by forces beyond their control as they make the confusing and sometimes perilous trip to manhood."[11] The milieu from which Black manhood springs is saturated with racist caricatures that all seem to legitimate the fear Americans have of Black men. The images and perceptions of Black men as dangerous to society, women, and themselves ultimately create a pattern of thinking that works to justify their seemingly inevitable deaths. The relationship between anti-Black racism (the hate of Blacks) and anti-Black chauvinism (the hate of Black males as the barbarous sex) is not adequately captured by a focus on the manhood denied to Black men and boys. Such positions erroneously depict Black men as purely mimetic creatures incapable of generating identities outside of the decadent tropes offered by white patriarchy. A more correct analysis of racism and chauvinism would understand that Black male oppression and death is rooted in an imposition of a deadly masculine caricature − a barbarism justifying multiple genocidal logics and encouraging a racist misandry throughout this society and the disciplines birthed from it. Ultimately, Black male suffering is made generic, thought to only be the function of "racism," so in an era pushing intellectuals and policy-makers alike to be anti-essentialist (problematizing racial explanations of inequality), Black men are deemed "unfit" for study.

The Black male is not born a patriarchal male. He is raced and sexed peculiarly, configured as barbaric and savage, imagined to be a violent animal, not a human being. His mere existence ignites the negrophobia taken to be the agreed upon justification for his death. Black male death lessens their economic competition with, as well as their political radicality against, white society. It is this fear of Black males that allows society to support the imposition of death on these bodies, and consent to the rationalizations the police state offer as their justifications for killing the Black-male-beast (the rapist, the criminal, and the deviant-thug). The young Black male's death, the death of Black boys, is merely an extension of this logic – the need to destroy the Black beast cub before it matures into full pathology. The Black boy, that child, is seen as the potential Nigger-beast. This anti-Black dynamic which specifically affects the Black boy has been referred to by Elaine Brown as a new kind of racism, a racism built upon the anti-Black mythology of America's Black males as the super-predator. This super-predator mythology not only acts to legitimize the violence responsible for the deaths of Black males, but inculcates the rationalization that given what Black males actually are, Black male death is necessary and an indispensable strategy for the safety and security of American society.[12] Overlooking the genocidal disposition of America towards Black males presents an incomplete diagnosis of the impetus behind the levels of violence and sanctions imposed upon Black communities (Black women, Black families) in an effort to control the lives of young Black males.[13]

Even childhood cannot protect young Black boys from the genocidal logics of American society. "Black boys are seen as more culpable for their actions (i.e., less innocent) within a criminal justice context than are their peers of other races."[14] Because Black boys are actually perceived as older as and hence more culpable for their behavior, there is an implicit dehumanization that "not only predicts racially disparate perceptions of Black boys but also predicts racially disparate police violence toward Black children in real-world settings."[15] Police often imagine the Black boy – a child – to be physically threatening; the manifestation of the savagery thought to be inherent to his Black maleness; a violent beast and predator. The association of Black males with animals, specifically apes and monkeys, diminishes our sympathies for their humanity; caricatures found to not only increase the propensity for, but also the acceptance of greater levels of violence directed towards them. Phillip A. Goff's implicit bias research has explained that the association between the Negro and ape is not simply an abstract and detached stereotype, but rather a historical trope used to justify the dehumanization of Black people which is "a method by which individuals and social groups are targeted for cruelty, social degradation, and state-sanctioned violence."[16] Black male death and dying is the result of this engineered societal program, and the machinations of this apparatus obscures and in many cases denies our ability to see the lives of Black men and boys as worthwhile.

## A Conclusion Gesturing Towards a Genre Study of Black Male Death and Dying

In "No Humans Involved," Sylvia Wynter urges the reader to consider the relationship between the paradigms of dehumanization that resulted in the genocide of Armenians by Turkish pan-nationalists, the holocaust inflicted upon Jews by the Germans, and the language used to describe Black men as a species deserving death. Because Black men are thought to be "not human," there is a tendency to embrace their sociological condition as their essential characteristics. Black males are thought to be the origins of their conditions rather than their conditions being the origin of their problems. The designation of Black males as problems in society, simultaneously enforced by our academic theories demanding the de-emphasis of their plight, allows such ideologies to operate without challenge. Such conceptualizations, contends Wynter, "while not overtly genocidal, are clearly serving to achieve parallel results: the incarceration and elimination of young Black males by ostensibly normal and everyday means."[17] Similarly, Huey P. Newton has argued in "Fear and Doubt" that "society responds to [the lower socioeconomic Black man] as a thing, a beast, a nonentity, something to be ignored or stepped on. He is asked to respect laws that do not respect him."[18] Ultimately, it is the Black men and boys who remain isolated, condemned, and ignored by theory that "have been made to pay the 'sacrificial costs' for the relatively improved conditions since the 1960s that have impelled many black Americans out of the ghettos and into the suburbs."[19] Black males are the depositories of the negativity traditionally associated with Blackness that makes transcendence, socially, politically and conceptually, possible for other Black bodies.

There is an eerie connection between the deaths of Black males in society and the erasure of Black men from the realm of theory. In reality, Black males are genre-ed as non-human and animalistic in the minds of whites,[20] but our theories relish assigning the death of Black males to the generic description of racism, a notion not thoroughly analyzed in identity scholarship and unable to adequately capture the specific kind of oppression and violence that defines Black male existence. Michael Brown was a victim; a display of the power white life has over this *kind* of Black existence – a demonstration of the seemingly endless limit of white individuals' power to enforce the anti-Black consensus of society towards these specific Black-male *kinds*. His death – *Black Male Death* – shows that racism is not simply racial antipathy, but the power whites assert over the world, thereby making Black life inconsequential in its rush to acquire ownership over reality; a dynamic creating the orders of knowledge as an extension of the order of society necessary to maintain anti-Blackness and preserve white supremacy. Because this racist societal architecture is de-emphasized, academic discourse(s) of race-class-gender – presupposing the infinite power of all male bodies – prefigures a conceptual calculus dedicated to eradicating the vulnerability of Black men because they are men. Black men are thought to be mimetic (white) patriarchs; an untenable theoretical position given the empirical evidence of Black male disadvantage, but one that serves to affirm society's assuredness in holding that *his* death is the only way to remedy the dangers *he* poses to society. We can see the corpse of Michael Brown, but do we really understand the vulnerability of Black boys enough to theorize his life?

## Study Questions

1. Describe and name the particular kind of racism that Curry thinks is imposed on black men and boys in the United States. Do you think shows like *Cops*, *Jail*, and *Lockup* could be called "cultural products" that distribute the kind of racism that Curry thinks is imposed on black men and boys?

2. Curry argues that there is a connection between the particular kind of racism imposed on black men in the US and police violence inflicted on black men and boys. What is this connection?

3. Assume, as Curry does, that there is a strong link between what he calls "anti-Black chauvinism" and police violence against black men. What do you think Curry would say about what needs to change in order to undo the root causes of police violence against black men?

4. Curry doesn't speak about women and the multiple kinds of brutal violence that they regularly face regardless of ethnicity or race. Why do you think that is?

## Notes

1 Trymaine Lee, "Eyewitness to Michael Brown Shooting Recounts His Friend's Death," MSNBC.com, 12 August 2014, http://www.msnbc.com/msnbc/eyewitness-michael-brown-fatal- shooting-missouri.

2 Frances Roble and Julie Bosman, "Autopsy Shows Michael Brown Was Struck at Least 6 Times," New York Times.com, 17 August 2014, http://www.nytimes.com/2014/08/18/us/michael-brown-autopsy-shows-he-was-shot- at-least-6-times.html?_r=0.

3 German Lopez, "Did Darren Wilson Have a Broken Eye Socket after His Encounter with Michael Brown?," Slate.com, 21 August 2014, http://www.vox.com/xpress/2014/8/21/6054237/source-to-cnn-darren-wilson-didnt-have-a-fractured-eye-socket. For a discussion of the robbery accusation, see Mark Peters and Ben Kensling, "Police: Officer Wasn't Aware Michael Brown Was Suspect in Alleged Robbery," Wall Street Journal.com, 15 August 2014, http://online.wsj.com/articles/police-name-darren-wilson-as-officer-in-ferguson-missouri-michael-brown- shooting-1408108371, and Trymaine Lee and Michele Richinick, "Police: Michael Brown Stopped because He Blocked Traffic," MSNBC.com, 15 August 2014, http://www.msnbc.com/msnbc/ferguson-police-name-michael-brown.

4 Paul Butler, "Black Male Exceptionalism: The Problems and Potential of Black Male Focused Interventions," *Du Bois Review* 12.2 (2013): 485–511, 503. Ironically, only Black men seem to be subject to this kind of analysis. We do not hear race-crits objecting to programs for white women on the basis of perpetuating white supremacy, nor do we hear objections to equal pay initiatives for women despite Black men holding less wealth and income than white women, and less education, social mobility, and income once we factor in zero employment and incarceration when compared to Black women (see Becky Pettit's *Invisible Men*).

5 Our current configurations of race, class, and gender blind us to the historic victimization of Black males by making certain types of oppression categorically attached to the female body. Black men were raped by white men and women, see Thomas Foster, "The Sexual Abuse of Black Men Under American Slavery," *Journal of the History of Sexuality* 20.3 (2011): 445–464, and eaten by whites in rituals of cannibalism – a ritual specific to the kind of raced thing the Black male was – see Vincent Woodard, *The Delectable Negro: Human Consumption and Homo-Eroticism within Slave Culture*, eds. Justin A. Joyce and Dwight McBride (New York: New York UP, 2014).

6 See T. Hasan Johnson, "From Amadou Diallo to Mike Brown: Challenging the Institutionalized Profitization of Black Male Hatred in Law Enforcement, Media, and Extremist Black Feminism," Black Masculinism and New Black Masculinities, last modified 16 August 2014, http://newblackmasculinities.wordpress.com/2014/08/16/hatred_of_black_men/.

7 Black men and boys are at the bottom of every demographic study. See James B. Stewart and Joseph W. Scott, "The Institutional Decimation of Black American Males," *Western Journal of Black Studies* (1978): 82–92 for the relationship between Black male incarceration and societal viability. For a discussion of how stereotypes about Black males being criminals and dishonest affect employment, see Ronald B. Mincy, eds., *Black Males Left Behind* (Washington DC: The Urban Institute P, 2006). For a discussion of how Black male incarceration and unemployment not only show that Black males have lower incomes than their female and racial counterparts, but also how incarceration creates sample bias across all datasets used to understand Black men and boys, see Becky Pettit, *Invisible Men: Mass Incarceration and the Myth of Black Progress*

(New York: Russell Sage Foundation, 2012). For Black male vulnerability to domestic abuse, see Carolyn M. West, "Partner Abuse in Ethnic Minority and Gay, Lesbian, Bisexual, and Transgender Populations," *Partner Abuse* 3.3 (2012): 336–57.

8  Historically, Black men have been the most disadvantaged in education; see Anne McDaniel et al., "The Black Gender Gap in Educational Attainment: Historical Trends and Racial Comparisons," *Demography* 48 (2011): 889–914.

9  See Becky Bratu, "After Zimmerman's Website Raises More than $200,000, Prosecution Asks Judge to Raise Bond," MSNBC.com, 27 April 2012, http://usnews.nbcnews.com/_news/2012/04/27/11427416-after-zimmermans- website-raises-more-than-200000-prosecution-asks-judge-to-raise-bond. Also see Natalie DiBlasio, "Cash Raised for Mo. Cop Surpasses Brown Donations," USAToday.com, 24 August 2014, http://www.usatoday.com/story/news/nation/2014/08/23/support-darren-wilson-rally/14495459/.

10  A.J. William-Myers, *Destructive Impulses: An Examination of an American Secret in Race Relations: White Violence* (Lanham: UP of America, 1995), 10.

11  Geoffrey Canada, *Reaching up for Manhood: Transforming the Lives of Boys in America* (Boston: Beacon P, 1998), xiii.

12  Elaine Brown, *The Condemnation of Lil B: New Age Racism in America* (Boston: Beacon P, 2002).

13  Our present configurations of race, class, and gender exclude material accounts of the role that criminogenic accounts have on the lives of Black people generally and how this affects Black women specifically. The death of Rekia Boyd for instance was the consequence of an off-duty cop (Dante Servin) shooting at Antonio Cross; see Erin Meyer, "Rekia Boyd's Friend Sues Chicago Cop Who Killed Unarmed Woman," DNAinfoChicago.com, 21 March 2013, http://www.dnainfo.com/chicago/20130321/chicago/rekia-boyds-friend-sues-chicago-cop-who-killed-unarmed-woman. The force used to apprehend Chauncey Owens similarly caused the death of Aiyana Stanley-Jones; see Diane Bukowski, "Owens Never Said Aiyana Jones Dad Gave Him the Gun Used in Teen's Killing," VoiceofDetroit.net, 23 May 2011, http://voiceofdetroit.net/2011/05/23/owens-never-said-aiyana-jones%E2%80%99-dad-gave-him-gun-used-in- teen%E2%80%99s-killing/.

14  Phillip Attiba Goff et al., "The Essence of Innocence: Consequences of Dehumanizing Black Children," *Journal of Personality and Social Psychology* 106.4 (2014): 526–45, 540.

15  Ibid.

16  Phillip Attiba Goff et al., "Not Yet Human: Implicit Knowledge, Historical Dehumanization, and Contemporary Consequences," *Journal of Personality and Social Psychology* 94.2 (2008): 292–306.

17  Sylvia Wynter, "No Humans Involved: An Open Letter to My Conception," *Voices of the African Diaspora: The CAAS Research Review* 8.2 (1992): 13–16, 14.

18  Huey P. Newton, "Fear and Doubt," in *Essays from the Minister of Defense* (USA: Black Panther Party), 15–18, 17.

19  Wynter, "No Humans Involved," 14.

20  In an "Interview in Proudflesh," *Proudflesh: New Afrikan Journal of Culture, Politics & Consciousness* 4 (2006): 1–36, Sylvia Wynter says, "I coined the word 'genre,' or I adapted it, because 'genre' and 'gender' come from the same root. They mean 'kind,' one of the meanings is 'kind.' Now what I am suggesting is that 'gender' has always been a function of the instituting of 'kind.' For example, in our order, which is a bourgeois order of kind, a bourgeois order of the human, the woman was supposed to be the housewife and the man was supposed to be the breadwinner. Each was as locked into their roles. By making the feminist movement into a bourgeois movement, what they've done is to fight to be equal breadwinners. This means that the breadwinning man and the breadwinning woman become a new class, so that the woman who remains in her role becomes a part of a subordinated class" (24).

# 3. Shari Collins-Chobanian, "Analysis of Paul Butler's Race-Based Jury Nullification and His Call to Black Jurors and the African American Community"

SHARI COLLINS-CHOBANIAN'S AREAS OF specialization include environmental ethics, business ethics, and applied ethics. In this article from the *Journal of Black Studies* (2009), she considers lawyer and professor Paul Butler's 1995 call to African American jurors to exercise their right to nullify cases brought to a jury when there are African American defendants who have been charged with nonviolent offenses and his call to African-American communities to help African Americans charged with nonviolent drug offences. He offered these proposals because African Americans are disproportionately affected by the criminal-justice system and therefore ought not to be further disadvantaged because of nonviolent offenses. Collins-Chobanian considers Butler's proposals in light of Andrew D. Leipold's criticisms of them. Leipold claims that Butler's race-based nullification proposal is overhasty, that he has not sufficiently taken into account the possibility that African-American communities are not equipped to treat or care for addicts, and that Butler's race-based nullification proposal, if acted on, would inspire racial bias. Collins-Chobanian responds to these criticisms and argues that Butler's race-based nullification proposal is reasonable and just.

---

PAUL BUTLER (1997B) noted,

> I wrote an academic article in which I suggested that black jurors ought to be thoughtful about who they send to prison. Murderers, rapists, robbers: absolutely yes, for the safety of the community. But when black people are prosecuted for drug offenses and other victimless crimes, I recommended that jurors consider nullification – their legal power to ignore the written-down law in favor of a broader notion of justice.
>
> All hell broke loose. One will never go broke overestimating the power of the black criminal to invoke America's wrath…. The article in the law review was featured on all the major network news programs … all for advocating the simple idea that when it comes to criminal justice, what is good enough for white people is good enough for African Americans. If whites are not … prosecuted … for certain conduct, blacks should not be either.
>
> That apparently is a radical notion. I had hoped my article would engender some debate in the academic community. I had not expected death threats. (pp. 12–13)

Butler (1995) received national attention for his article "Racially-Based Jury Nullification: Black Power in the Criminal Justice System." Therein he argues that African American jurors ought to exercise their right of nullification (a common law right of jurors to decide both matters of fact and law) when there are African American defendants of nonviolent crimes. That is, jurors should refuse to convict nonviolent African Americans or nullify the law under which they are being prosecuted, in part to make up for the oppression African Americans suffer at the hands of White society and in the racist criminal justice system and in part because he argues that the African American community can better address these defendants. Butler states that in the face of our current justice system, it is the "moral responsibility of black jurors to emancipate some guilty black outlaws" (p. 679). Butler points to the community to find ways to deal with their own "outlaws" and to develop true rehabilitative measures. Butler wrote this in 1995, and at that time, it was estimated that by the year 2000, 1 in 10 Black men would be in prison. The most recent statistics available from the US Department of Justice (2005) show that as of June 30, 2005, nearly 12% of Black males in their late 20s were in prison (Harrison and Beck, 2006).

In this article, I begin by defining and briefly discussing the history of jury nullification and some examples of its use. I then summarize Butler's call to African Americans to use jury nullification and critically review Leipold's (1996) dissenting response to Butler's race-based proposal. I argue that Butler's jury nullification proposal is a principled tool to use "in the meantime" while working to change disparate impact and treatment in the criminal justice system, and I address the somewhat problematic issue of returning nonviolent offenders back to the community....

**Part 1: Jury Nullification**

Jury nullification comes from common law and is considered a check on oppressive governments and policies and thus an important guarantor of our basic freedoms. Jury nullification occurs when the jury refuses to convict an obviously guilty defendant. The defendant has broken the law, but jurors either consider the law to be unjust, unfairly applied (especially to certain groups of people), anachronistic, or problematic in some way that justifies the release of the guilty defendant from the legal consequences of his or her action. Notably, before the US Civil War, in prosecutions under the fugitive slave law, jurors regularly practiced nullification (Marder, 1999).

Presently, jury nullification is often associated with juror prejudice and seen as illegitimate because of such cases where White jurors have freed White defendants guilty of crimes against Blacks. In the United States today, it has been assumed that the jury does not have a right to ignore the court's legal instructions, the jury is not informed of nullification, and counsel cannot argue for it. Courts refuse to inform juries of minimum mandatory sentences out of fear of nullification. It is still often used in death penalty cases when there is no sentencing discretion and when the law is perceived as unfair.

Farnham (1997) concludes that

> the schizophrenic approach to nullification has become the norm: the courts will not instruct on it and will not permit counsel to argue it because of fears of *jury lawlessness*. At the same time, judges acknowledge the important historical role it has played in the development of American freedoms. (p. 13)

It is clear that jurors can and do nullify for many reasons, or perhaps without reason. Nullification is a common law right, one that would benefit from public analysis, debate, and principled guidelines. Butler's model proposes just such a principled use of nullification.

**Part 2: Statistics and Cases**

Criminal Justice System Statistics

Before turning to his model for jury nullification, I will highlight a few of the statistics
he cites regarding African Americans in the
criminal justice system as well as many Jerome
Miller provides in *Search and Destroy: African
American Males in the Criminal Justice System.*

A National Center on Institutions and
Alternatives study (as cited in Butler, 1995)
found that in 1991, in Baltimore, Maryland,
56% of African Americans ages 18 to 35
were under the jurisdiction of the criminal
justice system, including probation, parole,
imprisonment, and awaiting trial. Miller's
study (as cited in Butler, 1995) pointed out
that the percentage was 42% in Washington,
DC. Tillman (as cited in Butler, 1995) notes
that in California, more than two thirds of
African American males between the ages
of 18 and 30 have been arrested at least once.
One sixth of California's Black men (age 16
and older) are arrested per year; 92% of the
Black men arrested by police on drug charges
were subsequently released for lack of evidence or inadmissible evidence (Miller, 1996,
p. 8). (This rate is contrasted with that of
Whites, which is 64%; 81% of Latino arrests
are not sustainable.) Nazario's study (as cited
in Miller, 1996) found that in 1992, 3% of
California's population was Black males, yet
40% of men entering state prisons were Black
(see also Barnes and Kingsnorth, 1996).

In 1991, there were 517,000 Black men in
college and 583,545 Black men in jail or under
the jurisdiction of correctional authorities.
Thus, more Black men were in jail or otherwise under jurisdiction than in college; in
2004, this still held true. Furthermore, for
every 100 Black men in jail, barely 1 Black man
graduates from college (Butler, 1997a). These
rates still hold and, in fact, have worsened.

Harrison and Beck (2006) reported that
as of June 30, 2005, Blacks constitute more
than half of all prison inmates, whereas they
constitute approximately 13% of the US
population. They noted that for every 100,000
people in each racial/ethnic category, there
were 709 White, 1,856 "Hispanic," and 4,682
Black inmates in state or federal prisons and
local jails. Of males age 25 to 29, 1.7% of
Whites versus 11.9% of Blacks are in prison
or jail. "In general, the incarceration rates
for black males of all ages were 5 to 7 times
greater than those for white males in the same
age groups" (Harrison and Beck, 2006, p. 10).
Furthermore, for the same crime, Blacks often
receive sentences that average 6 months longer than those of Whites (Miller, 1996).

Because many states bar felons from voting, approximately one in seven African
American men will lose the right to vote, further weakening representation in an already
compromised system, as well evidenced by
the racial discrimination documented in the
2000 presidential election (Palmer, 1999). In
addition, there are laws in all 50 states that
prevent former convicts from obtaining a state
license for everything from landscape architect to a driver's license, further entrenching
social and economic class (see "The Price of
Prisons," 2004).

Eckholm (2006) reports that incarceration
rates are climbing for Blacks despite the fact
that urban crime rates have declined. He further notes that neighborhoods with floods of
ex-offenders are having difficulty coping and
that the convicts are shunned by employers.
In response, many scholars and community
members are calling for a curb to the automatic incarceration of minor offenders. One
of the reasons there is such a disparate impact
in the criminal justice system is racial profiling. Racial profiling by law enforcement
continues, often defended as justified (see
Goldberg, 1999). A recent drug case makes

clear the depth and breadth of racism and profiling.

## Race, Drugs, and Incarceration

In 1999, in Tulia, Texas, nearly one 10th of the town's Black population of nearly 400 was arrested in a drug sting operation run by Thomas Coleman, a White man who

> now faces charges of lying under oath about stealing gasoline in 1998, when he was working as a sheriff's deputy in another county. His background includes [thousands] … in bad debts … skipping town in a previous job and failing to pay child support. (Hockstader, 2003, p. A03)

He also admits to the regular use of racial slurs. Thirteen of the 39 were imprisoned on severe sentences following trials in front of almost completely White juries whose evidence consisted of "no fingerprints, audio or video surveillance or corroborating witnesses, and the busts turned up no drugs, weapons, paraphernalia or other evidence of drug-dealing" (United Press International, 2003). When questioned, Coleman was incoherent and admitted to "scribbling crucial notes on his leg and stomach" (Hockstader, 2003, p. A03). After their story reached the press and the American Civil Liberties Union and the National Association for the Advancement of Colored People became involved, and after 4 years in prison, the 13 were released.

Additionally, there are odd discrepancies in the drug laws and sentences. For example, there is great disparity between sentences for cocaine, based on whether it is powder or crack cocaine. The first important element is that "most of the people who are arrested for crack cocaine are black; most arrested for powder cocaine are white" (Butler, 1995, p. 719). The next important element, made

evident by Thomas's article (as cited in Butler, 1995), is that "African Americans make up 13% of the nation's regular drug users, but they account for 35% of narcotics arrests, 55% of drug convictions, and 74% of those receiving prison sentences" (p. 719). The final important element is that the federal mandatory-minimum sentence for 50 grams of crack cocaine is 10 years. For the same sentence for powder cocaine, a defendant must have 10 times that amount, 500 grams. Crack and powder cocaine are pharmacologically identical. Despite a decade plus of debate, the disparate laws remain. For an historical and current account of differential punishment, see Alexander and Gyamerah (1997). As Butler (1995) states, in response to this, Blacks ask, "Is it justice, or Just us?" (p. 690).

## Part 3: Butler's Criminal Justice System Critiques

Butler (1995) classifies people into three types based on their perceptions of these statistics and knowledge about the criminal justice system. The first group holds a "liberal critique." People following this line of thought argue that the criminal justice system is an instrument of White people, who, either intentionally or negligently, are racist, and the higher percentage of African Americans in the penal system is due to racism (not guilt of Blacks). Butler does not find this credible and draws from his experience as a prosecutor to explain that the system is actually fairly good at catching criminals. He does not deny that the system is racist but does deny that all Blacks caught are innocent.

The second group holds a "radical critique." Those with this perspective argue that the criminal law is racist as an instrument of White supremacy. It is such an instrument because it has been developed by Whites to preserve and protect the interests of Whites, to maintain the status quo. Although those who hold this perspective see apprehended Blacks as guilty of breaking laws, this can only be understood in the larger social context of joblessness, disenfranchisement, poverty, and so forth. Many offenses, including drug use and crimes against other Blacks, are due to the internalization of a racist system. Under this perspective, despite the fact that Black defendants are guilty, attention is given to the fact that the system and the laws are discriminatory in both intent and effect. The radical critique is ballasted by many recent reports of police profiling and brutality and by widely publicized cases of unarmed Black men being shot to death by police (see Flynn, 1999; Fritsch, 2000; Goldberg, 1999; Harker, 2000; Herbert, 1999; Kocieniewski, 1999; Rashbaum, 2000; Roy, 2000; "U.S. Goes to War on Racial Profiling," 1999).

Butler cites a Gallup poll and states that approximately two thirds of African Americans are critical of the criminal justice system and fall under one of the above perspectives, whereas approximately one third are in the third group and hold a criminal "law enforcement enthusiast" position. Butler cites Randall Kennedy, a vocal African American who argues that Blacks want more law enforcement to prevent the most lethal danger to African Americans – the typically Black criminals who attack the most vulnerable Blacks. Kennedy further argues that we should not allow criminals to live unfettered in the community because it would harm the residents.

Butler falls most closely in the radical critique and wants African Americans to use the power they have now to redress the system, in part by encouraging Black jurors to refuse to convict Blacks guilty of nonviolent crimes. Butler argues that jury nullification is similar to civil disobedience, but lawful. He asks, "Why should the Black juror not

be color-conscious when the entire system is color-conscious?" The White privilege that perpetuates this systematic discrimination is inconsistent and, via disparate treatment, illegal. Butler's race-based jury nullification is a principled call requiring that jurors be moved by the injustice of the disparate treatment of African Americans under the law.

## Part 4: Butler's Call for Racially Based Jury Nullification

Butler (1995) focuses on the legal and social implications of racially based jury nullification and argues, "The race of a black defendant is sometimes a legally and morally appropriate factor for jurors to consider in refusing to vote for conviction" (p. 679). Butler also states, "Considering the costs of law enforcement to the black community and the failure of white lawmakers to devise nonincarcerative responses to black antisocial conduct, it is the *moral responsibility* of black jurors to emancipate some guilty black nonviolent outlaws" (p. 679). Butler's goal is the "subversion of the American criminal justice, at least as it now exists" (p. 680). And in advocating race-based jury nullification when the defendant is an African American nonviolent criminal, Butler states that he is calling for jurors to "dismantle the master's house with the master's tools" (p. 680).

### Butler's Model

His model for race-based jury nullification is as follows: In violent crimes such as rape and murder, jurors should consider the case only on the evidence, and if there is no reasonable doubt, then jurors should convict. In nonviolent "crimes such as theft and perjury," nullification should be an option for the juror to consider, although there is not a presumption in favor of nullification. In victimless crimes, such as narcotics offenses, "there should be a presumption in favor of nullification" (Butler, 1995, p. 715).

Butler (1995) assumes that drug crimes are victimless and cites literature to that end. I will address the issue of victimless crimes below, although I do not find it to be the crucial dividing line of Butler's argument but rather find the issue of violence to be critical. For example, when a drug crime turns violent, Butler no longer considers the defendant a candidate for nullification as the further risk(s) of (violent) harm to the community outweighs other concerns. Thus, the crucial issue in a drug crime is not its victim(s) but the presence or absence of violence associated with the crime.

Butler (1995) argues against violent offenders receiving nullification, for they pose further risk to the community. He states,

> Black people have a community that needs building, and children who need rescuing, and as long as a person will not hurt anyone, the community needs him there to help. Assuming that he actually will help is a gamble, but not a reckless one, for the "just" African American community will not leave the lawbreaker be: It will, for example, encourage his education and provide his health care (including narcotics dependency treatment).... If rehabilitation were a meaningful option in American criminal justice, I would not endorse nullification in any case. It would be counterproductive, for utilitarian reasons: The community is better off with the antisocial person cured than sick. (p. 718)

However, because our system is antirehabilitative, Butler advocates nullification as outlined above. He does not provide much guidance on how his race-based jury nullification model would be disseminated but suggests that it would be done through the Black community, including churches, popular culture, and the NAACP....

**Part 5: Responses to Leipold**

... Leipold doubts that race-based nullification has the same status as the historical uses of nullification, in part because there is not widespread outrage against the criminal justice system regarding nonviolent Black defendants. He argues that nullification has only worked when it reflected discontent already in place and cites statistics claiming that 76% of African Americans surveyed favored imposing more severe prison sentences, and 68% would approve of building more prisons so longer sentences could be given. This is almost the inverse of Butler's claims concerning where African Americans fall in their perceptions of the criminal justice system. As nullification requires one to respond to perceived injustice, this is an important point. However, if the survey question concerning the defendant had been worded "imposing more severe prison sentences on *Blacks*," there might not be differing statistics regarding attitudes in the African American community (W. Carter, personal communication, March 13, 2000).

Leipold's Call for Patience

Leipold (1996) also claims that implementing Butler's plan would cause further racism and further polarize a society already dealing with racial division. Regarding discrimination, he claims that "the tangible gains that have been made over the last few decades in reducing racial bias in the criminal justice system should not be so casually dismissed by those who are too impatient to continue on the current course" (p. 139).

What is the current course? The percentage

of Black men in jail reflects at best disparate impact and disparate treatment. Prison is a breeding ground for recidivism, rape, and AIDS. Why should they have patience? In *Letter from the Birmingham Jail*, Martin Luther King (1963) provides an excellent response to the issue of patience:

> For years now I have heard the word "Wait!" It rings in the ear of every Negro with piercing familiarity. This "Wait" has almost always meant "Never." It has been a tranquilizing thalidomide, relieving the emotional stress for a moment, only to give birth to an ill-formed infant of frustration. We must come to see with the distinguished jurist of yesterday that "justice too long delayed is justice denied." ... I guess it is easy for those who have never felt the stinging darts of segregation to say, "Wait." But when you have seen ... hate-filled policemen curse, kick, brutalize and even kill your black brothers and sisters with impunity; when you see the vast majority of your twenty million Negro brothers smoldering in an air-tight cage of poverty in the midst of an affluent society ... then you will understand why we find it difficult to wait.

Butler (1997c) also addresses the issue of waiting:

> African American people cannot afford to wait.... If the present rate of incarceration of African Americans continues, by the year 2010 the majority of African American men between the ages of 18 and 40 will be in prison, the majority. (p. 911)

On Race-Based Jury Nullification Causing Racism

Like affirmative action, race-based jury nullification did not create the problem of racism, and whether either exacerbates racism is an empirical question. I doubt that it does. For clarity, it is helpful to recall Wellman's (1993) definition of racism:

> Racism has various faces.... Sometimes it appears as a "personal prejudice" which ... is really a disguised way to defend privilege. Other times racism is manifested ideologically. Cultural and biological reasons are used as rationalizations and justifications for the superior position of whites. Racism is also expressed institutionally in the form of systematic practices that deny and exclude blacks from access to social resources. (p. 39)

Perhaps Leipold is referring to racism in the personal prejudice sense, where some Whites may become even more racist after being exposed to Butler's proposal. However, I agree with Wellman that this is a guise for defending (White) privilege, and I think very few Whites recognize this guise because recognition would entail admission of privilege. As of 2006, there will have been 42 years of legal freedom – freedom from legal discrimination based on race as the Civil Rights Act of 1964 ended 99 years of legal segregation, which were preceded by more than 350 years of slavery on US soil. These 42 years of legal freedom for Blacks has not resulted in an end to racism. We are color conscious; race matters. The system is racist, as evidenced by disparate impact and disparate treatment, both prima facie cases of discrimination.

I find Butler's principled call for nonviolent race-based jury nullification to be a justified tool to use "in the meantime" to fight existing racism in the criminal justice system, which would result in an end for the need to nullify based on race. I see this as justified from a legal and a utilitarian perspective. In light of the statistics, racism, and impact on

African Americans, incarcerating nonviolent African American defendants results in more harm than not doing so, especially when considering the nonrehabilitative nature of incarceration and the perpetuation of the status quo from the loss of voting rights, income, and potential. I agree with Butler that race-based jury nullification is consistent with the intent and history of jury nullification. Jury nullification is a juror's right; it does not operate outside the confines of law, but within the common law tradition, it nullifies specific applications of specific laws.

## Leipold's Community Critique

Leipold's (1996) most significant criticism involves the community when he asks the reader to consider how "the relevant actors – jurors, police, prosecutors, legislators, defendants, and community members – will respond" (p. 128). He argues that the community is not equipped to deal with the addicts, and if they were, why did they not do so proactively? This is a serious objection, especially if the community is partially responsible for the lack of support, options, and other necessities that contributed to or did not address the defendant's behavior and failed to rehabilitate him or her when he or she was there.

The community aspect of Butler's proposal is both the most troubling and the most intriguing part. It is troubling because he neither clearly articulates the African American community, nor how the community will address the nonviolent criminals. It is intriguing because of the many potential and extensive benefits to all of society if it were to be successful. Butler (1995) describes the African American community to which the acquitted defendant will go as a community that "will not leave the lawbreaker be: It will, for example, encourage his education and provide his health care (including narcotics dependency

treatment) and, if necessary, sue him for child support" (p. 717). Butler states that "jurors who engage in nullification might be morally obligated to participate in black self-help programs," such as Louis Farrakhan's request at the Million Man March to African American men to "adopt" a prison inmate (p. 717). As I have been called to jury duty multiple times and witnessed people irritably trying to get out of the duty, I am not optimistic that any jurors, including those who might nullify, would feel morally obligated to adopt a Black outlaw. However, there are many potential resources within the community that could "adopt" the inmate or defendant who is released via nullification.

Perhaps the "major institutional bulwarks against the pervasive meaninglessness and despair in Afro-America" that West (1993, p. 58) articulates, those found in Christian churches, Muslim mosques, and character-building schools, are sections of the community that could address these issues and provide the treatment, encourage education, and support family relationships. Marbley and Ferguson (2005) provide a more definitive map in their call for communities of color to address inmates of color. "There is an urgent need to have a systematic way of partnering with businesses, colleges and universities, faith-based institutions, and communities in an effort to reinstate reformed prisoners back into society as contributing, taxpaying citizens" (Marbley and Ferguson, 2005, p. 637). They point out that historically communities of color provided support systems that economically, politically, and educationally advanced their members. Furthermore, they continue,

> Based on the community's track record, it seems befitting that the African American community, for one, has the potential to become a vehicle for playing a key role in the transformation of inmates of color....

However, the communities of color must take a proactive role to save its members from prisons. (p. 645)

Marbley and Ferguson (2004) offer a systemic model that provides a rubric to follow for such proactive community action that includes mainstreaming nonviolent criminals, expungement of nonviolent criminal records, and integration with families and business resources, among others. They also illustrate one way in which funding could be provided. First, they note that incarcerating 15,000 nonviolent, low- or no-risk individuals costs $900 million. Next, they show that if this cost is coupled with the potential income of the same individuals, more than $1 million would be generated or saved; if, for example, these individuals are addicts, the $900 million could be used on rehabilitation programs and medical care, producing productive and healthy citizens rather than turning out untreated, unrehabilitated inmates subject to relapse and recidivism, thus potentially costing another $900 million.

However, as Butler (1995) points out, the breakdown of some African American communities has contributed to antisocial, illegal behavior. If the communities are a contributory cause at worst, or are neutral at best, then until and unless those problems are addressed, it is problematic (though still justified on a utilitarian basis) to nullify and send an offender back to the "community." In the absence of specifics, or more detail, Butler's proposal that defendants would receive attention in the community is unrealistic, and models such as Marbley and Ferguson's need to be instituted for the communities to effectively address defendants of color....

## Conclusion

I do not know whether race-based jury nullification will have a significant impact on racism in the criminal justice system or whether African American communities can better address nonviolent African Americans who break the law and whether these communities should be the place to which nonviolent criminals are returned. For these matters, the jury is still out. However, my verdict is that our society will be sentenced to continuing nullification if the system does not change to address its own myopic privilege and racism.

Some Black leaders have called the overrepresentation of Blacks in prison the most important issue in the African American community. Johnson (2000) states,

Statistics on the uses of prisons for minorities, when read together with firsthand accounts of the role of prisons in the life of African American communities since emancipation, point to social control and racial oppression as important and enduring functions of American prisons. (p. 8)

Others see it as another incarnation of slavery, especially when corporate interests can hire captive prisoners for less than minimum wage. Butler's call to use nullification to quell the incarceration of nonviolent Blacks will not solve the crisis, but until there is an effective redress of this injustice, race-based jury nullification can chip away at it, one defendant at a time.

## References

Alexander, R., Jr., and J. Gyamerah. (1997). "Differential Punishing of African Americans and Whites Who Possess Drugs: A Just Policy or a Continuation of the Past?" *Journal of Black Studies* 28(1): 97–111.

Barnes, C.W., and R. Kingsnorth. (1996). "Race, Drug, and Criminal Sentencing: Hidden Effects of the Criminal Law." *Journal of Criminal Justice* 24(1): 39–55.

Butler, P. (1995). "Racially Based Jury Nullification: Black Power in the Criminal Justice System." *Yale Law Journal* 105(3): 677–725.

_____. (1997a). "Affirmative Action and the Criminal Law." *University of Colorado Law Review* 68: 841–89.

_____. (1997b). "Brotherman: Reflections of a Reformed Prosecutor." In E. Cose (ed.), *The Darden Dilemma: 12 Black Writers on Justice, Race, and Conflicting Loyalties* (pp. 1–19). New York: HarperCollins.

_____. (1997c). "Symposium: The Role of Race-Based Jury Nullification in American Criminal Justice." *John Marshall Law Review* 30: 911–22. Retrieved March 6, 2002, from LexisNexis Academic Universe database.

Eckholm, E. (2006, March 20). "Plight Deepens for Black Men, Studies Warn." *The New York Times*, pp. A1, A18.

Farnham, D. (1997). "Jury Nullification: History Proves It's Not a New Idea." *Criminal Justice* 11: 5–14.

Flynn, K. (1999, December 1). "State Cites Racial Inequality in New York Police Searches." *The New York Times*, p. A22.

Fritsch, J. (2000, February 26). "Four Officers in Diallo Shooting Are Acquitted of All Charges." *The New York Times*, pp. A1, A 13.

Goldberg, J. (1999, June 20). "The Color of Suspicion." *The New York Times Magazine*, pp. 50–57, 64, 85, 87.

Harker, V. (2000, January 5). "Phoenix Police Sued over Beating: Black Resident Says Racial Profiling at Fault." *The Arizona Republic*, pp. A1, B7.

Harrison, P.M., and A.J. Beck. (2006). *Prison and Jail Inmates at Midyear 2005*. Retrieved June 30, 2006, from http://www.ojp.usdoj.gov/bjs/pub/pdf/pjim05.pdf.

Herbert, B. (1999, November 4). "Breathing while Black." *The New York Times*, p. A27.

Hockstader, L. (2003, June 16). "13 Imprisoned in Tulia Drug sweep to Be Freed Today; Racial Divide Still Deep in Texas Town." *The Washington Post*, p. A03. Retrieved August 2, 2004, from HighBeam Research database.

Johnson, R. (2000). "American Prisons and the African-American Experience: A History of Social Control and Racial Oppression." *Corrections Compendium* 25(9), 6, 8, 10, 28–30.

King, M.L. (1963). *Letter from Birmingham Jail*. Retrieved June 23, 2006, from http://www.stanford.edu/group/King/frequentdocslbirmingham.pdf.

Kocieniewski, D. (1999, December 23). "U.S. Will Monitor New Jersey Police on Race Profiling." *The New York Times*, pp. A1, A26.

Leipold, A.D. (1996). "The Dangers of Race-Based Jury Nullification: A Response to Professor Butler." *UCLA Law Review* 44(1), 109–41.

Marbley, A.F., and R. Ferguson. (2004). "Putting Back Together Our Communities of Color: A Systemic Model for Rehabilitation." *Journal of African American Studies* 7(4), 75–85.

_____. (2005). "Responding to Prisoner Reentry, Recidivism, and Incarceration of Inmates of Color: A Call to the Communities." *Journal of Black Studies* 35(5), 633–49.

Marder, N.S. (1999). "The Myth of the Nullifying Jury." *Northwestern University Law Review* 93(3), 877–959.

Miller, J. (1996). *Search and Destroy: African American Males in the Criminal Justice System*. New York: Cambridge UP.

Palmer, L.D. (1999, March 21). "More Blacks Serving Time in U.S. Prisons." *The Arizona Republic*, p. A19.

"The Price of Prisons." (2004, June 26). *The New York Times*, p. A26.

Rashbaum, W.K. (2000, March 17). "Unarmed Man Is Shot to Death in Scuffle with Three Undercover Detectives." *The New York Times*, p. A19.

Roy, Y. (2000, February 26). "Racial Profiling Is Center of Debate." *The Arizona Republic*, p. A25.

United Press International. (2003, June 2). "Tulia Defendants Freed by Texas Law." *Comtex* [online news network]. Retrieved August 2, 2004, from HighBeam Research database.

US Department of Justice, Bureau of Justice Statistics. (2003). *Prison Statistics*. Retrieved July 31, 2004, from http://www.ojp.usdoj.gov/bjs/prisons.htm.

"U.S. Goes to War on Racial Profiling." (1999, December 23). *The Arizona Republic*, p. A3.

Wellman, D.T. (1993). *Portraits of White Racism* (2nd ed.). New York: Cambridge UP.

West, C. (1993). *Race Matters*. Boston: Beacon.

## Study Questions

1. Given the criminal-justice system statistics that Collins-Chobanian provides, would you side with the "liberal critique" or the "radical critique" of the criminal-justice system as laid out by Paul Butler? Why?

2. In response to the concern that race-based jury nullification might cause racism, Collins-Chobanian writes:

> For clarity, it is helpful to recall Wellman's (1993) definition of racism:
>
>> Racism has various faces … Sometimes it appears as a "personal prejudice" which … is really a disguised way to defend privilege. Other times racism is manifested ideologically. Cultural and biological reasons are used as rationalizations and justifications for the superior position of whites. Racism is also expressed institutionally in the form of systematic practices that deny and exclude blacks from access to social resources. (p. 39)
>>
>> Perhaps Leipold is referring to racism in the personal prejudice sense, where some Whites may become even more racist after being exposed to Butler's proposal. However … [a]s of 2006, there will have been 42 years of legal freedom – freedom from legal discrimination based on race as the Civil Rights Act of 1964 ended 99 years of legal segregation, which were preceded by more than 350 years of slavery on US soil. These 42 years of legal freedom for Blacks has not resulted in an end to racism…. The system is racist, as evidenced by disparate impact and disparate treatment….

   What is the importance of this passage? How does it work to overcome the concern that race-based jury nullification might reinforce racist attitudes in whites?

3. Can you think of how Rawls's theory of justice might be used to argue for race-based jury nullification?

# 4.  Moya Lloyd, "Heteronormativity and/as Violence: The 'Sexing' of Gwen Araujo"

MOYA LLOYD'S WORKS INCLUDE *Judith Butler: From Norms to Politics* and *Beyond Identity Politics: Feminism, Power and Politics*. In this piece, from the journal *Hypatia* (2013), she considers the killing of 17-year-old Gwen Araujo, a transgender individual whose life has also been dramatized on film by Lifetime. Lloyd examines the concept of heteronormativity and argues for a subcategory of "heteronormative violence." She makes a case for varieties of heteronormative violence: one variety is physical violence inspired by one's nonconformance to gender norms; another occurs when one symptomizes or looks suspiciously upon the body or identity of someone who does not conform to heterosexual gender roles. Lloyd criticizes the "trans panic defense" that was used by the lawyers who defended Araujo's killers by asserting that it demonstrated the second kind of heteronormative violence. The trans panic defense and another version of it, the gay panic defense, attempt to win less serious convictions from a jury for those who kill transgender or gay individuals by arguing that some defendants react violently to, and experience temporary loss of self-control when encountering, LGBT individuals. Critics of the gay and trans panic defenses say that they devalue the integrity and humanity of LGBT individuals and assume heterosexism or homophobia to be a *defense* of someone's criminal actions, thus rationalizing violent crimes committed on account of heterosexism or homophobia. California was the first state to ban the defense in 2014. The American Bar Association approved of a resolution urging federal and state governments to restrict or ban the use of the defense; it can be read here: http://lgbtbar.org/wp-content/uploads/2014/02/Gay-and-Trans-Panic-Defenses-Resolution.pdf.

---

ON OCTOBER 3, 2002, seventeen-year-old Gwen Araujo was killed at a party in Newark, California by four men, who "kneed her in the face, slapped, kicked, and choked her, beat her with a can and a metal skillet, wrestled her to the ground, tied her wrists and ankles, strangled her with a rope, and hit her over the head with a shovel." They then "buried her in a shallow grave and went to McDonald's for breakfast" (Steinberg 2005, 499–500). The precipitating cause for this violent assault on Araujo, who had lived and identified as a woman from age 14, was the coerced revelation that she had male genitalia. (Araujo was held down in the bathroom by her assailants who forcibly removed her underwear.)[1]

Araujo was neither the first, nor indeed is she likely to be the last, transgender individual to die so violently. According to figures provided on the Transgender Day of Remembrance website, between March 1970 and October 2010 more than 300 transgender persons in the US suffered a similar fate. The site also publishes causes of death; this makes for grim reading. The list includes, among other equally horrific things: "Beat (*sic*) and sexually mutilated by members of a local street gang"; "42 stab wounds to the head, neck, face, and arm"; "Tortured for several hours, beaten to death, and beheaded"; "Stabbed repeatedly and castrated"; "Shot"; "Raped, hit in the head, and drowned"; and "Beaten with beer bottles, sexually assaulted with a broom handle, strangled with an electrical cord and then drowned in a bathtub. His body was later set on fire in a trash can behind a church" (St. Pierre 2011). Extrapolating from data such as this, the Human Rights Commission has estimated that "one out of every 1,000 homicides in the US is an anti-transgender hate crime" (Human Rights Commission 2011). The preliminary findings of a study organized by Transgender Europe, The Trans Murder Monitoring Project, indicate that worldwide "since the beginning of 2008 the murder of a trans person is reported every third day, on average" (Balzer 2009, 148).

It is not, specifically, the level of brutality involved in trans murder that interests me in this paper, though clearly it is significant. As the Organization for Security and Cooperation in Europe (OSCE) report for 2007 makes clear, "Homophobic hate crimes and incidents often show a high degree of cruelty and brutality" (OSCE 2007, 53–54; see also Balzer 2009, 149), with trans homicide and assault, in particular, likely to exhibit the characteristics of "overkill": the infliction of injuries in excess of those necessary to cause an individual's death.

The development in particular jurisdictions of hate crime enhancements or laws to prosecute the types of offenses committed against trans persons would appear to suggest that there has been some degree of official recognition of the seriousness of such acts. Yet trans murder is often not reported in the media, and many killers of trans individuals are never prosecuted. I am interested in what happens to those who are and, in particular, to those where the defense, with varying degrees of success, has attempted to have trans homicide reduced from murder to manslaughter through the deployment of an exculpatory legal strategy known as the "trans panic" defense.

Although the trans panic defense failed in the case I focus on – the prosecution of Gwen Araujo's killers – it has succeeded elsewhere.[2] It was the Araujo case, however, that has been credited with bringing the trans panic defense to "national consciousness" (Brigham 2006).[3] For my purposes, it is the "archive" of material available in this case that makes it so significant, for this material provides invaluable insight into what I will call the "heteronormative violence" at work in the construction of a trans panic defense and, in particular, in its deployment of gender norms.[4]

Accounts of gendered or sexual violence focus attention mainly on diverse forms of physical brutality, comprising rape, sexual abuse, domestic violence, "queer-bashing," "gay-bashing," and sexual assault. Here we might legitimately include the fatal assault on Araujo. When victims are gay or trans individuals, this violence is often categorized as either homophobic or transphobic respectively. Against this, I intend to characterize such species of violence as modes of *heteronormative* violence, that is, violence that constitutes and regulates bodies according to normative notions of sex, gender, and sexuality.[5]

To account fully for the violence that is heteronormativity, however, it is necessary, I will argue, to focus not only on gendered and sexualized physical harms of the kinds just listed, whether threatened or actual, though these certainly need to be attended to since the ability to recognize certain acts as "gendered" or "sexualized" violence is central to their prosecution and prevention. Attention must also be paid, however, to the *multiple* modalities through which heteronormativity performs its violence on, through, and against bodies and persons. This includes but is not limited to the violence of gender norms; the way those norms work to position certain bodies and persons outside the realm of "recognizable" violence; and, in this particular context, the kind of violence at stake in the use of the trans panic defense.

The paper thus begins with a brief contextualization of the trans panic defense. This is followed by an explanation of what is meant by heteronormative violence, drawing from work on heteronormativity as well as from the writings of Judith Butler and Michel Foucault. Examining reports of the trial of Araujo's killers as well as legal documents pertaining to the case, I then demonstrate the specific ways that heteronormative violence was enacted.

## The Trial

The prosecution of Araujo's killers was a complicated affair, involving two trials: the first ended in June 2004 when, after ten days of deliberations, the jury was unable to agree on a unanimous verdict.[6] Alameda County Superior Court Judge Harry Sheppard thus declared a mistrial (DeFao and St. John 2004). The second trial took place in September 2005. Initially, all four men involved in her killing (Jason Cazares, Michael Magidson, Jose Merel, and Jaron Nabors) were charged with first-degree murder with a hate crime enhancement, a crime carrying a sentence of twenty-five years to life with little prospect of parole. One of the four defendants, Nabors, however, pleaded guilty to voluntary manslaughter in return for testifying against his three friends; for this he received an eleven-year jail sentence.

As a result of the second trial, Magidson and Merel were both convicted of second-degree murder, with a sentence of fifteen years to life. The jury, however, was not willing to add hate crime enhancements to their convictions. Neither trial was able to determine the fate of Cazares, who denied involvement in Araujo's actual murder, claiming only to have assisted with her burial. He was eventually given a six-year prison term, after agreeing to

a plea of "no contest to voluntary manslaughter" (Baldman 2006).

At the preliminary hearing, lawyers for the defense attempted to have the charges against their clients downgraded from murder to manslaughter (Haddock 2004). They pursued a similar strategy at the two trials that followed. This strategy centered on attempting to persuade the jury that Araujo's slaying was not murder but rather "manslaughter in the heat of passion" (Thorman [defense lawyer], cited in Haddock 2004). The defense thus took the form of what has come to be known as the "trans panic defense," an exculpatory legal strategy designed to absolve killers of criminal responsibility for trans homicide by categorizing that crime as one committed in the "heat of the moment" (see Steinberg 2005; Lee 2008). It has its origins in two other related kinds of legal argument: the homosexual (or, more recently, gay) panic defense and the nonviolent homosexual advance argument (Chen 2000; Steinberg 2005).

"Acute homosexual panic" was initially categorized as a psychiatric disorder in the 1920s, at a time when homosexuality was widely considered to be a mental disease. The term was used to characterize feelings of extreme anxiety ostensibly exhibited by *latent homosexuals* in same-sex situations, feelings that often led to self-harm or even suicide, though not normally to violence against others (Howe 1997; Golder 2004). According to Cynthia Lee, from 1967 onward, however, the idea of homosexual panic began to be used in support of "mental defect" defenses (such as insanity or diminished capacity) in the hope of mitigating the nature of the crime *heterosexual* men had committed in cases where they were charged with murdering gay men; the contention was that "the victim's (homo) sexual advance triggered in them [the heterosexual men] a *violent psychotic reaction*" causing them to lose control temporarily and to resort to lethal force (Lee 2008, 491, my emphasis).

Although in some of these cases, defense teams fell back on the idea of latent homosexuality to explain the "panic" experienced by the defendant, once homosexuality ceased to be categorized as a mental disorder in 1973, when the American Psychiatric Association removed it as a mental illness from its *Diagnostic and Statistical Manual of Mental Disorders* (DSM-II), they could no longer do so. At this point, however, the legal strategy of "homosexual" or "gay panic" did not disappear as one might have expected; it was reconceptualized as a form of provocation defense.[7] Now it was asserted that "a non-violent homosexual advance reasonably provoked them [the defendants] into a heat of passion" such that they killed (Lee 2008, 500; see also Chen 2000, 210). It is this latter version of the panic defense based on *provocation* that informs the trans panic strategy. Here it is allegedly the discovery that sexual intimacy has taken place (or is about to take place) with a trans person that is adjudged to prompt the ostensible "panic" that leads to violence. The legal basis of the provocation, however, is that the victim has withheld information about their "true" sex from their assailant. This is precisely the logic employed by the defense team in the Araujo case.

Keen to establish that their clients were guilty only of manslaughter, defense lawyers claimed first that there was no premeditation in the killing of Araujo, and second that there was no hate crime involved. In fact, commenting on the case afterwards, William Du Bois (Merel's lawyer at the second trial) claimed that his client "had a real affection" for Araujo, being "almost in love with her" (cited in Szymanski 2006b). "This crime didn't occur because Mike had a bias," Magidson's attorney Michael Thorman told the jury at the first trial. "It happened because of *a discovery of what Eddie had done*" (cited in

Haddock 2004, my emphasis), "Eddie" being Araujo's birth name.[8]

What was it, though, that "Eddie" is alleged to have "done"? As Merel's lawyer at the first trial, Jack Noonan, put it, "he" was guilty of "sexual deceit" (cited in St. John 2004b). In the words of Thorman, Araujo had "lied to get them [Merel and Magidson] to engage in sex with her" (cited in St. John 2005). His client, Noonan claimed, had "had sex with a person who he thought was somebody else" (cited in St. John 2004b); he had been duped. It was the discovery of this "deception" that provoked the emotional reactions – "anger and rage and shock and revulsion" in the case of Magidson (Thorman, cited in Hoge 2004); an intensely tearful, emotional breakdown in the case of Merel – that caused Araujo's brutal homicide.[9] In short, as captured in the headline that appeared in *The San Francisco Chronicle*: "Teenager Provoked Own Killing, Attorney Says" (St. John 2005).

Panic-style defenses have been explored by a number of legal scholars (Howe 1997; Chen 2000; Golder 2004; Steinberg 2005; McDonald 2006; Lee 2008; and Tilleman 2010), concerned above all with their efficacy or suitability as vindications for murder. My main interest is not, however, in the legal viability of the trans panic defense; it is in how this defense functions to (re)instate a particular world view through the classificatory system it uses to position the sexed body of the trans individual. As Lucinda Finley points out, the "concepts, categories, and terms that law uses" have "a particularly potent ability to shape popular and authoritative understanding of situations." In this respect, legal language "reinforces certain world views and understandings of events" (Finley 1989, 888). With regard to the trans panic defense, the question is how does it function in support of a heteronormative understanding of transgender and trans murder? More specifically, how, in particular, does it operate as a mode of violence that parallels, though is distinct from, the lethal violence meted out by the killers of trans persons? In the next section, therefore, I set out what I mean by heteronormative violence before turning in the subsequent section to the question of how that violence was enacted at the trial of Araujo's killers.

**Heteronormative Violence**

Heteronormativity is a much-used though often ill-defined term. Originating in the work of queer theorist Michael Warner (Warner 1991; 1993), though clearly influenced by earlier feminist work on what has been variously called the "heterosexual contract" (Wittig), "compulsory heterosexuality" (Rich), or "obligatory heterosexuality" (Rubin; see Jackson 2006), heteronormativity has "become widely used," as Stevi Jackson observes, "as shorthand for the numerous ways in which heterosexual privilege is woven into the fabric of social life, pervasively and insidiously ordering everyday existence" (Jackson 2006, 108; see also Berlant and Warner 1998). Although there is disagreement, as Samuel Chambers reports, about how best to characterize this privilege, with some construing it in terms of "practices," others as "rules," and still others as a "system of binary gender" (Chambers 2009, 65), it has been most commonly defined in terms of "norms," the approach I will follow. Thus, Robert Corber and Stephen Valocchi surmise, "[h]eteronormativity" refers to "the set of norms that make heterosexuality seem natural or right and that organize homosexuality as its binary opposite" (Corber and Valocchi 2003, 4). But what does it mean to say that "within social life heterosexuality is constructed as a compulsory norm" (Beasley 2005, 251)?

"Norm" may, of course, be used in a variety of different ways. *The Oxford English Dictionary* defines a norm, deriving from the Latin *norma* (meaning carpenter's square, pattern, rule), as a "standard, a type; what is expected or regarded as normal; customary behaviour, appearance." Etymologically, "norm" links to "normal," its adjectival form connoting "constituting or conforming to a type or standard; regular, usual, typical; ordinary, conventional. Also, physically or mentally sound, healthy" (as well as "heterosexual"); to "normalize," a transitive verb meaning "to make normal or regular; cause to conform"; and to "normative," as in "establishing a norm or standard; of, deriving from, or implying a standard or norm; prescriptive." In social theory, norms have variously been viewed as the glue holding the social order together, an external constraint on the individual, constitutive of the self and, by extension, constitutive also of social action (Jackson 2006, 109). By contrast, according to Michel Foucault, norms are to be understood as both disciplinary and productive.

To contend that "heterosexuality *is* the norm, in culture, in society, in politics" (Chambers 2009, 35) might, therefore, be to make at least one of two claims: the first distributional, that statistically "heterosexuality" is the type of sexuality that occurs most frequently within the population; and the second normative, that heterosexuality is a prescribed mode of behavior, a regulatory standard, deviation from which is liable to censure, medical intervention, or worse. For the purposes of this paper, it is the latter conceptualization of norms that (as for Chambers, Beasley, et al.) is most pertinent to my argument; norms that establish heterosexuality as *the* default position in society (Warner 1993; Berlant and Warner 1998; Chambers 2009), where to be human is to "be" heterosexual (Warner 1993, xxiii) and where "heterosexual experience is *synonymous with* human experience" (Yep 2002, 167).

It is often assumed that the concept of

heterosexuality is "as old as procreation" (Katz 1995, 13). In fact it is of relatively recent historical origin. The term *heterosexuality* was, as Katz demonstrates, first used *publicly* in Germany in 1880, having been coined only some twelve years earlier in 1868 (54, 52), at which point it was differentiated from "'Normalsexualität,' normal sexuality" (52). At this time, 1868, Karl Maria Kertbeny (the originator of the term) saw heterosexuality and "normal sexuality," Katz notes, "as the innate form of sexual satisfaction of the majority of the population," with this stress on numbers as the basis of the "normal" signifying a "historical break with the old, qualitative, procreative standard" (52, 53) that preceded it. As late as the 1920s in the US, however, the label "heterosexual" was associated not with "normal sex, but with perversion," the hetero in heterosexual referring "*not* to their [the heterosexual's] interest in a *different sex*, but to their desire *for two different sexes*" (19–20, emphasis in original). A more thoroughgoing account of heteronormativity than that offered in this paper would thus need to acknowledge the historical conditions of possibility enabling the construction of heterosexuality as a norm in the sense that it operates today.[10]

As Sara Ahmed observes, heteronormativity refers to "more than simply the presumption that it is normal to be heterosexual," however historically specific that idea may be. "The 'norm,'" as she rightly notes, "is regulative" (Ahmed 2004, 149). Heteronormativity, I want to suggest, borrowing from Robyn Wiegman, is thus more accurately construed as *both* "the consequence as well as the sustaining force" (Wiegman 2006, 94) not just of norms of sexed anatomy that posit two (and only two) mutually exclusive but complementary kinds of bodies (one male, one female), most easily distinguishable by their different genitalia, but also, following Judith Butler, of norms of gender and sexuality (Butler 1990): specifically,

the norms of binary gender that dictate that biological maleness *naturally* gives rise to masculinity and femaleness to femininity, and the norms of sexuality that construe heterosexuality as the outcome of "normal" psychological development and that ordain that heterosexual sex is "natural" – or, to put it another way, the norms that "naturalize" heterosexuality.[11]

As Butler and others have pointed out, such (hetero-)norms constitute both the bodies that conform to them *as well as those that deviate from them* (Butler 2004, 42; see also Chambers 2007, 49 n. 17). This, of course, means that although as Corber and Valocchi remind us, phenomena such as intersex and transgender "provide graphic illustrations of the institutional and discursive power required to maintain the normative alignment of sex, gender, and sexuality" (Corber and Valocchi 2003, 9), heteronormativity also affects, though is *not necessarily co-extensive with*, heterosexuality. It conditions what it is acceptable to feel, who it is legitimate to be attracted to, and defines the kind of behavior attaching to heterosexual masculinity and femininity. In this sense, the impact of heteronormativity is both constitutive and regulatory.

What, though, is *violent* about heteronormativity understood in this way? Here I turn to Butler's work to explain. In the course of discussing Monique Wittig's work in *Gender Trouble*, Butler writes that (for Wittig) "'sex' is the reality-effect of a violent process that is concealed" by its (re)presentation of sex as an "objective datum of experience" (Butler 1990, 114). In "Contingent Foundations" (Butler 1992), she elaborates further on what she understands by her earlier statement that categorization effects a "material and physical violence against the bodies" it claims merely to describe (Butler 1990, 116). She notes:

Consider that most material of concepts, "sex," which Monique Wittig calls a thoroughly political category, and which Michel Foucault calls a regulatory and "fictitious unity." For both theorists, sex does not *describe* a prior materiality, but produces and regulates the *intelligibility* of the *materiality* of bodies. For both, and in different ways, the category of sex imposes a duality and a uniformity on bodies in order to maintain reproductive sexuality as a compulsory order.... I would like to suggest that this kind of categorization can be called a violent one, a forceful one, and that this discursive ordering and production of bodies in accord with the category of sex *is itself a material violence.* (17, my emphasis)

To talk of the categorization of bodies in terms of sex as "violent" may seem odd. Conventional approaches to violence usually conceive of it as "something done to bodies," entailing the "*rupturing* of the surface of the body, a wound" (Ross 2004, 2–4), "bruises, scratches, swellings ... broken bones ... loss of body parts, or death" (Keane 2004, 35); it is a phenomenon, in other words, that equates to "physical aggression" (Richard Felson, cited in Ray 2011, 9): violence, that is, of the kind Araujo was subjected to so lethally by her killers. As Sally Engle Merry reminds us, however, "violence as an act of injury cannot be understood outside the social and cultural systems which give it meaning" (Merry 2009, n.p.). The ability to "see" certain acts or phenomena as violent – and/or as particular kinds of violence – is socially and politically contingent. Here it is only necessary to recall the feminist campaign that constructed non-consensual sex within marriage as a form of gendered political violence.

Although in work on violence, it is common, even usual, to regard the body as existing *prior to* the violence it experiences, Butler, in calling on Wittig and Foucault,

contends by contrast that the categorization of the sexed body is itself *materially* violent. It is this particular insight I want to pursue here.

Understanding sex as an effect is not, of course, new. "Sex," as Foucault recognized, cannot be conceived of "*in itself*" (Foucault 1978, 152); it is, rather, "an artificial unity, anatomical elements, biological functions, conducts, sensations, and pleasures" (154). The idea that classifying bodies in accordance with the norm of sexual dimorphism is a mode of violence, however, is perhaps more controversial. In "Contingent Foundations," Butler describes this process in Derridean terms as the "violence of the letter" (Derrida 1974; Butler 1992, 17), "writing," or language, that "is violent in so far as it classifies and categorizes" (Howells 1999, 53).[12] In later work, however, she refers to it as "normative violence" (Butler 1999, xix–xx; see also Butler 2007; Chambers 2007; Jenkins 2007; Lloyd 2007; and Mills 2007) and to "gender norms ... as violations" (Butler 2004, 214).

I am not concerned in this paper with the details of these terminological shifts. It is what Butler's different accounts share that is of interest: namely, the idea that there is violence in the way that bodies are constituted and regulated as sexed, whether that violence operates through language or discourse (as implied by the violence of the letter), through norms (as suggested by normative violence), or through some as yet other undisclosed means. I refer, in this paper, to this understanding of violence as "heteronormative violence" rather than the more generic "normative violence" as adopted by, for instance, Chambers or Mills (Chambers 2007; Mills 2007). I do so to signal the *specificity* of the violence I am concerned with here – namely the violence enacted in the ordering and classification of bodies according to the norms of sex, gender, and sexuality denoted above – rather than to generalize about "the inherent violence of norms" *per se* (Chambers 2007, 49 n. 17; see also Mills 2007) as they relate to all manner of phenomena.[13]

According to Butler, "sex" is not made once and for all but is rather "an ideal construct ... forcibly materialized through time" (Butler 1993, 2), the effect of an "iterable process" (Butler 2007, 182). Logically, therefore, the violence productive of binary sex must itself also be *reiterative*. These various violent (re)iterations or materializations, I suggest, take different forms. One takes place when trans individuals are violently assaulted for being trans: when, that is, (to echo Butler) the "violent enforcement of a category violently constructed," occurs and the body of the trans individual is "reduced" (through physical violence) to its biological "sex" (Butler 1990, 166 n. 26). Another mode of violent materialization occurs, as I show in the next section, at trial each time the lawyers involved position trans women such as Gwen Araujo as "male."

## The Trans Panic Defense and/as Heteronormative Violence

In positing the idea of trans panic as a legitimate excuse or justification for murder, the law is engaged in the articulation of norms that "universalize particular modes of living, and specific identities and acts" (Bower 1997, 267). The law's relation to what Foucault calls "the things to be known," in this case the body of the trans individual, is one "of violence, domination, power, and force, a relation of violation" (Foucault 1994, 9). This violence is heteronormative in the case of the trans panic defense because the knowledge the law claims about the body of the victim is its "true sex," sex the law conceives of in binary terms. The assertions the law makes about binary morphology do not describe an objective truth about the sexed corpus, however; they forcibly constitute that body as "sexed." This

is evident in the defense's interpretation of the significance of the discovery that Araujo had male genitalia.

Although Araujo lived as a woman and so did not, in fact, misrepresent her *gender* to her killers, because her gender was feminine, in terms of sexed intelligibility she was immediately recuperated by the defense as "male" (see also Tilleman 2010, 1679). Indeed, the charge of deception used to ground cases of provocation in trans homicides rests on this very assumption: that the victim has hidden knowledge of her/his "real" sex from her/his assailants and has, thus, deceived them.[14] Instead of recognizing Araujo's own self-designation as a woman, lawyers in the two trials appropriated to themselves the authority to determine both Araujo's gender and sexed identity (Mackenzie and Marcel 2009). They did so by reiterating a heteronormative understanding of the body and of the "normal" relation assumed to obtain between anatomical sex and gender – namely, where genital sex is taken to be determinative of gender. Since Araujo had male sex organs, according to this logic, it could only mean that no matter how convincing her performance of femininity, she was really a man "pretending" to be a woman.

At issue in trans murder trials, however, is not just the relation between sex and gender. Since, according to the logic of heteronormativity, Araujo lacked the "biological credentials" (Schilt and Westbrook 2009, 456) that would confirm her sexual orientation as heterosexual (namely, a vagina), her sexuality was also put in question. Since she was "really" a "he" who had sex with men, then as far as the defendants and their lawyers were concerned, "Eddie" *must* be gay.[15] The exposure of Araujo's genitalia was seen as provocative not only because it revealed that she was male but, additionally, because it led her killers to "understand" the sexual relations they had engaged in with her as acts of *homosexual* sex, not the heterosexual sex they had believed them to be. The trans panic defense thus reveals what Andrew Sharpe refers to as "the legal anxiety over homosexuality" that appears when the parties to sexual relations share similar genitals, an anxiety heightened when *both* of those parties "assert heterosexual identity and desire" (Sharpe 2006, 628), as in the case under examination.

This anxiety is discernible in the stress placed on the impact the discovery of Araujo's "genital topography" (Sharpe 2006, 623) allegedly had on the defendants. Lawyers deployed testimony both from and about Merel that drew attention to the fact that he "threw up, disgusted that he had had sexual relations with a man"; became agitated at the thought that he might be gay "based on his belief that it was impossible for a heterosexual man to receive sexual pleasure from another man" (*People v. Merel*); and that, as he attacked Araujo, he repeated over and over the "sobbing mantra: 'I can't be ... gay'" (Haddock 2004; Lee 2004; Steinberg 2005, 520; and *People v. Merel*).

Steinberg also recounts how another of the defendants spoke about how "his illusion as to normality and the way things are supposed to be had been shattered" (Steinberg 2005, 520) when he learned Araujo was anatomically male. It was this that led Thorman to describe "what Eddie had done" (to recall his phrase) as a "theft of heterosexuality" (Szymanski 2006b). As he told the jury in closing arguments: "Sexuality, our sexual choices, are very important to us. They're private, they're personal ... and for young men, they form a substantial part of their identity.... That's why the deception in this case was such a substantial provocation – sexual fraud, a deception, a betrayal" (Thorman, cited in St. John 2004b) – because Araujo had enticed Merel and Magidson unknowingly into homosexual sex with "him," the disclosure of which tipped

them over the edge into violence.

The trans panic defense as articulated at the trial of Araujo's killers, and echoed in other parallel trials, enacts the violence that is heteronormativity in a number of different ways: in its assertion of binary sex, the "fact" of which, as Allen notes, is "taken as a fundamental a priori of legal reasoning" (cited in Howe 1997); in its (re) production of heterosexuality as the coupling of one anatomically male with one anatomically female body; when it posits the heterosexual male as a "real" man who prefers "real" women; and when it presents heterosexual masculinity as sexually predatory by nature but never sexually vulnerable (Lee 2008, 488). It does so, too, when it takes heterosexuality to be the "presumptive standard" (Chen 2000, 209) of reasonableness.[16] Heteronormative violence is further performed through the suggestion that the trans woman's body, the materiality of her sex, is provocation enough *in itself* to bring about her own demise: when it assumes that the corpus provides a sufficient reason – a "sexed" reason, as Butler might put it – for murder. It is manifest, finally, in the attempt to "disavow" the violence the transwoman suffers, as Fiona Jenkins writes in a different context, "in the name of a right to destroy that which threatens one's very existence" (Jenkins 2007, 166). When lawyers contend that lethal violence "should be *expected* or *excused* if it is committed in response to the discovery of a partner's transgender status" (Szymanski 2005, my emphasis), and when they claim, as Thorman did, that the "right" of "a heterosexual male ... to make choices for his life, and ... to choose the gender of his partners" trumps that of the victim "to be who she thinks she is" (cited in St. John 2004a), it is clearly normative heterosexuality that is being protected.

The trans panic defense draws (some of) its heteronormative "force" from its reiteration of the commonly held idea that there exists a natural sexual dimorphism, an idea that organizes its legal logic. But this forceful reiteration is also, and *crucially*, the means by which the trans panic defense *itself* operates forcibly to "sex" the bodies of trans individuals *and* to discipline and regulate them according to the gender norms productive of presumptive heterosexuality.[17] By actively "sexing" Araujo as male and by presenting her as a gender fraud, the defense team denied Araujo's own gender identification as feminine *and*, consequently, categorized the sexual relations she had with men as straightforwardly homosexual ones rather than as complexly heterosexual.[18]

### The Violence that Is Heteronormativity

My aim in this paper has been to explore heteronormative violence. This violence, I have argued, operates through a range of different modalities, two of which I have examined in this paper: the physical violence inflicted on Araujo's body by her murderers – the beating that killed her – and the violence of "categorization" (to borrow Butler's description) that inheres in the trans panic defense. Both are modes of heteronormative violence in that both reduce Araujo's body to its "sex"; both, that is, produce it *as male*, though each does so in a different way: one through sickening brutality, the other discursively, through a carefully crafted legal defense strategy. Heteronormative violence, in this case, I have suggested, was forcibly enacted through the circulation of a series of norms or purported "facts" of sex, foremost among which were the twin norms that bodies are sexually dimorphic, revealed by the presence or absence of particular genitalia, and that it is possible to read sexual orientation off that genitalia. In other words, that "heterosexual" desire is tied to body morphology (that a person with a vagina desires a person with a penis) rather than to gender identity (that someone feminine desires someone masculine)....

### References

Ahmed, Sara. 2004. *The Cultural Politics of Emotion*. Edinburgh, UK: Edinburgh UP.

Baldman, Anthony. 2006. "Bill Aims to Eliminate Gay/Trans Panic Strategies in Criminal Trials." *Gay and Lesbian Times*, January 19.

Balzer, Carsten. 2009. "Every Third Day the Murder of a Trans Person Is Reported." *Liminalis: Journal for Sex/Gender Emancipation and Resistance* 3: 147–59.

Beasley, Chris. 2005. *Gender and Sexuality: Critical Theories, Critical Thinkers*. London: Sage.

Berlant, Lauren, and Michael Warner. 1998. "Sex in Public." *Critical Inquiry* 24 (2): 547–66.

Bettcher, Talia Mae. 2006. "Appearance, Reality and Gender Deception: Reflections on Transphobic Violence and the Politics of Pretence." In *Violence, Victims, Justifications: Philosophical Approaches*, ed. Felix O'Murchadha. Oxford: Peter Lang.

——. 2007. "Evil Deceivers and Make-Believers: On Transphobic Violence and the Politics of Illusion." *Hypatia* 22 (3): 43–65.

Bower, L. 1997. "Queer Problems/Straight Solutions: The Limits of 'Official Recognition.'" In *Playing with Fire*, ed. Shane Phelan. London: Routledge.

Brigham, Roger. 2006. "TG Panic Bill Weakened." *The Bay Area Reporter*, 24 April.

Butler, Judith. 1990. *Gender Trouble: Feminism and the Subversion of Identity*. London: Routledge.

——. 1992. Contingent Foundations. In *Feminists Theorize the Political*, ed. Judith Butler and Joan Scott. London: Routledge.

——. 1993. *Bodies that Matter: On the Discursive Limits of "Sex."* London: Routledge.

_____. 1999. *Gender Trouble: Feminism and the Subversion of Identity.* Tenth anniversary edition. London: Routledge.

_____. 2004. *Undoing Gender.* London: Routledge.

_____. 2007. Reply from Judith Butler to Mills and Jenkins. *Differences: A Journal of Feminist Cultural Studies* 18 (2): 180–95.

Chambers, Samuel A. 2007. "Normative Violence after 9/11: Rereading the Politics of Gender Trouble." *New Political Science* 29 (1): 43–60.

_____. 2009. *The Queer Politics of Television.* London: I.B. Taurus.

Chen, Christina Pei-Lin. 2000. "Provocation's Privileged Desire: The Provocation Doctrine, 'Homosexual Panic,' and the Non-Violent Unwanted Sexual Advance Defense." *Cornell Journal of Law and Public Policy* 10: 195–235.

Corber, Robert J., and Stephen Valocchi, eds. 2003. *Queer Studies: An Interdisciplinary Reader.* Oxford: Blackwell Publishing.

DeFao, Janine, and Kelly St. John. 2004. "Retrial in Araujo Case Presents Challenges." *San Francisco Chronicle*, June 28.

Derrida, Jacques. 1974. *Of Grammatology.* Baltimore: Johns Hopkins UP.

Finley, Lucinda M. 1989. "Breaking Women's Silence in Law: The Dilemma of the Gendered Nature of Legal Reasoning." *Notre Dame Law Review* 64: 886–910.

Foucault, Michel. 1978. *History of Sexuality.* Volume 1. Harmondsworth, UK: Penguin.

_____. 1980. "The Confession of the Flesh." In *Michel Foucault: Power/Knowledge. Selected Interviews and Other Writings 1972–1977*, ed. Colin Gordon. Brighton: The Harvester P.

_____. 1994. "Truth and Juridical Forms." In *Michel Foucault: Power. Essential Works of Foucault 1954–1984*, vol. 3, ed. James D. Faubion. London: Penguin.

Golder, Ben. 2004. "The Homosexual Advance Defence and the Law/Body Nexus: Towards a Poetics of Law Reform." Murdoch University Electronic Journal of Law. http://papers.ssrn.com/sol3/papers.cfm?abstract_id=1351564 (accessed September 25, 2012).

Haddock, Vicki. 2004. "'Gay Panic' Defense in Araujo Case." *San Francisco Chronicle*, May 16.

Halberstam, Judith. 2005. *In a Queer Time and Place: Transgender Bodies, Subcultural Lives.* New York: New York UP.

Hernandez, Lance. 2009. "Wednesday: Closing Arguments." Andrade murder trial blog. http://www.thedenverchannel.com/news/19250576/detail.html (accessed November 5, 2011).

Hoge, Patrick. 2004. "Defense Calls Transgender Victim guilty of 'Deception and Betrayal.'" *San Francisco Chronicle*, April 16.

Howe, Adrian. 1997. "More Folk Provoke Their Own Demise (Homophobic Violence and Sexed Excuses – Rejoining the Provocation Law Debate, Courtesy of the Homosexual Advance Defence." *Sydney Law Review* 19 (3): 335–65.

Howells, Christina. 1999. *Derrida: Deconstruction from Phenomenology to Ethics.* Cambridge, UK: Polity.

Human Rights Commission. 2011. "How Do Transgender People Suffer from Discrimination?" http://2fwww.hrc.org/issues/1508.htm (accessed November 25, 2011).

Ingraham, Chrys, ed. 2005. *Thinking Straight: The Power, the Promise, and the Paradox of Heterosexuality.* London: Routledge.

Jackson, Stevi. 1999. *Heterosexuality in Question.* London: Sage.

_____. 2006. "Gender, Sexuality and Heterosexuality: The Complexity (and Limits) of Heteronormativity." *Feminist Theory* 7 (1): 105–21.

Jenkins, Fiona. 2007. "Toward a Nonviolent Ethics: Response to Catherine Mills." *Differences: A Journal of Feminist Cultural Studies* 18 (2): 157–79.

Katz, 1995. *The Invention of Heterosexuality.* Chicago: U of Chicago P.

Keane, John. 2004. *Violence and Democracy.* Cambridge, UK: Cambridge UP.

Lee, Cynthia. 2008. "The Gay Panic Defense." *University of California, Davis, Law Review* 42: 471–566.

Lee, Henry. 2004. "Araujo Begged for Mercy." *San Francisco Chronicle*, April 27.

Lieber, Sally. n.d. AB1160 Fact Sheet: The Gwen Araujo Justice for Victims Act. *Equality California*.

Lloyd, Moya. 2007. *Judith Butler: From Norms to Politics*. Cambridge, UK: Polity.

MacKenzie, Gordene, and Mary Marcel. 2009. "Media Coverage of the Murder of U.S. Transwomen of Color." In *Local Violence, Global Media: Feminist Analyses of Gendered Representations*, ed. Lisa M. Cuklanz and Sujata Moorti. New York: Peter Lang.

McDonald, Elisabeth. 2006. "No Straight Answer: Homophobia as Both an Aggravating and Mitigating Factor in New Zealand Homicide Cases." *Victoria University of Wellington Law Review* 37: 223–48.

Merry, Sally Engle 2009. *Gender Violence: A Cultural Perspective*. Oxford: Wiley-Blackwell. Kindle edition.

Mills, Catherine. 2007. "Normative Violence, Vulnerability, and Responsibility." *Differences: A Journal of Feminist Cultural Studies* 18 (2): 133–56.

Organization for Security and Cooperation in Europe (OSCE). 2007. "Hate Crimes in the OSCE Region: Incidents and Responses." Annual Report for 2006. Warsaw: OSCE.

*People v. Merel*, Cal: Court of Appeal, 1st Appellate Dist., 4th Div. 2009. http://scholar.google.co.uk/scholar_case?case=7219233048697743719&hl=en&as_sdt=2,7 (accessed October 8, 2012).

Ray, Larry. 2011. *Violence and Society*. London: Sage.

Richardson, Diane, ed. 1996. *Theorising Heterosexuality*. Maidenhead, UK: Open UP.

Ross, Daniel. 2004. *Violent Democracy*. Cambridge, UK: Cambridge UP.

Schilt, Kristen, and Laurel Westbrook. 2009. "Doing Gender, Doing Heteronormativity: 'Gender normals,' Transgender People, and the Social Maintenance of Heterosexuality." *Gender and Society* 23 (4): 440–64.

Sharpe, Andrew. 2006. "From Functionality to Aesthetics: The Architecture of Transgender Jurisprudence." In *The Transgender Studies Reader*, ed. Susan Stryker and Stephen Whittle. New York: Routledge.

St. John, Kelly. 2004a. "Nature of Killing Focus at End of Araujo Case: Was Transgender Teen Slain in Heat of Passion or Revenge?" *San Francisco Chronicle*, June 1.

_____. 2004b. "Defense in Araujo Trial Gives Final Argument." *San Francisco Chronicle*, June 3.

_____. 2005. "Teenager Provoked Own Killing, Attorney Says." *San Francisco Chronicle*, August 30.

St. Pierre, Ethan. 2011. "Statistics and Other Info." http://www.transgenderdor.org/?page_id=192 (accessed July 17, 2011).

Steinberg, Victoria L. 2005. "A Heat of Passion Offense: Emotions and Bias in 'Trans Panic' Mitigation Claims." *Boston College Third World Law Review* 25: 499–524.

Szymanski, Zak. 2005. "Two Murder Convictions in Araujo Case." *Bay Area Reporter*, September 15.

_____. 2006a. "Harris Announces 'Panic Defense' Conference." http://www.law.ucla.edu/williamsinstitute/press/HarrisAnnoucesPanicDefenseConference (accessed November 16, 2009).

_____. 2006b. "DA Convenes 'Panic' Conference." http://www.law.ucla/williamsinstitute/press/DAConvenesPanicConference.html (accessed November 17, 2009).

Tilleman, Morgan. 2010. "(Trans)forming the Provocation Defense." *Journal of Criminal Law and Criminology* 100 (4): 1659–88.

Warner, Michael. 1991. "Introduction: Fear of a Queer Planet." *Social Text* 29: 3–17.

_____, ed. 1993. *Fear of a Queer Planet: Queer Politics and Social Theory*. Minneapolis: U of Minnesota P.

Whaley, Monte. 2008. "Smile Called 'Provoking Act' in Transgender Case." *Denver Post*, September 19.

Wickberg, Daniel. 2000. "Homophobia: On the Cultural History of an Idea." *Critical Inquiry* 27 (1): 42–57.
Wiegman, Robyn. 2006. "Heteronormativity and the Desire for Gender." *Feminist Theory* 7 (1): 89–103.
Yep, Gust A. 2002. "From Homophobia and Heterosexism to Heteronormativity." *Journal of Lesbian Studies* 6 (3–4): 163–76.

## Study Questions

1. Based on Lloyd's descriptions, explain, as best you can, what "heteronormativity" (normative heterosexuality) is. How might "heteronormativity" be a form of cultural imperialism?

2. How is the concept of heteronormative violence broader than ordinary notions of violence that associate violence with acts of physical harm? Is this a useful way to think about violence?

3. Lloyd asserts that the trans panic defense and the murder of Gwen Araujo are *modes* of the same kind of violence. How are they both similar?

4. Can you think of an understanding of human sexuality that wouldn't be normatively violent?

## Notes

1  Since Araujo conceived of and presented herself as a woman, I will also refer to her by either her feminine name, Gwen, or by the feminine pronoun, except when quoting directly from other sources.

2  For example, the defense succeeded at the 1997 trial in Boston of William Palmer, who beat, strangled, and suffocated to death trans woman Chanelle Pickett. Palmer was acquitted of both first- and second-degree murder at his trial, *and* of manslaughter. He received a two-year sentence for assault and battery (Haddock 2004; Steinberg 2005, 521; Tilleman 2010, 1671). The same defense was also used in 2004 when Estanislao Martinez was sentenced to four years in prison for stabbing trans woman Joel Robles more than twenty times with a pair of scissors and killing her (Bettcher 2006, 183). A plea of "voluntary manslaughter" was accepted by the District Attorney in this case because the "prosecutor did not believe he could get a jury to convict for murder in that case" (Jennifer Muir, cited in Brigham 2006).

3  For instance, San Francisco District Attorney Kamala Harris convened a symposium on the "panic defense" that included a panel entitled "The Araujo Trial: A Case Study," featuring members of the defense team as well as Chris Lamiero, the lead prosecutor in the case (Szymanski 2006a). Furthermore, on September 28, 2006 the Gwen Araujo Justice for Victims Act (AB 1160) was signed into California state law by its then Governor, Arnold Schwarzenegger. This act, inspired by the killing of both Araujo and Robles, limits the use of "'panic strategies' to influence the proceedings of a criminal trial" (Lieber n.d.).

4  The term *archive* is Judith Halberstam's (Halberstam 2005, 23). The Araujo archive includes academic writing, legal documents, a film, and press reports. According to MacKenzie and

Marcel, 16,685 words were published by the press about this case in the first seven days after Araujo's murder compared to just 5,400 words for Pickett's murder for the same timeframe; this rose to over 392,000 published words between 2002 and April 2008 (MacKenzie and Marcel 2009, 103 n. 29).

5  As several commentators have noted, there is a problem with conceiving of attitudes toward nonnormative sexual minorities as individual phobias (Wickberg 2000, 45; Chambers 2009, 34) because doing so occludes the political, cultural, social, and legal arrangements (institutional, organizational, and ideological) that normalize heterosexuality and conceive of nonheterosexual modes of being, doing, or acting as nonnormative.

6  The jurors split 10–2 in favor of acquitting Merel and Cazares, and 7–5 in favor of convicting Magidson (DeFao and St. John 2004).

7  In legal terms, a shift took place from the homosexual panic defense (HPD) to the homosexual advance defense (HAD).

8  Using a transgender person's birth name rather than his or her preferred name, as MacKenzie and Marcel suggest, is a way "to undermine the transwoman's transgender identity, rather than representing her as a person with a legitimate gender and body" (MacKenzie and Marcel 2009, 83).

9  At the preliminary hearing at the trial of Allen Andrade, who murdered trans woman Angie Zapata, his lawyer defended him by arguing that: "At best, this is a case about passion," continuing, "When (Zapata) smiled at him, this was a highly provoking act, and it would cause someone to have an aggressive reaction" (Annette Kundelius, cited in Whaley 2008). In this case, the Colorado jury took two hours to convict Andrade of first-degree murder, with a three-year hate crime enhancement added to his conviction (Tilleman 2010, 1662).

10  Heteronormativity is perhaps best understood as functioning as a *dispositif* in Foucault's sense of the word: that is, as a complex ensemble of relations between (among other heterogeneous phenomena) discourses, institutions, laws, regulations, scientific propositions, and common sense beliefs that emerges at a particular historical moment in response to some kind of "urgent need" (Foucault 1980, 195).

11  For critical discussions of heterosexuality, see Richardson 1996; Jackson 1999; Ingraham 2005. For a critique of the relationship between heterosexuality and heteronormativity, see Jackson 2006.

12  Chambers provides an interesting discussion of the parallels between Derrida's and Butler's accounts of violence, though oddly he does not examine Butler's own discussion of the "violence of the letter" (Chambers 2007).

13  Although much of Chambers's actual discussion is on the link between "normative violence" and heteronormativity, his aim is to develop normative violence as a political concept that might be of interest to political theorists more generally (Chambers 2007, 49 n. 17). In discussing normative violence, however, Butler appears to argue *against* generalizing the concept too far (and, in particular, against assuming that "all normativity is founded in violence" [Butler 2007, 184]). I too want to reject the claim that norms or normativity *per se* are either necessarily or always violent. In this way I also keep my distance from those queer accounts of heteronormativity that apparently pathologize normativity as such (for further discussion of this point, see Wiegman 2006).

14  A similar charge of deception was laid against the victim in the Andrade trial (Hernandez 2009). As Andrade's lawyer told potential jurors at jury selection, "Angie was in fact Justin" (Kundelius, cited in Tilleman 2010, 1661). See Bettcher 2006, Bettcher 2007, and Schilt and Westbrook 2009 for articles exploring the association of transgender with gender deception.

15  Perversely, gay and lesbian activism may have done its work too well in this regard, in cementing the idea that same-sex desire essentially defines someone as homosexual.

16  Critics have argued that the standards of reasonableness operating in the US courts not only "reflect a male view of understandable homicidal violence" (Chen 2000, 195) but are predicated upon presumptive heterosexuality insofar as the courts have refused to postulate an alternative standard of "reasonableness" for male homosexuals or for women (straight or gay).

17  We could, in fact, go further and suggest that the logic of the trans panic defense also performs its violence against the defendants. Far from shoring up their heterosexuality, which had supposedly been threatened by the sexual encounters with Araujo, it actually destabilizes it, for if, according to its heteronormative logic, *being* a man is indicated by the presence of a penis and *being* gay by having a penis and having sex with men, then, by implication, the defendants must also *be* gay. I am grateful to one of the anonymous referees for *Hypatia* for prompting me to consider this inconsistency in the defense's logic, though I do not have the space here to pursue its implications any further.

18  In fact, the prosecutor in this case, Chris Lamiero, doubting he could convince the twelve jurors to "agree that Araujo was a woman" (Szymanski 2005), built his prosecution case on "the conduct of the defendants, not on the conduct of Gwen" (cited in Szymanski 2006b).

# 5. Catharine A. MacKinnon, "Sexual Harassment: Its First Decade in Court"

CATHARINE A. MACKINNON'S WORKS include *Only Words, Pornography and Civil Rights: A New Day for Women's Equality* (co-authored with Andrea Dworkin), *Women's Lives, Men's Laws, Toward a Feminist Theory of the State,* and *Sex Equality.* MacKinnon (b. 1946) assesses sexual harassment law in this chapter from her book *Feminism Unmodified: Discourses on Life and Law* (1987). MacKinnon explains that there was no language or law to name or address sexual harassment before it was legally recognized but that many women were, nevertheless, acquainted with its harm. Before sexual harassment law, the systematic abuse of creating a hostile work environment for women by subjecting them to unwelcome sexual advances or threatening women to provide sexual services in order to receive or keep a job was unnamed and was not considered a harm among men or by the courts. It was something women had to accept. In characterizing the division between the times before and after sexual harassment law, MacKinnon points to the necessity of feminist politics and jurisprudence that attempt to correct unspoken and entrenched patriarchal or sexist norms, privileges, and abuses in employment, education, law, and the family.

SEXUAL HARASSMENT, THE EVENT, is not new to women.[1] It is the law of injuries that it is new to. Sexual pressure imposed on someone who is not in an economic position to refuse it became sex discrimination in the midseventies,[2] and in education soon afterward.[3] It became possible to do something legal about sexual harassment because some women took women's experience of violation seriously enough to design a law around it, as if what happens to women matters. This was apparently such a startling way of proceeding that sexual harassment was protested as a feminist invention. Sexual harassment, the event, was not invented by feminists; the perpetrators did that with no help from us. Sexual harassment, the legal claim – the idea that the law should see it the way its victims see it – is definitely a feminist invention. Feminists first took women's experience seriously enough to uncover this problem and conceptualize it and pursue it legally. That legal claim is just beginning to produce more than a handful of reported cases. Ten years later, "[i]t may well be that sex harassment is the hottest present day Title VII issue."[4] It is time for a down-the-road assessment of this departure.

The law against sexual harassment is a practical attempt to stop a form of exploitation. It is also one test of sexual politics as feminist jurisprudence, of possibilities for social change for women through law. The existence of a law against sexual harassment has affected both the context of meaning within which social life is lived and the concrete delivery of rights through the legal system. The sexually harassed have been given a name for their suffering and an analysis that connects it with gender. They have been given a forum, legitimacy to speak, authority to make claims, and an avenue for possible relief. Before, what happened to them was all right. Now it is not.

This matters. Sexual abuse mutes victims socially through the violation itself. Often the abuser enforces secrecy and silence; secrecy and silence may be part of what is so sexy about sexual abuse. When the state also forecloses a validated space for denouncing and rectifying the victimization, it seals this secrecy and reenforces this silence. The harm of this process, a process that utterly precludes speech, then becomes all of a piece. If there is no right place to go to say, this hurt me, then a woman is simply the one who can be treated this way, and no harm, as they say, is done.

In point of fact, I would prefer not to have to spend all this energy getting the law to recognize wrongs to women as wrong. But it seems to be necessary to legitimize our injuries as injuries in order to delegitimize our victimization by them, without which it is difficult to move in more positive ways. The legal claim for sexual harassment made the events of sexual harassment illegitimate socially as well as legally for the first time. Let me know if you figure out a better way to do that.

At this interface between law and society, we need to remember that the legitimacy courts give they can also take. Compared with a possibility of relief where no possibility of relief existed, since women started out with nothing in this area, this worry seems a bit fancy. Whether the possibility of relief alters the terms of power that gives rise to sexual harassment itself, which makes getting away with it possible, is a different problem. Sexual harassment, the legal claim, is a demand that state authority stand behind women's refusal of sexual access in certain situations that previously were a masculine prerogative. With sexism, there is always a risk that our demand for self-determination will be taken as a demand for paternal protection and will therefore strengthen male power rather than undermine it. This seems a particularly valid concern because the law of sexual harassment began as case law, without legislative guidance or definition.

Institutional support for sexual self-determination is a victory; institutional paternalism reinforces our lack of self-determination. The problem is, the state has never in fact protected women's dignity or bodily integrity. It just says it does. Its protections have been both condescending *and* unreal, in effect strengthening the protector's choice to violate the protected at will, whether the protector is the individual perpetrator or the state. This does not seem to me a reason not to have a law against sexual harassment. It is a reason to demand that the promise of "equal protection of the laws" be *delivered upon* for us, as it is when real people are violated. It is also part of a larger political struggle to value women more than the male pleasure of using us is valued. Ultimately, though, the question of whether the use of the state for women helps or hurts can be answered only in practice, because so little real protection of the laws has ever been delivered.

The legal claim for sexual harassment marks the first time in history, to my knowledge, that women have defined women's injuries in a law. Consider what has happened with rape. We have never defined the injury of rape; men define it. The men who define it, define what they take to be this violation of women according to, among other things, what they think they don't do. In this way rape becomes an act of a stranger (they mean Black) committed upon a woman (white) whom he has never seen before.... Ask a woman if she has ever been raped, and often she says, "Well ... not really." In that silence between the well and the not really, she just measured what happened to her against every rape case she ever heard about and decided she would lose in court. Especially when you are part of a subordinated group, your own definition of your injuries is powerfully shaped by your assessment of whether you could get anyone to do anything about it, including anything official. You are realistic by necessity, and the voice of law is the voice in power. When the design of a legal wrong does not fit the wrong as it happens to you, as is the case with rape, that law can undermine your social and political as well as legal legitimacy in saying that what happened was an injury at all – even to yourself.

It is never too soon to worry about this, but it may be too soon to know whether the law against sexual harassment will be taken away from us or turn into nothing or turn ugly in our hands. The fact is, this law is working surprisingly well for women by any standards, particularly when compared with the rest of sex discrimination law. If the question is whether a law designed from women's standpoint and administered through this legal system can do anything for women – which always seems to me to be a good question – this experience so far gives a qualified and limited yes.

It is hard to unthink what you know, but there was a time when the facts that amount to sexual harassment did not amount to sexual harassment. It is a bit like the injuries of pornography until recently. The facts amounting to the harm did not socially "exist," had no shape, no cognitive coherence; far less did they state a legal claim. It just happened to you. To the women to whom it happened, it wasn't part of anything, much less something big or shared like gender. It fit no known pattern. It was neither a regularity nor an irregularity. Even social scientists didn't study it, and they study anything that moves. When law recognized sexual harassment as a practice of sex discrimination, it moved it from the realm of "and then he … and then he …," the primitive language in which sexual abuse lives inside a woman, into an experience with a form, an etiology, a cumulativeness – as well as a club.

The shape, the positioning, and the club – each is equally crucial politically. Once it became possible to do something about sexual harassment, it became possible to know more about it, because it became possible for its victims to speak about it. Now we know, as we did not when it first became illegal, that this problem is commonplace. We know this not just because it has to be true, but as documented fact. Between a quarter and a third of women in the federal workforce report having been sexually harassed, many physically, at least once in the last two years.[5] Projected, that becomes 85 per cent of all women at some point in their working lives. This figure is based on asking women "Have you ever been sexually harassed?" – the conclusion – not "has this fact happened? has that fact happened?" which usually produces more. The figures for sexual harassment of students are comparable.[6]

When faced with individual incidents of sexual harassment, the legal system's first question was, is it a personal episode? Legally, this was a way the courts inquired into whether the incidents were based on sex, as they had to be to be sex discrimination. Politically, it was a move to isolate victims by stigmatizing them as deviant. It also seemed odd to me that a relationship was either personal or gendered, meaning that one is not a woman personally. Statistical frequency alone does not make an event not personal, of course, but the presumption that sexual pressure in contexts of unequal power is an isolated idiosyncrasy to unique individual victims has been undermined both by the numbers and by their division by gender. Overwhelmingly, it is men who sexually harass women, a lot of them. Actually, it is even more accurate to say that men do this than to say that women have this done to them. This is a description of the perpetrators' behavior, not of the statisticians' feminism.

Sexual harassment has also emerged as a creature of hierarchy. It inhabits what I call hierarchies among men: arrangements in which some men are below other men, as in employer/employee and teacher/student. In workplaces, sexual harassment by supervisors of subordinates is common; in education, by administrators of lower-level administrators, by faculty of students. But it also happens among coworkers, from third parties, even by subordinates in the workplace, men who are women's hierarchical inferiors or peers. Basically, it is done by men to women regardless of relative position on the formal hierarchy. I believe that the reason sexual harassment was first established as an injury of the systematic abuse of power in hierarchies among men is that this is power men recognize. They comprehend from personal experience that something is held over your head if you do not comply. The lateral or reverse hierarchical examples[7] suggest something beyond this, something men don't understand from personal experience because they take its advantages for granted: gender is also a hierarchy. The courts do not use this analysis, but some act as though they understand it.[8]

Sex discrimination law had to adjust a bit to accommodate the realities of sexual harassment. Like many other injuries of gender, it wasn't written for this. For something to be based on gender in the legal sense means it happens to a woman as a woman, not as an individual. Membership in a gender is understood as the opposite of, rather than part of, individuality. Clearly, sexual harassment is one of the last situations in which a woman is treated without regard to her sex; it is because of her sex that it happens. But the social meaning attributed to women as a class, in which women are defined as gender female by sexual accessibility to men, is not what courts have considered before when they have determined whether a given incident occurred because of sex.

Sex discrimination law typically conceives that something happens because of sex when it happens to one sex but not the other. The initial procedure is arithmetic: draw a gender line and count how many of each are on each side in the context at issue, or, alternatively, take the line drawn by the practice or policy and see if it also divides the sexes. One by-product of this head-counting method is what I call the bisexual defense.[9] Say a man is accused of sexually harassing a woman. He can argue that the harassment is not sex-based because he harasses both sexes equally, indiscriminately as it were. Originally it was argued that sexual harassment was not a proper gender claim because someone could harass both sexes. We argued that this was an issue of fact to be pleaded and proven, an issue of did he do this, rather than an issue of law, of whether he could have. The courts accepted that, creating this kamikaze defense. To my knowledge, no one has used the bisexual defense since.[10] As this example suggests, head counting can provide a quick topography of the terrain, but it has proved too blunt to distinguish treatment whose meaning is based on gender from treatment that has other social hermeneutics, especially when only two individuals are involved.

Once sexual harassment was established as bigger than personal, the courts' next legal question was whether it was smaller than biological. To say that sexual harassment was biological seemed to me a very negative thing to say about men, but defendants seemed to think it precluded liability. Plaintiffs argued that sexual harassment is not biological in that men who don't do it have nothing wrong with their testosterone levels. Besides, if murder were found to have biological correlates, it would still be a crime. Thus, although the question purported to be whether the acts were based on sex, the implicit issue seemed to be whether the source of the impetus for doing the acts was relevant to their harmfulness.

Similarly structured was the charge that women who resented sexual harassment were oversensitive. Not that the acts did not occur, but rather that it was unreasonable to experience them as harmful. Such a harm would be based not on sex but on individual hysteria. Again shifting the inquiry away from whether the acts are based on sex in the guise of pursuing it, away from whether they occurred to whether it should matter if they did, the question became whether the acts were properly harmful. Only this time it was not the perpetrator's drives that made him not liable but the target's sensitivity that made the acts not a harm at all. It was pointed out that too many people are victimized by sexual harassment to consider them all hysterics. Besides, in other individual injury law, victims are not blamed; perpetrators are required to take victims as they find them, so long as they are not supposed to be doing what they are doing.

Once these excuses were rejected, then it was said that sexual harassment was not really an employment-related problem. That became hard to maintain when it was her job the woman lost. If it was, in fact, a personal relationship, it apparently did not start and stop there, although this is also a question of proof, leaving the true meaning of the events to trial. The perpetrator may have thought it was all affectionate or friendly or fun, but the victim experienced it as hateful, dangerous, and damaging. Results in such cases have been mixed. Some judges have accepted the perpetrator's view; for instance, one judge held queries by the defendant such as "What am I going to get for this?" and repeated importunings to "go out" to be "susceptible of innocent interpretation."[11] Other judges, on virtually identical facts, for example, "When are you going to do something nice for me?"[12]

have held for the plaintiff. For what it's worth, the judge in the first case was a man, in the second a woman.

That sexual harassment is sex-based discrimination seems to be legally established, at least for now.[13] In one of the few recent cases that reported litigating the issue of sex basis, defendants argued that a sex-based claim was not stated when a woman worker complained of terms of abuse directed at her at work such as "slut," "bitch," and "fucking cunt" and "many sexually oriented drawings posted on pillars and at other conspicuous places around the warehouse" with plaintiffs' initials on them, presenting her having sex with an animal.[14] The court said: "[T]he sexually offensive conduct and language used would have been almost irrelevant and would have failed entirely in its crude purpose had the plaintiff been a man. I do not hesitate to find that but for her sex, the plaintiff would not have been subjected to the harassment she suffered."[15] "Obvious" or "patently obvious" they often call it.[16] I guess this is what it looks like to have proven a point.

Sexual harassment was first recognized as an injury of gender in what I called incidents of quid pro quo. Sometimes people think that harassment has to be constant. It doesn't; it's a term of art in which once can be enough. Typically, an advance is made, rejected, and a loss follows.[17] For a while it looked as if this three-step occurrence was in danger of going from one form in which sexual harassment can occur into a series of required hurdles. In many situations the woman is forced to submit instead of being able to reject the advance: The problem has become whether, say, being forced into intercourse at work will be seen as a failed quid pro quo or as an instance of sexual harassment in which the forced sex constitutes the injury.

I know of one reported case in employment and one in education in which women who were forced to submit to the sex brought a sexual harassment claim against the perpetrator; so far only the education case has won on the facts.[18] The employment case that lost on the facts was reversed on appeal. The pressures for sex were seen to state a claim without respect to the fact that the woman was not able to avoid complying.[19] It is unclear if the unwanted advances constitute a claim, separate and apart from whether or not they are able to be resisted, which they should; or if the acts of forced sex would also constitute an environmental claim separate from any quid pro quo, as it seems to me they also should. In the education case, the case of Paul Mann, the students were allowed to recover punitive damages for the forced sex.[20] If sexual harassment is not to be defined only as sexual attention imposed upon someone who is not in a position to refuse it, who refuses it, women who are forced to submit to sex must be understood as harmed not less, but as much or more, than those who are able to make their refusals effective.

Getting recoveries for women who have actually been sexually violated by the defendant will probably be a major battle. Women being compensated in money for sex they *had* violates male metaphysics because in that system sex is what a woman is for. As one judge concluded, "[T]here does not seem to be any issue that the plaintiff did not desire to have relations with [the defendant], but it is also altogether apparent that she willingly had sex with him."[21] Now what do you make of that? The woman was not physically forced at the moment of penetration, and since it is sex she must have willed it, is about all you can make of it. The sexual politics of the situation is that men do not see a woman who has had sex as victimized, whatever the conditions. One dimension of this problem involves whether a woman who has been violated through sex has any credibility. Credibility is difficult to separate from the definition of the injury, since an injury in which the victim is not believed to have been injured *because she has been injured* is not a real injury, legally speaking.

The question seems to be whether a woman is valuable enough to hurt, so that what is done to her is a harm. Once a woman has had sex, voluntarily or by force – it doesn't matter – she is regarded as too damaged to be further damageable, or something. Many women who have been raped in the course of sexual harassment have been advised by their lawyers not to mention the rape because it would destroy their credibility! The fact that abuse is long term has suggested to some finders of fact that it must have been tolerated or even wanted, although sexual harassment that becomes a condition of work has also been established as a legal claim in its own right.[22] I once was talking with a judge about a case he was sitting on in which Black teenage girls alleged that some procedures at their school violated their privacy. He told me that with their sexual habits they had no privacy to lose. It seemed he knew what their sexual habits were from evidence in the case, examples of the privacy violations.

The more aggravated an injury becomes, the more it ceases to exist. Why is incomprehensible to me, but how it functions is not. Our most powerful moment is on paper, in complaints we frame, and our worst is in the flesh in court. Although it isn't much, we have the most credibility when we are only the idea of us and our violation in their minds. In our allegations we construct reality to some extent; face to face, their angle of vision frames us irrevocably. In court we have breasts, we are Black, we are (in a word) women. Not that we are ever free of that, but the moment we physically embody our complaint, and they can see us, the pornography of the process starts in earnest.

I have begun to think that a major reason

that many women do not bring sexual harassment complaints is that they know this. They cannot bear to have their personal account of sexual abuse reduced to a fantasy they invented, used to define them and to pleasure the finders of fact and the public. I think they have a very real sense that their accounts are enjoyed, that others are getting pleasure from the first-person recounting of their pain, and that is the content of their humiliation at these rituals. When rape victims say they feel raped again on the stand, and victims of sexual harassment say they feel sexually harassed in the adjudication, it is not exactly metaphor. I hear that they – in being publicly sexually humiliated by the legal system, as by the perpetrator – are pornography. The first time it happens, it is called freedom; the second time, it is called justice.

If a woman is sexually defined – meaning all women fundamentally, intensified by previous sexual abuse or identification as lesbian, indelible if a prostitute – her chances of recovery for sexual abuse are correspondingly reduced. I'm still waiting for a woman to win at trial against a man who forced her to comply with the sex. Suppose the male plaintiff in one sexual harassment case who rented the motel room in which the single sexual encounter took place had been a woman, and the perpetrator had been a man. When the relationship later went bad, it was apparently not a credibility problem for *him* at trial that he had rented the motel room. Nor was *his* sexual history apparently an issue. Nor, apparently, was it said when he complained he was fired because the relationship went bad, that he had "asked for" the relationship. That case was reversed on appeal on legal grounds, but he did win at trial.[23] The best one can say about women in such cases is that women who have had sex but not with the accused may have some chance. In one case the judge did not believe the plaintiff's denial of an affair with

another coworker, but did believe that she had been sexually harassed by the defendant.[24] In another, the woman plaintiff actually had "linguistic intimacy" with another man at work, yet when she said that what happened to her with the defendant was sexual harassment, she was believed.[25] These are miraculous. A woman's word on these matters is usually indivisible. In another case a woman accused two men of sexual harassment. She had resisted and refused one man to whom she had previously submitted under pressure for a long time. He was in the process of eliminating her from her job when the second man raped her. The first man's defense was that it went on so long, she must have liked it. The second man's defense was that he had heard that she had had sexual relations with the first man, so he felt this was something she was open to.[26] This piggyback defense is premised on the class definition of woman as whore, by which I mean what men mean: one who exists to be sexually done to, to be sexually available on men's terms, that is, a woman. If this definition of women is accepted, it means that if a woman has ever had sex, forced or voluntary, she can't be sexually violated.

A woman can be seen in these terms by being a former rape victim or by the way she uses language. One case holds that the evidence shows "the allegedly harassing conduct was substantially welcomed and encouraged by plaintiff. She actively contributed to the distasteful working environment by her own profane and sexually suggestive conduct."[27] She swore, apparently, and participated in conversations about sex. This effectively made her harassment-proof. Many women joke about sex to try to defuse men's sexual aggression, to try to be one of the boys in hopes they will be treated like one. This is to discourage sexual advances, not to encourage them. In other cases, judges have understood that "the plaintiffs did not appreciate the remarks and

... many of the other women did not either."[28]

The extent to which a woman's job is sexualized is also a factor. If a woman's work is not to sell sex, and her employer requires her to wear a sexually suggestive uniform, if she is repeatedly sexually harassed by the clientele, she may have a claim against her employer.[29] Similarly, although "there may well be a limited category of jobs (such as adult entertainment) in which sexual harassment may be a rational consequence of such employment," one court was "simply not prepared to say that a female who goes to work in what is apparently a predominantly male workplace should reasonably expect sexual harassment as part of her job."[30] There may be trouble at some point over what jobs are selling sex, given the sexualization of anything a woman does.

Sexual credibility, that strange amalgam of whether your word counts with whether or how much you were hurt, also comes packaged in a variety of technical rules in the sexual harassment cases: evidence, discovery, and burden of proof. In 1982 the EEOC held that if a victim was sexually harassed without a corroborating witness, proof was inadequate as a matter of law.[31] (Those of you who wonder about the relevance of pornography, get this: if nobody watched, it didn't happen.) A woman's word, even if believed, was legally insufficient, even if the man had nothing to put against it other than his word and the plaintiff's burden of proof. Much like women who have been raped, women who have experienced sexual harassment say, "But I couldn't prove it." They mean they have nothing but their word. Proof is when what you say counts against what someone else says – for which it must first be believed. To say as a matter of law that the woman's word is per se legally insufficient is to assume that, with sexual violations uniquely, the defendant's denial is dispositive, is proof. To say a woman's word is no proof amounts to saying a woman's word

is worthless. Usually all the man has is his denial. In 1983 the EEOC found sexual harassment on a woman's word alone. It said it was enough, without distinguishing or overruling the prior case.[32] Perhaps they recognized that women don't choose to be sexually harassed in the presence of witnesses.

The question of prior sexual history is one area in which the issue of sexual credibility is directly posed. Evidence of the defendant's sexual harassment of other women in the same institutional relation or setting is increasingly being considered admissible, and it should be.[33] The other side of the question is whether evidence of a victim's prior sexual history should be discoverable or admissible, and it seems to me it should not be. Perpetrators often seek out victims with common qualities or circumstances or situations – we are fungible to them so long as we are similarly accessible – but victims do not seek out victimization at all, and their nonvictimized sexual behavior is no more relevant to an allegation of sexual force than is the perpetrator's consensual sex life, such as it may be.

So far the leading case, consistent with the direction of rape law,[34] has found that the victim's sexual history with other individuals is not relevant, although consensual history with the individual perpetrator may be. With sexual harassment law, we are having to de-institutionalize sexual misogyny step by step. Some defendants' counsel have even demanded that plaintiffs submit to an unlimited psychiatric examination,[35] which could have a major practical impact on victims' effective access to relief. How much sexual denigration will victims have to face to secure their right to be free from sexual denigration? A major part of the harm of sexual harassment is the public and private sexualization of a woman against her will. Forcing her to speak about her sexuality is a common part of this process, subjection to which leads women to seek relief through the courts. Victims who choose to complain know they will have to endure repeated verbalizations of the specific sexual abuse they complain about. They undertake this even though most experience it as an exacerbation, however unavoidable, of the original abuse. For others, the necessity to repeat over and over the verbal insults, innuendos, and propositions to which they have been subjected leads them to decide that justice is not worth such indignity.

Most victims of sexual harassment, if the incidence data are correct, never file complaints. Many who are viciously violated are so ashamed to make that violation public that they submit in silence, although it devastates their self-respect and often their health, or they leave the job without complaint, although it threatens their survival and that of their families. If, on top of the cost of making the violation known, which is painful enough, they know that the entire range of their sexual experiences, attitudes, preferences, and practices are to be discoverable, few such actions will be brought, no matter how badly the victims are hurt. Faced with a choice between forced sex in their jobs or schools on the one hand and forced sexual disclosure for the public record on the other, few will choose the latter. This cruel paradox would effectively eliminate much progress in this area.[36]

Put another way, part of the power held by perpetrators of sexual harassment is the threat of making the sexual abuse public knowledge. This functions like blackmail in silencing the victim and allowing the abuse to continue. It is a fact that public knowledge of sexual abuse is often worse for the abused than the abuser, and victims who choose to complain have the courage to take that on. To add to their burden the potential of making public their entire personal life, information that has no relation to the fact or severity of the incidents complained of, is to make the law of this area implicitly complicit in the blackmail that keeps victims from exercising their rights and to enhance the impunity of perpetrators. In effect, it means open season on anyone who does not want her entire intimate life available to public scrutiny. In other contexts such private information has been found intrusive, irrelevant, and more prejudicial than probative.[37] To allow it to be discovered in the sexual harassment area amounts to a requirement that women be further violated in order to be permitted to seek relief for having been violated. I also will never understand why a violation's severity, or even its likelihood of occurrence, is measured according to the character of the violated, rather than by what was done to them.

In most reported sexual harassment cases, especially rulings on law more than on facts, the trend is almost uniformly favorable to the development of this claim. At least, so far. This almost certainly does not represent social reality. It may not even reflect most cases in litigation.[38] And there may be conflicts building, for example, between those who value speech in the abstract more than they value people in the concrete. Much of sexual harassment is words. Women are called "cunt," "pussy," "tits";[39] they are invited to a company party with "bring your own bathing suits (women, either half)";[40] they confront their tormenter in front of their manager with, "You have called me a fucking bitch," only to be answered, "No, I didn't. I called you a fucking cunt."[41] One court issued an injunction against inquiries such as "Did you get any over the weekend?"[42] One case holds that where "a person in a position to grant or withhold employment opportunities uses that authority to attempt to induce workers and job seekers to submit to sexual advances, prostitution, and pornographic entertainment, and boasts of an ability to intimidate those who displease him," sexual harassment (and intentional infliction of emotional distress) are pleaded.[43] Sexual harassment can also include pictures; visual as well as verbal pornography is commonly used as part of the abuse. Yet one judge found, apparently as a matter of law, that the pervasive presence of pornography in the workplace did not constitute an unreasonable work environment because, "For better or worse, modern America features open displays of written and pictorial erotica. Shopping centers, candy stores and prime time television regularly display naked bodies and erotic real or simulated sex acts. Living in this milieu, the average American should not be legally offended by sexually explicit posters."[44] She did not say she was offended, she said she was discriminated against based on her sex. If the pervasiveness of an abuse makes it nonactionable, no inequality sufficiently institutionalized to merit a law against it would be actionable.

Further examples of this internecine conflict have arisen in education. At the Massachusetts Institute of Technology pornography used to be shown every year during registration.[45] Is this *not* sexual harassment in education, as a group of women complained it was, because attendance is voluntary, both sexes go, it is screened in groups rather than individually, nobody is directly propositioned, and it is pictures and words? Or is it sexual harassment because the status and treatment of women, supposedly secured from sex-differential harm, are damaged, including that of those who do not attend, which harms individuals and undermines sex equality; therefore pictures and words are the media through which the sex discrimination is accomplished?

For feminist jurisprudence, the sexual harassment attempt suggests that if a legal initiative is set up right from the beginning, meaning if it is designed from women's real experience of violation, it can make some difference. To a degree women's experience can be written into law, even in some tension with the current doctrinal framework. Women who want to resist their victimization with legal terms that imagine it is not inevitable can be given some chance, which is more than they had before. Law is not everything in this respect, but it is not nothing either.[46] Perhaps the most important lesson is that the mountain can be moved. When we started, there was absolutely no judicial precedent for allowing a sex discrimination suit for sexual harassment. Sometimes even the law does something for the first time.

## Study Questions

1. In what ways does MacKinnon say one's own injuries are defined when one is a member of an oppressed group?

2. What several things does the legal recognition of sexual harassment give to women, and what is the historical significance of sexual harassment law, according to MacKinnon?

3. What does it mean to be a woman, according to MacKinnon? Why is this definition important to her discussion? Does it help to explain the idea that sexual harassment against women happens to them on account of their status as women?

4. Of what larger struggle does MacKinnon say equal protection for women under the law is part?

5. What, according to MacKinnon, causes sexual harassment against women to systematically take place?

6. How did the "bisexual defense" argue that sexual harassment was not a sex-based claim? What does MacKinnon say about this defense? What other arguments were made which claimed that sexual harassment as sex discrimination ought not to be legally recognized?

7. Why does MacKinnon think that a woman's claim of sexual violation can be discounted, even if the sex was forced?

8. What is the legal status of women's "sexual credibility"?

**Notes**

1 The original version of this speech was part of a panel on sexual harassment shared with Karen Haney, Pamela Price, and Peggy McGuiness at Stanford University, Stanford, California, April 12, 1983. It thereafter became an address to the Equal Employment Opportunities Section of the American Bar Association, New Orleans, Louisiana, May 3, 1984 and to a workshop for the national conference of the National Organization for Women, Denver, Colorado, June 14, 1986. The ideas developed further when I represented Mechelle Vinson as co-counsel in her US Supreme Court case in the spring of 1986. I owe a great deal to my conversations with Valerie Heller.

2 The first case to hold this was *Williams v. Saxbe*, 413 F. Supp. 654 (D. D.C. 1976), followed by *Barnes v. Costle*, 561 F.2d 983 (D.C. Cir. 1977).

3 *Alexander v. Yale University*, 459 F. Supp. 1 (D. Conn. 1977), aff'd, 631 F.2d 178 (2d Cir. 1980).

4 *Rabidue v. Osceola Refining*, 584 F. Supp. 419, 427 n.29 (E.D. Mich.1984).

5 U.S. Merit System Protection Board, *Sexual Harassment in the Federal Workplace: Is It a Problem?* (1981).

6 National Advisory Council on Women's Education Programs, Department of Education, *Sexual Harassment: A Report on the Sexual Harassment of Students* (1980); Joseph DiNunzio and Christina Spaulding, *Radcliffe Union of Students, Sexual Harassment Survey (Harvard/Radcliffe)* 20–29 (1984): 32 per cent of tenured female faculty, 49 per cent of nontenured female faculty, 42 per cent of female graduate students, and 34 per cent of female undergraduate students report some incident of sexual harassment from a person with authority over them; one-fifth of undergraduate women report being forced into unwanted sexual activity at some point in their lives. The Sexual Harassment Survey Committee, *A Survey of Sexual Harassment at UCLA* (185), finds 11 per cent of female faculty (N = 86), 7 per cent of female staff (N = 650), and 7 per cent of female students (N = 933) report being sexually harassed at UCLA.

7 If a superior sexually harasses a subordinate, the company and the supervisor are responsible if the victim can prove it happened. 29 C.F.R. 1604.ll(c). With coworkers, if the employer can be shown to have known about it or should have known about it, the employer can be held responsible. 29 C.F.R. 1604. ll(d). Sexual harassment by clients or other third parties is decided on the specific facts. *See* 29 C.F.R. 1604.ll(e).

8  The EEOC's requirement that the employer must receive notice in coworker cases suggests that they do not understand this point. 29 C.F.R. 1604.ll(d). One reasonable rationale for such a rule, however, is that a co-worker situation does not become hierarchical, hence actionable as *employment* discrimination, until it is reported to the workplace hierarchy and condoned through adverse action or inaction.

   In one inferior-to-superior case, staff was alleged to have sexually harassed a woman manager because of an interracial relationship. *Moffett v. Gene B. Glick Co., Inc.*, 621 F. Supp. 244 (D. Ind. 1985). An example of a third-party case that failed because of "positive proof" involved a nurse bringing a sex discrimination claim alleging she was denied a promotion that went to a less qualified female nurse because that other nurse had a sexual relationship with the doctor who promoted her. *King v. Palmer*, 598 F. Supp. 65, 69 (D.D.C. 1984). The difficulty of proving "an explicit sexual relationship between [plaintiff] and [defendant], each of whom vigorously deny it exists or even occurred," id., is obvious.

9  Catharine A. MacKinnon, *Sexual Harassment of Working Women* 203 (1979).

10 Dissenters from the denial of rehearing en banc in *Vinson v. Taylor* attempted a revival, however. *Vinson v. Taylor*, 760 F.2d 1330, 1333 n.7 (Circuit Judges Bork, Scalia, and Starr).

11 *Scott v. Sears & Roebuck*, 605 F. Supp. 1047, 1051, 1055 (N.D. Ill. 1985).

12 *Coley v. Consolidated Rail*, 561 F. Supp. 647, 648 (1982).

13 *Meritor Savings Bank, FSB v. Vinson*, 106 S.Ct. 2399 (1986); *Horn v. Duke Homes*, 755 F.2d 599 (7th Cir. 1985); *Crimm v. Missouri Pacific R.R. Co.*, 750 F.2d 703 (8th Cir. 1984); *Simmons v. Lyons*, 746 F.2d 265 (5th Cir. 1984); *Craig v. Y & Y Snacks*, 721 F.2d 77 (3d Cir. 1983); *Katz v. Dole*, 709 F.2d 251 (4th Cir. 1983); *Miller v. Bank of America*, 600 F.2d 211 (9th Cir. 1979); *Tomkins v. Public Service Electric & Gas Co.*, 568 F.2d 1044 (3d Cir. 1977); *Barnes v. Costle*, 561 F.2d 983 (D.C. Cir. 1977); *Bundy v. Jackson*, 641 F.2d 934 (D.C. Cir. 1981); *Henson v. City of Dundee*, 682 F.2d 897 (11th Cir.1982) (sexual harassment, whether quid pro quo or condition of work, is sex discrimination under Title VII). The court in *Rabidue* was particularly explicit on the rootedness of sexual harassment in the text of Title VII. *Rabidue v. Osceola Refining*, 584 F. Supp. 419, 427–29 (E.D. Mich. 1984). *Woerner v. Brzeczek*, 519 F. Supp. 517 (E.D. Ill. 1981) exemplifies the same view under the equal protection clause. Gender has also been found to create a class for a 42 U.S.C. § 1985(3) claim if the injury is covered by the Fourteenth Amendment. *Scott v. City of Overland Park*, 595 F. Supp. 520, 527–529 (D. Kansas 1984). *See also Skadegaard v. Farrell*, 578 F. Supp. 1209 (D.N.J. 1984). An additional question has been whether sexual harassment is intentional discrimination. Courts have been unimpressed with intent-related defenses like, he did it but "it was his way of communicating." *French v. Mead Corporation*, 333 FEP Cases 635, 638 (1983). Or, I did all of those things, but I am just a touchy person. Professor Sid Peck, in connection with the sexual harassment action brought against him by Ximena Bunster and other women at Clark University, reportedly stated that he exchanged embraces and kisses as greetings and to establish a feeling of safety and equality. *Worcester Magazine*, December 3, 1980, at 3; *Boston Phoenix*, February 24, 1981, at 6. But see *Norton v. Vartanian*, where Judge Zobel finds, inter alia, that the overtures were never sexually intended, so no sexual harassment occurred. 31 FEP Cases 1260 (D. Mass. 1983). The implicit view, I guess, is that the perpetrator's intent is beside the point of the harm, that so long as the allegations meet other requirements, the perpetrator does not need to intend that the sexual advances be discriminatory or even sex-based for them to constitute sex discrimination. *Katz v. Dole* holds that a showing of "sustained verbal sexual abuse" is sufficient to prove "the intentional nature of the harassment." 709 F. 2d, 255–56 esp. 256 n.7. As I understand it, this means that so long as the harassment is not credibly inadvertent, acts of this nature are facially discriminatory. Intentionality is inferred from the acts; the acts themselves, repeated after indications of disinclination and nonreceptivity, show the mental animus of bias. In short, the acts may not be intentionally discriminatory, yet still constitute intentional discrimination.

The upshot seems to be that sexual harassment allegations are essentially treated as facial discrimination.

14 *Zabkowicz v. West Bend Co.*, 589 F. Supp. 780, 782–83 (E.D. Wisc. 1984).

15 589 F. Supp., 784.

16 *Henson v. City of Dundee*, 29 FEP Cases 787, 793 (11th Cir. 1983). In *Huebschen v. Dept. of Health*, 32 FEP Cases 1582 (7th Cir. 1983), the facts were found not gender-based on a doctrinally dubious rationale. There a man was found to have been sexually harassed by his female superior. This result was reversed on the partial basis that it did not present a valid gender claim. Basically the court said that the case wasn't gender-based because it was individual. I remember this argument: the events were individual, not gender-based, because there was no employment problem until the relationship went sour. In my view, if the defendant is a hierarchical superior and the plaintiff is damaged in employment for reasons of sexual pressure vis à vis that superior, especially if they are a woman and a man, a claim is stated. It is one thing to recognize that men as a gender have more power in sexual relations in ways that may cross-cut employment hierarchies. This is not what the court said here. This case may have been, on its facts, a personal relationship that went bad, having nothing to do with gender. But these are not the facts as found at trial. The Court of Appeals did suggest that this plaintiff was hurt as an individual, not as a man, because the employment situation was fine so long as the sexual situation was fine – that is, until it wasn't. After which, because of which, the man was fired. Maybe men always stay individuals, even when women retaliate against them through their jobs for sexual refusals. But, doctrinally, I do not understand why this treatment does not state a gender-based claim. Not to, seems to allow employment opportunities to be conditional on the *continuing* existence of an undesired sexual relationship, where those opportunities would never be allowed to be conditioned on such a relationship's *initial* existence. Women have at times been gender female personally: "As Walter Scott acknowledges, he 'was attracted to her as a woman, on a personal basis. Her femaleness was a matter of attraction.'" *Estate of Scott v. deLeon*, 37 FEP Cases 563, 566 (1985).

17 *Barnes v. Costle* is the classic case. All of the cases in note 13 above are quid pro cases except *Vinson, Katz, Bundy*, and *Henson*. Note that the distinction is actually two poles of a continuum. A constructive discharge, in which a woman leaves the job because of a constant condition of sexual harassment, is an environmental situation that becomes quid pro quo.

18 In *Vinson v. Taylor*, 23 FEP Cases 37 (D.D.C. 1980), plaintiff accused defendant supervisor of forced sex; the trial court found, "If the plaintiff and Taylor did engage in an intimate or sexual relationship ... [it] was a voluntary one by plaintiff." At 42. Vinson won a right to a new trial for environmental sexual harassment. *Meritor Savings Bank, FSB v. Vinson*, 106 S. Ct. 2399 (1986). *See also Cummings v. Walsh Construction Co.*, 561 F. Supp. 872 (S.D. Ga. 1983) (victim accused perpetrator of consummated sex); *Micari v. Mann*, 481N.Y.S.2d967 (Sup. Ct. 1984) (students accused professor of forced sex as part of acting training; won and awarded damages).

19 *Vinson v. Taylor*, 753 F.2d 141 (D.C. Cir. 1985), *aff'd* 106 S. Ct. 2399 (1983).

20 *Micari v. Mann*, 481 N.Y.S.2d 967 (Sup. Ct. 1984).

21 *Cummings v. Walsh Construction Co.*, 31 FEP Cases 930, 938 (S. D. Ga. 1983).

22 *Bundy* and *Henson*, [note 13] above, establish environmental sexual harassment as a legal claim. Both that claim and the plaintiff's credibility in asserting it, since she was abused for such a long time, were raised in *Vinson v. Taylor* before the US Supreme Court.

23 *Huebschen v. Department of Health*, 547 F. Supp. 1168 (W.D. Wisc. 1982).

24 *Heelan v. Johns-Manville*, 451 F. Supp. 1382 (D. Colo. 1978). *See also Sensibello v. Globe Security Systems*, 34 FEP Cases 1357 (E.D. Pa. 1964).

25  *Katz v. Dole*, 709 F.2d 251, 254 n.3 (4th Cir. 1983) ("A person's private and consensual sexual activities do not constitute a waiver of his or her legal protections against unwelcome and unsolicited sexual harassment").

26  An attorney discussed this case with me in a confidential conversation.

27  *Gan v. Kepro Circuit Systems*, 28 FEP Cases 639, 641 (E.D. Mo. 1982). *See also Reichman v. Bureau of Affirmative Action*, 536 F. Supp. 1149, 1177 (M.D. Penn. 1982).

28  *Morgan v. Hertz Corp.*, 542 F. Supp. 123, 128 (W.D. Tenn. 1981).

29  *EEOC v. Sage Realty*, 507 F. Supp. 599 (S.D.N.Y. 1981).

30  *Pryor v. U.S. Gypsum Co.*, 585 F. Supp. 311, 316 n.3 (W.D. Mo. 1984). The issue here was whether the injuries could be brought under worker's compensation. The suggestion is that women who work in adult entertainment might be covered under that law for sexual harassment on their jobs.

31  EEOC Decision 82–13, 29 FEP Cases 1855 (1982).

32  Commission Decision 83–1, EEOC Decisions (CCH) 6834 (1983).

33  *Koster v. Chase Manhattan*, 93 F.R.D. 471 (S.D.N.Y. 1982).

34  *Priest v. Rotary*, 32 FEP Cases 1065 (N.D. Cal. 1983) is consistent with congressional actions in criminal rape, Fed. R. Evid., Rule 412, 124 *Cong. Rec.* H11944–11945 (daily ed. October 10, 1978) and 124 *Cong. Rec.* S18580 (daily ed. October 12, 1978) (evidence of prior consensual sex, unless with defendant, is inadmissible in rape cases) and with developments in civil rape cases. *Fults v. Superior Court*, 88 Cal. App. 3d 899 (1979).

35  *Vinson v. Superior Court*, Calif. Sup. SF 24932 (rev. granted, September 1985).

36  A further possibility – more political fantasy than practical – might be to insist that if the plaintiff's entire sexual history is open to inspection, the defendant's should be also: all the rapes, peeping at his sister, patronizing of prostitutes, locker-room jokes, use of pornography, masturbation fantasies, adolescent experimentation with boyfriends, fetishes, and so on.

37  *See, e.g., U.S. v. Kasto*, 584 F.2d 268, 271–72 (8th Cir. 1978), *cert. denied*, 440 U.S. 930 (1979); *State v. Bernier*, 491 A.2d 1000, 1004 (R.I. 1985).

38  Another reason women do not bring claims is fear of countersuit. The relationship between sexual harassment and defamation is currently unsettled on many fronts. *See, e.g., Walker v. Gibson*, 604 F. Supp. 916 (N.D. Ill. 1985) (action for violation of First Amendment will not lie against employer Army for hearing on unwarranted sexual harassment change); *Spisak v. McDole*, 472 N.E.2d 347 (Ohio 1984) (defamation claim can be added to sexual harassment claim); *Equal Employment Opportunity Commission v. Levi Strauss & Co.*, 515 F. Supp. 640 (N.D. Ill. 1981) (defamation action brought allegedly in response to employee allegation of sexual harassment is not necessarily retaliatory, if brought in good faith to vindicate reputation); *Arenas v. Ladish Co.*, 619 F. Supp. 1304 (E.D. Wisc. 1985) (defamation claim may be brought for sexual harassment in the presence of others, not barred by exclusivity provision of worker's compensation law); *Ross v. Comsat*, 34 FEP Cases 261 (D. Md. 1984) (man sues company for retaliation in discharge following his complaint against woman at company for sexual harassment). Education institutions have been sued for acting when, after investigation, the find the complaints to be true. *Barnes v. Oody*, 28 FEP Cases 816 (E.D. Tenn. 1981) (summary judgment granted that arbitrators' holding for women who brought sexual harassment claim collaterally estops defamation action by sexual harassment defendant; immunity applies to statements in official investigation). Although it is much more difficult to prove defamation than to defeat a sexual harassment claim, threats of countersuit have intimidated many victims.

39  *Rabidue v. Osceola Refining*, 584 F. Supp. 423 (E.D. Mich. 1984).

40  *Cobb v. Dufresne-Henry*, 603 F. Supp. 1048, 1050 (D. Vt. 1985).

41  *McNabb v. Cub Foods*, 352 N.W. 2d 378, 381 (Minn. 1984).

42  *Morgan v. Hertz Corp.*, 27 FEP Cases at 994.

43  *Seratis v. Lane*, 30 FEP 423, 425 (Cal. Super. 1980).

44  *Rabidue v. Osceola Refining*, 584 F. Supp. 419, 435 (E.D. Mich. 1984). This went to whether the treatment was sex-based. Note that the plaintiff did not say that she was offended but that she was discriminated against.

45  Women students at MIT filed a sexual harassment claim under Title IX, which was dismissed for lack of jurisdiction. *Baker v. M.I.T., U.S. Dept. Education Office of Civil Rights* #01–85–2013 (September 20, 1985).

46  Particularly given the formative contribution to the women's movement of the struggles against racial and religious stigma, persecution, and violence, it is heartening to find a Jewish man and a Black man recovering for religious and racial harassment, respectively, based on sexual harassment precedents. *Weiss v. U.S.*, 595 F. Supp. 1050 (E.D. Va. 1984) (pattern of anti-Semitic verbal abuse actionable based on *Katz* and *Henson*); *Taylor v. Jones*, 653 F.2d 1193, 1199 (8th Cir. 1981) (*Bundy* cited as basis for actionability of environmental racial harassment under Title VII).

# Section V:
# Environmental Ethics

A thing is right when it tends to preserve the integrity, stability, and beauty of the biotic community. It is wrong when it tends otherwise.

— Aldo Leopold, *A Sand County Almanac*

THE ENVIRONMENT IS THE basis for all life. Without air, water, and soil there is nothing to discuss, as there would be no life to do the discussing. Every human action is dependent on our finite natural environment – our ecosystems, the most taken-for-granted part of life. Consider the "Great Pacific Garbage Patch," a massive floating garbage dump (though not often visible from above) constituted primarily of plastic in various stages of degradation, twice the size of Alaska, and up to 80 feet deep. Plastic particles compete with, and in parts outnumber, plankton in the "Patch," which is devastating to the oceanic food chain; indeed, plastic has been found in harvested fish and dead sea birds.[1] It is widely considered impossible to clean up, and smaller garbage patches are also found in other oceans, including the Atlantic. How did we get here? Why did we get here? How are we to live ethically in our environment? Environmental ethicists address these questions.

Environmental ethics is the study of how we should live in relation to our environment and is the basis of our moral responsibilities toward that environment. There are two major approaches in environmental

ethics: anthropocentrism and ecocentrism (also known as biocentrism). Anthropocentrism is a human-centered approach wherein human concerns are paramount. Anthropocentrists assert that only humans have intrinsic value, and they see the environment and its species as instruments for human benefit; anthropocentrism thus entails (moral) duties only to human beings. Our legal system is replete with anthropocentric laws, such as the Clean Air Act of 1970, which addressed air pollution on a national level. Rather than determine the health of our ecosystems, the act was designed to "protect public health" (i.e., human health). It was subsequently amended under the first Bush administration to include pollution credits, and then again under the second Bush administration to allow for higher pollution levels and remove the requirement of costly pollution-controlling devices, not surprisingly benefiting companies that had made significant campaign contributions.[2] From this perspective, the environment is an instrument for humans, not a being with intrinsic value.

In contrast to anthropocentrism is ecocentrism. This approach is also called biocentrism or may also be familiar to some as "deep ecology." Ecocentrism is an ecosystem-centered approach in which humans are but one species of many: the ecosystem has intrinsic value, there are duties owed to other species and the environment, and human interests are not the only measure of an action. The quotation from Aldo Leopold that opened this introduction reflects ecocentrism, as the rightness of an action is spelled out in terms of ecosystem health, not human benefit. While the 2015 killing of Cecil the lion in Zimbabwe garnered worldwide attention that was generally ecocentric in nature, ecocentrism is widely absent from the US legal, political, economic, and consumer landscape.[3]

A key issue in ecocentrism (and also in anthropocentrism, but only insofar as it benefits humans) is biodiversity. Biodiversity is the variety of species that have evolved in an ecosystem. Edward O. Wilson, a Harvard biologist, wrote widely on biodiversity as well as "biophilia."[4] Biophilia is Wilson's term for the innate human attraction to the ecosystem and its species. It is not an untenable notion, as biophilia was clearly operating in the outrage over Cecil the lion. Wilson places environmental ethics in evolutionary time; that is, he urges us to take an evolutionary perspective to appreciate how species have evolved, with a resulting biodiversity that needs protecting. While there are "natural" extinctions of species, human activity has resulted in rates of extinction that are hundreds of thousands of times higher than the evolutionary record shows.[5] But why should humans care? Well, if biophilia isn't strong enough to answer that question, an anthropocentric answer is that without an intact biota, human existence on Earth would be, in Hobbesian terms, "nasty, brutish, and short."[6] And climate change is exacerbating the extinction rates, further threatening biodiversity.

Climate change is what was formerly called global warming. It refers to change in both regional and global climates that have been occurring since the middle of the twentieth century. Climate change involves both slow change and severe weather and is associated with the release of carbon dioxide in the atmosphere from the use of fossil fuels. The original term, global warming, referred to a general warming from the use of greenhouse gases. However, the warming trend is further associated with widespread climate change and effects that include drought, subsequent wildfires, tornadoes, rising oceanic levels, melting glaciers, and harsher winters. Strangely, there has been a significant amount of denial of both global warming and climate change, despite the evidence (both before and after the Industrial Revolution) of different atmospheric levels of carbon dioxide. Some who denied it have moved on to argue that it is "natural" and not generated by humans, while others – called "climate change deniers" – continue to deny it, despite the widely reported 97-per-cent level of scientific agreement that climate change is real and due to human fossil-fuel consumption. One peculiar aspect is that deniers generally fall to the right of the political spectrum in the United States; one Republican, Senator Jim Inhofe of Oklahoma, brought a snowball to the Senate floor and said that since it was cold enough for snow, "global warming" was not real.[7]

A much more hotly contested issue is that of "GMOs" (genetically modified organisms). The term itself is bit of a misnomer, because humans have been modifying natural evolutionary processes with seeds for 10,000 years, since the advent of agriculture, something that proponents of GMO biotechnology will happily point out. What people are referring to when the debate arises is transgenic agricultural biotechnology (TAB). TAB involves two or more species forcibly joined by inserting foreign genes into the target organism, which then takes up fragments of foreign DNA that subsequently transforms the genetic makeup of the recipient cell. For example, flounder genes have been put into tomatoes because the flounder has a natural antifreeze that was thought to allow for a longer growing season. But the most famous TAB is Monsanto's Roundup-Ready seed. This process allows for a heavier application of Monsanto's Roundup, the world's most-used pesticide. Indeed, most TABs are designed to allow for *more* pesticide application, because in the 1980s Green Revolution[8] pesticides began to lose their efficacy. While TAB companies, which often overlap with those previously providing pesticides for Green Revolution crops, claim that this technology will "feed the world," actual practice illustrates something much different. For example, Monsanto will not allow farmers, via the contract they sign when they purchase the seeds (and due to patents), to save seeds to be used the next season. And Roundup-Ready seeds mean that farmers have to make a double Monsanto purchase every season, as Monsanto sells the farmer both the seed and the pesticide. This is a much more expensive, and ecologically risky, practice, as farmers previously saved seeds that they had selected for the genetic traits produced in their particular locations. This was not only economically but also ecologically sound, as the seed had already adapted to the climate, soil, and water conditions. And it was free.

Another problem with TABs is that, through natural evolutionary processes, they can exchange genes with other plants. This gene exchange has been shown to take place, without there being any buffer zones (buffer zones are areas considered safe from pollinating birds and insects, wind and passing trucks) for crops grown in the open. This means that TABs can pollute adjacent farms and can also exchange genes with wild relatives. The fact that some TABs are designed to protect plants from pesticide application leads to the development of what are called "super weeds." This genetic pollution, unlike pesticides, replicates itself and permanently alters the genome of polluted plants. It is an especially significant risk to plants that are in their indigenous areas, as these areas are important resources for agriculture and are where the plant originally evolved.

Another aspect of TAB is what is known as "terminator technology." Terminator seeds are engineered to destroy the seed's fertility. "The Terminator" was developed jointly by the United States Department of Agriculture and Pine & Delta Land, and is patented. The Terminator caused an international uproar and was, in part, the genesis of many anti-GMO movements around the world. Think about this for a moment. Why engineer a seed to be infertile? Infertility means that a seed cannot be saved. Seed-saving is a centuries-old practice that ensures seeds adapted to that environment are available to grow the next season. To rob a seed of its fertility is not an act of addressing hunger. Terminator technology leads to food insecurity, not food security.

TAB has proceeded, nonetheless, and is now in products from wheat to soy to canola to corn, and it is not labeled. TAB proponents argue that TAB food is not any different from organic or traditional farmed-food and thus does not need labeling. This is an odd tactic, since if it's not different, then why is it patented? This also admits to it not being nutritionally superior. TAB opponents at least want to see labeling, and they have won that battle in over 60 nations including those in the European Union, Russia, China, Japan, and Australia.

Another aspect of our food – meat – is supplied overwhelmingly by factory or corporate farming, with over 90 per cent of our meat coming from this method. Factory farming of animals is also known as concentrated animal feeding operations, or CAFOs, which most often involve crowded indoor cages (especially for veal, chicken, and pork) where the animals do not get fresh air or sunlight. CAFOs also require the prophylactic use of antibiotics to prevent disease. These antibiotics are passed onto the consumer through meat and milk and are a major contributor to antibiotic resistance, where common antibiotics begin to lose their efficacy in human beings.

In addition to antibiotic resistance, the animals involved suffer extensively. Chickens are "de-beaked," a practice whereby their beaks are cut or burned off at the tip so that they are not able to injure each other in cages where they are so crowded that they cannot stretch their wings. In egg-producing CAFOs, male chicks are thrown away, often live, left to suffocate in trash bags. Pigs, if not restrained by metal bars,[9] stand on metal grates or concrete, over their waste, unable to roll in the mud or have straw for a cushion for their hooves. Suffering continues en route to slaughter, where pigs are so crowded in trailers that in cold temperatures they have frozen to the side of the transport trucks or become crushed even to the point of their entrails being forced out of their bodies. The waste from CAFOs is also extremely toxic, contaminated with heavy metals, E. coli, fecal coliform, Salmonella, and Cryptosporidium in levels up to 100 times of that of human feces, and is stored in large outside cesspools that leak in heavy rains.[10] These are just a few of the costs of factory farming. If people were to treat their pets, their dogs and cats especially, like factory-farmed animals, they would be charged with animal cruelty. It is curious that such a division exists, although appetites and profit continue to drive factory farming.

What if you could avoid contributing to, or partially funding, environmental degradation, climate change, TAB pollution, and harms from CAFOs? Every time we consume, we vote with our money. The United States makes up approximately five per cent of the world's population yet consumes far more than this, and it produces far more environmental pollution. One way to minimize one's environmental impact is to reduce consumption. For example, of the global carbon dioxide emissions from energy consumption of 32,310 million metric tons, the United States emits 5,270 million, or 16.3 per cent.[11] First one needs to become aware of one's consumption and have a desire to change. The essays in this section provide starting places for you to consider your environmental impact and to reflect upon how you can minimize contributing further harm to our ecosystem and its species.

## Reading Selections

In the first reading, Aldo Leopold notes that ethics has evolved to apply to all humans and that the next evolution should be to include the environment as morally considerable. He notes that in order for this change to occur we need to change our convictions, our loyalties, our affections, and our intellectual focus. Leopold takes us on this journey to evolve by placing humans in the biotic community, arguing that we need to change our role from environmental conqueror to environmental citizen. Leopold illuminates the land pyramid that is the result of evolution, with each species having a place dependent on what that species eats. Humans are not above other species, but rather they belong at the omnivore level, with pure carnivores at the "top" of the land pyramid. Relationships within this pyramid have been worked out through evolutionary history, and while changes have occurred (such as species extinctions) through this process, these "natural" changes are relatively slow and allow for resilience in the environment. Human changes to the pyramid can be sudden, swift, violent, and have destabilizing consequences. One of the changes humans make concerns population.

Carrying capacity is the amount of life that an ecosystem can support in the long term. Humans have stretched carrying capacity with the use of technology that allows them, at least in the short term (relatively speaking compared to evolutionary time) to exceed the carrying capacity for the number of human beings that can live in an ecosystem. This use of technology – from water delivery to imported food – has huge environmental costs and consequences. Eventually humans will exceed even the technologically enhanced carrying capacity as the land pyramid is a finite resource that cannot be exceeded to the point of destruction and still support life.

Leopold proposes an ethic for our relationship to the environment, an ethic that we should use to consider every action. This ethic appears at the end of the essay: "A thing is right when it tends to preserve the integrity, stability, and beauty of the biotic community. It is wrong when it tends otherwise." This is *the* land ethic, and it requires quite a lot of us in considering our actions. It requires us to give moral consideration to the ecosystem and its entire community. Thus, for example, if we want to clear land for human purposes, that desire has to be measured against ecosystem integrity and stability. This is a revolutionary ethic.

Naomi Klein acknowledges the debt the environmental movement owes Leopold as she turns our attention to climate change. She begins by telling the story of Nauru, a small island that was mined to death for fertilizer for industrial agriculture. The people living there are "home," but they live in a shell of what was and are homesick, even though they remain on the island. Klein then tells us that given climate change and the "new abnormal,"

we'll all feel homesick while home.

Klein also details how the Nauru people have suffered nearly every social and environmental ill and warns us that we are no different in kind as we continue to practice "extractivism," which is how we relate to the earth. Extractivism involves taking and dominance, and there is no giving in return. We have been in high extractivist mode ever since we became enamored with fossil fuel. Klein notes that we thought we had freed ourselves from our bond to nature, but instead we're all standing on Nauru.

Jeremy Baskin addresses climate change from the standpoint of questions of justice. He begins with the scientific position regarding the reality of climate change. First and foremost, climate change calls on us to immediately and significantly reduce greenhouse gases. This reduction needs to be informed by all of those involved, both historically (as developed countries generated disproportionate amounts of pollution) and presently (as countries like China "catch up" to developed countries). The reduction is a positive step – actions that we can carry out via positive action. He further calls for two "negative" aspects of climate justice in that he argues that a justice approach must neither further inequality nor increase intergenerational conflict.

Both Klein and Baskin urge us to stop ignoring the elephant in the room: climate change. Whether we're just having an extractivist party or choosing to not attend to climate change in denial does not matter. Our actions are those of affected ignorance, a description that Nancy Williams brings to our behavior in the next essay regarding factory farming, warning us that our "affected ignorance" is morally culpable. Affected ignorance means that people willfully do not learn about immoral and/or controversial practices that they contribute to (such as eating factory farmed meat). Williams argues that our affected ignorance in allowing factory farming to continue, as well as our consumption of factory-farmed animal products, places us at moral risk. She also asks us how we can remain ignorant and call ourselves "informed" moral agents. She draws from Montmarquet's virtues as those that could help lead us to responsible public debate regarding factory farming. These virtues closely resemble what "good" people assume about themselves, as responsible moral agents. For Williams, (affected) ignorance is not bliss; it is instead morally culpable.

Yet another area of affected ignorance is that of TAB. In her essay, Mae-Wan Ho takes on this topic and details its myriad harms to both the ecosystem and human bodies. Ho is one of many scientists who make clear that TAB is not about feeding the hungry; rather it is about profits and is unsustainable. Ho documents the numerous harms and risks, including loss of biodiversity, instability and pollution, and health hazards due to horizontal gene transfer and recombination. Ho argues that TAB not only does not meet our food needs but also worsens many of the problems it claims to solve. She calls for a drastic change toward conservation, sustainable development, and indigenous agricultural biodiversity protection.

Finally, Guy Claxton likens our material consumption (which could also be likened to extractivism above) to drug addiction, and thus consumers to addicts whose identity is all too often wrapped up in their material preferences. Claxton shows that in order to move away from addiction, one must go from first "wanting not to want" to "not wanting." It is not enough to provide facts, use willpower, and engage rational arguments to get there. He also discounts external means of intervention such as physical coercion, which includes rationing, reward and punishment, and something that resembles drug rehabilitation. What

he advocates is "mindfulness," a Buddhist practice that requires presence, reflection, and awareness so that one can engage at the psychological level necessary for internal change.

Claxton argues that we need to stop being human havings and return to (being) human beings. He acknowledges that unless there is a desire to leave the (over)consumptive lifestyle, his argument will not persuade. In order to change our addictive lifestyle, we need to engage our shadow and overcome our trap. The shadow is what dogs us into not doing what we intend or want to do to change. It is like knowing that I need to exercise, and having a desire to be healthier, but my involuntary impulses keep me from following through. This is like the drug addict who regrets her latest round of use, and wishes that she were not addicted, but returns to her addiction again and again.

Claxton notes that this is a deeply psychological issue that involves inertia, self-deception, and a massive, intricate belief system. The trap is our underlying system of beliefs: our worldview. And the trap is particularly resistant to change, partly because it is a belief system that operates in the background, and we are not forced to confront it as long as we are "using" or consuming. Imagine being sad or depressed or otherwise unhappy and knowing that a shopping fix can take you out of that. It is really no different from drug use. The fix is temporary, however, as it is an "outside" fix. It doesn't engage the trap. Also, things like a punishment/reward system, cold turkey, and rehab don't engage at the deep level. They are also outside source "solutions" and will only be temporary.

Claxton argues that humans need mindfulness in order to become human beings again. This means being present in a profound way, to be in the moment whatever the moment is, and to not medicate it away. This allows for one to see how one has linked identity and security with consumption. Above all, mindfulness requires presence in the moment. It is time that we took our place in the biotic community as informed moral agents.

## Notes

1 National Ocean Service, "What Is the Great Pacific Garbage Patch?," http://oceanservice.noaa.gov/facts/garbagepatch.html.
2 John Heilprin, "White House Loosens Clean Air Rules," *Associated Press*, November 22, 2002.
3 http://www.cbsnews.com/news/cecil-the-lion-killing-sparks-outrage-around-the-world/.
4 See Edward O. Wilson, *The Diversity of Life* (Cambridge, MA: Belknap P of Harvard UP, 1992).
5 See Sarah Kaplan, "Earth Is on Brink of a Sixth Mass Extinction," *Washington Post* 22 June 2015, http://www.washingtonpost.com/news/morning-mix/wp/2015/06/22/the-earth-is-on-the-brink-of-a-sixth-mass-extinction-scientists-say-and-its-humans-fault/.
6 A famous phrase from Thomas Hobbes's *Leviathan* (1651).
7 Steve Mirsky, "Climate Skeptic Senator Burned after Snowball Stunt," *Scientific American* 2 March 2015, http://www.scientificamerican.com/podcast/episode/climate-skeptic-senator-burned-after-snowball-stunt/.
8 The Green Revolution lasted from the 1930s into the 1970s and involved the implementation of monoculture hybrid crops which required heavy inputs of pesticides, artificial fertilizers, and water. Many people credit the Green Revolution for its increased crop yield which provided food for hungry masses. However, this came at a high environmental cost which includes pesticide pollution, and depleted ecosystems.
9 See Humane Society of the United States, "Crammed into Gestation Crates," n.d., http://www.humanesociety.org/issues/confinement_farm/facts/gestation_crates.html?referrer=https://www.google.com/.
10 See NRDC, "Livestock Production," n.d., http://www.nrdc.org/water/pollution/ffarms.asp.
11 http://www.eia.gov/cfapps/ipdbproject/iedindex3.cfm?tid=90&pid=44&aid=8 (accessed August 24, 2015).

# 1. Aldo Leopold, "The Land Ethic"

ALDO LEOPOLD (1887–1948) WAS one of the founding fathers of environmental ethics. In *A Sand County Almanac*, written over 65 years ago, he argues for an extension of our ethics to land, what he sees as the next step in our ethical progress (just as we have extended ethics from some men to now all humans). After all, humans are *part of* the ecosystem, or what he calls the biotic community, and should thus be biotic citizens, assuming our place *in* the land pyramid, not *above* it as a conqueror. Leopold provides an ethical principle, the "land ethic," whereby we can ethically judge our activities in the ecosystem. Insofar as our actions threaten the "integrity, stability, and beauty" of the ecosystem, they tend to be wrong; but when our actions tend to maintain the integrity, stability, and beauty of the ecosystem, they tend to be right. Given US consumption levels, which are rapidly being emulated and repeated around the globe, the land ethic is a significant challenge to human activity on this planet.

---

WHEN GODLIKE ODYSSEUS RE-TURNED from the wars in Troy, he hanged all on one rope a dozen slave-girls of his household whom he suspected of misbehavior during his absence.

This hanging involved no question of propriety. The girls were property. The disposal of property was then, as now, a matter of expediency, not of right or wrong.

Concepts of right and wrong were not lacking from Odysseus' Greece: witness the fidelity of his wife through the long years before at last his black-prowed galleys clove the wine-dark seas for home. The ethical structure of that day covered wives, but had not yet been extended to human chattels. During the three thousand years which have since elapsed, ethical criteria have been extended to many fields of conduct, with corresponding shrinkages in those judged by expediency only.

### The Ethical Sequence

This extension of ethics, so far studied only by philosophers, is actually a process in ecological evolution. Its sequences may be described in ecological as well as in philosophical terms.

An ethic, ecologically, is a limitation on freedom of action in the struggle for existence. An ethic, philosophically, is a differentiation of social from antisocial conduct. These are two definitions of one thing. The thing has its origin in the tendency of interdependent individuals or groups to evolve modes of co-operation. The ecologist calls these symbioses. Politics and economics are advanced symbioses in which the original free-for-all competition has been replaced, in part, by cooperative mechanisms with an ethical content.

The complexity of cooperative mechanisms has increased with population density, and with the efficiency of tools. It was simpler, for example, to define the anti-social uses of sticks and stones in the days of the mastodons than of bullets and billboards in the age of motors.

The first ethics dealt with the relation between individuals; the Mosaic Decalogue is an example. Later accretions dealt with the relation between the individual and society. The Golden Rule tries to integrate the individual to society; democracy to integrate social organization to the individual.

There is as yet no ethic dealing with man's

relation to land and to the animals and plants which grow upon it. Land, like Odysseus' slave-girls, is still property. The land-relation is still strictly economic, entailing privileges but not obligations.

The extension of ethics to this third element in human environment is, if I read the evidence correctly, an evolutionary possibility and an ecological necessity. It is the third step in a sequence. The first two have already been taken. Individual thinkers since the days of Ezekiel and Isaiah have asserted that the despoliation of land is not only inexpedient but wrong. Society, however, has not yet affirmed their belief. I regard the present conservation movement as the embryo of such an affirmation.

An ethic may be regarded as a mode of guidance for meeting ecological situations so new or intricate, or involving such deferred reactions, that the path of social expediency is not discernible to the average individual. Animal instincts are modes of guidance for the individual in meeting such situations. Ethics are possibly a kind of community instinct in-the-making.

## The Community Concept

All ethics so far evolved rest upon a single premise: that the individual is a member of a community of interdependent parts. His instincts prompt him to compete for his place in the community, but his ethics prompt him also to cooperate (perhaps in order that there may be a place to compete for).

The land ethic simply enlarges the boundaries of the community to include soils, waters, plants, and animals, or collectively: the land.

This sounds simple: do we not already sing our love for and obligation to the land of the free and the home of the brave? Yes, but just what and whom do we love? Certainly not

the soil, which we are sending helter-skelter downriver. Certainly not the waters, which we assume have no function except to turn turbines, float barges, and carry off sewage. Certainly not the plants, of which we exterminate whole communities without batting an eye. Certainly not the animals, of which we have already extirpated many of the largest and most beautiful species. A land ethic of course cannot prevent the alteration, management, and use of these "resources," but it does affirm their right to continued existence, and, at least in spots, their continued existence in a natural state.

In short, a land ethic changes the role of *Homo sapiens* from conqueror of the land-community to plain member and citizen of it. It implies respect for his fellow-members, and also respect for the community as such.

In human history, we have learned (I hope) that the conqueror role is eventually self-defeating. Why? Because it is implicit in such a role that the conqueror knows, *excathedra* [i.e., officially, just what makes the community clock tick, and just what and who is valuable, and what and who is worthless, in community life]. It always turns out that he knows neither, and this is why his conquests eventually defeat themselves.

In the biotic community, a parallel situation exists. Abraham knew exactly what the land was for: it was to drip milk and honey into Abraham's mouth. At the present moment, the assurance with which we regard this assumption is inverse to the degree of our education.

The ordinary citizen today assumes that science knows what makes the community clock tick; the scientist is equally sure that he does not. He knows that the biotic mechanism is so complex that its workings may never be fully understood.

That man is, in fact, only a member of a biotic team is shown by an ecological interpretation of history. Many historical events, hitherto explained solely in terms of human enterprise, were actually biotic interactions between people and land. The characteristics of the land determined the facts quite as potently as the characteristics of the men who lived on it....

## The Ecological Conscience

Conservation is a state of harmony between men and land. Despite nearly a century of propaganda, conservation still proceeds at a snail's pace; progress still consists largely of letterhead pieties and convention oratory. On the back forty we still slip two steps backward for each forward stride.

The usual answer to this dilemma is "more conservation education." No one will debate this, but is it certain that only the *volume* of education needs stepping up? Is something lacking in the *content* as well?

It is difficult to give a fair summary of its content in brief form, but as I understand it, the content is substantially this: obey the law, vote right, join some organizations, and practice what conservation is profitable on your own land; the government will do the rest.

Is not this formula too easy to accomplish anything worthwhile? It defines no right or wrong, assigns no obligation, calls for no sacrifice, implies no change in the current philosophy of values. In respect of land-use, it urges only enlightened self-interest. Just how far will such education take us? An example will perhaps yield a partial answer.

By 1930 it had become clear to all except the ecologically blind that southwestern Wisconsin's topsoil was slipping seaward. In 1933 the farmers were told that if they would adopt certain remedial practices for five years, the public would donate CCC labor to install them, plus the necessary machinery and materials. The offer was widely accepted, but the practices were widely forgotten when the five-year contract period was up. The farmers continued only those practices that yielded an immediate and visible economic gain for themselves.

This led to the idea that maybe farmers would learn more quickly if they themselves wrote the rules. Accordingly the Wisconsin Legislature in 1937 passed the Soil Conservation District Law. This said to farmers, in effect: *We, the public, will furnish you free technical service and loan you specialized machinery, if you will write your own rules for land-use. Each county may write its own rules, and these will have the force of law.* Nearly all the counties promptly organized to accept the proffered help, but after a decade of operation, *no county has yet written a single rule.* There has been visible progress in such practices as strip-cropping, pasture renovation, and soil liming, but none in fencing woodlots against grazing, and none in excluding plow and cow from steep slopes. The farmers, in short, have selected those remedial practices which were profitable anyhow, and ignored those which were profitable to the community, but not clearly profitable to themselves.

When one asks why no rules have been written, one is told that the community is not yet ready to support them; education must precede rules. But the education actually in progress makes no mention of obligations to land over and above those dictated by self-interest. The net result is that we have more education but less soil, fewer healthy woods, and as many floods as in 1937.

The puzzling aspect of such situations is that the existence of obligations over and above self-interest is taken for granted in such rural community enterprise as the betterment of roads, schools, churches, and baseball teams. Their existence is not taken for granted, nor as yet seriously discussed, in bettering the behavior of the water that falls on the land, or in the preserving of the beauty or diversity of the farm landscape. Land-use ethics are still governed wholly by economic self-interest, just as social ethics were a century ago.

To sum up: we asked the farmer to do what he conveniently could to save his soil, and he has done just that, and only that. The farmer who clears the woods off a 75 per cent slope, turns his cows into the clearing, and dumps its rainfall, rocks, and soil into the community creek, is still (if otherwise decent) a respected member of society. If he puts lime on his fields and plants his crops on contour, he is still entitled to all the privileges and emoluments of his Soil Conservation District. The District is a beautiful piece of social machinery, but it is coughing along on two cylinders because we have been too timid, and too anxious for quick success, to tell the farmer the true magnitude of his obligations. Obligations have no meaning without conscience, and the problem we face is the extension of the social conscience from people to land.

No important change in ethics was ever accomplished without an internal change in our intellectual emphasis, loyalties, affections, and convictions. The proof that conservation has not yet touched these foundations of conduct lies in the fact that philosophy and religion have not yet heard of it. In our attempt to make conservation easy, we have made it trivial.

### Substitutes for a Land Ethic

When the logic of history hungers for bread and we hand out a stone, we are at pains to explain how much the stone resembles bread. I now describe some of the stones which serve in lieu of a land ethic.

One basic weakness in a conservation system based wholly on economic motives is that most members of the land community have no economic value. Wildflowers and songbirds are examples. Of the 22,000 higher plants and animals native to Wisconsin, it is doubtful whether more than 5 per cent can be sold, fed, eaten, or otherwise put to economic use. Yet these creatures are members of the biotic community, and if (as I believe) its stability depends on its integrity, they are entitled to continuance.

When one of these non-economic categories is threatened, and if we happen to love it, we invent subterfuges to give it economic importance. At the beginning of the century songbirds were supposed to be disappearing. Ornithologists jumped to the rescue with some distinctly shaky evidence to the effect that insects would eat us up if birds failed to control them. The evidence had to be economic in order to be valid.

It is painful to read these circumlocutions today. We have no land ethic yet, but we have at least drawn nearer the point of admitting that birds should continue as a matter of biotic right, regardless of the presence or absence of economic advantage to us.

A parallel situation exists in respect of predatory mammals, raptorial birds, and fish-eating birds. Time was when biologists somewhat overworked the evidence that these creatures preserve the health of game by killing weaklings, or that they control rodents for the farmer, or that they prey only on "worthless" species. Here again, the evidence had to be economic in order to be valid. It is only in recent years that we hear the more honest argument that predators are members of the community, and that no special interest has the right to exterminate them for the sake of a benefit, real or fancied, to itself. Unfortunately this enlightened view is still in the talk stage. In the field the extermination of predators goes merrily on: witness the impending erasure of the timber wolf by fiat of Congress, the Conservation Bureaus, and many state legislatures.

Some species of trees have been "read out of the party" by economics-minded foresters because they grow too slowly, or have too low sale value to pay as timber crops: white cedar, tamarack, cypress, beech, and hemlock are examples. In Europe, where forestry is ecologically more advanced, the non-commercial tree species are recognized as members of the native forest community, to be preserved as such, within reason. Moreover some (like beech) have been found to have a valuable function in building up soil fertility. The interdependence of the forest and its constituent tree species, ground flora, and fauna is taken for granted.

Lack of economic value is sometimes a character not only of species or groups, but of entire biotic communities: marshes, bogs, dunes, and "deserts" are examples. Our formula in such cases is to relegate their conservation to government as refuges, monuments, or parks. The difficulty is that these communities are usually interspersed with more valuable private lands; the government cannot possibly own or control such scattered parcels. The net effect is that we have relegated some of them to ultimate extinction over large areas. If the private owner were ecologically minded, he would be proud to be the custodian of a reasonable proportion of such areas, which add diversity and beauty to his farm and to his community.

In some instances, the assumed lack of profit in these "waste" areas has proved to be wrong, but only after most of them had been done away with. The present scramble to re-flood muskrat marshes is a case in point.

There is a clear tendency in American conservation to relegate to government all necessary jobs that private landowners fail to perform. Government ownership, operation, subsidy, or regulation is now widely prevalent in forestry, range management, soil and watershed management, park and wilderness conservation, fisheries management, and migratory bird management, with more to come. Most of this growth in governmental conservation is proper and logical, some of it is inevitable. That I imply no disapproval of it is implicit in the fact that I have spent most of my life working for it. Nevertheless the question arises: What is the ultimate magnitude of the enterprise? Will the tax base carry its eventual ramifications? At what point will governmental conservation, like the mastodon, become handicapped by its own dimensions? The answer, if there is any, seems to be in a land ethic, or some other force which assigns more obligation to the private landowner.

Industrial landowners and users, especially lumbermen and stockmen, are inclined to wail long and loudly about the extension of government ownership and regulation to land, but (with notable exceptions) they show little disposition to develop the only visible alternative: the voluntary practice of conservation on their own lands.

When the private landowner is asked to perform some nonprofitable act for the good of the community, he today assents only with outstretched palm. If the act costs him cash this is fair and proper, but when it costs only forethought, open-mindedness, or time, the issue is at least debatable. The overwhelming growth of land-use subsidies in recent years must be ascribed, in large part, to the government's own agencies for conservation education: the land bureaus, the agricultural colleges, and the extension services. As far as I can detect, no ethical obligation toward land is taught in these institutions.

To sum up: a system of conservation based solely on economic self-interest is hopelessly lopsided. It tends to ignore, and thus eventually to eliminate, many elements in the land community that lack commercial value, but that are (as far as known) essential to its healthy functioning. It assumes, falsely, I think, that the economic parts of the biotic clock will function without the uneconomic parts. It tends to relegate to government many functions eventually too large, too complex, or too widely dispersed to be performed by government.

An ethical obligation on the part of the private owner is the only visible remedy for these situations.

## The Land Pyramid

An ethic to supplement and guide the economic relation to land presupposes the existence of some mental image of land as a biotic mechanism. We can be ethical only in relation to something we can see, feel, understand, love, or otherwise have faith in.

The image commonly employed in conservation education is "the balance of nature." For reasons too lengthy to detail here, this figure of speech fails to describe accurately what little we know about the land mechanism. A much truer image is the one employed in ecology: the biotic pyramid. I shall first sketch the pyramid as a symbol of land, and later develop some of its implications in terms of land-use.

Plants absorb energy from the sun. This energy flows through a circuit called the biota, which may be represented by a pyramid consisting of layers. The bottom layer is the soil. A plant layer rests on the soil, an insect layer on the plants, a bird and rodent layer on the insects, and so on up through various animal groups to the apex layer, which consists of the larger carnivores.

The species of a layer are alike not in where they came from, or in what they look like, but rather in what they eat. Each successive layer depends on those below it for food and often for other services, and each in turn furnishes food and services to those above. Proceeding upward, each successive layer decreases in numerical abundance. Thus, for every carnivore there are hundreds of his prey, thousands of their prey, millions of insects, uncountable plants. The pyramidal form of the system reflects this numerical progression from apex to base. Man shares an intermediate layer with the bears, raccoons, and squirrels which eat both meat and vegetables.

The lines of dependency for food and other services are called food chains. Thus soil-oak-deer-Indian is a chain that has now been largely converted to soil-corn-cow-farmer. Each species, including ourselves, is a link in many chains. The deer eats a hundred plants other than oak, and the cow a hundred plants other than corn. Both, then, are links in a hundred chains. The pyramid is a tangle of chains so complex as to seem disorderly, yet the stability of the system proves it to be a highly organized structure. Its functioning depends on the cooperation and competition of its diverse parts.

In the beginning, the pyramid of life was low and squat; the food chains short and simple. Evolution has added layer after layer, link after link. Man is one of thousands of accretions to the height and complexity of the pyramid. Science has given us many doubts, but it has given us at least one certainty: the trend of evolution is to elaborate and diversify the biota.

Land, then, is not merely soil; it is a fountain of energy flowing through a circuit of soils, plants, and animals. Food chains are the living channels which conduct energy upward; death and decay return it to the soil. The circuit is not closed; some energy is dissipated in decay, some is added by absorption from the air, some is stored in soils, peats, and long-lived forests; but it is a sustained circuit, like a slowly augmented revolving fund of life. There is always a net loss by downhill wash, but this is normally small and offset by the decay of rocks. It is deposited in the ocean and, in the course of geological time, raised to form new lands and new pyramids.

The velocity and character of the upward flow of energy depend on the complex structure of the plant and animal community, much as the upward flow of sap in a tree depends on its complex cellular organization. Without this complexity, normal circulation would presumably not occur. Structure means the characteristic numbers, as well as the characteristic kinds and functions, of the component species. This interdependence between the complex structure of the land and its smooth functioning as an energy unit is one of its basic attributes.

When a change occurs in one part of the circuit, many other parts must adjust themselves to it. Change does not necessarily obstruct or divert the flow of energy; evolution is a long series of self-induced changes, the net result of which has been to elaborate the flow mechanism and to lengthen the circuit. Evolutionary changes, however, are usually slow and local. Man's invention of tools has enabled him to make changes of unprecedented violence, rapidity, and scope.

One change is in the composition of floras and faunas. The larger predators are lopped off the apex of the pyramid; food chains, for the first time in history, become shorter rather than longer. Domesticated species from other lands are substituted for wild ones, and wild ones are moved to new habitats. In this worldwide pooling of faunas and floras, some species get out of bounds as pests and diseases, others are extinguished. Such effects are seldom intended or foreseen; they represent unpredicted and often untraceable readjustments in the structure. Agricultural science is largely a race between the emergence of new pests and the emergence of new techniques for their control.

Another change touches the flow of energy through plants and animals and its return to the soil. Fertility is the ability of soil to receive, store, and release energy. Agriculture, by overdrafts on the soil, or by too radical a substitution of domestic for native species in the superstructure, may derange the channels of flow or deplete storage. Soils depleted of their storage, or of the organic matter which anchors it, wash away faster than they form. This is erosion.

Waters, like soil, are part of the energy circuit. Industry, by polluting waters or obstructing them with dams, may exclude the plants and animals necessary to keep energy in circulation.

Transportation brings about another basic change: the plants or animals grown in one region are now consumed and returned to the soil in another. Transportation taps the energy stored in rocks, and in the air, and uses it elsewhere; thus we fertilize the garden with nitrogen gleaned by the guano birds from the fishes of seas on the other side of the Equator. Thus the formerly localized and self-contained circuits are pooled on a worldwide scale.

The process of altering the pyramid for human occupation releases stored energy, and this often gives rise, during the pioneering period, to a deceptive exuberance of plant and animal life, both wild and tame. These releases of biotic capital tend to becloud or postpone the penalties of violence.

This thumbnail sketch of land as an energy circuit conveys three basic ideas:

1. That land is not merely soil.

2. That the native plants and animals kept the energy circuit open; others may or may not.

3. That man-made changes are of a different order than evolutionary changes, and have effects more comprehensive than is intended or foreseen.

These ideas, collectively, raise two basic issues: Can the land adjust itself to the new order? Can the desired alterations be accomplished with less violence?

Biotas seem to differ in their capacity to sustain violent conversion. Western Europe, for example, carries a far different pyramid than Caesar found there. Some large animals are lost; swampy forests have become meadows or plowland; many new plants and animals are introduced, some of which escape as pests; the remaining natives are greatly changed in distribution and abundance. Yet the soil is still there and, with the help of imported nutrients, still fertile; the waters flow normally; the new structure seems to function and to persist. There is no visible stoppage or derangement of the circuit.

Western Europe, then, has a resistant biota. Its inner processes are tough, elastic, resistant to strain. No matter how violent the alterations, the pyramid, so far, has developed some new *modus vivendi* which preserves its habitability for man, and for most of the other natives.

Japan seems to present another instance of radical conversion without disorganization.

Most other civilized regions, and some as yet barely touched by civilization, display various stages of disorganization, varying from initial symptoms to advanced wastage. In Asia Minor and North Africa diagnosis is confused by climatic changes, which may have been either the cause or the effect of advanced wastage. In the United States the degree of disorganization varies locally; it is worst in the Southwest, the Ozarks, and parts of the South, and least in New England and the Northwest. Better land-uses may still arrest it in the less advanced regions. In parts of Mexico, South America, South Africa, and Australia a violent and accelerating wastage is in progress, but I cannot assess the prospects.

This almost world-wide display of disorganization in the land seems to be similar to disease in an animal, except that it never culminates in complete disorganization or death. The land recovers, but at some reduced level of complexity, and with a reduced carrying capacity for people, plants, and animals. Many biotas currently regarded as "lands of opportunity" are in fact already subsisting on exploitative agriculture, i.e., they have already exceeded their sustained carrying capacity. Most of South America is overpopulated in this sense.

In arid regions we attempt to offset the process of wastage by reclamation, but it is only too evident that the prospective longevity of reclamation projects is often short. In our own West, the best of them may not last a century.

The combined evidence of history and ecology seems to support one general deduction: the less violent the man-made changes, the greater the probability of successful readjustment in the pyramid. Violence, in turn, varies with human population density; a dense population requires a more violent conversion. In this respect, North America has a better chance for permanence than Europe, if she can contrive to limit her density.

This deduction runs counter to our current philosophy, which assumes that because a small increase in density enriched human life, that an indefinite increase will enrich it indefinitely. Ecology knows of no density relationship that holds for indefinitely wide limits. All gains from density are subject to a law of diminishing returns.

Whatever may be the equation for men and land, it is improbable that we as yet know all its terms. Recent discoveries in mineral and vitamin nutrition reveal unsuspected dependencies in the up-circuit: incredibly minute quantities of certain substances determine the value of soils to plants, of plants to animals. What of the down-circuit? What of the vanishing species, the preservation of which we now regard as an esthetic luxury? They helped build the soil; in what unsuspected ways may they be essential to its maintenance? Professor [John E.] Weaver [1884–1966] proposes that we use prairie flowers to reflocculate the wasting soils of the dust bowl; who knows for what purpose cranes and condors, otters and grizzlies may someday be used?

**Land Health and the A-B Cleavage**

A land ethic, then, reflects the existence of an ecological conscience, and this in turn reflects a conviction of individual responsibility for the health of the land. Health is the capacity of the land for self-renewal. Conservation is our effort to understand and preserve this capacity.

Conservationists are notorious for their dissensions. Superficially these seem to add up to mere confusion, but a more careful scrutiny reveals a single plane of cleavage common to many specialized fields. In each field one group (A) regards the land as soil and its function as commodity-production; another group (B) regards the land as a biota, and its function as something broader. How much broader is admittedly in a state of doubt and confusion.

In my own field, forestry, group A is quite content to grow trees like cabbages, with cellulose as the basic forest commodity. It feels no inhibition against violence; its ideology is agronomic. Group B, on the other hand, sees forestry as fundamentally different from agronomy because it employs natural species, and manages a natural environment rather than creating an artificial one. Group B prefers natural reproduction on principle. It worries on biotic as well as economic grounds about the loss of species like chestnut and the threatened loss of the white pines. It worries about a whole series of secondary forest functions: wildlife, recreation, watersheds,

wilderness areas. To my mind, Group B feels the stirrings of an ecological conscience.

In the wildlife field, a parallel cleavage exists. For Group A the basic commodities are sport and meat; the yardsticks of production are ciphers of take in pheasants and trout. Artificial propagation is acceptable as a permanent as well as a temporary recourse – if its unit costs permit. Group B, on the other hand, worries about a whole series of biotic side-issues. What is the cost in predators of producing a game crop? Should we have further recourse to exotics? How can management restore the shrinking species, like prairie grouse, already hopeless as shootable game? How can management restore the threatened rarities, like trumpeter swan and whooping crane? Can management principles be extended to wildflowers? Here again it is clear to me that we have the same A-B cleavage as in forestry.

In the larger field of agriculture I am less competent to speak, but there seem to be somewhat parallel cleavages. Scientific agriculture was actively developing before ecology was born, hence a slower penetration of ecological concepts might be expected. Moreover the farmer, by the very nature of his techniques, must modify the biota more radically than the forester or the wildlife manager. Nevertheless, there are many discontents in agriculture which seem to add up to a new vision of "biotic farming."

Perhaps the most important of these is the new evidence that poundage or tonnage is no measure of the food-value of farm crops; the products of fertile soil may be qualitatively as well as quantitatively superior. We can bolster poundage from depleted soils by pouring on imported fertility, but we are not necessarily bolstering food-value. The possible ultimate ramifications of this idea are so immense that I must leave their exposition to abler pens.

The discontent that labels itself "organic

farming," while bearing some of the earmarks of a cult, is nevertheless biotic in its direction, particularly in its insistence on the importance of soil flora and fauna.

The ecological fundamentals of agriculture are just as poorly known to the public as in other fields of land-use. For example, few educated people realize that the marvelous advances in technique made during recent decades are improvements in the pump, rather than the well. Acre for acre, they have barely sufficed to offset the sinking level of fertility.

In all of these cleavages, we see repeated the same basic paradoxes: man the conqueror *versus* man the biotic citizen; science the sharpener of his sword *versus* science the searchlight on his universe; land the slave and servant *versus* land the collective organism. [Edward Arlington] Robinson's [1869–1935] injunction to Tristram [1927] may well be applied, at this juncture, to *Homo sapiens* as a species in geological time:

Whether you will or not
You are a King, Tristram, for you are one
Of the time-tested few that leave the
        world,
When they are gone, not the same place
        it was.
Mark what you leave.

## The Outlook

It is inconceivable to me that an ethical relation to land can exist without love, respect, and admiration for land, and a high regard for its value. By value, I of course mean something far broader than mere economic value; I mean value in the philosophical sense.

Perhaps the most serious obstacle impeding the evolution of a land ethic is the fact that our educational and economic system is headed away from, rather than toward, an intense consciousness of land. Your true modern is separated from the land by many middlemen, and by innumerable physical gadgets. He has no vital relation to it; to him it is the space between cities on which crops grow. Turn him loose for a day on the land, and if the spot does not happen to be a golf links or a "scenic" area, he is bored stiff. If crops could be raised by hydroponics instead of farming, it would suit him very well. Synthetic substitutes for wood, leather, wool, and other natural land products suit him better than the originals. In short, land is something he has "outgrown."

Almost equally serious as an obstacle to a land ethic is the attitude of the farmer for whom the land is still an adversary, or a taskmaster that keeps him in slavery. Theoretically, the mechanization of farming ought to cut the farmer's chains, but whether it really does is debatable.

One of the requisites for an ecological comprehension of land is an understanding of ecology, and this is by no means co-extensive with "education"; in fact, much higher education seems deliberately to avoid ecological concepts. An understanding of ecology does not necessarily originate in courses bearing ecological labels; it is quite as likely to be labeled geography, botany, agronomy, history, or economics. This is as it should be, but whatever the label, ecological training is scarce.

The case for a land ethic would appear hopeless but for the minority which is in obvious revolt against these "modern" trends.

The "key-log" which must be moved to release the evolutionary process for an ethic is simply this: quit thinking about decent land-use as solely an economic problem. Examine each question in terms of what is ethically and esthetically right, as well as what is economically expedient. A thing is right when it tends to preserve the integrity, stability, and beauty of the biotic community. It is wrong when it tends otherwise.

It of course goes without saying that economic feasibility limits the tether of what can or cannot be done for land. It always has and it always will. The fallacy the economic determinists have tied around our collective neck, and which we now need to cast off, is the belief that economics determines *all* land-use. This is simply not true. An innumerable host of actions and attitudes, comprising perhaps the bulk of all land relations, is determined by the land-user's tastes and predilections, rather than by his purse. The bulk of all land relations hinges on investments of time, forethought, skill, and faith rather than on investments of cash. As a land-user thinketh, so is he.

I have purposely presented the land ethic as a product of social evolution because nothing so important as an ethic is ever "written." Only the most superficial student of history supposes that Moses "wrote" the Decalogue; it evolved in the minds of a thinking community, and Moses wrote a tentative summary of it for a "seminar," I say tentative because evolution never stops.

The evolution of a land ethic is an intellectual as well as emotional process. Conservation is paved with good intentions which prove to be futile, or even dangerous, because they are devoid of critical understanding either of the land, or of economic land-use. I think it is a truism that as the ethical frontier advances from the individual to the community, its intellectual content increases.

The mechanism of operation is the same for any ethic: social approbation for right actions: social disapproval for wrong actions.

By and large, our present problem is one of attitudes and implements. We are re-modeling the Alhambra with a steam-shovel, and we are proud of our yardage. We shall hardly relinquish the shovel, which after all has many good points, but we are in need of gentler and more objective criteria for its successful use.

## Study Questions

1. How does Leopold define an ethic both ecologically and philosophically? What does Leopold note is required for a change in ethics to come about? How likely do you think it is that these "internal" changes will actually take place? Do you think that we need more education, or will there be change only after an environmental crisis has become undeniable?

2. Leopold details "the land pyramid," which represents the ecosystem. Describe each layer of this pyramid, including explaining why it is shaped like a pyramid and where humans belong. The pyramid has a "carrying capacity," which is the long-term ability of the ecosystem to function and support the species within. What happens when the carrying capacity is exceeded? Has Earth's carrying capacity been exceeded? Why or why not?

3. Leopold details the workings of the (land-based) ecosystem as they have evolved. Evolutionary changes do occur, but generally the energy-circuit is sustained within this process that entails native species. Human changes differ from (non-human) evolutionary changes. Leopold states, "man-made changes are of a different order than evolutionary changes, and have effects more comprehensive than is intended or foreseen." Provide a brief explanation of this using the examples he provides.

4. *The Land Ethic* is described as follows: "A thing is right when it tends to preserve the integrity, stability, and beauty of the biotic community. It is wrong when it tends otherwise." This ethic is a significant challenge to the consumptive lifestyles of those in the "developed" countries, and is also a significant challenge to those "developing," especially in the image of the US. How would you embrace this ethic in your own life? What are the things that would have to change?

# 2. Naomi Klein, "Beyond Extractivism: Confronting the Climate Denier Within"

CANADIAN SOCIAL ACTIVIST NAOMI Klein (b. 1970) begins this selection, from her 2014 book *This Changes Everything*, with the example of Nauru, a small island ravaged by colonization and extraction. Extractivism is the practice of depleting natural resources in a nonreciprocal relationship between humans and the Earth. Klein argues that human extractivism of fossil fuels has not resulted in the assumed result of controlling nature; rather, the cumulative effects of fossil-fuel extraction and use have resulted in climate change. Our failure to live within environmental limits has made us all Nauruans.

---

The best thing about the Earth is if you poke holes in it oil and gas comes out.
— Republican US Congressman Steve Stockman, 2013[1]

The open veins of Latin America are still bleeding.
— Bolivian Indigenous leader Nilda Rojas Huanca, 2014[2]

It is our predicament that we live in a finite world, and yet we behave as if it were infinite. Steady exponential material growth with no limits on resource consumption and population is the dominant conceptual model used by today's decision makers. This is an approximation of reality that is no longer accurate and [has] started to break down.
— Global systems analyst Rodrigo Castro and colleagues, paper presented at a scientific modeling conference, 2014[3]

FOR THE PAST FEW years, the island of Nauru has been on a health kick. The concrete walls of public buildings are covered in murals urging regular exercise and healthy eating, and warning against the danger of diabetes. Young people are asking their grandparents how to fish, a lost skill. But there is a problem. As Nerida-Ann Steshia Hubert, who works at a diabetes center on the island, explains, life spans on Nauru are short, in part because of an epidemic of the disease. "The older folks are passing away early and we're losing a lot of the knowledge with them. It's like a race against time – trying to get the knowledge from them before they die."[4]

For decades, this tiny, isolated South Pacific island, just twenty-one square kilometers and home to ten thousand people, was held up as a model for the world – a developing country that was doing everything right. In the early 1960s, the Australian government, whose troops seized control of Nauru from the Germans in 1914, was so proud of its protectorate that it made promotional videos showing the Micronesians in starched white Bermuda shorts, obediently following lessons in English-speaking schools, settling their disputes in British-style courts, and shopping for modern conveniences in well-stocked grocery stores.[5]

During the 1970s and 1980s, after Nauru had earned independence, the island was periodically featured in press reports as a place of almost obscene riches, much as Dubai is invoked today. An Associated Press article from 1985 reported that Nauruans had "the world's highest per capita gross national product ... higher even than Persian Gulf oil Sheikdoms." Everyone had free health care, housing, and education; homes were kept cool with air-conditioning; and residents zoomed around their tiny island – it took twenty minutes to make the entire loop – in brand-new cars and motorcycles. A police chief famously bought himself a yellow Lamborghini. "When I was young," recalls Steshia Hubert, "we would go to parties where people would throw thousands of dollars on the babies. Extravagant parties – first, sixteenth, eighteenth, twenty-first, and fiftieth birthdays.... They would come with gifts like cars, pillows stuffed with hundred-dollar bills – for one-year-old babies!"[6]

All of Nauru's monetary wealth derived from an odd geological fact. For hundreds of thousands of years, when the island was nothing but a cluster of coral reefs protruding from the waves, Nauru was a popular pit stop for migrating birds, who dropped by to feast on the shellfish and mollusks. Gradually, the bird poop built up between the coral towers and spires, eventually hardening to form a rocky landmass. The rock was then covered over in topsoil and dense forest, creating a tropical oasis of coconut palms, tranquil beaches, and thatched huts so beatific that the first European visitors dubbed the island Pleasant Isle.[7]

For thousands of years, Nauruans lived on the surface of their island, sustaining themselves on fish and black noddy birds. That began to change when a colonial officer picked up a rock that was later discovered to be made of almost pure phosphate of lime, a valuable agricultural fertilizer. A German–British firm began mining, later replaced by a British–Australian–New Zealand venture.[8] Nauru started developing at record speed – the catch was that it was, simultaneously, committing suicide.

By the 1960s, Nauru still looked pleasant enough when approached from the sea, but it was a mirage. Behind the narrow fringe of coconut palms circling the coast lay a ravaged interior. Seen from above, the forest and top-soil of the oval island were being voraciously stripped away; the phosphate mined down to the island's sharply protruding bones, leaving behind a forest of ghostly coral totems. With the center now uninhabitable and largely infertile except for some minor scrubby vegetation, life on Nauru unfolded along the thin coastal strip, where the homes and civic structures were located.[9]

Nauru's successive waves of colonizers – whose economic emissaries ground up the phosphate rock into fine dust, then shipped it on ocean liners to fertilize soil in Australia and New Zealand – had a simple plan for the country: they would keep mining phosphate until the island was an empty shell. "When the phosphate supply is exhausted in thirty to forty years' time, the experts predict that the estimated population will not be able to live on this pleasant little island," a Nauruan council member said, rather stiffly, in a sixties-era black-and-white video produced by the Australian government. But not to worry, the film's narrator explained: "Preparations are being made now for the future of the Nauruan people. Australia has offered them a permanent home within her own shores.... Their prospects are bright; their future is secure."[10]

Nauru, in other words, was developed to disappear, designed by the Australian government and the extractive companies that controlled its fate as a disposable country.

It's not that they had anything against the place, no genocidal intent per se. It's just that one dead island that few even knew existed seemed like an acceptable sacrifice to make in the name of the progress represented by industrial agriculture.

When the Nauruans themselves took control of their country in 1968, they had hopes of reversing these plans. Toward that end, they put a large chunk of their mining revenues into a trust fund that they invested in what seemed like stable real estate ventures in Australia and Hawaii. The goal was to live off the fund's proceeds while winding down phosphate mining and beginning to rehabilitate their island's ecology – a costly task, but perhaps not impossible.[11]

The plan failed. Nauru's government received catastrophically bad investment advice, and the country's mining wealth was squandered. Meanwhile, Nauru continued to disappear, its white powdery innards loaded onto boats as the mining continued unabated. Meanwhile, decades of easy money had taken a predictable toll on Nauruans' life and culture. Politics was rife with corruption, drunk driving was a leading cause of death, average life expectancy was dismally low, and Nauru earned the dubious honor of being featured on a US news show as "the fattest place on Earth" (half the adult population suffers from type 2 diabetes, the result of a diet comprised almost exclusively of imported processed food). "During the golden era when the royalties were rolling in, we didn't cook, we ate in restaurants," recalls Steshia Hubert, a health care worker. And even if the Nauruans had wanted to eat differently, it would have been hard: with so much of the island a latticework of deep dark holes, growing enough fresh produce to feed the population was pretty much impossible. A bitterly ironic infertility for an island whose main export was agricultural fertilizer.[12]

By the 1990s, Nauru was so desperate for foreign currency that it pursued some distinctly shady get-rich-quick schemes. Aided greatly by the wave of financial deregulation unleashed in this period, the island became a prime money-laundering haven. For a time in the late 1990s, Nauru was the titular "home" to roughly four hundred phantom banks that were utterly unencumbered by monitoring, oversight, taxes, and regulation. Nauru-registered shell banks were particularly popular among Russian gangsters, who reportedly laundered a staggering $70 billion of dirty money through the island nation (to put that in perspective, Nauru's entire GDP is $72 million, according to most recent figures). Giving the country partial credit for the collapse of the Russian economy, a *New York Times Magazine* piece in 2000 pronounced that "amid the recent proliferation of money-laundering centers that experts estimate has ballooned into a $5 trillion shadow economy, Nauru is Public Enemy #1."[13]

These schemes have since caught up with Nauru too, and now the country faces a double bankruptcy: with 90 per cent of the island depleted from mining, it faces ecological bankruptcy; with a debt of at least $800 million, Nauru faces financial bankruptcy as well. But these are not Nauru's only problems. It now turns out that the island nation is highly vulnerable to a crisis it had virtually no hand in creating: climate change and the drought, ocean acidification, and rising waters it brings. Sea levels around Nauru have been steadily climbing by about 5 millimeters per year since 1993, and much more could be on the way if current trends continue. Intensified droughts are already causing severe freshwater shortages.[14]

A decade ago, Australian philosopher and professor of sustainability Glenn Albrecht set out to coin a term to capture the particular form of psychological distress that sets in when the homelands that we love and from which we take comfort are radically altered by extraction and industrialization, rendering them alienating and unfamiliar. He settled on "solastalgia," with its evocations of solace, destruction, and pain, and defined the new word to mean, "the homesickness you have when you are still at home." He explained that although this particular form of unease was once principally familiar to people who lived in sacrifice zones – lands decimated by open pit mining, for instance, or clear-cut logging – it was fast becoming a universal human experience, with climate change creating a "new abnormal" wherever we happen to live. "As bad as local and regional negative transformation is, it is the big picture, the Whole Earth, which is now a home under assault. A feeling of global dread asserts itself as the planet heats and our climate gets more hostile and unpredictable," he writes.[15]

Some places are unlucky enough to experience both local and global solastalgia simultaneously. Speaking to the 1997 UN climate conference that adopted the Kyoto Protocol, Nauru's then-president Kinza Clodumar described the collective claustrophobia that had gripped his country: "We are trapped, a wasteland at our back, and to our front a terrifying, rising flood of biblical proportions."[16] Few places on earth embody the suicidal results of building our economies on polluting extraction more graphically than Nauru. Thanks to its mining of phosphate, Nauru has spent the last century disappearing from the inside out; now, thanks to our collective mining of fossil fuels, it is disappearing from the outside in.

In a 2007 cable about Nauru, made public by WikiLeaks, an unnamed US official summed up his government's analysis of what went wrong on the island: "Nauru simply spent extravagantly, never worrying about tomorrow."[17] Fair enough, but that diagnosis is hardly unique to Nauru; our entire culture is extravagantly drawing down finite resources, never worrying about tomorrow. For a couple of hundred years we have been telling ourselves that we can dig the midnight black remains of other life forms out of the bowels of the earth, burn them in massive quantities, and that the airborne particles and gases released into the atmosphere – because we can't see them – will have no effect whatsoever. Or if they do, we humans, brilliant as we are, will just invent our way out of whatever mess we have made.

And we tell ourselves all kinds of similarly implausible no-consequences stories all the time, about how we can ravage the world and suffer no adverse effects. Indeed we are always surprised when it works out otherwise. We extract and do not replenish and wonder why the fish have disappeared and the soil requires ever more "inputs" (like phosphate) to stay fertile. We occupy countries and arm their militias and then wonder why they hate us. We drive down wages, ship jobs overseas, destroy worker protections, hollow out local economies, then wonder why people can't afford to shop as much as they used to. We offer those failed shoppers subprime mortgages instead of steady jobs and then wonder why no one foresaw that a system built on bad debts would collapse.

At every stage our actions are marked by a lack of respect for the powers we are unleashing – a certainty, or at least a hope, that the nature we have turned to garbage, and the people we have treated like garbage, will not come back to haunt us. And Nauru knows all about this too, because in the past decade it has become a dumping ground of another sort. In an effort to raise much needed revenue, it agreed to house an offshore refugee detention center for the government of Australia. In what has become known as "the Pacific Solution," Australian navy and customs

ships intercept boats of migrants and immediately fly them three thousand kilometers
to Nauru (as well as to several other Pacific
islands). Once on Nauru, the migrants – most
from Afghanistan, Sri Lanka, Iraq, Iran, and
Pakistan – are crammed into a rat-infested
guarded camp made up of rows of crowded,
stiflingly hot tents. The island imprisonment
can last up to five years, with the migrants in
a state of constant limbo about their status,
something the Australian government hopes
will serve as a deterrent to future refugees.[18]

The Australian and Nauruan governments
have gone to great lengths to limit information on camp conditions and have prevented
journalists who make the long journey to the
island from seeing where migrants are being
housed. But the truth is leaking out nonetheless: grainy video of prisoners chanting
"We are not animals"; reports of mass hunger strikes and suicide attempts; horrifying
photographs of refugees who had sewn their
own mouths shut, using paper clips as needles;
an image of a man who had badly mutilated
his neck in a failed hanging attempt. There
are also images of toddlers playing in the
dirt and huddling with their parents under
tent flaps for shade (originally the camp had
housed only adult males, but now hundreds
of women and children have been sent there
too). In June 2013, the Australian government
finally allowed a BBC crew into the camp in
order to show off its brand-new barracks – but
that PR attempt was completely upstaged one
month later by the news that a prisoner riot
had almost completely destroyed the new facility, leaving several prisoners injured.[19]

Amnesty International has called the camp
on Nauru "cruel" and "degrading," and a
2013 report by the United Nations High
Commissioner for Refugees concluded that
those conditions, "coupled with the protract-
ed period spent there by some asylum-seekers,
raise serious issues about their compatibility

with international human rights law, including the prohibition against torture and cruel,
inhuman or degrading treatment." Then, in
March 2014, a former Salvation Army employee named Mark Isaacs, who had been
stationed at the camp, published a tell-all
memoir titled *The Undesirables*. He wrote
about men who had survived wars and treacherous voyages losing all will to live on Nauru,
with one man resorting to swallowing cleaning fluids, another driven mad and barking
like a dog. Isaacs likened the camp to "death
factories," and said in an interview that it is
about "taking resilient men and grinding
them into the dust." On an island that itself
was systematically ground to dust, it's a harrowing image. As harrowing as enlisting the
people who could very well be the climate
refugees of tomorrow to play warden to the
political and economic refugees of today.[20]

Reviewing the island's painful history,
it strikes me that so much of what has gone
wrong on Nauru – and goes on still – has to
do with its location, frequently described as
"the middle of nowhere" or, in the words of
a 1921 *National Geographic* dispatch, "perhaps
the most remote territory in the world," a
tiny dot "in lonely seas." The nation's remote-
ness made it a convenient trash can – a place
to turn the land into trash, to launder dirty
money, to disappear unwanted people, and
now a place that may be allowed to disappear
altogether.[21]

This is our relationship to much that we
cannot easily see and it is a big part of what
makes carbon pollution such a stubborn problem: we can't see it, so we don't really believe
it exists. Ours is a culture of disavowal, of
simultaneously knowing and not knowing
– the illusion of proximity coupled with the
reality of distance is the trick perfected by the
fossil-fueled global market. So we both know
and don't know who makes our goods, who
cleans up after us, where our waste disappears

to – whether it's our sewage or electronics or our carbon emissions.

But what Nauru's fate tells us is that there is no middle of nowhere, nowhere that doesn't "count" – and that nothing ever truly disappears. On some level we all know this, that we are part of a swirling web of connections. Yet we are trapped in linear narratives that tell us the opposite: that we can expand infinitely, that there will always be more space to absorb our waste, more resources to fuel our wants, more people to abuse.

These days, Nauru is in a near constant state of political crisis, with fresh corruption scandals perpetually threatening to bring down the government, and sometimes succeeding. Given the wrong visited upon the nation, the island's leaders would be well within their rights to point fingers outward – at their former colonial masters who flayed them, at the investors who fleeced them, and at the rich countries whose emissions now threaten to drown them. And some do. But several of Nauru's leaders have also chosen to do something else: to hold up their country as a kind of warning to a warming world.

In *The New York Times* in 2011, for instance, then-president Marcus Stephen wrote that Nauru provides "an indispensable cautionary tale about life in a place with hard ecological limits." It shows, he claimed, "what can happen when a country runs out of options. The world is headed down a similar path with the relentless burning of coal and oil, which is altering the planet's climate, melting ice caps, making oceans more acidic and edging us ever closer to a day when no one will be able to take clean water, fertile soil or abundant food for granted." In other words, Nauru isn't the only one digging itself to death; we all are.[22]

But the lesson Nauru has to teach is not only about the dangers of fossil fuel emissions. It is about the mentality that allowed so many of us, and our ancestors, to believe that we could relate to the earth with such violence in the first place – to dig and drill out the substances we desired while thinking little of the trash left behind, whether in the land and water where the extraction takes place, or in the atmosphere, once the extracted material is burned. This carelessness is at the core of an economic model some political scientists call "extractivism," a term originally used to describe economies based on removing ever more raw materials from the earth, usually for export to traditional colonial powers, where "value" was added. And it's a habit of thought that goes a long way toward explaining why an economic model based on endless growth ever seemed viable in the first place. Though developed under capitalism, governments across the ideological spectrum now embrace this resource-depleting model as a road to development, and it is this logic that climate change calls profoundly into question.

Extractivism is a nonreciprocal, dominance-based relationship with the earth, one purely of taking. It is the opposite of stewardship, which involves taking but also taking care that regeneration and future life continue. Extractivism is the mentality of the mountaintop remover and the old-growth clear-cutter. It is the reduction of life into objects for the use of others, giving them no integrity or value of their own – turning living complex ecosystems into "natural resources," mountains into "overburden" (as the mining industry terms the forests, rocks, and streams that get in the way of its bulldozers). It is also the reduction of human beings either into labor to be brutally extracted, pushed beyond limits, or, alternatively, into social burden, problems to be locked out at borders and locked away in prisons or reservations. In an extractivist economy, the interconnections among these various objectified components of life are ignored; the consequences of severing them are of no concern.

Extractivism is also directly connected to the notion of sacrifice zones – places that, to their extractors, somehow don't count and therefore can be poisoned, drained, or otherwise destroyed, for the supposed greater good of economic progress. This toxic idea has always been intimately tied to imperialism, with disposable peripheries being harnessed to feed a glittering center, and it is bound up too with notions of racial superiority, because in order to have sacrifice zones, you need to have people and cultures who count so little that they are considered deserving of sacrifice. Extractivism ran rampant under colonialism because relating to the world as a frontier of conquest – rather than as home – fosters this particular brand of irresponsibility. The colonial mind nurtures the belief that there is always somewhere else to go to and exploit once the current site of extraction has been exhausted.

These ideas predate industrial-scale extraction of fossil fuels. And yet the ability to harness the power of coal to power factories and ships is what, more than any single other factor, enabled these dangerous ideas to conquer the world. It's a history worth exploring in more depth, because it goes a long way toward explaining how the climate crisis challenges not only capitalism but the underlying civilizational narratives about endless growth and progress within which we are all, in one way or another, still trapped.

**The Ultimate Extractivist Relationship**

If the modern-day extractive economy has a patron saint, the honor should probably go to Francis Bacon [1561–1626]. The English philosopher, scientist, and statesman is credited with convincing Britain's elites to abandon, once and for all, pagan notions of the earth as a life-giving mother figure to whom we owe respect and reverence (and more than a little fear) and accept the role as her dungeon master. "For you have but to follow and as it were hound nature in her wanderings," Bacon wrote in *De Augmentis Scientiarum* in 1623, "and you will be able, when you like, to lead and drive her afterwards to the same place again…. Neither ought a man to make scruple of entering and penetrating into these holes and corners, when the inquisition of truth is his sole object."[23] (Not surprisingly, feminist scholars have filled volumes analyzing the ex-Lord Chancellor's metaphor choices.)

These ideas of a completely knowable and controllable earth animated not only the Scientific Revolution but, critically, the colonial project as well, which sent ships crisscrossing the globe to poke and prod and bring the secrets, and wealth, back to their respective crowns. The mood of human invincibility that governed this epoch was neatly encapsulated in the words of clergyman and philosopher William Derham [1657–1735] in his 1713 book *Physico-Theology:* "We can, if need be, ransack the whole globe, penetrate into the bowels of the earth, descend to the bottom of the deep, travel to the farthest regions of this world, to acquire wealth."[24]

And yet despite this bravado, throughout the 1700s, the twin projects of colonialism and industrialization were still constrained by nature on several key fronts. Ships carrying both slaves and the raw materials they harvested could sail only when winds were favorable, which could lead to long delays in the supply chain. The factories that turned those raw materials into finished products were powered by huge water wheels. They needed to be located next to waterfalls or rapids which made them dependent on the flow and levels of rivers. As with high or low winds at sea, an especially dry or wet spell meant that working hours in the textile, flour, and sugar mills had to be adjusted accordingly – a mounting annoyance as markets expanded and became more global.

Many water-powered factories were, by necessity, spread out around the countryside, near bodies of fast-moving water. As the Industrial Revolution matured and workers in the mills started to strike and even riot for better wages and conditions, this decentralization made factory owners highly vulnerable, since quickly finding replacement workers in rural areas was difficult.

Beginning in 1776, a Scottish engineer named James Watt [1736–1819] perfected and manufactured a power source that offered solutions to all these vulnerabilities. Lawyer and historian Barbara Freese describes Watt's steam engine as "perhaps the most important invention in the creation of the modern world" – and with good reason.[25] By adding a separate condenser, air pump, and later a rotary mechanism to an older model, Watt was able to make the coal-fired steam engine vastly more powerful and adaptable than its predecessors. In contrast, the new machines could power a broad range of industrial operations, including, eventually, boats.

For the first couple of decades, the new engine was a tough sell. Water power, after all, had a lot going for it compared with coal. For one thing, it was free, while coal needed to be continually re-purchased. And contrary to the widespread belief that the steam engine provided more energy than water wheels, the two were actually comparable, with the larger wheels packing several times more horsepower than their coal-powered rivals. Water wheels also operated more smoothly, with fewer technical breakdowns, so long as the water was flowing. "The transition from water to steam in the British cotton industry did not occur because water was scarce, less powerful, or more expensive than steam," writes Swedish coal expert Andreas Malm. "To the contrary, steam gained supremacy *in spite of water being abundant, at least as powerful, and decidedly cheaper.*"[26]

As Britain's urban population ballooned, two factors tipped the balance in favor of the steam engine. The first was the new machine's insulation from nature's fluctuations: unlike water wheels, steam engines worked at the same rate all the time, so long as there was coal to feed them and the machinery wasn't broken. The flow rates of rivers were of no concern. Steam engines also worked anywhere, regardless of the geography, which meant that factory owners could shift production from more remote areas to cities like London, Manchester, and Lancaster, where there were gluts of willing industrial workers, making it far easier to fire troublemakers and put down strikes. As an 1832 article written by a British economist explained, "The invention of the steam-engine has relieved us from the necessity of building factories in inconvenient situations merely for the sake of a waterfall." Or as one of Watt's early biographers put it, the generation of power "will no longer depend, as heretofore, on the most inconstant of natural causes – on atmospheric influences."[27]

Similarly, when Watt's engine was installed in a boat, ship crews were liberated from having to adapt their journeys to the winds, a development that rapidly accelerated the colonial project and the ability of European powers to easily annex countries in distant lands. As the Earl of Liverpool put it in a public meeting to memorialize James Watt in 1824, "Be the winds friendly or be they contrary, the power of the Steam Engine overcomes all difficulties.... Let the wind blow from whatever quarter it may, let the destination of our force be to whatever part of the world it may, you have the power and the means, by the Steam Engine, of applying that force at the proper time and in the proper manner."[28] Not until the advent of electronic trading would commerce feel itself so liberated from the constraints of living on a planet bound by geography and governed by the elements.

Unlike the energy it replaced, power from fossil fuel always required sacrifice zones – whether in the black lungs of the coal miners or the poisoned waterways surrounding the mines. But these prices were seen as worth paying in exchange for coal's intoxicating promise of freedom from the physical world – a freedom that unleashed industrial capitalism's full force to dominate both workers and other cultures. With their portable energy creator, the industrialists and colonists of the 1800s could now go wherever labor was cheapest and most exploitable, and wherever resources were most plentiful and valuable. As the author of a steam engine manual wrote in the mid-1830s, "Its mighty services are always at our command, whether in winter or in summer, by day or by night – it knows of no intermission but what our wishes dictate."[29] Coal represented, in short, total domination, of both nature and other people, the full realization of Bacon's dream at last. "Nature can be conquered," Watt reportedly said, "if we can but find her weak side."[30]

Little wonder then that the introduction of Watt's steam engine coincided with explosive levels of growth in British manufacturing, such that in the eighty years between 1760 and 1840, the country went from importing 2.5 million pounds of raw cotton to importing 366 million pounds of raw cotton, a genuine revolution made possible by the potent and brutal combination of coal at home and slave labor abroad.[31]

This recipe produced more than just new consumer products. In *Ecological Economics*, Herman Daly and Joshua Farley point out that Adam Smith published *The Wealth of Nations* in 1776 – the same year that Watt produced his first commercial steam engine. "It is no coincidence," they write, "that the market economy and fossil fuel economy emerged at essentially the exact same time…. New technologies and vast amounts of fossil energy allowed unprecedented production of consumer goods. The need for new markets for these mass-produced consumer goods and new sources of raw material played a role in colonialism and the pursuit of empire. The market economy evolved as an efficient way of allocating such goods, and stimulating the production of even more."[32] Just as colonialism needed coal to fulfill its dream of total domination, the deluge of products made possible by both coal and colonialism needed modern capitalism.

The promise of liberation from nature that Watt was selling in those early days continues to be the great power of fossil fuels. That power is what allows today's multinationals to scour the globe for the cheapest, most exploitable workforce, with natural features and events that once appeared as obstacles – vast oceans, treacherous landscapes, seasonal fluctuations – no longer even registering as minor annoyances. Or so it seemed for a time.

\* \* \*

It is often said that Mother Nature bats last, and this has been poignantly the case for some of the men who were most possessed by the ambition of conquering her. A perhaps apocryphal story surrounds the death of Francis Bacon: in an attempt to test his hypothesis that frozen meat could be prevented from rotting, he traipsed around in chilly weather stuffing a chicken full of snow. As a result, it is said, the philosopher caught pneumonia, which eventually led to his demise.[33] Despite some controversy, the anecdote survives for its seeming poetic justice: a man who thought nature could be bent to his will died from simple exposure to the cold.

A similar story of comeuppance appears to be unfolding for the human race as a whole. Ralph Waldo Emerson called coal "a portable climate" – and it has been a smash success, carrying countless advantages, from longer life spans to hundreds of millions freed from hard labor.[34] And yet precisely because our bodies are so effectively separated from our geographies, we who have access to this privilege have proven ourselves far too capable of ignoring the fact that we aren't just changing our personal climate but the entire planet's climate as well, warming not just the indoors but the outdoors too. And yet the warming is no less real for our failure to pay attention.

The harnessing of fossil fuel power seemed, for a couple of centuries at least, to have freed large parts of humanity from the need to be in constant dialogue with nature, having to adjust its plans, ambitions, and schedules to natural fluctuations and topographies. Coal and oil, precisely because they were fossilized, seemed entirely possessable forms of energy. They did not behave independently – not like wind, or water, or, for that matter, workers. Just as Watt's engine promised, once purchased, they produced power wherever and whenever their owners wished – the ultimate nonreciprocal relationship.

But what we have learned from atmospheric science is that the give-and-take, call-and-response that is the essence of all relationships in nature was not eliminated with fossil fuels, it was merely delayed, all the while gaining force and velocity. Now the cumulative effect of those centuries of burned carbon is in the process of unleashing the most ferocious natural tempers of all.

As a result, the illusion of total power and control Watt and his cohorts once peddled has given way to the reality of near total powerlessness and loss of control in the face of such spectacular forces as Hurricane Sandy and Typhoon Haiyan. Which is just one of the reasons climate change is so deeply frightening. Because to confront this crisis truthfully is to confront ourselves – to reckon, as our ancestors did, with our vulnerability to the elements that make up both the planet and our bodies. It is to accept (even embrace) being but one porous part of the world, rather than its master or machinist, as Bacon long ago promised. There can be great well-being in that realization of interconnection, pleasure too. But we should not underestimate the depth of the civilizational challenge that this relationship represents. As Australian political scientist Clive Hamilton puts it, facing these truths about climate change "means recognizing that the power relation between humans and the earth is the reverse of the one we have assumed for three centuries."[35] …

## Some Warnings, Unheeded

There is one other group that might have provided a challenge to Western culture's disastrous view of nature as a bottomless vending machine. That group, of course, is the environmental movement, the network of organizations that exists to protect the natural world from being devoured by human activity. And yet the movement has not played this role, at least not in a sustained and coherent manner.

In part, that has to do with the movement's unusually elite history, particularly in North America. When conservationism emerged as a powerful force in the late nineteenth and early twentieth centuries, it was primarily about men of privilege who enjoyed fishing, hunting, camping, and hiking and who recognized that many of their favorite wilderness spots were under threat from the rapid expansion of industrialization. For the most part, these men did not call into question the frenetic economic project that was devouring natural landscapes all over the continent – they simply wanted to make sure that some particularly spectacular pockets were set aside for their recreation and aesthetic appreciation. Like the Christian missionaries who traveled with traders and soldiers, most early preservation-ists saw their work as a civilizing addendum to the colonial and industrial projects – not as a challenge to them. Writing in 1914, Bronx Zoo director William Temple Hornaday summed up this ethos, urging American educators to "take up their share of the white man's burden" and help to "preserve the wild life of our country."[36]

This task was accomplished not with dis-ruptive protests, which would have been unseemly for a movement so entrenched in the upper stratum of society. Instead, it was achieved through quiet lobbying, with well-bred men appealing to the noblesse oblige of other men of their class to save a cherished area by turning it into a national or state park, or a private family preserve – often at the direct expense of Indigenous people who lost access to these lands as hunting and fishing grounds.

There were those in the movement, how-ever, who saw in the threats to their country's most beautiful places signs of a deeper cultural crisis. For instance, John Muir [1838–1914], the great naturalist writer who helped found the Sierra Club in 1892, excoriated the industri-alists who dammed wild rivers and drowned beautiful valleys. To him they were heathens – "devotees of ravaging commercialism" who "instead of lifting their eyes to the God of the mountains, lift them to the Almighty Dollar."[37]

He was not the only heretic. A strain of radicalism drove some of the early Western ecological thinkers to argue for doing more than protecting isolated landscapes. Though frequently unacknowledged, these thinkers often drew heavily on Eastern beliefs about the interconnectedness of all life, as well as on Native American cosmologies that see all liv-ing creatures as our "relations."

In the mid-1800s, Henry David Thoreau [1817–62] wrote that, "The earth I tread on is not a dead, inert mass. It is a body, has a spirit, is organic, and fluid to the influence of its spirit, and to whatever particle of that spirit is in me."[38] This was a straight repudiation of Francis Bacon's casting of the earth as an inert machine whose mysteries could be mastered by the human mind. And almost a century after Thoreau, Aldo Leopold [1887–1948], whose book *A Sand County Almanac* [1949] was the touchstone for a second wave of envi-ronmentalists, similarly called for an ethic that "enlarges the boundaries of the community to include soils, waters, plants, and animals" and that recognizes "the individual is a member of a community of interdependent parts." A "land ethic," as he called it, "changes the role of *Homo sapiens* from conqueror of the land-community to plain member and citizen of it. It implies respect for his fellow-members, and also respect for the community as such."[39]

These ideas were hugely influential in the evolution of ecological thought, but unat-tached to populist movements, they posed little threat to galloping industrialization. The dominant worldview continued to see humans as a conquering army, subduing and mechanizing the natural world. Even so, by the 1930s, with socialism on the rise around the world, the more conservative elements of the growing environmental movement sought to distance themselves from Leopold's "radi-cal" suggestion that nature had an inherent value beyond its utility to man. If watersheds and old-growth forests had a "right to contin-ued existence," as Leopold argued (a preview of the "rights of nature" debates that would emerge several decades later), then an owner's right to do what he wished with his land could be called into question. In 1935, Jay Norwood "Ding" Darling [1876–1962], who would later help found the National Wildlife Federation, wrote to Leopold warning him, "I can't get away from the idea that you are getting us out into water over our depth by your new phi-losophy of wildlife environment. The end of that road leads to socialization of property."[40]

By the time Rachel Carson [1907–64] published *Silent Spring* in 1962, the attempts to turn nature into a mere cog in the American industrial machine had grown so aggressive, so overtly militaristic, that it was no longer possible to pretend that combining capitalism with conservation was simply a matter of protecting a few pockets of green. Carson's book boiled over with righteous condemnations of a chemical industry that used aerial bombardment to wipe out insects, thoughtlessly endangering human and animal life in the process. The marine biologist-turned-social-critic painted a vivid picture of the arrogant "control men" who, enthralled with "a bright new toy," hurled poisons "against the fabric of life."[41]

Carson's focus was DDT, but for her the problem was not a particular chemical; it was a logic. "The 'control of nature,'" Carson wrote, "is a phrase conceived in arrogance, born of the Neanderthal age of biology and philosophy, when it was supposed that nature exists for the convenience of man…. It is our alarming misfortune that so primitive a science has armed itself with the most modern and terrible weapons, and that in turning them against the insects it has also turned them against the earth."[42]

Carson's writing inspired a new, much more radical generation of environmentalists to see themselves as part of a fragile planetary ecosystem rather than as its engineers or mechanics, giving birth to the field of Ecological Economics. It was in this context that the underlying logic of extractivism – that there would always be more earth for us to consume – began to be forcefully challenged within the mainstream. The pinnacle of this debate came in 1972 when the Club of Rome published *The Limits to Growth*, a runaway best-seller that used early computer models to predict that if natural systems continued to be depleted at

their current rate, humanity would overshoot the planet's carrying capacity by the middle of the twenty-first century. Saving a few beautiful mountain ranges wouldn't be enough to get us out of this fix; the logic of growth itself needed to be confronted.

As author Christian Parenti observed recently of the book's lasting influence, "*Limits* combined the glamour of Big Science – powerful MIT computers and support from the Smithsonian Institution – with a focus on the interconnectedness of things, which fit perfectly with the new countercultural zeitgeist." And though some of the book's projections have not held up over time – the authors underestimated, for instance, the capacity of profit incentives and innovative technologies to unlock new reserves of finite resources – *Limits* was right about the most important limit of all. On "the limits of natural 'sinks,' or the Earth's ability to absorb pollution," Parenti writes, "the catastrophically bleak vision of *Limits* is playing out as totally correct. We may find new inputs – more oil or chromium – or invent substitutes, but we have not produced or discovered more natural sinks. The Earth's capacity to absorb the filthy byproducts of global capitalism's voracious metabolism is maxing out. That warning has always been the most powerful part of *The Limits to Growth*."[43]

And yet in the most powerful parts of the environmental movement, in the key decades during which we have been confronting the climate threat, these voices of warning have gone unheeded. The movement did not reckon with limits of growth in an economic system built on maximizing profits, it instead tried to prove that saving the planet could be a great new business opportunity.

The reasons for this political timidity have plenty to do with the themes already discussed: the power and allure of free market logic that usurped so much intellectual life in the late 1980s and 1990s, including large parts of the conservation movement. But this persistent unwillingness to follow science to its conclusions also speaks to the power of the cultural narrative that tells us that humans are ultimately in control of the earth, and not the other way around. This is the same narrative that assures us that, however bad things get, we are going to be saved at the last minute – whether by the market, by philanthropic billionaires, or by technological wizards – or best of all, by all three at the same time. And while we wait, we keep digging in deeper.

Only when we dispense with these various forms of magical thinking will we be ready to leave extractivism behind and build the societies we need within the boundaries we have – a world with no sacrifice zones, no new Naurus.

## Study Questions

1. What is the story of Nauru? How does Nauru serve as a cautionary tale for us all?

2. Klein argues that we have not harnessed nature with our extractivist methods of fossil fuels, thought to free us from natural constraints, but rather are experiencing dire consequences of climate change. Trace the history she provides to illustrate this phenomenon.

3. Klein considers the belief that we will be saved at the last minute – "by the market, by philanthropic billionaires, or by technological wizards" – to be "magical thinking." Briefly explain why she asserts that this magical thinking will not save us, and take a position on whether you agree.

## Notes

1 Steve Stockman, Twitter post, March 21, 2013, 2:33 p.m. ET, https://twitter.com.
2 Ben Dangl, "Miners Just Took 43 Police Officers Hostage in Bolivia," *Vice*, April 3, 2014.
3 Rodrigo Castro et al., "Human-Nature Interaction in World Modeling with Modelica," prepared for the Proceedings of the 10th International Modelica Conference, March 10–12, 2014, http://www.ep.liu.se.
4 Personal interview with Nerida-Ann Steshia Hubert, March 30, 2012.
5 Hermann Joseph Hiery, *The Neglected War: The German South Pacific and the Influence of World War I* (Honolulu: U of Hawai'i P, 1995), 116–25, 241; "Nauru," New Zealand Ministry of Foreign Affairs and Trade, updated December 9, 2013, http://wwww.mfat.govt.nz; "Nauru" (video), NFSA Australia, NFSA Films.
6 Charles J. Hanley, "Tiny Pacific Isle's Citizens Rich, Fat and Happy – Thanks to the Birds," Associated Press, March 31, 1985; Steshia Hubert interview, March 30, 2012.
7 "Country Profile and National Anthem," Permanent Mission of the Republic of Nauru to the United Nations, United Nations, http://www.un.int; Jack Hitt, "The Billion-Dollar Shack," *New York Times Magazine*, December 10, 2000.
8 Hiery, *The Neglected War*, 116–25, 241; "Nauru," New Zealand Ministry of Foreign Affairs and Trade.
9 Hitt, "The Billion-Dollar Shack"; David Kendall, "Doomed Island," *Alternatives Journal*, January 2009.

10 "Nauru" (video), NFSA Films.

11 Philip Shenon, "A Pacific Island Is Stripped of Everything," *New York Times*, December 10, 1995.

12 Hitt, "The Billion-Dollar Shack"; Robert Matau, "Road Deaths Force Nauru to Review Traffic Laws," *Islands Business*, July 10, 2013; "The Fattest Place on Earth" (video), *Nightline*, ABC, January 3, 2011; Steshia Hubert interview, March 30, 2012.

13 Hitt, "The Billion-Dollar Shack"; "Nauru," Country Profile, U.N. Data, http://data.un.org.

14 "Nauru," Overview, Rand McNally, http://education.randmcnally.com; Tony Thomas, "The Naughty Nation of Nauru," *The Quadrant*, January/February 2013; Andrew Kaierua et al., "Nauru," in *Climate Change in the Pacific, Scientific Assessment and New Research, Volume 2: Country Reports*, Australian Bureau of Meteorology and CSIRO, 2011, pp. 134, 140; "Fresh Water Supplies a Continual Challenge to the Region," Applied Geoscience and Technology Division, Secretariat of the Pacific Community, press release, January 18, 2011.

15 Glenn Albrecht, "The Age of Solastalgia," *The Conversation*, August 7, 2012.

16 Kendall, "Doomed Island."

17 "Nauru: Phosphate Roller Coaster; Elections with Tough Love Theme," August 13, 2007, via WikiLeaks, http://www.wikileaks.org.

18 Nick Bryant, "Will New Nauru Asylum Centre Deliver Pacific Solution?" BBC News, June 20, 2013; Rob Taylor, "Ruling Clouds Future of Australia Detention Center," *Wall Street Journal*, January 30, 2014; "Nauru Camp a Human Rights Catastrophe with No End in Sight," Amnesty International, press release, November 23, 2012; "What We Found on Nauru," Amnesty International, December 17, 2012; "Hundreds Continue 11-Day Nauru Hunger Strike," ABC News (Australia), November 12, 2012.

19 Bryant, "Will New Nauru Asylum Centre Deliver Pacific Solution?"; Oliver Laughland, "Nauru Immigration Detention Centre-Exclusive Pictures," *Guardian*, December 6, 2013; "Hundreds Continue 11-Day Nauru Hunger Strike," ABC News (Australia); "Police Attend Full-Scale Riot at Asylum Seeker Detention Centre on Nauru," ABC News (Australia), July 20, 2013.

20 "Nauru Camp a Human Rights Catastrophe with No End in Sight," Amnesty International, press release, November 23, 2012; "UNHCR Monitoring Visit to the Republic of Nauru, 7 to 9 October 2013," United Nations High Commissioner for Refugees, November 26, 2013; Mark Isaacs, *The Undesirables* (Richmond, Victoria: Hardie Grant Books, 2014), 99; Deborah Snow, "Asylum Seekers: Nothing to Lose, Desperation on Nauru," *Sydney Morning Herald*, March 15, 2014.

21 "The Middle of Nowhere," *This American Life*, December 5, 2003, http://www.thisamericanlife.org; Mitra Mobasherat and Ben Brumfield, "Riot on a Tiny Island Highlights Australia Shutting a Door on Asylum," CNN, July 20, 2013; Rosamond Dobson Rhone, "Nauru, the Richest Island in the South Seas," *National Geographic* 40 (1921): 571, 585.

22 Marcus Stephen, "On Nauru, a Sinking Feeling," *New York Times*, July 18, 2011.

23 Francis Bacon, *De Dignitate et Augmentis Scientiarum, Works*, ed. James Spedding, Robert Leslie Ellis, and Douglas Devon Heath, Vol. 4 (London: Longmans Green, 1870), 296.

24 William Derham, *Physico-Theology: or, A Demonstration of the Being and Attributes of God, from His Works of Creation* (London: Printed for Robinson and Roberts, 1768), 110.

25 Barbara Freese, *Coal: A Human History* (New York: Penguin, 2004), 44.

26 Emphasis in original. Many of the sources in this recounting were originally cited in Andreas Malm, "The Origins of Fossil Capital: From Water to Steam in the British Cotton Industry," *Historical Materialism* 21 (2013): 31.

27 J.R. McCulloch [unsigned], "Babbage on Machinery and Manufactures," *Edinburgh Review* 56 (January 1833): 313–32; François Arago, *Historical Eloge of James Watt*, trans. James Patrick Muirhead (London: J. Murray, 1839), 150.

28  C.H. Turner, *Proceedings of the Public Meeting Held at Freemasons' Hall, on the 18th June, 1824, for Erecting a Monument to the Late James Watt* (London: J. Murray, 1824), pp. 3–4, as cited in Andreas Malm, "Steam: Nineteenth-Century Mechanization and the Power of Capital," in *Ecology and Power: Struggles over Land and Material Resources in the Past, Present, and Future*, ed. Alf Hornborg, Brett Clark, and Kenneth Hermele (London: Routledge, 2013 ), 119.

29  M.A. Alderson, *An Essay on the Nature and Application of Steam: With an Historical Notice of the Rise and Progressive Improvement of the Steam-Engine* (London: Sherwood, Gilbert and Piper, 1834), 44.

30  Asa Briggs, *The Power of Steam: An Illustrated History of the World's Steam Age* (Chicago: U of Chicago P, 1982), 72.

31  Jackson J. Spielvogel, *Western Civilization: A Brief History, Volume II: Since 1500*, 8th ed. (Boston: Wadsworth, 2014), 445.

32  Herman E. Daly and Joshua Farley, *Ecological Economics: Principles and Applications* (Washington, DC: Island P, 2011), 10.

33  Rebecca Newberger Goldstein, "What's in a Name? Rivalries and the Birth of Modern Science," in *Seeing Further: The Story of Science, Discovery, and the Genius of the Royal Society*, ed. Bill Bryson (London: Royal Society, 2010), 120.

34  Ralph Waldo Emerson, *The Conduct of Life* (New York: Thomas Y. Crowell, 1903), 70.

35  Clive Hamilton, "The Ethical Foundations of Climate Engineering," in *Climate Change Geoengineering: Philosophical Perspectives, Legal Issues, and Governance Frameworks*, ed. Wil C.G. Burns and Andrew L. Strauss (New York: Cambridge UP, 2013), 58.

36  William T. Hornaday, *Wild Life Conservation in Theory and Practice* (New Haven: Yale UP, 1914), v–vi.

37  "Who Was John Muir?" Sierra Club, http://www.sierraclub.org; John Muir, *The Yosemite* (New York: Century, 1912), 261–62.

38  "In the morning I bathe my intellect in the stupendous and cosmogonal philosophy of the Bhagvat Geeta," wrote Thoreau in *Walden* of the famous Indian scripture. He continued, "I lay down the book and go to my well for water and lo! there I meet the servant of the Brahmin, priest of Brahma and Vishnu and Indra, who still sits in his temple on the Ganges reading the Vedas, or dwells at the root of a tree with his crust and water jug…. The pure Walden water is mingled with the sacred water of the Ganges."

39  Bradford Torrey, ed., *The Writings of Henry David Thoreau: Journal, September 16, 1851–April 30, 1852* (New York: Houghton Mifflin, 1906), 165; Aldo Leopold, *A Sand County Almanac* (Oxford: Oxford UP, 1949), 171; Henry David Thoreau, *Walden* (New York: Thomas Y. Crowell, 1910), 393–94.

40  Leopold, *A Sand Country Almanac*, 171; Jay N. Darling to Aldo Leopold, November 20, 1935, Aldo Leopold Archives, University of Wisconsin Digital Collections.

41  Rachel Carson, *Silent Spring* (New York: Houghton Mifflin, 1962), 57, 68, 297.

42  Ibid, 297.

43  Christian Parenti, "'The Limits to Growth': A Book That Launched a Movement," *The Nation*, December 5, 2012.

# 3.   Jeremy Baskin, "The Impossible Necessity of Climate Justice?"

JEREMY BASKIN, AN EXPERT on sustainable business, begins this 2009 article from the *Melbourne Journal of International Law* with the accepted scientific position that climate change is real. He moves from there to explore the issue of how we will achieve global climate justice given the range of impacts that climate change continues to have. Baskin identifies four factors regarding climate justice. The first two are positive: that climate justice requires significant reductions in greenhouse gases and their concentrations, and that it should take into account all involved, both historically and presently. The second two are negative: that neither inequality nor the potential for intergenerational conflict should be increased. Baskin acknowledges that the justice approach is considered naïve, that climate justice is the "elephant in the room," and that what is *right*, as in climate *justice*, must be a policy priority.

## I. Introduction

... BY "CLIMATE JUSTICE" I mean something both beyond and different from the notion of climate law. Climate law may not always be just; climate justice, on the other hand, involves looking at the extent to which our responses to climate change, whether by cutting emissions (mitigation) or by adapting to it, are fair and equitable. Although short on detail, the *United Nations Framework Convention on Climate Change*[1] recognizes that climate change should be tackled on the basis of equity and with "differentiated responsibilities." Similarly, the *Kyoto Protocol to the United Nations Framework Convention on Climate Change*[2] sets differential targets. The "climate justice" debate is, in part, an attempt to elaborate on what this entails. If there is a limited "budget" of carbon emissions which the atmosphere can tolerate, then how can this be allocated most equitably between nations and individuals? And if the costs of moving to a low-carbon economy are high, then who will bear them?

Approaches to climate justice vary. Some have called for "contraction and convergence" in which each country would end up with equal per capita emissions.[3] Others have framed the problem in the language of rights, calling for "greenhouse development rights."[4] This would entail greater cuts by the already industrialized countries, and allow for more limited cuts, and even growth in emissions in some instances, to give poorer countries and individuals the headroom to develop. Yet others have gone further in the direction of framing the issue as one of individual, rather than national, responsibility.[5] They argue that reductions should be required of the approximately one billion high emitters globally, regardless of where they live. I will examine these, and other proposals, shortly.

I start by unpacking the reasons why climate justice is important. I then argue that to assess whether a climate agreement or proposal is just, we need to pose four basic questions: does it lead to reductions in $CO_2$ concentrations?; does it involve an equitable sharing of the burden of change (both mitigating the problem and adapting to its inevitable and already visible consequences)?; does it increase inequality between nations and people?; and does it increase global conflict and insecurity? After outlining each of these components and why they are critical, I assess four broad proposals for dealing with climate change to see how they measure up against the requirements of climate justice.[6]

I conclude by suggesting that we find ourselves on the horns of a dilemma. On the one hand, we are unlikely to reach a climate agreement without a significant degree of justice. Equally, however, our experience suggests we cannot neglect the reality of global power and interests, nor the inertia or existing momentum of "business as usual." Being caught in this way, as a crisis looms, is a position familiar to international lawyers.

## II. Why Climate Justice?

Those arguing for the importance of "climate justice" rest their case on one or more of four, sometimes interrelated, arguments. The first argument addresses the disjuncture between *responsibility* for climate change and its *impact*. The fact is that industrialized countries have been overwhelmingly responsible for greenhouse gas emissions. This is true of current emissions and is even more marked in relation to historic emissions. And yet those likely to suffer the most as a result of climate change will not only be the poorest and most vulnerable, but also the least responsible for causing the problem. Whilst climate change will exact a price on most of humanity, it seems manifestly unjust that the "perpetrators" face a lesser penalty than the "victims."

The second argument is about *capacity;* that those most affected (the poorest people and poorest nations) lack the resources to make the necessary adaptations. They are likely to have the least resilience when faced with

food shortages, flooding and other extreme weather events, and the least capital to invest in protective infrastructure. The arguments about capacity, responsibility and impact are conceptually separate but are often combined in practice. For example, the Global Humanitarian Forum argues that:

> Those most vulnerable to climate change today are the world's poorest groups, since they lack the resources and means to cope with its impacts. It is also a clear injustice that these groups suffer the brunt of the impacts of climate change without any responsibility for having caused it.[7]

The third argument is about *development*. Poorer countries argue that their priority is development, and that this entails growing their economies and their capacity to meet the needs of their populations to enable them to emerge from poverty. "Our people have a right to economic and social development and to discard the ignominy of widespread poverty," argues Indian Prime Minister Manmohan Singh [2004–14], and "[f]or this we need rapid economic growth."[8] It is hard for rich countries to dispute this argument, as it is precisely the path that they have followed themselves. Almost by definition, such a trajectory involves a large increase in energy usage. In theory, this could be renewable energy but, to date, it has mainly involved the construction of coal-fired power stations, currently the cheapest available option.

The fourth argument is *pragmatic*. Greenhouse gas emissions are a transnational and trans-boundary problem. There is also insufficient atmospheric "space" to allow developing countries to emit anything like the carbon dioxide emitted by industrialized nations. Therefore, tackling climate change requires some form of global agreement and action. Such an agreement is unlikely to be reached unless it is perceived as "just" by all the major players. The *Greenhouse Development Rights Framework* links the "development" and "pragmatic" arguments: "The North cannot stabilize the climate without the full commitment of the South, and the South cannot make that commitment if doing so would even threaten to undermine its development."[9]

These arguments focus only on the North-South aspects of the climate justice debate. They do not address the added complexity of the intergenerational aspect, which will not be examined here.[10] All these arguments suggest why climate justice is important. What flows from this is a consideration of questions we need to ask of any global climate change agreement to see if it addresses the issue.

The *UNFCCC* recognizes the problem of climate justice but it is vague on the details of how it might be addressed. Article 3(1) states that "parties should protect the climate system ... on the basis of equity and in accordance with their common but differentiated responsibilities and respective capabilities." For this reason, it established at the outset a category of rich countries with obligations to reduce their emissions, without imposing obligations on the remainder of poor and medium-income countries.

Similarly, art 3(4) of the *UNFCCC* states that "parties have a right to, and should, promote sustainable development." However, we now know that "dangerous climate change" (to use the common expression) would *not* be avoided even if Annex I countries reduced their emissions to zero and other countries only took limited action. We also know that, in practice, the substantial economic growth that has occurred in the last two decades has rarely been ecologically sustainable. Something has to give. If we continue to increase the concentrations of greenhouse gases in the atmosphere, at a certain point we will face the prospect of "runaway" climate

change. This will undoubtedly be brutal, even fatal, for much of humanity. In such a scenario, justice, by any measure, will be hard to find.

## III. Climate Change Science

The science is clear.[11] Simply put, the increase in greenhouse gas emissions since the pre-industrial period has resulted in higher greenhouse gas concentrations in the atmosphere. This has already triggered a number of climatic changes, and there is a significant risk that, if emissions are not cut dramatically and rapidly, we may reach key "tipping points" and experience "runaway" climate change. This means a significant rise in average temperatures, above the current global average of around 15°C. Rising average temperatures are, in turn, associated with rising sea levels, more frequent extreme weather events, declining crop production and biodiversity, and many other serious effects which have been widely documented and reported.

Current atmospheric concentrations of $CO_2$ are around 388 parts per million ("ppm"), and above 460 ppm of $CO_2$ equivalent ("$CO_2$-e") if other greenhouse gases, such as methane, are included. Concentrations are rising at around 2 ppm annually, mainly as a result of the burning of fossil fuels. Greenhouse gases have the added problem that they remain in the atmosphere for long periods after they have been emitted. Worryingly, there are signs that the rate of increase in concentrations is rising as the ability of key "sinks," such as the oceans and forests, to re-absorb $CO_2$ declines.

The Intergovernmental Panel on Climate Change ("IPCC"), the "official" international authority on the science of climate change, estimated in 2007 that if concentrations could be stabilized at 450 ppm, we stand a 50 per cent chance of limiting temperature increases to 2°C.[12] These are not attractive odds, and even a 2°C change will come with many negative effects (such as the destruction of the Great Barrier Reef). More recent science, popularized by www.350.org, suggests that the IPCC's predictions may be too cautious and that 350 ppm – that is, below current concentrations – is required.[13] Neither goal is achievable under "business as usual" models.

Some policy analysts express the global solution in terms of a carbon budget. To have a balanced budget by 2050 implies that opting for limited cuts now will require sharper – and more expensive – cuts later. One such study, conducted by researchers from the University of Oxford and the Potsdam Institute for Climate Impact Research, argues that humanity should not emit more than one trillion tonnes of carbon into the atmosphere if we want a 50 per cent chance of limiting temperature increases to 2°C, or 750 billion tonnes for a 75 per cent chance. Over 500 billion tonnes have already been emitted. On current trends another 500 billion tonnes will be released in the next 40 years. To put these projections into perspective, burning only a quarter of existing oil, gas and coal reserves will result in us crossing the trillion tonnes threshold.[14]

According to the science, therefore, we can only avoid irreversible climate change if humanity can dramatically and rapidly reduce global greenhouse gas concentrations by upwards of 70–80 per cent, and by significantly more in industrialized countries.

### IV. Four Elements of Climate Justice

In this Part, I offer four considerations that are key to assessing the justice of any global climate action or successor agreements to the existing *UNFCCC*. I will examine each in turn.

The first consideration, effectively a threshold requirement, is that any agreement must result in a *substantial reduction in greenhouse gas emissions* and a stabilization of concentrations at a "safe" level. Concentrations of around 350 ppm are what the best current science seems to suggest is necessary for a decent chance of stabilization. It is impossible to overemphasize the magnitude of this change and its implications for our energy and production systems, our current carbon dependence, and our consumption patterns. Regardless of how it is done or who does it, without effectively addressing the core biophysical problem, at a certain point, we face the prospect of "runaway" climate change with severe consequences for much of humanity. In such circumstances, the question of climate justice will be moot. To put the matter starkly: climate action which cuts emissions dramatically, but is in all other respects unfair, will be a more just outcome than an ineffective agreement or no agreement at all.

The second consideration, and the most difficult to define, is that of substantive *fairness*. Procedural fairness in reaching an agreement may be relevant, but arguably the critical consideration is the substantive issue of whether the burden of change is effectively shared.[15] This must take into account both the capacity to shoulder the financial burden of adaptation, and the responsibility for both current and historical emissions. Poorer countries and individuals have relatively fewer resources at their disposal to invest in the technology and infrastructure needed to switch to renewable and low-carbon energy sources, or to invest in physical infrastructure to limit the effects of natural disasters such as storm surges and flooding, or to forgo, for example, cutting down forests to use the wood as fuel or the land cleared to grow crops. The *UNFCCC* recognizes this reality and assumes industrialized countries will need to provide financing and technology to developing countries to enable them to decarbonize their economies.

To date very little support and assistance has occurred and the main instrument developed, the Clean Development Mechanism ("CDM"), is widely regarded as being open to manipulation and ineffective at reducing greenhouse gas emissions significantly.

Historical responsibility is also relevant. Greenhouse gases remain in the atmosphere for a long time. High atmospheric concentrations are a function of past emissions, particularly those associated with the industrial revolution. The poorest 70 per cent of the world's population is estimated to be responsible for only 15 per cent of cumulative emissions.[16] In the 20th century, according to data analyzed by the World Resources Institute, the United States, Europe and the former Soviet Union were together responsible for around 70 per cent of all $CO_2$ emissions.[17]

Even ignoring historical responsibility, the responsibility for current emissions is highly differentiated. $CO_2$-e emissions in Australia in 2005 were around 27 tonnes per capita, comparable to the 23.5 tonnes recorded for the US, and greatly ahead of the 1.7 tonnes per capita of India.[18] China, which now has similar aggregate emissions to the US, still had estimated emissions of 5.5 tonnes per capita in 2005.[19] This is not only about a developed and developing country divide. If, for example, Australia cut its emissions by 60 per cent, it would still have per capita emissions higher than Sweden and similar to those of Japan today.

Complicating the issue of responsibility further still are a number of considerations. How far back into the past should responsibility stretch? Since the industrial revolution in the mid-19th century? Since the connection between greenhouse gas emissions and climate change became clear in the 1970s? Or since the UNFCCC was adopted in the early 1990s?

Even within poor countries, individual responsibility for emissions is highly differentiated. One report, *Hiding behind the Poor*, noted that whilst India's average emissions were below two tonnes per capita, the poorest people within the country emitted much less, whereas a large number of wealthy and middle-class families had consumption and emission patterns similar to those in developed countries.[20] Socolow makes a similar point when speaking of a study he co-authored with Chakravarty and others: "Rich people in poor countries," he is quoted as saying, "shouldn't be able to hide behind the poor people in those countries."[21]

A case can also be made that territorially-based emissions – the basis of the UNFCCC and current climate negotiations – do not take into account the role of trade or the "end user" of the emissions. The most striking example of this relates to China's emissions, much of which are associated with the manufacturing of products for consumption elsewhere. For example, are the emissions associated with the production of an iPod bought in Chicago really Chinese emissions? Indeed, it can be argued that the generally improving emissions efficiency of many developed countries, as opposed to their absolute emissions, are associated with the export of "dirty" industries to newly industrializing countries.

The current UNFCCC and *Kyoto Protocol* regime divides the world into Annex I (mainly rich) countries with obligations to reduce emissions, and non-Annex I (the rest) countries without reduction targets. This is an inadequate approach both because, absent significant voluntary targets by non-Annex I countries, it cannot lead to a sufficient level of emission reductions, and because it fails to differentiate between non-Annex I countries.[22]

In short, whilst there are some complexities associated with interpretation, in any conception of climate justice some account needs to be taken of both current and historical responsibility for emissions. And on both pragmatic and ethical grounds, some account must be taken of capacity. The reality is that fairness implies different obligations for different countries; the "common but differentiated" approach in the *UNFCCC's* formulation.

India, for example, has indicated that it rejects emissions targets but will commit to not exceeding the per capita emissions of the developed countries.[23] This is a rhetorically strong stance which emphasizes the inequity of the situation. But, it is of limited utility in practice as it avoids specifying what a meaningful per capita cap could be, or acknowledging how low it would need to be. The strongest candidates for the "fair" label are the "contract and converge" ("C&C") model (with rich and poor countries on different trajectories but converging on equal per capita emissions), and the "greenhouse development rights framework" (which calculates the share of the burden of global mitigation and adaptation which every country should bear based on an assessment of its responsibility and capacity). We will turn to these shortly.

The third consideration in taking into account the justice of any climate proposal is whether it increases the extent of material *inequality between nations and people*. Climate change will affect the existing patterns of economic power within and between nations, although the exact impacts are difficult to predict. In part, this is because the magnitude of economic change implied by a move to a low-carbon economy is hard to overstate. It calls into question the dominant assumption of endless growth. It challenges the "take-make-break" model of industrial production and forces us to think about sustainable consumption and production. This, in turn, has implications for existing patterns of trade and production. It compels us to think about how the inherent short-termism of markets can accommodate longer-term considerations and

constrain the externalizing impulses of profit-maximizing entities. It creates economic turbulence with "winners" and "losers" as some sectors decline and others emerge. Some countries, like Norway, may even benefit in the medium-term from some warming.

The Australian emissions trading system as initially proposed by Professor Ross Gamaut addressed the inequality issue in a domestic context, by proposing various cushioning subsidies for low-income families.[24] Climate policy cannot be expected to solve the problem of global inequality. However, any climate proposal which is likely to increase material inequality does not meet the climate justice test.

A fourth and final consideration relates to *global conflict and international stability*. Significant climate change raises major security concerns. These will be associated with potential conflict over scarce resources such as water and food, the possibility of extensive movement of people through migration or as climate refugees, or the emergence of border disputes (such as where glaciers define boundaries or over access to the ice-free Arctic). In the absence of a meaningful agreement to tackle climate change, we can expect the risk of conflict to rise dramatically. Not surprisingly, the security agencies of a number of countries are putting efforts into understanding this.[25]

Of course, one must be cautious about linking climate and security. As one study by the German Advisory Council on Global Change noted, such linkages can

> serve to legitimate new areas of military deployment.... In the context of North-South discourse ... [it can suggest] that the underdeveloped South poses a physical threat to the prosperous North, in that population explosion, migration and resource scarcity necessarily lead to

disputes over distribution and conflicts of interest that can be solved only by military means.[26]

And yet, as even that study noted, it seems undeniable that an issue as fundamental as climate change has implications for conflict and stability, as much as water access has resulted in conflicts between states. In such cases, the weaker parties are most likely to lose out. For this reason, I argue that any climate proposal which increases global insecurity and enhances the potential for conflict between states is unlikely to meet the climate justice test.

In summary then, there are four considerations which, taken together, can be considered essential to any proposal to tackle climate change that seeks to achieve some measure of climate justice. Two are positive: that it *should* involve dramatic reductions in greenhouse gas concentrations; and that it *should* be fair in that it takes into account both the varied current and historical responsibilities and the differing existing capacities of all involved. Two are negative: that it *should not* increase inequality; and that it *should not* increase the potential for interstate conflict....

## VI. Conclusion

I have not given space to considering a number of important issues relevant to climate justice. Can we ignore the mechanisms proposed to address climate change – whether market-based regulation (such as emissions trading) or more traditional mandate-type regulation? Should we be neutral about the mechanisms and focus on the ends? Or are there lessons from the dramatic failure of financial markets which are relevant to climate justice? Similarly, in relation to technology, does climate justice require environmentalists to rethink attitudes to nuclear power, "clean coal" and similar high-tech proposals? All

these questions are worth further exploration in relation to climate justice.

When considering climate change, it is easy to comply with the first part of Gramsci's famous dictum – "Pessimism of the intellect, optimism of the will." Finding the optimism is more difficult. Because it looks at climate justice, this think piece, perhaps inevitably, has focused on the costs and burdens of change. There are, of course, also significant opportunities for entrepreneurs with capital and the vision to imagine a low-footprint economy. And there is the attraction of imagining a much better world, one in which we have a more harmonious relationship with nature. In reality, the future is not as neatly predictable as the typology presented here may imply.

It is hard to imagine a unilateral solution to climate change which does not involve extensive re-engineering. And if we want an agreement then we will need to engage more deeply with climate justice than we have to date. Climate justice is the elephant in the room. A just solution is obviously the first prize in that it tackles climate change seriously and lays a basis for a more equitable global order able to operate within the limits of the biosphere. This in turn has a range of implications for existing power relations and patterns of consumption, production and trade.

A solution that significantly reduces greenhouse gas concentrations but which is unjust, is still, at the end of the day, a solution of sorts. At least it postpones our dash to the edge of the environmental cliff. No climate solution at all is a grim prospect.

It is generally regarded as naive, when considering international relations, to focus on justice, or to emphasize right over might. In this case – perhaps uniquely – even the powerful need a genuinely global solution, and agreement cannot be achieved without an engagement with justice. We have to hope that the pattern of millennia can be broken.

In this instance, might *needs* right. Climate justice is necessary and we can only hope it is possible. It needs to be higher up the policy agenda than it is currently.

## Study Questions

1. What is Baskin's definition of climate justice? What is the evidence he provides that illustrates the unjust distribution of the harms from greenhouse gasses (both historically and currently)?

2. Baskin gives evidence of the per capita differences in rich and poor countries; that is, the wealthy consume similarly regardless of where they are. Regarding cutting emissions – should it be per capita, or divided based on "developed" and "developing" countries? Why?

3. "Concentrations of around 350 ppm are what the best current science seems to suggest is necessary for a decent chance of" stabilization. This will require *drastic* change in our carbon consumption, change that has not even begun. Without such change, we risk "runaway climate change" that will bring severe consequences for most humans (and ecosystems and species). Because of this, Baskin states that even if there were unjust emission-cutting action, it would be better than no action at all. Grapple with this and provide a position from which you are faced with a scenario of unjust emission cutting. Who do you imagine will be the most harmed by such a scenario, given Baskin's data?

4. Baskin provides sound, ethical factors for ending climate injustice. Yet we are still globally consuming fossil fuels as if the elephant were not in the room, and we are witnessing the early signs of climate change. While we phased out CFCs and saw the resultant decrease in ozone depletion, we have yet to seriously address climate change. Draw from Guy Claxton's article later in this section (V.6, in which he argues that consumption is like addiction) to provide insight into this situation, and take a position on what you think will likely need to occur for global consumption of fossil fuels to drop to safe levels?

## Notes

1 Opened for signature 4 June 1992, 1771 UNTS 107 (entered into force 21 March 1994) ("*UNFCCC*").
2 Opened for signature 16 March 1998, 2303 UNTS 148 (entered into force 16 February 2005) ("*Kyoto Protocol*").
3 See Global Commons Institute, *Contraction and Convergence: A Global Solution to a Global Problem* (1996), available from http://www.gci.org.uk.
4 See Paul Baer et al., *The Greenhouse Development Rights Framework: The Right to Development in a Climate Constrained World* (Heinrich Boll Foundation Report, November 2008) http://gdrights.org/wp-content/uploads/2009/0I/thegdrsframework.pdf.

5  See Shoibal Chakravarty et al., "Sharing Global Co2 Emission Reductions among One Billion High Emitters" (2009) 106 *Proceedings of the National Academy of Sciences of the United States of America* II 884.

6  I will not focus on specific proposals for dealing with climate change as these are continually being developed and adapted, especially ahead of the Copenhagen Conference [in December 2009]. Rather, the emphasis here will be on broad-brush proposed "lines of march."

7  See Global Humanitarian Forum, *What Is Climate Justice?* (2009) http://www.ghfgeneva. org/ OurWork!RaisingAwareness/CiimateJustice/tabid/181/Default.aspx. The Forum goes on to say that "99% of the casualties due to climate change occur in developing countries, but 50 of the world's least developed nations account for less than 1% of greenhouse gas emissions that are the main cause of climate change." In a similar vein, in J. Timmons Roberts and Bradley Parks, *A Climate of Injustice: Global Inequality, North-South Politics, and Climate Policy* (2007) 7, the authors have referred to the "triple inequality" when describing the unequal vulnerability, unequal responsibility, and unequal mitigation and adaptation costs.

8  Prime Minister Singh goes on to say: "But I also believe that ecologically sustainable development need not be in contradiction to achieving our growth objectives": see Ministry of External Affairs, India, *The Road to Copenhagen: India's Position on Climate Change Issues* (Public Diplomacy Division, Ministry of External Affairs Report, 27 February 2009) 13 http://pmindia.nic.in/Ciimate%20Change_16.03.09.pdf.

9  Baer et al., above [note 4], 41.

10  The intergenerational argument is an important one and a key component of any sustainability worldview. It is not examined here for the sake of simplicity. It is philosophically extremely complex, hard to operationalize and, for our purposes, unlikely to be pragmatically important in working towards a global agreement. It does, however, lead to a view which favors deeper emissions cuts, as this reduces the risk of "runaway" climate change.

11  I simplify here. The science is clear regarding the fact of climate change occurring (including temperature and sea level rises); the link to greenhouse gas concentrations; and that these are largely linked to human activity (anthropogenic). The science is not fully clear on the exact nature of the linkages between different aspects of the climate system and on the resilience of the system as a whole. As a nonlinear system, it is difficult to predict exactly when key "tipping points" will occur. Empirical evidence, such as in relation to the melting of the Arctic, suggests that current modelling frequently underestimates the problem and that "tipping points" may be occurring sooner and at lower greenhouse gas concentrations than previously expected: see Stefan Rahmstorf et al., "Recent Climate Observations Compared to Projections" (2007) 316 *Science* 709.

12  Gerald Meehl et al., "Global Climate Projections: Supplementary Materials," in Working Group I, IPCC, *Climate Change 2007: The Physical Science Basis* (IPCC Fourth Assessment Report, 2007) 8, available from http://www.ipcc.ch.

13  James Hansen et al., "Target Atmospheric Co2: Where Should Humanity Aim?" (2008) 2 *Open Atmospheric Science Journal* 217, 229.

14  See Myles Allen and Malte Meinshausen, "The Trillion-Tonne 'Carbon Budget' We Can't Exceed" (2009) 202 *New Scientist* 4.

15  Shifting to a low-carbon economy is not only a matter of costs. There are also enormous opportunities for those developing substitute technologies and processes. Arguably the opportunities are less relevant to the justice debate, although access to new technologies linked to adaptation is, of course, critical.

16  Baer et al., above [note 4], 16.

17  See the world map showing the $CO_2$ emissions of countries and regions over the course of the 20th century: World Resources Institute, *Contributions to Global Warming: 1900–1999*, http://www.wri.org/map/contributions-to-global-warming.

18 These figures were derived from a database on the World Resources Institute website: World Resources Institute, *Total GHG Emissions in 2005* (2008), available from http://cait.wri.org/cait.php.

19 Ibid.

20 Guruswamy Ananthapadmanabhan, Krishnaswamy Srinivas and Vinuta Gopal, *Hiding behind the Poor* (Greenpeace India Report, October 2007) http://www.greenpeace.org/ raw/content/ india/press/reports/hiding-behind-the-poor.pdf.

21 Robert Socolow, Co-Director, Carbon Mitigation Initiative, cited in Douglas Fischer, "Solving the Climate Dilemma One Billion Emitters at a Time: Proposal Aims to Slice through Rich-Poor Divide on Global Emissions Targets," *The Daily Climate* (US) 6 July 2009, available from http://www.dailyclimate.org.

22 For example, both South Korea and Burkina Faso, who have vastly different emissions, fall into this category.

23 Ministry of External Affairs, India, above [note 20], 3.

24 See Ross Garnaut, *Garnaut Climate Change Review: Final Report* (2008) ch. 16.

25 Most of this information is not in the public domain. However, see the censored version of the report by the National Intelligence Council, US, *Global Trends to 2025* (US National Intelligence Council Report, November 2008) http://www.dni.gov/nic/PDF_2025/2025_Global_Trends_Final_Report.pdf. See also Ministry of Defence, UK, *DCDC Global Strategic Defence Programme: 2007–2036* (Development, Concepts and Doctrine Centre Report, 3rd ed., January 2007), available from http://www.dcdc-strategictrends.org.uk.

26 Renate Schubert et al., *Climate Change as a Security Risk* (German Advisory Council on Global Change Report, May 2007) 29–30.

# 4. Nancy M. Williams, "Affected Ignorance and Animal Suffering: Why Our Failure to Debate Factory Farming Puts Us at Moral Risk"

IN THIS 2008 ARTICLE from the *Journal of Agricultural and Environmental Ethics*, Nancy M. Williams argues that our choosing not to explore whether the details of a practice in which we participate are immoral (such as by consumption in the case of factory farming) places us at "moral risk." What allows people to remain "in the dark" about their moral risk is "affected ignorance." Williams outlines four types of affected ignorance and argues that this is what leads to the suffering of factory-farmed animals. She argues for epistemic conscientiousness, an intellectual virtue whereby one seeks truth and also seeks to avoid errors.

## I. Introduction

AFFECTED IGNORANCE, THE PHE-NOMENON of people choosing not to investigate whether some practice in which they participate might be immoral or rife with controversy, has received considerable attention recently from the philosophical community.[1] For the most part, the debate examines the conditions as to when it is reasonable to ascribe blame or moral exemption to average moral agents who fail to investigate or know the immoral status of conventional practices, values, and beliefs.[2] Are slave owners in ancient Greece or Nazis in 1930s Germany, for instance, morally responsible if they fail to debate the moral status of their socially accepted but immoral behavior? Any response to this question is philosophically complex because it is not clear whether one's failure to investigate emanates from an inability or a choice. In the former case, the agent is not culpable because the internalization of customary norms renders the individual morally blind.[3] In the latter case, however, the agent is morally culpable because the failure originates from a refusal to consider the

reasons for critical moral reflection. Failing to develop a critically reflective consciousness can perpetuate institutional systems, practices, and discourses that are cruel and corrupt. Discussions about affected ignorance, therefore, involve not only individual moral agency and responsibility, but concrete matters of social (in)justice.

In this paper, I argue that affected ignorance can help explain the lack of widespread public debate about the moral status of intensive animal farming practices. I contend, further, that this case involves the general failure to live up to certain intellectual virtues. Therefore, I consider James Montmarquet's [1993] account of virtue epistemology in order to extend a positive account of what it means to act as a responsible moral agent in a meat-eating culture, and to provide a theoretical model for the kind of debate I envision should occur. In order to set aside other questions, it is important to be clear about the scope of the paper. The debate about affected ignorance, whether implicit or explicit, involves two distinct questions: (1) are average moral agents culpable if they fail to know that a conventional practice is wrong? and (2) are average moral agents culpable if they fail to investigate whether a conventional practice is wrong? The first inquiry considers whether the agent is morally responsible for failing to *know* the objective moral status of conventional practices. In this case, one is responsible in the sense that one's moral beliefs or actions are in fact wrong. The second question, however, concerns the human capacity and responsibility to detect when a moral investigation is warranted. In this paper, I address the second question as it relates to factory farming practices.

## 2. Affected Ignorance

Affected ignorance is culpable. It is culpable because one is choosing to ignore something that is morally important. While it generally involves the refusal to consider if a practice in which one participates is immoral, affected ignorance has a variety of (sometimes overlapping) forms.[4] One form of affected ignorance occurs when people refuse to acknowledge the connection between their actions and the consequent suffering of their victims. Many times this form involves people masking the reality of their activities by carefully calculated language. Torturers often use deceptively benign phrases or euphemisms to describe their methods; for instance, some torture techniques are described as "the telephone" or the "parrots' swing" (Amnesty International, 1973). Hiding behind these verbal disguises is blameworthy because it is an active refusal to admit how one's actions contribute to insurmountable and unnecessary suffering.

In other cases, affected ignorance may involve asking not to be informed of the nature of the practice in question. Imagine the military commander who orders soldiers to retrieve information from captured prisoners of war by "any means possible," yet, later claims to "know nothing" about the torture that took place. By ignoring the culture in which the soldiers carried out their orders and by creating an environment where prisoner abuse would be overlooked, the commander is in some sense culpable when soldiers violate certain human rights conventions. The commander is culpable because he or she had a compelling reason and (we assume) the means to carefully monitor and investigate the soldiers' actions but failed to do so.

A third variety of affected ignorance is typically manifested in the readiness of some people to simply not ask questions. Suppose a mother suspects that her husband is sexually exploiting one of their daughters. She becomes suspicious after noticing sudden changes in her daughter's behavior, including unusual shyness, withdrawal, loss of appetite, nightmares and failing in school. Even more telling, were the recent changes in her daughter's behavior toward her husband. She would often appear fearful or unusually quiet in his presence. Yet, despite these behavioral signs, the mother refuses to investigate the matter. She represses her suspicions and the glimpse of knowledge she does have and remains "in the dark" about the abuse occurring in her home.

Finally, a fourth form of affected ignorance, and a particularly common one at that, is the widespread tendency to uncritically accept the dictates of custom and ideological constructions. It usually involves a dogmatic adherence to conventional rationalizations and the unwillingness to accept the possibility that majority opinions and widespread practices can be mistaken or cruel. As a result, this form of cultural and moral arrogance becomes an effective (psychological) mechanism to render oneself morally blind to the reasons or the evidence that would otherwise compel one to investigate. Hoagland (1993) examines those cases where approved prejudices or stereotypes enable members of dominant groups to understand instances of (cultural) resistance from oppressed persons as "confirmation" or "evidence" of their inferior nature and status rather than as reasons to question those prevailing stereotypes. She cites, for instance, the ways in which Southern slave owners would often dismiss acts of resistance as confirmation of their inherent inferiority:

> Consider the fact that white history depicts Black slaves (though not white indentured servants) as lazy, docile, and clumsy on such grounds as that slaves frequently broke tools. Yet a rational woman [sic] under slavery, comprehending that her situation is less than human, that she functions as an extension of the will of her master, will not run to pick up tools. She acts instead to differentiate herself from the will of her master, she breaks tools, carries on subversive activities – sabotage. Her master, in turn, perceiving her as subhuman and subrational, names her clumsy, childlike, foolish, perhaps, but not a saboteur. (1993: 92)

Within the confines of institutionalized slavery, no behavior, no set of actions, and no complaints count as reasons to question widely accepted notions about the inferiority of black slaves. Even if the slave was not breaking tools, but remained docile and obedient, this would also be used as "evidence" of their inferiority. Stereotypes such as these not only distort the reality of the situation, but they also maintain the conceptual framework in which slave owners can see themselves and their actions as legitimate and morally exempt. The point is blind adherence to conventional rationalizations about the legitimacy of a socially approved practice or industry can render reckless domination and systematic abuse as uncontroversial.

While it is possible that affected ignorance can take on more forms than the ones discussed here, in all its manifestations it is morally culpable because it involves a refusal to investigate rather than an inability to activate one's rational capacity to critically reflect. Affected ignorance points to those cases where people willingly turn away from something that is morally important and this seems to be the case when it comes to our collective silence regarding the ways in which pigs, cows, chickens, and many other animals suffer on factory farms so we can consume them.

## 3. Factory Farming

Many people want to believe that farm animals live a life full of the natural pleasures of animal existence without the hardships and constant struggle of living in the wild. Cows are left to graze on lush green fields while pigs live on quaint family farms. These comforting images, however, are far from reality. The vast majority of farm animals are reared on factory farms, also known as confined animal feeding operations (CAFOs) or intensive livestock operations (ILOs), and not the peaceful, idyllic family farms most people think of. Raising animals for mass food consumption has become a competitive business, managed and owned primarily by large corporations, which rely on animal confinement and assembly-line methods of production to maximize profit. Factory farming practices result in some of the lowest prices in the world for meat, eggs, and dairy products, but at a huge cost to the animals (as well as to the environment and human health). Yet, there is no vast public outcry about intensive rearing methods; most people find nothing controversial about the industry or the common practice that supports it: meat eating.[5] Dad's savory barbeque ribs and mom's juicy Thanksgiving turkey tend not to arouse acrimonious debates about the routine practices of chopping off piglets' tails

335

or how thousands of turkeys are packed into dark sheds with just over one square meter of space per bird.

Billions of animals are born, confined, biologically manipulated, transported, and ultimately slaughtered each year so that humans can consume them. The poultry industry, which includes chickens, ducks, geese, guinea fowl, pheasants, pigeons, quail, and turkeys, slaughters the majority of these animals. In egg "factories," for instance, hens are forced to live in battery cages stacked tier upon tier in huge warehouses. Confined seven to eight to a cage, they do not have enough room to turn around or spread their wings (Appleby et al., 2004). To prevent stress-induced behaviors caused by such extreme confinement, such as cannibalism, hens are typically kept in semi-darkness (witnessing natural sunlight only when transported to slaughter) and the ends of their sensitive beaks are cut off with hot blades without any anesthesia (Bauston, 1996). Undercover investigations into the broiler chicken industry have repeatedly revealed that birds were suffering from dehydration, respiratory diseases, bacterial infections, heart attacks, crippled legs, and other serious injuries (Weeks and Butterworth, 2004). Indeed, due to selective breeding for rapid growth, with scant attention given to leg and bone strength, 90% of broiler chickens have trouble walking (Kestin et al., 1992).

To maximize the use of space and minimize the need for maintenance, factory farms are notorious for encasing sows weighing between 180 and 230 kilos in iron crates that are just over 2m long and 56 cm wide (Weaver and Morris, 2004). Dysentery, cholera, trichinosis, and other diseases are common. Despite the Humane Slaughter Act that was passed by the United States Congress in 1958 and intended to ensure painless slaughter methods, a PETA (People for the Ethical Treatment of Animals) investigation found that workers at

an Oklahoma farm were killing pigs by slamming their heads against the floor and beating them with a hammer (Kaufman, 2001). Most beef cattle will spend their lives on huge feedlots, comprising hundreds of acres and housing more than one hundred thousand animals. At slaughter-houses, where the average kill rate is 400 animals per hour, the assembly line is not necessarily stopped even if the animal remains alive after being "stunned" (Eisnitz, 1997). In the end, it is fair to say that factory farming causes more harm to animals than does any other human institution or practice.

Given the realities of factory farming methods, and how they inflict acute pain onto billions of animals every year, what can explain the lack of extensive public debate regarding the moral status of these practices? While moral apathy and intellectual laziness can certainly play a role, so too does the preservation of self-interest. We can easily imagine the informed proponent of factory farming who adopts the classic point of view that human interest in animal products outweighs any animal interest at stake. The availability of inexpensive meat trumps animal pain and suffering and in this way, our informed proponent sees no reason to debate the issue. Financial profit (or greed), the convenience and ease of conforming to status quo values and practices as well as the resonant fear that one might be participating in an immoral practice can also generate the unwillingness to investigate. Akratic (or weak-willed) persons who continue to consume meat, dairy, and eggs, even though they believe factory farming methods are immoral, also do not debate the issue.[6] This paper, however, presents another possible explanation: many do not want to acknowledge the details of factory farming, and, in turn, they render themselves ignorant about the moral issues associated with this conventional practice. It addresses the critic who claims that the general failure to scrutinize these practices emerges from "genuine" ignorance or "honest" prejudice. To be sure, factory farming facilities (including large-scale feedlots, hog farms, chicken houses, and abattoirs) are far from public view, tucked away on remote country roads and, ultimately, sequestered from populated areas. Factory farmers are deeply indoctrinated in an agribusiness sub-culture. Therefore, on my critic's view, it is arduous and perhaps impossible for some individuals to even consider that there might be a moral issue at stake. These individuals have no reason (accessible to them) to investigate, and when this is the case, they are not culpable for their ignorance.

This argument, which removes moral responsibility from those who do not investigate, fails to consider that even in a meat-eating society it is not impossible for average moral agents to discern the reasons for debate. The meat industry is a powerful force in our culture and it prefers to sustain ignorance as the cultural norm when it comes to their practices; however, that is not to say that form of ignorance is inevitable. A careful examination reveals the possibility that some people are choosing to ignore important relevant information in this case. In particular, my critic overlooks the cultural opportunities for individuals to question whether modern farming methods infringe on established moral precepts concerning the wrongness of animal cruelty.

## 4. Animal Suffering and Affected Ignorance

Most of us have never visited a feedlot or hog farm, but that is not to say the general public has no inkling whatsoever that farmed animals may not be raised with their best interests in mind. Affected ignorance in this case arises from the deep-down suspicion that the animals we consume on a regular basis may have been mistreated somewhere along the way.

Driving behind a tractor trailer that is hauling hundreds of chickens in cramped wire-mesh cages or the all too common invasive stench from chicken houses ought to raise suspicions that food animals are not treated like many of our beloved pets. Celebrities and widely known animal-rights organizations such as PETA bring some degree of public awareness to factory farming issues. Outbreaks of related diseases such as Bovine Spongiform Encephalopathy (BSE), commonly known as Mad Cow disease, and Foot and Mouth disease send disturbing images of piles of animal corpses to living rooms around the country. National news reports about the threat of avian bird flu sometimes show farmers stuffing live birds in large plastic bags. Messages in major film releases like Babe and Chicken Run and the popular 2004 Internet spoof "The Meatrix," where explicit references are made to factory farming, ought to provoke one's moral sensibilities about the realities of meat production. Another opportunity for public dialogue lies in the increasing popularity of vegetarian/vegan diets. While vegetarians constitute a minority in most societies most people are aware to the extent that some find eating meat (or more precisely, animals) objectionable.[7] These fairly common experiences and societal tensions should propel one's imagination and moral curiosity into the realities of meat production; yet, ironically, it is these sorts of experiences that precipitate affected ignorance. For example, I am always struck by the way people admittedly avoid knowing the details of how their meat is produced. Most say, in effect, "If you know, please don't tell me. I don't want to hear the details because it would be too upsetting and would ruin my appetite." Knowledge about factory farming systems and animal suffering is knowledge most people do not want to have. We do not want to see or hear about what transpires on most hog or chicken farms, for we have a suspicion that this kind of information will be wrenching and interfere with human pleasure and privilege. Asking questions, we fear, might reveal an uncomfortable moral truth with respect to our role in perpetrating animal suffering; therefore, we choose not to ask questions and to remain uninformed about possible moral complexities. In his efforts to explain the parallels between public indifference in Nazi Germany concerning the treatment of Jews and our collective silence regarding the treatment of farm animals, Timothy M. Costelloe, in "The Invisibility of Evil: Moral Progress and the 'Animal Holocaust,'" writes,

> Like the camps on the edge of sleepy
> German towns whose presence was inte-
> grated into the rounds of daily routine,
> the realities of mass meat production are
> rendered invisible by a person's capacity to
> engage in an act of willful self-deception.
> Like ignoring the sudden disappearance
> of a neighbor, it is easy and convenient to
> cut into a pork chop when one "does not
> know" what is happening. (2003: 123)

There is a special sense of what it means "to know" in this case. Most people will claim that they do not know what is going on in factory farms and while this may be accurate to some extent, it is important to point out that this "lack of knowledge" is probably inspired by what they might guess is going on, although they do not know for sure. So in one sense people know but in another they do not know, could not afford to know, for their own moral sake. This is the essence of affected ignorance: it is a kind of ignorance generated by what one already knows. Whether it is a faint suspicion or a suggestive hint, affected ignorance entails this delicate form of knowledge, that which propels individuals to refrain from further moral inquiry.

Epistemological and moral tensions such as these, however, can be the impetus for social critique: a "place" where one can slip through normative structures and develop a reflective consciousness about those norms. When inner conflicts arise, individuals have opportunities to stand, if only for a moment, "outside" conventional attitudes and practices. My account takes its inspiration from Maria Lugones's work on individuals acquiring a liberatory sense of self despite the fact that their subjectivity remains fully immersed in an oppressive culture (Lugones, 1990). According to Lugones, every culture presents certain conditions for individuals to experience "an interstice from where one can most clearly stand critically toward different structures" (1990: 505). This cultural "place" allows the agent to slip through normative structures where she is able to forge a more critical understanding of "axiomatic" conventions. The inconsistency between the widespread declaration against practices that are cruel to animals and the simultaneous acceptance of factory farming represents the interstice Lugones speaks of. If responsible moral agents are obligated to do their best to form responsible beliefs, and avoid doxastic inconsistency when possible, then it is reasonable to expect them to examine why practices that are not morally permissible when they involve our pets are permissible when they involve other relevantly similar animals like cows, hogs, and chickens. Given the cultural opportunities for critical moral reflection, I believe the lack of extensive debate is the result of some people choosing not to be fully informed about modern factory farming practices (and subsequent animal suffering). To reinforce my point, let us consider the other forms of affected ignorance.

Recall the refusal to accept the connection between one's actions and the suffering of victims. By disavowing the relationship between meat eating and animal suffering, individuals can render themselves ignorant of their role in perpetuating practices that inevitably cause insurmountable suffering for billions of animals. Like the Nazis' egregious use of euphemisms, our language makes it all too convenient to find nothing controversial about meat eating. In agribusiness terms, farm animals are disguised as being-less "objects" by innocuous phrases such as "livestock," "protein harvester," "converting machines," "crops," and "biomachines." Trade reports on agricultural production do not mention animals, only pounds of meat and their market value, and it is fairly common for slaughterhouse workers to reference animals which they will slaughter by their inanimate names: chickens are "broilers," hens are "layers," and bulls are "beef." When animals are made into objects, "things" to be bought, transferred, sold, and then "processed," the connection between meat production and animal suffering dissolves. As consumers, we too rely on deceptive language to disassociate the once living, breathing animal from the "meat" on one's plate. Adams (2004) explains that in order for meat to exist, animals in name and body are made absent *as animals*:

> Animals are made absent through language that renames dead bodies before consumers participate in eating them … [W]hen we eat animals we change the way we talk about them, for instance, we no longer talk about baby animals but about veal or lamb … [T]he word *meat* has an absent referent, the dead animal. The absent referent permits us to forget the animal as an independent entity; it also enables us to resist efforts to make animals present. (2004: 51)

When the animal is made absent, so too is the possibility that one's actions may be linked to industrialized animal cruelty. In other words, verbal disguises shield us not only from the fact that it is dead (mostly baby) animals we are eating, but they also obscure the moral and epistemic obligation to know how our actions may contribute, in some way, to another's suffering.

Finally, the tendency to be satisfied with the legitimacy of whatever majority opinion dictates, despite conflicting evidence, is also evident in this case. In her provocative book, *The Dreaded Comparison* (1996), Speigel demonstrates how workers in an egg "factory" avoid the possibility that their socially approved actions are morally problematic:

> Question: Do you think about the chickens much?

> Answer: Usually I don't … the chickens here … know where their next meal is coming from, and they don't have to worry about predators …

> Q: It seems like a lot of their natural tendencies are inhibited though, in terms of expression, a pecking order, being able to mate …

> A: Well, no, they don't mate. They do, oh … they stretch; and they're happy. We see them, when we're walking through the place removing the dead … and they stretch. The pecking order: I think they have it in their individual cages.

> Q: Well, not being able to walk, or turn around, or scratch …

> A: Well on the other hand, if we were to put them out on the floor, it would take a lot more labor to gather the eggs. And eggs would cost a great deal more. What's the alternative, do we quit eating eggs?

Q: Why do you de-beak them?

A: The chickens will, in their pecking order, pick on the weakest chicken ... once they draw blood, then they just keep on going. They're quite cannibalistic.

Q: But when they are in a barnyard that usually doesn't happen.

A: No, but then the one who's being picked on can get away. (1996: 76–77)

Note the attempt to brush over the appalling conditions by unmitigated thoughtlessness, appeal to rationalizations, and false dichotomies. The worker refuses to see the animal's pain, anguish, and despair; instead, the cramped battery cage provides her with a "better" place. Because there is an unwillingness to see these animals as anything other than "egg-producers" or "layers," the worker sees no reason for critical moral reflection. In Schonfeld's and Alaux's provocative documentary, *The Animals' Film* (1981), a farmer, who keeps calves tethered for their entire lives so their flesh has the distinctive veal taste, also fails to acknowledge the cruelty of his socially approved actions:

> Some feel that it's rather cruel to the animals to keep them tied in there, but I point out that they're in a controlled environment they, uh, the weather is, they never get real hot, or in the winter time it's never zero weather, there's no fly problem. And as a result, really, they've got a pretty good life in there ... although they are chained.

This defense is yet another attempt to ignore the reality of oppressive situations. No confinement, no immobilization will count as evidence that one's socially accepted actions may be cruel. They do not count because the farmer does not want them to count. They do not count in an anthropocentric, profit-driven industry. To my critic who suggests that factory farmers are not in denial, as I claim, but rather a state of "honest" ignorance, I say this: the physical evidence of suffering in these cases is so obvious that only a sheer act of profound self-deception is required to make it disappear. This self-deception conceals the harm one is doing to others and thus makes it possible to continue to harm. The unwillingness to notice the calf's suffering allows the farmer to see what he wants to see: the calf is "fortunate" to have such a "good" life and "caretaker."

So far, I have argued that the general failure to debate animal farming practices can be explained by affected ignorance. In particular, people are refusing to acknowledge the connection between factory farming practices and animal suffering. Asking not to be informed of the nature of meat production (and subsequent animal suffering) and the readiness to not ask questions about the matter, despite compelling reasons to do so, is apparent in this case. Finally, the tendency to remain uncritical of established practices concerning the "welfare" of farm animals is clearly present.

## 5. Intellectual Virtues

Another facet, which has not been made explicit in related works, is the way in which affected ignorance runs counter to our commitment to conduct ourselves as responsible knowers. We are not only holding individuals accountable for their actions (or inaction as the case may be concerning affected ignorance), but also for those beliefs that influence such actions. Montmarquet (1993) has developed a concept of epistemology that gives certain character traits an important and fundamental role. For Montmarquet, critical examination and doxastic consistency are insufficient conditions for moral exemption.[8] Proper moral reflection should be structured by cogent ethical standards or certain intellectual virtues. Rather than thinking of intellectual virtues as cognitive faculties such as vision, memory, and introspection, Montmarquet conceives of them as personality traits that a person who desires the truth would want to have. The central intellectual virtue, according to Montmarquet, is epistemic conscientiousness. An epistemically conscientious person is someone "who tries her [sic] best to arrive at truth and to avoid error" (1993: 21). However, this desire (or love) for truth is insufficient, for one's desire must be appropriately regulated to protect against the possibility of enthusiastic agents forming dogmatic or fanatical beliefs. The desire to know the truth and avoid error must be situated within certain regulative virtues. Montmarquet classifies these under three main categories, two of which are particularly relevant. First, the virtues of intellectual impartiality, which include "an openness to the ideas of others, the willingness to exchange ideas with and learn from them, the lack of jealousy and a personal bias directed at their ideas, and the level sense of one's own fallibility" (1993: 21). The second set of virtues includes those of intellectual courage, "the willingness to conceive and examine alternatives to popularly held beliefs, perseverance in the face of opposition from others (until one is convinced that one is mistaken), and the determination required to see such a project through to completion."[9] We must promote *responsible* moral reflection; that is, responsible moral agents do their best to form reasonable beliefs and they are worthy of praise only when they confront the reasons for debate with intellectual impartiality and courage.

The kind of public debate I envision is inspired primarily by Montmarquet's normative approach to epistemology. Adherence to these virtues may promote a reasonable and thoughtful public dialogue about factory farming. Impartiality calls for an honest appraisal about the possibility that one's conventional beliefs and actions might be mistaken. When we keep aware of historical prejudices such as racism and sexism we are better equipped, I believe, to resist the all too common tendency to blindly conform to conventional beliefs like speciesism. In other words, one's willingness to exchange ideas with and learn from, say, vegetarians is demonstrative of a responsible knower. It is an intellectual virtue that promises to militate against dogmatism and moral arrogance. The virtues of intellectual courage – the willingness to conceive and examine alternatives to popular beliefs – relates to the person who, deep-down, suspects that factory farming practices violate our basic understanding regarding the wrongness of animal cruelty, but is too fearful to confront those suspicions. A responsible agent in this sense would welcome the opportunity for critical reflection because the failure to investigate one's suspicions could put one at moral risk of perpetuating unjust cultural norms. Montmarquet's intellectual virtues can serve as a conceptual model from which a responsible public debate ought to take place. They extend a positive account of what it means to act as a responsible moral agent in the face of cultural influences. I do not deny that this sort of debate is already taking place in limited circles or subgroups of moral experts; my point is, given the cultural conditions aforementioned, the general public has the rational capacity and an epistemic obligation to actively join that discussion in an intellectually responsible way.

## Conclusion

I have sought to provide an explanation as to why supporters of the meat, egg, and dairy industry may be at moral risk. I argued that the lack of extensive public debate about factory farming, and its corollary, extreme animal suffering, is probably due, in part, to affected ignorance. Despite the influence of cultural membership, I believe one can resist the tendency to affect ignorance. Cultures are not deterministic. Long standing (dietary) traditions and the meat industry's far-reaching influence can and should be challenged, deconstructed if you will, when average moral agents bravely confront their epistemic responsibility. Furthermore, one's failure to know the precise details of factory farming methods is not enough to vitiate responsibility. Indeed, as I have shown, societal tensions

and the established moral principle about animal cruelty ought to compel people to exercise their capacity to engage in responsible moral reflection and to reflect more deeply about the moral dimensions of factory farming and our peculiar relationship with animals. We need to take seriously our role as virtuous knowers and to do our best to judge whether the institution of factory farming is discriminatory (i.e., relies on speciesist assumptions) and unnecessarily cruel. Intensive animal rearing systems deserve greater public scrutiny because so much is at stake, including our epistemic and moral integrity and the well-being of 46 billion farm animals every year.

## References

Adams, C. (2004). *The Sexual Politics of Meat*. New York: Continuum P.

Amnesty International (1973). *Report on Torture*. London: Duckworth.

Appleby, M.C., J.A. Mench, and B.O. Hughes (2004). *Poultry Behavior and Welfare*. Wallingford: CABI Publishing.

Bauston G. (1996). *Battered Birds, Crated Herds: How We Treat the Animals We Eat*. Farm Sanctuary.

Calhoun, C. (1989). "Responsibility and Reproach." *Ethics* 99 (2): 389–406.

Costelloe, T. (2003). "The Invisibility of Evil: Moral Progress and the 'Animal Holocaust'." *Philosophical Papers* 32 (2): 109–31.

Eisnitz, G. (1997). *Slaughterhouse: The Shocking Story of Greed, Neglect, and Inhumane Treatment inside the U.S. Meat Industry*. New York: Prometheus Books.

Fischer, J. and M. Ravizza (eds.) (1993). *Perspectives on Moral Responsibility*. Ithaca, NY: Cornell UP.

Hoagland, S. (1993). "Femininity, Resistance, and Sabotage," in M. Pearsall (ed.), *Women and Values: Readings in Recent Feminist Philosophy*. Belmont, CA: Wadsworth.

Ikuenobe, P. (2004). "Culture of Racism, Self-Respect, and Blameworthiness." *Public Affairs Quarterly* 18 (1): 27–55.

Kaufman, M. (2001). "Ex-Pig Farm Manager Charged With Cruelty." *The Washington Post*, 9 September.

Kestin, S.C., T.G. Knowles, A.E. Tinch, and N.G. Gregory (1992). "Prevalence of Leg Weakness in Broiler Chickens and Its Relationship with Genotype." *Veterinary Record* 131: 190–94.

Levy, N. (2003). "Cultural Membership and Moral Responsibility." *The Monist* 86 (2): 145–63.

Lugones, M. (1990). "Structure/Antistructure and Agency under Oppression." *The Journal of Philosophy* 87 (10): 502–15.

Montmarquet, J. (1993). *Epistemic Virtue and Doxastic Responsibility*. Lanham: Rowan & Littlefield.

Moody-Adams, M. (1994). "Culture, Responsibility, and Affected Ignorance." *Ethics* 104: 291–309.

Regan, T. (2004). *Empty Cages: Facing the Challenge of Animal Rights*. Maryland: Rowan & Littlefield.

Schonfeld, V. and M. Alaux (1981). *The Animals' Film*, People for the Ethical Treatment of Animals.

Singer, P. (2001). *Animal Liberation*. New York: Harper Perennial.

Singer, P. and J. Mason (2006). *The Ethics of What We Eat: Why Our Food Choices Matter.* USA: Rodale Books.

Slote, M. (1982). "Is Virtue Possible?" *Analysis* 42: 70–76.

Speigel, M. (1996). *The Dreaded Comparison: Human and Animal Slavery.* New York: Mirror Books.

Weaver, S.A. and M.C. Morris (2004). "Science, Pigs, and Politics: A New Zealand Perspective on the Banning of Sow Stalls." *Journal of Agricultural and Environmental Ethics* 17: 51–66.

Weeks, C.A. and A. Butterworth (2004). *Measuring and Auditing Broiler Welfare.* Wallingford: CABI Publishing.

## Study Questions

1. What is affected ignorance? What are the four variations that Williams outlines? Can you think of any empirical examples of things (aside from factory farming) that people remain willfully ignorant about? Do you think that there is a limit to the amount of information one must seek about what one consumes – that is, given our limited time, can we be expected to be informed about everything we consume? Why or why not?

2. Williams details many harms and forms of suffering entailed in factory farming. Choose five of those harms and forms of suffering that are most salient to you, and list them. If any of us did to our pets some of the things that are done to factory farmed animals, we would be arrested and likely heavily punished. Why do you think this legal inconsistency is allowed?

3. Drawing from Montmarquet, Williams argues that our desire to know the truth and avoid errors should be "situated within certain regulative virtues." What are those regulative virtues and how would they contribute to "thoughtful public dialogue about factory farming"? Williams trusts that the general public is capable of this dialogue. First, do you agree that these regulative virtues would create thoughtful public dialogue? And second, do you think that the general public is capable of this dialogue? Why or why not?

## Notes

1  Cf. Moody-Adams (1994); Levy (2003); Slote (1982); Calhoun (1989); and Ikuenobe (2004).

2  "Average moral agents" is defined as normal adult human beings who can be held morally accountable for the acts they perform or fail to perform. Because they have the rational ability and agency to deliberate about which moral principles to act on, they can rightly be blamed or praised, criticized or condemned.

3  A theory of moral responsibility ought to consider at least two standard excusing conditions: a moral agent must have a reason to investigate and/or have access to viable alternatives in order to be morally responsible. Without a compelling reason, we cannot expect the agent to act otherwise. Cf. Fischer and Ravizza (1993).

4  Moody-Adams (1994) evaluates these forms as well.

5  For contemporary and engaging philosophical arguments about the immorality of factory farming, confer Singer (2001), Regan (2004), and Singer and Mason (2006).

6 See Aristotle's discussion on moral incontinence, or how one can knowingly do wrong, in *Nicomachean Ethics*, Sect. 3 of Book VII.

7 In addition to animal welfare reasons, some people choose vegetarianism or veganism because of human health, religious/spiritual, and environmental concerns.

8 People can perpetuate socially approved prejudices in spite of their reflective abilities. Imagine the reflective Nazi who, by using morally bad principles to justify other bad principles, is able to forge a consistent but immoral belief system regarding the inferiority of non-Aryans.

9 The third category is intellectual sobriety; as Montmarquet explains, "these are the virtues of the sober-minded inquirer: as opposed to the 'enthusiast' who is disposed, out of sheer love of truth, discovery, and the excitement of new and unfamiliar ideas, to embrace what is not really warranted, even relative to the limits of his own evidence" (1993: 21). It is not clear to me that this category captures the kind of intellectual failure that is taking place with regards to factory farming.

# 5. Mae-Wan Ho, "Perils amid Promises of Genetically Modified Foods"

IN THIS EXCERPT FROM her book *Genetic Engineering: Dream or Nightmare* (1998), geneticist Mae-Wan Ho (1941–2016) details existing food crises and directly addresses the transgenic agriculture (commonly called "GMOs" or genetically modified organisms) claims of addressing hunger and improving nutrition. Ho carefully sets out the transgenic science claims and argues against them, citing harms to the ecosystem and human health risks. She instead supports indigenous agricultural biodiversity as the only guarantee of sustainable food security.

## The Food "Crisis"

BY THE YEAR 2000, the world will need to consume over 2 billion tonnes a year of wheat, rice, maize, barley, and other crops – an increase of 25% compared with 1995 figures.[1] This view was echoed by the World Bank Report for the 1996 World Food Summit in Rome,[2] which warned that the world would have to double food production over the next 30 years. One major solution on offer to "feed the world" is agricultural biotechnology. This, it has been proposed, could be used to genetically modify crops for herbicide, pest, and disease resistance, to improve nutritional value and shelf-life, and also, for the future, to bring about promises of drought and frost resistance, nitrogen fixation,[3] and increased yield.[4]

Agricultural biotechnology is big business, and the mission to feed the world has the irresistible ring of a noble obligation. The same goes for improving the nutritional value of foods. Despite prices having dropped to the lowest on record, more than 800 million people still go hungry, and 82 countries – half of them in Africa – neither grow enough food, nor can afford to import it. Infant mortality rates – a sensitive indicator of nutritional stress – have been experiencing an upturn in recent years, reversing a long-term historical trend. Large numbers of children suffer from malnutrition in developing countries. In India alone, 85% of children under five are below the normal, acceptable state of nutrition.[5]

In view of the current crisis in food production, and the support for agricultural biotechnology as a solution to the crisis – as expressed by the World Bank Report and by Chapter 16 of Agenda 21 of the United Nations Convention on Biological Diversity – it is all the more important to examine the major claims and promises of the technology, as well as the uncertainties and hazards which are not adequately taken into account in existing practices and regulations.

### Can Genetically Modified Foods Feed the World or Improve Nutrition?

The Poverty Trap of Unequal Power Relationships

Undernutrition and malnutrition, found everywhere in the developing as well as the developed world, stem from poverty, as was admitted in the World Bank Report.

In the Third World, poverty was created, in large measure, by centuries of colonial and post-colonial economic exploitation under the free-trade imperative, and has been exacerbated since the 1970s by the introduction of the intensive, high-input industrial agriculture of the Green revolution.[6] The concentration on growing crops for export has benefited the corporate plant breeders and the elite of the Third World at the expense of ordinary people. In 1973, thirty-six of the nations most seriously affected by hunger and malnutrition exported food to the US – a pattern that continues to the present day.[7]

The "liberalization of trade" under the current World Trade Organization agreement will make things much worse.[8] While Southern countries are obliged to remove subsidies to their farmers, subsidies to Northern producers have remained untouched. This unequal competition will deprive millions of peasants of their livelihood. In addition, as part of the same WTO agreement, the intellectual property rights of corporate gene manipulators in the North will be protected, and that will restrict the use of indigenous varieties that were previously freely cultivated and sold. Thus, seeds protected by patents will no longer be able to be saved by farmers for replanting without annual royalties being paid to the company which owns them.

Another factor already adversely affecting agricultural biodiversity in Europe is the Seed Trade Act which makes it illegal to grow and sell noncertified seeds, produced by organic farmers from indigenous varieties, certification being biased towards the commercial varieties currently being used in agricultural biotechnology.[9] Far from providing cheaper food for all, agricultural biotechnology will further undermine the livelihoods of small organic farmers all over the world, resulting in increased loss of indigenous agricultural biodiversity.

Discussions on food supply are invariably linked to population growth in the Third World. But these discussions leave out the unequal power relations which exist between different countries and different groups of people. "Food scarcity," like "overpopulation," are both socially generated. While populations in the North are suffering from obesity, cardiovascular diseases, and diabetes from overconsumption, populations in the South are dying of starvation. Simplistic "solutions" which leave out the unequal power relations are oppressive, and ultimately "reinforce the very structures creating ecological damage and hunger."[10]

## Biological Diversity, Food Security, and Nutrition

Biological diversity and food security are intimately linked. Communities everywhere have derived livelihoods from natural diversity in wild and domesticated forms. Diversity is the basis of ecological stability.[11] Recent studies show that diverse ecological communities are more resilient to drought and other environmental disturbances which cause the population of individual species to fluctuate widely from year to year.[12] Species within an ecological community are interconnected in an intricate web of mutualistic as well as competitive interactions, of checks and balances that contribute to the survival of the whole. This has important implications for *in situ* conservation, particularly at a time when it is being estimated that 50,000 species will go extinct every year over the next decade.[13]

The same principles of diversity and stability operate in traditional agriculture.[14] Throughout the tropics, traditional agroforestry systems commonly contain well over 100 annual and perennial plant species per field. A profusion of varieties and land races are cultivated which are adapted to different local environmental conditions and possess a range of natural resistances to diseases and pests. Spatial diversity through mixed cropping is augmented by temporal diversity in crop rotation, ensuring the recycling of nutrients that maintain soil fertility. These practices have effectively prevented major outbreaks of diseases and pests and buffered food production from environmental exigencies.

The diversity of agricultural produce is also the basis of a balanced nutrition. Nutrition not only depends on the right balance of protein, carbohydrates, and fats, but also on a combination of vitamins, essential metabolites, cofactors, inorganic ions, and trace metals, which only a varied diet can provide. A major cause of malnutrition worldwide is the substitution of the traditionally varied diet for one based on monoculture crops. The transfer of an exotic gene into a monoculture crop can do little to make up for the dietary deficiencies of those suffering from monoculture malnutrition. The nutritional value of beans, or a combination of rice and beans, will always be greater than that of the transgenic rice with a bean gene.

## Monoculture and Transgenic Threats

It is now indisputable that monoculture crops introduced since the Green revolution have adversely affected biodiversity and food security all over the world. According to a FAO report, by the year 2000 the world will have lost 95% of the genetic diversity utilized in agriculture at the beginning of this century.[15] Monoculture crops are genetically uniform and, therefore, notoriously prone to disease and pest outbreaks. The corn belt of the United States was last devastated by corn blight in 1970–1971, while, in 1975, Indonesian farmers lost half a million acres of rice to leaf hoppers. Genetic modification for disease or pest resistance will not solve the problems, as intensive agriculture itself creates the conditions for new pathogens to arise.[16] In 1977, a variety of rice, IR-36, created to be resistant to 8 major diseases and pests, including

bacterial blight and tungro, was nevertheless attacked by two new viruses called "ragged stunt" and "wilted stunt." Thus, not only do new varieties have to be substituted every three years, they require heavy input of pesticides to keep pests at bay.

The high inputs of fertilizers, water, pesticides, and heavy mechanization required by monoculture crops have had devastating environmental effects.[17] Teddy Goldsmith, who started the ecology movement in Britain in 1970, has been a long-time critic of global financial institutions such as the World Bank and the International Monetary Fund for the antiecological projects they finance in the Third World, such as the construction of big dams for irrigation and roads which hasten the clearing of forests. Between 1981 and 1991, the world's agricultural base fell by some 7 per cent, primarily due to environmental degradation and water shortages. One-third of the world's croplands suffers from soil erosion, which could reduce agricultural production by a quarter between 1975 and the year 2000. In India, 800,000 square kilometers are affected, with many areas turning into scrub or desert. Deforestation has resulted in 8.6 million hectares of degraded land in Indonesia, which is unable to sustain even subsistence agriculture. Throughout the tropics, vast areas are vulnerable to flooding. Of the world's irrigated land, one-fifth – 40 million hectares – suffers from waterlogging or salination. The resultant pressures on agricultural land led to the further marginalization of small farmers, swelling the ranks of the dispossessed and hungry, while indigenous natural and agricultural biodiversity are eliminated at accelerated rates.

Transgenic crops are created from the same high-input monoculture varieties of the Green revolution, and are likely to make things worse. The greatest proportion of transgenic crop plants is now engineered to be resistant to herbicide, with companies engineering

347

resistance to their own herbicide to increase sales of herbicides with seeds.[18] The immediate hazard from herbicide-resistant crops is the spread of transgenes to wild relatives by cross-hybridization, creating super-weeds. Herbicide-resistant transgenic oilseed rape, released in Europe, has now hybridized with several wild relatives.[19]

There are yet other problems. Herbicide-resistant transgenic crops make it possible to apply powerful herbicides, killing many species, directly onto crops. This is so for Monsanto's Roundup®, which is lethal to most herbaceous plants. The US Fish and Wildlife Service has identified 74 endangered plant species threatened by the use of herbicides like glyphosate.[20] This product reduces the nitrogen-fixing activity of soils and is toxic to many species of mycorrhizal fungi which are vital for nutrient recycling in the soil. Glyphosate-type compounds are the third most commonly-reported cause of pesticide illness among agricultural workers. The use of this highly-toxic nondiscriminating herbicide will lead to the large-scale elimination of indigenous species and cultivated varieties, damaging soil fertility and human health besides. Herbicide-resistant transgenic crops also become weeds in the form of "volunteer plants" germinated from seeds after the harvest, so that other herbicides then have to be applied in order to eliminate them, with yet further impact on indigenous biodiversity.

## Food Security Depends on Agricultural Biodiversity

In order to counteract the crisis of environmental destruction, loss of agricultural land and indigenous biodiversity created by decades of intensive farming, there has been a global move towards holistic, organic farming methods that revive traditional practices. Previous promoters of the Green revolution are now calling for a shift to sustainable agriculture. Sustainable agriculture is promoted in Chapter 14 of Agenda 21 of the United Nations Convention in Biodiversity, signed by more than 140 countries. Large-scale implementation of biodynamic farming and sustainable agriculture is succeeding in the Philippines.[21] In Latin America, a number of nongovernment organizations have joined forces to form the Latin American Consortium on Agroecology and Development, to promote agroecological techniques which are sensitive to the complexities of local farming methods. Programs introducing soil conservation practices and organic fertilization methods tripled or quadrupled yields within a year.[22] Successive studies have highlighted the productivity and sustainability of traditional peasant farming in the Third World[23] as well as in the North, according to a report published by the US National Academy of Sciences.[24]

Many, if not all, southern countries still possess the indigenous genetic resources – requiring no further genetic modification – that can guarantee a sustainable food supply.

"Over centuries of agricultural practice, traditional societies have developed an incredible variety of crops and livestock. Some 200–250 flowering plants species have been domesticated, and genetic diversity amongst each of these is astonishing: in India alone, for instance, farmers have grown over 50,000 varieties of rice Oryza sativa. In a single village in northeast India, 70 varieties are being grown ... farmers (especially women) repeatedly used and enhanced some varieties which were resistant to disease and drought and flood, some which tasted nice, some which were colored and useful for ritual purposes, and some which were highly productive."[25]

In Brazil, hundreds of rural communities in the northeast are responding to the current crisis in food production by organizing communal seed banks to recover traditional indigenous varieties and to promote sustainable agricultural development, with little or no government support.[26]

It is significant that the World Bank is reported to be planning sharp changes in policy to concentrate its efforts on small farmers in developing countries.[27] It seems obvious that, in order to guarantee long-term food security and feed the world, we can do no better than take the aim of the Convention on Biological Diversity to heart, i.e., help to conserve and sustain existing indigenous agricultural diversity worldwide, and to develop this diversity as the basis of a secure and nutritious food base for all.

Thus, there is no need for genetically modified crops. On the contrary, they will undermine food security and biodiversity. Under the combined efforts of monopoly of transnational genetic manipulators' intellectual property rights and "free trade" agreements of the World Trade Organization, the livelihoods of small farmers will be further compromised, both by seed royalties and the restrictive practices of seed certification, and unfair competition from subsidized Northern produce. At the same time, the use of toxic, wide-spectrum herbicides with herbicide-resistant transgenic crops will result in irretrievable losses of indigenous agricultural and natural biologic diversity.

There are, in addition, problems and hazards inherent to the practice of the technology itself, which make the regulation of the technology, by a legally binding international Biosafety Protocol under the Convention of Biodiversity, a matter of urgency.

## Agricultural Biotechnology Is Misguided by Wilful Ignorance of Genetics

In a publication which aims to "provide consumers with clear and comprehensible information about products of the new [bio]

technology," we are told that: "Research scientists can now precisely identify the individual gene that governs a desired trait, extract it, copy it, and insert the copy into another organism. That organism (and its offspring) will then have the desired trait."[28]

This reaffirms the genetic determinist idea that one gene controls one character trait, and that transferring the gene results in the transfer of the corresponding trait to the genetically modified organism, which can then pass it on indefinitely to future generations. It presents the process of genetic modification as a precise and simple operation.

The above account – so typical of that found in publications promoting "public understanding" – is based on a simplistic assumption of genetics that both classical geneticists and plant breeders have rejected for many years, and which has been thoroughly invalidated by all the research findings in the new genetics. Unfortunately, most molecular geneticists, apart from being absorbed into industry, also lack training in classical genetics, and suffer from a severe molecular myopia that prevents them from appreciating the implications and broader perspective of the findings in their own discipline. Damages from intensive agricultural practices have indeed come about because they are based on the old reductionist paradigm, as Vandana Shiva has argued so convincingly.[29] For the same reason, agricultural biotechnology will bring new problems and hazards....

## Dangers of Ignoring the Interconnected Genetic Network

Because no gene ever functions in isolation, there will almost always be unexpected and unintended side-effects from the gene or genes transferred into an organism.

One major concern over transgenic foods is their potential to be toxic or allergenic, which has become a concrete issue since a transgenic soybean containing a brazil-nut gene was found to be allergenic.[30] Recent studies suggest that allergenicity in plants is connected to proteins involved in defense against pests and diseases. Thus, transgenic plants engineered for resistance to diseases and pests may have a higher allergenic potential than unmodified plants.[31]

New proteins from bacteria, such as the Bt toxin currently engineered into many transgenic crops, cannot be tested for allergenicity because allergic reactions depend on prior exposures. *This means that post-market monitoring and clear segregation and labelling of transgenic products are essential for proper consumer protection.* Most identified allergens are water-soluble and acid-resistant. Some, such as those derived from soya, peanut, and milk, are very heat-stable, and are not degraded during cooking, whereas fruit-derived allergenic proteins are heat-labile.[32]

A transgenic yeast was engineered for increased rate of fermentation with multiple copies of one of its own genes, which resulted in the accumulation of the metabolite methylglyoxal at toxic, multigenic levels.[33] This case should serve as a warning against applying the "familiarity principle" or "substantial equivalence" in risk assessment. We simply do not have sufficient understanding of the principles of physiological regulation to enable us to categorize, *a priori*, those genetic modifications that pose a risk and those that do not.

\* \* \*

## Danger of Ignoring the Ecology of Genes and Organisms

### Single Genes Impact on the Ecosystem

The most immediate and easily observable impacts of transgenic plants on the ecological environment are due to cross-pollination between transgenic crop-plants and their wild relatives to generate super-weeds. Field trials have shown that cross-hybridization has occurred between herbicide-resistant transgenic *Brassica napa* and its wild relatives: *B. campestris*,[34] *Hirschfeldia incana*,[35] and *Raphanus raphanistrum*.[36] These impacts have been predicted by ecologists such as Rissler and Mellon,[37] and arise from the introduction of any exotic species, whether genetically engineered or not.

Impacts which are generally underestimated are those due to transgenic soil bacteria. As very few molecular geneticists have any training in soil ecology, they will be ignorant of the important role played by the soil microbes in recycling nutrients for the growth of crop plants. Soil microbiologists Elaine Ingham and her student tested a common soil bacterium, *Klebsiella planticola*, engineered to produce ethanol from crop waste, in jars containing different kinds of soil in which a wheat seedling had been planted.[38] The experiments showed that, in all soil types, the growth of the wheat seedling was drastically inhibited. This was due to the ethanol produced, which had adverse effects on different microbes that were involved in recycling nutrients for the wheat seedling. Elaine has talked about this in several TWN-sponsored seminars, to great effect. She and her colleagues now run a consultancy and research firm for organic farming in the US, which is a marvelous way to resist the agrochemical biotechnological encroachment.

### The Instability of Transgenic Lines

Traditional breeding methods involve crossing closely-related varieties or species containing different forms of the same genes. Selection is then practiced over many generations under field conditions, so that the desired characteristics and the genes influencing those characteristics, *in the appropriate environment*, are tested and harmonized for stable expression over a range of genetic backgrounds. Different genetic combinations, moreover, will perform differently in different environments. This genotype-environment interaction is well-known in traditional breeding, so it is not possible to predict how a new variety will perform in untested environments. In many cases, new varieties will lose their characters in later generations as genes become shuffled and recombined, or as they respond to environmental changes.

In the new genetic modification, completely exotic genes are often introduced into organisms. In the case of plants, the genes are often introduced into plant cells in tissue culture, and transgenic plants are regenerated from the cells after selection in culture. The procedures inherently generate increased genetic instability in the resulting transgenic line.

First, the tissue culture technique itself introduces new genetic variations at high frequencies. These are known as *somaclonal variations*.[39] That is because the cells are removed from the internal, physiological environment of the plant which stabilize their gene expression and genetic complement *in vivo*. It is part of the spectrum of ecological interactions between organism and environment that keep gene expression, genes, and genome structure stable in the organism as a whole. Unilever used tissue culture techniques to regenerate oil palms for planting in Malaysia several years ago. This practice has now been abandoned as many plants have aborted in the field or failed to flower.[40] The second reason for increased instability of transgenic lines is that the process of gene insertion is random and a lot of secondary genetic effects can result, as mentioned earlier. Third, the extra DNA integrated into the transgenic organism's genome disrupts the structure of its chromosome, and can itself cause chromosomal rearrangement,[41] further affecting gene function. Finally, all species have cellular mechanisms which tend to eliminate or inactivate foreign DNA.[42] Transgene instability, particularly "gene-silencing"[43] – the inability of the introduced gene to become expressed in subsequent generations – has been discovered only within the past few years, and is now a recognized problem in both farm animals and plants.[44] In transgenic tobacco, 64% to 92% of the first generation of transgenic plants become unstable. Similarly, the frequency of transgene loss in *Arabidopsis* ranges between 50% and 90%. Instability arises both during the production of germ cells and in cell division during plant growth. The commonest cause is gene silencing due to the chemical modification of the introduced DNA by methylation – a reaction adding a methyl group, $-CH_3$, to the base cytosine or adenosine. Other causes are due to DNA rearrangements and excision of the transgene. The long-term agronomic viability of transgenic crops has yet to be proven. Calgene's Flavr Savr tomato, engineered for improved shelf life, was a financial disaster (as was the transgenic strawberry).[45] Apart from side effects, such as a skin too soft for the tomato to be successfully shipped, it also failed to grow in Florida, as it was created in California. At least in that regard, commercialization had been premature. In 1996/97, Monsanto's transgenic Bt-cotton crop, engineered to be resistant to the cotton bollworm, failed to live up to its promise in the field in both the USA and Australia, partly on account of transgene inactivation.[46] Farmers should beware.

By contrast, the long-established indigenous local varieties and land races are the most stable, as genes and environment have mutually adapted to reinforce the stable expression of desirable characteristics for hundreds, if not thousands, of years. There is no quick fix to establishing ecological balance, which must be restored in order to guarantee our long-term food security.

\* \* \*

## Hazards from Horizontal Gene Transfer and Recombination

The most underestimated hazards of agricultural biotechnology are from horizontal gene transfers. There is now abundant evidence that gene transfer vectors mediate horizontal gene transfer and recombination, spreading antibiotic resistance and generating new pathogens. Antibiotic resistance arose as the result of the profligate use of antibiotics in intensive farming, which predates genetic engineering. However, current transgenic plants often contain antibiotic-resistant marker genes. When released into the environment, these genes will exacerbate the spread of antibiotic resistance.

\* \* \*

### Viral Resistance Transgenes Generate Live Viruses

A major class of transgenic plants are now engineered for resistance to viral diseases by incorporating the gene for the virus's coat protein. Some molecular geneticists have expressed concerns that transgenic crops engineered to be resistant to viral diseases with genes for viral coat proteins might generate new diseases by several known processes. The first, *transcapsidation*, has already been detected, and involves the DNA/RNA of one virus being wrapped up in the coat protein of another so that viral genes can get into cells which otherwise exclude them. The second possibility is that the transgenic coat protein can help defective viruses

multiply by *complementation*. The third possibility, *recombination*, has been demonstrated in an experiment in which *Nicotiana benthamiana* plants, expressing a segment of a cowpea chlorotic mottle virus (CCMV) gene, were inoculated with a mutant CCMV, missing that gene. The infectious virus was indeed regenerated by recombination.[47] There is now also evidence that transgenic plants increase the frequency of viral recombination, owing to the continual expression of the viral coat protein gene.[48] As plant cells are frequently infected with several viruses, recombination events will occur and new and virulent strains will be generated. Viral recombination is well documented in animals and the resulting recombinant viruses are strongly implicated in causing diseases. As in animals, plant genomes also contain many endogenous proviruses and related elements which can potentially recombine with the introduced transgene.

Another strategy for viral resistance made use of benign viral "satellite RNAs" as transgenes, thereby attenuating the symptoms of viral infection. However, these were found to mutate to pathogenic forms at high frequencies.[49] These already documented pathogenic recombinants and mutants, regenerated from viral resistant transgenic plants, are particularly significant, as viruses are readily transmitted from one plant to another by many species of aphids and other insects that attack the plants. There is a distinct possibility of new broad-range recombinant viruses arising, which could cause major epidemics.

A potentially major source of new viruses arising from recombination has been pointed out by molecular geneticist Joe Cummins.[50] This is the powerful promoter gene from cauliflower mosaic virus (CaMV), which is routinely used to drive gene expression in transgenic crop plants for herbicide or disease resistance. Like the viral coat protein gene, this viral gene can also recombine with other viruses to generate new broad-range viruses. The CaMV has sequence homologies to human retroviruses such as the AIDS virus, human leukaemic virus, and human hepatitis B virus, and the promoter gene can drive the synthesis of these viruses as well. There is thus a possibility for the CaMV promoter to recombine with human viruses when ingested in food (see below).

## Vectors Can Infect Mammalian Cells and Resist Breakdown in the Gut

Among the important factors to consider in the safety of transgenic organisms used as food are the extent to which DNA, particularly vector DNA, can resist breakdown in the gut, and the extent to which it can infect the cells of higher organisms.

Studies made since the 1970s have documented the ability of bacterial plasmids carrying a mammalian virus to infect cultured mammalian cells, which then proceed to synthesize the virus, even though no eukaryotic signals for reading the genes are contained in the plasmid. This is because endogenous provirus and other elements can provide helper-functions which are missing. Similarly, bacterial viruses or baculavirus can also be taken up by mammalian cells.[51] Baculovirus is so effectively taken up by mammalian cells that it is now being developed as a gene transfer vector in human gene replacement therapy. At the same time, baculovirus is genetically engineered to kill insects more effectively, with genes encoding diuretic hormone, juvenile hormone, Bt endotoxin, mite toxins, and scorpion toxin. The recombinant virus is sprayed directly onto crop plants.[52] Recently, a recombinant baculovirus has even been made containing an anti-sense gene from a human cancer gene, c-myc. So, what happens when humans eat foods containing vectors and viral sequences?

It has long been assumed that our gut is full of enzymes which rapidly digest DNA. In a study designed to test the survival of viral DNA in the gut, mice were fed DNA from a bacterial virus, and large fragments were found to survive passage through the gut and to enter the bloodstream.[53] This research group has now shown that ingested DNA end up, not only in the gut cells of the mice, but also in spleen and liver cells as well as white blood cells. "In some cases, as much as one cell in a thousand had viral DNA."[54]

A group of French geneticists found that certain pathogenic bacteria have acquired the ability to enter mammalian cells directly by inducing their own internalization. They found invasive strains of *Shigella felxneri* and *E. coli* that had undergone lysis upon entering the mammalian cells because of an impairment in cell wall synthesis. The researchers developed these strains as DNA transfer systems into mammalian cells. This transfer was described as "efficient, of broad host cell range, and the replicative or integrative vectors so delivered are stably inherited and expressed by the cell progeny."[55] The researchers are totally unable to recognize the tremendous risks to health involved in developing such a vector. These cross-kingdom transfer vectors are extremely hazardous, as are transgenic vaccines constructed in plants and plants viruses, which are chimeras of animal viral genes inserted into plant viruses. These will have an increased propensity to invade cells, recombine with endogenous viruses and proviruses or insert themselves into the cell's genome.

Within the gut, vectors carrying antibiotic resistance markers may also be taken up by the gut bacteria, which would then serve as a mobile reservoir of antibiotic resistance genes for pathogenic bacteria. Horizontal gene transfer between gut bacteria has already been demonstrated in mice and chickens and in human beings.

In view of all this evidence, it would seem unwise to ingest transgenic foods, as foreign DNA can resist digestion. It can be taken up by gut bacteria, as well as by gut cells, and through the gut, into the blood stream and other cells. DNA uptake into cells can lead to the regeneration of viruses. If the DNA integrates into the cell's genome, a range of harmful effects can result, including cancer. Moreover, one cannot assume, without adequate data, that DNA is automatically degraded in *processed* transgenic foods, such as the Zeneca's tomato paste currently on sale in UK supermarkets, as well as the many foods containing processed transgenic soybean or maize. The public is already being experimented on, *without informed consent*. This is surely against the European BioEthics Convention. Yet, almost nothing can be learned, since it is, at present, impossible to collect relevant data when neither labeling nor post-market monitoring is required.

## Checklist of Hazards from Agricultural Biotechnology

As a summary, I shall reiterate the arguments on why agricultural biotechnology is unsustainable and poses unique hazards to health and biodiversity.

### a. Socio-Economic Impacts

1. Increased drain of genetic resources from South to North.
2. Increased marginalization of small farmers due to intellectual property rights, and other restrictive practices associated with seed certification.
3. Substitution of traditional technologies and produce.
4. Inherent genetic instability of transgenic lines resulting in crop failures.

### b. Hazards to Human and Animal Health

1. Toxic or allergenic effects due to transgene products or products from interactions with host genes.
2. Increased use of toxic pesticides with pesticide-resistant transgenic crops, leading to pesticide-related illnesses in farm workers, and the contamination of food and drinking water.
3. Vector-mediated spread of antibiotic resistance marker genes to gut bacteria and to pathogens.
4. Vector-mediated spread of virulence among pathogens across species by horizontal gene transfer and recombination.
5. Potential for vector-mediated horizontal gene transfer and recombination to create new pathogenic bacteria and viruses.
6. Potential of vector-mediated infection of cells after ingestion of transgenic foods, to regenerate disease viruses, or for the vector to insert itself into the cell's genome causing harmful or lethal effects including cancer.

### c. Hazards to Agricultural and Natural Biodiversity

1. Spread of transgenes to related weed species, creating super-weeds (e.g., herbicide resistance).
2. Increased use of toxic, nondiscriminating herbicides with herbicide-resistant transgenic plants leading to large-scale elimination of indigenous agricultural and natural species.
3. Increased use of other herbicides to control herbicide-resistant "volunteers," thus further impacting on indigenous biodiversity.
4. Increased use of toxic herbicides destroying soil fertility and yield.
5. Bioinsecticidal transgenic plants accelerating the evolution of biopesticide resistance in major insect pests, resulting in the loss of a biopesticide used by organic farmers for years.
6. Increased exploitation of natural biopesticides in transgenic plants, leading to a corresponding range of resistant insects, depriving the ecosystem of its natural pest controls and the ability to rebalance itself to recover from perturbation.

7. Vector-mediated horizontal gene transfer to unrelated species via bacteria and viruses, with the potential of creating many other weed species.

8. Vector recombination to generate new virulent strains of viruses, especially in transgenic plants engineered for viral resistance with viral genes.

9. The vectors carrying the transgene, unlike chemical pollution, can be perpetuated and amplified given the right environmental conditions. It has the potential to unleash cross-species epidemics of infectious plant and animal diseases that will be impossible to control or recall.

## Conclusion

The World Bank Report for the 1996 Food Summit advocated sustained support for research to develop new plants and technologies, but it also called for "whole new ways" of addressing the problem of the current food crisis, one of which was to concentrate on helping small farmers.

I have presented the reasons why agricultural biotechnology *cannot* alleviate the existing food crisis. On the contrary, *it is inherently unsustainable and extremely hazardous to biodiversity, human, and animal health.* A drastic change of direction is indeed required, targeted to supporting conservation and sustainable development of indigenous agricultural biodiversity. This would both satisfy the stated aims of the Biodiversity Convention and guarantee long-term food security for all.

## References

Allison, R. (1995). "RNA Plant Virus Recombination." Proceedings of USDA-APHIS/AIBS Workshop on Transgenic Virus-Resistant Plants and New Plant Viruses. April 20–21, Beltsville, Maryland.

Altieri, M.A. (1991). "Traditional Farming in Latin America." *The Ecologist* 21: 93–96.

Colman, A. (1996). "Production of Proteins in the Milk of Transgenic Livestock: Problems, Solutions and Successes." *American J. of Clinical Nutrition* 63: 639S–645S.

Cooking, E.C. (1989). "Plant Cell and Tissue Culture," In *A Revolution in Biotechnology*, ed. J.L. Marx, pp. 119–29. Cambridge, New York: Cambridge UP.

Cox, C. (1995). "Glyphosate, Part 2: Human Exposure and Ecological Effects." *J. of Pesticide Reform* 15 (4).

Courvain, P., S. Goussard, and C. Grillot-Courvain. (1995). "Gene Transfer from Bacteria to Mammalian Cells." *Comptes rendus de l'Académie des Sciences, Série III-Science de la vie* 318: 1207–12.

Cummins, J. (1994). "The Use of Cauliflower Mosaic Virus. 35S Promoter (CaMV) in Calgene's Flav Savr Tomato Creates Hazard." Available from the author at jcummins@julian.uwo.ca.

———. (1997). "Insecticide Viruses for Insect Control." Available from the author at jcummins@julian.uwo.ca.

Damency (1994). "The Impact of Hybrids between Genetically Modified Crop Plants and Their Related Species: Introgression and Weediness." *Molecular Ecology* 3: 37–40.

DeAngelis, D.L. (1992). *Dynamics of Nutrient Cycling and Food Webs.* London: Chapman and Hall.

Doerfler, W. (1991). "Patters of DNA Methylation: Evolutionary Vestiges of Foreign DNA Inactivation as a Host Defense Mechanism." *Biol. Chem. Hoppe-Seyler* 372: 557–64.

Eber, G., A.M. Chevre, A. Baranger, P. Vallee, X. Tanfuy, and M. Renard (1994). "Spontaneous Hybridization between a Male-Sterile Oilseed Rape and Two Weeds." *Theor. App. Gene.* 88: 362–68.

Finnegan, H., and McElroy (1994). "Transgene Inactivation Plants Fight Back!," *Bio/Technology* 12: 883–88.

Frank, S., and B. Keller (1995). "Produktesicherheit von krankheitsresistenten Nutzpflanzen: Toxikologie, allergens Potential, Sekundäreffekte und Markergene Eidg." Forschungsantalt für landwirtschaftlichen Pflanzenbau, Zürich.

Goldsmith, E. (1992). "Development: Fictions and Facts." *Ecoscript* 35. Foundation for Ecodevelopment, Amsterdam.

Goldsmith, E., and N. Hildyard (1991). "World Agriculture: Toward 2000, FAO's Plan to Feed the World." *The Ecologist* 21: 81–92.

Green, A.E., and R.F. Allison (1994). "Recombination between Viral RNA and Transgenic Plant Transcripts." *Science* 263: 1423.

Hardy, R.W.F. (1994). "Current and Next Generation Agricultural Biotechnology Products and Processes Considered from a Public Good Perspective." *NABC Report 6* "Agricultural Biotechnology and the Public Good," ed. J.F. MacDonald, pp. 43–50.

Heitman, D., and J.M. Lopes-Pila (1993). "Frequency and Conditions of Spontaneous Plasmid Transfer from *E. coli* to Cultured Mammalian Cells." *BiosSystems* 29: 37–48.

Hildyard, N. (1996). "Too Many for What? The Social Generation of Food 'Scarcity' and 'Overpopulation'." *The Ecologist* 26: 282–89.

Ho, M.-W., and P. Tappeser (1997). "Potential Contributions of Horizontal Gene Transfer to the Transboundary Movement of Living Modified Organisms Resulting from Modern Biotechnology." *Proceedings of Workshop on Transboundary Movement of Living Modified Organisms Resulting from Modern Biotechnology: Issues and Opportunities for Policy-Makers*, ed. K.J. Milongoy, pp. 171–93. International Academy of the Environment, Geneva.

Holmes, T.M., and E.R. Inghan (1995). "The Effects of Genetically Engineered Microorganisms on Soil Foodwebs." In *Supplement to Bulletin of Ecological Society of America 75/2, Abstracts of the 79th Annual ESA Meeting: Science and Public Policy*, Knoxville, Tennessee, 2–7 August 1994.

Inose, T., and K. Murata (1995). "Enhanced Accumulation of Toxic Compounds in Yeast Cells Having High Glycolytic Activity: A Case Study on the Safety of Genetically Engineered Yeast." *International J. of Food Science and Technology* 30: 141–46.

Jorgensen, R.B., and B. Andersen (1994). "Spontaneous Hybridization between Oilseed Rape (*Brassica napus*) and Weedy *B. campestris* (Brassicaceae): A Risk of Growing Genetically Modified Oilseed Rape." *Amer. Jour. Botany* 12: 1620–26.

Kothari, A. (1994). "The Need for a Protocol on Farmers' Rights and Indigenous Peoples." *Our Planet* 6: 36–40.

Lee, H.S., S.W. Kim., K.W. Lee, T. Ericksson, and J.R. Liu (1995). "Agrobacterium-Mediated Transformation of Ginseng (*Panax-ginseng*) and Mitotic Stability of the Inserted Beta-Glucuronidase Gene in Regenerants from Isolated Protoplasts." *Plant Cell Reports* 14: 545–49.

Lemke, P.A., and S.L. Taylor (1994). "Allergic Reactions and Food Intolerances," in *Nutritional Toxicology*, ed. F.N. Kotsonis, M. Mackay, and J.J. Hjelle, pp. 117–37. New York: Raven P.

Meister, I., and S. Mayer (1994). *Genetically Engineered Plants: Releases and Impacts on Less Developed Countries, A Green Peace Inventory*. Greenpeace International.

Mikkelsen, T.R., B. Andersen, and R.B. Jorgensen (1996). "The Risk of CropTransgene Spread." *Nature* 380: 31.

Moffat, A.S. (1996). "Biodiversity Is a Boon to Ecosystems, Not Species." *Science* 271: 1497.

Nordlee, J.A., S.L. Taylor, J.A. Townsend, L.A. Thomas, and R.K. Bush (1996). "Identification of a Brazil-Nut Allergen in Transgenic Soybeans." *The New England J. of Medicine* (March 14): 688–728.

Paulkaitis, P., and M.J. Roossinck (1996). "Spontaneous Change of a Benign Satellite RNA of Cucumber Mosaic Virus to a Pathogenic Variant." *Nature Biotechnology* 14: 1264–68.

356

Perlas, N. (1995). "Dangerous Trends in Agricultural Biotechnology." *Third World Resurgence* 38: 15–16.

Pimm, S.L. (1991). *Balance of Nature: Ecological Issues in the Conservation of Species and Communities.* Chicago: The U of Chicago P.

Raven, P. (1994). "Why It Matters." *Our Planet* 6: 5–8.

Rissler, J., and M. Mellon (1993). *Perils amidst the Promise: Ecological Risks of Transgenic Crops in a Global Market.* USA: Union of Concerned Scientists.

Schubbert, R., C. Lettmann, and W. Doerfler (1994). "Ingested Foreign (Phage M13) DNA Survives Transiently in the Gastrointestinal Tract and Enters the Bloodstream of Mice." *Mol. Gen. Genet.* 242: 495–504.

Shiva, V. (1993). *Monoculture of the Mind.* Penang: Third World Network.

Wahl, G.M., B.R. de Saint Vincent, and M.L. DeRose (1984). "Effect of Chromosomal Position on Amplification of Transfected Genes in Animal Cells." *Nature* 307: 516–20.

Watkins, K. (1996). "Free Trade and Farm Fallacies." *The Ecologist* 26: 244–55.

## Study Questions

1. As Leopold noted in "The Land Ethic" (V.1), ecological stability is a critical component of land health, and a critical component of ecological stability is ecological diversity, or biodiversity. The majority of what are called GMOs are introduced to "prop up" the failing Green Revolution pesticides, and the Green Revolution drew heavily on not only pesticides but also artificial fertilizers and water resources. However, the Green Revolution's largest ecological harm was the introduction of large-scale monoculture agriculture and the resultant displacement of indigenous agricultural biodiversity. Ho argues that what is needed to feed hungry people is indigenous agricultural biodiversity, the very thing that GMOs displace via monoculture, and more so by risk of genetic pollution. Trace her argument, and provide an explanation of how the biodiversity she advocates is in keeping with Leopold's Land Ethic.

2. Due to factory farming's widespread use of antibiotics in livestock, antibiotic resistance has become a critical issue facing us today. Ho details how transgenic agriculture further contributes to antibiotic resistance. First, trace the process by which this occurs. Next, reflect upon the difference between the agriculture Ho advocates and transgenic agriculture. Given the further risk of antibiotic resistance, and the empirical evidence that transgenic food has neither increased nutrition nor significantly addressed existing hunger, provide an analysis of why it is undertaken.

3. Corporations that are highly invested in transgenic agricultural biotechnology have spent extraordinary amounts of money to prevent farmers from saving seeds (a time-honored method of addressing hunger), patent infringement, labeling initiatives, and independent research on transgenic seeds (see, for example, Monsanto's contract when Roundup-Ready seeds are purchased[56]). These same corporations also receive huge investments via the United States Department of Agriculture. In contrast, national seed banks, also paid for by taxes, used to give viable heirloom seeds away for free. Addressing the harms Ho lists from transgenic agricultural biotechnology, especially

permanent ecosystem pollution, and the empirical facts about exactly how transgenic agricultural corporations have conducted business (including not feeding the hungry or advancing nutrition), take a position on whether this technology should be allowed.

## Notes

1 See *Food for Our Future, Food and Biotechnology* (Food and Drink Federation, London, 1995).
2 Geoffrey Lean, "And still the children go hungry," *Independent on Sunday* 10 November, 1996, p. 12.
3 Hardy, 1994.
4 See A. Aslan, "Food-population: Experts want to break wheat's yield barrier," *Inter Press Service*, October 18, 1996.
5 Lester Brown of the World Watch Institute, quoted in Goldsmith and Hildyard, 1991.
6 Goldsmith, 1992.
7 N. Hildyard, An open letter to Edouard Saouma, Director-General of the Food and Agricultural Organization of the United Nations. *The Ecologist* 21 (1991): 43–46.
8 Watkins, 1996.
9 E. Beringer, "Seed Action in Germany," *Landmark* July/August, p. 13.
10 Hildyard, 1996, p. 282.
11 See DeAngelis, 1992; Pimm, 1991.
12 Moffat, 1996.
13 Raven, 1994.
14 Altieri, 1991.
15 C. Emerson, "Throwing Out the Baby with the Bathwater," *On the Ground*, September, p. 2.
16 Shiva, 1993.
17 See Goldsmith, 1992; Shiva, 1993.
18 Meister and Mayer, 1994.
19 Mikkelsen et al., 1996; see also Ho and Tappeser, 1997.
20 Cox, 1995.
21 Perlas, 1994.
22 See note 14 [Altieri, 1991].
23 Shiva, 1993, Introduction; see also note 2 [Lean].
24 *Alternative Agriculture, Report of the National Academy of Sciences*, Washington, DC, 1989.
25 Kothari, 1994.
26 "Seed action in Brazil," *Landmark* July/August 1996, p. 10.
27 See note 2 [Lean].
28 See Food and Drink Federation, *Food for Our Future; Food and Biotechnology*, London, 1995, p. 5.
29 Shiva, 1993.
30 Nordlee et al., 1996.
31 Frank and Keller, 1995.
32 Lemke and Taylor, 1994.
33 Inose and Murata, 1995.
34 See Jorgensen and Anderson, 1994; Mikkelsen et al., 1996.
35 See Eber et al., 1994; Darmency, 1994.
36 Eber et al., 1994.
37 Rissler and Mellon, 1993.
38 See Holmes and Ingham, 1995.
39 See Cooking, 1989.

40 Reported by Perlas, 1995.

41 Wahl et al., 1984.

42 See Doerfler, 1992.

43 Finnegan and McElroy, 1994.

44 See Colman, 1996; Lee et al., 1995, and references therein.

45 Vicki Brower, "Monsanto Swallows Calgene Whole," *Nature Biotechnology* 15, 213, 1997.

46 See "Pests Eat Monsanto's Profits," *GenEthics News* 13, p. 1, 1996; also "Bt cotton fiascos in the US and Australia," *Biotechnology Working Group: Briefing Paper Number 2*, BSWG, Montreal, Canada, May 1997.

47 Green and Allison, 1994.

48 Allison, 1995.

49 Paulkaitis and Rossinck, 1996.

50 Cummins, 1994.

51 Heitman and Lopes-Pila, 1993.

52 Cummins, 1997. I thank the author for sending this article to me.

53 Schubbert et al., 1994.

54 Cited in Phillip Cohen, "Can DNA in Food Find Its Way into Cells?," *New Scientist* 4 (January 1997), p. 14.

55 Courvain et al., 1995, p. 1207.

56 Center for Food Safety, *Monsanto vs. U.S. Farmers*, 2004, http://www.centerforfoodsafety.org/files/cfsmonsantovsfarmerreport11305.pdf.

# 6. Guy Claxton, "Involuntary Simplicity: Changing Dysfunctional Habits of Consumption"

IN THIS 1994 ARTICLE from the journal *Environmental Values*, cognitive scientist Guy Claxton (b. 1947) likens our material consumption to drug addiction, and thus likens consumers to addicts whose identity is all too often wrapped up in their material preferences. Claxton illuminates that in order to move away from addiction, one must go from first "wanting not to want" to "not wanting." It is not enough to provide facts, use willpower, and engage rational arguments to get there. He also discounts external means of intervention such as physical coercion, which includes rationing, reward and punishment, and something that resembles drug rehabilitation. What he advocates is "mindfulness," a Buddhist practice that requires presence, reflection, and awareness so that one can engage at the psychological level necessary for internal change.

---

When our ruling passion is no longer survival it becomes comfort. To someone whose passion *is* survival our preoccupation with comfort is ignoble and trivial; there is no way it can be justified. It can't even be understood.

— Nicholas Freeling, *A City Solitary*

IN NON-ABUNDANT SOCIETIES, WHERE the prerogative of survival leaves little room for choice, people's patterns of consumption are predominantly dictated by the nature of their circumstances. When there is little to eat, how one acts is largely determined by agricultural or ecological forces beyond individual control. But in the affluent countries of the North, what people consume, what they waste, what long and short-term considerations are or are not taken into account in making consumption decisions – these betray the powerful influence of the cultural and individual assumptions and beliefs that are resident in people's minds. And if dysfunctional habits of consumption are driven by psychological factors, then a satisfactory solution is not going to be found in either technological innovation or in ecopolitical reorganization, but in the liberation of individuals, in their millions, from the sway of an unconsciously self-destructive worldview.

This obvious starting-point for any discussion about ways of averting further ecological catastrophes is summed up by Laszlo (1989):

There are hardly any world problems that cannot be traced to human agency and which could not be overcome by appropriate changes in human behavior. The root cause even of physical and ecological problems are the inner constraints on our vision and values…. Living on the threshold of a new age, we squabble among ourselves to acquire or retain the privileges of bygone times. We cast about for innovative ways to satisfy obsolete values. We manage individual crises while heading towards collective catastrophes. We contemplate changing almost anything on this earth except ourselves…. A new insight must dawn on people: you do not solve world problems by applying technological fixes within the framework of narrowly self-centered values and short-sighted national institutions. Coping with mankind's current predicament calls for inner changes, for a human and human-istic revolution mobilizing new values and aspirations, backed by new levels of personal commitment and political will. (pp. 46–47)

## Voluntary Simplicity

Those who have seen that this individual pro-cess of *reprioritization* is the nub of the problem have tended to take two routes. One involves making explicit the tacit dysfunctional beliefs that have driven heedless overconsumption and waste (as Laszlo does), in the hope that "making the unconscious conscious" (in Freud's famous phrase) will do the trick. The other relies more on extolling the virtues of "voluntary simplicity." Elgin (1981), who coined the phrase, has argued irrefutably *why* changes in personal lifestyle are vital for plan-etary well-being, and has persuasively shown how such changes can be construed not as sacrifice but as a joyous reorientation of life away from "having" and towards "being" (cf. Fromm, 1978). "To live more frugally on the material side of life is to be enabled to live more abundantly on the psychological and spiritual side of life" (Elgin, ibid). And he offers in his book plenty of good, practical ad-vice, not just about what we should be doing, but about how to get started and put it into effect. He has recently (Elgin, 1992) returned to the theme, and the mixture is as before: scary facts and prognostications acting as the "stick"; glowing exhortations about the joys of frugality to provide the "carrot"; and tips as to how to do it. ·

Yet while the spirit, as a result of reflecting on these considerations, may, for many people,

be willing, the flesh remains often and indu-bitably weak. In this area of personal lifestyle, as in many others such as dieting or giving up smoking, to *know* what to do, to *agree* that it is a good idea, even to *want* to change, seem over and over again to be insufficient. A new course of action is enthusiastically embraced, but somehow, as T.S. Eliot (1962) said in "The Hollow Men," "between the idea and the re-ality, between intention and the act, falls the Shadow." That which is adopted *voluntarily* has, it seems, little power to resist being shoul-dered aside by a deeper impulse that remains involuntary. The vital tactical question, then, in considering any attempt to save human-kind from itself, focuses not on information or exhortation, but on the resilience of habits and beliefs that are "embodied," in the face of contrary principles that are "espoused." One *wants,* and one *wants not to want*; the problem is how to translate the *wanting not to want* into *not wanting.*

To see how to enable oneself to change it is necessary to understand the psychology of ad-diction, for people's involuntary rejection of their "better natures" can be seen as reflecting an addiction to luxury, or comfort, that relies on the psychological (though not of course the same physiological) dynamics as that of heroin addicts, whose need may require them, in the heat of the moment, continually to over-ride their aversion to lying to, and stealing from, those they love. In the long run it may be no less destructive – to the sustainability of the planet, if not to individual well-being – to be unable to give up flushing the toilet after every visit, or to drop the attachment to being able to pop into town on a whim, which creates the addiction to the second car. For neither the drug addict nor the comfort addict is the combination of *voluntary* effort – "will-power" – self-talk and guilt adequate to the task.

## Traps

This problem arises when the dysfunctional habit is locked in place by an underlying system of belief which determines, to a significant extent, a person's worldview. Such a belief system is called by Stolzenberg (1984) a "trap," which he defines as:

> a closed system of attitudes, beliefs and habits of thought for which one can give an objective demonstration that certain of the beliefs are incorrect, and in which certain of the attitudes and habits of thought prevent this from being recognized.

Such a system constitutes, in effect, one's vantage point; while the system is operating "upstream" of perception, its assumptions are built in to the "reality" that is experienced, and its constituents are not visible, and not open to question. One might say that the word-processing program that is currently installed on my computer is a "trap" in the same sense. Its instructions and sub-routines are nowhere to be seen; yet they determine absolutely the "reality" that appears on the screen in front of me. Unless I become aware (as in fact I am) that the "belief system" embodied by WordPerfect 5.1 is simply one amongst many, and that there are many alternative "realities" that my laptop is potentially capable of revealing to me, then I am "trapped" into confusing the view according to WordPerfect with the way things "really" (i.e., inevitably, unquestionably) are. It is possible (as I am about to do) to type, in Word Perfect, a "heretical" statement like "I wish I could be working in Microsoft Word; it's so much better." But whatever I type *within* WordPerfect can have absolutely no effect on the program itself.

Just so, when the mind habitually runs a particular belief system, and when that belief system is instrumental in creating (editing, selecting, interpreting) *experience*, then everything that happens can only be understood in terms of the presuppositions of the system – or it cannot be understood at all. As the programmers say, "it does not compute." To quote Stolzenberg (ibid.) again:

> A belief system has this one distinguishing feature: all acts of observation, judgment etc., are performed solely from the particular standpoint of the system itself. Therefore, once any belief or operating principle has been accepted, that is, is seen as "being so," any argument for not accepting it will be rejected unless it can be shown that there is something "wrong" with it from the standpoint of the system itself.... And any such demonstration would collapse as soon as it had been given because its force would depend upon the correctness of the very methodology that has just been found to be incorrect.
>
> When an outside observer is in a position to see that such a system contains an incorrect belief and also that no proof of its incorrectness can be given in terms of the system itself, then he is in a position to say that this system has become a trap. In such a situation, the outside observer will see those within as being dogmatic, while those on the inside will see the observer as someone who refuses to accept what is "obviously so." And, in fact, both will be right. (pp. 269, 272)

## The Trap of Competitive Needs

We might argue that comfort-addicts are in exactly this situation. Their view of the world embodies a nest of assumptions that link together identity, preference and material comfort in such a way that denial of preference is experienced as a mortal blow to personal efficacy, and discomfort is experienced as a threat to physical survival. Xenos (1989), for example, shows how Europeans' "normal" experience of themselves – and their experience of themselves as "normal" – was shifted, in the eighteenth century, by the rise of manufacturing industry and the invention of fashion, towards a constant state of relativized need or scarcity. One's sense of self, and self-worth, came to depend on possession and consumption. As fashions changed, so those one aspired to be like threatened to pull further away, while the hot breath of those one was striving *not* to be like could perpetually be felt on the back of one's neck.

Needs that are conceived to be naturally based, such as needs for food, shelter, sex. etc., can be approached discretely.... But when these needs become intertwined with a fluid, ever-changing social world of emulation and conspicuous consumption, they become transformed into an indiscrete desire constantly shifting its focus from one unpossessed object to another.

Among the social needs constitutive of modern commercial societies are those of recognition and prestige, and even if some of them run up against absolute limits to their satisfaction, others, particularly those tied to fashion, are capable of apparently infinite expansion. Thus the boundlessness of desire is realized in the proliferation of social needs. For us, the denizens of this world of desire, it is no longer a question of episodic insufficiency; out of our affluence we have created a social world of scarcity. (Xenos, ibid., pp. 5, 10)

Put simply, "individual consumerism" has become a cornerstone of modern Northern/ Western identity, so that living in a spiral of escalating affluence is no longer experienced as a fortunate option, but as a matter of absolute necessity. This belief installs consumption at the heart of human identity, as a core trait that is now not the servant, but the master, of survival. The idea of *not* being able to continue to consume in the style, and at the rate, that has been prescribed, therefore, can *only* be experienced as loss, sacrifice and threat, because the perceptual apparatus has been programmed to see that way.

This is true even when the conscious, voluntary mind is espousing alternative values and dispositions. One can *try* to cut down consumption, but if underneath the intention to live frugally there is the buried belief that "I shop; therefore I am," the commitment to the conscious intention will be fragile and half-hearted, and can only manifest as a "gesture" that may placate the espoused belief while, on a deeper level, validating the embodied belief. I *know* I should be buying recycled toilet paper, but somehow, when I get home from the supermarket, I find, almost to my surprise, that yet again it is the softer, whiter product that I have actually bought.

Whilst the underlying trap is in place, the attempt to live frugally is bound to be experienced, however faintly, as *painful*, as a deprivation of what is "needed," and as soon as this occurs, the system as a whole seeks to rectify the situation. The lack of comfort or of choice becomes an itch that demands scratching; and because the "motive" is still in place, there are no good-enough grounds for resisting the urge to "scratch." The Buddhist monk Nanavira Thera (1987) uses again the analogy of the drug addict:

If (the addict) decides that he must give up his addiction to the drug (it is too expensive; it is ruining his reputation or his career; it is undermining his health; and so on) he will make the decision only when he is in a fit state to consider the matter, that is to say *when he is drugged*;

and it is from this (for him, *normal*) point of view that he will envisage the future. But as soon as the addict puts his decision into effect and stops taking the drug he ceases to be "normal," and decisions taken when he was normal now appear in quite a different light – and this will include his decision to stop taking the drug. *Either,* then, he abandons his decision as invalid ("How could I possibly have decided to do such a thing? I must have been off my head.") and returns to his drug-taking, *or* (though he approves the decision) he feels it urgently necessary to return to the state in which he originally took the decision (which was when he was drugged) *in order to make the decision seem valid again.* In both cases the result is the same – a return to the drug. And so long as the addict takes his "normal" drugged state for granted at its face value – i.e., *as* normal – the same thing will happen whenever he tries to give up his addiction. (pp. 205–06)

The foregoing discussion has tried to make clear that any espousal of "voluntary simplicity" is doomed if it is overlaid on an embodied belief system to which it is antithetical. It follows that encouraging people to see voluntary simplicity as a "good idea," and offering them advice as to how to put it into practice, is a waste of time if, for the vast majority of the audience, the underlying addiction is not treated. But how is this to be done? How can one truly experience the value of simplicity, when one's experience itself is the product of a belief in the necessity of luxury?

### Getting Out of Jail

There are a number of possible methods for escaping from the trap. One is to *require* people to behave in a way that respects ecological values. If they are prevented from retreating into the familiar, sensible, normal, comfortable way, when the going gets tough, and are forced to put up with the withdrawal symptoms (to "go cold turkey"), without any apparent hope of returning to "the good (bad) old days," then a shift in underlying assumptions and priorities can take place which makes it possible for the value of simplicity to be experienced and appreciated. The problems and risks with this eco-dictatorial solution are, however, too numerous and too obvious to make it either a viable or a sensible option.

Another strategy is to engage a different motivation, so that the discomfort of acting *as if* one were un-trapped is made worth bearing. Like the first method, the idea is to arrange things so that people will for a sustained period act in line with the espoused belief rather than the embodied one. As the benefit of the new way of acting cannot be experienced to begin with, and therefore cannot act as the *reward* for putting up with the disruption and discomfort, some *other* form of reward can be used to keep the new behavior going while it "takes root."

These rewards may be either positive or negative, and there are risks associated with each. Lepper and Greene (1975), in their studies of the so-called "undermining effect," have shown that when people are positively reinforced for doing something that they themselves would have voluntarily undertaken anyway, the habit can be "appropriated" by the extrinsic reinforcement, and when the reward stops, the original motivation is now no longer strong enough to keep the behavior going. So giving people money back on returnable bottles, to encourage them to recycle, is a self-limiting expedient if it turns out that as soon as you stop the cash everybody stops recycling. This of course is why Elgin and others have emphasized that the simplification of lifestyles should be "voluntary." The use of negative reinforcement – punishment – on the other hand, tends towards the eco-fascist option, which we have already discarded.

A third option is to create a special context within which the value of a simplified lifestyle can be experienced; a context within which people's purpose or activity is framed in such a way that the materialistic trap is weakened or unactivated. On a camping holiday, or a meditation retreat, for example, one's expectations and habits of consumption may be radically different from those that are compulsive within the normal routines of life. The problem with this is that there is often little or no carry-over from one context to the other. We seem to be constructed psychologically in such a way that we can happily manifest different priorities in different contexts without feeling obliged to achieve any reconciliation (e.g., Lave, 1988). As Sheldrake (1990) has pointed out, many people sense no contradiction between working all week for a multinational oil company or a merchant bank, and on Friday evening dashing down the M4 in the Range Rover to a country home where the pin-stripe is immediately exchanged for working jeans, and Nature is celebrated, respected (and occasionally, without any felt contradictions, shot) for a couple of days.

This analysis of the causes of resistance to lifestyle changes makes the role of "self-help" and "support" groups very clear. Normal relationships, and the normal routines or life, readily reinforce both each other *and* the beliefs that underpin normal habits of consumption. But the power of *example* and *support*, in the suspension of this package of self-fulfilling, mutually-reinforcing life structures, is formidable, and certainly much greater than rational assent or individual resolve. Religious communities have long known the value of congregation and of *sangha* (Rahula, 1967), but in the lay world this kind

of support has often been seen as a comforting *addition* to other strategies for life change, rather than as one of the few strategies that actually addresses the heart of the psychological difficulty.

The final approach to making voluntary simplicity a reality which I shall discuss here is the cultivation of *mindfulness*, a term which Elgin (1981) has borrowed from Buddhist scripture. I have argued elsewhere (Claxton, 1994) that sharpening awareness of the immediate present is a prerequisite for the uncovering of tacit presuppositions. It is only an acquired (and therefore reversible) habit of perceptual imprecision that allows these unrecognized assumptions to be continually dissolved in the process whereby experience is fabricated. We can "leap to conclusions," and mistake those conclusions for "reality," only if we do not see that "leaping to conclusions" is what we are doing. By attending precisely to the minute detail of experience, the nest of assumptions that link identity, security and consumption can be brought to light – not just in intellectual fashion, but within the realm of spontaneous perceptions and dispositions.

## Conclusions

The main conclusion of this analysis, then, is that those who wish to promote what they see as healthier lifestyles, and more sustainable patterns of consumption, must acknowledge that giving information, advice and encouragement have to be seen as just one component of a much wider strategy. To write your book, and then stand back in puzzled confusion while the mass of enthusiastic readers continue much as before, is only possible given an ignorance of the depth of the psychological challenge which a change of lifestyle poses. To become either angry, despondent or exhausted are the reactions of one who has grievously underestimated the magnitude and subtlety of the problem.

The second conclusion is that the practical wisdom that is often associated with spiritual traditions such as Buddhism is "wise" not because it relies on a particular theology, but because it understands the psychological dynamics of inertia, denial and self-deception, and is designed to engage with the issue at the requisite depth (see Fox, 1990). The Three Jewels of Buddhism – Buddha, Dharma and Sangha – represent the power of inspiration and living example, the power of mindfulness, and the power of supportive friendship, respectively. Advocacy of "voluntary simplicity," or any other significant lifestyle change, which does not understand that what is required is not *just* a change of habits, but that these habits are the visible tip of a massive and intricate belief system, is bound to increase frustration, guilt, hostility, and thereby to generate heat and friction – in the manner of one who releases the clutch, only to depress simultaneously the accelerator and the brake – but not much motion.

## References

Claxton, G.L. 1994. *Noises from the Darkroom: The Science and Mystery of the Mind*. London: HarperCollins/Aquarian P.

Elgin, D. 1981. *Voluntary Simplicity: Toward a Way of Life That Is Outwardly Simple, Inwardly Rich*. New York: Morrow.

_____. 1992. "Ecological Living and the New American Challenge." *Elmwood Quarterly* 8(1): 11–12.

Eliot, T.S. 1962. *Selected Poems*. London: Faber & Faber.

Fox, W. 1990. *Toward a Transpersonal Ecology*. London and Boston: Shambhala.

Fromm, E. 1978. *To Have or to Be*. London: Cape.

Laszlo, E. 1989. *The Inner Limits of Mankind*. London: One-World Publications.

Lave, J. 1988 *Cognition in Practice*. Cambridge: Cambridge UP.

Lepper, M, and D. Greene. 1975. "Turning Play into Work," *Journal of Personality and Social Psychology* 31: 479–86.

Nanavira Thera. 1987. *Clearing the Path*. Colombo, Sri Lanka: Path P.

Rahula, W. 1967. *What the Buddha Taught*. London: Gordon Fraser.

Sheldrake, R. 1990. *The Rebirth of Nature*. London: Century.

Stolzenberg, G. 1984. "Can an Inquiry into the Foundations of Mathematics Tell Us Anything Interesting about Mind?," in *The Invented Reality*, ed. P. Watzlawick. New York: W.W. Norton.

Xenos, N. 1989. *Scarcity and Modernity*. New York: Routledge.

## Study Questions

1. What is "the Shadow" and how does it operate in a consumer's life? What is the "trap" and how does it operate in a consumer's life? Why won't "voluntary simplicity" help one avoid this trap?

2. Claxton illuminates how consumption has come to be "escalating affluence," whereby people see that consumption not only as a part of their identity but as an absolute necessity as well. This can be stated, as Claxton puts it, as "I shop; therefore I am." First, explain how he sets out how this came to be. Next, reflect upon this: Is your identity

tied to what you consume? Do you consider consumption, at the level of escalating affluence, to be a basic freedom and liberty?

3. Claxton quotes Xenos regarding needs versus wants. What are the differences between needs and wants?

4. Claxton advocates mindfulness as the way out of our consumption addiction. First, explain what mindfulness is. Next, explain how mindfulness would work in practice regarding over-consumption. Finally, do you think that mindfulness would be an effective remedy for consumption addiction? Why or why not?

# Section VI: Re-Conceiving (Issues in) Reproductive Ethics

REPRODUCTIVE ETHICS ENTAILS A wide array of topics, from the most typical, abortion, to the ones that are a product of our ever-evolving technology: cloning, stem-cell research, gamete donation, and birth control, among others. Because of the ubiquitous nature of the abortion issue, a section on reproductive ethics would be remiss not to discuss it. However, in this section you will find aspects of the abortion debate not often discussed in other applied ethics books: questions concerning the role of a prospective father in an abortion decision, whether the pro-choice and pro-life communities are damaging their positions and arguments by failing to take into account the valid points of the other side, and whether it is possible to be pro-choice and still demonstrate respect for the loss of fetal life. It would be equally remiss, though, to limit a section on reproductive ethics to just abortion. In this section, therefore, you will also find articles on such topics as the ethical dimensions that come with using reproductive technologies that increase the chances for multiple births, and whether gamete donation (i.e., the donation of sperm and ova) is morally permissible.

## Abortion

The 1973 case *Roe v. Wade* did far more than legalize abortion in the United States – it set off a divisive debate that has permeated American culture for the last four decades. One study illustrates that abortion is such an emotional and partisan issue that it has caused "pro-life Democrats and pro-choice Republicans to switch parties."[1] Needless to say, abortion is a dichotomizing subject. Those who deny that women have a right to choose abortion are branded as religious fundamentalists who simply wish to oppress women and banish them back into the home. Those who are in favor of abortion rights are branded as baby killers who support female promiscuity without consequences. Neither stereotype is an accurate indication of the typical "pro-lifer" or "pro-choicer." Moreover, such labels hardly capture the general American stance on this issue. A May 2010 poll by the Virginia Commonwealth University of Life Sciences found that 44 per cent of individuals polled thought that abortion should be legal, but only in some circumstances. This indicates that the majority of people hold a conditional position, as 37 per cent responded that abortion should be legal in any circumstance, and 15 per cent responded that it should be illegal in all circumstances.

Philosophical literature has tended to follow this trend. Typically, arguments about the ethical dimensions of abortion have involved arguing either in favor of or against it, with very little acknowledgment of the difficult grey areas in between. Philosophers and ethicists who argue against the moral permissibility of abortion usually maintain that the fetus's biological humanity is sufficient for bestowing upon it the same moral and legal rights as any other human being.[2] Some philosophers reject this biological view of moral status and, instead, argue that abortion is morally wrong because it deprives the fetus of its valuable future. This is the main thesis in Don Marquis's "Why Abortion Is Immoral" – an essay that is quite possibly the best secular argument against the general moral permissibility of abortion.

Philosophers and ethicists who defend abortion rights typically argue that human fetuses are missing the qualities that are necessary for personhood (e.g., rationality, self-consciousness, or moral agency) and that they therefore lack moral status.[3] As such, they lack moral rights, and therefore killing them violates no rights at all. Typically, philosophers who argue in this way assume a tacit moral premise: because the fetus lacks moral status, the fetus lacks any moral import at all. Mary Anne Warren, for example, has argued that because the human fetus lacks certain cognitive capacities, such as self-consciousness, sentience, and agency, it has no more moral value than a guppy. However, many pro-choice philosophers have maintained that it is not necessary to deny fetal personhood in order to make a case in favor of abortion rights. Even if the fetus were granted full rights, because no human being has a right to forcibly use another person's body for sustenance, the fetus cannot be granted this right either. This is Judith Jarvis Thomson's argument in "A Defense of Abortion" – one of the most influential pro-choice essays ever written.

Both defenders and detractors of abortion usually debate the issue in terms of rights: the rights of the fetus are contrasted with the rights of the pregnant woman. They are portrayed as intrinsically adversarial, with the rights of one yielding to the rights of the other. Either the woman's body, autonomy, health, or future desires for her life are erased in exchange for preserving the fetus's life, or the fetus is dehumanized, dismissed as unimportant or mere tissue, and erased from the discussion altogether by rendering it a nonperson. This dichotomy has prevented a deeper and more nuanced understanding of the reality of abortion in the lives of the women who procure them. If, as is argued by many on the pro-choice side, the fetus were mere tissue, then there would be no reason to regard abortion as a weighty issue. Yet many women who procure abortions *do* agonize over the decision, and the procedure, to them, is not akin to merely obtaining a haircut or removing an organ. In her book *The Abortion Myth*, Leslie Cannold relays various stories of women who procure an abortion. Most of the women have no regrets about their decision, yet it still disturbs them to hear the fetus disparaged. One woman comments: "The whole handling of the abortion issue is wrong. You don't toss it in the garbage. I mean, I've had an abortion, it was an incredibly painful experience. I didn't toss it in the garbage. And I find it really distressing to hear it referred to in that way."[4] On the other hand, women who procure abortions are equally dismissed by many on the pro-life side, stereotyped as promiscuous women who simply wish to kill their "babies" and skirt their responsibilities.

Of course, the truth runs deeper than this. In the United States, by the age of 45, one-third of women will have procured at least one abortion. Sixty per cent of women obtaining abortions are already mothers. And, despite the pictures often depicted during pro-life protests, 89 per cent of abortions take place during the first trimester.[5] One common reason for women waiting longer involves a lack of access to abortion services (for example, due to financial reasons or because they live in an area of the country with limited abortion services).

Clearly, then, some traditional philosophical literature is out of touch with the reality of abortion. Some philosophers have talked about abortion in ways that transcend the discussion of rights and have acknowledged, first, that the status of the human fetus is not as clear as decreeing it a person or nonperson, and, second, that the reasons women wish to obtain abortions are multi-layered and complex. However, most of the philosophical literature has, until recently, presented a bifurcated conception of the issue. Yet within the past few years, the debate over reproductive rights, and the moral dimensions of issues such as abortion, has evolved. Pro-choice advocates are beginning to understand that the value of fetal life can no longer be ignored or thrown by the wayside. Dr. Lisa Harris, a professor of women's studies and obstetrics/gynecology, and an abortion-rights advocate, writes that "the pro-choice movement has not owned or owned up to the reality of the fetus ... [it] is usually neglected entirely, becomes unimportant or nothing."[6] A 2010 article in *Newsweek* magazine entitled "Remember Roe!" quotes Nancy Keenan, president of NARAL Pro-Choice America (originally called "National Association for the Repeal of Abortion Laws"), commenting that pro-choice advocates' "reluctance to address the moral complexity of this debate is no longer serving our cause or our country well." Francis Kissling's essay "Is There Life after *Roe*? How to Think about the Fetus" is an attempt to do just this. Although Kissling herself is pro-choice, she argues that other members of the pro-choice community do not bestow proper respect upon nascent human life. Any defense of the pro-choice perspective, she argues, should be filtered through a lens that accords fetal life value, not one that ignores or dismisses it.

On the other side, many pro-life advocates have urged their constituents to address the reality of what leads women to obtain abortions. The stereotypical picture of a woman who procures an abortion as irresponsible, promiscuous, and uncaring of the life inside her is seriously questioned when one reads the personal stories of women who obtain abortions, and also when one learns the disturbing, at times gruesome, details about illegal abortions before *Roe* was legalized. Steve Tracy's essay "Abortion, the Marginalized, and the Vulnerable: A Social Justice Perspective for Reducing Abortion" represents a pro-life voice that acknowledges the difficult realties that lead so many women to procure abortions. Instead of dismissing women as immoral or callous for obtaining abortions, Tracy calls upon the pro-life community to fight in favor of several social justice reforms in an earnest effort to reduce abortion rates.

Moreover, the viewpoint of prospective fathers, long thought to be irrelevant when it comes to abortion, is beginning to be increasingly acknowledged. In 2006, Matthew Dubay and his ex-girlfriend Lauren Wells went to court in a case that has come to be known as *Roe v. Wade for Men* (*Dubay v. Wells*). According to Dubay, while they were dating, he made it clear to Wells that he had no desire to become a father. According to Dubay, Wells assured him that she was taking oral contraceptives and that she suffered from physical conditions that made pregnancy unlikely. After they separated, Wells informed Dubay that she was pregnant. She decided to keep the baby, and sued Dubay for child-support payments. The case questioned whether men should be forced to pay child support for children they did not intend to have, and therefore whether they should be obligated to be fathers against their will, when women are able to reject motherhood via either abortion or adoption. That is, if women are given a "second chance," so to speak, after becoming pregnant to decide whether they want to become mothers, why aren't men granted a corollary right? Another relevant concern is what voice, if any, should be given to a man who desperately wants to keep a fetus that his partner wants to abort? Should he be allowed to seek an injunction against the woman from procuring the abortion? Should he not have *some* say, given that the fetus is, genetically, 50 per cent his own? This latter concern is addressed by Bertha Alvarez Manninen in "Pleading Men and Virtuous Women: Considering the Role of the Father in the Abortion Debate," where she argues that although women have a right to obtain an abortion even against the prospective father's consent, there is still room in the discussion for men's voices, and that the normative ethical theory of virtue ethics helps us to have this conversation.

**Artificial Reproductive Technologies**

On 25 July 1978, Louise Joy Brown, the world's first "test tube baby," was born. Brown was the first live human birth from in vitro fertilization (IVF), the process in which an embryo is fertilized in a Petri dish outside the womb (rendering the term "test tube baby" a misnomer) and then implanted back into a woman's uterus for possible implantation and gestation. Four years later, her sister Natalie Brown was born, the 40th baby in the world conceived via the use of IVF. The Brown sisters would have probably never been born without the use of IVF technology, given that their mother, Lesley Brown, suffered from blocked fallopian tubes. Because an embryo conceived via the use of IVF is implanted directly into a woman's uterus, there is no need for it to travel through the fallopian tube. For women who are afflicted with blocked, scarred, or non-functioning fallopian tubes, the advent and development of IVF allowed them to finally have genetic children of their own. Moreover, IVF helped to overcome certain forms of male infertility, those usually related to low sperm count or defective sperm quality. In conjunction with IVF, intracytoplasmic sperm injection can be used, where a sperm cell is injected directly into an ovum and then the fertilized embryo is transferred into the uterus.

In addition to providing a means for overcoming some instances of infertility, the (increasingly frequent) use of IVF carries with it a host of unique ethical issues. Because IVF entails fertilization outside the body and the re-implantation of the embryo in the uterus, for the first time it was possible for a woman to gestate an embryo that was not genetically hers (if another woman's ovum was used), or not genetically her sexual partner's (if donor sperm was used), or genetically unrelated to either of them. A baby born through IVF could have as many as five distinct "parents": two genetic parents (the gamete donors), a gestational mother (although at times she may also be the genetic mother), and two social parents who undertake the task of raising the child. This scenario forces us to ask these questions: What defines parenthood? Who are the child's "real" parents?

Related to the issues that come with surrogacy, gamete donation has also been the focus of some ethical concerns. Some common issues include the rights of the gamete donors (e.g., do they have a right to remain anonymous or the right to relinquish all responsibilities for any consequent offspring?), the rights of the gamete recipients (e.g., do they have a right to know sensitive information about the donors, such as predisposition to genetic diseases?), and the rights of the children born from gamete donation (e.g., do they, like adopted children, have a right to know the identity of the donors?). Particularly complicated situations arise when those rights conflict, that is, when the right to donor anonymity conflicts with the child's right to know about his or her genetic heritage. There are also concerns with the issue of compensation for gamete donation, especially among women. Because women are paid several thousands of dollars for ova donation, there is a worry that the donors will be mostly women of low socioeconomic backgrounds, while the women who receive the donation will come from more affluent backgrounds. Some of these concerns are addressed by Shari Collins and Eric Comerford in their essay "Anonymous Sperm Donation: A Case for Genetic Heritage and Wariness for Contractual Parenthood," where they argue that children born from gamete donations have a right to knowledge about their genetic parentage.

In addition to IVF, other forms of artificial reproductive technology present ethical problems of their own. Intrauterine insemination (IUI) is a type of artificial insemination where sperm is inserted directly into the uterus in order to increase the possibility of successful conception. Like IVF, IUI raises questions concerning parentage, since a woman can be inseminated with the sperm of someone other than her sexual partner (adding to the number of ways in which a child can have a "faceless" parent). Additionally, IUI in conjunction with oral and injectionable types of ovulation induction, such as Clomiphene and Pergonal, is responsible for the almost five-fold increase in higher-order multiple births (or HOMBs, defined as pregnancies with three or more fetuses) in the past four decades.[7]

Media attention usually focuses on the successful aspects of HOMBs while ignoring its often tragic consequences. Arlene Judith Klotzko's "Medical Miracle or Medical Mischief? The Saga of the McCaughey Septuplets" details the ethical concerns brought about by HOMBs by focusing on the case of the 1997 birth of the McCaughey septuplets. The infants were born in Des Moines, Iowa, after their mother was prescribed the fertility drug Metrodin. Because of their Christian faith, they declined selective reduction, a form of abortion in multifetal pregnancies. Two of their seven children, Alexis and Nathan, now suffer from cerebral palsy, and Nathan has undergone spinal surgery in order to combat his walking difficulties. In 1985, in Orange, California, after her use of the ovulation drug Pergonal, Patti Frustaci's ultrasound revealed that they had conceived septuplets, but she and her husband Sam refused selective abortion. One baby was stillborn and three babies died shortly after their births, all having succumbed to hyaline membrane disease. The remaining three children have cerebral palsy and are mentally disabled. Despite these consequences, the Frustacis were not deterred from using fertility drugs again; in 1990, Patti gave birth to healthy twins after using Pergonal once more. The Morrison sextuplets were born in Minneapolis, Minnesota, in 2007. They too were products of fertility drugs and were born prematurely at twenty-three weeks gestational age. Five of the six children died within two months of their birth. In England in 1996, Mandy Allwood was pregnant with eight fetuses after taking fertility drugs. She was offered a large amount of money by a British tabloid for the exclusive rights to cover the birth of all eight babies. Because of the

offer, she refused selective reduction. The oc-
tuplets, six boys and two girls, all died within
an hour of their birth. In August 2009, the
Stansel sextuplets were born in Houston,
Texas, as a result of ovulation induction and
IUI. Against the advice of their doctor, the
Stansels refused to selectively abort any of the
fetuses. Only two of the six survived, each
suffering from their own set of health prob-
lems even after spending five months in the
Neonatal Intensive Care Unit of the Texas
Women's Hospital.

On 26 January 2009, Nadya Suleman gave
birth to eight babies, all of whom survived
and appear, for now, to be in good health.
The Suleman infants are the first set of surviving octuplets in the United States. Keeping
true to form, the media initially celebrated
the birth of the octuplets. However, upon the
revelation that Suleman was a single mother,
with no steady income, and that she already
had six children under the age of eight, three
of whom suffer from disabilities of varying
degrees of severity, she came to be known,
derogatorily, as "Octomom," with the media
and the general public turning against her. All
fourteen of Suleman's children were conceived
through the use of IVF (because of her scarred
fallopian tubes, IVF was the only chance
Suleman had at conceiving). According to
Suleman, the birth of the octuplets resulted
when she asked that the last six embryos from

her previous fertility treatment be implanted,
and two of the embryos twinned (this account
has been called into question as the children
grew, since none of them appear to be identical twins). One of the most concerning
aspects of this case is Suleman's confession that
in *each* of her six fertility treatments, she was
implanted with six embryos.[8]

Gestating multiple fetuses can result in dire
consequences for them. They can be miscarried or stillborn, or they can die shortly after
birth. When they do survive, they are often
born prematurely and with a low birth weight.
Because of their prematurity, these infants
can suffer from a variety of physical impair-
ments and are also more likely to suffer from
respiratory distress syndrome and intracranial
hemorrhage. Gestating multiple fetuses also
leads to increased health risks for the woman,
who is more likely to suffer from high blood
pressure during gestation and is at risk for
potentially fatal blood clots. She is also more
likely to suffer from anemia, hypertension,
preterm labor, and postpartum hemorrhage.
In addition, the cost to keep premature and
low birth weight infants alive is substantial,
averaging about $3,500 per day, per infant.[9]
Consequently, at least under these present
harms and economic burdens, we must consider whether it is morally permissible to engage
in reproductive technology that increases the
risk of a higher-order multiple birth.

## Notes

1   Mitchell Killian and Clyde Wilcox, "Do Abortion Attitudes Lead to Party Switching?"
    *Political Research* 61.4 (2008): 561.
2   For example, see John T. Noonan, "An Almost Absolute Value in History," in *The Morality of
    Abortion: Legal and Historical Perspectives* (Cambridge, MA: Harvard UP, 1970), 1–59.
3   See Peter Singer, *Practical Ethics* (New York: Cambridge UP, 1993); Michael Tooley, "Abortion
    and Infanticide," *Philosophy and Public Affairs* 2.1 (1972): 37–65; and Mary Anne Warren, "On
    the Moral and Legal Status of Abortion," *The Monist* 57.1 (1973): 43–61.
4   David Boonin, *A Defense of Abortion* (New York: Cambridge UP, 2003), 36.
5   Guttenmacher Institute, "Facts about Induced Abortion," 2010, http://www.guttmacher.org/
    pubs/fb_induced_abortion.html.

6  Lisa Harris, "Second Trimester Abortion Provision: Breaking the Silence and Changing the Discourse," *Reproductive Health Matters* 16.31 (2008): 77.

7  Karen Hammond, "Multifetal Pregnancy Reduction," *Journal of Obstetric, Gynecologic, & Neonatal Nursing* 27.3 (1997): 338–43.

8  Associated Press, "Medical Society Probes Octuplets' Conception," MSNBC, 10 February 2009, http://www.msnbc.msn.com/id/29123731/.

9  Jonathan Muraskas and Kayhan Parsi. 2008. "The Cost of Saving the Tiniest Lives: NICUs versus Prevention." *AMA Journal of Ethics*, 10.10: 655–58.

# 1.  Don Marquis, "Why Abortion Is Immoral"

IT IS CONSIDERED UNCONTROVERSIAL that murder is morally wrong and that humans have a *prima facie* right to life. But *why* is murder morally wrong – what is the primary wrong-making feature of killing? In this 1989 article from the *Journal of Philosophy*, Don Marquis (b. 1935) argues that what makes killing *any* being (human or not) morally questionable is that death entails the eradication of that being's future. The higher the quality of the future, the worse the deprivation and, therefore, the act of killing increases in its moral gravity. Therefore, whereas the act of killing an ant would be negligible according to Marquis, the act of killing a standard fetus, whom you are depriving of the kind of future typical to human persons, deprives it of a lot more. Therefore, because killing a fetus denies it the kind of future life typical to human persons, it is as wrong to kill the fetus as it is to kill any other human person.

---

THE VIEW THAT ABORTION is, with rare exceptions, seriously immoral has received little support in the recent philosophical literature. No doubt most philosophers affiliated with secular institutions of higher education believe that the anti-abortion position is either a symptom of irrational religious dogma or a conclusion generated by seriously confused philosophical argument. The purpose of this essay is to undermine this general belief. This essay sets out an argument that purports to show, as well as any argument in ethics can show, that abortion is, except possibly in rare cases, seriously immoral, that it is in the same moral category as killing an innocent adult human being....

## I.

... [A] necessary condition of resolving the abortion controversy is a more theoretical account of the wrongness of killing. After all, if we merely believe, but do not understand, why killing adult human beings such as ourselves is wrong, how could we conceivably show that abortion is either immoral or permissible?

## II.

In order to develop such an account, we can start from the following unproblematic assumption concerning our own case: it is wrong to kill *us*. Why is it wrong? Some answers can be easily eliminated. It might be said that what makes killing us wrong is that a killing brutalizes the one who kills. But the brutalization consists of being inured to the performance of an act that is hideously immoral; hence, the brutalization does not explain the immorality. It might be said that what makes killing us wrong is the great loss others would experience due to our absence. Although such hubris is understandable, such an explanation does not account for the wrongness of killing hermits, or those whose lives are relatively independent and whose friends find it easy to make new friends.

A more obvious answer is better. What primarily makes killing wrong is neither its effect on the murderer nor its effect on the victim's friends and relatives, but its effect on the victim. The loss of one's life is one of the greatest losses one can suffer. The loss of one's life deprives one of all the experiences, activities, projects, and enjoyments that would otherwise have constituted one's future. Therefore, killing someone is wrong, primarily because the killing inflicts (one of) the greatest possible losses on the victim. To describe this as the loss of life can be misleading, however. The change in my biological state does not by itself make killing me wrong. The effect of the loss of my biological life is the loss to me of all those activities, projects, experiences, and enjoyments which would otherwise have constituted my future personal life. These activities, projects, experiences, and enjoyments are either valuable for their own sakes or are means to something else that is valuable for its own sake. Some parts of my future are not valued by me now, but will come to be valued by me as I grow older and as my values and capacities change. When I am killed, I am deprived both of what I now value which would have been part of my future personal life, but also what I would come to value. Therefore, when I die, I am deprived of all of the value of my future. Inflicting this loss on me is ultimately what makes killing me wrong. This being the case, it would seem that what makes killing *any* adult human being prima facie seriously wrong is the loss of his or her future.[1]

How should this rudimentary theory of the wrongness of killing be evaluated? It cannot be faulted for deriving an "ought" from an "is," for it does not. The analysis assumes that killing me (or you, reader) is prima facie seriously wrong. The point of the analysis is to establish which natural property ultimately explains the wrongness of the killing, given that it is wrong. A natural property will ultimately explain the wrongness of killing, only if (1) the explanation fits with our intuitions about the matter and (2) there is no other natural property that provides the basis for a better explanation of the wrongness of killing. This analysis rests on the intuition that what makes killing a particular human or animal wrong is what it does to that particular human or animal. What makes killing wrong is some natural effect or other of the killing....

The claim that what makes killing wrong is the loss of the victim's future is directly supported by two considerations. In the first place, this theory explains why we regard killing as one of the worst of crimes. Killing is especially wrong, because it deprives the victim of more than perhaps any other crime. In the second place, people with AIDS or cancer who know they are dying believe, of course, that dying is a very bad thing for them. They believe that the loss of a future to them that they would otherwise have experienced is what makes their premature death a very bad thing for them. A better theory of the wrongness of killing would require a different natural property associated with killing which better fits with the attitudes of the dying. What could it be?

The view that what makes killing wrong is the loss to the victim of the value of the victim's future gains additional support when some of its implications are examined. In the first place, it is incompatible with the view that it is wrong to kill only beings who are biologically human. It is possible that there exists a different species from another planet whose members have a future like ours. Since having a future like that is what makes killing someone wrong, this theory entails that it would be wrong to kill members of such a species. Hence, this theory is opposed to the claim that only life that is biologically human has great moral worth, a claim which many anti-abortionists have seemed to adopt. This opposition, which this theory has in common with personhood theories, seems to be a merit of the theory.

In the second place, the claim that the loss of one's future is the wrong-making feature of one's being killed entails the possibility that the futures of some actual nonhuman mammals on our own planet are sufficiently like ours that it is seriously wrong to kill them also. Whether some animals do have the same right to life as human beings depends on adding to the account of the wrongness of killing some additional account of just what it is about my future or the futures of other adult human beings which makes it wrong to kill us. No such additional account will be offered in this essay. Undoubtedly, the provision of such an account would be a very difficult matter. Undoubtedly, any such account would be quite controversial. Hence, it surely should not reflect badly on this sketch of an elementary theory of the wrongness of killing that it is indeterminate with respect to some very difficult issues regarding animal rights.

In the third place, the claim that the loss of one's future is the wrong-making feature of one's being killed does not entail, as sanctity of human life theories do, that active euthanasia is wrong. Persons who are severely and incurably ill, who face a future of pain and despair, and who wish to die will not have suffered a loss if they are killed. It is, strictly speaking, the value of a human's future which makes killing wrong in this theory. This being so, killing does not necessarily wrong some persons who are sick and dying. Of course, there may be other reasons for a prohibition of active euthanasia, but that is another matter. Sanctity-of-human-life theories seem to hold that active euthanasia is seriously wrong even in an individual case where there seems to be good reason for it independently of public policy considerations. This consequence is most implausible, and it is a plus for the claim that the loss of a future of value is what makes killing wrong that it does not share this consequence.

In the fourth place, the account of the wrongness of killing defended in this essay does straightforwardly entail that it is prima facie seriously wrong to kill children and infants, for we do presume that they have futures of value. Since we do believe that it is wrong to kill defenseless little babies, it is important that a theory of the wrongness of killing easily account for this. Personhood theories of the wrongness of killing, on the other hand, cannot straightforwardly account for the wrongness of killing infants and young children.[2] Hence, such theories must add special ad hoc accounts of the wrongness of killing the young. The plausibility of such ad hoc theories seems to be a function of how desperately one wants such theories to work. The claim that the primary wrong-making feature of a killing is the loss to the victim of the value of its future accounts for the wrongness of killing young children and infants directly; it makes the wrongness of such acts as obvious as we actually think it is. This is a further merit of this theory. Accordingly, it seems that this value of a future-like-ours theory of the wrongness of killing shares strengths of both sanctity-of-life and personhood accounts while avoiding weaknesses of both. In addition, it meshes with a central intuition concerning what makes killing wrong.

The claim that the primary wrong-making feature of a killing is the loss to the victim of the value of its future has obvious consequences for the ethics of abortion. The future of a standard fetus includes a set of experiences, projects, activities, and such which are identical with the futures of adult human beings and are identical with the futures of young children. Since the reason that is sufficient to explain why it is wrong to kill human beings after the time of birth is a reason that also applies to fetuses, it follows that abortion is prima facie seriously morally wrong.

This argument does not rely on the invalid inference that, since it is wrong to kill persons, it is wrong to kill potential persons also. The category that is morally central to this analysis is the category of having a valuable future like ours; it is not the category of personhood. The argument to the conclusion that abortion is prima facie seriously morally wrong proceeded independently of the notion of person or potential person or any equivalent....

Of course, this value of a future-like-ours argument, if sound, shows only that abortion is prima facie wrong, not that it is wrong in any and all circumstances. Since the loss of the future to a standard fetus, if killed, is, however, at least as great a loss as the loss of the future to a standard adult human being who is killed, abortion, like ordinary killing, could be justified only by the most compelling reasons. The loss of one's life is almost the greatest misfortune that can happen to one. Presumably abortion could be justified in some circumstances, only if the loss consequent on failing to abort would be at least as great. Accordingly, morally permissible abortions will be rare indeed unless, perhaps, they occur so early in pregnancy that a fetus is not yet definitely an individual. Hence, this argument should be taken as showing that abortion is presumptively very seriously wrong, where the presumption is very strong – as strong as the presumption that killing another adult human being is wrong....

## IV.

The analysis of the previous section suggests that alternative general accounts of the wrongness of killing are either inadequate or unsuccessful in getting around the anti-abortion consequences of the value of a future-like-ours argument. A different strategy for avoiding these anti-abortion consequences involves limiting the scope of the value of a future argument. More precisely, the strategy involves arguing that fetuses lack a property that is essential for the value-of-a-future argument (or for any anti-abortion argument) to apply to them.

One move of this sort is based upon the claim that a necessary condition of one's future being valuable is that one values it. Value implies a valuer. Given this one might argue that, since fetuses cannot value their futures, their futures are not valuable to them. Hence, it does not seriously wrong them deliberately to end their lives.

This move fails, however, because of some ambiguities. Let us assume that something cannot be of value unless it is valued by someone. This does not entail that my life is of no value unless it is valued by me. I may think, in a period of despair, that my future is of no worth whatsoever, but I may be wrong because others rightly see value – even great value – in it. Furthermore, my future can be valuable to me even if I do not value it. This is the case when a young person attempts suicide, but is rescued and goes on to significant human achievements. Such young people's futures are ultimately valuable to them, even though such futures do not seem to be valuable to them at the moment of attempted suicide. A fetus's future can be valuable to it in the same way. Accordingly, this attempt to limit the anti-abortion argument fails....

## V.

In this essay, it has been argued that the correct ethic of the wrongness of killing can be extended to fetal life and used to show that there is a strong presumption that any abortion is morally impermissible. If the ethic of killing adopted here entails, however, that contraception is also seriously immoral, then there would appear to be a difficulty with the analysis of this essay.

But this analysis does not entail that contraception is wrong. Of course, contraception prevents the actualization of a possible future of value. Hence, it follows from the claim that futures of value should be maximized that contraception is prima facie immoral. This obligation to maximize does not exist, however; furthermore, nothing in the ethics of killing in this paper entails that it does. The ethics of killing in this essay would entail that contraception is wrong only if something were denied a human future of value by contraception. Nothing at all is denied such a future by contraception, however.

Candidates for a subject of harm by contraception fall into four categories: (1) some sperm or other, (2) some ovum or other, (3) a sperm and an ovum separately, and (4) a sperm and an ovum together. Assigning the harm to some sperm is utterly arbitrary, for no reason can be given for making a sperm the subject of harm rather than an ovum. Assigning the harm to some ovum is utterly arbitrary, for no reason can be given for making an ovum the subject of harm rather than a sperm. One might attempt to avoid these problems by insisting that contraception deprives both the sperm and the ovum separately of a valuable future like ours. On this alternative, too many futures are lost. Contraception was supposed to be wrong, because it deprived us of one future of value, not two. One might attempt to avoid this problem by holding that contraception deprives the combination of sperm and ovum of a valuable future like ours. But here the definite article misleads. At the time of contraception, there are hundreds of millions of sperm, one (released) ovum and millions of possible combinations of all of these. There is no actual combination at all. Is the subject of the loss to be a merely possible combination? Which one? This alternative does not yield an actual subject of harm either. Accordingly, the immorality of contraception is not entailed by the loss of a future-like-ours argument simply because there is no nonarbitrarily identifiable subject of the loss in the case of contraception.

**VI.**

The purpose of this essay has been to set out an argument for the serious presumptive wrongness of abortion subject to the assumption that the moral permissibility of abortion stands or falls on the moral status of the fetus. Since a fetus possesses a property, the possession of which in adult human beings is sufficient to make killing an adult human being wrong, abortion is wrong. This way of dealing with the problem of abortion seems superior to other approaches to the ethics of abortion, because it rests on an ethics of killing which is close to self-evident, because the crucial morally relevant property clearly applies to fetuses, and because the argument avoids the usual equivocations on "human life," "human being," or "person." The argument rests neither on religious claims nor on Papal dogma. It is not subject to the objection of "speciesism." Its soundness is compatible with the moral permissibility of euthanasia and contraception. It deals with our intuitions concerning young children.

Finally, this analysis can be viewed as resolving a standard problem – indeed, *the* standard problem – concerning the ethics of abortion. Clearly, it is wrong to kill adult human beings. Clearly, it is not wrong to end the life of some arbitrarily chosen single human cell. Fetuses seem to be like arbitrarily chosen human cells in some respects and like adult humans in other respects. The problem of the ethics of abortion is the problem of determining the fetal property that settles this moral controversy. The thesis of this essay is that the problem of the ethics of abortion, so understood, is solvable.

## Study Questions

1   Explain Marquis's argument against abortion, focusing on the "future-like-ours" principle. Marquis maintains that his principle is significantly different from typical arguments focusing on the potential of the fetus as a basis for its right to life. Why does Marquis maintain this, and do you agree with him that the principles are different?

2   Marquis argues that, while it is wrong to kill a "standard" fetus because of its valuable future, it may not be wrong to euthanize someone (upon her request) if she faces a future fraught with pain and suffering. This concession presents a problem for Marquis when trying to navigate the difficult questions surrounding therapeutic abortions – at what point is a fetus so sick that killing it qualifies more as euthanasia and less as abortion? How can we delineate what standards of health must be met in order to maintain that a fetus (or any other human being) possesses a future of value?

3   Suppose that, one day, we perfect cloning, making it so that every single cell in my body could be used to create a new human being. Would the "future-like-ours" principle apply to each cell in my body? If so, does this mean that destroying any cell in my body would be morally equivalent to abortion? If not, what are the significant differences between a clonable cell and a human fetus, such that Marquis's argument can successfully defend the right to life of the latter but not the former?

4   If you disagree with Marquis's argument concerning the essential wrong-making features of killing, what do you think makes killing morally wrong? Do these reasons apply to human embryos and fetuses? Why or why not?

## Notes

1   I have been most influenced on this matter by Jonathan Glover, *Causing Death and Saving Lives* (New York: Penguin, 1977), ch. 3; and Robert Young, "What Is So Wrong with Killing People?" *Philosophy* 54:210 (1979): 515–28.

2   Feinberg, Tooley, Warren, and Engelhardt have all dealt with this problem. [Joel Feinberg, "Abortion," *Matters of Life and Death: New Introductory Essays in Moral Philosophy*, ed. Tom Regan (New York: Random House, 1986), 256–93; Michael Tooley, "Abortion and Infanticide," *Philosophy and Public Affairs* 2.1 (1972): 37–65; Michael Tooley, *Abortion and Infanticide* (New York: Oxford, 1984); Mary Anne Warren, "On the Moral and Legal Status of Abortion," *The Monist* 57.1 (1973): 43–61; H. Tristram Engelhardt, "The Ontology of Abortion," *Ethics* 84.3 (1974): 217–34.]

# 2.  Judith Jarvis Thomson, "A Defense of Abortion"

TYPICALLY, PRO-LIFE ARGUMENTS STRESS the humanity and personhood of the fetus, maintaining that its right to life trumps any right a woman may have to bodily autonomy. In this 1971 article from the journal *Philosophy and Public Affairs*, Judith Jarvis Thomson (b. 1929) argues that this is not so. Even if the fetus is granted every single right typically granted to all persons, because no person has a right to use the body of another for sustenance, the fetus cannot be granted this right either. For example, even though patients in dire need of a bone marrow transplant are clearly persons with rights, their need does not mean that another person can be forced to donate bone marrow in order to sustain them. Therefore, granting that fetuses are persons does not entail that abortion is morally impermissible. Although this is the most important aspect of Thomson's argument, two other points are notable. First, she draws a distinction between moral justice and moral decency, arguing that although no abortion is ever unjust (because the woman always retains the right to retract aid from the fetus in terms of bodily sustenance), not all exercises of abortion are morally decent. Second, toward the end of the essay, Thomson argues that if a fetus were able to survive without the continued use of the woman's body, she would retain a right to remove it, but not to kill it. This point presents possible arguments in favor of restricting abortions once the fetus is viable and in favor of treatment and care for fetuses who survive abortions.

---

MOST OPPOSITION TO ABORTION relies on the premise that the fetus is a human being, a person, from the moment of conception.[1] The premise is argued for, but, as I think, not well. Take, for example, the most common argument. We are asked to notice that the development of a human being from conception through birth into childhood is continuous; then it is said that to draw a line, to choose a point in this development and say "before this point the thing is not a person, after this point it is a person" is to make an arbitrary choice, a choice for which in the nature of things no good reason can be given. It is concluded that the fetus is, or anyway that we had better say it is, a person from the moment of conception. But this conclusion does not follow. Similar things might be said about the development of an acorn into an oak tree, and it does not follow that acorns are oak trees, or that we had better say they are. Arguments of this form are sometimes called "slippery slope arguments" – the phrase is perhaps self-explanatory – and it is dismaying that opponents of abortion rely on them so heavily and uncritically.

I am inclined to agree, however, that the prospects for "drawing a line" in the development of the fetus look dim. I am inclined to think also that we shall probably have to agree that the fetus has already become a human person well before birth. Indeed, it comes as a surprise when one first learns how early in its life it begins to acquire human characteristics. By the tenth week, for example, it already has a face, arms and legs, fingers and toes; it has internal organs, and brain activity is detectable.[2] On the other hand, I think that the premise is false, that the fetus is not a person from the moment of conception. A newly fertilized ovum, a newly implanted clump of cells, is no more a person than an acorn is an oak tree. But I shall not discuss any of this. For it seems to me to be of great interest to ask what happens if, for the sake of argument, we allow the premise. How, precisely, are we supposed to get from there to the conclusion that abortion is morally impermissible? Opponents of abortion commonly spend most of their time establishing that the fetus is a person, and hardly any time explaining the step from there to the impermissibility of abortion. Perhaps they think the step too simple and obvious to require much comment. Or perhaps instead they are simply being economical in argument. Many of those who defend abortion rely on the premise that the fetus is not a person, but only a bit of tissue that will become a person at birth; and why pay out more arguments than you have to? Whatever the explanation, I suggest that the step they take is neither easy nor obvious, that it calls for closer examination than it is commonly given, and that when we do give it this closer examination we shall feel inclined to reject it.

I propose, then, that we grant that the fetus is a person from the moment of conception. How does the argument go from here? Something like this, I take it. Every person has a right to life. So the fetus has a right to life. No doubt the mother has a right to decide what shall happen in and to her body; everyone would grant that. But surely a person's right to life is stronger and more stringent than the mother's right to decide what happens in and to her body, and so outweighs it. So the fetus may not be killed; an abortion may not be performed.

It sounds plausible. But now let me ask you to imagine this. You wake up in the morning and find yourself back to back in bed with an unconscious violinist. A famous unconscious violinist. He has been found to have a fatal kidney ailment, and the Society of Music Lovers has canvassed all the available medical records and found that you alone have the

right blood type to help. They have therefore kidnapped you, and last night the violinist's circulatory system was plugged into yours, so that your kidneys can be used to extract poisons from his blood as well as your own. The director of the hospital now tells you, "Look, we're sorry the Society of Music Lovers did this to you — we would never have permitted it if we had known. But still, they did it, and the violinist now is plugged into you. To unplug you would be to kill him. But never mind, it's only for nine months. By then he will have recovered from his ailment, and can safely be unplugged from you." Is it morally incumbent on you to accede to this situation? No doubt it would be very nice of you if you did, a great kindness. But do you *have* to accede to it? What if it were not nine months, but nine years? Or longer still? What if the director of the hospital says, "Tough luck, I agree, but you've now got to stay in bed, with the violinist plugged into you, for the rest of your life. Because remember this. All persons have a right to life, and violinists are persons. Granted you have a right to decide what happens in and to your body, but a person's right to life outweighs your right to decide what happens in and to your body. So you cannot ever be unplugged from him." I imagine you would regard this as outrageous, which suggests that something really is wrong with that plausible-sounding argument I mentioned a moment ago.

In this case, of course, you were kidnapped; you didn't volunteer for the operation that plugged the violinist into your kidneys. Can those who oppose abortion on the ground I mentioned make an exception for a pregnancy due to rape? Certainly. They can say that persons have a right to life only if they didn't come into existence because of rape; or they can say that all persons have a right to life, but that some have less of a right to life than others, in particular, that those who came into existence because of rape have less. But these statements have a rather unpleasant sound. Surely the question of whether you have a right to life at all, or how much of it you have, shouldn't turn on the question of whether or not you are the product of a rape. And in fact the people who oppose abortion on the ground I mentioned do not make this distinction, and hence do not make an exception in case of rape.

Nor do they make an exception for a case in which the mother has to spend the nine months of her pregnancy in bed. They would agree that would be a great pity, and hard on the mother; but all the same, all persons have a right to life, the fetus is a person, and so on....

Some won't even make an exception for a case in which continuation of the pregnancy is likely to shorten the mother's life; they regard abortion as impermissible even to save the mother's life....

Where the mother's life is not at stake, the argument I mentioned at the outset seems to have a much stronger pull. "Everyone has a right to life, so the unborn person has a right to life." And isn't the child's right to life weightier than anything other than the mother's own right to life, which she might put forward as ground for an abortion?

This argument treats the right to life as if it were unproblematic. It is not, and this seems to me to be precisely the source of the mistake.

For we should now, at long last, ask what it comes to, to have a right to life. In some views having a right to life includes having a right to be given at least the bare minimum one needs for continued life. But suppose that what in fact *is* the bare minimum a man needs for continued life is something he has no right at all to be given? If I am sick unto death, and the only thing that will save my life is the touch of Henry Fonda's cool hand on my fevered brow, then all the same, I have no right

to be given the touch of Henry Fonda's cool hand on my fevered brow. It would be frightfully nice of him to fly in from the West Coast to provide it. It would be less nice, though no doubt well meant, if my friends flew out to the West Coast and carried Henry Fonda back with them. But I have no right at all against anybody that he should do this for me. Or again, to return to the story I told earlier, the fact that for continued life that violinist needs the continued use of your kidneys does not establish that he has a right to be given the continued use of your kidneys. He certainly has no right against you that *you* should give him continued use of your kidneys. For nobody has any right to use your kidneys unless you give him such a right; and nobody has the right against you that you shall give him this right — if you do allow him to go on using your kidneys, this is a kindness on your part, and not something he can claim from you as his due. Nor has he any right against anybody else that *they* should give him continued use of your kidneys. Certainly he had no right against the Society of Music Lovers that they should plug him into you in the first place. And if you now start to unplug yourself, having learned that you will otherwise have to spend nine years in bed with him, there is nobody in the world who must try to prevent you, in order to see to it that he is given something he has a right to be given.

Some people are rather stricter about the right to life. In their view, it does not include the right to be given anything, but amounts to, and only to, the right not to be killed by anybody. But here a related difficulty arises. If everybody is to refrain from killing that violinist, then everybody must refrain from doing a great many different sorts of things. Everybody must refrain from slitting his throat, everybody must refrain from shooting him — and everybody must refrain from unplugging you from him. But does he have a right against everybody that they shall refrain from unplugging you from him? To refrain from doing this is to allow him to continue to use your kidneys. It could be argued that he has a right against us that *we* should allow him to continue to use your kidneys. That is, while he had no right against us that we should give him the use of your kidneys, it might be argued that he anyway has a right against us that we shall not now intervene and deprive him of the use of your kidneys. I shall come back to third-party interventions later. But certainly the violinist has no right against you that *you* shall allow him to continue to use your kidneys. As I said, if you do allow him to use them, it is a kindness on your part, and not something you owe him.

The difficulty I point to here is not peculiar to the right to life. It reappears in connection with all the other natural rights; and it is something which an adequate account of rights must deal with. For present purposes it is enough just to draw attention to it. But I would stress that I am not arguing that people do not have a right to life – quite to the contrary, it seems to me that the primary control we must place on the acceptability of an account of rights is that it should turn out in that account to be a truth that all persons have a right to life. I am arguing only that having a right to life does not guarantee having either a right to be given the use of or a right to be allowed continued use of another person's body – even if one needs it for life itself. So the right to life will not serve the opponents of abortion in the very simple and clear way in which they seem to have thought it would.

There is another way to bring out the difficulty. In the most ordinary sort of case, to deprive someone of what he has a right to is to treat him unjustly. Suppose a boy and his small brother are jointly given a box of chocolates for Christmas. If the older boy takes the box and refuses to give his brother any of the chocolates, he is unjust to him, for the brother has been given a right to half of them. But suppose that, having learned that otherwise it means nine years in bed with that violinist, you unplug yourself from him. You surely are not being unjust to him, for you gave him no right to use your kidneys, and no one else can have given him any such right. But we have to notice that in unplugging yourself, you are killing him; and violinists, like everybody else, have a right to life, and thus in the view we were considering just now, the right not to be killed. So here you do what he supposedly has a right you shall not do, but you do not act unjustly to him in doing it.

The emendation which may be made at this point is this: the right to life consists not in the right not to be killed, but rather in the right not to be killed unjustly. This runs a risk of circularity, but never mind: it would enable us to square the fact that the violinist has a right to life with the fact that you do not act unjustly toward him in unplugging yourself, thereby killing him. For if you do not kill him unjustly, you do not violate his right to life, and so it is no wonder you do him no injustice.

But if this emendation is accepted, the gap in the argument against abortion stares us plainly in the face: it is by no means enough to show that the fetus is a person, and to remind us that all persons have a right to life – we need to be shown also that killing the fetus violates its right to life, i.e., that abortion is unjust killing. And is it?

I suppose we may take it as a datum that in a case of pregnancy due to rape the mother has not given the unborn person a right to the use of her body for food and shelter. Indeed, in what pregnancy could it be supposed that the mother has given the unborn person such a right? It is not as if there were unborn persons drifting about the world, to whom a woman who wants a child says "I invite you in."

But it might be argued that there are other ways one can have acquired a right to the use of another person's body than by having been invited to use it by that person. Suppose a woman voluntarily indulges in intercourse, knowing of the chance it will issue in pregnancy, and then she does become pregnant; is she not in part responsible for the presence, in fact the very existence, of the unborn person inside her? No doubt she did not invite it in. But doesn't her partial responsibility for its being there itself give it a right to the use of her body?[3] If so, then her aborting it would be more like the boy's taking away the chocolates, and less like your unplugging yourself from the violinist – doing so would be depriving it of what it does have a right to, and thus would be doing it an injustice.

And then, too, it might be asked whether or not she can kill it even to save her own life: If she voluntarily called it into existence, how can she now kill it, even in self-defense?

The first thing to be said about this is that it is something new. Opponents of abortion have been so concerned to make out the independence of the fetus, in order to establish that it has a right to life, just as its mother does, that they have tended to overlook the possible support they might gain from making out that the fetus is *dependent* on the mother, in order to establish that she has a special kind of responsibility for it, a responsibility that gives it rights against her which are not possessed by any independent person – such as an ailing violinist who is a stranger to her.

On the other hand, this argument would give the unborn person a right to its mother's body only if her pregnancy resulted from a voluntary act, undertaken in full knowledge of the chance a pregnancy might result from it. It would leave out entirely the unborn person whose existence is due to rape. Pending the availability of some further argument, then, we would be left with the conclusion that unborn persons whose existence is due to rape have no right to the use of their mothers' bodies, and thus that aborting them is not depriving them of anything they have a right to and hence is not unjust killing.

And we should also notice that it is not at all plain that this argument really does go even as far as it purports to. For there are cases and cases, and the details make a difference. If the room is stuffy, and I therefore open a window to air it, and a burglar climbs in, it would be absurd to say, "Ah, now he can stay, she's given him a right to the use of her house – for she is partially responsible for his presence there, having voluntarily done what enabled him to get in, in full knowledge that there are such things as burglars, and that burglars burgle." It would be still more absurd to say this if I had had bars installed outside my windows, precisely to prevent burglars from getting in, and a burglar got in only because of a defect in the bars. It remains equally absurd if we imagine it is not a burglar who climbs in, but an innocent person who blunders or falls in. Again, suppose it were like this: people-seeds drift about in the air like pollen, and if you open your windows, one may drift in and take root in your carpets or upholstery. You don't want children, so you fix up your windows with fine mesh screens, the very best you can buy. As can happen, however, and on very, very rare occasions does happen, one of the screens is defective; and a seed drifts in and takes root. Does the person-plant who now develops have a right to the use of your house? Surely not – despite the fact that you voluntarily opened your windows, you knowingly kept carpets and upholstered furniture, and you knew that screens were sometimes defective. Someone may argue that you are responsible for its rooting, that it does have a right to your house, because after all you *could* have lived out your life with bare floors and furniture, or with sealed windows and doors. But this won't do – for by the same token anyone can avoid a pregnancy due to rape by having a hysterectomy, or anyway by never leaving home without a (reliable!) army.

It seems to me that the argument we are looking at can establish at most that there are *some* cases in which the unborn person has a right to the use of its mother's body, and therefore *some* cases in which abortion is unjust killing. There is room for much discussion and argument as to precisely which, if any. But I think we should side-step this issue and leave it open, for at any rate the argument certainly does not establish that all abortion is unjust killing.

There is room for yet another argument here, however. We surely must all grant that there may be cases in which it would be morally indecent to detach a person from your body at the cost of his life. Suppose you learn that what the violinist needs is not nine years of your life, but only one hour: all you need do to save his life is to spend one hour in that bed with him. Suppose also that letting him use your kidneys for that one hour would not affect your health in the slightest. Admittedly you were kidnapped. Admittedly you did not give anyone permission to plug him into you. Nevertheless it seems to me plain you *ought* to allow him to use your kidneys for that hour – it would be indecent to refuse.

Again, suppose pregnancy lasted only an hour, and constituted no threat to life or health. And suppose that a woman becomes pregnant as a result of rape. Admittedly she did not voluntarily do anything to bring about the existence of a child. Admittedly she did nothing at all which would give the unborn person a right to the use of her body. All the same it might well be said, as in the newly emended violinist story, that she *ought* to allow it to remain for that hour – that it would be indecent in her to refuse....

A further objection to so using the term "right" that from the fact that A ought to do a thing for B, it follows that B has a right against A that A do it for him, is that it is going to make the question of whether or not a man has a right to a thing turn on how easy it is to provide him with it; and this seems not merely unfortunate, but morally unacceptable. Take the case of Henry Fonda again. I said earlier that I had no right to the touch of his cool hand on my fevered brow, even though I needed it to save my life. I said it would be frightfully nice of him to fly in from the West Coast to provide me with it, but that I had no right against him that he should do so. But suppose he isn't on the West Coast. Suppose he has only to walk across the room, place a hand briefly on my brow – and lo, my life is saved. Then surely he ought to do it, it would be indecent to refuse. Is it to be said "Ah, well, it follows that in this case she has a right to the touch of his hand on her brow, and so it would be an injustice in him to refuse"? So that I have a right to it when it is easy for him to provide it, though no right when it's hard? It's rather a shocking idea that anyone's rights should fade away and disappear as it gets harder and harder to accord them to him.

So my own view is that even though you ought to let the violinist use your kidneys for the one hour he needs, we should not conclude that he has a right to do so – we should say that if you refuse, you are, like the boy who owns all the chocolates and will give none away, self-centered and callous, indecent in fact, but not unjust. And similarly, that even supposing a case in which a woman pregnant due to rape ought to allow the unborn person to use her body for the hour he needs, we should not conclude that he has a right to do so; we should conclude that she is self-centered, callous, indecent, but not unjust, if she refuses. The complaints are no less grave; they are just different. However, there is no need to insist on this point. If anyone does wish to deduce "he has a right" from "you ought," then all the same he must surely grant that there are cases in which it is not morally required of you that you allow that violinist to use your kidneys, and in which he does not have a right to use them, and in which you do not do him an injustice if you refuse. And so also for mother and unborn child. Except in such cases as the unborn person has a right to demand it – and we were leaving open the possibility that there may be such cases – nobody is morally *required* to make large sacrifices, of health, of all other interests and concerns, of all other duties and commitments, for nine years, or even for nine months, in order to keep another person alive.

We have in fact to distinguish between two kinds of Samaritan: the Good Samaritan and what we might call the Minimally Decent Samaritan. The story of the Good Samaritan, you will remember, goes like this:

> A certain man went down from Jerusalem to Jericho, and fell among thieves, which stripped him of his raiment, and wounded him, and departed, leaving him half dead.
>
> And by chance there came down a certain priest that way; and when he saw him, he passed by on the other side.
>
> And likewise a Levite, when he was at the place, came and looked on him, and passed by on the other side.
>
> But a certain Samaritan, as he journeyed, came where he was; and when he saw him he had compassion on him.
>
> And went to him, and bound up his wounds, pouring in oil and wine, and set him on his own beast, and brought him to an inn, and took care of him.
>
> And on the morrow, when he departed, he took out two pence, and gave them to the host, and said unto him, "Take care of him; and whatsoever thou spendest more, when I come again, I will repay thee."
>
> (Luke 10:30–35)

The Good Samaritan went out of his way, at some cost to himself, to help one in need of it. We are not told what the options were, that is, whether or not the priest and the Levite could have helped by doing less than the Good Samaritan did, but assuming they could have, then the fact they did nothing at all shows they were not even Minimally Decent Samaritans, not because they were not Samaritans, but because they were not even minimally decent.

These things are a matter of degree, of course, but there is a difference, and it comes out perhaps most clearly in the story of Kitty Genovese, who, as you will remember, was murdered while thirty-eight people watched or listened, and did nothing at all to help her.[4] A Good Samaritan would have rushed out to give direct assistance against the murderer. Or perhaps we had better allow that it would have been a Splendid Samaritan who did this, on the ground that it would have involved a risk of death for himself. But the thirty-eight not only did not do this, they did not even trouble to pick up a phone to call the police. Minimally Decent Samaritanism would call for doing at least that, and their not having done it was monstrous.

After telling the story of the Good Samaritan, Jesus said "Go, and do thou likewise." Perhaps he meant that we are morally required to act as the Good Samaritan did. Perhaps he was urging people to do more than is morally required of them. At all events it seems plain that it was not morally required of any of the thirty-eight that he rush out to give direct assistance at the risk of his own life, and that it is not morally required of anyone that he give long stretches of his life – nine years or nine months – to sustaining the life of a person who has no special right (we were leaving open the possibility of this) to demand it.

Indeed, with one rather striking class of exceptions, no one in any country in the world is *legally* required to do anywhere near as much as this for anyone else. The class of exceptions is obvious. My main concern here is not the state of the law in respect to abortion, but it is worth drawing attention to the fact that in no state in this country is any man compelled by law to be even a Minimally Decent Samaritan to any person; there is no law under which charges could be brought against the thirty-eight who stood by while Kitty Genovese died. By contrast, in most states in this country women are compelled by law to be not merely Minimally Decent Samaritans, but Good Samaritans to unborn persons inside them. This doesn't by itself settle anything one way or the other, because it may well be argued that there should be laws in this country – as there are in many European countries – compelling at least Minimally Decent Samaritanism.[5] But it does show that there is a gross injustice in the existing state of the law. And it shows also that the groups currently working against liberalization of abortion laws, in fact working toward having it declared unconstitutional for a state to permit abortion, had better start working for the adoption of Good Samaritan laws generally, or earn the charge that they are acting in bad faith.

I should think, myself, that Minimally Decent Samaritan laws would be one thing, Good Samaritan laws quite another, and in fact highly improper. But we are not here concerned with the law. What we should ask is not whether anybody should be compelled by law to be a Good Samaritan, but whether we must accede to a situation in which somebody is being compelled – by nature, perhaps – to be a Good Samaritan. We have, in other words, to look now at third-party interventions. I have been arguing that no person is morally required to make large sacrifices to sustain the life of another who has no right to demand them, and this even where the

sacrifices do not include life itself; we are not morally required to be Good Samaritans or anyway Very Good Samaritans to one another. But what if a man cannot extricate himself from such a situation? What if he appeals to us to extricate him? It seems to me plain that there are cases in which we can, cases in which a Good Samaritan would extricate him. There you are, you were kidnapped, and nine years in bed with that violinist lie ahead of you. You have your own life to lead. You are sorry, but you simply cannot see giving up so much of your life to the sustaining of his. You cannot extricate yourself, and ask us to do so. I should have thought that in light of his having no right to the use of your body it was obvious that we do not have to accede to your being forced to give up so much. We can do what you ask. There is no injustice to the violinist in our doing so.

Following the lead of the opponents of abortion, I have throughout been speaking of the fetus merely as a person, and what I have been asking is whether or not the argument we began with, which proceeds only from the fetus' being a person, really does establish its conclusion. I have argued that it does not.

But of course there are arguments and arguments, and it may be said that I have simply fastened on the wrong one. It may be said that what is important is not merely the fact that the fetus is a person, but that it is a person for whom the woman has a special kind of responsibility issuing from the fact that she is its mother. And it might be argued that all my analogies are therefore irrelevant – for you do not have that special kind of responsibility for that violinist, Henry Fonda does not have that special kind of responsibility for me. And our attention might be drawn to the fact that men and women both *are* compelled by law to provide support for their children.

I have in effect dealt (briefly) with this argument in section 4 above; but a (still briefer)

389

recapitulation now may be in order. Surely we do not have any such "special responsibility" for a person unless we have assumed it, explicitly or implicitly. If a set of parents do not try to prevent pregnancy, do not obtain an abortion, and then at the time of birth of the child do not put it out for adoption, but rather take it home with them, then they have assumed responsibility for it, they have given it rights, and they cannot *now* withdraw support from it at the cost of its life because they now find it difficult to go on providing for it. But if they have taken all reasonable precautions against having a child, they do not simply by virtue of their biological relationship to the child who comes into existence have a special responsibility for it. They may wish to assume responsibility for it, or they may not wish to. And I am suggesting that if assuming responsibility for it would require large sacrifices, then they may refuse. A Good Samaritan would not refuse – or anyway, a Splendid Samaritan, if the sacrifices that had to be made were enormous. But then so would a Good Samaritan assume responsibility for that violinist; so would Henry Fonda, if he is a Good Samaritan, fly in from the West Coast and assume responsibility for me.

My argument will be found unsatisfactory on two counts by many of those who want to regard abortion as morally permissible. First, while I do argue that abortion is not impermissible, I do not argue that it is always permissible. There may well be cases in which carrying the child to term requires only Minimally Decent Samaritanism of the mother, and this is a standard we must not fall below. I am inclined to think it a merit of my account precisely that it does *not* give a general yes or a general no. It allows for and supports our sense that, for example, a sick and desperately frightened fourteen-year-old schoolgirl, pregnant due to rape, may *of course* choose abortion, and that any law which rules this out is an insane law. And it also allows for and supports our sense that in other cases resort to abortion is even positively indecent. It would be indecent in the woman to request an abortion, and indecent in a doctor to perform it, if she is in her seventh month, and wants the abortion just to avoid the nuisance of postponing a trip abroad. The very fact that the arguments I have been drawing attention to treat all cases of abortion, or even all cases of abortion in which the mother's life is not at stake, as morally on a par ought to have made them suspect at the outset.

Secondly, while I am arguing for the permissibility of abortion in some cases, I am not arguing for the right to secure the death of the unborn child. It is easy to confuse these two things in that up to a certain point in the life of the fetus it is not able to survive outside the mother's body; hence removing it from her body guarantees its death. But they are importantly different. I have argued that you are not morally required to spend nine months in bed, sustaining the life of that violinist; but to say this is by no means to say that if, when you unplug yourself, there is a miracle and he survives, you then have a right to turn round and slit his throat. You may detach yourself even if this costs him his life; you have no right to be guaranteed his death, by some other means, if unplugging yourself does not kill him. There are some people who will feel dissatisfied by this feature of my argument. A woman may be utterly devastated by the thought of a child, a bit of herself, put out for adoption and never seen or heard of again. She may therefore want not merely that the child be detached from her, but more, that it die. Some opponents of abortion are inclined to regard this as beneath contempt – thereby showing insensitivity to what is surely a powerful source of despair. All the same, I agree that the desire for the child's death is not one which anybody may gratify, should it turn out to be possible to detach the child alive.

At this place, however, it should be remembered that we have only been pretending throughout that the fetus is a human being from the moment of conception. A very early abortion is surely not the killing of a person, and so is not dealt with by anything I have said here.

## Study Questions

1. What is the function of the violinist example? How is it supposed to be analogous with typical cases of pregnancy? Is the analogy a strong or weak one?

2. Thomson's main point is that no one's right to life (including a fetus's) entails that someone else has a moral obligation to use her body to sustain that life. Thomson is, in general, right about this. For example, no one can be compelled to donate blood or bone marrow, even if someone's else's life were dependent on it. In what ways is pregnancy similar to these cases? In what ways is it different? Why should a fetus be given a right to use someone else's body for sustenance if no other person has such a right?

3. Many people argue that if a woman concedes to voluntary sexual intercourse and becomes pregnant, she should take responsibility for the fetus's existence and allow it continued gestation. The underlying assumption is the following: If I do action x knowing that consequence y may ensue, I am morally responsible for y and should accept responsibility for y. In some cases this principle is clearly true; for example, if I get into a car under the influence of alcohol knowing I may crash and hurt someone, I am morally responsible for the consequences if I do hit someone. Yet in some cases this principle is clearly false: if I walk down the street of a crime-infested neighborhood knowing I may be raped, this does not mean that I should accept responsibility for being raped. In one case carelessness or negligence makes me responsible for a consequence, but not in the other case. Thomson clearly thinks unwanted pregnancy is an example of the latter, as is evident by her burglar and people-seeds example. Is she right? In which category of responsibility should voluntary sexual intercourse lie?

4. Thomson argues that, although there is no such thing as an unjust abortion, there is such a thing as an "indecent" abortion. What do you think Thomson means by an "indecent" abortion? Do you agree with this distinction? What do you think constitutes an "indecent" abortion? In contrast, what would constitute a "decent" one?

## Notes

1 I am very much indebted to James Thomson for discussion, criticism, and many helpful suggestions.
2 Daniel Callahan, *Abortion: Law, Choice and Morality* (New York, 1970), p. 373. This book gives a fascinating survey of the available information on abortion. The Jewish tradition is surveyed in David M. Feldman, *Birth Control in Jewish Law* (New York, 1968), Part 5, the Catholic

tradition in John T. Noonan Jr., "An Almost Absolute Value in History," in *The Morality of Abortion*, ed. John T. Noonan Jr. (Cambridge, MA, 1970).

3 The need for a discussion of this argument was brought home to me by members of the Society for Ethical and Legal Philosophy, to whom this paper was originally presented.

4 Kitty Genovese was stabbed to death outside her New York City apartment in 1964. There is some controversy, however, about the number of bystanders who purportedly did nothing while Genovese was being murdered.

5 For a discussion of the difficulties involved, and a survey of the European experience with such laws, see *The Good Samaritan and the Law*, ed. James M. Ratcliffe (New York, 1966).

# 3.   Frances Kissling, "Is There Life after *Roe*? How to Think about the Fetus"

IN THIS ESSAY, FRANCES Kissling (b. 1943), the former president of Catholics for a Free Choice and an active member of the feminist pro-choice community, calls out fellow pro-choice advocates for what appears to be a callous dismissal of the value of fetal life. In this article from a 2004 edition of the Catholic news journal *Conscience*, Kissling argues that the pro-choice community is gradually losing the public-relations battle because of "the lack of adequate and clear expressions of respect for fetal life." Individuals who insist that fetuses be acknowledged as entities of value are not "enemies of choice," she argues, but, rather, they wish to avoid "a coarsening of humanity that can result from the taking of life." While it may be easier to hold to a pro-choice stance if the fetus is dismissed as a nonperson, regarding the fetus as an entity worthy of respect affixes a layer of depth and complexity to the pro-choice side that is commensurate with how most people (including women who procure abortions) regard abortion.

---

[…]

### Rights and Values

I believe women have a basic human right to decide what to do about a pregnancy. Other well-established human rights concepts bolster this argument including bodily integrity, the right to health, the right to practice one's religion (or not) and the right to be free from religious laws in modern democratic societies. Despite the assertions of some very intelligent prolifers[1] that the abortion issue is a question of the human rights of the fetus, the human rights community is moving steadily towards recognizing a woman's right to choose and there is no countervailing view in this community that even considers the question of whether or not fetuses are rights-bearing entities.

But the abortion issue is not one in which only rights are at stake. There are at least three central values that need to be part of the public conversation about abortion and, as appropriate, influence behavior, if not law. They are:

i)   The human right of women to decide whether or not to continue a pregnancy.

ii)  A respect for human life that takes the form of what Daniel Callahan called more than 30 years ago a moral presumption in favor of life.

iii) A commitment to ensure that provisions which permit the taking of life (whether it be fetal, animal or plant) not coarsen the overall fabric of society and our attitudes toward each other as well as toward developing human life.

First, and I would say primary, is our obligation to respect in law and social thought the right of women to bodily autonomy. Generally speaking, nobody should be forced to carry a pregnancy to term without their consent. I am revolted by the thought that a law banning most or all abortions would, if it were to be more than a rhetorical exercise, require an enforcement mechanism that actively forces women to continue pregnancies that they believe to be antithetical to their needs or identities. But the right to choose abortion is not absolute, and in practice and law even those of us most ardently prochoice do not demand absolutism....

## Valuing Fetal Life

This brings us to the second value of a good society: respect for life, including fetal life. Why should we allow this value to be owned by those opposed to abortion? Are we not capable of walking and chewing gum at the same time; of valuing life and respecting women's rights? Have we not ceded too much territory to antiabortionists by not articulating the value of fetal life? In an important op-ed in the *New York Times*, author William Saletan claimed that "supporters of abortion rights ... still don't know how to articulate the value of unborn human life." Saletan makes a good point, but he does not pursue it and offers no suggestions for how we could articulate this value.

Such an effort will take a lot of work and involve exposing deep differences among supporters of choice regarding our views on the inherent value of fetal life on its own terms and in relation to women's rights. An interesting thought exercise might help to clarify what prochoice (and antiabortion) leaders believe about fetal value. Imagine a world in which it was possible to remove fetuses prior to viability from women's bodies and allow them to develop in a nonuterine environment. Perhaps they could be implanted in men or

other women who want them; perhaps they could develop in a specially equipped nursery? In this world, medicine is so far advanced that this could be accomplished painlessly and without risking the health of either the woman or the fetus. Of course, this is at present largely a fantasy and by that time we would have found the ideal, risk-free, failure-free contraceptive; but let's pretend.

What are the first five concerns and reactions that come to your mind? Is one of them the fact that this would mean fetuses need not die? My own experience in presenting this option to both advocates and opponents of abortion is that the fetus's life is rarely a consideration. Among the most interesting reactions of those who are prochoice is a concern that some women might find the continued existence of the fetus painful for them or that women have a right to ensure that their genetic material does not enter the world. Abortion in this sense becomes the guarantee of a dead fetus, if desired, rather than the removal of the fetus from an unwilling host, the woman. To even offer women such an option is, some think, cruel. For some the right to choose abortion seems to include the right to be protected from thinking about the fetus and from any pain that might result from others talking about the fetus in value-laden terms. In this construct, it is hard to identify any value fetal life might have.

This level of sensitivity to protecting women from their feelings takes other forms. For example, some prochoice advocates have objected to public discussion of abortion that includes concern for the number of abortions that occur in the US or has as its goal reducing the number of abortions. Some bristled at President [Bill] Clinton's formula that abortion should be "safe, legal and rare." If abortion is justifiable why should it be rare? Even the suggestion that abortion is a moral matter as well as a legal one has caused concern that such a statement might make women feel guilty. Words like "baby" are avoided, not just because they are inaccurate, but because they are loaded.

In a society where women have long been victims of moral discourse, these concerns are somewhat understandable, but they do not contribute much towards convincing people that when prochoice people say they value fetal life it is more than lip service.

The reaction of antiabortionists to the idea that a fetus could be removed from the body of an unwilling woman is as troubling. Again, one rarely hears cries of joy that fetal lives would be saved. The focus also is on the woman. But here, the view that women are, by their nature, made for childbearing dominates. Women have an obligation to continue pregnancies, to suffer the consequences of their sexuality. It is unnatural to even think that fetuses could become healthy and happy people if they did not spend nine months in the womb of a woman. One is led to believe that, for those opposed to abortion, it is not saving fetuses that matters but preserving a social construct in which women breed.

## Thinking about Messages

Thought exercises, however, have their limits and there is much that could be done to balance women's rights with an expression of fetal value without resorting to science fiction. A first step might be a conversation among prochoice leaders that explored what we think about the value of fetal life. You cannot talk cogently about things you have not thought about or discussed. And not thinking leads to mistakes. At times there is a kind of prochoice triumphalism in operation. Abortion is a serious matter; it is a woman's right and no woman needs to apologize for making this decision. On the other hand, no woman needs to brag about her choice and the

decision of one prochoice organization to sell T-shirts announcing, "I had an abortion" was in poor taste and diminished the seriousness of the act of abortion.

A second step might include care not to confuse legal arguments with moral messages. Too often the legal arguments that win in a court of law are the very arguments that lose in the court of public opinion. Antiabortion legislators have played on this tendency by introducing legislation that appears unrelated to abortion, but "protects" the fetus. The most emotionally charged legislation was the Unborn Victims of Violence Act which introduced an extra penalty for anyone convicted of harming a fetus during the commission of certain federal crimes (separate from penalties related to the injury or death of the pregnant woman). It gave separate legal status to a fertilized egg, embryo or fetus, even if the woman did not know she was pregnant. Crafted in the wake of the death of Laci and Conner Peterson,[2] the legislation captured people's sympathy. Prochoice responses that focused on the fact that the legislation was not needed or that argued that it was a back door attempt to eviscerate the right to abortion made us seem heartless. As difficult as it may be, this may have been one piece of legislation we could have tolerated. In the war of ideas, not every hill is worth climbing.

Up to now, the conventional wisdom in the prochoice movement has been that talking about fetal life is counterproductive. In the polarized climate created by absolutists opposed to legal abortion, a siege mentality has developed. Prochoice advocates fear that any discussion of fetal value will strengthen the claim that if the fetus has value, abortion must be prohibited in all or most circumstances.

An interesting example of the way in which some opponents of legal abortion are taking a different approach (which may make prochoice people more comfortable talking about this question) is the current debate in Great Britain about reducing the time limit for abortion from 24 weeks to 20. The impetus for this comes from a minority view on the prochoice side, including Sir David Steel who introduced prochoice legislation in the parliament in 1966. Some in the prolife movement think that the best thing they can do is to sit it out, suggesting that the bishops should not intervene and the more absolutist antiabortion groups should permit this conversation to go on among prochoice people. Perhaps, they speculate, if not threatened by the notion that any restrictive change in abortion laws is part of an antichoice campaign to make all abortions illegal, some moderate change might happen. In citing this example, I am not suggesting that it would be a good thing to reduce the time limit on abortions in Britain, nor do I want to overstate the extent of a prochoice discussion on the matter. Within the organized British prochoice movement there is little if any support for such a move and much distress that some who are prochoice would even consider it. But it does represent an attempt by some who are prochoice to address new information about potential fetal capacity that does not automatically reject thinking about these issues as "antiabortion propaganda."

In addition to the fear that acknowledging fetal life as valuable would lead to making abortion illegal is the reality that the ethical discussion about when the fetus becomes a person (whether theological, legal, sociological or medical) seems abstract to most people. In theology, the question has traditionally focused on when is it most likely that God gives the developing fetus a soul, a discourse pretty much abandoned by both traditional and innovative theologians; in sociology, most often the capacity for relationships is central – when can one say a meaningful relationship exists between the fetus and society; in medicine,

the weight is on viability and on the physical and mental capacity of the fetus – when could it survive outside the womb, when is there higher brain development. Fascinating speculation, but similar to arguments over the number of angels that could dance on a pinhead. The precise moment when the fetus becomes a person is less important than a simple acknowledgement that whatever category of human life the fetus is, it nonetheless has value, it is not nothing.

In this context the various ad hoc remarks of Senator John Kerry are interesting, if flawed. Kerry has said that he "opposes abortion, personally. I don't like abortion. I believe life does begin at conception." When later pressed on this he said, "Within weeks, you look and see the development of it, but that's not a person yet, and it's certainly not what somebody, in my judgment, ought to have the government of the United States intervening in." Kerry's statements reflect what most people think. Personhood is a code word for extent of value, not a fine scientific fact. What those who favor abortion rights are saying is that whatever value fetal life has – from none to much – it is not the moral equivalent of those of us who have been born. In fact, prochoicers argue, there are a number of values greater than the fetus that justify answering the "Who Decides?" question strongly in favor of the woman.

However, once one moves away from the narrow question of when the fetus becomes a person to the more meaningful question of what value does the fetus have and when that value emerges, it becomes difficult to develop an ethical formula for assigning value and asserting the obligations that flow from that value. There is a wide range of respectable opinion on these questions and few hard and fast conclusions.

### An Urgent Task

But the need to offer some answers from a prochoice perspective is both morally and politically urgent. Those opposed to abortion have moved aggressively for laws that depend on the recognition of the fetus as a person, as a rights-bearing entity. At the same time, there are scientific advances that affect the way we think about the fetus and indeed make it more present among us. For some, these realities lead to a greater connection to fetal life; perhaps not as a person, but as part of the continuum of what we are, of humanity. Examples include 3-D and 4-D pictures of fetuses in utero that appear to be awake, asleep, walking, yawning – engaging in activities that are related to human identity – and the few, very few, very premature babies who struggle and appear to have a great determination to live. Even the reality that pre-embryos used to create stem cells that may ultimately save the lives of thousands makes the embryo more human and more valuable – it can give as well as receive, even at a stage of development that bears little resemblance to even fetal life. Of course, there is an element of my ode to the embryo that is poetic and romantic, even anthropomorphic, as the embryo does not consciously "give"; it is instead useful, but nonetheless that usefulness is a positive quality that should not be feared, but appreciated.

The fetus is indeed a wondrous part of our humanity; we are drawn to it as part of the ongoing mystery of who we are. Do we not question our own value and why we are here, what we contribute and what we take from the world? There is of course a danger in over-romanticizing fetal life or in defining its value primarily in relation to ourselves. For an infertile couple who deeply want a child, someone else's fetus is very precious and potentially their child. For a woman who has been raped, that fetus may well be seen as a monster. The relation of value to wantedness is complex and at times troubling. Antiabortionists have countered the "Every child a wanted child" message by pointing out that if wantedness is what gives us value and a right to life, then who among the unwanted will be the next to be declared disposable – the sick, the disabled, the poor or the unemployed?

### Too Hard?

Such concerns should not be quickly dismissed. I am deeply struck by the number of thoughtful, progressive people who have been turned off to the prochoice movement by the lack of adequate and clear expressions of respect for fetal life, people who are themselves grappling with the conflict between upholding women's rights and the right to conscience and respecting the value of nascent human life. A recent article by John Garvey in *Commonweal* put it well. Struggling with his inability to cast a vote for George [W.] Bush for all the usual liberal reasons and his distaste for what he saw as Kerry's – and by extension the prochoice movement's – inability to acknowledge one iota of value in fetal life, he said: "Our attitude toward life at this stage has much to say about what we believe about humanity as a whole: this is where we all come from, and at no point does it mean nothing." Garvey suggests that perhaps there has been a "hardening of the heart" resulting from the prochoice position.

The John Garveys of the world have a point. They are not the enemies of choice. They occupy the middle ground that we seek to convince that being prochoice is morally sound and they sometimes express the wisdom that flows from those who can see different sides in a moral dilemma.

Garvey's comments are suggestive of the last of the three values I believe must be included in an ethical prochoice perspective:

avoiding a coarsening of humanity that can result from the taking of life. Prochoice advocates may bristle at such a claim; we see ourselves as deeply compassionate and good people who are working hard to alleviate women's pain and to create a world in which children are wanted and loved. How could anyone suggest that our sensibilities could become coarsened by exposure to the taking of fetal life that is currently a necessary component of abortion?

And, while little research has been done on this question, it and history point to no coarsening of respect for persons as a result of legal abortion. Those countries with long-standing liberal abortion laws have been among the most supportive of life. Japan, for example, widely uses abortion as a method of birth control. Yet the respect the Japanese show for the elderly is great and their love of children renowned. While abortion is common in Japan, there are rituals of respect for both aborted and miscarried fetuses that express value. The Scandinavian countries have liberal abortion laws and some of the most people-friendly social policies in the world. There is more evidence that denying women the right to choose abortion leads to a coarsening of attitudes toward children than permitting it does. In [former leader Nicolae] Ceausescu's Romania, abortion was strictly forbidden and women's pregnancies monitored closely to prevent abortion. The resulting massive abandonment of children is well known. Likewise, studies of what happens to children born after their mothers were denied abortion in the former Czechoslovakia and several Scandinavian countries show that these children have a significantly higher rate of crime, mental illness and problems in school.[3]

For me, a more troubling question is whether or not regular exposure to the taking of life in abortion or the defense of a right to choose abortion would, if not addressed, lead to a coarsening of attitude toward fetal life. The inability of prochoice leaders to give any specific examples of ways in which respect for fetal life can be demonstrated or to express any doubt about any aspect of abortion suggests that such a hardening of the heart is possible. This concern or possibility does not lead me to say that abortion should become illegal, more restricted, more stigmatized. It does lead me to believe that we would do well as prochoice people to present abortion as a complex issue that involves loss – and to be saddened by that loss at the same time as we affirm and support women's decisions to end pregnancies. Is there not a way to simply say, "Yes, it is sad, unfortunate, tragic (or whatever word you are comfortable with) that this life could not come to fruition. It is sad that we live in a world where there is so little social and economic support for families that many women have no choice but to end pregnancies. It is sad that so many women do not have access to contraception. It is sad that this fetus was not healthy enough to survive and it was good that this woman had the right to make this choice for herself and her family, to avoid suffering, and to act on her values and her sense of what her life should be." ...

**Honoring Law and Morality**

It has long been a truism of the abortion debate that those who are prochoice have rights and those who are against legal abortion have morality; that those who support abortion rights concentrate on women and those opposed focus on the fetus. After 30 years of legal abortion and a debate that shows no signs of ending and has no clear winner – is it not time to try and combine rights and morality, to consider both women and developing human life? Ultimately, abortion is not a political question and politics will not end the enormous conflict over abortion. Abortion is a profoundly moral question and any movement that fails to grapple with and respect all the values at stake in crafting a social policy about abortion will be inadequate in its effort to win the support of the majority of Americans.

## Study Questions

1. In what ways is Kissling's piece a departure from traditional pro-choice arguments? Do you think it is consistent to hold simultaneously that there should be abortion rights, but also that a fetus ought to be respected given its value as nascent human life?

2. According to Kissling, it seems as if there has been a "hardening of the heart" when it comes to pro-choice advocates' general reluctance to admit that fetal life has value. Do you agree with her? If so, from where does this reluctance originate? If not, why do you think Kissling has interpreted the pro-choice movement in this way?

3. How can a pro-choice advocate incorporate respect for fetal life into his/her pro-choice philosophy? What would this respect look like, and how can one maintain this respect in the face of also maintaining that women have a right to decide whether to terminate a pregnancy?

4. Kissling argues that pro-choice advocates "would do well ... to present abortion as a complex issue that involves loss – and to be saddened by that loss at the same time as we affirm and support women's decisions to end pregnancies." How do you feel about this suggestion? If you are sympathetic to the pro-choice perspective, do you believe Kissling is right that such a view should be adopted? If you are sympathetic to the pro-life perspective, how would you view such a change in pro-choice philosophy?

## Notes

1 A word about terminology. Any thoughtful article on abortion runs afoul of what to call opponents and proponents of legal abortion. Generally I try to use the more specific terms "those who support" or "those who oppose" legal abortion. Occasionally it seems fair to describe some groups and individuals as prolife, if their position is broader and includes opposition to war and capital punishment as well as supporting social and political measures that enable people to lead healthy and productive lives. At the same time, I am convinced that few opponents of legal abortion are truly motivated by a deep respect for fetal life. If they were, they would, as Randall Terry, the founder of Operation Rescue, said many years ago, "act as if abortion were murder." The example of the Catholic bishops is most illuminating. I would expect that if bishops really believed that abortion was murder, they would individually and collectively make far more sacrifices to ensure that abortions did not happen. While the bishops provide very little detailed information about their expenditures, it is clear that the amount of money spent on preventing abortions is very little. The bishops claim that abortion is the greatest moral issue of our time, that Catholics cannot vote for candidates who are prochoice and that prochoice Catholic legislators are committing a grave sin by supporting legal abortion. This is a weak rhetorical response to "murder." How can any bishop or parish priest justify spending one penny on anything discretionary rather than on helping the many

women who would continue their pregnancies if they had the resources to bear and raise a child? No dinners, no business class plane tickets, no vacations, no flowers on the altar as long as one penny is needed to prevent abortions. The same standard should be applied to the lay Catholics speaking out against abortion. Few of them are doing anything other than attacking prochoice Catholic politicians and supporting the Republican Party. Nothing short of austerity and sacrifice is called for if you believe that abortion is the greatest evil facing humanity.

2  Laci Peterson went missing in 2002 while she was eight months pregnant with her son Connor. On April 13, 2003, Laci's body was found on the shores of the San Francisco Bay; she had been decapitated and several of her limbs were missing. The body of her baby, Connor, was also found with tape wrapped around his neck and several cuts to his body. On March 16, 2005, Scott Peterson – Laci's husband and Connor's father – was convicted of first degree murder and sentenced to death.

3  See for example, Henry P. David et al., eds., *Born Unwanted: Developmental Effects of Denied Abortion* (Springer Publishing Company, 1988).

# 4. Steve Tracy, "Abortion, the Marginalized, and the Vulnerable: A Social Justice Perspective for Reducing Abortion"

IN WHAT CAN ALMOST be described as a companion piece to Frances Kissling's article (a pro-choice perspective that nevertheless claims that some pro-choice advocates turn their backs on the worth of fetal life), Steve Tracy, a pro-life theologian, argues that some pro-life advocates largely ignore the impact that poverty and lack of social support have on increasing abortion rates. Tracy argues, in this 2010 article from the journal *Cultural Encounters*, that in order to remain consistent, pro-life advocates must do more to emphasize social justice concerns in their pro-life philosophy. He stresses that both pro-life and pro-choice advocates share the common goal of wanting to reduce the prevalence of abortion and that, therefore, they could perhaps find common ground in taking an interest in the implementation of social justice factors that would help to achieve this goal.

## I. Abortion, Human Rights, and Social Justice[1]

I HAVE BEEN ACTIVE PROFESSIONALLY with the issue of abortion for many years. I became involved in the pro-life movement as a young minister and seminarian. This flowed from my conviction that all life is sacred and should be valued and protected, particularly those who are most marginalized and vulnerable. This is a historical Christian conviction, one that caused Christians over the centuries to risk their lives to protect the defenseless and weak and to fight against oppression. I was, and am, deeply concerned at the individual[2] and societal[3] harm that comes from devaluing any human life, particularly "the other" – those different from us. History is replete with tragic examples of what happens when those with greater power determine that a certain race, age, caste, religious group, or gender is of less value and hence can be marginalized, exploited, or even exterminated. I have witnessed firsthand the results of genocide, exploitation of the poor,

and horrific gender violence in East Africa, particularly in the Democratic Republic of the Congo. And often, injustice that is created by devaluing and dehumanizing one specific group in one specific manner will unleash a host of additional unanticipated injustices. Dr. Martin Luther King Jr.'s words written from jail were brilliant and prescient: "Injustice anywhere is a threat to justice everywhere."[4]

This leads us to the tragic irony of much of the abortion debate. And there is tragic irony on both sides of the issue. I will start with the pro-choice camp. At the heart of historical pro-choice ideology is the commitment to liberate and protect women in the context of male oppression. (And there is overwhelming evidence that patriarchal-inspired oppression of women has been, and continues to be, one of the greatest scourges of human history.[5]) In a world where since the dawn of history those rights have been systematically threatened and denied through male oppression and

401

patriarchal systems which devalue women, the legal right to abortion is seen as inextricably connected with women's basic human right to self-determination, particularly over their bodies, health, and sexuality.[6] Andrea Dworkin articulates this plainly:

> [T]he practical reality is that as long as sex is forced on women, women must have the right to abortion, absolutely, no matter what it means, no matter what you think it means. Abortion is ideologically central to understanding women's condition. What abortion means is the absolute right to control the reproductive functions of our bodies.[7]

Thus, abortion is seen as a social justice issue. Recent "third wave" feminism has enlarged social justice concerns to non-Caucasian women. This is reflected in the argument that outlawing or restricting abortion unjustly impacts minorities.

There are many tragic ironies in this type of pro-choice application of social justice to abortion. I'll note just a few. African-Americans have experienced as much or more egregious injustice than any ethnic group in America, with an estimated five million perishing just from the process of being shipped to the New World as slaves.[8] Yet currently more African Americans are killed by abortion than the other seven leading causes of death combined.[9] African American women have almost five times the abortion rate as compared with white women, in large part due to their lower socioeconomic status, limited resources, and marginalization.[10]

In much of the world, particularly Asia, abortion has often been utilized as an expression of patriarchal devaluing of women with astoundingly destructive consequences for females and the broader society. For instance, due to the overwhelming preference for males,

who are considered more desirable, there are an estimated one hundred million "missing females" in the world, primarily because they were aborted or killed shortly after birth, leading to great gender disparities particularly in India and China.[11] This gender birth disparity has particularly increased among the more affluent who have access to ultrasound technology and hence can choose to abort female fetuses. A recent Chinese Academy of Sciences report warned that at the current trajectory, one in five young Chinese men will be unable to find a bride in the next decade because there will be thirty to forty million more young men than women.[12] In other words, China may soon have a young male population the size of the whole young male population of America with little prospect of marriage because their female peers have been killed since they were not considered to have as much value as males. We are already seeing this gender disparity in China and elsewhere in Asia lead to increased physical violence, rape, and global sex trafficking.[13] Injustice anywhere is a threat to justice everywhere.

Let's now move to the pro-life camp. The pro-life movement has also been driven by a commitment to human rights in the face of perceived egregious injustice. In this case, the taking of an innocent human life by someone with more power who simply determined that unborn life was of lesser value. In human rights terms, we pro-lifers see abortion as the strong devaluing, marginalizing, and violating the weak, denying them their basic human rights in a most complete and final manner.

Yet tragic social justice ironies are not limited to the pro-choice movement. "Pro-life" means the valuing of all human life whatsoever, giving particular attention to the care and protection of the weak and marginalized. Yet all too often it means "valuing only the lives I deem valuable." I confess that for many years my understanding of being pro-life was minimalistic. I prided myself on placing a high value on the life of the unborn, but didn't extend the same concern and value to babies once they were born, particularly the poor and ethnic minorities. All too often those of us in the pro-life movement are, at best, known for only being anti-abortion, and, at worst, for being anti-social justice.[14] For instance, of the 113 members of Congress that the nonpartisan Children's Defense Fund identified as "the worst" for children, all are pro-life.[15]

Many pro-lifers have been scathing in their criticism of President Obama, in particular noting that one of his first executive orders overturned the "Mexico City Policy" which had barred federal funds from going to international organizations that performed or promoted abortions. I was also deeply disturbed by this action. But these same pro-life critics have been glaringly mute in acknowledging that one of President Obama's first executive actions was robustly pro-life. He ordered an immediate ban on the use of torture to interrogate enemy prisoners.[16]

This pro-life schizophrenia is particularly acute here in Arizona. I could give various examples related to our current pro-life elected officials, but I will offer just one. Joe Arpaio has been the Maricopa County Sheriff since 1992, having been elected to this office five times in a row. He has been extremely popular with pro-life social conservatives. He has won particular respect from pro-lifers for going (unsuccessfully) all the way to the Supreme Court in his efforts to restrict county prisoners from getting abortions. So how "pro-life" are adults treated in Arpaio's jails?

He boasts about being "America's toughest Sheriff" for his "tough on crime" approach, which has included chain gangs, pink underwear for male prisoners, a tent city (where prisoners are housed year-round outdoors in tents even in the summer when temperatures can reportedly reach 150 degrees in the top bunks), and for extremely aggressive pursuit of undocumented immigrants.[17] John Dickerson, one of my seminary students (who for the record is a social conservative and strongly pro-life) while a journalist for the *New York Times*, wrote a carefully researched investigative article on Sheriff Arpaio and the living conditions in the Maricopa County jails. This award-winning article was entitled "The Price of Inhumanity." Dickerson documented numerous chronic, life-threatening conditions in the county jails, resulting in Sheriff Arpaio having had fifty times as many lawsuits filed against his jail system as the New York, Los Angeles, Chicago, and Houston jail systems combined, costing taxpayers over forty-one million dollars. Dickerson cited the findings of an independent auditor who stated "[t]he current correctional healthcare program at Maricopa County is not in compliance with the basic healthcare rights provided to inmates under the US Constitution" and constitutes "cruel and unusual punishment." Dickerson concluded that "at least 11 inmate deaths have directly resulted from Arpaio's refusal to heed such warnings." The unborn have seemingly more value and deserve human rights that we persistently deny to unworthy prisoners. Injustice anywhere is a threat to justice everywhere.

But a proper and robust pro-life posture is that every human being has intrinsic value and possesses innate human rights regardless of age, gender, ethnicity, or social status. This should apply to the born as well as the unborn, citizens and immigrants, rich and poor, pro-life proponents as well as abortion providers and post-abortive women. And we should be particularly careful to protect the human rights of the vulnerable and marginalized. Thankfully, more and more American religious pro-lifers are developing this broader social justice understanding of what pro-life means.[18]

At the same time, more pro-choice advocates are recognizing that pro-life human rights concerns must not be entirely dismissed, that there are numerous negative consequences of abortion; thus, we need to reduce its frequency. Naomi Wolf, a pro-choice feminist, argues,

> I will maintain that we need to contextualize the fight to defend abortion rights within a moral framework that admits that the death of a fetus is a real death; that there are degrees of culpability, judgment, and responsibility involved in the decision to abort a pregnancy ... and that we need to be strong enough to acknowledge that this country's high rates of abortion – which ends more than a quarter of all pregnancies – can only be rightly understood as what Dr. Henry Foster was brave enough to call it: "a failure."[19]

Clearly pro-life and pro-choice adherents have very different understandings of how social justice should be applied to abortion, particularly whose rights take precedence. But the good news is that in spite of our weighty, passionate differences on the legality and morality of abortion, both sides are driven by a concern for social justice. And both sides want to see abortions reduced. And therein lies fertile ground for united efforts to reduce abortion in America.

## II. Applying Social Justice to Reduce Abortion Prevalence

I would now like briefly to suggest three broad social justice activities to reduce abortion rates. It would take extensive analysis to develop the application of these categories, so I will simply seek to provide "big picture" suggestions supported by the literature.

### A. Material (Physical) Assistance

Abortion is a serious procedure with serious consequences. I believe most women who have abortions know this all too well, but feel they lack any other viable option. As Frederica Mathewes-Green, a pro-life feminist puts it, "no one wants an abortion as she wants an ice-cream cone or a Porsche. She wants an abortion as an animal, caught in a trap, wants to gnaw off its own leg."[20] Providing material assistance in the form of financial and healthcare resources demonstrably reduces abortions. The latter also reduces unplanned pregnancies, which are highly correlated with abortions – 40 per cent of unplanned pregnancies in the United States are terminated by abortion.[21] In terms of health care, we should note that the United States has the highest abortion rates in the developed world, much higher than countries such as Japan, Germany, and Britain where there is widespread public acceptance of abortion, far fewer practicing Roman Catholics or conservative Protestants, and where abortions are provided for free. T.R. Reid has demonstrated that the critical difference is that all of these other countries provide some form of affordable universal health care.[22]

The correlation between poverty and elevated abortion rates is undisputable. The abortion rate among women living below the federal poverty level is more than four times that of women above 300 per cent of the poverty level.[23] Thus, it is not surprising that surveys of women who have had abortions reveal the vast majority did so because they felt they lacked the resources to have a child, or having a child would compromise their existing and future economic resources. Roughly three-fourths of the women felt they could not afford a baby at that time, were concerned they would not be able to finish school, or were concerned that a baby would seriously impede their employment.[24] Political scientist Joseph Wright has taken this much further and through careful socioeconomic analysis quantified the impact of economic assistance on abortion rates. He found that a two standard deviation increase in economic assistance to low-income families (roughly $100 per person) was correlated with a 20 per cent drop in abortion rates in the 1990s. Nationally, this translated into approximately 200,000 fewer abortions. Additionally, 4 per cent higher male employment was associated with a 21 per cent lower abortion rate.[25]

## B. Social Support

Material assistance and social support are closely related and equally important. They are social justice activities because they both relate to the provision of necessities that women facing crisis pregnancies often lack. Social support is a pivotal and complex need often misunderstood by those who have little experience working with women facing an unwanted pregnancy. Since pro-life adherents view the unborn as vulnerable, valuable, tiny children who should be preserved and protected, we might glibly draw the conclusion that most women who have abortions simply don't value children. The facts suggest otherwise. In reality, the factors that motivate a woman to have an abortion are frequently complex and multifaceted. Often, women with an unwanted pregnancy are conflicted because they value children, but feel they do not have the emotional or other resources to care for a child (or an additional child) properly. Sixty per cent of women who have abortions already have at least one child.[26] They may in turn feel shame over this very conflict. This helps explain why so many women apparently feel they cannot resolve the conflict created by an unwanted pregnancy through giving the child up for adoption.

For instance, in surveys of almost two hundred pregnancy center directors across the United States, out of twenty-seven possible responses, the number one reason the directors gave for their clients having abortions was "adoption appears too difficult" (emotionally or practically).[27]

Women facing an unwanted pregnancy are often conflicted over the negative impact having a child might have on their other relationships. It is particularly difficult when a pregnant woman feels that continuing her pregnancy will imperil her relationships with the most important people in her life or that those people will be unwilling or unable to assist her in the demands of parenting. Such relational conflicts are primary factors in abortions. When Mathewes-Green went around the country and conducted "post-abortion listening groups" and talked with women about the factors that led to their abortion, the number one reason cited was their relationship with the baby's father, and the second leading factor was pressure from parents.[28] In surveys of pregnancy center directors, the second most common reason cited for abortion was the husband or partner was "absent, undependable, or insufficiently supportive."[29]

These findings demonstrate the tremendous need women facing a crisis pregnancy have for strong social support. Material assistance will be of very limited long-term value, and could prove counter-productive, if it is not tied to social support. This is the area where pro-life advocates have perhaps done some of their best work by providing counseling, mentoring, life coaching, etc., for women in crisis pregnancies and for young mothers.

## C. Addressing Abuse

Pro-life discussions of abortion have frequently assessed it as a form of child abuse, but few have assessed abortion as a result of abuse.

This is most unfortunate, since research shows there is an astounding correlation between physical and sexual abuse and elevated abortion rates. For instance, in one study of clients in an abortion clinic, the majority of women (50.8 per cent) self-reported that at some time in their life they had experienced physical or sexual abuse.[30] When they become pregnant, women who are experiencing intimate partner violence are much more likely than non-abused women to have an abortion.[31] Childhood sexual abuse, in particular, has been shown to greatly increase rates of sexual promiscuity, which in turn greatly elevates unplanned pregnancy rates, which in turn leads to greatly elevated abortion rates.[32] For males, having experienced or witnessed abuse in childhood is also directly related to increased rates of abortion because this dramatically increases the likelihood that these males will impregnate a teenage girl. For instance, compared to adult peers who report no childhood abuse, males who experienced sexual abuse at ten years of age or younger are 80 per cent more likely to get a teenage girl pregnant. Males who were sexually abused in childhood and experienced or witnessed physical violence in the home are 110 per cent more likely to get a teenage girl pregnant.[33]

Finally, it is important to note that abuse is not only highly correlated with first time abortions, but plays an increasingly significant role in subsequent abortions. One study found that "women presenting for a second or subsequent abortion were more than 2.5 times as likely as those seeking a first abortion to report a history of physical abuse by a male partner or a history of sexual abuse or violence."[34]

### III. Final Case Study

In an article on how to reduce abortions, evangelical ethicist Glen Stassen uses a case study from his former community in Louisville, Kentucky.[35] His wife and one of his parishioners were nurses at Louisville and Jefferson County's Teenage Parents Program (TAPP) for pregnant teenage students. In 1998, the year of this study, the Centers for Disease Control and Prevention reported that in Louisville 75 per cent of pregnant teenagers younger than fifteen years old, and 39 per cent of teenagers fifteen to nineteen years old, had abortions. In contrast, only 1 per cent of the twelve to nineteen year-old girls at TAPP had abortions. Furthermore, these girls had much lower school dropout, drug abuse, and suicide rates than their peers. Almost none of the girls got pregnant again while they were still in school. How did they achieve these stunning results? Stassen explains, "TAPP gave pregnant teenagers a way to continue school while taking care of their babies, and while building an economically viable future. The clear result was that they chose not to have abortions." TAPP provided child care while the girls were in class. The girls each worked one class period each day in the nursery, receiving hands-on expert child care instruction. Social workers provided counseling and helped the girls address individual needs and plan their future. Nurses and doctors provided OB/GYN care and medical counseling. If this case study is any indication, providing material assistance, social support, and addressing abuse are proven ways to dramatically reduce abortions.

### Conclusion

Pro-life and pro-choice adherents have very different understandings of how social justice should be applied to abortion, particularly whose rights take precedence. Yet, in spite of our weighty and passionate differences on the legality and morality of abortion, both sides are driven by a concern for social justice, and both sides want to see abortions reduced.

Therein lies fertile ground for united efforts to reduce abortions in America. Thus, I suggest the three broad social justice activities I outlined above to reduce abortion rates: material (physical) assistance, social support, and addressing abuse. I, like many of you, have devoted my life to social justice causes because I believe that injustice anywhere is a threat to justice everywhere. I am sustained by the flip side of this principle, which I also believe to be true: justice anywhere challenges injustice everywhere. May we work together to assist those in need to reduce the number of abortions in America.

## Study Questions

1. In what ways is Tracy's piece a departure from traditional pro-life arguments? Do you think it is inconsistent, as Tracy argues, to be simultaneously against abortion rights and yet also against the social welfare programs that have been shown to reduce the prevalence of abortion?

2. Tracy argues that "all too often those of us in the pro-life movement are, at best, known for only being anti-abortion and, at worst, for being anti-social justice." What do you think of Tracy's assessment here? Is he correct that typical pro-choice advocates ignore violations of social justice elsewhere in society?

3. Although abortion rights are often considered an aspect of social justice, Tracy argues that abortion access has also been used in ways that target the poor and minorities. What do you think of Tracy's assessment in this regard? Is there a way to support abortion choice while also condemning certain uses for, and instances of, abortion?

4. Tracy argues that pro-life advocacy needs to extend beyond defending fetal life and into recognizing the intrinsic value of all human life "regardless of age, gender, ethnicity, or social status … born as well as unborn, citizens and immigrants, rich and poor." What do you think of this expanded definition of what it means to be pro-life? If Tracy's position is accepted, what would this entail for issues such as the ethics of war, the death penalty, and our treatment of criminals, minorities, and immigrants?

## Notes

1 As a biblical ethicist, I derive my understanding of "social justice" primarily from biblical teaching on "justice" and "mercy." "Mercy" is an active commitment to alleviate human suffering regardless of the cause. "Justice" is an active commitment to insure that all humans, particularly those with the least status and power (since they are most often recipients of injustice) are treated with value, respect, and fairness. It also means standing with the oppressed, fighting against oppression, and confronting oppressors. On biblical definitions of "justice" and "mercy" see Christopher J.H. Wright, *Old Testament Ethics for the People of God* (Downers Grove, IL: InterVarsity, 2004), 235–80; and Ron Sider, "Justice, Human Rights, and Government: Toward an Evangelical Perspective," in *Toward an Evangelical Public Policy*, ed. Ronald J. Sider and Diane Knippers (Grand Rapids, MI: Baker, 2005), 163–93.

There is a growing body of evangelical scholarship demonstrating that justice and mercy, especially for the vulnerable, oppressed, and broken, is a canon-wide moral priority in Scripture. See Ron Sider, *Rich Christians in an Age of Hunger*, 5th ed. (Nashville, TN: W Publishing Group, 2005); Glen H. Stassen and David Gushee, *Kingdom Ethics: Following Jesus in Contemporary Context* (Dowers Grove, IL: InterVarsity, 2003); John Stott, *Human Rights and Human Wrongs: Major Issues for a New Century*, 3rd ed. (Grand Rapids, MI: Baker, 1999); and Nicholas Wolterstorff, *Until Justice and Peace Embrace* (Grand Rapids, MI: Eerdmans, 1983). The following summarizes the biblical data supporting this thesis. (1.) It encapsulates what God desires of his people (Mi 6:8; Jas 1:27) and "what it means to know God" (Jer 22:3, 13–17). (2.) It offers some of the surest evidence of conversion and godliness (Jb 29:12–17; Ez 18:5–17; Mt 25:31–46). (3.) It forms the criteria for particularly rich blessings (Is 33:14–17; Lk 14:12–14) and harsh judgment (Ex 22:22–24; Ez 22:27–31). (4.) It lay at the heart of Jesus' ministry and message (Lk 4:18–21).

2   This is most obviously true for the approximately 1.2 million fetuses that are aborted annually in the United States, but abortion also causes grave consequences for the women who undergo them, their family and partners, as well as those who perform and assist with the procedure itself. On the rarely discussed emotional trauma experienced by those who work in the abortion care industry, see Rachel M. MacNair, *Prism Magazine* 16 (November/December 2009): 8–16.

3   There is considerable evidence that legalized abortion not only harms the millions of unborn children who are aborted, but devalues life for the living. For instance, Vincent Rue documents the increase in child homicide and abuse since abortion has been legal in America, and summarizes the research, stating, "acceptance of abortion erodes instinctual parent-child bonding, increases parental aggressiveness against their defenseless offspring, and thereby increases the probability of subsequent child abuse," "Death by Design of Handicapped Newborns," *Issues in Law and Medicine* 1 (1985): 207.

4   Martin Luther King Jr., "Letter from a Birmingham Jail," April 16, 1963. See also King, *Why We Can't Wait* (New York: New American Library, 1964).

5   There is so much careful documentation from multiple disciplines applied historically from every corner of the globe that I will merely cite two recent non-academic sources here: Nicholas D. Kristof and Sheryl WuDunn, *Half the Sky: Turning Oppression into Opportunity for Women Worldwide* (New York: Knopf, 2009); and Ron Sider, "Gender and Justice Today," *Priscilla Papers* 21 (2007): 4–8.

6   For a concise defense of abortion as a basic human right, see Center for Reproductive Rights, "Women Have the Right to Abortion," in *Feminism: Opposing Viewpoints*, Christina Fisanick, ed. (New York: Gale Group, 2008), 110–17.

7   Andrea Dworkin, *Letters from a War Zone* (Brooklyn, NY: Lawrence Hill Books, 1993), 144.

8   Marcus Rediker, *The Slave Ship: A Human History* (New York: Penguin Books, 2008), 5. For an analysis of the issue of mortality rates surrounding the Atlantic slave trade, see Herbert S. Klein and Stanley L. Engerman, "Long-Term Trends in African Mortality in the Transatlantic Slave Trade," *Slavery & Abolition* 18 (1997): 36–48.

9   Heidi Unruh, "Life, Hope and a Future: Healthcare and Abortion," Evangelicals for Social Action, available at: http://www.worddeednetwork.org/Article. asp?RecordKey=4EBB5E0F-65E6-4412-8750- DE210BA4CDA.

10  Ibid. Susan A. Cohen, "Abortion and Women of Color: The Bigger Picture," *Guttmacher Policy Review* 11 (2008): 2. It should be noted that Dr. Alveda King, Dr. Martin Luther King Jr.'s niece, is heavily involved in the pro-life movement and helps direct Priests for Life African-American Outreach (http://www.priestsforlife.org/africanamerican).

11  Amartya Sen, "Missing Women – Revisited: Reduction in Female Mortality Has Been Counterbalanced by Sex-Selective Abortions," *British Medical Journal* 327 (2003): 1297–98.

12  "Gendercide: The Worldwide War on Baby Girls," *The Economist*, March 4, 2010; Wei Xing Zhu, Li Lu, and Therese Hesketh, "China's Excess Males, Sex Selective Abortion and One Child Policy," *British Medical Journal* 338 (2009): 1211.

13  "Gendercide: The Worldwide War on Baby Girls"; Laura J. Lederer, "Female Feticide and Its Impact on Human Trafficking," *Prism Magazine* 18 (March/April 2010): 8–12.

14  Glenn Beck, an influential conservative talk show host and author, provides an extreme, recent example of this. Beck, who is staunchly pro-life, told his listeners in March of 2010 that if their pastor spoke of social justice from the pulpit, they should immediately leave that church for those are merely "code words" for socialism and fascism. For an excellent rebuttal from a leading evangelical social justice ethicist, see David P. Gushee, "Glenn Beck vs. God: The Bible Speaks for Itself," *The Huffington Post*, March 17, 2010.

15  Cristina Page, *How the Pro-Choice Movement Saved America: Freedom, Politics and the War on Sex* (New York: Perseus, 2006), 45. This Children's Defense Fund congressional scorecard can be found at: http://www.childrensdefense.org/child-research-data- publications/data/2004-cdfac-congressional-scorecard.pdf. This reflects data from a 2004 scorecard, but the current situation remains virtually unchanged.

16  Ironically, the pro-life [George W.] Bush administration was willing to use "harsh interrogation tactics" on enemy combatants, including techniques such as waterboarding, which had previously been prosecuted by the United States in war-crimes trials after World War II; see Scott Shane and Mark Mazzetti, "In Adopting Harsh Tactics, No Look at Past Use," *New York Times*, April 22, 2009. For an excellent evangelical ethical assessment of the immorality and ineffectiveness of torturing prisoners, see David P. Gushee, *The Future of Faith in American Politics: The Public Witness of the Evangelical Center* (Waco, TX: Baylor UP, 2008), 121–39.

17  On Sheriff Arpaio's response to immigrants, see Ryan Gabrielson and Paul Giblin, "Reasonable Doubt," *East Valley Tribune*, July 9–13, 2008. Gabrielson and Giblin received a Pulitzer Prize for this five-part investigative series which concluded that the Sheriff 's immigration program, particularly his saturation patrols launched in immigrant neighborhoods, "has brought MCSO into violation of federal rules on racial profiling, caused 911 response times to soar, and pushed the agency into financial crisis."

18  See for instance the recent column by Nicholas Kristof, "Learning from the Sin of Sodom," *New York Times*, February 28, 2010. Two significant works which support and reflect this thesis are: David Gushee, *The Future of Faith in American Politics* and Ronald J. Sider and Diane Knippers, eds., *Toward an Evangelical Public Policy*.

19  Naomi Wolf, "Our Bodies, Our Souls," in *The Ethics of Abortion*, 3rd ed., ed. Robert M. Baird and Stuart E. Rosenbaum (Amherst, NY: Prometheus Books, 2001), 180.

20  Frederica Mathewes-Green, *Real Choices: Listening to Women: Look for Alternatives to Abortion* (Ben Lomond, CA: Conciliar P, 1997), 11. This statement was quickly embraced and cited by both sides of the debate – Planned Parenthood in its Public Affairs Action Letter and by the Pro-Choice Network Newsletter as its quote of the month.

21  "Facts on Induced Abortion in the United States," Washington, DC: Guttmacher Institute, July 2008.

22  T.R. Reid, "Universal Health Care Tends to Cut the Abortion Rate," *The Washington Post*, March 14, 2010.

23  "Facts on Induced Abortion in the United States," Guttmacher Institute.

24  Lawrence B. Finer et al., "Reasons U.S. Women Have Abortions: Quantitative and Qualitative Perspectives," *Perspectives on Sexual and Reproductive Health* 37 (2005): 110–18; Mathews-Green, *Real Choices*, 189–201. Similarly, worldwide studies find that the second most common reason women report for having an abortion are socioeconomic; Akinrinola Bankole, Susheela Singh, and Taylor Haas, "Reasons Why Women Have Induced Abortions: Evidence from 27 Countries," *International Family Planning Perspectives* 24 (1998): 117–27.

25 Joseph Wright, "Reducing Abortion in America: The Effect of Economic and Social Supports," *Catholics in Alliance for the Common Good* (November 2008): 7; http://catholic-sinalliance.org/files/ CACG_Final.pdf (accessed March 18, 2010).

26 "Facts on Induced Abortion in the United States," Guttmacher Institute.

27 Mathewes-Green, *Real Choices*, 12.

28 Ibid., 173.

29 Ibid., 12.

30 Anna Whitehead, and Janet Fanslow, "Prevalence of Family Violence Amongst Women Attending an Abortion Clinic in New Zealand," *Australian & New Zealand Journal of Obstetrics & Gynaecology* 45 (2005): 321.

31 Dore Hollander, "Does Abuse Lead to Abortion?" *Family Planning Perspectives* 30 (1998): 203; N.N. Sarkar, "The Impact of Intimate Partner Violence on Women's Reproductive Health and Pregnancy Outcome," *Journal of Obstetrics & Gynaecology* 28 (2008): 266–71; Lena Widding Hedin and Per Olof Janson, "Domestic Violence during Pregnancy," *Acta Obstetricia & Gynecologica Scandinavica* 79 (2000): 625–30.

32 Joseph M. Boden, David M. Fergusson, and John L. Horwood, "Experience of Sexual Abuse in Childhood and Abortion in Adolescence and Early Adulthood," *Child Abuse & Neglect* 33 (2009): 870–76; Thea van Roode et al., "Child Sexual Abuse and Persistence of Risky Sexual Behaviors and Negative Sexual Outcomes Over Adulthood: Findings from a Birth Cohort," *Child Abuse & Neglect* 33, Issue 3 (2009): 161–72.

33 Robert F. Anda et al., "Abused Boys, Battered Mothers, and Male Involvement in Teen Pregnancy," *Pediatrics* 107 (2001): 19.

34 William A. Fisher et al., "Characteristics of Women Undergoing Repeat Induced Abortion," *Canadian Medical Association Journal* 172 (2005): 640.

35 Glen Stassen, "What Actually Works: The Right Supports Can Reduce Abortion Rates," *Sojourners Magazine* (June 2009), 18–20.

# 5. Bertha Alvarez Manninen, "Pleading Men and Virtuous Women: Considering the Role of the Father in the Abortion Debate"

AFFECTED BY THE EMOTIONAL toll that an unwanted abortion had on a male student, philosopher Bertha Alvarez Manninen reflects on what role a prospective father's voice should be given by women in the abortion decision. In the longer version of this 2007 essay, from the *International Journal of Applied Philosophy*, she argues that the final say on whether a woman gestates needs to remain with her alone. Yet, she further argues, this is not the end to the question, but, rather, the beginning of a very complicated and often-ignored topic: what is the best way to ensure that the right to an abortion is exercised virtuously? Particularly, what is the responsible or virtuous way to exercise such a right in the case of a dissenting prospective father who very desperately wishes to keep the baby? This is the topic of this selection. Manninen uses virtue ethics and care ethics to navigate through this difficult question, concluding that there are times that an adherence to these theories may entail that a woman should consider not aborting in the face of a dissenting prospective father. That is, although the abortion right remains in women's hands, a virtuous exercise of that right entails giving a more prominent position to the voices of the men involved.

## Introduction

WHEN JOHN[1] CAME TO me to tell me he would be missing a week of class, I did not expect to hear the excuse he offered me. He told me that he did not think he could stand listening to lectures for a whole week on the ethics of abortion. A year prior, John and his girlfriend found out that she was pregnant, and they had planned to marry and raise the baby. An amniocentesis had revealed that the fetus, a boy, was afflicted with Down's syndrome, and John's girlfriend decided to have an abortion. John pleaded with her, cried to her, and offered to take full responsibility for the infant once he was born. He was even willing to quit college and take on a full-time job to provide for the child on his own, and his family was more than willing to help. John's girlfriend had the abortion against his pleas,

and here he was, one year later, telling me that he still suffered from it. John did end up going to class that week after all, and I admired him for it. But I have not been able to shake the image out of my head of a nineteen-year-old man, who was willing to give up everything to raise his baby alone, and how this was taken away from him. It is because of him that I felt the need to write this paper.

For a man that may feel a lingering sense of grief after his female partner has procured an abortion, there is no socially sanctioned way for him to express his sorrow. In our society, there is a cultural expectation that a man is to sever all emotional ties that he may have towards the fetus if his female partner chooses to obtain an abortion and be completely supportive of such a decision. Any dissent that he expresses against the abortion may be viewed as an attempt to interfere with a woman's right to bodily autonomy. Men, however, can (and often times do) suffer emotional strains due to their partner's abortion decision, and "the emotional toll can manifest itself in low-self-esteem, substance abuse, failed relationships and sexual dysfunction."[2] One man describes the experience as something that "seeps into the subconscious and always stays with you."[3] One study found that "adult men who experienced a partner's having undergone an abortion during the teen years reported markedly more distress in early adulthood than peers who had not experienced a partner's abortion."[4] ...

In this paper, I argue that, legally and morally speaking, a man does not have the right to veto a woman's abortion decision.[5] ...

Yet the debate ought not to end here. Although a woman ought to have the ultimate say regarding whether she will terminate a pregnancy (as delineated by *Roe v. Wade*), even against her partner's wishes, this does not entail that any exercise of this right would be a virtuous one. With the sanctification of a woman's right to choose what happens to her body when it comes to the gestation of a fetus, there comes a responsibility to use that legal and moral right virtuously, particularly in situations where a man may find himself in John's position and desperately wants to have the baby. To have an abortion in these circumstances will probably result in great emotional harm for the man, for it robs him of the child he so desperately desires. As women, we must understand that we have great power over men in this area, and thus we should try to ensure that we exercise this power in the most virtuous manner possible. Given this, I will argue that it is in the realm of virtue ethics, and also to some extent care ethics, where a man's voice in the abortion debate can best be accommodated....

## Pleading Men and Virtuous Women

### A Brief Explanation of Virtue and Care

... The virtues are certain traits of character, dispositions to act and feel in certain ways, which are necessary in order for a human being to live well; to achieve a *eudaimonistic*, or a flourishing, life. Examples of virtuous character traits, which are particularly important for the subject at hand, are: responsibility, selflessness, compassion, empathy, and justice or fairness. A virtuous person consistently acts in a manner which manifests these character traits; her main concern is not just doing the right thing, but also being a good person, and the two cannot be divorced. Aristotle argues that virtue is not an abstract concept that can be learned merely by reading or studying; one must actually perform virtuous and good actions in order to become a virtuous and good person. For example, one does not become compassionate and honest (two virtuous character traits) by simply reading about compassion and honesty in philosophy books. Instead, one must go out into the world, interact and engage with others, and act towards them in compassionate and honest ways.[6] After we repeatedly act in such ways, eventually the traits of compassion and honesty will become part of our fixed character. This, in turn, ensures that we will continue to act in compassionate and honest ways.

A virtuous character is manifested by engaging in virtuous actions. The way we can tell whether a certain individual is, for example, an honest individual is because she consistently engages in honest actions, i.e., she consistently tells the truth. However, being an honest person does not mean that lying is out of the question. A virtuous person is sensitive to context and the particulars of a situation, and realizes that differing situations require differing actions. For example, consider a nurse working in a hospital or institution that cares for patients afflicted with Alzheimer's disease. One of her patients often raves to others about his successful son, and doing so adds joy to his otherwise difficult existence. In truth, however, his son has died long before, and every time he is reminded of this the patient undergoes extreme emotional agony until he once again forgets. The nurse may decide that continuing to remind the patient of his son's death is not only fruitless (since he is bound to forget again), but also extremely detrimental to his well-being, which is already suffering enough due to the disease. Thus, she decides to no longer do so. She may even continue to tell him that his son plans to visit him some time soon, for the prospect alone fills the patient with happiness and he never seems to notice that the visit does not materialize. In fact, the nurse may even go so far as to humor her patient when he raves about his son's last visit, enforcing his false belief that the son visits him often. Given these very special circumstances, an honest person may legitimately conclude that continuing to tell the patient the truth is not the right thing to do. In this instance, or any relevantly similar instance, lying does not impugn on an honest person's character. Thus, being an honest person does not mean *always* telling the truth, but rather it means understanding when telling the truth is called for, and when it may not be....

... Care ethics is related to virtue ethics, though not reducible to nor subsumed by it.[7] The behaviors espoused by care ethicists (care, compassion, and selflessness, amongst others) are themselves virtuous character traits, of course, but virtue ethicists are concerned with cultivating other character traits as well, whereas care ethicists are primarily concerned with these traits as the foundation of their moral theory. Care ethicists approach moral issues by emphasizing certain character traits, or relating to others in ways which are stereotypically thought to be female in nature. Caring about others properly involves engaging them in a caring relationship, feeling concern for others, and manifesting certain emotions. Care ethicists are less concerned with following rigid rules or principles, which can be rather impersonal, and are more concerned with relating to others in a personal and caring manner. Care ethicists emphasize the importance of relationships, love, trust, and human bonding; they do not want to do away with rules or obligations, but rather wish to merge them with a consideration of the importance of personal human relationships.

The practice of care ethics involves "engagement with another's will."[8] According to Hilde Lindemann, this means that we must interact with another person

> as someone with wants, intention, and desires of his own. You don't high-handedly impose your own will on your charge, riding roughshod over his wishes, because that would be an abuse of the power you have over him ... [care ethicists] practice *engrossment*, which consists of such close attention to the feelings, needs, ideas, or wants of their charges that the caregivers' own needs and wants are displaced.[9]

According to Nel Noddings, engrossment

> is receptive ... [w]hen I care, my motive energy begins to flow toward the needs and wants of the cared-for. This does not mean that I will always approve of what the other wants, nor does it mean that I will never try to lead him or her to a better set of values, but I must take into account the feelings and desires that are actually there and respond as positively as my values and capacities allow.[10]

*Prima facie*, however, engrossment poses a

problem. It seems that complete engrossment entails what Lindemann calls a "problem of integrity ... what are you supposed to do when a conflict arises between your charge's wants and purposes and your own sense of what's right? Does the ethics of care require you to sacrifice your own integrity?"[11] Hence, it seems, at first, that the practice of care and engrossment requires always yielding one's priorities and needs to others. No ethical theory should entail that one human agent (man or woman) is required to sacrifice her own personal integrity and needs and allow herself to be completely subsumed by the wants and needs of others.

But being a caring person and engrossing oneself in the feelings or needs of others does not equate to losing one's integrity or allowing oneself to be exploited. It is necessary to walk a delicate tightrope here. A caring person knows when to be selfless and when to be selfish, just like the honest individual knows when to tell the truth and when to lie. Such a person knows how to balance her own desires and wants with the desires and wants of others affected by her actions and her decisions. Caring well entails caring for others *and* caring for oneself. Hence, some care ethicists, as Lindemann writes, "have proposed [building] self-care into the ethics of care so that it doesn't become an ethics of self-erasure.... Care arises from *engaging* with another's will — not sacrificing your own."[12] ...

### Attempting to Make Sense of the Quagmire: How Virtue and Care Ethics Can Help

... We ... know that being a virtuous person can be difficult and intricate because we must be sensitive to the particulars of a situation in order to correctly determine what the virtuous thing to do in that situation would be. For the case at hand, I can think of, at least, the following particulars that may make a

relevant difference concerning whether or not it would be virtuous for a woman to abort a fetus against the father's consent.

• Was the fetus a product of consensual sex, or did the man commit a violent act against the woman that resulted in her pregnancy?

• Would gestating the fetus cause many emotional or physical burdens on the woman, so that self-preservation may entail aborting the fetus?

• How close were the potential parents; did they have an intimate relationship already built on trust and love?

• Can the father really care for the infant in the manner that he says he can?

• Will the pregnant woman suffer any emotional or long-term damage as a result of giving the infant up for adoption?

I will address all of these to some extent below and illustrate how each of them can play a salient role for determining when it would be non-virtuous for a woman to exercise her right to an abortion in the face of a dissenting man, or when gestating a fetus unwanted by her in order to provide the man with his child may manifest virtue.

One of the first things I want to emphasize is that if a man expresses an interest in having a child, caring for a child, and being a loving father to a child, this is an interest that is of great moral worth, and one that ought to be taken seriously. Within the context of virtue ethics, the man himself is displaying virtuous character traits: responsibility, adoration towards his offspring, and the willingness to engage in the self-sacrifice common to almost any individual that chooses to become a parent. A man who wishes to become a *good* parent understands that, as Hursthouse writes, "parenthood in general … [is] intrinsically worthwhile [and] among the things that can be correctly thought to be partially constructive of a flourishing life."[13] Rewarding and supporting someone who is himself acting virtuously is in itself a virtuous thing to do: it manifests compassion, respect, and empathy towards the father of the fetus.[14] Thus, while a man cannot be given equal rights over the fetus while it is in the womb without violating a woman's dignity and freedom, if a woman chooses to give a certain man who desires to be a virtuous parent a voice in the abortion decision, she would be expressing compassion and empathy towards her male partner.

In a situation where the man genuinely and whole-heartedly desires the future baby, from a care ethics perspective, he has already engrossed himself with this fetus and in the future baby's existence and welfare. John, for example, was already engaging in a caring relationship with the fetus; he already saw himself as the fetus' care-giver and it as his charge. This is one of the reasons he begged his girlfriend not to abort the fetus; "to me," he told me, "this was not just a fetus; this was my son, and I had a responsibility to try to protect him in any way that I could." In relevantly similar situations, we have a man already engrossed and engaging in a caring relationship with a being he considers his child, and we have a woman who is not engrossed to the same extent, if at all. For anyone that desires to be a virtuous person, a key issue to always consider and always keep in the forefront of your mind is how your actions affect the welfare of others, for a virtuous person would never engage in wantonly harming others and is always aware of the impact her actions can make in the lives of others. A derivative, and pertinent, question that a woman needs to ask herself in this difficult situation is whether it would be morally virtuous to abort a fetus with whom the father is already deeply engrossed; is it virtuous to forcibly sever that engrossment (for if a woman does decide to do so, this would no doubt harm the man who already has a deep and emotional attachment to the fetus)?

With all this in mind, I proceed by considering three instances when a woman would *not* be manifesting a non-virtuous character if she exercises her abortion rights in the face of a dissenting father, in addition to one situation when she very obviously would be. Considering these situations will help us shed some light on the salient particulars that will help to determine whether the exercise of the abortion right in the face of a dissenting man is virtuous.

*The rape or abuse victim.* Suppose a woman was raped and is pregnant as a result. Perhaps the rapist is genuinely apologetic for what he has done, and he now begs the woman to not abort the fetus and let him raise the infant instead. George W. Harris describes a similar situation in his article "Fathers and Fetuses," and he argues that when a fetus is "forced upon a woman she is not required to view the fetus as a legitimate object of interest for him…. Although procreation is a morally legitimate object of interest that men can have, the pursuit of this interest is restricted by the requirement that men respect the autonomy of women in this regard."[15] If a woman has been sexually assaulted, the pregnancy is the result of a violent and involuntary invasion of her body. In this case, the man has voided any possible claim he has to the fetus when he decided to impose his will violently upon the woman against her consent. The violence done unto her nullifies any requirement on her to regard the man's feelings or interests concerning the termination of the fetus.

When it comes to assessing her actions using virtue ethics, as abovementioned, the appropriate question she needs to ask herself is: "If I obtain an abortion now, would I be acting callously, unjustly, or in a light-minded fashion?" Given the violent manner in which the fetus was conceived, and the emotional and physical trauma that often results from being sexually assaulted, a woman would not be manifesting a callous attitude if she did not make the concession to carry the fetus to term in order to appease the man who raped her. The same would seem to hold true if the woman was in a relationship with a man who was physically, mentally, or emotionally abusive throughout the course of their union. Indeed, it would be difficult to maintain that a failure to appease any individual who has violated your rights or harmed you is a morally reprehensible or callous way for you to act towards your assailant.

*Conflict with health.* Consider a situation where pregnancy would cause a great burden to the woman (beyond what it normally causes her), so much so that her physical, emotional, or mental health may be at risk. For example, consider the case of Andrea Yates. After battling severe depression and psychosis, she was advised by her psychiatrist not to have any more children, since pregnancy and childbirth would almost certainly result in a relapse of her depression and psychotic behavior. Shortly after the birth of her fifth child, Yates drowned all five of her children in the family's bathtub. Had she decided to abort her fifth child in the interest of retaining her mental and emotional health, even in the face of her husband's protests, it does not seem to me that she would have been manifesting any non-virtuous character traits. Approaching it from a care ethics perspective, she may rightly opt for self-care (and the care and protection of her other children) rather than conceding to her husband's desire to have a fifth child. Indeed, if a man asks a woman to gestate a fetus, knowing the harm that can come to the woman as a result, it is he who is engaging in

selfish or callous behavior, for he is then putting his own desire for a baby (no matter how genuine or strong that desire may be) over and above the very basic welfare interest a woman has in mental, emotional, or physical health.

If a woman were to ask herself in this situation: "Would I be acting in a callous, light-minded, or in any other non-virtuous manner by choosing to abort a fetus in order to preserve my mental, emotional, or physical health?" the answer seems to be an emphatic no, especially when there are four other children to care for, as was Yates's case. When there are other children in the picture that need consideration, the woman is acting in a responsible manner toward them in wanting to preserve her well-being; for they are already here, and they are in need of a healthy mother. Yet even if there weren't any other children to consider, prioritizing herself and her health over and above the man's desire for an infant does not seem to impugn on a woman's character. Similar to the honest individual who knows when it is permissible to lie, this is one of those instances where it would be permissible for her to think of herself before she considers others.

*Compromising one's career.* Suppose that a woman's much sought-after career would be compromised as a result of being pregnant for nine months. For example, say she was a professional athlete or she was in the internship phase of medical school, which required her to work over seventy hours a week with very little sleep. It seems to me that in these cases, carrying a fetus to term would result in a great sacrifice for her. The career that constitutes a great part of her character and that she has worked so hard to attain may be permanently compromised. I would not at all think it heartless or light-minded of her to choose to abort against the wishes of her partner in these, or relevantly similar, circumstances. A woman's ulterior interest in preserving her much sought-after career seems to me to be as important as a man's ulterior interest in being a father to this specific offspring.

Consider the case of one of Carol Gilligan's subjects in a famous experiment she conducted at Harvard University concerning the differing moral attitudes between women and men. Her subject was a woman in her late twenties who had decided to procure an abortion. She was a musician who maintained that "her choice for abortion was selfish because it was for her 'survival,' but she meant surviving in her work, which, she said, was 'where I derive the meaning of what I am.'"[16] In this situation, it seems that denying herself the opportunity to continue her career would have constituted a type of self-erasure. A woman may be sympathetic to a man's desires and interest in her carrying the fetus to term, but it does not seem at all callous for her to want to preserve the career she has worked so hard for and would be devastating to her to lose. In cases where respect for the man's interest in becoming a father and preserving the woman's much sought after career may be mutually exclusive, it would not strike me as necessarily callous, heartless, or light-minded to have an abortion in the face of the dissenting father.

*Vengeance.* An obvious case where a woman *would* be acting non-virtuously (and even viciously) when obtaining an abortion against her partner's wishes is if she uses the abortion as a method of exacting revenge upon the man, or out of spite. For example, say that after a bitter separation from her husband or partner (for non-abusive reasons, let's suppose) a woman learns she is pregnant and informs her partner of it. Her partner displays great joy at the prospect of having the child, despite the failed relationship, and in an attempt to hurt him she exercises her right to an abortion. In this case, if she were to ask herself: "By having this abortion, would I be acting in a spiteful, callous, or selfish manner?" her answer here

would be that she is indeed acting in such a manner. According to the care ethicist, this woman is refusing to engage in any caring relationship with this man whatsoever; she is completely neglecting any engagement with the will or desires of the man. She is, in effect, unilaterally imposing her own will upon him, neglecting his wishes or needs completely, and declining to be empathetic in any possible way. In essence, she is "riding roughshod over his wishes"[17] and thus she is abusing the power she has over him in this regard. None of these are actions that a virtuous person or caring person would indulge in.

But, granted, the cases I have cited may be less than ordinary. So how can we approach the more common instances of dissent: cases where the man is a good person, who is already engrossed in the welfare of a being he perceives as his child, and will most likely be a good father who would care for and nurture his child, but the woman simply does not want to go through with the pregnancy because she does not want there to *be* a child? Let me begin approaching this question with the following experiment in empathy and compassion, which are two character traits absolutely essential for any virtuous or caring person to possess.

To my female readers: imagine how you would feel if you were told you were going to be a parent and were thrilled at the prospect. You begin to envision what this child will look like, what she will grow up to become, and all the milestones that you will share with her. You picture hugging and kissing her, reading to her, watching her walk or speak for the first time, or just looking into her eyes and feeling that there is no greater love than the love a parent has for his or her child. You imagine her future needs to become an integral part of your needs. You already engage in a care-giver/charge relationship with the fetus: you eat healthy, exercise regularly, take vitamins, read to her, talk to her, and already start a savings account for her college education. No matter what stage of development the fetus is at, even if it is a very young one and intrinsically nothing more than, as Noddings puts it, "an information speck," you nevertheless "confer sacredness upon it … [you] cannot, will not, destroy it … [your] decision is an ethical one born of the nature of caring."[18]

After this intimate engagement in the existence and welfare of your fetus, someone then informs you that, for some reason, he is going to take her away from you. Suddenly, the dream that you were falling in love with is in danger of collapsing. You beg and plead with that person not to do it, that you would be perfectly willing to care for the child on your own, if it meant that she or he could live. Imagine the feelings of helplessness, loss, and emptiness that would ensue when your connection with this fetus is forcibly severed, and you are powerless to do anything at all about it. Picture the suffering that would result, and then ask yourself: under what circumstances should you be willing to inflict this kind of suffering upon another human being?

As abovementioned, obtaining an abortion would not be manifesting a non-virtuous character if gestating the fetus may result in a severe physical or mental health risk for the woman, for these interests, being welfare interests, are more vital than the man's ulterior interest in procreation in this specific instance. It would also not be non-virtuous to abort a fetus that was a product of rape, even if the rapist desires to keep and raise the resulting infant. And it would not necessarily be non-virtuous to abort a fetus in the face of a dissenting father when the alternative is for a woman to compromise her much sought-after, possibly identity-defining, career.

However, in a situation where a woman and a man shared, or continue to share, an intimate relationship, when a man is engrossed

in the existence and welfare of his future child (as the individual in the above example is), and when gestating a fetus may not necessarily result in a compromise of career, health, continued existence, or any other integral aspect of a woman's life, then I propose that she ought to seriously consider gestating the fetus to term for the sake of respecting the man's interest in being a father to this specific child that is his biological child and in the interest of not inflicting upon him the emotional pain described before. A woman could approach this as an opportunity to give a man a great gift, as parenthood often is. She would be acknowledging what seems to be a very obvious, and yet constantly overlooked, fact: that the fetus, even while in the woman's womb, is also his progeny, half his own, and thus that his interest in the fetus is legitimate. She would be rewarding a man who desperately wants to experience fatherhood, an attitude that, as a society, we commonly wish to propagate in other men.

From a virtue ethics perspective, a woman needs to ask herself: "Would it be virtuous to forcibly sever his engrossment towards this fetus; would I be acting in a non-virtuous manner if I did?" In order to successfully answer this question, again, the particulars of the situation must be taken into account. For example, although the woman may no longer be engrossed with the man, nor with the fetus she is currently gestating, the fact that there was a mutual past engrossment may play a salient role here; she would need to ask herself: "What type of person would I be if I chose to completely ignore and disregard the pain I would be causing to this man with whom I used to share an intimate relationship?" It would seem to impugn more on her character, perhaps make her more callous, if she would be willing to completely disregard the interests, desires, and the pains of a man with whom she used to share a loving and healthy relationship than with a man whom she met for one night at a bar, or shared a brief fling with. It would seem much more callous of me to abort my soon-to-be ex-husband's fetus against his pleas, after a relatively healthy and loving marriage that came apart because we grew apart or became different, irreconcilable, people, than to abort the fetus of a man whom I knew for a month and with whom I shared no intimate bond at all.[19] Another salient particular, for example, may concern whether the man who desires the future infant really *can* care for the baby in a decent manner. Perhaps the woman knows that he has the best of intentions to raise the child, but she also knows that he suffers from a drug and alcohol problem, or that, at times, he may be prone to violence. It would certainly not seem to be callous of her if she aborts the fetus against his pleas because she genuinely believes that he cannot be the father he wants to be. Indeed, in certain situations, her inability to care about the fetus coupled with his inability to care for it may mean that aborting the fetus is the responsible thing to do.

Suppose, however, that a woman concedes to gestating a fetus that she does not want for a responsible and caring man with whom she used to share a bond and who has the ability to care for the future baby because she feels that it would be indecent for her to abort in this situation, or relevantly similar ones. Here, she would be manifesting several virtuous character traits. As the above experiment illustrates, she would be exercising the virtues of empathy and compassion, allowing herself to see the situation from a man's point of view and treating him, perhaps, in a manner that she would herself like to be treated if the tables were turned. She would be acting in a kind and fair manner by allowing a man a voice in the abortion debate and in the fate of his future child, even though she is absolutely under no legal obligation or compulsion to do so.

She would also be acting in one of the most selfless ways possible, for giving up a child for adoption is never easy (as I will discuss below), and women who voluntarily do so are often looked upon as courageous and selfless. In this case, not only is she giving the infant a chance to live, she is also giving her partner the opportunity to be a father, which he obviously very much desires to be. A woman who brings a fetus, whom she initially wanted to abort, to term in order to give a good man a chance to be a good father is courageous, fair, kind, empathetic, selfless, and very noble indeed.

In some situations, then, where the woman wants to abort the fetus but the man dissents and wants to raise the baby, the minimally virtuous thing for a woman to do would be to carefully consider the man's point of view, his wishes, and his ability to care for this future child. She should also acknowledge that the fetus does partially, biologically speaking, belong to the man, and that therefore his interest in the fetus' survival is legitimate. She should then take these salient aspects and ask herself what it would mean for her character if she exercised her right to an abortion, and she may conclude that procuring the abortion would manifest a non-virtuous character. However, that is not to say that she should *always* make this concession. Perhaps after much deliberation and consideration of the man's position, a woman may still decide that she cannot face the prospect of adopting out her child, even if it is to the infant's father. Perhaps she knows that if she does continue to gestate, she too would become engrossed in the fetus and in the future child, and this is *precisely* what she does not want. As Margaret Olivia Little poignantly puts it, a woman who chooses abortion over adoption (even to the infant's father) may know that:

[t]o give up a child would be for [her] a life long trauma…. Gestation, she knows,

is likely to reshape her heart and soul, transforming her into a mother emotionally, not just officially; and it is precisely that transformation she does not want to undergo. It is because continuing pregnancy brings with it this new identity and, likely, relationship, then, that many feel it is legitimate to decline ... whether one rears the child or lets it go – to continue a pregnancy means that a piece of one's heart, as the saying goes, will forever walk outside one's body.[20]

The woman's desire not to become engrossed with an embryo or fetus she wishes to abort, her desire not to have her "heart and soul" transformed, can indeed be a salient factor. On the other hand, after carefully considering the man's wishes and desires, she may decide to make one of the most ultimate sacrifices imaginable in order to concede to his wishes. If she does choose to go this route, there is no doubt that making this very difficult concession to a man in order to retain a virtuous character would be a fine [kalos] and noble thing to do.[21]

## Conclusion

... [T]he best way to explain what I want to say in this paper is the following. Women have all the cards when it comes to the issue of gestating a fetus, and I have argued in the first part of the paper that, when discussing legal and moral rights, it ought to stay that way. However, we should be conscientious and judicious about how we play these cards, and we should take it upon ourselves to share these cards with (good and decent) men as much as possible, especially when the fate of his future as a father to this specific child lies unilaterally in our hands. In some cases, a woman may decide that she will bring a fetus to term and give the man his much desired wish of fatherhood. In other cases, a woman, after carefully considering the man's interests, feelings, and desires, may still not be able to make the concession to gestate. In the end, what truly matters is that women should always approach similar instances of dissent in the most virtuous way possible.

## References

Coleman, Priscilla K., and Eileen S. Nelson. 1999. "Abortion Attitudes as Determinates of Perceptions Regarding Male Involvement in Abortion Decisions." *Journal of American College of Health*, Vol. 47, No. 4. 164–72.

Dworkin, Ronald. 1993. *Life's Dominion: An Argument about Abortion, Euthanasia, and Individual Freedom*. New York: Random House.

Harris, George W. 1986. "Fathers and Fetuses." *Ethics*, Vol. 96, No. 3. 594–603.

Hursthouse, Rosalind. 1991. "Virtue Theory and Abortion." *Philosophy and Public Affairs*, Vol. 20, No. 3. 223–46.

Kalish, Stacey. 2004. "Lingering Thoughts about Abortion: Male Grief Is Hidden." *Psychology Today*, Vol. 37, Issue 3. 14–5.

Lindemann, Hilde. 2006. *An Invitation to Feminist Ethics*. Boston: McGraw Hill.

Little, Margaret Olivia. 2003. "The Morality of Abortion." *Biomedical Ethics*, ed. Thomas A. Mappes and David DeGrazia, New York: McGraw Hill, 2005. 479–83.

Noddings, Nel. 1984. *Caring: A Feminine Approach to Ethics and Moral Education*. Berkley: U of California P.

____. 2005. "Caring in Education." *The Encyclopedia of Informal Education*. Accessed on February 9, 2007. http://www.infed.org/biblio/noddings_caring_in_education.htm.

Rosenwasser, Shirley Miller, Loyd S. Wright, and R. Bruce Barber. "The Rights and
    Responsibilities of Men in Abortion Situations." *Journal of Sex Research*, Vol. 23, No. 1. 97–104.
Sander-Staudt, Maureen. 2006. "The Unhappy Marriage of Care Ethics and Virtue Ethics,"
    *Hypatia*, Vol. 21, No. 4. 21–39.

## Study Questions

1. Manninen maintains that women cannot be forced to gestate a fetus for the sake of the prospective father's desire to have a baby. Do you agree with her in this regard? What reasons could be given in favor of blocking a woman's abortion decision on behalf of the prospective father? Ultimately, do you believe that there should be a legal means to force women to gestate for the sake of the prospective father? What would be the practical consequences of such laws?

2. Aside from the examples given in the essay, can you think of any circumstances where it would be unvirtuous for a woman to choose abortion if the fetus's father wanted to care for it? Can you think of any circumstances where it would *not* be unvirtuous for a woman to choose abortion if the fetus's father wanted to care for it? How did you arrive at your answer?

3. Manninen states that there is no "socially-sanctioned" way for men to express grief after an abortion; however, this seems true for both genders. Why do you think this is? Why are people (both women and men) hesitant about expressing any feelings of grief after an abortion? Japanese culture has funeral rites for aborted or miscarried babies (called *mizuko kuyo* rites) even though abortion is legal – would something like this be beneficial in US culture?

4. Explain how virtue and care ethics are used in Manninen's argument as a way of understanding how a prospective father's voice may come into play in an abortion decision. What do you think of these two theoretical models for interpreting ethical decisions? What other moral dilemmas can you think of that would benefit from an analysis using these theories?

## Notes

1. This is not the student's real name; I have changed it in order to protect his privacy.
2. Kalish, "Lingering Thoughts about Abortion: Male Grief is Hidden" (2004), 14.
3. Kalish, 15.
4. Coleman and Nelson, "Abortion Attitudes as Determinates of Perceptions Regarding Male Involvement in Abortion Decisions" (1999), 164.
5. In March 2001, a British man named Stephen Hone went to court in an attempt to stop his ex-girlfriend, Claire Hansell, from aborting their mutually created fetus. He initially won a partial victory, with the High Court in London ruling that Hansell needed to secure a second opinion from another physician before the abortion was allowed to proceed. A week later,

Hansell defied the court ruling and procured an abortion from another clinic. The remains of the fetus were discarded even though Hone had asked for them in order to give the fetus a burial. Hone and his family did end up having a burial for the fetus – but they buried an empty coffin. Although I cannot condone a legal ruling that would have compelled Hansell to carry an unwanted fetus to term, the pain felt by Hone after the abortion of his fetus convinces me that ethics needs to find some room for his voice, and for relevantly similar voices, in the abortion debate.

6   Aristotle, *Nicomachean Ethics*, 1103a15–1103b.

7   Care ethics and virtue ethics share some commonalities; for example, advocates of both theories contend that good and caring motivations, and our relationships to others, are essential for a flourishing, *eudamonistic*, life. However, there has been a resistance to collapse care ethics into virtue ethics, or to consider care ethics as nothing but an offshoot of virtue ethics. Although care is a virtue, it is certainly not the *only* virtue, and so care ethics cannot be fully captured as a version of virtue ethics. For an excellent discussion on this issue, see Sander-Staudt, "The Unhappy Marriage of Care Ethics and Virtue Ethics," (2006), 21–39.

8   Lindemann, *An Invitation to Feminist Ethics*, 93.

9   Ibid.

10  Noddings, "Caring in Education" (2005), http://www.infed.org/biblio/noddings_caring_in_education.htm.

11  Lindemann, 96.

12  Lindemann, 96–97; emphasis in the original.

13  Hursthouse, 241.

14  I am assuming, of course, that the man is of sound character; that he is not, for example, an abuser or adulterer, which I think nullifies any possible consideration a woman should give him when it comes to the abortion decision. Surely I cannot advocate that a woman ought to, in some circumstances, consider sacrificing her body for nine months for a child she does not want in order to consider the wishes of a man who has previously beaten her or disrespected her gravely in some respect.

15  Harris, "Fathers and Fetuses" (1986), 597.

16  Dworkin, *Life's Dominion*, 59.

17  Lindemann, 93.

18  Noddings, *Caring*, 87–88.

19  The level of intimacy in a relationship seems to shape public opinion concerning the extent a man's dissent should be taken to heart by a woman considering abortion. In one study, a survey containing questions concerning the role of a man in the abortion decision was given to college students between eighteen and twenty-three years of age. The study found that the students considered

> the man's opinion … more important in more intimate versus less intimate relationships … [p]articipants were more likely to think that the woman should have the right to have an abortion in spite of the man's opinion in the less intimate situations, namely the "dating 6 months" condition and the "one-time encounter" than the married and engaged conditions. Also, students were more likely to agree that the man should be able to legally block the abortion in the more intimate situations … than in the less intimate situations. Finally, in the less intimate situations such as "dating 6 months" condition or the "one-time encounter," students were more likely than for the more intimate situations to agree with the statement that Sarah should consider Rick's opinion, but that the final decision should be hers. (Rosenwasser, Wright, and Barber, "The Rights and Responsibilities of Men in Abortion Situations" [1987], 103)

George Harris's article "Fathers and Fetuses" (see n. 15 [21]) can be appealed to in order to shed more light on the complexities of this issue. Harris delineates several hypothetical cases in which men and women dissent concerning the abortion decision, each case differing in the levels of intimacy and the levels of wrongdoing that one party has committed against the other (e.g., the level of deceit involved on the woman's behalf in convincing her partner that she wanted children when she really did not). His argument concerning whether it would be morally impermissible for a woman to abort, however, is more dependent on the differing levels of wrongdoing than the differing levels of intimacy. Nevertheless, this is certainly an issue I would like to expand on in subsequent versions of this paper.

20  Little, "The Morality of Abortion" (2003), 480–81.

21  It may be objected that the Kantian formula of humanity prevents such an analysis; the imperative maintains that we cannot treat either others or *ourselves* solely as a means to an end, and it seems that I am here arguing that there are times that a woman ought to subjugate herself to such a role. I suppose one *could* interpret my argument as maintaining that a virtuous woman would, at times, concede to being used as a mere incubator in order to satisfy a man's interests. I choose, however, to see it differently. Instead of seeing women as incubators when it comes to an impasse between men and women in the abortion decision, I am choosing to see women as the sole bringers and facilitators of a special gift for those men who are themselves manifesting a virtuous character in wanting so much to be loving fathers, and who indeed have a legitimate interest in the fetus she carries because it is, biologically, half his own. In these situations, a woman has an opportunity to be selfless, empathetic, and to give a man a voice in the life of his child even though she is not at all legally required to do so; that is, women have the opportunity to act in a virtuous manner.

# 6. Shari Collins and Eric Comerford, "Anonymous Sperm Donation: A Case for Genetic Heritage and Wariness for Contractual Parenthood"

IN THIS ESSAY, FROM a 2012 issue of the *International Journal of Applied Philosophy*, Shari Collins and Eric Comerford tackle the issue of gamete donation, especially from the perspective of the resulting children who yearn for a connection with their biological origins (the article concentrates mainly on sperm donation, but the authors' points apply equally to ova donation). Collins and Comerford first explore will and interest theory regarding the desire to be familiar with one's genetic heritage, and they argue that both theories entail a right of offspring to have access to this knowledge. Then they look at the issue of donor contracts and argue that an inconsistency exists between the capacities of donors to eschew parental responsibility and those of men who become biological fathers through sexual reproduction. Collins and Comerford conclude that offspring have a right to their genetic heritage and call for caring reproductive technological practices that ensure children of donors this right.

WE WERE MOTIVATED TO write this paper after hearing accounts of sperm donor-conceived offspring searching for their biological fathers. Some donor-conceived offspring have sued courts, sued their parents, written articles in newspapers, made their stories known to magazines and talk shows – all claiming that it should be their right to know at least something about their biological father. Until fairly recently, conversations about whether those born by anonymous sperm donation should have a right to information concerning their donors has made its way into public and medical discourse, and even into law in the Netherlands in 2004.

While there is no official national count of children born from these banks, it is estimated that nearly 30,000 children are born each year in the United States through donor insemination, with about one million currently living in the United States.[1] Others estimate that 60,000 are born each year.[2] The reason why these statistics are unknown is because there is no federal accounting of those born by sperm donation.[3] Because most donor insemination occurs under donor anonymity, many of these children are deprived from knowing about the conditions of their birth, namely, as it concerns their biological father. Yet to act on these interests conflicts with the donor's right to remain anonymous, and so the issue becomes one of whose right is to be favored.

In this paper, we discuss two significant aspects of anonymous sperm donation. The first is the question of whether donor-conceived offspring have a right to know of their genetic heritage. It is argued that a right to know of one's genetic heritage can be inferred from two general theories concerning the formation of rights: will and interest theory. The second is the issue of parental responsibility in light of anonymous sperm donor contracts. The contract between the sperm donor (seller), the bank, and the mother exempts the donor from all rights and responsibilities a biological father has in the production of a child, a procedure that is not allowed elsewhere. We question this process, and identify that it upholds an unequal application of rights to biological fathers and children. Lastly, it is encouraged that reproductive ethics emphasize not only how births can occur in moral and healthy ways, but also urge that respectful and caring practices surrounding reproductive technology be met in a social sense as well.

## The Right to Genetic Heritage

There is no requirement in the United States for any information concerning one's donor to be given to those born by anonymous sperm donation, even when they are of legal age. While this was once considered immaterial, the implications have become less ethically confident. Joanna Scheib, for instance, a professor of psychology at the University of California, Davis, has researched this topic and found that "genetic relatedness is important to these offspring and there was some urgency for this group to learn the identity of their donor within the month that they turned 18, when self-identity is developing."[4] Her study included 142 donor-conceived individuals from ages eighteen to twenty-five, and confirmed that 82 per cent of the volunteers had requested to find out information about their donor when they turned eighteen.[5] It was also found that those surveyed desired "first and foremost" to see a picture of their biological father.[6] Desiring to know information concerning one's donor often peaks at eighteen, but also can arise later in life as well. This was found by Wendy Kramer, founder of the Donor Sibling Registry, in a study with a team from Cambridge University.[7] Another study carried out by Patricia Mahlstedt, a psychologist, found that of 85 donor-conceived offspring, 90 per cent of them desired to find out identifying information concerning their donors, and 60 per cent of them believed that

donor-conceived offspring should be allowed to access information about their donor.[8] Dr. Mahlstedt has identified that donor-conceived offspring "hope that providers such as sperm banks, physicians, and nurses will come to regard sperm donation as a positive option, with no need for secrecy, and that they will encourage the use of donors who provide identifying information."[9] And a study released by the Commission on Parenthood's Future found that two-thirds of the 485 donor-conceived adults surveyed around the US from ages eighteen to forty-five agreed that "[m]y sperm donor is half of who I am."[10] In another study, two psychologists at Surrey University found that of 16 volunteers conceived by anonymous sperm donation from the US, UK, Canada, and Australia, between ages twenty-six to fifty-five, all of them thought they had a right to know of their donor.[11]

Taking these kinds of matters into account (and others as well), countries such as Sweden, the UK (in 2005), and Austria have banned anonymous sperm donation. The Netherlands has a law that donor-conceived offspring have a right to access identifying information about their donor[12] and the UK's law affords these offspring the right to access identifying or non-identifying information. What unites these laws is that they regard the child's interests or desires as more substantial than the donor's.

Beyond the studies recounted above, there are first-hand accounts from the children themselves. Many who are born by anonymous insemination have criticized the practice for numerous reasons, but those who voice such concerns commonly agree that they should have a right to access information concerning their donor. So as to frame these concerns in terms of a right, we now discuss how those rights might be conceived, and determine where a right to know of one's genetic heritage might be established.

There are historically two general ways to speak of the genesis of rights and what they do. These are the will theory and interest theory. The will theory dictates that the will – wishes or preferences – of rational adults be considered, and when legitimate, observed in the form of a right. An important stipulation on this is that, as rights come from will, only rational wills are considered as legitimately recognized. This means only competent adults are included in this theory. The function of these rights is twofold: (1) others have a duty to observe them and (2) the right-holder can exercise the right by either demanding that the right be fulfilled or can waive the right's observance if so desired. This being the case, if one has such a right, she has the power to command how others act, that is, command that others act in accordance with the right. This theory connects rights with the idea that they are instituted norms that others are obliged to follow.

Contrasting this is the interest theory, which holds that rights act to benefit people, and derive from those concerns. Rights here come from some principled rule that acts on behalf of people's interests. Given that one can potentially act on behalf of anyone, interest theory allows that rights be allocated to any of those non-rational beings in the world: the criminally insane, children, and infants for example. Interest theory accounts for how many tend to think that non-rational beings do have rights. This is opposed to the will theory, where any such inclusions are disallowed....

To bring this distinction of rights into the milieu of anonymous sperm donation, the right to genetic heritage can be argued for by way of either of these two theories. If the will approach is taken, the wills or preferences of those who desire to know of their genetic heritage is coming from many rational adults. This may just oblige us to act in ways that recognize

their preferences in terms of a right, where they can access genetic heritage information, or waive that right if desired. Will theory could also justify coercing donors to give up information about themselves, as will theory connects an individual's rights with corresponding obligations for others. What must be considered under the will approach is how strong, exact, widespread or significant these wishes might be, along with how rational and reasonably enforced they might be. Once one takes on this task, she soon realizes that many desire to know of their donor, and that these desires are widespread, specific, and are taken with personal seriousness. This is perhaps most readily observed by noting that there are Internet registry sites where donor-conceived offspring attempt to find "matches" with their siblings or donor. One of those sites, the Donor Sibling Registry, founded by Wendy Kramer, attempts to connect donor-conceived offspring with their donors, and has gained over 25,000 members internationally.[13] Another major registry site is www.donoroffspringmatches.com. The website SearchingForMySpermDonor Father.org (which is international) allows donor-conceived offspring to publish information about themselves in hopes that their possible donor might one day answer back. The site UK DonorLink.org was established to allow for the exchange of information between donor-conceived offspring and sperm donors in a discreet but revealing way. One may also consider how some individuals born by anonymous sperm donation are particularly outspoken about the fact that they are denied a full genetic heritage. In Canada, where anonymous sperm donation is practiced, Olivia Pratton in British Columbia was so driven to discover her genetic heritage that she sued the BC Supreme Court, claiming that donor-conceived children who turn 19 should have a right to access information about their donors.[14] In America, Kathleen Ruby LaBounty, also conceived under donor anonymity, has fiercely spoken publicly for a donor-conceived offspring's rights to a genetic heritage. She has told her story to *Oprah*, *The Today Show*, New York Public Radio, and to *People*, among others. The following is a portion of her time on *Oprah*.

> Now 26, Kathleen says having no information about the donor's medical history, heritage or family has been frustrating. She isn't even sure if her donor father knows she exists. "To me, it feels like the death of my biological father and half of my family. I've been searching, and I can't find them." Kathleen's search has centered on the few facts she knows about her donor dad – he was enrolled in medical school at Baylor College in 1981. Over the years, she's written 600 letters to men who fit that description and received 220 responses. Despite 15 DNA tests in one year, she still doesn't have any answers. Over the years, Kathleen says her feelings about not knowing her biological father have changed. "When I was younger, it was more of the curiosity, like why am I who I am and what did I get from my biological father? How am I like him? How am I different from him?" Kathleen says. "Then as I got older, it became more grief and more anger, and I just feel like it should be my right to know who this man is." Finding the donor, Kathleen says, would make a big difference in her life. "I feel like it would put the pieces of my life together and it would provide information about who I am that many people just take for granted."[15]

The following is an autobiographical account taken from the website TangledWebs UK, an organization whose mission is "supporting the rights of donor-conceived people in the UK and across the world."[16]

> To cut a much longer story short, everything turned around for me one day in 2005, when I found out from UK Donor Link the name of several half-siblings, including the natural son of my donor and, thereby, my donor's identity. Although I was in a much stronger frame of mind by then (owing to a relentless pursuit of sanity and wholeness!), it is almost impossible to describe the explosively powerful effect that this had on me. In one moment everything changed. I felt more solid, and the shame slid off me. No longer did I feel apologetic about my appearance, or the workings of my mind. Ironically, it has been much easier to handle the relationship with my social father since learning my natural father's identity, as I can operate from the base of who I am and it is easier, so much easier to cope with our differences. Getting hold of the truth has done a lot to make being donor conceived palatable. Not knowing donor identity is like being lost in the middle of a great, featureless ocean. Now that I know who he was (and, of course, I have a relationship with my half-siblings) my life has form and landmarks.[17]

Katrina Clark wrote as an undergraduate these poignant remarks in *The Washington Post* in 2006:

> I was angry at the idea that where donor conception is concerned, everyone focuses on the "parents" – the adults who can make choices about their own lives. The recipient gets sympathy for wanting to have a child. The donor gets a guarantee of anonymity and absolution from any responsibility for the offspring of his "donation." As long as these adults are

happy, then donor conception is a success, right? Not so. The children born of these transactions are people, too. Those of us in the first documented generation of donor babies – conceived in the late 1980s and early 1990s, when sperm banks became more common and donor insemination began to flourish – are coming of age, and we have something to say…. We offspring are recognizing the right that was stripped from us at birth – the right to know who both our parents are. And we're ready to reclaim it.[18]

These are not trivial desires, but are self-conscious, articulate, authentic, and serious ones that will theory can be persuaded to take as considerable enough in order to justify limiting the donor's rights, along with granting the child the power to accommodate her desires over the donor's. One attractive aspect of taking the will approach to the right to genetic heritage is that similar wills have been taken into account before, with adopted children (and matching wills have been taken into account in other countries). Donor-conceived adults and adult adoptees have historically expressed similar wills in desiring to obtain genetic heritage information. Yet despite similarities in will, adult adoptees have the right in the US to obtain genetic heritage information and those born by anonymous sperm donation are legally barred from this. However, if we accept that these wishes are similar, and appreciate the fact that the wishes of adult adoptees have been legally acknowledged, we cannot fairly deny those born by sperm bank donation a similar right. Granting similar rights to those born by sperm donation would address what amounts to an uneven application of these rights.[19] To state this more formally, the following argument could be made: (1) For many years adult adoptees have struggled for rights to access information about their genetic

heritage, and for many years this was denied. However, these wishes were eventually taken into account, and this led to changes in adoption policy: Not only does the child have a right to access information about her parents, but the parent who gave the child up for adoption does not have a right to privacy insofar as remaining a secret to his or her child. (2) Those born by anonymous sperm donation want to know about their genetic heritage as well, and their desires, compared to adult adoptees, are nearly identical. (3) Like wishes (especially when similar in end and nature) entail like rights. (4) Adult adoptees have a right to obtain information about their genetic heritage. (5) Therefore, those born by sperm donation should have a right to obtain information about their genetic heritage. So long as adult adoptees' right to access genetic heritage is legally enforceable and considered legitimate, there is an unequal application of rights with respect to these two categories of children. These concerns could even come under the scope of the Equal Protection Clause, for as everyone is equal under the law, so should genetic heritage rights be equally awarded.

The interest theory, on the other hand, allows that rights come from acting on behalf of people's interests, and there are several ways to frame the right to genetic heritage under this prerequisite. It is clearly in one's interest to obtain medical information about one's donor. There was a case in 2006 where a man passed on a rare and dangerous genetic disease to five children by sperm donation.[20] If only medical and genetic history are considered adequate to act in one's interests, then only non-identifying information would be included in the right to genetic heritage. However, if emotional or psychological benefits were included, this could make a case for identifying information as well. By emotional and psychological benefits, we mean that some studies have suggested that donor-conceived offspring suffer from not knowing about their genetic heritage, and hence, providing them with identifying information or robust non-identifying information could help alleviate those possible harms. For example, Lynne W. Spencer, herself a donor child, found through testimonial research that donor-conceived children often experienced troubled emotions, e.g., they felt nonexistent, struggled with their identity, felt a sense of injustice, and a deep-rooted sense of loss.[21]

Information that would help mitigate these feelings would likely have to be more "emotional" than medical, e.g., knowing about the biological father's hobbies, talents, place of origin, ethnicity, and learning about his physical features, among others. Juliet Guichon, a medical bioethics professor at the University of Calgary in Alberta, has held that those conceived by anonymous sperm donation may suffer from comparable kinds of psychological pain due to not knowing their genetic heritage and may also experience difficulties with establishing an identity.[22]

A study published in 2000 in the journal *Human Reproduction* found that when those conceived by anonymous sperm donation find out about the conditions of their birth, they can suffer from an identity crisis along with having feelings of abandonment and loss.[23]

The same journal published a study in 2007, concluding that theoretically and clinically, "secrecy in families compromises functioning" as related to topic avoidance when children are donor-conceived.[24]

And Derek Morgan, a professor of genetic and bioengineering law at Queensland University of Technology, has held that "genetic anger" and "a real resentment" can result when information about one's biological father or mother is being withheld from people born by artificial reproduction.[25] To act on these interests probably means allowing donor-conceived offspring to obtain meaningful information about their donor, which speaks of their biological father's personality. Also, consider the UN Convention on the Rights of the Child. Article 8 has identified that it is in one's interest to "preserve his or her identity, including nationality, name and family relations as recognized by law without unlawful interference."[26] It is further in one's own interest, and the interests of the state, that donor-conceived offspring avoid sibling intermarriage. Consider the following research from Walter Wadlington:

> on balance the lack of donor recordkeeping is perhaps unparalleled anywhere in medical practice … the pertinent … information typically is never even recorded. If genetic or medical informational needs and the avoidance of sibling intermarriage requires detailed donor records, the legislature must consider the problems of controlling access to these records and the access rights of artificially conceived children.[27]

At the least, information about one's siblings should be given to the biological children of sperm donors. And perhaps this should be a matter of course for the sake of public health, instead of voluntarily accessed. Either way, as Wadlington illustrates, clinics will have to take on new levels of responsibility in documentation than currently invested if they take into account such concerns. Invoking interest theory can also argue for overturning the donor's right to anonymity based on either a version of the Harm Principle, or by mention of the Welfare Principle. One's liberty may be justifiably controlled to act in certain ways by others when doing so prevents harm, which has a "negative" interest in benefiting others. And one's liberty may also be constrained to act in certain ways to protect others from harm.

So both theories of rights provide justification for a right to genetic heritage. Combining the empirical and ethical concerns is compatible under these approaches. As new sperm bank children come into the world, they should be able to claim, without struggle, a birthright that has thus far been denied to many in the past.

## Power of the Contract and Parental Responsibility

We now look at the source of the donor's right to anonymity, which is the anonymous sperm donor contract. The above considerations aside, the moral legitimacy of the contract itself is questioned in this section. In this way, anonymous sperm donation can be challenged on two independent levels: the right to genetic heritage, and the proposition that the contract may not earn moral or legal recognition (for reasons unrelated to genetic heritage). So what does the contract do? It is assumed sufficient to excuse the biological father from any legal or familial obligations he might have, and also denies his parental rights, which are given to the mother. The contract also acts to cover all potential children from the use of the seller's sperm. This may be identified as contractual parenthood: the ability of biological parents to ratify or render inoperative parenthood for one party or another through a contract. The result of contractual parenthood in this case affords rights to biological fathers that are not granted to other biological fathers by allowing some to withdraw from paternal responsibility by contract and prohibiting others to do the same thing in other situations. This also delivers an uneven application of rights to children insofar as some children are entitled to child support from their biological fathers and others are not, when their biological father happens to be a donor.

Such irregularities have also been exposed in the courts. For example, the Pennsylvania Supreme Court determined in 2008 that a sperm donor does not have to pay child support and this per a verbal agreement.[28] In another decision conflicting with this one, the United States Court of Appeals, Sixth Circuit, voted down similar rights for the biological father in a verbal agreement. In the case of *Dubay v. Wells*,[29] Mr. Dubay insisted that he made it clear to Ms. Wells that he did not want to have children, and she assured him of similar intentions by telling him that she was taking oral contraceptives and that pregnancy was unlikely due to certain physical conditions. After they separated from dating each other, Wells informed Dubay that she was pregnant, and, after deciding to keep the baby, Wells sued Dubay for child support. Despite Dubay's explicit intentions made known to Wells about not wanting to have a child, and her agreement to these terms, the appeals court ruled in favor of the mother. But by using the sperm donor contract as a model and legal precedent, might not the court be bound to rule otherwise in this case were a written contract involved?

That is, using the sperm donor contract as a model, what if Dubay had written out a sexual contract, which Wells had agreed to? The contract would carry out the same end, and provide the same right to the same individual, the biological father, excusing him from paternal responsibility and renouncing his paternal rights. Suppose he carefully stated his intent, which is to not have children, and is therefore to not be liable as a parent if happenstance proved otherwise. He could include the language from a donor contract in this adapted model:

> Each party acknowledges and agrees that the MALE LOVER is providing his [love through] … said [intercourse] and does so with the clear understanding that

he will not demand, request, or compel any guardianship, custody, or visitation rights with any child(ren) resulting … [and] the RECIPIENT, through this AGREEMENT, has relinquished any and all rights that she might otherwise have to hold the MALE LOVER legally, financially, or emotionally responsible for any child(ren) that result from … [intercourse].[30]

Similar interests do call for similar rights, that is, for biological fathers, so why allow the donor to use the contract to multiply his seed without legal or moral consequence and disallow others or even a one-night stand father to enjoy such a right? This is not about a notion of parental responsibility that is genetically based (or not). Rather this is about an unequal application of rights, and this moves us to three main options. In the interest of being fair, we could disallow biological parents to engage in contracts that determine parental responsibility. Or, in the interest of being fair, we could allow all biological parents to engage in contracts that determine parental responsibility. Thirdly, we could uphold the status quo. Now the status quo is undesirable because, as mentioned, it upholds an unequal application of rights to biological fathers and to children. The option of allowing all biological parents to engage in a contract that determines parental responsibility would be a cumbersome project, and undo our legal paradigm that presumes that parental responsibility is an involuntary, not elective, duty that is enacted despite one's inclinations to be or not be a parent. So the first option seems the best, to equalize these rights by deflating the validity of determining parental responsibility by contract.[31] …

So how might the moral argument against the donor contract and the rights argument against the donor contract be acknowledged in the legal sphere? And how could it be done by respecting the prospective mother's reproductive autonomy and choice in obtaining sperm, and also respect the biological father's interests in donating? Consider that when parents of adopted children give up their parental rights, it is accomplished through court procedures and is only completed after the child has been born. In contrast to this, the biological fathers who remove their parental rights and responsibilities by way of the donor contract give up those rights as they pertain to possibly numerous children, before they are born. Taking this into account, one possible answer to this question might be to hold sperm donors responsible in a similar way wherein parental rights must be terminated in a manner akin to a biological parent releasing a child for adoption. Donors could still obtain financial reward for selling their reproductive material and would not be held liable for child support afterward, and prospective mothers could still obtain sperm, but the donors would have to remove their parental rights through the courts for each child actually born by their sperm. Assuredly, this is an investment, but it would, to some degree, even out the rights assigned to parents and children, by assuming parental responsibility as legally enforceable instead of voluntarily rejected, and would also bring to light the magnitude and responsibility involved in one deciding to produce a child. Parental responsibility would not be an item that one could contractually avoid before a child is born. Under this provision, biological fathers would be presumed responsible and would be required to give up their parental rights in a way similar to the removal of parental rights for adoption. It would not be one's inclinations against being a parent that would remove parental responsibility. It would certainly be in the donor's interest then to know how many biological children he had, as child support could be enforceable until his parental rights were properly removed for any one child.

## On Signing Papers as a Sufficient Meeting of Parental Responsibility

Signing adoption papers is no small, legalistic gesture. It is a sobering acknowledgment of one's responsibility and an acknowledgement of the child brought into existence from one's own genetic material. The present cavalier method of sperm depositing and never looking back does not properly address the depth of one's connection to, and responsibility for, the child. If donors had to sign adoption papers it is our assertion that they would experience a moral pause and most likely emotional difficulties....

The mere depositing of sperm, often by young men, carries an aura of nonchalant irresponsibility. If a potential donor knew that he would have to sign away his rights at the birth of his issue, he would certainly be given serious pause as opposed to the circumstances now. This procedure would be even more austere if he were to see the child in court. His actions would no longer be hypothetical, there would be empirical evidence of his role in creating another human being....

## Reproductive Ethics in the Public Domain: Respect and Care

In conclusion, while reproductive ethics is concerned with many essential problems, there could be more concern with the point of view of offspring born by reproductive technology by looking at how the social rules around that technology affect them in emotional or legal ways. Doing so, we submit, would require ethicists to encourage that due care and respect be allotted to these offspring. As Joan Hollinger, an expert on adoption law at the University of California, Berkeley, said, "There isn't anyone at the table assigned to think about the needs of any resulting children" from sperm donation.[32] However, some are trying to articulate such needs. Dr. Ian Mitchell, a professor of pediatrics and bioethics at the University of Calgary and Juliet Guichon, a professor of medical bioethics professor at the same university, have worked on a book that concerns the rights for those born by reproductive technology.[33] Both have been concerned with how anonymous sperm donation severs people from their genetic heritage, and how this might adversely affect them. Taking donor-conceived offspring as a moral precedent, this could help articulate what other children born by artificial reproduction might be entitled to after they are born. Doing so would involve reproductive ethics in two fields: the moral concerns involved in attaining or ending fetal life, and also issues of social justice for those born by artificial reproduction. Realizing that reproductive technology manifestly involves social components compels us to conceive a reproductive socio-bioethics. At any rate, we no longer should think of artificial reproduction without thinking of the children it produces, and what they need....

## Study Questions

1. Collins and Comerford argue that there is an inconsistency between allowing donors to relinquish parental responsibility but compelling those who become parents through sexual reproduction to take responsibility for the resulting offspring. Do you agree with their argument? How would you propose to eradicate this inconsistency? Do you agree with their proposals?

2. Do children of gamete donors have a right to know their genetic ancestry? If so, does this interfere with donors' rights to anonymity? Is there a way to reconcile the two, or are Collins and Comerford correct that the rights of the offspring trump the rights of the donor?

3. The Supreme Court has constantly recognized a right to procreative liberty (that is, people cannot be forced to have children, nor can they be prevented from having children). Some have argued that restricting gamete donations would violate this right. Do you believe this to be the case? If Collins and Comerford are correct that children have a right to know their genetic heritage, and therefore that there should be restrictions on gamete donation, could this interfere with procreative liberty? Why or why not?

4. Why do you think children of gamete donors desire knowledge about their genetic parents? How much of our identity is related to our genes and our genetic history? What implications does this question have for other areas of reproductive ethics, e.g., cloning, genetic engineering, and even transracial adoption?

## Notes

1  Parrish Anne Protheroe, "Conceived Via Anonymous Donor Insemination: Understanding What It Means to Be a Donor Offspring" (PhD Thesis, The University of Connecticut, 2005).
2  Cheryl Wetzstein, "Report: Sperm-Donor Offspring Support Idea but They Also Have Concerns about Father, Half-Siblings," *The Washington Times*, June 1, 2010, http://www.washingtontimes.com/news/2010/jun/1/report-sperm-donor-offspring-support-idea/ (accessed June 30, 2010).
3  Ibid.
4  Kate Johnson, "ASRM: Pressure Builds for Open-Identity Sperm Donation in the U.S." *medpage TODAY*, November 14, 2008, http://www.medpagetoday.com/MeetingCoverage/ASRM/11783 (accessed June 30, 2010).
5  Ibid.
6  Margaret Talbot, "THE YEAR IN IDEAS: A TO Z; Open Sperm Donation," *The New York Times*, December 9, 2001, http://www.nytimes.com/2001/12/09/magazine/the-year-in-ideas-a-to-z-open-sperm-donation.html?scp=1&sq=sperm+donation+anonymous&st=nyt (accessed June 30, 2010).
7  Johnson, "ASRM: Pressure Builds for Open-Identity Sperm Donation in the U.S."
8  Ibid.
9  Ibid.
10 Elizabeth Marquardt, Norval D. Glenn, and Karen Clark, "Pathbreaking Study Finds Adults Conceived through Sperm Donation Suffer Substantial Harm," *Family Scholars*, May 2010, http://www.familyscholars.org/assets/Donor_pressrelease.pdf (accessed June 30, 2010).
11 Sarah Boseley, "Children Born by Donated Sperm 'Liable to Suffer Identity Crisis' Researchers Claim," *The Guardian*, August 31, 2000, http://www.guardian.eo.uk/uk/2000/aug/31/sarahboscley (accessed June 30, 2010).
12 P.M.W. Janssens, A.H.A Simons, R.J. van Kooij, E. Blokzijl, and G.A.J. Dunselman, "A New Dutch Law Regulating Provision of Identifying Information of Donors to Offspring: Background, Content and Impact," *Human Reproduction* 21.4 (2005): 852–56.

13  Roger Collier, "Disclosing the Identity of Sperm Donors," *Canadian Medical Association Journal*, February 23, 2010, http://www.cmaj.ca/cgi/content/full/182/3/232 (accessed June 30, 2010).

14  Ibid.

15  *The Oprah Winfrey Show*, "Donor-Conceived Children Search for Answers," aired March 14, 2008.

16  http://www.tangledwebs.org.uk/tw /.

17  *TangledWebs UK*, "Louise's Story," n.d, http://www.tangledwebs.org.uk/tw/Stories/ Louise/ (accessed July 2, 2010).

18  Katrina Clark," My Father Was an Anonymous Sperm Donor," *The Washington Post*, December 17, 2006, http://www.washingtonpost.com/wp-dyn/content/article/2006/12/15/ AR2006121501820.html (accessed June 10, 2010).

19  Note that genetic heritage information awarded to adult adoptees varies from state to state: some are entitled to more information, others less, and some find existing law still too narrow. For example, the organization "Bastard Nation" is campaigning so that adult adoptees have unrestricted access to their birth records.

20  Roxanne Khamsi, "Children with Gene Disorder Share Sperm Donor Dad," *New Scientist*, May 23, 2006, http://www.newscientist.com/article/dn9208-children-with-gene-disorder-share-sperm-donor-dad.html (accessed July 28, 2010).

21  Lynne W. Spencer, "Sperm Donor Offspring: Identity and Other Experiences" (PhD Thesis, self published, 2007).

22  Collier, "Disclosing the Identity of Sperm Donors."

23  Boseley, "Children Born by Donated Sperm."

24  Marilyn S. Paul and Roni Berger, "Topic Avoidance and Family Functioning in Families Conceived with Donor Insemination," *Human Reproduction* 22.9 (2007): 2566–71.

25  Australian Broadcasting Corporation, "7.30 Report-23/11/2006: IVF Youth Experiencing Genetic Anger," November 23, 2006, http://www.abc.net.au/7.30/content/2006/ s1796095.htm (accessed July 2, 2010).

26  UN General Assembly, Office of the UN High Commissioner for Human Rights, *Convention on the Rights of the Child*, November 20, 1989, United Nations, http://www2.ohchr.org/english/law/crc.htm (accessed July 2, 2010).

27  Walter Wadlington, "Artificial Conception: The Challenge for Family Law," *Virginia Law Review* 69.3 (1983): 465–514.

28  Associated Press, "Sperm Donor Wins Child Support Battle: Mother Can't Renege on Payment Deal, Pa. Supreme Court Rules," *msnbc.com*, January 3, 2008, http://www.msnbc.msn.com/id/22488113/ (accessed June 30, 2010).

29  *Dubay v. Wells*, 506 F.3d 422 (6th Cir.2007).

30  "Sample Known-Donor Contract," *Maia Midwifery and Preconception Services*. 2005, http:// http://www.maiamidwifery.com/downloads/Sample_Known_Donor_Agreement.pdf (accessed June 3, 2010).

31  The Supreme Court of Ireland ruled in favor of this understanding in December of 2009, making it so that "Lesbians and other recipients of donor sperm cannot rely on pre-existing contracts that say the birth father has little or no role in their children's lives. Men's biology and parenthood matters and, as a result of the unanimous Supreme Court ruling, sperm donors have the status of a natural father." *Irish Independent*, "Constitution Holds Sway in Definition of the Family Unit," December 11, 2009, http://www.independent.ie/opinion/analysis/constitution-holds-sway-in-definition-of-the-family-unit-1971190.html (accessed July 2, 2010).

32   Amy Harmon, "Are You My Sperm Donor? Few Clinics Will Say," *The New York Times*, January 20, 2008, http://query.nytimes.com/gst/fullpage.html?res=9403E1DB123FF933A15752 COA9609C8B63&sec=health&spon=&pagewanted=2 (accessed June 30, 2010).

33   Collier, "Disclosing the Identity of Sperm Donors."

# 7. Arlene Judith Klotzko, "Medical Miracle or Medical Mischief? The Saga of the McCaughey Septuplets"

THE AMERICAN MEDIA, AND its audience, is enamored with the birth of multiples. When the McCaughey septuplets were born in 1997, the family was inundated by media, well-wishers, and donations, all fascinated by the successful birth and survival of seven infants. Television shows such as *Jon and Kate Plus 8*, *Table for Twelve*, and *Raising Sextuplets* contribute to the celebration, giving a seemingly ideal picture of families that are stressed out by a brood of healthy, active, and adorable multiples. However, the reality, as bioethicist Arlene Judith Klotzko emphasizes in this 1998 *Hastings Center Report* essay, is not as idyllic. Infants who result from higher-order multiple births (defined as a pregnancy with three or more fetuses) are often born prematurely and sometimes die within days or weeks of their birth. When they do survive, they can face a host of health problems: for example, bowel obstructions, intracranial hemorrhages, respiratory distress syndrome, and cerebral palsy. What are the moral dimensions to using reproductive technology that increases the chances of higher-order multiple births? Would selective abortion be morally permissible in these cases or, indeed, even morally required? Klotzko discusses all these questions in her article and argues that these ethical issues must be addressed if we are to responsibly engage in reproductive technology.

---

THE STORY OF THE McCaughey septuplets is a quintessentially American story, combining many ingredients of modern life. The oftentimes uncritical celebration of dramatic, medical technological breakthroughs, the romanticization of life in middle America, and the growing influence of fundamentalist Christianity, along with its close relative, the anti-abortion movement. And in the later stages of the story, the growing visibility of bioethics and bioethicists.

On 19 November, after thirty-one weeks gestation, the seven babies – dubbed "the magnificent seven" by wide-eyed reporters – were born within six minutes. Their weights ranged from two pounds five ounces to three pounds four ounces. A team of forty nurses, respiratory therapists, perinatologists, neonatologists, and anesthesiologists officiated at the delivery. All the septuplets were placed on ventilator support for some days, but by the end of November they were breathing on their own.

The birth that captured and held the attention of the American media took place at Iowa Methodist Medical Center, just ten miles from the small midwestern town of Carlisle, Iowa, population 3,240. Carlisle is the home of Bobbi McCaughey, a twenty-nine-year-old seamstress, and her husband, Kenny, twenty-seven, a billing clerk at a local automobile dealership. They shared their small two-bedroom house with a daughter, Mikayla, aged two. Since the septuplets' birth, the Governor of Iowa made good his promise to build them a new – and much larger – house.

This was the most generous of a bewildering assortment of gifts showered upon the family, including seven years of cable TV, university scholarships for all the children, ten years of portrait photographs, and a lifetime supply of Pampers. And there were more meaningful and less tangible gifts. According to *Time* magazine (1 December 1997), the response of the other inhabitants of Carlisle "bespoke a neighborliness that seems to have vanished from much of America…. A brigade of neighbors and friends has coordinated meal preparation, laundry, transportation, baby sitting, and housecleaning. 'They say it takes a village to raise children,' says city administrator Neil Ruddy. 'We just didn't know it would be our village.'" Lonely city sophisticates on both coasts turned green with envy.

Bobbi had been born with a malfunctioning pituitary gland that produced too little follicle stimulating hormone (FSH) that normally prompts a few eggs to mature every month. She wanted very much to have a child and sought fertility treatment. After one year without success, her doctors prescribed a stronger drug, Metrodin, which is rich in FSH. Mikayla, a single child, was the result. When the little girl was sixteen months old, the McCaugheys decided that she should have a brother or sister. Reluctant to wait a year, they asked that Metrodin be administered without delay.

What happened next is somewhat unclear. There have been conflicting reports, but it seems that Bobbi was given a shot of human chorionic gonadotropin (HCG), which helped release her eggs and enabled them to unite with her husband's sperm. Bobbi became pregnant on the first try and six weeks later an ultrasound revealed that she was carrying seven fetuses. A failure of medical judgment – or at least medical management – seems to have occurred, but much of the media resolutely kept its eyes off this aspect of the story.

Most Americans believe that the McCaugheys faced an inevitable choice between the risks of this multiple pregnancy and what was for this family, as fundamentalist Christians, the morally untenable option of selective abortion. But abortion is a retrospective solution, and prospective remedies are always better. This multiple pregnancy simply did not have to happen. Good medical practice mandates ultrasound scans for women who have taken fertility drugs in order to monitor accurately the number of eggs they produce. If the number is too high and the risks of multiple pregnancy too great, the patient should be advised to refrain from sexual activity and try again later.

Moreover, when the ultrasound scan reveals a large number of eggs, in vitro fertilization (IVF) can be used. Bobbi McCaughey's physicians could have removed some of her eggs, fertilized them outside her body, and then implanted a maximum of three embryos. In some ways – as wonderful as it most certainly is that Bobbi McCaughey and her children are doing so well – the birth of septuplets should be seen not as a great success of modern medical technology, but as a failure.

Dr. Mark Sauer, Chief of Reproductive Endocrinlogy at Columbia Presbyterian Medical Center in New York, told the *Washington Post* (21 November 1997) that "it would have been obvious that her ovaries had overreacted to the drug…. She must have had a dozen or more eggs going, and if she was being monitored correctly they had to know she was grossly overstimulated before she got her HCG shot." Voices such as his were drowned out, however, as the celebration of a happy outcome for the McCaughey family quickly metamorphosed into a celebration of technology.

Two days after the birth, critical voices were raised once more. Bioethicists participated in two of the three major Sunday news programs. Dr. Sauer appeared as well, characterizing the birth of the septuplets as an example of the overzealous use of fertility drugs. This inappropriate use, he said, has resulted in widespread iatrogenic fetal reduction. And a shocking number of multiple births – since 1971, the number of multiple births in the United States has quadrupled.

It has resulted, as well, in mothers and babies being exposed to great – and avoidable – risk. Ovarian over-stimulation carries dangers of swelling and bleeding of the ovaries and severe fluid retention. In rare cases this can lead to heart failure. Women carrying multiple fetuses are at risk for potentially fatal blood clots during pregnancy and delivery. Children born in numbers greater than three often suffer from illnesses including chronic lung disease, strokes, mental retardation, and blindness. Once medical management has failed, however, the only remedy is selective reduction.

Selective abortion, as this practice is usually called in the United States, inspires a great deal of controversy. There is a large measure of irony here as well. As Dr. Sauer said, the practice is an emblem of medical failure. But that failure is due in no small part to the absence of a comprehensive regulatory scheme for IVF and embryo research in the United States. And the cause of that effect is the political power of the anti-abortion movement. Human IVF has developed in the private sector. Several hundred clinics operate with no government money and little government oversight. Guidelines have been developed by the industry, but compliance is voluntary. There is also a set of ethical considerations, published by The American Society for Reproductive Medicine in 1994.

It could well be that this entrepreneurial atmosphere has in itself encouraged the inappropriate use of fertility drugs. In the American culture – where the customer is always right – the customer in this case wants to become pregnant. And if possible, she will choose the clinic that has the highest pregnancy rate. One way of securing a competitive advantage is to overuse fertility drugs. In the United States the costs of fertility treatments are usually not covered by insurance; they must be borne by the patient. Thus there is even more pressure for a quick success – and, as a result, more and more multiple births.

In many respects, the situation in Britain provides an interesting and illuminating comparison. In the United Kingdom assisted reproduction is regulated by the Human Fertilisation and Embryology Act. The Act's Code of Practice for physicians providing infertility treatment limits the number of embryos that can be implanted to three. Any more would pose unacceptable dangers for mother and babies. But there are gaps in even the best legislative scheme. The administration of fertility drugs is not covered by UK legislation. Hence the infamous case of Mandy Allwood, a case that both shocked and fascinated the British public in 1996.

Even though she had conceived naturally several times, Mandy applied for and was given fertility drugs. After an ultrasound revealed the presence of an unsafe number of eggs, she ignored her physician's advice not to have intercourse. Mandy became pregnant with eight fetuses. She refused to have selective abortion, but it soon became apparent that her decision probably had a pecuniary rather than a moral basis. Reportedly, a tabloid – the *News of the World* – had agreed to pay her £1,000,000 if all eight babies were born. But Mandy could not sustain her pregnancy and after nineteen weeks she lost all eight fetuses. She had literally gambled and lost.

Bobbi McCaughey gambled as well, but according to both the family and the media, she had a powerful ally. *As Time* magazine put it, "The McCaugheys' faith, plus a gamble on fertility drugs, won them a seven-figure jackpot." *People* magazine (8 December 1997) said that, "defying the medical odds, Bobbi and Kenny McCaughey clung to their faith and were rewarded – times seven." This religious vocabulary was certainly apt for the McCaugheys. Fundamentalist Christian religion is central to their lives, and to the life of the town of Carlisle. And it is not out of place in much – but not all – of contemporary America.

Ronald Dworkin has described the profound ambivalence of Americans on the subject of religion. Despite a constitutionally mandated separation of church and state, the United States is among the most religious of modern western democracies. And in the tone of its most powerful religious groups, by far the most fundamentalist. With its opposition to abortion and to euthanasia, the Catholic church has played an important role, as have fundamentalist Christians – particularly in regard to abortion, fetal tissue research, and embryo research. For the McCaugheys, selective reduction "just wasn't an option," Kenny told reporters. "We were trusting in the Lord for the outcome."

For those of a more secular turn of mind, several troublesome moral issues are raised by this case. And they are certainly not peculiar to the American scene.

First, the role and responsibility of the media, a role that was pivotal in the Allwood case. The offer of one million pounds from the *News of the World* may well have affected her decision not to have selective reduction. But more often, as in the McCaughey case, the media plays a less direct role. When they report a story such as this one in a way that emphasizes the positive side and de-emphasizes the risks, they are behaving irresponsibly. Indeed, the celebratory tenor of the septuplet coverage raises a real danger that giving birth to seven babies all at once will be seen as the medical state of the art to be emulated for fame or for profit.

Second, the stigmatization of infertility as a disease and not, as Tristram Engelhardt might call it, an unfortunate result of life's lottery. If Bobbi McCaughey was willing to go to such lengths to become a mother, are those with less strength of purpose or less success somehow flawed?

Third, the matter of eligibility and access. Mandy Allwood had conceived naturally several times and Bobbi McCaughey already had one child. What are morally permissible criteria for eligibility? And who decides? In the United States it is the market. Fertility drugs seem to be the poor person's remedy, while IVF is reserved for those with means or very good insurance. The McCaugheys are economically in the lower middle class. One can only wonder about the care Bobbi McCaughey would have received at a more state of the art – and expensive – program.

In Britain, in theory, the physician decides who should have treatment. The Code of Practice of the Human Fertilisation and Embryology Act gives broad discretion to physicians to make eligibility determinations based on the best interests of potential children. But the so-called "internal market" may be distorting the process. Fertility clinics in the United Kingdom provide services according to contractual arrangements made with the particular patient's local or regional health authority. Some contracts contain criteria that are more stringent than others. Thus while some women must be infertile or at least childless to qualify for treatment, others need not meet such qualifications. Such discrepancies seem both arbitrary and grossly unfair.

Fourth, the question of cost – both human and economic. The former relates to the risk of harm to mother and baby, the latter to the identity of the payer. In the United Kingdom patients have IVF on the National Health Service, but also privately. Should the identity of the payer – the state or private funds – change the moral calculus in regard to eligibility? If the government pays, thus expending a communal resource, should eligibility be restricted to those who are childless or married? In the United States, although the costs of fertility treatment are seldom covered by insurance, the exorbitant cost of caring for multiple premature newborns – in this case estimated at upwards of $1,500,000 – is a covered expense. Society must bear these costs in one way or another. Do people have the right to inflict costs like these on others?

Fifth, some difficult informed consent questions. Many practitioners consider selective reduction to be a fall-back position to be used when fertility treatment goes wrong. What is to be done if the patient, like the McCaugheys, simply refuses? Is it morally permissible to build this decision into the informed consent process and if the woman will not acquiesce in advance, deny her treatment? Can a document be drafted that would lock a patient into agreeing to selective reduction if there were a certain number of embryos? For both legal and ethical reasons, certainly not.

Sixth, the question of the propriety of selective reduction itself. If we could save some lives only by taking others, could it somehow be more ethical to allow all to perish? It certainly seems not, but selective reduction is performed in circumstances in which there is no way to know which fetus is more likely to be normal or to flourish. Does this veil of ignorance make selective reduction more morally problematic than abortion for reasons of defect?

What are the circumstances in which we should allow or even recommend selective reduction? Should this option be limited to situations of great risk to mother or baby, or can its use be more discretionary? In the United States the right to an abortion is a fundamental right under the Constitution and cannot be infringed upon in any way during the first trimester of pregnancy. The current abortion law in Britain is also quite broad. But what of morally troublesome cases like the recent instance, in Britain, of selective reduction of a twin for social reasons – for the convenience of an upper middle class working mother?

Finally, it is crucial that the humanity in human interest stories such as the tale of the McCaughey septuplets does not obscure the key moral issues. There are many. They are compelling. And they must be addressed. Bioethicists have been seen, but have they really been heard?

## Study Questions

1. List some of the concerns that Klotzko discusses about higher-order multiple births. Given these concerns, what should couples facing infertility do with respect to utilizing artificial reproductive technologies? That is, what are some of the morally responsible ways of using this technology?

2. Is the selective reduction of multifetal pregnancies a case of morally permissible abortion? Were the McCaugheys right in refusing to abort some of the fetuses as a means to assure the health of the others? Given their voluntary participation in reproductive medicine and their refusal to abort, are they morally responsible for the disabilities of their children?

3. Some countries, for example the UK and Italy, have placed legal restrictions on how many embryos can be transferred into a womb during IVF procedures. Would such restrictions be appropriate in the United States? Why or why not?

4. As Klotzko notes, the American media often focus on successful cases of higher-order multiple births (for example, the McCaugheys and the Gosselins) without also highlighting cases where the infants either die or suffer a lifetime of severe disabilities. Do you agree with Klotzko that the media are "behaving irresponsibly" when they do this? What moral obligations, if any, do the media have in reporting cases of higher-order multiple births in more honest, and less sensationalistic, ways?

# Section VII:
# Living and Dying Well:
# Health Care and Euthanasia

Every nation must now develop an overriding loyalty to mankind as a whole in order to preserve the best in their individual societies. This call for a worldwide fellowship that lifts neighborly concern beyond one's tribe, race, class, and nation is in reality a call for an all-embracing, unconditional love for all men. This oft misunderstood and misinterpreted concept, so readily dismissed by the Nietzsches of the world as a weak and cowardly force, has now become an absolute necessity for the survival of mankind.

— Dr. Martin Luther King Jr., *Why I Am Opposed to the Vietnam War*

DR. SAMUEL METZ, A private-practice anesthesiologist in Portland, Oregon, wrote a piece in *Anesthesiology Today* in 2015, explaining that

> Americans pay twice as much as citizens in the average industrialized nation – our health care is the most expensive on earth. Yet our public health is a disgrace. There are 60 other countries where a pregnant woman and her baby have better chances of surviving the pregnancy. American diabetics are more likely to suffer a foot amputation from an untreated ulcer than are diabetics living anywhere else where you can drink the tap water. Our infant mortality rates are the highest in the civilized world…. Our life expectancy ranks 30 to 35 in the world, even after

correcting for trauma, traffic accidents, racial disparity and smoking. And each year, 44,000 Americans die of treatable diseases because they lack money for treatment.[1]

Dr. Metz argues in the above commentary, both from an economic/administrative and a health-care delivery perspective, that the United States desperately needs to learn lessons about health care from other countries that have less waste and better outcomes. We can also react to the 2009 statistic of 44,000 Americans dying of treatable diseases a year because they lack money for treatment by asking whether, as a matter of principle, it is just to deny people life-saving medical therapies simply because they lack money for treatment. One way to raise this question is to ask whether the "exclusively American" phenomenon of "medical bankruptcy" is just. As Dr. Metz writes,

> Adding insult to the injury of expensive care and dismal outcomes is that medical debt is the leading cause of personal bankruptcy in the United States. Most of those bankrupt families owned an insurance policy when the medical crisis began – so much for insurance policies protecting access to health care. A further insult is that "medical bankruptcy" is an exclusively American disease. In no other country will you lose your home, your foot or your life if you can't pay for health care.[2]

Is it just that someone should have to "choose" between having a place to live and being able to live? Should life-saving treatments or services benefit those who can afford them and be denied to those who can't? Should expensive medical treatments be distributed as luxury cars are distributed? Should health care be treated as just another commodity, or is there something morally distinctive and important about health care that means it ought to be conceived of as a right? International moral discourse created in response to the desecration of human life in World War II and the need to try those who carried out crimes against humanity sees health care as a right. Section 1 of Article 25 of the 1948 UN Declaration of Human Rights reads:

> Everyone has the right to a standard of living adequate for the health and well-being of himself and of his family, including food, clothing, housing and medical care and necessary social services, and the right to security in the event of unemployment, sickness, disability, widowhood, old age or other lack of livelihood in circumstances beyond his control.[3]

And Article 12 of the International Covenant on Economic, Social and Cultural Rights (1966) reads:

> The States Parties to the present Covenant recognize the right of everyone to the enjoyment of the highest attainable standard of physical and mental health. The steps to be taken by the States Parties to the present Covenant to achieve the full realization of this right shall include those necessary for: (a) The provision for the reduction of the stillbirth-rate and of infant mortality and for the healthy development of the child; (b) The improvement of all aspects of environmental and industrial hygiene; (c) The prevention, treatment and control of epidemic, endemic, occupational and other diseases; (d) The creation of conditions which would assure to all medical service and medical attention in the event of sickness.[4]

The 2009 statistic of 44,000 Americans dying a year from treatable diseases because they lack money for treatment may well change, given the US Supreme Court decision on the Affordable Care Act on 25 June 2015, which, as Adam Gaffney states, had the practical consequence of ensuring that "[m]any Americans – some 8.2 million, according to an estimate from the Urban Institute – no longer need to worry about being unceremoniously dumped into the ranks of the uninsured. It has been estimated that a ruling in favor of the plaintiffs could have cost between 8,000 and 9,800 lives a year."[5] Yet this has to be considered in light of a 2014 study which found that

> One-quarter of people with healthcare coverage are paying so much for deductibles and out-of-pocket expenses that they are considered underinsured.... An

SECTION VII: LIVING AND DYING WELL: HEALTH CARE AND EUTHANASIA

estimated 31 million insured people are not adequately protected against high medical costs, a figure that has doubled since 2003.... Rising deductibles – even under ObamaCare – are the biggest problem for most people who are considered underinsured.... "The steady growth in the proliferation and size of deductibles threatens to increase under-insurance in the years ahead," the report warns. The data is an early warning sign for the Obama administration, which has promised that the millions of people who gained insurance under the president's law would have affordable access to healthcare. The survey found that millions of people are paying into the insurance system but are largely unable to reap the benefits. People who purchase the lowest-quality health insurance are also less likely to see a doctor when they are ill or injured because they fear their high out-of-pocket costs.[6]

Clearly, issues relating to how the US health-care system should be run have not been settled. But neither have issues relating to health-care justice. How might we go about settling among ourselves distributive issues pertaining to how health-care dollars should be socially spent? Consider for a moment the procedure that John Rawls claims allows rules pertaining to social cooperation to be justly asked, evaluated, and resolved. He writes:

Imagine a society of persons amongst whom a certain system of practices is *already* well established. Now suppose that by and large they are mutually self-interested; their allegiance to their established practices is normally founded on the prospect of self-advantage.... Now suppose also that these persons are rational....

Finally, assume that these persons have roughly similar needs and interests, or needs and interests in various ways complementary, so that fruitful cooperation amongst them is possible; and suppose that they are sufficiently equal in power and ability to guarantee that in normal circumstances none is able to dominate the others.... Since these persons are conceived as engaging in their common practices, which are already established, there is no question of our supposing them to come together to deliberate as to how they will set these practices up for the first time. Yet we can imagine that from time to time they discuss with one another whether any of them has a legitimate complaint against their established institutions. Such discussions are perfectly natural in any normal society. Now suppose that they have settled on doing this in the following way. They first try to arrive at the principles by which complaints, and so practices themselves, are to be judged. Their procedure for this is to let each person propose the principles upon which he wishes his complaints to be tried with the understanding that, if acknowledged, the complaints of others will be similarly tried, and that no complaints will be heard at all until everyone is roughly of one mind as to how complaints are to be judged. They each understand further that the principles proposed and acknowledged on this occasion are binding on future occasions.... Each person knows that he will be bound by [the principle] in future circumstances the peculiarities of which cannot be known, and which might well be such that the principle is then to his disadvantage. The idea is that everyone should be required to make in *advance* a firm commitment, which others also may reasonably be expected to make, and that no one be given the opportunity to tailor the canons of a legitimate complaint to fit his own special condition, and then to discard them when they no longer suit his purpose.... In this way one can see how the acceptance of the principles of justice might come about....[7]

Could not health-care distribution questions be publicly discussed and resolved following these ostensibly reasonable conditions of just deliberation? Could not citizens come together, with such assurances of just deliberation in place, in order to justly and democratically determine how health-care resources should be socially used? Leonard M. Fleck, in his 2009 book *Just Caring: Health Care Rationing and Democratic Deliberation*, argues that health-care decisions that determine how health-care resources are distributed should be made upon the basis of public discussions that are generally regulated by Rawlsian conditions of just deliberation, whereby, for example, the following five conditions hold: a) people involved in such discussions understand that they will be bound by the decisions they make even though they cannot know what medical or economic circumstances they will face in the future; b) discussions are carried out rationally, such that only reasons, and not power or money, are relied on in order to determine the desirability of options; c) conditions are put in place to correct for power inequalities between groups, such that no group is able to dominate other groups; d) discussants come together with the aim and purpose of working together to discover what distributive decisions they think merit public confirmation, based on relevant considerations of justice; and e) discussants are self-assured that the procedures and conditions under which complaints are evaluated and heard are fair.[8]

But why would one advocate such a position in the first place? First, in any health-care system, rationing decisions are inevitable because, as Fleck writes, "we have only limited resources to meet virtually unlimited health care needs."[9] There are limits to what can be afforded in order to meet health-care needs, and this is exacerbated by the continual production of life-saving and expensive drugs and treatments that can add years to life. Second, people are affected by health-care coverage decisions made by private insurers and yet they have no knowledge of when these decisions are made or of the rationales behind them. Taking these two facts into account, we can then ask how inevitable rationing decisions pertaining to health-care expenditures should be made – democratically, or behind closed doors by private insurers? In order to answer this question, we can consider which decision procedure would more likely rule out unjust rationing decisions and which one would be better able to hide possibly unjust rationing decisions from the public. Fleck holds that if rationing decisions were made upon the basis of democratic deliberation, the outcomes would be more just than outcomes determined by private insurers. Articulating this position and explaining why medical rationing decisions should be made upon the basis of democratic deliberation, Fleck writes:

rationing decisions are more likely to be just and caring if they are self-imposed through a process of rational democratic deliberation....The public must receive a fair representation of the problem of health care cost escalation, the role of advancing medical technology in driving those costs higher, and the often very marginal benefits we collectively purchase with our health care dollars, as well as the opportunity to think through trade-offs and priority setting for a very large range of health care needs in the framework of a set budget. I believe the public is capable of this sort of thinking.[10]

Fleck points out that health-care rationing decisions can be agreed to by the public only if the public is included in the decision-making process and if it authorizes or imposes those decisions upon the basis of rational democratic deliberation. In the absence of democratically achieved consensus about how health-care dollars should be spent, there will be, in Fleck's view, a legitimacy gap between health-care rationing policy and those to whom it applies. Further, Fleck holds that democratic deliberation (or what is sometimes called "public deliberation") is more likely to achieve just outcomes in the distribution of health-care resources than in any other procedure. He holds this, most generally, because more just outcomes are likely to be achieved when representative interests are included in making decisions that everyone involved understands will be applied to all. You may think about this in Kantian terms: if the real interests of those who might be affected by a health-care rationing decision are included in discussions that lead to policy, and if all of the discussants understand that their policy decisions or recommendations will apply to everyone – that, by way of comparison, the universalized maxims that they formulate *will be* universal law – then the outcomes following this decision-making procedure are more likely to be just than any other decision procedure.

To investigate the issue of democratic deliberation and health care, we include in this section a piece by Erika Blacksher et al. entitled "What Is Public Deliberation?" and a piece by Stephanie Solomon and Julia Abelson entitled "Why and When Should We Use Public Deliberation?" Blacksher et al. examine the concept of democratic deliberation, while Solomon and Abelson explain the purposes for which public deliberation could

be used and why it would be morally desirable and fitting in the context of health-care policy.

Shifting our focus from how health-care decisions should be made to the question of whether health care ought to be conceived of as a socially guaranteed right, we include a piece by Thomas J. Papadimos entitled "Healthcare Access as a Right, Not a Privilege: A Construct of Western Thought." Papadimos argues that numerous western traditions can lend philosophical support to the idea that health care is a right. He draws on Aristotle, Immanuel Kant, Thomas Hobbes, Thomas Paine, Hannah Arendt, and John Rawls. Papadimos is also concerned about health inequalities in the US. He references the work of Norman Daniels, who has argued that liberal democratic states should seek to contribute to the "normal functioning" of individuals so that equality of opportunity is protected.[11] If some groups do not possess such normal functioning, then they do not have the same chances as others in obtaining positions, income, social respect, and the like. Daniels and colleagues have also argued that because social and economic factors control the health of certain groups of people, what is called the "social determinants of health" should be distributed in society fairly so as to protect people's health and to in turn protect equality of opportunity. With respect to the social determinants of health, Daniels, Kennedy, and Kawachi write that research over the course of 150 years has shown

that an individual's chances of life and death are patterned according to social class: the more affluent and educated people are, the longer and healthier their lives. These patterns persist even when there is universal access to health care…. [R]ecent cross-national evidence suggests that the greater the degree of socioeconomic inequality that exists within a society, the steeper the *gradient* of health inequality. As a result, middle-income groups in a less equal society will have worse health than comparable or even poorer groups in a society with greater equality ... it is not unreasonable to talk here about the social "determinants" of health.[12]

The term thus generally suggests that the more inegalitarian a society is, the greater health disparities there will be between social classes. There are, according to Daniels and his co-authors, four main findings that research on the social determinants of health has uncovered:

First, the income/health gradients ... are not the result of some fixed or determinate laws of economic development, but are influenced by policy choices. Second, the income/health gradients are not just the result of the deprivation of the poorest groups. Rather, a gradient in health operates across the whole socioeconomic spectrum within societies, such that the slope or steepness of the income/health gradient is affected by the degree of inequality in a society. Third, relative income or socioeconomic status (SES) is as important as, and may be more important than, the absolute level of income in determining health status.... Fourth, there are identifiable social and psychosocial pathways through which inequality produces its effects on health.[13]

The first finding indicates that a state's social policies are a key social determinant of health, while the second points out that socially produced health disparities can and do exist in industrially advanced societies and that one main contributor to health disparity in

societies, developed or not, is class. The third finding indicates that annual income and one's social standing in society play a role in determining the likely status of one's health, while the fourth shows that there are clear causal links between social disparities and health disparities.

Thus once we start thinking of health care as a right, we cannot confine the conversation to access to health care alone. Indeed, as Papadimos explains, when the Johns Hopkins Urban Health Institute was established in East Baltimore in 2000, its working groups had identified that making health care available to the medically needy would not alone be sufficient to improve the health of residents. This is because social and economic regularities in a society make a difference in determining the health of groups. Health care as a right speaks to justice as a right too. If, as a matter of justice, we are concerned about the fair distribution of social opportunity, then we need to also be concerned about the fair distribution of the social determinants of health. And if we are concerned about significant health disparities between groups living in the same society, then we also need to be concerned about how well social structures support equal opportunity for all.

If we use Hobbes's political theory alone to argue that health care is a right, then that right applies only to those who have transferred their right of nature over to a sovereign in order to live in a state of sworn peace with one another. If we use Kant's moral theory alone to argue that health care is a right, then that right applies to all human beings. If health care is a universal right that people are owed by virtue of their worth as rational beings, then the conversation about health care as a right cannot be confined to the context of signatories of a social contract. It must be expanded to include everyone.

Paul Farmer is the co-founder of Partners

In Health, which is an organization that delivers first-rate health care to the world's poorest, including life-saving and often expensive drugs that they otherwise would not have access to. He believes the world has the obligation to provide "a preferential option for the poor," which is the moral judgment, as Tracy Kidder writes, that first-rate drugs and services ought not to be withheld from anyone and that medical technologies and drugs should be distributed by "identifying the patients in gravest danger and giving them priority."[14] In his article in this section, "Pathologies of Power: Rethinking Health and Human Rights," he argues that the orthodox framework of human rights is blind to violations that occur by way of state power and social inequalities. He thinks that human rights should be framed in the context of social and economic rights and that instead of focusing on single violations, human-rights discourse and agencies should focus on exercises of state power, the global economic order, and social inequalities that contribute to the human-rights violations of hundreds as

an obstacle to their right to health.

Finally in this section, we include two selections that help us think morally about end-of-life treatment. James Rachels's piece, "Active and Passive Euthanasia," assesses the position that passive euthanasia is morally permissible whereas active euthanasia is not. Rachels asserts that both forms of euthanasia cause death and that the active form can be more humane than the passive. He argues that the difference between "letting die" and killing is morally unimportant even while, in the United States, it is thought to be of great, even inviolable, moral significance in standard medical practice. Rachels's point is that, while there is a descriptive difference between killing and letting die, morally there is no difference. Margaret P. Battin's piece, "Euthanasia: The Way We Do It, the Way They Do It," illustrates three Western models of dying and argues that none is fitting for or morally acceptable in the social and political context of the United States. She concludes that physician-assisted suicide for terminal illness is the best option for the United States.

## Notes

1  Samuel Metz, "The U.S. Health Care System: Really the Best?" *Anesthesiology News*, June 2015, http://www.anesthesiologynews.com/ViewArticle. aspx?d=Commentary&d_id=449&i=June+2015&i_id=1194&a_id=32591.
2  Ibid.
3  United Nations General Assembly, "The Universal Declaration of Human Rights," 1948, http://www.un.org/en/documents/udhr/index.shtml.
4  United Nations General Assembly, "International Covenant on Economic, Social and Cultural Rights," 1966, http://www.ohchr.org/EN/ProfessionalInterest/Pages/CESCR.aspx.
5  Adam Gaffney, "America's Health Care System is Still Broken: Why Single-Payer is the Only Thing that will ever fix it," *Salon* 26 June 2015, http://www.salon.com/2015/06/26/americas_health_care_system_is_still_broken_why_single_payer_is_the_only_thing_that_will_ever_fix_it/.
6  Sarah Ferria, "Study: 'Underinsured' Population has doubled to 31 Million," *The Hill*, 10 May 2015, http://thehill.com/policy/healthcare/242584-study-underinsured-population-has-doubled-to-31-million.
7  John Rawls, "Justice as Fairness," *The Philosophical Review* 67.2 (1958): 164–94, at 169–73.
8  Leonard M. Fleck, *Just Caring: Health Care Rationing and Democratic Deliberation* (New York: Oxford UP, 2009).

9   Ibid., p. vii.

10  Leonard M. Fleck, "The Costs of Caring: Who Pays? Who Profits? Who Panders?" *Hastings Center Report*, 36.3 (2006): 13–17, at 15–16.

11  Norman Daniels, *Just Health* (Cambridge: Cambridge UP, 1985).

12  Norman Daniels, Bruce P. Kennedy, and Ichiro Kawachi, "Why Justice Is Good for Our Health: The Social Determinants of Health Inequalities," *Daedalus* 128.4 (1999): 215–51, at 215.

13  Ibid., p. 218.

14  Tracy Kidder, *Mountains Beyond Mountains: The Quest of Dr. Paul Farmer, A Man Who Would Cure the World* (New York: Random House, 2004) p. 286.

# 1. Erika Blacksher, Alice Diebel, Pierre-Gerlier Forest, Susan Dorr Goold, and Julia Abelson, "What Is Public Deliberation?"

THIS ARTICLE, FROM A 2012 *Hastings Center Report*, examines the concept of public deliberation, which has recently been proposed as a form of public engagement to inform health-care policy decision making. The authors propose a minimal definition of public deliberation and discuss the purposes for which public deliberation could be used. They emphasize that public deliberation is a fact-based and inclusive learning process that occurs through listening, exchange, and reflecting on empirical data and diverse viewpoints with participants. If done correctly, it is always an enlightening process. The authors also contend that an important benefit of public deliberation is cultivating "respect and reciprocity among citizens." It can promote democratic action in society and, in so doing, strengthen bonds between citizens. They further look into how public deliberation ought to be conducted.

THE IDEA THAT ORDINARY people should have an opportunity to participate in important policy matters is as old as democracy itself. Today, this idea prevails in contemporary democratic theory and has made significant inroads in public policy.[1] Deliberations to address social challenges in health, science, education, and the environment are proliferating around the globe. Deliberative processes have been used, for example, to strengthen local government and civil society in Bolivia; promote growth and sustainability in Perth, Australia; and advise health ministries in Canada on new health technologies.[2]

Yet despite the widespread appeal of and volumes of ink devoted to this idea, there is no settled account of what constitutes public deliberation in theory or in practice. Deliberative processes go by a variety of names (deliberative democracy, deliberative politics, participatory governance) and take diverse forms (citizen juries, national issue forums, deliberative opinion polls, participatory budgeting). The purposes, processes, and products of deliberation are all subject to debate. Here we propose and defend a minimum definition of public deliberation offered in the spirit of continued debate.

In its most general usage, public deliberation refers to a form of public discussion that seeks collective solutions to challenging social problems. The term *"public"* refers to ordinary people with an emphasis on the inclusion of groups whose voices are marginalized in political processes and in daily life. This feature of deliberation reflects both a belief in citizens' abilities to understand and communicate about complex social issues and a view of citizens as equal participants in civic life.[3]

*"Deliberation"* refers to a discussion that is informed, value-based, and transformative. Participants should have access to balanced, factual information that improves their understanding of the topic and fosters reasoned engagement. Public deliberation is value-based in that it seeks to determine what *ought* to be done in response to a particular issue – a challenge that requires citizens to identify,

clarify, and weigh the tensions among their views and the values underlying them; justify them to others; and set priorities.[4] This exchange – an iterative process of talking and listening – is potentially transformative. People learn from one another, gain insight into their own and alternative positions, and may revise their views as a result.

Public deliberation need not achieve consensus. It should leave citizens better informed about the issue and their fellow citizens. It may also promote ownership of public programs and cultivate a civic sensibility among participants.[5] All these benefits may lend legitimacy to policy decisions, political institutions, and democracy itself. Citizens may find public decisions more acceptable and fairer when they are subject to an open, inclusive discussion that carefully considers competing claims, even if they disagree with the decision.[6] The last point alludes to a final, yet central, goal of public deliberation: respect and reciprocity among citizens.[7] These goals – an informed citizenry, public spiritedness, legitimacy, and mutual respect – suggest some of the rationales for public deliberation.

Public deliberation differs from another popular form of public participation, public consultation. This type of engagement also seeks to learn what people think about important social issues, but it does not create the conditions for reasoned deliberation about what a collective (a city, state, nation, or particular population) should do. Public consultation captures individual opinions, often via interviews, that in the aggregate reflect current public opinion about an issue, but it does not create conditions in which those opinions might evolve and change. Thus, public consultation lacks the "transformative" feature of public deliberation and cannot yield considered collective judgments.

In general, then, public deliberation engages ordinary citizens with diverse perspectives in reasoned and respectful discussion about important social issues in search of well-informed proposals that deliberators will view as legitimate. This much is likely to be uncontroversial. Closer inspection reveals a highly contested concept.

A fundamental debate about public deliberation concerns its purpose. Why deliberate? Four answers are commonly given: (1) to help citizens become better informed about important issues; (2) to locate common ground and points that all participants can live with, if not agree with; (3) to inform policy decisions and legislation; and (4) to unearth different perspectives to ensure inclusivity.[8] Debate surrounds the merits of these goals, as well as how to determine what they are and who should do this. Complicating matters further, the choice of one goal may preclude other goals or compromise critical features of deliberative practice. For example, public deliberation that aims for common ground may stifle minority views by neglecting perspectives on the margins of discussion.

This point hints at the question of representation, a second area of lively debate. Are everyone's interests represented, and what does it mean to represent an interest? Are participants expected to speak on behalf of a particular social, ethnic, or gender group, or as individuals? Closely related are questions about how to overcome power inequalities associated with race and ethnicity, social class, and position and privilege.

Some commentators argue that an emphasis on particular forms of reasoning, consensus, and the common good privilege dominant groups' forms of communication, suppress minority views, and define deliberation's goals in terms likely to represent majority interests.[9] To remedy these biases, some recommend that deliberative processes intentionally seek conflict and difference[10] rather than consensus or common ground, and they encourage the use of alternative forms of communication, such as testimony and storytelling.[11] Still others recommend giving disadvantaged groups the opportunity to deliberate among themselves before deliberating with other participants. Some evidence suggests that so-called enclave deliberation may broaden the spectrum of views captured in a deliberative process – particularly minority views – thus enhancing its legitimacy.[12]

A third area of debate relates to the products of deliberation. If the deliberative exercise is designed to inform policy, then how should the link between deliberation and policy action be understood? Perhaps the most dominant approach treats deliberative outcomes as input that policy-makers should take into consideration but not be bound by. Another approach holds public officials accountable to the deliberators' decisions, informing the legislative process and moving deliberation into the realm of politics. Good reasons can be marshaled for and against each approach. The higher the stakes, the more motivated citizens may be to undertake this time-consuming activity and to take it seriously. Citizens who have participated in public deliberation may become cynical if their advice is ignored in policy decisions. But the more focused on political action deliberation becomes, the less likely it is to reveal a diversity of viewpoints.[13]

None of these questions are settled. And … the context-specific nature of public deliberation does not lend itself to uniformity or consensus. Nonetheless, identifying the core elements of "public deliberation" – the features that any deliberative process should have – will help advance the state of the debate and research in the field.

We propose a minimum definition that encompasses three essential elements: (1) the provision of balanced, factual information that improves participants' knowledge of the issue; (2) the inclusion of diverse perspectives to counter the well-documented tendency of better educated and wealthier citizens to participate disproportionately in deliberative opportunities and to identify points of view and conflicting interests that might otherwise go untapped; and (3) the opportunity to reflect on and discuss freely a wide spectrum of viewpoints and to challenge and test competing moral claims. None of these standards is easily achieved. But when they are met, deliberation supports three normative goals we take to be definitive of public deliberation: an informed citizenry, reciprocity and mutual respect, and public-spirited proposals that locate common ground (if not a common good). These goals support individuals' capacities to act as citizens – an overarching end that motivates the deliberative enterprise.

Public processes that lack these characteristics may be useful in the policy realm and to democracy more generally. But they would not constitute public deliberation as we understand it. We strongly support deliberative processes that not only educate but also inform policy decisions. But we also recognize that deliberation can yield benefits in the absence of direct impact. Other features of deliberation may enhance the deliberative process, depending on the goals and context of deliberation. As our discussion illustrates …, the purposes, processes, and products of deliberation are interrelated and need to be considered as a whole.

## Study Questions

1. Do some research on your own and identify differences between representative democracy and deliberative democracy. What practical and political consequences follow from each model of democracy?

2. What is the definition of public deliberation that Blacksher et al. provide? Take into account the function and aim of public deliberation, its minimal components according to the authors, and the civic and political benefits it is supposed to yield.

3. What problems do Blacksher et al. identify about public deliberation, and what recommendations do they make in order to address these problems?

4. What are the four possible purposes of public deliberation, according to Blacksher et al.? Outline how public deliberation could be used, addressing specific issues, according to each purpose.

## Notes

1  S. Chambers, "Deliberative Democratic Theory," *Annual Review of Political Science* 6 (2003): 307–26; S. Elstub, "The Third Generation of Deliberative Democracy," *Political Studies Review* 8 (2010): 291–307; J. Abelson et al., "Deliberations about Deliberation: Issues in the Design and Evaluation of Public Participation Processes," *Social Science Medicine* 57 (2003): 239–51.

2  *Participedia*, an open-source Web site established in 2009, documents the diversity and volume of experiments, at http://www.parricipedia.net.

3  A. Wildavsky, "Citizens as Analyst," in *Speaking Truth to Power: The Art and Craft of Policy Analysis*, 2nd ed. (New Brunswick, NJ: Transaction Publishers, 1987), 252–79.

4  The Charles F. Kettering Foundation, "Public Deliberation in Democracy" (Dayton, OH: The Charles F. Kettering Foundation, 2008).

5  S. Dorr Goold et al., "Choosing Healthplans All Together: A Deliberative Exercise for Allocating Limited Health Care Resources," *Journal of Health Politics, Policy, and Law* 30.4 (2005): 563–601.

6  S. Freeman, "Deliberative Democracy: A Sympathetic Comment," *Philosophy and Public Affairs* 29.4 (2000): 371–418.

7  A. Gutmann and D. Thompson, *Democracy and Disagreement* (Cambridge, MA: Harvard UP, 1996).

8  M. Button and K. Mattson, "Deliberative Democracy in Practice: Challenges and Prospects for Civic Deliberation," *Polity* 31.4 (1999): 609–37; A. Fung, "Recipes for Public Spheres: Eight Institutional Design Choices and Their Consequences," *Journal of Political Philosophy* 11.3 (2003): 338–67.

9  J.J. Mansbridge et al., "Norms of Deliberation: An Inductive Study," *Journal of Public Deliberation* 2.1 (2006): 1–47.

10  I.M. Young, *Inclusion and Democracy* (New York: Oxford UP, 2000).

11  J. Gastil, *Political Communication and Deliberation* (Thousand Oaks, CA: Sage, 2008).

12  C.F. Karpowitz, C. Raphael, and A.S. Hammond, "Deliberative Democracy and Inequality: Two Cheers for Enclave Deliberation among the Disempowered," *Politics and Society* 37.4 (2009): 576–615.

13  D.M. Ryfe, "Does Deliberative Democracy Work?" *Annual Review of Political Science* 8 (2005): 49–71.

# 2. Stephanie Solomon and Julia Abelson, "Why and When Should We Use Public Deliberation?"

IN AN ARTICLE FROM the same *Hastings Center Report* as the Blacksher et al. reading above, Stephanie Solomon and Julia Abelson work to gain clarity on when a policy issue is suited for public deliberation. They contend that health-care policy is a suitable issue for public deliberation. They also claim that if public deliberation were used to inform health-care policy, it could make for more accountable and inclusive policy because people's experiences and knowledge of their health, health concerns, and interactions with medical facilities and insurance, if brought into policy discussions, would make for better and more informed health-care policy. They further consider the issue of how influential public deliberation should be in the making of policy decisions.

---

PUBLIC DELIBERATION IS AN approach policy-makers can use to tackle public policy problems that require the consideration of both values and evidence. However, there is much uncertainty about why and when to choose it rather than more familiar approaches, such as public opinion polls or expert panels. With guidance on the why and when of public deliberation, policy-makers can use it appropriately to inform public policy.

To answer the "why" question, we emphasize the importance of matching the method to purpose. Public deliberation is not right for all policy issues. Polls, surveys, and focus groups are appropriate when the aim is to access the "top of mind" or "general attitudes" of the public, and when the issue is one that people think about or have experience with in their everyday lives. In addition, there are purely technical or scientific matters for which experts alone should be consulted, such as determining which flu viruses should be used to make next year's vaccine.

But for an increasing number of public policy problems, neither of these approaches is adequate. For these issues, public deliberation can contribute to more legitimate policy decisions than other approaches; it can yield recommendations that are more feasible, better framed, more accountable, more inclusive, more just, and more balanced. Public deliberation may also have intrinsic value, increasing public-spiritedness, buy-in, and trust in governing institutions and their decisions, which are also central goals for policy-makers.[1]

The "when" question has two parts: *When* is a policy question most suited for public deliberation, and *when* in the policy-making process should the public deliberate? Both questions are important.

## When Is a Policy Issue Most Suited for Public Deliberation?

Policy issues that are well suited to public deliberation have one or more of the following characteristics: conflicting public values, high controversy, combined expert and real-world-knowledge, and low trust in government. The deliberation process can help members of the public work through the complexity of the issues and build trust in the policymaking process.

*Decisions reflecting conflicting values about the public good.* Most, if not all, public policy decisions involve competing values about what is good for individuals. But those that also involve competing values about what is good for a community, country, or society stand to benefit most from public deliberation. For example, setting policies for population biobanking requires weighing "privacy and consent against ease of research and outputs; and individual control over biobanks against benefits and risks to communities and unconsenting individuals."[2] The value of moving the science of population genetics forward efficiently and effectively, as well as the value of using this knowledge to develop improved medical treatments, must be weighed against the values of genetic privacy and security and of limiting controversial genetic research that is at odds with religious, cultural, or other belief systems.

More obviously, in health care and public health, where resources are limited and rationing may be necessary, policymakers must weigh difficult trade-offs among funding for preventive care, emergency care, specialty care, mental health services, and myriad other options. While there are reasons to prioritize some of these options over others, there is no absolute hierarchy of their importance. The answer depends on what the public values or finds relevant to its collective health and well-being. While medical and economic data can illuminate the implications of different choices, the choices themselves require normative evaluation of priorities and acceptable compromises.[3]

The kinds of value judgments required for policy decisions must also be considered. The aggregation of individual preferences toward specific public policies provides a limited

perspective. Rather, we are interested in an aggregate of the values that individuals hold *about a public good.* One strength of public deliberation is its ability to shift participants from the "what would/should I do?" response often elicited by surveys to the "what would/ should *we* do?" reasoning more appropriate to many policy decisions. When citizens with various perspectives gather to ask these questions, the diverse impacts of public policy decisions are explicitly addressed in public decision-making.

*Controversial and divisive topics.* While public values are relevant to many public policy decisions, not all of these values are highly controversial and divisive. Policy-makers are often cautious about consulting the public about controversial topics, such as genetically modified foods, stem cell research, gene therapy, and public health coverage. These types of issues are likely to produce standoffs if they are posed to the public without appropriate background information, framing, and facilitated discussion.

There has been considerable debate among public deliberation theorists over whether deliberation processes tend to generate more agreement on controversial issues[4] or lead instead to more heterogeneous and diverse positions.[5] While public deliberation need not produce a consensus, it has the unique capability to bring divergent views to the table and into conversation with the goal of collectively addressing thorny problems. In our view, well-designed and moderated public deliberation that respects divergent views and seeks to articulate the values underlying them is more likely than other methods of public consultation to yield a set of collective policy responses, even if individuals do not agree on the particular issues. Even in cases where consensus cannot be reached, the positions that result from public deliberation are better articulated and justified than those that participants began with, since all participants must acknowledge and engage with opposing views and provide reasons to support their own positions.

As such, public deliberation is particularly useful in domains where individuals must reflect on highly divisive and controversial issues that impact broad populations and communities, such as priority-setting in health reform where professional turf is at stake and the outcomes are perceived to produce winners and losers. While most people agree that the uninsured should have some level of basic coverage, there is much disagreement about where to draw the line between essential and nonessential health care needs, as well as the moral valence to some aspects of health care, such as mental health and addiction services, reproductive health, and cosmetic medicine. A model public deliberation exercise called CHAT (Choosing Healthplans All Together), which has been implemented throughout the United States and abroad, found that citizens tended to draw a strong line between services that are needed to survive and those that improve quality of life. The activity showed much less division between socioeconomic groups than between individuals. Moreover, while public rhetoric often revolves around the importance of freedom of choice in health care (of doctors, providers, hospitals, and so on), when faced with a discussion of the trade-off between less restricted networks and more access to particular health services, more than half of the participants reluctantly sacrificed their freedoms.[6]

*Hybrid topics: Combining technical and real-world knowledge.* Unlike purely technical decisions that require consultation with experts, hybrid topics require a more general reflection on cultural and practical knowledge and on how particular decisions would impact people's lives. Decisions about health insurance coverage, vaccination mandates, clinical trial design, and biobanking policies are examples of hybrid topics.

The consequences of neglecting to account for cultural knowledge in decision-making are difficult to ignore. Had University of Arizona researchers held a public deliberation to ascertain the knowledge of social risks and harms posed by pursuing ancestry, mental health, and addiction research on the Havasupai tribe, they might have avoided years of lawsuits, bad publicity, and loss of trust in the research enterprise.[7] Similarly, a recent public deliberation to inform recommendations for colorectal cancer screening in Ontario, Canada, revealed real-world knowledge that an expert panel had not considered. While expert panelists focused on the clinical benefits and cost-effectiveness of different screening modalities, public deliberation widened the lens to show that citizens had broader concerns about the lack of information provided to the public about the full range of screening options and the vulnerability they would expose themselves to within their patient-provider relationships if they were to resist the screening option.[8] These concerns were incorporated into the expert panel's final recommendation, demonstrating that without the lived experience of relevant members of the public, technically informed decisions on hybrid topics are likely to lack relevance and efficacy. In addition, public exposure to the technical knowledge associated with complex topics yields a richer and more informed set of views that are likely to result in more viable policy recommendations. In this way, public deliberation is uniquely suited to hybrid topics.

*Low-trust issues.* Public deliberation can also be useful for issues over which the public and the government are at odds. Public health crises – such as mad cow disease, severe acute respiratory syndrome (SARS), and influenza pandemics – are situations in which governments, depending on their response, can earn, retain, or lose the public's trust and counter challenges to scientific or governmental legitimacy.[9] Public trust is complex, however, and the result of multiple factors, both local (do we trust the decision-makers in this particular context?) and global (do we trust our government?).[10] As such, public deliberation on low-trust issues should not be perceived as a solution to the multiple causes of low trust, but rather, if conducted appropriately, as a means to increase transparency and accountability between policy-makers and the public. This can, in turn, promote increased trust.

Moreover, public deliberation that is geared toward improving trust must walk a fine line. If performed with the intention of honestly involving the public, it can contribute to increased public trust. If deliberation is not implemented carefully, however, or if the public sees the exercise as being only for show, it can backfire and even lead to decreased trust. For example, the public deliberations carried out in the United Kingdom on the issue of genetically modified crops were intended to increase trust in the government policies. Yet, as a result of a poorly implemented process, they were co-opted by interest groups that were against genetically modified crops, and the fallout from the deliberations ultimately increased the polarity of the public's positions and the severity of policy, rather than leading to fruitful and trusting solutions.[11]

## When in the Policy Process?

Many argue that public deliberation is most likely to have a direct impact on policy decisions when it is undertaken in close proximity to the decision being made. At that point, because policy-makers know which options are available, participants are only given choices that are legitimately on the table. Thus, those who argue that public deliberation should only be undertaken when it can have a concrete impact on policy are committed to public deliberation taking place only downstream.

However, some argue that deliberation held just prior to a policy decision has already been framed by dominant groups, which limits the opportunity for the public to entertain and provide truly alternative views and options.[12] In other words, the practical policy choices provided to deliberators downstream may not accurately reflect the spectrum of the public's views on the issues. While participants may not have a direct voice in the final decision if engaged upstream, they may feel their participation is more significant because it shaped the policy questions themselves. Critics of upstream deliberation worry that participants will expect that their voices will be heeded, and when they do not see any direct results of their time and energy, they will be less likely to engage in the future.

Our view is that both upstream and downstream public deliberation is crucial, but that their effectiveness depends on the clarity with which expectations are established from the start. If people are engaged only downstream, they can never challenge the fundamental questions and options of policy decisions; they can only choose among pre-established options. If people are only engaged upstream, they have the chance to express their views, but they are less likely to directly influence real policy choices. Groups considering public deliberation should weigh these trade-offs. If possible, both upstream and downstream engagement should be utilized. If not, the implications of either choice should be made clear to participants.

Those who want to make the best public policy recommendations and decisions are faced with a multitude of approaches, from public polls, expert panels, surveys, and, increasingly, public deliberation. The choice of when to use which strategy should reflect the types of policy issues at hand, the state of the public's trust at the time, and the timing and pace of the policy-making process associated with the given issues.

## Acknowledgments

Stephanie Solomon's work on this essay was supported by federal grant UL1RR024992 from the National Center for Research Resources, National Institutes of Health.

## Study Questions

1. Why do Solomon and Abelson think public deliberation is especially suited to address health-care rationing? Carefully trace their argument under the subsection "decisions reflecting conflicting values about the public good." Do you agree with this argument?

2. A major claim that Solomon and Abelson make is that "[p]ublic deliberation can contribute to more legitimate policy decisions and yield recommendations that are more feasible, better framed, more accountable, more inclusive, more just, and more balanced." Identify the various examples and reasons that the authors give to support this claim. How well do you think they support this claim?

3. Solomon and Abelson write that "[u]nlike purely technical decisions that require consultation with experts, hybrid topics require a more general reflection on cultural and practical knowledge and on how particular decisions would impact people's lives. Decisions about health insurance coverage, vaccination mandates, clinical trial design, and biobanking policies are examples of hybrid topics." What do you think about this distinction? Do "purely technical decisions" not have an impact on people's lives? If technical decisions do have an impact on people's lives, why should only experts be the ones to make such decisions? Can you think of technical decisions that might very well have an impact on people's lives?

4. Solomon and Abelson present a case of how public deliberation was used to inform recommendations for colorectal cancer screening. And they conclude that public deliberation improved the "relevance and efficacy" of the final recommendations. Can you think, more broadly, about how including the lived experiences of the public would improve the "relevance and efficacy" of other policy decisions?

## Notes

1 A. Gutmann and D. Thompson, "Deliberating about Bioethics," *Hastings Center Report* 27.3 (1997): 38–41.
2 S. MacLean and M.M. Burgess, "In the Public Interest: Assessing Expert and Stakeholder Influence in Public Deliberation about Biobanks," *Public Understanding of Science* 19.4 (2010): 486.
3 P. Muhlberger, *Researching Public Deliberation on Health Care, Environmental, and Bioethical Issues: A Primer* (Ann Arbor: U of Michigan P, 2010).

4 J. Habermas and T. McCarthy, *The Theory of Communicative Action: Reason and the Rationalization of Society* (Boston, MA: Beacon P, 1985); J. Rawls, "The Idea of Public Reason," in *Deliberative Democracy: Essays on Reason and Politics*, ed. J. Bohman and W. Rehg (Cambridge, MA: The MIT P, 1997), 93–139.

5 C.R. Sunstein, "The Law of Group Polarization," *Journal of Political Philosophy* 10.2 (2002): 175–95.

6 M. Ginsburg, S.D. Goold, and M. Danis, "(De)constructing 'Basic' Benefits: Citizens Define the Limits of Coverage," *Health Affairs* 25.6 (2006): 1648.

7 M.M. Mello and L.E. Wolf, "The Havasupai Indian Tribe Case – Lessons for Research Involving Stored Biologic Samples," *New England Journal of Medicine* 363 (2010): 204–07.

8 Y. Bombard et al., "Eliciting Ethical and Social Values in Health Technology Assessment: A Participatory Approach," *Social Science and Medicine* 73.1 (2011): 135–44.

9 P. Muhlberger, *Researching Public Deliberation on Health Care, Environmental, and Bioethical Issues: A Primer* (Ann Arbor: U of Michigan P, 2010); S.M. Cox, M. Kazubowski-Houston, and J. Nisker, "Genetics on Stage: Public Engagement in Health Policy Development on Preimplantation Genetic Diagnosis," *Social Science and Medicine* 68.8 (2009): 1472–80; C.Y. Deng and C.L. Wu, "An Innovative Participatory Method for Newly Democratic Societies: The 'Civic Groups Forum' on National Health Insurance Reform in Taiwan," *Social Science and Medicine* 70.6 (2010): 896–903.

10 J. Pen, "Public Engagement to Build Trust: False Hopes?" *Journal of Risk Research* 11.6 (2008): 821–35.

11 T. Horlick-Jones et al., *The GM Debate: Risk, Politics and Public Engagement* (Oxford: Routledge, 2007).

12 I.M. Young, "Activist Challenges to Deliberative Democracy," *Political Theory* 29.5 (2001): 670–90.

# 3. Thomas J. Papadimos, "Healthcare Access as a Right, Not a Privilege: A Construct of Western Thought"

IN THIS 2007 ESSAY, from the journal *Philosophy, Ethics, and Humanities in Medicine*, Thomas J. Papadimos surveys certain constructs of Western thought and argues that they each provide philosophical support in favor of health care being a right. What he strives to demonstrate is that health care as a right is not a foreign concept to Western thought but is, instead, integral to it. He considers how Aristotle, Hobbes, Kant, and Rawls can each argue for health care as a right. He goes on to consider health inequalities in the US and explains why health-care access is not alone sufficient to respond to the health needs of those who are underinsured or who are in need of medical resources.

## Background

THE HEALTH OF PEOPLE in different socioeconomic strata is disparate whether measured by education, type of employment, or income level [1], but those living in poverty exhibit the worst health status [2,3]. In the United States there are over 45 million uninsured or underinsured people who by definition have restricted access to healthcare [4]. Although not all of them are unemployed, or underemployed, there is no doubt that occupational status affects insurance status, which affects health status, and there is convincing evidence that low socioeconomic status causes poor health [5], as does race [6].

Having established that there are people who have a lack of healthcare access due to multi-factorial etiologies, the question arises as to whether the intervention necessary to assist them is something that should be considered as a privilege, or a right. I will posit in this dialectic that access to healthcare is a right, not a privilege.

## Discussion

### Aristotle and the Soul

Many have argued on behalf of the existence of "the soul," a concept perpetuated in many religions and philosophies. Aristotle (384–322 BCE) hypothesized the existence, content, and necessary conditions of the soul [7]. His arguments as to the existence of a soul, and what it is, will serve as the initial kernel in the examination of access to healthcare as a right.

Aristotle argues that there are natural bodies, some are living and others are not. In his argument Aristotle calls attention to the fact that whatever has a soul, in the human sense, displays life. The soul is the first entelechy (the real existence of a thing; not merely its theoretical existence; in some philosophies it is a life-giving force believed to be responsible for the development of all living things). Aristotle believed that a besouled natural body could grow, decay and at the same time provide itself with nutrition; the soul is further characterized by the powers of sensation (that allow pain and pleasure, which lead to desire), thinking (besouled beings have the power of thought, calculation, and imagination), and motivity [7]. The soul is a substance that is the definitive essence of a thing. Aristotle claimed soul and body were not the same, "the body cannot be soul; the body is subject or matter, not what is attributed to it. Hence there must be a substance in the sense of the form of a natural body having life potentially within it" [7]. Aristotle illustrates the relationship of the body to the soul by remarking that:

If the whole body was one vast eye, sight would be its soul. As the eye is a tool for seeing with, but a living tool which is part of ourselves, so the body is like a tool or instrument for living with. Hence we may say of the soul that it is the "end" of the body, the activity to which the body is instrumental, as seeing the "end" to which the eye is instrumental. [8]

Putting aside the concepts of good and evil, and having determined that souls need nourishment, have sensation (pain, pleasure, desire) and that they can think, calculate, and imagine, would it not be right and prudent to assist this entity called "soul" (that moves through a society by using a body which needs nutrition/nurture to slow or prevent its decay) to endure and persist as long as possible in the midst of others like itself? To press the argument further, would humankind not be better off if the vehicle of social interaction (body with soul) was cared for and nourished, not only by itself, but assisted and nurtured by other such vehicles in a society? Would there not be an alteration in its growth, perception, calculation and imagination that resulted in a higher probability of positive (good) consequences or actions?

For the soul to be fulfilled it must be nourished and grow. Therefore, healthcare access is necessary for the soul to attain its fullest growth, to nurture its intellect as a thinker and a citizen. While the soul is the first entelechy, good health is needed to reach the final entelechy, "a life of intelligence and character actively functioning" [8].

Theology, politics and economics aside, respecting, nurturing, and caring for human beings and their "essence," whatever that may be, can only help a society grow and prosper. To lead an "intelligent life" and to be an "actively functioning" member of society a body, whether one believes Aristotle's arguments about souls pertain to it or not, needs access to healthcare.

## Kant and the Force of Morality

Aristotle argues that for a soul to exist and to grow it needs nourishment to allow it to think (imagine), sense (pain and pleasure), and desire (thus we have a human being). Everyone on earth, according to Immanuel Kant (1724–1804), "exists as an end in himself, not merely as a means for arbitrary use by this or that will: he must in all his actions, whether they are directed to himself or to other rational beings, always be viewed at the same time as an end" [9].

The existence of humans is not for their use only as a means to accomplish a task. We are not, "a means to someone else's pleasure or well-being and our personhood consists in our status as a rational agent of worth" [9]. If people should not be treated as things, then it must be recognized that all people have an absolute worth simply because they exist, therefore you must "act in such a way that you always treat humanity whether in your own person or in the person of any other, never simply as a means, but at the same time as an end" [9]. This statement has been called the Formula of Humanity [9]. Kant explains that society depends upon interactions between people: we all serve each other's interests at one time or another, but we are never to be treated only as a means. Everyone has worth.

If every human needs nourishment, thinks, senses, and has an absolute value (worth), and if Kant's categorical imperative addressing people as an end-in-themselves is accepted (the Formula of Humanity), then we have established a force of morality in that: (1) all living natural bodies having needs, sensations/desires, and intelligence are thus human, and (2) as natural bodies they (humans) have an absolute worth that makes it necessary that all humans treat each other as one wishes to be treated. This moral force is irresistible.

In regard to this force of morality (as it concerns people as ends-in-themselves) Kant claims:

> The motive of morality is quite different from that of interest or desire. It rules us absolutely and necessarily; we feel its power even when we are most defying it. It is not one consideration to be balanced against others, but rather a compelling dictate that can be ignored, but never refuted. [10]

We can politically ignore the force of morality, but it will always be there. The question of healthcare access for all people will be a persistent moral and politico-economic interrogative.

## Hobbes and Covenants

We have established that natural living bodies (humans) should be treated as ends-in-themselves (all persons have absolute value, or worth). Humans have worth that must be preserved. This preservation of life can be argued to be sacred, or important, whether it is viewed religiously, socially, economically, or militarily. Religions universally value the preservation of life and the soul from the perspective of immortality. Socially, we need preservation of life so that we have like beings with which to interact. Economically, we need taxpayers and workers. Even the military places an extremely high value on its personnel because of the costs of training and the necessary numbers needed for its interventions. Thomas Hobbes (1588–1679) felt that reason would allow man to figure out what must be done to preserve life. To this end, in his epic work, *Leviathan*, he presents his rules, or Laws of Nature, and explains, "A law of nature (lex naturalis) is a precept or general rule, found out by reason, by which a man is forbidden to do that which is destructive of his life or taketh away the means of preserving the same, and to omit that by which he thinketh it may be best preserved" [11].

Hobbes reasoned that every person has a "Right of Nature" in that, "every man has a right to everything, even to one another's body" [11]. In other words, anybody can do anything. However, as soon as we come to our senses we realize there are laws of nature that rein in this liberty. These laws that are put into place give us the concept of "obligation."

Hobbes presents three important laws of nature that cause us obligation in regard to our actions. Hobbes's laws involve (1) seeking peace, (2) laying down the right of nature and making covenants, and (3) performance of covenants. In following Hobbes's laws to their conclusion an argument can be made that a covenant exists between members of a society, though unwritten, to provide security or well being for one another. Furthermore, since "we the people" are the government, such a covenant may actually exist between the members of a society and the government as to the provision of access to healthcare.

Hobbes's first law is to seek peace, "that every man, ought to endeavor peace, as farre as he has hope of obtaining it; and when he cannot obtain it, that he may seek, and use, all helps, and the advantages of warre" [11]. He follows this statement with the advisory that society should "seek peace, and follow it," and if a society cannot get peace, they must defend themselves.

In regard to healthcare, seeking peace and defending one's self can be manifested in the form of negotiations and the use of the electoral process to gain a favorable hearing on the argument that healthcare is a right to be shared by or available to all. However, this becomes difficult for the uninsured or the underinsured to pursue because they are without economic strength, many times they are racial minorities and can be marginalized by the political process.

Hobbes's second law, "lay down the right of nature," also applies and is extremely important. Here Hobbes indicates that we should lay down our right "to do anything" if others are willing to do the same. The rule "requires each of us to be satisfied with as much liberty toward other human beings as we are willing to allow them with respect to ourselves" [12]. When we give up liberty (or portions thereof) we can:

Renounce this right or transfer it to someone else. In engaging in either of these acts, we are removing an impediment to someone else's use of those same things or someone else's exercise of their right to them. In this way we are bestowing benefits on these other people. If we care not who receives the benefit, we are said to renounce our right; if we wish the benefit to accrue to some one or more particular persons, we are to speak of transferring our right to them, which amounts to a gift. We may, then, either abandon our right or give it away to other people. [12]

Whether a right is renounced or transferred a promise is made (commitment) and thus an obligation is incurred (by us). Hobbes considers the obligation created by "laying down the right of nature" as the origin of morality [12]. Nature does not require commitment, i.e., one can do whatever he or she pleases (there is no morality in nature according to Hobbes). However any commitment to an ideal, or situation, incurs an obligation on my part. Thus there is justice in my promise of commitment and injustice is my breaching of a promise of commitment [12]. The "implication" here is that in "laying down the right of nature" all members of a society obligate themselves to one another, to live in peace among one another, and thus to provide mutual security for one another.

This second law leads to the concept of contracts, or covenants. When people renounce or transfer the "right of nature" a contract, or covenant, is made. Covenants may "not be explicitly conveyed and acknowledged by words. The sign or indication of a contract may be by inference, and be implicit, or covert" [12]. Hobbes claims that, "generally a signe by inference of any contract is whatsoever sufficiently argues the will of the contractor" [11]. The "right" at stake here is the right of the medically needy to "transfer" their need (per Hobbes's theory) for healthcare to a society in which all of its members have pledged mutual cooperation by agreeing to Hobbes's second law. This acquiescence to Hobbes's second law has in fact occurred in our society although it seems not to have been acknowledged. Applying Kant's thoughts to this condition, this implicit covenant may be ignored politically, but it has a force of morality that cannot be refuted. Even though Hobbes thinks that the moral life is not constitutive of human nature [12], he would probably agree with Kant's thoughts on the basis of social, political, and economic reasoning.

Hobbes's third law regards the performance of covenants. When a covenant is made it is important that "men perform their covenants made: without which, covenants are in vain, and but empty words, and the right of all men to all things remaining, wee are still in the condition of warre" [13]. If we have agreed to live in mutual security then we must make good on our promises, implied or otherwise.

The concept of "inference" or "implicitness," regarding Hobbes's second law, and the obligation of performance of covenants regarding the third law, are very important. The citizens of the United States have come to hope and expect availability of healthcare access. The growing number of persons that are uninsured, or underinsured, have a limited access to prompt and adequate healthcare. The provision of healthcare is an implied covenant that the medically needy have hoped and expected society to embrace.

## Paine and the Rights of Man

Hobbes spoke of natural laws. Thomas Paine (1737–1809) spoke of natural rights [14]. Such rights are those that pertain to a person in relation to his or her right to exist. These rights are of two kinds: the first kind regards intellectual rights (rights of the mind, including religion), and the second involves a person's right to pursue comfort and happiness as long as the rights of others are not injured.

These natural rights act as a foundation for civil rights. A member of society does not have enough individual power to pursue these rights (civil), which are all those that relate to security and protection. Therefore, natural rights are:

Those in which power to execute is perfect in the individual as the right itself ... The natural rights that are not retained, are all those in which, though the right is perfect in the individual, the power to execute them is defective. They answer

not his purpose. A man, by natural right, has a right to judge his own cause; and so far as the right of the mind is concerned, he never surrenders it: but what availeth it him to judge, if he has not power to redress? He therefore deposits this right in the common stock of society, and takes the arm of society, of which he is a part, in preference and in addition to his own. [15]

From this line of reasoning Paine concludes that all civil rights grew out of natural rights; that civil power is an aggregation of people's natural rights and this is so because the individual is ineffective to pursue security and protection alone, but together the will of the many is "competent to the purpose of every one" [15]; and that this imperfect individual ability to secure collective security, when given to a central power (government), cannot be used to disarm a person of their natural rights. Paine concludes that, "Every man is a proprietor in society, and draws on the capital as a matter of right" [15].

In view of the aging baby boomer generation, shrinking urban tax bases, and projected shortages in skilled labor there is some reason to think that Paine would consider healthcare access in today's society a matter of security, personal and national. All people in a society today surrender their natural rights to a central power. Every person expects security and benefit from the common good, thus an argument can be made that individuals may draw on the capital of collective security in regard to healthcare access, "as a matter of right" [15].

## Arendt and the Human Condition: Speech, Action, Power and the Space of Appearance

*The Human Condition* (1958) by Hannah Arendt (1906–75) is as relevant now as it was at the time of its publication [16]. Her thoughts and process of reasoning are insightfully cutting and are applicable to the topic of the process of acquiring healthcare access.

Humans, having absolute worth, having made an implicit covenant with one another for their mutual good, and having surrendered their natural rights to a central power for their collective security, must by definition be equals, and in addition to being equals, they are distinct:

> Human plurality, the basic condition of both action and speech, has the twofold character of equality and distinction. If men were not equal, they could neither understand each other and those who came before them nor plan for the future and foresee the needs of those who will come after them. If men were not distinct, each human being distinguished from any other who is, was, or will ever be, they would need neither speech nor action to make themselves understood. Signs and sounds to communicate immediate, identical needs and wants would be enough. [17]

Humans' speech and action make them distinct, "Through them, men distinguish themselves instead of being merely distinct; they are modes in which human beings appear to each other, not indeed as physical objects, but qua men" [17]. This distinctness rests on what people say (speech) and what initiative they exhibit (action). Some forms of speech make people better known and some forms of action make some people rich and others poor, disabled, or even dead. Such variety among humans does cause "distinctness," but it does not change equality.

All humans are equals, all humans are different (distinctive), and all humans are heroes. However, heroes have no distinctive qualities; "the word 'hero' originally, that is, in Homer, was no more than a name given each free man who participated in the Trojan enterprise and about whom a story could be told" [17]. Courage, something we identify with a hero, according to Arendt, is nothing more than being willing to act, speak, and insert one's self into society and to begin one's own "story." Arendt's concept of courage has nothing to do with suffering; it has everything to do with:

> Leaving one's private hiding place and showing who one is, in disclosing and exposing one's self. The extent of this original courage, without which action and speech and therefore, according to the Greeks, freedom, would not be possible at all, is not less great and may even be greater if the "hero" happens to be a coward. [17]

In other words, a hero is a human being who awakens each morning and inserts himself, or herself, into society. All men and women are therefore heroes; all are equal, yet distinct. They may vary in height, weight, race, wealth, sex, age, or religion, etc., but they all are heroes who insert themselves into the world and begin their story.

The space of appearance is "the space where I appear to others as others appear to me, where men exist not merely like other living or inanimate things but make their appearance explicitly" [17]. The space of appearance is not like a room or a building, it comes into being when people interact in speech and action and it disappears with the dispersal of people, such as with wars and natural disasters [17]. It is a public space that endures through the rule of law and people sharing their lives together. It is the place where speech and action come to bear upon society. It can also be called the public realm.

Power is an actuality that occurs between people when they speak and act together,

"Power is what keeps the public realm, the potential space of appearance between acting and speaking men, in existence" [17]. It too disappears when people disperse. Power cannot be held in reserve like tanks and weapons of mass destruction, it exists only when actualized by men and women. Power is a potential and is actualized where words and actions, "have not parted company ... where words are not empty and deeds not brutal, where words are not used to veil intentions but to disclose realities, and deeds are not used to violate and destroy but to establish relations and create new realities" [17].

The medically needy are usually those of a disadvantaged socioeconomic status [2,3,5,6]. To actualize the power referred to above the medically needy would have to interact in the space of appearance. The space of appearance cannot be occupied by all of the people all of the time, but some people, such as the medically needy, may never enter it:

> This space does not always exist, and although all men are capable of deed and word, most of them – like the slave, the foreigner, and the barbarian in antiquity, like the laborer or the craftsman prior to the modern age, the jobholder or businessman in our world – do not live in it. No man, moreover, can live in it all the time. To be deprived of it means to be deprived of reality, which, humanly and politically speaking is the same as appearance. [17]

There are times when others may need to come forward and speak for those who have no power and cannot enter the space of appearance; even better, they should secure the entrance of the powerless so that they may be heard, "To men the reality of the world is guaranteed by the presence of others ..." [17]. Every human must be able to partake of the space of appearance at some time (and thus the sharing of power), even though he or she cannot partake of it at all times. To deny this is to deny the soul of its nutrition, morality of its force, and the existence of any covenant of, or right to, mutual security.

## The Presence of Others: Rawls and Daniels and the Application of Justice to Healthcare

While navigating the pathway of healthcare access as a right, emphasis has been placed upon Aristotle's view of the soul, Kant's regard for the absolute worth of humans, Hobbes's position on covenants, Paine's support of rights (both intellectual and in the pursuit of happiness), and Arendt's eloquence on the human condition. Now a juncture in the argument is reached where Arendt's desire for others to come forward and speak for those who have no power is addressed. John Rawls (1921–2002) and Norman Daniels [b. 1942] have championed justice and its application to healthcare access.

John Rawls's work on "Justice as Fairness" [18] and Norman Daniels's framing of the argument for universal healthcare by using Rawls's principles to demonstrate that there are social determinants of health affecting the health achieved by societies [19,20], complete a Kantian thread that runs throughout this dialectic.

John Rawls believed that,

> Each person possesses an inviolability founded on justice that even the welfare of a society as a whole cannot override. Therefore in a just society the rights secured by justice are not subject to political bargaining or the calculus of social interests. [18]

While Rawls's work was not directly related to healthcare access it provided principles that Daniels uses to illuminate the "just distribution of the social determinants of health" [20]. Rawls argued two principles. The first principle addressed an equal claim by all citizens to equal rights and freedoms. The second principle was in two parts. The first part of the second principle states that there must be equality of opportunity provided by social structures so all citizens may have the same chance of gaining income, wealth, position, and social advantages. The second part of the second principle states that inequalities will be tolerated only when such inequalities work to the advantage of society's most disadvantaged [18].

Daniels emphasizes that people in wealthy countries live longer and that within a particular country's social structure, government policies and national/regional cultures contribute to health variation within each country. He further argues that a country's health depends not only on its economy, but how the wealth is distributed. Wealthy countries may demonstrate better health than poorer countries, but wealthy nations also demonstrate variability in health along lines of income distribution. This variability within a country, or socioeconomic gradient, can be identified throughout all ranges of income distribution. Additionally, Daniels explains that what is invested by a country/government in its society, education for example, benefits the health of a nation. This not only varies from country to country, but in the United States it varies from state to state. Thus politics and public policy begin to play large roles. Investments in education, the workplace, health and immunizations, and nutrition, can provide a major advantage to those in need. In other words, health inequities need to be addressed through the correction of economic inequities. So while the United States engages in a debate on healthcare reform, interested parties need to understand that while there may be a "focus on healthcare at the point of delivery,"

the battle for healthcare access may also need to be addressed along the lines of the social determinants of health.

## Academic Medical Centers (AMCs): A Space of Appearance for Power and Action

The reality of this world, indeed, is guaranteed by the presence of others. While "others" have provided the theoretical basis for healthcare as a right, and "others" have been political proponents of such a right, what vehicle can be the conduit for championing such a right? The natural conduit for providing access to healthcare is the AMC; the necessary space of appearance can be provided by AMCs. Why should AMCs champion healthcare access, and what role should they play?

Historically, AMCs have been at the epicenter of providing healthcare for the disadvantaged. Eli Ginzberg's excellent treatise, "Teaching Hospitals and the Urban Poor," provides an enlightening historical review [21]. Many well-known AMCs established themselves in the 19th century. These centers were a union of teaching hospitals with medical schools established through philanthropy. They provided care to those in the neighborhood that were ill, specifically to those urban residents affected by intermittent epidemics that plagued population centers. The vast majority of these patients were poor. The acute care hospital was not used by the middle and upper classes until the very late 19th and 20th centuries.

AMCs have treated a disproportionate number of the uninsured for years. There is a Kantian force of morality regarding the historical mission of AMCs. This backdrop of the health plight (urban and rural) does not fade easily; it comes to the foreground. It is an irresistible moral force. This force of morality, as mentioned previously, can be ignored, but never refuted [10]. AMCs are further championed in this dialectic because of their (1) locations (usually urban), (2) expertise (subspecialty, research, and otherwise), and (3) educational mission (training of physicians, nurses, researchers, and allied health providers) [21]. Therefore, from a historical, geographic, expert, educational, and moral perspective AMCs are naturally selected conduits to argue for a right to access healthcare.

However, AMCs cannot be expected to shoulder the brunt of health needs of urban and rural America without financial assistance. Such help must come from local, state, and federal governments. Unfortunately, such an outlay of resources needs more than a moral will, it needs a political will that is increasingly difficult to muster in the face of the extended conflicts in Iraq and Afghanistan and the continued trade deficit and national debt of the United States. With a limited source of funding, what should be provided and how?

AMCs treat many uninsured patients in their emergency departments. The emergency department for the uninsured and underinsured is not an ideal field in which to address the order of battle when combating the problem of healthcare access. Intervening early in the course of an illness is better, but ideally, disease prevention through the modification of social determinants that may be initiators of disease, including early access to healthcare, is a more worthy course of action for AMCs.

A noteworthy example of an AMC's attempt to address the need for healthcare among the socially disadvantage was the establishment of The Johns Hopkins Urban Health Institute. It "was established with the mission to marshal the resources of the university and external groups to improve the health and well being of the residents of East Baltimore" [3]. While the United States has been a country of medical breakthroughs and advancements the vulnerable segments of its

society have experienced inadequate delivery of healthcare [3,22].

Urban health in East Baltimore had been extremely poor in the 1990s. Besides poverty and violence (near the top in the USA) this part of the city had 12% of its first graders with asthma, 18% of all its births had complications secondary to low birth weight, sexually transmitted disease rates that were the highest in the country, and a rate of syphilis that was the highest of any city in the developed world [3]. There were also very high rates of diabetes, human immunodeficiency virus, substance abuse, pulmonary, cardiovascular, and cerebrovascular disease [3].

In 1999 several working groups determined there were 13 obstacles to improving the health of East Baltimore: poverty; a drug-based economy; abandonment of the economically mobile to the suburbs; lack of education; lack of economic and political power; economic and environmental pressures that divert people from health lifestyles; issues of race and discrimination; lack of continuity of care; lack of community health workers; lack of health insurance; mistrust of the AMC, government and the local community; a lack of coordination between research projects and clinical care; and concerns about privacy of health information [3]. The institute was established soon after these obstacles were identified (2000). Its three strategic goals were, (1) strengthening and enhancing urban health research and learning both locally and nationally, (2) reducing disparities in health and healthcare for East Baltimore residents, and (3) promoting economic growth in the area. Goal 1 was addressed through university support for community-based research. Funding of projects such as "The Amazing Grandmothers," support services to grandmothers who cared for children whose parents were no longer caring for them because of drug abuse; and "Spirituality, Substance Abuse, and Mental illness," a service improvement project for those with co-existing substance abuse disorders and mental illness. Goal 2 was an active practice of medical intervention against HIV/AIDS through testing, counseling, and placement in appropriate care; and the development of a local, university-supported primary care system aimed at: (a) impacting East Baltimore health, (b) encouraging community involvement, (c) educating university medical staff in urban health, (d) decreasing emergency department visits and the need for tertiary care, and (e) providing evidence-based proof that primary care can improve the health of urban citizens. Goal 3 was promoted by providing East Baltimore residents with technical training and computer skills so that they can earn a living in the current market through the East Baltimore Technology Resource Center, a new community entity [3].

This action by Johns Hopkins University was the realization that:

> Even though the "best care in the world" may literally be next door, poor urban residents experience some of the worst health conditions, live in some of the least healthy environments, and have some of the worst health indices of any population group in the nation – in some instances comparable to those found in developing nations. [3]

Nearly all AMCs make some effort to provide healthcare access to the medically needy. Can all AMCs do what Johns Hopkins University did? Maybe not, but, nonetheless, every AMC should make an ongoing, informed, intentional effort to direct a certain amount of resources/effort toward improving healthcare access or correcting social determinants affecting a people's health or ability to access healthcare. If there are no resources available, then an effort should be made to acquire the necessary resources. Each AMC and their area partners can decide what their local priorities should be. Interventions may be broad or narrow, i.e., if a health system cannot provide an entire primary care program, they may wish to target less comprehensive projects such as providing vaccines, nutrition education, or access to tertiary services. A cooperative effort by AMCs and their partners can help identify targets and strategies within defined financial parameters, i.e., pick what you can do and how you can do it with the money you have available. AMCs have a moral obligation for such actions.

Action is needed to secure the health of the body and soul. Action is needed to secure the mutual well being of individuals and the preservation of a "normal" society where safety, education, economic opportunity, and access to healthcare would have at least some small chance to flourish. In short, AMCs must be the leaders in this effort. AMCs must use their power, through speech and action in the space of appearance, to secure the entrance of the powerless into the space of appearance so that healthcare access is available to all members of society.

## Conclusion

Once healthcare access is a right, difficulties will invariably ensue. Do the elderly receive liver transplants? Can a morbidly obese person receive a reoperation for coronary artery bypass grafting? Can a diabetic receive a second kidney transplant? How much is enough healthcare access? Will healthcare delivery become a tiered process? Are we wise enough to make the necessary and correct decisions? Who will be society's proxy to make such decisions? There are no clear answers.

Some may think these decisions simply cannot be made. The argument presented here begs the opposite. Situations such as those found in East Baltimore, MD were amenable to interventions. The conditions regarding the ability of the medically needy to access healthcare can be resolved. As Hannah Arendt insightfully reminded us:

The new always happens against the overwhelming odds of statistical laws and their probability, which for all practical, everyday purposes amounts to a certainty; the new therefore always appears in the guise of a miracle. The fact that man is capable of action means the unexpected can be expected from him, that he is able to perform what is infinitely improbable. [17]

## References

1. Anderson RT, Sorlie P, Backlund E, Johnson N, Kaplan GA: Mortality effects of community socioeconomic status. *Epidemiology* 1997, 8:42–47.
2. Marmot MG, Smith GD, Stansfield S, Patel C, North F, Head J, White I, Brunner E, Feeney A: Health inequalities among British civil servants: the Whitehall II study. *Lancet* 1991, 337:1387–93.
3. Fox CE, Morford TG, Fine A, Gibbons MC: The Johns Hopkins Urban Institute: a collaborative response to urban health issues. *Acad Med* 2004, 79:1169–74.
4. US Census [http://www.census.gov/prod/2004pubs/p60-226.pdf].
5. Fiscella K, Williams DR: Health disparities based on socioeconomic inequities: implications for urban health care. *Acad Med* 2004, 79:1139–47.
6. Williams DR, Collins C: Racial residential segregation: a fundamental cause of racial disparities in health. *Public Health Rep* 2001, 116:404–16.
7. Aristotle: *The Soul* Edited by: Smith JA. Whitefish: Kessinger Publishing; 2005.
8. Taylor AE: *Aristotle* Toronto: Dover Publications; 1955.
9. Arrington RL: Kant. In *Western Ethics* Edited by: Arrington RL. Malden: Blackwell Publishers; 1998:261–94.
10. Scruton R: *Kant: a very short introduction* Oxford: Oxford UP; 1996.
11. Hobbes T: Chapter XIV. In *Leviathan* Edited by: Tuck R. Cambridge: Cambridge UP; 1996:91–100.
12. Arrington RL: Hobbes. In *Western Ethics* Edited by: Arrington RL. Malden: Blackwell Publishers; 1998:157–83.
13. Hobbes T: Chapter XV. In *Leviathan* Edited by: Tuck R. Cambridge: Cambridge UP; 1996:100–11.
14. Paine T: *Rights of Man* Mineola: Dover Publications; 1999.
15. Paine T: Rights of Man. In *Rights of Man* Mineola: Dover Publications; 1999:7–64.
16. Arendt H: *The Human Condition* Chicago: U of Chicago P; 1958.
17. Arendt H: Action. In *The Human Condition*. Chicago: U of Chicago P; 1958:175–247.
18. Rawls J: *A Theory of Justice* Cambridge: Harvard UP; 1999.
19. Daniels N: *Just Health* Cambridge: Cambridge UP; 1985.
20. Justice is good for our health [http://bostonreview.net/BR25.1/daniels.html].
21. Ginzberg E: *Teaching Hospitals and the Urban Poor* New Haven: Yale UP; 2000.
22. Prewitt E: Inner city health care. *Ann Intern Med* 1997, 26:485–90.

**Study Questions**

1. Which figure discussed by Papadimos do you think would make the most persuasive case for health care being a right? Can you explain your answer by pointing out why the others make a less persuasive case for health care being a right?

2. Papadimos says that John Rawls's theory of justice can be used to defend the idea that health care is a right. How would you explain to a friend the argument Papadimos makes in this regard?

3. Look over Papadimos's article carefully and identify differences between Paine's natural rights and Hobbes's natural law. Identify, for example, where obligation comes from for both of them. Which theory of rights do you think Westerners are more familiar with? Which theory of rights makes more sense to you?

4. How did The John Hopkins Urban Health Institute address the 13 obstacles to improving the health of residents in East Baltimore? What broader implications does this have?

# 4. Paul Farmer, "Pathologies of Power: Rethinking Health and Human Rights"

IN THIS 1999 ESSAY from the *American Journal of Public Health*, Paul Farmer (b. 1959) explains the relevance of health in human-rights law. He argues that violations to the right to health occur not most significantly by way of the actions of individual persons but by way of large-scale structures of power that can be national or international. Only by looking at the dynamics of power can human-rights organizations gain proper information about and respond adequately to human-rights abuses in the area of health and health care. Farmer concludes by proposing an agenda plan that would make health central to human-rights advocacy and research.

MEDICINE AND THE ALLIED health sciences have long been peripherally involved in work on human rights. Fifty years ago, the door to greater involvement was opened by Article 25 of the Universal Declaration of Human Rights, which underlined social and economic rights: "Everyone has the right to a standard of living adequate for the health and well-being of himself and his family, including food, clothing, housing, and medical care and necessary social services, and the right to security in the event of unemployment, sickness, disability, widowhood, old age or other lack of livelihood in circumstances beyond his control."[1]

But the intervening decades have seen little progress in the press for social and economic rights, even though we may point with some pride to gains in civil or legal rights. That these distinctions are crucial is made clear by a visit to a Russian prison. The Russian Federation has traditionally been the United States' only serious competitor in the race to be the country with the highest rates of incarceration. With its current political and economic disruption, Russia has pulled ahead: some 700 per 100,000 citizens are currently in jail or prison. (In much of the rest of Europe,

that figure is about one fifth as high.[2])

In the full-to-bursting pretrial detention centers in which hundreds of thousands of Russian detainees await due process, many fall ill with tuberculosis (TB). Convicted prisoners who are diagnosed with TB are sent to one of more than 50 "TB colonies." Imagine a Siberian prison in which the cells are as cramped as cattle cars, the fetid air thick with tubercle bacilli. Imagine a cell in which most of the prisoners are coughing and all are said to have active TB. Let the mean age of the inmates be less than 30 years. Finally, imagine that many of these young men are receiving ineffective therapy for their disease – given drug toxicity, worse than receiving placebo – even though they are the beneficiaries of directly observed therapy with first-line antituberculous agents, delivered by European humanitarian organizations and their Russian colleagues.[3]

For many, the therapy is ineffective because the strains of TB that are epidemic within the prisons are resistant to the drugs being administered. Various observers, including some from international human rights organizations, have averred that these prisoners have "untreatable forms" of TB, even though treatment with the standard of care used elsewhere in Europe and in North America can cure the great majority of such cases.[4] TB has again become the leading cause of death among Russian prisoners – even among those receiving treatment. Similar situations may be found throughout the former Soviet Union.

Are human rights violated in this dismal scenario? Conventional views of human rights would lead one to focus on a single violation: prolonged pretrial detention, which currently has the accused detained for up to a year before making a court appearance. In many documented cases, young detainees died of prison-acquired TB before their cases ever went to trial. Such detention is in clear violation not only of Russian law, but of several human rights charters to which the country is signatory. And Russian and international human rights activists have indeed focused on this problem, demanding that all detainees be brought quickly to trial. An impasse is quickly reached when the underfunded Russian courts wearily respond that they are working as fast as they can. The Ministry of Justice agrees and is now interested in amnesty for prisoners and alternatives to imprisonment.

But let us reconsider TB in Russian prisons as a question of social and economic rights. Such an exercise yields a far longer list of violations – and a longer list of possible interventions. First, as noted, pretrial detention is illegally prolonged, and conditions are deplorable. The directors of the former gulag do not dispute this point. The head of the federal penitentiary system, speaking to Amnesty International, described the prisoners as living in "conditions amounting to torture."[5] Some of the more astute prison administrators remind their critics that the dismantling of the Soviet economy has led to a sharp rise in petty crime – "People now have to steal for food," in the words of one official[6] – which has swamped the prison system even as

"economic restructuring" planned with the help of Western economic advisors has slashed budgets for prison health.[7]

Second, the detainees are subjected to conditions in which they are guaranteed increased exposure to multidrug-resistant strains of TB (MDR-TB). In other words, increased TB risks should be seen as a violation of rights; TB, as a form of punishment.[8] This is due to overcrowding, ineffective infection control measures, tardy diagnosis, and ineffective or interrupted treatment of the disease once diagnosed.

Third, the prisoners are denied not only adequate food but also medical care. But again, where does the blame lie? Interview medical staff in these prisons and you will find them distraught about the funding cuts that have followed the restructuring and collapse of the Russian economy. In the words of one physician: "I have spent my entire medical career caring for prisoners with TB. And although we complained about shortages in the eighties, we had no idea how good we had it then. Now it's a daily struggle for food, drugs, lab supplies, and even heat and electricity."[9]

Fourth, prisoners are dying of *ineffectively treated* MDR-TB. Article 27 of the Universal Declaration of Human Rights, which insists that everyone has a right "to share in scientific advancement and its benefits," would have us raise questions about the fact that representatives of wealthy donor nations – relief workers – are giving prisoners drugs to which their infecting TB strains have documented resistance. Thus are the rights of the prisoners violated by the logic of cost-efficacy, which says that the appropriate drugs are too expensive for use in "the developing world," to which post-perestroika Russia has been demoted. All the prison rights activism in the world will come to naught if prisoners are guaranteed the right to treatment but given the wrong prescription. In short, conventional legal views on recrudescent TB in Russian prisons fail to recognize much of the problem.

## Questioning "Immodest Claims of Causality"

As complicated as this picture is, even more complicated are the competing explanations offered by various actors on the scene. Some international health experts insist that the heart of the problem lies with Russian physicians, who have failed to adopt modern approaches to TB control.[10] Others, basing their arguments on technical or cost-efficacy grounds, argue that MDR-TB is untreatable in such settings. Experts from the international public health community have argued that it is not necessary to treat MDRTB – the "untreatable form" in question – in this region, because the necessary second-line drugs are too expensive. These experts argue that all patients should be treated with the same doses of the same drugs and that MDR-TB would disappear if such strategies were adopted.[11] Other experts, both Russian and international, have claimed that the reason for poor treatment outcomes lies with the prisoners, who are said to refuse treatment.[12]

How many of these claims are true? First, it seems an immodest claim of causality to lay the blame for a burgeoning TB epidemic on Russia's hapless TB specialists, given that the nation's public health infrastructure has crumbled because of economic restructuring rather than ill-advised clinical management strategies. Second, cost-efficacy arguments against treating drug-resistant TB almost always fail to note that most of the drugs necessary for such treatment have been off-patent for years. Also incorrect is the claim that MDR-TB is untreatable. My colleagues and I have done work in Peru and Haiti showing that MDR-TB can be cured in resource-poor settings.[13] We also know from painful experience in New York prisons that failure to identify and treat MDR-TB will lead to outbreaks of disease throughout the prison system, and thence on to the public hospitals and beyond. Claims that the problem would be eliminated by low-cost, short-course chemotherapy are thus dangerously incorrect.[14]

There is reason to suspect that the other assertion, that prisoners refuse treatment, is also false. How might this claim be assessed? One option would be to ask the concerned parties. "How many of you," I asked one group of Siberian prisoners with TB, "want to be treated?" All hands went up. "Why, then, is it so widely rumored that you refuse treatment?" "Hearsay," came one quick reply. "Just not true," came another. "But we want treatment that will cure us."

Clearly, the veracity of competing claims about a matter as delicate as epidemic MDR-TB cannot be assessed by a show of hands. MDR-TB in Russian prisons is an example of a complex human rights problem that requires the application of epidemiology, subspecialty clinical medicine, and a critical sociology of knowledge. The social sciences can help to reveal the immodest claims of causality that fill any explanatory void. Facile claims about the nature of excess deaths among prisoners are to be expected; such claims are patterned and predictable. The analysis also calls for an international political economy of relief work – that is, a critical look, from a political science perspective, at the way in which humanitarian work is conducted.

But what, more specifically, does the focus on health bring to the struggle for human rights? In this article I argue that an exclusive focus on a legal approach to health and human rights can obscure the nature of violations, thereby hobbling our best responses to them. Casting prison-based TB epidemics in terms of social and economic rights offers an entrée for public health and medicine, an important step in the process that could halt these epidemics. Conversely, failure to consider social and economic rights can prevent the allied health professions and the social sciences from making a significant contribution to the struggle for human rights.

## Asking New Questions about Health and Human Rights

Public health and access to medical care are social and economic rights; they are every bit as critical as civil rights. One of the great ironies of the global era, in which public health has increasingly sacrificed equity for efficacy, has been the rejection by the poor of separate standards of care. In our professional journals, these subaltern voices have been heard most clearly with regard to access to antiviral therapy for HIV disease, but the destitute sick are increasingly clear on one point: promoting social and economic rights is the key goal for health and human rights in the 21st century.

I will not discuss, except in passing and to set the stage, the covenants and conventions that constitute the key documents of the human rights movement. The goal of this article is to raise, and to answer, some questions relevant to health and human rights, and in so doing to identify promising directions for future work in this field.

Allow me to say at the outset that although I am an anthropologist, I do not embrace the rigidly particularist and relativist tendencies popularly associated with the discipline.[15] That is, I believe that violations of human dignity are not to be dismissed merely because they are buttressed by local ideology or long-standing tradition. But anthropology – in common with sociologic and historical perspectives in general – allows us to place in broader contexts both human rights abuses and the discourses (and other responses) they generate.[16] Furthermore, these disciplines permit us to ground our understanding of

human rights violations in broader analyses of power and social inequality. Whereas a purely legal view of human rights tends to obscure the dynamics of human rights violations, the contextualizing disciplines reveal them to be "pathologies of power." Social inequalities based on race or ethnicity, gender, religious creed, and – above all – social class are the motive force behind most human rights violations. In other words, violence against individuals is usually embedded in entrenched "structural violence."[17]

In exploring the relationships between structural violence and human rights, I will also draw on my own experience serving the destitute sick in settings such as Haiti and Chiapas, where human rights violations are a daily concern; I have already discussed Russia, where increasing structural violence is not yet recognized as a human rights issue. I do this not to make too much of my personal acquaintance with other people's suffering, but rather to ground a theoretical discussion in the very real experiences that have shaped my views on health and human rights. Each of these situations calls not only for our recognition of the relationship between structural violence and human rights violations, but also for what might be termed pragmatic solidarity: the rapid deployment of our tools and resources to improve the health of those who are victimized by this violence.

### How Far Has the Human Rights Movement Come?

The field of health and human rights, most would agree, is in its infancy. Attempting to define a new field is necessarily a treacherous enterprise: sometimes we appear to step on the toes of those who have long been at work when we mean instead to stand on their shoulders. Human rights law, which focuses on civil and legal rights, is much older than human rights medicine. And if vigor is assessed in the typical academic style – by length of bibliography – human rights law is the more robust field, too. That legal documents and scholarship dominate the human rights literature is unsurprising, note Steiner and Alston, given that the human rights movement has "struggled to assume so law-like a character."[18]

Even in legal terms, the international human rights movement is essentially a modern phenomenon, beginning, some argue, with the Nuremberg trials.[19] It is this movement that has led, most recently, to the constitution of international tribunals to judge war crimes in the Balkans and in Rwanda. It is 50 years after the Universal Declaration of Human Rights, 50 years after the 4 Geneva Conventions. What do we have to show for these efforts? Do we have some sense of outcomes? Aryeh Neier, former executive director of Human Rights Watch, recently reviewed the history of various treaties and covenants from Nuremberg to the Convention against Torture and Other Cruel, Inhuman or Degrading Treatment or Punishment. "Nations have honored these obligations," he concludes, "largely in the breach."[20]

Certainly, it would be difficult to correlate a steep rise in the publication of human rights documents with a statistically significant drop in the number of human rights abuses. Rosalyn Higgins says pointedly (emphasis in the original):

No one doubts that there exists a norm prohibiting torture. No state denies the existence of such a norm; and, indeed, it is widely recognized as a customary rule of international law by national courts. But it is equally clear from, for example, the reports of Amnesty International, that *the great majority* of states systematically engage in torture. If one takes the view that noncompliance is relevant to the retention of normative quality, are we to conclude that there is not really any prohibition of torture under customary international law?[21]

Whether these laws are binding or largely hortatory constitutes a substantial debate in the legal literature, but such debates seem academic in the face of overwhelming evidence of persistent abuses. When we expand the concept of rights to include social and economic rights, the gap between the ideal and reality is even wider.

Local and global inequalities mean that the fruits of medical and scientific advances are stockpiled for some and denied to others. The dimensions of this inequality are staggering, and the trends are bad. To cite just a few examples: by 1995, the total wealth of the top 358 "global billionaires" equaled the combined income of the world's 2.3 billion poorest people.[22] In 1998, Michael Jordan earned from Nike the equivalent of 60,000 years' salary for an Indonesian footwear assembly worker. Haitian factory workers, most of them women, make 28 cents per hour sewing Pocahontas pajamas, while Disney's US-based chief executive officer makes $97,000 for each hour he toils.[23]

The pathogenic effects of such inequality per se are now recognized.[24] Many governments, including our own, refuse to redress inequalities in health, while others are largely powerless to address them.[25] But although the reasons for failure are many and varied, even optimists allow that these charters and covenants have not brought an end to – and may not even have slowed – egregious abuses of human rights, however they are defined. States large and small violate civil, economic, and social rights, and inequality both prompts and covers these violations.

There are, of course, exceptions; victories have been declared. But none of them are very encouraging on close scrutiny. Haiti, the case I know best, offers a humbling example. First, the struggle for social and economic rights in Haiti has been dealt lethal blows. Such basic entitlements, the centerpiece of the popular movement that in 1990 brought the first democratically elected president to power, were buried under an avalanche of human rights violations after the military coup of 1991. And although human rights groups were among those credited with helping to restore constitutional rule in Haiti, this was accomplished, to a large extent, by sacrificing the struggle for social and economic rights.[26] Today, the steam has also run out of the movement to bring to justice those responsible for the murder and mayhem that have made Haiti such a difficult place to live.

Or take Argentina, considered by some to be a successful chapter in the struggle against impunity. The gruesome details of the "dirty war" are familiar to many.[27] Seeking what Aryeh Neier has chillingly termed "a better mousetrap of repression," the Argentine military government began "disappearing" (as Latin Americans said in the special syntax crafted for the occasion) people it identified as leftists.[28] Many people know, now, about the death flights that took place every Wednesday for 2 years: thousands of citizens the government deemed subversive, many of them students and most of them having survived torture, were flown from a military installation out over the Atlantic, stripped, and shoved out of the plane. A better mouse-trap, indeed.

What happened next is well documented, although it is a classic instance of the half-empty, half-full glass. Those who say the glass is half-full note that an elected civilian government subsequently tried and convicted high-ranking military figures, including the generals who spelled one another in the presidential office. Those who say the glass is half-empty note that the prompt pardoning and release of the criminals meant that, once again, no one was held accountable for thousands of murders.[29] Similar stories abound in Guatemala, El Salvador, the state of Chiapas in Mexico, and elsewhere in Latin America, as the record shows.[30]

These painful experiences are, of course, no reason to declare legal proceedings ineffective. On the contrary, they remind us that what was previously hidden away is now more out in the open. Disclosure is often the first step in the struggle against impunity, and human rights organizations – almost all of them nongovernmental – have at times forced unwilling governments to acknowledge what really happened. These efforts should serve as a rallying cry for those who now look to constitute international criminal tribunals.

Still, the results to date suggest that we would be unwise to put all of our eggs in the legal-struggle basket. Complementary strategies and new openings are critically needed. The health and human rights "angle" can provide new opportunities and new strategies at the same time that it lends strength to a movement sorely in need of buttressing.

### Can One Merely Study Human Rights Abuses?

A few years ago, the French sociologist Pierre Bourdieu [1930–2002] and his colleagues pulled together a compendium of testimonies from those the French term "the excluded" in order to bring into relief la misère du monde. Bourdieu and colleagues qualify their claims for the role of scholarship in addressing this misery: "To subject to scrutiny the mechanisms which render life painful, even untenable, is not to neutralize them; to bring to light contradictions is not to resolve them."[31]

It is difficult to merely study human rights abuses. We know with certainty that rights are being abused at this very moment. And the fact that we study, rather than endure, these abuses is a reminder that we too are implicated in and benefit from the increasingly global structures that determine, to an important extent, the nature and distribution of assaults on dignity.

Ivory-tower engagement with health and human rights can, often enough, reduce us to seminar-room warriors. At worst, we stand revealed as the hypocrites that our critics in many parts of the world have not hesitated to call us. Anthropologists have long been familiar with these critiques; specialists in international health, including AIDS researchers, have recently had a crash course.[32] It is possible, usually, to drown out the voices of those demanding that we stop studying them, even when they go to great lengths to make sure we get the message. Social scientists have documented a rich trove of graffiti, songs, demonstrations, tracts, and broadsides on the subject. A hit record album in Haiti was called *International Organizations*. The title cut includes the following lines: "International organizations are not on our side. They're there to help the thieves rob and devour…. International health stays on the sidelines of our struggle."

In the context of long-standing international support for sundry Haitian dictatorships, one could readily see the gripe with international organizations. The international community's extraordinary largesse to the Duvalier regime has certainly been well documented.[33] Subsequent patterns of giving, relying as they did on sundry Duvalierist military juntas, did nothing to improve the reputation of US foreign aid or the international organizations. Such critiques are not specific to Haiti, although Haitians have pronounced them with exceptional frankness and richness of detail. These accusations have been echoed and amplified throughout what

some are beginning to call the global geoculture.[34] A full decade before the AIDS research debates of the past year, it was possible to collect a bookful of such commentary.[35]

It is in this context of globalization, "mediatization," and growing inequality that we are forging the new field of health and human rights. These contextual factors are particularly salient when we think about social and economic rights, as Steiner and Alston have noted: "An examination of the concept of the right to development and its implications in the 1990s cannot avoid consideration of the effects of the globalization of the economy and the consequences of the near-universal embrace of the market economy."[36] It is in this context that we must define our research agenda. We are leaving behind the terra firma of double-blinded, placebo-controlled studies, of cost-efficacy, and of sustainability.

What, then, is the role of the First World university, of researchers and health care professionals, in all of this? We can agree, perhaps, that these centers are places from which to conduct research, to document, and to teach. A university does not have the same obligations or constraints as an international institution such as the United Nations, or as organizations such as Amnesty International or Physicians for Human Rights. Such institutions afford a unique and privileged space in which to conduct research and engage in critical assessment.

In human rights work, however, research and critical assessment are necessary but not sufficient. No more adequate, for all their virtues, are denunciation and exhortation, whether in the form of press conferences or reports or harangues directed at students. To confront, as an observer, ongoing abuses of human rights is to be faced with a moral dilemma. The increasingly baroque codes of research ethics generated by institutional review boards will not help us out of this dilemma, nor will medical ethics, which are lost, so often, in the quandary ethics of the individual. But certain models of engagement are not irrelevant. If the university-based human rights worker is in a peculiar position, it is not entirely unlike that of the clinician researcher. Both study suffering; both are bound to relieve it; neither is in possession of a tried-and-true remedy. Both the human rights specialist and the clinician researcher have blind spots, too.

To push the analogy further, it could be argued that there are, in both lines of work, obligations regarding the standard of care. Once a reasonably effective intervention has been identified, it – and not placebo – is considered the standard against which a new remedy must be tested. Of course, pushing for higher standards for the victims is always a utopian enterprise. Many factors may limit feasibility, but that didn't stop the authors of the Universal Declaration from setting high goals. That we have failed to meet them does not imply that the next step is to lower our sights, although this has been the default logic in many instances. The next step is to try new approaches and to hedge our bets with indisputably effective interventions.

Providing pragmatic services to the afflicted is one obvious response to the critiques that we ignore at our peril. In other words, social and economic rights cannot be excluded from the campaign for health and human rights. Again, my own experience in Haiti, which began in 1983, made this clear. The [Jean-Claude "Baby Doc"] Duvalier dictatorship [1971–86] was then in power, seemingly immovable. Its chief source of external financial aid was the United States and various international institutions, many of them ostensibly charitable in nature. The local director of the United States Agency for International Development at the time had often opined that if Haiti was underdeveloped, the causes were to be sought in

Haitian culture.[37] Popular cynicism regarding these transnational institutions was at its peak when my colleagues and I began working in Haiti, and that is precisely why we chose to work through community-based organizations and for a group of rural peasants who had been dispossessed of their land. Although we conducted research and published it, research did not figure on the wish list of the people we were trying to serve. *Services* were what they asked for, and as people who had been displaced by political and economic violence, they regarded these services as the rightful remedy for what they had suffered. In other words, social and economic rights were deemed central to the Haitian struggle for human rights.

The same has been true of the struggle in Chiapas. The Zapatista rebellion was launched on the day the North American Free Trade Agreement was signed, and the initial statement of the rebellion's leaders put their demands in terms of social and economic rights:

> We are denied the most elementary education so that they can use us as cannon fodder and plunder our county's riches, uncaring that we are dying of hunger and curable diseases. Nor do they care that we have nothing, absolutely nothing, no decent roof over our heads, no land, no work, no health, no food, no education. We do not have the right to freely and democratically elect our own authorities, nor do we have peace or justice for ourselves and our children.[38]

It is in settings such as these that we must decide how health professionals might make common cause with the destitute sick, whose rights are violated daily. Helping governments shore up failing public health systems may or may not be wise. In Chiapas, for example, many communities simply refuse to use government health services. In village after village, we heard the same story. To quote one health worker, "The government uses health services against us. They persecute us if they think we are on the side of the rebels." In some "autonomous zones," the Mexican Army – one third of which, or 70,000 troops, is now stationed in Chiapas – has entered these villages and destroyed health records and what meager infrastructure had been developed. Our own investigations have been amply confirmed by others, including Physicians for Human Rights:

> At best, [Mexican] Government health and other services are subordinate to Government counterinsurgency efforts. At worst, these services are themselves components of repression, manipulated to reward supporters and to penalize and demoralize dissenters. In either case, Government health services in the zone are discriminatory, exacerbate political divisions, and fail utterly to address the real health needs of the population.[39]

What Is the Difference, in Human Rights Work, Between Analysis and Strategy?

If we accept the need to think in both theoretical and instrumental terms, there is a difference, in human rights work, between analysis and strategy. Failure to recognize this difference has often hobbled interventions designed to prevent or allay human rights violations. In this arena, analysis means bringing out the truth, no matter how clumsy or embarrassing or inexpedient. It means documenting, as Aryeh Neier recently put it, "Who did what to whom, and when?" Strategy asks a different question: What is to be done?

For example, high-minded charters are utopian strategies that may become laws to be flouted or obeyed; they are not analysis. The notion that everyone shares the risk of having his or her rights violated is reminiscent of catchy public health slogans such as "AIDS is for everyone." These slogans may be useful for social marketing, but they are redolent of the most soft-headed thinking. The distribution of AIDS is strikingly patterned; so is that of human rights abuses. There is considerable overlap between the groups at risk: if you are likely to be tortured or otherwise abused, you are also likely to be in the AIDS risk group composed of the poor and the defenseless.[40]

Human rights can and should be declared universal, but the risk of having one's rights violated is not universal. Moreover, not every offense should be automatically classed as a human rights violation. Sticks and stones, we know, may break bones; but although it is not true that "names will never hurt me," there is wisdom in this adage. The often parochial identity politics of our time and place have indeed sought to extend the reach of rights language. But the risk of such universalization of the concept of rights is that obscene inequalities of risk will be drowned in a rising tide of petty complaint.[41]

Only careful comparative analysis gives us a sense of scale; only careful analysis brings mechanisms into relief. We have seen brisk debate about a hierarchy of human rights abuses and about whether or not it makes sense to consider some rights "fundamental." The struggle for recognition of social and economic rights has engendered even more acrimony.[42] But this debate has been legal in nature – centered in and destined toward law, where it is customary to speak of inalienable rights and to wait decades or centuries to see them vindicated. The public health and medical communities are accustomed to triage and to assessment of gravity; it makes sense, in my view, to distinguish between the harm done by receiving 6 lashes for vandalism – when meted out to a US citizen abroad, a cause cé-lèbre, to judge by inches of newspaper copy – and that done by a lifetime of institution-alized racism.[43] It makes sense to distinguish between a struggle for access to control of power – breaking the gendered "glass ceiling" of transnational corporations, say – and access to basic primary health care, especially if these same corporations can be shown to be linked to deepening inequity between rich and poor. To make distinctions between genocide and censorship of intellectuals is not to declare the latter trivial. But our job of telling the truth as best we can compels us to weight those wrongs differently.

Merely telling the truth, of course, often calls for exhaustive research. In the 20th century, human rights violations are usually both local and global; telling who did what to whom and when becomes a complicated affair. Take the case of Chouchou Louis, a young man tortured to death in Haiti in early 1992. I have told his story elsewhere in lurid detail; here I will say merely that I was called to see him after he was cast out of police head-quarters to die in the street. He did just that: I was too late, too unequipped, medically, to save his life. Documenting what had hap-pened to him was the least I could do.

Was I to document only the "distal" events? Although all present were terrified, it was possible to obtain the names of those who arrested and tortured Chouchou Louis. But the chain of command, I learned, kept reaching higher. At the time, US officialdom's explanation of human rights abuses in Haiti, including the torture and murder of people like Chouchou Louis, focused almost exclusively on local actors and local factors. One heard of the "culture of violence" that rendered this and similarly grisly deaths comprehensible. Such official analyses, constructed through the conflation of structural violence and cul-tural difference, were distancing tactics.

Innumerable immodest claims of causality, such as attributing a sudden upsurge in torture of persons in police custody to longstanding local custom, play into the convenient alibi that refuses to follow the chain of events to their source, that keeps all the trouble local. Such alibis obscure the fact that the modern Haitian military was created by an act of the US Congress during our 20-year occupa-tion (1915–1934) of Haiti. These analyses did not discuss generous US assistance to the post-Duvalier military: over $200 million in aid passed through the hands of the Haitian military in the 18 months after Jean-Claude Duvalier left Haiti on a US cargo plane in 1986. Bush administration statements, and their faithful echoes in the establishment press, failed to mention that many of the command-ers who issued the orders to detain and torture were trained in Fort Benning, Georgia.[44]

The masking of the mechanisms of human rights violations is seen elsewhere. When my coworkers and I visited autonomous commu-nities in Chiapas in November 1997, it was clear that paramilitary groups linked tightly with the Mexican government were respon-sible for the bulk of intimidation and violence in these villages.[45] But, as in Haiti, federal authorities insisted that such violence was due to "local inter-community and interparty tension" or to ethnic rivalry.[46]

Immodest claims of causality are not always so flagrantly self-serving as those prof-fered to explain Haiti's agony or the violence in Chiapas. But only careful analysis allows us to rebut them with any confidence.

## What Can a Focus on Health Bring to the Struggle for Human Rights?

Medicine and public health, and also the social sciences relevant to these disciplines, have much to contribute to the great, often rancorous debates on human rights. But what, precisely, might be our greatest contribution? Rudolph Virchow saw doctors as "the natural attorneys of the poor."[47] A "health angle" can promote a broader human rights agenda in unique ways. In fact, the health part of the formula may prove critical to the success of the human rights movement. The honor in which public health and medicine are held affords us openings – again, a space of privilege – enjoyed by few other professions. For example, it is unlikely that my colleagues and I would have been welcomed so warmly into Russian prisons as social scientists or as human rights investigators. We went, instead, as TB specialists, and we suspected, without egotism, that a visiting group of doctors might be able to do more for the rights of these prisoners than a delegation from a conventional human rights organization. It is important to get the story straight: the leading cause of death among young Russian detainees is TB, not torture or starvation.

Medicine benefits from an extraordinary symbolic capital that is, so far, sadly underutilized in human rights work. No one made this point more clearly and persistently than the late Jonathan Mann. In an essay written with Daniel Tarantola, Mann noted that AIDS "has helped catalyze the modern health and human rights movement, which leads far beyond AIDS, for it considers that promoting and protecting health and promoting and protecting human rights are inextricably connected."[48]

But have we gone far beyond AIDS? Is it not a human rights issue that Russian prisoners are exposed, often during illegally prolonged pretrial detention, to epidemic MDR TB and then denied effective treatment? Is it not a human rights issue that international expert opinion has mistakenly informed Russian prison officials that treatment with second-line drugs is not cost-effective or that it is just plain unnecessary?

Standing on the shoulders of giants – from the authors of the Universal Declaration to Jonathan Mann – we can recognize prison epidemics as human rights issues. But what, precisely, is to be done? Russian penal codes *already* prohibit overcrowding, long pretrial detention, and undue risk from malnutrition and communicable disease. Prison officials *already* regard the TB problem as a top priority; that's why they let TB specialists in there. In a recent interview, one high-ranking prison official told me that the ministry saw their chief problems as lack of resources, over-crowding, and TB.[49] And the pièce de résistance might be that Boris Yeltsin had *already* declared 1998 "the year of human rights."

The Haitian military coup leaders were beyond the pale. But how about Chiapas? Instruments to which Mexico is already signatory include the Geneva Conventions of 1949; the International Covenant on Civil and Political Rights; the International Covenant on Economic, Social and Cultural Rights; the International Labor Organization Convention 169; the American Convention on Human Rights; the Maastricht Guidelines on Violations of Economic, Social and Cultural Rights; and the Convention on the Elimination of All Forms of Discrimination Against Women. Each of these is flouted each day in Chiapas.

As the Haitians say, "Laws are made of paper; bayonets are made of steel." The law alone is not up to the tasks of relieving such immense suffering. Louis Henkin has reminded us that international law is fundamentally a set of rules and norms designed to protect the interests of states, not their citizens. "Until recently," he observed in 1989, "international law took no note of individual human beings."[50] And states, as we have seen, honor human rights law largely in the breach – sometimes through intention, and sometimes through sheer impotence. This chief irony of human rights work – that states will not or cannot obey the treaties to which they are signatory – can lead to despair or to cynicism, if all one's eggs are in the international-law basket.

Laws are not science; they are normative ideology, and tightly tied to power.[51]

Biomedicine and public health, though also vulnerable to ideological deformations, serve different imperatives, ask different questions. They do not ask whether an event or process violates an existing rule; they ask whether that event or process can be shown to have ill effects on a patient or on a population. They ask whether such events can be prevented or remediated. This approach would have, I would argue, a salutary effect on many human rights debates.

To return to the case of prisoners with MDR-TB, the best way to protect their rights is to cure them of their disease; the best way to protect the rights of other prisoners is to prevent transmission by treating the sick. A variety of strategies, from human rights arguments to epidemiologic scare tactics, have been used to make headway in raising the funds necessary to treat these and other prisoners. In the end, then, the health angle on human rights may prove more pragmatic than approaching the problem as one of penal reform alone. Previously closed institutions have opened their doors to international collaboration designed to halt prison epidemics. This approach – pragmatic solidarity – may lead to penal reform as well. I will return to this approach in proposing new agendas for health and human rights, but proceed under the assumption that there are many pitfalls – moral, strategic, and analytic – to any approach to human rights that regards research as an end in and of itself.[52]

## Some New Agendas for Health and Human Rights?

To summarize the argument so far: We have a long way to go in the struggle for health and human rights; it isn't really possible to merely study the topic without meaningful and pragmatic interventions; it is important to distinguish between our best analysis and our best strategies; and the health angle offers a critical new dimension to human rights work and is still a largely untapped vein of resources and passion and goodwill.

What about new agendas? First, is it grandiose to seek to define new agendas? When one reads the powerfully worded statutes, conventions, treaties, and charters stemming from international revulsion over the crimes of the Third Reich, it would seem pointless to call for better instruments of this sort. Yet events in the former Yugoslavia and in Rwanda serve as a powerful rebuke to undue confidence in these approaches: "That it should nevertheless be possible for Nazi-like crimes to be repeated half a century later in full view of the whole world," remarks Aryeh Neier, "points up the weakness of that system – and the need for fresh approaches."[53] Steiner and Alston, similarly, call for "heightened attention to the problems of implementation and enforcement of the new ideal norms. The old techniques," they conclude, "simply won't work."[54]

A corollary question, then: Does a coherent agenda spring from the critique inherent in the answers to the questions presented here? If so, is this agenda compatible with existing approaches and documents, including the Universal Declaration of Human Rights? To those who believe that social and economic rights must be central to the health and human rights agenda, the answers to these questions are "Yes" and "Of course, yes." This agenda is coherent, pragmatic, and informed by careful scholarship. It builds on 5 decades of work within the traditional human rights framework: articles 25 and 27 of the Universal Declaration inspire the vision of this emerging agenda, which would rely on tighter links between universities, medical providers, and both nongovernmental and community-based organizations.

## What Can Be Done?

How might we proceed with this effort, if most reviews of the effects of international laws and treaties designed to protect human rights raise serious questions of efficacy, to say the least? What can be done to advance new agendas of health and human rights? I offer 6 suggestions, which are intended to complement ongoing efforts.

### Make Health and Healing the Symbolic Core of the Agenda

If we make health and healing the symbolic core of the agenda, we tap into something truly universal – concern for the sick – and, at the same time, engage medicine, public health, and the allied health professions, including the basic sciences. Although many global health indicators show significant improvement, we still have endless work to do before we can claim to have made the slightest headway in ensuring the highest possible level of health for all. In fact, several studies suggest that inequalities in health outcomes are growing in many places.[55]

Put another way, we need to throw the full weight of the medical and scientific communities behind a noble cause. There is no hostility, in these communities, to this cause; quite the contrary. What has been lacking, with some notable exceptions (such as Physicians for Human Rights) has been concerted efforts to engage health professionals in human rights work.

### Make the Provision of Services Central to the Agenda

We need to listen to the sick and abused and to those most likely to have their rights violated. Whether they are nearby or far away, we know, often enough, who they are. The abused offer, to those willing to listen, critiques far sharper than my own. They are not asking for new centers of study and reflection. They have not commissioned new studies of their suffering. That means we need new programs in addition to the traditional ventures of a university or a research center (journals, books, articles, courses, conferences, research). Law schools have clinics, and so do medical schools. Programs promoting health and human rights should not have only legal clinics. With help from a broad range of health professionals, it would be possible to establish, for example, referral clinics for those subjected to torture and other human rights abuses as classically defined.

But a far larger group calls for our pragmatic solidarity. We need to hedge our moral bets with programs designed to remediate inequalities of access. If everyone has a right "to share in scientific advancement and its benefits," where are our pragmatic efforts to improve the spread of these advances? Such efforts exist, but, again, the widening "outcome gap" stands as the sharpest rebuke to the health and human rights community: even as our biomedical interventions become more effective, our capacity to distribute them equitably is further eroded. The world's poor and otherwise marginalized people currently constitute a vast control group of the untreated, and even cursory examination of the annual tally of victims reminds us that this sector also constitutes the group most likely to have their rights violated.

How can we make services – pragmatic solidarity – central to the work of health and human rights programs? Our own group, Partners in Health, has worked largely with community-based organizations in Haiti and Peru whose express goal has been to remediate inequalities of access. This community of providers and scholars believes that "the vitality of practice" lends a corrective strength to our research and writing.[56] The possibilities for programmatic collaboration range, we have learned, from Russian prison officials to peasant collectives in the autonomous zones of Chiapas. In Chiapas, it is possible to hedge bets by supporting health promoters working within autonomous zones, which have been singled out for particularly brutal reprisals for alleged support of rebels. Novel collaborations of this sort are certainly necessary if we are to address the increasing inequalities of access here in wealthy, inegalitarian countries such as the United States. Relying exclusively on nation-states' compliance with a social-justice agenda is naive at best.

These questions of new collaboration are raised at a time of increasing globalization, yet our action agenda has stayed parochial. We lag behind trade and finance, since we are still at the first steps in the press for universal rights while the "masters of the universe" are already "harmonizing" their own standards and practices. Fifteen years of work in the most difficult field conditions have taught my group that it is difficult, perhaps impossible, to meet the highest standards of health care in every situation. But it is an excellent idea to try to do so. Projects striving for excellence – rather than, say, "cost-efficacy" or "sustainability," which are often at odds with social-justice approaches to medicine and public health – are not merely misguided quests for personal efficacy. Such projects respond to widespread demands for equity in health care. The din around AIDS research in the Third World is merely the latest manifestation of a rejection of low standards as official policy. That these

are widely seen as violating human rights is no surprise for those interested in social and economic rights. Efficacy cannot trump equity in the field of health and human rights.

## Establish New Research Agendas

We need to make room in the academy for serious scholarly work on the multiple dynamics of health and human rights, on the health effects of war and political-economic disruption, and on the pathogenic effects of social inequalities, including racism, gender inequality, and the growing gap between rich and poor. By what mechanisms, precisely, do such noxious events and processes become embodied as adverse health outcomes? Why are some at risk and others spared?

Here again, we lag far behind. As Nancy Krieger notes, "epidemiologic research explicitly focused on discrimination as a determinant of population health is in its infancy."[57] To answer the questions posed above, we require a new level of cooperation between disciplines ranging from social anthropology to molecular epidemiology. We need a new sociology of knowledge that can pick apart a wide body of commentary and scholarship: complex international law; the claims and disclaimers of officialdom; postmodern relativist readings of suffering; clinical and epidemiologic studies of the long-term effects of, say, torture.[58] And because such research would be linked to service, we need operational research by which we can gauge the efficacy of interventions quite different from those measured in the past.

## Assume a Broader Educational Mandate

Human rights work usually has a suasive component. If the primary objective is to set things right, education is central to our task. But the educational mandate should not be conventional in either of the 2 most likely ways: we must not limit ourselves to teaching a select group of students with an avowed interest in health and human rights, nor must we limit ourselves to trying to teach lessons to recalcitrant governments. Jonathan Mann signaled to us the limitations of the latter approach: "Support for human rights-based action to promote health ... at the level of declarations and speeches is welcome, and useful in some ways, but the limits of official organizational support for the call for societal transformation inherent in human rights promotion must be recognized."[59] A broader educational mandate would mean engaging students from *all* faculties, but also, as noted, engaging the members of these faculties. Beyond the university and various governmental bodies lies the broader public, for whom the connections between health and human rights have not even been traced.

Achieve Independence from Governments and Bureaucracies

We need to be untrammeled by obligations to powerful states and international bureaucracies. What is the central irony of human rights law? That it consists largely of appeals to the perpetrators. After all, most crimes against human rights are committed by states, not by rogue factions or gangs or cults or terrorists. That makes it difficult for institutions accountable to states to take their constituents to task. When in 1994 the UN created the post of High Commissioner for Human Rights, the $700,000 annual budget was paltry even by the standards of a nongovernmental organization. The results were predictable: "With denunciation of those responsible for abuses the only means available for carrying out his mission," the first commissioner "managed to go through his first year in his post without publicly criticizing a single government

anywhere in the world."[60] In Chiapas, the displacement and massacre of presumed Zapatista supporters by paramilitary groups tightly tied to the government has been documented by numerous observers: "State and federal authorities have permitted these groups to act with impunity, and state Public Security Police have not only failed to protect victims, but have sometimes participated in the evictions."[61]

In the end, university- and hospital-based programs may hope to be, along with the efforts of nongovernmental organizations, independent, well designed, pragmatic, and feasible. The imprimatur of medicine and public health would afford even more weight and independence. And only a failure of imagination has led us to ignore the potential of collaboration with community-based organizations and with communities in resistance to ongoing violations of human rights.

Secure More Resources for Health and Human Rights

"Growth is wildly uneven, inequality is immense, anxiety is endemic," says Todd Gitlin of our era. "The state, as a result, is continually urged to do more but deprived of the means to do so."[62] The halting but ineluctable spread of the global economy is linked to an evolving human rights irony: states become less able to help their citizens attain social and economic rights, even though they retain, often enough, their ability to violate human rights. Even where reforms have led to the enjoyment of basic political rights, the right to freedom from want may be eroded as new economic policies are implemented. This is particularly true of many developing countries, as Steiner and Alston note:

> Civil and political rights have been
> greatly strengthened in many countries.

Nonetheless, related contemporary phenomena – including privatization, deregulation, the expanded provision of incentives to entrepreneurial behavior, structural adjustment programs and related pressures from international financial institutions and developed countries – have had mixed, and sometimes seriously adverse, effects on the enjoyment of economic and social rights.[63]

Of course, it's easy to demand more resources, harder to produce them. But if social and economic rights are acknowledged as such, then foundations, governments, businesses, and international financial institutions – many of which are awash in resources – may be called to prioritize human rights endeavors that reflect the paradigm shift advocated here.

## Conclusion

Regardless of where one stands on the process of globalization, it has important implications for efforts to promote health and human rights. As states weaken, it is easy to discern an increasing role for nongovernmental institutions, including universities and medical centers. How will we live up to the challenge to promote the highest possible level of health for all? Universities and medical centers, we have argued, should conduct research, and the subject – health and human rights – demands complementary services. Linking research to service costs money. But if we lack ambition, we should expect the next 50 years to yield a harvest of shame.

The experience of my own group suggests that ambitious goals can be met even without a large springboard. Over the past decade and against a steady current of naysaying, we have channeled significant resources to the destitute sick in Haiti, Peru, Mexico, and Boston. We didn't argue that it was "cost-effective," nor did we promise that such efforts would be replicable. We argued that it was the right thing to do. It was the human rights thing to do.

Claims that we live in an era of limited resources fail to mention that these resources happen to be less limited now than ever before in human history. Arguing that it is too expensive to treat MDR-TB among prisoners in Russia, say, sounds nothing short of ludicrous when this world contains at least one individual worth more than $60 billion. Arguments against treating HIV disease in precisely those areas in which it exacts its greatest toll warn us that misguided notions of cost-efficacy have already trumped equity. Arguing that nominal legal rights are the best we can hope for will mean that members of the healing professions will have their hands tied. We will be forced to stand by as the rights and dignity of the poor and marginalized undergo further sustained and deadly assault.

## Acknowledgments

An essay shouldn't incur a great deal of debt, unless it's about a matter of life and death. Three groups of people have helped me write this paper: friends engaged in asking hard questions about health and human rights; friends who work each day to prevent human rights abuses; and those who have endured human rights abuses. In the first category, I thank Mercedes Becerra, Didi Bertrand, Ophelia Dahl, Jennifer Furin, Howard Hiatt, Jim Yong Kim, Carole Mitnick, June Osborn, Joyce Millen, Aaron Shakow, David Walton, Noam Chomsky, Alex Goldfarb, Betty Levin, Mary Northridge, Vivien Stem, Heman Reyes, Mia Nitchun, Haun Saussy, and Kedar Mate. For sending me to Russia, special thanks to Aryeh Neier. The second group is too long to list, but it includes Blanca Jimenez, Loune Viaud, Titid, and coworkers from Haiti, Peru, and Chiapas. Of course, one learns bitter lessons from the sacrifice of those who have paid the ultimate price. This essay is dedicated gratefully to Armando, Chouchou, and Jean-Marie.

## Works Cited

Alston P. "Conjuring Up New Human Rights: A Proposal for Quality Control." *American Journal of International Law.* 1984;78:607–21.

Amnesty International. *Torture in Russia.* London, England: Amnesty International; 1997.

Asad T, ed. *Anthropology and the Colonial Encounter.* London, England: Ithaca Press and Humanities; 1975.

Asad T. "On Torture, or Cruel, Inhuman, and Degrading Treatment." In: Kleinman A, Das V, Lock M, eds. *Social Suffering.* Berkeley: U of California P; 1997:285–308.

Bedjaoui M. "The Right to Development." In: Bedjaoui M, ed. *International Law: Achievements and Prospects.* Paris, France: United Nations Educational, Scientific, and Cultural Organization; 1991:1177–92.

Berreman GD. "Bringing It All Back Home. Malaise in Anthropology." In: Hymes D, ed. *Reinventing Anthropology.* New York, NY: Random House; 1974:83–98.

Bourdieu P, ed. *La Misère du Monde.* Paris, France: Seuil; 1993.

Campbell D. "Herskovits, Cultural Relativism and Metascience." In: Herskovits M, ed. *Cultural Relativism: Perspectives in Cultural Pluralism.* New York, NY: Random House; 1972:289–315.

Chomsky N. *Turning the Tide: U.S. Intervention in Central America and the Struggle for Peace.* Boston, MA: South End P; 1985.

Ciancaglini S, Granovsky M. *Nada Más que la Verdad: El Juicio a las Juntas.* Buenos Aires, Argentina: Planeta; 1995.

Comisión Nacional Sobre la Desaparición de Personas. *Nunca Más: The Report of the Argentine National Commission on the Disappeared.* New York, NY: Farrar Straus & Giroux; 1986.

Dlugy Y. "The Prisoners' Plague." *Newsweek.* July 5,1999:18–20.

Dussel I, Finocchio S, Gojman S. *Haciendo Memoria en el Pais de Nunca Mils.* Buenos Aires, Argentina: Eudeba; 1997.

Eisenberg L. "Rudolf Ludwig Karl Virchow, Where Are You Now that We Need You?" *American Journal of Medicine.* 1984;77:524–32.

Farmer PE. *AIDS and Accusation: Haiti and the Geography of Blame.* Berkeley: U of California P; 1992.

Farmer PE. "Cruel and Unusual: Drug-Resistant Tuberculosis as Punishment." In: Stern V, Jones R, eds. *Sentenced to Die? The Problem of TB in Prisons in East and Central Europe and Central Asia.* London: Prison Reform International; 1999.

Farmer PE. "Haiti's Lost Years: Lessons for the Americas." *Current Issues in Public Health.* 1996;2:143–51.

Farmer PE. *Infections and Inequalities: The Modern Plagues.* Berkeley: U of California P; 1999.

Farmer PE. "The Significance of Haiti." In: North American Congress on Latin America. *Haiti: Dangerous Crossroads.* Boston, MA: South End P; 1995:217–30.

Farmer PE. "On Suffering and Structural Violence: A View from Below." *Daedalus.* 1996;125(1):261–83.

Farmer PE. "TB Superbugs: The Coming Plague on All Our Houses." *Natural History.* April 1999:46–53.

Farmer PE. *The Uses of Haiti.* Monroe, ME: Common Courage P; 1994.

Farmer PE. "A Visit to Chiapas." *America.* 1998; 178(10):14–18.

Farmer PE, Bayona J, Becerra M, et al. "The Dilemma of MDR-TB in the Global Era." *International Journal of Tuberculosis and Lung Disease.* 1998;2(11):1–8.

Farmer PE, Bayona J, Shin S, et al. "Preliminary Results of Community-Based MDR-TB Treatment in Lima, Peru." *International Journal of Tuberculosis and Lung Disease.* 1998;2(11):S371.

Geertz C. "Anti-Anti-Relativism." *American Anthropologist.* 1984;86:263–78.

Gitlin T. *The Twilight of Common Dreams.* New York, NY: Metropolitan Books; 1995.

Glendon MA. "Rights Talk." *The Impoverishment of Political Discourse.* New York, NY: The Free P; 1991.

Guillermoprieto A. *The Heart that Bleeds: Latin America Now.* New York, NY: Alfred A. Knopf; 1994.

Hancock G. *The Lords of Poverty: The Power, Prestige, and Corruption of the International Aid Business.* New York, NY: Atlantic Monthly P; 1989.

Harrison L. "Voodoo Politics." *The Atlantic Monthly.* June 1993:101–08.

Hatch E. *Culture and Morality: The Relativity of Values in Anthropology.* New York, NY: Columbia UP; 1983.

Henkin L. *International Law: Politics. Values and Functions: General Course on Public International Law.* Boston, MA: M. Nijhoff Publishers; 1990. Collected Courses of the Hague Academy of International Law 1989; 216(4).

Henkin L. *Right v. Might: International Law and the Use of Force.* New York, NY: Council on Foreign Relations; 1991.

Hochschild A. *King Leopold's Ghost.* New York, NY: Houghton Mifflin; 1998.

Hughes R. *Culture of Complaint: The Fraying of America.* New York, NY: Oxford UP; 1993.

Hymes D. "The Use of Anthropology: Critical, Political, Personal." In: Hymes D, ed. *Reinventing Anthropology.* New York, NY: Random House; 1974:3–79.

Jacoby R. *Dogmatic Wisdom: How the Culture Wars Divert Education and Distract America.* New York, NY: Doubleday; 1994.

Kawachi I, Kennedy BP, Lochner K, et al. "Social Capital, Income Inequality, and Mortality." *American Journal of Public Health.* 1997;87:1491–98.

Keegan V. "Highway Robbery by the Super-Rich." *The Guardian.* July 22, 1996:16.

Krieger N. "Embodying Inequality: A Review of Concepts, Measures, and Methods for Studying Health Consequences of Discrimination." *Int J Health Serv.* 1999;29(2):295–352.

LaFeber W. *Inevitable Revolutions: The United States in Central America.* New York, NY: WW Norton; 1984.

Mann J. "AIDS and Human Rights: Where Do We Go from Here?" *Health and Human Rights.* 1998;3(1):143–49.

Mann J, Tarantola D. "Responding to HIV/AIDS: A Historical Perspective." *Health and Human Rights.* 1998;2(4):5–8.

Mason TA. *Harlan Fiske Stone: Pillar of the Law.* New York, NY: Viking P; 1956.

Millen JV, Holtz T. "Labor, Environmental, and Marketing Practices of Transnational Corporations and the Health of the Poor." In: Millen JV, Kim JY, Gershman J, Irwin A, eds. *Dying for Growth: Global Restructuring and the Health of the Poor.* Monroe, ME: Common Courage P; 1999.

Millen JV, Kim JY, Gershman J, Irwin A, eds. *Dying for Growth: Global Inequality and the Health of the Poor.* Monroe, ME: Common Courage P; 1999.

Neier A. *War Crimes: Brutality, Genocide, Terror, and the Struggle for Justice.* New York, NY: Times Books; 1998.

Neier A. "What Should Be Done about the Guilty?" *New York Review of Books.* February 1, 1990:32.

Physicians for Human Rights. *Health Care Held Hostage: Human Rights Violations and Violations of Medical Neutrality in Chiapas, Mexico.* Boston, MA: Physicians for Human Rights; 1999.

Renteln AD. "Relativism and the Search for Human Rights." *American Anthropologist.* 1988;90:56–72.

Reyes H, Coninx R. "Pitfalls of Tuberculosis Programmes in Prisons." *British Medical Journal.* 1997;315:1447–50.

Schachter O. *International Law in Theory and Practice.* Boston, MA: M. Nijhoff Publishers; 1991.

Schmidt PF. "Some Criticisms of Cultural Relativism." *Journal of Philosophy.* 1955;70:780–91.

Skogly S. "Structural Adjustment and Development: Human Rights – An Agenda for Change." *Human Rights Quarterly.* 1993;15:751–78.

Steadman KJ. "Struggling for a 'Never Again': A Comparison of the Human Rights Reports in Post-Authoritarian Argentina and Chile" [bachelor's thesis]. Cambridge, MA: Harvard University; 1997.

Steiner HJ, Alston P. *International Human Rights in Context: Law, Politics, Morals.* New York, NY: Oxford UP; 1996.

Stern V. *A Sin against the Future: Imprisonment in the World.* London, England: Penguin; 1998.

Subcomandante Marcos. *Shadows of Fury. Letters and Communiqués of Subcomandante Marcos and the Zapatista Army of National Liberation.* New York, NY: Monthly Review P; 1995.

Telzak EE, Sepkowitz K, Alpert P, et al. "Multi-Drug-Resistant Tuberculosis in Patients without HIV Infection." *New England Journal of Medicine.* 1995;333:907–11.

Varmus H, Satcher D. "Complexities of Conducting Research in Developing Countries." *New England Journal of Medicine.* 1997;337:1003–05.

Virchow RLK. *Die Einheitsrebungen in der Wissenschaftlichen Medicin.* Berlin, Germany: Druck und Verlag von G. Reimer; 1849.

Wallerstein I. "The Insurmountable Contradictions of Liberalism: Human Rights and the Rights of Peoples in the Geoculture of the Modern World-System." *South Atlantic Quarterly.* 1995;46:1161–78.

Wedel JR. *Collision and Collusion. The Strange Case of Western Aid to Eastern Europe 1989–1998.* New York, NY: St. Martin's P; 1998.

Whitehead M, Scott-Samuel A, Dahlgren G. "Setting Targets to Address Inequalities in Health." *Lancet.* 1998;351:1279–82.

Wilkinson RG. *Unhealthy Societies: The Afflictions of Inequality.* London, England: Routledge; 1997.

## Study Questions

1. What are the four reasons that Farmer provides to defend the idea that Russian "TB colonies" violate the human rights of inmates?

2. What does it mean to expand the concept of rights to include social and economic rights? What does this expansion make visible?

3. Farmer rebuts three main "immodest claims of causality" that mean to explain why Russian prisoners die from TB. Why does he call them "immodest"? If these claims are causally inadequate to explain why prisoners die from TB, what causal connections do they fail to identify? What conclusion does Farmer work toward by showing that these claims are explanatorily deficient?

4. Explain how Farmer problematizes the orthodox framework or "purely legal view" of human rights. How does social anthropology, the concept of "structural violence,"

focusing on exercises of state power and social inequalities, and prioritizing social and economic rights in the struggle for human rights, all help to remedy the defects of the orthodox framework of human rights?

5. Explain what Farmer means by the term "structural violence." What examples of structural violence does Farmer provide? If you were to provide a definition of the term, what would it be? If you were to identify conceptually necessary aspects of structural violence, what would they be?

## Notes

1 Universal Declaration of Human Rights, GA res 217A (III), UN Doc A/810 at 71 (1948).
2 Stern, 12.
3 For a more detailed depiction of these prisons, see Farmer, "TB Superbugs."
4 Telzak et al., 911.
5 Amnesty International.
6 Ivan Nikitovich Simonov, Chief Inspector of Prisons (now with the Chief Board of Punishment Execution), Ministry of Internal Affairs, Russian Federation; interview by author, Moscow, June 4, 1998.
7 Wedel, 5.
8 Farmer, "Cruel and Unusual."
9 Dr. Natalya Vezhina, Medical Director, TB Colony 33, Mariinsk, Kemerovo, Russian Federation; interview by author, Mariinsk, June 1, 1998.
10 Dlugy.
11 See, for example, "Money Isn't the Issue; It's (Still) Political Will." *TB Monitor.* May 1998: 53.
12 This topic is discussed in Reyes and Coninx.
13 Farmer, Bayona, Shin, et al.
14 For a rebuttal of these claims, see Farmer, Bayona, Becerra, et al.
15 Most anthropologists do not. Cultural relativism as a "metaethical theory" has its role and, contrary to popular belief, is not incompatible with universal values. Although I cannot review the topic here, my thinking on these matters has been informed most by my fieldwork in Haiti, but also by others in and outside anthropology. See, for example, Campbell; Geertz; Hatch; Renteln; and Schmidt.
16 See, for example, Asad's recent discussion of torture: "Although the phrase 'torture or cruel, inhuman, or degrading treatment' serves today as a cross-cultural criterion for making moral and legal judgements about pain and suffering, it nevertheless derives much of its operative sense historically and culturally" (285).
17 The concept of structural violence, and its relation to human rights, is explored in Farmer, "On Suffering and Structural Violence."
18 Steiner and Alston, vi.
19 A notable exception is to be found in the multinational mobilization against King Léopold's brutal seizure of the Congo. See Hochschild's gripping account of "the first great international human rights movement of the twentieth century" (2).
20 Neier, *War Crimes,* 75. Why are states signatory to human rights accords that they do not intend to respect? In 1989, Louis Henkin wrote: "One can only speculate as to why States accepted these norms and agreements, but it may be reasonable to doubt whether those developments authentically reflected sensitivity to human rights generally. States attended to what

occurred inside another State when such happenings impinged upon their political-economic interests" (quoted in Steiner and Alston, 114).

21  Quoted in Steiner and Alston, 141.

22  Keegan.

23  Millen and Holtz.

24  On the pathogenic effects of inequality, see Farmer, "Cruel and Unusual"; Wilkinson; and Kawachi et al. A similar point was underscored in the constitution of the World Health Organization: "Unequal development in different countries in the promotion of health and control of disease, especially communicable disease, is a common danger" (July 22, 1946).

25  A growing number of public health practitioners and physicians have been pushing for a concerted effort to reduce inequalities in health. For a recent review, see Whitehead et al.

26  I am, of course, glossing a very complicated process in simple terms. The defeat of the Aristide government's social-justice agenda, which explicitly endorsed the "right to development," seemed complete by the time the Haitian government signed on to a structural adjustment project endorsed by the World Bank and the US government; see Farmer, "Significance of Haiti," for a more in-depth discussion of this process. The concept of development as a new human right, most eloquently endorsed by Judge Mohammed Bedjaoui, president of the International Court of Justice, has been hotly contested by the United States, which Steiner and Alston (1113) qualify as "an implacable opponent of the right to development." For more in-depth discussion of the relationship between human rights and structural adjustment projects, see Skogly.

27  Nunca Más, the report of the Alfonsin-appointed Sábato commission (Comisión Nacional Sobre la Desaparición de Personas), remains the best text on the subject. Its English translation is introduced by Ronald Dworkin, who writes of a "system of licensed sadism." See also Dussel et al.; Steadman; and Ciancaglini and Granovsky.

28  Neier, War Crimes, 33.

29  This view is compellingly defended by Neier, who wonders "why the Argentine prosecution of crimes against human rights started so promisingly and why it ended so badly" ("What Should Be Done"; see also War Crimes).

30  For overviews, see Guillermoprieto; Chomsky; and LaFeber.

31  Bourdieu, 944.

32  For an overview of critiques of anthropology as a colonial project, see Asad. See also the essays by Hymes and by Berreman. These debates resonate with recent critiques of US-funded AIDS research in the developing world. For her comparison of placebo studies on HIV-infected mothers in Africa with the Tuskegee experiments on African Americans, New England Journal of Medicine editor Marcia Angell was taken to task by prominent figures in the scientific community (see, e.g., Varmus and Satcher), and 2 influential AIDS specialists resigned from the editorial board of the journal in protest (see Richard Saltus, "Journal Departures Reflect AIDS dispute," Boston Globe, October 16, 1997, A11). The debate continued with a front-page exploration of the ironies of US-funded AIDS research in the Ivory Coast (see Howard French, "AIDS Research in Africa: Juggling Risks and Hopes," New York Times, October 10, 1997, A1, A14). Angell justified her analogy by making a point-by-point comparison between the AIDS trials and the infamous syphilis study in "Tuskegee Revisited," Wall Street Journal, October 28, 1997, A22.

33  See Farmer, Uses of Haiti, and Hancock for overviews of the type and extent of international aid to these regimes.

34  See Wallerstein.

35  Farmer, AIDS and Accusation.

36  Steiner and Alston, 1110.

37  Harrison, 102. For a discussion, see Farmer, Uses of Haiti, 57.

38  Subcomandante Marcos, 54.

39  Physicians for Human Rights, 4.

40  Farmer, "On Suffering and Structural Violence."

41  This trend has already occasioned much commentary in the popular and scholarly literature. See, for example, Gitlin; Glendon; Hughes; and Jacoby. Gitlin (236) noted trenchantly that "the politics of identity is silent on the deepest sources of social misery: the devastation of the cities, the draining of resources away from the public and into the private hands of the few. It does not organize to reduce the sickening inequality between rich and poor."

42  See Steiner and Alston, 128–31, for an overview of the legal controversy over a hierarchy of rights. See also Alston's 1984 discussion of the proliferation of proposed rights, which have ranged from the "right to sleep" to the "right to tourism."

43  I refer here to the case of Michael Fay, an 18-year-old US citizen convicted of vandalizing cars and tearing down traffic signs in Singapore. According to the *New York Times* (April 5, 1994, A6), "Amnesty International sees the Fay case as one more reason to refocus international attention on the inhumaneness of flogging." But "many Americans," noted the article, "are surprisingly unsympathetic to the plight of the Ohio youth." The piece went on to note that letters to the editor of the *Dayton Daily News*, Fay's hometown newspaper, were "running against the youth," and the Singapore embassy in Washington, DC, attested that the majority of mail it received was in support of Singapore's position.

44  The passion of Chouchou Louis is recounted in chapter 7 of Farmer, *The Uses of Haiti.* Precisely the same pattern has been well documented in El Salvador and Guatemala. See chapter 5 of *Uses* for a comparison between these countries and Haiti. With the help of courageous colleagues in Haiti, it was possible for North Americans to work in solidarity on several levels. For example, an account of the murder of Chouchou Louis appeared under David Nyhan's name in the *Boston Globe* ("Murder in Haiti," March 19, 1992, A17); subsequent accounts appeared in a political magazine and in *The Uses of Haiti.* Pax Christi visited central Haiti in the spring of 1992 and interviewed torture victims and the families of the disappeared, including the widow of Chouchou Louis (see *Pax Christi Newsletter,* April 1992). The effects of the coup d'état of 1991 on the health of the local population are explored in Farmer, "Haiti's Lost Years" and "On Suffering and Structural Violence."

45  Farmer, "Visit to Chiapas."

46  Physicians for Human Rights, 4.

47  Virchow wrote: "For if medicine is really to accomplish its great task, it must intervene in political and social life. It must point out the hindrances that impede the normal social functioning of vital processes, and effect their removal" (48). See also Eisenberg.

48  Mann and Tarantola, 8.

49  Ivan Nikitovich Simonov, Chief Inspector of Prisons (now with the Chief Board of Punishment Execution), Ministry of Internal Affairs, Russian Federation; interview by author, Moscow, June 4, 1998.

50  Henkin, 1990, 208.

51  Oscar Schachter (6) has observed: "International law must also be seen as the product of historical experience in which power and the 'relation of forces' are determinants. Those States with power (i.e., the ability to control the outcomes contested by others) will have a disproportionate and often decisive influence in determining the content of rules and their application in practice. Because this is the case, international law, in a broad sense, both reflects and sustains the existing political order and distribution of power." Furthermore, legal commentary often reminds us of the power of normative, procedural thinking. During and after the Nuremberg trials, there was debate – again, cast in legal terms – as to whether the trials themselves were legal. Some key trial documents were published in 1947 in the *American Journal of International Law*: "It was urged on behalf of the defendants that a fundamental

principle of all law – international and domestic – is that there can be no punishment of crime without a pre-existing law…. It was submitted that ex post facto punishment is abhorrent to the law of all civilized nations." (See International Military Tribunal [Nuremberg]. Judgment and sentences. *American Journal of International Law.* 1947;41[174]:19). In other words, some legalists seemed to argue that, had there been no law against genocide or "aggressive war" on the books before the fact, it was illegitimate to prosecute the Nazis for these actions. Those arguing the illegality of the Nuremberg trials were not fringe elements. Citing such concerns, Chief Justice Harlan Fiske Stone referred to the "high-grade lynching party in Nuremberg" (quoted in Mason, 746).

52 I do not refer here to historical investigation, which is crucial to an understanding of the dynamics of structural violence. The study of human rights abuses in the slave trade, say, is quite different from an investigation of ongoing, documentable suffering.

53 Neier, *War Crimes*, xiii.

54 Steiner and Alston, viii.

55 For a review, see Millen et al.

56 For an overview of this group and its "vitality of practice," see the chapter by that name in Farmer, *Infections and Inequalities.*

57 Krieger, 295.

58 An example of this approach is to be found in Asad's recent discussion of torture and modem human rights discourse. He notes: "If cruelty is increasingly represented in the language of rights (and especially of human rights), this is because perpetual legal struggle has now become the dominant mode of moral engagement in an interconnected, uncertain, and rapidly changing world" (304–05).

59 Mann, 145–46.

60 Neier, *War Crimes*, 23–24.

61 Physicians for Human Rights, 12.

62 Gitlin, 224.

63 Steiner and Alston, 1140.

# 5.  James Rachels, "Active and Passive Euthanasia"

IN THIS CLASSIC ARTICLE from a 1975 issue of the *New England Journal of Medicine*, American philosopher James Rachels (1941–2003) argues that the intrinsic moral distinction between letting die and killing cannot be rationally supported and therefore ought not to be decisive in the making of end-of-life decisions as it typically is in the United States. He first argues that letting someone die and refusing to actively euthanize can be "so patently cruel as to require no further refutation." He then argues that when passive but not active euthanasia is considered permissible, this can allow others to make decisions on irrelevant grounds about letting someone die, which allows those making the decision to skirt the real issue at hand. Rachels goes on to show that killing and letting die are not morally distinguishable because the intentional or physical differences between the two actions do not change the moral quality of either action. He concludes by illustrating how lines of reasoning that have been used to support the moral distinguishability between killing and letting die break down once reflected upon.

---

THE DISTINCTION BETWEEN ACTIVE and passive euthanasia is thought to be crucial for medical ethics. The idea is that it is permissible, at least in some cases, to withhold treatment and allow a patient to die, but it is never permissible to take any direct action designed to kill the patient. This doctrine seems to be accepted by most doctors, and it is endorsed in a statement adopted by the House of Delegates of the American Medical Association on 4 December 1973:

> The intentional termination of the life of one human being by another – mercy killing – is contrary to that for which the medical profession stands and is contrary to the policy of the American Medical Association.
>
> The cessation of the employment of extraordinary means to prolong the life of the body when there is irrefutable evidence that biological death is imminent is the decision of the patient and/ or his immediate family. The advice and judgment of the physician should be freely available to the patient and/or his immediate family.

However, a strong case can be made against this doctrine. In what follows, I will set out some of the relevant arguments, and urge doctors to reconsider their views on this matter.

To begin with a familiar type of situation, a patient who is dying of incurable cancer of the throat is in terrible pain, which can no longer be satisfactorily alleviated. He is certain to die within a few days, even if present treatment is continued, but he does not want to go on living for those days since the pain is unbearable. So he asks the doctor for an end to it, and his family joins in the request.

Suppose the doctor agrees to withhold treatment, as the conventional doctrine says he may. The justification for his doing so is that the patient is in terrible agony, and since he is going to die anyway, it would be wrong to prolong his suffering needlessly. But now notice this – If one simply withholds treatment, it may take the patient longer to die, and so he may suffer more than he would if more direct action were taken and a lethal injection given. This fact provides strong reason for thinking that, once the initial decision not to prolong his agony has been made, active euthanasia is actually preferable to passive euthanasia, rather than the reverse. To say otherwise is to endorse the option that leads to more suffering rather than less, and is contrary to the humanitarian impulse that prompts the decision not to prolong his life in the first place.

Part of my point is that the process of being "allowed to die" can be relatively slow and painful, whereas being given a lethal injection is relatively quick and painless. Let me give a different sort of example. In the United States about one in 600 babies is born with Down's syndrome. Most of these babies are otherwise healthy – that is, with only the usual pediatric care, they will proceed to an otherwise normal infancy. Some, however, are born with congenital defects such as intestinal obstructions that require operations if they are to live. Sometimes, the parents and the doctor will decide not to operate, and let the infant die. Anthony Shaw describes what happens then:

> When surgery is denied [the doctor] must try to keep the infant from suffering while natural forces sap the baby's life away. As a surgeon whose natural inclination is to use the scalpel to fight off death, standing by and watching a salvageable baby die is the most emotionally exhausting experience I know. It is easy at a conference, in a theoretical discussion, to decide that such infants should be allowed to die. It is altogether different to stand by in the nursery and watch as dehydration and infection wither a tiny being over hours and days. This is a terrible ordeal for me and the hospital staff – much more so than for the parents who never set foot in the nursery.[1]

I can understand why some people are opposed to all euthanasia, and insist that such infants must be allowed to live. I think I can also understand why other people favor destroying these babies quickly and painlessly. But why should anyone favor letting "dehydration and infection wither a tiny being over hours and days"? The doctrine that says a baby may be allowed to dehydrate and wither, but may not be given an injection that would end its life without suffering, seems so patently cruel as to require no further refutation. The strong language is not intended to offend, but only to put the point in the clearest possible way.

My second argument is that the conventional doctrine leads to decisions concerning life and death made on irrelevant grounds.

Consider again the case of the infants with Down's syndrome who need operations for congenital defects unrelated to the syndrome to live. Sometimes, there is no operation, and the baby dies, but when there is no such defect, the baby lives on. Now an operation such as that to remove an intestinal obstruction is not prohibitively difficult. The reason why such operations are not performed in these cases is, clearly, that the child has Down's syndrome and the parents and the doctor judge that because of that fact it is better for the child to die.

But notice that this situation is absurd, no matter what view one takes of the lives and potentials of such babies. If the life of such an infant is worth preserving what does it matter if it needs a simple operation? Or, if one thinks it better that such a baby should not live on, what difference does it make that it happens to have an unobstructed intestinal tract? In either case, the matter of life and death is being decided on irrelevant grounds. It is the Down's syndrome, and not the intestines, that is the issue. The matter should be decided, if at all, on that basis, and not be allowed to depend on the essentially irrelevant question of whether the intestinal tract is blocked.

What makes this situation possible, of course, is the idea that when there is an intestinal blockage, one can "let the baby die," but when there is no such defect there is nothing that can be done, for one must not "kill" it. The fact that this idea leads to such results as deciding life or death on irrelevant grounds is another good reason why the doctrine would be rejected.

One reason why so many people think that there is an important moral difference between active and passive euthanasia is that they think killing someone is morally worse than letting someone die. But is it? Is killing, in itself, worse than letting die? To investigate this issue, two cases may be considered that are exactly alike except that one involves killing whereas the other involves letting someone die. Then, it can be asked whether this difference makes any difference to the moral assessments. It is important that the cases be exactly alike, except for this one difference, since otherwise one cannot be confident that it is this difference and not some other that accounts for any variation in the assessments of the two cases. So, let us consider this pair of cases.

In the first, Smith stands to gain a large inheritance if anything should happen to his six-year-old cousin. One evening while the child is taking his bath, Smith sneaks into the bathroom and drowns the child, and then arranges things so that it will look like an accident.

In the second, Jones also stands to gain if anything should happen to his six-year-old cousin. Like Smith, Jones sneaks in, planning to drown the child in his bath. However, just as he enters the bathroom Jones sees the child slip and hit his head, and fall face down in the water. Jones is delighted; he stands by, ready to push the child's head back under if it is necessary, but it is not necessary. With only a little thrashing about, the child drowns all by himself, "accidentally," as Jones watches and does nothing.

Now Smith killed the child, whereas Jones "merely" let the child die. That is the only difference between them. Did either man behave better, from a moral point of view? If the difference between killing and letting die were in itself a morally important matter, one should say that Jones's behavior was less reprehensible than Smith's. But does one really want to say that? I think not. In the first place, both men acted from the same motive, personal gain, and both had exactly the same end in view when they acted. It may be inferred from Smith's conduct that he is a bad man, although that judgment may be withdrawn or modified if certain further facts are learned about him – for example, that he is mentally deranged. But would not the very same thing be inferred about Jones from his conduct? And would not the same further considerations also be relevant to any modification of this judgment? Moreover, suppose Jones pleaded, in his own defense, "After all, I didn't do anything except just stand there and watch the child drown. I didn't kill him; I only let him die." Again, if letting die were in itself less bad than killing, this defense should have at least some weight. But it does not. Such a "defense" can only be regarded as a grotesque perversion of moral reasoning. Morally speaking, it is no defense at all.

Now, it may be pointed out, quite properly, that the cases of euthanasia with which doctors are concerned are not like this at all. They do not involve personal gain or the destruction of normal healthy children. Doctors are concerned only with cases in which the patient's life is of no further use to him, or in which the patient's life has become or will soon become a terrible burden. However, the point is the same in these cases: The bare difference between killing and letting die does not, in itself, make a moral difference. If a doctor lets a patient die, for humane reasons, he is in the same moral position as if he had given the patient a lethal injection for humane reasons. If his decision was wrong – if, for example, the patient's illness was in fact curable – the decision would be equally regrettable no matter which method was used to carry it out. And if the doctor's decision was the right one, the method used is not in itself important.

The AMA policy statement isolates the crucial issue very well; the crucial issue is "the intentional termination of the life of one human being by another." But after identifying this issue, and forbidding "mercy killing," the statement goes on to deny that the cessation of treatment is the intentional termination of a life. This is where the mistake comes in, for what is the cessation of treatment, in these circumstances, if it is not "the intentional termination of the life of one human being by another"? Of course it is exactly that, and if it were not, there would be no point to it.

Many people will find this judgment hard to accept. One reason, I think, is that it is very easy to conflate the question of whether killing is, in itself, worse than letting die, with the very different question of whether most actual cases of killing are more reprehensible than most actual cases of letting die. Most actual cases of killing are clearly terrible (think, for example, of all the murders reported in the newspapers), and one hears of such cases every day. On the other hand, one hardly ever hears of a case of letting die, except for the actions of doctors who are motivated by humanitarian reasons. So one learns to think of killing in a much worse light than of letting die. But this does not mean that there is something about killing that makes it in itself worse than letting die, for it is not the bare difference between killing and letting die that makes the difference in these cases. Rather, the other

factors – the murderer's motive of personal gain, for example, contrasted with the doctor's humanitarian motivation – account for different reactions to the different cases.

I have argued that killing is not in itself worse than letting die; if my contention is right, it follows that active euthanasia is not any worse than passive euthanasia. What arguments can be given on the other side? The most common, I believe, is the following:

> The important difference between active and passive euthanasia is that, in passive euthanasia, the doctor does not do anything to bring about the patient's death. The doctor does nothing, and the patient dies of whatever ills already afflict him. In active euthanasia, however, the doctor does something to bring about the patient's death: he kills him. The doctor who gives the patient with cancer a lethal injection has himself caused his patient's death; whereas if he merely ceases treatment, the cancer is the cause of death.

A number of points need to be made here. The first is that it is not exactly correct to say that in passive euthanasia the doctor does nothing, for he does do one thing that is very important: He lets the patient die. "Letting someone die" is certainly different, in some respects, from other types of action – mainly in that it is a kind of action that one may perform by way of not performing certain other actions. For example, one may let a patient die by way of not giving medication, just as one may insult someone by way of not shaking his hand. But for any purpose of moral assessment, it is a type of action nonetheless. The decision to let a patient die is subject to moral appraisal in the same way that a decision to kill him would be subject to moral appraisal: It may be assessed as wise or unwise, compassionate or sadistic, right or wrong. If a doctor deliberately let a patient die who was suffering from a routinely curable illness, the doctor would certainly be to blame for what he had done, just as he would be to blame if he had needlessly killed the patient. Charges against him would then be appropriate. If so, it would be no defense at all for him to insist that he didn't "do anything." He would have done something very serious indeed, for he let his patient die.

Fixing the cause of death may be very important from a legal point of view, for it may determine whether criminal charges are brought against the doctor. But I do not think that this notion can be used to show a moral difference between active and passive euthanasia. The reason why it is considered bad to be the cause of someone's death is that death is regarded as a great evil – and so it is. However, if it has been decided that euthanasia – even passive euthanasia – is desirable in a given case, it has also been decided that in this instance death is no greater an evil than the patient's continued existence. And if this is true, the usual reason for not wanting to be the cause of someone's death simply does not apply.

Finally, doctors may think that all of this is only of academic interest – the sort of thing that philosophers may worry about but that has no practical bearing on their own work. After all, doctors must be concerned about the legal consequences of what they do, and active euthanasia is clearly forbidden by the law. But even so, doctors should also be concerned with the fact that the law is forcing upon them a moral doctrine that may be indefensible, and has a considerable effect on their practices. Of course, most doctors are not now in the position of being coerced in this matter, for they do not regard themselves as merely going along with what the law requires. Rather, in statements such as the AMA policy statement that I have quoted, they are endorsing this doctrine as a central point of medical ethics. In that statement, active euthanasia is condemned not merely as illegal but as "contrary to that for which the medical profession stands," whereas passive euthanasia is approved. However, the preceding considerations suggest that there is really no difference between the two, considered in themselves (there may be important moral differences in some cases in their *consequences*, but as I pointed out, these differences may make active euthanasia, and not passive euthanasia, the morally preferable option). So, whereas doctors may have to discriminate between active and passive euthanasia to satisfy the law, they should not do any more than that. In particular, they should not give the distinction any added authority and weight by writing it into official statements of medical ethics.

**Study Questions**

1. Looking over Rachels's piece as a whole, what would you say, for him, is the main moral notion that causes the most confusion for those who think that letting die is less reprehensible than killing?

2. Rachels provides a counterargument to his thesis and provides several objections to this counterargument. Identity the responses he provides to this counterargument and say which one you think is the most convincing.

3. Rachels states that most of us come to believe that killing is worse than letting die because of the sensational way in which media covers murder headlines. Do you agree?

4. Explain, as best you can, the several ways in which Rachels demonstrates that the understanding that passive euthanasia is morally better than active euthanasia can lead to pernicious forms of ethical reasoning or decision making.

## Note

1 Anthony Shaw, "Doctor, Do We Have a Choice?" *The New York Times Magazine*, 30 January, 1972, p. 54.

# 6. Margaret P. Battin, "Euthanasia: The Way We Do It, the Way They Do It: End-of-Life Practices in the Developed World"

IN THIS 1991 ARTICLE from the *Journal of Pain and Symptom Management*, Margaret P. Battin (b. 1940) examines how the United States, the Netherlands, and Germany historically dealt with dying, pointing out their philosophical and palliative differences. What characterized the American practice of dealing with dying was "withholding or withdrawing various forms of treatment." The Dutch courts had developed guidelines allowing physicians to euthanize patients upon request, and Germany had moved to allow for assisted suicide. Battin raises objections to each model of dealing with dying and finds the American practice to be especially problematic. After considering a variety of alternatives to the American practice, and ruling each one out, Battin proposes that "physician-assisted suicide" would be the best practice for the American context. Currently, physician-assisted suicide is legal in several states in the United States and in the Netherlands, Germany, and other countries around the world.

## Introduction

BECAUSE WE TEND TO be rather myopic in our discussions of death and dying, especially about the issues of active euthanasia and assisted suicide, it is valuable to place the question of how we go about dying in an international context. We do not always see that our own cultural norms may be quite different from those of other nations, and that our background assumptions and actual practices differ dramatically. Thus, I would like to examine the perspectives on end-of-life dilemmas in three countries, Holland, (West) Germany,[1] and the USA.

Holland, Germany, and the United States are all advanced industrial democracies. They all have sophisticated medical establishments and life expectancies over 70 years of age; their populations are all characterized by an increasing proportion of older persons. They are all in what has been called the fourth stage of the epidemiologic transition[2] – that stage of societal development in which it is no longer the case that most people die of acute parasitic or infectious diseases. In this stage, most people do not die of diseases with rapid, unpredictable onsets and sharp fatality curves; rather, the majority of the population – as much as perhaps 70%–80% – dies of degenerative diseases, especially delayed degenerative diseases, that are characterized by late, slow onset and extended decline. Most people in highly industrialized countries die from cancer, atherosclerosis, heart disease (by no means always suddenly fatal), chronic obstructive pulmonary disease, liver, kidney or other organ disease, or degenerative neurological disorders. Thus, all three of these countries are alike in facing a common problem: how to deal with the characteristic new ways in which we die.

## Dealing with Dying in the United States

In the United States, we have come to recognize that the maximal extension of life-prolonging treatment in these late-life degenerative conditions is often inappropriate. Although we could keep the machines and tubes – the respirators, intravenous lines, feeding tubes – hooked up for extended periods, *we* recognize that this is inhumane, pointless and financially impossible. Instead, as a society we have developed a number of mechanisms for dealing with these hopeless situations, all of which involve withholding or withdrawing various forms of treatment.

Some mechanisms for withholding or withdrawing treatment are exercised by the patient who is confronted by such a situation or who anticipates it; these include refusal of treatment, the patient-executed DNR order, the Living Will, and the Durable Power of Attorney. Others are mechanisms for decision by second parties about a patient who is no longer competent or never was competent. The latter are reflected in a long series of court cases, including *Quinlan, Saikewicz, Spring, Eichner, Barber, Bartling, Conroy, Brophy,* the trio *Farrell, Peter* and *Jobes,* and *Crown.* These are cases that attempt to delineate the precise circumstances under which it is appropriate to withhold or withdraw various forms of therapy, including respiratory support, chemotherapy, antibiotics in intercurrent infections, and artificial nutrition and hydration. Thus, during the past 15 years or so, roughly since *Quinlan* (1976), we have developed an impressive body of case law and state statute that protects, permits, and facilitates our characteristic American strategy of dealing with end-of-life situations. These cases provide a framework for withholding or withdrawing treatment when we believe there is no medical or moral point in going on. This is sometimes termed *passive euthanasia*; more

often, is it simply called *allowing to die*, and is ubiquitous in the United States.

For example, a recent study by Miles and Gomez indicates that some 85% of deaths in the United States occur in health-care institutions, including hospitals, nursing homes, and other facilities, and of these, about 70% involve electively withholding some form of life-sustaining treatment.[3] A 1989 study cited in the *Journal of the American Medical Association* claims that 85%–90% of critical care professionals state that they are withholding and withdrawing life-sustaining treatments from patients who are "deemed to have irreversible disease and are terminally ill."[4] Still another study identified some 115 patients in two intensive-care units from whom care was withheld or withdrawn; 110 were already incompetent by the time the decision to limit care was made. The 89 who died while still in the intensive care unit accounted for 45% of all deaths there.[5] It is estimated that 1.3 million American deaths a year follow decisions to withhold life support;[6] this is a majority of the just over 2 million American deaths per year. Withholding and withdrawing treatment is the way we in the USA go about dealing with dying, and indeed "allowing to die" is the only legally protected alternative to maximal treatment recognized in the United States. We do not legally permit ourselves to actively cause death.

## Dealing with Dying in Holland

In the Netherlands, voluntary active euthanasia is also an available response to end-of-life situations. Although active euthanasia remains prohibited by statutory law, it is protected by a series of lower and supreme court decisions and is widely regarded as legal, or, more precisely, *gedoeken*, legally "tolerated." These court decisions have the effect of protecting the physician who performs euthanasia from prosecution, provided the physician meets a rigorous set of guidelines.

These guidelines, variously stated, contain five central provisions:

1. that the patient's request be voluntary;

2. that the patient be undergoing intolerable suffering;

3. that all alternatives acceptable to the patient for relieving the suffering have been tried;

4. that the patient has full information;

5. that the physician has consulted with a second physician whose judgment can be expected to be independent.

Of these criteria, it is the first which is central: euthanasia may be performed only at the voluntary request of the patient. This criterion is also understood to require that the patient's request be a stable, enduring, reflective one – not the product of a transitory impulse. Every attempt is to be made to rule out depression, psychopathology, pressures from family members, unrealistic fears, and other factors compromising voluntariness. Of physicians responding to a national survey in 1985 and 1986, 48% reported that they had received one or more requests for active euthanasia, and of these cases, 37% of the patients' requests had been honored.[7] In general, pain is not the basis for euthanasia, since pain can, in most cases, be effectively treated; "intolerable suffering," understood to mean suffering that is in the patient's (rather than the physician's) view intolerable, may also include fear of or unwillingness to endure *entluisterung*, or that gradual effacement and loss of personal identity that characterizes the end stages of many terminal illnesses. It is also required that euthanasia

be performed only by a physician; it may not be performed by a nurse, family member, or other party.

It is expected that the physician who performs euthanasia report it to the judicial authorities; in 1990, 454 cases were so reported and reviewed by the Ministry of Justice. None were prosecuted, and all were dismissed immediately. However, it is believed that the reported cases represent only a small fraction of the actual cases; the current estimate of frequency is somewhere between 3000 and 4000 cases a year: some 1000–2000 in hospitals, less than 100 in nursing homes, and perhaps 2000 in the patients' home.[8] Four thousand deaths by euthanasia per year would represent, in a country with a population of 14.9 million and an annual mortality of 125,000, just 3.2% of the total deaths per year. If euthanasia deaths were distributed equally (which they are not) among Holland's 30,000 physicians, then this would mean that only 1 in every 7 or 8 physicians would perform a case of euthanasia in a given year, or that a given physician would perform euthanasia once or at most twice in a decade of practice. Because most cases are not actually reported, no accurate figures are available, but euthanasia appears to be comparatively rare. Nevertheless, it is a conspicuous alternative to terminal illness well known to both physicians and the general public. Surveys of public opinion show growing public support for a liberal euthanasia policy (increasing from 40% in 1966 to 81% in 1988), and whereas there is a vocal minority opposed to the practice (including a group of about 1000 physicians), it is apparent that both the majority of the population in Holland and the majority of Holland's physicians support it.

In Holland, many hospitals now have protocols for the performance of euthanasia; these serve to ensure that the court-established guidelines have been met. However, it is believed that most euthanasia is practiced in the patient's home, typically by the *huisarts* or general practitioner who is the patient's long-term family physician. Euthanasia is usually performed after aggressive hospital treatment has failed to arrest the patient's terminal illness; the patient has come home to die, and the family physician is prepared to ease this passing. Whether practiced at home or in the hospital, it is believed that euthanasia usually takes place in the presence of the family members, perhaps the visiting nurse, and often, the patient's pastor or priest. Many doctors say that performing euthanasia is never easy, but that it is something they believe a doctor ought to do for his or her patient, when nothing else can help.

Thus, in Holland a patient facing the end of life has an option not openly practiced in the United States: to ask the physician to bring his or her life to an end. Although not everyone does so – indeed, at least 95% of people who die in a given year do not – it is a choice widely understood as available.

## Facing Death in Germany

In part because of its very painful history of Nazism, Germany appears to believe that doctors should have no role in causing death. Although societal generalizations are always risky, it is fair, I think, to say that there is vigorous and nearly universal opposition in Germany to the notion of active euthanasia. Euthanasia is viewed as always wrong, and the Germans view the Dutch as stepping out on a dangerously slippery slope.

However, it is an artifact of German law that, whereas killing on request (including voluntary euthanasia) is prohibited, assisting suicide – where the person committing suicide is determined to do so – is not a violation of the law. Taking advantage of this situation, there has developed a private organization, the *Deutsches Gesellschaft für Humanes Sterben* (DGHS), or German Society for Humane Dying, which provides support to its very extensive membership in choosing suicide as an alternative to terminal illness. The DGHS provides information about suicide; it assists in gaining access to the means for suicide; and, if requested, then it provides *Begleitung* or "accompaniment" for the person about to commit suicide, sending someone to be with the person who takes a fatal dose, especially if that person is alone or does not have a family supportive of such a choice. The DGHS runs regular ads in the popular magazines, and apparently is familiar to a sizeable proportion of the populace. I do not know how frequent are suicides assisted by the DGHS, as distinct from suicides in terminal illness generally, but it seems fair to say that the option of self-produced death is more clearly open in Germany than in Holland or in the United States.

## Objections to the Three Models of Dying

In response to the dilemmas raised by the new circumstances of death, in which the majority of the population in each of the advanced industrial nations dies of degenerative diseases after an extended period of terminal deterioration, different countries develop different practices. The United States legally permits only withholding and withdrawal of treatment, though of course active euthanasia and assisted suicide do occur. Holland also permits voluntary active euthanasia, and although Germany rejects euthanasia, it tolerates assisted suicide. But there are serious moral objections to be made to each of these practices, objections to be considered before resolving the issue of which practice our own culture ought to adopt.

## Objections to the German Practice

German law does not prohibit assisting suicide, but postwar German culture discourages physicians from taking any active role in death. This gives rise to distinctive moral problems. For one thing, it appears that there is little professional help or review provided for patients' choices about suicide; because the patient makes this choice essentially outside the medical establishment, medical professionals are not in a position to detect or treat impaired judgment on the part of the patient, especially judgment impaired by depression. Similarly, if the patient must commit suicide assisted only by persons outside the medical profession, there are risks that the patient's diagnosis and prognosis are inadequately confirmed, that the means chosen for suicide will be unreliable or inappropriately used, that the means used for suicide will fall into the hands of other persons, and that the patient will fail to recognize or be able to resist intrafamilial pressures and manipulation. The DGHS policy for providing assistance requires, I believe, that the patient be terminally ill and have been a member of the DGHS for at least 1 year in order to make use of its services (the latter requirement intended, I assume, to provide evidence of the stability of such a choice), but these minimal requirements are hardly sufficient to answer the charge that suicide decisions, which are made for medical reasons but must be made without medical help, may be rendered under less than ideally informed and voluntary conditions.

## Objections to the Dutch Practice

The Dutch practice of physician-performed active voluntary euthanasia also raises a number of ethical issues, many of which have been discussed vigorously both in the Dutch press and in commentary on the Dutch practices

from abroad. For one thing, it is sometimes said that the availability of physician-performed euthanasia creates a disincentive for providing good terminal care. I have seen no evidence that this is the case; on the contrary, Peter Admiraal, the anesthesiologist who is perhaps Holland's most vocal proponent of voluntary active euthanasia, insists that pain should rarely or never be the occasion for euthanasia, as pain (in contrast to suffering) is comparatively easily treated.[9] Instead, it is a refusal to endure the final stages of deterioration, both mental and physical, that motivates requests.

It is also sometimes said that active euthanasia violates the Hippocratic Oath. Indeed, it is true that the original Greek version of the Oath prohibits the physician from giving a deadly drug, even when asked for it; but the original version also prohibits performing surgery and taking fees for teaching medicine, neither of which prohibitions has survived into contemporary medical practice. Dutch physicians often say that they see performing euthanasia – where it is genuinely requested by the patient and nothing else can be done to relieve the patient's condition – as part of their duty to the patient, not as a violation of it.

The Dutch are also often said to be at risk of starting down the slippery slope, that is, that the practice of voluntary active euthanasia for patients who meet the criteria will erode into practicing less-than-voluntary euthanasia on patients whose problems are not irremediable, and perhaps by gradual degrees develop into terminating the lives of people who are elderly, chronically ill, handicapped, mentally retarded, or otherwise regarded as undesirable. This risk is often expressed in vivid claims of widespread fear and wholesale slaughter, claims that are repeated in the Right-to-Life press in both Holland and the USA; however, these claims are simply not true. However, it is true that the Dutch are now beginning to agonize over the problems of the incompetent patient, the mentally ill patient, the newborn with serious deficits, and other patients who cannot make voluntary choices, though these are largely understood as issues about withholding or withdrawing treatment, not about direct termination.[10]

What is not often understood is that this new and acutely painful area of reflection for the Dutch – withholding and withdrawing treatment from incompetent patients – has already led in the United States to the development of a vast, highly developed body of law: namely, that series of cases just cited, beginning with *Quinlan* and culminating in *Cruzan*. Americans have been discussing these issues for a long time, and have developed a broad set of practices that are regarded as routine in withholding and withdrawing treatment. The Dutch see Americans as much further out on the slippery slope than they are, because Americans have already become accustomed to second-party choices about other people. Issues involving second-party choices are painful to the Dutch in a way they are not to us precisely because *voluntariness* is so central in the Dutch understanding of choices about dying. Concomitantly, the Dutch see the Americans' squeamishness about first-party choices – voluntary euthanasia, assisted suicide – as evidence that we are not genuinely committed to recognizing *voluntary* choice after all. For this reason, many Dutch commentators believe that the Americans are at a much greater risk of sliding down the slippery slope into involuntary killing than they are. I fear, I must add, that they are right about this.

## Objections to the American Practice

There may be moral problems raised by the German and the Dutch practices, but there are also moral problems raised by the American practice of relying on withholding and

withdrawal of treatment in end-of-life situations. The German, Dutch, and American practices all occur within similar conditions – in industrialized nations with highly developed medical systems, where a majority of the population dies of illnesses exhibiting characteristically extended downhill courses – but the issues raised by our own response to this situation may be even more disturbing than those of the Dutch or the Germans. We often assume that our approach is "safer" because it involves only letting someone die, not killing him or her; but it too raises very troubling questions.

The first of these issues is a function of the fact that withdrawing and especially withholding treatment are typically less conspicuous, less pronounced, less evident kinds of actions than direct killing, even though they can equally well lead to death. Decisions about nontreatment have an invisibility that decisions about directly causing death do not have, even though they may have the same result, and hence there is a much wider range of occasions in which such decisions can be made. One can decline to treat a patient in many different ways, at many different times – by not providing oxygen, by not instituting dialysis, by not correcting electrolyte imbalances, and so on – all of which will cause the patient's death; open medical killing also brings about death, but is a much more overt, conspicuous procedure. Consequently, letting die also invites many fewer protections. In contrast to the earlier slippery slope argument which sees killing as riskier than letting die, the slippery slope argument warns that because our culture relies primarily on decisions about nontreatment, grave decisions about living or dying are not as open to scrutiny as they are under more direct life-terminating practices, and hence, are more open to abuse.

Second, and closely related, reliance on withholding and withdrawal of treatment invites rationing in an extremely strong way, in part because of the comparative invisibility of these decisions. When a healthcare provider does not offer a specific sort of care, it is not always possible to discern the motivation; the line between believing that it would not provide benefit to the patient and that it would not provide benefit worth the investment of resources in the patient can be very thin. This is a particular problem where health care financing is highly decentralized, as in the United States, and where rationing decisions without benefit of principle are not always available for easy review.

Third, relying on withholding and withdrawal of treatment can often be cruel. It requires that the patient who is dying from one of the diseases that exhibits a characteristic extended, downhill course (as the majority of patients in Holland, Germany, and the US do) must in effect wait to die until the absence of a certain treatment will cause death. For instance, the cancer patient who forgoes chemotherapy or surgery does not simply die from this choice: he or she continues to endure the downhill course of the cancer until the tumor finally destroys some crucial bodily function or organ. The patient with amyotrophic lateral sclerosis who decides in advance to decline respiratory support does not die at the time this choice is made, but continues to endure increasing paralysis until breathing is impaired and suffocation occurs. We often try to ameliorate these situations by administering pain medication or symptom control at the same time we are withholding treatment, but these are all ways of disguising the fact that we are letting the disease kill the patient rather than directly bringing about death. But the ways diseases kill people are far more cruel than the ways physicians kill patients when performing euthanasia or assisting in suicide.

## The Problem: A Choice of Cultures

Thus we see three similar cultures and countries and three similar sets of circumstances, but three quite different basic practices in approaching death. All three of these practices generate moral problems; none of them, nor any others we might devise, is free of moral difficulty. But the question that faces us is this: which of these practices is best?

It is not possible to answer this question in a less-than-ideal world without some attention to the specific characteristics and deficiencies of the society in question. In asking which of these practices is best, we must ask which is best *for us*. That we currently employ one set of these practices rather than others does not prove that it is best for us: the question is, would practices developed in other cultures or those not yet widespread in any be better for our own culture, than that which has developed here? Thus, it is necessary to consider the differences between our own society and these European cultures that have real bearing on which model of approach to dying we ought to adopt.

First, notice that different cultures exhibit different degrees of closeness between physicians and patients – different patterns of contact and involvement. The German physician is sometimes said to be more distant and more authoritarian than the American physician; on the other hand, the Dutch physician is sometimes said to be closer to his or her patients than either the American or the German is. In Holland, basic primary care is provided by the *huisarts*, the general practitioner or family physician, who typically lives in the neighborhood, makes house calls frequently, and maintains an office in his or her own home. The *huisarts* is usually the physician for the other members of the patient's family, and will remain the family's physician throughout his or her practice. Thus, the patient for whom euthanasia becomes an issue – say, the terminal cancer patient who has been hospitalized in the past but who has returned home to die – will be cared for by the trusted family physician on a regular basis. Indeed, for a patient in severe distress, the physician, supported by the visiting nurse, may make house calls as often as once a day, twice a day, or more (after all, it is right in the neighborhood), and is in continuous contact with the family. In contrast, the traditional American institution of the family doctor who makes house calls is rapidly becoming a thing of the past, and whereas some patients who die at home have access to hospice services and house calls from their long-term physician, many have no such long-term care and receive most of it from staff at a clinic or house staff rotating through the services of a hospital. The degree of continuing contact the patient can have with a familiar, trusted physician clearly influences the nature of his or her dying, and also plays a role in whether physician-performed active euthanasia, assisted suicide, and/or withholding and withdrawing treatment is appropriate.

Second, the United States has a much more volatile legal climate than either Holland or Germany; our medical system is increasingly litigious, much more so than that of any other country in the world. Fears of malpractice action or criminal prosecution color much of what physicians do in managing the dying of their patients. We also tend to evolve public policy through court decisions, and to assume that the existence of a policy puts an end to any moral issue. A delicate legal and moral balance over the issue of euthanasia, as is the case in Holland, would not be possible here.

Third, we in the United States have a very different financial climate in which to do our dying. Both Holland and Germany, as well as every other industrialized nation except South Africa, have systems of national health insurance or national health care. Thus the patient is not directly responsible for the costs of treatment, and consequently the patient's choices about terminal care and/or euthanasia need not take personal financial considerations into account. Even for the patient who does have health insurance in the United States, many kinds of services are not covered, whereas the national health care or health insurance programs of many other countries variously provide many sorts of relevant services, including at home physician care, home nursing care, home respite care, care in a nursing home or other long-term facility, dietician care, rehabilitation care, physical therapy, psychological counseling, and so on. The patient in the United States needs to attend to the financial aspects of dying in a way that patients in many other countries do not, and in this country both the patient's choices and the recommendations of the physician are very often shaped by financial considerations.

There are many other differences between the USA on the one hand and Holland and Germany, with their different models of dying, on the other. There are differences in degrees of paternalism in the medical establishment and in racism, sexism, and ageism in the general culture, as well as awareness of a problematic historical past, especially Nazism. All of these and the previous factors influence the appropriateness or inappropriateness of practices such as active euthanasia and assisted suicide. For instance, Holland's tradition of close physician/patient contact, its absence of malpractice-motivated medicine, and its provision of comprehensive health insurance, together with its comparative lack of racism and ageism and its experience in resistance to Nazism, suggest that this culture is able to permit the practice of voluntary active euthanasia, performed by physicians, without risking abuse. On the other hand, it is sometimes said that Germany still does not trust its physicians, remembering the example of

Nazi experimentation, and given a comparatively authoritarian medical climate in which the contact between physician and patient is quite distanced, the population could not be comfortable with the practice of active euthanasia. There, only a wholly patient-controlled response to terminal situations, as in non-physician-assisted suicide, is a reasonable and prudent practice.

But what about the United States? This is a country where 1) sustained contact with a personal physician is decreasing, 2) the risk of malpractice action is increasing, 3) much medical care is not insured, 4) many medical decisions are financial as well, 5) racism is on the rise, and 6) the public is naive about direct contact with Nazism or similar totalitarian movements. Thus, the United States is in many respects an untrustworthy candidate for practicing active euthanasia. Given the pressures on individuals in an often atomized society, encouraging solo suicide, assisted if at all only by nonprofessionals, might well be open to considerable abuse too.

However, there is one additional difference between the United States and both Holland and Germany that may seem relevant here. At first, it appears to be a trivial, superficial difference – the apparent fact that we Americans are the biggest consumers of "pop psychology" in the world. While of course things are changing and our cultural tastes are widely exported, the fact remains that the ordinary American's cultural diet contains more in the way of do-it-yourself amateur psychology and self-analysis than anyone else's. This long tradition of pop psychology and self-analysis may put us in a better position for certain kinds of end-of-life practices than many other cultures – despite whatever other deficiencies we have, just because we live in a culture that encourages us to inspect our own motives, anticipate the impact of our actions on others, and scrutinize our own relationships with others, including our physicians. What, then, is appropriate for our own cultural situation? Physician-performed euthanasia, though not in itself morally wrong, is morally jeopardized where the legal, time allotment, and especially financial pressures on both patients and physicians are severe; thus, it is morally problematic in our culture in a way that it is not in Holland. Solo suicide outside the institution of medicine (as in Germany) is problematic in a culture (like the United States) that is increasingly alienated, offers deteriorating and uneven social services, is increasingly racist, and in other ways imposes unusual pressures on individuals. Reliance only on withholding and withdrawing treatment (as in the United States) can be, as we've seen, cruel, and its comparative invisibility invites erosion under cost containment and other pressures. These are the three principal alternatives we've considered; but none of them seems wholly suited to our actual situation for dealing with the new fact that most of us die of extended-decline, deteriorative diseases. However, permitting physicians to supply patients with the means for ending their own lives still grants physicians some control over the circumstances in which this can happen – only, for example, when the prognosis is genuinely grim and the alternatives for symptom control are poor – but leaves the fundamental decision about whether to use these means to the patient alone. It is up to the patient then, and his or her advisors, including family, clergy, physician, other health-care providers, and a raft of pop-psychology books, to be clear about whether he or she really wants to use these means or not. Thus, the physician is involved, but not directly; and it is the patient's choice, but the patient is not alone in making it. We live in a quite imperfect world, but, of the alternatives for facing death – which we all eventually must – I think that the practice of permitting physician-assisted suicide is the one most nearly suited to the current state of our own somewhat flawed society. This is a model not yet central in any of the three countries examined here – Holland, Germany, or the United States – but it is the one I think suits us best.

## Study Questions

1. Review each model of dying that Battin provides. See which, if any, ethical theory or theories each model relies on.

2. Review each objection that Battin provides to the American model of dying. Compare her objections to Rachels's objections to the practice of "letting die."

3. Explain how Battin arrives at the judgment that none of the models she describes is best for dealing with end-of-life matters in the United States context. Do you agree with her reasoning?

4. Do some research on current state laws in the United States that allow for physician-assisted suicide. What reasons are given to defend these laws? To what extent do these reasons resemble the reasons Battin provides in defense of physician-assisted suicide?

## Notes

1 As the medical care system in the German Democratic Republic (East Germany) was structurally different and was faced with many unique problems, especially in terms of shortages in high-tech equipment, I will only be referring to what was known as the Federal Republic of (West) Germany up until 1990.

2 Olshansky SJ, Ault AB. The fourth stage of the epidemiological transition: the age of delayed degenerative diseases. *Milbank Memorial Fund Quarterly/Health and Society* 1986;64:355–91.

3 Miles S, Gomez C. *Protocols for Elective Use of Life-Sustaining Treatment.* New York: Springer-Verlag, 1988.

4 Sprung CL. "Changing Attitudes and Practices in Foregoing Life-Sustaining Treatments." *JAMA* 1990;263:2213.

5 Smedira NG et al. "Withholding and Withdrawal of Life Support from the Critically Ill." *N Engl J Med* 1990;322:309–15.

6 *New York Times,* July 23, 1990, p. A13.

7 de Wachter MAM. "Active Euthanasia in the Netherlands." *JAMA* 1989;262:3316–19.

8 Borst-Eilers E. "Controversies in the Care of Dying Patients." University of Florida conference held in Orlando, Florida, February 14–16, 1991.

9 Admiraal P. "Euthanasia in a General Hospital." Address to the Eighth World Congress of the International Federation of Right-to-Die Societies, Maastricht, Holland, June 8, 1990.

10 ten Have H. "Coma: Controversy and Consensus." *Newsletter of the European Society for Philosophy of Medicine and Health Care.* May 1990;8: 19–20.

# Section VIII:
# War and Terrorism

I am tired and sick of war. Its glory is all moonshine. It is only those who have neither fired a shot nor heard the shrieks and groans of the wounded who cry aloud for blood, for vengeance, for desolation. War is hell.

– William Tecumesh Sherman

Terrorism is a psychological warfare. Terrorists try to manipulate us and change our behavior by creating fear, uncertainty, and division in society.

– Patrick J. Kennedy

PEACE, OR THE ABSENCE of war, is a highly desired yet elusive human value. What, then, justifies human beings engaging in widespread conflict resulting in killing each other? Theologians, philosophers, ethicists, and politicians, among others, have long debated war and its various justifications. Is self-defense, whereby one extrapolates from defending oneself to a particular group, nation, or group of nations defending themselves, a viable justification? Are there conditions that make war "just," such that the nearly universal prohibition against murder is overcome and replaced with justified killing? Given finite resources, what can justify war when those resources could go to assist the poor, feed the hungry, house the homeless, educate children, and meet other human needs?

The costs of war – environmental, human life and limb, animal habitat, psychological, emotional, family, educational, economic – are outrageously high. Before turning to what might justify such costs, it is enlightening to

look at recent costs in the United States' wars in Afghanistan and Iraq. Consider economic costs: "The decade-long American wars in Afghanistan and Iraq would end up costing as much as $6 trillion, the equivalent of $75,000 for every American household," and "this accounted for roughly 20 per cent of the total amount added to the US national debt between 2001 and 2012…. the US 'has already paid $260 billion in interest on the war debt,' and future interest payments would amount to trillions of dollars."[1] Just for perspective, consider the following estimate of how much it would cost to make public colleges and universities tuition-free in the United States: $62.6 billion.[2] For further perspective, consider that in February of 2014, Congress approved a bill to cut food-stamp programs, $8 billion over ten years, and this at a time when demand for these programs has risen.[3]

Next, consider human costs: US deaths (not from suicide) since 2001, 6,853; total deaths in Iraq, Afghanistan, and Pakistan,

298,000–354,000.[4] Among suicides in the United States in 2015, nearly one-quarter were veterans, and 22 veterans commit suicide every day,[5] a figure that translates into over 8,000 a year. Compare this to the combat total above. PTSD (post-traumatic stress disorder) is often cited as a major contributing factor, if not the most important. This is a horrific human cost of war, and a cost that is likely underreported, as full suicide statistics (especially of those who commit suicide while on duty) are difficult to acquire. There are other human costs from families torn apart by combat death and suicide, to psychological struggles, to loss of limbs.

Given the enormous economic and human costs, why engage in war? Pacifists and those committed to nonviolence would answer that there is no justification. Pacifists are not passive; rather, they are committed to finding nonviolent ways to end conflict. Mohandas K. Gandhi (1869–1948) is perhaps the most famous advocate of nonviolence. Gandhi was successful, without weapons or violence, in leading India out from the shadow of British colonialism. Gandhi argues, in an article in this section, that the means are as morally important as the ends, such that both the means and the ends must be just. Pacifists accept significant costs for their nonviolent means, from arrests to incarceration to assassination. Gandhi was assassinated, as was another well-known pacifist, Martin Luther King Jr. (1929–68), who led many in demonstrations and nonviolent actions that brought about significant changes in recognizing the civil rights of African Americans.

In light of the great desire for peace, and given the effectiveness of pacifist movements, what then can justify war? The most common justification is what is known as "just war theory." From the Latin *jus bellum iustum*, this theory is a standard doctrine used by philosophers, theologians, and ethicists (particularly those interested in military ethics) that outlines the necessary conditions for ensuring morally just acts of war. The doctrine is further subdivided into two categories: *jus ad bellum* denotes the conditions under which it is just *to go to* war, and *jus in bello* denotes the criteria for just conduct *within* a war. Just war theory is offered by those who reject both moral nihilism (the claim that all war is neither moral nor immoral, but more typically understood as simply necessary or not for the purposes of national interest) and pacifism. Pacifism is most often rejected by offering cases such as World War II, for which the claim is made that someone must oppose the violence of others as a means of either self-defense or defense of those who cannot protect themselves.

Although St. Thomas Aquinas's writings — a selection of his work opens this section — are some of the most popular incarnations of just war doctrine, they are not the first. For example, as far back as the ninth century, Arabic philosophers were concerned with putting ethical constraints on acts of war. Moreover, Augustine was one of the first Christian scholars to break from Christian pacifism. As you read through Aquinas's text and consider the conditions he delineates in order to render a particular act of war justifiable, ask yourself whether our more recent conflicts in Iraq and Afghanistan meet these conditions. For example, in regard to the second war in Iraq, the official stance of the Catholic Church is that it does not meet the criteria for being labeled a just war. Regardless of the 2003 capture of Saddam Hussein, a Vatican official claimed that "the war was useless, and served no purpose."[6] Regardless of whether we agree with this stance, it does allow us the opportunity to question what greater good, if any, justifies the loss of life and economic costs that come with war.

In addition to the costs of war itself, there

are also costs in the aftermath of war. In his article in this section, Brian Orend examines justice after war in light of just war theory. The aftermath includes first, how the aggression is to end. Orend makes clear that if this is not done carefully, and justly, then there will certainly be future bloodshed. Further important post-war considerations include determining the criteria for trials for war crimes, and rehabilitation of the war-torn locale. Anthony Burke, for his part, questions whether there can be a just war, especially the assumptions that strategic violence and brute force can be justified for bringing about the desired ends. Burke especially argues against the way in which just war theory does not hold agents responsible for avoidable harm in the pursuit of war. Burke finds just war theory outdated and unable to address the multicultural and international discourse that exists today.

Larry Minear's essay explores the ethical difficulties of being a conscientious objector when one is already an active military serviceperson. Minear highlights the concerning ways in which these soldiers are treated while in the military, and he encourages us to listen to the voices of individuals who actually have to do our fighting in order to begin a national conversation on the wars and conflicts in which our governments engage.

Terrorism is an act that is meant, as the name suggests, to strike terror in those being affected by the act. While one could be terrorized by many acts, however, not all terrorizing acts are considered acts of terrorism.

Terrorism is usually associated with political, religious, or national groups that are engaged in forcing change in their favor and/or eliminating their enemies. While the term has been used extensively since the late twentieth century, what counts as terrorism and what makes a terrorist are both extremely subjective. For example, many have criticized the fact that white men who bomb or massacre get characterized as rogues rather than as terrorists, while people of color, especially of Middle East descent, are immediately tagged as terrorists. In his essay below, Samuel Scheffler asks whether terrorism is morally distinctive, and argues that it is, as its goal is to disrupt social order and remove the stability that people find in it. Terrorism accomplishes this by using terror to strike fear in citizens, whether it is carried out by the state or cells or individuals. Others would consider all, or nearly all, war to be terrorism, while yet others, such as Claudia Card, whose essay is also included in this section, call for the notion of terrorism to be expanded to include such acts as environmental racism, rape, and domestic violence. Certainly the acts that Card highlights strike fear in citizens and also disrupt their existing social order.

Terrorism, like war, is a fact of life for countless people and seems to be an intractable part of the human condition. Whether elusive peace will ever be attained may well be a matter of how committed future generations are to the security and dignity of life, as well as to the ideal of peace.

## Notes

1 http://www.globalresearch.ca/us-wars-in-afghanistan-iraq-to-cost-6-trillion/5350789. Emphasis in original.
2 Jordan Weissman, "Here's Exactly How Much the Government Would Have to Spend to Make Public College Tuition Free," *Atlantic* 3 January 2014, http://www.theatlantic.com/business/archive/2014/01/heres-exactly-how-much-the-government-would-have-to-spend-to-make-public-college-tuition-free/282803/.

3   Mark Trumbull, "Does Slicing $8 Billion from Food Stamps Cut to
    Bone or Just Trim Some Flab?," *Christian Science Monitor* 4 February 2014,
    http://www.csmonitor.com/USA/Politics/DC-Decoder/2014/0204/
    Does-slicing-8-billion-from-food-stamps-cut-to-bone-or-just-trim-some-flab-video.

4   http://watson.brown.edu/costsofwar/figures/2015/
    direct-war-death-toll-iraq-afghanistan-and-pakistan-2001.

5   Department of Veterans Affairs, *Suicide Data Report, 2012,* http://www.va.gov/opa/docs/
    Suicide-Data-Report-2012-final.pdf.

6   "Saddam's capture may bring peace, doesn't excuse war, cardinal says," 2003, http://www.
    americancatholic.org/News/JustWar/Iraq/.

# 1. St. Thomas Aquinas, "Whether It Is Always Sinful to Wage War?"

IN THE THIRTEENTH CENTURY, St. Thomas Aquinas (1225–74), drawing inspiration from the writings of St. Augustine of Hippo (354–430), outlined, in his *Summa Theologica*, three necessary conditions that all instances of war must meet in order to be considered morally defensible. According to Aquinas, war is considered morally just if, first, it is declared by a legitimate authority – individuals, or groups of individuals who do not constitute a governmental power, cannot wage war on others. Second, the reasons for going to war must be just: those who are attacked must "deserve it on account of some fault," and the actions taken against them must be in proper proportion to their offense. Third, those who wage war should ensure that their intentions are just, and the final goal must be the attainment or advancement of peace (waging war to satisfy a thirst for power, for example, would fail to meet this criterion). Part of this third aspect is that war should be waged only as a last resort, only when all other peaceful prospects are exhausted. Reading Aquinas's *Summa Theologica* may be tricky for those who are not familiar with his methodology. He begins all his sections by outlining some prospective difficulties with a certain thesis, and reveals his own arguments while responding to these objections. In this section, therefore, Aquinas's interlocutor is someone who is opposed to any act of war at all, declaring that all acts of war are sinful. Aquinas refutes this stance by outlining his three proposed criteria.

---

WE MUST NOW CONSIDER war, under which head there are four points of inquiry:

1. Whether some kind of war is lawful?
2. Whether it is lawful for clerics to fight?
3. Whether it is lawful for belligerents to lay ambushes?
4. Whether it is lawful to fight on holy days?

## Whether It Is Always Sinful to Wage War?

**Objection 1**: It would seem that it is always sinful to wage war. Because punishment is not inflicted except for sin. Now those who wage war are threatened by Our Lord with punishment, according to [Matthew] 26:52: "All that take the sword shall perish with the sword." Therefore all wars are unlawful.

**Objection 2**: Further, whatever is contrary to a Divine precept is a sin. But war is contrary to a Divine precept, for it is written ([Matthew] 5:39): "But I say to you not to resist evil"; and ([Romans] 12:19): "Not revenging yourselves, my dearly beloved, but give place unto wrath." Therefore war is always sinful.

**Objection 3**: Further, nothing, except sin, is contrary to an act of virtue. But war is contrary to peace. Therefore war is always a sin.

**Objection 4**: Further, the exercise of a lawful thing is itself lawful, as is evident in scientific exercises. But warlike exercises which take place in tournaments are forbidden by the Church, since those who are slain in these trials are deprived of ecclesiastical burial. Therefore it seems that war is a sin in itself.

**On the contrary**, Augustine [of Hippo] says in a sermon on the son of the centurion [Ep. ad Marcel. cxxxviii[1]]: "If the Christian Religion forbade war altogether, those who sought salutary advice on the Gospel would rather have been counselled to cast aside their arms, and to give up soldiering altogether. On the contrary, they were told: 'Do violence to no man … and be content with your pay' [Luke] 3:14]. If he commanded them to be content with their pay, he did not forbid soldiering."

**I answer that**, In order for a war to be just, three things are necessary. First, the authority of the sovereign by whose command the war is to be waged. For it is not the business of a private individual to declare war, because he can seek for redress of his rights from the tribunal of his superior. Moreover it is not the business of a private individual to summon together the people, which has to be done in wartime. And as the care of the common weal is committed to those who are in authority, it is their business to watch over the common weal of the city, kingdom or province subject to them. And just as it is lawful for them to have recourse to the sword in defending that common weal against internal disturbances, when they punish evil-doers, according to the words of the Apostle ([Romans] 13:4): "He beareth not the sword in vain, for he is God's minister, an avenger to execute wrath upon him that doth evil"; so too, it is their business to have recourse to the sword of war in defending the common weal against external enemies. Hence it is said to those who are in authority (Ps[alm] 81:4): "Rescue the poor: and deliver the needy out of the hand of the sinner"; and for this reason Augustine says (Contra Faust.[2] xxii, 75): "The natural order conducive to peace among mortals demands that the power to declare and counsel war should be in the hands of those who hold the supreme authority."

**Secondly**, a just cause is required, namely that those who are attacked, should be attacked because they deserve it on account of some fault. Wherefore Augustine says (Questions. in Hept.,[3] qu. x, super Jos.): "A just war is wont to be described as one that avenges wrongs, when a nation or state has to be punished, for refusing to make amends for the wrongs inflicted by its subjects, or to restore what it has seized unjustly."

**Thirdly**, it is necessary that the belligerents should have a rightful intention, so that they intend the advancement of good, or the avoidance of evil. Hence Augustine says (De Verb. Dom. [The words quoted are to be found not in St. Augustine's works, but Can. Apud. Caus. xxiii, qu. 1][4]): "True religion looks upon as peaceful those wars that are waged not for motives of aggrandizement, or cruelty, but with the object of securing peace, of punishing evil-doers, and of uplifting the good." For it may happen that the war is declared by the legitimate authority, and for a just cause, and yet be rendered unlawful through a wicked intention. Hence Augustine says (Contra Faust. xxii, 74): "The passion for inflicting harm, the cruel thirst for vengeance, an unpacific and relentless spirit, the fever of revolt, the lust of power, and such like things, all these are rightly condemned in war."

**Reply to Objection 1**: As Augustine says (Contra Faust. xxii, 70): "To take the sword is to arm oneself in order to take the life of anyone, without the command or permission of superior or lawful authority." On the other hand, to have recourse to the sword (as a private person) by the authority of the sovereign or judge, or (as a public person) through zeal for justice, and by the authority, so to speak, of God, is not to "take the sword," but to use it as commissioned by another, wherefore it does not deserve punishment. And yet even those who make sinful use of the sword are not always slain with the sword, yet they always perish with their own sword, because, unless they repent, they are punished eternally for their sinful use of the sword.

**Reply to Objection 2**: Such like precepts, as Augustine observes (De Serm. Dom. in Monte[5] i, 19), should always be borne in readiness of mind, so that we be ready to obey them, and, if necessary, to refrain from resistance or self-defense. Nevertheless it is necessary sometimes for a man to act otherwise for the common good, or for the good of those with whom he is fighting. Hence Augustine says (Ep. ad Marcellin. cxxxviii): "Those whom we have to punish with a kindly severity, it is necessary to handle in many ways against their will. For when we are stripping a man of the lawlessness of sin, it is good for him to be vanquished, since nothing is more hopeless than the happiness of sinners, whence arises a guilty impunity, and an evil will, like an internal enemy."

**Reply to Objection 3**: Those who wage war justly aim at peace, and so they are not opposed to peace, except to the evil peace, which Our Lord "came not to send upon earth" ([Matthew] 10:34). Hence Augustine says (Ep. ad Bonif. clxxxix[6]): "We do not seek peace in order to be at war, but we go to war that we may have peace. Be peaceful, therefore, in warring, so that you may vanquish those whom you war against, and bring them to the prosperity of peace."

**Reply to Objection 4**: Manly exercises in warlike feats of arms are not all forbidden, but those which are inordinate and perilous, and end in slaying or plundering. In olden times warlike exercises presented no such danger, and hence they were called "exercises of arms" or "bloodless wars," as [St.] Jerome [c. 347–420] states in an epistle.

## Study Questions

1. Consider, individually, each of Aquinas's criteria and whether you agree that any act of war needs to meet that condition in order to be morally defensible. Which ones do you agree with? Which ones do you disagree with? Are there any additional conditions for ensuring a just war that you believe Aquinas may have overlooked? Offer a defense of any additional criteria. How do you think Gandhi (VIII.2 below) would react to Aquinas, given Gandhi's defense of pacifism?

2. Given what you know about the wars or conflicts in which the United States has been involved, do you believe some, all, or none have met the standards of just war theory? How did you determine this? If you believe that some of these conflicts did not meet these standards, what is your moral assessment of that particular war or conflict (perhaps you believe it was still morally permissible given the additional criteria you proposed in question one, but perhaps you do not)?

3. What are some possible difficulties with determining whether a particular war or conflict meets Aquinas's standards? For example, how do we determine whether "those who are attacked … deserve it," how do we determine whether the cause of war is considered sufficiently "just," and how can we know that "the belligerents"

have the "rightful intention" when declaring war? Given these difficulties, do you think it is possible to really determine whether a particular act of war meets Aquinas's conditions?

4. Later in this section (VIII.5), Larry Minear's "Conscience and Carnage in Afghanistan and Iraq" discusses the issue of how conscientious objectors to war are treated in the military. One point he highlights is that philosophical or moral objection to a *particular* war is not typically deemed sufficient to release one from duty as a conscientious objector; one must be against *all* war as a general principle. How would Aquinas react to this, given that he does think some wars can be morally just, but not others? Do you think a soldier should be given conscientious objector status, and thus released of his/her duties, if (s)he believes that a particular act of war fails to meet the just war criteria? Why or why not?

## Notes

1  *Letter 138 to Marcellinus.*
2  *Reply to Faustus the Manichean.*
3  *Questions on the Heptateuch.*
4  The parenthetical comment states that the quoted words are not from Augustine's *De verbo domini* (*On the Word of God*), but rather from Gratian, *Decretum*, Part II, case XXIII, question 1, canon 6.
5  *Our Lord's Sermon on the Mount.*
6  *Letter 189 to Boniface.*

# 2.  Mohandas K. Gandhi, *Hind Swaraj or Indian Home Rule*

IN HIS 1909 BOOK *Hind Swaraj or Indian Home Rule*, Mohandas K. Gandhi (1869–1948) lays out two main ways in which goals can be achieved: the way of passive resistance and the way of brute force. He argues that passive resistance is the better of the two approaches to action/ conflict resolution and is, in the last analysis, absolutely better. Gandhi also seeks to demonstrate how thinking that force is sometimes necessary and morally acceptable to achieve ends is a product of shortsightedness and unscrupulous reasoning that artificially separates means from ends and gives undeserved superiority to ends over means. He thus indirectly calls into question the assumptions of just war theory. Gandhi further claims that passive resistance is proper to Indian civilization in that it reserved for members of society the right to passively resist laws that they found to be against their conscience. Gandhi contrasts Indian civilization with modern, Western civilization primarily in terms of how each culture thinks ends should be achieved. Modern civilization has obtained power, resources and privilege by following the path of force. It sees, in principle, no problem with using force to attain ends, whereas Indian civilization cultivates in its members the understanding that the use of force to attain ends is contrary to the ends of social life.

---

## VI. Civilization

### XIII. What Is True Civilization?

... CIVILIZATION IS THAT MODE of conduct which points out to man the path of duty. Performance of duty and observance of morality are convertible terms. To observe morality is to attain mastery over our mind and our passions. So doing, we know ourselves....

If this definition be correct, then India, as so many writers have shown, has nothing to learn from anybody else, and this is as it should be. We notice that the mind is a restless bird; the more it gets the more it wants, and still remains unsatisfied. The more we indulge our passions the more unbridled they become. Our ancestors, therefore, set a limit to our indulgences. They saw that happiness was largely a mental condition. A man is not necessarily happy because he is rich, or unhappy because he is poor. The rich are often seen to be unhappy, the poor to be happy.

Millions will always remain poor. Observing all this, our ancestors dissuaded us from luxuries and pleasures. We have managed with the same kind of plough as existed thousands of years ago. We have retained the same kind of cottages that we had in former times and our indigenous education remains the same as before. We have had no system of life-corroding competition. Each followed his own occupation or trade and charged a regulation wage. It was not that we did not know how to invent machinery, but our forefathers knew that, if we set our hearts after such things, we would become slaves and lose our moral fibre. They, therefore, after due deliberation decided that we should only do what we could with our hands and feet. They saw that our real happiness and health consisted in a proper use of our hands and feet. They further reasoned that large cities were a snare and a useless encumbrance and that people would not be happy in them, that there would be gangs of thieves and robbers, prostitution and vice flourishing in them and that poor men would be robbed by rich men. They were, therefore, satisfied with small villages. They saw that kings and their swords were inferior to the sword of ethics, and they, therefore, and the sovereigns of the earth to be inferior to the Rishis and the Fakirs.[1] A nation with a constitution like this is fitter to teach others than to learn from. This nation had courts, lawyers and doctors, but they were all within bounds. Everybody knew that these professions were not particularly superior; moreover, these vakils and vaids[2] did not rob people; they were considered people's dependants, not their masters. Justice was tolerably fair. The ordinary rule was to avoid courts. There were no touts to lure people into them. This evil, too, was noticeable only in and around capitals. The common people lived independently and followed their agricultural occupation. They enjoyed true Home Rule.

And where this cursed modern civilization has not reached, India remains as it was before. The inhabitants of that part of India will very properly laugh at your newfangled notions. The English do not rule over them, nor will you ever rule over them. Those in whose name we speak we do not know, nor do they know us. I would certainly advise you and those like you who love the motherland to go into the interior that has yet been not polluted by the railways and to live there for six months; you might then be patriotic and speak of Home Rule.

Now you see what I consider to be real civilization. Those who want to change conditions such as I have described are enemies of the country and are sinners....

## XVI. Brute Force

... READER:[3] Will you not admit that you are arguing against yourself? You know that what the English obtained in their own country they obtained by using brute force.[4] I know you have argued that what they have obtained is useless, but that does not affect my argument. They wanted useless things and they got them. My point is that their desire was fulfilled. What does it matter what means they adopted? Why should we not obtain our goal, which is good, by any means whatsoever, even by using violence? Shall I think of the means when I have to deal with a thief in the house? My duty is to drive him out anyhow. You seem to admit that we have received nothing, and that we shall receive nothing by petitioning. Why, then, may we do not so by using brute force? And, to retain what we may receive we shall keep up the fear by using the same force to the extent that it may be necessary. You will not find fault with a continuance of force to prevent a child from thrusting its foot into fire. Somehow or other we have to gain our end.

EDITOR: Your reasoning is plausible. It has deluded many. I have used similar arguments before now. But I think I know better now, and I shall endeavour to undeceive you. Let us first take the argument that we are justified in gaining our end by using brute force because the English gained theirs by using similar means. It is perfectly true that they used brute force and that it is possible for us to do likewise, but by using similar means we can get only the same thing that they got. You will admit that we do not want that. Your belief that there is no connection between the means and the end is a great mistake. Through that mistake even men who have been considered religious have committed grievous crimes. Your reasoning is the same as saying that we can get a rose through planting a noxious weed. If I want to cross the ocean, I can do so only by means of a vessel; if I were to use a cart for that purpose, both the cart and I would soon find the bottom. "As is the God, so is the votary," is a maxim worth considering. Its meaning has been distorted and men have gone astray. The means may be likened to a seed, the end to a tree; and there is just the same inviolable connection between the means and the end as there is between the seed and the tree. I am not likely to obtain the result flowing from the worship of God by laying myself prostrate before Satan. If, therefore, anyone were to say: "I want to worship God; it does not matter that I do so by means of Satan," it would be set down as ignorant folly. We reap exactly as we sow. The English in 1833 obtained greater voting power by violence. Did they by using brute force better appreciate their duty? They wanted the right of voting, which they obtained by using physical force. But real rights are a result of performance of duty; these rights they have not obtained. We, therefore, have before us in English the force of everybody wanting and insisting on his rights, nobody thinking of his duty. And, where everybody wants rights, who shall give them to whom? I do not wish to imply that they do no duties. They don't perform the duties corresponding to those rights; and as they do not perform that particular duty, namely, acquire fitness, their rights have proved a burden to them. In other words, what they have obtained is an exact result of the means they adapted. They used the means corresponding to the end. If I want to deprive you of your watch, I shall certainly have to fight for it; if I want to buy your watch, I shall have to pay you for it; and if I want a gift, I shall have to plead for it; and, according to the means I employ, the watch is stolen property, my own property, or a donation. Thus we see three different results from three different means. Will you still say that

means do not matter?

Now we shall take the example given by you of the thief to be driven out. I do not agree with you that the thief may be driven out by any means. If it is my father who has come to steal I shall use one kind of means. If it is an acquaintance I shall use another; and in the case of a perfect stranger I shall use a third. If it is a white man, you will perhaps say you will use means different from those you will adopt with an Indian thief. If it is a weakling, the means will be different from those to be adopted for dealing with an equal in physical strength; and if the thief is armed from top to toe, I shall simply remain quiet. Thus we have a variety of means between the father and the armed man. Again, I fancy that I should pretend to be sleeping whether the thief was my father or that strong armed man. The reason for this is that my father would also be armed and I should succumb to the strength possessed by either and allow my things to be stolen. The strength of my father would make me weep with pity; the strength of the armed man would rouse in me anger and we should become enemies. Such is the curious situation. From these examples we may not be able to agree as to the means to be adopted in each case. I myself seem clearly to see what should be done in all these cases, but the remedy may frighten you. I therefore hesitate to place it before you. For the time being I will leave you to guess it, and if you cannot, it is clear you will have to adopt different means in each case. You will also have seen that any means will not avail to drive away the thief. You will have to adopt means to fit each case. Hence it follows that your duty is not to drive away the thief by any means you like.

Let us proceed a little further. That well-armed man has stolen your property; you have harboured the thought of his act; you are filled with anger; you argue that you want to punish that rogue, not for your own sake, but for the good of your neighbours; you have collected a number of armed men, you want to take his house by assault; he is duly informed of it, he runs away; he too is incensed. He collects his brother robbers, and sends you a defiant message that he will commit robbery in broad daylight. You are strong, you do not fear him, you are prepared to receive him. Meanwhile the robber pesters your neighbours. They complain before you. You reply that you are doing all for their sake, you do not mind that your own goods have been stolen. Your neighbours reply that the robber never pestered them before, and that he commenced his depredations only after you declared hostilities against him. You are between Scylla and Charybdis.[5] You are full of pity for the poor men. What they say is true. What are you to do? You will be disgraced if you now leave the robber alone. You therefore, tell the poor men: "Never mind. Come, my wealth is yours, I will give you arms, I will teach you how to use them; you should belabour the rogue; don't you leave him alone." And so the battle grows; the robbers increase in numbers; your neighbours have deliberately put themselves to inconvenience. Thus the result of wanting to take revenge upon the robber is that you have disturbed your own peace; you are in perpetual fear of being robbed and assaulted; your courage has given place to cowardice. If you will patiently examine the argument, you will see that I have not overdrawn the picture. This is one of the means. Now let us examine the other. You set this armed robber down as an ignorant brother; you intend to reason with him at a suitable opportunity: you argue that he is, after all, a fellow-man; you do not know what prompted him to steal. You, therefore, decide that, when you can, you will destroy the man's motive for stealing. Whilst you are thus reasoning with yourself, the man comes again to steal. Instead of being angry with him you take pity on him. You

think that this stealing habit must be a disease with him. Henceforth, you, therefore, keep your doors and windows open, you change your sleeping-place, and you keep your things in a manner most accessible to him. The robber comes again and is confused as all this is new to him; nevertheless, he takes away your things. But his mind is agitated. He inquires about you in the village, he comes to learn about your broad and loving heart, he repents, he begs your pardon, returns you your things, and leaves off the stealing habit. He becomes your servant, and you find for him honourable employment. This is the second method. Thus, you see, different means have brought about totally different results. I do not wish to deduce from this that robbers will act in the above manner or that all will have the same pity and love like you, but I only wish to show that fair means alone can produce fair results, and that, at least in the majority of cases, if not indeed in all, the force of love and pity is infinitely greater than the force of arms. There is harm in the exercise of brute force, never in that of pity.

Now we will take the question of petitioning. It is a fact beyond dispute that a petition, without the backing of force is useless. However, the late Justice [Mahadev Govind] Ranade [1842–1901] used to say that petitions served a useful purpose because they were a means of educating people. They give the latter an idea of their condition and warn the rulers. From this point of view, they are not altogether useless. A petition of an equal is a sign of courtesy; a petition from a slave is a symbol of his slavery. A petition backed by force is a petition from an equal and, when he transmits his demand in the form of a petition, it testifies to his nobility. Two kinds of force can back petitions. "We shall hurt you if you do not give this," is one kind of force; it is the force of arms, whose evil results we have already examined. The second kind of force can thus be stated; "If you do not concede our demand, we shall be no longer your petitioners. You can govern us only so long as we remain the governed; we shall no longer have any dealings with you." The force implied in this may be described as love-force, soul-force, or, more popularly but less accurately, passive resistance. This force is indestructible. He who uses it perfectly understands his position. We have an ancient proverb which literally means; "One negative cures thirty-six diseases." The force of arms is powerless when matched against the force of love or the soul.

Now we shall take your last illustration, that of the child thrusting its foot into fire. It will not avail you. What do you really do to the child? Supposing that it can exert so much physical force that it renders you powerless and rushes into fire, then you cannot prevent it. There are only two remedies open to you – either you must kill it in order to prevent it from perishing in the flames, or you must give your own life because you do not wish to see it perish before your very eyes. You will not kill it. If your heart is not quite full of pity, it is possible that you will not surrender yourself by preceding the child and going into the fire yourself. You, therefore, helplessly allow it to go into the flames. Thus, at any rate, you are not using physical force. I hope you will not consider that it is still physical force, though of a low order, when you would forcibly prevent the child from rushing towards the fire if you could. That force is of a different order and we have to understand what it is.

Remember that, in thus preventing the child, you are minding entirely its own interest, you are exercising authority for its sole benefit. Your example does not apply to the English. In using brute force against the English you consult entirely your own, that is the national, interest. There is no question here either of pity or of love. If you say that

the actions of the English, being evil, represent fire, and that they proceed to their actions through ignorance, and that therefore they occupy the position of a child and that you want to protect such a child, then you will have to overtake every evil action of that kind by whomsoever committed and, as in the case of the evil child, you will have to sacrifice yourself. If you are capable of such immeasurable pity, I wish you well in its exercise.

XVII. Passive Resistance

READER: Is there any historical evidence as to the success of what you have called soul-force or truth-force? No instance seems to have happened of any nation having risen through soul-force. I still think that the evildoers will not cease doing evil without physical punishment.

EDITOR: The [Hindu] poet Tulsidas [1532–1623] has said: "Of religion, pity, or love, is the root, as egotism of the body. Therefore, we should not abandon pity so long as we are alive." This appears to me to be a scientific truth. I believe in it as much as I believe in two and two being four. The force of love is the same as the force of the soul or truth. We have evidence of its working at every step. The universe would disappear without the existence of that force. But you ask for historical evidence. It is, therefore, necessary to know what history means. The Gujarati equivalent means: "It so happened." If that is the meaning of history, it is possible to give copious evidence. But, if it means the doings of the kings and emperors, there can be no evidence of soul-force or passive resistance in such history. You cannot expect silver ore in a tin mine. History, as we know it, is a record of the wars of the world, and so there is a proverb among Englishmen that a nation which has no history, that is, no wars, is a happy nation. How kings played, how they became enemies of one another, how they murdered one another, is found accurately recorded in history, and if this were all that had happened in the world, it would have been ended long ago. If the story of the universe had commenced with wars, not a man would have been found alive today. Those people who have been warred against have disappeared as, for instance, the natives of Australia of whom hardly a man was left alive by the intruders. Mark, please, that these natives did not use soul-force in self-defence, and it does not require much foresight to know that the Australians will share the same fate as their victims. "Those that take the sword shall perish by the sword." With us the proverb is that professional swimmers will find a watery grave.

The fact that there are so many men still alive in the world shows that it is based not on the force of arms but on the force of truth or love. Therefore, the greatest and most unimpeachable evidence of the success of this force is to be found in the fact that, in spite of the wars of the world, it still lives on.

Thousands, indeed tens of thousands, depend for their existence on a very active working of this force. Little quarrels of millions of families in their daily lives disappear before the exercise of this force. Hundreds of nations live in peace. History does not and cannot take note of this fact. History is really a record of every interruption of the even working of the force of love or of the soul. Two brothers quarrel; one of them repents and reawakens the love that was lying dormant in him; the two again begin to live in peace; nobody takes note of this.

But if the two brothers, through the intervention of solicitors or some other reason take up arms or go to law – which is another form of the exhibition of brute force – their doings would be immediately noticed in the press, they would be the talk of their neighbours and would probably go down to history. And

what is true of families and communities is true of nations. There is no reason to believe that there is one law for families and another for nations. History, then, is a record of an interruption of the course of nature. Soul-force, being natural, is not noted in history.

READER: According to what you say, it is plain that instances of this kind of passive resistance are not to be found in history. It is necessary to understand this passive resistance more fully. It will be better, therefore, if you enlarge upon it.

EDITOR: Passive resistance is a method of securing rights by personal suffering; it is the reverse of resistance by arms. When I refuse to do a thing that is repugnant to my conscience, I use soul-force. For instance, the Government of the day has passed a law which is applicable to me. I do not like it. If by using violence I force the Government to repeal the law, I am employing what may be termed body-force. If I do not obey the law and accept the penalty for its breach, I use soul-force. It involves sacrifice of self.

Everybody admits that sacrifice of self is infinitely superior to sacrifice of others. Moreover, if this kind of force is used in a cause that is unjust, only the person using it suffers. He does not make others suffer for his mistakes. Men have before now done many things which were subsequently found to have been wrong. No man can claim that he is absolutely in the right or that a particular thing is wrong because he thinks so, but it is wrong for him so long as that is his deliberate judgment. It is therefore meet that he should not do that which he knows to be wrong, and suffer the consequence whatever it may be. This is the key to the use of soul-force.

READER: You would then disregard laws – this is rank disloyalty. We have always been considered a law-abiding nation. You seem to be going even beyond the extremists. They say that we must obey the laws that have been passed, but that if the laws be bad, we must drive out the lawgivers even by force.

EDITOR: Whether I go beyond them or whether I do not is a matter of no consequence to either of us. We simply want to find out what is right and to act accordingly. The real meaning of the statement that we are a law-abiding nation is that we are passive resisters. When we do not like certain laws, we do not break the heads of lawgivers but we suffer and do not submit to the laws. That we should obey laws whether good or bad is a newfangled notion. There was no such thing in former days. The people disregarded those laws they did not like and suffered the penalties for their breach. It is contrary to our manhood if we obey laws repugnant to our conscience. Such teaching is opposed to a religion and means slavery. If the Government were to ask us to go about without any clothing, should we do so? If I were a passive resister, I would say to them that I would have nothing to do with their law. But we have so forgotten ourselves and become so compliant that we do not mind degrading law....

To use brute force, to use gunpowder, is contrary to passive resistance, for it means that we want our opponent to do by force that which we desire but he does not. And if such a use of force is justifiable, surely he is entitled to do likewise by us. And so we should never come to an agreement. We may simply fancy, like the blind horse moving in a circle round a mill, that we are making progress. Those who believe that they are not bound to obey laws which are repugnant to their conscience have only the remedy of passive resistance open to them. Any other must lead to disaster.

READER: From what you say I deduce that passive resistance is a splendid weapon of the weak, but that when they are strong they may take up arms.

EDITOR: This is gross ignorance. Passive resistance, that is, soul-force, is matchless. It is superior to the force of arms. How, then, can it be considered only a weapon of the weak? Physical-force men are strangers to the courage that is requisite in a passive resister. Do you believe that a coward can ever disobey a law that he dislikes? Extremists are considered to be advocates of brute force. Why do they, then, talk about obeying laws? I do not blame them. They can say nothing else. When they succeed in driving out the English and they themselves become governors, they will want you and me to obey their laws. And that is a fitting thing for their constitution. But a passive resister will say he will not obey a law that is against his conscience, even though he may be blown to pieces at the mouth of a cannon....

This however, I will admit: that even a man weak in body is capable of offering this resistance. One man can offer it just as well as millions. Both men and women can indulge in it. It does not require the training of an army; it needs no jiujitsu. Control over the mind is alone necessary, and when that is attained, man is free like the king of the forest and his very glance withers the enemy.

Passive resistance is an all-sided sword, it can be used anyhow; it blesses him who uses it and him against whom it is used. Without drawing a drop of blood it produces far-reaching results. It never rusts and cannot be stolen. Competition between passive resisters does not exhaust. The sword of passive resistance does not require a scabbard. It is strange indeed that you should consider such a weapon to be a weapon merely of the weak.

READER: You have said that passive resistance is a speciality of India. Have cannons never been used in India?

EDITOR: Evidently, in your opinion, India means its few princes. To me it means its teeming millions on whom depends the existence of its princes and our own.

Kings will always use their kingly weapons.

To use force is bred in them. They want to command, but those who have to obey commands do not want guns; and these are in a majority throughout the world. They have to learn either body-force or soul-force. Where they learn the former, both the rulers and the ruled become like so many mad-men: but where they learn soul-force, the commands of the rulers do not go beyond the point of their swords, for true men disregard unjust commands. Peasants have never been subdued by the sword, and never will be. They do not know the use of the sword, and they are not frightened by the use of it by others. That nation is great which rests its head upon death as its pillow. Those who defy death are free from all fear. For those who are labouring under the delusive charms of brute-force, this picture is not overdrawn. The fact is that, in India, the nation at large has generally used passive resistance in all departments of life. We cease to cooperate with our rulers when they displease us. This is passive resistance.

I remember an instance when, in a small principality, the villagers were offended by some command issued by the prince. The former immediately began vacating the village. The prince became nervous, apologized to his subjects and withdrew his command. Many such instances can be found in India. Real Home Rule is possible only where passive resistance is the guiding force of the people.

Any other rule is foreign rule.

READER: Then you will say that it is not at all necessary for us to train the body?

EDITOR: I will certainly not say any such thing. It is difficult to become a passive resister unless the body is trained. As a rule, the mind, residing in a body that has become weakened by pampering, is also weak, and where there is no strength of mind there can be no strength of soul. We shall have to improve our physique by getting rid of infant marriages and luxurious living. If I were to ask a man with a shattered body to face a cannon's mouth I should make a laughingstock of myself.

READER: From what you say, then, it would appear that it is not a small thing to become a passive resister, and, if that is so, I should like you to explain how a man may become one.

EDITOR: To become a passive resister is easy enough but it is also equally difficult. I have known a lad of fourteen years become a passive resister; I have known also sick people do likewise: and I have also known physically strong and otherwise happy people unable to take up passive resistance. After a great deal of experience it seems to me that those who want to become passive resisters for the service of the country have to observe perfect chastity, adopt poverty, follow truth, and cultivate fearlessness....

## Study Questions

1. Gandhi writes, "History is really a record of every interruption of the even working of the force or love or of the soul." Elaborate on the meaning of this sentence as Gandhi understands it. Consider how violence or the use of force might interrupt the soul and how the force of love might constitute, rather than interrupt, the soul. Also, what do you think Gandhi would say about how force or violence affects a society, based on your prior considerations?

2. Explain what Gandhi means when he says, "The real meaning of the statement that we are a law-abiding nation is that we are passive resisters." How can passively resisting law exemplify law-abidingness?

3. Identify all the ways in which Gandhi thinks nonaggression is absolutely superior to the use of force.

4. In describing how one arrives at the idea that the use of force is sometimes necessary and morally permissible, Gandhi writes, "Shall I think of the means when I have to deal with a thief in the house? My duty is to drive him out anyhow. You seem to admit that we have received nothing, and that we shall receive nothing by petitioning. Why, then, may we do not so by using brute force? And, to retain what we may receive we shall keep up the fear of using the same force to the extent that it may be necessary. You will not find fault with a continuance of force to prevent a child from thrusting its foot into fire. Somehow or other we have to gain our end." Whose voice do you think this is and what is the protest? Identify the objections Gandhi provides to the above line of reasoning. Do you think the criticisms he offers in response to it could apply to just war theory? Do you think the above line of reasoning mirrors just war thinking?

## Notes

1 Hindu ancient sages were Rishis, and Fakirs were Rishis who went naked, with tangled hair. See http://www.sikhiwiki.org/index.php/Kanga.

2 A *vakil* or *vaid* is a lawyer or counselor. See http://www.oxforddictionaries.com/us/definition/american_english/vakil.

3 Gandhi set this up as a dialogue between the reader, who is the Indian countryman, and the editor, who is himself.

4 Gandhi argues that brute force is the modus operandi of the British and is foreign to India.

5 From Greek mythology (specifically in Homer's *Odyssey*), referring to having to choose between two evils.

# 3. Brian Orend, "Justice after War"

IN THIS 2002 ARTICLE from *Ethics and International Affairs*, Brian Orend (b. 1971) explores a gap in just war theory, namely justice after war (*jus post bellum*). Drawing from Michael Walzer (b. 1935), he first outlines the "right reasons" (*jus ad bellum*) and the "right methods" (*jus in bello*) for war. Orend proposes conditions for the end of a just war, including how to end aggression, criteria for war-crime trials, and rehabilitation.

SADLY, THERE ARE FEW restraints on the endings of wars.[1] There has never been an international treaty to regulate war's final phase, and there are sharp disagreements regarding the nature of a just peace treaty. There are, by contrast, restraints aplenty on starting wars, and on conduct during war. These restraints include: political pressure from allies and enemies; the logistics of raising and deploying force; the United Nations, its Charter and Security Council; and international laws like the Hague and Geneva Conventions. Indeed, in just war theory – which frames moral principles to regulate wartime actions – there is a robust set of rules for resorting to war (*jus ad bellum*) and for conduct during war (*jus in bello*) but not for the termination phase of war.[2] Recent events in Afghanistan, and the "war against terrorism," vividly underline the relevance of reflecting on this omission, and the complex issues related to it.

The international community should remedy this glaring gap in our ongoing struggle to restrain warfare. The following facts bear this out:

- Recent armed conflicts – in the Persian Gulf, Bosnia, Rwanda, and Kosovo – demonstrate the difficulty, and illustrate the importance, of ending wars in a full and fair fashion. We know that when wars are wrapped up badly, they sow the seeds for future bloodshed.[3]

- To allow unconstrained war termination is to allow the winner to enjoy the spoils of war. This is dangerously permissive, as winners have been known to exact peace terms that are draconian and vengeful. The Treaty of Versailles, terminating World War I, is often mentioned in this connection.[4]

- Failure to regulate war termination may prolong fighting on the ground. Since they have few assurances regarding the nature of the settlement, belligerents will be sorely tempted to keep using force to jockey for position. Many observers felt that this reality plagued the Bosnian civil war, which saw many failed negotiations and a three-year "slow burn" of continuous violence as the very negotiations took place.[5]

- Allowing war termination to be determined without normative restraints leads to inconsistency and confusion. First, how can we try to regulate the first two phases of war – the beginning and middle – yet not the end? Second, the lack of established norms to guide the construction of peace treaties leads to patchwork "solutions," mere ad hoc arrangements that may not meet well-considered standards of prudence and justice.

Peace treaties should still, of course, remain tightly tailored to the historical realities of the particular conflict in question. But admitting this is not to concede that the search for general guidelines, or universal standards, is futile or naive. There is no inconsistency, or mystery, in holding particular actors in complex local conflicts up to more general, even universal standards of conduct. Judges and juries do that daily, evaluating the factual complexities of a given case in light of general principles. We should do the same regarding war termination.

This article will consider what participants should do as they move to wrap up a war. It will do so while drawing on the resources contained within the just war tradition, particularly its reworking offered by Michael Walzer.[6] Since just war theory has played a constructive role thus far in its influence on political and legal discourse concerning launching and carrying out war, there is reason to believe it has light to shed on war termination. My goal is to construct a general set of plausible principles to guide communities seeking to resolve their armed conflicts fairly.

### The Ends of a Just War

The first step is to answer the question: What may a participant rightly aim for with regard to a just war? What are the goals to be achieved by the settlement of the conflict? We need some starting assumptions to focus our thoughts on these issues. First, this article will consider classical cases of interstate armed conflict to provide a quicker, cleaner route to the general set of postwar principles sought after. I hope to show that the resulting set can then be applied more broadly, not only to civil wars but also to unconventional armed conflicts involving complex mixtures of state and nonstate actors. For instance, I believe the

forthcoming principles are as meaningful for the current "war against terrorism" as they were for World War II. Next, the set of postwar principles is being offered as guidance to those participants who want to end their wars in a fair, justified way. Not all participants do, of course, and to the extent they fail to do so, they act unjustly during the termination phase. A related assumption is that there is no such thing as "victor's justice." The raw fact of military victory in war does not of itself confer moral rights upon the victor, nor duties upon the vanquished. In my judgment, it is only when the victorious regime has fought a just and lawful war, as defined by international law and just war theory, that we can speak meaningfully of rights and duties, of both victor and vanquished, at the conclusion of armed conflict.[7]

Such a just and lawful war is defined by just war theorists as one that was begun for the right reasons, and that has been fought appropriately. The resort to war was just (*jus ad bellum*), and only the right methods were used during the war (*jus in bello*). A war begun for the right reasons is a war fought in response to aggression, defined by Walzer as "any use of force or imminent threat of force by one state against the political sovereignty or territorial integrity of another."[8] Such state rights are themselves founded, ultimately, upon individual human rights to life and liberty. The most obvious example of an act of international aggression would be an armed invasion by one state bent on taking over another, much as Iraq did to Kuwait in August 1990. But this requirement of just cause, in terms of resisting aggression, is not the only rule just war theorists insist on prior to beginning war. They also stipulate that the war in question be launched as a last resort, be publicly declared by a proper authority, have some probability of success, be animated by the right intention of resisting aggression, and also be expected to produce at least a proportionality of benefits to costs. These general norms have worked their way into various pieces of international law.[9]

A war begun justly must also be fought appropriately. For just war theorists, this means that a state's armed forces obey at least three rules of right conduct: they must discriminate between combatant (military) and noncombatant (civilian) targets and direct their armed force only at the former; they may attack legitimate military targets only with proportionate force; and they are not to employ methods which, in Walzer's words, "shock the moral conscience of mankind." Examples of such heinous methods include the deployment of weapons of mass destruction, and the use of mass rape campaigns as instruments of war. These principles of *jus in bello*, alongside those of *jus ad bellum*, offer a coherent set of plausible values to draw on while developing an account of just war settlement.[10]

It is often contended that the just goal of a just war is the proverbial status quo ante bellum: the victorious regime ought simply to reestablish the state of affairs that obtained before the war broke out. Restore the equilibrium disturbed by the aggressor, traditionalists advise. As Walzer points out, however, this assertion makes little sense: one ought not to aim for the literal restoration of the status quo ante bellum because that situation was precisely what led to war in the first place. Also, given the sheer destructiveness of war, any such literal restoration is empirically impossible. War simply changes too much. So the just goal of a just war, once won, must be a more secure and more just state of affairs than existed prior to the war. This condition Walzer refers to as one of "restoration plus."[11] What might such a condition be?

The general answer is a more secure possession of our rights, both individual and collective. The aim of a just and lawful war is the resistance of aggression and the vindication of the fundamental rights of political communities, ultimately on behalf of the human rights of their individual citizens. The overall aim is, in Walzer's words, "to reaffirm our own deepest values" with regard to justice, both domestic and international. It is not implausible to follow John Rawls in claiming that, in our era, no deeper, or more basic, political values exist than those human rights that justify a reasonable set of social institutions and ultimately enable a satisfying political existence.[12]

From this general principle, that the proper aim of a just war is the vindication of those rights whose violation grounded the resort to war in the first place, more detailed commentary needs to be offered. For what does such "vindication" of rights amount to: what does it include; what does it permit; and what does it forbid? The last aspect of the question seems the easiest to answer, at least in abstract terms: The principle of rights vindication forbids the continuation of the war after the relevant rights have, in fact, been vindicated. To go beyond that limit would itself become aggression: men and women would die for no just cause. This bedrock limit to the justified continuance of a just war seems required in order to prevent the war from spilling over into something like a crusade, which demands the utter destruction of the demonized enemy. The very essence of justice of, in, and after war is about there being firm limits, and constraints, upon its aims and conduct. Unconstrained fighting, with its fearful prospect of degenerating into barbarity, is the worst-case scenario – regardless of the values for which the war is being fought.

This emphasis on the maintenance of limits in wartime has the important consequence that there can be no such thing as a morally mandated unconditional surrender. This is so because, as Walzer observes, "conditions inhere in the very idea of international relations, as they do in the idea of human relations." The principles vindicated successfully by the just state themselves impose outside constraints on what can be done to an aggressor following its defeat. This line of reasoning might spark resistance from those who view favorably the Allied insistence on unconditional surrender during the closing days of World War II. But we need to distinguish here between rhetoric and reality. The policy of unconditional surrender followed by the Allies was not genuinely unconditional; there was never any insistence that the Allies be able to do whatever they wanted with the defeated nations. Churchill himself, for example, said: "We are bound by our own consciences to civilization. [We are not] entitled to behave in a barbarous manner."[13] At the very most, the policy the Allies pursued was genuinely unconditional vis-à-vis the governing regimes of the Axis powers, but not vis-à-vis the civilian populations in those nations.

Such a discriminating policy on surrender may be defensible in extreme cases, involving truly abhorrent regimes, but is generally impermissible. For insistence on unconditional surrender is disproportionate and will prolong fighting as the defeated aggressor refuses to cave in, fearing the consequences of doing so. Walzer believes this was the case during the Pacific War, owing to America's insistence on Japan's unconditional surrender. It is thus the responsibility of the victor to communicate clearly to the losing aggressor its sincere intentions for postwar settlement, intentions that must be consistent with the other principles of postwar justice here developed.[14]

What does the just aim of a just war — namely, rights vindication, constrained by a proportionate policy on surrender — precisely include or mandate? The following seems to be a plausible list of propositions regarding what would be at least permissible with regard to a just settlement of a just war:

- The aggression needs, where possible and proportional, to be rolled back, which is to say that the unjust gains from aggression must be eliminated. If, to take a simple example, the aggression has involved invading and taking over a country, then justice requires that the invader be driven out of the country and secure borders reestablished. The equally crucial corollary to this principle is that the victim of the aggression is to be reestablished as an independent political community, enjoying political sovereignty and territorial integrity.

- The commission of aggression, as a serious international crime, requires punishment in two forms: compensation to the victim for at least some of the costs incurred during the fight for its rights; and war crimes trials for the initiators of aggression. I will later argue that these are not the only war crimes trials required by justice in war's aftermath.

- The aggressor state might also require some demilitarization and political rehabilitation, depending on the nature and severity of the aggression it committed and the threat it would continue to pose in the absence of such measures. "One can," Walzer avers, "legitimately aim not merely at a successful resistance but also at some reasonable security against future attack."[15] The question of forcible, forward-looking rehabilitation is one of the most controversial and interesting surrounding the justice of settlements.

Metaphorically, one might say that a just war, justly prosecuted, is something like radical surgery: an extreme yet necessary measure to be taken in defense of fundamental values, like human rights, against serious, lethal threats to them, such as violent aggression. And if just war, justly prosecuted, is like radical surgery, then the justified conclusion to such a war can only be akin to the rehabilitation and therapy required after the surgery, in order to ensure that the original intent – namely, defeating the threat and protecting the rights – is effectively secured and that the patient is materially better off than before the exercise. The "patient" in this case is, in the first instance, the victim(s) of aggression. Secondarily, the term refers to the international community generally – including even the aggressor(s) or at least the long term interests of the civilians in aggressor(s).[16]

Sufficient comment has already been offered on what the first proposition requires and why: aggression, as a crime that justifies war, needs to be rolled back and have its gains eliminated as far as is possible and proportional; and the victim of aggression needs to have the objects of its rights restored. This principle seems quite straightforward, one of justice as rectification. But what about compensation, "political rehabilitation," and war crimes trials?

**Compensation and Discrimination**

Since aggression is a crime that violates important rights and causes much damage, it is reasonable to contend that, in a classical context of interstate war, the aggressor nation, "Aggressor," owes some duty of compensation to the victim of the aggression, "Victim." This is the case because, in the absence of aggression, Victim would not have to reconstruct itself following the war, nor would it have had to fight for its rights in the first place, with all the death and destruction that implies. Walzer says that the deepest nature of the wrong an aggressor commits is to make people fight

for their rights, that is, make them resort to violence to secure those things to which they have an elemental entitlement, and which they should enjoy as a matter of course. To put the issue bluntly, Aggressor has cost Victim a considerable amount, and so at least some restitution is due. The critical questions are how much compensation, and by whom in Aggressor is the compensation to be paid out?

The "how much" question, clearly, will be relative to the nature and severity of the act of aggression itself, alongside considerations of what Aggressor can reasonably be expected to pay. Care needs to be taken not to bankrupt Aggressor's resources, if only for the reason that the civilians of Aggressor still, as always, retain their claims to human rights fulfillment, and the objects of such rights require that resources be devoted to them.[17] There needs, in short, to be an application of the principle of proportionality here. The compensation required may not be draconian in nature. We have some indication, from the financial terms imposed on Germany at the Treaty of Versailles, that to beggar thy neighbor is to pick future fights.[18]

This reference to the needs of the civilians in Aggressor gives rise to important considerations of discrimination with regard to answering the "from whom" question: When it comes to establishing terms of compensation, care needs to be taken by the victorious Victim, and/or any third-party "Vindicators" who fought on behalf of Victim, not to penalize unduly the civilian population of Aggressor for the aggression carried out by their regime. This entails, for example, that any monetary compensation due to Victim ought to come, first and foremost, from the personal wealth of those political and military elites in Aggressor who were most responsible for the crime of aggression. Walzer seems to disagree when he suggests that such a discriminating policy on reparations "can hardly" raise the needed amount. But he ignores the fact that, historically, those who launch aggressive war externally have very often abused their power internally to accumulate personal fortunes. In light of this supposed shortfall, Walzer argues that, since "reparations are surely due the victims of aggressive war," they should be paid from the taxation system of the defeated Aggressor. There ought to be a kind of postwar poll tax on the population of Aggressor, with the proceeds forwarded to Victim. In this sense, he says, "citizenship is a common destiny."[19] I believe, however, that this fails to respect the discrimination principle during war termination. Though Walzer insists that "the distribution of costs is not the distribution of guilt," it is difficult to see what that is supposed to mean here: Why not respond by asking why civilians should be forced, through their tax system, to pay for the damage if they are not in some sense responsible for it? Respect for discrimination entails taking a reasonable amount of compensation only from those sources that can afford it and that were materially linked to the aggression in a morally culpable way. If such reparations "can hardly" pay for the destruction Aggressor meted out on Victim, then that fiscal deficiency does not somehow translate into Victim's moral entitlement to tax everyone in Aggressor. The resources for reconstruction simply have to be found elsewhere.[20]

An application to recent events can be seen through consideration of the following question: Should the United States levy a postwar poll tax on the citizens of Afghanistan to increase the funds available to compensate and care for those who lost loved ones during the 9-11 strikes, or else to rebuild New York's financial district? The principles just developed would seem to argue against such a tax, as there is a serious question of affordability in Afghanistan and an even sharper

one regarding responsibility, as the available evidence points to a collusion between the now-routed Taliban regime and the al-Qaeda network as the source of the attacks. Commendably, there has been little talk of any such punitive measure on Afghanistan, and Americans have instead turned toward each other to raise the needed reconstruction resources. Indeed, it is Afghanistan's interim government that has formally requested American resources to help rebuild its broken social and physical infrastructure.

A further implication of respect for discrimination in settlements is a ban on sweeping socioeconomic sanctions. The reasoning is clear: Sanctions that cut widely and deeply into the well-being of the civilian population are not only punitive, they surely end up punishing some who do not deserve such treatment. Such sanctions are properly condemned as inappropriately targeted and morally wrongheaded. Great controversy, of course, surrounds the issue of whether American-led sanctions on Iraq, following the Persian Gulf War, count as such sanctions or not. There is a vocal and apparently growing community of thought that commends instead sanctions that target elites, for instance by freezing personal assets, blocking weapons trade, and banning foreign travel.[21] The assets of some organizations alleged to be involved in terrorism have been frozen since 9-11; it will be interesting to see whether further sanctions in the war against terrorism will be applied, for instance, to entire countries, and, if so, what kind.

### Rehabilitation

The notion under this heading is that, in the postwar environment, Aggressor may be required to demilitarize, at least to the extent that it will not pose a serious threat to Victim – and other members of the international community – for the foreseeable future. The appropriate elements of such demilitarization will clearly vary with the nature and severity of the act of aggression, along with the extent of Aggressor's residual military capabilities following its defeat, But they may, and often do, involve: the creation of a demilitarized "buffer zone" between Aggressor and Victim (and any Vindicator), whether it be on land, sea or air; the capping of certain aspects of Aggressor's military capability; and especially the destruction of Aggressor's weapons of mass destruction. Once more, proportionality must be brought to bear upon this general principle: The regime in Aggressor may not be so demilitarized as to jeopardize its ability to fulfill its function of maintaining law and order within its own borders, and of protecting its people from other countries who might be tempted to invade if they perceive serious weakness in Aggressor. Another way this requirement could be met would be for the victors to provide reliable security guarantees to the people of Aggressor.

The imposition of some substantial requirement of political rehabilitation seems the most serious and invasive measure permitted a just regime, following its justified victory over Aggressor. As Walzer asserts, the "outer limit" of any surrender by Aggressor to Victim, and any Vindicator, is the construction and maintenance of a new kind of domestic political regime within Aggressor, one more peaceable, orderly, and pro-human rights in nature. It is probably correct to agree with him, however, when he cautions that, as a matter of proportionality, such measures are in order only in the most extreme cases, such as Nazi Germany at the close of World War II.[22]

If the actions of Aggressor during the war were truly atrocious, or if the nature of the regime in Aggressor at the end of the war is still so heinous that its continued existence poses a serious threat to international justice and human rights, then – and only then – may such a regime be forcibly dismantled and a new, more defensible regime established in its stead. But we should be quick to note, and emphasize, that such construction necessitates an additional commitment on the part of Victim and any Vindicators to assist the new regime in Aggressor with this enormous task of political restructuring. This assistance would be composed of seeing such "political therapy" through to a reasonably successful conclusion – which is to say, until the new regime can stand on its own, as it were, and fulfill its core functions of providing domestic law and order, human rights fulfillment, and adherence to the basic norms of international law, notably those banning aggression. The rehabilitations of the governing structures of both West Germany and Japan following World War II, largely by the United States, seem quite stellar and instructive examples in this regard.[23] They also illustrate the profound and costly commitments that must be borne by any Victim or Vindicator seeking to impose such far-reaching and consequential terms on the relevant Aggressor following defeat.

One open question concerns whether we "probably" should agree with Walzer that rehabilitation be reserved only for the most grave cases of aggression, like Nazi Germany. Why shouldn't we impose at least some rehabilitative measures on any aggressor? Given the serious nature of any act of aggression – so serious that, by Walzer's own lights, it justifies war – why should we refrain from imposing political reform upon the defeated aggressor, unless its regime is as bad as that of the Nazis? After all, the immediate postwar environment would seem the perfect opportunity to pursue such reform, and presumably it would contribute to a more peaceful world order in the long run. The German and Japanese examples might even be cited as evidence in favor of this. Some cited such cases in 1991, while arguing that the allies in the Gulf War should have moved on to change the regime in Iraq, and not "merely" to have pushed it out of Kuwait. The reason Walzer hesitates to affirm this more expansive view on forcible rehabilitation is because of the great value he attaches to political sovereignty, to shared ways of life, and to free collective choice – even if these end up failing to express the degree of domestic human rights fulfillment that we in Western liberal democracies might prefer. He cautions against "the terrible presumption" behind external powers' deliberately changing domestic social institutions, even in aggressors.[24]

My judgment is that Walzer's caution here may be too cautious, and that his reluctance to permit institutional restructuring may reveal the limitations of his strong commitment to national sovereignty. I suggest that there should be a presumption in favor of permitting rehabilitative measures in the domestic political structure of a defeated aggressor. But such rehabilitation does need to be proportional to the degree of depravity inherent in the political structure itself. This way, complete dismantling and constitutional reconstruction – like the sea change from totalitarian fascism to liberal democracy – will probably be reserved for exceptional cases similar to those Walzer cites. But comparatively minor renovations – like human rights education programs, police and military retraining programs, reform of the judiciary and bureaucracy into accountable institutions, external verification of subsequent election results, and the like – are permitted in any defeated aggressor, subject to need and proportionality. It is worthy of notice that many of the most recent peace treaties – like that ending the Bosnian civil war – have included this more permissive principle in favor of political rehabilitation. Political activity here seems to be outpacing political theory, leaving

some of the strictures of sovereignty behind in favor of augmenting adherence to international values.[25]

It is interesting to reflect on Afghanistan in connection with these issues. A more representative interim government has been formed in the Taliban's wake, and there has been talk of partially secularizing and modernizing the education system, for instance by permitting the participation of girls and women. Foreign peacekeepers, though, currently serve as the effective enforcers of law and order, external humanitarian aid is still needed simply to feed people, and much of the country's infrastructure has been ruined – by conflicts that started well before the US-led campaign. Moreover, the exact details regarding the move from a merely "interim" government to a more stable system have yet to be clarified, and the support of some important communal leaders in parts of the country has yet to be secured.

We should also expect, to return to rehabilitation in general, a formal apology by Aggressor to Victim and any Vindicator for its aggression, While it is right to agree with Walzer that "official apologies somehow seem an inadequate, perhaps even a perfunctory, way" of atoning for aggression,[26] this is no reason to rule such an apology out of the terms of the peace. For even though formal apologies cannot of themselves restore territory, revive casualties, or rebuild infrastructure, they do mean something real to us. If not, why do formal apologies, and victims' campaigns to secure such apologies, generate considerable political and media attention? If not, why do informed people know that Germany has apologized profusely for its role in World War II whereas Japan has hardly apologized at all? Walzer must concede that we expect wrongdoers eventually to admit their wrongdoing and to express their regret for it. We feel that victims of wrongdoing are owed that kind of respect and that aggressors must at least show recognition of the moral principles they violated. Apologies are a nontrivial aspect of a complete peace treaty.[27]

This perspective on rehabilitation – calling for disarmament, institutional reform, political transformation, infrastructure investments, and official apologies – brings into focus important questions. Does it follow from the above that the imposition of rehabilitation on an aggressor is itself a legitimate war aim? Can a just state set out, from the start of the war, not only to vindicate its violated rights, but, in addition, to impose institutional therapy upon the aggressor? If so, what does that imply in terms of the use of force during war, since being in a position to impose institutional therapy after the war is at least linked to, and may even depend on, the achievement of a certain degree of military superiority at war's end? The therapy requires the strength to see it through.[28] My sense is that the imposition of institutional therapy on an aggressor is consistent with, even implied by, the overall goal of a justified war argued for previously, namely, rights vindication constrained by a proportionate policy on surrender. The therapy is justly invoked when required to prevent future aggression and to enable the defeated community to meet international commitments to law and order, and basic human rights. In terms of war fighting, having rehabilitation as a war end does not somehow diminish the responsibility to fight in accord with the *jus in bello* rules of right conduct. The importance of the end does not lessen the constraints just communities face when they vindicate their rights by force. Will insistence on rehabilitation as part of war settlement itself prolong the fighting? While it might do so as a matter of fact, relative to a less stringent or unjust settlement offer, seeing it through is not wrong provided the fighting continues to respect *jus in bello*. The duty falls on Aggressor to agree to reasonable terms of

rehabilitation, not on Victim/Vindicator to avoid seeking those means necessary to secure adherence to them.

It is an implication of this discussion that the three sets of just war principles – of, in, and after war – must not be applied sequentially as each phase arises but, rather, considered together right from the start. There needs to be a consistent commitment that encompasses, from the outset, all three stages of a military engagement. Potential participants in armed conflict should consider in advance whether it is likely that the requirements of all three sets of just war principles can be satisfied prior to engaging in political violence.[29]

## War Crimes Trials

This leaves the vexed topic of war crimes trials, perhaps the one issue of justice after war that has already received searching attention. The normative need for such trials follows from Walzer's dictum: "There can be no justice in war if there are not, ultimately, responsible men and women."[30] Individuals who play a prominent role during wartime must be held accountable for their actions and what they bring about. There are, of course, two broad categories of war crimes: those that violate *jus ad bellum* and those that violate *jus in bello*.

*Jus ad bellum* war crimes have to do with "planning, preparing, initiating and waging" aggressive war. Responsibility for the commission of any such crime falls on the shoulders of the political leader(s) of the aggressor regime. Such crimes, in the language of the Nuremberg prosecutors, are "crimes against peace."[31] What this principle entails is that, subject to proportionality, the leaders of Aggressor are to be brought to trial before a public and fair international tribunal and accorded full due process rights in their defense. Why subject this principle of punishment to proportionality constraints? Why concur with Walzer when he says that "it isn't always true that their leaders ought to be punished for their crimes"?[32] The answer is that sometimes such leaders, in spite of their moral decrepitude, retain considerable popular legitimacy, and thus bringing them to trial could seriously destabilize the polity within Aggressor. NATO forces, for example, held off for a long time on the seizure of prominent persons charged with war crimes in the former Yugoslavia, presumably for reasons including this one. Care needs to be taken, as always, that appeal to proportionality does not amount to rewarding aggressors, or to letting them run free and unscathed despite their grievous crimes. Yet this care does not vitiate the need to consider the destruction and suffering that might result from adhering totally to what the requirements of justice as retribution demand.

Should political leaders on trial for *jus ad bellum* violations be found guilty, through a public and fair proceeding, then the court is at liberty to determine a reasonable punishment, which will obviously depend upon the details of the relevant case. Perhaps the punishment will only consist of penalizing the leaders financially for the amount of compensation owed to Victim, as previously discussed. Or perhaps, should the need for political rehabilitation be invoked, such leaders will need to be stripped of power and barred from political participation, or even jailed. Some figures in the Bosnian Serb community were, for instance, barred from seeking office in the first postwar election.[33] It is not possible, a priori, to stipulate what exactly is required with regard to such personal punishments. The point here is simply that the principle itself, of calling those most responsible for the aggression to task for their crimes, must be respected as an essential aspect of justice after war. It is relevant to add that the actual enforcement of this principle might constitute a nontrivial deterrent to future acts of aggression on the part of ambitious heads of state. If such figures have good reason to believe that they will themselves, personally, pay a price for the aggression they instigate and order, then perhaps they will be less likely to undertake such misadventures in the first place.

Important progress has recently been made on this front. First, the former prime minister of Rwanda in late 1998 was found guilty of war crimes and crimes against humanity in connection with the brutal civil war that consumed that country in the summer of 1994. Moreover, Serbian president Slobodan Milosevic was formally indicted by an international tribunal for committing war crimes in May 1999, the first time a sitting head of state has faced such a charge. In June 2001, after losing power, Milosevic was taken under arrest and transported to The Hague for trial.[34]

*Jus ad bellum* war crimes trials are not the only ones mandated by international law and just war theory: attention must also, in the aftermath of conflict, be paid to trying those accused of *jus in bello* war crimes. Such crimes include: deliberately using indiscriminate or disproportionate force; failing to take due care to protect civilian populations from lethal violence; using weapons that are themselves intrinsically indiscriminate and/ or disproportionate, such as those of mass destruction; employing intrinsically heinous means, like rape campaigns; and treating surrendered prisoners of war in an inhumane fashion, for example, torturing them. Primary responsibility for these war crimes must fall on the shoulders of those soldiers, officers, and military commanders who were most actively involved in their commission. Officers and commanders carry considerable moral burdens of their own during wartime. They are duty-bound not to issue orders that violate any aspect of the laws of war. Furthermore, they must plan military campaigns so that foreseeable civilian casualties are minimized, and must teach and train their soldiers not only about combat but also about the rules of just war theory and the laws of armed conflict.[35]

Something of note here is that, unlike *jus ad bellum* war crimes, *jus in bello* war crimes can be, and usually are, committed by all sides in the conflict. So, care needs to be taken that Victim and any Vindicator avoid the very tempting position of punishing only *jus ad bellum* war crimes. In order to avoid charges of applying a double standard and exacting revenge, the justified side must – despite the justice of its cause in fighting – also be willing to submit members of its military for the commission of *jus in bello* war crimes to an impartially constructed international tribunal. We know that, in 1998, the international community voted in Rome to establish at The Hague a permanent court for the prosecution of war crimes and other crimes against humanity. Ratification of the Treaty of Rome is close at hand, and before the end of 2002 an important new international institution should be born. [The International Criminal Court, for prosecuting war crimes, was established in July 2002.]

### Publicity

Do the terms of the settlement, as thus far discussed, need to be public? On the one hand, war settlements often exert deep impact on people's lives. They are thus entitled to know the substance of peace settlements, and especially how such are predicted to affect them. Immanuel Kant, for one, was vehement about this publicity requirement in his famous writings on war.[36] But someone might challenge this publicity principle, for instance, by citing a counterexample. We know that part of the reason why the Soviet Union backed down

during the Cuban Missile Crisis was because of John F. Kennedy's secret assurances that the United States would remove missiles from Turkey shortly after the Soviets removed theirs from Cuba.[37] But this instance does not deal with a full-blown war, much less a postwar period, and so it is not directly analogous. People who have suffered through a war deserve to know what the substance of the settlement is.

This does not mean that the people must explicitly and immediately endorse the proposed settlement, for instance through a plebiscite. Nor does it mean that the settlement must be drafted up in a formal treaty. Both things are clearly permissible, and perhaps desirable as well: a show of popular support for a settlement might bolster its endurance; and writing out the peace terms can enhance the clarity of everyone's understandings and expectations. But it seems needlessly stringent to insist that both phenomena must be there for the settlement to be legitimate. We can imagine numerous practical difficulties with running a plebiscite in the immediate postwar period, and we can imagine communities that come to an understanding on the settlement – even going so far as to adhere to it – without nailing down every possible contingency in a detailed legal document.

### Summary of the Set

Perhaps it would be helpful to list the proffered set of settlement principles. A just state, seeking to terminate its just war successfully, ought to be guided by all of the following norms:

> Proportionality and Publicity. The peace settlement should be both measured and reasonable, as well as publicly proclaimed. To make a settlement serve as an instrument of revenge is to make a volatile bed one may be forced to sleep in later.

In general, this rules out insistence on unconditional surrender.

Rights Vindication. The settlement should secure those basic rights whose violation triggered the justified war. The relevant rights include human rights to life and liberty and community entitlements to territory and sovereignty. This is the main substantive goal of any decent settlement. Respect for rights is a foundation of civilization, whether national or international. Vindicated rights, not vindictive revenge, is the order of the day.

Discrimination. Distinction needs to be made between the leaders, the soldiers, and the civilians in the country one is negotiating with. Civilians are entitled to reasonable immunity from punitive postwar measures. This rules out sweeping socioeconomic sanctions as part of postwar punishment.

Punishment #1. When the defeated country has been a blatant, rights-violating aggressor, proportionate punishment must be meted out. The leaders of the regime, in particular, should face fair and public international trials for war crimes.

Punishment #2. Soldiers also commit war crimes. Justice after war requires that such soldiers, from all sides of the conflict, likewise be held accountable at trial.

Compensation. Financial restitution may be mandated, subject to both proportionality and discrimination. A postwar poll tax on civilians is impermissible, and enough resources need to be left so that the defeated country can begin its reconstruction. To beggar thy neighbor is to pick future fights.

Rehabilitation. The postwar environment provides a promising opportunity to reform decrepit institutions in an aggressor regime. Such reforms are permissible but they must be proportional to the degree of depravity in the regime. They may involve: demilitarization and disarmament; police and judicial retraining; human rights education; and even deep structural transformation toward a peaceable liberal democratic society.

Any serious defection, by any participant, from these principles of just war settlement should be seen as a violation of the rules of just war termination, and so should be punished. At the least, violation of such principles mandates a new round of diplomatic negotiations – even binding international arbitration – between the relevant parties to the dispute. At the very most, such violation may give the aggrieved party a just cause – but no more than a just cause – for resuming hostilities. Full recourse to the resumption of hostilities may be made only if all the other traditional criteria of *jus ad bellum* are satisfied in addition to just cause.

### Conclusion: An Ethical "Exit Strategy"

The topic of justice after war, or *jus post bellum*, has been somewhat neglected, yet has recently become prominent, even pressing, in international relations. This article offers one plausible set of just war settlement norms, which communities seeking to conclude their just wars properly ought to obey. The terms of a just peace should satisfy the requirements listed above in the summary. There needs to be an ethical "exit strategy" from war, and it deserves at least as much thought and effort as the purely military exit strategy so much on the minds of policy planners and commanding officers.

One final aspect merits consideration: To what extent can these principles of just war settlement, developed mainly in a conventional interstate context, be applied to nontraditional intrastate conflicts? This question gains sharpness when we note that most recent conflicts seem to have been of the latter sort: brutal civil wars in Rwanda and Bosnia; multifaction wars in central Africa; armed insurrection in Chechnya; and forcible armed intervention in Somalia and Kosovo. The short answer is that the extension of these principles is another project.[38] It remains important, though, to get the principles right in the more conventional case, before moving on to the nonconventional, and arguably more complex, ones. The longer answer to the question is that, with modifications, the principles developed here no doubt serve as a compelling moral blueprint for application to these other cases. Indeed, some attempt was made here to do just that, in connection with the "war against terrorism" in Afghanistan. The principles offered here deal with the core controversies involved in any use of mass political violence, and they capture precisely those values and concepts we all employ to reflect on and speak intelligently about, the ethics of war and peace.

## Study Questions

1. Just war theory provides for war to be instigated "for the right reasons" and for war to be fought with "the right methods." What are the right reasons and the right methods? Take a position on whether there are "right methods" in fighting a "just" war.

2. Orend explores a gap in just war theory – justice after war. What are the conditions he proposes for justice after war?

3. When does Orend allow for forcible dismantling of the regime against whom the Aggressor waged war? Take a position on whether forcible dismantling is justified after a just war, or if it violates national sovereignty.

4. Orend, in closing, turns to intrastate conflict, stating that it is a topic for another project. Take this on and apply his principles for justice after war to either Somalia or Kosovo. What ease or difficulty do you have in doing this?

## Notes

1  Thanks to the editors of *Ethics & International Affairs*, especially Christian Barry. Thanks, too, to Michael Walzer and some anonymous reviewers who commented on an earlier draft.
2  On just war theory in general, see Michael Walzer, *Just and Unjust Wars*, 3rd ed. (New York: Basic Books, 2000) and Brian Orend, *Michael Walzer on War and Justice* (Cardiff: U of Wales, 2000).
3  David E. Decosse, ed., *But Was It Just? Reflections on the Morality of the Persian Gulf War* (New York: Doubleday, 1992); David Rieff, *Slaughterhouse: Bosnia and the Failure of the West* (New York: Simon and Schuster, 1995); Gerard Prunier, *The Rwanda Crisis: History of a Genocide* (New York: Columbia UP, 1995); and Brian Orend, "Crisis in Kosovo: A Just Use of Force?" *Politics* 19.3 (1999), pp. 125–30.

4   Manfred F. Boemeke, Gerald D. Feldman, and Elisabeth Glaser, eds., *The Treaty of Versailles: A Reassessment after 75 Years* (Cambridge: Cambridge UP, 1998).

5   Rieff, *Slaughterhouse.*

6   This is not to deny the importance of the robust conflict-resolution literature. Much of that literature is relevant to the present concern, but not much of it is located within the explicitly ethical values and commitments of just war theory, whereas this piece is. For more on conflict resolution in general. see Stephen J. Cimbala, ed., *Strategic War Termination* (New York: Praeger, 1986); Paul R. Pillar, *Negotiating Peace: War Termination as a Bargaining Process* (Princeton: Princeton UP, 1983); Stuart Albert and Edward Luck, eds., *On the Endings of Wars* (Port Washington, NY: Kennikat P, 1980); A.J.P. Taylor, *How Wars End* (London: Hamilton, 1985); and Fen Osier Hampson, *Nurturing Peace: Why Peace Settlements Succeed or Fail* (Washington, DC: U.S. Institute of Peace, 1996).

7   Adam Roberts and Richard Guelff, eds., *Documents on the Laws of War* (Oxford: Oxford UP, 1999).

8   Walzer, *Just and Unjust Wars*, p. 62.

9   For more on *jus ad bellum*, see Walzer, *Just and Unjust Wars*, pp. 3–33 and 51–125; and David Luban, "Just War and Human Rights," *Philosophy and Public Affairs* 9 (1980), pp. 160–81. On law, see Roberts and Guelff, eds., *Documents on the Laws of War.*

10  For more on *jus in bello*, see Walzer, *Just and Unjust Wars*, pp. 34–50 and 127–224 (quote at p. 107); Thomas Nagel, "War and Massacre," *Philosophy and Public Affairs* 1 (1972), pp. 123–45: Robert K. Fullinwinder, "War and Innocence," *Philosophy and Public Affairs* 5 (1975), pp. 90–97: and Geoffrey Best, *War and Law Since 1945* (Oxford: Oxford UP, 1994).

11  Walzer, *Just and Unjust Wars*, pp. xx, 119.

12  Walzer, *Just and Unjust Wars*, pp. 110, 117, 123; John Rawls, "The Law of Peoples," in Steven Shute and Susan Hurley, eds., *On Human Rights* (New York: Basic Books, 1993), pp. 40–80.

13  Churchill quoted in Walzer, *Just and Unjust Wars*, p. 112.

14  Walzer, *Just and Unjust Wars*, pp. 113, 263–68.

15  Walzer, *Just and Unjust Wars*, p. 118.

16  This image of just war as radical surgery, and just settlement as the subsequent therapy, came to mind while reading Nissan Oren, "Prudence in Victory," in Nissan Oren, ed., *Termination of War: Processes, Procedures and Aftermaths* (Jerusalem: Hebrew UP, 1982), pp. 147–64.

17  James Nickel, *Making Sense of Human Rights* (Berkeley: U of California P, 1987).

18  Boemeke, Feldman, and Glaser, eds., *The Treaty of Versailles.*

19  One of my reviewers concurred with Walzer, drawing on the analogy of shareholders being collectively responsible, at least in financial terms, for corporate wrongdoing even when such was committed by management only. But I'm not sure that analogy holds: shareholders lose money they risked voluntarily in pursuit of capital gains, whereas citizenship is less voluntary and far weightier.

20  Walzer, *Just and Unjust Wars*, p. 297.

21  See Ramsey Clark, *The Children are Dying: The Impact of Sanctions on Iraq* (New York: World View Forum, 1996); Anthony Arnove and Ali Abunimah, eds., *Iraq Under Siege: The Deadly Impact of Sanctions and War* (London: South End P, 2000); Albert Pierce, "Just War Principles and Economic Sanctions," *Ethics & International Affairs* 10 (1996), pp. 99–113; and the multi-essay exchange on the issue between Joy Gordon and George Lopez, *Ethics & International Affairs* 13 (1999), pp. 123–50.

22  Walzer, *Just and Unjust Wars*, pp. 113, 119, 267–68.

23  Leon V. Sigal, *Fighting to the Finish: The Politics of War Termination in the United States and Japan, 1945* (Ithaca: Cornell UP, 1989); Howard B. Schonberger, *Aftermath of War: Americans and the Remaking of Japan, 1945–1952* (Ohio: Kent State UP, 1989); Michael Schaller, *The American*

*Occupation of Japan* (Oxford: Oxford UP, 1987); and Eugene Davidson, *The Death and Life of Germany: An Account of the American Occupation* (St. Louis: U of Missouri P, 1999).

24  Walzer, *Just and Unjust Wars*, pp. xvii–xx.

25  On Bosnia, see Rieff, *Slaughterhouse*; and the text of the Dayton Peace Agreement itself, at www.state.gov/www/regions/eurlbosnialbosagree.html, which ended the war in November 1995. See also the text of the Ahtisaari Accord, at www.nato/int/usa/policy/d 990609.htm, Serbia's initial agreement in May 1999 to NATO's terms on ending its armed intervention in favor of the Kosovars. Also relevant is Alcira Kreimer et al., *Bosnia and Herzegovina: Post-Conflict Reconstruction* (Washington, DC: World Bank, 2000); and Ruti G. Teitel, *Transitional Justice* (Oxford: Oxford UP, 2000).

26  Walzer, "Untitled," *Dissent* (1995), p. 330.

27  Walzer, *Just and Unjust Wars*, p. 20.

28  I owe these questions to Michael Walzer.

29  Christian Barry rightly pushed me to point this out.

30  Walzer, *Just and Unjust Wars*, p. 288. See also W. Michael Reisman and Chris T. Antoniou, eds., *The Laws of War* (New York: Vintage, 1994), pp. 317–405.

31  Walzer, *Just and Unjust Wars*, pp. 292–301.

32  Ibid., p. 123.

33  The Dayton Peace Agreement, www.stat.e.gov/www/regions/eur/bosnia/bosagree.html.

34  For more on war crimes trials, see Reisman and Antoniou, eds., *The Laws of War*, pp. 317–405. See also Juan E. Méndez, "National Reconciliation, Transnational Justice, and the International Criminal Court," pp. 25–44, and Thomas Pogge, "Achieving Democracy," pp. 3–23, both in *Ethics & International Affairs* 15, no. 1 (2001).

35  Walzer, *Just and Unjust Wars*, pp. 304–28.

36  Immanuel Kant, *The Metaphysics of Morals*, trans. Mary Gregor (Cambridge: Cambridge UP, 1995), pp. 114–24; and Brian Orend, *War and International Justice: A Kantian Perspective* (Waterloo: Wilfrid Laurier UP, 2000).

37  Martin Walker, *The Cold War: A History* (New York: Henry Holt, 1995), pp. 160–83.

38  See Nigel Biggar, ed., *Burying the Past: Making Peace and Doing Justice After Civil Conflict* (Washington, DC: Georgetown UP, 2001).

# 4.  Anthony Burke, "Just War or Ethical Peace? Moral Discourses of Strategic Violence after 9/11"

ANTHONY BURKE'S 2004 ESSAY, from the journal *International Affairs*, criticizes just war theory. One of his main criticisms is that just war moralizes strategic violence, what Gandhi would call "brute force," under the assumption that brute force is a reasonable and sometimes necessary means to obtain ends. Burke (b. 1966) argues that this assumption not only conceptually underlies just war theory but is also stimulated by it. The assumption, he says, can be found in the just war rule of proportionality, which holds that the means of violence must be proportionate to the ends to be secured, such that excessive force cannot be used to achieve ends. He is also critical of the rule of proportionality because it leaves open too much range as to what counts as "excessive" and because it relieves agents of war of liability when human deprivation or destruction was unintentional. As an alternative, Burke thinks just war theory should be modified with, for example, enforceable laws of war that criminalize the production of avoidable harm. This would be accompanied by the ideal of eliminating violence from international relations and of supporting international disarmament efforts.

Burke also argues that just war theory is too abstract to be an acceptable standard for deciding when to use brute force against others. For example, it hides the political reality that the United States doesn't currently understand war as an idiosyncratic, unfortunate, and morally necessary response to secure national security or justice, but as policy. It also can hide the atrocity of war and the moral burden of deciding to use brute force against others by fixing the declaration to use brute force against others in clean and non-concrete, moralistic language. Just war discourse can place authority in the hands of states instead of the international community; it is thus too outdated to be compatible with contemporary international human-rights discourse and law. Burke is also assured that just war criteria have failed to prevent the avoidable deaths of innocents. He also criticizes just war thinking because he thinks it easily colludes with war propaganda produced by politicians, which equates strategic violence with justice and the upholding of Western values.

---

The kindness of the enthroned Gods contains an element of force.

– Aeschylus[1]

… there are now reasons of state for fighting justly.

– Michael Walzer[2]

IN 1973 THE STRATEGIST and estranged member of the "nuclear priesthood" Bernard Brodie wrote in his book *War and Politics* that "the morality or immorality of acts of war is not a popular subject among the military and their civilian associates, nor for that matter among writers on strategy. It makes the military uneasy and defensive, ready to dismiss the troubling issue whenever it arises, either by asserting its irrelevancy or by falling back on some convenient sophistry."[3] This sad observation is hardly news, but we would be wrong to infer from it that a discourse on morality is entirely missing from questions of strategy and war. Brodie hints at this when he goes on to point out that the training of soldiers in the "conviction that the all-important goal is to win" does have a moral quality: in the general's view, "whatever contributes to his overall victory usually diminishes overall casualties, especially his own. It is therefore self-evident to him that any device or tactic that hastens victory represents the highest morality."[4]

For those who assume that the application of morality to foreign policy or war-making implies a radical critique of strategic violence – one that seeks to abolish it or at least to control its use – it may be surprising that moral convictions can be placed in its service. Yet in the wake of the attacks of September 11, 2001, and the development of the cybernetically controlled, mediated and "limited" forms of violence James DerDerian has termed "virtuous war," we are faced with a prospect of morality being deployed, imagined and evaded in the process of planning and waging the war on terror.[5] In however bizarre and unsatisfactory a fashion, moral discourses and judgements permeate the war on terror, many of them in its justification. In the light of this experience we may be forced to conclude that "amorality" does embody powerful moral assumptions; that in the view of many, strategic violence is and can be "moral"; that we must see a moral position implicit in George Kennan's self-consciously amoral view that "the interests of the national society for which government has to concern itself are basically those of its military security, the integrity of its political life, and the well-being of its people."[6]

Moral discourses and justifications permeated the sense of outrage and violation felt by Americans after 9/11, soaked its media coverage and public debate, and were smoothly deployed to justify military action against Afghanistan. Rhetorics of justice and injustice, humanity and inhumanity, civilization and barbarism, were repeatedly invoked by US officials in the tragedy's wake. Moral discourses have been used to brush aside concerns about the disproportionately high level of civilian casualties incurred during US and Northern Alliance operations against the Taliban and Al-Qaeda, as they were similarly used to play down the casualties of the war against Iraq. Moral arguments – including, incredibly, "just war" arguments – have even been used to support waging war against Iraq.[7] In their wake, we face the sobering realization that moral discourses are part of the warrior's political armoury; they are part of war's machinery, not a rod in its wheels. As Vivienne Jabri has written, "strategic and normative (just war) discourses ... constitute together the structuring language of war ... [they] share that element of destruction which is the defining characteristic of war."[8] In short, moral rules about war's justification, process and restraint may function not so much as limitations on war as tools for its liberation.

## Moral Trouble / Moral War

My argument is not that moral discourses on war do not sometimes work to limit strategic violence, particularly when they have been codified in the law of war and internalized in military operations. However, it is arguable that the law of war is flawed and extremely difficult to enforce – which throws the focus back on to its voluntary observance by governments and militaries, who nonetheless remain largely unaccountable for violations. We can point to a large number of possible violations of the laws of war (and other important international human rights laws) by the US and its allies in the course of the war on terror, few if any of which can be prosecuted and all of which the internalization of legal or moral rules sadly failed to prevent....

Death can be commuted not only through technological distancing, media spin and military jargon, but also in theory – which works to control its ethical disturbance through the creation of abstract moral and political rules that claim to fix truth, enable justice and provide a sure guide for policy. "Just war" theory now plays this role, especially as a way of controlling and managing the question of *responsibility* raised by Der Derian. The moralizing of just war advocates has come into renewed prominence since 9/11 as a legitimizing framework for the war on terror, in terms of providing both justifications for military action (*jus ad bellum*) and moral limits on its conduct (*jus in bello*).[9] ...

... [J]ust war arguments generally map out no essential role for international law and have often been deployed to justify its evasion, preferring instead their own (strikingly malleable) criteria for the waging and conduct of war. On the other hand, in the recent writings of Jean Bethke Elshtain just war doctrine blurs into and in fact *sanctifies* "reason of state" as she simultaneously lays claim to a "Christian tradition [that] tells us government is instituted by God" and "an Augustinian realism that resists sentimentalism and insists on ethical restraint."[10] ... Michael Walzer makes a significant point in his recent admission that "there are now reasons of state for fighting justly" – even if I see it as a problem and he as a potential virtue.[11]

In the face of this interweaving and proliferation of moral discourses *in favour* of strategic violence, a number of important questions arise. Are our moral discourses – whether they are couched in realist, "just war" or liberal/legal terms – adequate to the problem and phenomenon of war, and especially war against terror? Where they set out rules, criteria and restraints, are those provisions observed and enforced? Are they adequate as

moral standards *in themselves*, or can they be criticized in these terms? Do they adequately understand either war *or* terror, and will war against terror ever succeed in eliminating either from our world? Do they unfairly colonize the possible space of discourse about morality, ethics and strategic violence – and what alternative ways of thinking might be possible were we to shake off their constraints?

I will address these questions with a particular focus on "just war" rhetoric and theory as they have been mobilized in the United States after 9/11. My exploration arises out of what I had originally thought of as a tangential project examining the influence of instrumental reason on strategic discourse and war – until it became clear that moral discourses are closely intertwined with instrumental/rational processes of strategic calculation, even as their result might be forms of violence many consider to be morally unacceptable. The no-man's-land that joins these discourses and processes is my analytical terrain; a land where, as the phrase suggests, morally acceptable slaughter, suffering and chaos are described as "regrettable," but occur because they are "unintentional," "collateral" or "necessary." Is an international community based on modern liberal principles really willing to treat this as morally acceptable, and leave its theories, laws and systems of enforcement untouched? One of my conclusions is that moral discourses of strategic violence have ... internalized the instrumental ... assumption that war is both a normal and a rational pursuit of political ends. This is what unites and underpins the various moral discourses of war – realist, liberal and neo-Augustinian: the conviction that has made war such a pervasive modern phenomenon, that war "is a mere continuation of policy by other means."[12]

Following this, another important conclusion underpins the argument of this article. If war is seen as policy, we must do what so many just war thinkers fail to do: treat war as part of a historical and policy continuum, rather than an isolated event limited to the conduct of high-intensity military operations whose impact can somehow be limited in time, scope and spatial reach.[13] This continuum must include mechanisms such as diplomacy, covert operations, sanctions, coups, economic relationships, foreign aid and international law enforcement, and moral responsibility must extend across the entire gamut of social, political and humanitarian circumstances which precede, generate, shape and follow conflict. Given the complex array of interconnected threats, processes and conflicts tied into the 9/11 attacks and the war on terror – among them the Israeli–Palestinian conflict, the 1982 Israeli invasion of Lebanon and the involvement of Iran and Syria there, the *Mujahedin* war against Soviet forces in Afghanistan, the development of radical Islamist movements in Egypt and other African and Middle Eastern states, and Iraq's war against Iran and its aftermath in the invasion of Kuwait, Operation Desert Storm, UN sanctions and CIA covert operations – we need a moral and analytical framework which can better deal with historical and geopolitical complexity.

The article concludes by speculating that our frameworks for the moral justification (and limitation) of strategic violence have failed us; and, moreover, that they have failed at a cost of thousands of innocent lives and at the risk of creating a future in which we are not free of terror but condemned to its permanent presence. It shifts the normative ideal from just war to *ethical peace*, an ethics that eschews abstract moral theory in favour of a context-sensitive ethical orientation that is concerned with the *outcomes* of decisions and the *avoidance* of suffering. While strategic violence will be difficult to eliminate, and may be necessary in strictly limited situations before the achievement of ethical peace, its acceptance can only be *conditional*, and under conditions far more stringent, enforceable and morally consistent than have so far been provided by either realism, just war theory or international law. Against the claustrophobic and divided moral communities imagined by both realism and just war theory, ethical peace imagines a universal moral community in which no ethical obligation can be traded away in times of emergency, and no humans can be put in mortal danger so that others may be safe.

**Moralizing the "War on Terror"**

American anger in the wake of September 11 was expressed in two interwoven languages: morality and war. As Jean Bethke Elshtain describes it, "from George W. Bush to the average man and woman on the street, Americans since September 11 have invoked the language of justice to characterize their collective response to the despicable deeds perpetrated against innocent men, women and children."[14] George W. Bush told Congress that on September 11 "enemies of freedom committed an act of war against our country" and promised that "whether we bring our enemies to justice, or bring justice to our enemies, justice will be done." He claimed that the war against terror was "the fight of all who believe in progress and pluralism, tolerance and freedom," and that "we are in a fight for our principles, and our first responsibility is to live by them. No one should be singled out for unfair treatment or unkind words because of their ethnic background or religious faith."[15]

This, unmistakably, is a language of morality allied to a declaration and promise of war: a declaration of the immorality of the attacks and their perpetrators, of the tolerance, fairness and purity of the United States and its allies, and of its moral duty to seek and live by principles of justice through military and other counterterrorist action. It is a language which creates an irrevocably divided moral universe, in which all virtue lies with the US and all iniquity with "the terrorists," set out starkly in the President's description of Al-Qaeda and the Taliban as "the heirs of all the murderous ideologies of the twentieth century ... fascism, and Nazism, and totalitarianism."[16] It is a language which sees force not merely as a rational response to a threat to American national security, but as a moral response to an act of injustice – a response which it is moral to make, and which he implies should also be made in a moral way. In short, Bush's address to Congress imagines a martial universe and a moral universe, and then unites them. What are the implications of doing so? How does it drive or enable policy, and what expectations might we have of that policy once it is couched in these terms?

The answers are complex and disturbing. Elshtain's argument is that, by invoking the language of justice, Americans "tap into a complex tradition called 'just war.'" In her view the war on terror is both a just cause and being fought according to just war principles:

> When a wound as grievous as that of September 11 has been inflicted on a body-politic, it would be the height of irresponsibility – a dereliction of duty, a flight from the serious vocation of politics – to fail to respond ... A *political* ethic is an ethic of responsibility. The just war tradition gives us a way of exercising that responsibility.[17]

Elshtain is firm in her belief that the war on terror – even extended to Iraq – measures up to the standards of "just war," in both its justification and its execution. Her argument is significant for the evaluation of the just war discourse, even though it can be challenged

on a number of grounds, such as the reluctance of the US to explore alternatives to a war against Afghanistan, the conduct of US operations, and the naivety of her belief that the just war framework is the one actually being applied by the Bush administration. As Nicholas Wheeler notes, the administration tapped into more than the just war "tradition" both in designing and in justifying its response; just war, he argues, jostled for space with "alternative moral theories that challenge the idea of restraint in war" such as the "realist doctrine of necessity," and the "supreme emergency" and "war is hell" arguments discussed by just war theorist Michael Walzer.[18] Bush's own rhetoric betrays this ambiguity, as when he stated in the address to Congress that "whether we bring our enemies to justice, or bring justice to our enemies, justice will be done."[19] "Bringing our enemies to justice" implies using legal processes and neutral/universal standards of judgement; "bringing justice to our enemies" suggests the use of extralegal means both to deal with a threat and to achieve "justice." They are not the same, and the latter suggests that the use of extralegal violence or coercion (killing at a distance on the basis of minimal evidence or suspect intelligence, highly coercive interrogation techniques, and the long-term detention of suspects outside domestic or international law) may be both morally necessary and morally legitimate. The US has put great emphasis on this approach, as shown by the indefinite detention of prisoners at Camps Delta and X-Ray, the creation of special military tribunals to try terrorist suspects in the US (rather than either using its own civil courts or creating an international one), the bombing of Taliban and Al-Qaeda hideouts and positions, and the use of an unmanned Predator drone armed with Hellfire missiles to assassinate six Al-Qaeda "leaders" in Yemen.[20]

On the other hand, as Wheeler suggests,

the US did employ some restraints on its bombing and targeting during Operation Enduring Freedom – even if, as I will shortly suggest, these failed to prevent a disturbingly high number of civilian casualties and other potential violations of the laws of war. He argues that, "as in the Gulf War and Kosovo, collateral damage concerns were an integral part of the targeting process. Lawyers in the Pentagon and at the Combined Air Operations Centre at Prince Sultan Air Base in Saudi Arabia scrutinized targets for their legality under international humanitarian law."[21] This no doubt saved many lives, but we can reasonably suggest that comparisons with Operation Allied Force in Kosovo are misleading. As a Project on Defense Alternatives study (discussed below) shows, both total casualty rates and casualty rates per sortie were much higher in Afghanistan.[22]

The conduct of US and allied forces in Afghanistan and Iraq is analyzed in detail below. What becomes clear from this examination is that "bringing justice to our enemies" was the administration's and the Pentagon's primary response; a response characterized by Michael Byers as part of an evolving pattern in which the US "is attempting to create new, exceptional rules for itself alone" and by Abdullahi Ahmed An-Na'im as an "institutional and procedural failure of international legality" that "promotes the cause of militant Islamic fundamentalism and undermines prospects of support for international peace and universal human rights in Islamic societies."[23] Such a disregard for international law is built upon a particularly claustrophobic idea of moral community; a bifurcated moral universe which casts the US and its allies as virtuous and its enemies as ineradicably threatening and evil. As Wheeler points out, the administration's rhetoric equating Al-Qaeda and the Taliban with Nazism suggested that they were being constructed as such a threat to human values, as did Vice-President Cheney's statement that "We cannot deal with terror ... the struggle can only end with their complete and permanent destruction."[24]

[...]

### Just War, before and after 9/11

Just war theory claims to limit and control strategic violence in two ways: by limiting the circumstances under which one can resort to war (*jus ad bellum*), and by limiting the ways it can be fought (*jus in bello*). These roughly correspond with similar categories in international law (as laid out in the UN Charter and the Geneva Conventions) but cannot be reduced to them; furthermore, just war advocates do not require that states be accountable to international law. In her book *Women and War* Elshtain sets out the moral tests of just war as follows:

(1) that a war be the last resort to be used only after all other means have been exhausted; (2) that a war be clearly an act of redress of rights actually violated or defense against unjust demands backed by the threat of force; (3) that war be openly and legally declared by properly constituted governments; (4) that there be a reasonable prospect of victory; (5) that the means be proportionate to the ends; (6) that a war be waged in such a way as to distinguish between combatants and non-combatants; (7) that the victorious nation not require the utter humiliation of the vanquished.[25]

Just war advocates oppose force being used aggressively, for the purposes of national aggrandizement or imperialism; they oppose the preventive use of force, but are ambiguous about pre-emptive strikes; they advocate the use of peaceful efforts to deal with threats before war is tried; and they advocate the principles of "proportionality" and "non-combatant immunity" to limit the impact of war on civilians.

It is these last principles that, for me, are most controversial. Proportionality and non-combatant immunity are welcome brakes on the limitless application of force, but they are also beset with problems. First, the demand that means be matched to ends exposes a[n] … instrumentalism hiding in the interstices of just war theory, which accepts that (under more limited circumstances) war is a rational and controllable means to political ends. Second, the principle of non-combatant immunity is qualified by a judgement that "non-combatants must not be the *intended* targets of violence."[26] There is enormous scope for abuse here, compounded by an implicit assumption that decisions and acts of war are limited in space and time – that moral judgements about particular circumstances can be quarantined from the history preceding, or a future beyond, the cessation of high-intensity military operations. Once we begin to question these assumptions, morally neat arguments about the justice of strategic violence begin to unravel.

We can begin to test just war theory by examining the judgements its advocates have made about the legitimacy of armed force in the conflicts that have surrounded, preceded and followed the tragedy of 9/11: the Arab–Israeli conflict; the war against Soviet forces in Afghanistan; Operation Desert Storm; the sanctions and weapons inspection regime imposed on Iraq after 1990; and the post-9/11 wars against Afghanistan and Iraq. Focusing on two of the most influential theorists (Walzer and Elshtain), however, it is difficult to find a just war position that is consistent either between them, across examples or through time. For example, of Iraq Walzer

argues that much of the 1991 bombing was unjust: that "shielding civilians would certainly have excluded the destruction of electricity networks and water purification plants."[27] In 1995 Elshtain argued that just war principles should have governed the postwar situation in Iraq as well, and that the imposition of sanctions that were causing enormous suffering was not "ethically pristine … the rush to use embargoes and sanctions that target whole populations, harming the least powerful first, requires more justification than it has received from past and current policymakers."[28] Yet by 2003 she was marshalling just war arguments *in support* of the Bush administration's plans for war in Iraq, parroting administration propaganda that Iraq possessed a large arsenal of threatening weapons of mass destruction and supported Al-Qaeda, and arguing that "when a state destroys or is prepared to destroy its own citizens and propels its violence outside its own borders, it becomes a criminal entity."[29]

Elshtain's argument came with the usual *jus in bello* caveats about "proportionality" and "non-combatant immunity," but Walzer differed from her in arguing that there was no justification (*jus ad bellum*) for war with Iraq by 2003. Even though he supported immediate pre-emptive attacks in the case of Israel's 1967 war, he suggested that "the [Iraq] war that is being discussed is preventive, not pre-emptive – it is designed to respond to a more distant threat."[30] Elshtain counters that "imminent threat does not necessarily mean one that is just around the comer" but refers "to murderous capabilities that an outlaw regime is in the process of developing."[31] Walzer argues that the restoration of the weapons inspections is the best way to deal with such concerns, and that it is superior to preventive war "because the dangers to which it alludes are not only distant but speculative, whereas the costs of a preventive war are near, certain and usually terrible."[32] To this prospect Elshtain offers crocodile tears: "in any conflict non-combatants will fall in harm's way. But it is forbidden to knowingly and maliciously target them."[33]

The arguments of both here are replete with problems, at both the *jus in bello* and *jus ad bellum* levels. In relation to *jus ad bellum*, Elshtain stands on disappearing ground: months after the conclusion of the fighting, *no* weapons of mass destruction have yet been found, and no links to Al-Qaeda proven.[34] Then there is the pile of documentary and anecdotal evidence, dating back to a presidential finding signed by George Bush senior in 1992, that successive US governments had really been driven by an overriding policy aim to remove Saddam Hussein from power, and that influential neo-conservatives began to argue publicly in 1998 that CIA-directed covert operations should be abandoned in favour of a military invasion.[35] To this can be added the way the regime-change policy muddied the inspection waters, given the clear views of US officials that sanctions should remain until Saddam Hussein was removed from power, *even if the UN resolutions were complied with* – a scandalous position for a veto-wielding UN Security Council member to take.[36] Larger strategic objectives for control of the Middle East dating back to 1975 – the establishment of military bases in the Persian Gulf and Central Asia, removal of regimes in Iran and Syria, the strengthening of Israel and the control of Gulf oil supplies – also rank as plausible motives for the invasion of Iraq.[37] These facts shake both Elshtain's argument for the enforcement of UN resolutions with war in 2003, and Walzer's view that

> there was a just and necessary war waiting to be fought back in the 1990s when Saddam was playing hide-and-seek with the inspectors ... an internationalist war, a war of enforcement, and its justice would

have derived, first, from the justice of the system it was enforcing and, second, from its likely outcome: the strengthening of the UN and the global legal order.[38]

Not only are their analyses willfully naive about the cynical realism of US and European foreign policy with regard to Iraq – the double standard of states that had helped create Iraq's WMD capability before 1990 demanding compliance in its removal,[39] while remaining unwilling to disarm themselves – but they are silent about the crime against humanity perpetrated by the powers on the UN Security Council as they claimed to be enforcing its resolutions. Just war talk of "proportionality," "non-combatant immunity" and "the protection of innocents" is worth recalling here, when against the fear of Iraq's future use of WMD is balanced the death of more than a million Iraqi citizens as a result of sanctions which US officials, contrary to UN Resolutions 661 and 687, insisted should stay in place until Saddam Hussein was removed from power.[40] This was the "justice of the system it was enforcing": a crime against humanity perpetrated by the UN itself – an image of "justice" angrily purloined by Osama bin Laden in his 1998 interview with ABC and then directed, with terrifying intensity, into the heart of the United States three years later.[41] The continuing spectacle of western assumptions of moral superiority in relation to Iraq is deeply unsettling, when what would be more appropriate is the kind of soul-searching that accompanied postwar revelations of the Nazi Holocaust.

We are not to know whether or not Elshtain and Walzer believe that the impact of the sanctions amounted to a major international crime, but they have both used arguments that the death of civilians cannot be criminal if *jus ad bellum* conditions are met and the killing was *unintentional*. Indeed, in a combative 2003

*Public Interest* article Elshtain cites Walzer's attack on critics of the war against Afghanistan to press home this point. Against what he describes as "leftist" claims that the similarity of the death tolls on September 11 and in Afghanistan undermines the justice of the war, Walzer counters that this "denies one of the most basic and best understood moral distinctions between premeditated murder and unintentional killing."[42] Even if we were to accept this distinction (which seems to me to be a stunning evasion of responsibility), it is not as if the US were willing to make its armed forces accountable for their targeting decisions, having refused to place its forces under the jurisdiction of the International Criminal Court (ICC), which is currently the only body able to prosecute violations of the laws of war. In the absence of that accountability we are forced to rely on the arbitrary judgements of just war intellectuals, among whom Elshtain is convinced that "no group in the US pays more attention to ethical restraint on the use of force than does the US military" and that "the real dissenters in American intellectual life are likely to be those who, at least in part, defend the foreign policy of the United States."[43]

## Justice and "Proportionality": Killing Civilians in Afghanistan and Iraq

The distinction between intentional and unintentional killing is enshrined both in just war theory and in the Geneva Conventions as the "proportionality" rule. Article 51(5)(b) of Protocol 1 to the Conventions prohibits operations which "may be expected to cause incidental loss of civilian life, injury to civilians, damage to civilian objects, or a combination thereof, which would be excessive in relation to the concrete and direct military advantage anticipated." Nicholas Wheeler criticizes international humanitarian

law for being imprecise about what "constitutes 'excessive' civilian casualties or 'concrete and direct military advantage' in specific cases"; this imprecision, he argues, leaves "the door ... sufficiently wide open under Protocol 1 that states can justify the killing of innocent civilians as an unintended consequence of attacks against legitimate military targets" – a problem compounded by the fact that these provisions have rarely (if ever) been tested in a court. In this light, I can only agree with Wheeler's conclusion that "the proportionality rule is the Achilles heel of just war theory."[44]

Contrary to Elshtain's defensive protestations about the "ethical restraint" of the US military, its war-fighting strategies in Afghanistan and Iraq have both tested the (legal) limits of the proportionality rule and exposed its utter ethical inadequacy. The study conducted of Operation Enduring Freedom by the Project on Defense Alternatives (PDA), for example, conclusively refutes claims that the US fought with care to avoid harming civilians. Using deliberately conservative figures, its author Carl Conetta concluded that despite the US navy and air force flying *64 per cent fewer sorties* over Afghanistan than NATO in the Kosovo war, it caused *two to three times more direct civilian deaths* – the respective sortie/casualty ratios being approximately 4,700/1,000–1,300 in Afghanistan versus 13,000/500 in Yugoslavia (i.e., a civilian was killed every twenty-six sorties in Yugoslavia and every three or four sorties in Afghanistan).[45]

In the first half of 2002 *New York Times* reporters visited eleven locations where civilians were said to have been killed in US airstrikes, verifying the killing of nearly 400 people and the wounding of many more. These episodes included six massacres in which 50 or more were killed – including the death of 52 people in Niazi Qala in December 2001 after US planes bombed an ammunition dump moved there by Taliban forces, and the killing of 65 people at a mosque in Khost in November 2001, when a bomb aimed at a residence containing a Taliban leader went off course. Reporters who visited Niazi Qala wrote of seeing "bloodied children's shoes and shirts," "the scalp of a woman with braided grey hair," and the "severed shoe" of a child. In another atrocity a US AC-130 gunship attacked four villages near Kakrak in July 2002, killing 54 and wounding 120, during an operation aimed at hunting down and killing Al-Qaeda and Taliban leaders. Afterwards, "American soldiers found villagers gathering up the limbs of their neighbours."[46] Other events which ought to trouble both just war advocates and those concerned with US observance of international law include the targeting of civilian infrastructure, the deliberate bombing of the Al-Jazeera bureau in Kabul, the execution and mistreatment of prisoners in Northern Alliance hands, the enormous death and suffering attributable to the broader impact of US military operations, and the state of instability and crisis that was allowed to develop in Afghanistan following the fall of the Taliban.

Numerous reports attest to the killing and mistreatment of as many as 800 Taliban prisoners of war by Northern Alliance militias, including the execution of approximately 600 prisoners at Mazar-i-Sharif, many of them suffocated in sealed shipping containers.[47] US forces destroyed or damaged the main telephone exchange in Kabul, the electrical grid in Kandahar and the hydro-electric power station near the Kajaki dam, which would have exacerbated an already difficult humanitarian situation.[48] The PDA estimates that from mid-September 2001 to mid-January 2002, between 8,000 and 18,000 Afghanis died from starvation, injuries sustained as they fled combat zones, or exposure and associated illnesses. Of these 40 per cent (between 3,200

and 7,200) "are attribut[able] to the effects of the crisis and war." At the outset of the war the UN was estimating that 1.5 million people were at extreme risk; the military operations exacerbated this crisis by generating some 560,000 refugees, disrupting national-level food deliveries by 40 per cent in October 2001, and completely interrupting local food and aid deliveries for two to three months (and sometimes longer) in many places. At a time of enormously increased and desperate humanitarian need, this "more than doubled the size of the gap between the supply of aid and the need for it."[49]

How are these awful facts to be treated by the advocates of just war, given their concern for the proportional use of force, and the injunction that innocent life not be taken or maimed intentionally? Both Walzer and Elshtain have given Operation Enduring Freedom the imprimatur of a "just war" and aggressively challenged its critics. The allied forces, apparently, are guilty of no crimes – the death they caused was *unintentional*. Is *carelessness* really a defence? Carelessness, when civilians are killed in the course of aerial assassination operations based on poor intelligence and extra-legal principles, prosecuted in such an indiscriminate way as to leave entire villages filled with the dead and wounded? Carelessness, when an ammunition dump is seen as such a threat to allied troops as to justify its detonation, from the air, in the midst of a densely populated area? Carelessness, when it was highly predictable that thousands of vulnerable people would die fleeing areas where force was being deployed in such an indiscriminate manner and supplies of desperately needed aid disrupted? A more genuine test for the just warriors, and international law, would be whether *avoidable* death and suffering are condemned and prosecuted[50] – a test they refuse to accept, perhaps because it would undermine the sovereign prerogative of states to use force; it might begin genuinely to constrain war rather than liberate it.

Another profound flaw in just war theory is exposed by the suffering and instability faced by the people of Afghanistan following the fall of the Taliban. Afghanistan has been left with an enormous humanitarian crisis, damaged and deteriorated infrastructure, a vacuum of legitimate authority outside Kabul that has been filled by warlords (many allied with the US), and a massive resumption of opium production. While the Bonn Agreement on a new democratic framework for Afghanistan was welcome, it has been undermined by the precarious nature of the interim government's authority and by the refusal of the US and Russia to encourage the creation of a nationwide peacekeeping force that might challenge warlord power. The 4,500 troops of the International Security Assistance Force (ISAF) are a shadow of the 30,000 the PDA estimated would be needed to have "mitigated the challenges faced by the interim government, dampened the potential for internecine violence, and facilitated humanitarian relief efforts." Such a force could also have "served to support disarmament efforts and train a new national army," which along with a large civilian police force is seen as essential to re-establishing security; but observers now say that "it will take a number of years for a fully functional national army and police force to be developed."[51] Peter Marsden rightly insists that "security is regarded by all as the absolute prerequisite for a successful reconstruction process," but by making deals with warlords to enable continued military operations against Al-Qaeda and the Taliban to take place, the US appears (in a typically realist fashion) to have valued its own security over that of the Afghan people.[52] While the adoption of a new constitution in late 2003 and planned elections for 2004 are extremely positive developments, continuing warlord power and a resurgence of

Taliban attacks suggest to many that the basic stability necessary to secure Afghanistan's political future may never be achieved.[53]

Security failures have been matched by a failure to provide adequate aid: even though a joint study prepared for the January 2002 meeting of donors in Tokyo estimated that reconstruction costs would range from $14.6 billion to $18.1 billion over ten years, donors pledged only $5.2 billion, a third of the per capita amount allocated to the Balkans, Palestine and East Timor after recent emergencies. As of 25 September 2002 only $960 million had been disbursed, in comparison with an estimated $3.8 billion for the first three months of US military operations.[54] No one could plausibly deny that by waging war against Afghanistan in its own interests the West did not also contract a responsibility for the country's future; yet such a failure of responsibility and justice is of little matter to just war theory because it limits its moral system, in time and space, to high-intensity war. Walzer does appear troubled by this, advocating the development of a theory of "justice-in-endings" and saying that "once we have acted in ways that have significant negative consequences for other people (even if there were positive consequences) we cannot just walk away ... the work of the virtuous is never finished."[55] He criticized the US for abandoning Afghanistan after the defeat of the Soviet-backed regime, and in a *Ha'aretz* interview said that US post-Taliban policy was "shameful ... if you fight such a war, you have a responsibility to create a minimum of law and order in the country which you have invaded."[56]

The war in Iraq, begun 18 months after the September 11 attacks, raises the same problems for just war theory and international law, but even more intensely. There are similar problems of violation of *jus in bello* rules and postwar instability, compounded by a globally accepted view that the war was illegal under international law (and thus an act of aggression) and also failed to satisfy just war's *jus ad bellum* criteria.[57] As such, the death of every single Iraqi combatant, not merely those of "innocent" civilians, must be considered a crime. Iraqi military deaths, while hard to assess, have been estimated by Jonathon Steele at between 3 and 10 per cent of functioning units, or between 13,500 and 45,000 individuals; completely outmatched by US technology, Iraqi troops died under volleys of cluster rockets, fire from helicopter gunships and carpets of bombs from B-52s.[58] The civilian death toll is also extremely high, and climbing. At the time of writing, in January 2004, the website "Iraq Body Count" estimated a minimum civilian death toll attributable to the invasion and subsequent counterinsurgency operations of 8,014 and a maximum of 9,852.[59] Another casualty tracking project by the PDA has not compiled total estimates, but cites a number of incidents and surveys which make very disturbing reading.[60]

A *Knight-Ridder* newspapers survey of 19 Baghdad hospitals after the fall of the city estimated that at least 1,101 civilians and another 1,255 who were "probably civilians" were killed after the war began on 19 March, while a *Los Angeles Times* survey of 27 hospitals concluded that at least 1,700 were killed and 8,000 injured, not counting "hundreds" of "undocumented civilian deaths" reported by "Islamic burial societies and humanitarian groups that are trying to trace those missing in the conflict," and "dozens of deaths that doctors indirectly attributed to the conflict … pregnant women who died of complications while giving birth at home … and chronically ill people, such as cardiac or dialysis patients, who were unable to obtain needed care while fighting raged." High numbers of civilian (and some military) deaths were reported by hospitals in other cities, such as Basra (400), Hilla

(250), Najaf (378) and Nasiriyah (250). When these totals are added to the *Knight-Ridder* survey of hospitals in Baghdad, the death toll is approximately 3,634, the vast majority of the dead civilians. The PDA also cites another 37 reports of mid-war incidents in which at least 650 civilians were killed, a report from Najaf cemetery suggesting 2,000 excess burials during the fighting, and, following the liberation, 200 deaths from unexploded ordnance and 34 civilians killed by US forces during protests and civil disturbances.[61]

These shockingly high casualty figures were incurred during bombing, missile strikes, artillery, mortar and small arms fire, cluster bombing, and attacks from helicopter gunships – all in the face of claims in glossy State Department documents about the "strategic imperative" of the US air force paying close attention to the law of armed conflict using technologies such as laser-guided bombs and collateral damage assessment software.[62] In the vast majority of the incidents allied forces used indiscriminate force against targets which were civilian in nature or were close to heavily populated civilian areas.[63] The humanitarian crisis the war provoked was compounded by airstrikes against electricity generators and telephone exchanges, and widespread looting after the liberation (which US troops stood by and watched, while ensuring the Iraqi Oil Ministry was secure). Some hospitals were forced to close, or could not gain access to power or water, while patients were deterred from seeking help because of the general insecurity.[64] Some of the more notorious incidents included jittery US troops shooting child weapons collectors and firing on vehicles approaching checkpoints, and airstrikes on the Al-Shaab and Al-Nasser marketplaces in Baghdad which killed 76 and injured 77. Journalists were also murdered in a US airstrike on the Al-Jazeera office and tank fire on the Palestine Hotel: clear and chilling violations of the laws of war.[65]

Nothing in the Iraq experience justifies the faith that Elshtain and others have placed in the US military's responsibility and restraint; indeed, as in Afghanistan, that experience reveals the just warriors' excuse that the killing was "unintentional" to be little more than a moral smokescreen for the indiscriminate application of strategic violence. Likewise, the idea that "proportionality" would suffice to balance the suffering, instability and chaos caused by the invasion against some greater "social good" drives just war theory "perilously close to moral incoherence," as Wheeler remarked of its faith in such a "double effect."[66] Ironic, then, that in justifying the war Elshtain wrote that "it is better to put one's own combatants in danger than stand by as the innocent are slaughtered" – this, when a US soldier at Kerbala was quoted as saying: "I think they thought we wouldn't shoot kids. But we showed them that we don't care. We are going to do what we have to do to stay alive and keep ourselves safe."[67]

In her June 2002 *Boston Globe* article and the November 2002 *Statement of Principles* on Iraq published by the Institute for American Values (also signed by Francis Fukuyama, Robert Putnam and Theda Skocpol), Elshtain relied on the enforcement of UN resolutions to justify war against Iraq.[68] However, by May 2003, relying on the "double effect," she had shifted register to focus on the liberation of Iraqis from the brutal Hussein regime: "Are we just going to provide iodine and band aids or might it be necessary, as Bonhoeffer put it, to 'cut off the head of the snake'?"[69] We could ask why, if it was so genuinely concerned by the suffering of the Iraqi people, the US supported Hussein through his gassing of Kurds and Iranian troops; why it helped cause the death of a million Iraqis through sanctions while claiming to be so opposed to their oppressor; and why it does not support the ICC

and the indictment of terrorists and torturers everywhere.

This new, humanitarian justification for the war also raises another question of the advocates who have stolen the robes of the judge: *who* gets to wage just war? Does every sufferer of harm and injustice, or merely those who have the power and the means, and who can turn their justifications into truth? Surely, if the just warriors are right, the Palestinian people had a right to wage just war on Israel after its 1982 invasion of Lebanon and the massacres in Sabra and Shatila which the Israel Defense Force helped to organize and enable?[70] Surely the Palestinians had the right to invade Israel, remove its government and impose one which would create a just peace and right the historic wrong imposed on them after 1948? Surely, as Elshtain says of Iraq, they had a "claim to have coercive force deployed [on their] behalf to stop the Lions before they crush and devour all the Lambs"?[71] However, such an argument would rightly disturb those who, whatever its flaws, wish to support Israeli democracy and halt the awful cycle of violence and retribution that has driven this conflict for decades, and who believe that the conflict must be resolved with a measure of security and justice for both peoples. In short, the weak do not get to wage just war. Their "innocence" goes undefended....

## Ethical Peace

The manifest failures of just war theory, of current systems of international law relating to armed conflict, of operational military restraint, and of so much western defence and foreign policy demand the imagination of alternatives that better reflect the near-universal view that the use of force should be subject to moral restraint. I want to outline these alternatives tentatively here under a set of principles I term "ethical peace." I do this with a respectful refusal of Nicholas Rengger's appeal against abandoning the just war tradition, preferring instead to pick up his challenge to "start afresh and think our own ideas on how to legitimate and justify force." I will, however, try to build upon his anxiety about the way in which the context-based "casuistical" mode of practical reasoning represented by the earlier just war tradition was reified into a modernist (scientistic) *theory* "to be used as a kind of moral slide rule from which legitimate instances of the use of force can be read off whenever necessary."[72]

Ethical peace differs from "just war" by rejecting the latter's prima facie acceptance of the legitimacy of strategic violence, and by making peace – however complex, difficult and delayed – its central normative goal. Ethical peace refuses to provide legitimacy to strategic policy and strategic violence, even as it accepts that the prevalence of such violence means that it cannot be quickly eliminated. Important questions of national security and strategic stability necessitate a coordinated and gradual approach to the elimination of force from international life, accompanied by sustained and imaginative efforts to promote disarmament and resolve conflict. In this respect, the appalling double standards over weapons of mass destruction – in which it is illegal for North Korea, Iran or Iraq to possess them but fine for the US, Israel, Russia, the UK, France and China – must be eliminated.[73] Ethical peace also accepts that humanitarian intervention may be necessary and valuable at times, but that continuous debate over the conditions, experience and practice of such intervention is needed, given the very problematic experiences of recent years in Somalia, Bosnia and Herzegovina, East Timor, Rwanda, Kosovo and Cambodia.[74] The use of humanitarian arguments for an imperialist war against Iraq, and the subversion of effective peacekeeping in post-Taliban Afghanistan by US priorities, have muddied these waters even further.

Ethical peace assumes that if the short- to medium-term existence of strategic violence is to be accepted, it must only be *conditional*, and used only under conditions far more stringent, enforceable and morally consistent than have so far been provided by either just war theory or international law. The first step is to ensure that the international legal frameworks provided by the United Nations Charter, the law of armed conflict and the covenants on human rights form the starting point for decisions about coercion and the use of armed force (while also acknowledging that decisions of the UN Security Council are sometimes tainted by power play, and that its voting structures and membership need reform). Embodied in international law are important liberal and humanitarian principles that forbid armed aggression and the abuse of human rights, legitimate the resort to force only after all other alternatives have been exhausted, and impose legal restraints on the use of that force. The UN also provides frameworks which allow for the creation of enforcement and judicial bodies, both on a permanent basis (such as the ICC) and on an ad hoc basis (such as the International Criminal Tribunal for the Former Yugoslavia).[75] If the US had asked the Security Council to create an international criminal tribunal to try the perpetrators of the African embassy bombings and the 9/11 attacks, it might have set in motion the creation of an enduring, impartial legal framework to punish, deter and delegitimate the very lethal forms of terrorism that have emerged in recent years. Instead, just warriors find themselves defending violent, extralegal approaches which undermine international humanitarian law and create a level of global anger that cannot but manifest itself in future atrocities.

Ethical peace would also demand that

action be taken to ensure that existing international law relating to human rights and armed conflict was consistently enforced – that resources be devoted to the ICC to enable it to prosecute violations, that the UN Human Rights Commission be reformed and given the ability to launch investigations and prosecutions, and that UN member states agree to make their policy-makers and soldiers accountable to international law. The Geneva Conventions also need reforming – not to remove constraints on armed forces, but to tighten them.[76] The principles of "proportionality" and "unintentional" killing, which have created loopholes that have cost thousands of civilian lives in recent conflicts, need to be abandoned in favour of a principle that declares the illegality of *avoidable* harm....

The capricious attitude of just war theorists to international law – enforce it here, ignore or undermine it there – mirrors that of the most cynical realists, and is particularly egregious given their claim to provide a universal moral theory of force. Too often, just warriors seek to enshrine their isolated and partisan advocacy as moral truth, to steal for themselves the "tragic vocation of the judge" rather than submit the decisions they exonerate from blame to international structures of judgement that can be debated, scrutinized and enforced....

[E]thical peace makes no claims to be a universal political or ethical theory, but *would* be driven by a view that the protection of innocent life is a universally applicable principle – unlike just war theory which, even as it asserts that it has universal moral validity, uses concepts like "proportionality" and the "double effect" to remove thousands of people from the space of moral concern....

## Study Questions

1. Describe the components of "ethical peace" as Burke lays them out. How might these standards differ from just war criteria in deciding when to use brute force against others?

2. What main thesis is Burke attempting to support in regard to the adequacy of just war theory by reviewing the killing of civilians in Afghanistan and Iraq?

3. What assumption, according to Burke, has made war such a "pervasive modern phenomenon"? Can you name examples, such as speeches, committee hearings, or news reports, which communicate with this assumption in mind?

4. Both Orend and Burke draw extensively on Walzer. What are the similarities and differences in Orend's and Burke's applications of Walzer's principles?

## Notes

1 Phillip Vellacott, "Introduction," in *Prometheus Bound, The Suppliants, Seven Against Thebes and The Persians* (London: Penguin, 1961), p. 7.
2 Michael Walzer, "The Triumph of Just War Theory (and the Dangers of Success)," *Social Research* 69:4, Winter 2002, pp. 925–46.

3   Bernard Brodie, *War and Politics* (London: Cassell, 1973), pp. 45–46. My thanks to Alex Bellamy and Marianne Hanson, organizers of the "Ethics and Foreign Policy" symposium at the University of Queensland, July 2003, for which this article was drafted.

4   Ibid., p. 46.

5   James Der Derian, *Virtuous War: Mapping the Military-Industrial Media Entertainment Network* (Boulder: Westview, 2001).

6   As David Campbell and Michael Shapiro suggest, "far from being a principle that keeps morality at bay, reason of state constitutes the realist problematic as a moral argument in which the claim is that 'the reasons for overriding the constraints of ordinary morality in emergency situations are themselves moral.'" David Campbell and Michael Shapiro, eds., "Introduction," in *Moral Spaces: Rethinking Ethics and World Politics* (Minneapolis: Minnesota UP, 1999), p. vii.

7   See Jean Bethke Elshtain, "A Just War?," *Boston Globe*, 10 June 2002.

8   Vivienne Jabri, *Discourses on Violence* (Manchester: Manchester UP, 1996), pp. 104–07. See also Martin Shaw, *War and Genocide* (Cambridge: Polity, 2003), p. 103.

9   Nicholas Rengger, "On the Just War Tradition in the Twenty-First Century," *International Affairs* 78: 2, April 2002, p. 358.

10  Jean Bethke Elshtain, "How to Fight a Just War," in Ken Booth and Tim Dunne, eds, *Worlds in Collision: Terror and the Future of Global Order* (Hampshire and New York: Palgrave Macmillan, 2002), p. 264 and cited in Carlin Romano, "Case for Justice in War on Iraq," *Philadelphia Inquirer*, 16 March 2003.

11  Walzer, "The Triumph of Just War Theory," part I.

12  Carl von Clausewitz, *On War*, ed. Anatole Rapoport (London: Penguin, 1982). p. 118.

13  Michael Walzer appears to recognize this problem when he argues that recent wars raise stability, reconstruction and continuing humanitarian crisis as issues for the further development of just war theory. Importantly, he acknowledges that just war theorists are yet to do this; more problematically, his argument suggests that, should militaries begin to resolve this problem, it will be easier to pronounce future wars as "just." Walzer, "The Triumph of Just War Theory," part II.

14  Elshtain, "How to Fight a Just War," p. 263.

15  George W. Bush, "Address to a Joint Session of Congress and the American People," 20 September 2001, http://www.whitehouse.gov/news/releases/2001/Q9/20010920--8.html.

16  Ibid.

17  Elshtain, "How to Fight a Just War," p. 264.

18  Nicholas Wheeler, "Dying for 'Enduring Freedom': Accepting Responsibility for Civilian Casualties in the War against Terrorism," *International Relations* 16: 2, 2002, p. 206.

19  Bush, "Address to a Joint Session of Congress."

20  On Camp X-Ray see Suvendrini Perera, "What Is a Camp?," *Borderlands e-journal* I: I, 2002, http:// www.borderlandsejournal.adelaide.edu.au/; the Predator attack is described in Fred Kaplan, "Bush's Army – or Bill's?," *Slate*, 2 May 2003, http://slate.msn.com/.

21  Wheeler, "Dying for 'Enduring Freedom,'" p. 211.

22  Carl Conetta, *Operation Enduring Freedom: Why a Higher Rate of Civilian Bombing Casualties?*, Briefing Report no. 11, Commonwealth Institute Project on Defense Alternatives, Cambridge, MA, Jan. 2002, http://www.comw.org/pda/0201oef.html.

23  Michael Byers, "Terror and the Future of International Law" and Abdullahi Ahmed An-Na'im, "Upholding International Legality against Islamic and American Jihad," both in Booth and Dunne, eds, *Worlds in Collision*, pp. 118–27 and 162–71.

24  Wheeler, "Dying for 'Enduring Freedom,'" p. 216.

25  Elshtain, *Women and War*, p. 150.

26  Elshtain, "How to Fight a Just War," p. 263.

27  Walzer, "The Triumph of Just War Theory," part I.

28  Elshtain, *Women and War*, p. 265.

29  Elshtain, "A Just War?"

30  Michael Walzer, "No Strikes – Inspectors Yes, War No," *New Republic*, 30 September 2002, p. 19.

31  Elshtain, "A Just War?"

32  Walzer, "No Strikes – Inspectors Yes, War No."

33  Elshtain, "A Just War?"

34  Nicholas D. Kristof, "Missing in Action: Truth," *New York Times*, 6 May 2003, http://www.nytimes.com/2003IOs/o6/opinion/o6KRIS.htm.

35  Andrew and Patrick Cockburn, *Saddam Hussein: an American Obsession* (London: Verso, 2002), p. 31; Transcript, "American Dreamers," *ABC Four Corners*, 10 March 2003, http://www.abc.net.au/4comers/content/2003 /transcripts/ s8or 456.htm.

36  US Deputy National Security Advisor Robert Gates said in May 1991 that economic sanctions would remain in place and that "Iraqis will pay the price" while Saddam remained in power. Cockburn and Cockburn, *Saddam Hussein*, p. 114.

37  Robert Dreyfuss, "The Thirty-Year Itch," *Mother Jones*, 1 March 2003, http://motherjones.com/news/feature/200J/Io/ma_273_0I.html.

38  Walzer, "No Strikes – Inspectors Yes, War No."

39  See the arguments made by Phyllis Bennis of the Institute for Policy Studies that a US company, the American Type Culture Collection, sold Iraq the seed stock for *E. coli*, anthrax and botulism: "American Dreamers."

40  By the end of 1995 alone the UN Food and Agriculture Organization estimated that 576,000 children had died as a result of sanctions, and the World Health Organization estimated that 90,000 Iraqis were dying in hospitals every year over and above normal mortality rates. Cockburn and Cockburn, *Saddam Hussein*, p. 137.

41  Bin Laden specifically mentioned the sanctions toll in Iraq and claimed that US failure to distinguish between civilians and combatants justified Al-Qaeda in targeting American and Jewish civilians: "We believe that the biggest thieves in the world and the terrorists are the Americans. The only way for us to fend off these assaults is to use similar means." John Miller, "Talking with Terror's Banker," May 1998, http://www.ABCNews.com/.

42  Jean Bethke Elshtain, "Intellectual Dissent and the War on Terror," *Public Interest*, Spring 2003, p. 93.

43  Ibid., p. 95.

44  Wheeler, "Dying for 'Enduring Freedom,'" p. 209.

45  Conetta suggests a range of reasons for the change: the differing objectives of the operations (coercive diplomacy versus regime change and destruction of enemy personnel); a greater reliance on cluster bombs and GPS-guided bombs such as the Joint Direct Attack Munition QDAM) as opposed to laser-guided weapons; a heavy reliance on bombers such as the B-1 and B-52 (rather than the B-2 in Yugoslavia), which resulted in 40 per cent of attacks being with unguided ("dumb") weapons and another 40 per cent with the less accurate GPS-guided weapons; bombing activity being concentrated in heavily populated areas where "the fronts of the ethnic war … tended to form"; the higher number of opportunistic attacks using dumb weapons based on real-time intelligence; and the reliance on suspect intelligence supplied by Northern Alliance militias, which saw US bombers being co-opted into murderous local rivalries. Conetta, *Operation Enduring Freedom: Why a Higher Rate of Civilian Bombing Casualties?*

46  Dexter Filkins, "Flaws in US Air War Left Hundreds of Civilians Dead," *New York Times*, 21 July 2002; Fairness and Accuracy in Reporting, "Action Alert: NYT Buries Story of Airstrikes on Afghan Civilians', 9 January 2002, http://www.fair.org/activism/nyt-niazi-kala.html.

47 Carl Conetta, *Strange Victory: A Critical Appraisal of Operation Enduring Freedom and the Afghanistan War*, Project on Defense Alternatives Research Monograph no. 6, January 2002, http://www.comw.org/pda/020isttangevic. html; "600 Bodies Discovered in Mazar-al-Sharif: ICRC," Agence France Presse, 22 Nov. 2001; "International Red Cross Investigating Reports of Taliban Prisoner Container Deaths," AP Worldstream, 11 December 2001.

48 Wheeler, "Dying for 'Enduring Freedom,'" p. 213.

49 Conetta, *Strange Victory*.

50 For example, in a post-9/11 essay Andrew Linklater writes of the "challenge of ensuring that efforts to protect innocent civilians from terrorist attacks do not damage the moral ideal of freeing all human beings from unnecessary suffering ... that the 'civilising' process of eradicating indefensible violence does not have the paradoxical effect of creating 'de-civilising processes' that cause many human beings avoidable distress and injury." Andrew Linklater, "Unnecessary Suffering," in Booth and Dunne, eds, *Worlds in Collision*, p. 303.

51 Peter Marsden, "Afghanistan: the Reconstruction Process," *International Affairs* 79: 1, January 2003, p. 103; Conetta, *Strange Victory*, part 4.3; William Maley, "The Reconstruction of Afghanistan," in Booth and Dunne, eds, *Worlds in Collision*, pp. 184–93.

52 Marsden, "Afghanistan: The Reconstruction Process," p. 103.

53 Sam Zia-Zarifi, "Losing the Peace in Afghanistan," *World Report 2004: Human Rights and Armed Conflict* (New York: Human Rights Watch, 2004), pp. 61–92; Pamela Constable, "Afghan Militia Leaders Sign Truce; 50 Slain in Fighting; Rivalry Still Threatens Plan for Disarmament," *Washington Post*, 10 October 2003, p. A21.

54 Marsden, "Afghanistan: The Reconstruction Process," p. 93; Connetta, *Strange Victory*, part 1.2.

55 Walzer, "The Triumph of Just War Theory," part II.

56 Yair Sheleg, "Splitting Hairs on War," *Ha'aretz*, 26 June 2003.

57 Editorial, "Fruits of Disorder," *Boston Globe*, 20 May 2003; Ellen Goodman, "Conned into Conflict," *Boston Globe*, 18 May 2003; Seymour Hersh, "Selective Intelligence," *New Yorker*, 12 May 2003; Sydney Schanberg, "Let Us Count the Lies on the Road to War," *Village Voice*, 2–8 April 2003, http://www.villagevoice.com/issues/ 0314/schanberg.php.

58 Jonathon Steele, "Body Counts," *Guardian*, 28 May 2003; Lindsay Murdoch, "'We Shoot Them Down like the Morons They Are': US general," *Sydney Morning Herald*, 9 April 2003.

59 Iraq Body Count, http://www.iraqbodycount.net. The methodology used by this project involves, in their words, "cross-checking reports of casualties based on a comprehensive survey of online media reports and eyewitness accounts. Where these sources report differing figures, the range (a minimum and a maximum) are given and factored into totals." Incidents credited by the project must be reported by at least two distinct sources, and the compilers seem careful to use later investigations of incidents to correct sometimes erroneous early reporting. Of a number of projects attempting to amass statistics for civilian casualties, this appears to be the most careful and comprehensive; however, the limitations of its sourcing approach must be taken into account. Its figures, in my view, may be relied upon as a strong but not definitive guide to the true picture.

60 Melissa Murphy and Carl Conetta, *Civilian Casualties in the 2003 Iraq War: A Compendium of Accounts and Reports*, Project on Defense Alternatives, 21 May 2003.

61 Ibid.

62 David Anthony Benny, "US Air Force Uses New Tools to Minimize Civilian Casualties," US Department of State International Information Programs, http://usinfo.state.gov/regional/ nea/Iraq/0J03 I 804.html.

63 Suzanne Goldenberg, "A Picture of Killing Inflicted on a Sprawling City – and It Grew More Unbearable by the Minute," *Guardian*, 9 April 2003.

64 Cahal Milmo and Andrew Buncombe, "Surgeons Using Headache Pills instead of Anaesthetic," *Independent*, 9 April 2003; Murphy and Conetta, *Civilian Casualties in the 2003 Iraq War*; editorial, "Fruits of Disorder," *Boston Globe*, 20 May 2003; "Joy and Chaos," *Mother Jones*, 11 April 2003.

65 Craig Nelson, "The Killer Attack Journalists Never Saw Coming," *Sydney Morning Herald*, 10 April 2003; Reuters, "Killing a Child: 'I Did What I Had to Do,'" *Sydney Morning Herald*, 8 April 2003; Robert Fisk, "Is There Some Element in the US Military that Wants to Take Out Journalists?," *Independent*, 9 April 2003.

66 Jean Bethke Elshtain, "Commentary: Thinking about War and Justice," Religion and Culture Web Forum, May 2003, Martin Marty Center, http://marty-center.uchicago.edu/webforum/05200J/commentary.shtml; Wheeler, "Dying for 'Enduring Freedom,'" p. 208.

67 Elshtain, "A Just War?," Reuters, "Killing a Child."

68 Institute for American Values, "Pre-emption, Iraq, and Just War: a Statement of Principles," 14 November 2002, http://www.americanvalues.org/html/I b_pre-emption.html.

69 Elshtain, "Commentary: Thinking about War and Justice."

70 See Robert Fisk, *Pity the Nation: Lebanon at War* (Oxford: Oxford UP, 2001), pp. 243–400; Avi Shlaim, *The Iron Wall: Israel and the Arab World* (London: Penguin, 2000), pp. 415–17.

71 Elshtain, "Commentary: Thinking about War and Justice."

72 Rengger, "On the Just War Tradition," pp. 363, 360.

73 Roland Bleiker, "A Rogue Is a Rogue Is a Rogue: US Foreign Policy and the Korean Nuclear Crisis," *International Affairs* 79: 4, July 2003.

74 Nicholas J. Wheeler, *Saving Strangers: Humanitarian Intervention in International Society* (Oxford: Clarendon, 2000); Alex Bellamy, *Kosovo and International Society* (London: Palgrave Macmillan, 2002); Mary Kaldor, *New and Old Wars* (Cambridge: Polity, 1998).

75 Geoffrey Robertson, *Crimes against Humanity: the Struggle for Global Justice* (London: Penguin, 2000), pp. 285–367.

76 In the wake of the Iraq war, right-wing US law professors such as Alfred P. Rubin and Kenneth Anderson have been arguing that the Geneva Conventions are not "realistic," especially in their assumption that "military planners can easily differentiate between civilians and combatants." See Susan Milligan and Ross Kerber, "Geneva Conventions: Viability of WWII-Era Rules of War Questioned," *Boston Globe*, 2 April 2003.

# 5. Larry Minear, "Conscience and Carnage in Afghanistan and Iraq: US Veterans Ponder the Experience"

IN THIS 2014 ESSAY from the *Journal of Military Ethics*, Larry Minear (b. 1936) uses the recent experiences of men and women in uniform fighting in the Iraq and Afghanistan wars to revisit the ethically challenging issues that come with conscientious objection. A conscientious objector (CO) is someone who refuses to engage in military service on the grounds that doing so profoundly violates his or her moral and/or religious beliefs. Typically, CO status is granted to those seeking complete recuse from military service (often because they have been drafted). However, Minear addresses the complexities that arise when individuals already in the military face difficult ethical challenges given several factors: for example, direct and consistent exposure to violence and carnage, especially when it relates to the death of innocent civilians; objections to the dehumanizing treatment of the "enemy"; the constant suspension of the Rules of Engagement (which relaxes the conditions under which a person may be killed); and the perceived violation of trust in the soldier–state compact. Minear highlights the troubling ways in which COs are treated in the military, and encourages all of us, as a society, to use the unique ethical issues raised by the Iraq and Afghanistan wars as an avenue for encouraging soldiers to voice their moral concerns about the conflicts for which they are expected to fight and die. This, in turn, may incite a needed national dialogue about the ethical dimensions of the wars our governments wage in our name.

## Introduction

IN MY SCORES OF interviews beginning in late 2006 with US veterans of the Afghanistan and Iraq wars, the subject of conscientious objection was conspicuous by its relative absence. If mentioned at all, it was usually noted in passing. The infrequent mention seemed anomalous since the wars in Afghanistan and Iraq created many well-documented problems of conscience for those involved.

The research questions are legion. How many conscientious objectors (hereafter, COs) were there in the two conflicts? What did they find most inimical to their consciences? How were they viewed and treated by the military? Why would persons who enlist in

the now all-voluntary US armed forces refuse to bear arms in Afghanistan or Iraq – and why would their refusal be accepted? What impact, if any, did persons granted military discharges for reasons of conscience have on the conduct of the wars and on their peers? What are the implications of their experience for future US national security policy?

[...]

In the last several years, my efforts to publicize my findings have often taken the form of panel discussions that have included veterans who invariably express strong personal views about disquieting aspects of their service. I began to realize that many of those who articulated serious doubts about an entire range of *ius* [i.e., *jus*] *ad bellum* and *ius in bello* issues, while not classified as COs, were posing questions similar to those raised by soldiers who received (or were denied) discharges from the military on grounds of conscience.

In short, today's prototypical CO is not the bespectacled Quaker ambulance driver in the First World War France or the soft-spoken Mennonite performing alternative service on the home front as a school janitor in the Second World War. It is the young Marine, still in his (or often her) 20s or early 30s, heavily tattooed, angry, and eloquent in struggling to make sense of the war experience. Augmenting the ranks of recognized COs were many others, often hiding in plain sight.

[...]

**Carnage**

Most of the 2.5 million US troops who deployed to Afghanistan and Iraq witnessed carnage of colossal magnitude and fierce intensity. Judging from the accounts of veterans, it was – beyond the casualties sustained by the troops themselves – the deaths of civilians and the destruction of civilian infrastructure that caused the most profound revulsion in the ranks against the wars. Even those with backgrounds in emergency medical care and trauma treatment were unprepared for what they saw.

In his 13 years as a policeman, Sgt. Greg Mayfield had seen "two people die in front of my face." On duty in Iraq, by contrast, "we sat and watched three people die in an hour" (Minear 2010: 63). Kevin Shangraw of the New Hampshire National Guard recalls seeing the remains of a woman who had been struck by a convoy being zipped into a body bag. "I'll remember that for the rest of my life," he said. "The Iraqi people are who we are there to help and we just killed one of them" (Minear 2010: 81). Josh Barber, who witnessed a suicide bombing in 2004 that killed 22 people in Iraq, told his wife that he would "never be free of the smell of death." He took his own life in 2008 (Minear 2010: 57).

By 2007, the New Hampshire National Guard had established a correlation between the duration and intensity of conflict experienced and the likelihood of post-traumatic stress disorder (PTSD) (Minear 2010: 151). The more frequent and intense the deployments, the more likely PTSD. Already in 2006, the coordinator of PTSD centers for the Veterans Administration, Dr. Matthew J. Friedman, was expressing his judgment that "the wars in Afghanistan and Iraq are likely to produce a new generation of veterans with chronic mental health problems associated with participation in combat. Most people who have survived this experience will be changed by it, whether crossing some psychiatric threshold or not" (Minear 2010: 159).[1]

Many soldiers found the violence against children particularly unsettling. According to one study published in 2004, some 46 per cent of the US troops stationed in Afghanistan and 69 per cent of those in Iraq had seen wounded children and women whom they were unable to help (Hoge et al. 2004). In fact, the Rules of Engagement in some areas specified that drivers of US military vehicles not stop for children on the roads for fear of ambush.

Children were indeed part of the conflict. Some were curious bystanders, but others served as spotters of military convoys, providing detailed information to the insurgents. How could soldiers tell the difference? One analyst observed:

If you're looking at a kid on the side of the road with something in his hand, if it's a grenade and he throws it and kills someone in your unit, you've failed your comrade. But if it's a rock, you've just shot a kid with a rock. (Freedman 2013)[2]

Soldiers were frequently forced to make life-and-death decisions in split seconds and then left to ponder the results.

Capt. Ed Hrivnak, a veteran of Rwanda, Somalia, Bosnia and Operation Desert Storm, recalls a conversation with a fellow soldier whom he was medevacing (evacuating for medical reasons) following an injury. The wounded American confided that:

he had witnessed some Iraqi children get run over by a convoy. He was in the convoy and they had strict orders not to stop. If a vehicle stops, it is isolated and an inviting target for a rocket-propelled grenade…. But the convoys do not stop. He tells me that dealing with that image is worse than the pain of his injury. (Minear 2010: 81)

Violence engulfing children also stirred memories of the soldiers' own children, separated from them by the war. After veterans returned home, images of the wars remained vivid. Experiences with children imperiled by combat also affected relationships between veterans and their own families. Some spouses were unwilling to leave their husbands at home alone with their children….

Such carnage, however troubling for some, does not correlate directly with the incidence of conscientious objection. Some soldiers were surrounded by mayhem but did not become COs. Others became COs without ever participating in military operations. Many, however, were affected by the violence in which they, too, were participants. They became indelibly aware of what young 2nd Lt. Wilfred Owen of the Artists' Rifles group, writing from the trenches of the First World War, called "war and the pity of war."[3]

## Policy and Practice

The Department of Defense (DoD) has a clear policy recognizing the legitimacy of conscientious objection. A DoD Instruction defines conscientious objection as "a firm, fixed, and sincere objection to participation in war in any form or the bearing of arms, by reason of religious training and/or belief."[4] The Instruction stipulates that "administrative discharge due to conscientious objection prior to the completion of an obligated term of service is discretionary with the Military Department concerned, based on a judgment of the facts and circumstances in the case."[5] The military acknowledges that an individual, for reasons of conscience, may seek to be relieved of his or her duties and accepts its obligation to give such a person a fair hearing.

In the US, exemption from military service on grounds of conscience has been a relative constant over the years. However, Congress and the courts have generally treated conscientious objection as a privilege rather than as a right. "Exemption from military service is a matter of legislative grace," observed one federal court opinion, "and not a matter of right."[6] The courts have held that in raising and equipping armies, Congress has no specific obligation to exempt any individual from military service for any reason. However, once it decides to allow exceptions, it must frame all exceptions with equity and consistency. In some other industrialized countries, conscientious objection enjoys the firmer status of a right. At the international level as well, conscientious objection is widely recognized as a right.[7]

[...]

The military sometimes makes life difficult for those who apply for discharge on grounds of conscience.[8] The first non-commissioned officer to resist the Iraq war publicly was Camilo Mejía, Nicaraguan-born leader of a US infantry squad who served five months in combat. His unit ran a 48-hour sleep deprivation program in an Iraqi detention facility. Home on leave, he decided not to return to Iraq. He explained:

> This soldier went AWOL because this soldier does not think that this is a good war. I remember my platoon sergeant saying that [the sleep deprivation program] doesn't meet Red Cross or Geneva Conventions standards. There were no medical people around except the platoon's medic, and God knows how many other violations were found.

Sgt. Mejía was "thinking of calling the Red Cross, but was told that if he did, he would piss off the commander and mess up his career" (Minear 2010: 77).

The violations, in Mejía's view, were flagrant. "By Geneva Convention standards, you were not supposed to conduct missions near hospitals, mosques, schools, or residential areas. We broke every rule there was" (Mejía 2007). "To me there is no military contract and no military duty that's going to justify being a part of that war," he explained. He received a bad-conduct discharge and forfeited his benefits. The military had extended his time beyond the agreed eight years even though his green card had expired during that period and notwithstanding US treaties with his native Nicaragua and Costa Rica forbidding forced military service (Fantina 2006: 196–97).[9]

In uniform at the time of the Gulf War but never called up, Sgt. Kevin Benderman re-enlisted after 9/11 because "I kind of felt like I hadn't fulfilled my obligation." Posted to Iraq during the initial month of the US invasion, he became jarred by the war's impact on civilians. The terrain in Iraq, he explained, placed soldiers in a no-win situation. With civilians, whether by default or design, located throughout the field of battle, a soldier has to "put aside your humanity to survive in a war zone." "You see all that stuff," he said, recalling an incident in which a young girl was badly wounded by gunfire, "and you see how it affects you, and you see how it affects everyone around you, and you just say, 'You know what? Why are we even doing this anymore?'" Benderman was court-martialed and detained at Fort Stewart, Georgia after his unit returned to Iraq. A 10-year military man, he received a jail sentence of 15 months and a dishonorable discharge. The intent, he concluded, was to send an unmistakable message to everyone in the ranks that "You don't do this" (Benderman 2007).[10]

Sgt. Aidan Delgado came to his assignment at Abu Ghraib prison from an American diplomat's family (his father was a Foreign Service officer), early education at a school in Cairo where he learned Arabic, and convictions about killing that reflected his exposure to Buddhism in Thailand and his study of Buddhism while in the military. He found treatment of inmates at the prison unconscionable. Most, he concluded, were petty criminals rather than dangerous terrorists. In keeping with his Buddhist principles, he explained: "I can't make the leap to think of the enemy as subhuman. But it is the nature of war to set the other apart, because you can't kill someone who's like yourself." His honorable discharge credits him with surviving "over 26 enemy attacks by mortar, small arms fire, rocket, RPG [rocket-propelled grenade], IED [improvised explosive device], and vehicle-borne IED." Learning of his discharge request, however, his superiors reclaimed his body armor, leaving him, he said, more exposed to injury in performing his motor pool duties. His successful CO claim, he noted, which took 18 months to process, "did not shorten my time in Iraq by a single minute."[11]

Acknowledging that the review of CO claims by the authorities must be rigorous, Col. Herman Keizer, Jr. (retired) observes that:

> ... in my 34 years as an Army chaplain, I was deeply disturbed by the atmosphere of disdain heaped on the objector. The objectors' patriotism was questioned and challenged as well as their courage. The worst challenge was the questioning of the objectors' faith. I have seen commanders, non-commissioned officers and some fellow chaplains try to reason and argue against the faith statements of the objector. I would remind those who issued the challenges that the Department of Defense honored conscientious objection by publishing a directive and designing a process to honor the conscientious objector and it was their duty to live in the spirit of the directive and the process. (Weinberg and Ryan 2008)

Indeed, the experience of applicants for discharge on grounds of conscience – reviewed at greater length in a subsequent section – suggests that the military's treatment of COs was often at variance with stated Pentagon policy.

[...]

## Concerns of Conscience

Many of the concerns raised by COs in Afghanistan and Iraq were related to the Rules of Engagement (ROE). The ROE:

> describe the circumstances and limitations under which forces will begin or continue to engage in combat.... ROE ensure that the use of force in an operation occurs in accordance with national policy goals, mission requirements, and the rule of law. (Powers n.d.)

Failure to observe the ROE is punishable under the Universal Code of Military Justice. While some soldiers raised questions about the rightness of the wars, it was typically the ways in which wars were conducted that generated issues of conscience.

While the ROE sought to describe the mission and the enemy, the situation on the ground defied precise formulation. Army Sgt. James R. Welch recalled:

> [Distinguishing the enemy from the civilian population] was the really hard part. A lot of what we did as infantry is, we'd go into cities and towns, but we didn't know who the enemy was. Civilians and the enemy looked exactly alike. As far as what our soldiers on the ground knew, if they were a bad guy, they were a bad guy. (Minear 2010: 66)

Things had changed profoundly since the Cold War, mused Sgt. Todd Walton, when "it was very simple: if they carried an AK, they were bad; if they carried an [M]16, they were good. That's a good old cheat sheet," he concluded, but it no longer holds. It has been overtaken by events, including changes in the nature of warfare (Minear 2010: 169).

In the Afghanistan and Iraq theaters, ROE were revised from time to time to reflect the changing military and political scene. For example, in a rapidly deteriorating situation in Fallujah in 2004, recalled Marine Sgt. Adam Kokesh, after four Blackwater security guards had been killed and their bodies hung from a bridge, "we changed Rules of Engagement more often than we changed our underwear." There, as elsewhere, soldiers carried a breast-pocket card that said "Nothing on this card prevents you from using deadly force to defend yourself" as long as you have "reasonable certainty... that your target is a legitimate military target" (Kokesh 2008: 42).

"During the invasion of Iraq, during the push north to Baghdad," Sgt. Jason Wayne Lemieux recalled, "the rules given to me were gradually reduced to nonexistence." He was speaking at Winter Soldier Iraq and Afghanistan, a gathering of anti-war veterans seeking to highlight alleged US war crimes on the fifth anniversary of the US invasion of Iraq:

> When we first crossed the Kuwait–Iraq border at Azubad in March 2003, we were operating under Geneva Convention guidelines and, with the exception of medical and religious personnel, we were authorized to shoot anyone wearing a military uniform unless they surrendered. By the time we got to Baghdad, however, I was explicitly told by my chain of command that I could shoot anyone who came closer to me than I felt comfortable with. [The general attitude was] "better them than us," and we were given guidance that reinforced that attitude across the ranks. I watched that attitude intensify throughout my three tours. (IVAW and Glantz 2008: 17)

During Lemieux's second deployment, his commander treated "everyone on the streets [as] an enemy combatant." On his third tour, the ROE were stricter "but they only existed," he believed, "so that the command could say there were ROEs that were being followed." After describing several shootings of civilians who were no apparent threat to his unit, Lemieux concluded that:

with no way to identify their attackers, and no clear mission worth dying for, marines viewed the ROE as either a joke or a technicality to be worked around so that they could bring each other home alive. Not only are the misuses of the ROE in Iraq indicative of supreme strategic incompetence, they are also a moral disgrace. (IVAW and Glantz 2008: 18–19)

"We had gotten our Rules of Engagement brief at Camp Ramadi," recalled Marine Lance Corporal Jon Michael Turner in a presentation at the same venue. Turner's 1st Sergeant then took the platoon aside and said: "If you feel threatened in any way, shape, or form, take care of the threat and we will deal with it later." That being said, Turner commented: "Mistakes were made on several occasions." A heavily decorated machine-gunner thoroughly frustrated and enraged by his Iraq experience, Turner ripped off his Purple Heart medal at the Winter Soldier meeting and threw it away (IVAW and Glantz 2008: 23–27).

[...]

In the wake of the international furor unleashed by the revelation of the abusive treatment of captured enemy prisoners by US personnel in the Abu Ghraib prison, the military staged crash briefings on the law of war and Geneva Conventions. Interviews and other data suggest, however, that over the long haul, the international legal framework exercised at best an uneven influence on the conduct of US military operations and personnel. Thanks as well to the confused situation on the ground and flagrant violations by the enemy, the international rules may have been honored largely in the breach.

Violations of the law of war were often cited as contributing to the decisions of persons to seek discharge on grounds of conscience. Such was the case with Lance Corporal Chris Magaoay, an American of Filipino extraction who grew up in Hawaii and enlisted in the Marine Corps. Having completed basic training and with his deployment to Iraq looming, he decided he could not participate in the war and fled to Canada, where he became a prominent voice in the anti-war movement. He remembers calling his father to explain his decision:

> I told him I couldn't fight because of what I believe in, that what we were doing was wrong. [My father] understood the idea behind fighting for what is right and what is wrong. When he started to understand that civilians were dying and what my sergeant showed me about lighting a cigarette off a charred body in Iraq, he started to understand. (Gutmann and Lutz 2010: 157)

In retrospect, Magaoay wondered whether he should have expressed his views from within the ranks rather than going AWOL. That, he concluded, would have meant a prison sentence and jail time:

> I don't want to spend a single day in prison for something I didn't do wrong. I don't think I should be the one in prison. I think the guy who ordered me over there [President George W. Bush] should be in prison. I think soldiers who are going over and killing civilians should be the ones in prison, not the guy who said he won't be part of it. (Gutmann and Lutz 2010: 182)

[...]

One final issue of concern to COs in Afghanistan and Iraq is the purpose of each of the wars and their likelihood of success.

Many found the declaration of war against Afghanistan in September 2001 an appropriate and measured response to the 9/11 attacks and the country harboring their architect, Osama bin Laden. But some viewed as far less supportable the expansion of the war in March 2003 to Iraq. The Iraq invasion seemed more tangential to US national interests and also lacked the UN imprimatur enjoyed by the Afghanistan intervention. Failure to discover any weapons of mass destruction in Iraq, the stated rationale for the invasion, added to the doubts. For a time, too, difficulties in the Iraq war eroded support for the mission in Afghanistan.

> Army Spec. Tina Garnanez, an emergency medical technician who served in Iraq, said: I'm not in favor of this war. I believe it's illegal and immoral, a bunch of lies from start to finish. Now that I'm out of the service, I've made it my mission to speak out. This war is not about what they say it's about. It's not about terrorism or spreading freedom or democracy. If it were, I'd be all for it. Honestly, I feel it's about oil. (Minear 2010: 35)

"Even if the president conceded tomorrow it was about oil," countered Army 1st Lt. Derek Sutton, "you are still there and you do what you have to do" (Minear 2010: 35).

[...]

### The Evolution of Conscientious Objection

In one respect, the jurisprudential context for conscientious objection has become more solicitous of the views of COs from the two current wars. Changes in the selective service legislation shortly after the Second World War specified that objections to military service be based on "religious training and belief," understood to include "an individual's belief in relation to a Supreme Being involving duties superior to those arising from any human relation."[12] The law was challenged by Daniel A. Seeger, a Vietnam War draftee who espoused "belief in and devotion to goodness and virtue for their own sakes, and a religious faith in a purely ethical creed." Many religions and believers, he pointed out, do not affirm belief in a supreme being. To require such, he argued, violated his First and Fifth Amendment rights.

After losing in the federal district court, Seeger's challenge was sustained by a federal circuit court of appeals and then by the Supreme Court. Writing for a unanimous high court, Justice Thomas C. Clark articulated a more expansive understanding of the religious roots of conscientious objection than prevailed at the time. Applicants needed to demonstrate "a sincere and meaningful belief which occupies in the life of its possessor a place parallel to that filled by the God of those admittedly qualifying for the exemption." In the case of Seeger, Justice Clark wrote, the beliefs that prompted his objection "occupy the same place in his life as the beliefs in a traditional deity hold in the lives of his friends, the Quakers."[13] In the years since the 1965 judgment and its "place parallel" provision – the process took eight years from challenge to exoneration – the company of COs has reached beyond members of the historic peace churches to include persons embracing a variety of moral and ethical, as well as religious, beliefs.

If the Seeger verdict broadened the allowable rationale for refusing to take up arms, the case of Elliott Ashton Welsh II five years later recognized that individual consciences may legitimately forbid participating in war as an institution on other than religious grounds. The law expressly denied CO status to persons whose opposition to participation in war was based on "essentially political, sociological or philosophical views or a merely personal moral code." Yet, a majority on the high court concluded that Welsh, an individual who

deeply and sincerely holds beliefs that are purely ethical or moral but that nevertheless impose upon him a duty of conscience to refrain from participating in any war at any time ... is as much entitled to a "religious" conscientious objector exemption... as is someone who derives his conscientious opposition to war from traditional religious convictions.[14]

The Seeger and Welsh opinions acknowledged that convictions beyond those associated with traditional religion may legitimately constrain individuals from participating in good conscience in any and all wars.

Many objectors nowadays still base their claims on religious training and belief, with or without reference to a supreme being. Yet COs now hail from more diverse faith backgrounds than the peace churches and mainstream faith groups. There is often still a religious underpinning – whether Christian, Judaic, or, increasingly, Islamic[15] – to participation in wars. However, an individual's religious faith and upbringing nowadays often play a secondary role. Maria Santelli of the Center on Conscience and War, which counsels persons of all backgrounds and persuasions, observes:

In addition to the continuing presence of religious objectors, we now see people raising really strong objections on moral but secular grounds. For example, their objections today might be based on concerns about civilian casualties or the impact of the war on the environment.[16]

Indeed, the values that COs articulate resonate with a broader vision affirmed by progressive elements in contemporary international civil society. Beyond traditional anti-war views, they share a global justice agenda comprised of elements such as concern for the rule of law, human rights, humanitarian relief and access, refugee protection, environmental protection and sustainability, global warming, nuclear proliferation and global governance. In the language of the Seeger verdict, individuals are finding more and more "places parallel," that is, reasons to conclude that "war is not the answer" to many of the issues for which the military is being pressed into service.

### The Non-Evolving Element

Current law requires that COs be opposed to all wars. "Selective" conscientious objection – an arrangement that would allow a given soldier to pick and choose the wars that he or she will fight – is not allowed. The still-prevailing view of selective objection is evident in the 1971 case of Guy Peter Gillette, who refused to report for duty when drafted for Vietnam. He did not oppose all military force: he was willing to defend the US in the event of an attack and to serve in a UN peacekeeping force. His opposition was specifically to the Vietnam War, which he viewed as "unnecessary and unjust."[17]

A Supreme Court majority held that Gillette did not qualify as a CO. To rule otherwise, wrote Justice Thurgood Marshall for the majority, would "open the doors to a general theory of selective disobedience to law." With Congress having voted by a clear majority to proceed with the Vietnam War, Gillette's view might "jeopardize the binding quality of democratic decisions." How would the state be able to function, Marshall asked, if individuals for whatever reason were allowed to second-guess the judgment of Congress on a matter as fundamental as declaring war?[18]

A dissenting opinion by Justice William O. Douglas affirmed Gillette's objection and argued for legitimizing not only selective objection but also objections of conscience based on other-than-religious affirmations. He wrote:

> Conscience is often the echo of religious faith. But, as this case illustrates, it may also be the product of travail, meditation, or sudden revelation related to a moral comprehension of the dimensions of a problem, not to a religion in the ordinary sense.[19]

[...]

The requirement that a soldier oppose all wars seems particularly anachronistic in the case of Afghanistan and Iraq. A number of soldiers with ad bellum or *in bello* reservations had already been deployed in other conflicts or had expressed their willingness to serve elsewhere. Some had completed assignments in theaters such as Haiti, Somalia and the former Yugoslavia, either as members of US forces or under the aegis of UN peacekeeping missions. Their objection was not to war as an institution but to what they viewed as the immoral and unjust wars being waged by the US in Afghanistan and/or Iraq.

... [However,] could an army function effectively if deployment accommodated an individual's willingness to serve in Afghanistan but not Iraq, Korea but not Vietnam, Bosnia but not Grenada, Libya but not Syria, Yugoslavia but not Israel or the occupied Palestinian territories? "I love being a soldier," remarked Zack Bazzi. "The only bad thing about the army is you can't pick your war" (Minear 2010: 37–38). Accommodating individual consciences, opponents of selective objection point out, might soon undercut the basic effectiveness and esprit de corps of the fighting force.

[...]

Arguably, the fact that a system that allowed selective conscientious objection might prove more difficult to administer should not in and of itself deny the well-reasoned claims of individuals to constitutional protection. Nor should the idea of allowing an individual who serves in an all-volunteer army to express a geographical preference for deployment be rejected out of hand.

## Sincerity

Adjudging the sincerity of persons applying for discharge from the military as COs, whether selective or universal, has always been a challenge. What are the safeguards against those who, pleading the stirrings of conscience, might try to "game the system"? How does the system differentiate between a "death bed conversion" by a soldier suddenly afraid for his own safety and a genuinely "crystalizing" moment in which all war, or a particular war, is seen to be wrong? The issue seems particularly charged in the case of those who have volunteered and are facing, or resisting, deployment into combat.

The experience in Afghanistan and Iraq broadly confirms the GAO's observation that exposure to conflict may constitute an experience that fundamentally alters one's religious, ethical and/or moral beliefs. Indeed, some soldiers link late-blooming changes in their convictions to exposure (or anticipated exposure) to combat in those theaters. Jeff Paterson explained:

> From my personal experience, I can tell you that it is one thing to think about the "what ifs" of life, but it is another when you are actually faced with killing someone in the very immediate sense. And naturally it is easier to crystalize

your opinions when you're really faced with something you're going to have to do the next day. (Jamail 2009: 105)

While sincerity is clearly a legitimate concern, it has not been an issue in most cases making their way into the federal courts. An exception is the case of Spec. Agustin Aguayo, who applied for CO status but was sent to Iraq while his request was being processed. He received several awards as a medic in Tikrit in 2004, where he performed his duties without carrying a loaded weapon. "No matter what," he explained, "I cannot take a life." With a second deployment looming and his request for discharge from the Army turned down, he went AWOL. His court-martial found him guilty of desertion; he was demoted, deprived of benefits and served 160 days in jail. His request went up the chain of command from battalion commander to brigade commander to division commander, with staff judge advocate and the Department of the Army Conscientious Objector Review Board (DAYCORB) also involved. The military found "an attempt to remedy the anxiety all soldiers face during an extended deployment in a combat theater of operations." The federal courts upheld the Army's decision.[20]

## The Soldier–State Compact

Raising and maintaining an all-volunteer military establishes a different relationship between soldier and state than does a system of conscription. Sgt. Aidan Delgado, who had happened to enlist in the Army Reserve on 11 September 2001, explained:

> When I volunteer, and I think when most soldiers volunteer, they have the understanding that there is some kind of social compact that they will be used in a responsible way. When that trust is violated,

in my opinion, the entire contract is morally nullified. (Laufer 2006: 157)

An individual soldier is of course hardly an equal partner with the US DoD. Yet, the contractual nature of the relationship is so fundamental that, as Mark Zelcer observed in a recent *Journal of Military Ethics* article:

> the further a military engagement veers from the nation's legitimate and vital interests, the more a mission is selflessly humanitarian, for example, or, the more an operation is to make a political point not for the obvious betterment of the nation, the more the government is in breach of the soldiers' "contracts." (Zelcer 2012: 341)

Some soldiers believe that in Afghanistan and Iraq, the military violated the compact regularly and with impunity. Examples most frequently cited involve lack of necessary equipment (including body and vehicle armor), inadequate training, premature return of injured personnel to the battlefield, pre-emption of state National Guard units from domestic tasks to reinforce active-duty units abroad, and "stop loss," the unilateral extension of tours beyond statutory limits to offset manpower shortages.

In this context, the punitive treatment of some soldiers seeking discharge on grounds of conscience seems designed to send a negative message to other would-be objectors and the rank and file. The perception of many COs and of the career military chaplain quoted earlier suggests that the military's attitude toward COs reflects a pervasive institutional bias. That bias, if it exists, doubtless reflects the armed forces' overall mission and its difficulties, especially in unpopular wars such as Vietnam, Afghanistan and Iraq, of raising and maintaining an effective fighting force.

One way of promoting fairer treatment for COs might be for military officials outside the chain of command to handle such determinations. A similar recalibration of the command structure was suggested in 2013 in response to the widespread incidence of sexual abuse. Some such fundamental change may now also be needed to ensure prompt and even-handed adjudication of CO claims, acknowledging that in judging the merits of an individual's application for discharge, his or her commanding officer is hardly a neutral party.

More mutuality in the contract between soldier and state might also facilitate the recovery and re-entry process of many veterans. That was the view of Sgt. Dax Carpenter, an Arkansas marine who returned from service in both Afghanistan and Iraq with both PTSD and traumatic brain injury. He said: "I fought for two years all the way to Washington to get the 40 per cent disability rating from the Marine Corps so they'd put me on a temporary retired list." He had expected a different response from the bureaucracy:

> It should've been, "OK you're hurting. We see that. You've done more than your fair share on it. Here's your benefits and your family's benefits. You have a nice day, sir, and if you need anything, don't hesitate to call." (Minear 2010: 149)[21]

Others believe that the armed forces should make life difficult for those who seek discharge, keeping them in the ranks as punishment rather than releasing them and giving them an opportunity to rally opposition to the war.[22] Still others point out that soldiers with strong personal convictions bring vitality to the military as an institution and to the nation whose values the military espouses and defends.

[...]

## Conclusion

... The military should become less punitive in its approach to those raising questions of conscience. As the wars in Afghanistan and Iraq wind down, as the troops resume peacetime routines, and as time allows for processing their experiences, issues of conscience may well come into sharper focus.... The nation should seize the present moment to reflect on the issues of conscience involved. How can space be preserved amid the carnage of today's warfare for the multifarious expressions of conscience? Should the nation moderate the levels of mayhem in its war-making to accommodate dictates of conscience? Should those who volunteer to serve be given greater discretion in choosing their conflicts? Should the body politic be more selective in embracing military solutions to complex problems? With the tumult abating, veterans have more time and space to share and reflect on their experiences – and we with them....

## References

Benderman, Kevin. (2007) *Letters from Fort Lewis Brig: A Matter of Conscience* (Guilford, CT: Lyons P).

Fantina, Robert. (2006) *Desertion and the American Soldier, 1776–2006* (New York: Algora).

Freedman, Samuel G. (2013) "Tending to Veterans' Afflictions of the Soul," The New York Times Online, 11 January 2013, accessed 18 July 2014, available at: http://www.nytimes.com/2013/01/12/us/12religion.html?_r=0; Internet.

Gutmann, Matthew and Catherine Lutz. (2010) *Breaking Ranks: Iraq Veterans Speak out against the War* (Berkeley, CA: U of California P).

Hoge, C.W., C.A. Castro, S.C. Messer, D. McGurk, D.I. Cotting, and R.L. Koffman. (2004) "Combat Duty in Iraq and Afghanistan: Mental Health Problems and Barriers to Care," *New England Journal of Medicine* 351: 13–22.

IVAW (Iraq Veterans against the War) and Aaron Glantz (eds). (2008) *Winter Soldier: Iraq and Afghanistan: Eyewitness Accounts of the Occupation* (Chicago, IL: Haymarket Books).

Jamail, Dahr. (2009) *The Will to Resist: Soldiers Who Refuse to Fight in Iraq and Afghanistan* (Chicago, IL: Haymarket Books).

Kokesh, Adam. (2008) "Rules of Engagement," in Iraq Veterans against the War and Aaron Glantz (eds), *Winter Soldier: Iraq and Afghanistan. Eyewitness Accounts of the Occupation*, pp. 42–46 (Chicago, IL: Haymarket Books).

Laufer, Peter. (2006) *Mission Rejected: US Soldiers Who Say No to Iraq* (White River Junction, VT: Chelsea Green).

Mejía, Camilo. (2007) *The Road from Ar Ramadi: The Private Rebellion of Staff Sergeant Mejía* (New York: The New P).

Minear, Larry. (2010) *Through Veterans' Eyes: The Iraq and Afghanistan Experience* (Washington, DC: Potomac).

Powers, Rod. (n.d.) "Law of Armed Conflict," accessed 18 July 2014, available at: http://usmilitary.about.com/cs/wars/a/loac.htm; Internet.

Weinberg, Gary and Catherine Ryan (dirs). (2008) *Soldiers of Conscience* [TV documentary] (New York, NY: Luna Productions).

**Study Questions**

1. In this essay, Minear highlights one very troubling way in which warfare has changed: it is now much harder for soldiers to discern between innocent civilians and individuals who pose a legitimate threat. Consequently, many soldiers are faced with the reality of having killed the former, some of whom have been children. What kinds of ethical challenges do you think are posed by this inability to easily identify enemy combatants? How should we regard the innocent civilians who are killed as a result of these blurred lines? What steps can we take to try to minimize the death of innocent civilians? Does this make it more difficult for a particular war or conflict to meet the requirements of just war theory?

2. Traditionally, CO status has only been granted to individuals who have an objection to all instances of war, or to war as a kind of general practice. Minear suggests that we revisit this, and consider selective conscientious objection, although he also recognizes that doing so raises difficulties of its own. Do you think selective conscientious objection should be allowed? If so, how would you deal with the difficulties Minear raises, particularly concerning whether the military could effectively function if soldiers were allowed to opt out of individual conflicts? If not, how would you respond to someone like St. Thomas Aquinas, as well as to some of the soldiers Minear cites in the essay, who do not have a general opposition to war, but recognize that some will fail to meet basic standards of justice?

3. Do you agree with the treatment of COs within the military? What is your response to Corporal Chris Magaoay's claim that he does not think it is morally right to subject soldiers who go AWOL due to issues of conscience to prison terms? Moreover, how do you regard his claim that soldiers who kill innocent civilians are more deserving of jail time than soldiers who refuse to go into war precisely to avoid killing innocent civilians?

4. Consider the consequences that may arise with forcing soldiers to fight in wars or conflicts that they deem deeply immoral. For example, what may be the psychological repercussions during their service, and also once they resume their peacetime lives? What effects could there be on their performance while in active duty? Are there any benefits, or positive consequences, to compelling their participation? After weighing the possible harms versus the possible benefits, apply the utilitarian moral theory in order to assess Minear's conclusion that "the military should become less punitive in its approach to those raising questions of conscience."

## Notes

1 Interview with the author, White River Junction, VT, 13 November 2006.
2 The statement is by Dr. Rita Nakashima Brock, who directs the Soul Repair program of Brite Divinity School in Fort Worth, TX, designed to assist soldiers suffering from "moral injury."
3 The phrase is taken from Owen's poem "Strange Meeting," which is set to music by Benjamin Britten in his *War Requiem*.
4 DoD Instruction 1300.6, Section 3, Para 3.1., 5 May 2007.
5 DoD Instruction 1300.6, Section 4.1.
6 D.C. N.Y, 1963. *U.S. v. Seeger*, 216 F. Supp. 516. The sentence in the *Seeger* opinion is quoted from *Korte v. United States*, 260 F.2d at 635.
7 For a recent discussion of the issue among governments, see "Analytical Report on Conscientious Objection to Military Service," UN High Commissioner for Human Rights, A/HRC/23/22 (2013).
8 When a system of conscription was in place, COs who had been drafted could opt to work in alternative service in civilian institutions or under military aegis as non-combatants. Since the current all-voluntary military does not offer the civilian option and only a limited number of genuinely non-combatant positions exist in today's war theaters, soldiers unwilling to fight for reasons of conscience typically apply for discharge from military service altogether.
9 For an account of his experiences, see Mejía (2007), Jamail (2009) and also Fantina (2006: 189, 196–97). Mejía's defense team included former Attorney General Ramsey Clark.
10 Benderman's struggle between his military commitment and his conscience is depicted in Weinberg and Ryan (2008). See also Jamail (2009: 200) and Fantina (2006: 190, 197–200).
11 Delgado is one of the soldiers featured in Weinberg and Ryan (2008). See also Laufer (2006).
12 Title 50, U.S.C. Appendix 456(j).
13 380 U.S. 163, 85 S. Ct. 850 865.
14 *Elliott Ashton Welsh II v. U.S.*, 398 U.S. 333 (1970). One justice on a deeply divided high court opined that his colleagues had expanded CO protections so significantly as to have performed a "lobotomy" on the existing statute.
15 The locus of conflicts in which the USA has recently engaged in areas of the world with large Muslim populations poses particular problems for US Muslims.
16 Interview with the author, 12 September 2012.
17 *Gillette v. United States*, 401 U.S. at 465, quoting *U.S. v. Macintosh*, 293 U.S. 605, 635 (1931).
18 The judgment in the Gillette case drew on the 1967 report of the National Advisory Commission on Selective Service, which had opposed selective conscientious objection.
19 *Gillette v. United States*, 466.
20 Jamail (2009: 97–100).
21 Carpenter eventually received a 100 per cent disability rating. Retired from the service, he has served as an advocate with the federal veterans' bureaucracy on behalf of other returned veterans.
22 Soldiers like Mejía, Delgado, Benderman and Magoay following their discharges went on to become leaders in the anti-war movement.

# 6. Samuel Scheffler, "Is Terrorism Morally Distinctive?"

THROUGH AN ANALYSIS OF the role of fear in our lives, Samuel Scheffler (b. 1951) argues in this 2006 article from the *Journal of Political Philosophy* that terrorism is indeed morally distinctive because it uses terror to destabilize an existing social order. He contrasts this use of fear with what he refers to as "state terror," in which fear is used to stabilize an existing social order. He claims in both cases, though, that social life is undermined. Though he uses the term "state terror," he is quick to point out that he does not mean that only states can engage in this type of activity, just as he begins his discussion by pointing out that terrorism could be (but wouldn't have to be) carried out by state power.

---

THE TERM "TERRORISM" MAY by now have become too ideologically freighted to have any analytic value. If the term is to be an aid to understanding, two opposed but complementary ways of employing it will have to be resisted. On the one hand, there is the tendency, among the representatives and defenders of governments facing violent threats from non-state groups and organizations, to use the term to refer to all forms of political violence perpetrated by non-state actors. On the other hand, there is the tendency, among the representatives and defenders of non-state actors engaged in political violence, to insist that "the real terrorists" are the officials or the military forces of those states with which they are locked in conflict. Under the combined influence of these two tendencies, the word "terrorism" is in danger of becoming little more than a pejorative term used to refer to the tactics of one's enemies.

... I will proceed on the assumption that the concept of terrorism retains more content than that, and that we recognize a use of the term in which it refers to a special kind of phenomenon or class of phenomena. My primary aim will not be to produce a definition of the term but rather to consider whether there is anything morally distinctive about the type of phenomenon to which it refers. Clearly, it will be impossible to do this without making some attempt to characterize the phenomenon. Still, my aim is not to produce a definition of the term "terrorism" or to identify necessary and sufficient conditions for its application.[1] What I will do instead is to describe a certain familiar pattern to which terrorist actions often conform, and to argue that instances of terrorism which fit this pattern do indeed have a morally distinctive character....

Two other caveats are in order. First, I will assume that terrorism is a prima facie evil, and that the use of terrorist tactics is presumptively unjustified, but I will remain agnostic on the question of whether there can ever be circumstances in which such tactics may nevertheless be justified, all things considered. Second, I take it to be obvious that, although terrorism is a prima facie evil and its use is presumptively unjustified, it may sometimes be a response to policies that are also unjustified and which may be as objectionable as the terrorist response itself. Furthermore, the fact that terrorism is unjustified does not mean that all of the measures used to oppose it are themselves justified. In short, I assume that terrorism is a prima facie evil and my concern is with the kind of evil it is.

[...]

... I think it is a mistake to begin an inquiry into the morality of terrorism by endorsing a broad definition. Such a starting point may lead us to overlook relevant distinctions and to give an oversimplified description of the moral terrain. I prefer to begin, not by trying to settle on a definition, but rather by thinking about certain familiar forms of violence that most people would not hesitate, prior to analysis, to classify as instances of terrorism. I want to ask whether there is anything morally distinctive about these specific patterns of activity. As I hope will emerge from my discussion, this relatively narrow focus will serve to highlight some morally salient features and distinctions that might otherwise be easier to overlook. And, as I will try to make clear, such a focus need not import an uncritical pro-state bias, both because state activity can fall within the narrower sphere of activity on which I will concentrate and because many forms of violence that do not fall within that sphere nevertheless deserve severe condemnation, whether or not they are classified, in the end, as instances of terrorism.

[...]

A number of contemporary writers on terrorism have found it natural to situate their discussions in relation to the traditional theory of the just war.[2] For my purposes, it will be helpful to begin instead with the pre-eminent philosopher of fear in our tradition, Thomas Hobbes. It is striking that, in his famous catalogue of the "incommodities" of the state of nature, Hobbes describes fear as the worst incommodity of all. The state of nature, he says, is characterized by a war of "every man against every man," and such a war comprises not merely actual battles but an extended "tract of time" in which "the will to contend by battle is sufficiently known."[3] This means that, in the war of every man against every man, a

condition of general insecurity prevails for an extended period. "In such condition," he says, "there is no place for industry, because the fruit thereof is uncertain; and consequently no culture of the earth; no navigation, nor use of the commodities that may be imported by sea; no commodious building; no instruments of moving and removing such things as require much force; no knowledge of the face of the earth; no account of time; no arts; no letters; no society; *and which is worst of all, continual fear, and danger of violent death*. And the life of man, solitary, poor, nasty, brutish, and short" (Ch. 13, para. 9, pp. 95–96, emphasis added).

Hobbes makes at least three points in this passage and the surrounding text that are relevant to our topic. First, there is his insistence on how bad a thing fear is. Continual fear – not momentary anxiety but the grinding, unrelenting fear of imminent violent death – is unspeakably awful. It is, he suggests, worse than ignorance. It is worse than the absence of arts, letters and social life. It is worse than being materially or culturally or intellectually impoverished. Fear dominates and reduces a person. A life of continual fear is scarcely a life at all. Someone who is in the grip of chronic terror is in a state of constant distress; he "hath his heart all the day long gnawed on by fear of death, poverty, or other calamity and has no repose, nor pause of his anxiety, but in sleep" (Ch. 12, para. 5, p. 82).

The second point is that fear is incompatible with social life. On the one hand, sustained fear undermines social relations, so that in addition to being worse than various forms of poverty and deprivation it also contributes to them, by destroying the conditions that make wealth and "commodious living" possible. Fearful people lead "solitary" lives. Alone with their fears, trusting no one, they cannot sustain rewarding forms of interpersonal exchange. On the other hand, the establishment of society offers relief from fear and, in Hobbes's view, it is to escape from fear that people form societies. The fear of death, he says, is the first of "the passions that incline men to peace" (Ch. 13, para. 14, p. 97). Indeed, and this is the third point, it is only within a stable political society that the miserable condition of unremitting fear can be kept at bay. In addition to being incompatible with social life, sustained fear is the inevitable fate of pre-social human beings.

Terrorists take these Hobbesian insights to heart. In a familiar range of cases, at least, they engage in violence against some people in order to induce fear or terror in others, With the aim of destabilizing or degrading (or threatening to destabilize or degrade) an existing social order. Without meaning to beg the very questions of definition that I said I would not be addressing, I will call these "the standard cases." I do so in part on the boringly etymological ground that these cases preserve the link between the idea of terrorism and the root concept of terror. But I will also go on to argue – indeed, it is my primary thesis – that the etymology points us to something morally interesting which might otherwise be easier to overlook.

In "the standard cases," terrorists undertake to kill or injure a more or less random group of civilians or noncombatants;[4] in so doing, they aim to produce fear within some much larger group of people, and they hope that this fear will in turn erode or threaten to erode the quality or stability of an existing social order. I do not mean that they aim to reduce the social order to a Hobbesian state of nature, but only that they seek to degrade or destabilize it, or to provide a credible threat of its degradation or destabilization, by using fear to compromise the institutional structures and disrupt the patterns of social activity that help to constitute and sustain that order. The fear that terrorism produces may, for example, erode confidence in the government, depress the economy, distort the political process, reduce associational activity and provoke destructive changes in the legal system. Its ability to achieve these effects derives in part from the fact that, in addition to being intrinsically unpleasant to experience, the fear that terrorism produces may inhibit individuals' participation in a wide range of mundane activities on which a polity's social and economic health depends. In some cases people may become mistrustful of the other participants in the activity (one of the other passengers may be a hijacker or suicide bomber), while in other cases they may fear that the activity will be targeted by terrorists who are not participants (someone may toss a hand grenade into the night club or movie theater). In the various ways I have mentioned and others that I will describe, the fear that is generated by terrorism can lead to significant changes in the character of society and the quality of daily life, and at the extremes these changes can destabilize a government or even the social order as a whole. In the standard cases, then, terrorists use violence against some people to create fear in others, with the aim of degrading the social order and reducing its capacity to support a flourishing social life – or at least with the aim of credibly threatening to produce these effects.[5]

Terrorist violence may, of course, have many other aims as well, even in the standard cases.[6] The terrorists may hope that their violent acts will attract publicity for their cause, or promote their personal ambitions, or provoke a response that will widen the conflict, or enhance their prestige among those they claim to represent, or undermine their political rivals, or help them to achieve a kind of psychological or metaphysical liberation. Nor need they conceive of their actions exclusively in instrumental terms. They may also be seeking to express their rage. Or they may believe that their victims are not in the relevant sense innocent, despite being civilians or noncombatants, and they may think of themselves as administering forms of deserved punishment or retribution.

There are many other respects in which what I am calling standard cases of terrorism can differ from one another. But they all have the following minimum features: 1) the use of violence against civilians or noncombatants, 2) the intention that this use of violence should create fear in others, including other civilians and noncombatants, and 3) the further intention that this fear should destabilize or degrade an existing social order, or at any rate that it should raise the specter of such destabilization or degradation. The destabilization or degradation of the social order may itself have many different aims. Among other things, it may be intended a) as a prelude to the imposition of a different social order or the reconstitution of the existing order on different terms, b) as a way of effecting some change in the policy of an existing state or society, c) as a form of deserved punishment, and hence as an end in itself, or d) as some combination of these.

What makes terrorism of the standard kind possible is the corrosive power of fear. As Hobbes suggests, sustained or continual fear is a regressive force both individually and socially. It can induce the unraveling of an individual's personality and, as we have already seen, its cumulative effects on large numbers of people can degrade the social order and diminish the quality of social life. Its capacity to achieve these effects is enhanced by the infectiousness of fear, the fact that it can so easily be transmitted from one person to another, even when the second person is unaware of the reasons for the first person's fear.... [T]errorism ... benefits from the infectiousness of fear, because the fact that something has frightened one person may itself frighten another person, and the fearful attitudes of different people can exert mutually reinforcing and intensifying effects. In this age of instant communication, moreover, the capacity of terrorist acts to cause fear, and to exploit the phenomena of mutual reinforcement and intensification, is greatly increased. The news media can be counted on to provide graphic coverage of each terrorist outrage, so that a bomb blast anywhere can generate fear and insecurity everywhere. These attitudes in turn become newsworthy and are dutifully reported by the media, thus contributing to the syndrome of mutual reinforcement.

I said earlier that, in the standard cases, terrorist violence is usually directed against a "more or less random" group of civilians or noncombatants. It is difficult to be more precise. Sometimes virtually any civilians will do. At other times, terrorists will select a particular population group, defined by occupation or ethnicity or religion or social class, and will target people indiscriminately within that group. Or they will select a symbolic target (the World Trade Center), and those who are killed or injured will be those who happen to be in the chosen location at the wrong time. Even when the target class is maximally wide, the victimization is random in the sense that it is indiscriminate within that class but not in the sense that it is pointless or irrational. And even when the target class is relatively narrow, there is an advantage in preserving some degree of indiscriminateness within that class. In both cases, the randomness or indiscriminateness has the same point. It is to maximize (within the relevant parameters) the numbers of people who identify with the victims, thus subverting the defensive ingenuity with which people seize on any feature that distinguishes them from the victims of misfortune to preserve their own sense of invulnerability. In this way, the appearance of randomness is used to exploit the psychic economy of identification in such a way as to maximize the spread of fear.

This is not to say that it is always easy to achieve one's aims using terrorist tactics. In fact, it is usually difficult for terrorist acts to destabilize an otherwise stable social order. This is not merely because such acts can backfire, and reduce support for the terrorists' goals. Nor is it merely because of the large armies, police forces and intelligence services that stable societies normally have available to fight those who employ terrorism. Just as important is the fact that stable societies, and individuals raised in such societies, have substantial social and psychological resources with which to resist the destructive effects of fear. People can be remarkably tenacious in their determination to preserve the lives they have made for themselves in society, and if fear can be infectious so too can courage and the determination to persevere in the face of great danger. These too have mutually reinforcing and intensifying effects.

But terrorism does not need to destabilize a social order altogether in order to transform and degrade it and, as we have seen, often such transformation and degradation will suffice to enable those who employ terrorist tactics to achieve some or all of their aims. The problem is that living with fear can have corrosive effects even for those who are courageous and determined to persevere. One might put the point provocatively and say that courage itself – or the need to sustain it over long periods of time – can be corrosive.

Living each day with the vivid awareness that one's children may be killed whenever they leave home, or that a decision to meet one's friends at a restaurant or café may result in violent death, or that an ordinary bus ride on a sunny day may end with lumps of flesh raining down on a previously peaceful neighborhood, exacts a cost. Nor is this true only if one yields to one's fears and keeps one's children at home, gives up socializing and avoids public transportation. It is also true if one

grits one's teeth and resolves to carry on as normal. People often say, in explaining their determination to maintain a normal routine in the face of terrorist activities or threats, that to do otherwise would be to "give the terrorists what they want." This is not wrong, but it understates the problem. Maintaining one's normal routine does not suffice to preserve normalcy. Terrorism undermines normalcy almost by definition. One cannot, simply through an act of will, immunize oneself against the effects of continual fear and danger on one's state of mind or on the quality of one's life. These effects are distressingly easy for groups that use terrorist tactics to achieve and distressingly difficult for the members of targeted populations to avoid.

This is one reason why terrorism is so popular, even if it is not always ultimately successful. Apologists for terror often claim that it is the weapon of the weak, who have no other tools available for fighting back against their oppressors. This may be true in some circumstances. As far as I can see, however, those who engage in terrorism rarely invest much time in exploring the availability of other tools. All too often terrorism is the tool of choice simply because the perceived advantages it offers are so great. It costs relatively little in money and manpower. It has immediate effects and generates extensive and highly sensationalized publicity for one's cause. It affords an emotionally satisfying outlet for feelings of rage and the desire for vengeance. It induces an acute sense of vulnerability in all those who identify with its immediate victims. And insofar as those victims are chosen randomly from among some very large group, the class of people who identify with them is maximized, so that an extraordinary number of people are given a vivid sense of the potential costs of resisting one's demands. Figuratively and often literally, terrorism offers the biggest bang for one's buck.

If what I have said to this point is on the right track, then it does seem that terrorism is morally distinctive, at least insofar as it conforms to the pattern of what I have been calling "the standard cases." In these cases, at least, it differs from other kinds of violence directed against civilians and noncombatants. By this I do not mean that it is worse, but rather that it has a different moral anatomy. By analogy: humiliation is morally distinctive, and so too are torture, slavery, political oppression and genocide. One can investigate the moral anatomy of any of these evils without taking a position on where it stands in an overall ranking of evils. Many people are pluralists about the good. We can be pluralists about the bad as well.

In the "standard cases," some people are killed or injured (the primary victims), in order to create fear in a larger number of people (the secondary victims), with the aim of destabilizing or degrading the existing social order for everyone. The initial act of violence sets off a kind of moral cascade: death or injury to some, anxiety and fear for many more, the degradation or destabilization of the social order for all. Nor is this simply a cascade of harms. It is, instead, a chain of intentional abuse, for those who employ terrorist tactics do not merely produce these harms, they intentionally aim to produce them. The primary victims are used – their deaths and injuries are used – to terrify others, and those others are used – their fear and terror are used – to degrade and destabilize the social order.

The fact that the secondary victims' fear and terror are used in this way is one thing that distinguishes the standard cases from other cases in which civilians are deliberately harmed in order to achieve some military or political objective. In other cases of deliberate, politically-motivated violence against civilians, the perpetrators display a callous disregard not only for the lives of their victims but also for the misery and suffering of the people who care about or identify with them. Since those who commit such acts are willing to kill or injure their victims, it is hardly surprising that they should be indifferent to the intensely painful human reactions – fear, horror and grief – that their acts are liable to produce in others. In the "standard cases," however, the primary victims are killed or injured precisely in order to elicit such reactions – precisely in order to elicit fear, horror and grief – so that those reactions can in turn be exploited to promote the perpetrators' ultimate, destabilizing objectives.

Using Kantian terminology, we might say that the primary victims are treated not just as means to an end but as means to a means: that is, they are treated as means to the end of treating the secondary victims as means to an end. Those who engage in this kind of terrorism do not merely display callous indifference to the grief, fear and misery of the secondary victims; instead, they deliberately use violence to cultivate and prey on these reactions. This helps to explain why there is something distinctively repellent about terrorism, both morally and humanly.[7]

As I have said, not all instances of terrorism fit the description of the "standard cases." Sometimes, for example, terrorist tactics may be employed not to destabilize or degrade an entire social order but rather to make the place of a particular social group or class within that order insecure, as in cases where the ambition is to drive the members of the targeted group into another country or territory ("ethnic cleansing"). In cases like this, the description of the "moral cascade" will differ somewhat, but the moral anatomy of these cases will still bear a clear and recognizable relation to that of the standard cases. Other instances in which the term "terrorism" is likely to be employed may differ more substantially from the standard cases. An example might be a situation in which violence is directed against civilians solely for the purpose of provoking a response and thereby producing an escalation in the level of a conflict; the fact that the violence also generates fear, although predictable and not unwelcome, is no part of the perpetrators' aim. In a similar vein, insurgents might take civilian hostages simply as a way of pressuring a government to release some of their imprisoned comrades, and not for the purpose of spreading fear, although fear may be one predictable effect of their actions. Still other examples, meanwhile, may seem sufficiently different from the standard cases that the propriety of the term "terrorism" becomes doubtful, even if it is often applied to them. This may be true, for example, of targeted political assassinations or acts of sabotage.

In general, we should be sensitive to the wide variety of actual cases we are likely to encounter, and we should avoid theory-driven oversimplifications of the phenomena…. [T]he fact that some form of conduct is not best thought of as amounting to terrorism does not mean that there is no objection to it. As the doctrine of the pluralism of the bad reminds us, there are many different kinds of atrocities and many different forms of horrific behavior, and we learn more by attending to the differences among them than by assimilating them all to a single category. One of the many unsettling features of the Bush administration's post-9/11 moral discourse, with its frequent references to "evildoers" and "bad guys," is that it uses moral categories to inhibit rather than to promote moral understanding. It relies on simplifying dichotomies that appeal to psychologically primitive sources of moral motivation and, in so doing, it encourages a dangerously reductive conception of the moral domain.

As I noted at the outset, the term "terrorism" is sometimes used, by representatives and defenders of governments facing violent threats from non-state groups and organizations, to refer to all forms of political violence perpetrated by non-state actors. This makes it impossible by definition for states to engage in terrorism. Although I have not endorsed this – or any other – definition, my narrow focus on the standard cases and my emphasis on terrorism's destabilizing aims may seem to imply that it can only be the tactic of insurgents or other non-state actors. But this is not in fact a consequence of my view. States can certainly employ terrorist tactics in the manner I have described as a way of destabilizing other societies. They can do this in wartime, through the use of such tactics as "terror bombing," or in peacetime, through covert operations targeting another country's civilian population. And domestically, a government might use such tactics in order to create a limited degree of instability, with the aim of discrediting its opponents or generating increased support for repressive policies. Of course, it is crucial in such cases that the government should not appear to be the perpetrator of the terrorist acts, since its aim is precisely to ascribe those acts to others. Still, the fact remains that governments can engage in terrorism both against other societies and, with the qualification just mentioned, domestically as well.

Governments may also use terror as an instrument of policy without this amounting to terrorism of the "standard" type. Indeed, here I am prepared to engage in at least partial, stipulative definition, and to say that governments may use terror as an instrument of policy without this amounting to terrorism at all. This will be true, in my view, when a government uses terror internally – and is willing to be seen as doing so – in order to stifle dissent and opposition, to maintain its grip on power and to preserve the established order. I will use the term "state terror" to describe this phenomenon, and in the usage I have stipulated there is an important contrast

SCHEFFLER: IS TERRORISM MORALLY DISTINCTIVE?

between state terror and terrorism, even terrorism that is perpetrated by states. The point of the stipulation is not to suggest that one of these phenomena is better or worse than the other, but rather to highlight what I take to be a significant distinction between two different political uses to which terror may be put. Terrorism, as I understand it, standardly involves the use of violence to generate fear with the aim of destabilizing or degrading an existing social order. State terror, as I understand it, standardly involves the use or threat of violence to generate fear with the aim of stabilizing or preserving an existing social order. Of course, other people may use the terms "terrorism" and "state terror" in different ways, but the point is not merely terminological, and anyone whose use of the relevant terminology differs from mine needs to find some other way of expressing the contrast I have described.

It is an interesting fact that fear and terror can be used either to undermine an existing social order or to preserve one. They can be made to serve not only revolutionary but also conservative purposes. How is this possible? How, in particular, is it possible that fear and terror can be used to preserve a social order if, as I said earlier, they undermine social life? Hobbes, who certainly understood the second of these points, also emphasized the first. He wrote: "Of all passions, that which inclineth men least to break the laws is fear. Nay, excepting some generous natures, it is the only thing (when there is appearance of profit or pleasure by breaking the laws) that makes men keep them" (Ch. 27, para. 19, p. 222). For Hobbes, fear can be used to preserve order because it is a passion "that relate[s] to power" (Ch. 31, para. 9, p. 269). In the state of nature – in the war of all against all – each person has sufficient power to pose a threat to every other person. Hence each person has reason to fear every other person, and this undermines the

conditions of social life. But the concentration of power in a sovereign produces a redistribution of the capacity to inspire fear, and this makes social life possible. On the one hand, people's attitudes toward one another need no longer be dominated by fear and mistrust, and so the development of social relations is no longer inhibited. On the other hand, everyone has reason to fear the sovereign's power, and hence to obey the sovereign's laws, and so the social order is stabilized.

But this suggests that fear does not, after all, undermine social life, at least not in all cases. It undermines social life only when, in the absence of a common authority, fear is radically decentralized, and each person has reason to fear every other person. There is something to this, but as stated it overlooks the differences between ordinary political authority and a regime of state terror. In a decent society that is governed by the rule of law, crimes are punished and the fear of punishment can be said to provide individuals with a reason for obeying the laws. Here the phrase "fear of punishment" functions as a way of characterizing a certain kind of reason for action; people's presumed desire to avoid punishment is a consideration that counts in favor of obedience. But this does not mean that people are actually afraid or that they lead lives full of fear.[8] On the contrary, one of the primary advantages of the rule of law, and of a predictable, publicly promulgated and impartially administered system of punishments and sanctions, is that it enables people to avoid fear. By structuring their lives in accordance with what the law allows, they can predictably avoid the punishments and sanctions attached to violations. Of course, people who break the law, or are accused or suspected of doing so, may find themselves genuinely fearing punishment. But, leaving aside false accusations and unwarranted suspicions, law-abiding citizens need not actually experience any fear of the state, even if we can truly say that the fear of punishment gives them a reason to obey. In a well-functioning state, the "fear of punishment" is not normally a condition of fear at all. For this reason, it provides no obstacle to the development of rich social relations, and indeed helps to facilitate them. For the very same reason, however, it also provides no counterexample to the thesis that a state of continual fear undermines social life.

Things are very different under a regime of state terror. Here the state deliberately keeps people afraid as a way of maintaining its grip on power and preserving the established system. In order to do this, it deliberately eliminates the features of impartiality and predictability associated with the rule of law. Power is exercised and laws are administered arbitrarily. Although there may be forms of conduct that can reliably be expected to result in arrest and punishment, there are few if any reliable ways of avoiding such outcomes. Networks of secret agents and informers may denounce people for any reason or none, and there is no independent judiciary or regime of rights to protect those who are accused. People may be imprisoned, or lose their jobs, or have their property confiscated, or be tortured or killed, without ever knowing why. Since citizens have no basis for confidence in their ability to avoid such calamities, they are kept perpetually fearful, uncertain, anxious. And since they have no way of knowing who may be an informer or an agent of the state, they are kept perpetually wary and mistrustful of one another. The point of inducing this Hobbesian condition of ongoing mutual mistrust is precisely to restrict the development of social relations and to inhibit the cooperative and solidaristic attitudes that accompany them. A regime that rules by terror recognizes these relations and attitudes as potential threats. By using fear to constrict and impoverish social life, it confirms both that fear undermines social relations and that a free social life is the antidote to fear.

Thus, the fact that genuine terror can be used to preserve an established order does not falsify the observation that fear undermines social life, for social relations are indeed inhibited under a regime of terror. Notwithstanding the existence of centralized rule and a set of rigidly constrained social and economic institutions, such a regime has as much in common with the Hobbesian state of nature as it does with a political society that is subject to the rule of law.[9]

I have drawn the contrast between a regime of terror and the rule of law starkly, but I do not mean to deny that there can be intermediate cases. On the one hand, even the most brutal totalitarian states may need to provide selective relief from terror for certain groups of people in order to achieve their aims.[10] On the other hand, even relatively decent governments may find it irresistible at times to use fear as a way of deflecting criticism or deflating political opposition. A judiciously administered dose of alarm can do wonders in inducing a compliant frame of mind and encouraging people to rally round their leaders. Ironically, the fear of terrorism – which is in part to say the fear of fear – seems to be a particularly effective tool for this purpose. This is one reason why governments are so eager to label their enemies as terrorists; in addition to discrediting them, the very use of the label may help to induce a state of timid docility in an otherwise restive population. But none of this undermines the argument I have been developing.

The upshot of that argument is that there are two different ways in which fear might be said to be capable of contributing to the preservation of order. Although Hobbes, to the detriment of his political theory, did not distinguish between them, neither of them falsifies the claim that fear undermines social life. It is true that, when the rule of law prevails, the fear of punishment gives people a reason to obey, yet social life is not inhibited. But since the "fear of punishment" is not, in these circumstances, a condition of actual fear, the idea that fear undermines social life remains intact. Under a regime of terror, by contrast, genuine fear is indeed used to preserve order, but since social relations are severely restricted under such a regime, the tendency of fear to compromise social life is confirmed rather than disconfirmed.

... [S]tate terror typically aims to stabilize more than just the existing political configuration. It also seeks to preserve a set of tightly controlled social and economic institutions, and in this sense it aims to stabilize an entire social order – albeit a severely constrained one – and not merely a government. Despite the fact that it uses fear to inhibit certain kinds of social relations and thus to restrict social life, in other words, it does nevertheless seek to preserve a rigidly constrained social order, in the sense just specified. To be sure, the fact that social life is so severely compromised under such a regime means that the social order that is preserved is bound to be a grim and dystopian one. Still, I think it would be a mistake to deny that it is a social order at all or to ignore the fact that the regime aims to stabilize and preserve it.[11]

If this is correct, then it is possible to reaffirm and to expand upon my earlier observations about the relationship between terrorism and state terror. In the standard cases, I have said, terrorism involves the use or threat of violence to generate fear, with the aim of degrading or destabilizing an existing social order. State terror, on the other hand, standardly involves the use or threat of violence to generate fear, with the aim of stabilizing or preserving an existing social order – albeit a grim and tightly controlled one. There is, accordingly, a significant difference between terrorism – even terrorism perpetrated by a state – and state terror. They represent different ways of using terror for political purposes. But they exploit a common mechanism: the capacity of fear to undermine social life. As I have argued, terrorism of the standard kind uses this mechanism to degrade the institutional structures and patterns of activity that help to constitute and sustain an existing social order.

State terror, by contrast, uses the same mechanism to subvert or prevent the emergence of cooperative social relationships that might pose a threat to the power of the state or to the character of the prevailing social and economic arrangements. People are kept chronically fearful and mistrustful of one another so that, even if they have the resources and opportunities to do so, they will be unwilling or unable to form the kinds of groups, associations and social networks that might become independent centers of influence, facilitate the emergence of critical voices and perspectives, or in other ways challenge the status quo.

Under a regime of state terror, fear is used by the state to keep social relations impoverished so that a rigidly constrained social and economic order can be preserved and protected from challenge.

I think that this contrast helps to explain why terrorist violence is so often calculated to attract maximum publicity, whereas so much of the violence associated with state terror is carried out in secret. Terrorists aim to promote chaos and disarray as a way of subverting the social fabric. They want people running for cover. The perpetrators of state terror want to promote order and regimentation. They want people marching in step. Spectacular acts of public violence are designed to produce disruption and panic. The shadowy operations of secret police and paramilitary groups are designed to produce silence, conformity and the desire to make oneself inconspicuous, to attract no notice.[12]

One additional complication should be noted. I have been distinguishing between terrorism and state terror: between the use of fear to degrade or destabilize an existing order and the use of fear to stabilize or preserve an existing order. But I have emphasized that states can engage in both forms of activity. It is natural to wonder whether the reverse is also true. Can non-state groups use fear to stabilize an existing order? Although the label "state terror" is obviously not appropriate to such cases, I believe that the answer is yes. For example, non-state groups may use violence to terrorize an oppressed or subordinated population, with the aim of reinforcing an established system of caste or hierarchy or defeating attempts to dismantle such a system. (Think, for example, of the Ku Klux Klan.) We can think of these as cases of "sub-state terror," in which fear is used to police the boundaries of a social hierarchy, to block the development of new social movements, or to inhibit social change. The use of fear to stabilize an existing order is no more the exclusive province of the state than the use of fear to destabilize such an order is the exclusive province of non-state actors. The reason for distinguishing between terrorism, on the one hand, and state or sub-state terror, on the other, is to highlight the distinction between these two different uses of fear, and not to suggest a distinction between two different categories of agents.

## Conclusion

The title of this paper poses a question. The answer that has emerged from my discussion is as follows. Terrorism is morally distinctive insofar as it seeks to exploit the nexus of violence and fear in such a way as to degrade or destabilize an existing social order. Terrorist acts may have many functions other than the degradation of the social order, and the degradation of the social order may itself be intended to serve different purposes. But insofar as it conforms to the "standard" pattern I have described, terrorism has a morally distinctive character, whatever other functions and purposes individual instances of it may also serve. If, as is often the case, the term is applied more widely, then one consequence may be that terrorism so understood is not always morally distinctive....

I do not take these considerations as reasons for insisting on a definition of terrorism that limits it to the standard cases. But I do think that the word "terrorism" is morally suggestive precisely because "terror" is its linguistic root, and that if we define the term in a way that effaces or even breaks the connection between terrorism and terror, as the definitions just mentioned do, then we are liable to miss some of the moral saliences toward which the word "terrorism" gestures.[13] The currency of that particular word, which adds to the already rich vocabulary we have for describing violence of various kinds, testifies to the power of fear and to the peculiar moral reactions evoked by its deliberate use for political ends....

## Study Questions

1. Based on this reading, in what specific ways is fear such a bad thing? Why is it "incompatible with social life"? According to Scheffler, how does forming societies help people to escape from fear? Do you agree with these claims?

2. What are the minimum features of what Scheffler refers to as the "standard cases" of terrorism? What distinguishes the use of terror in these situations, according to the author?

3. In the next selection, Claudia Card argues that the US war on terrorism is a form of terrorism itself. Using Scheffler's distinction between terrorism and state terror, what arguments can be given to support the claim that the war on terrorism is terrorism, state terror, or neither?

## Notes

1 Many different definitions have been proposed. For discussion, see C.A. Coady, "Terrorism and Innocence," *Journal of Ethics* 8 (2004), 37–58, and Jenny Teichman, "How to Define Terrorism," *Philosophy* 64 (1989), 505–17.

2 See also the symposia on terrorism published in special issues of *Ethics* (Volume 114, Number 4) and *The Journal of Ethics* (Volume 8, Number 1) in 2004. See, for example, C.A. Coady, "The Morality of Terrorism," *Philosophy* 60 (1984), 47–69; "Terrorism and Innocence"; "Terrorism, Morality, and Supreme Emergency," *Ethics* 114 (2004), 772–89; David Rodin, "Terrorism without Intention," *Ethics* 114 (2004), 752–71. See also E.M. Kamm, "Failures of Just War Theory: Terror, Harm, and Justice," *Ethics* 114 (2004), 650–92, and Noam Zohar, "Innocence and Complex Threats: Upholding the War Ethic and the Condemnation of Terrorism," *Ethics* 114 (2004), 734–51. The pioneering contemporary revival of just war theory is, of course, Michael Walzer's *Just and Unjust Wars* (New York: Basic Books, 1977). Walzer devotes one chapter of that book to terrorism, and he also discusses terrorism in several of the essays included in *Arguing about War* (New Haven, CT: Yale UP, 2004). The application of just war theory to terrorism is vigorously criticized by Robert Goodin in *What's Wrong with Terrorism?* (Cambridge: Polity P, forthcoming).

3 Thomas Hobbes, *Leviathan*, chapter 13, paragraph 8. Quotation taken from the edition edited by A.P. Martinich (Peterborough, ON: Broadview P, 2002), p. 95. Subsequent references, including chapter, paragraph, and page number in the Martinich edition, will be given parenthetically in the text.

4 The relevance of civilian or noncombatant status to the definition of terrorism is contested, but since I am setting aside questions of definition I will not address the issue. For pertinent discussion, see Coady, "The Morality of Terrorism" and "Terrorism and Innocence"; Robert Fullinwider, "Terrorism, Innocence, and War," in Gehring ed., *War after September 11* (Lanham, MD: Rowman and Littlefield, 2003); Virginia Held, "Terrorism, Rights, and Political Goals," in Frey and Morris eds., *Violence, Terrorism, and Justice* (New York: Cambridge UP, 1991), pp. 59–85; Virginia Held, "Terrorism and War," *Journal of Ethics* 8 (2004), 59–75; Igor Primoratz, "The Morality of Terrorism," *Journal of Applied Philosophy* 14 (1997), 221–33; Noam Zohar, "Innocence and Complex Threats." There is, of course, a large literature on the principle of noncombatant immunity in wartime.

5 For a related discussion, see Jeremy Waldron, "Terrorism and the Uses of Terror," *Journal of Ethics* 8 (2004), 5–35, at pp. 22–23.

6 Waldron has a good discussion of many of these aims in "Terrorism and the Uses of Terror," Section 6.

7 There are three misunderstandings to be avoided. First, in saying that there is "something distinctively repellent" about terrorism, I am not saying that it is more repellent than any other type of atrocity. I am saying only that some of the reasons why it is repellent are distinctive.

Second, I am not saying that all of the reasons why terrorism is repellent are distinctive; obviously, it is also repellent for some of the same reasons that other types of unjustified violence are. Finally, I am not claiming that what is distinctively repellent about terrorism is also what is morally worst about it. What is distinctively repellent about terrorism is, roughly, that it treats the primary victims as means to a means, but what is morally worst about it may simply be that it involves (for example) the unjustified killing of the innocent.

8  This is related to Jeremy Waldron's distinction between "Jack Benny-style coercion" and "Arendtian terrorization." See Waldron, "Terrorism and the Uses of Terror," pp. 15–16.

9  My discussion in this paragraph is indebted to Waldron, "Terrorism and the Uses of Terror," pp. 18–20.

10  Indeed, just as terrorist tactics are sometimes used, not to destabilize the entire social order but rather to make the place of a particular group within that order insecure, so too the apparatus of state terror is sometimes used against a subset of the population rather than against the population as a whole. Of course, such limitations tend to be unstable. Once terror is put to political use, it is hard to keep it within bounds.

11  I am grateful to Jay Wallace and to an anonymous referee for prompting me to clarify these points.

12  Of course, show trials and public executions can also help to produce these effects, and they too are familiar devices of state terror. But silence and conformity are not normally achieved by setting off bombs in public places or by using other standard terrorist tactics.

13  Many other writers have insisted on the importance of fear for an understanding of the morality of terrorism. See, for example, Robert Goodin, *What's Wrong with Terrorism?*, Jeremy Waldron, "Terrorism and the Uses of Terror," and Carl Wellman, "On Terrorism Itself," *Journal of Value Inquiry* 13 (1979), 250–58.

# 7. Claudia Card, "Recognizing Terrorism"

IN THIS 2007 ARTICLE from *The Journal of Ethics*, Claudia Card (1940–2015) argues for an expansion of what is typically categorized as terrorism to include issues such as oppressive regimes, racist environments, rape, and domestic violence. In doing so, she analyzes two existing models for understanding terrorism and illustrates the ways in which these other activities relate to them as well. Card calls for recognition of these forms of "publicly invisible terrorism."

---

... EVERYDAY LIVES UNDER OPPRESSIVE regimes, in racist environments, and of women, children, and elders everywhere who suffer violence in their homes seldom capture public attention as high drama. But there is real terrorism in many of these lives. A genuine war on terrorism might well begin with such domestic issues. But first it is necessary to be able to recognize terrorism.

To recognize terrorism in the everyday lives of people who may never make headlines, and at the same time deepen our appreciation of terrorism in more high-profile cases, it is helpful to be able to identify imaginatively with not only potential targets but also potential terrorists....

My aim ... is to justify an expanded range of paradigms of terrorism that is not limited to high-profile cases and to do this without diluting the moral seriousness of the concept. The importance of this project is twofold. On one hand, we gain greater insight into what is distinctive about terrorism and what kind of moral significance it has. On the other, we realize that many cases of publicly invisible terrorism deserve to be taken as seriously as the widely recognized high-profile cases involving governments and other public policy-makers.

I neither begin nor conclude this project with a definition of terrorism in the sense of a set of necessary and sufficient conditions.

Nor do I take a final position on whether terrorism is ever justifiable. The conception of terrorism that emerges from this investigation suggests, however, that for the relatively powerless oppressed, and especially for those who are coerced into a relationship from which they cannot extricate themselves by ordinary lawful means, the question of justification is a serious one, and its answer is not obvious.

... I begin with two models of terrorism that fit high-profile paradigms. Let us call them the "the coercion model" and the "group target model." Each model has appealed to philosophers. Each emerges from important histories. Even if, ultimately, one model might absorb the other, both are useful in that they encourage identification with different parties.

## 1. Two Models of Terrorism

[...] The coercion model was persuasively developed by Carl Wellman nearly three decades ago.[1] It focuses on the logic of terrorism, how the terrorist thinks, what the terrorist hopes to achieve. Ultimately, it encourages inquiry into why such drastic means would be chosen to achieve those objectives. On this model, terrorism typically has two targets. One target is direct but secondary in importance. The indirect target is primary in that it is the intended recipient of a message containing the terrorist's demands, which are sent by way of violence (or the threat of violence) to the direct target. Direct targets can be people, property, or both. An example captured by this model is bombing a public building (direct but secondary target) to pressure a government (indirect but primary target) to release prisoners or alter policies. The message, often implicit, is "accede to our demands, or there will be further bombings." The building and any occupants may be treated as "throwaways." Their survival may not matter to achievement of the terrorist's objective, whereas survival of the primary target can be essential to that end.

Other examples, arguably captured by the coercion model, include hostage-taking (Munich, 1972), kidnap for ransom (the Lindbergh baby), airplane hijackings (or carjackings), some forms of witness intimidation, some forms of extortion practiced by organized crime, ... some drive-by shootings by inner city gangs, and cross-burnings by the Ku Klux Klan. Wellman gives armed holdups as an example of terrorist coercion. But that example requires a little tampering with the model, since the same person is ordinarily both the primary and secondary target, a matter to which I return. Likewise, hijacking methods are typically coercive (armed holdups), even if the plane or vehicle is not used for further coercion.

A shortcoming of the coercion model is that it restricts terrorist objectives to coercion to comply with demands. But the same basic pattern characteristic of the coercion model, namely, two targets (direct and indirect) and a message (to the indirect but primary target), is compatible with objectives other than coercion and messages other than demands. Other objectives might be, for example, those of demonstration, protest, revenge, or disruption.

Actions of partisans and of resistance fighters in World War II, such as bombing trains headed for Poland, are often cited in raising the question whether terrorism can be justified.[2] Such actions appear not to fit the coercion model in that they do not present the primary target with a demand or offer a choice. Still, they send messages: to the Allies, "watch these trains" and to Nazis, "we will not just stand by but will do all in our power to stop you," an urgent message in the context of widespread acquiescence to Nazi policies. The pattern of a direct and indirect target and a message remains, even if coercion drops out. Coercion may not be an option for those extremely lacking in power. But some can still use terrorist means to send messages.

[...]

In presenting the coercion model, Wellman did not defend terrorism. Yet it may be no accident that he found that model apt in the 1970s. Popular paradigms of terrorism in the US then included an array of morally and politically motivated non-lethal violent crimes (mainly property destruction) committed by otherwise ordinary citizens, some from well-off and highly respected families.[3] These crimes ranged from bombings by members of the Weather Underground to "monkey-wrenching" by environmental activists (such as sabotage of off-road vehicles used in projects destructive of natural habitats).[4] Many sent clear demands to stop specific activities. Their objectives evoked some sympathy from social critics on the left.[5]

If the coercion model gets us to focus on terrorist reasoning, the group target model, in contrast, gets us to focus on target predicaments. The group target model appears to be at work in Michael Walzer's widely cited chapter on terrorism in *Just and Unjust Wars*.[6] Although Walzer describes terrorist violence as targeting victims randomly ("its method is the random murder of innocent people"), what he appears to have in mind is randomness within a group, as he also characterizes terrorism as "the systematic terrorizing of whole populations" in order "to destroy the morale of a nation or a class."[7] Again there is a primary target, often less obvious than the immediate (direct) targets. The primary target here is a group, a "class," which presumably might be racial, ethnic, or religious, not only national. Immediate targets appear (at least, to members of the target group) to be randomly chosen members of the group, vulnerable not for their conduct (in that sense "innocent") but simply on account of their identity as members of the group. Immediate targets could also be persons or property presumed to be of value to the group, targeted for that reason. The apparent objective is to hurt the group (demoralization, as Walzer puts it); harm to immediate targets is part of or a means to that end. Terrorism so understood fits what have come to be (long since Walzer's book appeared) common definitions of hate crime, according to which victims are selected at least partly on the basis of their membership in an ethnic, racial, religious, or national group. In contrast, terrorism understood on the coercion model need not be a hate crime.

The group target model makes sense of some ethnic, racist, and religious harassment that apparently goes beyond coercion. An example might be the physical beating of Jewish students on their way to school by groups of Christian students on examination days, as recounted by Simon Wiesenthal in his memoir *The Sunflower*.[8] The immediate aim was to hinder Jewish students from passing examinations. Yet there was no evident demand satisfaction of which would have ended the harassment. Were it not exams, it would likely have been something else. The aim seemed to be to harm the Jewish community; coercion, a means.

... The coercion model might be made compatible with the group target model by the supposition that there is at least an implicit coercive demand for the entire group to get out. But terrorists can be expected to know that the demand is unrealistic when there is no place for those expelled to go. Demoralization may be a more realistic goal of terrorism that targets a group.

A shortcoming of the group target model is that it does not encourage inquiry into why assailants wish to harm the group. Perhaps the assumption is that it does not matter: people should not be harmed on the basis of their identity as members of such groups, whatever the reason. But failure to look for a rationale can mislead us about who the primary target is. When we discover animating objectives, we sometimes identify the primary target differently, often more (or less) specifically, as I argue below (Section 4) with respect to rape terrorism.

Even if neither model entirely absorbs the other, many terrorist deeds seem to fit both. On both, individuals may be deliberately harmed regardless of whether they have done anything to provoke attack. Yet neither a lack of scruple regarding who is harmed nor the actual infliction of harm is central to the coercion model (threats may suffice). On both, targets may be coerced into acceding to terrorists' demands. Yet that aim is not central to the group target model (terrorism may continue even though some demands are met). The two models also incorporate some of the same features. On both, there is an absence of procedural justice in target selection. On both, there is, if not major harm or an attempt at it, at least a credible threat of major harm.

Yet there are also important differences. On the group target model, terrorism lies on a continuum of hate crime, at one extreme end of which is genocide. The coercion model does not put terrorism on that continuum.

On the contrary, the coercion model suggests grounds for relative optimism regarding terrorists' potential amenability to dialogue and argument. Coercive terrorists may hope to succeed in relying on threats and avoid ever having to carry them out. It is the group target model, however, that makes sense of much popular thinking about terrorism in the United States today, which would have us identify not only *with* but *as* potential direct targets who have done nothing to provoke attack. It is no accident that this model enjoys popularity now, following the 1993 bombing of the World Trade Center and the massively lethal attacks of the Oklahoma City and 9/11 bombings.... These deeds, along with recent bombings of embassies and ships, are the paradigms that underlie and inform the current G. W. Bush administration's "war on terrorism."

## 2. War on Terrorism

The Bush administration's war on terrorism appears not only to *invoke* the group target model as applicable to the enemy, it also appears to *exemplify* that model in the way it treats those it regards as the enemy. It views terrorism as a special form of combat or violence, distinguishable on one hand from conventional warfare (terrorists need not be agents of states bound by treaties or international conventions) and on the other from ordinary violent civilian crime (terrorist harm is often on a greater scale and for larger purposes). The upshot is that restrictions applying to conventional warfare and to the treatment of civilian criminals are bypassed. As noted by David Luban, persons arrested and detained as suspected terrorists enjoy neither Prisoner of War (POW) protections nor civil rights.[9] This situation leaves them vulnerable to suffering many forms of terrorism. It can easily seem right, however, to distinguish terrorism from both conventional warfare and ordinary

crime and to treat terrorists differently from POWs and from civilian criminals. First, the discrimination principle (from the "*jus in bello*" part of "just war theory"), which prohibits direct targeting of non-combatants, appears to be increasingly a scruple that is not recognized by terrorists.[10] Second, criminal violence is usually motivated by personal, family, or business interests rather than by political concerns, whereas terrorists are more often politically motivated. Third, criminal violence is also commonly clandestine, whereas terrorists are often politically motivated and sometimes take responsibility publicly.

Yet these distinctions are not firm. On both models, terrorism overlaps substantially with conventional warfare and with ordinary crime. First, in the 20th century, conventional warfare also increasingly departed from the *jus in bello* discrimination principle until by its end, over 80% of war casualties were civilians.[11] That statistic makes dubious whether the old *jus in bello* discrimination principle is any longer even *governing* such warfare. The World War II saturation bombings of Dresden and Tokyo, for example, directly targeted civilians with conventional weapons, aiming to coerce German and Japanese capitulation, sending the message that otherwise more cities would be destroyed.[12]

Second, domestic hate crimes do have political motives, whereas terrorism is often *not* political. Hostages are often taken for private gain.... Taking tellers as hostages is criminal terrorism to coerce law enforcement into letting robbers escape with their loot.

Finally, ordinary crime need not be clandestine. Some bank robbers act in broad daylight.... The Tokyo and Dresden fire bombings were not isolated incidents in the Allied conduct of the war. Less well known than it deserves to be is the massive area bombing by British forces throughout Germany and by US forces in the Pacific.[13] This is terrorism in modern conventional war. Closer to the present, the conduct of US soldiers in Iraq in rounding up detainees indiscriminately as "insurgents" illustrates routine military terrorism. Mark Danner in *Torture and Truth: America, Abu Ghraib, and the War on Terror* quotes a Red Cross report:

Arresting authorities entered houses usually after dark, breaking down doors, waking up residents roughly, yelling orders, forcing family members into one room under military guard while searching the rest of the house and further breaking doors, cabinets, and other property. They arrested suspects, tying their hands in the back with flexi-cuffs, hooding them, and taking them away. Sometimes they arrested all adult males present in a house, including elderly, handicapped or sick people ... pushing people around, insulting, taking aim with rifles, punching and kicking and striking with rifles.[14]

He quotes further:

In almost all instances ..., arresting authorities provided no information about who they were, where their base was located, nor did they explain the cause of arrest. Similarly, they rarely informed the arrestee or his family where he was being taken and for how long, resulting in the de facto "disappearance" of the arrestee.... Many families were left without news for months, often fearing that their relatives were dead.[15]

The Red Cross then notes that military intelligence officers said that "in their estimate between *70 per cent* and *90 per cent of the persons deprived of their liberty in Iraq had been arrested by mistake* [emphasis added by Danner]."[16]

"Mistakes" that occur 90% of the time are not mistakes. This is terrorism. The group target model appears to fit. The ostensible purpose was to coerce information from detainees. But people were selected for round-up on the basis of their identity, not on the basis of prior evidence that they had information. Terrorism was an expedient and a weapon. It may not be clear whether the message-to-others aspect of the coercion model also fits. There could be an implied message in the disappearances – a possible form of hostage-taking – that anyone else who knows anything had better come forward, or their families would be subjected to similar treatment. But even without that message, this activity fits the group target model.

Active opposition to terrorism *as such* would reject not only saturation bombing of cities but tactics described in this Red Cross report. Such a campaign would also publicly expose and aggressively oppose *as terrorist* many kinds of domestic criminal violence: disappearances engineered by oppressive regimes, witness intimidation, drive-by shootings, and even stalking, rape, and intimate relationship violence. I select for special attention ... the cases of oppressive regimes and the often doubly domestic crimes of rape and relationship violence, which have in common that their targets tend to be relatively low-profile.

Perhaps it will be objected that because domestic violence is small-scale compared with mass killings in the bombing of buildings or even ships, calling them "terrorist" alters the meaning and dilutes the seriousness of the concept of terrorism. Yet the appearance of a small scale comes from looking only at individual episodes or at episodes with a single victim. Victims of domestic violence are more spread out in time and space than victims in bombed buildings. Collectively, domestic violence victims are not less numerous.

Individually, many of them suffer equally serious harms and fatalities. Because those who suffer violence in the home need not be prominent individuals, such as government officials, or even individuals about whom prominent people can be expected to care particularly, their cases are better described as "low-profile" than as "small-scale."

[...]

The *group* target model appears inapt to make the case that stalking and intimate relationship violence (relationship violence, for short) can be terrorist, as their *primary* targets are specific individuals. And for the coercion model to fit, as in the case of hold-ups, we need to collapse the two targets. Yet stalking and relationship violence bear relevant similarities to rape terrorism, which fits both models. The two models bring us closer to an intuitive recognition of terrorism in rape when it becomes a practice, whether in war or during times of so-called peace....

### 3. Rape Terrorism

Mass rape of civilians by soldiers and militias during the 1990s wars in the former Yugoslavia and in Rwanda has been publicly exposed as a weapon that was used in a deliberate and calculated manner.[17] It is now widely and officially acknowledged that military rape is not simply a case of "a few bad apples" but has been a matter of policy. War rape directly targets women and girls of all ages, even pregnant women, menstruating women, disabled women, injured women, sick women, even infants. The most salient feature of these targets is their gender, and so the crime initially appears misogynist and in that way to fit the group target model. Were the primary target females, war would simply offer a context in which it is easy to commit misogynist crimes

with impunity. That would not make rape, any more than looting, a weapon. When rape is a weapon, it is not simply a gigantic hate crime against women that happens to be perpetrated by soldiers, even if misogynist soldiers do the actual raping most readily. A military objective of the toleration and encouragement of war rape in the former Yugoslavia was to get Muslim families to leave the territory. That made rape a coercive weapon.

As military policy, war rape appears to fit both the coercion and group target models of terrorism. On the coercion model, the *primary* target is not women and girls; they are the *direct* targets. The *primary* target is an entire people. A coercive threat (message) is aimed at those who resist or who might resist leaving, a slightly more specific target than the people as a whole.[18] Insofar as the objective is not simply to harm the group but to expel it, harm can seem secondary, which makes the coercion model appear right. The basis for selecting direct victims is that, because they are members of the group, publicized abuse of them can intimidate others into leaving.

Rape as a weapon of war is arguably not just coercive, however, but genocidal, insofar as a reasonably foreseeable consequence, if not a major purpose, is the irreversible destruction of families and cultural practices that define a people. So understood, harm is not just instrumental but part of the end sought. Still, military rape can appear more coercive than genocidal if individuals and families who leave can relocate successfully without being pursued and hunted down to be destroyed, as the Nazis did with Jews who fled to other countries. The rape/death camps in the former Yugoslavia imprisoned people who were captured right there, who were unable or unwilling to flee. Genocide may have been a fallback, in the event that coercion to disperse was unsuccessful.

It is less widely appreciated that much

civilian rape is also not simply a matter of rotten apples but is part of a widespread coercive practice or institution.[19] Feminist scholars have long argued that women and girls are targeted for rape not for the most part because they are pretty, flirtatious, or teasing but because they happen to be vulnerable and female.[20] The group target model makes sense of that claim and of the idea that rape harms all women and girls, not just those who are raped. But the group target model also leaves us *mystified*, as in Susan Griffin's report of her childhood perception of the threat of rape, in the observations opening her classic essay "Rape: The All-American Crime":

> I have never been free of the fear of rape.
> From a very early age I, like most women,
> have thought of rape as part of my natural
> environment – something to be feared
> and prayed against like fire or lightning.
> I never asked why men raped; I simply
> thought it one of the many mysteries of
> human nature.[21]

What Griffin describes seems so far to fit the group target model. Yet a few pages later, she proposes an answer to the question of why men rape, invoking the coercion model to dispel the mystery. As in the case of war rape, the coercion model suggests a new identification of the primary target and a new view of the harm rape does even to females who are not raped:

> In the system of chivalry, men protect
> women against men. This is not unlike the
> protection relationship which [organized
> crime] established with small businesses
> in the early part of this [20th] century.
> Indeed, chivalry is an age-old protection
> racket which depends for its existence on
> rape.[22]

The idea is that even men who profess to abhor rape but nevertheless trade "protection" for domestic services (including sexual service) can have an interest in the continued existence of the threat of rape, hence in not having rapists prosecuted zealously. Although individually less powerful, they can play a role, as can others who judge that a woman was "asking for it," analogous to that of military officers who make it evident that rapists will not be prosecuted or will not receive very harsh treatment if they are. It is the intentions of men in these roles, rather than the intentions of individual rapists, that reveal the nature of rape as a coercive practice. How many ordinary men listen with what must appear to be vicarious pleasure, raising no objection, to tales of rape by friends, relatives, acquaintances? One reason men rape is they can. They usually get away with it. That could change with less peer tolerance.

Any woman or girl can become a direct target of civilian rape, if she can be made to appear afterward to have "asked for it," not a difficult task. Rules of the practice make it nearly impossible to prosecute successfully "simple rape" (not aggravated – for example, by threats with a weapon).[23] Again, the group target model appears to fit. But Griffin's analogy with organized crime invokes the context of a practice of extortion, defined by rules that include those of chivalry. Insofar as the message is "good girls don't get raped (they get put on pedestals)," it appears to be directed to females who may be insufficiently attached to, deferential to, or supportive of male "protectors." Again, this is the message apt to be sent by those who could but do not take serious steps to prosecute rapists or discourage rape, who blame the victim, and so on. These are the parties whose roles are analogous to those of military officers and others who choose not to discourage or investigate war rape or treat it seriously. Individual rapists, however, often target specific individuals, not just "a woman" (not to deny that for some – or for many, under some conditions – any woman will do). Although rape as a practice is more about violence than about sex, the individual rapist engages in a sexual performance and may be able to do that only to certain women. Hence, victims need not appear from the rapist's perspective to be randomly selected (although there may be no way for the victim to have predicted the choice, and so, the selection may well appear random from her perspective). Nor need the rapist have any interest in supporting a protection racket (although he may). For these reasons, one may resist the idea that rape as a civilian crime is a form of terrorism.

The claim I wish to defend, however, is more specific: that civilian rape, when supported by a protection racket, is a form of terrorism. It does not matter what the individual rapist's intentions are, in civil society any more than in war. What matters is how he is used. It is only at the level of rules mandating female attachment to male protectors that it becomes possible to see rape as a coercive practice creating an atmosphere of terror for women who would, or who might, violate the rules. Allowing rape, both preemptively and punitively, is the sanction of the rules. And those who back the rules include women, not just men. The very few rapists who are caught and punished are scapegoats that allow the protection racket to continue.

On the coercion model, civilian rape terrorism makes extremely ineligible female independence, assertiveness, or a lifestyle in which a woman's most intimate and enduring primary attachments are to other women. Who, then, is really the primary target? The message now appears directed to lesbians and any women who might prefer not to embrace, defer to, and serve men.[24] Perhaps the primary target really is females in general, conceived as potential lesbians or marriage resisters and other potential trouble-makers for patriarchal politics.

It is an empirical question whether a rape protection racket exists in a particular locale, just as it is an empirical question whether rape is a weapon in a particular war. Rape as a war weapon is now recognized as terrorist; protection racket rape should be so recognized, also.

The coercion and the group target models bring war and civilian rape policies intuitively closer to more widely recognized paradigms of terrorism, such as extortionist practices in organized crime and mass destruction in war. They highlight comparable harms and injustices. They reveal coercion and a lack of due process. Neither model yet makes explicit what is specifically terrorist in these policies (for that, see Section 5)....

## 4. Beyond the Two Models

Restricting terrorism to political violence aimed at groups seems arbitrary, as does restricting it to political violence with a coercive aim. Emma Goldman and Michael Walzer have discussed instances of political violence, including assassinations, that were not aimed at groups.[25] Were they not terrorist? Many 19th- and early 20th-century political activists aimed their violence at specific individuals who occupied positions of public trust and could affect public policy. Walzer notes that some assassins who killed in public apparently had scruples against allowing children to be killed, even as "collateral damage." The lack of randomness leads Walzer to distinguish such political violence from terrorism.

[...]

Like many rapists, stalkers and abusers in intimate relationships target specific individuals. Still, it might seem that the group target model captures these cases. For it appears that most victims are female. A good case can be made for the view that women who suffer domestic abuse are targeted not for who they are or for what they are like as individuals but because they are female, because they are easily accessible by their partners, and because any penalty for the abuse is likely not to be high.

[...]

Although the group target model is not clearly apt, many cases of relationship violence and stalking do appear to fit the coercion model, at least somewhat.... First, both the direct and the indirect targets are usually the same person, whom it is more natural to call "the target." In intimate relationships, as in punishment by the state, the message "do this or else" is usually sent to the same person who will suffer the "or else" if the demand is not met.

Second, what is coercive is more the whole relationship than a series of specific demands, and even the demands are often implicit and vague or general rather than explicit and clear or specific.[26] There are, of course, coercive episodes: batterers escalate violence when a partner attempts to leave, or to get a restraining order, or to report prior violence to friends, doctors, or police. But not every threat, act of violence, or other deed that contributes to a coercive pattern need come with its own demand. Some threats and violent episodes display dominance – show who is boss or demonstrate the futility of resistance – rather than manipulate particular choices.[27] Yet they are part of a pattern that manipulates a partner's attitudes toward the batterer and toward possibilities of resistance. Many episodes that pretend to be punishments (coercive) are better construed as dominance displays, since the "offense" that ostensibly provoked them could not reasonably have been predicted in advance to be an offense

and will not necessarily provoke "punishment" next time. Abused partners are often forced to use imagination and ingenuity to anticipate what will displease or provoke and what will please or pacify.

If assassinations, stalkings, and relationship violence have primary targets that are more focused than groups, terrorist *regimes* can be less discriminating than even the group target model ordinarily allows. In oppressive regimes, harm is aimed by a ruling body, or its representatives, against its own people, or rather against a subset of them that defies definition.[28] Oppressive regimes are notorious for cannibalizing themselves. The French Revolution and ensuing Terror of 1793–1794 (which bequeathed us the concept of terrorism) ostensibly targeted the privileged – royalty, nobility, and clergy who supported them. In practice, however, it targeted *anyone who was perceived as insufficiently supportive of the revolution*, which included former leaders of the revolution. Likewise, Joseph Stalin and Pol Pot (and closer to home, former US Senator Joseph McCarthy and former FBI Director J. Edgar Hoover) targeted anyone who fell into political disfavor.

For terrorist regimes, the group target model is both unhelpful and misleading. The regime's alleged principles do not really explain why many individuals are targeted. They do not yield a group the members of which could have been identified in advance. It may appear that primary targets are certain groups – homosexuals, Communists, Capitalists. In practice, however, those groups are like the targets of the French Terror: anyone who falls into political disfavor. Victims may come to be branded "queer," "Communists," or "Capitalists" *after* the fact (after they have been targeted). People who never identified themselves as members of such groups may be so "identified" by others, for any number of reasons, and treated accordingly. Hence, the terror.

The message not to do anything that would bring one into political disfavor is unhelpful, as there is no reliable way to predict what would stave off political disfavor. Regime violence is often better understood as a dominance display and as coercive in many of the same ways as relationship violence. Some demands, such as "do not even attempt to leave," are specific. Citizens who tried to escape the Soviet Union by going over the Berlin Wall were shot, as are many battered women who try to leave a partner. But targets must often use imagination and ingenuity to avoid being harmed. What they are coerced into is, basically, maintaining a relationship, just as abused intimate partners are, although the relationship is a different one.

Neither model is an entirely satisfactory fit for the cases of oppressive regimes and relationship violence. But the coercion and group target models are best treated not as *definitive* of terrorism but as invitations to *understand* terrorism by identifying with different parties to a relationship that at least one of them perceives as terrorist. That thought experiment is the project of the final section. Applied to low-profile violence, such as intimate relationship violence, that experiment should enable us to recognize terrorism in many of those cases.

## 5. How Terrorism Works

Following the lead of the coercion model, which takes us inside the terrorist's head, suppose we consider what circumstances and objectives might drive one to use terrorist methods, make them appear attractive or tempting. What advantage might terrorist methods offer, as compared with alternatives? Similarly, following the lead of the group target model, which invites us to identify with a potential target, suppose we consider what, if anything, is distinctive about what potential targets have reason to fear, under what circumstances one becomes liable to such fears, and what the fears can do to those who have them, what is so terrifying.

Let us begin with the perspective of targets. Not all terror is a product of terrorism. Nor does terrorism always succeed in arousing terror. But terrorism creates an atmosphere of grave uncertainty, often in the face of what could be imminent danger, which makes fears *reasonable* and can sometimes make terror a natural response. People who belong to an ethnic group, members of which appear to have been targeted just because of their group identity, *have reason* to fear for their own safety. For all they know, they could be next. And next might be any time. There may be nothing they can effectively do to avoid that danger.[29]

Knowing that one is a member of a deliberately targeted group is not the only kind of basis for grave uncertainty. Terrorists' willingness to do "collateral damage" also creates reason for many who are not members of a targeted group to fear being next – caught in the crossfire. Other potential sources of equally grave uncertainty can be created by terrorists. We have reason to fear being next when we cannot predict what instruments are apt to be used as weapons, or when we cannot detect instruments or carriers of danger (an issue with chemical and biological weapons), when we cannot predict *where* the sources of danger may be located (what streets, cities, or airlines to avoid), or if we do not know *when* or for *how long* to be alert. For there may then appear nothing we can do effectively to escape, protect or defend ourselves, or even get braced to withstand assault. Our sense of helplessness is aggravated by the thought that these uncertainties are deliberately created by malevolent parties who are monitoring us while we are unable to monitor them, that they are in control and we are not.

Grave uncertainty about whether one might be next is brought to prominence in the group target model. On that model, all that keeps uncertainty alive is the hope that not all members of the group will eventually become direct targets. Without that hope, resignation can take over. The term "terrorism" suggests the perspective of a target who is not resigned but is still vulnerable to fear and hope.

The coercion model incorporates a different strategy to keep uncertainty alive, to stave off resignation (which can defeat terrorists' ends) and also keep fear manageable. If demands are met, the threat of harm may be withdrawn, or so terrorists would have targets believe. In reality, as the target should know, demands may escalate as a result of success.[30] Hence, uncertainty, and the instability of a fear that is in danger of passing over into resignation – which presents a challenge for the terrorist. But, again, that is getting ahead of the story. The point to note here is that there appears to be something a potential direct target of coercive terrorism can do, namely, pressure a primary target to accede to demands, a task that keeps hope, and thereby uncertainty, alive.

Such atmospheres of uncertainty are common predicaments of unarmed potential targets of bombings, targets of stalking and intimate relationship violence, and targets of oppressive regimes. Unlike most members of hated groups and citizens of oppressive regimes, many targets of stalkers and violent partners know specifically that they are direct targets. They do not have to wonder *who* will be next. But they often cannot predict *when* an assault will be triggered, *what* will trigger it, what *places*, topics of conversation, or potentially offending behaviors to avoid, and so on. If they can predict timing and triggers, they often remain uncertain what instruments will become weapons or what torture the next assault will inflict.

"Reason to *fear*" understates a terrorist target's predicament. Fear need not amount to terror. Fear can be advantageous for mobilizing self-protection. Terror makes us less able to resist. It focuses our energies nonproductively, interferes with our ability to think and plan, undermines competence. It is a panic response. Uncertainty in confronting imminent danger does not always actually produce panic. But it makes us vulnerable to panic, irrationality, imprudence....

[...]

Just as evils are most likely to be so called by victims and seldom by perpetrators, terrorism is apt to be called something else by those whom others identify as terrorists: "freedom fighting," "enforcing discipline," "romantic pursuit," "eliminating traitors," "war," even "war on terrorism."[31] Public perception tends to be controlled more by regimes and dominant partners in intimate relationships, which is surely a factor in why deeds of regimes and of dominant partners in intimate relationships are less widely recognized as terrorist than are deeds that target states or prominent men.

[...]

Consider more fully the position of the terrorist. Like interrogational torture, terrorism can be an expedient. But torture assaults a victim who has already been rendered defenseless (tied up naked on a table or rack, for example).[32] Terrorists, in contrast, often attack targets who are anything but defenseless in terms of their power positions and the resources to which they have access. Terrorism offers the advantage over more conventional modes of attack that it is able to make strategic use of the element of *surprise*, or at least unpredictability, to make up for either or both of two serious sources of disadvantage in a struggle. One source of disadvantage is that of being on the short end of a gross *power disparity*, as is ordinarily the case with individual citizens in relation to their government. The other source of disadvantage is that of being unable to *justify* one's demands to those of whom they are made, as is typically the case with an intimate abuser and with oppressive governments. Although a terrorist can be at both disadvantages simultaneously, often it is one or the other. Intimate abusers, like governments, for example, often do have power but are unable to justify their demands and secure the voluntary cooperation of those they terrorize. If terrorism is ever justifiable, it seems most likely in the case of those who use it to overcome a severe power disadvantage and least likely in the case of those who use it because they are simply unable to justify their demands.

For terrorists who are relatively poor in resources or who are relatively powerless politically, the surprise element has the advantage of giving victims no chance to mobilize their greater resources for protection and defense. To the terrorist, it may not matter whether targets actually feel terror or even whether they are surprised, as long as they are placed in a situation of grave uncertainty that renders them unable to defend or protect themselves against threatened harm. Panic does tend to increase defenselessness. But it can also make a target less prudent, which would be a disadvantage for many coercive terrorists.

The surprise of terrorism is created in various ways. One, captured by the group target model, is arbitrary selection of members of an ethnic, racial, national, or religious group. The surprise in rape terrorism is often of this sort: one is not surprised to learn that a woman was raped, but one is often surprised to learn who it was and who did it. Other ways of creating surprise, which produce a sense of betrayal, include turning against people instruments

they have come to depend on in daily life and regard as benign (box cutters, kitchen knives) or attacking when it is least expected or in circumstances under which people are likely to have let down their guard (in the middle of the night when they are sleeping, for example, which is when terrorist regimes tend to arrest people, when US soldiers in Iraq arrested detainees, when the Chicago police raided the apartment of Fred Hampton).[33] Surprise in rape terrorism can include unexpected betrayal as well, as in some cases of marital rape, war rape by neighbors, and the rape of children by guardians.

Yet, it may be objected, surprise need not be a problematic strategy. In many contests, it is perfectly acceptable for contestants to aim to surprise opponents in order to win. Surprise is a strategy that opponents expect others will try to use against them. What, then, is distinctive about the use of surprise in terrorism?

The answer, I think, is that terrorists strike (or threaten to strike) not just to win but in such a manner that the target cannot even mount a defense. "Winning" is not really the right concept here. "Beating" comes closer. It is tempting to say that terrorism is not so much a mode of fighting as a response that makes fighting unnecessary, which can explain why it is resorted to by those who lack the resources to fight or who are incapable of justifying their aims. Terrorism allows its targets no opportunity to mobilize what forces or resources they have to put up a fight, try to hide, or try to escape. Yet a general presumption exists, not only in morality but even in law and politics, that everyone should be allowed a decent opportunity for self-defense. When assailants appear to violate that presumption, their activity may be perceived, ... depending on the level and seriousness of the violation, as *terrorist*.

Traditions of just war theory and rules of International Humanitarian Law attempt to define distinctions between acceptable and unacceptable ways to take advantage of an enemy's vulnerabilities. They rule out, as "hitting below the belt," the kinds of surprise on which terrorists rely to gain advantage over adversaries. It should be as difficult to justify terrorism, if terrorism is ever justifiable, as it is to justify hitting below the belt. Perhaps the best case is made for those who confront genuine evils against which they can defend themselves no other way. It is true that modern warfare has been unclear about where the belt lies. The old *jus in bello* discrimination principle no longer appears to help very much to pick it out. Nevertheless, it is widely agreed that biological and chemical weapons strike below. In civil society, likewise, criminal offenses become terrorist when a violent perpetrator takes unthinkable advantage of others' vulnerabilities, as in the case of the Washington, DC snipers, Lee Boyd Malvo and John Allen Muhammad, in 2002.[34] Lawbreakers who take hostages also cross that line.

The 9/11 bombers exploited the element of surprise, attacking in broad daylight, literally out of the blue, using as weapons, we are told, civilian transport planes and box cutters. The planners of these attacks, whoever they were, turned against the US its own resources and technology. If *The 9/11 Commission Report*'s identification of the agents is accurate, they also turned against the US its history of trust and goodwill toward immigrants who came to pursue an education or occupational training.[35] Suicide bombers in many parts of the world disguise themselves as ordinary pedestrians, customers, clients, or passengers, exploiting the trust of everyday life that is so much of the glue that holds a society together. What make their deeds terrorist is as much these elements as their principles of target selection or the use of some targets to coerce others. All contribute to creating atmospheres of grave uncertainty, inability to protect or

defend, vulnerability to panic, and the sense that basic trust has been betrayed.

World Trade Center Twin Towers workers were citizens of many nations, members of many racial, ethnic, and religious groups. The Towers may have been targeted in part because of this diversity. Compatibly with the account of *The 9/11 Commission Report* on who the perpetrators were, the message may not have been just "Americans, take note!" but more generally, "anyone who benefits from, supports, or condones those who kill Muslims or endangers Islamic communities, take note!" – a "group" apt to be constituted more like the targets of Stalin or the French Terror than like the targets of racist or homophobic hate crimes. There is no need to understand such terrorism in a manner that would put it on a continuum with genocide.

[...]

For terrorists who occupy positions of political power, and for dominant partners in abusive relationships, surprise violence has special advantages. When one cannot justify one's objectives rationally to others or secure voluntary cooperation, surprise violence has the advantage of removing any need to argue or justify. But in allowing targets no time to think, plan, or respond, it also removes decent opportunities for them to defend themselves. It intimidates potential questioners and keeps them occupied with urgencies. Like terrorist governments, terrorists in intimate relationships use unpredictability to keep targets walking on eggshells, ready to defer. Terrorists in the home can be as creative as the 9/11 bombers in the use of betrayal and surprise to create atmospheres of grave uncertainty, taking advantage of targets' special vulnerabilities.[36] They strike below the belt, not just figuratively. Surprise is an advantage also for governments who must deceive a public, as it gives victims no time to let others know what is being done to them or where they are being taken.

The current US war on terrorism is philosophically misleading with respect to the project of arriving at an adequate, realistic understanding of terrorism because that war was never meant to target terrorists in general. It ignores the terrorism of rape, of violence in intimate relationships, and of terrorist regimes and military policies, such as those described by the Red Cross regarding the US treatment of Arab detainees. A conception of terrorism guided solely by the objective of making sense of the usual suspects, or of the war on terrorism, risks leaving out the commonest, most pervasive forms of terrorism in the world, perpetuating their public invisibility. Even if it remains true that most preventable suffering and death are caused not by terrorism …, an enormous amount of preventable suffering and death, globally, is caused by terrorism against targets who have lacked a public voice.

And how much suicidal terrorism directed against those in positions of power is a desperate, last-ditch attempt also to gain a public voice?[37]

## Study Questions

1. Describe the two models of terrorism that Card discusses. Briefly explain what kinds of activities might be included in each model. Are there types of activities that would be considered terrorism under one model but not the other? Does the fact that there are at least two competing models of understanding terrorism support the idea that there may be many other cases of terrorism that are not recognized as such?

2. What is the argument that Card gives to support the idea that the US war on terrorism is actually a form of terrorism itself? What are the criteria she is using? How does the war on terrorism fit into these criteria? Do you agree with her assessment? What would you consider to be acceptable and unacceptable ways to combat terrorism?

3. Explain how Card sees rape during times of peace to be analogous to war rape. What intentions do the war rapist and the civilian rapist share, and how are those intentions revealed by the way in which they react to instances of rape?

4. If we accept that rape and domestic violence are forms of terrorism, as Card is arguing, what are the benefits to this categorization? That is, presumably rape and domestic violence are already seen as unethical actions by the general public, so how might we think of them differently if they are perceived of specifically as terrorist acts?

## Notes

1 Carl Wellman, "On Terrorism Itself," *Journal of Value Inquiry* 13 (1978), pp. 250–58. This is a model I have relied on and found useful in the past.
2 See, for example, R.M. Hare, "Terrorism," *Journal of Value Inquiry* 13 (1978), pp. 241–49.

3 Susan Braudy, *Family Circle: The Boudins and the Aristocracy of the Left* (New York: Knopf, 2003) details the career and background of Kathy Boudin, member of the Weather Underground, who eventually served 22½ years in prison for complicity in a bank hold-up.

4 See Edward Abbey, *The Monkey Wrench Gang* (Philadelphia: Lippincott, 1975).

5 See documentary film *The Weather Underground*, Bill Seigel and Sam Green (II), (dirs.), 2003 (DVD 2004) and Abbey, *The Monkey Wrench Gang*.

6 Michael Walzer, *Just and Unjust Wars: A Moral Argument with Historical Illustrations* (New York: Basic Books, 1977), pp. 197–206. A version of the coercion model is also currently being developed persuasively by Reitan in "Defining Terrorism," unpublished paper presented at the Pacific Division meetings of the American Philosophical Society, March 2004; cited with permission.

7 Walzer, *Just and Unjust Wars*, p. 197.

8 Simon Wiesenthal, *The Sunflower: On the Possibilities and Limits of Forgiveness*, revised and expanded edition, H.A. Pichler (trans.) (New York: Schocken, 1997), pp. 18–20.

9 David Luban, "The War on Terrorism and the End of Human Rights," *Philosophy and Public Policy Quarterly* 22 (2002), pp. 9–14.

10 Reitan argues that terrorism is distinguished from conventional war in being governed by a variant principle of target selection: target directly only members of the target group ("Defining Terrorism"). A useful introduction to just war theory is William V. O'Brien, *The Conduct of Just and Limited War* (New York: Praeger, 1981).

11 Mary Kaldor, *New and Old Wars: Organized Violence in a Global Era, with an Afterword January 2001* (Stanford: Stanford UP, 1999, 2001), p. 100.

12 There is in addition the claim made by some critics of the bombings of Hiroshima and Nagasaki that a deterrent message was also intended for the Soviet Union.

13 See A.C. Grayling, *Among the Dead Cities: The History and Moral Legacy of the WWII Bombing of Civilians in Germany and Japan* (New York: Walker and Company, 2006).

14 Mark Danner, *Torture and Truth: America, Abu Ghraib, and the War on Terror* (New York: New York Review Books, 2004), p. 2.

15 Danner, *Torture and Truth*, p. 2.

16 Danner, *Torture and Truth*, p. 3.

17 The film *Hotel Rwanda* (Metro-Goldwyn-Mayer, Terry George (dir.), 2004; DVD 2005), excellent in most respects, showed the machetes but failed to convey that mass rape was also a weapon in the Rwandan genocide. For an account of the mass rape in Rwanda, including interviews with survivors, see Human Rights Watch, *Rwanda: Shattered Lives–Sexual Violence during the Rwandan Genocide and its Aftermath* (New York: Human Rights Watch, 1996).

18 On war rape in the former Yugoslavia, see Alexandra Stiglmayr (ed.), *Mass Rape: The War against Women in Bosnia-Herzegovina*, Marion Faber (trans.) (Lincoln: U of Nebraska P, 1994), and Beverly Allen, *Rape Warfare: The Hidden Genocide in Bosnia-Herzegovina and Croatia* (Minneapolis: U of Minnesota P, 1996).

19 Following Rawls, I use the terms "practice" and "institution" interchangeably, understanding them to refer to forms of activity defined by rules that create and distribute powers and opportunities, liabilities, responsibilities for consequences, and so forth.

20 Scholarship on rape in the "Second Wave" of feminism begins with Barbara Mehrhof and Pamela Kearon, "Rape: An Act of Terror," in Anne Koedt, Ellen Levine, and Anita Rapone (eds.), *Radical Feminism* (New York: Quadrangle, 1973), pp. 228–33; Andra Medea and Kathleen Thompson, *Against Rape: A Survival Manual* (New York: Farrar, Straus, Giroux, 1974); and Susan Brownmiller, *Against Our Will: Men, Women, and Rape* (New York: Simon and Schuster, 1975). Other early philosophical classics include four essays (by Susan Griffin, Carolyn M. Shafer and Marilyn Frye, Pamela Foa, and Susan Rae Peterson) in Mary Vetterling-Braggin, Frederick Elliston, and Jane English (eds.), *Feminism and Philosophy*

(Totowa: Littlefield, Adams, 1977), pp. 313–71; Angela Davis, *Women, Race, and Class* (New York: Vintage, 1981), pp. 172–201; Lorenne M.G. Clark and Debra J. Lewis, *Rape: The Price of Coercive Sexuality* (Toronto: The Women's P, 1977). Also influential is Menachem Amir, *Patterns in Forcible Rape* (Chicago: The U of Chicago P, 1971).

21 Griffin, "Rape: The All-American Crime," *Ramparts* (September, 1971), pp. 26–35, reprinted in Vetterling-Braggin et al. (eds.), *Feminism and Philosophy*, pp. 313–32.

22 Griffin, "Rape: The All-American Crime," p. 320.

23 On the rules of rape, see Claudia Card, *The Unnatural Lottery: Character and Moral Luck* (Philadelphia: Temple UP, 1996), pp. 97–117. See, also, Susan Estrich, *Real Rape* (Cambridge: Harvard UP, 1987).

24 For development of the idea that heterosexuality is made compulsory by social practices, see Adrienne Rich, "Compulsory Heterosexuality and Lesbian Existence," *Signs* 5 (1980), pp. 631–60.

25 Walzer, *Just and Unjust Wars*, pp. 197–206; Emma Goldman, *Anarchism and Other Essays* (New York: Dover, 1969), pp. 79–108. See, also, Goldman's autobiography, *Living My Life*, 2 volumes (New York: Knopf, 1931). Goldman was vilified as a terrorist on the basis of her alleged connections with an assassination (President McKinley) and an attempted assassination (Henry Clay Frick).

26 I have discussed this issue at greater length in Claudia Card, *Lesbian Choices* (New York: Columbia UP, 1995), pp. 110–15.

27 For an excellent discussion that makes this point, using Amnesty International's Chart of Coercion, see Ann Jones, *Next Time She'll Be Dead: Battering and How to Stop It* (Boston: Beacon, 1994), pp. 90–91.

28 For accounts of the French Revolution and the Terror of 1793–94, I have relied on Will and Ariel Durant, *The Age of Napoleon* (New York: Simon & Schuster, 1975), pp. 13–87, and Thomas Carlyle, *The French Revolution*, Volume 3 (London: J. Fraser, 1837).

29 This point is made very well by Reitan ("Defining Terrorism").

30 Alan Dershowitz argues that terrorism continues because it succeeds. See Dershowitz, *Why Terrorism Works: Understanding the Threat, Responding to the Challenge* (New Haven: Yale UP, 2002).

31 See Robert E. Goodin, *What's Wrong with Terrorism?* (Cambridge: Polity P, 2006) for development of the idea that governments who cultivate a climate of terror as part of their response to terror may be undermining the autonomy of citizens just as those whom they call "terrorists."

32 See Henry Shue, "Torture," *Philosophy and Public* Affairs 7 (1978), pp. 124–43.

33 On FBI involvement in the Chicago police raid of Hampton's apartment, fatal to Hampton, who died in his bed, see Curt Gentry, *J. Edgar Hoover: The Man and the Secrets* (New York: Plume, 1992), pp. 620–22.

34 See Sari Horwitz and Michael E. Ruane, *Sniper: Inside the Hunt for the Killers Who Terrorized the Nation* (New York: Random House, 2003).

35 There has, of course, been nothing like a trial to confirm the identities of those said to be agents of the 9/11 bombings. For sketches of some of those named as agents, see *The 9/11 Commission Report: Final Report of the National Commission on Terrorist Attacks Upon the United States*, Authorized edition (New York: Norton, n.d.), pp. 145–73.

36 For examples of intimate terrorist creativity, see the film *What Ever Happened to Baby Jane?* Robert Aldrich (dir.), 1962. The film *Sleeping with the Enemy*, Joseph Ruben (dir.), 1991, portrays the use of surprise but fails to capture the inventiveness of abusers in creating it.

37 Thanks to Alison Jaggar, Paula Gottlieb, Mohammed Abed, Vivi Atkin, Sara Gavrell, Fred Harrington, Alan Rubel, and to audiences at the Rocky Mountain Philosophy Conference in Boulder (2006) and at the University of Victoria Lansdowne lecture (2006) for helpful comments, reflections, and suggestions.

# Section IX:
# Caring for the "Other"

Human suffering anywhere concerns men and women everywhere.

– Elie Wiesel, *Night*

ONE COMMON CRITICISM AMONGST fans of the *Star Wars* films is that the Stormtroopers are often very precise in their shooting – except when they are actually shooting at the film's heroes. Then, their aim suddenly becomes extremely bad. This *prima facie* inconsistency is addressed by the comedic website Cracked.com, with the conclusion that this "plot hole" can be easily explained by appealing to what psychological studies tell us about the process of dehumanization. Because the heroes' faces are clearly visible to the Stormtroopers, they have a more difficult time killing them because they see them clearly as persons, whereas our heroes do not experience similar difficulties killing the Stormtroopers because they wear helmets, obfuscating their faces. This is relevant because "when you remove human qualities from a person, you make it much easier to justify acts of violence towards them. Han, Leia, and Luke don't see a person giving his life for the empire, because he thinks it's the right thing to do, or because he was grown in a vat for it and never had a chance to choose – they see an anonymous, faceless, evil robot. No different from the three million other identical soldiers standing next to him."[1]

When we dehumanize others, we tend not to regard them as persons worthy of moral consideration – we end up erasing them from our moral radar. The consequences of this can be severe. When a person is dehumanized, they become "deindividuated, [they] lose the capacity to evoke compassion and moral emotions, and may be treated as [a] means toward vicious ends."[2] When we elect not to see others as sufficiently "like us," we dull our ability to empathize with their perspective or their suffering. Gordon Allport explains this further:

> There is a good reason why out-groups are often chosen as the object of hate and aggression rather than individuals. One human being is, after all, pretty much like another – like oneself. One can scarcely help but sympathize with the victim. To attack him would be to arouse some pain in ourselves. Our own "body image" would be involved, for his body is like our own body. But there is no body image in a group. It is more abstract, more impersonal.... We are less likely to consider [the subject] an individual, and more likely to think of him only as an out-group member.[3]

Indeed, dehumanizing others can so deeply impact our psyche that it may have neurological effects. One study found that

> members of extreme out-groups are so dehumanized that they may not even be encoded as social beings. When participants viewed targets from highly stigmatized social groups (e.g., homeless people and drug addicts) who elicit disgust, the region of the brain typically recruited for social perception (the medial prefrontal cortex) was not recruited. Those who are the least valued in the culture were not deemed worthy of social consideration on a neurological level ... there is a neurological correlate to extreme social devaluation and moral exclusion. When taken together, contemporary research on dehumanization suggests that privileging the "humanity" of one's own group is a common occurrence.[4]

A study by Adam Waytz and Nicholas Epley examined the consequences of social connections for dehumanizing behavior. They concluded that when strong connections are made with others whom we deem to be part of "our" group, the more likely we are to dehumanize those who we perceive as being outside of the group: "the clearest examples of dehumanization arise in intergroup settings in which ingroup members dehumanize outgroup members ... [it] can increase the perceived distance between us and them."[5]

Certain uses of language can have powerful dehumanizing effects. One common way in which this occurs is through the use of racial or ethnic slurs – words that are used to lump all individual members of a community into a single faceless group that is then derided. Several studies have illustrated that the use of slurs reinforces stereotypes and discrimination in the minds of those who

employ them.[6] Richard Delgado writes that "the racial insult remains one of the most pervasive channels through which discriminatory attitudes are imparted. Such language injures the dignity and self-regard of the person to whom it is addressed, communicating the message that distinctions of race are distinctions of merit, dignity, status, and personhood."[7] This kind of prejudicial attitude toward "the other" is typically resistant to any new information that challenges a preconceived narrative. Individuals who really believe, for example, that all Hispanics or African Americans are criminals, or that all Muslims are terrorists, are unlikely to be persuaded by information that illustrates the contrary view, or even by meeting members of the group who don't conform to the stereotype (in those cases, these individuals are typically regarded as the "exception that proves the rule"). Interestingly enough, in what amounts to a "real-world" example of the Stormtrooper phenomenon discussed above, when meeting an actual member of a hated group – when forced to "remove the mask," so to speak, and view the "other" as a *person* rather than as a mere member of an abstract group – the prejudiced person will "often act fairly and even kindly toward individual members of the group."[8]

A contemporary example of the violent consequences of dehumanization can be seen in the anti-Muslim sentiment that has permeated American culture since the attacks of September 11, 2001 – even against individuals who are *perceived* as Muslim. In 2012, a man viciously beat a Sikh taxi driver while shouting anti-Muslim slurs; that same year a gunman killed worshippers at a Sikh temple in Milwaukee, Wisconsin, mistaking them for Muslim. According to one study, since 9/11 the Federal Bureau of Investigation has reported a 1,700% increase in crimes against Muslims.

Dehumanizing others, however, need not always result in such blatant forms of violence. Another consequence, one that is arguably far more pervasive, is simply apathy. Holocaust survivor Elie Wiesel (1928–2016) powerfully makes this point: "The opposite of love is not hate, it's indifference. The opposite of art is not ugliness, it's indifference. The opposite of faith is not heresy, it's indifference. And the opposite of life is not death, it's indifference."[9] Most of us will probably never engage in the kind of violence so far described, but far more of us are simply apathetic to the plights of those who are distant from us. For example, Collin Allen attributes our indifference to the problem of homelessness in the United States to our tendency to dehumanize those we consider to be on the outskirts of society:

> If someone is deemed "homeless," that sole attribute takes priority over all other descriptors, and immediately we start to subconsciously conceptualize what that person looks like, what their social worth is, etc. We can dismiss someone as homeless, which is a lot easier and more pleasant than thinking about how terrible his or her life actually is and thinking about how he or she got there and what can be done to help. As long as they are treated like "non-people," they will continue to be "non-people."[10]

The first step to battling both violence and apathy is to force ourselves to look at each other without helmets – to concentrate on our common humanity. As you read in Section I, this is a vital component of Immanuel Kant's moral philosophy: *all* persons, in virtue of their common rational nature, are worthy of intrinsic dignity and respect, and as such they must always be treated as ends in themselves. Another version of this can be seen in John Stuart Mill's utilitarian philosophy:

the interests of *all* sentient beings, not just the ones we prefer or like the most, must be taken into account in our moral calculations, because all sentient beings can be harmed (or benefitted) from our actions. Yet others will argue that simply *acting* in ways that emphasize commonality is insufficient – we must cultivate the actual sentiments that should accompany those actions. If I have to decide whether I should save a drowning child in a pond, it is not enough that I do so out of an abstract sense of duty, or because my moral calculations suggest that it would result in the best consequences. I should do it because I actually *care* about the welfare of the child. This is part of Nel Noddings's criticism of traditional normative ethics, like utilitarianism and deontology: these theories "approach moral matters in ... mathematical way[s].... Many persons who live moral lives do not approach moral problems this way."[11]

Noddings, whose work is excerpted in this section, is clear that truly caring for others entails acting for their benefit; that is, just *saying* that you care about someone or something is mere lip-service: "When we see another's reality as a possibility for us, we must act to eliminate the intolerable, to reduce the pain, to fill the need, to actualize the dream."[12] Genuinely caring for the welfare of other human beings, even those who lie outside your immediate social circle, is a vital first step toward combatting the apathy that contributes to so many tragedies in the world. This caring involves breaking down the us/them distinction and "[a]pprehending the other's reality."[13]

In the New Testament of the Bible, the person of Jesus Christ repeatedly commands that we must "love thy neighbor as thy self." A similar sentiment appears in the Qur'an: "O mankind! Allah created you from a single (pair) of a male and a female, and made you into nations and tribes, that you may know each other (not that you despise each other)" (49:13). The Old Testament also has similar commands (e.g., Leviticus 19:18). Danish philosopher Søren Kierkegaard, who wrote mainly about Christian ethics, the status of the Church, and the relationship between God and the individual, was particularly interested in understanding the command-ment from a Christian perspective, and this was the subject of his book *Works of Love*, a selection from which appears in this section. Kierkegaard argues that the term "neighbor" refers to *every single human being*, for all humans share in God's "eternal likeness." Kierkegaard draws a distinction between "preferential love" and "unconditional love." The former is the way most human beings practice love; that is, we tend to love only those whom we prefer in some way: *our* children, *our* parents, *our* friends, *our* spouses, *our* fellow country-men. But this kind of love remains selfish because we base it solely on these individuals' relationship to *us*. We don't love *all* children, only *our* children; we don't love *all* parents, only *our* parents. This kind of love still retains our self as the center of our moral universe. Instead, Kierkegaard argues that the biblical commandment forces us to apply this kind of self-love to *all* human beings, to concentrate on our similarities to each other in light of our relationship to God, rather than on our super-ficial differences. Another New Testament verse is relevant here. In Matthew 25:40, Jesus chastises his disciples for not feeding or cloth-ing him. When the disciples protest, saying that they never rejected him, Jesus points to the many others they have rejected, and says to them: "Truly I tell you, whatever you did for one of the least of these brothers and sisters of mine, you did for me."

Kierkegaard's interpretation entails a radical egalitarianism, especially for those who agree with his religious world views. However, this is not to say that his position has no secular moral force; a Kantian appeal to the commonality of our rational nature could work just as well, as could an appeal to our common sentient nature or our com-mon biological humanity. With this in mind, let us take a brief look at the other topics that will be discussed in this section, and how taking seriously the moral imperative to care for others, even distant others, could deeply influence how we deal with moral atrocities. While all these problems may appear over-whelming, and the singular person may feel absolutely powerless to stop them, it is im-perative to remember that in a representative democracy, the people have the power to in-fluence those in charge, who, in turn, possess the resources to intervene and effect real and positive change.

## Genocide

The term *genocide* typically refers to the de-liberate killing of groups of persons based on their race, religion, or ethnicity, often with the goal of eradicating the whole group from ex-istence. When most people think of genocide, they immediately think of the Holocaust. In addition to this moral atrocity, however, there have been many other instances of genocide throughout world history. During World War I, from 1915 to 1923, the Ottoman Empire ini-tiated the Armenian genocide, which horribly massacred over a million men, women, and children of this Christian minority (although the Turkish government has refused to use the term "genocide" to denote the massacre). Armenian people were also sent to concentra-tion camps, where, as in the Holocaust, many were killed through the use of poisonous gas, in addition to often being burned alive. Many Armenian children were killed when they were injected with typhoid fever. During the Iraq–Iran War in 1988, Saddam Hussein initi-ated the Anfal Campaign, killing thousands of Kurds with the use of chemical weapons. After the fall of the Soviet Union in the early 1990s, Muslims in Bosnia were targeted and massacred in an attempt to "ethnically cleanse" the area.

If we are tempted to think that these kinds of atrocities occur only in other parts of the world, we only have to remember the genocide of the Native Americans during the 1800s, and the suffering caused by their forced relocation in what is now known as the Trail of Tears, the route that the Natives took during their ejection. President Andrew Jackson's Indian Removal Act of 1830 led to the starvation, disease, and death of thousands of Cherokees. In 1864, Navajo tribes were deported from their homes (known as the Long Walk of the Navajo), and thousands of them were placed in internment camps in New Mexico, suffering deplorable and inhumane conditions. Indeed, it has been said that Hitler modeled many of the German concentration camps after the US Native American internment camps.[14]

In 1994, for one hundred days, the members of the Hutu majority in the East African state of Rwanda murdered approximately one million members of the Tutsi minority, as well as any Hutu perceived to be sympathetic to the Tutsis. Hutu extremists massacred Tutsis as they were trying to leave their homes, or set up road blocks where Tutsis were immediately gunned down. Tutsi women were systematically raped and often kept as sex slaves before they were murdered. The Hutu militia would attack orphanages with Tutsi children and would murder them with machetes. One of the most notable aspects of the Rwandan genocide is how little the international community did to try to stop it, even though they were fully aware that it was happening. The United States was hesitant to get involved in another conflict within Africa after their 1993 peacekeeping mission in Somalia resulted in

the death of 18 US Army Rangers. However, in a 2013 interview, former president Bill Clinton admitted that "if we'd gone in sooner, I believe we could have saved at least a third of the lives that were lost.... [I]t had an enduring impact on me."[15] President Clinton's feelings of remorse can incite a conversation over the moral responsibility of the bystander in cases of genocide, particularly bystanders with political, monetary, and military power who can intervene in order to halt or prevent incidences of mass extermination.

The fact that so many genocides have occurred, and will likely continue to occur, can be partially blamed on widespread apathy. This is captured in a single line in the film *Hotel Rwanda*, a fictionalized account of the Rwandan genocide. After a videographer captures footage of Tutsis being massacred, hotel manager Paul Rusesabagina (who in real life used the privileges of his position to save over 1,200 Tutsi refugees at the Hotel Mille Collines) states that he is happy the world will see the video, so that they will be incited to intervene. In response, the videographer somberly tells him: "I think, if people see this footage, they'll say 'Oh my God, that's horrible!' then they go on eating their dinners."[16] Arne Johan Vetlesen's essay below discusses what moral obligations bystanders possess to help prevent genocide, and highlights the psychological repercussions of the "us vs. them" mentality that contributes not only to acts of genocide but also to the apathy that allows such atrocities to occur.

## Global Health Care Disparities

Currently, the United States of America stands almost entirely alone amongst industrialized first-world countries in not offering some sort of universal medical coverage program to its citizens. Despite President Barack Obama's implementation of the Affordable Care Act in

2010, millions of Americans remain without health insurance. A 2013 study found that medical bills remain the largest contributor to bankruptcy in the United States.[17] And yet the US spends over 50 per cent of the entire world's health resources on 5 per cent of the world's population.[18] Developing countries that consistently battle abject poverty often face an incredible disparity in health care. While here in the United States, the debate over the safety of childhood vaccines rages, with an increasing number of parents electively opting out of vaccinating their children, the World Health Organization estimates that in 2013 alone, 21.8 million children in poverty-stricken countries such as Ethiopia, India, Kenya, and Pakistan (amongst others) did not receive basic immunizations. Currently 1.5 million children die from vaccine-preventable illnesses every year in developing countries.[19]

In 2014, the United States experienced a brief scare as American medical workers who had contracted Ebola while helping patients in West Africa made their way home. Out of the handful of cases reported, two patients died. The others who were treated in the US fully recovered, and (as of this writing) no new cases have been reported since December 2014. In contrast, poverty-stricken West African countries have experienced a widespread epidemic of Ebola, with a fatality rate as high as 70 per cent in Guinea, Liberia, and Sierra Leone.[20] Ebola is spread via exposure to an infected person's bodily fluids. The cadaver of a person who died from Ebola must be treated with great care in order to avoid contamination, but the burial practices in these countries often include close contact with the body without the necessary precautions. And to compound the problem, the medical resources needed to treat Ebola are paltry in many African countries. Daniel Bausch, an associate professor of public health and medicine who provided Ebola care in West Africa, explains the conditions within which medical staff must work:

If you're in a hospital in Sierra Leone or Guinea, it might not be unusual to say, "I need gloves to examine this patient," and have someone tell you, "We don't have gloves in the hospital today," or "We're out of clean needles," – all the sorts of things you need to protect against Ebola…. [I would] walk into the hospital in the morning and find patients on the floor in pools of vomit, blood, and stool. They had fallen out of their beds during the night, and they were delirious. "What should happen is that a nursing staff or sanitation officer would come and decontaminate the area," he said. "But when you don't have that support, obviously it gets more dangerous." So the disease spreads.[21]

In one of the most comprehensive studies conducted on this issue, the correlation between poverty and health disparities was confirmed. Childhood mortality and maternal malnutrition, for example, is correlated with economic status:

Among all of the countries included in the study, a child from the poorest wealth quintile is twice as likely on average as a child in the richest quintile to die before age 5. The disparity is similar in maternal nutrition, with women in the poorest quintile about twice as likely as those in the wealthiest to be malnourished, and more pronounced in stunting (low height for age) among children.[22]

Resources that we take for granted in the developed world, such as clean water and proper sanitation facilities, are severely lacking in developing countries. In Africa, approximately

358 million people lack access to safe drinking water, and in Latin America there are about 36 million without access. This is in contrast to 9 million people across *all* of the developed countries, including the United States and all of Europe. Lack of access to proper sanitation services contributes to over 800,000 deaths per year across the globe.[23] Repeated studies have illustrated the connection between poverty and poor health, not only between the developed and developing countries, but even within the residents of the former: "the poorest people in most societies almost always experience higher morbidity levels, die younger (on average), and experience higher levels of child and maternal mortality."[24] Clearly, if we are to take seriously the moral imperative to care for others, and claim to harbor a universal respect for human life, it is unacceptable that this state of affairs continues to run rampant. In their essay in this section, Solomon Benatar, Abdallah Daar, and Peter Singer focuses on various issues pertaining to global health-care disparities and their relationship to poverty and free-market forces. The very first step, they argue, is to acknowledge, in earnest, the intrinsic value of all human life, regardless of people's location, nationality, ethnicity, or race, and to take active policy steps to show that we acknowledge that value.

## Issues in Economic Injustice

Here in the United States, homelessness and childhood poverty are on the rise and have reached troublesome levels. A 2013 study illustrated that 14.3 per cent of households in the United States (a total of 17.5 million households) struggle with food insecurity, meaning that they lack "consistent, dependable access to enough food for active, healthy living."[25] A 2012 study saw the homeless population in New York City rise to 43,000, including 17,000 children. The rates of homelessness were "the worst for New York City ... since the Great Depression. And one of the major reasons is that, for the first time since modern homelessness began, the City provides no housing assistance to help homeless children and adults move from shelters to permanent housing."[26] In 2013, the Community Partnership for the Prevention of Homelessness conducted a survey in Washington, DC, and counted a total of 6,865 homeless persons for that year alone (though this was noted to be a 1.4-per-cent decrease from the year before). In a testament to the impact that state-sponsored programs can have for curbing homelessness, that same year, 643 families had been found stable shelter due to the Prevention and Rapid Re-Housing programs funded by the DC Department of Human Services and the Department of Veteran Affairs.[27]

Moreover, the facts on global poverty are deeply disconcerting. In addition to the lack of clean water and sanitation that plagues so many developing countries, over three billion people in the world live on less than $2.50 per day; 80 per cent live on less than $10 a day. In 2013, an estimated 22,000 children died *per day* across the world due to the consequences of poverty, and approximately "27–28 per cent of all children in developing countries are estimated to be underweight or stunted."[28] There are approximately 2.2 billion children in the world, and almost half of them live in poverty. As mentioned above, although basic childhood vaccines are plentiful in the United States, there are approximately 22 million infants in the world who are not vaccinated. The American Academy of Pediatrics maintains that the cost of immunizing every single child in the world from pneumonia, diarrhea, polio, and measles would be only $20 per child.[29] Two of the biggest supporters of universal childhood vaccinations are Bill and Melinda Gates who, through their Foundation, have donated billions of dollars to vaccination supply and access to the poorest parts of the world. Peter Singer has been highlighting the plight of the impoverished, and the moral obligations we have as citizens in first-world countries to help alleviate it, since the publication of his 1971 essay "Famine, Affluence, and Morality." In the essay reprinted here, "What Should a Billionaire Give and What Should You?," Singer applies the utilitarian moral theory to argue that individuals who have money left over for luxury items have a moral obligation to help others obtain their most basic necessities. Many of us, often unwittingly, have contributed to the plights of the poor in other countries by benefitting from the goods produced in sweatshops and other factories with ethically questionable labor practices. In 2010, eighteen employees working for the company Foxconn in China attempted suicide while at their jobs – fourteen succeeded. All of the employees were young, no older than 25, and the surviving ones pointed toward the inhumane and abhorrent labor conditions they had to endure. Foxconn has business ties with companies that produce many of the products we routinely use in the US: Dell, Nokia, Sony, and Apple – indeed, one of their factories in Longhua makes about 137,000 Apple iPhones per day.[30] One of the workers who attempted suicide, Tian Yu, was 17 when she jumped out of a window, and although she survived, she is now a paraplegic. Her personal narrative is a window into the working conditions she endured:

> I woke up at 6:30 am, attended an unpaid morning meeting at 7:20 am, started work at 7:40 am, went to lunch at 11, and then usually skipped the evening meal to work overtime until 7:40 pm ... There seemed to be no way for me to say 'no' to overtime ... Toilet breaks during the working hours are also restricted ... I had to ask permission from the assistant line leaders to leave my seat ... [I worked] twelve-hour days with a single day off every second week ... Friendly chit-chat among co-workers is not very common even during the break; everyone rushes to queue up for lunch and eat quickly. The company prohibits conversation in the workshop ... After work, all of us – more than 100 people – are sometimes made to stay behind. This happens whenever a worker is punished. A girl is forced to stand at attention to read aloud a statement of self-criticism ... After I had worked a month, when it was time to distribute wages, everyone got their wage debit cards, but I did not.[31]

In response to the suicides, the company hired counselors for their workers – and installed nets to catch anyone else who attempted to jump.

These companies are not alone in their dubious labor practices. A 2006 report by the National Labor Committee found approximately 200 children, many younger than eleven, making clothing in Bangladesh for companies such as Walmart, Hanes, and JCPenney. The children "report being routinely slapped and beaten, sometimes falling down from exhaustion, forced to work 12 to 14 hours a day, even some all-night, 19- to 20-hour shifts, often seven days a week, for wages as low as 6 ½ cents an hour. The wages are so wretchedly low that many of the child workers get up at 5:00 am each morning to brush their teeth using just their finger and ashes from the fire, since they cannot afford a toothbrush or toothpaste."[32] The Disney Company has also come under fire for using sweatshop labor to create their clothing and toys; for example, one company, also in Bangladesh, has been accused of inhumane practices such as paying workers only five cents per article of clothing sewn, and as little as $5.28 a week; not providing any health insurance and no physician on site to care for injuries; workers only having access to dirty drinking water, and being forced to work anywhere between 35–42 hours of overtime a week, often with little or no overtime pay. Women are routinely denied any maternity benefit. There are no vacation days. Workers are not allowed to talk during working hours and must meet excessive quotas (such as ironing 100 pieces of garments in one hour). A plant in Nigeria that makes Disney products "routinely holds back paying wages by an additional week or two." In one instance, when the workers demanded their wages, they were beaten, imprisoned, and then fired.[33]

As Kant argued, it is morally wrong to dehumanize a person to the extent that (s)he is treated as mere means to some end. A strong case can be made that sweatshop workers are clearly being treated in a way that violates this imperative. This is the argument made by Denis Arnold and Norman Bowie in "Sweatshops and Respect for Persons," reprinted in this section. They defend the thesis that respecting the dignity of these workers involves providing a liveable wage, safe working environments, and protections under a rule of law designed to ensure their rights.

W.D. Ross argues that one of the *prima facie* duties we possess to each other is the duty of reparation – the duty to make up for any injuries that we have caused against others. Given that so many of us in the developed world contribute to the systematic subjugation and humiliation of workers in sweatshops by purchasing the products made in these factories, our duty of reparation requires that we be more conscientious about the companies we support. The group United Students against Sweatshops has worked to convince several universities to sever their business relationships with corporations using sweatshop labor to produce college apparel. Because of their efforts, in 2014 Cornell University stopped conducting business with JanSport after the company failed to sign an agreement to improve the labor conditions of their Bangladesh factories, despite the deaths of hundreds of workers in 2013 after one of their garment factories collapsed. Other universities, including American University, Boston University, Macalester College, the University of Michigan, and Pennsylvania State University, have followed suit.

These changes are a testament to what can be achieved when the public becomes educated and decides to use their consumer power to make a positive impact in the lives of others. The first step to "re-humanizing" and caring for the "other" is the realization that, in the end, they are not really "others" after all.

## Notes

1  Karl Smallwood. 2010. "The Biggest Star Wars Plot Hole, Explained by Science." Cracked. com. http://www.cracked.com/article_18858_the-biggest-star-wars-plot-hole- explained-by-science.html.

2  Nick Haslam, "Dehumanization: An Integrative Review," *Personality and Social Psychology Review* 10 (2006): 255.

3  Gordon Allport, "The Nature of Hatred," in *Hatred, Bigotry, and Prejudice*, ed. Robert M. Baird and Stuart E. Rosenbaum (Amherst, NY: Prometheus Books, 1979), p. 91.

4  Phillip Goff, Jennifer L. Eberhardt, Melissa J. Williams, and Matthew Christian Jackson, "Not Yet Human: Implicit Knowledge, Historical Dehumanization, and Contemporary Consequences," *Journal of Personality and Social Psychology* 94 (2008): 293–94.

5  Adam Waytz and Nicholas Epley, "Social Connection Enables Dehumanization," *Journal of Experimental Social Psychology* 28 (2012): 71, 75.

6  See, for example, Martin Reisig and Ruth Wodak, *Discourse and Discrimination: Rhetorics of Racism and Anti-Semitism* (New York: Routledge, 2001); Teun van Dijk, *Elite Discourse and Racism* (London: SAGE Series on Race and Ethnic Relations, 1993).

7  Richard Delgado, "Words that Wound: A Tort Action for Racial Insults, Epithets, and Name-Calling," *Harvard Civil Rights-Civil Liberties Law Review* 17 (1982): 135–36.

8  Allport, "The Nature of Hatred," p. 92.

9  Elie Wiesel, *US News & World Report* 27 October 1986.

10  Colin Allen, "Parallel Dualisms: Understanding America's Apathy for the Homeless through the Sociological Imagination," *Human Architecture: Journal of Sociology of Self-Knowledge* 5.2 (2007): 5.

11  Nel Noddings, *Caring: A Feminine Approach to Ethics and Moral Education* (Berkeley: U of California P, 1984), p. 8.

12  Noddings 1984, p. 14.

13  Noddings 1984, p. 16.

14  See John Toland, *Adolf Hitler: The Definitive Biography* (New York: Anchor Books, 1976).

15  Interview with President Bill Clinton, *CNBC*, http://www.cnbc.com/id/100546207#.

16  *Hotel Rwanda*, dir. Terry George, MGM/United Artists, 2004.

17  Christina LaMontagne, "NerdWallet Health finds Medical Bankruptcy Accounts for Majority of Personal Bankruptcies," 26 Mar. 2014, http://www.nerdwallet.com/blog/health/2014/03/26/medical-bankruptcy/.

18  Barry Bloom, "The Future of Public Health," *Nature* 402 (1999): Supplement, C63–64.

19  World Health Organization, "Global Immunization Data," 2014, http://www.who.int/immunization/monitoring_surveillance/global_immunization_data.pdf?ua= 1.

20  WHO Ebola Response Team, "Ebola Virus Disease in West Africa – The First 9 Months of the Epidemic and Forward Projections," *The New England Journal of Medicine* 371 (2014): 1481–95.

21  Julia Belluz, "Seven Reasons Why This Ebola Epidemic Spun out of Control," 4 September 2014, http://www.vox.com/2014/9/4/6103039/Seven-reasons-why-this-ebola-virus-outbreak- epidemic-out-of-control.

22  Population Reference Bureau, "Improving the Health of the World's Poorest People," April 2004, http://www.prb.org/pdf04/improvingtheHealthbrief_Eng.pdf.

23  "Facts about Water and Sanitation," n.d., http://water.org/water-crisis/water-facts/water/.

24  Ursula Grant, "Health and Poverty Linkages: Perspectives of the Chronically Poor," February 2005, http://www.chronicpoverty.org/uploads/publication_files/CPR2_Background_Papers_Grant_05.pdf.

25  United States Department of Agriculture, "Household Food Security in the United States in 2013," September 2014, http://www.ers.usda.gov/media/1565410/err173_summary.pdf.

26  Patrick Markee, "State of the Homeless in 2012," 8 June 2012, http://www.coalitionfortheehomeless.org//uploads/2013/03/StateoftheHomeless2012.pdf.

27  The Community Partnership for the Prevention of the Homelessness, "Homelessness in the Distinct of Columbia," 2013, http://www.community-partnership.org/facts-and-figures.

28  Anup Shah, "Poverty Facts and Stats," http://www.globalissues.org/article/26/poverty-facts-and-stats.

29  American Academy of Pediatrics, "Global Immunizations," http://www2.aap.org/international/immunization/pdf/GlobalImmunizations_FactSheet.pdf.

30  Aditya Chakrabortty, "The Woman Who Nearly Died Making Your iPad." *The Guardian*, 5 August 2013, http://www.theguardian.com/commentisfree/2013/aug/05/woman-nearly-died- making-ipad.

31  Jenny Chan, "A Suicide Survivor: The Life of a Chinese Worker," *New Technology, Work, and Employment* 28.2 (2013): 88–90.

32  Labor and Worklife, "Children Found Sewing Clothing For Wal-Mart, Hanes & Other U.S. & European Companies," http://www.law.harvard.edu/programs/lwp/NLC_childlabor.html.

33  Global Labor Rights, "Disney Sweatshop in Bangladesh," http://www.globallabourrights.org/reports/document/0403-IGLHR-DisneySweatshopInBangladeshNiagra.pdf.

# 1.   Nel Noddings, *Caring*

IN THIS EXCERPT FROM her widely influential book *Caring: A Feminine Approach to Ethics and Moral Education* (1984), Nel Noddings (b. 1929) outlines the moral theory of care ethics, which emphasizes the importance of dependencies, empathy, compassion, motivations that stem from care, and the relationship between the "cared-for" and the "one-caring." Most relevant for the aims of this section, Noddings focuses on the ethical responsibilities we have for each other, what it means to care for the "other," and the phenomenology of both the person being cared for and the one doing the caring. One thing to keep in mind while reading is Noddings's assertion that an ethic of care is predominantly a feminine approach to ethics. While she does *not* claim that men are incapable of care, she does believe that men tend to approach moral dilemmas more like a math problem that needs to be solved (what she calls the "rational-cognitive approach"), while women are more focused on feelings, engrossment with others, and the ethical responsibilities that arise from relationships. It is worth thinking about whether this analysis is accurate and, if it is, from where those differences arise.

---

### 1. Why Care about Caring?

The Fundamental Nature of Caring

... IT SEEMS OBVIOUS IN an everyday sense why we should be interested in caring. Everywhere we hear the complaint "Nobody cares!" and our increasing immersion in bureaucratic procedures and regulations leads us to predict that the complaint will continue to be heard. As human beings we want to care and to be cared for. *Caring* is important in itself. It seems necessary, however, to motivate the sort of detailed analysis I propose; that is, it is reasonable in a philosophical context to ask: Why care about caring?

If we were starting out on a traditional investigation of what it means to be moral, we would almost certainly start with a discussion of moral judgment and moral reasoning. This approach has obvious advantages. It gives us something public and tangible to grapple with – the statements that describe our thinking on moral matters. But I shall argue that this is not the only – nor even the best – starting point. Starting the discussion of moral matters with principles, definitions, and demonstrations is rather like starting the solution of a mathematical problem formally. Sometimes we can and do proceed this way, but when the problematic situation is new, baffling, or especially complex, we cannot start this way. We have to operate in an intuitive or receptive mode that is somewhat mysterious, internal, and nonsequential. After the solution has been found by intuitive methods, we may proceed with the construction of a formal demonstration or proof. As the mathematician Gauss put it: "I have got my result but I do not know yet how to get (prove) it."[1] A difficulty in mathematics teaching is that we too rarely share our fundamental mathematical thinking with our students. We present everything ready-made as it were, as though it springs from our foreheads in formal perfection. The same sort of difficulty arises when we approach the teaching of morality or ethical behavior from a rational-cognitive approach. We fail to share with each other the feelings, the conflicts, the hopes and ideas that influence our eventual choices. We share only the justification for our acts and not what motivates and touches us.

I think we are doubly mistaken when we approach moral matters in this mathematical way. First, of course, we miss sharing the heuristic processes in our ethical thinking just as we miss that sharing when we approach mathematics itself formally. But this difficulty could be remedied pedagogically. We would not have to change our approach to ethics but only to the teaching of ethical behavior or ethical thinking. Second, however, when we approach moral matters through the study of moral reasoning, we are led quite naturally to suppose that ethics is necessarily a subject that must be cast in the language of principle and demonstration. This, I shall argue, is a mistake.

Many persons who live moral lives do not approach moral problems formally. Women, in particular, seem to approach moral problems by placing themselves as nearly as possible in concrete situations and assuming personal responsibility for the choices to be made. They define themselves in terms of *caring* and work their way through moral problems from the position of one-caring.[2] This position or attitude of caring activates a complex structure of memories, feelings, and capacities. Further, the process of moral decision making that is founded on caring requires a process of concretization rather than one of abstraction; An ethic built on caring is, I think, characteristically and essentially feminine – which is not to say, of course, that it cannot be shared by men, any more than we should care to say that traditional moral systems cannot be embraced by men. But an ethic of caring arises, I believe, out of our experience as women, just as the traditional logical approach to ethical problems arises more obviously from masculine experience.

One reason, then, for conducting the comprehensive and appreciative investigation of caring to which we shall now turn is to capture conceptually a feminine – or simply an alternative – approach to matters of morality.

## What Does It Mean To Care?

Our dictionaries tell us that "care" is a state of mental suffering or of engrossment: to care is to be in a burdened mental state, one of anxiety, fear, or solicitude about something or someone. Alternatively, one cares for something or someone if one has a regard for or inclination toward that something or someone. If I have an inclination toward mathematics, I may willingly spend some time with it, and if I have a regard for you, what you think, feel, and desire will matter to me. And, again, to care may mean to be charged with the protection, welfare, or maintenance of something or someone.

These definitions represent different uses of "care" but, in the deepest human sense, we shall see that elements of each of them are involved in caring. In one sense, I may equate "cares" with "burdens"; I have cares in certain matters (professional, personal, or public) if I have burdens or worries, if I fret over current and projected states of affairs. In another sense, I *care* for someone if I feel a stir of desire or inclination toward him. In a related sense, I *care* for someone if I have regard for his views and interests. In the third sense, I have the care of an elderly relative if I am charged with the responsibility for his physical welfare. But, clearly, in the deep human sense that will occupy us, I cannot claim to care for my relative if my caretaking is perfunctory or grudging.

We see that it will be necessary to give much of our attention to the one-caring in our analysis. Even though we sometimes judge caring from the outside, as third-persons, it is easy to see that the essential elements of caring are located in the relation between the one-caring and the cared-for. In a lovely little book, *On Caring*, Milton Mayeroff describes caring largely through the view of one-caring. He begins by saying: "To care for another person, in the most significant sense, is to help him grow and actualize himself."[3] ...

... When my caring is directed to living things, I must consider their natures, ways of life, needs, and desires. And, although I can never accomplish it entirely, I try to apprehend the reality of the other.

This is the fundamental aspect of caring from the inside. When I look at and think about how I am when I care, I realize that there is invariably this displacement of interest from my own reality to the reality of the other. (Our discussion now will be confined to caring for persons.) Kierkegaard has said that we apprehend another's reality as *possibility*.[4] To be touched, to have aroused in me something that will disturb my own ethical reality, I must see the other's reality as a possibility for my own. This is not to say that I cannot try to see the other's reality differently. Indeed, I can. I can look at it objectively by collecting factual data; I can look at it historically. If it is heroic, I can come to admire it. But this sort of looking does not touch my own ethical reality; it may even distract me from it. As Kierkegaard put it:

> Ethically speaking there is nothing so conducive to sound sleep as admiration of another person's ethical reality. And again ethically speaking, if there is anything that can stir and rouse a man, it is a possibility ideally requiring itself of a human being.[5]

But I am suggesting that we do not see only the direct possibilities for becoming better than we are when we struggle toward the reality of the other. We also have aroused in us the feeling, "I must do something." When

we see the other's reality as a possibility for us, we must act to eliminate the intolerable, to reduce the pain, to fill the need, to actualize the dream. When I am in this sort of relationship with another, when the other's reality becomes a real possibility for me, I care....

Apprehending the other's reality, feeling what he feels as nearly as possible, is the essential part of caring from the view of the one-caring. For if I take on the other's reality as possibility and begin to feel its reality, I feel, also, that I must act accordingly; that is, I am impelled to act as though in my own behalf, but in behalf of the other. Now, of course, this feeling that I must act may or may not be sustained. I must make a commitment to act. The commitment to act in behalf of the cared-for, a continued interest in his reality throughout the appropriate time span, and the continual renewal of commitment over this span of time are the essential elements of caring from the inner view....

... As I think about how I feel when I care, about what my frame of mind is, I see that my caring is always characterized by a move away from self....

The one cared-for sees the concern, delight, or interest in the eyes of the one-caring and feels her warmth in both verbal and body language. To the cared-for no act in his behalf is quite as important or influential as the attitude of the one-caring.... When the attitude of the one-caring bespeaks caring, the cared-for glows, grows stronger, and feels not so much that he has been given something as that something has been added to him....

## Caring and Acting

... Our motivation in caring is directed toward the welfare, protection, or enhancement of the cared-for. When we care, we should, ideally, be able to present reasons for our action/inaction which would persuade a reasonable, disinterested observer that we have acted in behalf of the cared-for. This does not mean that all such observers have to agree that they would have behaved exactly as we did in a particular caring situation. They may, on the contrary, see preferred alternatives. They may experience the very conflicts that caused us anxiety and still suggest a different course of action; or they may proceed in a purely rational-objective way and suggest the same or a different course. But, frequently, and especially in the case of inaction, we are not willing to supply reasons to an actual observer; our ideal observer is, and remains, an abstraction. The reasons we would give, those we give to ourselves in honest subjective thinking, should be so well connected to the objective elements of the problem that our course of action clearly either stands a chance of succeeding in behalf of the cared-for, or can have been engaged in only with the hope of effecting something for the cared-for.

Caring involves stepping out of one's own personal frame of reference into the other's. When we care, we consider the other's point of view, his objective needs, and what he expects of us. Our attention, our mental engrossment is on the cared-for, not on ourselves. Our reasons for acting, then, have to do both with the other's wants and desires and with the objective elements of his problematic situation....

To act as one-caring, then, is to act with special regard for the particular person in a concrete situation. We act not to achieve for ourselves a commendation but to protect or enhance the welfare of the cared-for. Because we are inclined toward the cared-for, we want to act in a way that will please him. But we wish to please him for his sake and not for the promise of his grateful response to our generosity....

My concern is for the ethical ideal, for my own ethical ideal and for whatever part of it others in my community may share. Ideally, another human being should be able to request, with expectation of positive response, my help and comfort. If I am not blinded by fear, or rage, or hatred, I should reach out as one-caring to the proximate stranger who entreats my help....

The duty to enhance the ethical ideal, the commitment to caring, invokes a duty to promote skepticism and noninstitutional affiliation. In a deep sense, no institution or nation can be ethical. It cannot meet the other as one-caring or as one trying to care. It can only capture in general terms what particular ones-caring would like to have done in well-described situations. Laws, manifestos, and proclamations are not, on this account, either empty or useless; but they are limited, and they may support immoral as well as moral actions. Only the individual can be truly called to ethical behavior, and the individual can never give way to encapsulated moral guides, although she may safely accept them in ordinary, untroubled times.

Everything depends, then, upon the will to be good, to remain in caring relation to the other....

## Study Questions

1. Noddings would argue that deontology and utilitarianism (in their various incarnations) are normative ethical theories that mostly adhere to the "rational-cognitive approach" to moral dilemmas. Given what you learned in Section I, and in this reading as well, do you agree or disagree with her assessment of these theories? Noddings further argues that, because of this approach, these theories fail to appreciate some

important aspects of our ethical lives, ones that care ethics does a much better job of capturing. Do you believe that this is true? If so, what are these aspects?

2. Noddings argues that care ethics is "characteristically and essentially feminine ... an ethic of care arises, I believe, out of our experiences as women." Notice that she does not say that men are not capable of caring, but that, in general, focusing more on care, compassion, empathy, and relationships when facing moral dilemmas is more associated with a feminine viewpoint, whereas men tend to approach ethics in a more calculated manner (again, see Kant's and Mill's respective writings). Why do you believe she says this? Do you agree? If not, why not? If so, why do you think these differences in perspectives exist between men and women?

3. Noddings argues that to truly engage in a caring relationship with others, we have to step outside our own perspectives and "apprehend the reality of the other." This precludes any attempt to dehumanize others, to see them as less worthy of dignity and respect than you are. Noddings calls this "engrossment" – the genuine attempt to see the world through the eyes of another; to gain a better understanding of him or her. What do you think of her claim that being a caring individual requires genuine engrossment with others? What changes in the world do you think would occur if people tried to engross themselves with one another? Can you think of a time when your ethical perspective was altered because you practiced engrossment?

4. Throughout the rest of this section you will be reading about ethical issues that may benefit from an analysis that incorporates engrossing oneself in the realities of others – in particular others with whom we may fail to typically identify due to class differences, ethnic or racial differences, or simply distance. Pick one of those topics and filter your ethical analysis of it through an ethics of care. How would that analysis differ (if it all) from applying a deontic or utilitarian approach? Can implementing care ethics when approaching ethical issues help enact social change? Why or why not?

## Notes

1  Gauss's remark is quoted by Morris Kline, *Why Johnny Can't Add* (New York: Vintage Books, 1974), p. 58.
2  See Carol Gilligan, "In a Different Voice: Women's Conception of the Self and of Morality," *Harvard Education Review* 47 (1977), 481–517. Also, "Woman's Place in Man's Life Cycle," *Harvard Education Review* 49 (1979), 431–46. Also, *In a Different Voice* (Cambridge, MA: Harvard UP), 1982.
3  Milton Mayeroff, *On Caring* (New York: Harper and Row, 1971), p. 1.
4  Søren Kierkegaard, *Concluding Unscientific Postscript*, trans. David F. Swenson and Walter Lowrie (Princeton: Princeton UP, 1941).
5  Ibid., p. 322.

## 2. Søren Kierkegaard, *Works of Love*

DANISH PHILOSOPHER SØREN KIERKEGAARD (1813–55) is widely regarded as the father of existentialism. In *Works of Love* (1847), Kierkegaard's main focus is to examine the commandment in Matthew 22:39 of the New Testament: "You shall love the neighbor as yourself." What, Kierkegaard asks, could God have meant by this command? This excerpt highlights two aspects of Kierkegaard's analysis that are pertinent for the purpose of this section. First, he maintains that the term "neighbor" refers to *every single human being*, rather than just our family, friends, fellow countrymen, etc. This leads to the second point: the purpose of the commandment is to get human beings to move beyond what Kierkegaard calls "preferential love" (loving only those with whom we have a relationship, and thus those whom we *prefer*) toward "unconditional love" (love toward all human beings in virtue that all are created in God's image). It is important to consider the radical change in our social and ethical lives if we were to genuinely try to adopt Kierkegaard's words; it would entail concentrating on our universal similarities rather than our differences.

---

### You Shall Love

Matthew 22:39. But the second commandment is like it: You shall love your neighbor as yourself.

EVERY DISCOURSE, PARTICULARLY A section of a discourse, usually presupposes something that is the starting point. Someone who wishes to deliberate on the discourse or statement therefore does well to find this presupposition first in order then to begin with it. Our quoted text also contains a presupposition that, although it comes last, is nevertheless the beginning. When it is said, "You shall love your neighbor ... as yourself," this contains what is presupposed, that every person loves himself.... [I]t is Christianity's intention to wrest self-love away from us human beings.

In other words, this is implied in loving oneself; but if one is to love the neighbor *as oneself*, then the commandment, as with a pick, wrenches ... open the lock of self-love and wrests ... it away from a person. If the commandment about loving the neighbor were expressed in any other way than with this little phrase, *as yourself*, which simultaneously is so easy to handle and yet has the elasticity of eternity, the commandment would be unable to cope with self-love in this way. This *as yourself* does not vacillate in its aim, and therefore, judging with the unshakableness of eternity, it penetrates into the innermost hiding place where a person loves himself; it does not leave self-love the slightest little excuse, the least little way of escape. How amazing! Long and discerning addresses could be delivered on how a person ought to love his neighbor, and when the addresses had been heard, self-love would still be able to hit upon excuses and find a way of escape, because the subject had not been entirely exhausted, all circumstances had not been taken into account, because something had continually been forgotten or something had not been accurately and bindingly enough expressed and described. But this *as yourself* – indeed, no wrestler ... can wrap himself around the one he wrestles as this commandment wraps itself around self-love, which cannot move from the spot.....

*Who, then, is one's neighbor?* The word is obviously derived from "nearest" ... thus the neighbor is the person who is nearer to you than anyone else, yet not in the sense of preferential love, since to love someone who in the sense of preferential love is nearer than anyone else is self-love – "do not the pagans also do the same?" The neighbor, then, is nearer to you than anyone else. But is he also nearer to you than you are to yourself? No, that he is not, but he is just as near, or he ought to be just as near to you. The concept "neighbor" is actually the redoubling of your own self; "the neighbor" is what thinkers call "the other," that by which the selfishness in self-love is to be tested.... To be sure, "neighbor" in itself is a multiplicity, since "the neighbor" means "all people," and yet in another sense one person is enough in order for you to be able to practice the Law....

In this way *the neighbor* comes as close to self-love as possible. If there are only two people, the other person is the neighbor; if there are millions, everyone of these is the neighbor, who in turn is closer than *the friend* and *the beloved*, inasmuch as they, as the objects of preference, more or less hold together with the self-love in one. Usually a person is aware of the existence of the neighbor and of his being so close when he thinks he has privileges in relation to him or is able to claim something from him. If someone with this view asks, "Who is my neighbor?" then that reply of Christ to the Pharisee will contain an answer only in a singular way, because in the answer the question is actually first turned around, whereby the meaning is: how is a person to ask the question. That is, after having told the parable of the merciful Samaritan, Christ says to the Pharisee (Luke 10:36), "Which of these three seems to you to have been the neighbor to the man who had fallen among robbers?" and the Pharisee answers *correctly*, "The one who showed mercy on him" – that is, by acknowledging your duty you easily discover who your neighbor is. The Pharisee's answer is contained in Christ's question, which by its form compelled the Pharisee to answer in that way. The one to whom I have a duty is my neighbor, and when I fulfill my duty I show that I am a neighbor. Christ does not speak about knowing the neighbor but about becoming a neighbor oneself, about showing oneself to be a neighbor just as the Samaritan showed it by his mercy. By this he did not show that the assaulted man was his neighbor but that he was a neighbor of the one assaulted. The Levite and the priest were in a stricter sense the victim's neighbor, but they wished to ignore it. The Samaritan, on the other hand, who because of prejudice was predisposed to misunderstanding, nevertheless correctly understood that he was a neighbor of the assaulted man. To choose a beloved, to find a friend, yes, this is a complicated business, but one's neighbor is easy to recognize, easy to find if only one will personally – acknowledge one's duty.

The commandment said, "You shall love your neighbor as yourself," but if the commandment is properly understood it also says the opposite: *You shall love yourself in the right way....* To love yourself in the right way and to love the neighbor correspond perfectly to one another; fundamentally they are one and the same thing. When the Law's *as yourself* has wrested from you the self-love that Christianity sadly enough must presuppose to be in every human being, then you have actually learned to love yourself. The Law is therefore: You shall love yourself in the same way as you love your neighbor when you love him as yourself....

## You Shall Love the Neighbor

Go, then, and do this, take away dissimilarity and its similarity so that you can love the neighbor. Take away the distinction of preferential love so that you can love the neighbor. But you are not to cease loving the beloved because of this – far from it. If in order to love the neighbor you would have to begin by giving up loving those for whom you have preference, the word "neighbor" would be the greatest deception ever contrived. Moreover, it would even be a contradiction, since inasmuch as the neighbor is all people surely no one can be excluded – should we now say, least of all the beloved? No, because this is the language of preference. Thus, it is only the preferential love that should be taken away – and yet it is not to be introduced in turn into the relation to the neighbor so that with twisted preference you would love the neighbor in contrast to the beloved....

Do not delude yourself into thinking that you could bargain, that by loving some people, relatives and friends, you would be loving the neighbor.... No, love the beloved faithfully and tenderly, but let love for the neighbor be the sanctifying element in your union's covenant with God. Love your friend honestly and devotedly, but let love for the neighbor be what you learn from each other in your friendship's confidential relationship with God! Death, you see, abolishes all dissimilarities, but preference is always related to dissimilarities; yet the way to life and to the eternal goes through death and through the abolition of dissimilarities – therefore only love for the neighbor truly leads to life. Just as Christianity's joyful message is contained in the doctrine of humanity's inherent kinship with God, so is Christianity's task humanity's likeness to God. But God is Love, and therefore we can be like God only in loving, just as we also, according to the words of the apostle,

can only be *God's co-workers-in love.* Insofar as you love the beloved, you are not like God, because for God there is no preference, something you have reflected on many times to your humiliation, but also many times to your rehabilitation. Insofar as you love your friend, you are not like God, because for God there is no distinction. But when you love the neighbor, then you are like God.

Therefore, go and do likewise. Forsake the dissimilarities so that you can love the neighbor. Alas, perhaps it is not even necessary to say this to you; perhaps you found no beloved in this world, no friend along the way, so that you are walking alone. Or perhaps God took from your side and gave you the beloved, but death took and took her from your side; it took again and took your friend but gave you none in return, so that now you walk alone, have no beloved to cover your weak side and no friend on your right side. Or perhaps life separated the two of you, even if you both remained unchanged-in the solitariness of separation. Alas, perhaps change separated the two of you, so that you walk sorrowfully alone because you did find but in turn found what you found – changed! How disconsolate! ...

... [W]hatever your fate was in erotic love and friendship, whatever your lack, whatever your loss was, ... the highest still remains: love the neighbor! As already shown, him you can easily find; him, as already shown, you can unconditionally always find; him you can never lose. The beloved can treat you in such a way that he is lost, and you can lose a friend; but whatever the neighbor does to you, you can never lose him. To be sure, you can also continue to love the beloved and the friend no matter how they treat you, but you cannot truly continue to call them the beloved and friend if they, sorry to say, have really changed. No change, however, can take the neighbor from you; because it is not the neighbor who holds you fast, but it is your love that holds the neighbor fast. If your love for the neighbor remains unchanged, then the neighbor also remains unchanged by existing.

Death cannot deprive you of the neighbor, for if it takes one, life immediately gives you another. Death can deprive you of a friend, because in loving a friend you actually hold together with the friend, but in loving the neighbor you hold together with God; therefore death cannot deprive you of the neighbor. If therefore, you have lost everything in erotic love and friendship, if you have never had any of this happiness — you still retain the best in loving the neighbor....

... [I]f someone is truly to love his neighbor, it must be kept in mind at all times that his dissimilarity is a disguise. As previously said, Christianity has not wanted to storm forth to abolish dissimilarity, neither the dissimilarity of distinction nor of lowliness; nor has it wished to effect in a worldly way a worldly compromise among the dissimilarities; but it wants the dissimilarity to hang loosely on the individual, as loosely as the cape the king casts off in order to show who he is, as loosely as the ragged costume in which a supranatural being has disguised himself. In other words, when the dissimilarity hangs loosely in this way, then in each individual there continually glimmers that essential other, which is common to all, the eternal resemblance, the likeness....

## Study Questions

1. Kierkegaard argues that loving others based on preference is still an instance of "selfish love," mainly because you are making your love for them contingent upon their relationship to you. Instead, to love the neighbor as you love yourself is to take your own self-love and expand it to include every single human being (since all humans are neighbors). Do you agree with Kierkegaard that loving based on preference is selfish? What ethical consequences arise when we choose to care only for the people whom we prefer (whether it be friends, family, or others that are related to us in ways we deem significant)?

2. Is it possible for human beings to practice unconditional love in the way Kierkegaard implores us? If you share Kierkegaard's religious beliefs, do you believe God would command humans to do something that was unattainable? If you do not share Kierkegaard's religious beliefs, do you believe humans are psychologically capable of unconditionally loving all? If we are capable, why don't we love like this more often? If we aren't capable, why do you think that is?

3. It seems as if many of our moral problems in the world have their roots in our tendency to dehumanize each other, particularly those with whom we disagree or who fail to share our ethical or religious worldview. How would this change if we allowed our dissimilarities to "hang loosely on the individual" and, instead, concentrate on what "is common to all"? Even if you do not believe that it is possible to love like this all the time, is it possible to love like this more than we do now? How could you implement Kierkegaard's analysis in your own life?

4. How do you interpret the commandment to "love thy neighbor as thy self"?

# 3. Arne Johan Vetlesen, "Genocide: A Case for the Responsibility of the Bystander"

WHAT MORAL RESPONSIBILITY DO bystanders – individuals who could help prevent atrocities but do not – incur when they let genocide go unchallenged? In this article from a 2000 issue of the *Journal of Peace Research*, Norwegian philosopher Arne Johan Vetlesen (b. 1960) uses historical examples to argue that bystanders (which he categorizes into groups) do indeed incur some level of moral responsibility when they fail to stop genocide, albeit to different degrees. Vetlesen presents a philosophical argument that failing to prevent genocide when one can act to prevent it (an act of omission) is, in itself, a morally objectionable action. One notable aspect of Vetlesen's article is how he details the subtle ways in which "perpetrator" groups convince members of the general public that certain acts of genocide are permissible – for example, by establishing an "us" vs. "them" mentality between the victimized group and the rest of society. It is imperative to keep these tactics in mind as a way of helping to prevent future instances of persecution and genocide.

## Introduction: Defining Genocide

AFTER AFFIRMING THAT GENOCIDE is a crime under international law whether committed in time of peace or war, the 1948 Convention on the Prevention and Punishment of the Crime of Genocide defines genocide as

> any of the following acts committed with intent to destroy, in whole or in part, a national, ethnic, racial or religious group, as such: killing members of the group; causing serious bodily or mental harm to members of the group; deliberately inflicting on the group conditions of life calculated to bring about its physical destruction in whole or in part; imposing measures intended to prevent births within the group; forcibly transferring children of the group to another group. (Gutman and Rieff, 1999: 154)

In addition to the crime of genocide itself, the 1948 Convention provides that the following acts shall be punishable: conspiracy to commit genocide, direct and public incitement to commit genocide, attempts to commit genocide, and complicity in genocide. The Genocide Convention imposes a general duty on States that are parties to the convention "to prevent and to punish" genocide. In addition to individual criminal responsibility for genocide, the convention also establishes State responsibility, i.e., international legal responsibility of the State itself for breaching its obligations under the convention. It is crucial to bear in mind that the main criterion of genocide is that it is directed at individuals "not in their capacities as individuals but as members of the national [or ethnic, racial or religious] group" (Helsinki Watch, 1992: 2; Sells, 1996: 24).

The term "genocide" was coined as recently as the mid-1930s by the Polish scholar Raphael Lemkin, who fashioned the term from the Greek word *genos*, meaning race or tribe, and the Latin term for killing, *cide*. Lemkin pointed out that, generally speaking, genocide does not necessarily mean the immediate destruction of a nation. It is intended rather to signify

> a coordinated plan of different actions aiming at the destruction of essential foundations of the life of national groups, with the aim of annihilating the groups themselves. (Gutman and Rieff, 1999: 155)

Lemkin observed that genocide has two phases:

> one, destruction of the national pattern of the oppressed group; the other, the imposition of the national pattern of the oppressor. This imposition, in turn, may be made upon the oppressed population which is allowed to remain, or upon the territory alone, after removal of the population and colonization of the area by the oppressor's own nationals. (ibid.)

Before proceeding, let me briefly note the problems created for nations of a genuinely *multinational* and *multireligious* kind by the conceptual nationalist bias implicit in the Lemkin-inspired Genocide Convention. In a state such as Bosnia, there is not one – homogeneous – national group that is being threatened. As David Campbell argues, because a "national" group has to be ethnically, racially, or religiously specific to have status according to the Convention, a multicultural state, in order to protect itself from partition, would have to "[submit] itself to the very identity politics and territorial division it is seeking to resist" (Campbell, 1998: 108). What the bias in favor of homogeneous, exclusivist identity built into the very premises of the Genocide Convention cannot accommodate,

then, are threats to a hybrid, multicultural polity, one where each person is the carrier of multiple identities, thus defying any one-criterion identity mark.

It is important to have this in mind when, in what follows, I invoke empirical material from the war in Bosnia (1992–95). My purpose is to raise the issue of responsibility for genocide, in particular with regard to *incitement* to genocide and *complicity* in genocide....

## A Typology of Bystanders to Genocide

Most often, in cases of genocide, for every person directly victimized and killed there will be hundreds, thousands, perhaps even millions, who are neither directly targeted as victims nor directly participating as perpetrators. The moral issues raised by genocide, taken as the illegal act *par excellence*, are not confined to the nexus of agent and victim. Those directly involved in a given instance of genocide will always form a minority, so to speak. The majority to the event will be formed by the contemporary bystanders. Such bystanders are individuals; in their private and professional lives, they will belong to a vast score of groups and collectives, some informal and closely knit, others formal and detached as far as personal and emotional involvement are concerned. In the loose sense intended here, every contemporary citizen cognizant of a specific ongoing instance of genocide, regardless of where in the world, counts as a bystander.

Bystanders in this loose sense are cognizant, through TV, radio, newspapers, and other publicly available sources of information, of ongoing genocide somewhere in the world, but they are not – by profession or formal appointment – involved in it. Theirs is a passive role, that of onlookers, although what starts out as a passive stance may, upon decision, convert into active engagement in the events at hand. I shall label this category *passive bystanders*.

This group should be distinguished from bystanders by *formal appointment*: the latter bystanders have been professionally engaged as a "third party" to the interaction between the two parties directly involved in acts of genocide. The stance of this third party to an ongoing conflict, even one with genocidal implications, is in principle often seen as one of impartiality and neutrality, typically high-lighted by a determined refusal to "take sides." This manner of principled non-involvement is frequently viewed as highly meritorious (Vetlesen, 1998). A case in point would be UN personnel deployed to monitor a ceasefire between warring parties, or (as was their task in Bosnia) to see to it that the civilians within a UN-declared "safe area" are effectively guaranteed "peace and security," as set down in the mandate to establish such areas. By virtue of their assigned physical presence on the scene and the specific tasks given to them, such (groups of) bystanders may be referred to as *bystanders by assignment*.

What does it mean to be a contemporary bystander? To begin with, let us consider this question not from the expected viewpoint – that of the bystander – but from the two viewpoints provided by the parties directly involved in the event.

To put it as simply as possible: From the viewpoint of an agent of genocide, bystanders are persons possessing a potential (one needing to be estimated in every concrete case) to halt his ongoing actions. The perpetrator will fear the bystander to the extent that he has reason to believe that the bystander will intervene to halt the action already under way, and thereby frustrate the perpetrator's goal of eliminating the targeted group. That said, we immediately need to differentiate among the different categories of bystanders introduced above. It is obvious that the more knowledgeable and

otherwise resourceful the bystander, the more the perpetrator will have reason to fear that the potential for such resistance will translate into action, meaning a more or less direct intervention by military or other means deemed efficient to reach the objective of halting the incipient genocide. Of course, one should distinguish between bystanders who remain inactive and those who become actively engaged. Nonetheless, the point to be stressed is that, in principle, even the most initially passive and remote bystander possesses a potential to cease being a mere onlooker to the events unfolding. Outrage at what comes to pass may prompt the judgment that "this simply must be stopped" and translate into action promoting that aim.

But is not halting genocide first and foremost a task, indeed a duty, for the victims themselves? The answer is simple: The sheer fact that genocide is happening shows that the targeted group has proven itself unable to prevent it. This being so, responsibility for halting what is now unfolding cannot rest with the victims alone; it must also be seen to rest with the party not itself affected but which is knowledgeable about – which is more or less literally *witnessing* – the genocide that is taking place. So whereas for the agent, bystanders represent the potential of resistance, for the victims they may represent the only source of hope left. In ethical terms, this is borne out in the notion of responsibility of Emmanuel Levinas (1991), according to which responsibility grows bigger the weaker its addressee.

Of course, agents of genocide may be caught more or less *in delicto flagrante*. But in the age of television – with CNN being able to film and even interview doers as well as victims on the spot, and broadcast live to the entire television-watching world (such as was the case in the concentration camp Omarska in Bosnia in August 1992) (see Gutman, 1993)

– physical co-presence to the event at hand is almost rendered superfluous. One need not have been there in order to have known what happened. The same holds for the impact of the day-to-day reporting from the ground by newspaper journalists of indisputable reputation. In order to be knowledgeable about ongoing genocide, it suffices to watch the television news or read the front pages of a daily newspaper.

But, to be more precise, what exactly does it mean to act? What is to count as an action? We need to look briefly at the philosophical literature on the notion of action – as well as the notion of agent responsibility following from it – in order to get a better grasp of the moral issues involved in being a bystander to genocide, whether passive or active.

## Acting – and Deciding Not To

"I never forget," says Paul Ricoeur in *Oneself as Another*, "to speak of humans as acting and suffering. The moral problem," he continues, "is grafted onto the recognition of this essential dissymmetry between the one who acts and the one who undergoes, culminating in the violence of the powerful agent." To be the "sufferer" of a given action in Ricoeur's sense need not be negative; either "the sufferer appears as the beneficiary of esteem or as the victim of disesteem, depending on whether the agent proves to be someone who distributes rewards or punishments." Since there is to every action an agent and a sufferer in the sense given), action is interaction; its structure is interpersonal (Ricoeur, 1992: 145).

But this is not the whole picture. Actions are also omitted, endured, neglected, and the like; and Ricoeur takes these phenomena to remind us that

> on the level of interaction, just as on that of subjective understanding, not acting is

still acting: neglecting, forgetting to do something, is also letting things be done by someone else, sometimes to the point of criminality. (Ricoeur, 1992: 157)

Ricoeur's systematic objective is to extend the theory of action from acting to suffering beings; again and again he emphasizes that "every action has its agents and its patients" (1992: 157).

Ricoeur's proposed extension certainly sounds plausible. Regrettably, his proposal stops halfway. The vital insight articulated, albeit not developed, in the passages quoted is that *not acting is still acting*. Brought to bear on the case of genocide as a reported, ongoing affair, the inaction making a difference is the inaction of the bystander to unfolding genocide. The failure to act when confronted with such action, as is involved in accomplishing genocide, is a failure which carries a message to both the agent and the sufferer: the action may proceed. Knowing, yet still not acting, means granting acceptance to the action. Such inaction entails "letting things be done by someone else" – clearly, in the case of acknowledged genocide, "to the point of criminality," to invoke one of the quotes from Ricoeur. In short, inaction here means complicity; accordingly, it raises the question of responsibility, guilt, and shame on the part of the inactive bystander, by which I mean the bystander who *decides* to remain inactive....

To repeat, not all bystanders are equal. In particular, with regard to the question of complicity raised above, some bystanders carry greater responsibility than others. If we continue to confine ourselves to bystanders in the present tense, i.e., to bystanders to contemporary, ongoing events, it is clear that some bystanders will be closer to the event than others. "Closer" does not have to denote spatially closer; it may denote closeness by virtue of professional assignment as well, or by virtue of one's knowledge as an intellectual. Indeed, the spatial notion of responsibility and its proper scope is hopelessly out of tune with the moral issues prompted by acts facilitated by context-transcending modern technology (Jonas, 1979). Today, ethics in world politics must take the form of a deterritorialization of responsibility (Campbell and Shapiro, 1999).

Is degree of responsibility directly proportionate to degree of closeness to the event? The answer will hinge on how we conceptualize not only agency but responsibility as well.

To clarify what is at stake here, some distinctions made by Larry May in his book *Sharing Responsibility* may be helpful. A famous quote from Edmund Burke sets the stage for May's discussion: All that is necessary for evil to triumph in the world is for good people to do nothing. May goes on to observe that

> just as a person's inaction makes him or her at least partially responsible for harms that he or she could have prevented, so collective inaction of a group of persons may make the members of that group at least partially responsible for harms that the group could have prevented. (1992: 105)

He then defines "collective omission" as the failure of a group that collectively chooses not to act; by contrast, "collective inaction" refers to the failure to act of "a collection of people that did not choose *as a group* to remain inactive but that could have acted as a group" (1992: 107). The latter case of collective inaction is particularly salient with respect to what May speaks of as "putative groups," in which "people are sometimes capable of acting in concert but in which no formal organization exists and, as a result, there is no decision-making apparatus" (1992: 109). The fundamental premise informing May's

discussion is that "once one is aware of the things that one could do, and one then does not do them, then lack of action is something one has chosen" (1992: 119).

For my purposes, the central question is whether the harm (read genocide) that took place in Bosnia *could* have been prevented, or at least halted, by the contemporary bystanders to it. Employing the distinction made above between passive bystanders and bystanders by assignment, we shall explore the extent to which both categories can be held responsible for *failing to prevent* ongoing and well-documented cases of genocide.

## Collectivizing Human Agency and Moral Responsibility: A Look at Genocidal Logic

So far we have described the nature of genocide only by reference to its juridical definition as coined by Raphael Lemkin and employed by the UN and international humanitarian law. In order to answer the question about responsibility among different types of bystanders, we need to take a more phenomenological look at what characterizes the practice of genocide.

Genocide is a collective action. By this, I mean that genocide is contemplated, thought out, planned, organized, and carried out by a specific organized collective, by a *group*. The defined target of genocide is another group. As a piece of action, genocide is the interaction taking place between a perpetrator group and a target group.

Typically, the perpetrator group will define itself by reference to the individual member's common identity, be it defined by reference to nation, race, ethnicity, religion, or sex. The target group will be defined by the perpetrator group by the same set of (collectivist, often essentialist) criteria. The antagonism that is produced by this type of identificatory reference takes the form of a one-to-one

631

relationship: if the perpetrator group focuses its identificatory attention upon the *racial* identity of the target group, the ideological message conveyed is that the race identity of one's own group is what is first and foremost threatened by the other group. Similarly, if the *ethnic* identity of the target group provides the primary focus, the ethnic identity of the perpetrator group is likely to prevail as what is threatened most directly by the other group.

Political scientist Espen Barth Eide (1997) has noted a principle at work in all the documented instances of genocide in the 20th century: namely, that "a war of words precedes a war of bodies." Genocide does not occur without preparation, by which is meant not only practical, logistical, strategic preparation, and the like, but primarily *ideological* preparation, the chief objective of which is to mobilize support for the action that will later ensue. This includes first and foremost support among members of the in-group, in which some people will be direct participants to the event and others passive and more or less distant bystanders. This preparation often also aims at garnering support from the outside world and thus from among the audience of bystanders in the common sense of the word as non-party, outsiders, to the event. The crucial part played by ideological preparation is captured in Article III of the Genocide Convention of 1948. Here, it is stated that "direct and public incitement to commit genocide" is punishable....

Not something spontaneous, genocide is reactive, indeed reactive in the strong sense of *imitation*. If there is one *Gedankenfigur*[1] that is common to most well-known instances of genocide, it is this: the perpetrator group does exactly what it castigates the target for having done (in some remote or recent past) or for being just now about to do toward one's own group. To imitate means to legitimize — when the focus of attention is on past wrongs

caused by the target group, legitimation of the action now taken assumes the form of *retaliation*; when the selected focus is on the wrongs (allegedly) planned and about to be performed by the target group, legitimation assumes the form of *pre-emption*. In both cases, the ideologically produced upshot is that the action taken by one's own group has the character of *self-defense*. Self-defense provides a moral justification for acts of aggression; it is invoked as a license to kill precisely those *deserving* to be killed.

Doing unto the other what one holds the other to have done, or is contemplating doing, unto oneself: this is often the logic of imitation characteristic of genocide. We noted that genocide is not spontaneous. This entails that genocide never occurs in a social, historical, or cultural vacuum. In particular, the historical past is manipulated so as to become thoroughly mythologized. Thus gestalted, the past is transformed into an arena of *collective*, not individual, agency. In this fashion, the Muslims living in Bosnia today are deemed guilty for what their forefathers are said to have done some 600 years ago, given that Serb ideologues have picked the battle against the Ottomans (Turks) at Kosovo Polje in 1389 as their "chosen trauma." The categories of agency, including guilt and complicity, are set loose from the original contextuality of events and travel freely as it were through the centuries that have passed. Once collectivized, human agency in all its moral (as well as spatio-temporal) dimensions is conceived of in such a way that the individual is compelled to answer for everything "his" group does, has done, or is held to be about to do; conversely, the group is made to answer for everything a single individual member does, has done, or is held to be about to do. Collectivizing human agency in the manner typical of genocidal ideologues is tantamount to obliterating the morally and legally crucial distinction between individual and group. In a word, it creates a logic that completely undermines the enactment of law. For law to be (re)enacted, disaggregation is required so as to reinstall agency as a property of individuals as distinct from collectivities.

[...]

## Conclusion: Three Lessons and One Question

... [I]s there one lesson in particular that needs to be learned here? I believe there are three important lessons. The first is that the bystander is the one who decides whether the harm wrought by the aggressor is permitted to stand unrectified or not. The bystander who reacts with non-reaction, with silence in the face of killing, helps legitimize that very killing. When nothing is done in the face of what is unfolding, and when what unfolds is, beyond doubt, killing of a genocidal nature, the message to the agent as well as to the direct victim is that such killing may continue. Knowing, yet deciding not to act when action would have been possible, entails complicity – that is to say, on general grounds, it counts as moral complicity (Unger, 1996), though we need to inquire further to settle the question of strict *legal* – meaning punishable – complicity. I return to this below.

The second lesson is that there is every reason *not* to downplay but instead take extremely seriously any statement – be it oral or written, broadcast in the mass media or published in journals and books – about specific groups if such statements will contribute to actions which will rob such groups of their humanity and right to live under decent conditions. To allude to Hegel, discourses of *misrecognition* are likely to constitute a phase of ideological preparation for the carrying out of a politics of enforced removal, humiliation, and perhaps eventually downright annihilation of the abused individuals. Deeds follow upon words. Generally speaking, due among other things to their comprehensive reading, traveling, and contacts abroad, intellectuals in different countries, although outsiders to such developments within a given state (religion), have a duty to sound the alarm bell upon learning about the spreading of hate speech. This is *especially* true in cases where the hate speech is authorized by the authorities, and even more so if the authorities are undemocratic or downright totalitarian. Although we still await the first indictment of journalists on the charge of incitement to genocide in the former Yugoslavia, Rwanda represents a historic precedent. In 1995, Ferdinand Nahimana, a well-known historian who served as the director of the most popular Rwandan radio station, RTLM, was arrested and delivered to the Arusha tribunal, where he will have to answer to the charge of "incitement to genocide." It is now an established view that this radio station, in the two months in the spring of 1994 when up to one million Rwandans were slaughtered, had one single aim: to incite the Hutu masses to exterminate their Tutsi neighbors (Gutman and Rieff, 1999: 192).

The third lesson is that the failure to act when knowledgeable about ongoing genocide corrupts the bystander – the more so the greater his or her potential for acting. Not only are the victims those people falling prey to slaughter, but also the individual bystanders who *decide* to remain inactive and allow what is happening to continue. Ever since Hugo Grotius's *De Jure Belli ac Pacis* from 1625 (the treatise inspiring the principles behind humanitarian intervention to this day), a central criterion to justify the use of force is that the crime must be excessively cruel so as to shock the society of mankind. Every one of us is an embodiment of the society thus able to be shocked, to be morally outraged at what befalls other human beings – even if it be those unknown and far off. The idea is that we inflict evil upon ourselves – and not only upon the victims slaughtered – when we willfully remain passive bystanders. In the spirit of Grotius, Mark Huband writes that, since the UN knew that genocide was being planned and once the genocide began nothing was done, this makes what took place in Rwanda in 1994 "more than a crime. It was an event that shamed humanity" (Gutman and Rieff, 1999: 314). I believe the same point can be made with regard to Bosnia. Indeed, when professional bystanders (which I have earlier called *bystanders by assignment*) to a violent conflict eschew responsibility for the victimized, deciding – precisely – to *stand by* and watch as the slaughter unfolds, giving priority instead to their own security and to that alone, the consequence is that humanity is shamed....

## References

Barth Eide, Espen, 1997. *Conflict Entrepreneurship.* Oslo: NUPI.

Campbell, David, 1998. *National Deconstruction: Violence, Identity, and Justice in Bosnia.* Minneapolis: U of Minnesota P.

Campbell, David and Michael J. Shapiro, eds., 1999. *Moral Spaces: Rethinking Ethics and World Politics.* Minneapolis: U of Minnesota P.

Gutman, Roy, 1993. *Witness to Genocide.* Shaftesbury: Element.

Gutman, Roy and David Rieff, eds., 1999. *Crimes of War.* New York: W.W. Norton.

Helsinki Watch, 1992. *War Crimes in Bosnia-Herzegovina.* New York: Human Rights Watch.

Jonas, Hans, 1979. *Das Prinzip Verantwortung.* [The Principle of Responsibility]. Frankfurt am Main: Suhrkamp.

Levinas, Emmanuel, 1991. *Otherwise than Being or Beyond Essence:* Dordrecht: Kluwer.

May, Larry, 1992. *Sharing Responsibility.* Chicago: U of Chicago P.

Ricoeur, Paul, 1992. *Oneself as Another,* trans. Kathleen Blamey. Chicago: U of Chicago P.

Sells, Michael, 1996. *The Bridge Betrayed: Religion and Genocide in Bosnia.* Berkeley: U of California P.

Unger, Peter, 1996. *Living High and Letting Die.* Oxford: Oxford UP.

Vetlesen, Arne Johan, 1998. "Impartiality and Evil," *Philosophy and Social Criticism* 24(5): 1–35.

## Study Questions

1. Vetlesen argues that, although typically lauded, non-involvement or neutrality by bystanders by assignment (for example UN workers) is morally objectionable. This is because bystanders are still "persons possessing a potential ... to halt ongoing actions." Do you agree with his assessment here? If you do, how does this affect your views of US foreign policies when we have elected to remain uninvolved in acts of genocide in other countries (for example, in Rwanda)? If you do not, what justification could there be for being fully able to prevent an act of genocide, but choosing not to?

2. One common response against intervening in a foreign country's affairs, including instances of genocide, is that the people in that country have to learn to take responsibility for their own welfare. However, Vetlesen brings up the following point concerning victims of genocide: "the sheer fact that genocide is happening shows that the targeted group has proven itself unable to prevent it." How can victims of genocide

be considered capable of caring for themselves? If they are, indeed, as incapable of preventing genocide as Vetlesen maintains, how does this affect the argument against foreign intervention in these countries?

3. Vetlesen argues that, in cases where bystanders can effect change, failing to act against violence (acts of omission) is morally liable because "inaction here means complicity." Explain his argument here. Do you agree with him that, in general, failing to act to prevent an atrocity (whether it is genocide or otherwise) is morally objectionable? Is it *as* morally objectionable as committing the action itself? That is, are acts of omission morally equivalent to acts of commission?

4. Vetlesen mentions various psychological tools that the "perpetrator" group uses against victims of genocide in order to make it seem as if the violence is justifiable. What are these various psychological tools? Have similar tools been used in public discourse against any group in the United States? Why is it important to be aware of the psychological effects of such discourse?

**Note**

1 Figure of thought.

# 4. Solomon Benatar, Abdallah Daar, and Peter Singer, "Global Health Ethics: The Rationale for Mutual Caring"

SOLOMON BENATAR, ABDALLAH DAAR, and Peter Singer's 2003 essay, from the journal *International Affairs*, on global health ethics highlights the consequences of an overly individualistic world view, one that does not take into account the welfare and needs of the distant "other," especially those who live in the kind of abject poverty that those of us in the "First World" can scarcely imagine. The authors focus on disparities in health among the poor and the consequences of linking health care to purely free-market forces, amongst other considerations. The focus of this article, however, is to suggest ways in which we can move forward with improving the health status of all human beings, and the authors argue that the first step toward doing so is recognizing the intrinsic dignity and worth of all persons, regardless of their location, nationality, ethnicity, or economic status. That is, we need to increase "our sensitivity (empathy) to the pain, suffering and humiliation of others."

DESPITE SPECTACULAR PROGRESS IN science and technology during the twentieth century, as we enter the twenty-first the world is more inequitable than it was 50 years ago.[1] Disparities in wealth and health within and between nations are widening inexorably, and the rapidly expanding global economy has failed to reduce poverty and improve health for all. This is evident both in terms of access to health care for individuals, and in relation to the health of whole populations. Billions of people live in degrading poverty with little if any access to health care, and the Universal Declaration of Human Rights remains an unrealized aspiration for the majority of the world's people.[2] ...

A set of values that combines genuine respect for the dignity of all people with a desire to promote the idea of human development beyond that conceived within the narrow, individualistic, "economic" model of human flourishing, could serve to promote peaceful and beneficial use of new knowledge and power. A global agenda must extend beyond the rhetoric of universal human rights to include greater attention to duties, social justice and interdependence. Health and ethics provide a framework within which such an agenda could be developed and promoted across national borders and cultures....

## The Context of Global Health Ethics

The context within which global health ethics needs to be developed highlights the importance of the problems for which ethical solutions must be sought. We begin here by describing key elements that frame the context for an unstable world increasingly at risk of massive rebellion and violence from those who are excluded from the benefits of progress and who have nothing to lose from destroying what others thoughtlessly or selfishly enjoy.

## Advances in Science and Technology

Twentieth-century developments in science and technology have transformed health care and improved the lives of many people.[3] Most recently, the rapid acquisition of biological knowledge has surpassed all past theoretical and technological achievements. Advances in genomics and genome-related biotechnology could, *if applied correctly*, transform medicine and health care in the next few decades, and perhaps even reduce inequities in global health both between and within countries.[4]

Health professionals will have the opportunity to investigate genetic determinants in relation to individually expressed responses to environmental influences; use gene therapy to correct genetic defects; and use new molecular biology techniques to design more specific therapeutic agents. Plants could be genetically engineered to manufacture or incorporate vaccines, nutrients and drugs of major public health significance, which could then be purified and packaged as pharma- or agri-ceuticals (this area covers such initiatives as molecular farming, nutraceuticals, functional foods). Alternatively, and more alluringly, the same desired products could be grown in commonly eaten foods to become edible vaccines, nutrients and drugs, with potentially impressive public health benefits. The underlying technology, once developed and validated by industry or public research institutions, might be easily transferable even to the poorest of developing countries, where fertile land may be readily available to grow the biomass needed, and where public health needs are the greatest. Local harvesting could drastically reduce transportation, refrigeration and storage costs.

However, the social implications of these advances must be anticipated before stakeholders' positions become deeply entrenched. Used inappropriately and unwisely, the new power of genome-related biotechnologies may, like other forms of power, benefit only a privileged minority and actually increase inequities in global health.[5] It is salutary to consider that we have not yet wisely applied already proven drugs and vaccines, or our accumulated impressive knowledge, to improve the health of people across the world.

Ethical evaluation and the widespread promotion of ethical values that are truly universal must go hand-in-hand with new discovery, not lag behind. An extended bioethics discourse should involve the public and help create a new social contract between science and society.[6] However, it is also necessary to acknowledge that science is not value free and has deep social foundations.[7] The extent to which the scientific endeavor is driven by social priorities is revealed by several facts. For example, 66 per cent of US government expenditure on research and development is devoted to military research,[8] and 90 per cent of global expenditure on medical research is on diseases causing 10 per cent of the global burden of disease.[9] Moreover, of 1,223 new drugs developed between 1975 and 1997, only 13 were for the treatment of tropical diseases. It is evident from these facts that the questions posed by scientists are not necessarily determined by the need for knowledge. The interests of powerful nations, those who fund research and perhaps even the interests of many researchers often outweigh the interests of research subjects or society as a whole. It is also fair to note that the value placed on acquiring new knowledge exceeds that placed on how best to apply existing knowledge.[10]

The global social context of research thus needs to be understood in order to unravel the values that drive the scientific quest.[11] The emphasis on military research and the neglect of diseases that afflict billions of people living in abject misery reflects a value system that marginalizes and devalues with impunity the

637

lives of more than half the world's population. It is also important to make the point that saving lives in poor countries is not dependent predominantly on medical research. Just as mortality rates for tuberculosis and measles fell precipitously with improved living conditions before specific treatments became available,[12] so many lives could be saved now by economic and social policies that would improve basic living conditions.

In his presidential address to the US National Academy of Sciences in 2000, Bruce Alberts emphasized the responsibility of the scientific community for making social progress.[13] Science cannot be focused solely on acquiring new knowledge. It must also examine the ethical implications of the application of such knowledge in an international context in order to form legitimate public policy and promote ways to ameliorate the miserable conditions in which the majority of the world's people live.

## Disparities in Health

In spite of unprecedented advances in science, technology and medicine, marked disparities in health persist. Life expectancy has improved dramatically worldwide during the twentieth century, but in recent years this trend has been reversed in the poorest countries. For example, life expectancy in Canada is 80 years and rising, but in some countries in Africa it is 40 years and dropping. It is expected to fall to as low as 30 in Botswana by 2010 if the trend is not checked and reversed.[14] Disparities in health and life expectancy, posing threats to the lives of all, are linked to wealth and poverty, within and between rich and poor nations. Moreover, "Among the developed countries it is not the richest societies which have the best health, but those that have the smallest income differences between rich and poor."[15]

The challenge of achieving improved health for a greater proportion of the world's population is one of the most pressing problems of our time and is starkly illustrated by the threat of infectious diseases. A few decades ago there was hope that the major infectious diseases plaguing humankind could be eliminated. The World Health Organization's unprecedented success with smallpox was a remarkable model. However, the recrudescence of tuberculosis and malaria in multi-drug resistant forms, and the appearance of HIV infection (and other new infectious diseases) have dashed such expectations and illustrated the limitations of a narrowly focused scientific approach to public health.[16] We cannot ignore the adverse historical, political and economic factors that contribute to the ecological conditions conducive to the rise and spread of these diseases.[17] Communicable diseases continue to be the leading causes of loss of human life and potential. Their control is not merely a problem for individual nations but rather one for the whole world.[18] Infections have no respect for geographical boundaries, particularly in an era of extensive and rapid transportation allowing easy transmission of infectious agents....

## Widening Economic Disparities and Extreme Poverty

Changes in the world economy during the past century have generated great wealth that has enhanced the lives of many. However, neoliberal global economic trends are both widening the gap between rich and poor and exacerbating extreme poverty,[19] defined as "a condition of life so limited by malnutrition, illiteracy, disease, squalid living conditions, high infant mortality, and low life expectancy as to be beneath any reasonable definition of human decency."[20] At the beginning of the twentieth century, the income of the richest

20 per cent of the world's population was nine times that of the poorest 20 per cent. By 1960, it was 30 times as large; and since then the gap has widened ever more rapidly, to the point where at the end of the century the richest fifth had an income 80 times that of the poorest fifth.... Today, 2 billion people live on less than US$2 per day, and more than a quarter of the world's population lives under conditions of "absolute poverty"....

## Patterns of Expenditure on Health Care and Research

With modern advances in medicine, and many causes of wasted resources in the provision of health care, the proportion of GNP spent on health care has escalated rapidly in many industrialized countries. The United States alone spends above 50 per cent (US$1.2 trillion) of the total health care expenditure in the world (approximately US$2.2 trillion a year) – on 5 per cent of the world's population.[21] In some developing countries per capita GDP has been declining steadily over the past 20 years, and with this the proportion of GDP spent on health care has also diminished markedly. For example, in sub-Saharan Africa, per capita GDP fell from US$590 in 1980 to US$500 in 1997; over the same period, government expenditure on health care fell from 5.8 per cent to 1.6 per cent of GDP.[22]

Regrettably, medicine is becoming increasingly linked to and influenced by market forces, with consequent conflicts of interest and dilution of professionalism.[23] Loss of public trust in the medical profession undermines society by threatening the effective and equitable delivery of valued social services.[24] The moral dilemma for wealthy nations and multinational pharmaceutical companies that make vast profits has been powerfully portrayed in relation to lack of treatment for HIV/AIDS in poor countries.[25] ...

## Values for Global Health Ethics

We contend that all of the values we review below must be fostered to form a basis for global health ethics. Although none can stand alone, the most important for global health ethics is *solidarity*. Without solidarity it is inevitable that we shall ignore distant indignities, violations of human rights, inequities, deprivation of freedom, undemocratic regimes, and damage to the environment. However, if a spirit of mutual caring can be developed between those in wealthy countries and those in developing countries, constructive change is possible.

### Respect for All Human Life and Universal Ethical Principles

The idea of respect for human life springs partly from the long-standing religious belief, common to many cultures, that "man is made in the image of God." Given the diversity of religions and the unfortunate tendency to highlight only their differences, imaginative approaches are needed to promote respect for human dignity on these grounds. Hans Küng argues that, despite their wide range, all religions have many common elements that can be used to promote a sense of spiritual kinship while respecting a diversity of customs and rituals. His global ethic for humankind, offered as a means of promoting peaceful progress in a world divided by religious (and other) differences,[26] has been a major achievement and it is regrettable that it has not achieved a higher action profile (box 1).

In the secular sphere, for the past 50 years respect for human dignity, expressed through the Universal Declaration of Human Rights (UDHR), has achieved a high profile and many highly significant and valued results. However, its successes are difficult to quantify and many regard them as limited. For

---

**Box 1: Declaration Made by the World Conference of the Religions of Peace, Kyoto, Japan, 1970**

Bahai, Buddhist, Confucian, Christian, Hindu, Jain, Jew, Muslim, Shintoist, Sikh, Zoroastrian and others – we have come together in peace out of a common concern for peace.

As we sat down together facing the overriding issues of peace we discovered that the things which unite us are more important than the things that divide us. We found that we share:

- a conviction of the fundamental unity of the human family, of the equality and dignity of all human beings;
- a sense of the sacredness of the individual person and his conscience;
- a sense of the value of the human community;
- a belief that love, compassion, unselfishness and the force of inner truthfulness and of the spirit have ultimately greater power than hate, enmity and self-interest;
- a sense of obligation to stand on the side of the poor and the oppressed as against the rich and the oppressors;
- a profound hope that good will finally prevail.

*Source*: H. Küng, *Global Responsibility: In Search of a New World Ethic* (New York: Continuum P, 1993), p. 63.

---

example, many oppressive regimes continue to participate with relative impunity in international activities, and the United States has both failed to ratify several crucial international agreements and refused to accept humanitarian treaties on landmines and the International Criminal Court. In addition, as Richard Falk has noted, the United States is widely perceived as using its diplomatic strength to protect its friends from well-deserved allegations of abuse of human rights, and has used force unilaterally – all of which undermine its advocacy for human rights.[27] ...

## Human Rights, Responsibilities and Needs

"Human rights," as a secular concept for promoting human dignity, has the potential to transcend religions, national borders and cultures. In recent decades the human rights movement has flourished and more countries seem to be accepting universal human rights as a "civilizational" standard.[28] ...

Inadequate attention has been paid to the fact that rights and duties are intimately connected; that the conceptual logic of rights entails corresponding duties. Thus duty bearers need to be identified to ensure the realization of rights. If all claim rights but none is willing to bear duties, rights will not be satisfied. Our ability to enjoy rights is thus determined by our willingness to accept our responsibilities....

The recently proposed Declaration of Universal Duties could further strengthen the rights approach.[29] A focus on duties would expose the responsibility of developed nations not to act in ways that may abrogate the rights of people in developing countries. It could also promote recognition of the role developing countries themselves play in causing and perpetuating the misery of their peoples.

The application of human rights must thus extend beyond civil and political rights to include social, cultural and economic rights and their close integration with the reciprocal responsibilities required to ensure that rights are honoured and basic needs are met.[30] Just as the concept of "political citizenship" requires non-discriminatory enfranchisement of all, so the concept of "social citizenship" requires access to the basic requirements for survival and potential flourishing – a requirement of modern democracy....

## Equity

"Equity" is another concept that could transcend national borders and cultures. Equity can be defined as the provision of equal shares for equal needs, or the allocation of unequal shares for unequal needs as long as proportionality is maintained.

However, proportionality is difficult to assess because of incommensurability.[31] Some inequalities in wealth, health and disease are inevitable aspects of life.

Eliminating all inequalities is not possible. In addition, not all inequality is inequitable. Inequity refers to those inequalities that are considered to arise from unfairness.

Inequitable disparities in health have become a major focus of attention in recent years. The Global Health Equity Initiative (GHEI) funded by the Rockefeller Foundation is based on the idea that advocacy, capacity building and a focus on specific product initiatives can effectively harness the new sciences to counter health-product market failures. Its work includes accelerating the development and distribution of vaccines and drugs to fight the diseases that afflict those who are poor and who are bypassed by commercial research and development, notably AIDS, malaria and tuberculosis. For example, market failure to develop new drugs

for tuberculosis will be dealt with through the Global Alliance for TB drug development (GATB). The GATB is seeking a minimum of 50 per cent government funding and the balance from private sources. Its social mission is to establish immediate equitable access to new innovative treatments for tuberculosis, including strains that are resistant to many drugs, and to disseminate a directly observed therapy strategy (DOTS) using innovative approaches to public relations, transfer of technology and capacity building.[32]

However, it is unlikely that inequitable disparities in health will be reduced merely through changes in the health sector alone. As the achievement of good health requires more than the provision of health care services, so attention needs to be directed towards the forces that drive and perpetuate economic inequity: for example, to the forces that in recent years have shifted much of the discourse in international health policy debates away from considerations of equity towards an efficiency-driven perspective. While this market influence, which reflects a narrow, direct approach to health, has value, it also has considerable potential to damage the equity valued by more egalitarian approaches.[33]

Instead of taking a direct approach that focuses on equity in health (a difficult concept to define) as an end in itself, Fabienne Peter has suggested an indirect approach that sees the pursuit of health as embedded in the broader pursuit of social justice (as an important determinant of health) in general.[34] This approach emphasizes the concept of agency and well-being (defined as "having the capabilities that a person can achieve") and the freedom (see next section) to pursue one's own life goals within a pluralistic world.[35] It also provides space to address the "politics of need [for food, shelter, education and protection from harm] in the context of the modern welfare state in general and in relation to public health in particular."[36] ...

## Freedom

Freedom is another highly prized value. This includes "freedom from" as well as "freedom to." Good health and satisfying lives are determined both by the freedom from want (of basic subsistence and educational needs) and by the freedom to undertake activities of one's choice to achieve personal goals. In Amartya Sen's view, action should be focused on ensuring the opportunities to undertake these activities (defined by him as 'capabilities'), as he believes that equality can be best promoted by enhancing the capabilities of individuals.[37] Freedom from want (dependent at least to some extent on the actions of others) is essential to achieving these goals. Ian Gough and Len Doyal argue on moral grounds that the freedom to develop one's potential must be coupled to "freedom from" through security of person and access to first-order biological needs – food, clean water, shelter, etc. – as the essentials for decent lives. A sense of empowerment and control over ourselves is, in their view, essential for human flourishing.[38] Respect for the basic needs and dignity of others, respect for the full range of human rights, belief in the rule of just law, willingness to take responsibility for one's actions and societal well-being, deriving satisfaction from work well done, contributing to new knowledge, and the freedom to develop one's full potential are essential for the achievement of personal fulfilment and human flourishing....

## Democracy

Democracy, coupled with the capitalist free-market system, has been an essential and well-recognized feature of progress during the twentieth century. Less widely recognized are the tensions between democracy and capitalism. Democracy, a concept that has evolved considerably since its inception in ancient Greece,[39] should be more than either mere procedural democracy ("free and fair elections") or constitutional democracy (with its focus on legislated civil and political rights). It should also include more accountable decision-making and mechanisms for dealing with the inequities that are created and exacerbated by social and economic structures and processes.

Although there may be no true democracies, modern democracies aim to provide equal rights to a reasonable income, access to education for children and adequate health-care facilities. The fact that few societies can meet these requirements within the system of resource distribution operative under the current capitalist system (the US health care system, which excludes about 20 per cent of its population from health coverage, is a prime example) reveals the difficulty of achieving the goals of true modern democracy even in developed nations.[40] ...

## Environmental Ethics

As realization grows of the impact on the planet of the six-fold increase in world population and the 30-fold increase in annual energy consumption over the past 150 years, respect for our common environment is another value that is increasingly becoming accepted. Globalization of the world economy adversely affects the environment by encouraging the unrestrained use of natural resources and through pollution of rivers, soil and air in countries where legislation is less stringent or is not enforced. Such environmental abuse has potentially profoundly adverse effects on health and human well-being.[41] In this context the perspective of public health ethics must be extended beyond the local to include the global.[42] Environmental and ecological ethics thus have important contributions to make to the study of global bioethics, as originally recognized by Van Renselaar Potter.[43]

Now more than ever before, the *cooperative instinct* will need to supplement the *competitive forces* that promoted magnificent progress over several centuries but that now threaten to annihilate life on our planet. An alteration in the spectrum of concern from one narrowly focused on ourselves (an anthropocentric ethic) towards a broader spectrum that embraces concern for the environment on which all life depends (an ecocentric ethic) has become crucial. The challenge is to prevent an unmitigated, market-driven, global monoculture, that treats life and nature (including animals) as exploitable, from eclipsing a broader moral vision of the good life.[44] The emergence of bovine spongiform encephalopathy and epidemics of foot and mouth disease requiring the mass slaughter of animals is a sad reflection of failed human stewardship of nature.

### Solidarity

... Richard Rorty argues that solidarity is not discovered by reflection and reasoning, but rather by increasing our sensitivity (empathy) to the pain, suffering and humiliation of others. Such sensitivity, he argues, would make it difficult to marginalize "the other."[45] Progress towards achieving solidarity requires humility. Humility and arrogance involve general attitudes to one's place in the world and to whether or not one considers oneself subject to the same constraints of morality as other rational beings. Superior intelligence, exquisite beauty, great wealth and high social status, as well as fundamentalist religious beliefs, can lead to the arrogant attitudes that allow some to try to impose their will or way of life on others. In a world characterized more by arrogance than by humility, a world in which the lives of some are considered to be of infinite value while the lives of others are considered

irrelevant and dispensable, there is a great need for empathy and humility in order to promote solidarity and mutual caring.[46] This realization, and the description by Jonathan Glover of how moral imagination is needed to protect our moral identity and to prevent moral human responses to atrocities from being eclipsed by ideology, tribalism or distance,[47] brings us back full circle to the respect for dignity and universal ethical principles with which this section began.

## The Way Forward for Global Health Ethics

### Developing a Global State of Mind

Developing a global state of mind about the world and our place in it is perhaps the most crucial element in the development of an ethic for global health....

... [T]he current paradigm emphasizes relationships characterized by exclusion, confrontation, domination and enmity; diplomacy that is adversarial, intransigent, unilateral, vengeful and exploitative; power that is used to maintain superiority through compulsion and punishment; and ideas of security that are based on inequality, deterrence, coercion and national interests....

... [A]chieving the new paradigm will require shifts towards relationships characterized by inclusion, détente and engagement; diplomacy that is cooperative, compromising, multilateral, magnanimous and reciprocal; new attitudes to power that would foster persuasion and reward; and security at an international level pursued through reassurance and cooperation on a global scale....

... The impetus for change comes from growing recognition of the unsustainability of exclusively individualistic approaches to human health and the pressing need also to improve health at the level of whole populations.[48] ...

643

Such considerations raise the perennial problem of how to strike a balance between the rights (and needs) of individuals and the common good of societies. While the focus on individual rights is vital and necessary for the well-being of individuals, and contributes substantially to the well-being of societies, such a focus is not sufficient for the achievement of improved public health.

New paradigms of thinking that could be widely shared would allow extension of the conception of human rights beyond civil and political rights to include social, economic and cultural rights and their close integration with the reciprocal responsibilities required to ensure that rights are honoured and basic needs are met....

## Promoting Long-Term Self-Interest

In arguing that it is both desirable and necessary to develop a global mindset in health ethics, we also suggest that this change need not be based merely on altruism, but could be founded on long-term self-interest. For example, it has been shown by mathematical modelling for hepatitis B that the resources needed to prevent one carrier in the United Kingdom could prevent 4,000 carriers in Bangladesh of whom, statistically, four might be expected to migrate to the UK. Thus it would be four times more cost-effective for the UK to sponsor a vaccination programme against hepatitis B in Bangladesh than to introduce its own universal vaccination programme.[49]

Perhaps the clearest example of self-interest in the face of mutual interdependence is the threat posed by the HIV/AIDS epidemic. Recent information about the origin of HIV/AIDS highlights the importance of new ecological niches in the genesis of epidemics. HIV/AIDS is only one of several microbial threats.[50]

Microbial antibiotic resistance, as in the case of tuberculosis, is on the upswing, and the underlying social and economic reasons for this must be understood and countered if future and potentially more devastating plagues are to be avoided.[51]

Acknowledgement by the United States that health has important security implications for US foreign policy has provided space for an argument that improving the health status of people in developing countries makes both moral and strategic sense. In the past, security has focused on striving for competitive advantage. With the development of nuclear and other weapons of mass destruction it became evident that humankind could destroy all life on the planet in the quest for superiority by one group over others. In this context, it would be prudent to assume that genuine security can be achieved only through cooperation and not through "mutually assured destruction" doctrines. This goal requires a shift in mindset towards seeing ourselves as intricately linked to the lives and well-being of others and to the state of the global environment, on which we are crucially dependent. Such a mindset is more likely to promote the self-interest of all and less likely to damage the global commons. We also have a biological imperative to recognize that we are of one species and that this fact requires a collective interest in species-wide survival....

## Conclusions

... Achieving human development globally requires more than economic growth. It also requires confronting the current challenging context of global health, developing a global mindset, basing a response on shared values, and adopting transformational approaches in governance, global political economy and capacity strengthening. Education and the development of such human values as empathy, generosity, solidarity, civic responsibility, humility and self-effacement require an inter-disciplinary space to thrive. We propose that global health ethics offers such a space, and that it can help to catalyse crucial improvements in global health.

## Study Questions

1. Benatar, Daar, and Singer point out that "among the developed countries, it is not the richest societies which have the best health, but those that have the smallest income differences between rich and poor." By some accounts, the United States has one of the largest income inequality gaps amongst its citizens (http://fortune.com/2014/10/31/inequality-wealth-income-us/). Given this, what do you think the health consequences are for the United States as a nation?

2. Benatar, Daar, and Singer highlight a common assumption in ethical theory – rights and duties are correlates of each other. That is, if someone has a right to x, someone has a duty to provide x to her. What do you think of this proposed correlation? If there is indeed a relationship between rights and duties, and if there is a basic standard of health to which all human beings have a right, what moral obligations does this incur amongst those in developed nations (especially in light of the fact that the United States spends 50 per cent of the world's health resources on 5 per cent of the world's population)?

3. One of the values most cherished by those of us who live in the United States is freedom. However, we rarely stop to ask ourselves what this term actually means, and what it means to protect the freedom of persons. Benatar, Daar, and Singer argue that one key aspect of freedom is "freedom from want (of basic subsistence and educational need)." Do you agree with them? What moral obligations do we incur toward our poor, and the poor in other countries, if we agree that this is an important aspect to valuing freedom?

4. Benatar, Daar, and Singer argue that one of the key reasons such health disparities exist throughout the world is because we have failed to adopt a "global mindset" – one that perceives all human beings as persons with intrinsic value and dignity. Do you agree that our tendency to emphasize the "otherness" of people who are different from us – that is, our tendency to participate in their dehumanization – has the kind of consequences described in this article? What are some other consequences of such dehumanization?

## Notes

1 The authors thank Lou Pauly and James Orbinski for constructive comments on an earlier draft of this article.

2  S.R. Benatar, "Global Disparities in Health and Human Rights," *American Journal of Public Health* 88, 1998, pp. 295–300.

3  R. Porter, *The Greatest Benefit to Mankind: A Medical History of Humanity from Antiquity to the Present* (London: HarperCollins, 1997).

4  P.A. Singer and A.S. Daar, "Harnessing Genomics and Biotechnology to Improve Global Health Equity," *Science* 294, 2001, pp. 87–98.

5  S.R. Benatar, "A Perspective from Africa on Human Rights and Genetic Engineering," in J. Burley, ed., *The Genetic Revolution and Human Rights* (Oxford: Oxford UP, 1999); S.R. Benatar, "Human Rights in the Biotechnology Era: A Story of Two Lives and Two Worlds," in G.S. Bhatia, J.S. O'Neil, G.L. Gall and P.D. Bendin, eds, *Peace, Justice and Freedom: Human Rights Challenges in the New Millennium* (Edmonton: U of Alberta P, 2000), pp. 245–57.

6  M. Gibbons, "Science's New Social Contract with Society," *Nature* 402, 1999 (supplement), pp. C81–84.

7  National Academy of Sciences, National Academy of Engineering and Institute of Medicine, *On Being a Scientist* (Washington, DC: National Academy P, 1995).

8  R.L. Sivard, *World Military and Social Expenditures*, 16th ed., *1996* (Washington, DC: World Priorities P, 1996).

9  World Health Organization, *Investing in Health Research and Development: Report of the Ad Hoc Committee on Health Research Relating to Future Intervention Options* (Geneva: WHO, 1999).

10  N. Maxwell, *From Knowledge to Wisdom: A Revolution in the Aims and Methods of Science* (Oxford: Blackwell, 1984).

11  E. Hobsbawm, *The Age of Extremes: A History of the World 1914–1991* (New York: Pantheon, 1994).

12  L.A. Sagan, *The Health of Nations* (New York: Basic Books, 1987).

13  B. Alberts, "Science and Human Needs," presidential address, 137th annual meeting of the US National Academy of Sciences, Washington, DC, 1 May 2000.

14  "HIV/AIDS in Africa," http://www.securethefuture.com/aidsin/data/aidsin.htm.

15  R.G. Wilkinson, *Unhealthy Societies: The Afflictions of Inequality* (New York: Routledge, 1996).

16  S.R. Benatar, "Prospects for Global Health: Lessons from Tuberculosis," *Thorax* 50, 1995, pp. 487–89.

17  K. Lee and A.B. Zwi, "A Global Political Economy Approach to AIDS: Ideology, Interests and Implications," *New Political Economy* 1, 1996, pp. 355–73.

18  L. Garrett, *The Coming Plague: Newly Emerging Diseases in a World Out of Balance* (New York: Farrar, Straus and Giroux, 1994).

19  R. Falk, *Predatory Globalization: A Critique* (Cambridge: Polity P, 1999); R. Barnet and J. Cavanagh, *Global Dreams: Imperial Corporations and the New World Order* (New York: Simon & Schuster, 1994).

20  *World Military and Social Expenditures 1996*.

21  B.R. Bloom, "The Future of Public Health," *Nature* 402, 1999, Supplement, 2 Dec., pp. C63–64.

22  R. Sandbrook, *Closing the Circle: Democratisation and Development in Africa* (London: Zed Books, 2000).

23  R.G. Spece, D.S. Shimm and A.E. Buchanan, *Conflicts of Interest in Clinical Practice and Research* (New York: Oxford UP, 1997).

24  E. Freidson, *Professionalism: The Third Logic* (Chicago: U of Chicago P, 2001).

25  P. Bond, "Globalisation, Pharmaceutical Pricing and South African Health Policy," *International Journal of Health Sciences* 29: 4, 1999, pp. 765–92.

26  H. Küng, *A Global Ethic for Global Politics and Economics* (Oxford: Oxford UP 1997).

27  R.A. Falk, *Human Rights Horizons: The Pursuit of Justice in a Globalising World* (New York: Routledge, 2000).

28  J. Donnelly, "Human Rights: A New Standard of Civilization?," *International Relations* 74, 1998, pp. 1–24.

29  Trieste Declaration of Universal Duties, Trieste UP, 1997.

30  Together with the Civil and Political Rights Covenant, the General Assembly of the United Nations adopted in 1966 the International Covenant on Economic, Social and Cultural Rights, obliging governments to protect the rights of all their citizens to labor, social, economic and cultural rights.

31  By incommensurability is meant the impossibility of weighing and balancing values that cannot be measured against each other on any common scale – for example, additional years of normal life against years of disabled life.

32  http://www.rockfound.org/rocktext/t_99prog/t_health/t_indicators.html.

33  L. Gilson, "In Defence and Pursuit of Equity," *Social Science and Medicine* 47/12, 1998, pp. 1981–96.

34  F. Peter and T. Evans, "Ethical Dimensions of Health Equity," in T. Evans, M. Whitehead, F. Diderichsen, A. Bhuyia and M. Wirth, eds, *Challenging Inequities in Health: From Ethics to Action* (New York: Oxford UP, 2001), pp 24–33.

35  A. Sen, *Development as Freedom* (New York: Anchor Books, 1999).

36  A. Robertson, "Critical Reflection on the Politics of Need: Implications for Public Health," *Social Science and Medicine* 47: 10, 1998, pp. 1419–30.

37  Sen, *Development as Freedom.*

38  L. Doyal and I. Gough, *A Theory of Human Need* (London: Macmillan, 1991).

39  J. Dunne, ed., *Democracy: The Unfinished Journey, 508 BC–AD 1993* (Oxford: Oxford UP, 1992).

40  I. Wallerstein, *The End of the World as We Know It: Social Science for the 21st Century* (Minneapolis: U of Minnesota P, 1999).

41  C.P. Howson, H.V. Fineberg, and B.R. Bloom, "The Pursuit of Global Health: The Relevance of Engagement for Developing Countries," *Lancet* 351, 1998, pp. 586–90.

42  P. Beaglehole and R. Bonita, "Public Health at the Crossroads: Which Way Forward?," *Lancet* 351, 1998, pp. 590–92.

43  V.R. Potter, *Global Bioethics: Building on the Leopold Legacy* (East Lansing: Michigan State UP, 1998).

44  M.W. Fox, B.E. Rolin, *Bringing Life to Ethics: Global Bioethics for a Humane Society* (New York: State University of New York P, 2001).

45  R. Rorty, *Contingency, Irony and Solidarity* (Cambridge: Cambridge UP, 1989).

46  B. Gert, *Morality* (New York: Oxford UP, 1988).

47  J. Glover, *Humanity: A Moral History of the Twentieth Century* (New Haven, CT: Yale UP, 2001).

48  S.R. Benatar, "Global Disparities in Health and Human Rights: A Critical Commentary," *American Journal of Public Health* 88, 1998, pp. 295–300; S.R. Benatar, "Millennial Challenges for Medicine and Modernity," *Journal of the Royal College of Physicians* 32, 1998, pp. 160–65.

49  N.J. Gay and W.J. Edmunds, "Developed Countries Should Pay for Hepatitis B Vaccine in Developing Countries," *British Medical Journal* 316, 1998, p. 1457.

50  Garrett, *The Coming Plague.*

51  S.R. Benatar, "The Coming Catastrophe in International Health," *International Journal* LV 1: 4, 2001, pp. 611–31.

# 5.   Peter Singer, "What Should a Billionaire Give – and What Should You?"

AS YOU LEARNED FROM the readings in Section I, one of the key tenets of utilitarianism is that we should generally act in a manner that yields the most benefit and the least harm to all sentient beings affected by our decisions. In this article from the *New York Times* in December 2006, noted philosopher Peter Singer (b. 1946) applies utilitarianism to the issue of global poverty and examines what moral obligations exist for us to use our excess money to help others attain basic necessities (particularly those in foreign countries who live in abject poverty). In particular, Singer's analysis focuses on the moral obligations that the very wealthy have in alleviating global poverty, but his principles can be easily applied to many of our own lives as well. When I choose to use my money to purchase luxuries, I am making a conscious choice to value those material objects over the lives of the human beings I could be helping instead. Although if we were asked, Singer acknowledges that most of us would agree that human life is of the utmost value; our practices, both as a country and individually, do not reflect this belief.

---

WHAT IS A HUMAN life worth? You may not want to put a price tag on it. But if we really had to, most of us would agree that the value of a human life would be in the millions. Consistent with the foundations of our democracy and our frequently professed belief in the inherent dignity of human beings, we would also agree that all humans are created equal, at least to the extent of denying that differences of sex, ethnicity, nationality and place of residence change the value of a human life.

With Christmas approaching, and Americans writing checks to their favorite charities, it's a good time to ask how these two beliefs – that a human life, if it can be priced at all, is worth millions, and that the factors I have mentioned do not alter the value of a human life – square with our actions. Perhaps this year [2006] such questions lurk beneath the surface of more family discussions than usual, for it has been an extraordinary year for philanthropy, especially philanthropy to fight global poverty.

For Bill Gates, the founder of Microsoft, the ideal of valuing all human life equally began to jar against reality some years ago, when he read an article about diseases in the developing world and came across the statistic that half a million children die every year from rotavirus, the most common cause of severe diarrhea in children. He had never heard of rotavirus. "How could I never have heard of something that kills half a million children every year?" he asked himself. He then learned that in developing countries, millions of children die from diseases that have been eliminated, or virtually eliminated, in the United States. That shocked him because he assumed that, if there are vaccines and treatments that could save lives, governments would be doing everything possible to get them to the people who need them. As Gates told a meeting of the World Health Assembly in Geneva last year, he and his wife, Melinda, "couldn't escape the brutal conclusion that

– in our world today – some lives are seen as worth saving and others are not." They said to themselves, "This can't be true." But they knew it was.

Gates's speech to the World Health Assembly concluded on an optimistic note, looking forward to the next decade when "people will finally accept that the death of a child in the developing world is just as tragic as the death of a child in the developed world." That belief in the equal value of all human life is also prominent on the Web site of the Bill and Melinda Gates Foundation, where under Our Values we read: "All lives – no matter where they are being led – have equal value."

We are very far from acting in accordance with that belief. In the same world in which more than a billion people live at a level of affluence never previously known, roughly a billion other people struggle to survive on the purchasing power equivalent of less than one US dollar per day. Most of the world's poorest people are undernourished, lack access to safe drinking water or even the most basic health services and cannot send their children to school. According to Unicef, more than 10 million children die every year – about 30,000 per day – from avoidable, poverty-related causes.

Last June the investor Warren Buffett took a significant step toward reducing those deaths when he pledged $31 billion to the Gates Foundation, and another $6 billion to other charitable foundations. Buffett's pledge, set alongside the nearly $30 billion given by Bill and Melinda Gates to their foundation, has made it clear that the first decade of the 21st century is a new "golden age of philanthropy." On an inflation-adjusted basis, Buffett has pledged to give more than double the lifetime total given away by two of the philanthropic giants of the past, Andrew Carnegie and John D. Rockefeller, put together. Bill and Melinda Gates's gifts are not far behind.

Gates's and Buffett's donations will now be put to work primarily to reduce poverty, disease and premature death in the developing world. According to the Global Forum for Health Research, less than 10 per cent of the world's health research budget is spent on combating conditions that account for 90 per cent of the global burden of disease. In the past, diseases that affect only the poor have been of no commercial interest to pharmaceutical manufacturers, because the poor cannot afford to buy their products. The Global Alliance for Vaccines and Immunization (GAVI), heavily supported by the Gates Foundation, seeks to change this by guaranteeing to purchase millions of doses of vaccines, when they are developed, that can prevent diseases like malaria. GAVI has also assisted developing countries to immunize more people with existing vaccines: 99 million additional children have been reached to date. By doing this, GAVI claims to have already averted nearly 1.7 million future deaths.

Philanthropy on this scale raises many ethical questions: Why are the people who are giving doing so? Does it do any good? Should we praise them for giving so much or criticize them for not giving still more? Is it troubling that such momentous decisions are made by a few extremely wealthy individuals? And how do our judgments about them reflect on our own way of living?

Let's start with the question of motives. The rich must – or so some of us with less money like to assume – suffer sleepless nights because of their ruthlessness in squeezing out competitors, firing workers, shutting down plants or whatever else they have to do to acquire their wealth. When wealthy people give away money, we can always say that they are doing it to ease their consciences or generate favorable publicity. It has been suggested – by, for example, David Kirkpatrick, a senior editor at Fortune magazine – that Bill Gates's turn to philanthropy was linked to the anti-trust problems Microsoft had in the US and the European Union. Was Gates, consciously or subconsciously, trying to improve his own image and that of his company?

This kind of sniping tells us more about the attackers than the attacked. Giving away large sums, rather than spending the money on corporate advertising or developing new products, is not a sensible strategy for increasing personal wealth. When we read that someone has given away a lot of their money, or time, to help others, it challenges us to think about our own behavior. Should we be following their example, in our own modest way? ...

... [There are] questions about whether there is an obligation for the rich to give, and if so, how much they should give. A few years ago, an African-American cabdriver taking me to the Inter-American Development Bank in Washington asked me if I worked at the bank. I told him I did not but was speaking at a conference on development and aid. He then assumed that I was an economist, but when I said no, my training was in philosophy, he asked me if I thought the US should give foreign aid. When I answered affirmatively, he replied that the government shouldn't tax people in order to give their money to others. That, he thought, was robbery. When I asked if he believed that the rich should voluntarily donate some of what they earn to the poor, he said that if someone had worked for his money, he wasn't going to tell him what to do with it.

At that point we reached our destination. Had the journey continued, I might have tried to persuade him that people can earn large amounts only when they live under favorable social circumstances, and that they don't create those circumstances by themselves. I could have quoted Warren Buffett's acknowledgment that society is responsible for much of his wealth. "If you stick me down in the middle of Bangladesh or Peru," he said, "you'll find out how much this talent is going to produce in the wrong kind of soil." ...

In any case, even if we were to grant that people deserve every dollar they earn, that doesn't answer the question of what they should do with it. We might say that they have a right to spend it on lavish parties, private jets and luxury yachts, or, for that matter, to flush it down the toilet. But we could still think that for them to do these things while others die from easily preventable diseases is wrong. In an article I wrote more than three decades ago, at the time of a humanitarian emergency in what is now Bangladesh, I used the example of walking by a shallow pond and seeing a small child who has fallen in and appears to be in danger of drowning. Even though we did nothing to cause the child to fall into the pond, almost everyone agrees that if we can save the child at minimal inconvenience or trouble to ourselves, we ought to do so. Anything else would be callous, indecent and, in a word, wrong. The fact that in rescuing the child we may, for example, ruin a new pair of shoes is not a good reason for allowing the child to drown. Similarly if for the cost of a pair of shoes we can contribute to a health program in a developing country that stands a good chance of saving the life of a child, we ought to do so.

Perhaps, though, our obligation to help the poor is even stronger than this example implies, for we are less innocent than the passer-by who did nothing to cause the child to fall into the pond. Thomas Pogge, a philosopher at Columbia University, has argued that at least some of our affluence comes at the expense of the poor. He bases this claim not simply on the usual critique of the barriers that Europe and the United States maintain against agricultural imports from developing countries but also on less familiar aspects of our trade with developing countries. For example, he points out that international corporations are willing to make deals to buy natural resources from any government, no matter how it has come to power. This provides a huge financial incentive for groups to try to overthrow the existing government. Successful rebels are rewarded by being able to sell off the nation's oil, minerals or timber.

In their dealings with corrupt dictators in developing countries, Pogge asserts, international corporations are morally no better than someone who knowingly buys stolen goods – with the difference that the international legal and political order recognizes the corporations, not as criminals in possession of stolen goods but as the legal owners of the goods they have bought. This situation is, of course, beneficial for the industrial nations, because it enables us to obtain the raw materials we need to maintain our prosperity, but it is a disaster for resource-rich developing countries, turning the wealth that should benefit them into a curse that leads to a cycle of coups, civil wars and corruption and is of little benefit to the people as a whole.

In this light, our obligation to the poor is not just one of providing assistance to strangers but one of compensation for harms that we have caused and are still causing them. It might be argued that we do not owe the poor compensation, because our affluence actually benefits them. Living luxuriously, it is said, provides employment, and so wealth trickles down, helping the poor more effectively than aid does. But the rich in industrialized nations buy virtually nothing that is made by the very poor. During the past 20 years of economic globalization, although expanding trade has helped lift many of the world's poor out of poverty, it has failed to benefit the poorest 10 per cent of the world's population....

The remedy to these problems, it might reasonably be suggested, should come from the state, not from private philanthropy. When aid comes through the government, everyone who earns above the tax-free threshold contributes something, with more collected from those with greater ability to pay. Much as we may applaud what Gates and Buffett are doing, we can also be troubled by a system that leaves the fate of hundreds of millions of people hanging on the decisions of two or three private citizens. But the amount of foreign development aid given by the US government is, at 22 cents for every $100 the nation earns, about the same, as a percentage of gross national income, as Portugal gives and about half that of the UK. Worse still, much of it is directed where it best suits US strategic interests – Iraq is now by far the largest recipient of US development aid, and Egypt, Jordan, Pakistan and Afghanistan all rank in the Top 10. Less than a quarter of official US development aid – barely a nickel in every $100 of our GNI – goes to the world's poorest nations.

Adding private philanthropy to US government aid improves this picture, because Americans privately give more per capita to international philanthropic causes than the citizens of almost any other nation. Even when private donations are included, however, countries like Norway, Denmark, Sweden and the Netherlands give three or four times as much foreign aid, in proportion to the size of their economies, as the US gives – with a much larger percentage going to the poorest nations....

Aid has always had its critics. Carefully planned and intelligently directed private philanthropy may be the best answer to the claim that aid doesn't work. Of course, as in any large-scale human enterprise, some aid can be ineffective. But provided that aid isn't actually counterproductive, even relatively inefficient assistance is likely to do more to advance human wellbeing than luxury spending by the wealthy.

The rich, then, should give. But how much should they give? Gates may have given away nearly $30 billion, but that still leaves him sitting at the top of the Forbes list of the richest Americans, with $53 billion. His 66,000-square-foot high-tech lakeside estate near Seattle is reportedly worth more than $100 million. Property taxes are about $1 million. Among his possessions is the Leicester Codex, the only handwritten book by Leonardo da Vinci still in private hands, for which he paid $30.8 million in 1994. Has Bill Gates done enough? More pointedly, you might ask: if he really believes that all lives have equal value, what is he doing living in such an expensive house and owning a Leonardo Codex? Are there no more lives that could be saved by living more modestly and adding the money thus saved to the amount he has already given?

Yet we should recognize that, if judged by the proportion of his wealth that he has given away, Gates compares very well with most of the other people on the Forbes 400 list, including his former colleague and Microsoft co-founder, Paul Allen. Allen, who left the company in 1983, has given, over his lifetime, more than $800 million to philanthropic causes. That is far more than nearly any of us will ever be able to give. But Forbes lists Allen as the fifth-richest American, with a net worth of $16 billion. He owns the Seattle Seahawks, the Portland Trailblazers, a 413-foot oceangoing yacht that carries two helicopters and a 60-foot submarine. He has given only about 5 per cent of his total wealth.

Is there a line of moral adequacy that falls between the 5 per cent that Allen has given away and the roughly 35 per cent that Gates has donated? Few people have set a personal example that would allow them to tell Gates that he has not given enough, but one who could is Zell Kravinsky. A few years ago,

when he was in his mid-40s, Kravinsky gave almost all of his $45 million real estate fortune to health-related charities, retaining only his modest family home in Jenkintown, near Philadelphia, and enough to meet his family's ordinary expenses. After learning that thousands of people with failing kidneys die each year while waiting for a transplant, he contacted a Philadelphia hospital and donated one of his kidneys to a complete stranger.

After reading about Kravinsky in The New Yorker, I invited him to speak to my classes at Princeton. He comes across as anguished by the failure of others to see the simple logic that lies behind his altruism. Kravinsky has a mathematical mind – a talent that obviously helped him in deciding what investments would prove profitable – and he says that the chances of dying as a result of donating a kidney are about 1 in 4,000. For him this implies that to withhold a kidney from someone who would otherwise die means valuing one's own life at 4,000 times that of a stranger, a ratio Kravinsky considers "obscene."

What marks Kravinsky from the rest of us is that he takes the equal value of all human life as a guide to life, not just as a nice piece of rhetoric. He acknowledges that some people think he is crazy, and even his wife says she believes that he goes too far. One of her arguments against the kidney donation was that one of their children may one day need a kidney, and Zell could be the only compatible donor. Kravinsky's love for his children is, as far as I can tell, as strong as that of any normal parent. Such attachments are part of our nature, no doubt the product of our evolution as mammals who give birth to children, who for an unusually long time require our assistance in order to survive. But that does not, in Kravinsky's view, justify our placing a value on the lives of our children that is thousands of times greater than the value we place on the lives of the children of strangers. Asked if he would allow his child to die if it would enable a thousand children to live, Kravinsky said yes. Indeed, he has said he would permit his child to die even if this enabled only two other children to live. Nevertheless, to appease his wife, he recently went back into real estate, made some money and bought the family a larger home. But he still remains committed to giving away as much as possible, subject only to keeping his domestic life reasonably tranquil.

Buffett says he believes in giving his children "enough so they feel they could do anything, but not so much that they could do nothing." That means, in his judgment, "a few hundred thousand" each.... But even if Buffett left each of his three children a million dollars each, he would still have given away more than 99.99 per cent of his wealth. When someone does that much – especially in a society in which the norm is to leave most of your wealth to your children – it is better to praise them than to cavil about the extra few hundred thousand dollars they might have given.

Philosophers like Liam Murphy of New York University and my colleague Kwame Anthony Appiah at Princeton contend that our obligations are limited to carrying our fair share of the burden of relieving global poverty. They would have us calculate how much would be required to ensure that the world's poorest people have a chance at a decent life, and then divide this sum among the affluent. That would give us each an amount to donate, and having given that, we would have fulfilled our obligations to the poor.

What might that fair amount be? One way of calculating it would be to take as our target, at least for the next nine years, the Millennium Development Goals, set by the United Nations Millennium Summit in 2000. On that occasion, the largest gathering of world leaders in history jointly pledged to meet, by 2015, a list of goals that include:

Reducing by half the proportion of the world's people in extreme poverty (defined as living on less than the purchasing-power equivalent of one US dollar per day).

Reducing by half the proportion of people who suffer from hunger.

Ensuring that children everywhere are able to take a full course of primary schooling.

Ending sex disparity in education.

Reducing by two-thirds the mortality rate among children under 5. Reducing by three-quarters the rate of maternal mortality.

Halting and beginning to reverse the spread of HIV/AIDS and halting and beginning to reduce the incidence of malaria and other major diseases.

Reducing by half the proportion of people without sustainable access to safe drinking water.

Last year a United Nations task force, led by the Columbia University economist Jeffrey Sachs, estimated the annual cost of meeting these goals to be $121 billion in 2006, rising to $189 billion by 2015. When we take account of existing official development aid promises, the additional amount needed each year to meet the goals is only $48 billion for 2006 and $74 billion for 2015.

Now let's look at the incomes of America's rich and superrich, and ask how much they could reasonably give. The task is made easier by statistics recently provided by Thomas

Piketty and Emmanuel Saez, economists at the École Normale Supérieure, Paris-Jourdan, and the University of California, Berkeley, respectively, based on US tax data for 2004. Their figures are for pretax income, excluding income from capital gains, which for the very rich are nearly always substantial. For simplicity I have rounded the figures, generally downward. Note too that the numbers refer to "tax units," that is, in many cases, families rather than individuals.

Piketty and Saez's top bracket comprises 0.01 per cent of US taxpayers. There are 14,400 of them, earning an average of $12,775,000, with total earnings of $184 billion. The minimum annual income in this group is more than $5 million, so it seems reasonable to suppose that they could, without much hardship, give away a third of their annual income, an average of $4.3 million each, for a total of around $61 billion. That would still leave each of them with an annual income of at least $3.3 million.

Next comes the rest of the top 0.1 per cent (excluding the category just described, as I shall do henceforth). There are 129,600 in this group, with an average income of just over $2 million and a minimum income of $1.1 million. If they were each to give a quarter of their income, that would yield about $65 billion, and leave each of them with at least $846,000 annually.

The top 0.5 per cent consists of 575,900 taxpayers, with an average income of $623,000 and a minimum of $407,000. If they were to give one-fifth of their income, they would still have at least $325,000 each, and they would be giving a total of $72 billion.

Coming down to the level of those in the top 1 per cent, we find 719,900 taxpayers with an average income of $327,000 and a minimum of $276,000. They could comfortably afford to give 15 per cent of their income. That would yield $35 billion and leave them

with at least $234,000.

Finally, the remainder of the nation's top 10 per cent earn at least $92,000 annually, with an average of $132,000. There are nearly 13 million in this group. If they gave the traditional tithe 10 per cent of their income, or an average of $13,200 each – this would yield about $171 billion and leave them a minimum of $83,000....

Obviously, the rich in other nations should share the burden of relieving global poverty.. The US is responsible for 36 per cent of the gross domestic product of all Organization for Economic Cooperation and Development nations. Arguably, because the US is richer than all other major nations, and its wealth is more unevenly distributed than wealth in almost any other industrialized country, the rich in the US should contribute more than 36 per cent of total global donations. So somewhat more than 36 per cent of all aid to relieve global poverty should come from the US. For simplicity, let's take half as a fair share for the US. On that basis, extending the scheme I have suggested worldwide would provide $808 billion annually for development aid. That's more than six times what the task force chaired by Sachs estimated would be required for 2006 in order to be on track to meet the Millennium Development Goals, and more than 16 times the shortfall between that sum and existing official development aid commitments.

If we are obliged to do no more than our fair share of eliminating global poverty, the burden will not be great....

For more than 30 years, I've been reading, writing and teaching about the ethical issue posed by the juxtaposition, on our planet, of great abundance and life-threatening poverty. Yet it was not until, in preparing this article, I calculated how much America's Top 10 per cent of income earners actually make that I fully understood how easy it would be for the world's rich to eliminate, or virtually eliminate, global poverty. (It has actually become much easier over the last 30 years, as the rich have grown significantly richer.) I found the result astonishing. I double-checked the figures and asked a research assistant to check them as well. But they were right. Measured against our capacity, the Millennium Development Goals are indecently, shockingly modest. If we fail to achieve them – as on present indications we well might – we have no excuses. The target we should be setting for ourselves is not halving the proportion of people living in extreme poverty, and without enough to eat, but ensuring that no one, or virtually no one, needs to live in such degrading conditions. That is a worthy goal, and it is well within our reach.

## Study Questions

1. Singer tells the story of a cab driver he encountered who maintained that if someone earned their money, he had no right to tell them what to do with it. Singer does not argue that individuals should be *forced* to donate money, but he *does* argue that there are still moral standards for how we should use our money. That is, he argues that there is a distinction between what we have a *right* to do, and what are the most morally virtuous ways of *exercising* those rights. Elaborate on this distinction. What other examples can you think of that concern morally questionable ways of using our rights? Do you agree with Singer that how we choose to use our excess money can be subject to moral assessment?

2. Consider Singer's example: suppose a child drowns in a pond, and as it turns out I could have easily waded into the water and pulled him out. When the police question me, I answer that I didn't save the child because I didn't want to ruin my new pair of name-brand boots. Is my answer morally satisfactory? According to Singer, this example is morally comparable to the decision to spend money on luxury items rather than helping others attain basic needs, for in both cases we are prizing our material goods over the lives of human beings. Is this a good analogy? If not, what are the relevant dissimilarities in the examples? If so, what are the moral implications of his argument for the spending practices of those living in first-world countries?

3. One example Singer offers of someone who has devoted much of his life to giving to others is that of Zell Kravinsky, who even donated one of his kidneys to a stranger because he didn't think that he could justify valuing his own life at "4,000 times that of a stranger." He also admitted that, though he loves his children, he would allow them to die in exchange for the lives of thousands of children. In what way do Kravinsky's answers indicate a utilitarian framework? How (if at all) does this affect your view of utilitarianism as a moral theory?

4. As Singer calculates, the price to be paid for eradicating global poverty is "shockingly modest." Given the fact that global poverty *isn't* eradicated, what do you think it reveals about our values when we allow immense human suffering to continue when it would, collectively, take modest effort to combat it?

# 6.  Denis Arnold and Norman Bowie, "Sweatshops and Respect for Persons"

FEW OF US STOP and think about the origins of the products we so easily purchase. Often, the creation of these products is outsourced to other countries, where the production conditions of workers in sweatshops are frequently deplorable. In this 2003 article from the *Business Ethics Quarterly*, Denis Arnold and Norman Bowie apply Immanuel Kant's moral philosophy, explored in Section I, to argue that respect for the personhood and dignity of these workers requires a change in their treatment and labor conditions, resulting not only in higher salaries but also in the absence of psychological coercion, the creation of safe working environments, and a guarantee that their treatment will follow the rule of law designed to protect all employees. Although the authors focus mainly on the moral obligations that multinational enterprises have toward their workers, it is also worth considering what moral obligations consumers have in holding companies accountable. As Arnold and Bowie briefly mention, public pressure has resulted in companies improving the condition of their employees. Therefore, it seems as if consumers are also morally obliged, at the very minimum, to educate themselves about sweatshop labor and to help lobby on behalf of workers who are in vulnerable positions and are easily exploited.

---

IN RECENT YEARS LABOR and human rights activists have been successful at raising public awareness regarding labor practices in both American and off-shore manufacturing facilities.[1] Organizations such as Human Rights Watch, United Students Against Sweatshops, the National Labor Coalition, Sweatshop Watch, and the Interfaith Center on Corporate Responsibility have accused multinational enterprises (MNEs), such as Nike, Wal-Mart, and Disney, of the pernicious exploitation of workers. Recent violations of American and European labor laws have received considerable attention.[2] However, it is the off-shore labor practices of North American and European based MNEs and their contractors that have been most controversial. This is partly due to the fact that many of the labor practices in question are legal outside North America and Europe, or are tolerated by corrupt or repressive political regimes. Unlike the recent immigrants who toil in the illegal sweatshops of North America and Europe, workers in developing nations typically have no recourse to the law or social service agencies. Activists have sought to enhance the welfare of these workers by pressuring MNEs to comply with labor laws, prohibit coercion, improve health and safety standards, and pay a living wage in their global sourcing operations. Meanwhile, prominent economists wage a campaign of their own in the opinion pages of leading newspapers, arguing that because workers for MNEs are often paid better when compared with local wages, they are fortunate to have such work. Furthermore, they argue that higher wages and improved working conditions will raise unemployment levels.

One test of a robust ethical theory is its ability to shed light on ethical problems. One of the standard criticisms of Immanuel Kant's ethical philosophy is that it is too abstract and formal to be of any use in practical decision making. We contend that this criticism is mistaken and that Kantian theory has much to say about the ethics of sweatshops.[3] We argue that Kant's conception of human dignity provides a clear basis for grounding the obligations of employers to employees. In particular, we argue that respecting the dignity of workers requires that MNEs and their contractors adhere to local labor laws, refrain from coercion, meet minimum safety standards, and provide a living wage for employees. We also respond to the objection that improving health and safety conditions and providing a living wage would cause greater harm than good.

## 1. Respect for Persons

Critics of sweatshops frequently ground their protests in appeals to human dignity and human rights. Arguably, Kantian ethics provides a philosophical basis for such moral pronouncements. The key principle here is Kant's second formulation of the categorical imperative: "Act so that you treat humanity, whether in your own person or in that of another, always as an end and never as a means only."[4] The popular expression of this principle is that morality requires that we respect people. One significant feature of the idea of respect for persons is that its derivation and application can be assessed independently of other elements of Kantian moral philosophy. Sympathetic readers need not embrace all aspects of Kant's system of ethics in order to grant the merit of Kant's arguments for the second formulation of the categorical imperative.[5] This is because Kant's defense of respect for persons is grounded in the uncontroversial claim that humans are capable of rational, self-governing activity. We believe that individuals with a wide range of theoretical commitments can and should recognize the

force of Kant's arguments concerning respect for persons.

Kant did not simply assert that persons are entitled to respect, he provided an elaborate argument for that conclusion. Persons ought to be respected because persons have dignity. For Kant, an object that has dignity is beyond price. Employees have a dignity that machines and capital do not have. They have dignity because they are capable of moral activity. As free beings capable of self-governance they are responsible beings, since freedom and self-governance are the conditions for responsibility. Autonomous responsible beings are capable of making and following their own laws; they are not simply subject to the causal laws of nature. Anyone who recognizes that he or she is free should recognize that he or she is responsible (that he or she is a moral being). As Kant argues, the fact that one is a moral being entails that one possesses dignity.

> Morality is the condition under which
> alone a rational being can be an end
> in himself because only through it is it
> possible to be a lawgiving member in the
> realm of ends. Thus morality, and human-
> ity insofar as it is capable of morality,
> alone have dignity.[6]

As a matter of consistency, a person who recognizes that he or she is a moral being should ascribe dignity to anyone who, like him or herself, is a moral being.

Although it is the capacity to behave morally that gives persons their dignity, freedom is required if a person is to act morally. For Kant, being free is more than freedom from causal necessity. This is negative freedom. Freedom in its fullest realization is the ability to guide one's actions from laws that are of one's own making. Freedom is not simply a spontaneous event. Free actions are caused, but they are caused by persons acting from laws they themselves have made. This is positive freedom....

When we act autonomously we have the capacity to act with dignity. We do so when we act on principles that are grounded in morality rather than in mere inclination. Reason requires that any moral principle that is freely derived must be rational in the sense that it is universal. To be universal in this sense means that the principle can be willed to be universally binding on all subjects in relevantly similar circumstances without contradiction. The fact that persons have this capability means that they possess dignity. And it is as a consequence of this dignity that a person "exacts respect for himself from all other rational beings in the world."[7] As such, one can and should "measure himself with every other being of this kind and value himself on a footing of equality with them."[8] Respecting people requires honoring their humanity; which is to say it requires treating them as ends in themselves. In Kant's words,

> Humanity itself is a dignity; for a man cannot be used merely as a means by any man ... but must always be used at the same time as an end. It is just in this that his dignity ... consists, by which he raises himself above all other beings in the world that are not men and yet can be used, and so over all *things*.[9]

... Kant argues that respecting people means that we cannot be indifferent to them. Indifference is a denial of respect.[10] He also argues that we have an obligation to be concerned with the physical welfare of people and their moral well-being. Adversity, pain, and want are temptations to vice and inhibit the ability of individuals to develop their rational and moral capacities.[11] It is these rational and moral capacities that distinguish people from mere animals. People who are not free to develop these capacities may end up leading lives that are closer to animals than to moral beings. Freedom from externally imposed adversity, pain, and want facilitate the cultivation of one's rational capacities and virtuous character. Thus, treating people as ends in themselves means ensuring their physical well-being and supporting and developing their rational and moral capacities.

With respect to the task at hand, what does treating the humanity of persons as ends in themselves require in a business context – specifically in the context of global manufacturing facilities? ... To fully respect a person one must actively treat his or her humanity as an end. This is an obligation that holds on every person *qua* person, whether in the personal realm or in the marketplace. As Kant writes, "Every man has a legitimate claim to respect from his fellow men and is *in turn* bound to respect every other."[12] There are, of course, limits to what managers of MNEs can accomplish. Nonetheless, we believe that the analysis we have provided entails that MNEs operating in developing nations have an obligation to respect the humanity of their employees....

It is noteworthy that an application of the doctrine of respect for persons to the issue of the obligations of employers to employees in developing economies results in conclusions similar to the capabilities approach developed by Amartya Sen.[13] Over the last twenty years Sen has argued that development involves more than an increase in people's incomes and the GNP of the country. He argues that we should be concerned with certain basic human capabilities, the most important of which is freedom. Sen's perspective is similar in important respects to our own because both are concerned with providing work that enhances the positive freedom of the worker. The United Nations utilizes both the Kantian view and the capabilities view as a dual theoretical foundation for its defense of human rights. Among the rights identified by the UN are freedom from injustice and violations of the rule of law; freedom to decent work without exploitation; and the freedom to develop and realize one's human potential. It argues that all global actors, including MNEs, have a moral obligation to respect basic human rights.[14] This general approach to poverty and development has recently been embraced by the World Bank.[15] James Wolfensohn, President of The World Bank, writes:

> A better quality of life for the poor
> calls for higher incomes. This requires
> sound economic policies and institutions
> conducive to sustained growth. Achieving
> higher incomes and a better quality of life
> also calls for much more improved and
> more equitable opportunities for educa-
> tion and jobs, better health and nutrition,
> a cleaner and more sustainable natural
> environment, an impartial judicial and
> legal system, greater civilian and politi-
> cal liberties, trustworthy and transparent
> institutions, and freedom of access to a
> rich and diverse cultural life....[16]

Significantly, The World Bank has recognized "crucial gaps" in its efforts to encourage development and eliminate poverty through market liberalization. What has been missing is "adequate attention to the quality and sustainability of growth." The World Bank now explicitly acknowledges that all major stakeholders have important roles to play in this process. "Functioning markets and liberalization are crucial" to poverty reduction. "But so is acknowledging the limits of the market and an essential role for governments *and other stakeholders* in the reform process."[17] MNEs have a significant interest in developing nations as sources of natural resources and

inexpensive labor, and as emerging markets. As such, The World Bank properly recognizes MNEs as stakeholders with important moral obligations in the global reform process.

## II. Outsourcing and the Duties of MNEs

One significant feature of globalization that is of particular relevance to our analysis is the increase in outsourcing by MNEs. Prior to the 1970s most foreign production by MNEs was intended for local markets. In the 1970s new financial incentives led MNEs to begin outsourcing the production of goods for North American, European, and Japanese markets to manufacturing facilities in developing countries. Encouraged by international organizations such as The World Bank and the International Monetary Fund, developing nations established "free trade zones" to encourage foreign investment via tax incentives and a minimal regulatory environment. In the 1980s the availability of international financing allowed entrepreneurs to set up production facilities in developing economies in order to meet the growing demand by MNEs for offshore production.[18] ...

Outsourcing has been especially popular in consumer products industries, and in particular in the apparel industry. Nike, for example, outsources all of its production.

Are MNEs responsible for the practices of their subcontractors and suppliers? We believe that they are. Michael Santoro has defended the view that MNEs have a moral duty to ensure that their business partners respect employees by ensuring that human rights are not violated in the workplace. Santoro argues as follows:

> [M]ultinational corporations are morally
> responsible for the way their suppliers
> and subcontractors treat their workers.
> The applicable moral standard is similar

to the legal doctrine of *respondeat superior*, according to which a principal is "vicariously liable" or responsible for the acts of its agent conducted in the course of the agency relationship. The classic example of this is the responsibility of employers for the acts of employees. Moreover, ignorance is no excuse. Firms must do whatever is required to become aware of what conditions are like in the factories of their suppliers and subcontractors, and thereby be able to assure themselves and others that their business partners don't mistreat those workers to provide a cheaper source of supply.[19]

We concur with Santoro's judgment and offer the following two-fold justification for the view that MNEs have a duty to ensure that the dignity of workers is respected in the factories of subcontractors. First, an MNE, like any other organization, is composed of individual persons and, since persons are moral creatures, the actions of employees in an MNE are constrained by the categorical imperative. This means MNE managers have a duty to ensure that those with whom they conduct business are properly respected.[20] Second, as Kant acknowledges, individuals have unique duties as a result of their unique circumstances. One key feature in determining an individual's duties is the power they have to render assistance. For example, Kant famously argues that a wealthy person has a duty of charity that an impoverished person lacks. Corollary duties apply to organizations. Researchers have noted that the relationship of power between MNEs and their subcontractors and suppliers is significantly imbalanced in favor of MNEs:

[A]s more and more developing countries have sought to establish export sectors, local manufacturers are locked in fierce competitive battles with one another.

The resulting oversupply of export factories allows US companies to move from one supplier to another in search of the lowest prices, quickest turnaround, highest quality and best delivery terms, weighted according to the priorities of the company. In this context, large US manufacturer-merchandisers and retailers wield enormous power to dictate the price at which they will purchase goods.[21]

MNEs are well positioned to help ensure that the employees of its business partners are respected because of this imbalance of power. In addition, MNEs can draw upon substantial economic resources, management expertise, and technical knowledge to assist their business partners in creating a respectful work environment.

## III. The Rule of Law

Lawlessness contributes to poverty[22] and is deeply interconnected with human and labor rights violations. One important role that MNEs can play to help ensure that the dignity of workers is properly respected is encouraging respect for the rule of law. The United Nations has emphasized the importance of ensuring that citizens in all nations are not subject to violations of the rule of law.

The rule of law means that a country's formal rules are made publicly known and enforced in a predictable way through transparent mechanisms. Two conditions are essential: the rules apply equally to all citizens, and the state is subject to the rules. How state institutions comply with the rule of law greatly affects the daily lives of poor people, who are very vulnerable to abuses of their rights.[23]

It is commonplace for employers in developing

nations to violate worker rights in the interest of economic efficiency and with the support of state institutions. Violations of laws relating to wages and benefits, forced overtime, health and safety, child labor, sexual harassment, discrimination, and environmental protection are legion. Examples include the following:

1   Human Rights Watch reports that in Mexican maquiladoras, or export processing zones, US companies such a Johnson Controls and Carlisle Plastics require female job applicants to submit to pregnancy screening; women are refused employment if they test positive. Employment discrimination based on pregnancy is a violation of Mexican law.[24]

2   A Guatemalan Ministry of the Economy study found that less than 30 per cent of maquiladora factories that supply MNEs make the legally required payments for workers into the national social security system which gives workers access to health care. The report was not made public by the Ministry of the Economy due to its "startling" nature.[25]

3   An El Salvadoran Ministry of Labor study funded by the United States Agency for International Development found widespread violation of labor laws, including flagrant violation of the freedom to organize and unionize, in maquiladora factories that supply MNEs. The report was suppressed by the Ministry of Labor after factory owners complained.[26]

4   In North and Central Mexico widespread violation of Mexican environmental laws by MNEs and their contractors has been documented by both US and Mexican nongovernmental organizations, and local Mexican governmental officials.[27]

5   In Haiti apparel manufacturers such as L.V. Myles Corporation, producing clothing under license with the Walt Disney Company in several contract factories, paid workers substantially less than the Haitian minimum wage. These clothes were sold in the US at Wal-Mart, Sears, JCPenney and other retailers. This practice continued until the National Labor Committee documented and publicized this violation of Haitian law.[28]

Furthermore, in many nations in which MNEs operate those responsible for administering justice are violators of the law. Factory workers frequently have no legal recourse when their legal rights are violated.

The intentional violation of the legal rights of workers in the interest of economic efficiency is fundamentally incompatible with the duty of MNEs to respect workers. Indifference to the plight of workers whose legal rights are systematically violated is a denial of respect. At a minimum, MNEs have a duty to ensure that their offshore factories, and those of their suppliers and subcontractors, are in full compliance with local laws. Failure to honor the dignity of workers by violating their legal rights – or tolerating the violation of those rights – is also hypocritical. In Kantian terms, it constitutes a pragmatic contradiction. A pragmatic contradiction occurs when one acts on a principle that promotes an action that would be inconsistent with one's purpose if everyone were to act upon that principle. In this case, the principle would be something like the following: "It is permissible to violate the legal rights of others when doing so is economically efficient." MNEs rely on the rule of law to ensure, among other things, that their contracts are fulfilled, their property is secure, and their copyrights are protected. When violations of the legal rights of MNEs take place, MNEs and business organizations protest vociferously. Thus, MNEs rely on the rule of law to ensure the protection of their own interests. Without the rule of law, MNEs would cease to exist. Therefore, it is inconsistent for an MNE to permit the violation of the legal rights of workers while at the same time it demands that its own rights be protected.

**IV. Coercion**

... Coercion is prima facie wrong because it treats the subjects of coercion as mere tools, as objects lacking the rational capacity to choose for themselves how they shall act.

Are sweatshops in violation of the no coercion requirement? An answer to this question depends both on the definition of the concepts in question and on the facts of the particular case.... Physical coercion occurs when one's bodily movements are physically forced. In cases where one person (P) physically coerces another person (Q), Q's body is used as an object or instrument for the purpose of fulfilling P's desires. We assume that readers of this essay will agree that using physical coercion to keep people working in sweatshops against their will is disrespectful and morally wrong. While comparatively rare, physical coercion, or the threat of physical coercion, does take place. For example, at a shoe factory in Guangdong, China, it is reported that 2,700 workers were prevented from leaving the factory by 100 live-in security guards that patrolled the walled factory grounds.[29] ...

In typical cases, people work in sweatshops because they believe they can earn more money working there than they can in alternative employment, or they work in sweatshops because it is better than being unemployed. In many developing countries, people are moving to large cities from rural areas because agriculture in those areas can no longer support the population base. When people make a choice that seems highly undesirable because

there are no better alternatives available, are those people coerced? ... [H]aving to make a choice among undesirable options is not sufficient for coercion. We therefore assume that such persons are not coerced even though they have no better alternative than working in a sweatshop.

Nonetheless, the use of psychological coercion in sweatshops appears widespread. For example, coercion is frequently used by supervisors to improve worker productivity. Workers throughout the world report that they are forced to work long overtime hours or lose their jobs. In Bangladesh factory workers report that they are expected to work virtually every day of the year. Overtime pay, a legal requirement, is often not paid. Employees who refuse to comply are fired.[30] ...

Bangladesh, El Salvador, and other developing economies lack the social welfare programs that workers in North America and Europe take for granted. If workers lose their jobs, they may end up without any source of income. Thus, workers are understandably fearful of being fired for noncompliance with demands to work long overtime hours. When a worker is threatened with being fired by a supervisor unless she agrees to work overtime, and when the supervisor's intention in making the threat is to ensure compliance, then the supervisor's actions are properly understood as coercive. Similar threats are used to ensure that workers meet production quotas, even in the face of personal injury. For example, a 26-year-old worker who sews steering wheel covers at a Mexican maquila owned by Autotrim reports the following:

> We have to work quickly with our hands, and I am responsible for sewing 20 steering wheel covers per shift. After having worked for nine years at the plant, I now suffer from an injury in my right hand.

I start out the shift okay, but after about three hours of work, I feel a lot of sharp pains in my fingers. It gets so bad that I can't hold the steering wheel correctly. But still the supervisors keep pressuring me to reach 100 per cent of my production. I can only reach about 70 per cent of what they ask for. These pains began a year ago and I am not the only one who has suffered from them. There are over 200 of us who have hand injuries and some have lost movement in their hands and arms. The company has fired over 150 people in the last year for lack of production. Others have been pressured to quit ...[31]

We do not claim that production quotas are inherently coercive. Given a reasonable quota, employees can choose whether or not to work diligently to fill that quota. Employees who choose idleness over industriousness and are terminated as a result are not coerced. However, when a supervisor threatens workers who are ill or injured with termination unless they meet a production quota that either cannot physically be achieved by the employee, or can only be achieved at the cost of further injury to the employee, the threat is properly understood as coercive. In such cases the employee will inevitably feel compelled to meet the quota. Still other factory workers report being threatened with termination if they seek medical attention. For example, when a worker in El Salvador who was three months pregnant began hemorrhaging she was not allowed to leave the factory to receive medical attention. She subsequently miscarried while in the factory, completed her long work day, and took her fetus home for burial.[32] Other workers have died because they were not allowed to leave the factory to receive medical attention.[33] In cases where workers suffer miscarriages or death, rather than risk

termination, we believe that it reasonable to conclude that the workers are coerced into remaining at work.

... Respecting workers requires that they be free to decline overtime work without fear of being fired. It also requires that if they are injured or ill – especially as a result of work related activities – they should be allowed to consult healthcare workers and be given work that does not exacerbate their illnesses or injuries. Using coercion as a means of compelling employees to work overtime, to meet production quotas despite injury, or to remain at work while in need of medical attention, is incompatible with respect for persons because the coercers treat their victims as mere tools....

## V. Working Conditions

Critics of MNEs argue that many workers are vulnerable to workplace hazards such as repetitive motion injuries, exposure to toxic chemicals, exposure to airborne pollutants such as fabric particles, and malfunctioning machinery. One of the most common workplace hazards concerns fire safety. In factories throughout the world workers are locked in to keep them from leaving the factory. When fires break out workers are trapped. This is what happened in 1993 when a fire broke out at the Kader Industrial Toy Company in Thailand. More than 200 workers were killed and 469 injured. The factory had been producing toys for US companies such as Hasbro, Toys "R" Us, JCPenney, and Fisher-Price.[34] In Bangladesh alone, there have been seventeen fires that have resulted in fatalities since 1995. A recent fire at Chowdhury Knitwears claimed 52 lives.[35]

Workers are also exposed to dangerous toxic chemicals and airborne pollutants. For example, a Nike-commissioned Ernst & Young Environmental and Labor Practices

Audit of the Tae Kwang Vina factory outside Ho Chi Minh City, Vietnam, was leaked to the press. Among the many unsafe conditions reported by Ernst & Young at this 10,000 person facility was exposure to toluene (a toxic chemical used as a solvent in paints, coatings, adhesives, and cleaning agents) at amounts 6 to 177 times that allowed by Vietnamese law.[36] The US Environmental Protection Agency identifies the following acute effects of toluene exposure:

> The central nervous system is the primary target organ for toluene toxicity in both humans and animals for acute (short-term) and chronic (long-term) exposures. CNS dysfunction (which is often reversible) and narcosis have been frequently observed in humans acutely exposed to low or moderate levels of toluene by inhalation; symptoms include fatigue, sleepiness, headaches, and nausea. CNS depression and death have occurred at higher levels of exposure. Cardiac arrhythmia has also been reported in humans acutely exposed to toluene.[37]

In addition to toluene, workers at the Tae Kwang Vina factory were exposed to airborne fabric particles and chemical powders at dangerous levels. It is implausible to think that the (mainly) young women who work in the Tae Kwang Vina factory were informed about these health risks before they were hired. Ernst & Young reports that the employees received no training concerning the proper handling of chemicals after they were hired. Since that time Nike has overseen substantial health and safety improvements at the Tae Kwang Vina factory, and at the other Southeast Asian factories with which it contracts. Nonetheless, available evidence indicates that unsafe workplace conditions remain common among MNE factories.[38] ...

If our analysis is correct, then those MNEs that tolerate such health and safety risks have a duty to improve those conditions. Lax health and safety standards violate the moral requirement that employers be concerned with the physical safety of their employees. A failure to implement appropriate safeguards means that employers are treating their employees as disposable tools rather than as beings with unique dignity....

## VI. Wages

One of the most controversial issues concerning sweatshops is the demand that employers raise the wages of employees in order to provide a "living wage." Workers from all over the world complain about low wages. For example,

> [E]mployees of a maquiladora in Ciudad Acuna, Mexico, owned by the Aluminum Company of America (Alcoa), calculated that to buy the most basic food items needed by a factory worker – items such as beans, tortilla, rice, potatoes, onions and cooking oil, and excluding such "luxuries" as milk, meat, vegetables and cereal – cost US $26.87 per week. At the time, weekly wages at the plant ranged only from $21.44 to $24.60.[39]

... It is our contention that, at a minimum, respect for employees entails that MNEs and their suppliers have a moral obligation to ensure that employees do not live under conditions of overall poverty by providing adequate wages for a 48 hour work week to satisfy both basic food needs and basic non-food needs. Doing so helps to ensure the physical well-being and independence of employees, contributes to the development of their rational capacities, and provides them with opportunities for moral development.

This in turn allows for the cultivation of self-esteem.[40] It is difficult to specify with precision the minimum number of hours per week that employees should work in order to receive a living wage. However, we believe that a 48 hour work week is a reasonable compromise that allows employees sufficient time for the cultivation of their rational capacities while providing employers with sufficient productivity. In addition, MNEs and their suppliers have an obligation to pay appropriate host nation taxes and meet appropriate codes and regulations to ensure that they contribute in appropriate ways to the creation and maintenance of the goods, services, and infrastructure necessary for the fulfillment of human capabilities. Anything less than this means that MNEs, or their suppliers, are not respecting employees as ends in themselves.

## VII. Economic Considerations

The failure of many MNEs to meet the standards required by the application of the doctrine of respect for persons has not gone unnoticed. Through consumer boycotts, letter writing campaigns, opinion columns, and shareholder resolutions, activists have been successful in persuading some MNEs to implement changes. For example, Nike recently created the position of Vice President for Corporate Social Responsibility, hired a public affairs specialist to fill the position, and began to aggressively respond to activist complaints. In a recent open letter to its critics Nike concedes that "Several years ago, in our earlier expansion into certain countries, we had lots to learn about manufacturing practices and how to improve them."[41] However, Nike reports that it has fully embraced the goals of higher wages, the elimination of child labor, and the creation of better working conditions. In short, Nike's response to its critics is "... guess what? You've already succeeded!"[42]

Asked whether or not Nike would have made improvements without public pressure, a Nike official responded "Probably not as quickly, probably not to the degree."[43] Thus, ethical theory and a significant number of citizens of good will stand as one on this issue....

... Companies such as Levis Strauss [sic], Motorola, and Mattel have expended considerable resources to ensure that employees in their global sourcing operations work in healthy and safe environments. For example, Levis Strauss & Company stipulates that "We will only utilize business partners who provide workers with a safe and healthy environment."[44] Levis is known for acting in a manner consistent with this policy. Motorola explicitly endorses the idea of respect for persons in their Code of Business Conduct. The Code is built on two foundations:

> *Uncompromising integrity* means staying true to what we believe. We adhere to honesty, fairness and "doing the right thing" without compromise, even when circumstances make it difficult.

> *Constant respect for people* means we treat others with dignity, as we would like to be treated ourselves. Constant respect applies to every individual we interact with around the world.[45]

The physical instantiation of these principles can be seen at Motorola's factory in Tianjin, China:

> In the company cafeteria, workers queue up politely for a variety of free and nutritious meals. One area is set aside for a pregnancy well-care program. A booth is open at which appointments can be made with the company medical staff. There is a bank branch dedicated to employee needs. It is a scene that one might expect

665

on a Fortune 500 corporate campus in the United States. The overwhelming sense is of a pleasant, orderly place in which people are fulfilled in their work.[46]

Recently Mattel announced the creation of a global code of conduct for its production facilities and contract manufacturers. It has spent millions of dollars to upgrade its manufacturing facilities in order to improve worker safety and comfort. Furthermore, it has invited a team of academics led by S. Prakash Sethi to monitor its progress in complying with its self-imposed standards and to make their findings public.[47]

This is believed to be the first time that a major MNE has voluntarily submitted to external monitoring. The examples set by Levis, Motorola, and Mattel provide evidence that MNEs are capable of improving worker health and safety without causing further hardship in the communities in which they operate.

... With regard to the lowest paid formal sector wage earners in developing countries, the assumption that productivity is independent of wage levels is dubious.

As exceptionally low wages are raised, there may be increases in productivity either because of induced management improvements or because of greater labour efficiency due to a decrease in wasteful labour turnover and industrial disputes and to improvements in workers morale and nutrition resulting, in turn, in an increase in the workers' willingness and capacity to work and a reduction in the incidence of debilitating diseases, time off due to illness and accidents caused by fatigue. If higher wages, at least over a certain range, are accompanied by certain improvements in labour productivity, it is conceivable that labour costs could decrease rather

than increase and to such an extent that employment would not fall.[48]

Put simply, workers whose minimum daily caloric intakes are met, and who have basic non-food needs met, will have more energy and better attitudes at work; will be less likely to come to work ill; and will be absent with less frequency. Workers are thus likely to be more productive and loyal. Economists refer to a wage that if reduced would make the firm worse off because of a decrease in worker productivity as the efficiency wage. Empirical evidence supports the view that increased productivity resulting from better nutrition offsets the cost of higher wages.[49] Thus, if workers are being paid less than the efficiency wage in a particular market there are good economic reasons, in addition to moral reasons, for raising wages. Higher productivity per hour could also help alleviate the need for overtime work and facilitate a 48 hour work week....

... [There is the concern] that increased labor costs will inevitably result in higher unemployment in competitive markets.... However, this view has been challenged in recent years. In their recent influential book-length study of the impact of minimum wage increases on employment, David Card and Alan Krueger argue that their reanalysis of the evidence from the Unites States, Canada, the United Kingdom, and Puerto Rico indicates that the existing data does not provide compelling evidence for the textbook view.[50] In addition, Card and Krueger analyzed new data for recent increases in the minimum wage in the US. Their analysis is complex, but the results of their analysis are straightforward. "In every case ... the estimated effect of the minimum wage was either zero or positive."[51] ... After evaluating recent work on the impact of minimum wages, economists William Spriggs and John Schmitt reached a more determinate conclusion: "The overwhelming weight of recent evidence supports the view that low-wage workers will benefit overwhelmingly from a higher federal minimum."[52] ...

## VIII. Conclusion

As Kant argues, it is by acting in a manner consistent with human dignity that persons raise themselves above all things. Insofar as we recognize the dignity of humanity, we have an obligation to respect both ourselves and others.[53] We have argued that MNE managers who encourage or tolerate violations of the rule of law; use coercion; allow unsafe working conditions; and provide below subsistence wages, disavow their own dignity and that of their workers. In so doing, they disrespect themselves and their workers. Further, we have argued that this moral analysis is not undermined by economic considerations. Significantly, MNEs are in many ways more readily able to honor the humanity of workers. This is because MNEs typically have well defined internal decision structures that, unlike individual moral agents, are not susceptible to weakness of the will.[54] For this reason, MNE managers who recognize a duty to respect their employees, and those of their subcontractors, are well positioned to play a constructive role in ensuring that the dignity of humanity is respected.

## Study Questions

1. There have been several examples of students in various universities across the country (for example, Purdue University, University of Iowa, University of Illinois-Chicago, University of Texas-Austin, Rutgers University, and Virginia Tech) protesting the deplorable conditions of sweatshop workers. As a result, some universities have cut ties with the targeted companies, resulting in a huge loss of revenue, or the companies have taken steps to improve worker conditions. This indicates that consumers are indeed influential and that they, with enough collective pressure, can help create the kinds of changes that Arnold and Bowie support in their essay. Given this, what moral responsibilities do you believe you have in helping to alleviate the working conditions in sweatshops? Is your responsibility greater, less, or equivalent to that of multinational enterprises?

2. As was discussed in the introduction to this section, in 2010, 14 employees of the Foxconn corporation in China, which manufactures products for Apple, Hewlett-Packard, Dell, and Sony, among others, committed suicide as a result of inhumane working conditions and several instances of labor abuses. According to Arnold and Bowie, what moral responsibility do these companies bear for the suicide of these workers and in improving their working conditions? As a consumer, what responsibilities, if any, do you bear?

3. In Section VI, Steve Tracy's article "Abortion, the Marginalized, and the Vulnerable" emphasizes the need for a more comprehensive pro-life approach – one that focuses not only on fetal welfare but also on the welfare of all human persons, particularly

those who are in vulnerable positions. Put Tracy's article in dialogue with Arnold and Bowie's essay. What commonalities do you see? In what ways can Tracy's article influence the moral assessment of sweatshop working conditions?

4. Arnold and Bowie point out that what would often be considered labor abuses in the United States are legally tolerated in other countries (and, in cases where the conditions are not legal, they are overlooked when it comes to sweatshop labor). This brings to the surface an important discussion between what is legal and what is moral, and how often the two fail to intersect. What other cases can you think of where what is legal may not necessarily be what is moral? What are the implications of this when it comes to the moral responsibilities of citizens, especially those who live in free and democratic societies?

**Notes**

1  Earlier versions of this essay were presented to the Annual Meeting of the Society for Business Ethics, Washington, DC, August, 2001; and the American Philosophical Association 100th Anniversary Conference, "Morality in the 21st Century," Newark, DE., October, 2001. We are grateful to audience members for their comments on those occasions. Thanks also to George Brenkert, Heather Douglas, Laura Hartman, John McCall, Sara Arnold, and an anonymous reviewer for helpful comments on earlier drafts of this essay. Special thanks to Ian Maitland and Norris Peterson for detailed written comments; although we continue to disagree with them on some matters, their comments led to several improvements in this essay.

2  See, for example, Susan Chandler, "Look Who's Sweating Now," *BusinessWeek*, October 16, 1995; Steven Greenhouse, "Sweatshop Raids Cast Doubt on an Effort By Garment Makers to Police the Factories," *New York Times*, July 18, 1997; and Gail Edmondson et al., "Workers in Bondage," *Business Week*, November 27, 2000.

3  For the purposes of this paper we define the term as any workplace in which workers are typically subject to two or more of the following conditions: income for a 48 hour work week less than the overall poverty rate for that country (see Table 1 below); systematic forced overtime; systematic health and safety risks that stem from negligence or the willful disregard of employee welfare; coercion; systematic deception that places workers at risk; and underpayment of earnings.

4  Immanuel Kant, *Foundations of the Metaphysics of Morals*, trans. Lewis White Beck (New York: Macmillan, 1990), 46.

5  In making this claim we explicitly reject the conclusion reached by Andrew Wicks that one must either "fully embrace Kant's metaphysics" or "break from the abstract universalism of Kant." See Andrew Wicks, "How Kantian a Theory of Capitalism," *Business Ethics Quarterly*, The Ruffin Series: Special Issue 1 (1998): 65.

6  Kant, *Foundations of the Metaphysics of Morals*, 52.

7  Immanuel Kant, *The Metaphysics of Morals*, trans. Mary Gregor (Cambridge: Cambridge UP, 1991), 230.

8  Ibid.

9  Ibid., 255.

10  Ibid., 245.

11  Ibid., 192–93 and 196–97.

12  Ibid., 255.

13  His latest book is *Development as Freedom* (New York: Anchor Books, 1999). Martha Nussbaum
    has developed her own version of the capabilities approach, one that pays particular attention
    to the unique circumstances of women's lives. *Women and Human Development: The Capabilities
    Approach* (Cambridge: Cambridge UP, 2000).

14  United Nations Development Programme, *Human Development Report 2000* (New York:
    Oxford UP, 2000).

15  See, for example, Vinod Thomas et al., *The Quality of Growth* (Washington, DC: The World
    Bank, 2000); Deepa Narayan et al., *Voices of the Poor: Crying Out for Change* (Washington, DC:
    The World Bank, 2000); and Deepa Narayan et al., *Voices of the Poor: Can Anyone Hear Us?*
    (Washington, DC: The World Bank, 2000).

16  Thomas et al., *The Quality of Growth*, xiv.

17  Ibid., xvii–xviii (italics added by authors).

18  Pamela Varley, ed., *The Sweatshop Quandary: Corporate Responsibility on the Global Frontier*
    (Washington, DC, Investor Responsibility Research Center, 1998), 185–86.

19  Michael A. Santoro, *Profits and Principles: Global Capitalism and Human Rights in China* (Ithaca:
    Cornell UP, 2000), 161.

20  For a fuller discussion of this matter see Bowie, *Business Ethics: A Kantian Perspective*, esp. chap.
    2.

21  Varley, ed., *The Sweatshop Quandary*, 95.

22  Better rule of law is associated with higher per capita income. See *World Development Report
    2000/2001: Attacking Poverty* (New York: Oxford UP, 2000), 103.

23  Ibid., 102. See also the United National Development Programme's *Human Development Report
    2000* (New York: Oxford UP, 2000), esp. 37–38.

24  Human Rights Watch, "A Job or Your Rights: Continued Sex Discrimination in Mexico's
    Maquiladora Sector," volume 10, no. 1(B) December 1998. Available at http://www.hrw.org/
    reports98/women2/.

25  Varley, ed., *The Sweatshop Quandary*, 131.

26  Republic of El Salvador, Ministry of Labor, Monitoring and Labor Relations Analysis Unit,
    "Monitoring Report on Maquilas and Bonded Areas," (July 2000). Available at http://www.
    nlcnet.org/elsalvador/040 1/translation.htm.

27  Edward J. Williams, "The Maquiladora Industry and Environmental Degradation in the
    United States-Mexican Borderlands," paper presented at the annual meeting of the Latin
    American Studies Association, Washington, DC, September, 1995. Available at http://
    www.natlaw.com/pubs/williams.htm. See also Joan Salvat, Stef Soetewey, and Peter Breuls,
    *Free Trade Slaves*, 58 min. (Princeton, NJ: Films for the Humanities and Sciences, 1999),
    videocassette.

28  National Labor Committee, "The U.S. in Haiti: How To Get Rich on 11 Cents an Hour,"
    1995. Available at http://www.nlcnet.org/Haiti/0 196/index.htm.

29  Varley, ed., *The Sweatshop Quandary*, 12.

30  Barry Bearak, "Lives Held Cheap In Bangladesh Sweatshops," *New York Times*, April 15, 2001.

31  Varley, ed., *The Sweatshop Quandary*, 68.

32  Salvat et al., *Free Trade Slaves*.

33  Ibid.

34  Varley, ed., *The Sweatshop Quandary*, 61.

35  Bearak, "Lives Held Cheap in Bangladesh Sweatshops."

36  "Ernst & Young Environmental and Labor Practice Audit of the Tae Kwang Vina Industrial
    Ltd. Co., Vietnam." Available at http://www.corpwatch.org/trac/nike/ernst/audit.html.

37  United States Environmental Protection Agency, Office of Air Quality, Planning, and
    Standards, "Toluene." Available at http://www .epa.gov/ttnuatw 1/hlthef/toluene.html.

38  See, for example, Varley, ed., *The Sweatshop Quandary*, esp. 59–398.

39  After the complaint was raised in a shareholder meeting Alcoa raised the wages of the workers by 25%. Pamela Varley, ed., *The Sweatshop Quandary*, 63.

40  Self-esteem is grounded in the conscious recognition of one's dignity as a rational being.

41  Nike, "An Open Letter Response to USAS Regarding Their National Protest of Nike through August 16, 2000." Available at http://nikebiz.com/labor/usas_let.shtml.

42  Ibid.

43  Frank Denton, "Close Look at Factory for Nikes," *Wisconsin State Journal*, July 30, 2000.

44  Maitland, "The Great Non-Debate Over International Sweatshops," 539.

45  Motorola, "Code of Business Conduct." Available at http://www.motorola.com/code/code.html.

46  Santoro, *Profits and Principles*, 6.

47  S. Prakash Sethi, "Codes of Conduct for Multinational Corporations: An Idea Whose Time Has Come," *Business and Society Review* 104 (1999): 225–41.

48  Gerald Starr, *Minimum Wage Fixing* (Geneva: International Labour Organization, 1981), 157.

49  C.J. Bliss and N.H. Stern, "Productivity, Wages, and Nutrition, 2: Some Observations." *Journal of Development Economics* 5 (1978): 363–98. For theoretical discussion see C.J. Bliss and N.H. Stern, "Productivity, Wages, and Nutrition, 1: The Theory," *Journal of Development Economics* 5 (1978): 331–62.

50  See David Card and Alan B. Krueger, *Myth and Measurement: The New Economics of the Minimum Wage* (Princeton: Princeton UP, 1995). See also the special symposium on *Myth and Measurement* in *Industrial & Labor Relations Review* (July 1995) with contributions by Charles Brown, Richard Freeman, Daniel Hamermesh, Paul Osterman, and Finis Welch; David Neumark and William Wascher, "Minimum Wages and Employment: A Case Study of the Fast-Food Industry in New Jersey and Pennsylvania: Comment," *The American Economic Review* (December 2000): 1362–96; and David Card and Alan B. Krueger, "Minimum Wages and Employment: A Case Study of the Fast-Food Industry in New Jersey and Pennsylvania: Reply," *The American Economic Review* (December 2000): 1397–1420. For a discussion of the living wage issue in the context of the US economy see Robert Pollin and Stephanie Luce, *The Living Wage: Building a Fair Economy* (New York: The New P, 1998).

51  Card and Krueger, *Myth and Measurement*, 389.

52  William Spriggs and John Schmitt, "The Minimum Wage: Blocking the Low-Wage Path," in *Reclaiming Prosperity: A Blueprint for Progressive Economic Reform*, Todd Schafer and Jeff Faux (Armonk, NY: ME Sharpe, 1996), 170.

53  Kant, *Foundations of the Metaphysics of Morals*, 255.

54  For a fuller defense of this position see Peter A. French, *Corporate Ethics* (Fort Worth, TX: Hartcourt Brace, 1995), 79–87.

# Permissions Acknowledgments

Aristotle. Excerpts from *Nicomachean Ethics*, second edition, translated by Terence Irwin. Hackett Publishing Company, Inc., copyright © 1999. Reprinted with the permission of the publisher.

Denis Arnold and Norman Bowie. "Sweatshops and Respect for Persons," from *Business Ethics Quarterly*, Volume 13, Issue 2, April 2003. Copyright © Society for Business Ethics 2003. Reprinted with the permission of Cambridge University Press.

Jeremy Baskin. "The Impossible Necessity of Climate Justice?," from *The Melbourne Journal of International Law*, Volume 10, 2009. Reprinted with the permission of The Melbourne Journal of International Law and Jeremy Baskin, Associate, Melbourne Sustainable Society Institute, University of Melbourne.

Margaret P. Battin. "The Way We Do It, the Way They Do It: End-of-Life Practices in the Developed World," from *Journal of Pain and Symptom Management*, July 6 (5): 298–305, 1991. Copyright © 1991. Reprinted with permission from Elsevier.

Solomon Benatar, Abdallah Daar, and Peter Singer. Excerpt from "Global Health Ethics: The Rationale for Mutual Caring," in *International Affairs*, Volume 79, Issue 1, pp. 107–38, January 2003. Royal Institute of International Affairs. DOI: 10.1111/1468-2346.00298. Reprinted with the permission of John Wiley and Sons, via Copyright Clearance Center, Inc.

Erika Blacksher, Alice Diebel, Pierre-Gerlier Forest, Susan Dorr Goold, and Julia Abelson. "What Is Public Deliberation?," from *Hastings Center Report* 42, no. 2 (2012): 14–16. Copyright © 2012 by The Hastings Center. Reprinted with the permission of John Wiley and Sons via Copyright Clearance Center, Inc.

Susan J. Brison. Excerpts from "Outliving Oneself," in *Aftermath: Violence and the Remaking of a Self*. Princeton: Princeton University Press, 2002. Republished with the permission of Princeton University Press via Copyright Clearance Center, Inc.

Anthony Burke. "Just War or Ethical Peace? Moral Discourses of Strategic Violence after 9/11," from *International Affairs*, Volume 8, Number 2, Israeli-Palestinian Conflict (March 2004), pp. 329–53. Copyright © 2004, John Wiley and Sons. Reprinted with the permission of John Wiley and Sons, via Copyright Clearance Center, Inc.

Loren Cannon. "Trans-Marriage and the Unacceptability of Same-Sex Marriage Restrictions," from *Social Philosophy Today*, Volume 25, 2009. DOI: 10.5840/socphiltoday2009257. Reprinted with the permission of the Philosophy Documentation Center.

Claudia Card. "Recognizing Terrorism," from *The Journal of Ethics* (2007) 11:1–29. DOI: 10.1007/s10892-006-9008-x. Copyright © 2006, Springer Science+Business Media B.V. Reprinted with the permission of Springer via Copyright Clearance Center, Inc.

Guy Claxton. "Involuntary Simplicity: Changing Dysfunctional Habits of Consumption," from *Environmental Values*, Volume 3, Number 1 (Spring 1994), pp. 71–78. Reprinted with the permission of White Horse Press, www.whpress.co.uk.

Shari Collins and Eric Comerford. "Anonymous Sperm Donation: A Case for Genetic Heritage and Wariness for Contractual Parenthood," from *International Journal of Applied Philosophy*,

Volume 26, Issue 2, Fall 2012. DOI: 10.5840/ijap201226216. Reprinted with the permission of the Philosophy Documentation Center.

Shari Collins-Chobanian. "Analysis of Paul Butler's Race-Based Jury Nullification and His Call to Black Jurors and the African American Community," from *Journal of Black Studies*, Volume 39, Number 4 (March 2009): 508–27 (http://jbs.sagepub.com/content/39/4/508.abstract). Reprinted with permission.

Tommy J. Curry. "Michael Brown and the Need for a Genre Study of Black Male Death and Dying," from *Theory and Event* 17:3 Supplement (2014). Copyright © 2014 Tommy J. Curry and the Johns Hopkins University Press. Reprinted with the permission of Johns Hopkins University Press.

Michelle Madden Dempsey. Excerpt from "How to Argue about Prostitution," in *Criminal Law and Philosophy*, Volume 6, Issue 1, 2012, pp 65–80. DOI: 10.1007/s11572-011-9129-6. Reprinted with the permission of Springer.

David DiRamio and Kathryn Jarvis. "Crisis of Identity? Veteran, Civilian, Student," *ASHE Higher Education Report*, 37.3, 2011. Special Issue: *Veterans in Higher Education*. Republished with the permission of John Wiley and Sons via Copyright Clearance Center, Inc.

Paul Farmer. "Pathologies of Power: Rethinking Health and Human Rights," from *The American Journal of Public Health*, Volume 89, Number 10, October 1999: 1486–96. Reprinted with the permission of The American Public Health Association via The Sheridan Press.

Mohandas K. Gandhi. Excerpts from Chapter VI: "Civilisation," Chapter XIII: "What Is True Civilisation?," Chapter XVI: "Brute Force," Chapter XVII: "Passive Resistance," in *Hind Swaraj or Indian Home Rule*, 1909. Translated by Mohandas K. Gandhi, 1910. Reprinted 1919 by Ganesh & Co., Madras.

Raja Halwani. "Casual Sex, Promiscuity, and Temperance," from *Sex and Ethics: Essays on Sexuality, Virtue, and the Good Life*. Palgrave Macmillan, 2007. Reprinted with the permission of Palgrave Macmillan.

Axel Honneth. Excerpt from "Integrity and Disrespect: Principles of a Conception of Morality Based on the Theory of Recognition," in *Political Theory*, May 1992. Copyright © 1992 by Sage Publications. Reprinted with the permission of Sage Publications via Copyright Clearance Center, Inc.

Mae-Wan Ho. "Perils amid Promises of Genetically Modified Foods," from *Genetic Engineering: Dream or Nightmare? The Brave New World of Bad Science and Big Business*. Gateway Books, 1998, 1999. Reprinted with the permission of Dr. Mae-Wan Ho.

bell hooks (Gloria Watkins). Excerpt from "Theory as Liberatory Practice," Chapter 5 of *Teaching to Transgress*. Copyright © 1994 Gloria Watkins. Reprinted with the permission of Taylor and Francis Group LLC, a division of Informa plc, via Copyright Clearance Center, Inc.

Immanuel Kant. Excerpt from *Groundwork for the Metaphysics of Morals*, edited by Lara Denis. Copyright © 2005 by Lara Denis. Broadview Press, 2005.

Søren Kierkegaard. Excerpts from *Kierkegaard's Writings, XVI: Works of Love*, edited and translated by Howard V. Hong and Edna H. Hong. Princeton University Press, 1998. Reprinted with the permission of Princeton University Press, via Copyright Clearance Center, Inc.

Frances Kissling. "Is There Life after *Roe*? How to Think about the Fetus," from *Conscience: The News Journal of Catholic Opinion* 25 (3), Winter 2004–2005. Reprinted with the permission of Frances Kissling and Catholics for Choice.

Naomi Klein. "Beyond Extractivism: Confronting the Climate Denier Within," from *This Changes Everything: Capitalism vs. the Climate*. Copyright © 2014 by Naomi Klein. All rights reserved. Reprinted in the United States with the permission of Simon & Schuster, Inc. Reprinted in Canada with the permission of Alfred A. Knopf Canada, a division of Penguin Random House Canada Limited.

W.D. Ross. "What Makes Right Acts Right?," Chapter II of *The Right and the Good*, second edition, edited by Philip Stratton-Lake. Copyright © Oxford University Press, 1930, 2002. Reprinted with the permission of Oxford University Press.

Jean-Paul Sartre. "The Look," from *Being and Nothingness*, translated by Hazel E. Barnes. New York: Washington Square Press, 1966. Reprinted with the permission of the Philosophical Library, New York.

Samuel Scheffler. "Is Terrorism Morally Distinctive?," from *The Journal of Political Philosophy*, Volume 14, Number 1, 2006, pp. 1–17. Copyright © 2006, John Wiley and Sons. Reprinted with the permission of John Wiley and Sons via Copyright Clearance Center, Inc.

Peter Singer. "What Should a Billionaire Give—and What Should You?," from *The New York Times*, December 17, 2006. Copyright © 2006 The New York Times. All rights reserved. Used by permission and protected by the Copyright Laws of the United States. The printing, copying, redistribution or retransmission of this Content without express written permission is prohibited.

Stephanie Solomon and Julia Abelson. "Why and When Should We Use Public Deliberation?," from *Hastings Center Report* 42, no. 2 (2012): 17–20. Copyright © 2012 by The Hastings Center. Reprinted with the permission of John Wiley and Sons via Copyright Clearance Center, Inc.

Charles Taylor. Excerpts from "The Politics of Recognition," in *Multiculturalism*, edited by Amy Gutmann. Copyright © 1994 by Princeton University Press. Reprinted with the permission of Princeton University Press via Clearance Center, Inc.

Judith Jarvis Thomson. Excerpt from "A Defense of Abortion," in *Philosophy and Public Affairs*, Volume 1, Number 1, 1971: pp. 47–66. Reprinted with the permission of Blackwell Publishing Inc., via Copyright Clearance Center, Inc.

Steve Tracy. "Abortion, the Marginalized, and the Vulnerable," from *Cultural Encounters* 6 (2), 2010: 23–33. Reprinted with the permission of The Institute for the Theology of Culture: New Wine, New Wineskins; reprinted with the permission of Steve Tracy.

Arne Johan Vetlesen. Excerpts from "Genocide: A Case for the Responsibility of the Bystander," in *Journal of Peace Research*, July 2000, Volume 37, Number 4, 519–32. Copyright © 2000 by Sage Publications, Ltd. Reprinted by permission of Sage Publications, Ltd., via Copyright Clearance Center, Inc.

Michael Warner. "The Ethics of Sexual Shame," Chapter 1 of *The Trouble with Normal: Sex, Politics, and the Ethics of Queer Life*. Copyright © 1999 by Michael Warner. Reprinted with the permission of Free Press, a Division of Simon & Schuster, Inc. All rights reserved.

Nancy M. Williams. "Affected Ignorance and Animal Suffering: Why Our Failure to Debate Factory Farming Puts Us at Moral Risk," from *Journal of Agricultural and Environmental Ethics* 21 (4): 371–84 (2008). Copyright © Springer Science+Business Media B.V. 2008. Reprinted with permission of Springer.

Iris Marion Young. Excerpts from "Five Faces of Oppression," Chapter 2 of *Justice and the Politics of Difference*. Princeton University Press, 1990. Republished with the permission of Princeton University Press via Copyright Clearance Center, Inc.